W9-BSW-366

SOCIOLOGICAL THEORY

ORIGIN 1897

FOUNDERS Émile Durkheim, Robert Ezra Park, Ernest Burgess, Clifford Shaw, Walter Reckless, Frederic Thrasher

MOST IMPORTANT WORKS Durkheim, *The Division of Labor in Society* (1893), and *Suicide: A Study in Sociology* (1897); Park, Burgess, and John McKenzie, *The City* (1925); Thrasher, *The Gang* (1926); Shaw et al., *Delinquency Areas* (1925); Edwin Sutherland, *Criminology* (1924)

CORE IDEAS A person's place in the social structure determines his or her behavior. Disorganized urban areas are the breeding ground of crime. A lack of legitimate opportunities produces criminal subcultures. Socialization within the family, the school, and the peer group controls behavior.

MODERN OUTGROWTHS Strain Theory, Cultural Deviance Theory, Social Learning Theory, Social Control Theory, Social Reaction Theory, Labeling Theory

Émile Durkheim

Corbis/Bettmann

MULTIFACTOR/INTEGRATED THEORY

ORIGIN About 1930

FOUNDERS Sheldon and Eleanor Glueck

MOST IMPORTANT WORKS Sheldon and Eleanor Glueck: *Five Hundred Delinquent Women* (1934); *Later Criminal Careers* (1937); *Criminal Careers in Retrospect* (1943); *Juvenile Delinquents Grown Up* (1940); *Unraveling Juvenile Delinquency* (1950)

CORE IDEAS Crime is a function of environmental, socialization, physical, and psychological factors. Each makes an independent contribution to shaping and directing behavior patterns. Deficits in these areas of human development increase the risk of crime. People at risk for crime can resist antisocial behaviors if these traits and conditions can be strengthened.

MODERN OUTGROWTHS Developmental Theory, Life Course Theory, Latent Trait Theory

Harvard Law School Library
Sheldon and Eleanor Glueck

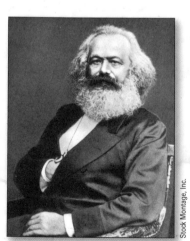
Stock Montage, Inc.
Karl Marx

MONEY NUMBERS

EVENING

1934   1839

1969

1951

0876

8904

1234

6085

0786

0639

MED

367

713

786

247

347

819

TENTH EDITION

CRIMINOLOGY
THEORIES, PATTERNS, AND TYPOLOGIES

Larry J. Siegel
University of Massachusetts, Lowell

WADSWORTH
CENGAGE Learning™

Australia • Brazil • Japan • Korea • Mexico • Singapore • Spain • United Kingdom • United States

WADSWORTH
CENGAGE Learning™

Criminology: Theories, Patterns, and Typologies, **Tenth Edition**
Larry J. Siegel

Senior Acquisitions Editor, Criminal Justice:
Carolyn Henderson Meier

Development Editor: Shelley Murphy

Assistant Editor: Meaghan Banks

Editorial Assistant: John Chell

Technology Project Manager: Bessie Weiss

Marketing Manager: Michelle Williams

Marketing Assistant: Jillian Myers

Marketing Communications Manager:
Tami Strang

Project Manager, Editorial Production:
Jennie Redwitz

Creative Director: Rob Hugel

Art Director: Maria Epes

Print Buyer: Becky Cross

Permissions Editor: Bobbie Broyer

Production Service: Linda Jupiter Productions

Text Designer: Tani Hasegawa

Photo Researcher: Linda Rill

Copy Editor: Lunaea Weatherstone

Proofreader: Debra Gates

Indexer: Medea Minnich

Illustrator: Scientific Illustrators

Cover Designer: Yvo Riezebos, Riezebos
Holzbaur Design Group

Cover Image: Naoki Okamoto/SuperStock

Compositor: International Typesetting and
Composition

For product information and technology assistance, contact us at
Cengage Learning Customer & Sales Support, 1-800-354-9706.

For permission to use material from this text or product,
submit all requests online at **www.cengage.com/permissions**.
Further permissions questions can be e-mailed to
permissionrequest@cengage.com.

Library of Congress Control Number: 2008932091

Student Edition:

ISBN-13: 978-0-495-60013-8
ISBN-10: 0-495-60013-X

Loose-Leaf Edition:

ISBN-13: 978-0-495-60030-5
ISBN-10: 0-495-60030-X

Wadsworth
10 Davis Drive
Belmont, CA 94002-3098
USA

Cengage Learning is a leading provider of customized learning solutions with office locations around the globe, including Singapore, the United Kingdom, Australia, Mexico, Brazil, and Japan. Locate your local office at **www.cengage.com/international**.

Cengage Learning products are represented in Canada by Nelson Education, Ltd.

To learn more about Wadsworth, visit **www.cengage.com/wadsworth**.

Purchase any of our products at your local college store or at our preferred online store **www.ichapters.com**.

Printed in China by China Translation & Printing Services Limited
2 3 4 5 6 7 12 11 10

ABOUT THE AUTHOR

Larry J. Siegel was born in the Bronx in 1947. While living on Jerome Avenue and attending City College of New York in the 1960s, he was swept up in the social and political currents of the time. He became intrigued with the influence contemporary culture had on individual behavior: Did people shape society or did society shape people? He applied his interest in social forces and human behavior to the study of crime and justice. After graduating CCNY, he attended the newly opened program in criminal justice at the State University of New York at Albany, earning both his M.A. and Ph.D. degrees there. After completing his graduate work, Dr. Siegel began his teaching career at Northeastern University, where he was a faculty member for nine years. After leaving Northeastern, he held teaching positions at the University of Nebraska–Omaha and Saint Anselm College in New Hampshire. He is currently a professor at the University of Massachusetts–Lowell. Dr. Siegel has written extensively in the area of crime and justice, including books on juvenile law, delinquency, criminology, criminal justice, and criminal procedure. He is a court certified expert on police conduct and has testified in numerous legal cases. The father of four and grandfather of three, Larry Siegel and his wife, Terry, now reside in Bedford, New Hampshire, with their two dogs, Watson and Cody.

BRIEF CONTENTS

CONTENTS

■■■■■■ **PART TWO**

THEORIES OF CRIME CAUSATION 93

Cc

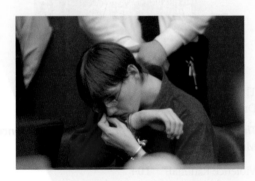

CHAPTER 11
Political Crime and Terrorism 334

CHAPTER 12
Property Crime 368

CHAPTER 13
Enterprise Crime: White-Collar and Organized Crime   394

CHAPTER 14
Public Order Crime: Sex and Substance Abuse   424

CHAPTER 15
Cyber Crime and Technology 466

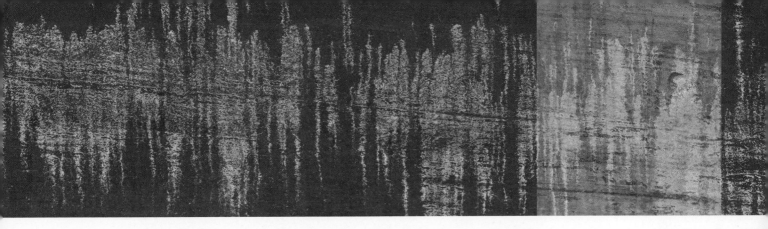

Introducing the Wadsworth Cengage Learning Criminal Justice Advisory Board

The entire Criminal Justice team at Wadsworth Cengage Learning wishes to express its sincere gratitude to the hardworking members of our Criminal Justice Advisory Board. This group of skilled, experienced instructors comes together once a year to further their driving mission, which can be summed up as follows:

> *This collaborative group of publishing professionals and instructors from traditional and nontraditional educational institutions is designed to foster development of exceptional educational and career opportunities in the field of criminal justice by providing direction and assistance to the faculty and administrators charged with training tomorrow's criminal justice professionals. The Advisory Board offers peer support and advice, consults from both the academic and publishing communities, and serves as a forum for creating and evolving best practices in the building of successful criminal justice programs.*

The members of our Advisory Board have the wisdom, expertise, and vision to set goals that empower students, setting them up to capitalize on the field's tremendous growth and expanding job opportunities. According to the U.S. Bureau of Labor Statistics, employment for correctional officers, law enforcement officers, investigators, and security officers is projected to increase at a rate of 9–26 percent over the next eight years. Add to that the growing number of jobs available in other parts of the criminal justice system—case officer, youth specialist, social services, and more—and one can begin to get a true sense of the vast employment opportunities in the field. Helping today's students unlock the door to exciting and secure futures is the ultimate goal of everyone associated with the Wadsworth Cengage Learning Criminal Justice Advisory Board.

Included on the board are faculty and administrators from schools such as:

Brown College

Florida Metropolitan University

Globe University/Minnesota School of Business

Hesser College

Kaplan University

Keiser University

John Jay College of Criminal Justice

Rasmussen College

South University

Western Career College

Western Carolina University

Westwood College

Again, the Wadsworth Cengage Learning Criminal Justice Team would like to extend our personal and professional thanks for all that the Advisory Board has enabled us to accomplish over the past few years. We look forward to continuing our successful collaboration in the years ahead.

We are always looking to add like-minded instructors to the Advisory Board; if you would like to be considered for inclusion on the Board, please contact Michelle Williams (michelle.williams@cengage.com).

Preparing Students for a Lifetime of Service

PREFACE

For the past year or so, my family and I, along with the rest of the nation, have debated the behavior of Michael Vick. On August 27, 2007, the star quarterback pleaded guilty to charges of criminal conspiracy stemming from his involvement in a dog-fighting ring. Vick had been accused of torturing and executing dogs who lost their matches. My family, dog lovers all, was shocked and dismayed by the accusations. As we debated the case over dinner, my wife and some of my kids glanced over at our two beloved cockapoos, Watson and Cody, and demanded that Vick receive the harshest punishment possible. My son Andrew sagely observed that we were eating cheeseburgers at the time. "Isn't it a bit hypocritical to consume the flesh of dead animals, killed for our pleasure, and condemn the behavior of someone accused of killing animals?" And, he went on to note, some of our friends in New Hampshire are hunters who routinely shoot and kill moose and deer. "Why is it legal to hunt and kill defenseless animals if we are so concerned about animal welfare?" My wife, Terry, was swayed by the argument and announced that she was becoming a vegan. The conversation turned to fishing, fox hunting, raising chinchillas for fur coats, bull fighting, and boiling lobsters alive (the latter activity a staple of New England culture). Why were these practices, which involved the killing of innocent creatures, legal while dog fighting was condemned and its practitioners imprisoned? While some have argued that it is the method of killing that counts, I am not sure that the victims would agree.

The Vick case raises many important issues. As our dinner-time debate suggests, there are still many questions on the definition of what is legal versus criminal, moral versus immoral. Who defines morality? Where do you draw the line between legal and criminal activity, and who gets to draw it? Even if Vick engaged in conduct that is widely considered immoral, should he have been punished as a criminal and sent to prison? One of the richest athletes in the United States before his conviction, on July 7, 2008, Vick was forced to file for bankruptcy. Is being ruined financially and forced to serve time in prison fair and just punishment? Before you answer, be aware that the latest federal data indicates that almost half of all people convicted of violent felonies did not go to prison; about 24 percent spent time in a local jail and another 20 percent were allowed to remain in the community on probation; 30 percent of drug offenders got a

© AP Images/Gerald Herbert

probation-only sentence. If murders, rapists, and drug traffickers are granted probation, should Vick have gone to prison? And when he is eventually released, should he be allowed to return to the NFL? Can someone like Vick be restored to society and, if so, does he deserve restoration?

In addition, the Vick case raises questions about the motivation and cause of crime: Why would a talented football star such as Michael Vick, who had recently signed a contract for more than $100 million, risk everything in an illegal and depraved dog-fighting scheme? Was it a product of a troubled childhood? Improper and damaged socialization? An impulsive personality? Or had he simply chosen to engage in risky and reckless behavior because he thought he was above the law?

The general public is greatly concerned by cases such as the Michael Vick incident. I too share this concern. For the past 38 years I have been able to channel my personal interest into a career as a teacher of criminology. In 1971, fresh out of grad school, I began as an assistant professor at Northeastern University in Boston. I first stepped into a classroom at the ripe old age of 23 and have been teaching ever since. This semester I have 160 students in my crim class at UML. My goal in writing this text is to help my students and others generate the same curiosity about issues of crime and justice. What could be more fascinating than a field of study that deals with such wide-ranging topics as the motivation for mass murder, the effects of violent media on young people, drug abuse, and organized crime? Criminology changes constantly with the release of major research studies,

Supreme Court rulings, and governmental policy. Its dynamism and diversity make it an important and engrossing area of study.

Because interest in crime and justice is so great and so timely, this text is designed to review these ongoing issues and cover the field of criminology in an organized and comprehensive manner. It is meant as a broad overview of the field, designed to whet the reader's appetite and encourage further and more in-depth exploration. Several major themes recur throughout the book.

Competing Viewpoints In every chapter an effort is made to introduce students to the diversity of thought that characterizes the discipline. One reason that the study of criminology is so important is that debates continue over the nature and extent of crime and the causes and prevention of criminality. Some experts view criminal offenders as society's victims, unfortunate people who are forced to violate the law because they lack hope of legitimate opportunity. Others view aggressive, antisocial behavior as a product of mental and physical abnormalities, present at birth or soon after, which are stable over the life course. Still another view is that crime is a function of the rational choice of greedy, selfish people who can only be deterred though the threat of harsh punishments. All chapters explore how different theoretical frameworks cover different aspects of criminology. Students are helped in this regard by Concept Summaries that compare different viewpoints, showing both their main points and their strengths.

Critical Thinking It is important for students to think critically about law and justice and to develop a critical perspective toward the social institutions and legal institutions entrusted with crime control. Throughout the book, students are asked to critique research highlighted in boxed material and to think outside the box. To aid in this task, each chapter ends with a Thinking Like a Criminologist section, which presents a scenario that can be analyzed with the help of material found in the chapter.

Diversity Diversity is a key issue in criminology, and the text attempts to integrate issues of racial, ethnic, gender, and cultural diversity throughout. The book includes material on international issues, such as the use of the death penalty abroad, as well as gender issues such as the rising rate of female criminality. To help with the coverage of diversity issues, Race, Culture, Gender, and Criminology boxes focus on diversity issues. For example, in Chapter 10 there is a feature on the honor killing of women and girls that discusses how young girls are victimized because of cultural values that may seem cruel and unusual. Comparative Criminology boxes focus on criminological issues abroad or compare the justice process in the United States with that of other nations. For example, in Chapter 1 there is a feature covering international crime trends.

Currency and Immediacy Throughout the book, every attempt is made to use the most current research and to cover the most immediate topics. The idea is to show students the major trends in criminological research and justice

policy. Most people who use the book have told me that this is one of its strongest features. I have attempted to present current research in a balanced fashion, though this sometimes can be frustrating to students. For example, while some experts find that defendants' race negatively affects sentencing in the criminal courts, other criminologists reach an opposing stance, concluding that race has little influence. Which position is correct? While it is comforting to reach an unequivocal conclusion about an important topic, sometimes it is simply not possible. In an effort to be objective and fair, each side of important criminological debates is presented in full. Throughout the text, Criminological Enterprise boxes review important research in criminology. For example, in Chapter 2 a box entitled "Explaining Crime Trends" discusses research that helps explain why crime rates rise and fall.

Social Policy A focus on social policy throughout the book helps students see how criminological theory has been translated into crime prevention programs. To support this theme, Policy and Practice in Criminology boxes are included throughout the text. These features show how criminological ideas and research can be put into action. For example, in Chapter 15 there is a box entitled "Biometric Technology" which discusses the use of technology to identify criminal suspects.

In sum, the primary goals in writing this text are as follows:

1. To provide students with a thorough knowledge of criminology and show its diversity and intellectual content

2. To be as thorough and up to date as possible

3. To be objective and unbiased

4. To describe current theories, crime types, and methods of social control, and analyze their strengths and weaknesses

5. To show how criminological thought has influenced social policy

TOPIC AREAS

The tenth edition has undergone significant revision, one important facet of which being a new chapter covering political crime and terrorism. The book is divided into three major parts.

Part One provides a framework for studying criminology. The first chapter defines the field and discusses its most basic concepts: the definition of crime, the component areas of criminology, the history of criminology, the concept of criminal law, and the ethical issues that confront the field. Chapter 2 covers criminological research methods and the nature, extent, and patterns of crime. Chapter 3 is devoted to the concept of victimization, including the nature of victims, theories of victimization, and programs designed to help crime victims.

Part Two contains six chapters that cover criminological theory: why do people behave the way they do? Why do they commit crimes? Theories that attempt to answer these questions focus on choice (Chapter 4); biological and psychological traits (Chapter 5); social structure and culture (Chapter 6); social process and socialization (Chapter 7); social conflict (Chapter 8); and human development (Chapter 9).

Part Three is devoted to the major forms of criminal behavior. The chapters in this section cover violent crime (Chapter 10); political crime and terrorism (Chapter 11); common theft offenses (Chapter 12); white-collar and organized crimes (Chapter13); public order crimes, including sex offenses and substance abuse (Chapter 14); and cyber crime (Chapter 15).

GOALS AND OBJECTIVES

The tenth edition has been carefully structured to cover relevant material in a comprehensive, balanced, and objective fashion. Every attempt has been made to make the presentation of material interesting and contemporary. No single political or theoretical position dominates the text; instead, the many diverse views that are contained within criminology and characterize its interdisciplinary nature are presented. While the text includes analysis of the most important scholarly works and scientific research reports, it also includes a great deal of topical information on recent cases and events, such as recent cyber scams, the Virginia Tech shooting, and the effects of excessive CEO pay.

NEW IN THE TENTH EDITION

■ **Chapter 1, Crime and Criminology,** now begins with the story of Douglas Richard Stevens, who used the Internet to arrange sexual meetings with underage minors. The chapter contains new developments in law and theory, including research on the falsely convicted. There is a new Profiles in Crime box entitled "The Mother of All Snakeheads," which talks about the activities of Cheng Chui Ping, one of the most powerful underworld figures in New York.

■ **Chapter 2, The Nature and Extent of Crime,** begins with a discussion of Tommy Henderson, a career criminal whose crime spree resulted in multiple deaths. Killers such as Henderson convince the public that crime is a major social problem despite a decade-long drop in the crime rate. A Profiles in Crime box details the fraud schemes of Ronald and Mary Evano, who turned dining in restaurants into a profitable, albeit illegal, scam. There are new sections on data collection techniques in criminology, including data mining and systematic review. UCR, NCVS, and self-report data are all updated, and recent trends in crime explored.

■ **Chapter 3, Victims and Victimization,** begins with the tragic story of Imette St. Guillen, a young graduate student who was killed after stopping in for a late-night drink in The Falls bar, a popular New York City nightspot. The chapter contains new information on the suffering experienced by rape survivors and the long-term stress experienced by crime victims. In addition, it covers the Justice for All Act of 2004, Stand Your Ground laws, and victims' rights in Europe. A Profiles in Crime box looks at Jesse Timmendequas and Megan's Law.

■ **Chapter 4, Rational Choice Theory,** begins with the story of Michael Pickens, son of a billionaire, who got involved in a fraudulent stock market scheme. The Profiles in Crime box "Looting the Public Treasury" tells the story of Albert Robles, a mayor, councilman, and deputy city manager of South Gate, California, who used his position for personal gain. A Comparative Criminology feature called "Reducing Crime through Surveillance" discusses the use of mechanical devices such as closed-circuit TV to control crime. There is new material on selecting the targets of crime, whether murder can be rational, and situational crime prevention efforts including how efforts to ban alcohol influence DWI arrests. Research looks at how perception of risk shapes criminal choices and the effect of deterrence strategies on crime rates.

■ **Chapter 5, Trait Theories,** begins with the story of Seung-Hui Cho, who methodically took the lives of 32 people— 27 students and 5 professors—at Virginia Tech before taking his own life. A Profiles in Crime box looks at the case of Andrea Yates, a young mother who killed her children in a fit of depression. New information on international studies measuring the effects of diet on crime is included, as is recent research on the effects of maternal smoking and alcohol consumption on children's development. There is also new research on the effects of environmental pollution on behavior, and new studies on the effect of depression and mental illness on crime are discussed.

■ **Chapter 6, Social Structure Theories,** begins with a vignette on gangs in Los Angeles. There is a Profiles in Crime box on life in the drug trade, as well as information on the neighborhood context of policing and the association of neighborhood structure and parenting processes. There are new data on the evolving wealth structure of society and the issue of race and poverty. Recent research on the effects of exposure to community violence and neighborhood disadvantage is reported. And the chapter covers the latest research on topics such as fear of crime, and collective and street efficacy.

■ **Chapter 7, Social Process Theories,** opens with a vignette on the case of Genarlow Wilson, a young man imprisoned for consensual sex with a minor. There is a Profiles in Crime box on Jesse James Hollywood, whose story was made into a motion picture called *Alpha Dog*. Two new Criminological Enterprise features are presented: "When Being Good is Bad," which is an expansion of neutralization theory, and "Storylines," which looks at the stories criminals tell to understand their motivations. There is new research on childhood predictors of criminality, the effects of bad parenting, parent–adolescent processes and reduced risk for delinquency, and the influence of fathers on male delinquency.

- **Chapter 8, Social Conflict, Critical Criminology, and Restorative Justice,** begins with a vignette on executive pay trends. There is a Profiles in Crime box on Mumia Abu-Jamal, an activist accused of a murder many supporters believe he did not commit; a Comparative Criminology feature on restoration programs around the world; and new research on genocide, feminist criminology, and race and crime.

- **Chapter 9, Developmental Theories: Life Course and Latent Trait,** now opens with a vignette focusing on Troy Victorino, the notorious Xbox Killer. New research covers such issues as the effects of family instability, self-control and victimization, cultural invariance, and the development of self-control.

- **Chapter 10, Interpersonal Violence,** now focuses squarely on interpersonal violence, including common law crimes such as murder and rape, and emerging forms of violence such as work place violence, hate crimes, and stalking. It begins with a vignette on the Duke Lacrosse scandal, in which three young men were charged with a rape they did not commit but which still made national headlines. There is a new Race, Culture, Gender, and Criminology box on the honor killing of women and girls. The chapter includes new research on violence and residential choice, the violent brain, and men who sexually abuse their own partners. A new analysis of the roots of serial murder and stalking is provided, as well as new sections on psychological and social learning views of rape causation. The section on rape law changes has been updated with a new section on consent.

- **Chapter 11, Political Crime and Terrorism,** is a new chapter added because of the topic's salience and importance. It begins with a vignette on the assassination of Benazir Bhutto. There are two Profiles in Crime features, one on Adam Gadahn, also known as Azzam the American, the first American to be charged with treason in nearly 50 years, and another on spymaster Aldrich Hazen Ames. There is a Criminological Enterprise feature on the use of torture. Some of the new sections cover such political crimes as voter fraud, espionage, and treason. The coverage of the nature and cause of terrorism is expansive, and the chapter delves into material on the history of terrorism, comparing terrorists to guerillas and insurgents, and what is being done to thwart terror attacks.

- **Chapter 12, Property Crime,** begins with the story of a thief who specialized in stealing rare maps. Two Profiles in Crime boxes have been added, one called "Invasion of the Body Snatchers" about people who stole body parts from corpses for resale, and another on credit card cons. There is a new Criminological Enterprise feature on the confessions of a dying thief. The

chapter contains new material on street life and auto theft and on embezzlement. A new section called "Planning to Burgle" shows how burglars decide to commit their crimes.

- **Chapter 13, Enterprise Crime: White-Collar and Organized Crime,** has expanded coverage and more focus on white-collar crime than in the previous edition. We begin the chapter with a new vignette on Medicare fraud, and there is a new Profiles in Crime box called "When the Flu Bug Bites" about a scam to sell fake flu shots. We discuss the federal government's Operation Bullpen, aimed at stopping chiseling in the sports memorabilia industry (including photos with fake autographs), as well as international bribery used to secure business contracts. There is new material on influence peddling in government and an update on the Tyco and Enron cases. Lastly, a new section covers health care fraud and the rationalization/neutralization theory of white-collar crime.

- **Chapter 14, Public Order Crime: Sex and Substance Abuse,** now opens with the story of Eliot Spitzer, former governor of New York, and his involvement with a high-priced call girl ring. There is more information on the international trade in prostitution and the coercion of women from the former Soviet Union into prostitution. A Profiles in Crime covers John Evander Couey and the Jessica Lunsford murder case. And the data on drug use and abuse and drug control strategies have all been updated. A Policy and Practice in Criminology box reviews drug courts.

- **Chapter 15, Cyber Crime and Technology,** begins with a new vignette that tells of an international Internet fraud scheme. Biometric identification is the topic of a Policy and Practice in Criminology box. There are new sections on cyber bullying, computer fraud, distribution of illegal sexual material, distribution of dangerous drugs, cyber spying, international treaties to control cyber crime, using the Internet to fund terrorist activities, and whether cyber terrorism is a real threat. There is a new Concept Summary on types of cyber crime. New exhibits cover the most common Internet fraud schemes and the crimes of reshipping and swatting. The entire section on law enforcement technology has been updated with a section titled "Contemporary IT Programs."

FEATURES

This text contains different kinds of pedagogy to help students analyze material in greater depth and also link it to other material in the book.

- **Profiles in Crime** are new to the tenth edition and are designed to present students with case studies of actual criminals and crimes to help illustrate the position or views within the chapter. Among the cases covered are those of super spy Aldrich Ames in Chapter 11 and "When the Flu Bug Bites" in Chapter 13, which discusses a scheme to sell fake flu shots to unsuspecting victims.

▌ **The Criminological Enterprise** boxes review important issues in criminology and reflect the major sub-areas of the field: measuring crime, creating theory, crime typologies, legal theory, and penology. For example, in Chapter 5, a Criminological Enterprise box focuses on the important issue of whether there is a link between violent media and violent crime.

▌ **Policy and Practice in Criminology** boxes show how criminological ideas and research can be put into action. For example, in Chapter 2, "Should Guns Be Controlled?" examines the pros and cons of the gun control debate, an issue that is being re-examined in the aftermath of the Virginia Tech killings.

▌ **Race, Culture, Gender, and Criminology** boxes cover issues of racial, sexual, and cultural diversity. For example, in Chapter 6 "There Goes the Neighborhood" discusses the work and thoughts of William Julius Wilson, one of the nation's leading sociologists.

▌ **Comparative Criminology** boxes compare criminological policies, trends, and practices in the United States and abroad. For example, in Chapter 13 a Comparative Criminology box looks at Russian organized crime.

▌ **Critical Thinking** questions accompany each of the boxed features, and more are presented at the end of each chapter to help students develop their analytical abilities.

▌ **Connections** are short inserts that help link the material to other areas covered in the book. For example, a Connections box in Chapter 14 links media violence to the material in the Chapter 5 discussion of whether watching violent media causes violence.

▌ **Chapter Outlines** provide a roadmap to text coverage and serves as a useful review tool.

▌ **Chapter Objectives** are presented at the beginning of each chapter to help students get the most out of the chapter coverage.

▌ **Thinking Like a Criminologist** sections at the end of each chapter present challenging questions or issues that students must use their criminological knowledge to answer or confront. Applying the information learned in the text will help students begin to "think like criminologists." Each of these applications now includes a **Writing Exercise.**

▌ **Doing Research on the Web** sections also accompany every Thinking Like a Criminologist and guide students to web pages that will help them answer the criminological questions posed.

▌ Each chapter ends with a **Chapter Summary** and a list of **Key Terms.**

ANCILLARIES

A number of supplements are provided by Wadsworth to help instructors use *Criminology: Theories, Patterns, and Typologies* in their courses and to aid students in preparing for exams. Supplements are available to qualified adopters. Please consult your local sales representative for details.

For the Instructor

Instructor's Resource Manual with Test Bank An improved and completely updated *Instructor's Resource Manual with Test Bank* has been developed by Joanne Ziembo-Vogl of Grand Valley State University. The manual includes learning objectives, a chapter summary, detailed chapter outlines, key terms, an explanation of the chapter's themes, class discussion exercises, and worksheets. Each chapter's test bank contains questions in multiple-choice, true-false, fill-in-the-blank, and essay formats, with a full answer key. The test bank is coded to the learning objectives that appear in the main text, and includes the page numbers in the main text where the answers can be found. Finally, each question in the test bank has been carefully reviewed by experienced criminal justice instructors for quality, accuracy, and content coverage. Our Instructor Approved seal, which appears on the front cover, is our assurance that you are working with an assessment and grading resource of the highest caliber.

Lesson Plans New to this edition, the instructor-created lesson plans bring accessible, masterful suggestions to every lesson. Created by Joanne Ziembo-Vogl of Grand Valley State University, each lesson plan includes a sample syllabus, learning objectives, lecture notes, discussion topics, in-class activities, tips for classroom presentation of chapter material, a detailed lecture outline, and assignments. Lesson plans are available on the PowerLecture resource and the instructor website, or by e-mailing your local representative and asking for a download of the eBank files.

Power Lecture with JoinIn™ and ExamView® This one-stop digital library and presentation tool includes preassembled Microsoft® PowerPoint® lecture slides created by Sharon Tracy at Georgia Southern University. In addition to the full *Instructor's Resource Manual with Test Bank,* PowerLecture also includes JoinIn, ExamView, lesson plans, and video and image libraries.

WebTutor™ ToolBox on Blackboard® and WebCT® Jumpstart your course with customizable, rich, text-specific content within your Course Management System. Whether you want to Web-enable your class or put an entire course online, WebTutor delivers. WebTutor offers a wide array of resources including media assets, test bank, practice quizzes, and additional study aids. Visit www.cengage.com/webtutor to learn more.

Companion Website The book-specific website at www .cengage.com/criminaljustice/siegel offers students a variety of study tools and useful resources such as quizzing, web links, Internet exercises, glossary, flash cards, and more.

Wadsworth Criminal Justice Video Library The Library offers an exciting collection of videos to enrich lectures. Qualified adopters may select from a wide variety of professionally prepared videos covering various aspects of policing, corrections, and other areas of the criminal justice system. The selections include videos from *Films for the Humanities and Sciences*, *Court TV* videos that feature provocative one-hour court cases to illustrate seminal high-profile cases in depth, *A&E American Justice Series* videos, *National Institute of Justice: Crime File* videos, *ABC®* News videos, and *Moments in Time: The Oral History of Criminology and Criminal Justice*.

For the Student

Study Guide An extensive study guide has been developed and updated for this edition by Joanne Ziembo-Vogl of Grand Valley State University. Because students learn in different ways, the guide includes a variety of pedagogical aids to help them, as well as integrated art and figures from the main text. Each chapter is outlined and summarized, major terms and figures are defined, and worksheets and self-tests are provided.

CengageNOW™ CengageNOW is an easy-to-use online resource that helps students study in less time to get the grade they want—NOW. CengageNOW Personalized Study (a diagnostic study tool containing valuable text-specific resources) lets students focus on just what they don't know and learn more in less time to get a better grade. If the textbook does not include an access code card, students can go to www.ichapters.com to purchase CengageNOW.

Audio Study Tools Now students have a quick, convenient, and enjoyable way to study—and they can do it while doing all the other things they need to do. In just ten minutes, students can review each assigned chapter of the textbook. Audio practice quizzes help students figure out what they know and what they don't. Audio Study Tools will be available for sale at www.ichapters.com, both in complete versions and by the chapter or concept.

Current Perspectives: Readings from InfoTrac® College Edition These readers, designed to give students a closer look at special topics in criminal justice, include free access to InfoTrac College Edition. The timely articles are selected by experts in each topic from within InfoTrac College Edition. They are available for free when bundled with the text and include the following titles:

- *Cyber Crime*
- *Victimology*
- *Juvenile Justice*

- *Racial Profiling*
- *White-Collar Crime*
- *Terrorism and Homeland Security*
- *Public Policy and Criminal Justice*
- *New Technologies and Criminal Justice*
- *Ethics in Criminal Justice*
- *Forensics and Criminal Investigation*

Crime Scenes: An Interactive Criminal Justice CD-ROM, Version 2.0 Recipient of several *New Media Magazine* Invision Awards, this interactive CD-ROM allows students to take on the roles of investigating officer, lawyer, parole officer, and judge in excitingly realistic scenarios. An instructor's manual for the CD-ROM is also available.

Careers in Criminal Justice Website *Expands students' careers knowledge*! The site includes new video interviews and profiles, and also gives students access to current information on job requirements, training, salary, and benefits for CJ's hottest new careers.

Seeking Employment in Criminal Justice and Related Fields Written by J. Scott Harr and Kären Hess, this practical book helps students develop a search strategy to find employment in criminal justice and related fields. Each chapter includes "insider's views," written by individuals in the field and addressing issues such as promotions and career planning.

Guide to Careers in Criminal Justice This concise 60-page booklet provides a brief introduction to the exciting and diverse field of criminal justice. Students can learn about opportunities in law enforcement, courts, and corrections and how they can go about getting these jobs.

Internet Guide for Criminal Justice, Second Edition Internet beginners will appreciate this helpful booklet. With explanations and the vocabulary necessary for navigating the Web, it features customized information on criminal justice–related websites and presents Internet project ideas.

Internet Activities for Criminal Justice, Second Edition This completely revised 96-page booklet shows how to best utilize the Internet for research through searches and activities.

Criminology: An Introduction Using MicroCase ExplorIt, Fourth Edition This book features real data to help students examine major criminological theories such as social disorganization, deviant associations, and others. It has 12 one-hour exercises and five independent projects in all, covering dozens of topic areas and offering an exciting view of criminological research.

ACKNOWLEDGMENTS

The preparation of this text would not have been possible without the aid of my colleagues, who helped by reviewing the previous editions and giving me important suggestions for improvement. Reviewers for the tenth edition were:

Richard Dewey, *Indian River Community College*
Richard Felson, *Pennsylvania State University*
Darrell Mills, *Pima Community College*
David Murphy, *Western Oregon University*
Craig Robertson, *University of North Alabama*
Deanna Shields, *Fairmont Banks University*
Tracey Steele, *Wright State University*
Ronald Thrasher, *Oklahoma State University*
Michael Witkowski, *University of Detroit Mercy*

My colleagues at Wadsworth Cengage Learning did their typically outstanding job of aiding me in the preparation of the text and gave me counseling and support. My editor, Carolyn Henderson Meier, is a real pro and gave me a lot of TLC, while I only gave her GRIEF. The fantastic Shelley Murphy is a terrifically superb development editor who is always there for me. I really could not do another edition without her. My photo editor and friend Linda Rill did a thorough, professional job in photo research as usual. I have worked with Linda Jupiter, the book's production editor, many times, and she is always great and also a close friend and confidant. The fabulous Jennie Redwitz somehow pulls everything together as production manager, and Michelle Williams is the quintessential marketing manager. All in all a terrific team!

Larry Siegel
Bedford, New Hampshire

CONCEPTS OF CRIME, LAW, AND CRIMINOLOGY

How is crime defined? How much crime is there, and what are the trends and patterns in the crime rate? How many people fall victim to crime, and who is likely to become a crime victim? How did our system of criminal law develop, and what are the basic elements of crimes? What is the science of criminology all about?

These are some of the core issues that will be addressed in the first three chapters of this text. Chapter 1 introduces students to the field of criminology: its nature, area of study, methodologies, and historical development. Concern about crime and justice has been an important part of the human condition for more than 5,000 years, since the first criminal codes were set down in the Middle East. Although criminology—the scientific study of crime—is considered a modern science, it has existed for more than 200 years. Chapter 1 introduces students to one of the key components of criminology—the development of criminal law. It also discusses the social history of law, the purpose of law, and how law defines crime. Chapter 2 focuses on the acquisition of crime data, crime rate trends, and observable patterns within the crime rate. Chapter 3 is devoted to victims and victimization. Topics include the affects of victimization, the cause of victimization, and efforts to help crime victims.

Crime and Criminology

On December 7, 2005, Douglas Richard Stevens, 53, of Ontario, Canada, began communicating online with "Jane," whom he believed had a ten-year-old daughter named Mary. Using the screen name "ontm4momanddaughter," Stevens told "Jane" that he wanted to engage in sexual acts with "Mary" and bragged about previous conquests of girls he met online. He arranged to meet "Jane" and "Mary" in Atlanta so that he could sexually molest "Mary." When he arrived, federal law enforcement agents arrested Stevens in a restaurant parking lot. "Jane" and "Mary" never existed and were in fact identities created and used by an undercover FBI agent working as part of the FBI's Safe Child Task Force, designed to lure predators such as Stevens. He was indicted by a federal grand jury in January 2006 on charges that included using a computer to entice a minor to engage in sexual activity and traveling across state lines to engage in sexual acts with the minor. Stevens pleaded guilty to both counts and on June 9, 2006, he was sentenced to 12 years in prison.[1]

The Stevens case illustrates the evolution of criminal behavior in contemporary society. The computer and Internet have enabled people to engage in criminal activities unknown a decade ago. Besides crimes like the one Stevens committed, these range from identity theft to online securities fraud.

The reach of crime has become truly international, creating new challenges for law enforcement authorities. The questions about crime and its control raised by the Stevens case and others have spurred interest in criminology, an academic discipline that uses the scientific method to study the nature, extent, cause, and control of criminal behavior. Unlike political figures and media commentators—whose opinions about crime may be colored by personal experiences, biases, and election concerns—criminologists remain objective as they study crime and its consequences.[2]

Criminology is a multidisciplinary science. In addition to criminology, criminologists hold degrees in a variety of diverse fields, including sociology, criminal justice, political science, psychology, public policy, economics, and the natural sciences.

For most of the twentieth century, criminology's primary orientation was sociological, but today it can be viewed as an integrated approach to the study of criminal behavior. How this field developed, its major components, and its relationship to crime law and deviance are some of the topics discussed in this chapter.

This text analyzes criminology and its major subareas of inquiry. It focuses on the nature and extent of crime, the causes of crime, and patterns of criminal behavior. This chapter introduces and defines criminology: What are its goals? What is its history? How do criminologists define crime? How do they conduct research? What ethical issues face those wishing to conduct criminological research?

WHAT IS CRIMINOLOGY?

Criminology is the scientific approach to studying criminal behavior. In their classic definition, preeminent criminologists Edwin Sutherland and Donald Cressey state:

> Criminology is the body of knowledge regarding crime as a social phenomenon. It includes within its scope the processes of making laws, of breaking laws, and of reacting toward the breaking of laws. . . . The objective of criminology is the development of a body of general and verified principles and of other types of knowledge regarding this process of law, crime, and treatment.[3]

Sutherland and Cressey's definition includes some of the most important areas of interest to criminologists:

- *Crime as a social phenomenon.* Although some criminologists believe that individual traits and characteristics may play some role in the cause of criminals' antisocial behavior, most believe that social factors play a role in the cause of crime. Even the most disturbed people are influenced by their environment, social interactions, and personal relationships.
- *The processes of making laws.* Sutherland and Cressey's definition recognizes the association between crime and the criminal law and shows how the law defines crime. How and why laws are created and why some are strengthened and others eliminated is of great interest to criminologists.
- *Of breaking laws and reacting toward the breaking of laws.* At its core, the purpose of criminology is to understand both the onset of crime and the most effective methods for its elimination. Why do people commit illegal acts, and what can be done to convince them—and others who are contemplating crime—that it is in their best interests to turn their back on criminality? These concepts are naturally bound together: it is impossible to effectively control crime unless we understand its cause.
- *Development of a body of general and verified principles.* Sutherland and Cressey recognize that criminology is a social science and criminologists must use the scientific method when conducting research. Criminologists are required to employ valid and reliable experimental designs and sophisticated data analysis techniques or else lose standing in the academic community.

Criminology and Criminal Justice

Although the terms *criminology* and *criminal justice* may seem similar, and people often confuse the two or lump them together, there are major differences between these fields of study. Criminology explains the etiology (origin), extent, and nature of crime in society, whereas criminal justice refers to the study of the agencies of social control—police, courts, and corrections. While criminologists are mainly concerned with identifying the suspected cause of *crime*, criminal justice scholars spend their time identifying effective methods of *crime control*.

Since both fields are crime-related, they do overlap. Some criminologists devote their research to justice and social control and are concerned with how the agencies of justice operate, how they influence crime and criminals, and how justice policies shape crime rates and trends. Conversely, criminal justice experts often want to design effective programs of crime prevention or rehabilitation and to do so must develop an understanding of the nature of crime and its causation. It is common, therefore, for criminal justice programs to feature courses on criminology and for criminology courses to evaluate the agencies of justice.

Criminology and Deviance

Criminology is also related to the study of deviant behaviors—those actions that depart from social norms, values, and beliefs. Included within the broad spectrum of deviant acts are behaviors ranging from violent crimes to joining a nudist colony. However, significant distinctions can be made between these two areas of study because many crimes are not unusual or deviant, and many deviant acts are neither illegal nor criminal.

Take, for instance, substance abuse. Selling and/or possessing recreational drugs, such as marijuana, may be illegal, but can it actually be considered deviant? A significant percentage of the population have used or are using drugs; more than half of all high school students have tried drugs before they graduate.[4] Therefore, it is erroneous to argue that all crimes are deviant behaviors that depart from the norms of society.

CRIMINOLOGY: CRIMINAL JUSTICE AND DEVIANCE

Criminology explores the etiology (origin), extent, and nature of crime in society. Criminologists are concerned with identifying the nature, extent, and cause of crime.

Criminal Justice

Criminal justice refers to the agencies of social control that handle criminal offenders. Criminal justice scholars engage in describing, analyzing, and explaining operations of the agencies of justice, specifically the police departments, courts, and correctional facilities. They seek more effective methods of crime control and offender rehabilitation.

Overlapping Areas of Concern

Criminal justice experts cannot begin to design effective programs of crime prevention or rehabilitation without understanding the nature and cause of crime. They require accurate criminal statistics and data to test the effectiveness of crime control and prevention programs.

Deviance

Deviance refers to the study of behavior that departs from social norms. Included within the broad spectrum of deviant acts are behaviors ranging from violent crimes to joining a nudist colony. Not all crimes are deviant or unusual acts, and not all deviant acts are illegal.

Overlapping Areas of Concern

Under what circumstances do deviant behaviors become crimes? When does sexually oriented material cross the line from merely suggestive to obscene and therefore illegal? If an illegal act becomes a norm, should society reevaluate its criminal status? There is still debate over the legalization and/or decriminalization of abortion, recreational drug use, possession of handguns, and assisted suicide.

Similarly, many deviant acts are not criminal even though they may be both disturbing and shocking to the conscience. Suppose a passerby witnesses someone floundering in the ocean and makes no rescue attempt. Most people would condemn the onlooker's coldhearted behavior as callous, immoral, and deviant. However, no legal action could be taken since a private citizen is not required by law to risk his or her own life to save another's. There is no legal requirement that a person rush into a burning building, brave a flood, or jump into the ocean to save someone from harm. They may be deviant and not share commonly held values, but according to the law, they are not criminals.

In sum, criminologists are concerned with the concept of deviance and its relationship to criminality, whereas those sociologists who study deviant behaviors often want to understand and/or identify the line that separates criminal from merely unusual behaviors. The shifting definition of deviant behavior is closely associated with our concepts of crime. The relationships among criminology, criminal justice, and deviance are illustrated in Concept Summary 1.1.

www The principal purpose of the **Office on National Drug Control Policy (ONDCP)** is to establish policies, priorities, and objectives for the nation's drug control program, the goals of which are to reduce illicit drug use, manufacturing, and trafficking; reduce drug-related crime and violence; and reduce drug-related health consequences. To read more about their efforts, access their website via academic.cengage.com/criminaljustice/siegel.

A BRIEF HISTORY OF CRIMINOLOGY

How did the study of criminology develop? It is actually a relatively new field of study. Although written criminal codes have existed for thousands of years, these were restricted to defining crime and setting punishments. What motivated people to violate the law remained a matter for conjecture.

During the early Middle Ages (1200–1400), superstition and fear of satanic possession dominated thinking. People who violated social norms or religious practices were believed to be witches or possessed by demons. The prescribed method for dealing with the possessed was burning at the stake, a practice that survived into the seventeenth century. Beginning in the mid-thirteenth century, the jurisdiction of central governments reached a significantly broader range of social behaviors. Human problems and conflicts began to be dealt with in a formalized and legal manner.[5] Nonetheless, superstition and harsh punishments did not end quickly. The authorities were on guard against Satan's offspring, who engaged in acts ranging from witchcraft to robbery. Between 1581 and 1590, Nicholas Remy, head of the Inquisition in the French province of Lorraine, ordered 900 sorcerers and witches burned to death; likewise, Peter Binsfield, the bishop of the German city of Trier, ordered the death of 6,500 people. An estimated 100,000 people were prosecuted throughout Europe for witchcraft during the sixteenth and seventeenth centuries. It was also commonly believed that some families produced offspring who were unsound or unstable and that social misfits were inherently damaged by reason of their "inferior blood."[6] It was common practice to use cruel tortures to extract confessions, and those convicted of violent or theft crimes suffered extremely harsh penalties, including whipping, branding, maiming, and execution. Almost all felons were punished with death; the law made little distinction between thieves and murderers.

Classical Criminology

During the eighteenth century, social philosophers such as Jeremy Bentham began to embrace the view that human behavior was a result of rational thought processes. According to Bentham's utilitarianism, people choose to act when, after weighing costs and benefits, they believe that their actions will bring them an increase in pleasure and a reduction of pain. It stands to reason that criminal behavior could be eliminated or controlled if would-be law violators could be convinced that the pain of punishment exceeds the benefits of crime. Cesare Beccaria (1738–1794) applied these principles to criminal behavior in his famous treatise, "On Crimes and Punishment." He agreed that people want to achieve pleasure and avoid pain. He suggested that harsh punishments and routine use of torture were inappropriate and excessive. If every felon were punished with death, he reasoned, there would be little incentive for criminals not to escalate the severity of their crimes. To deter crime, the pain of punishment must be administered in a fair, balanced, and proportionate amount, just enough to counterbalance the pleasure obtained from crime. Beccaria stated his famous theorem like this:

> In order for punishment not to be in every instance, an act of violence of one or many against a private citizen, it must be essentially public, prompt, necessary, the least possible in the given circumstances, proportionate to the crimes, and dictated by the laws.[7]

The writings of Beccaria and his followers form the core of what today is referred to as classical criminology. As originally conceived in the eighteenth century, classical criminology theory had several basic elements:

▌ In every society people have free will to choose criminal or lawful solutions to meet their needs or settle their problems.

▌ Criminal solutions can be very attractive because for little effort they hold the promise of a huge payoff.

▌ A person will choose not to commit crime only if they believe that the pain of expected punishment is greater than the promise of reward. This is the principle of deterrence.

During the Middle Ages, superstition and fear of satanic possession dominated thinking. People who violated social norms or religious practices were believed to be witches or possessed by demons. The prescribed method for dealing with the possessed was burning at the stake, a practice that survived into the seventeenth century. This painting, *The Trial of George Jacobs, August 5, 1692* by T. H. Matteson (1855), depicts the ordeal of Jacobs, a patriarch of Salem, Massachusetts. During the witch craze, he had ridiculed the trials, only to find himself accused, tried, and executed.

The Trial of George Jacobs, August 5, 1692 by T. H. Matteson (1855). Oil on Canvas 39×53 inches. #1.246 Peabody Essex Museum, Salem, MA

▌ In order to be an effective crime deterrent, punishment must be severe, certain, and swift enough to convince potential criminals that "crime does not pay."

This classical perspective influenced penal practices for more than 200 years. The law was made proportionate to crime so that the most serious offenses earned the harshest punishments. Executions were still widely used but slowly began to be employed for only the most serious crimes. The catchphrase was "let the punishment fit the crime."

As the nineteenth century was coming to a close, a new vision of the world challenged the validity of classical theory and presented an innovative way of looking at the causes of crime.

Nineteenth-Century Positivism

During the late nineteenth century, the scientific method was beginning to take hold in Europe. Rather than rely on pure thought and reason, contemporary scientists began to use careful observation and analysis of natural phenomena in their experiments. This movement inspired new discoveries in biology, astronomy, and chemistry. Charles Darwin's (1809–1882) discoveries on the evolution of man encouraged a nineteenth-century "cult of science." Darwin's discoveries encouraged other scholars to be certain that all human activity could be verified by scientific principles. If the scientific method could be applied to the study of the natural world, then why not use it to study human behavior?

Auguste Comte (1798–1857), considered the founder of sociology, applied scientific methods to the study of society. According to Comte, societies pass through stages that can be grouped on the basis of how people try to understand the world in which they live. People in primitive societies consider inanimate objects as having life (for example, the sun is a god); in later social stages, people embrace a rational, scientific view of the world. Comte called this final stage the positive stage, and those who followed his writings became known as positivists.

As we understand it today, positivism has two main elements:

▌ All true knowledge is acquired through direct observation and not through conjecture or belief. Statements that cannot be backed up by direct observation—for instance, "all babies are born innocent"—are invalid and worthless.

▌ The scientific method must be used if research findings are to be considered valid. This involves such steps as identifying problems, collecting data, forming hypotheses, conducting experiments, and interpreting results (see Exhibit 1.1).

According to the positivist tradition, social processes are a product of the measurable interaction between relationships and

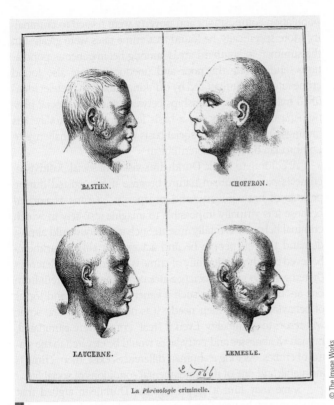

La *Phrénologie* criminelle.

Early positivists believed the shape of the skull was a key determinant of behavior. These drawings from the nineteenth century illustrate "typical" criminally shaped heads.

EXHIBIT 1.1

Elements of the Scientific Method

Observation
Identify problem and collect data and facts

Hypothesis
Develop a reasonable explanation to account for or predict the data observed and the facts collected

Test Hypothesis
Test hypothesis using control groups and experimental methods

Interpretation
Analyze data using accepted statistical techniques

Conclusion
Interpret data and verify or disprove accuracy of hypothesis

---

events. Human behavior therefore is a function of a variety of forces. Some are social, such as the effect of wealth and class; others are political and historical, such as war and famine. Other forces are more personal and psychological, such as an individual's brain structure and his or her biological makeup or mental ability. Each of these influences and shapes human behavior. People are neither born "good" nor "bad," and are neither "saints" nor "sinners." They are a product of their social and psychological traits, influenced by their upbringing and environment.

Biological Positivism The earliest "scientific" studies applying the positivist model to criminology were conducted by **physiognomists**, such as J. K. Lavater (1741–1801), who studied the facial features of criminals to determine whether the shape of ears, nose, and eyes and the distance between them were associated with antisocial behavior. **Phrenologists**, such as Franz Joseph Gall (1758–1828) and Johann K. Spurzheim (1776–1832), studied the shape of the skull and bumps on the head to determine whether these physical attributes were linked to criminal behavior. Phrenologists believed that external cranial characteristics dictate which areas of the brain control physical activity. The brain, they suggested, has 30 different areas or faculties that control behavior. The size of a brain could be determined by inspecting the contours of the skull—the larger the organ, the more active it was. The relative size of brain organs could be increased or decreased through exercise and self-discipline.[8] Though phrenology techniques and methods

are no longer practiced or taken seriously, these efforts were an early attempt to use a "scientific" method to study crime.

By the early nineteenth century, abnormality in the human mind was being linked to criminal behavior patterns.[9] Philippe Pinel (1745–1826), one of the founders of French psychiatry, claimed that some people behave abnormally even without being mentally ill. He coined the phrase *manie sans delire* to denote what today is referred to as a **psychopathic personality**. In 1812, an American, Benjamin Rush (1745–1813), described patients with an "innate preternatural moral depravity."[10] Another early criminological pioneer, English physician Henry Maudsley (1835–1918), believed that insanity and criminal behavior were strongly linked. He stated: "Crime is a sort of outlet in which their unsound tendencies are discharged; they would go mad if they were not criminals, and they do not go mad because they are criminals."[11] These early research efforts shifted attention to brain functioning and personality as the keys to criminal behavior. When Sigmund Freud's (1856–1939) work on the unconscious gained worldwide notoriety, the psychological basis of behavior was forever established.

In Italy, Cesare Lombroso (1835–1909), a physician who served much of his career in the Italian army, was studying the cadavers of executed criminals in an effort to scientifically determine whether law violators were physically different from people of conventional values and behavior.[12] Lombroso believed that serious offenders—those who engaged in repeated assault- or theft-related activities—were "born criminals" who had inherited a set of primitive physical traits that he referred to as **atavistic anomalies**. Physically, born criminals were throwbacks to more primitive savage people. Among the crime-producing traits Lombroso identified were enormous jaws and strong canine teeth common to carnivores and savages who devour raw flesh. These criminogenic traits can be acquired through *indirect heredity*, from a degenerate family whose members suffered from such ills as insanity, syphilis, and alcoholism, or *direct heredity*—being the offspring of criminal parents.

Lombroso's version of criminal anthropology was brought to the United States via articles and textbooks that adopted his ideas. He attracted a circle of followers who expanded on his vision of biological determinism. His scholarship helped stimulate interest in a criminal anthropology.[13] Ironically, his work was actually more popular in the United States than it was in Europe, and by the turn of the century, American social thinkers were discussing "the science of penology" and "the science of criminology."[14]

Lombroso's version of strict biological determinism is no longer taken seriously (later in his career even he recognized that not all criminals were biological throwbacks). Today, those criminologists who suggest that crime has some biological basis also believe that environmental conditions influence human behavior. Hence, the term biosocial theory has been coined to reflect the assumed link between physical and mental traits, the social environment, and behavior.

Social Positivism At the same time that biological positivists were conducting their experiments, other positivists were using social data to scientifically study the major changes that were taking place in nineteenth-century society and in so doing helping to create the field of sociology.

Sociology seemed an ideal perspective from which to study society. After thousands of years of stability, the world was undergoing a population explosion. The population estimated at 600 million in 1700 had risen to 900 million by 1800. People were flocking to cities in ever-increasing numbers. Manchester, England, had 12,000 inhabitants in 1760 and 400,000 in 1850; during the same period, the population of Glasgow, Scotland, rose from 30,000 to 300,000.

The development of machinery such as power looms had doomed cottage industries and given rise to a factory system in which large numbers of people toiled for extremely low wages. The spread of agricultural machines increased the food supply while reducing the need for a large rural workforce; these excess laborers further swelled city populations. At the same time, political, religious, and social traditions continued to be challenged by the scientific method.

Quetelet and Durkheim The application of sociological concepts to criminology can be traced to the works of pioneering sociologists L. A. J. (Adolphe) Quetelet (1796–1874) and (David) Émile Durkheim (1858–1917). Quetelet instigated the use of data and statistics in performing criminological research. Durkheim, considered one of the founders of sociology, defined crime as a normal and necessary social event.[15] These two perspectives have been extremely influential on modern criminology. L. A. J. (Adolphe) Quetelet was a Belgian mathematician who began (along with a Frenchman, Andre-Michel Guerry) what is known as the cartographic school of criminology.[16] This approach made use of social statistics that were being developed in Europe in the early nineteenth century. Statistical data provided important demographic information on the population, including density, gender, religious affiliations, and wealth.

Quetelet studied data gathered in France (called the *Comptes generaux de l'administration de la justice*) to investigate the influence of social factors on the propensity to commit crime. In addition to finding a strong influence of age and sex on crime, Quetelet also uncovered evidence that season, climate, population composition, and poverty were related to criminality. More specifically, he found that crime rates were greatest in the summer, in southern areas, among heterogeneous populations, and among the poor and uneducated. He also found crime rates to be influenced by drinking habits.[17] Quetelet identified many of the relationships between crime and social phenomena that still serve as a basis for criminology today. His findings that crime had a social basis were a direct challenge to Lombrosian biological determinism.

According to Émile Durkheim's vision of social positivism, crime is part of human nature because it has existed during periods of both poverty and prosperity.[18] Crime is *normal* because it is virtually impossible to imagine a society in which criminal behavior is totally absent. Such a society would almost demand that all people be and act exactly alike. Durkheim believed that the inevitability of crime is linked to the differences (heterogeneity) within society. Since people are so different from one another and employ such a variety of methods and forms of behavior to meet their needs, it is not surprising that some will resort to criminality. Even if "real" crimes were eliminated, human weaknesses and petty vices would be elevated to the status of crimes. As long as human differences exist, then, crime is inevitable and one of the fundamental conditions of social life.

Some may find it surprising, but Durkheim argued that crime can even be useful and, on occasion, healthy for society. He held that the existence of crime paves the way for social change and indicates that the social structure is not rigid or inflexible. Put another way, if such differences did not exist, it would mean that everyone behaved the same way and agreed on what is right and wrong. Such universal conformity would stifle creativity and independent thinking. To illustrate this concept, Durkheim offered the example of the Greek philosopher Socrates, who was considered a criminal and put to death for corrupting the morals of youth simply because he expressed ideas that were different from what people believed at that time.

Durkheim reasoned that another benefit of crime is that it calls attention to social ills. A rising crime rate can signal the need for social change and promote a variety of programs designed to relieve the human suffering that may have caused crime in the first place. In his influential book, *The Division of Labor in Society*, Durkheim described the consequences of the shift from a small, rural society, which he labeled "mechanical," to the more modern "organic" society with a large urban population, division of labor, and personal isolation.[19] From this shift flowed anomie, or norm and role confusion, a powerful sociological concept that helps describe the chaos and disarray accompanying the loss of traditional values in modern society. Durkheim's research on suicide indicated that anomic societies maintain high suicide rates; by implication, anomie might cause other forms of deviance as well.

The Chicago School and Beyond

The primacy of sociological positivism as the intellectual basis of criminology was secured by research begun in the early twentieth century by Albion W. Small (1854–1926), who organized the famed sociology department at the University of Chicago.

Referred to as the **Chicago School**, urban sociologists such as W. I. Thomas (1863–1947), Robert Ezra Park (1864–1944), Ernest W. Burgess (1886–1966), and Louis Wirth (1897–1952) pioneered research on the **social ecology** of the city. In 1915, Robert Ezra Park called for anthropological methods of description and observation to be applied to urban life.[20] He was concerned about how neighborhood structure developed, how isolated pockets of poverty formed, and what social policies could be used to alleviate urban problems. In response, Chicago School sociologists carried out an ambitious program of research and scholarship on urban topics, including criminal behavior patterns. Harvey Zorbaugh's *The Gold Coast and the Slum*,[21] Frederick Thrasher's *The Gang*,[22] and Louis Wirth's *The Ghetto*[23] are classic examples of objective, highly descriptive accounts of urban life. Park, with Ernest Burgess, studied the social ecology of the city and found that some neighborhoods formed so-called natural areas of wealth and affluence, while others suffered poverty and disintegration.[24] Regardless of their race, religion, or ethnicity, the everyday behavior of people living in these areas was controlled by the social and ecological climate.

This body of research inspired a generation of scholars to conclude that social forces operating in urban areas create "natural areas" for crime.[25] These urban neighborhoods maintain such a high level of poverty that critical institutions of socialization and control, such as the school and the family, begin to break down. While normally these social institutions can apply the social control necessary to restrain deviant behaviors, because they are weak, people are free to engage in exciting and enticing law-violating behaviors. As crime rate soars and residents are afraid to leave their homes at night, the neighborhood becomes *socially disorganized*—unable to apply social control. It can no longer muster the cohesion needed to protect its residents from crime, drug abuse, and violence. Criminal behavior is not then a function of personal traits or characteristics but is linked to environmental conditions that fail to provide residents with proper human relations and development.

The Chicago School sociologists initiated the view that crime and social ecological conditions were linked. Neighborhood conditions, and not individual pathologies, influence and shape the direction of crime rates.

Social-Psychological Views

During the 1930s and 1940s, another group of sociologists began to link social-psychological interactions to criminological behavior. Sociological **social psychology** (also known as psychological sociology) is the study of human interactions and relationships, and emphasizes such issues as group dynamics and socialization.

According to this school of thought, an individual's relationship to important social processes, such as education, family life, and peer relations, is the key to understanding human behavior. Poverty and social disorganization alone are not sufficient to cause criminal activity because, after all, many people living in the most deteriorated areas never commit criminal offenses. Something else was needed. Research seemed to show that children who grow up in homes wracked by conflict, attend inadequate schools, and/or associate with deviant peers become exposed to pro-crime forces.

In this view, **socialization**, rather than social structure, is key to understanding crime. But what element of socialization had the greatest effect? To Edwin Sutherland, the preeminent American criminologist, it was the learning of criminal attitudes from older, more experienced law violators. Crime was a learned behavior similar to any other, such as driving and playing sports. Another view, developed by Chicago-trained sociologist Walter Reckless, was that crime occurs when children develop an inadequate self-image, rendering them incapable of controlling their own misbehavior. Criminologists seized upon this concept of control and suggested that it was a key element in a criminal career: people became crime prone when social forces proved inadequate to control their behavior.

Both of these views—learning and control—link criminality to the failure of socialization, the interactions people have with the various individuals, organizations, institutions, and processes of society that help them mature and develop.

By mid-century, most criminologists had embraced either the structural/**ecological view** or the socialization view of crime. However, these were not the only positions on how social institutions influence human behavior. In Europe, the writings of another social thinker, Karl Marx (1818–1883), had pushed the understanding of social interaction in another direction and sowed the seeds for a new approach in criminology.[26]

Conflict and Crime

In his *Communist Manifesto* and other writings, Marx described the oppressive labor conditions prevalent during the rise of industrial capitalism. His observations of the economic structure convinced Marx that the character of every civilization is determined by its mode of production—the way its people develop and produce material goods (materialism). The most important relationship in industrial culture is between the owners of the means of production—the capitalist **bourgeoisie**—and the people who do the actual labor, the **proletariat**. The economic system controls all facets of human life; consequently, people's lives revolve around the means of production. The exploitation of the working class, he believed, would eventually lead to class conflict and the end of the capitalist system.

Though these writings laid the foundation for a Marxist-based criminology, decades passed before the impact of Marxist theory was realized. In the United States during the 1960s, social and political upheaval was fueled by the Vietnam War, the development of an antiestablishment counterculture movement, the civil rights movement, and the women's movement. Contemporary sociologists interested in applying Marx's principles to the study of crime began to analyze the socioeconomic conditions in the United States that promoted class conflict and crime. What emerged from this intellectual ferment was a Marxist-based critical criminology that indicted the capitalist economic system as producing the conditions that support a high crime rate. The critical view of crime developed in the 1960s has played a significant role in criminology ever since.

Integrating Diverse Perspectives: Developmental Criminology

During the twentieth century some criminologists began to integrate sociological, psychological, and economic elements into more complex developmental views of crime causation. Hans Eysenck published *Crime and Personality* in 1964 and proclaimed that antisocial behavior was linked to psychological conditions that were a product of heredity.[27] His controversial theory integrated social, biological, and psychological factors, a vision that upset the sociologists who controlled the field at that time.[28]

However, it is Sheldon (1896–1980) and Eleanor (1898–1972) Glueck who are today considered founders of the developmental branch of criminological theory. While at Harvard University in the 1930s, they conducted research on the careers of known criminals to determine the factors that predicted persistent offending, making extensive use of interviews and records in their elaborate comparisons of criminals and noncriminals.

connections

Because Eysenck's theory is essentially psychological, there will be more on his views in our Chapter 5 discussion of individual traits that produce crime. The Gluecks are revisited in Chapter 9, Developmental Theories, because they are more closely associated with that area of scholarship.

The Gluecks' research focused on early onset of delinquency as a harbinger of a criminal career: "[T]he deeper the roots of childhood maladjustment, the smaller the chance of adult adjustment."[29] They also noted the stability of offending careers: children who are antisocial early in life are the most likely to continue their offending careers into adulthood.

The Gluecks identified a number of personal and social factors related to persistent offending, the most important of which was family relations. This factor was considered in terms of quality of discipline and emotional ties with parents. The adolescent raised in a large, single-parent family of limited economic means and educational achievement was the most vulnerable to delinquency. Not restricting their analysis to social variables, the Gluecks measured such biological and psychological traits as body type, intelligence, and personality, and found that physical and mental factors also played a role in determining behavior. Children with low intelligence, who had a background of mental disease, and who had a powerful ("mesomorph") physique were the most likely to become persistent offenders.

Integrating biological, social, and psychological elements, the Gluecks' research suggested that the initiation and continuity of a criminal career was a developmental process influenced by both internal and external situations, conditions, and circumstances. While impressive, their research was heavily criticized by sociologists such as Edwin Sutherland who wanted to keep criminology within the field of sociology and feared or disparaged efforts to integrate biological or psychological concepts into the field.[30] Following Sutherland's critique, the Gluecks' work was ignored for quite some time until criminologists began to revisit their data and use contemporary methods to reanalyze their results. Today, upon reflection, it is now considered one of the foundations for the developmental theory model that is influential in the field today. Developmental models track the natural history of a criminal career. Rather than limiting their purpose to finding the root cause of crime, developmental criminologists examine the life course of a criminal career and ponder such issues as why people begin to commit crime, why they escalate their criminal activities, why they stop committing crime, and if they do stop, why some begin again. Contemporary developmental theories will be discussed in Chapter 9.

Contemporary Criminology

The various schools of criminology developed over the past 200 years. Though they have evolved, each continues to have an impact on the field. For example, classical theory has evolved into rational choice and deterrence theories. Rational choice theorists today argue that criminals are rational and use available information to decide if crime is a worthwhile undertaking. A sub-branch of rational choice theory, deterrence theory, holds that this choice is structured by the fear of punishment. Biological positivism has undergone similar transformation.

Although criminologists no longer believe that an inherited characteristic can by itself determine the course of behavior, some are convinced that behavior is altered when an individual's biological and psychological traits interact with environmental influences. Biological and psychological criminologists study the association between criminal behavior and such traits as diet, hormonal makeup, personality, and intelligence.

The sociological tradition, linked back to Quetelet and Durkheim, maintains that individuals' lifestyles and living conditions directly control their criminal behavior. Contemporary structural and social ecological theory holds that (a) a person's place in the social structure controls his or her behavioral choices, and (b) due to the ecological conditions they face, those at the bottom of the social structure, cannot achieve success and instead experience anomie, strain, failure, and frustration.

Sociological social psychology theories remain influential with contemporary criminologists. In their modern incarnation, they suggest that individuals' learning experiences and socialization directly control their behavior. In some cases, children learn to commit crime by interacting with and modeling their behavior after others they admire, whereas other criminal offenders are people whose life experiences have shattered their social bonds to society. These current social process theories will be discussed in Chapter 7.

The writings of Marx and his followers also continue to be influential. Many criminologists still view social and political conflict as the root cause of crime. The inherently unfair economic structure of the United States and other advanced capitalist countries is the engine that drives the high crime rate. Critical criminology, the contemporary form of Marxist/conflict theory, will be discussed further in Chapter 8. The developmental, multifaceted views of the Gluecks have morphed into a developmental criminology that has received a great deal of attention from contemporary criminologists; these views of crime are

CRIMINOLOGICAL PERSPECTIVES

The major perspectives of criminology focus on individual (biological, psychological, and choice theories), social (structural and process theories), political and economic (conflict theory), and multiple (developmental theory) factors.

Classical/Choice Perspective

Situational forces. Crime is a function of free will and personal choice. Punishment is a deterrent to crime.

Biological/Psychological Perspective

Internal forces. Crime is a function of chemical, neurological, genetic, personality, intelligence, or mental traits.

Structural Perspective

Ecological forces. Crime rates are a function of neighborhood conditions, cultural forces, and norm conflict.

Process Perspective

Socialization forces. Crime is a function of upbringing, learning, and control. Peers, parents, and teachers influence behavior.

Conflict Perspective

Economic and political forces. Crime is a function of competition for limited resources and power. Class conflict produces crime.

Developmental Perspective

Multiple forces. Biological, social-psychological, economic, and political forces may combine to produce crime.

---

analyzed in Chapter 9. Each of the major perspectives is summarized in Concept Summary 1.2.

WHAT CRIMINOLOGISTS DO: THE CRIMINOLOGICAL ENTERPRISE

Regardless of their theoretical orientation, criminologists are devoted to the study of crime and criminal behavior. As two noted criminologists, Marvin Wolfgang and Franco Ferracuti, put it: "A criminologist is one whose professional training, occupational role, and pecuniary reward are primarily concentrated on a scientific approach to, and study and analysis of, the phenomenon of crime and criminal behavior."[31]

Because criminologists have been trained in diverse fields, including sociology, criminal justice, political science, psychology, economics, and the natural sciences, criminology is today an interdisciplinary science. As a result, several subareas, reflecting different orientations and perspectives, are now contained within the broader arena of criminology. Taken together, these subareas make up the criminological enterprise. Criminologists may specialize in a subarea in the same way that psychologists might specialize in a subfield of psychology, such as cognition, development, perception, personality, psychopathology, or sexuality. Some of the more important criminological specialties are described next and summarized in Concept Summary 1.3 on page 16.

Criminal Statistics and Research Methodology

Those criminologists who devote themselves to criminal statistics and research methodology engage in a number of different tasks, including:

- Devising accurate methods of collecting crime data
- Using these tested methods to measure the amount and trends of criminal activity
- Using valid crime data to determine who commits crime and where it occurs
- Measuring the effect of social policy and social trends on crime rate changes
- Using crime data to design crime prevention programs and then measuring their effectiveness

The media loves to sensationalize crime and report on lurid cases of murder and rape. The general public is influenced by these stories, becoming fearful and altering their behavior to avoid victimization.[32] These news accounts, proclaiming crime waves, are often driven by the need to sell newspapers and/or increase TV viewership. Media accounts can be biased and inaccurate, and it is up to criminologists to set the record straight. Criminologists therefore try to create valid and reliable measurements of criminal behavior. They create techniques to access the records of police and court agencies and use sophisticated statistical methods to understand underlying patterns and trends. They develop survey instruments and then use them with large samples to determine the actual number of crimes being committed and the number of victims who suffer criminal violations: How many people are victims of crime, and what percentage reports the crime to police?

Criminologists are also interested in helping agents of the criminal justice system develop effective crime control policies that rely on accurate measurement of crime rates. A recent (2007) analysis by Jacqueline Cohen and her associates used advanced statistical techniques to predict where crime will take place, based on past criminal activities. Police departments can allocate patrol officers based on these predictions.[33]

The development of valid methods to measure crime and the accuracy of crime data are crucial aspects of the criminological enterprise. Without valid and reliable crime data sources, efforts to conduct research on crime and create criminological theories would be futile. It is also important to determine why crime rates vary across and within regions in order to gauge the association between social and economic forces and criminal activity. Criminal statistics may be used to make international comparisons in order to understand why some countries are crime free while others are beset by antisocial activities. This is the topic of the Comparative Criminology box "International Crime Trends" on the next page.

INTERNATIONAL CRIME TRENDS

In 1981, there were 88 residential burglaries per 1,000 households in the United States, compared with 41 per 1,000 households in England (including Wales). Ten years later, the U.S. rate had decreased to 54 per 1,000 households, but the English rate had increased to 68 per 1,000 households.

The English experience is not unique. Crime rates appear to be increasing around the world even as they decline in the United States. Asian countries now report an upswing in serious criminal activities. Cambodian officials are concerned with drug production/trafficking and human trafficking. Drugs produced in neighboring countries are being trafficked into Cambodia for local consumption, and drug traffickers routinely use Cambodia as a transit country for distributing narcotics around the world. The trafficking of Cambodian women into Thailand for sexual activities and the presence of a large number of Vietnamese women in Cambodia who are engaged in prostitution are also major concerns. Even Japan, a nation renowned for its low crime rate, has experienced an upswing in crime linked to its economy. Japan's economic bubble burst in 1990 and more than 15 years of economic stagnation has resulted in climbing numbers of reported crime.

Similarly, China, another relatively safe nation, has experienced an upswing in violent crime. Chinese police handled almost 5 million criminal cases in 2005, and though this number was down slightly from the previous year, the decline comes after years of steady increases. And though crime declined in general, theft and robbery remain a serious problem, especially in public places such as railway stations, long-distance bus stations, and passenger docks. The Chinese Ministry of Public Security reports these trends:

- Criminals are targeting richer people and/or entities.
- Car theft is on the rise.
- Criminal cases happen more often in public spaces—meaning that the streets are becoming less safe than they used to be.
- The average age of criminals is lowering—more kids are involved in illegal activities.
- New types of criminal activities are emerging: blackmailing, cons, and prostitution via the Web.

Though these trends are alarming, making international comparisons is often difficult because the legal definitions of crime vary from country to country. There are also differences in the way crime is measured. For example, in the United States, crime may be measured by counting criminal acts reported to the police or by using victim surveys, whereas in many European countries crime is measured by the number of cases solved by the police. Despite these problems, valid comparisons can still be made about crime across different countries using a number of reliable data sources. The United Nations Survey of Crime Trends and Operations of Criminal Justice Systems (UNCJS) is the most well known source of information on cross-national data. The International Crime Victims Survey (ICVS) is conducted in 60 countries and managed by the Ministry of Justice of the Netherlands, the Home Office of the United Kingdom, and the United Nations Interregional Crime and Justice Research Institute. INTERPOL, the international police agency, collects data from police agencies in 179 countries. The World Health Organization (WHO) has conducted surveys on global violence. The *European Sourcebook of Crime and Criminal Justice Statistics* provides data from police agencies in 36 European nations.

International Crime Rates

What do these various sources tell us about international crime rates?

Homicide

Many nations, especially those experiencing social or economic upheaval, have murder rates much higher than the United States. Colombia has about 63 homicides per 100,000 people and South Africa has 51, compared to fewer than 6 in the United States. During the 1990s there were more homicides in Brazil than in the United States, Canada, Italy, Japan, Australia, Portugal, Britain, Austria, and Germany taken together. Why are murder rates so high in nations like Brazil? Law enforcement officials link the upsurge in violence to drug trafficking, gang feuds, vigilantism, and disputes over trivial matters in which young, unmarried, uneducated males are involved. Others find that local custom and practice underpin the homicide rate. India has experienced a shocking form of violence against women known as bride burning. A woman may be burned to death if her family fails to provide the expected dowry to the groom's family or if she is suspected of premarital infidelity. Many Indian women commit suicide to escape the brutality of their situation.

Rape

Until 1990, U.S. rape rates were higher than those of any Western nation, but by 2000, Canada took the lead. Violence against women is related to economic hardship and the social status of women. Rates are high in poor nations in which women are oppressed. Where women are more emancipated, the rates of violence against women are lower.

For many women, sexual violence starts in childhood and adolescence and may occur in the home, school, and community. Studies conducted in a wide variety of nations ranging from the Cameroon to New Zealand found high rates of reported forced sexual initiation. In some nations, as many as 46 percent of adolescent women and 20 percent of adolescent men report sexual coercion at the hands of family members, teachers, boyfriends, or strangers.

Sexual violence has significant health consequences, including suicide, stress, mental illnesses, unwanted pregnancy, sexually transmitted diseases, HIV/AIDS, self-inflicted injuries, and, in the case of child sexual abuse, adoption of high-risk behaviors such as multiple sexual partners and drug use.

Robbery

Countries with more reported robberies than the United States include England and Wales, Portugal, and Spain. Countries with fewer reported robberies include Germany, Italy, and France, as well as Middle Eastern and Asian nations.

Burglary

The United States has lower burglary rates than Australia, Denmark, Finland, England and Wales, and Canada. It has higher reported burglary rates than Spain, Korea, and Saudi Arabia.

Vehicle Theft

Australia, England and Wales, Denmark, Norway, Canada, France, and Italy now have higher rates of vehicle theft than the United States.

Child Abuse

A World Health Organization report found that child physical and sexual abuse takes a significant toll around the world. In a single year, about 57,000 children under 15 years are murdered. The homicide rates for children aged 0 to 4 years are over twice as high as rates among children aged 5 to 14 years. Many more children are subjected to nonfatal abuse and neglect; 8 percent of male and 25 percent of female children up to age 18 experience sexual abuse of some kind.

Why the Change?

Why are crime rates increasing around the world while leveling off in the United States? Some conservative commentators reason that the get-tough crime control policies instituted in the United States have resulted in increases in conviction and punishment rates—an outcome that may help lower crime rates. In 1981 it was estimated that 15 in every 1,000 U.S. burglary offenders were convicted, compared with 28 in every 1,000 English burglary offenders. Ten years later, the U.S. conviction rate had increased to 19 per 1,000 offenders, while the English rate had decreased to 10 per 1,000 offenders. In addition, the death penalty is commonly employed in the United States, whereas it has been abolished in many European nations.

Crime rates may be spiraling upward abroad because nations are undergoing rapid changes in their social and economic makeup. In eastern Europe, the fall of Communism has brought about a transformation of the family, religion, education, and economy. These changes increase social pressures and result in crime rate increases. Some Asian societies, such as China, are undergoing rapid industrialization, urbanization, and social change. The shift from agricultural to industrial and service economies has produced political turmoil and a surge in their crime rates. For example, the island of Hong Kong, long a British possession but now part of the People's Republic of China, is experiencing an upsurge in club drugs. Tied to the local dance scene, ecstasy and ketamine use has skyrocketed, in synch with the traditional drug of choice, heroin. In sum, the crime problems we experience at home are not unique to the United States.

CRITICAL THINKING

1. While risk factors at all levels of social and personal life contribute to violence, people in all nations who experience change in societal-level factors—such as economic inequalities, rapid social change, and the availability of firearms, alcohol, and drugs—seem the most likely to get involved in violence. Can anything be done to help alleviate these social problems?

2. The United States is notorious for employing much tougher penal measures than Europe. Do you believe our tougher measures explain why crime is declining in the United States while increasing abroad?

Sources: James Finckenauer and Ko-lin Chin, *Asian Transnational Organized Crime and Its Impact on the United States* (Washington, DC: National Institute of Justice, 2007); Zhu Zhe, "Nationwide Crime Rate Shows Drop," *China Daily News,* 20 January 2006, www.chinadaily.com.cn/english/doc/2006–01/20/content_513862.htm (accessed March 14, 2007); Mauro Marescialli, "Crime in China: Some Statistics," Danwei Organization, www.danwei.org/ip_and_law/crime_in_china_some_statistics.php (accessed March 14, 2007); Dag Leonardsen, "Crime in Japan: Paradise Lost?" *Journal of Scandinavian Studies in Criminology and Crime Prevention* 7 (2006): 185–210; Karen Joe Laidler, "The Rise of Club Drugs in a Heroin Society: The Case of Hong Kong," *Substance Use and Misuse* 40 (2005): 1,257–1,279; Virendra Kumar and Sarita Kanth, "Bride Burning," *Lancet* 364 (2004): 18–19; Etienne Krug, Linda Dahlberg, James Mercy, Anthony Zwi, and Rafael Lozano, *World Report on Violence and Health* (Geneva: World Health Organization, 2002); Gene Stephens, "Global Trends in Crime: Crime Varies Greatly Around the World, Statistics Show, but New Tactics Have Proved Effective in the United States. To Keep Crime in Check in the Twenty-First Century, We'll All Need to Get Smarter, Not Just Tougher," *The Futurist* 37 (2003): 40–47; David P. Farrington, Patrick A. Langan, and Michael Tonry, *Cross-National Studies in Crime and Justice* (Washington, DC: Bureau of Justice Statistics, 2004); Pedro Scuro, *World Factbook of Criminal Justice Systems: Brazil* (Washington, DC: Bureau of Justice Statistics, 2003).

Law and Society: The Sociology of Law

The sociology of law, also referred to as the study of law and society, is a subarea of criminology concerned with the role social forces play in shaping criminal law and, concomitantly, the role of criminal law in shaping society. Criminologists interested in studying the social aspects of law focus on such topics as:

■ The history of legal thought

■ How social forces shape the definition and content of the law

■ The impact of legal change on society

■ The relationship between law and social control

■ The effect of criminalization/legalization on behaviors

Some criminologists who study law and society consider the role of law in the context of criminological theory. They try to understand how legal decision making influences individuals, groups, and the criminal justice system. Others try to identify alternatives to traditional legal process—for example, by designing nonpunitive methods of dispute resolution. Some seek to describe the legal system and identify and explain patterns of behavior that guide its operation. Others use the operations of law as a perspective for understanding culture and social life.[34]

Because the law is constantly evolving, criminologists are often asked to determine whether legal change is required and what shape it should take. Computer fraud, airplane hijacking, ATM theft, and cyber stalking did not exist when the nation was founded. Consequently, the law must be revised to reflect cultural, societal, and technological changes. In fact, the Supreme Court has often considered empirical research supplied by criminologists on such topics as racial discrimination in the death penalty before it renders an opinion.[35] The research conducted by criminologists then helps shape the direction of their legal decision making.

Theory Construction and Testing

Social theory can be defined as a systematic set of interrelated statements or principles that explain some aspect of social life. At their core, theories should serve as models or frameworks for understanding human behavior and the forces that shape its content and direction.

Because, ideally, theories are based on verified *social facts*—readily observed phenomenon that can be consistently quantified and measured—criminological theorists use the scientific method to test their theories. They gather data, derive *hypotheses*—testable expectations of behavior that can be derived from the theory—and then test them using valid empirical research methods. For example, general deterrence theory (see Chapter 4) states that the more people fear punishment the less willing they are to commit crime. If this statement is accurate, then logically there should be a significant association between police levels and crime. To test this theory, a number of hypotheses can be derived:

H1: The greater the number of police on the street, the lower the crime rate.

H2: Cities with the most police officers per capita will also have the lowest crime rates.

H3: Adding more police officers to the local force will cause the crime rate to decline.

H4: Cities that reduce the size of their police forces will experience an upsurge in criminal activity.

The validity of the theory would be damaged if research data showed that cities with large police forces had crime rates similar to those with smaller per capita forces, or that cities that have added police officers experience little decline in their crime rate. In contrast, if research shows that adding police reduces crime and this effect could be observed at different times in a number of different locales, then the theory might eventually become an accepted element of social thought.

Sometimes criminologists use innovative methods to test theory. When Dennis Wilson sought to determine whether adding police would deter crime, he used data from the National Hockey League to test the hypothesis that adding an enforcement agent (i.e., an additional referee) would deter law violations (i.e., penalties). His analysis of game data supported the theory that adding police would bring the crime rate down: as the number of refs in a hockey game increase, serious penalties that are potentially harmful decline![36]

Criminal Behavior Systems and Crime Typologies

Criminologists who study criminal behavior systems and crime typologies focus their research on specific criminal types and patterns: violent crime, theft crime, public order crime, and organized crime. Numerous attempts have been made to describe and understand particular crime types. Marvin Wolfgang's famous 1958 study, *Patterns in Criminal Homicide*—considered a landmark analysis of the nature of homicide and the relationship between victim and offender—found that victims often precipitate the incident that results in their death.[37] Edwin Sutherland's analysis of business-related offenses helped coin a new phrase—white-collar crime—to describe economic crime activities.

Criminologists also conduct research on the links between different types of crime and criminals. This is known as a **crime typology**. Some typologies focus on the criminal, suggesting the existence of offender groups, such as professional criminals, psychotic criminals, amateur criminals, and so on. Others focus on the crimes, clustering them into categories such as property crimes, sex crimes, and so on.

Research on criminal behavior systems and crime types is important because it enables criminologists to understand why people commit specific sorts of crime, and using this information, gives them the tools to devise crime reduction strategies. In one recent study, Arielle Baskin-Sommers and Ira Sommers analyzed the relationship between methamphetamine use and violence among young adults. To understand the association, Sommers and Sommers conducted in-depth life history interviews with

New York City Police Department Sergeant Rafi Ovanessian checks the contents of a commuter's backpack as he goes into the subway at 96th Street. New York ramped up security on its subway system after receiving a specific threat of a terrorist attack. Some criminologists focus their attention on a specific crime problem such as terrorism in order to understand its nature and extent and to help plan programs that can control or eliminate its occurrence.

more than 100 individuals who used methamphetamine for a minimum of three months. They found that about one-third committed violent acts while under the influence of methamphetamine. Incidents included domestic, drug, and gang related violence. Although the association between drug use and violence is strong, about two-thirds of the meth users remained nonviolent. Consequently, Sommers and Sommers conclude that while methamphetamine use is a *risk factor*, violence is not an inevitable outcome of even chronic methamphetamine use.[38] These results show that violence reduction policies should not be limited to reducing drug abuse since most abusers are nonviolent.

Penology and Social Control

The study of penology involves the correction and control of known criminal offenders; it is the segment of criminology that overlaps criminal justice. Criminologists conduct research that is designed to evaluate justice initiatives in order to determine their efficiency, effectiveness, and impact. For example, should capital punishment continue to be employed or is its use simply too risky? To explore this issue, Samuel Gross and his colleagues looked at death row inmates who were later found to be innocent. His sample of 340 death row inmates (327 men and

13 women), exonerated after having served years in prison, indicated that about half (144 people) were cleared by DNA evidence. Collectively, they had spent more than 3,400 years in prison for crimes they did not commit—an average of more than ten years each. Gross and his colleagues found that exonerations from death row are more than 25 times more frequent than exonerations for other prisoners convicted of murder, and more than 100 times more frequent than for all imprisoned felons.[39] How many wrongful convictions might be uncovered if all criminal convictions were given the same degree of scrutiny as death penalty cases? The Gross research illustrates how important it is to evaluate penal measures in order to determine their effectiveness and reliability.

Victimology: Victims and Victimization

In two classic criminological studies, one by Hans von Hentig and the other by Stephen Schafer, the critical role of the victim in the criminal process was first identified. These authors were the first to suggest that victim behavior is often a key determinant of crime and that victims' actions may actually precipitate crime. Both men believe that the study of crime is not complete unless the victim's role is considered.[40] For those studying the role of the victim in crime, these areas are of particular interest:

- Using victim surveys to measure the nature and extent of criminal behavior not reported to the police

- Calculating the actual costs of crime to victims

- Measuring the factors that increase the likelihood of becoming a crime victim

- Studying the role of the victim in causing or precipitating crime

- Designing services for the victims of crime, such as counseling and compensation programs

The study of victims and victimization has uncovered some startling results. For one thing, criminals have been found to be at greater risk for victimization than noncriminals.[41] Rather than being the passive receptors of criminal acts who are in the "wrong place at the wrong time," crime victims may engage in high risk lifestyles that increase their own chance of victimization and make them highly vulnerable to crime. The various elements of the criminological enterprise are summarized in Concept Summary 1.3.

connections

In recent years, criminologists have devoted ever-increasing attention to the victim's role in the criminal process. It has been suggested that a person's lifestyle and behavior may actually increase the risk that he or she will become a crime victim. Some have suggested that living in a high-crime neighborhood increases risk; others point at the problems caused by associating with dangerous peers and companions. For a discussion of victimization risk, see Chapter 3.

HOW CRIMINOLOGISTS VIEW CRIME

Professional criminologists usually align themselves with one of several schools of thought or perspectives in their field. Each perspective maintains its own view of what constitutes criminal behavior and what causes people to engage in criminality. This diversity of thought is not unique to criminology; biologists, psychologists, sociologists, historians, economists, and natural scientists disagree among themselves about critical issues in their fields. Considering the multidisciplinary nature of the field of criminology, fundamental issues such as the nature and definition of crime itself is cause for disagreement among criminologists.

A criminologist's choice of orientation or perspective depends, in part, on his or her definition of crime. This section discusses the three most common concepts of crime used by criminologists.

The Consensus View of Crime

According to the **consensus view**, crimes are behaviors believed to be repugnant to all elements of society. The **substantive criminal law**, which is the written code that defines crimes and their punishments, reflects the values, beliefs, and opinions of society's mainstream. The term "consensus" is used because it implies that there is general agreement among a majority of citizens on what behaviors should be outlawed by the criminal law and henceforth viewed as crimes. As the eminent criminologists Edwin Sutherland and Donald Cressey put it:

> *Criminal behavior is behavior in violation of the criminal law. . . . [I]t is not a crime unless it is prohibited by the criminal law [which] is defined conventionally as a body of specific rules regarding human conduct which have been promulgated by political authority, which apply uniformly to all members of the classes to which the rules refer, and which are enforced by punishment administered by the state.*[42]

This approach to crime implies that it is a function of the beliefs, morality, and rules established by the existing legal power structure. According to Sutherland and Cressey's statement, criminal law is applied "uniformly to all members of the classes to which the rules refer." This statement reveals the authors' faith in the concept of an "ideal legal system" that deals adequately with all classes and types of people. Laws prohibiting theft and violence may be directed at the neediest members of society, whereas laws that sanction economic acts such as insider trading, embezzlement, and corporate price-fixing are aimed at controlling the wealthiest. The reach of the criminal law is not restricted to any single element of society.

Social Harm The consensus view of crime links illegal behavior to the concept of **social harm**. Though people generally enjoy a great deal of latitude in their behavior, it is agreed that behaviors that are harmful to other people and society in general must be controlled. Social harm is what sets strange, unusual, or **deviant behavior**—or any other action that departs from social norms—apart from criminal behaviors.[43]

connections

The associations among crime, social harm, and morality are best illustrated in efforts to criminalize acts considered dangerous to the public welfare because they involve behaviors that offend existing social values. These so-called public order crimes include pornography, prostitution and drug use. Though "victims" are often willing participants, some people believe it is society's duty to save them from themselves. To read more about crime, morality, and social harm, see Chapter 14.

This position is not without controversy. Although it is clear that rape, robbery, and murder are inherently harmful and their control justified, behaviors such as drug use and prostitution are more problematic because the harm they inflict is only on those who are willing participants. According to the consensus view, society is justified in controlling these so-called victimless crimes because public opinion holds that they undermine the social fabric and threaten the general well-being of society. Society has a duty to protect all its members—even those who choose to engage in high-risk behaviors.

The consensus view of crime suggests that most people agree on what acts cause social harm and should therefore be outlawed. Here, rug store owner Bob Rue stands in front of his shop, which is adorned with graffiti that warns looters to keep away, in New Orleans in September 2005. There was widespread looting in the aftermath of Hurricane Katrina, and Rue wanted to make sure people realized that society frowns on such behavior.

The Conflict View of Crime

The **conflict view** depicts society as a collection of diverse groups—owners, workers, professionals, students—who are in constant and continuing conflict. Groups able to assert their political power use the law and the criminal justice system to advance their economic and social position. Criminal laws, therefore, are viewed as acts created to protect the haves from the have-nots. Critical criminologists often compare and contrast the harsh penalties exacted on the poor for their "street crimes" (burglary, robbery, and larceny) with the minor penalties the wealthy receive for their white-collar crimes (securities violations and other illegal business practices), though the latter may cause considerably more social harm. While the poor go to prison for minor law violations, the wealthy are given lenient sentences for even the most serious breaches of law. Rather than being class neutral, criminal law reflects and protects established economic, racial, gendered, and political power and privilege.[44]

Crime, according to this definition, is a political concept designed to protect the power and position of the upper classes at the expense of the poor. Even crimes prohibiting violent acts, such as armed robbery, rape, and murder, may have political undertones. Banning violent acts ensures domestic tranquility and guarantees that the anger of the poor and disenfranchised classes will not be directed at their wealthy capitalist exploiters. According to this conflict view of crime, "real" crimes would include the following acts:

- Violations of human rights due to racism, sexism, and imperialism
- Unsafe working conditions
- Inadequate child care
- Inadequate opportunities for employment and education
- Substandard housing and medical care
- Crimes of economic and political domination

- Pollution of the environment
- Price-fixing
- Police brutality
- Assassinations and war-making
- Violations of human dignity
- Denial of physical needs and necessities, and impediments to self-determination
- Deprivation of adequate food
- Blocked opportunities to participate in political decision making[45]

The Interactionist View of Crime

The **interactionist view** of crime traces its antecedents to the symbolic interaction school of sociology, first popularized by pioneering sociologists George Herbert Mead, Charles Horton Cooley, and W. I. Thomas.[46]

This position holds that (a) people act according to their own interpretations of reality, through which they assign meaning to things; (b) they observe the way others react, either positively or negatively; and (c) they reevaluate and interpret their own behavior according to the meaning and symbols they have learned from others.

According to this perspective, there is no objective reality. People, institutions, and events are viewed subjectively and labeled either good or evil according to the interpretation of the evaluator. Some people might consider the hit film *Borat: Cultural Learnings of America for Make Benefit Glorious Nation of Kazakhstan* as obscene, degrading, and offensive, while others view the same film as a laugh riot. The same interactions help define crime:

- The content of the criminal law and consequently the definition of crime often depend on human interaction and perceptions. Alcohol is legal, marijuana is not. It could easily be the other way around. Gay marriage is legal in some jurisdictions, illegal in others.

- Deciding whether an individual act is considered a crime is also a function of interaction and labeling. When an argument results in the death of one of the participants, a jury may be asked to decide whether it was murder, self-defense, or merely an accidental fatality. Each person on the jury may have their own interpretation of what took place, and whether the act is labeled a crime depends on their interpretation of events.

- The process in which people are defined or labeled as criminal is also subjective. One person is viewed as an unrepentant hard-core offender and sent to a maximum security prison. Another, who has committed essentially the same crime, is considered remorseful and repentant and given probation in the community. Though their acts are similar the treatment they receive is quite different.

According to the interactionist view, the definition of crime reflects the preferences and opinions of people who hold social

Defining Crime

It is possible to take elements from each school of thought to formulate an integrated definition of crime, such as this one:

Crime is a violation of societal rules of behavior as interpreted and expressed by a criminal legal code created by people holding social and political power. Individuals who violate these rules are subject to sanctions by state authority, social stigma, and loss of status.

This definition combines the consensus position that the criminal law defines crimes with the conflict perspective's emphasis on political power and control and the interactionist concept of labeling and stigma. Thus crime, as defined here, is a political, social, and economic function of modern life.

CRIME AND THE CRIMINAL LAW

No matter which definition of crime we embrace, criminal behavior is tied to the criminal law. It is therefore important for all criminologists to have some understanding of the development of criminal law, its objectives, its elements, and how it evolves.

The concept of criminal law has been recognized for more than 3,000 years. Hammurabi (1792–1750 BCE), the sixth king of Babylon, created the most famous set of written laws of the ancient world, known today as the Code of Hammurabi. Preserved on basalt rock columns, the code established a system of crime and punishment based on physical retaliation ("an eye for an eye"). The severity of punishment depended on class standing: if convicted of an unprovoked assault, a slave would be killed, whereas a freeman might lose a limb.

More familiar is the Mosaic Code of the Israelites (1200 BCE). According to tradition, God entered into a covenant or contract with the tribes of Israel in which they agreed to obey his law (the 613 laws of the Old Testament, including the Ten Commandments), as presented to them by Moses, in return for God's special care and protection. The Mosaic Code is not only the foundation of Judeo-Christian moral teachings but also a basis for the U.S. legal system. Prohibitions against murder, theft, and perjury, preceded, by several thousand years, the same laws found in the modern United States.

Though ancient formal legal codes were lost during the Dark Ages, early German and Anglo-Saxon societies developed legal systems featuring monetary compensation for criminal violations. Guilt was determined by two methods. One was compurgation, in which the accused person swore an oath of innocence with the backing of 12 to 25 oath helpers, who would attest to his or her character and claims of innocence. The second was trial by ordeal, which was based on the principle that divine forces would not allow an innocent person to be harmed. It involved such measures as having the accused place his or her hand in boiling water or hold a hot iron. If the wound healed, the person was found innocent; if the wound did not heal, the accused was deemed

power in a particular legal jurisdiction. These people use their influence to impose their definition of right and wrong on the rest of the population. Conversely, criminals are individuals people choose to label or stigmatize as outcasts or deviants because they have violated social rules. In a classic statement, sociologist Howard Becker argued, "The deviant is one to whom that label has successfully been applied; deviant behavior is behavior people so label."[47] Crimes are outlawed behaviors because society defines them that way, not because they are inherently evil or immoral acts.

The interactionist view of crime is similar to the conflict perspective; both suggest that behavior is outlawed and considered criminal when it offends people who hold social, economic, and political power. However, unlike the conflict view, the interactionist perspective does not attribute capitalist economic and political motives to the process of defining crime. Instead, interactionists see the criminal law as conforming to the beliefs of "moral crusaders" or moral entrepreneurs, who use their influence to shape the legal process in the way they see fit.[48] Laws against pornography, prostitution, and drugs are believed to be motivated more by moral crusades than by economic values.

The three main views of crime are summarized in Concept Summary 1.4.

guilty. Another version, trial by combat, allowed the accused to challenge his accuser to a duel, with the outcome determining the legitimacy of the accusation. Punishments included public flogging, branding, beheading, and burning.

Common Law

After the Norman conquest of England in 1066, royal judges began to travel throughout the land, holding court in each shire several times a year. When court was in session, the royal administrator, or judge, would summon a number of citizens who would, on their oath, tell of the crimes and serious breaches of the peace that had occurred since the judge's last visit. The royal judge would then decide what to do in each case, using local custom and rules of conduct as his guide. Courts were bound to follow the law established in previous cases unless a higher authority, such as the king or the pope, overruled the law.

The present English system of law came into existence during the reign of Henry II (1154–1189), when royal judges began to publish their decisions in local cases. Judges began to use these written decisions as a basis for their decision making, and eventually a fixed body of legal rules and principles was established. If a new rule was successfully applied in a number of different cases, it would become a precedent. These precedents would then be commonly applied in all similar cases—hence the term **common law**. Crimes such as murder, burglary, arson, and rape are common-law crimes whose elements were initially defined by judges. They are referred to as *mala in se*, or inherently evil and depraved. When the situation required, the English parliament enacted legislation to supplement the judge-made common law. Crimes defined by Parliament, which reflected existing social conditions, were referred to as *mala prohibitum*, or **statutory crimes**.

Before the American Revolution, the colonies, then under British rule, were subject to the common law. After the colonies acquired their independence, state legislatures standardized common-law crimes such as murder, burglary, arson, and rape by putting them into statutory form in criminal codes. As in England, whenever common law proved inadequate to deal with changing social and moral issues, the states and Congress supplemented it with legislative statutes, creating new elements in the various state and federal legal codes. Table 1.1 lists a number of crimes that were first defined in common law.

Contemporary Criminal Law

Criminal laws are now divided into felonies and misdemeanors. The distinction is based on seriousness: a felony is a serious offense; a misdemeanor is a minor or petty crime. Crimes such as murder, rape, and burglary are felonies; they are punished with long prison sentences or even death. Crimes such as unarmed assault and battery, petty larceny, and disturbing the peace are misdemeanors; they are punished with a fine or a period of incarceration in a county jail.

Regardless of their classification, acts prohibited by the criminal law constitute behaviors considered unacceptable and impermissible by those in power. People who engage in these acts are eligible for severe sanctions. By outlawing these behaviors, the government expects to achieve a number of social goals:

- *Enforcing social control.* Those who hold political power rely on criminal law to formally prohibit behaviors believed to threaten societal well-being or to challenge their authority. For example, U.S. criminal law incorporates centuries-old prohibitions against the following behaviors harmful to others: taking another person's possessions, physically harming another person, damaging another person's property, and cheating another person out of his or her possessions. Similarly, the law prevents actions that challenge the legitimacy of the government, such as planning its overthrow, collaborating with its enemies, and so on.

- *Discouraging revenge.* By punishing people who infringe on the rights, property, and freedom of others, the law shifts the burden of revenge from the individual to the state. As Oliver Wendell Holmes stated, this prevents "the greater evil of private retribution."[49] Although state retaliation may offend the sensibilities of many citizens, it is greatly preferable to a system in which people would have to seek justice for themselves.

- *Expressing public opinion and morality.* Criminal law reflects constantly changing public opinions and moral values. *Mala in se* crimes, such as murder and forcible rape, are almost universally prohibited; however, the prohibition of legislatively created *mala prohibitum* crimes, such as traffic offenses and gambling violations, changes according to social conditions and attitudes. Criminal law is used to codify these changes.

- *Deterring criminal behavior.* Criminal law has a social control function. It can control, restrain, and direct human behavior through its sanctioning power. The threat of punishment associated with violating the law is designed to prevent crimes before they occur. During the Middle Ages, public executions drove this point home. Today criminal law's impact is felt through news accounts of long prison sentences and an occasional execution.

- *Punishing wrongdoing.* The deterrent power of criminal law is tied to the authority it gives the state to sanction or punish offenders. Those who violate criminal law are subject to physical coercion and punishment.

- *Maintaining social order.* All legal systems are designed to support and maintain the boundaries of the social system they serve. In medieval England, the law protected the feudal system by defining an orderly system of property transfer and ownership. Laws in some socialist nations protect the primacy of the state by strictly curtailing profiteering and individual enterprise. Our own capitalist system is also supported and sustained by criminal law. In a sense, the content of criminal law is more a reflection of the needs of those who control the existing economic and political system than a representation of some idealized moral code.

Some of the elements of the contemporary criminal law are discussed in The Criminological Enterprise feature "The Elements of Criminal Law," on page 22.

Table 1.1 Common-Law Crimes

Crime	Description	Example
Crimes Against the Person		
First-Degree Murder	Unlawful killing of another human being with malice aforethought and with premeditation and deliberation.	A woman buys poison and pours it into a cup of coffee her husband is drinking, intending to kill him for the insurance benefits.
Voluntary Manslaughter	Intentional killing committed under extenuating circumstances that mitigate the killing, such as killing in the heat of passion after being provoked.	A husband coming home early from work finds his wife in bed with another man. The husband goes into a rage and shoots and kills both lovers with a gun he keeps by his bedside.
Battery	Unlawful touching of another with intent to cause injury.	A man seeing a stranger sitting in his favorite seat in a cafeteria goes up to that person and pushes him out of the seat.
Assault	Intentional placing of another in fear of receiving an immediate battery.	A student aims an unloaded gun at her professor and threatens to shoot. He believes the gun is loaded.
Rape	Unlawful sexual intercourse with a female without her consent.	After a party, a man offers to drive a young female acquaintance home. He takes her to a wooded area and, despite her protests, forces her to have sexual relations with him.
Robbery	Wrongful taking and carrying away of personal property from a person by violence or intimidation.	A man armed with a loaded gun approaches another man on a deserted street and demands his wallet.
Inchoate (Incomplete) Offenses		
Attempt	An intentional act for the purpose of committing a crime that is more than mere preparation or planning of the crime. The crime is not completed, however.	A person places a bomb in the intended victim's car so that it will detonate when the ignition key is used. The bomb is discovered before the car is started. Attempted murder has been committed.
Conspiracy	Voluntary agreement between two or more persons to achieve an unlawful object or to achieve a lawful object using means forbidden by law.	A doctor conspires with a con man to fake accidents and then bring the false "victims" to his office so he can collect medical fees from an insurance company.
Solicitation	With the intent that another person engage in conduct constituting a felony, a person solicits, requests, commands, or otherwise attempts to cause that person to engage in such conduct.	A terrorist approaches a person he believes is sympathetic to his cause and asks him to join in a plot to blow up a government building.
Crimes Against Property		
Burglary	Breaking and entering of a dwelling house of another in the nighttime with the intent to commit a felony.	Intending to steal some jewelry and silver, a young man breaks a window and enters another's house at 10 P.M.
Arson	Intentional burning of a dwelling house of another.	A worker, angry that her boss did not give her a raise, goes to her boss's house and sets it on fire.
Larceny	Taking and carrying away the personal property of another with the intent to keep and possess the property.	While shopping, a woman sees a diamond ring displayed at the jewelry counter. When no one is looking, the woman takes the ring, places it in her pocket, and walks out of the store without paying.

Source: Developed by Therese J. Libby, J.D.

THE MOTHER OF ALL SNAKEHEADS

Cheng Chui Ping was one of the most powerful underworld figures in New York. Known as "the Mother of all Snake-heads"—meaning she was top dog in the human smuggling trade—to her friends in Chinatown she was "Sister Ping."

Cheng was an illegal immigrant herself. Born in 1949 in the poor farming village of Shengmei in Fujian province, she left her husband and family behind and set out for the West, traveling via Hong Kong and Canada before ending up in New York in 1981.

She opened a grocery store and started other ventures that became fronts for her people trafficking business. For more than a decade, Cheng smuggled as many as 3,000 illegal immigrants from her native China into the United States—charging upwards of $40,000 per person. To ensure her clients paid their smuggling fees, Sister Ping hired members of the Fuk Ching, Chinatown's most feared gang, to transport and guard them in the United States.

In addition to running her own operation, Sister Ping helped other smugglers by financing large vessels designed for human cargo. She also ran a money transmitting business out of her Chinatown variety store. She used this business to collect smuggling fees from family members of her own "customers," and also collected ransom money on behalf of other alien smugglers.

Conditions aboard the smuggling vessels were often inhumane. The voyages were dangerous, and on at least one occasion a boat capsized while offloading people to a larger vessel and fourteen of her "customers" drowned. The *Golden Venture*, a smuggling ship Sister Ping helped finance for others, was intentionally grounded off the coast of Rockaway, Queens, in early June 1993 when the offloading vessel failed to meet it in the open sea. Many of the passengers could not swim and ten drowned.

Cheng Chui Ping was indicted in 1994 when members of the Fuk Ching gang cooperated with federal agents. After her indictment, Cheng fled to China, where she continued to run a smuggling operation. In April 2000, Hong Kong police arrested her at the airport. Cheng fought extradition but was eventually delivered to the United States in July 2003. She was convicted in New York less than two years later on multiple counts, including money laundering, conspiracy to commit alien smuggling, and other smuggling-related offenses, and was sentenced to 35 years in prison.

The activities of Sister Ping illustrate how the law must evolve to confront newly emerging social problems such as illegal immigration. Other areas include cyber crime, drug importation, and terrorism. Unfortunately, the law is sometimes slow to change, and change comes only after conditions have reached a crisis. How might laws be changed to reduce illegal immigration? Should people caught entering the country illegally be charged with a felony and imprisoned?

Sources: FBI News release, "Sister Ping Sentenced to 35 Years in Prison for Alien Smuggling, Hostage Taking, Money Laundering and Ransom Proceeds Conspiracy," 16 March 2006, http://newyork.fbi.gov//dojpressrel/pressrel06/sispter_ping031606.htm (accessed March 14, 2007); BBC news, "Cheng Chui Ping: 'Mother of snakeheads,'" http://news.bbc.co.uk/2/hi/americas/4816354.stm (accessed March 14, 2007).

The Evolution of Criminal Law

The criminal law is constantly evolving in an effort to reflect social and economic conditions. Sometimes legal changes are prompted by highly publicized cases that generate fear and concern. A number of highly publicized cases of celebrity stalking, including Robert John Bardo's fatal shooting of actress Rebecca Schaeffer on July 18, 1989, prompted more than 25 states to enact **stalking statutes** that prohibit "the willful, malicious, and repeated following and harassing of another person."[50] Similarly, after 7-year-old Megan Kanka of Hamilton Township, New Jersey, was killed in 1994 by a repeat sexual offender who had moved into her neighborhood, the federal government passed legislation requiring that the general public be notified of local pedophiles (sexual offenders who target children).[51] California's sexual predator law, which took effect on January 1, 1996, allows people convicted of sexually violent crimes against two or more victims to be committed to a mental institution after their prison terms have been served.[52]

The criminal law may also change because of shifts in culture and social conventions, reflecting a newfound tolerance of behavior condemned only a few years before. In an important 2003 case, *Lawrence v. Texas*, the Supreme Court declared that laws banning sodomy were unconstitutional because they

The Criminological Enterprise

THE ELEMENTS OF CRIMINAL LAW

Although each state and the federal government have unique methods of defining crime, there are significant uniformities and similarities that shape the essence of almost all criminal law codes. Although the laws of California, Texas, and Maine may all be somewhat different, the underlying concepts that guide and shape their legal systems are universal. The question remains: regardless of jurisdictional boundaries, what is the legal definition of a crime—and how does the criminal law deal with it?

Legal Definition of a Crime

Today, in all jurisdictions, the legal definition of a crime involves the elements of the criminal acts that must be proven in a court of law if the defendant is to be found guilty. For the most part, common criminal acts have both mental and physical elements, both of which must be present if the act is to be considered a legal crime. In order for a crime to occur, the state must show that the accused committed the guilty act, or *actus reus*, and had the *mens rea*, or criminal intent, to commit the act. The *actus reus* may be an aggressive act, such as taking someone's money, burning a building, or shooting someone; or it may be a failure to act when there is a legal duty to do so, such as a parent's neglecting to seek medical attention for a sick child. The

mens rea (guilty mind) refers to an individual's state of mind at the time of the act or, more specifically, the person's intent to commit the crime.

Actus Reus

To satisfy the requirements of *actus reus*, guilty actions must be voluntary. Even though an act may cause harm or damage, it is not considered a crime if it was done by accident or was an involuntary act. For example, it would not be a crime if a motorist obeying all the traffic laws hit a child who ran into the street. If the same motorist were drinking or speeding, then his action would be considered a vehicular crime because it was a product of negligence. Similarly, it would not be considered a crime if a babysitter accidentally dropped a child and the child died. However, it would be considered manslaughter if the sitter threw the child down in anger or frustration and the blow caused the child's death. In some circumstances of *actus reus*, the use of words is considered criminal. In the crime of sedition, the words of disloyalty constitute the *actus reus*. If a person falsely yells "fire" in a crowded theater and people are injured in the rush to exit, that person is held responsible for the injuries, because the use of the word in that situation constitutes an illegal act.

Typically, the law does not require people to aid others in distress, such as entering a burning building to rescue people trapped by a fire. However,

failure to act is considered a crime in certain instances:

- **Relationship of the parties based on status.** Some people are bound by relationship to give aid. These relationships include parent/child and husband/wife. If a husband finds his wife unconscious because she took an overdose of sleeping pills, he is obligated to save her life by seeking medical aid. If he fails to do so and she dies, he can be held responsible for her death.

- **Imposition by statute.** Some states have passed laws requiring people to give aid. For example, a person who observes a broken-down automobile in the desert but fails to stop and help the other parties involved may be committing a crime.

- **Contractual relationships.** These relationships include lifeguard and swimmer, doctor and patient, and babysitter or au pair and child. Because lifeguards have been hired to ensure the safety of swimmers, they have a legal duty to come to the aid of drowning persons. If a lifeguard knows a swimmer is in danger and does nothing about it and the swimmer drowns, the lifeguard is legally responsible for the swimmer's death.

Mens Rea

In most situations, for an act to constitute a crime, it must be done with criminal

violated the due process rights of citizens because of their sexual orientation. In its decision, the Court said:

> *Although the laws involved . . . here . . . do not more than prohibit a particular sexual act, their penalties and purposes have more far-reaching consequences, touching upon the most private human conduct, sexual behavior, and in the most private of places, the home. They seek to control a personal relationship that, whether or not entitled to formal recognition in the law, is within the liberty of persons to choose without being punished as criminals. The liberty protected by the Constitution allows homosexual persons the right to choose to enter upon relationships in the confines of their homes and their own private lives and still retain their dignity as free persons.*

As a result of the decision, all sodomy laws in the United States are now unconstitutional and therefore unenforceable.[53]

The future direction of U.S. criminal law remains unclear. Certain actions, such as crimes by corporations and political corruption, will be labeled as criminal and given more attention. Other offenses, such as recreational drug use, may be reduced in importance or removed entirely from the criminal law system. In addition, changing technology and its ever-increasing global and local roles in our lives will require modifications in criminal law. Such technologies as automatic teller machines and cellular phones have already spawned a new generation of criminal acts such as identity theft and software piracy. The globalization of crime will present even more intent, or *mens rea*. Intent, in the legal sense, can mean carrying out an act intentionally, knowingly, and willingly. However, the definition also encompasses situations in which recklessness or negligence establishes the required criminal intent.

Criminal intent also exists if the results of an action, although originally unintended, are certain to occur. When Timothy McVeigh planted a bomb in front of the Murrah Federal Building in Oklahoma City, he did not intend to kill any particular person in the building. Yet the law would hold that McVeigh or any other person would be substantially certain that people in the building would be killed in the blast, and McVeigh therefore had the criminal intent to commit murder.

Strict Liability

Though common-law crimes require that both the *actus reus* and the *mens rea* must be present before a person can be convicted of a crime, several crimes defined by statute do not require *mens rea*. In these cases, the person accused is guilty simply by doing what the statute prohibits; intent does not enter the picture. These strict liability crimes, or public welfare offenses, include violations of health and safety regulations, traffic laws, and narcotic control laws. For example, a person stopped for speeding is guilty of breaking the traffic laws regardless of whether he or she intended to go over the speed limit or did it by accident.

The underlying purpose of these laws is to protect the public; therefore, intent is not required.

Criminal Defenses

When people defend themselves against criminal charges, they must refute one or more of the elements of the crime of which they have been accused. A number of different approaches can be taken to create this defense.

First, defendants may deny the *actus reus* by arguing that they were falsely accused and that the real culprit has yet to be identified. Second, defendants may claim that although they engaged in the criminal act of which they are accused, they lacked the *mens rea* (intent) needed to be found guilty of the crime.

If a person whose mental state is impaired commits a criminal act, it is possible for the person to excuse his or her criminal actions by claiming that he or she lacked the capacity to form sufficient intent to be held criminally responsible. Insanity, intoxication, and ignorance are types of excuse defenses. A defendant might argue that because he suffered from a mental impairment that prevented him from understanding the harmfulness of his acts, he lacked sufficient *mens rea* to be found guilty as charged.

Another type of defense is justification. Here the individual usually admits committing the criminal act but maintains that he or she should not be held

criminally liable because the act was justified. Among the justification defenses are necessity, duress, self-defense, and entrapment. A battered wife who kills her mate might argue that she acted out of duress; her crime was committed to save her own life.

Persons standing trial for criminal offenses may thus defend themselves by claiming that they did not commit the act in question, that their actions were justified under the circumstances, or that their behavior can be excused by their lack of *mens rea*. If either the physical or mental elements of a crime cannot be proven, then the defendant cannot be convicted.

CRITICAL THINKING

1. Should the concept of the "guilty mind" be eliminated from the criminal law and replaced with a strict liability standard? (If you do the crime, you do the time.)

2. Some critics believe that current criminal defenses, such as the battered wife defense or the insanity defense, allow people to go free even though they committed serious criminal acts and are actually guilty as charged. Do you agree?

Sources: Joshua Dressler, *Cases and Materials on Criminal Law* (American Casebook Series) (Eagan, MN: West Publishing, 2003); Joel Samaha, *Criminal Law* (Belmont, CA: Wadsworth Publishing, 2001).

challenges, as the Profiles in Crime feature "The Mother of All Snakeheads" illustrates on page 21.

ETHICAL ISSUES IN CRIMINOLOGY

A critical issue facing students of criminology involves recognizing the field's political and social consequences. All too often, criminologists forget the social responsibility they bear as experts in the area of crime and justice. When government

agencies request their views of issues, their pronouncements and opinions become the basis for sweeping social policy. The lives of millions of people can be influenced by criminological research data.

Debates over gun control, capital punishment, and mandatory sentences are ongoing and contentious. Some criminologists have successfully argued for social service, treatment, and rehabilitation programs to reduce the crime rate, but others consider them a waste of time, suggesting instead that a massive prison construction program coupled with tough criminal sentences can bring the crime rate down. By accepting their roles as experts on law-violating behavior, criminologists place themselves in a position of power; the potential consequences of their actions are enormous. Therefore, they must be aware of the ethics of their profession and be prepared to defend their work in the light of public scrutiny. Major ethical issues include these:

▌ What to study?

▌ Whom to study?

▌ How to study?

What to Study?

Under ideal circumstances, when criminologists choose a subject for study, they are guided by their own scholarly interests, pressing social needs, the availability of accurate data, and other similar concerns. Nonetheless, in recent years, a great influx of government and institutional funding has influenced the direction of criminological inquiry. Major sources of monetary support include the Justice Department's National Institute of Justice, the National Science Foundation, and the National Institute of Mental Health. Private foundations, such as the Edna McConnell Clark Foundation, have also played an important role in supporting criminological research.

Though the availability of research money has spurred criminological inquiry, it has also influenced the direction research has taken. State and federal governments provide a significant percentage of available research funds, and they may also dictate the areas that can be studied. In recent years, for example, the federal government has spent millions of dollars funding long-term cohort studies of criminal careers. Consequently, academic research has recently focused on criminal careers. Other areas of inquiry may be ignored because there is simply not enough funding to pay for or sponsor the research.

A potential conflict of interest may arise when the institution funding research is itself one of the principal subjects of the research project. Governments may be reluctant to fund research on fraud and abuse of power by government officials. They may also exert a not-so-subtle influence on the criminologists seeking research funding: if criminologists are too critical of the government's efforts to reduce or counteract crime, perhaps they will be barred from receiving further financial help. This situation is even more acute when we consider that criminologists typically work for universities or public agencies and are under pressure to bring in a steady flow of research funds or to maintain the continued viability of their agency. Even when criminologists maintain discretion of choice, the direction of their efforts may not be truly objective. The objectivity of research may be questioned if studies are funded by organizations that have a vested interest in the outcome of the research. For example, a study on the effectiveness of the defensive use of handguns to stop crime may be tainted if the funding for the project comes from a gun manufacturer whose sales may be affected by the research findings. Efforts to show that private prisons are more effective than state correctional facilities might be tainted if the researchers received a research grant from a corporation that maintains private prisons.

Whom to Study?

A second major ethical issue in criminology concerns who will be the subject of inquiries and study. Too often, criminologists focus their attention on the poor and minorities while ignoring the middle-class criminal who may be committing white-collar crime, organized crime, or government crime. Critics have charged that by "unmasking" the poor and desperate, criminologists have justified any harsh measures taken against them. For example, a few social scientists have suggested that criminals have lower intelligence quotients than the average citizen, and that because minority group members have lower than average IQ scores, their crime rates are high.[54] This was the conclusion reached in *The Bell Curve*, a popular though highly controversial book written by Richard Herrnstein and Charles Murray.[55] Although such research is often methodologically unsound, it brings to light the tendency of criminologists to focus on one element of the community while ignoring others. The question that remains is whether it is ethical for criminologists to publish biased or subjective research findings, paving the way for injustice.

How to Study?

Ethics are once again questioned in cases where subjects are misled about the purpose of the research. When white and African American individuals are asked to participate in a survey of their behavior or an IQ test, they are rarely told in advance that the data they provide may later be used to prove the existence of significant racial differences in their self-reported crime rates. Should subjects be told about the true purpose of a survey? Would such disclosures make meaningful research impossible? How far should criminologists go when collecting data? Is it ever permissible to deceive subjects to collect data? Criminologists must take extreme care when they select subjects for their research studies to ensure that they are selected in an unbiased and random manner.[56]

When criminological research efforts involve experimentation and treatment, care must be taken to protect those subjects who have been chosen for experimental and control groups. For example, it may be unethical to provide a special treatment program for one group while depriving others of the same opportunity. Conversely, criminologists must be careful to protect subjects from experiments that may actually cause them harm. An examination of the highly publicized Scared Straight program, which brought youngsters into contact with hard-core prison inmates who gave them graphic insights into prison life (to scare them out of a life of crime), discovered that the young subjects may have been harmed by their experience. Rather than being frightened into conformity, subjects actually increased their criminal behavior.[57]

THINKING LIKE A CRIMINOLOGIST

You have been experimenting with various techniques to identify a sure-fire method to predict violence-prone behavior in delinquents. Your procedure involves brain scans, DNA testing, and blood analysis. When used with samples from incarcerated adolescents, your procedure has been able to distinguish with 80 percent accuracy between youths with a history of violence and those who are exclusively property offenders.

Your research indicates that if any youth were tested with your techniques, potentially violence-prone career criminals easily could be identified for special treatment. For example, children in the local school system could be tested, and those who are identified as violence prone carefully monitored by teachers. Those at risk for future violence could be put into special programs as a precaution.

Some of your colleagues argue that this type of testing is unconstitutional because it violates the subjects' Fifth Amendment right against self-incrimination. There is also the problem of error: Some kids may be falsely labeled as violence prone.

 Writing Exercise Write a brief paper (two double-spaced pages) explaining how you would answer your critics. Is it fair and/or ethical to label people as "potentially" criminal and violent even though they have not yet exhibited any antisocial behaviors? Do the risks of such a procedure outweigh its benefits?

 Doing Research on the Web To help answer your critics, review these Web-based resources:

▪ Read about the "DNA Testing of Criminals" prepared by Angela Blann.
▪ Learn more about "Arresting Developments in DNA Typing" by Phillip B. C. Jones.
▪ Read Nicole Rafter's take on biological theories of crime to learn more about the biological testing of criminals.
▪ Learn more about the effects of stigma as it pertains to mental health.

These websites can be accessed via academic.cengage.com/criminaljustice/siegel.

SUMMARY

▪ Criminology is the scientific approach to the study of criminal behavior and society's reaction to law violations and violators. It is essentially an interdisciplinary field; many of its practitioners were originally trained as sociologists, psychologists, economists, political scientists, historians, and natural scientists.

▪ Criminology has a rich history, with roots in the utilitarian philosophy of Beccaria, the biological positivism of Lombroso, the social theory of Durkheim, and the political philosophy of Marx.

▪ The criminological enterprise includes subareas such as criminal statistics, the sociology of law, theory construction, criminal behavior systems, penology, and victimology.

▪ When they define crime, criminologists typically hold one of three perspectives: the consensus view, the conflict view, or the interactionist view.

▪ The consensus view holds that criminal behavior is defined by laws that reflect the values and morals of a majority of citizens.

▪ The conflict view states that criminal behavior is defined in such a way that economically powerful groups can retain their control over society.

▪ The interactionist view portrays criminal behavior as a relativistic, constantly changing concept that reflects society's current moral values. According to the interactionist view, behavior is labeled as criminal by those in power; criminals are people society chooses to label as outsiders or deviants.

- The criminal law is a set of rules that specify the behaviors society has outlawed.

- The criminal law serves several important purposes. It represents public opinion and moral values; it enforces social controls; it deters criminal behavior and wrongdoing; it punishes transgressors; and it banishes private retribution.

- The criminal law used in U.S. jurisdictions traces its origin to the English common law. In the U.S. legal system, lawmakers have codified common-law crimes into state and federal penal codes.

- Every crime has specific elements. In most instances, these elements include both the *actus reus* (guilty act) and the *mens rea* (guilty mind)—the person's state of mind or criminal intent.

- At trial, a defendant may claim to have lacked *mens rea* and, therefore, to not be responsible for a criminal action. One type of defense is excuse for mental reasons, such as insanity, intoxication, necessity, or duress. Another type of defense is justification by reason of self-defense or entrapment.

- The criminal law is undergoing constant reform. Some acts are being decriminalized—their penalties are being reduced—while penalties for others are becoming more severe.

- Ethical issues arise when information-gathering methods appear biased or exclusionary. These issues may cause serious consequences because research findings can significantly impact individuals and groups.

- CENGAGENOW™ is an easy-to-use online resource that helps you study in less time to get the grade you want—Now. CengageNOW™ Personalized Study (a diagnostic study tool containing valuable text specific resources) lets you focus on just what you don't know and learn more in less time to get a better grade. If your textbook does not include an access code card, you can go to www.ichapters.com to purchase CengageNOW™.

KEY TERMS

criminology *(4)*
criminologists *(4)*
criminal justice *(4)*
scientific method *(4)*
justice *(4)*
utilitarianism *(5)*
classical criminology *(6)*
positivism *(6)*
physiognomist *(7)*
phrenologist *(7)*
psychopathic personality *(7)*
atavistic anomalies *(7)*
biological determinism *(8)*
criminal anthropology *(8)*

biosocial theory *(8)*
cartographic school of criminology *(8)*
anomie *(8)*
Chicago School *(9)*
social ecology *(9)*
social psychology *(9)*
socialization *(9)*
ecological view *(9)*
bourgeoisie *(9)*
proletariat *(9)*
rational choice *(10)*
criminological enterprise *(11)*
crime typology *(14)*
consensus view *(16)*

substantive criminal law *(16)*
social harm *(16)*
deviant behavior *(16)*
conflict view *(17)*
interactionist view *(17)*
stigmatize *(18)*
moral entrepreneurs *(18)*
common law *(19)*
mala in se *(19)*
mala prohibitum *(19)*
statutory crimes *(19)*
stalking statutes *(21)*

CRITICAL THINKING QUESTIONS

1. Beccaria argued that the threat of punishment controls crime. Are there other forms of social control? Aside from the threat of legal punishments, what else controls your own behavior?

2. What research method would you employ if you wanted to study drug and alcohol abuse at your own school?

3. Would it be ethical for a criminologist to observe a teenage gang by "hanging" with them, drinking, and watching as they steal cars? Should he report that behavior to the police?

4. Can you identify behaviors that are deviant but not criminal? What about crimes that are illegal but not deviant?

5. Do you agree with conflict theorists that some of the most damaging acts in society are not punished as crimes? If so, what are they?

6. If you could change the criminal law, what behaviors would you legalize? What would you criminalize? What might be the consequences of your actions—in other words, are there any hidden drawbacks?

NOTES

1. FBI, news release, "Canadian Man Pleads Guilty to Traveling to Georgia to Engage in Sexual Activity with a 10-Year-Old Girl," March 15, 2006, Department of Justice News Release, "Canadian Man Sentenced for Traveling to Georgia to Engage in Sexual Activity with a 10-Year-Old Girl," www.usdoj.gov/usao/gan/press/2006/03-15-06.pdf (accessed May 11, 2007).

2. John Hagan and Alberto Palloni, "Sociological Criminology and the Mythology of Hispanic Immigration and Crime," *Social Problems* 46 (1999): 617–632.

3. Edwin Sutherland and Donald Cressey, *Principles of Criminology*, 6th ed. (Philadelphia: J. B. Lippincott, 1960), p. 3.

4. Monitoring the Future, "Teen Drug Use Continues Down in 2006, Particularly among Older Teens; but Use of Prescription-Type Drugs Remains High," December 21, 2006, www.monitoringthefuture.org/pressreleases/06drugpr.pdf.

5. Alan Harding, *Medieval Law and the Foundations of the State* (New York: Oxford University Press, 2002).

6. Eugen Weber, *A Modern History of Europe* (New York: W. W. Norton, 1971), p. 398.

7. Marvin Wolfgang, *Patterns in Criminal Homicide* (Philadelphia: University of Pennsylvania Press, 1958).

8. Nicole Rafter, "The Murderous Dutch Giddler: Criminology, History and the Problem of Phrenology," *Theoretical Criminology* 9 (2005): 65–97.

9. Nicole Rafter, "The Unrepentant Horse-Slasher: Moral Insanity and the Origins of Criminological Thought," *Criminology* 42 (2004): 979–1,008.

10. Described in David Lykken, "Psychopathy, Sociopathy, and Crime," *Society* 34 (1996): 29–38.

11. See Peter Scott, "Henry Maudsley," in *Pioneers in Criminology,* ed. Hermann Mannheim (Montclair, NJ: Prentice Hall, 1981).

12. To read about Lombroso, go to http://jahsonic.com/Lombroso.html (accessed May 11, 2007).

13. Nicole Hahn Rafter, "Criminal Anthropology in the United States," *Criminology* 30 (1992): 525–547.

14. Ibid., p. 535.

15. See, generally, Robert Nisbet, *The Sociology of Émile Durkheim* (New York: Oxford University Press, 1974).

16. L. A. J. Quetelet, *A Treatise on Man and the Development of His Faculties* (Gainesville, FL: Scholars' Facsimiles and Reprints, 1969), pp. 82–96.

17. Ibid., p. 85.

18. Émile Durkheim, *Rules of the Sociological Method,* reprint ed., trans. W. D. Halls (New York: Free Press, 1982).

19. Émile Durkheim, *The Division of Labor in Society,* reprint ed. (New York: Free Press, 1997).

20. Robert E. Park, "The City: Suggestions for the Investigation of Behavior in the City Environment," *American Journal of Sociology* 20 (1915): 579–583.

21. Harvey Zorbaugh, *The Gold Coast and the Slum* (Chicago: University of Chicago Press, 1929).

22. Frederick Thrasher, *The Gang* (Chicago: University of Chicago Press, 1927).

23. Louis Wirth, *The Ghetto* (Chicago: University of Chicago Press, 1928).

24. Robert Park, Ernest Burgess, and Roderic McKenzie, *The City* (Chicago: University of Chicago Press, 1925).

25. Ibid.

26. Karl Marx and Friedrich Engels, *Capital: A Critique of Political Economy,* trans. E. Aveling (Chicago: Charles Kern, 1906); Karl Marx, *Selected Writings in Sociology and Social Philosophy,* trans. P. B. Bottomore (New York: McGraw-Hill, 1956). For a general discussion of Marxist thought, see Michael Lynch and W. Byron Groves, *A Primer in Radical Criminology* (New York: Harrow and Heston, 1986), pp. 6–26.

27. Hans Eysenck, *Crime and Personality* (London: Methuen, 1964).

28. Nicole Hahn Rafter, "H. J. Eysenck in Fagin's Kitchen: The Return to Biological Theory in 20th-Century Criminology," *History of the Human Sciences* 19 (2006): 37–56.

29. Sheldon Glueck and Eleanor Glueck, *Unraveling Juvenile Delinquency* (Cambridge: Harvard University Press, 1950), p. 48.

30. John Laub and Robert Sampson, "The Sutherland-Glueck Debate: On the Sociology of Criminological Knowledge," *The American Journal of Sociology* 96 (1991): 1,402–1,440.

31. Marvin Wolfgang and Franco Ferracuti, *The Subculture of Violence* (London: Social Science Paperbacks, 1967), p. 20.

32. Mirka Smolej and Janne Kivivuori, "The Relation between Crime News and Fear of Violence," *Journal of Scandinavian Studies in Criminology and Crime Prevention* 7 (2006): 211–227.

33. Jacqueline Cohen, Wilpen Gorr, and Andreas Olligschlaeger, "Leading Indicators and Spatial Interactions: A Crime-Forecasting Model for Proactive Police Deployment," *Geographical Analysis* 39 (2007): 105–127.

34. The Sociology of Law Section of the American Sociological Association, www.departments.bucknell.edu/soc_anthro/soclaw/textfiles/Purpose_soclaw.txt (accessed March 21, 2007).

35. Rosemary Erickson and Rita Simon, *The Use of Social Science Data in Supreme Court Decisions* (Champaign, IL : University of Illinois Press, 1998).

36. Dennis Wilson, "Additional Law Enforcement as a Deterrent to Criminal Behavior: Empirical Evidence from the National Hockey League," *Journal of Socio-Economics* 34 (2005): 319–330.

37. Wolfgang, *Patterns in Criminal Homicide.*

38. Arielle Baskin-Sommers and Ira Sommers, "Methamphetamine Use and Violence among Young Adults," *Journal of Criminal Justice* 34 (2006): 661–674.

39. Samuel Gross, Kristen Jacoby, Daniel Matheson, Nicholas Montgomery, and Sujata Patil, "Exonerations in the United States, 1989 through 2003," *Journal of Criminal Law and Criminology* 95 (2005): 523–559.

40. Hans von Hentig, *The Criminal and His Victim* (New Haven: Yale University Press, 1948); Stephen Schafer, *The Victim and His Criminal* (New York: Random House, 1968).

41. Linda Teplin, Gary McClelland, Karen Abram, and Darinka Mileusnic, "Early Violent Death among Delinquent Youth: A Prospective Longitudinal Study," *Pediatrics* 115 (2005): 1,586–1,593.

42. Edwin Sutherland and Donald Cressey, *Criminology,* 8th ed. (Philadelphia: J. B. Lippincott, 1960), p. 8.

43. Charles McCaghy, *Deviant Behavior* (New York: MacMillan, 1976), pp. 2–3.

44. Michael Lynch, Raymond Michalowski, and W. Byron Groves, *The New Primer in Radical Criminology: Critical Perspectives on Crime, Power and Identity,* 3rd ed. (Monsey, NY: Criminal Justice Press, 2000), p. 59.

45. Michael Lynch and W. Byron Groves, *A Primer in Radical Criminology* (Albany, NY: Harrow and Heston, 1989).

46. See Herbert Blumer, *Symbolic Interactionism* (Englewood Cliffs, NJ: Prentice Hall, 1969).

47. Howard Becker, *Outsiders: Studies in the Sociology of Deviance* (New York: Free Press, 1963), p. 9.

48. Ibid.

49. Oliver Wendell Holmes, *The Common Law,* ed. Mark De Wolf (Boston: Little, Brown, 1881), p. 36.

50. National Institute of Justice, *Project to Develop a Model Anti-stalking Statute* (Washington, DC: National Institute of Justice, 1994).

51. "Clinton Signs Tougher 'Megan's Law,'" *CNN News Service,* 17 May 1996.

52. Associated Press, "Judge Upholds State's Sexual Predator Law," *Bakersfield Californian,* 2 October 1996.

53. *Lawrence et al. v. Texas,* No. 02-102. June 26, 2003.

54. See, for example, Michael Hindelang and Travis Hirschi, "Intelligence and Delinquency: A Revisionist Review," *American Sociological Review* 42 (1977): 471–486.

55. Richard Herrnstein and Charles Murray, *The Bell Curve* (New York: Free Press, 1994).

56. Victor Boruch, Timothy Victor, and Joe Cecil, "Resolving Ethical and Legal Problems in Randomized Experiments," *Crime and Delinquency* 46 (2000): 330–353.

57. Anthony Petrosino, Carolyn Turpin-Petrosino, and James Finckenauer, "Well-Meaning Programs Can Have Harmful Effects! Lessons from Experiments of Programs Such as Scared Straight," *Crime and Delinquency* 46 (2000): 354–379.

2

The Nature and Extent of Crime

Tommy Henderson liked to settle scores with a gun, and he didn't like snitches or witnesses to his crimes—"Dead men tell no tales," he would say. Henderson's history of violence began way back in May 1981 when he killed Ron Beauford, a man who had beaten him up in a fight. Another man happened to be with Beauford at the time of his murder, so Henderson killed him too. Later, Henderson traveled to Florida with a woman named Ecolia Johnson on a mission to kill a witness planning to testify against a fellow criminal named Bobby Bass. On the way to Florida for the hit, Henderson's car broke down in Macon, Georgia, where, to kill some time, he robbed a bank. After hiring two men to drive him home, he paid one to kill the other (again cutting down on witnesses). Unfortunately for him, Henderson was recognized in a bank surveillance photo. Ecolia Johnson, who had purchased a police scanner right before the bank robbery, was also located and arrested. Later she and Bobby Bass (the man Henderson was going to kill for) implicated Henderson in the bank robbery and another previous murder. Faced with their testimony, Henderson pleaded guilty and served 14 years.

But his time behind bars did not mellow Tommy Henderson. Intent on revenge against those who put him there, he found and killed Bobby Bass in 1995 and two years later shot Ecolia Johnson four times as she left for work. Because there was not enough evidence linking him to these murders, Henderson was still on the street, but his crime spree, which involved six murders, was not yet over. He got involved in drug dealing, weapons, and other crimes and by 2001 was once again behind bars. There he began to plot revenge against the assistant U.S. attorney, a former state prosecutor, who was responsible for his conviction. Aware of the plot, federal agents began to monitor his phone calls, a maneuver that yielded important evidence. Reluctant witnesses were persuaded to step forward. With this evidence, Henderson was found guilty of murdering Bass and Johnson and on June 26, 2007, was sentenced to life in prison without parole.[1]

Stories about career criminals such as Tommy Henderson help convince most Americans that we live in a violent society. When people read headlines about a violent crime spree such as Henderson's, they begin to fear crime and take steps to protect themselves, perhaps avoiding public places and staying at home in the evening.[2] When asked if they fear walking in their neighborhood at night, more than one-third of all American citizens say yes.[3] About one-quarter say they have bought a gun for self-protection, and more than 10 percent claim they carry guns for defense.[4]

Are Americans justified in their fear of crime? Should they barricade themselves behind armed guards? Are crime rates actually rising or falling? And where do most crimes occur and who commits them? To answer these and similar questions, criminologists have devised elaborate methods of crime data collection and analysis. Without accurate data on the nature and extent of crime, it would not be possible to formulate theories that explain the onset of crime or to devise social policies that facilitate its control or elimination. Accurate data collection is also critical in order to assess the nature and extent of crime, track changes in the crime rate, and measure the individual and social factors that may influence criminality.

In this chapter, we review how crime data are collected on criminal offenders and offenses and what this information tells us about crime patterns and trends. We also examine the concept of criminal careers and discover what available crime data can tell us about the onset, continuation, and termination of criminality. We begin with a discussion of the primary sources of crime data: official record and victim/criminal behavior surveys.

PRIMARY SOURCES OF CRIME DATA: RECORD DATA

The primary sources of crime data routinely used by criminologists around the globe are surveys and official records collected, compiled, and analyzed by government agencies such as the federal government's Bureau of Justice Statistics or the Federal Bureau of Investigation (FBI). Criminologists use these techniques to measure the nature and extent of criminal behavior and the personality, attitudes, and background of criminal offenders. It is important to understand how these data are collected to gain insight into how professional criminologists approach various problems and questions in their field. What are these primary sources, how are they collected, and how valid are their findings?

Official Record Research

In order to understand more about the nature and extent of crime, criminologists use the records of government agencies such as police departments, prisons, and courts. Official record data can be used to examine crime rates and trends.

It can also be analyzed to uncover the individual and social forces that affect crime: to study the relationship between crime and poverty, criminologists might use income and family data from the United States Census Bureau and then cross-reference this information with crime data collected by local police departments. The most important crime record data are collected from local law enforcement agencies by the FBI and published yearly in their Uniform Crime Report (UCR). The following section is devoted to an analysis of this important source of crime data.

The Uniform Crime Report

The Federal Bureau of Investigation's Uniform Crime Report (UCR) is the best known and most widely cited source of official criminal statistics.[5] The UCR includes both crimes reported to local law enforcement departments and the number of arrests made by police agencies. The FBI receives and compiles records from more than 17,000 police departments serving a majority of the U.S. population. Its major unit of analysis involves index crimes, or Part I crimes: murder and nonnegligent manslaughter, forcible rape, robbery, aggravated assault, burglary, larceny, arsons, and motor vehicle theft. Exhibit 2.1 defines these crimes.

The FBI tallies and annually publishes the number of reported offenses by city, county, standard metropolitan statistical area, and geographical divisions of the United States. In addition to these statistics, the UCR shows the number and characteristics (age, race, and gender) of individuals who have been arrested for these and all other crimes, except traffic violations; these are referred to as Part II crimes.

Compiling the Uniform Crime Report The methods used to compile the UCR are quite complex. Each month law enforcement agencies report the number of index crimes known to them. These data are collected from records of all crime complaints that victims, officers who discovered the infractions, or other sources reported to these agencies.

Whenever criminal complaints are found through investigation to be unfounded or false, they are eliminated from the actual count. However, the number of actual offenses known is reported to the FBI whether or not anyone is arrested for the crime, the stolen property is recovered, or prosecution ensues.

The UCR uses three methods to express crime data. First, the number of crimes reported to the police and arrests made are expressed as raw figures (e.g., an estimated 17,034 persons were murdered nationwide in 2006). Second, crime rates per 100,000 people are computed. That is, when the UCR indicates that the murder rate was 5.7 in 2006, it means that almost 6 people in every 100,000 were murdered between January 1 and December 31 of 2006. This is the equation used:

$$\frac{\text{Number of Reported Crimes}}{\text{Total U.S. Population}} \times 100{,}000 = \text{Rate per } 100{,}000$$

Third, the FBI computes changes in rate of crime over time. The number of murders increased 1.8 percent between 2005

Part I Index Crime Offenses

Criminal Homicide

Murder and Nonnegligent Manslaughter The willful (nonnegligent) killing of one human being by another. Deaths caused by negligence, attempts to kill, assaults to kill, suicides, accidental deaths, and justifiable homicides are excluded. Justifiable homicides are limited to (1) the killing of a felon by a law enforcement officer in the line of duty and (2) the killing of a felon, during the commission of a felony, by a private citizen.

Manslaughter by Negligence The killing of another person through gross negligence. Traffic fatalities are excluded. Although manslaughter by negligence is a Part I crime, it is not included in the crime index.

Forcible Rape

The carnal knowledge of a female forcibly and against her will. Included are rapes by force and attempts or assaults to rape. Statutory offenses (no force used—victim under age of consent) are excluded.

Robbery

The taking or attempting to take anything of value from the care, custody, or control of a person or persons by force or threat of force or violence and/or by putting the victim in fear.

Aggravated Assault

An unlawful attack by one person upon another for the purpose of inflicting severe or aggravated bodily injury. This type of assault usually is accompanied by the use of a weapon or by means likely to produce death or great bodily harm. Simple assaults are excluded.

Burglary/Breaking or Entering

The unlawful entry of a structure to commit a felony or a theft. Attempted forcible entry is included.

Larceny/Theft (except motor vehicle theft)

The unlawful taking, carrying, leading, or riding away of property from the possession or constructive possession of another. Examples are thefts of bicycles or automobile accessories, shoplifting, pocket picking, or the stealing of any property or article that is not taken by force and violence or by fraud. Attempted larcenies are included. Embezzlement, con games, forgery, worthless checks, and so on are excluded.

Motor Vehicle Theft

The theft or attempted theft of a motor vehicle. A motor vehicle is self-propelled and runs on the surface and not on rails. Specifically excluded from this category are motorboats, construction equipment, airplanes, and farming equipment.

Arson

Any willful or malicious burning or attempt to burn, with or without intent to defraud, a dwelling house, public building, motor vehicle, or aircraft, personal property of another, or the like.

Source: FBI, Uniform Crime Report, 2006, www.fbi.gov/ucr/cius2006/ (accessed June 25, 2008).

---

and 2006 and decreased 1.1 percent between December 31, 2006, and June 2007.

Clearance Rates In addition, each month law enforcement agencies also report how many crimes were cleared. Crimes are cleared in two ways: (1) when at least one person is arrested, charged, and turned over to the court for prosecution; or (2) by exceptional means, when some element beyond police control precludes the physical arrest of an offender (i.e., the offender leaves the country). Data on the number of clearances involving the arrest of only juvenile offenders, data on the value of property stolen and recovered in connection with Part I offenses, and detailed information pertaining to criminal homicide are also reported.

Traditionally, slightly more than 20 percent of all reported index crimes are cleared by arrest each year (Figure 2.1).

Not surprisingly, as Figure 2.1 shows, more serious crimes such as murder and rape are cleared at much higher rates than less serious property crimes such as larceny. What factors account for this clearance rate differential?

▌ The media gives more attention to serious violent crimes and as a result local and state police departments are more likely to devote time and spend more resources on their investigations.

▌ There is more likely to be a prior association between victims of violent/serious crimes and their attackers, a fact that aids police investigations.

▌ Even if they did not know one another beforehand, violent crime victims and offenders interact so that identification is facilitated.

▌ Serious violent crimes often produce physical evidence, such as blood, body fluids, or fingerprints, which can be used to identify suspects.

The Profiles in Crime feature "A Pain in the Glass" shows how one atypical crime was solved.

Validity of the Uniform Crime Report Despite criminologists' continued reliance on the UCR, its accuracy has been suspect. The three main areas of concern are reporting practices, law enforcement practices, and methodological problems.

1. *Reporting practices.* Some criminologists claim that victims of many serious crimes do not report these incidents to police; therefore, these crimes do not become part of the UCR. The reasons for not reporting vary. Some victims do not trust the police or have confidence in their ability to solve crimes. Others do not have property insurance and therefore believe it is useless to report theft. In other cases, victims fear reprisals from an offender's friends or family or, in the case of family violence, from their spouse, boyfriend, and/or girlfriend.[6]

   According to surveys of crime victims, less than 40 percent of all criminal incidents are reported to the police.

Figure 2.1 Crime Clearances: Crimes Cleared by Arrest

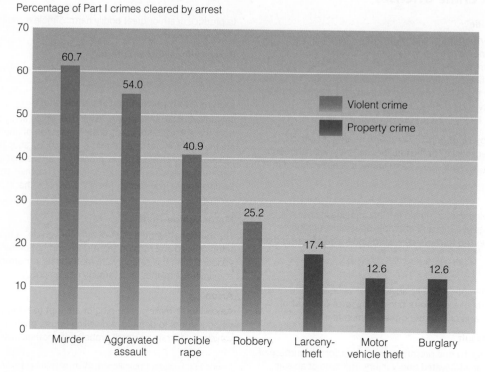

Percentage of Part I crimes cleared by arrest

Violent crime
Property crime

Murder: 60.7
Aggravated assault: 54.0
Forcible rape: 40.9
Robbery: 25.2
Larceny-theft: 17.4
Motor vehicle theft: 12.6
Burglary: 12.6

Source: FBI, Crime in the United States, 2006, www.fbi.gov/ucr/cius2006/offenses/clearances/ (accessed June 26, 2008).

Some of these victims justify not reporting by stating that the incident was "a private matter," that "nothing could be done," or that the victimization was "not important enough."[7] These findings indicate that the UCR data may significantly underreport the total number of annual criminal events.

2. *Law enforcement practices.* The way police departments record and report criminal and delinquent activity also affects the validity of UCR statistics. Some police departments define crimes loosely—reporting a trespass as a burglary or an assault on a woman as an attempted rape—whereas others pay strict attention to FBI guidelines. These reporting practices may help explain interjurisdictional differences in crime.[8] Arson is seriously underreported because many fire departments do not report to the FBI, and those that do define many fires that may well have been set by arsonists as "accidental" or "spontaneous."[9]

Some local police departments make systematic errors in UCR reporting. They may count an arrest only after a formal booking procedure, although the UCR requires arrests to be counted even if the suspect is released without a formal charge. One survey of arrests found an error rate of about 10 percent in every Part I offense category.[10] More serious allegations claim that in some cases police officials may deliberately alter reported crimes to improve

their department's public image. Police administrators interested in lowering the crime rate may falsify crime reports by classifying a burglary as a nonreportable trespass.[11] An audit of the Atlanta Police Department, which included confidential interviews with police officers, concluded that the department consistently underreported crimes for years. The reason? To improve the city's image for tourism.[12]

Ironically, boosting police efficiency and professionalism may actually help increase crime rates: as people develop confidence in the police, they may be more motivated to report crime. A New York City police program provided special services (such as follow-up visits and education) to a select sample of domestic violence victims.[13] Evaluation of the program showed that households that received the extra attention were more likely to report new incidences of violence than those that received no special services. Although it is possible that the follow-ups encouraged violence, a more realistic assessment is that the interventions increased citizens' confidence in the ability of the police to handle domestic assaults and encouraged greater crime reporting.

Higher crime rates may occur when police adopt more sophisticated computer technology and hire better-educated, better-trained employees. Crime rates also may be altered based on the way law enforcement agencies

A PAIN IN THE GLASS

From 1997 to 2005, Ronald and Mary Evano turned dining in restaurants into a profitable albeit illegal scam. They used the "waiter, there is glass in my food" ruse in restaurants and supermarkets stretching from Boston to Washington, D.C. While crude, their efforts paid big dividends. They allegedly swindled insurance companies out of $200,000 and conned a generous helping of food establishments and hospitals along the way. And to top it off, in order to look authentic, the Evanos actually did eat glass.

How did the Evanos pull off their scam? After ordering or buying food at restaurants, hotel bars, or supermarkets, either Ronald or May would "discover" glass in his or her food. They would then complain of the incident to management and fill out a report.

After leaving the food establishment, they would check into the emergency room at the local hospital complaining of severe stomach pain. After presenting fake IDs and Social Security cards to hospital staff, they'd allow doctors to examine them. In some cases, x-rays would show actual pieces of glass in their stomachs (but none of it came from the food they purchased). Once released from the hospital,

the couple would continue getting medical treatment for stomach pain. After racking up several thousand dollars in bills, they would file an insurance claim for their extensive "pain and suffering."

The scheme unraveled when the Insurance Fraud Bureau of Massachusetts noticed a pattern of glass-eating claims in the state. The private industry organization eventually realized that most claims were being filed by the same couple and contacted federal authorities who then traced the couple's trail of insurance fraud across three states and the District of Columbia.

On March 16, 2006, the Evanos were indicted on mail fraud, identity theft, Social Security fraud, and making false statements on health care matters. Ronald was arrested less than a month later, but Mary—his partner in crime—is still on the lam.

Sources: Department of Justice Press Release, "Man Arrested in Glass-Eating Fraud Scheme," http://boston.fbi.gov/dojpressrel/pressrel06/evanoranald_indict.htm (accessed June 25, 2008); Federal Bureau of Investigation, "Bizarre Meal Ticket: The Couple Who Ate Glass," November 8, 2006, www.fbi.gov/page2/nov06/glass110806.htm (accessed June 25, 2008); "Mass. Couple Charged in Glass-Eating Insurance Fraud," *Insurance Journal*, April 17, 2006, www.insurancejournal.com/news/east/2006/04/17/67327.htm (accessed June 25, 2008).

process UCR data. As the number of employees assigned to dispatching, record keeping, and criminal incident reporting increases, so too will national crime rates. What appears to be a rising crime rate may be simply an artifact of improved police record-keeping ability.[14]

3. *Methodological issues.* Methodological issues also contribute to questions pertaining to the UCR's validity. The most frequent issues include the following:

▌ No federal crimes are reported.

▌ Reports are voluntary and vary in accuracy and completeness.

▌ Not all police departments submit reports.

▌ The FBI uses estimates in its total crime projections.

▌ If an offender commits multiple crimes, only the most serious is recorded. Thus, if a narcotics addict rapes, robs, and murders a victim, only the murder is recorded. Consequently, many lesser crimes go unrecorded.

▌ Each act is listed as a single offense for some crimes but not for others. If a man robs six people in a bar, the offense is listed as one robbery; but if he assaults

or murders them, it is listed as six assaults or six murders.

▌ Incomplete acts are lumped together with completed ones.

▌ Important differences exist between the FBI's definition of certain crimes and those used in a number of states.[15]

In addition to these issues, the complex scoring procedure used in the UCR program means that many serious crimes are not counted. If during an armed bank robbery, the robber strikes a teller with the butt of a handgun, runs from the bank, and steals an automobile at the curb, he has technically committed robbery, aggravated assault, and motor vehicle theft, which are three Part I offenses. However, the UCR only records the most serious crime; hence, the robbery would be the only one recorded in the UCR.[16]

National Incident-Based Reporting System (NIBRS)
Clearly there must be a more reliable source for crime statistics than the UCR as it stands today. Beginning in 1982, a five-year redesign effort was undertaken to provide more comprehensive

and detailed crime statistics. The effort resulted in the National Incident-Based Reporting System (NIBRS), a program that collects data on each reported crime incident. Instead of submitting statements of the kinds of crime that individual citizens report to the police and summary statements of resulting arrests, the new program requires local police agencies to provide at least a brief account of each incident and arrest, including the incident, victim, and offender information. Under NIBRS, law enforcement authorities provide information to the FBI on each criminal incident involving forty-six specific offenses, including the eight Part I crimes, that occur in their jurisdiction; arrest information on the forty-six offenses plus eleven lesser offenses is also provided in NIBRS. These expanded crime categories include numerous additional crimes, such as blackmail, embezzlement, drug offenses, and bribery; this allows a national database on the nature of crime, victims, and criminals to be developed. Other collected information includes statistics gathered by federal law enforcement agencies, as well as data on hate or bias crimes. When fully implemented NIBRS will provide:

- Expansion of the number of offense categories included

- Detail on individual crime incidents (offenses, offenders, victims, property, and arrests)

- Linkage between arrests and clearances to specific incidents or offenses

- Inclusion of all offenses in an incident rather than only the most serious offense

- The ability to distinguish between attempted and completed crimes

- Linkages between offense, offender, victim, property, and arrestee variables that permit examination of interrelationships[17]

Thus far more than 20 states have implemented the NIBRS program, and 12 others are in the process of finalizing their data collections. When this program is fully implemented and adopted across the nation, it should bring about greater uniformity in cross-jurisdictional reporting and improve the accuracy of official crime data. Whether it can capture cases missing in the UCR remains to be seen.[18]

PRIMARY SOURCES OF CRIME DATA: SURVEY RESEARCH

The second primary source of crime/victimization measurement is through surveys in which people are asked about their attitudes, beliefs, values, characteristics, as well as their experiences with crime and victimization.

Surveys typically involve sampling, which refers to the process of selecting for study a limited number of subjects who are representative of entire groups sharing similar characteristics,

called the population. To understand the social forces that produce crime, a criminologist might interview a sample of 3,000 prison inmates drawn from the population of more than 2 million inmates in the United States. It is assumed that the characteristics of people or events in a carefully selected sample will be quite similar to those of the population at large. If the sampling was done correctly, the responses of the 3,000 inmates should represent the entire population of U.S. inmates.

In some circumstances criminologists may want the survey to be representative of all members of society; this is referred to as a cross-sectional survey. A survey of all students who attend the local public high school would be considered a cross-sectional survey since all members of the community, both rich and poor, male and female, go to high school. Cross-sectional surveys are useful and cost-effective technique for measuring the characteristics of large numbers of people:

- Because questions and methods are standardized for all subjects, responses are unaffected by the perceptions or biases of the person gathering the data.

- Carefully drawn samples enable researchers to generalize their findings from small groups to large populations.

- Though surveys measure subjects at a single point in their life span, questions can elicit information on subjects' past behavior as well as expectations of future behaviors.[19]

The National Crime Victimization Survey (NCVS)

Because more than half of all victims do not report their experiences to the police, the UCR cannot measure all the annual criminal activity. To address the nonreporting issue, the federal government's Bureau of Justice Statistics sponsors the National Crime Victimization Survey (NCVS), a comprehensive, nationwide survey of victimization in the United States. Begun in 1973, the NCVS provides a detailed picture of crime incidents, victims, and trends.[20]

connections

Victim surveys provide information not only about criminal incidents that have occurred but also about the individuals who are most at risk of falling victim to crime, and where and when they are most likely to become victimized. Data from recent NCVS surveys will be used in Chapter 3 to draw a portrait of the nature and extent of victimization in the United States.

How is the NCVS conducted? At the present time, about 76,000 households and 135,300 individuals age 12 or older are interviewed for the NCVS. Households stay in the sample for three years. New households are rotated into the sample on an ongoing basis. The NCVS collects information on crimes suffered by individuals and households, whether or not those crimes were reported to law enforcement. It estimates the proportion of each crime type reported to law enforcement, and it summarizes the reasons that victims give for reporting or not reporting. In 1993, the survey was redesigned to provide detailed information on the frequency and nature of the crimes of rape, sexual assault, personal robbery, aggravated and simple assault, household burglary, theft, and motor vehicle theft. In 2006, the techniques used were once again changed so that results are not fully comparable to those in previous years (see below for more on the changes).[21]

The survey provides information about victims (age, sex, race, ethnicity, marital status, income, and educational level), offenders (sex, race, approximate age, and victim–offender relationship), and the crimes (time and place of occurrence, use of weapons, nature of injury, and economic consequences). Questions also cover the experiences of victims with the criminal justice system, self-protective measures used by victims, and possible substance abuse by offenders. Supplements are added periodically to the survey to obtain detailed information on topics such as school crime.

NCVS: Advantages and Problems The greatest advantage of the NCVS over official data sources such as the UCR is that it can estimate the total amount of annual crimes and not only those that are reported to police. Nonreporting is a significant issue: during 2006, only 49 percent of all violent victimizations and 38 percent of all property crimes were reported to the police. As a result, the NCVS data provide a more complete picture of the nation's crime problem. Also, because some crimes are significantly underreported, the NCVS is an indispensable measure of their occurrence. Take for example the crime of rape and sexual assault, of which only about 41 percent of incidents are reported to police. The UCR shows that in 2006 slightly more than 92,000 rapes or attempted rapes occurred, as compared to the 270,000 uncovered by the NCVS. In addition, the NCVS helps us understand why crimes are not reported to police and whether the type and nature of the criminal event influences whether the police will ever know it occurred. With the crime of rape, research shows that victims are much more likely to report rape if it is accompanied by another crime such as robbery than they are if it is a stand-alone event. Official data alone cannot provide that type of information.[22]

While its utility and importance are unquestioned, the NCVS may also suffer from some methodological problems. As a result, its findings must be interpreted with caution. Among the potential problems are the following:

▌ Overreporting due to victims' misinterpretation of events. A lost wallet may be reported as stolen or an open door may be viewed as a burglary attempt.

▌ Underreporting due to the embarrassment of reporting crime to interviewers, fear of getting in trouble, or simply forgetting an incident.

▌ Inability to record the personal criminal activity of those interviewed, such as drug use or gambling; murder is also not included, for obvious reasons.

▌ Sampling errors, which produce a group of respondents who do not represent the nation as a whole.

▌ Inadequate question format that invalidates responses. Some groups, such as adolescents, may be particularly susceptible to error because of question format.[23]

The Future of the NCVS For the past 30 years, the NCVS (along with the UCR) has served as one of the two major indicators of crime and victimization in the United States. It now faces some important challenges. A recent analysis conducted by the National Research Council found that its effectiveness has been undermined by budget limitations.[24]

To keep going in spite of tight resources, the survey's sample size and methods of data collection have been altered. Although the current sample size is valid for its purpose, victimization is still a relatively rare event, so that when contacted many respondents do not have incidents to report. Consequently the NCVS now has to combine multiple years of data in order to comment on change over time, which is less desirable than an annual measure of year-to-year change.

Reflecting these issues, in 2006 significant changes were made to the way the NCVS is collected so that victimization estimates are not totally comparable to previous years. The methodological changes included a new sampling method, a change in the method of handling first-time interviews with households, and a change in the method of interviewing. Some selected areas were dropped from the sample while others were added. Finally, computer-assisted personal interviewing (CAPI) replaced paper and pencil interviewing (PAPI). While these issues are critical, there is no substitute available that provides national information on crime and victimization with extensive detail on victims and the social context of the criminal event.

Self-Report Surveys

While the NCVS is designed to measure victimization directly and criminal activity indirectly, participants in **self-report surveys** are asked to describe, in detail, their recent and lifetime participation in criminal activity. Self-reports are generally given anonymously in groups, so that the people being surveyed are assured that their responses will remain private and confidential. Secrecy and anonymity are essential to maintain the honesty and validity of responses. Self-report survey questions might ask:

▌ How many times in the past year have you stolen something worth more than $50?

▌ How many times in the past year did you hurt someone so badly that they needed medical care?

▌ How many times in the past year did you vandalize or damage school property?

▌ How many times in the past year did you use marijuana?

While most self-report studies have focused on juvenile delinquency and youth crime, they can also be used to examine the offense histories of select groups such as prison inmates, drug users, and even police officers.[25]

Self-report data can be used to gauge the extent of gang membership in areas where gangs are not assumed to exist. Here, Robert Ryales (front) and Thaddeus Manzano, both 16, stand in the front door of Ryales's house in A Pocono Country Place, a gated community near Tobyhanna, Pennsylvania. A few doors down, police say a reputed Crip gang member stabbed a reputed Blood gang member. Authorities say gang members from New York City and its suburbs have quietly taken up residence in some of the private, gated communities of the Poconos, where they can stake out new drug turf with little interference from municipal or state police.

In addition to crime-related items, most self-report surveys also contain questions about attitudes, values, and behaviors. There may be questions about a participant's substance abuse history and their family relations, such as, "Did your parents ever strike you with a stick or a belt?" By correlating the responses, criminologists are able to analyze the relationship between personal factors and criminal behaviors. Statistical analysis of the responses can be used to determine whether people who report being abused as children are also more likely to use drugs as adults. When psychologist Christiane Brems and her associates used this approach to collect data from 274 women and 556 men receiving drug detoxification services, they found that 20 percent of men and more than 50 percent of women reported childhood physical or sexual abuse. Individuals who self-report an abuse history also reported earlier age of onset of drinking, more problems associated with use of alcohol/drugs, more severe psychopathology, and more lifetime arrests.[26]

Self-Report Patterns One of the most important sources of self-report data is the Monitoring the Future (MTF) study, which researchers at the University of Michigan Institute for Social Research (ISR) have been conducting annually since 1978. This national survey typically involves more than 2,500 high school seniors.[27] The MTF is considered the national standard to measure substance abuse trends among American teens.

connections

MTF data on patterns and trends in teenage substance abuse will be analyzed in Chapter 13. Despite public perception to the contrary, teen drug use seems to be on the decline.

The MTF data indicate that the number of people who break the law is far greater than the number projected by official statistics. Almost everyone questioned is found to have violated a law at some time, including truancy, alcohol abuse, false ID use, shoplifting or larceny under $50, fighting, marijuana use, and damage to the property of others. Furthermore, self-reports dispute the notion that criminals and delinquents specialize in one type of crime or another; offenders seem to engage in a mixed bag of crime and deviance.[28]

Validity of Self-Reports Critics of self-report studies frequently suggest that it is unreasonable to expect people to candidly admit illegal acts. This is especially true of those with official records, who may be engaging in the most criminality. At the same time, some people may exaggerate their criminal acts, forget some of them, or be confused about what is being asked. Some surveys contain an overabundance of trivial offenses, such as shoplifting small items or using false identification to obtain alcohol, often lumped together with serious crimes to form a total crime index. Consequently, comparisons between groups can be highly misleading.

The "missing cases" phenomenon is also a concern. Even if 90 percent of a school population voluntarily participate in a self-report study, researchers can never be sure whether the few who refuse to participate or are absent that day comprise a significant portion of the school's population of persistent high-rate offenders. Research indicates that offenders with the most extensive prior criminality are also the most likely "to be poor historians of their own crime commission rates."[29] It is also unlikely that the most serious chronic offenders in the teenage population are willing to cooperate with criminologists administering self-report tests.[30] Institutionalized youths, who are not generally represented in the self-report surveys, are not only more delinquent than the general youth population, but are also considerably more misbehaving than the most delinquent youths identified in the typical self-report survey.[31] Consequently, self-reports may measure only nonserious, occasional delinquents while ignoring hard-core chronic offenders who may be institutionalized and unavailable for self-reports.

connections

Criminologists suspect that a few high-rate offenders are responsible for a disproportionate share of all serious crime. Results would be badly skewed if even a few of these chronic offenders were absent or refused to participate in schoolwide self-report surveys. For more on chronic offenders, see the Chronic Offenders/Criminal Careers section near the end of this chapter.

Finally, there is evidence that reporting accuracy differs among racial, ethnic, and gender groups. It is possible that some groups are more worried about image than others and less willing to report crime, deviance, and/or victimization for fear that it would make them or their group look bad. Take these cases, for instance:

▮ One recent study found that while girls were usually more willing than boys to disclose drug use, Latino girls significantly underreport their drug usage. Such gender- and ethnic-based differences in reporting might provide a skewed and inaccurate portrait of criminal and/or delinquent activity—in this case, the self-report data would falsely show that Latino girls use fewer drugs than other females.[32]

▮ African Americans have been found to be less willing to report traffic stops than Caucasians, a phenomenon that prevents accurate assessments of racial profiling by police. Because Black motorists are reluctant to report traffic stops, it is possible that the "driving while black" phenomenon is worse than research surveys indicate.[33]

To address these criticisms, various techniques have been used to verify self-report data.[34] The "known group" method compares youths who are known to be offenders with those who are not to see whether the former report more delinquency. Research shows that when kids are asked if they have ever been arrested or sent to court their responses accurately reflect their true life experiences.[35]

While these studies are supportive, self-report data must be interpreted with some caution. Asking subjects about their past behavior may capture more serious crimes but miss minor criminal acts—for instance, people remember armed robberies and rapes better than they do minor assaults and altercations.[36] In addition, some classes of offenders, such as substance abusers, may have a tough time accounting for their prior misbehavior.[37]

Evaluating the Primary Sources of Crime Data

The UCR, NCVS, and self-reports are the standard sources of data used by criminologists to track trends and patterns in the crime rate. Each has its own strengths and weaknesses. The UCR contains information on the number and characteristics of people arrested, information that the other data sources lack. Some recent research indicates that for serious crimes, such as drug trafficking, arrest data can provide a meaningful measure of the level of criminal activity in a particular neighborhood environment, which no other data sources can provide. It is also the source of information on particular crimes such as murder, which the other data sources cannot provide.[38] It remains the standard unit of analysis upon which most criminological research is based. However, UCR data omit many criminal incidents that victims choose not to report to police, and they are subject to the reporting caprices of individual police departments.

The NCVS includes unreported crime and important information on the personal characteristics of victims. However, the data consist of estimates made from relatively limited samples of the total U.S. population, so that even narrow fluctuations in the rates of some crimes can have a major impact on findings. They also rely on personal recollections that may be inaccurate. However, the NCVS does not include data on important crime patterns, including murder and drug abuse.

Self-report surveys can provide information on the personal characteristics of offenders—such as their attitudes, values, beliefs, and psychological profiles—that is unavailable from any other source. Yet, at their core, self-reports rely on the honesty of criminal offenders and drug abusers, a population not generally known for accuracy and integrity.

Although their tallies of crimes are certainly not in sync, the crime patterns and trends they record are often quite similar (see Concept Summary 2.1).[39] Each of the sources of crime data agree about the personal characteristics of serious criminals (such as age and gender) and where and when crime occurs (such as urban areas, nighttime, and summer months). In addition, the problems inherent in each source are consistent over time. Therefore, even if the data sources are incapable of providing an exact, precise, and valid count of crime at any given time, they are reliable indicators of changes and fluctuations in yearly crime rates.

www Go to academic.cengage.com/criminaljustice/siegel to learn more about the following services:

- The **Bureau of Justice Statistics**
- The **National Incident-Based Reporting System (NIBRS)**
- The Princeton University Survey Research Center, one of a number of academic institutes devoted to **survey research**
- **Monitoring the Future**

SECONDARY SOURCES OF CRIME DATA

In addition to these main sources of crime data, a number of other techniques are used by criminologists to gather data on specific crime problems and trends, to examine the lives of criminal offenders, and to assess the effectiveness of crime control efforts.

Cohort Research

Cohort research involves observing a group of people who share a like characteristic over time. For example, researchers might select all girls born in Albany, New York, in 1970 and then follow their behavior patterns for 20 years. The research data might include their school experiences, arrests, hospitalizations, and information about their family life (divorces, parental relations). The subjects might be given repeated intelligence and physical exams; their diets might be monitored.

Data may be collected directly from subjects during interviews and meetings with family members. Criminologists might also examine records of social organizations, such as hospitals, schools, welfare departments, courts, police departments, and prisons. School records contain data on students' academic performance, attendance, intelligence, disciplinary problems, and teacher ratings. Hospitals record incidents of drug use and suspicious wounds, which may be indicative of child abuse. Police files contain reports of criminal activity, arrest data, personal information on suspects, victim reports, and actions taken by police officers. Court records enable researchers to compare the personal characteristics of offenders with the outcomes of their court appearances, conviction rates, and types of sentence. Prison records contain information on inmates' personal characteristics, adjustment problems, disciplinary records, rehabilitation efforts, and length of sentence served. If the cohort is carefully drawn, it may be possible to determine which life experiences produce criminal careers.

Because it is extremely difficult, expensive, and time-consuming to follow a cohort over time, another approach is to take an intact cohort from the past and collect data from their educational, family, police, and hospital records. This format is known as **retrospective cohort study**.[40] For example, a cohort of girls who were in grade school in 1980 could be selected from school attendance records. A criminologist might then acquire their police and court records over the proceeding two decades to determine (a) which ones developed a criminal record and (b) whether school achievement predicts adult criminality.

connections

Some critical criminological research has been based on cohort studies, such as the important research conducted by University of Pennsylvania criminologist Marvin Wolfgang and his colleagues. Their findings have been instrumental in developing an understanding about the onset and development of a criminal career. Wolfgang's cohort research, which is discussed later in this chapter, helped identify the chronic criminal offender.

Experimental Research

Sometimes criminologists are able to conduct controlled experiments to collect data on the cause of crime. They may wish to directly test whether (a) watching a violent TV show will (b) cause viewers to act aggressively. This test requires experimental research. To conduct experimental research, criminologists manipulate or intervene in the lives of their subjects to see the outcome or the effect of the intervention. True experiments usually have three elements: (1) random selection of subjects, (2) a control or comparison group, and (3) an experimental condition. Using this approach to find out the effects of viewing violent media content, a criminologist might have one group of randomly chosen subjects watch an extremely violent and gory film (such as *Hostel* or *Saw*) while another randomly selected group views something more mellow (such as *The Princess Diaries* or *Wall-E*). If the subjects who watched the violent film were significantly more aggressive than those who watched the nonviolent film, an association between media content and behavior would be supported. The fact that both groups were randomly selected would prevent some preexisting condition from invalidating the results of the experiment.

Because it is sometimes impossible to randomly select subjects or manipulate conditions, criminologists may be forced to rely on what is known as a *quasi-experimental design*. A criminologist may want to measure whether kids who were abused as children are more likely to become violent as teens. Of course, it is impossible to randomly select youth, assign them to two independent groups, and then purposely abuse members of one group in order to gauge their reactions. To get around this dilemma, a criminologist may follow a group of kids who were abused and compare them with a matched group who, though similar in every other respect, were never abused, in order to discover if the battered kids were more likely to become violent teens. Because the subjects were not randomly assigned, it is impossible to know whether there was something in the abused group that made them more crime prone than the kids who were not abused.

Sometimes criminologists focus their research on relatively few subjects, interviewing them in depth or observing them as they go about their activities. Doreen McGloughlin, a convicted cocaine user and dealer, talks about how she spent a large part of her life on cocaine and how in prison she got a lucky break when she was moved from the state women's prison in Framingham, Massachusetts, to a treatment program known as Women in Transition in Salisbury, Massachusetts.

True criminological experiments are relatively rare because they are difficult and expensive to conduct; they involve manipulating subjects' lives, which can cause ethical and legal roadblocks; and they require long follow-up periods to verify results. Nonetheless, they have been an important source of criminological data.

Observational and Interview Research

Sometimes criminologists focus their research on relatively few subjects, interviewing them in depth or observing them as they go about their activities. This research often results in the kind of in-depth data absent in large-scale surveys. In one such effort Claire Sterk-Elifson focused on the lives of middle-class female drug abusers.[41] The 34 interviews she conducted provide insight into a group whose behavior might not be captured in a large-scale survey. Sterk-Elifson found that these women were introduced to cocaine at first "just for fun": "I do drugs," one 34-year-old lawyer told her, "because I like the feeling. I would

never let drugs take over my life."[42] Unfortunately, many of these subjects succumbed to the power of drugs and suffered both emotional and financial stress.

Another common criminological method is to observe criminals firsthand to gain insight into their motives and activities. This may involve going into the field and participating in group activities, as was done in sociologist William Whyte's famous study of a Boston gang, *Street Corner Society*.[43] Other observers conduct field studies but remain in the background, observing but not being part of the ongoing activity.[44]

Meta-Analysis and Systematic Review

Meta-analysis involves gathering data from a number of previous studies. Compatible information and data are extracted and pooled together. When analyzed, the grouped data from several different studies provide a more powerful and valid indicator of relationships than the results provided from a single study. A systematic review is another widely accepted means of evaluating the effectiveness of public policy interventions. It involves collecting the findings from previously conducted scientific studies that address a particular problem, appraising and synthesizing the evidence, and using the collective evidence to address a particular scientific question.

Through these well-proven techniques, criminologists can identify what is known and what is not known about a particular problem and use the findings as a first step for carrying out new research. Criminologists David Farrington and Brandon Welsh used a systematic review and meta-analysis to study the effects of street lighting on crime.[45] After identifying and analyzing thirteen relevant studies, Farrington and Welsh found evidence showing that neighborhoods that improve their street lighting do in fact experience a reduction in crime rates. Their findings should come as no great surprise. It seems logical that well-lit streets would have fewer robberies and thefts because (a) criminals could not conceal their efforts under the cover of darkness, and (b) potential victims could take evasive action if they saw a suspicious-looking person lurking about. However, the analysis produced an unusual finding: improving lighting caused the crime rate to go down during the day just as much as it did during the night! Obviously, the crime-reducing effect of streetlights had little to do with illuminating the streets. Farrington and Welsh speculate that improved street lighting increases community pride and solidarity, and the result of this newfound community solidarity is a lowered crime rate, during both the day and evening.

Data Mining

A relatively new criminological technique, data mining, uses multiple advanced computational methods, including artificial intelligence (the use of computers to perform logical functions), to analyze large data sets usually involving one or more data sources. The goal is to identify significant and recognizable patterns, trends, and relationships that are not easily detected

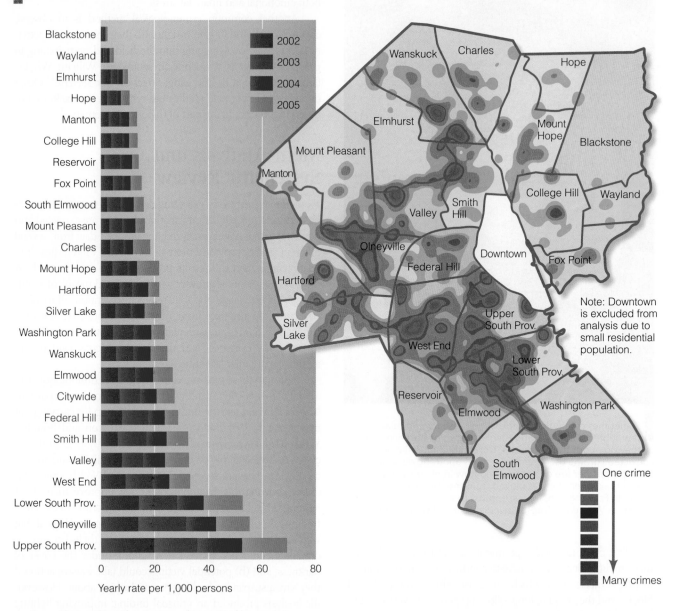

Figure 2.2 Violent Crime in Providence, Rhode Island

Note: Downtown is excluded from analysis due to small residential population.

Source: The Providence Plan, www.provplan.org. Used by permission.

through traditional analytical techniques alone.[46] Criminologists then use this information for various purposes, such as the prediction of future events or behaviors.

Data mining might be employed to help a police department allocate resources to combat crime based on offense patterns. To determine if such a pattern exists, a criminologist might employ data mining techniques with a variety of sources, including calls for service data, crime or incident reports, witness statements, suspect interviews, tip information, telephone toll analysis, or Internet activity.

Data mining permits proactive or "risk-based" deployment of police resources, a procedure that can increase public safety by optimizing the allocation of resources. For example, Richmond, Virginia, has experienced frequent random gunfire

on New Year's Eve that has long presented a challenge to local law enforcement agencies. Through the use of data mining, the Richmond Police Department identified and targeted locations associated with increased random gunfire during the previous New Year's Eve holiday and deployed additional police resources to these areas. The results were extremely positive: there was a 49 percent reduction in the number of random gunfire complaints, with a concomitant increase in seized weapons of 246 percent. Using data mining to target resources, the Richmond Police Department required fewer police personnel than originally anticipated, which permitted the release of approximately 50 sworn employees. Data mining yielded a cost savings of approximately $15,000 during the eight-hour initiative. The Richmond Police Department's initiative demonstrated the ability to do more with less through the use of data mining and risk-based deployment strategies in the public safety arena.[47]

Crime Mapping

Criminologists are now using crime maps to create graphic representations of the spatial geography of crime. Computerized crime maps allow criminologists to analyze and correlate a wide array of data to create immediate, detailed visuals of crime patterns. The most simple maps display crime locations or concentrations and can be used, for example, to help law enforcement agencies increase the effectiveness of their patrol efforts. More complex maps can be used to chart trends in criminal activity. For example, criminologists might be able to determine if certain neighborhoods in a city have significantly higher crime rates than others—so-called "hot spots" of crime.[48] Figure 2.2 illustrates a typical crime map.

One innovative mapping program, CATCH—the Crime Analysis Tactical Clearing House—is a federal program that supports local law enforcement agencies in analyzing crime series and patterns. The CATCH staff use a number of crime mapping and analysis software applications and techniques to help agencies analyze identified crime series. CATCH is based on next-event forecasting, which differs from geographic profiling. Geographic profiling analyzes the locations of a series of crimes to determine where the offender most likely resides. Next-event forecasting looks at where previous crimes occurred to predict where the next crime will happen. So far CATCH has had several successes. In one case, the Savannah-Chatham, Georgia, police department was baffled by a series of nine kidnappings and rapes. CATCH staff mapped the crime locations along with other variables and created a timeline. Because the victims were kidnapped and then taken to isolated locations and assaulted, the mapping was complex. Using movement-analysis techniques, CATCH team members projected probable locations where the offender had targeted the victims and provided a list of recommendations for disrupting the series. These forecasts and recommendations backed up conclusions by the Savannah authorities, who initiated a public awareness campaign about the crimes. The

Savannah-Chatham police department arrested the offender following an attack in an area targeted for increased surveillance.[49]

CRIME TRENDS

Crime is not new to this century.[50] Studies have indicated that a gradual increase in the crime rate, especially in violent crime, occurred from 1830 to 1860. Following the Civil War, this rate increased significantly for about fifteen years. Then, from 1880 up to the time of the First World War, with the possible exception of the years immediately preceding and following the war, the number of reported crimes decreased. After a period of readjustment, the crime rate steadily declined until the Depression (about 1930), when another crime wave was recorded. As measured by the UCR, crime rates increased gradually following the 1930s until the 1960s, when the growth rate became much greater. The homicide rate, which had actually declined from the 1930s to the 1960s, also began a sharp increase that continued through the 1970s.

By 1991 police recorded about 14.6 million crimes. Since then the number of crimes has been in decline; in 2006 about 11.4 million crimes were reported to the police. Figure 2.3 illustrates crime rate trends between 1960 and the first six months of 2007, the last data available. As the figure shows, there has been a significant downward trend in the rate of crime for more than a decade. Even teenage criminality, a source of national concern, has been in decline during this period, decreasing by about one-third over the past 20 years.[51] The factors that help explain the upward and downward movements in crime rates are discussed in The Criminological Enterprise feature "Explaining Crime Trends."

Trends in Violent Crime

The violent crimes reported by the FBI include murder, rape, assault, and robbery. About 1.4 million violent crimes are now being reported to police. The estimated rate of violent crime was 474 per 100,000 inhabitants (a 1 percent increase when the 2006 and 2005 rates were compared).

- Nationwide, there were an estimated 1,417,745 violent crimes reported in 2006.

- Of the violent crimes, the estimated number of murders and nonnegligent manslaughters increased 2 percent, and the estimated number of robberies increased 7 percent in 2006 when compared with 2005 data. The estimated number of aggravated assaults decreased 0.2 percent, and the estimated number of forcible rapes declined 2 percent.[52]

Figure 2.3 Crime Rate Trends

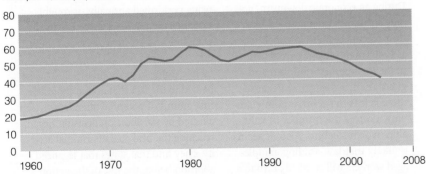

Rate per 1,000 population

Source: FBI, *Crime in the United States, 2006,* updated with preliminary 2007 data.

EXPLAINING CRIME TRENDS

Crime experts have identified a variety of social, economic, personal, and demographic factors that influence crime rate trends. Although crime experts are still uncertain about how these factors impact these trends, directional change seems to be associated with changes in crime rates.

Age Structure of Society

Because teenagers have extremely high crime rates, crime experts view change in the age structure of society as having a significant influence on crime trends. As a general rule, the crime rate follows the proportion of teens in the population: more kids, more crime! And because adolescents who commit a lot of crime early in childhood are also the ones most likely to continue to commit crime into adulthood, the more children in the population, the greater the likelihood of having a significant number of persistent offenders.

With the "graying" of society in the 1980s and a decline in the birthrate, it is not surprising that the overall crime rate has been in decline. The number of juveniles should be increasing over the next decade, and some crime experts fear that this will signal a return to escalating crime rates. However, the number of senior citizens is also expanding, and their presence in the population may have a moderating effect on crime rates (seniors do not commit much crime), offsetting the effect of teens.

The State of the Economy

Crime rates may also be influenced by changes in the economic environment. The decline in the burglary rate over the past decade may be explained in part by the abundance and subsequent decline in price of commonly stolen merchandise such as DVD players, laptops, cell phones, flat screen TVs, and digital cameras. Improving home and commercial security devices may also discourage would-be burglars, convincing them to turn to other forms of crime such as theft from motor vehicles. On the other hand, new targets may increase crime rates: subway crime increased in New York when thieves began targeting people carrying iPods and expensive cell phones such as the iPhone. While the association between crime and the economy may seem straightforward, there is still significant debate over its direction and effect. There are four different views on the association between the economy and crime rates:

1. **Bad economy/increased crime rates.** When the economy turns down, people who are underemployed or unemployed will become motivated to commit property crimes to obtain desperately needed resources. In contrast, a strong economy, such as the one we had in the 1990s, will bring the crime rate down. When people perceive that the economy is doing well and that there is positive consumer sentiment, the rate of property crimes such as burglary, larceny, and motor vehicle theft decline.

2. **Good economy/higher crime rates.** A good economy requires that more people be hired, including teens. Unfortunately, some criminologists believe that kids with after-school jobs are more likely to engage in antisocial activities. Since teens commit more crimes than adults, increasing their employment will have an adverse effect on the overall crime rate.

3. **Bad economy/lower crime rate.** During an economic downturn, not only are fewer kids employed, but their parents begin to lose their jobs as well. Unemployed parents are at home to supervise children and guard their possessions. Because there is less to spend, a poor economy reduces the number of valuables worth stealing. Also, it seems unlikely that law-abiding, middle-aged workers will suddenly turn to a life of crime if they are laid off during an economic downturn.

4. **Crime and the economy are unrelated.** It is also possible that the state of the economy and crime rates are unrelated. Research conducted by Gary Kleck and Ted Chiricos shows that the relationship between unemployment and crime rates is insignificant. Unemployed people are not likely to stick up gas stations, banks, and drug stores, nor are they more likely to engage in nonviolent property crimes such as shoplifting, residential burglary, theft of motor vehicle parts, and theft of automobiles, trucks, and motorcycles.

One reason for all this confusion may simply be methodological: measuring the association between variables such as jobs, the economy, and crime is often quite difficult. There are significant economic differences at the state, county, community, and neighborhood level. While people in one area of the city are doing quite well, their neighbors living in another part of town may be suffering unemployment. Crime rates may even vary by street, an association that is difficult to detect.

Abortion

In a controversial work, John J. Donohue III and Steven D. Levitt found empirical evidence that the recent drop in the crime rate can be attributed to the availability of legalized abortion. In 1973, *Roe v. Wade* legalized abortion nationwide. Within a few years of *Roe v. Wade*, more than 1 million abortions were being performed annually, or roughly one abortion for every three live births. Donohue and Levitt suggest that the crime rate drop, which began approximately eighteen years later in 1991, can be tied to the fact that at that point the first groups of potential offenders affected by the abortion decision began reaching the peak age of criminal activity. They find that states that legalized abortion before the rest of the nation were the first to experience decreasing crime rates and that states with high abortion rates have seen a greater fall in crime since 1985.

It is possible that the link between crime rates and abortion is the result of two mechanisms: (1) selective abortion on the part of women most at risk to have children who would engage in criminal activity, and (2) improved child-rearing or environmental circumstances caused by better maternal, familial, or fetal care because women are having fewer children. According to Donohue and Levitt, if abortion were illegal, crime rates might increase by 10 to 20 percent. If these estimates are correct, legalized abortion can explain about half of the recent fall in crime. All else equal, the researchers predict that crime rates will continue to fall slowly for an additional 15 to 20 years as the full effects of legalized abortion are gradually felt.

Guns

The availability of firearms may influence the crime rate: as the number of guns in the population increases, so do violent crime rates. While some gun advocates suggest that criminals who kill obtain guns illegally and therefore are immune from gun control efforts, recent (2007) research by Matthew Miller and his associates found that states with higher rates of household firearm ownership had significantly higher homicide victimization rates of men, women, and children. Contrary to popular belief, their findings suggest that the household may be an important source of firearms used to kill men, women, and children in the United States.

Handguns are especially dangerous if they fall into the hands of teens. There is evidence that more guns than ever before are finding their way into the hands of young people. Surveys of high school students indicate that between 6 and 10 percent carry guns at least some of the time. Guns also cause escalation in the seriousness of crime. As the number of gun-toting students increases, so too does the seriousness of violent crime, as a schoolyard fight turns into murder.

Gangs

Another factor that affects crime rates is the explosive growth in teenage gangs. Surveys indicate that there may be about 800,000 gang members in the United States. Data collected by the National Youth Gang Center show that gang members are responsible for a large proportion of all violent offenses committed during the adolescent years:

- One study conducted with Rochester gang members found that they commit 68 percent of all adolescent violent offenses reported to police in that community.

- A Seattle survey found that gang members (15 percent of the sample surveyed) reported committing 85 percent of all adolescent robberies.

- A Denver study found that gang members (14 percent of the sample) reported committing 79 percent of all serious violent adolescent offenses reported to the police.

Boys who are members of gangs are far more likely to possess guns than non-gang members; criminal activity increases when kids join gangs. According to Alfred Blumstein, gangs involved in the urban drug trade recruit juveniles because they work cheaply, are immune from heavy criminal penalties, and are daring and willing to take risks. Arming themselves for protection, these drug-dealing children present a menace to their community, which persuades non–gang-affiliated neighborhood adolescents to arm themselves as well. The result is an arms race that produces an increasing spiral of violence. As gangs become more organized, so too does their level of violence and drug dealing.

The decade-long decline in the crime rate may be tied to changing gang values. Some streetwise kids have told researchers that they now avoid gangs because of the "younger brother syndrome"—they have watched their older siblings or parents caught in gangs or drugs and want to avoid the same fate. However, there has been a recent upswing in gang violence, a phenomenon that may herald an overall increase in violent crime.

Drug Use

Some experts tie increases in the violent crime rate between 1985 and 1993 to the crack epidemic, which swept the nation's largest cities, and to drug-trafficking gangs that fought over drug turf. These well-armed gangs did not hesitate to use violence to control territory, intimidate rivals, and increase market share. As the crack epidemic subsided, so too did the violence rates in New York City and other metropolitan areas where crack use was rampant. Alfred Blumstein's research helps define what happened. He finds that the rapid rise in violence between 1985 and 1993 was attributable largely to the recruitment of young people, armed with handguns, into the crack markets as replacements for those sent to prison. When violent crime declined between 1993 and 2000, there was a significant drop in the demand for crack by new users, and so the young people were no longer needed, but they could be absorbed into the robust economy. A sudden increase in drug use, on the other hand, may be a harbinger of future increases in the crime rate, especially if guns are easily obtained and the economy is weak.

Media

Some experts argue that violent media can influence the direction of crime rates. As the availability of media with a violent theme skyrocketed with the introduction of home video players, DVDs, cable TV, computer and video games, and so on, so too did teen violence rates. According to Brad Bushman and Craig Anderson, watching violence on TV is correlated to aggressive behaviors, especially for people with a preexisting tendency toward crime and violence.

(continued)

(continued)

This conclusion is bolstered by research showing that the more kids watch TV, the more often they get into violent encounters. Jeffrey Johnson and his associates at Columbia University found that 14-year-old boys who watched less than 1 hour of TV per day later got into an average of 9 fights resulting in injury. In contrast, adolescent males watching 1 to 3 hours of TV per day got into an average of 28 fights; those watching more than 3 hours of TV got into an average of 42 fights. Of those watching 1 to 3 hours per day, 22.5 percent later engaged in violence, such as assaults or robbery, in their adulthood; 28.8 percent of kids who regularly watched more than 3 hours of TV in a 24-hour period engaged in violent acts as adults.

Medical Technology

Some crime experts believe that the presence and quality of health care can have a significant impact on murder rates. According to research conducted by Anthony Harris and his associates, murder rates would be up to five times higher than they are today without medical breakthroughs in treating victims of violence developed over the past forty years. They estimate that the United States would suffer between 50,000 to 115,000 homicides per year as opposed to the current number,

which has fluctuated at around 17,000. Looking back more than forty years, they found that the aggravated assault rate has increased at a far higher pace than the murder rate, a fact they attribute to the decrease in mortality of violence victims in hospital emergency rooms. The big breakthrough occurred in the 1970s when technology developed to treat injured soldiers in Vietnam was applied to trauma care in the nation's hospitals. Since then, fluctuations in the murder rate can be linked to the level and availability of emergency medical services.

Justice Policy

Some law enforcement experts have suggested that a reduction in crime rates may be attributed to adding large numbers of police officers and using them in aggressive police practices that target "quality of life" crimes such as panhandling, graffiti, petty drug dealing, and loitering. By showing that even the smallest infractions will be dealt with seriously, aggressive police departments may be able to discourage potential criminals from committing more serious crimes. Michael White and his associates have recently shown that cities employing aggressive, focused police work may be able to lower homicide rates in the area.

It is also possible that tough laws imposing lengthy prison terms on drug

dealers and repeat offenders can affect crime rates. The fear of punishment may inhibit some would-be criminals and place a significant number of potentially high-rate offenders behind bars, lowering crime rates. As the nation's prison population has expanded, the crime rate has fallen.

However, justice policy can sometimes backfire and actually lift crime rates. Take for instance the long-term effect of incarceration. The imprisonment boom has resulted in more than 2 million people behind bars. While this policy may take some dangerous offenders off the street, eventually most get out. About 600,000 inmates are now being released each year, and many return back to their communities without marketable skills or resources. The number of releasees will rise for the foreseeable future as more and more sentences bestowed during the high crime rate 1990s are completed. The recidivism rate of paroled inmates is quite high, averaging about 40 percent for those released from federal penitentiaries and 67 percent for those released from state custody. Inmates reentering society may have a significant effect on local crime rates.

Social and Cultural Conditions

Cultural macro-level conditions such as the number of single-parent families, high school dropout rates, racial conflict,

---

While these data are disturbing, it is too soon to tell whether crime rates are once again increasing. Law enforcement agencies throughout the nation reported a decrease of 2 percent in the number of violent crimes in the first half of 2007 so it is possible that the downward trend in violent crime is about to resume once again.

Trends in Property Crime

The property crimes reported in the UCR include larceny, motor vehicle theft, and arson. The estimated volume of property crime decreased 2 percent in 2006 when compared with 2005 figures; the rate of property crime was 3,334 per 100,000 inhabitants (a 3 percent decline). Property crime rates have

declined in recent years, though the drop has not been as dramatic as that experienced by the violent crime rate. Between 1995 and 2006, the total number of property crimes declined more than 15 percent, and the property crime rate declined 25 percent. Preliminary 2007 data indicates that the property crime rate has continued to fall so that the overall crime rate is still in decline.

Trends in Victimization Data (NCVS Findings)

According to the latest NCVS survey, during 2006, U.S. residents age 12 and older experienced an estimated 25 million crimes of violence and theft. Also during that year, the violent crime rate and the prevalence of teen pregnancies exert a powerful influence on crime rates. High levels of race- and ethnicity-based income inequality have been shown to impact on crime rates. Areas where there is both intra- and intergroup inequality experience more violent crimes than neighborhoods in which most residents are doing equally well.

Immigration

Immigration has become one of the most controversial issues in American society due in part to the belief that immigrants have high crime rates and therefore should be prevented from entering the country. Contradicting such concern have been data showing that immigrants commit less crime and are far less likely to be incarcerated than the native born. Robert Sampson has found that immigrants are actually less violent than the general population, especially when they live in concentrated immigrant areas. Sampson and his colleagues found that Mexican immigrants experienced lower rates of violence compared to their native-born counterparts. Ramiro Martinez and his colleagues examined the influence on drug crimes and violence produced by recent immigration in Miami and San Diego and found that immigration has a *negative* effect on overall levels of homicides and on drug-related homicides specifically. This

research indicates that as the number of immigrants in the population increases, crime rates may decline.

CRITICAL THINKING

While crime rates have been declining in the United States, they have been increasing in Europe. Is it possible that factors that correlate with crime rate changes in the United States have little utility in predicting changes in other cultures? What other factors may increase or reduce crime rates?

Sources: Robert Sampson and Lydia Bean, "Cultural Mechanisms and Killing Fields: A Revised Theory of Community-Level Racial Inequality," in *The Many Colors of Crime: Inequalities of Race, Ethnicity, and Crime in America*, ed. Ruth D. Peterson, Lauren Krivo, and John Hagan (New York: New York University Press, 2006): 8–36; Ramiro Martinez, Jr., and Matthew Amie Nielsen, "Local Context and Determinants of Drug Violence in Miami and San Diego: Does Ethnicity and Immigration Matter?" *International Migration Review* 38:131–157 (2004); Scott Decker, Charles Katz, and Vincent Webb, "Understanding the Black Box of Gang Organization: Implications for Involvement in Violent Crime, Drug Sales, and Violent Victimization, *Crime and Delinquency* 54 (2008): 153–172; Robert Apel, Shawn Bushway, Robert Brame, Amelia Haviland, Daniel Nagin, and Ray Paternoster, "Unpacking the Relationship between Adolescent Employment and Antisocial Behavior: A Matched Samples Comparison," *Criminology* 45 (2007): 67–97; Richard Rosenfeld, Robert Fornango, and Andres Rengifo, "The Impact of Order-Maintenance Policing on New York City Homicide and Robbery Rates: 1988–2001," *Criminology* 45 (2007): 355–384; John Hipp, "Income Inequality, Race, and Place: Does the Distribution of Race and Class within

Neighborhoods Affect Crime Rates?" *Criminology* 45 (2007): 665–697; National Youth Gang Center, "What Proportion of Serious and Violent Crime Is Attributable to Gang Members?" www.iir.com/nygc/faq.htm#r50 (accessed June 26, 2008); Richard Rosenfeld and Robert Fornango, "The Impact of Economic Conditions on Robbery and Property Crime: The Role of Consumer Sentiment," *Criminology* 45 (2007): 735–769; Martin Killias, "The Opening and Closing of Breaches: A Theory on Crime Waves, Law Creation and Crime Prevention," *European Journal of Criminology* 3 (2006): 11–31; Matthew Miller, David Hemenway, and Deborah Azrael, "State-Level Homicide Victimization Rates in the U.S. in Relation to Survey Measures of Household Firearm Ownership, 2001–2003," *Social Science and Medicine* 64 (2007), 656–664; Alfred Blumstein, "The Crime Drop in America: An Exploration of Some Recent Crime Trends," *Journal of Scandinavian Studies in Criminology and Crime Prevention* 7 (2006): 17–35; Thomas Arvanites and Robert Defina, "Business Cycles and Street Crime," *Criminology* 44 (2006): 139–164; Gary Kleck and Ted Chiricos, "Unemployment and Property Crime: A Target-Specific Assessment of Opportunity and Motivation as Mediating Factors," *Criminology* 40 (2002): 649–680; Michael Brick, "An iPod Crime Wave? How Terrible. On Second Thought . . .", *New York Times*, 2 May 2005; Steven Levitt, "Understanding Why Crime Fell in the 1990s: Four Factors That Explain the Decline and Six That Do Not," *Journal of Economic Perspectives* 18 (2004): 163–190; Jeffrey Johnson, Patricia Cohen, Elizabeth Smailes, Stephanie Kasen, and Judith Brook, "Television Viewing and Aggressive Behavior During Adolescence and Adulthood," *Science* 295 (2002): 2,468–2,471; Brad Bushman and Craig Anderson, "Media Violence and the American Public," *American Psychologist* 56 (2001): 477–489; Anthony Harris, Stephen Thomas, Gene Fisher, and David Hirsch, "Murder and Medicine: The Lethality of Criminal Assault 1960–1999," *Homicide Studies* 6 (2002): 128–167; John J. Donohue and Steven D. Levitt, "The Impact of Legalized Abortion on Crime," *Quarterly Journal of Economics* 116 (2001): 379–420.

was about 25 victimizations per 1,000 persons age 12 or older; for property crimes it was 160 per 1,000 households.[53]

As Figures 2.4 and 2.5 show, like the official UCR data, the NCVS indicates that the rate of both violent and property victimizations has been in decline, stabilizing a bit in the past few years.

Trends in Self-Reporting

Self-report results appear to be more stable than the UCR. When the results of recent self-report surveys are compared with various studies conducted over a 20-year period, a uniform pattern emerges: The use of drugs and alcohol increased markedly in the 1970s, leveled off in the 1980s, and then

began to increase in the mid-1990s until 1997, when the use of most drugs began to decline. Theft, violence, and damage-related crimes seem more stable. Although a self-reported crime wave has not occurred, neither has there been any visible reduction in self-reported criminality. Table 2.1 contains data from the most recent (2007) Monitoring the Future (MTF) survey. A surprising number of these *typical* teenagers reported involvement in serious criminal behavior. About 13 percent reported hurting someone badly enough that the victim needed medical care (7 percent said they did it more than once); about 27 percent reported stealing something worth less than $50, and another 9 percent stole something worth more than $50; 28 percent reported shoplifting; 13 percent reported damaged school property.

Figure 2.4 Trends in Violent Crime Victimizations

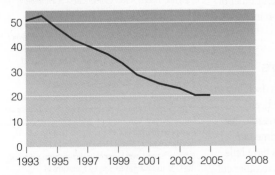

Violent victimizations per
1,000 population age 12 or over

Source: National Crime Victimization Survey, www.ojp.usdoj.gov/bjs/pub/
pdf/cv05.pdf (accessed June 26, 2008).

Figure 2.5 Trends in Property Crime Victimizations

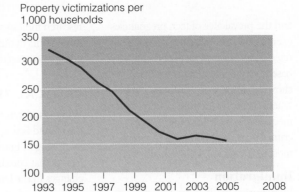

Property victimizations per
1,000 households

Source: National Crime Victimization Survey, www.ojp.usdoj.gov/bjs/pub/
pdf/cv05.pdf (accessed June 26, 2008).

If the MTF data are accurate, the crime problem is much greater than FBI data would lead us to believe. There are approximately 40 million youths between the ages of 10 and 18. Extrapolating from the MTF findings, this group accounts for more than 100 percent of all theft offenses reported in the UCR. More than 3 percent of the students said they used a knife or a gun in a robbery. At this rate, high school students commit 1.2 million armed robberies per year. In comparison, the UCR tallied about 230,000 armed robberies for all age groups. Over the past decade, the MTF surveys indicate that, with a few exceptions, self-reported participation in theft, violence, and damage-related crimes seems to be more stable than the trends reported in the UCR arrest data.

What the Future Holds

It is risky to speculate about the future of crime trends because current conditions can change rapidly, but some criminologists believe that crime rates may eventually rise as the number of teens in the population increases.

Not all criminologists believe we are in for an age-driven crime wave. Some, such as Steven Levitt, dispute the fact that the population's age makeup contributes as much to the crime rate as others have suggested.[54] Even if teens commit more crime in the future, he finds that their contribution may be offset by the aging of the population, which will produce a large number of senior citizens and elderly, a group with a relatively low crime rate.

Criminologists Darrell Steffensmeier and Miles Harer predict a much more moderate increase in crime than previously believed possible.[55] Steffensmeier and Harer agree that the age structure of society is one of the most important determinants of crime rates, but they believe the economy, technological change, and social factors help moderate the crime rate.[56] They note that American culture is being transformed because baby boomers, now in their late 50s and 60s, are exerting a significant influence on the nation's values and morals. As a result, the narcissistic youth culture that stresses materialism is being replaced by more moralistic cultural values.[57] Positive social values have a "contagion effect";

Table 2.1 Survey of Criminal Activity of High School Seniors, 2007

Crime	*Percentage Engaging in Offenses*	
	Committed at Least Once	Committed More Than Once
Set fire on purpose	2	2
Damaged school property	6	5
Damaged work property	3	3
Auto theft	3	2
Auto part theft	2	2
Break and enter	12	13
Theft, less than $50	12	15
Theft, more than $50	5	5
Shoplift	11	14
Gang fight	9	8
Hurt someone badly enough to require medical care	6	5
Used force or a weapon to steal	2	2
Hit teacher or supervisor	1	2
Participated in serious fight	7	5

Source: Monitoring the Future, 2006 (Ann Arbor, MI: Institute for Social Research, 2006).

those held by the baby boomers will have an important influence on the behavior of all citizens, even crime-prone teens. The result may be a moderation in the potential growth of the crime rate.

Such prognostication is reassuring, but there is, of course, no telling what changes are in store that may influence crime rates either up or down. Technological developments such as e-commerce on the Internet have created new classes of crime. Concern about the environment in rural areas may produce a rapid upswing in environmental crimes ranging from vandalism to violence.[58] A financial crisis or energy supply disruption may have an impact on crime. Although crime rates have trended downward, it is too early to predict that this trend will continue into the foreseeable future.

CRIME PATTERNS

Criminologists look for stable crime rate patterns to gain insight into the nature of crime. The cause of crime may be better understood by examining the rate. If, for example, criminal statistics consistently show that crime rates are higher in poor neighborhoods in large urban areas, then the cause of crime would be linked to poverty and neighborhood decline. The link between crime and economic factors would be broken if crime rates are spread evenly across society, and were found to be equal in both poor and affluent neighborhoods. If crime was spread evenly across the social structure then its cause might be linked to socialization, personality, intelligence, or some other trait unrelated to class position or income. In this section we examine traits and patterns that may influence the crime rate.

The Ecology of Crime

Patterns in the crime rate seem to be linked to temporal and ecological factors. Some of the most important of these are discussed here.

Day, Season, and Climate Most reported crimes occur during the warm summer months of July and August. During the summer, teenagers, who usually have the highest crime levels, are out of school and have greater opportunity to commit crime. People spend more time outdoors during warm weather, making themselves easier targets. Similarly, homes are left vacant more often during the summer, making them more vulnerable to property crimes. Two exceptions to this trend are murders and robberies, which occur frequently in December and January (although rates are also high during the summer).

Crime rates also may be higher on the first day of the month than at any other time. Government welfare and Social Security checks arrive at this time, and with them come increases in such activities as breaking into mailboxes and accosting recipients on the streets. Also, people may have more disposable income at this time, and the availability of extra money may relate to behaviors associated with crime such as drinking, partying, gambling, and so on.[59]

Temperature Weather effects (such as temperature swings) may have an impact on violent crime rates. Traditionally, the association between temperature and crime was thought to resemble an inverted U-shaped curve: crime rates increase with rising temperatures and then begin to decline at some point (85 degrees) when it may be too hot for any physical exertion.[60] However, criminologists continue to debate this issue:

- Some believe that crime rates rise with temperature (i.e., the hotter the day, the higher the crime rate).[61]
- Others have found evidence that the curvilinear model is correct.[62]
- Some research shows that a rising temperature will cause some crimes to continually increase (such as domestic assault), while others (such as rape) will decline after temperatures rise to an extremely high level.[63]

If in fact there is an association between temperature and crime, how can it be explained? The relationship may be due to the stress and tension caused by extreme temperature. The human body generates stress hormones (adrenaline and testosterone) in response to excessive heat; hormonal activity has been linked to aggression.[64]

© AP Images/Tucson Police Department

Crime rates peak during the summer months in most areas and then decline in the fall and winter. A surveillance camera tape shows David Willingham (right) and Megan Franklin as they rob a convenience store in Tucson, Arizona, in August 2005. The couple, who robbed the store while wearing clown suits, was sentenced to three years in prison each. What does this seasonal effect tell us about the cause of crime?

Figure 2.6 Regional Crime Rates for Violent and Property Crimes

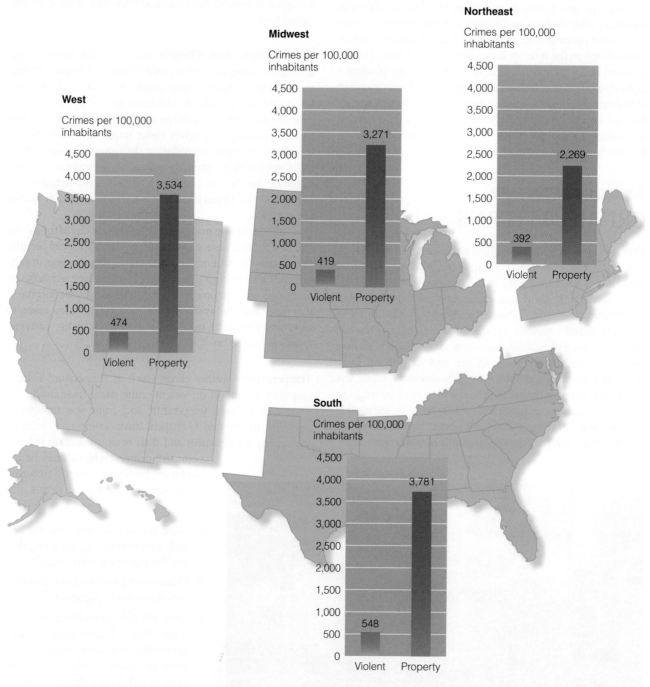

West

Crimes per 100,000 inhabitants

3,534

474

Violent   Property

Midwest

Crimes per 100,000 inhabitants

3,271

419

Violent   Property

Northeast

Crimes per 100,000 inhabitants

2,269

392

Violent   Property

South

Crimes per 100,000 inhabitants

3,781

548

Violent   Property

Source: FBI, Crime in the United States, 2006, www.fbi.gov/ucr/cius/about/crime_map.html (accessed June 26, 2008).

One way to combat the temperature–crime association: turn off your air conditioner! James Rotton and Ellen Cohn found that assaults in air-conditioned settings increased as the temperature rose; assaults in non–air-conditioned settings decline after peaking at moderately high temperatures.[65]

Regional Differences Large urban areas have by far the highest violence rates; rural areas have the lowest per capita crime rates. Exceptions to this trend are low population resort areas with large transient or seasonal populations—such as Atlantic City, New Jersey. Typically, the western and southern states have had consistently higher crime rates than the Midwest and Northeast (Figure 2.6). This pattern has convinced some criminologists that regional cultural values influence crime rates; others believe that regional differences can be explained by economic differences.

Use of Firearms

Firearms play a dominant role in criminal activity. According to the NCVS, firearms are typically involved in about 20 percent of robberies, 10 percent of assaults, and more than 5 percent of rapes. According to the UCR, about two-thirds of all murders involve firearms; most of these weapons are handguns.

Because of these findings, there is an ongoing debate over gun control. International criminologists Franklin Zimring and Gordon Hawkins believe the proliferation of handguns and the high rate of lethal violence they cause is the single most significant factor separating the crime problem in the United States from the rest of the developed world.[66] Differences between the United States and Europe in nonlethal crimes are only modest at best—and getting smaller over time[67]

In contrast, some criminologists believe that personal gun use can actually be a deterrent to crime. Gary Kleck and Marc Gertz have found that as many as 400,000 people per year use guns in situations in which they later claim that the guns "almost certainly" saved lives. Even if these estimates are off by a factor of 10, it means that armed citizens may save 40,000 lives annually. Although Kleck and Gertz recognize that guns are involved in murders, suicides, and accidents, which claim more than 30,000 lives per year, they believe their benefit as a crime prevention device should not be overlooked.[68] Because this is so important, the Policy and Practice in Criminology feature "Should Guns Be Controlled?" discusses this issue in some detail.

Social Class, Socioeconomic Conditions, and Crime

It makes sense that crime is inherently a lower-class phenomenon. After all, people at the lowest rungs of the social structure have the greatest incentive to commit crimes and those people who are undergoing financial difficulties are the ones most likely to become their targets.[69] It seems logical that people who are unable to obtain desired goods and services through conventional means may consequently resort to theft and other illegal activities—such as selling narcotics—to obtain them. These activities are referred to as instrumental crimes. Those living in poverty are also believed to engage in disproportionate amounts of expressive crimes, such as rape and assault, as a result of their rage, frustration, and anger against society. Alcohol and drug abuse, common in impoverished areas, help fuel violent episodes.[70]

When measured with UCR data, official statistics indicate that crime rates in inner-city, high-poverty areas are generally higher than those in suburban or wealthier areas.[71] Surveys of prison inmates consistently show that prisoners were members of the lower class and unemployed or underemployed in the years before their incarceration.

An alternative explanation for these findings is that the relationship between official crime and social class is a function of law enforcement practices, not actual criminal behavior patterns. Police may devote more resources to poor areas, and consequently apprehension rates may be higher there. Similarly, police may be more likely to formally arrest and prosecute lower-class citizens than those in the middle and upper classes, which may account for the lower class's overrepresentation in official statistics and the prison population.

Class and Self-Reports Self-report data have been used extensively to test the class–crime relationship. Surprisingly, early self-report studies conducted in the 1950s, specifically those conducted by James Short and F. Ivan Nye, did not find a direct relationship between social class and youth crime.[72] They found that socioeconomic class was related to official processing by police, courts, and correctional agencies but not to the actual commission of crimes. In other words, although lower- and middle-class youth self-reported equal amounts of crime, the lower-class youths had a greater chance of being arrested, convicted, and incarcerated and becoming official delinquents. In addition, factors generally associated with lower-class membership, such as broken homes, were found to be related to institutionalization but not to admissions of delinquency. Other studies of this period reached similar conclusions.[73]

For more than 20 years after the use of self-reports became widespread, a majority of self-report studies concluded that a class–crime relationship did not exist: if the poor possessed more extensive criminal records than the wealthy, this difference was attributable to differential law enforcement and not to class-based behavior differences. That is, police may be more likely to arrest lower-class offenders and treat the affluent more leniently.[74] One problem with using self-reports to measure the class–crime relationship is that the methods employed to measure social class vary widely. Some methods of measuring social class in self-report studies, such as items asking about father's occupation and education, are only weakly related to self-reported crime, but others, such as unemployment or receiving welfare, are more significant predictors of criminality.[75]

It is also possible that the association between class and crime is quite complex and cannot be explained with a simple linear relationship (i.e., the poorer you are, the more crime you commit).[76] Class and economic conditions may affect some crimes and some people differently than they affect others. Some subgroups in the population (e.g., women, African Americans) seem more deeply influenced by economic factors than others (e.g., males, whites).[77] Job loss seems to affect young adults more than it does teens. Younger adults are affected not only when they experience job loss but when only low-wage jobs are available.[78]

Evaluating the Class–Crime Association

While the true relationship between class and crime is difficult to determine, the weight of recent evidence seems to suggest that serious, official crime is more prevalent among the lower classes, whereas less serious and self-reported

SHOULD GUNS BE CONTROLLED?

The association between guns and crime has spurred many Americans to advocate controlling the sale of handguns and banning the cheap mass-produced handguns known as Saturday night specials. In contrast, gun advocates view control as a threat to personal liberty and call for severe punishment of criminals rather than control of handguns. They argue that the Second Amendment of the U.S. Constitution protects the right to bear arms. The debate was recently addressed by the Supreme Court when, in *District of Columbia v. Heller*, it ruled that the Second Amendment protects an individual's right to own weapons for self-defense—and that gun ownership was not merely a right related to membership in a "well-regulated militia." While the Court recognized the right to own guns, its decision still allows for the registration and regulation of handguns.

Efforts to control handguns have come from many different sources. States and many local jurisdictions have laws restricting sales or possession of guns; some regulate dealers who sell guns. The Federal Gun Control Act of 1968, which is still in effect, requires that all dealers be licensed, fill out forms detailing each trade, and avoid selling to people prohibited from owning guns such as minors, ex-felons, and drug users. Dealers must record the source and properties of all guns they sell and carefully account for their purchase. Gun buyers must provide identification and sign waivers attesting to their ability to possess guns. Unfortunately, the resources available to enforce this law are meager.

On November 30, 1993, the Brady Handgun Violence Prevention Act was enacted, amending the Gun Control Act of 1968. The bill was named after former

Press Secretary James Brady, who was severely wounded in the attempted assassination of President Ronald Reagan by John Hinckley in 1981. The Brady Law imposes a waiting period of five days before a licensed importer, manufacturer, or dealer may sell, deliver, or transfer a handgun to an unlicensed individual. The waiting period applies only in states without an acceptable alternate system of conducting background checks on handgun purchasers. Beginning November 30, 1998, the Brady Law changed, providing an instant check on whether a prospective buyer is prohibited from purchasing a weapon. Federal law bans gun purchases by people convicted of or under indictment for felony charges, fugitives, the mentally ill, those with dishonorable military discharges, those who have renounced U.S. citizenship, illegal aliens, illegal drug users, and those convicted of domestic violence misdemeanors or who are under domestic violence restraining orders (individual state laws may create other restrictions). The Brady Law now requires background approval not just for handgun buyers but also for those who buy long guns and shotguns. In addition, the Federal Violent Crime Control and Law Enforcement Act of 1994 banned a group of military-style semiautomatic firearms (that is, assault weapons). However, this ban on assault weapons was allowed to lapse in 2004.

Although gun control advocates see this legislation as a good first step, some question whether such measures will ultimately curb gun violence. When Jens Ludwig and Philip Cook compared two sets of states—32 that installed the Brady Law in 1994 and 18 states plus the District of Columbia that already had similar types of laws prior to 1994—they found that there was no evidence that implementing the Brady Law contributed to a reduction in homicide. However,

there is evidence that legislation targeting specific crimes can bring positive results. A number of states have instituted laws restricting access to firearms by individuals who are subject to a restraining order or have been convicted of a domestic violence misdemeanor, or allowing law enforcement officers to confiscate firearms at a domestic violence scene. Research indicates that taking guns out of the hands of domestic abusers can lower rates of intimate partner homicides.

Another approach is to severely punish people caught with unregistered handguns. The most famous attempt to regulate handguns using this method is the Massachusetts Bartley-Fox Law, which provides a mandatory one-year prison term for possessing a handgun (outside the home) without a permit. A detailed analysis of violent crime in Boston after the law's passage found that the use of handguns in robberies and murders did decline substantially (in robberies by 35 percent and in murders by 55 percent in a two-year period). However, these optimistic results must be tempered by two facts: rates for similar crimes dropped significantly in comparable cities that did not have gun control laws, and the use of other weapons, such as knives, increased in Boston.

Can Guns Be Outlawed?

Even if outlawed or severely restricted, the government's ability to control guns is problematic. If legitimate gun stores were strictly regulated, private citizens could still sell, barter, or trade handguns. Unregulated gun fairs and auctions are common throughout the United States; many gun deals are made at gun shows with few questions asked. People obtain firearms illegally through a multitude of unauthorized sources, including unlicensed dealers, corrupt licensed dealers, and "straw" purchasers (people who buy guns for those who cannot purchase them legally).

If handguns were banned or outlawed, they would become more valuable; illegal importation of guns might increase as it has for other controlled substances (for instance, narcotics). Increasing penalties for gun-related crimes has also met with limited success because judges may be reluctant to alter their sentencing policies to accommodate legislators. Regulating dealers is difficult, and tighter controls on them would only encourage private sales and bartering. Relatively few guns are stolen in burglaries, but many are sold to licensed gun dealers who circumvent the law by ignoring state registration requirements or making unrecorded or misrecorded sales to individuals and unlicensed dealers. Even a few corrupt dealers can supply tens of thousands of illegal handguns.

Is There a Benefit to Having Guns?

Not all experts are convinced that strict gun control is a good thing. Some, such as Gary Kleck, a leading advocate of gun ownership, argue that guns may actually inhibit violence. He finds that Americans use guns for defensive purposes more than 2 million times a year. While this figure seems huge, it must be viewed in the context of gun ownership: almost 50 million households own a gun; more than 90 million, or 49 percent of the adult U.S. population, live in households with guns; and about 59 million adults personally own guns. Considering these numbers it is not implausible that 3 percent of the people (or 2.5 million people) with access to guns could have used one defensively in a given year.

Guns have other uses. In many assaults, Kleck reasons, the aggressor

does not wish to kill but only scare the victim. Possessing a gun gives aggressors enough killing power so that they may actually be inhibited from attacking. Guns may also enable victims to escape serious injury. Victims may be inhibited from fighting back without losing face; it is socially acceptable to back down from a challenge if the opponent is armed with a gun. Guns then can deescalate a potentially violent situation. The benefits of gun ownership, he concludes, outweigh the costs.

Does Defensive Gun Use Really Work?

While this research is persuasive, many criminologists are still skeptical about the benefits of carrying a handgun. Tomislav Kovandzic and his colleagues used data for all large (population over 100,000) U.S. cities to examine the impact of right-to-carry concealed handgun laws on violent crime rates from the period 1980 to 2000 and found that carry laws have little effect on local crime rates. And while Kleck's research shows that carrying a gun can thwart crimes, other research shows that defensive gun use may be more limited than he believes: people who carry guns may be at greater risk of victimization than those who do not. Even people with a history of violence and mental disease are less likely to kill when they use a knife or other weapon than when they employ a gun. Nor is the death of others the only problem associated with possessing a weapon: suicides now account more than half of all firearm-related deaths. Gun-related suicides have outnumbered firearm homicides and accidents for 20 of the past 25 years.

Do guns kill people or do people kill people? Research indicates that even the most dangerous people are less likely to

resort to lethal violence if the gun is taken out of their hands.

CRITICAL THINKING

1. Do you agree with the Heller decision? Or should the sale and possession of handguns be banned? Would you uphold such a law if you had a vote?

2. Which of the gun control methods discussed do you feel would be most effective in deterring crime?

Sources: District of Columbia v. Heller (07-290), 2008; Mike Stobbe, "Gun Owners More Often Kill Themselves Than Others," Denver Post, 1, July 2008, www.denverpost.com/breakingnews/ci_9747969 (accessed July 2, 2008); E. R Vigdor and J. A. Mercy, "Do Laws Restricting Access to Firearms by Domestic Violence Offenders Prevent Intimate Partner Homicide?" Evaluation Review 30 (2006): 313–346; Gary Kleck and Jongyeon Tark, "Resisting Crime: The Effects of Victim Action on the Outcomes of Crimes," Criminology 42 (2005): 861–909; Robert Martin and Richard Legault, "Systematic Measurement Error with State-Level Crime Data: Evidence from the 'More Guns, Less Crime' Debate," Journal of Research in Crime and Delinquency 42 (2005): 187–210; Tomislav Kovandzic, Thomas Marvell, and Lynne Vieraitis, "The Impact of 'Shall-Issue' Concealed Handgun Laws on Violent Crime Rates: Evidence from Panel Data for Large Urban Cities," Homicide Studies 9 (2005): 292–323; Tomislav Kovandzic and Thomas Marvell, "Right-to-Carry Concealed Handguns and Violent Crime: Crime Control through Gun Control?" Criminology and Public Policy 2 (2003): 363–396; Lisa Hepburn and David Hemenway, "Firearm Availability and Homicide: A Review of the Literature," Aggression and Violent Behavior 9 (2004): 417–440; Matthew Miller, Deborah Azrael, and David Hemenway, "Rates of Household Firearm Ownership and Homicide across U.S. Regions and States, 1988–1997," American Journal of Public Health 92 (2002): 1,988–1,993; John Lott, Jr., "More Guns, Less Crime: Understanding Crime and Gun-Control Laws," Studies in Law and Economics, 2nd ed. (Chicago: University of Chicago Press, 2001); Anthony A. Braga and David M. Kennedy, "The Illicit Acquisition of Firearms by Youth and Juveniles," Journal of Criminal Justice 29 (2001): 379–388; Gary Kleck and Marc Gertz, "Armed Resistance to Crime: The Prevalence and Nature of Self-Defense with a Gun," Journal of Criminal Law and Criminology 86 (1995): 150–187; Jens Ludwig and Philip Cook, "Homicide and Suicide Rates Associated with the Implementation of the Brady Violence Prevention Act," Journal of the American Medical Association 284 (2000): 585–591.

Supporters of gun rights hold up their banners outside the Supreme Court in Washington, D.C., on June 26, 2008, after the court ruled that Americans have a constitutional right to keep guns in their homes for self-defense. This ruling was the justices' first major pronouncement on gun control in U.S. history. Do you think that the proliferation of guns promotes criminal behavior or allows potential victims to protect themselves against it?

Age and Crime

There is general agreement that age is inversely related to criminality. Criminologists Travis Hirschi and Michael Gottfredson state, "Age is everywhere correlated with crime. Its effects on crime do not depend on other demographic correlates of crime."[86] Regardless of economic status, marital status, race, sex, and so on, younger people commit crime more often than their older peers. Research shows that on average, kids who are persistent offenders begin committing crime in their childhood, rapidly increase their offending activities in late adolescence and then begin a slowdown in adulthood. Early starters tend to commit more crime and are more likely to continue to be involved in criminality over a longer period of time. [87]

While it has been long assumed that most kids commit crime in groups, and that peer support encourages offending in adolescence, the most recent research disputes the "co-offending" hypothesis and suggests the great bulk of youth crime is a solo act.[88] Though juvenile criminals may be lone operators, kids who assume an outlaw persona find that their antisocial acts bring them increased social status among peers who admire their risk-taking behaviors. While the "good kids" may shun young criminals, those who do poorly in school may be looking for an avenue of behavior that improves their peer group standing.[89]

crime is spread more evenly throughout the social structure.[79] Income inequality, poverty, and resource deprivation are all associated with the most serious violent crimes, including homicide and assault.[80] Members of the lower class are more likely to suffer psychological abnormality, including high rates of anxiety and conduct disorders, conditions that may promote criminality.[81]

Contemporary research shows that community level indicators of social inequality are significantly related to crime rates. While a particular individual who is poor may not commit crime, groups of people living in communities that lack economic and social opportunities are influenced by their neighborhood disadvantage.[82] These community conditions also produce high levels of frustration; residents believe they are relatively more deprived than residents in more affluent areas and may then turn to criminal behavior to relieve their frustration.[83] Family life is disrupted, and law-violating youth groups thrive in a climate that undermines adult supervision.[84] Conversely, when the poor are provided with economic opportunities via welfare and public assistance, crime rates drop.[85]

connections

If class and crime are unrelated, then the causes of crime must be found in factors experienced by members of all social classes—psychological impairment, family conflict, peer pressure, school failure, and so on. Theories that view crime as a function of problems experienced by members of all social classes are reviewed in Chapter 7.

connections

Hirschi and Gottfredson have used their views on the age–crime relationship as a basis for their General Theory of Crime. This important theory holds that the factors that produce crime change little after birth and that the association between crime and age is constant. For more on this view, see the section on the General Theory of Crime in Chapter 9.

Official statistics tell us that young people are arrested at a disproportionate rate to their numbers in the population; victim surveys generate similar findings for crimes in which assailant age can be determined. Whereas youths under 18 collectively make up about 6 percent of the total U.S. population, they account for about 25 percent of serious crime arrests and 17 percent of arrests for all crimes. As a general rule, the peak age for property crime is believed to be 16, and for violence 18 (Figure 2.7). In contrast, adults 45 and over, who make up about a third of the population, account for only 7 percent of serious crime arrests. The elderly are particularly resistant to the temptations of crime; they make up more than 14 percent of the population and less than 1 percent of arrests. Elderly males 65 and over are predominantly arrested for alcohol-related matters (e.g., public drunkenness

Figure 2.7 Relationship between Age and Serious Crime Arrests

Arrest rate per 100,000 persons

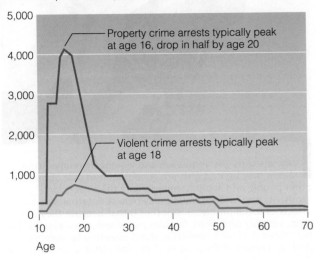

Property crime arrests typically peak at age 16, drop in half by age 20

Violent crime arrests typically peak at age 18

Source: FBI, *Uniform Crime Report, 2005.*

other adults who enforce conventional standards of morality and behavior. They have a new sense of energy and strength and are involved with peers who are similarly vigorous and frustrated.

In adulthood, people strengthen their ability to delay gratification and forgo the immediate gains that law violations bring. They also start wanting to take responsibility for their behavior and to adhere to conventional mores, such as establishing long-term relationships and starting a family.[96] Getting married, raising a family, and creating long-term family ties provide the stability that helps people desist from crime.[97]

connections

Those who oppose the Hirschi and Gottfredson view argue that although most people age out of crime, a small group continues into old age as chronic or persistent offenders. It is possible that the population may contain different sets of criminal offenders: one group whose criminality declines with age; another whose criminal behavior remains constant through maturity. This issue will be discussed in greater detail in Chapter 9.

and drunk driving) and elderly females for larceny (e.g., shoplifting). The elderly crime rate has remained stable for the past 20 years.[90]

Aging Out of Crime Most criminologists agree that people commit less crime as they age.[91] Crime peaks in adolescence and then declines rapidly thereafter. According to criminologist Robert Agnew, this peak in criminal activity can be linked to essential features of adolescence in modern, industrial societies. Because adolescents are given most of the privileges and responsibilities of adults in these cultures, they also experience:

▌ A reduction in supervision

▌ An increase in social and academic demands

▌ Participation in a larger, more diverse, peer-oriented social world

▌ An increased desire for adult privileges

▌ A reduced ability to cope in a legitimate manner and increased incentive to solve problems in a criminal manner[92]

Adding to these incentives is the fact that young people, especially the indigent and antisocial, tend to discount the future.[93] They are impatient, and because their future is uncertain, they are unwilling or unable to delay gratification. As they mature, troubled youths are able to develop a long-term life view and resist the need for immediate gratification.[94] Aging out of crime may be a function of the natural history of the human life cycle.[95] Deviance in adolescence is fueled by the need for money and sex and reinforced by close relationships with peers who defy conventional morality. At the same time, teenagers are becoming independent from parents and

Gender and Crime

Male crime rates are much higher than those of females. Victims report that their assailant was male in more than 80 percent of all violent personal crimes. The most recent *Uniform Crime Report* arrest statistics (2006) indicate that males account for more than 80 percent of all arrests for serious violent crimes and almost 70 percent of the arrests for serious property crimes; murder arrests are 8 males to 1 female. MTF data also show that young men commit more serious crimes, such as robbery, assault, and burglary, than their female peers (see Table 2.2). However, although the patterns in self-reports parallel official

Table 2.2 Percentage of High School Seniors Admitting to at Least One Offense during the Past 12 Months, by Gender

Delinquent Acts	Males	Females
Serious fight	14	9
Gang fight	21	16
Hurt someone badly	17	5
Used a weapon to steal	5	2
Stole less than $50	30	25
Stole more than $50	13	7
Shoplift	25	25
Breaking and entering	27	22
Arson	4	2
Damaged school property	17	6

Source: *Monitoring the Future, 2006* (Ann Arbor, MI: Institute for Social Research, 2007).

CHAPTER 2 The Nature and Extent of Crime   **53**

data, the ratios are smaller. In other words, males self-report more criminal behavior than females, but not to the degree suggested by official data. How can these differences be explained?

Explaining Gender Differences in the Crime Rate Early criminologists pointed to emotional, physical, and psychological differences between males and females to explain the differences in crime rates. Cesare Lombroso's 1895 book, *The Female Offender*, argued that a small group of female criminals lacked "typical" female traits of "piety, maternity, undeveloped intelligence, and weakness."[98] In physical appearance as well as in their emotional makeup, delinquent females appeared closer to men than to other women. Lombroso's theory became known as the masculinity hypothesis; in essence, a few "masculine" females were responsible for the handful of crimes women commit.

Another early view of female crime focused on the supposed dynamics of sexual relationships. Female criminals were viewed as either sexually controlling or sexually naive, either manipulating men for profit or being manipulated by them. The female's criminality was often masked because criminal justice authorities were reluctant to take action against a woman.[99] This perspective is known as the chivalry hypothesis, which holds that much female criminality is hidden because of the culture's generally protective and benevolent attitude toward women.[100] In other words, police are less likely to arrest, juries are less likely to convict, and judges are less likely to incarcerate female offenders.

Although these early writings are no longer taken seriously, some criminologists still believe that gender-based traits are a key determinant of crime rate differences. Among the suspected differences include physical strength and hormonal influences. According to this view, male sex hormones (androgens) account for more aggressive male behavior and that gender-related hormonal differences explain the gender gap in the crime rate.[101]

Why are girls less aggressive and violent than boys? One reason may be that girls are encouraged to care about other people and avoid harming them; their need for sensitivity and understanding may help counterbalance the effects of social problems. Another is that because they are more verbally proficient, females may develop social skills that help them deal with conflict without resorting to violence. And, as a result of these social skills, females are generally less belligerent than their males counterparts.

© David De Lossy/Photodisc/Getty Images

connections

Gender differences in the crime rate may be a function of androgen levels. These hormones cause areas of the brain to become less sensitive to environmental stimuli, making males more likely to seek high levels of stimulation and to tolerate more pain in the process. Chapter 5 discusses the biosocial causes of crime and reviews this issue in greater detail.

Socialization and Development Although there are few gender-based differences in aggression during the first few years of life, girls are socialized to be less aggressive than boys and are supervised more closely by parents.[102] Differences in aggression become noticeable between ages 3 and 6 when children are first socialized into organized peer groups such as the day care center or school. Males are more likely then to display physical aggression whereas girls display relational aggression—excluding disliked peers from playgroups, gossiping, and interfering with social relationships.

Males are taught to be more aggressive and assertive and less likely to form attachments to others. They often view their aggression as a gender-appropriate means to gain status and power, either by joining deviant groups and gangs or engaging in sports. Even in middle-class suburbs, they may seek approval by knocking down or running through peers on the playing field, while females literally cheer them on. The male search for social approval through aggressive behavior may make them more susceptible to criminality, especially when the chosen form of aggression is antisocial or illegal. Recent research by Jean Bottcher found that young boys perceive their roles as being more dominant than young girls.[103] Male perceptions of power, their ability to have freedom and hang with their friends, helped explain the gender differences in crime and delinquency.

In contrast, girls are encouraged to care about other people and avoid harming them; their need for sensitivity and understanding may help counterbalance the effects of poverty and family problems. And because they are more verbally proficient, many females may develop social skills that help them deal with conflict without resorting to violence. Females are taught to be less aggressive and to view belligerence as a lack of self-control—a conclusion that is unlikely to be reached by a male.

Girls are usually taught—directly or indirectly—to respond to provocation by feeling anxious and depressed, whereas boys are encouraged to retaliate. Overall, when they are provoked, females are much more likely to feel distressed than males, experiencing sadness, anxiety, and uneasiness. Although females may get angry as often as males, many have been taught to blame themselves for harboring such negative feelings. Females are therefore much more likely than males to respond to anger with feelings of depression, anxiety, fear, and shame. Although females are socialized to fear that their anger will harm valued relationships, males react with "moral outrage," looking to blame others for their discomfort.[104]

Cognitive Differences Psychologists note significant cognitive differences between boys and girls that may impact on their antisocial behaviors. Girls have been found to be superior to boys in verbal ability, whereas boys test higher in visual-spatial performance. Girls acquire language faster, learning to speak earlier and faster with better pronunciation. Girls are far less likely to have reading problems than boys, whereas boys do much better on standardized math tests. (This difference is attributed by some experts to boys receiving more attention from math teachers.) In most cases these cognitive differences are small, narrowing, and usually attributed to cultural expectations. When given training, girls demonstrate an ability to increase their visual-spatial skills to the point that their abilities become indistinguishable from the ability of boys.

Cognitive differences may contribute to behavioral variations. Even at an early age, girls are found to be more empathic than boys—that is, more capable of understanding and relating to the feelings of others.[105] Empathy for others may help shield girls from antisocial acts because they are more likely to understand a victim's suffering. Girls are more concerned with relationship and feeling issues, and they are less interested than boys are in competing for material success. Boys who are not tough and aggressive are labeled sissies and cry babies. In contrast, girls are expected to form closer bonds with their friends and share feelings. When faced with conflict, women might be more likely to attempt to negotiate, rather than to either respond passively or to physically resist, especially when they perceive increased threat of harm or death.[106]

Feminist Views In the 1970s, liberal feminist theory focused attention on the social and economic roles of women in society and their relationship to female crime rates.[107] This view suggested that the traditionally lower crime rate for women could be explained by their "second-class" economic and social position. As women's social roles changed and their lifestyles became more like men's, it was believed that their crime rates would converge. Criminologists, responding to this research, began to refer to the "new female criminal." The rapid increase in the female crime rates, especially in what had traditionally been male-oriented crimes (such as burglary and larceny), supports the feminist view. In addition, self-report studies seem to indicate that (a) the pattern of female criminality, if not its frequency, is quite similar to that of male criminality; and (b) the factors that predispose male criminals to crime have an equal impact on female criminals.[108]

connections

Critical criminologists view gender inequality as stemming from the unequal power of men and women in a capitalist society and the exploitation of females by fathers and husbands. This perspective is considered more fully in Chapter 8.

Is Convergence Likely? Although male arrest rates are still considerably higher than female rates, female arrest rates seem to be increasing at a faster pace; it is possible that they may eventually converge. Women are committing more crime and young girls are joining gangs in record numbers.[109]

Although these trends indicate that gender differences in the crime rate may be eroding, some criminologists remain skeptical about the data. They find that gender-based crime rate differences are still significant; the "emancipation of women" may have had relatively little influence on female crime rates.[110] For one thing, many female criminals come from the socioeconomic class least affected by the women's movement; their crimes seem more a function of economic inequality than women's rights. For another, the offense patterns of women are still quite different from those of men. Though males still commit a disproportionate share of serious crimes such as robbery, burglary, murder, and assault, most female criminals are still engaging in petty property crimes such as welfare and credit card fraud, and public order crimes such as prostitution.[111] How then can increases in female arrest rates be explained? According to Darrell Steffensmeier and his associates, these arrest trends may be explained more by changes in police activity than in criminal activity: police today may be more willing to arrest girls for minor crimes; police are making more arrests for crimes that occur at school and in the home; police are responding more vigorously to public demands for action and therefore are less likely to use their discretion to help females.[112] Police may also be abandoning their traditional deference toward women in an effort to be to be "gender neutral." In addition, changing laws such as dual arrest laws in domestic cases, which mandate both parties be taken into custody, result in more women suffering arrest in domestic incidents.[113]

Race and Crime

Official crime data indicate that minority group members are involved in a disproportionate share of criminal activity. African Americans make up about 12 percent of the general population, yet they account for almost 40 percent of Part I violent crime arrests and 30 percent of property crime arrests. They also are responsible for a disproportionate number of Part II arrests (except for alcohol-related arrests, which detain primarily white offenders).

It is possible that these data reflect true racial differences in the crime rate, but it is also likely that they reflect bias in the justice process. We can evaluate this issue by comparing racial differences in self-report data with those found in official delinquency records. Charges of racial discrimination in the justice process would be substantiated if whites and blacks self-reported equal numbers of crimes, but minorities were arrested and prosecuted far more often.

Early efforts by noted criminologists Leroy Gould in Seattle, Harwin Voss in Honolulu, and Ronald Akers in seven midwestern states, found virtually no relationship between race and self-reported delinquency.[114] These research efforts supported a case for police bias in the arrest decision. Other, more recent self-report studies that use large national samples of youths have

Empirical evidence shows that, in at least some jurisdictions, young African American males are treated more harshly by the criminal and juvenile justice systems than are members of any other group. Elements of institutional racism have become so endemic that terms such as "DWB" (driving while black) are now part of the vernacular, used to signify the fact that young African American motorists are routinely stopped by police.

also found little evidence of racial disparity in crimes committed.[115] Monitoring the Future data indicate that, if anything, black youths self-report less delinquent behavior and substance abuse than whites.[116] These and other self-report studies seem to indicate that the delinquent behavior rates of black and white teenagers are generally similar and that differences in arrest statistics may indicate a differential selection policy by police.[117] Suspects who are poor, minority, and male are more likely to be formally arrested than suspects who are white, affluent, and female.[118]

Racial differences in the crime rate remain an extremely sensitive issue. Although official arrest records indicate that African Americans are arrested at a higher rate than members of other racial groups, self-report data, which indicates greater equality between the races, suggest arrest rate differences are an artifact of justice system bias.[119] Some critics charge that police officers routinely use "racial profiling" to stop African Americans and search their cars without probable cause or

reasonable suspicion. Police officers, they glibly suggest, have created a new form of traffic offense called DWB, "driving while black."[120] National surveys of driving practices show that young black and Latino males are more likely to be stopped by police and suffer citations, searches, and arrests, as well as be the target of force, even though they are no more likely to be in the possession of illegal contraband than white drivers.[121]

Although the official statistics (such as UCR arrest data) may reflect discriminatory justice system practices, African Americans are arrested for a disproportionate amount of serious violent crime, such as robbery and murder, and it is improbable that police discretion and/or bias *alone* could account for these proportions. It is doubtful that police routinely release white killers, robbers, and rapists while arresting violent black offenders who commit the same offenses.[122] How can these racial differences in serious crimes be explained?

Racism and Discrimination To explain racial and ethnic differences in the violent crime rate, criminologists focus on the impact of economic deprivation and the legacy of racism discrimination on personality and behavior.[123] The fact that U.S. culture influences African American crime rates is underscored by the fact that black violence rates are much lower in other nations—both those that are predominantly white, such as Canada, and those that are predominantly black, such as Nigeria.[124]

Some criminologists view black crime as a function of socialization in a society where the black family was torn apart and black culture destroyed in such a way that recovery has proven impossible. Early experiences, beginning with slavery, have left a wound that has been deepened by racism and lack of opportunity.[125] Children of the slave society were thrust into a system of forced dependency and ambivalence and antagonism toward one's self and group.

In an important work, *All God's Children: The Bosket Family and the American Tradition of Violence,* crime reporter Fox Butterfield chronicles the history of the Boskets, a black family, through five generations.[126] He focuses on Willie Bosket, who is charming, captivating, and brilliant. He is also one of the worst criminals in the New York State penal system. By the time he was in his teens, he had committed more than 200 armed robberies and 25 stabbings. Butterfield shows how early struggles in the South, with its violent slave culture, led directly to Willie Bosket's rage and violence on the streets of New York City. Beginning in South Carolina in the 1700s, the southern slave society was a place where white notions of honor demanded immediate retaliation for the smallest slight. According to Butterfield, contemporary black violence is a tradition inherited from white southern violence. The need for respect has turned into a cultural mandate that can provoke retaliation at the slightest hint of insult.

The Racial Threat Hypothesis It is possible that the minority crime rate is relatively high because racism is still an element of daily life in the minority community and police behavior and decision making reflect a racial bias. Because the white population fears minorities, they demand that police exercise strict social control, arrest minorities for acts that would not result in official action if committed by whites, and devote more attention and resources to minority neighborhoods, resulting in higher arrest rates.

Collectively these beliefs have produced the **racial threat hypothesis**: as the percentage of minorities in the population increases so too does the amount of social control that police direct at minority group members.[127]

Those criminologists who find that the racial threat hypothesis holds traction point to the significant body of research showing that the justice system may be racially biased.[128] On an individual level, research shows that black and Latino adults are less likely to receive bail in violent crime cases than whites, and that minority group members are more likely to be kept in detention pending trial.[129] There is also evidence that African Americans, especially those who are indigent or unemployed, receive longer prison sentences than whites with the same employment status. It is possible that judges impose harsher punishments on minority group members because they view them as "social dynamite," considering them more dangerous and more likely to recidivate than white offenders.[130] Yet when African Americans are victims of crime, their predicaments receive less public concern and media attention than that afforded white victims.[131] Murders involving whites (and females) are much more likely to be punished with death than those whose victims are black males, a fact not lost on the minority population.[132]

On an institutional level, the racial threat hypothesis maintains that police are more likely to aggressively patrol minority neighborhoods, suspect, search, and arrest minority group members, and make arrests for minor infractions, helping to raise the minority crime rate. The racial threat hypothesis has been applied to Hispanics as well as African Americans. Research now shows that relatively poor Hispanics living in the United States are viewed as a threat that results in higher police expenditures. In the Southwest, especially in border communities, police maintain order and reinforce the physical and social isolation of poor barrio residents. As minority poverty becomes concentrated, relatively affluent citizens may mobilize politically to demand greater numbers of police to control the comparatively poor.[133]

The racial threat effect does not end with the police. As the percentage of minorities in a state jurisdiction increases, so too does the use of draconian sentencing practices. Take for instance the use of habitual offender statutes that provide very long sentences for a second or third conviction (i.e., "three strikes and you're out"). One recent study (2008) by Matthew Crow and Kathrine Johnson looked at the use of habitual sentencing practices in Florida and reached the conclusion that race and ethnicity still matter: minority drug and violent offenders are viewed as particular threats to dominant, mainstream values and are more likely to be charged as habitual offenders than European Americans.[134]

Disparities in justice policy result in the widely disproportionate makeup of the prison population. As Figure 2.8 shows, the percentage of minority men and women who are behind bars is far higher than the percentage of European Americans. It is not surprising then that African Americans of all social classes hold negative attitudes toward the justice system and view it as an arbitrary and unfair institution.[135]

Economic and Social Disparity Racial and ethnic differentials in crime rates may also be tied to economic and social disparity. Racial and ethnic minorities are often forced to live in high crime areas where the risk of victimization is significant. People who witness violent crime and are victimized may themselves engage in violence.[136]

Racial and ethnic minorities face a greater degree of social isolation and economic deprivation than the white majority, a condition that has been linked by empirical research to high violence rates.[137] Not helping the situation is the fact that during tough economic times, blacks and whites may find themselves competing for shrinking job opportunities. As economic competition between the races grows, interracial homicides do likewise; economic and political rivalries lead to greater levels of interracial violence.[138]

Even during times of economic growth, lower-class African Americans are left out of the economic mainstream, a fact that meets with a growing sense of frustration and failure.[139] As a result of being shut out of educational and economic opportunities enjoyed by the rest of society, this population may be susceptible to the lure of illegitimate gain and criminality. African Americans living in lower-class inner-city areas may be disproportionately violent because they are exposed to more violence in their daily lives than other racial and economic groups.[140] Many black youths are forced to attend essentially segregated schools that are underfunded and deteriorated, a condition that elevates the likelihood of their being incarcerated in adulthood.[141]

connections

The concept of relative deprivation refers to the fact that people compare their success to those with whom they are in immediate contact. Even if conditions improve, they still may feel as if they are falling behind. A sense of relative deprivation, discussed in Chapter 6, may lead to criminal activity.

Family Dissolution Family dissolution in the minority community may be tied to low employment rates among African American males, which places a strain on marriages. The relatively large number of single, female-headed households in these communities may be tied to the high mortality rate among African American males, due in part to their increased risk of early death by disease or violence.[142] When families are weakened or disrupted, their social control is compromised. It is not surprising, then, that divorce and separation

Figure 2.8 Who's Behind Bars

As of January 1, 2008, more than one in every one hundred adults is behind bars. For the most part, incarceration is heavily concentrated among men, racial and ethnic minorities, and 20- and 30-year-olds. Among men, the highest rate is among black males aged 20 to 34; among women, it's with black females aged 35 to 39.

Men

All men ages 18 or older: **1 in 54**

White men ages 18 or older: **1 in 106**

Hispanic men ages 18 or older: **1 in 36**

Black men ages 18 or older: **1 in 15**

Black men ages 20–34: **1 in 9**

Women

All women ages 35–39: **1 in 265**

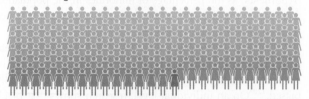

White women ages 35–39: **1 in 355**

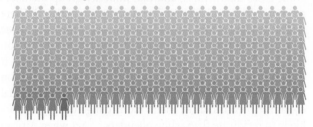

Hispanic women ages 35–39: **1 in 297**

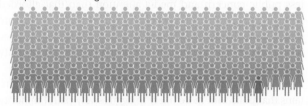

Black women ages 35–39: **1 in 100**

Source: The Pew Center on the States, One in 100: Behind Bars in America 2008 (Washington, DC: Pew Foundation, 2008), www.pewcenteronthestates.org/uploadedFiles/8015PCTS_Prison08_FINAL_2-1-1_FORWEB.pdf, p. 6 (accessed July 10, 2008).

rates are significantly associated with homicide rates in the African American community.[143]

connections

According to some criminologists, racism has created isolated subcultures that espouse violence as a way of coping with conflict situations. Exasperation and frustration among minority group members who feel powerless to fit into middle-class society are manifested in aggression. This view is discussed further in Chapter 10, which reviews the subculture of violence theory.

Is Convergence Possible? Considering these overwhelming social problems, is it possible that racial crime rates will soon converge? One argument is that if economic conditions improve in the minority community, then differences in crime rates will eventually disappear.[144] A trend toward residential integration, underway since 1980, may also help reduce crime rate differentials.[145] Convergence in crime rates will occur if economic and social obstacles can be removed.

In sum, the weight of the evidence shows that although there is little difference in the self-reported crime rates of racial groups, Hispanics and African Americans are more likely to be arrested for serious violent crimes. The causes of minority crime have been linked to poverty, racism, hopelessness, lack of

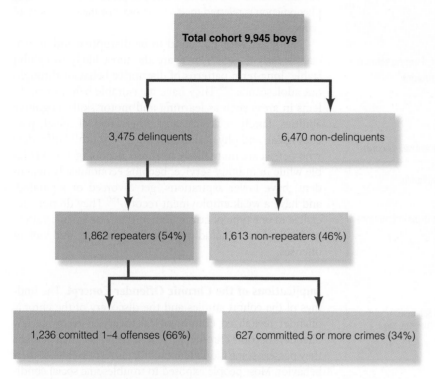

Figure 2.9 Distribution of Offenses in the Philadelphia Cohort

Total cohort 9,945 boys

3,475 delinquents

6,470 non-delinquents

1,862 repeaters (54%)

1,613 non-repeaters (46%)

1,236 comitted 1–4 offenses (66%)

627 committed 5 or more crimes (34%)

Source: Marvin Wolfgang, Robert Figlio, and Thorsten Sellin, *Delinquency in a Birth Cohort* (Chicago: University of Chicago Press, 1972).

opportunity, and urban problems experienced by all too many African American citizens.

Chronic Offenders/Criminal Careers

Crime data show that most offenders commit a single criminal act and upon arrest discontinue their antisocial activity. Others commit a few less-serious crimes. A small group of criminal offenders, however, account for a majority of all criminal offenses. These persistent offenders are referred to as **career criminals** or **chronic offenders**. The concept of the chronic or career offender is most closely associated with the research efforts of Marvin Wolfgang, Robert Figlio, and Thorsten Sellin.[146] In their landmark 1972 study, *Delinquency in a Birth Cohort,* they used official records to follow the criminal careers of a cohort of 9,945 boys born in Philadelphia in 1945 from the time of their birth until they reached 18 years of age in 1963. Official police records were used to identify delinquents. About one-third of the boys (3,475) had some police contact. The remaining two-thirds (6,470) had none. Each delinquent was given a seriousness weight score for every delinquent act.[147] The weighting of delinquent acts allowed the researchers to differentiate between a simple assault requiring no medical attention for the victim and serious battery in which the

victim needed hospitalization. The best-known discovery of Wolfgang and his associates was that of the so-called chronic offender. The cohort data indicated that 54 percent (1,862) of the sample's delinquent youths were repeat offenders, whereas the remaining 46 percent (1,613) were one-time offenders. The repeaters could be further categorized as non-chronic recidivists and chronic recidivists. The former consisted of 1,235 youths who had been arrested more than once but fewer than five times and who made up 35.6 percent of all delinquents. The latter were a group of 627 boys arrested five times or more, who accounted for 18 percent of the delinquents and 6 percent of the total sample of 9,945 (see Figure 2.9).

The chronic offenders (known today as "the chronic 6 percent") were involved in the most dramatic amounts of delinquent behavior: they were responsible for 5,305 offenses, or 51.9 percent of all the offenses committed by the cohort. Even more striking was the involvement of chronic offenders in serious criminal acts. Of the entire sample, the chronic 6 percent committed 71 percent of the homicides, 73 percent of the rapes, 82 percent of the robberies, and 69 percent of the aggravated assaults.

Wolfgang and his associates found that arrests and court experience did little to deter the chronic offender. In fact, punishment was inversely related to chronic offending: the more stringent the sanction chronic offenders received, the more likely they would be to engage in repeated criminal behavior.

In a second cohort study, Wolfgang and his associates selected a new, larger birth cohort, born in Philadelphia in 1958, which contained both male and female subjects.[148] Although the proportion of delinquent youths was about the same as that in the 1945 cohort, they again found a similar pattern of chronic offending. Chronic female delinquency was relatively rare—only 1 percent of the females in the survey were chronic offenders. Wolfgang's pioneering effort to identify the chronic career offender has been replicated by a number of other researchers in a variety of locations in the United States.[149] The chronic offender has also been found abroad.[150]

What Causes Chronicity? As might be expected, kids who have been exposed to a variety of personal and social problems at an early age are the most at risk to repeat offending, a concept referred to as **early onset**. One important study of delinquent offenders in Orange County, California, conducted

Characteristics that Predict Chronic Offending

School Behavior/Performance Factor

- Attendance problems (truancy or a pattern of skipping school)
- Behavior problems (recent suspensions or expulsion)
- Poor grades (failing two or more classes)

Family Problem Factor

- Poor parental supervision and control
- Significant family problems (illness, substance abuse, discord)
- Criminal family members
- Documented child abuse, neglect, or family violence

Substance Abuse Factor

- Alcohol or drug use (by minors in any way but experimentation)

Delinquency Factor

- Stealing pattern of behavior
- Runaway pattern of behavior
- Gang member or associate

Source: Michael Schumacher and Gwen Kurz, *The 8% Solution: Preventing Serious Repeat Juvenile Crime* (Thousand Oaks, CA: Sage, 1999).

by Michael Schumacher and Gwen Kurz, found several factors (see Exhibit 2.2) that characterized the chronic offender, including problems in the home and at school.[151] Other research studies have found that involvement in criminal activity (getting arrested before age 15), relatively low intellectual development, and parental drug involvement are key predictive factors for chronicity.[152] Offenders who accumulate large debts, use drugs, and resort to violence are more likely to persist.[153] In contrast, those who spend time in a juvenile facility and later in an adult prison are more likely to eventually desist in their adulthood.[154]

connections

It is evident that chronic offenders suffer from a profusion of social problems. Some criminologists believe that accumulating a significant variety of these social deficits is the key to understanding criminal development. For more on this topic, see the discussion on problem behavior syndrome in Chapter 9.

Persistence: The Continuity of Crime One of the most important findings from the cohort studies is that persistent juvenile offenders are the ones most likely to continue their criminal careers into adulthood.[155] Paul Tracy and Kimberly Kempf-Leonard followed up all subjects in the second 1958 cohort and found that two-thirds of delinquent offenders

desisted from crime, but those who started their delinquent careers early and who committed serious violent crimes throughout adolescence were the most likely to persist as adults.[156] This phenomenon is referred to as **persistence** or the **continuity of crime**.[157]

Children who are found to be disruptive and antisocial as early as age 5 or 6 are the most likely to exhibit stable, long-term patterns of disruptive behavior throughout adolescence.[158] They have measurable behavior problems in areas such as learning and motor skills, cognitive abilities, family relations, and other areas of social, psychological, and physical functioning.[159] Youthful offenders who persist are more likely to abuse alcohol, get into trouble while in military service, become economically dependent, have lower aspirations, get divorced or separated, and have a weak employment record.[160] They do not specialize in one type of crime; rather, they engage in a variety of criminal acts, including theft, use of drugs, and violent offenses.

Implications of the Chronic Offender Concept The findings of the cohort studies and the discovery of the chronic offender revitalized criminological theory. If relatively few offenders become chronic, persistent criminals, then perhaps they possess some individual trait that is responsible for their behavior. Most people exposed to troublesome social conditions, such as poverty, do not become chronic offenders, so it is unlikely that social conditions alone can cause chronic offending. Traditional theories of criminal behavior have failed to distinguish between chronic and occasional offenders. They concentrate more on explaining why people begin to commit crime and pay scant attention to why people stop offending. The discovery of the chronic offender 30 years ago forced criminologists to consider such issues as persistence and desistance in their explanations of crime; more recent theories account for not only the onset of criminality but also its termination.

The chronic offender has become a central focus of crime control policy. Apprehension and punishment seem to have little effect on the offending behavior of chronic offenders and most repeat their criminal acts after their correctional release.[161] Because chronic offenders rarely learn from their mistakes, sentencing policies designed to incapacitate chronic offenders for long periods of time without hope of probation or parole have been established. Incapacitation rather than rehabilitation is the goal. Among the policies spurred by the chronic offender concept are mandatory sentences for violent or drug-related crimes, "three strikes" policies, which require people convicted of a third felony offense to serve a mandatory life sentence, and "truth in sentencing" policies, which require that convicted felons spend a significant portion of their sentence behind bars. Whether such policies can reduce crime rates or are merely "get tough" measures designed to placate conservative voters remains to be seen.

THINKING LIKE A CRIMINOLOGIST

The planning director for the State Department of Juvenile Justice has asked for your advice on how to reduce the threat of chronic offenders. Some of the more conservative members of her staff seem to believe that these kids need a strict dose of rough justice if they are to be turned away from a life of crime. They believe juvenile delinquents who are punished harshly are less likely to recidivate than youths who receive lesser punishments, such as community corrections or probation. In addition, they believe that hard-core, violent offenders deserve to be punished; excessive concern for offenders and not their acts ignores the rights of victims and society in general.

The planning director is unsure whether such an approach can reduce the threat of chronic offending. Can tough punishment produce deviant identities that lock kids into a criminal way of life? She is concerned that a strategy stressing punishment will have relatively little impact on chronic offenders and, if anything, may cause escalation in serious criminal behaviors. She has asked you for your professional advice.

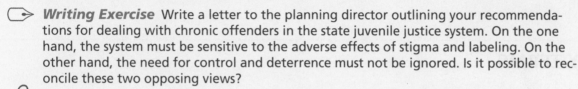

Writing Exercise Write a letter to the planning director outlining your recommendations for dealing with chronic offenders in the state juvenile justice system. On the one hand, the system must be sensitive to the adverse effects of stigma and labeling. On the other hand, the need for control and deterrence must not be ignored. Is it possible to reconcile these two opposing views?

Doing Research on the Web To help formulate your answer to the question above, you might want to review some of these web-based resources:

▮ Eric B. Schnurer and Charles R. Lyons, "Turning Chronic Juvenile Offenders into Productive Citizens: Comprehensive Model Emerging."

▮ For an international view, see "Juvenile Offending: Predicting Persistence and Determining the Cost-Effectiveness of Intervention."

These websites can be accessed via academic.cengage.com/criminaljustice/siegel.

SUMMARY

▮ Criminologists use various research methods to gather information that will shed light on criminal behavior. These include surveys, cohort studies, official record studies, experiments, observations, and meta-analysis/systematic reviews.

▮ The FBI's *Uniform Crime Report* is an annual tally of crime reported to local police departments. It is the nation's official crime database.

▮ The National Crime Victimization Survey (NCVS) uses nationally drawn samples to estimate the total number of victimizations, including those not reported to police.

▮ Self-report surveys ask respondents about their own criminal activity. They are useful in measuring crimes rarely reported to police, such as drug usage.

▮ Each data source has its strengths and weaknesses, and although different from one another, they actually agree on the nature of criminal behavior.

▮ Crime rates peaked in the early 1990s and have been in sharp decline ever since. While there has been some stabilization in recent years, the rates of most crimes are now lower than they were a decade ago.

▮ A number of factors are believed to influence the crime rate, including the economy, drug use, gun availability, and crime control policies such as adding police and putting more criminals in prison.

▮ It is difficult to gauge future trends. Some experts forecast an increase in crime, while others foresee a long-term decline in the crime rate.

▮ The data sources show stable patterns in the crime rate.

- Ecological patterns show that some areas of the country are more crime prone than others, that there are seasons and times for crime, and that these patterns are quite stable.

- There is also evidence of gender and age gaps in the crime rate: Men commit more crime than women, and young people commit more crime than the elderly. Crime data show that people commit less crime as they age, but the significance and cause of this pattern is not completely understood.

- Similarly, racial and class patterns appear in the crime rate. However, it is unclear whether these are true differences or a function of discriminatory law enforcement. Some criminologists suggest that institutional racism, such as police profiling, accounts for the racial differences in the crime rate. Others believe that high African American crime rates are a function of living in a racially segregated society.

- One of the most important findings in the crime statistics is the existence of the chronic offender, a repeat criminal responsible for a significant amount of all law violations. Chronic offenders begin their careers early in life and, rather than aging out of crime, persistently offend into adulthood. The discovery of the chronic offender has led to the study of developmental criminology—why people persist, desist, terminate, or escalate their deviant behavior.

- **CENGAGENOW** is an easy-to-use online resource that helps you study in less time to get the grade you want—NOW. CengageNOW™ Personalized Study (a diagnostic study tool containing valuable text-specific resources) lets you focus on just what you don't know and learn more in less time to get a better grade. If your textbook does not include an access code card, you can go to www.ichapters.com to purchase CengageNOW™.

KEY TERMS

Uniform Crime Report (UCR) *(30)*
index crimes *(30)*
Part I crimes *(30)*
Part II crimes *(30)*
cleared crimes *(31)*
National Incident-Based Reporting System (NIBRS) *(34)*
sampling *(34)*
population *(34)*
cross-sectional survey *(34)*

National Crime Victimization Survey (NCVS) *(34)*
self-report survey *(35)*
cohort research *(38)*
retrospective cohort study *(38)*
meta-analysis *(39)*
systematic review *(39)*
instrumental crimes *(49)*
expressive crimes *(49)*
aging out *(53)*

masculinity hypothesis *(54)*
chivalry hypothesis *(54)*
liberal feminist theory *(55)*
racial threat hypothesis *(57)*
career criminals *(59)*
chronic offenders *(59)*
early onset *(59)*
persistence *(60)*
continuity of crime *(60)*
three strikes *(60)*

CRITICAL THINKING QUESTIONS

1. Would you answer honestly if a national crime survey asked you about your criminal behavior, including drinking and drug use? If not, why not? If you would not answer honestly, do you question the accuracy of self-report surveys?

2. How would you explain gender differences in the crime rate? Why do you think males are more violent than females?

3. Assuming that males are more violent than females, does that mean crime has a biological rather than a social basis (because males and females share a similar environment)?

4. The UCR reports that crime rates are higher in large cities than in small towns. What does that tell us about the effects of TV, films, and music on teenage behavior?

5. What social and environmental factors do you believe influence the crime rate? Do you think a national emergency would increase or decrease crime rates?

NOTES

1. FBI, "Never Say Die: The Relentless Pursuit of a Killer," August 13, 2007, www.fbi.gov/page2/august07/henderson081307.htm (accessed June 26, 2008).
2. Mirka Smolej and Janne Kivivuori, "The Relation Between Crime News and Fear of Violence," *Journal of Scandinavian Studies in Criminology and Crime Prevention* 7 (2006), 211–227.
3. The Gallup Organization, Inc., *The Gallup Poll*, www.gallup.com/poll/1603/Crime.aspx (accessed June 26, 2008).
4. Data provided by the *Sourcebook of Criminal Justice Statistics*, Hindelang Criminal Justice Research Center, State University of New York at Albany, 2008, www.albany.edu/sourcebook/pdf/t2402007.pdf (accessed June 26, 2008).

5. Federal Bureau of Investigation, *Crime in the United States, 2006* (Washington, DC: U.S. Government Printing Office, 2007), www.fbi.gov/ucr/cius2006/ (accessed June 26, 2008). Herein cited in notes as FBI, Uniform Crime Report, and referred to in text as Uniform Crime Report or UCR. When possible, data has been updated with preliminary 2007 preliminary results: www.fbi.gov/ucr/prelim2007/ (accessed June 26, 2008).

6. Richard Felson, Steven Messner, Anthony Hoskin, and Glenn Deane, "Reasons for Reporting and Not Reporting Domestic Violence to the Police," *Criminology* 40 (2002): 617–648.

7. Shannan Catalano, *Criminal Victimization 2003* (Washington, DC: Bureau of Justice Statistics, 2004). Herein cited as NCVS, 2003.

8. Duncan Chappell, Gilbert Geis, Stephen Schafer, and Larry Siegel, "Forcible Rape: A Comparative Study of Offenses Known to the Police in Boston and Los Angeles," in *Studies in the Sociology of Sex*, ed. James Henslin (New York: Appleton Century Crofts, 1971), pp. 169–193.

9. Patrick Jackson, "Assessing the Validity of Official Data on Arson," *Criminology* 26 (1988): 181–195.

10. Lawrence Sherman and Barry Glick, "The Quality of Arrest Statistics," *Police Foundation Reports* 2 (1984): 1–8.

11. David Seidman and Michael Couzens, "Getting the Crime Rate Down: Political Pressure and Crime Reporting," *Law and Society Review* 8 (1974): 457.

12. Ariel Hart, "Report Finds Atlanta Police Cut Figures on Crimes," *New York Times,* 21 February 2004, p. A3.

13. Robert Davis and Bruce Taylor, "A Proactive Response to Family Violence: The Results of a Randomized Experiment," *Criminology* 35 (1997): 307–333.

14. Robert O'Brien, "Police Productivity and Crime Rates: 1973–1992," *Criminology* 34 (1996): 183–207.

15. Leonard Savitz, "Official Statistics," in *Contemporary Criminology*, eds. Leonard Savitz and Norman Johnston (New York: Wiley, 1982), pp. 3–15.

16. FBI, *UCR Handbook* (Washington, DC: U.S. Government Printing Office, 1998), p. 33.

17. Bureau of Justice Statistics, "About Incident-Based Statistics and the National Incident-Based Reporting System (NIBRS)," www.ojp.usdoj.gov/bjs/ibrs.htm (accessed June 26, 2008).

18. Lynn Addington, "The Effect of NIBRS Reporting on Item Missing Data in Murder Cases," *Homicide Studies* 8 (2004): 193–213.

19. Michael Gottfredson and Travis Hirschi, "The Methodological Adequacy of Longitudinal Research on Crime," *Criminology* 25 (1987): 581–614.

20. Bureau of Justice Statistics, "The Nation's Two Crime Measures," www.ojp.usdoj.gov/bjs/pub/html/ntcm.htm (accessed June 26, 2008).

21. Michael Rand and Shannan Catalano, *Criminal Victimization, 2006* (Washington, DC: Bureau of Justice Statistics, 2007), www.ojp.usdoj.gov/bjs/pub/pdf/cv06.pdf (accessed July 2, 2008).

22. Lynn Addington and Callie Marie Rennison, "Rape Co-occurrence: Do Additional Crimes Affect Victim Reporting and Police Clearance of Rape?" *Journal of Quantitative Criminology* 24 (2008): 205–226.

23. L. Edward Wells and Joseph Rankin, "Juvenile Victimization: Convergent Validation of Alternative Measurements," *Journal of Research in Crime and Delinquency* 32 (1995): 287–307.

24. Robert M. Groves and Daniel L. Cork, *Surveying Victims: Options for Conducting the National Crime Victimization Survey* (Washington, DC: National Research Council, 2008), www.nap.edu/catalog/12090.html (accessed June 26, 2008).

25. Saul Kassin, Richard Leo, Christian Meissner, Kimberly Richman, Lori Colwell, Amy-May Leach, and Dana La Fon, "Police Interviewing and Interrogation: A Self-Report Survey of Police Practices and Beliefs," *Law and Human Behavior* 31 (2007): 381–400.

26. Christiane Brems, Mark Johnson, David Neal, and Melinda Freemon, "Childhood Abuse History and Substance Use among Men and Women Receiving Detoxification Services," *American Journal of Drug and Alcohol Abuse* 30 (2004): 799–821.

27. Lloyd Johnston, Patrick O'Malley, and Jerald Bachman, *Monitoring the Future, 2006* (Ann Arbor, MI: Institute for Social Research, 2006).

28. D. Wayne Osgood, Lloyd Johnston, Patrick O'Malley, and Jerald Bachman, "The Generality of Deviance in Late Adolescence and Early Adulthood," *American Sociological Review* 53 (1988): 81–93.

29. Leonore Simon, "Validity and Reliability of Violent Juveniles: A Comparison of Juvenile Self-Reports with Adult Self-Reports Incarcerated in Adult Prisons," paper presented at the annual meeting of the American Society of Criminology, Boston, November 1995, p. 26.

30. Stephen Cernkovich, Peggy Giordano, and Meredith Pugh, "Chronic Offenders: The Missing Cases in Self-Report Delinquency Research," *Journal of Criminal Law and Criminology* 76 (1985): 705–732.

31. Terence Thornberry, Beth Bjerregaard, and William Miles, "The Consequences of Respondent Attrition in Panel Studies: A Simulation Based on the Rochester Youth Development Study," *Journal of Quantitative Criminology* 9 (1993): 127–158.

32. Julia Yun Soo Kim, Michael Fendrich, and Joseph S. Wislar, "The Validity of Juvenile Arrestees' Drug Use Reporting: A Gender Comparison," *Journal of Research in Crime and Delinquency* 37 (2000): 419–432.

33. Donald Tomaskovic-Devey, Cynthia Pfaff Wright, Ronald Czaja, and Kirk Miller, "Self-Reports of Police Speeding Stops by Race: Results from the North Carolina Reverse Record Check Survey," *Journal of Quantitative Criminology* 22 (2006): 279–297,

34. See Spencer Rathus and Larry Siegel, "Crime and Personality Revisited: Effects of MMPI Sets on Self-Report Studies," *Criminology* 18 (1980): 245–251; John Clark and Larry Tifft, "Polygraph and Interview Validation of Self-Reported Deviant Behavior," *American Sociological Review* 31 (1966): 516–523.

35. Mallie Paschall, Miriam Ornstein, and Robert Flewelling, "African-American Male Adolescents' Involvement in the Criminal Justice System: The Criterion Validity of Self-Report Measures in Prospective Study," *Journal of Research in Crime and Delinquency* 38 (2001): 174–187.

36. Jennifer Roberts, Edward Mulvey, Julie Horney, John Lewis, and Michael Arter, "A Test of Two Methods of Recall for Violent Events," *Journal of Quantitative Criminology* 21 (2005): 175–193.

37. Lila Kazemian and David Farrington, "Comparing the Validity of Prospective, Retrospective, and Official Onset for Different Offending Categories," *Journal of Quantitative Criminology* 21 (2005): 127–147.

38. Barbara Warner and Brandi Wilson Coomer, "Neighborhood Drug Arrest Rates: Are They a Meaningful Indicator of Drug Activity? A Research Note," *Journal of Research in Crime and Delinquency* 40 (2003): 123–139.

39. Alfred Blumstein, Jacqueline Cohen, and Richard Rosenfeld, "Trend and Deviation in Crime Rates: A Comparison of UCR and NCVS Data for Burglary and Robbery," *Criminology* 29 (1991): 237–248. See also Michael Hindelang, Travis Hirschi, and Joseph Weis, *Measuring Delinquency* (Beverly Hills: Sage, 1981).

40. See generally David Farrington, Lloyd Ohlin, and James Q. Wilson, *Understanding and Controlling Crime* (New York: Springer-Verlag, 1986), pp. 11–18.

41. Claire Sterk-Elifson, "Just for Fun? Cocaine Use among Middle-Class Women," *Journal of Drug Issues* 26 (1996): 63–76.

42. Ibid., p. 63.

43. William F. Whyte, *Street Corner Society* (Chicago: University of Chicago Press, 1955).

44. Herman Schwendinger and Julia Schwendinger, *Adolescent Subcultures and Delinquency* (New York: Praeger, 1985).

45. David Farrington and Brandon Welsh, "Improved Street Lighting and Crime Prevention," *Justice Quarterly* 19 (2002): 313–343.

46. Colleen McCue, Emily Stone, and Teresa Gooch, "Data Mining and Value-Added Analysis," *FBI Law Enforcement Bulletin* 72 (2003): 1–6.

47. Colleen McCue, "Using Data Mining to Predict and Prevent Violent Crimes," presentation made to SPSS Incorporated, 2004, www.spss.com/dirvideo/richmond .htm (accessed June 26, 2008).

48. Jerry Ratcliffe, "Aoristic Signatures and the Spatio-Temporal Analysis of High Volume Crime Patterns," *Journal of Quantitative Criminology* 18 (2002): 23–43.

49. *TechBeat*, National Law Enforcement and Corrections Technology Center, "A Good Catch," www.nlectc.org/techbeat/ spring2006/AGoodCatch.pdf; www .crimeanalysts.net/catch.htm (both sites accessed June 26, 2008). For general information about the CMAP initiative, visit www.crimeanalysts.net (accessed June 26, 2008).

50. Clarence Schrag, *Crime and Justice: American Style* (Washington, DC: U.S. Government Printing Office, 1971), p. 17.

51. Thomas Bernard, "Juvenile Crime and the Transformation of Juvenile Justice: Is There a Juvenile Crime Wave?" *Justice Quarterly* 16 (1999): 336–356.

52. FBI, "FBI Releases its 2006 Crime Statistics," September 24, 2007, www.fbi .gov/ucr/cius2006/about/crime_summary .html (accessed June 26, 2008).

53. Michael Rand and Shannan Catalano, *Criminal Victimization, 2006* (Washington, DC: Bureau of Justice Statistics), www.ojp .usdoj.gov/bjs/pub/pdf/cv06.pdf (accessed June 26, 2008).

54. Steven Levitt, "The Limited Role of Changing Age Structure in Explaining Aggregate Crime Rates," *Criminology* 37 (1999): 581–599.

55. Darrell Steffensmeier and Miles Harer, "Did Crime Rise or Fall during the Reagan Presidency? The Effects of an 'Aging' U.S. Population on the Nation's Crime Rate," *Journal of Research in Crime and Delinquency* 28 (1991): 330–339.

56. Darrell Steffensmeier and Miles Harer, "Making Sense of Recent U.S. Crime Trends, 1980 to 1996/1998: Age Composition Effects and Other Explanations," *Journal of Research in Crime and Delinquency* 36 (1999): 235–274.

57. Ibid., p. 265.

58. Ralph Weisheit and L. Edward Wells, "The Future of Crime in Rural America," *Journal of Crime and Justice* 22 (1999): 1–22.

59. Ellen Cohn, "The Effect of Weather and Temporal Variations on Calls for Police Service," *American Journal of Police* 15 (1996): 23–43.

60. R. A. Baron, "Aggression as a Function of Ambient Temperature and Prior Anger Arousal," *Journal of Personality and Social Psychology* 21 (1972): 183–189.

61. Brad Bushman, Morgan Wang, and Craig Anderson, "Is the Curve Relating Temperature to Aggression Linear or Curvilinear? Assaults and Temperature in Minneapolis Reexamined," *Journal of Personality and Social Psychology* 89 (2005): 62–66.

62. Paul Bell, "Reanalysis and Perspective in the Heat-Aggression Debate," *Journal of Personality and Social Psychology* 89 (2005): 71–73.

63. Ellen Cohn, "The Prediction of Police Calls for Service: The Influence of Weather and Temporal Variables on Rape and Domestic Violence," *Journal of Environmental Psychology* 13 (1993): 71–83.

64. John Simister and Cary Cooper, "Thermal Stress in the U.S.A.: Effects on Violence and on Employee Behaviour," *Stress and Health* 21 (2005): 3–15.

65. James Rotton and Ellen Cohn, "Outdoor Temperature, Climate Control, and Criminal Asault," *Environment and Behavior* 36 (2004): 276–306.

66. See generally Franklin Zimring and Gordon Hawkins, *Crime Is Not the Problem: Lethal Violence in America* (New York Oxford University Press, 1997).

67. Ibid., p. 36.

68. Gary Kleck and Marc Gertz, "Armed Resistance to Crime: The Prevalence and Nature of Self-Defense with a Gun," *Journal of Criminal Law and Criminology* 86 (1995): 219–249.

69. Felipe Estrada and Anders Nilsson, "Segregation and Victimization: Neighbourhood Resources, Individual Risk Factors and Exposure to Property Crime," *European Journal of Criminology* 5 (2008): 193–216.

70. Robert Nash Parker, "Bringing 'Booze' Back In: The Relationship between Alcohol and Homicide," *Journal of Research in Crime and Delinquency* 32 (1995): 3–38.

71. Victoria Brewer and M. Dwayne Smith, "Gender Inequality and Rates of Female Homicide Victimization across U.S. Cities," *Journal of Research in Crime and Delinquency* 32 (1995): 175–190.

72. James Short and F. Ivan Nye, "Extent of Unrecorded Juvenile Delinquency, Tentative Conclusions," *Journal of Criminal Law, Criminology, and Police Science* 49 (1958): 296–302.

73. Ivan Nye, James Short, and Virgil Olsen, "Socio-Economic Status and Delinquent Behavior," *American Journal of Sociology* 63 (1958): 381–389; Robert Dentler and Lawrence Monroe, "Social Correlates of Early Adolescent Theft," *American Sociological Review* 63 (1961): 733–743. See also Terence Thornberry and Margaret Farnworth, "Social Correlates of Criminal Involvement: Further Evidence of the Relationship between Social Status and Criminal Behavior," *American Sociological Review* 47 (1982): 505–518.

74. Charles Tittle, Wayne Villemez, and Douglas Smith, "The Myth of Social Class and Criminality: An Empirical Assessment of the Empirical Evidence," *American Sociological Review* 43 (1978): 643–656.

75. David Brownfield, "Social Class and Violent Behavior," *Criminology* 24 (1986): 421–439.

76. Douglas Smith and Laura Davidson, "Interfacing Indicators and Constructs in Criminological Research: A Note on the Comparability of Self-Report Violence Data for Race and Sex Groups," *Criminology* 24 (1986): 473–488.

77. R. Gregory Dunaway, Francis Cullen, Velmer Burton, and T. David Evans, "The Myth of Social Class and Crime Revisited: An Examination of Class and Adult Criminality," *Criminology* 38 (2000): 589–632.

78. Lauren Krivo and Ruth D. Peterson, "Labor Market Conditions and Violent Crime among Youth and Adults," *Sociological Perspectives* 47 (2004): 485–505.

79. Judith Blau and Peter Blau, "The Cost of Inequality: Metropolitan Structure and Violent Crime," *American Sociological Review* 147 (1982): 114–129; Richard Block, "Community Environment and Violent Crime," *Criminology* 17 (1979): 46–57; Robert Sampson, "Structural Sources of Variation in Race-Age-Specific Rates of Offending across Major U.S. Cities," *Criminology* 23 (1985): 647–673.

80. Chin-Chi Hsieh and M. D. Pugh, "Poverty, Income Inequality, and Violent Crime: A Meta-Analysis of Recent Aggregate Data Studies," *Criminal Justice Review* 18 (1993): 182–199.

81. Richard Miech, Avshalom Caspi, Terrie Moffitt, Bradley Entner Wright, and Phil Silva, "Low Socioeconomic Status and Mental Disorders: A Longitudinal Study of Selection and Causation during Young Adulthood," *American Journal of Sociology* 104 (1999): 1,096–1,131; Marvin Krohn, Alan Lizotte, and Cynthia Perez, "The Interrelationship between Substance Use and Precocious Transitions to Adult Sexuality," *Journal of Health and Social Behavior* 38 (1997): 87–103, at 88; Richard Jessor, "Risk Behavior in Adolescence: A Psychosocial Framework for Understanding and Action," in *Adolescents at Risk: Medical and Social Perspectives,* eds. D. E. Rogers and E. Ginzburg (Boulder, CO: Westview, 1992).

82. Ramiro Martinez, Jacob Stowell, and Jeffrey Cancino, "A Tale of Two Border Cities: Community Context, Ethnicity, and Homicide," *Social Science Quarterly* 89 (2008): 1–16.

83. Robert Agnew, "A General Strain Theory of Community Differences in Crime Rates," *Journal of Research in Crime and Delinquency* 36 (1999): 123–155.

84. Bonita Veysey and Steven Messner, "Further Testing of Social Disorganization Theory: An Elaboration of Sampson and Groves's Community Structure and Crime," *Journal of Research in Crime and Delinquency* 36 (1999): 156–174.

85. Lance Hannon and James DeFronzo, "Welfare and Property Crime," *Justice Quarterly* 15 (1998): 273–288.

86. Travis Hirschi and Michael Gottfredson, "Age and the Explanation of Crime," *American Journal of Sociology* 89 (1983): 552–584, at 581.

87. Misaki Natsuaki, Xiaojia Ge, and Ernst Wenk, "Continuity and Changes in the Developmental Trajectories of Criminal Career: Examining the Roles of Timing of First Arrest and High School Graduation," *Journal of Youth and Adolescence* 37 (2008): 431–444.

88. Lisa Stolzenberg and Stewart D'Alessio, "Co-Offending and the Age-Crime Curve," *Journal of Research in Crime and Delinquency* 45 (2008): 65–86.

89. Derek Kreager, "When It's Good to Be 'Bad': Violence and Adolescent Peer Acceptance," *Criminology* 45 (2007): 893–923.

90. For a comprehensive review of crime and the elderly, see Kyle Kercher, "Causes and Correlates of Crime Committed by the Elderly," in *Critical Issues in Aging Policy,* eds. E. Borgatta and R. Montgomery (Beverly Hills: Sage, 1987), pp. 254–306; Darrell Steffensmeier, "The Invention of the 'New' Senior Citizen Criminal," *Research on Aging* 9 (1987): 281–311.

91. Hirschi and Gottfredson, "Age and the Explanation of Crime."

92. Robert Agnew, "An Integrated Theory of the Adolescent Peak in Offending," *Youth and Society* 34 (2003): 263–302.

93. Margo Wilson and Martin Daly, "Life Expectancy, Economic Inequality, Homicide, and Reproductive Timing in Chicago Neighbourhoods," *British Journal of Medicine* 314 (1997): 1,271–1,274.

94. Edward Mulvey and John LaRosa, "Delinquency Cessation and Adolescent Development: Preliminary Data," *American Journal of Orthopsychiatry* 56 (1986): 212–224.

95. James Q. Wilson and Richard Herrnstein, *Crime and Human Nature* (New York: Simon & Schuster, 1985): 126–147.

96. Ibid., p. 219.

97. Ryan King, Michael Massoglia, and Ross Macmillan, "The Context of Marriage and Crime: Gender, the Propensity to Marry, and Offending in Early Adulthood," *Criminology* 45 (2007): 33–65.

98. Cesare Lombroso, *The Female Offender* (New York: Appleton, 1920), p. 122.

99. Otto Pollack, *The Criminality of Women* (Philadelphia: University of Pennsylvania, 1950).

100. For a review of this issue, see Darrell Steffensmeier, "Assessing the Impact of the Women's Movement on Sex-Based Differences in the Handling of Adult Criminal Defendants," *Crime and Delinquency* 26 (1980): 344–357.

101. Alan Booth and D. Wayne Osgood, "The Influence of Testosterone on Deviance in Adulthood: Assessing and Explaining the Relationship," *Criminology* 31 (1993): 93–118.

102. This section relies on the following sources: Kristen Kling, Janet Shibley Hyde, Carolin Showers, and Brenda Buswell, "Gender Differences in Self-Esteem: A Meta Analysis," *Psychological Bulletin* 125 (1999): 470–500; Rolf Loeber and Dale Hay, "Key Issues in the Development of Aggression and Violence from Childhood to Early Adulthood," *Annual Review of Psychology* 48 (1997): 371–410; Darcy Miller, Catherine Trapani, Kathy Fejes-Mendoza, Carolyn Eggleston, and Donna Dwiggins, "Adolescent Female Offenders: Unique Considerations," *Adolescence* 30 (1995): 429–435; John Mirowsky and Catherine Ross, "Sex Differences in Distress: Real or Artifact?" *American Sociological Review* 60 (1995): 449–468; Anne Campbell, *Men, Women and Aggression* (New York: Basic Books, 1993); Ann Beutel and Margaret Mooney Marini, "Gender and Values," *American Sociological Review* 60 (1995): 436–448; John Gibbs, Velmer Burton, Francis Cullen, T. David Evans, Leanne Fiftal Alarid, and R. Gregory Dunaway, "Gender, Self-Control, and Crime," *Journal of Research in Crime and Delinquency* 35 (1998): 123–147; David Rowe, Alexander Vazsonyi, and Daniel Flannery, "Sex Differences in Crime: Do Means and Within-Sex Variation Have Similar Causes?" *Journal of Research in Crime and Delinquency* 32 (1995): 84–100.

103. Jean Bottcher, "Social Practices of Gender: How Gender Relates to Delinquency in the Everyday Lives of High-Risk Youths," *Criminology* 39 (2001): 893–932.

104. Daniel Mears, Matthew Ploeger, and Mark Warr, "Explaining the Gender Gap in Delinquency: Peer Influence and Moral Evaluations of Behavior," *Journal of Research in Crime and Delinquency* 35 (1998): 251–266.

105. Lisa Broidy, Elizabeth Cauffman, and Dorothy Espelage, "Sex Differences in Empathy and Its Relation to Juvenile Offending," *Violence and Victims* 18 (2003): 503–516.

106. Debra Kaysen, Miranda Morris, Shireen Rizvi, and Patricia Resick, "Peritraumatic Responses and Their Relationship to Perceptions of Threat in Female Crime Victims," *Violence Against Women* 11 (2005): 1,515–1,535.

107. Freda Adler, *Sisters in Crime* (New York: McGraw-Hill, 1975); Rita James Simon, *The Contemporary Woman and Crime* (Washington, DC: U.S. Government Printing Office, 1975).

108. David Rowe, Alexander Vazsonyi, and Daniel Flannery, "Sex Differences in Crime: Do Mean and Within-Sex Variation Have Similar Causes?" *Journal of Research in Crime and Delinquency* 32 (1995): 84–100; Michael Hindelang, "Age, Sex, and the Versatility of Delinquency Involvements," *Social Forces* 14 (1971): 525–534; Martin Gold, *Delinquent Behavior in an American City* (Belmont, CA: Brooks/Cole, 1970); Gary Jensen and Raymond Eve, "Sex Differences in Delinquency: An Examination of Popular Sociological Explanations," *Criminology* 13 (1976): 427–448.

109. Finn-Aage Esbensen and Elizabeth Piper Deschenes, "A Multisite Examination of Youth Gang Membership: Does Gender Matter?" *Criminology* 36 (1998): 799–828.

110. Darrell Steffensmeier and Renee Hoffman Steffensmeier, "Trends in Female Delinquency," *Criminology* 18 (1980): 62–85; see also Darrell Steffensmeier and Renee Hoffman Steffensmeier, "Crime and the Contemporary Woman: An Analysis of Changing Levels of Female Property Crime, 1960–1975," *Social Forces* 57 (1978): 566–584; Joseph Weis, "Liberation and Crime: The Invention of the New Female Criminal," *Crime and Social Justice* 1 (1976): 17–27; Carol Smart, "The New Female Offender: Reality or Myth," *British Journal of Criminology* 19 (1979): 50–59; Steven Box and Chris Hale, "Liberation/Emancipation, Economic Marginalization or Less Chivalry," *Criminology* 22 (1984): 473–478.

111. Anne Campbell, Steven Muncer, and Daniel Bibel, "Female–Female Criminal Assault: An Evolutionary Perspective," *Journal of Research in Crime and Delinquency* 35 (1998): 413–428.

112. Darrell Steffensmeier, Jennifer Schwartz, Hua Zhong, and Jeff Ackerman, "An Assessment of Recent Trends in Girls' Violence Using Diverse Longitudinal Sources: Is the Gender Gap Closing?" *Criminology* 43 (2005): 355–406.

113. Susan Miller, Carol Gregory, and Leeann Iovanni, "One Size Fits All? A Gender-Neutral Approach to a Gender-Specific Problem: Contrasting Batterer Treatment Programs for Male and Female Offenders," *Criminal Justice Policy Review* 16 (2005): 336–359.

114. Leroy Gould, "Who Defines Delinquency: A Comparison of Self-Report and Officially Reported Indices of Delinquency for Three Racial Groups," *Social Problems* 16 (1969): 325–336; Harwin Voss, "Ethnic Differentials in Delinquency in Honolulu," *Journal of Criminal Law, Criminology, and Police Science* 54 (1963): 322–327; Ronald Akers, Marvin Krohn, Marcia Radosevich, and Lonn Lanza-Kaduce,

"Social Characteristics and Self-Reported Delinquency," in *Sociology of Delinquency*, ed. Gary Jensen (Beverly Hills: Sage, 1981), pp. 48–62.

115. David Huizinga and Delbert Elliott, "Juvenile Offenders: Prevalence, Offender Incidence, and Arrest Rates by Race," *Crime and Delinquency* 33 (1987): 206–223. See also Dale Dannefer and Russell Schutt, "Race and Juvenile Justice Processing in Court and Police Agencies," *American Journal of Sociology* 87 (1982): 1,113–1,132.

116. Institute for Social Research, *Monitoring the Future* (Ann Arbor, MI: Author, 2001).

117. Paul Tracy, "Race and Class Differences in Official and Self-Reported Delinquency," in *From Boy to Man, from Delinquency to Crime,* eds. Marvin Wolfgang, Terence Thornberry, and Robert Figlio (Chicago: University of Chicago Press, 1987), p. 120.

118. Miriam Sealock and Sally Simpson, "Unraveling Bias in Arrest Decisions: The Role of Juvenile Offender Type-Scripts," *Justice Quarterly* 15 (1998): 427–457.

119. Phillipe Rushton, "Race and Crime: An International Dilemma," *Society* 32 (1995): 37–42; for a rebuttal, see Jerome Neapolitan, "Cross-National Variation in Homicides: Is Race a Factor?" *Criminology* 36 (1998): 139–156.

120. "Law Enforcement Seeks Answers to 'Racial Profiling' Complaints," *Criminal Justice Newsletter* 29 (1998): 5.

121. Robin Shepard Engel and Jennifer Calnon, "Examining the Influence of Drivers' Characteristics during Traffic Stops with Police: Results from a National Survey," *Justice Quarterly* 21 (2004): 49–90.

122. Daniel Georges-Abeyie, "Definitional Issues: Race, Ethnicity and Official Crime/Victimization Rates," in *The Criminal Justice System and Blacks*, ed. D. Georges-Abeyie (New York: Clark Boardman, 1984), p. 12; Robert Sampson, "Race and Criminal Violence: A Demographically Disaggregated Analysis of Urban Homicide," *Crime and Delinquency* 31 (1985): 47–82.

123. Barry Sample and Michael Philip, "Perspectives on Race and Crime in Research and Planning," in *The Criminal Justice System and Blacks,* ed. Georges-Abeyie, pp. 21–36.

124. Candace Kruttschnitt, "Violence by and against Women: A Comparative and Cross-National Analysis," *Violence and Victims* 8 (1994): 4.

125. James Comer, "Black Violence and Public Policy," in *American Violence and Public Policy,* ed. Lynn Curtis (New Haven: Yale University Press, 1985), pp. 63–86.

126. Fox Butterfield, *All God's Children: The Bosket Family and the American Tradition of Violence* (New York: Avon, 1996).

127. Hubert Blalock Jr., *Toward a Theory of Minority-Group Relations* (New York: Capricorn Books, 1967).

128. Karen Parker, Brian Stults, and Stephen Rice, "Racial Threat, Concentrated Disadvantage and Social Control: Considering the Macro-Level Sources of Variation in Arrests," *Criminology* 43 (2005): 1,111–1,134; Lisa Stolzenberg, J. Stewart D'Alessio, and David Eitle, "A Multilevel Test of Racial Threat Theory," *Criminology* 42 (2004) 673–698.

129. Michael Leiber and Kristan Fox, "Race and the Impact of Detention on Juvenile Justice Decision Making," *Crime and Delinquency* 51 (2005): 470–497; Traci Schlesinger, "Racial and Ethnic Disparity in Pretrial Criminal Processing," *Justice Quarterly* 22 (2005): 170–192.

130. Tracy Nobiling, Cassia Spohn, and Miriam DeLone, "A Tale of Two Counties: Unemployment and Sentence Severity," *Justice Quarterly* 15 (1998): 459–486.

131. Alexander Weiss and Steven Chermak, "The News Value of African-American Victims: An Examination of the Media's Presentation of Homicide," *Journal of Crime and Justice* 21 (1998): 71–84.

132. Jefferson Holcomb, Marian Williams, and Stephen Demuth, "White Female Victims and Death Penalty Disparity Research," *Justice Quarterly* 21 (2004): 877–902.

133. Malcolm Holmes, Brad Smith, Adrienne Freng, and Ed Muñoz, eds., "Minority Threat, Crime Control, and Police Resource Allocation in the Southwestern United States" *Crime and Delinquency* 54 (2008): 128–152.

134. Matthew Crow and Kathrine Johnson, "Race, Ethnicity, and Habitual-Offender Sentencing: A Multilevel Analysis of Individual and Contextual Threat," *Criminal Justice Policy Review* 19 (2008): 63–83.

135. Ronald Weitzer and Steven Tuch, "Race, Class, and Perceptions of Discrimination by the Police," *Crime and Delinquency* 45 (1999): 494–507.

136. Joanne Kaufman, "Explaining the Race/Ethnicity–Violence Relationship: Neighborhood Context and Social Psychological Processes," *Justice Quarterly* 22 (2005): 224–251.

137. Karen Parker and Patricia McCall, "Structural Conditions and Racial Homicide Patterns: A Look at the Multiple Disadvantages in Urban Areas," *Criminology* 37 (1999): 447–469.

138. David Jacobs and Katherine Woods, "Interracial Conflict and Interracial Homicide: Do Political and Economic Rivalries Explain White Killings of Blacks or Black Killings of Whites?" *American Journal of Sociology* 105 (1999): 157–190.

139. Melvin Thomas, "Race, Class and Personal Income: An Empirical Test of the Declining Significance of Race Thesis, 1968–1988," *Social Problems* 40 (1993): 328–339.

140. Mallie Paschall, Robert Flewelling, and Susan Ennett, "Racial Differences in Violent Behavior among Young Adults: Moderating and Confounding Effects," *Journal of Research in Crime and Delinquency* 35 (1998): 148–165.

141. Gary LaFree and Richard Arum, "The Impact of Racially Inclusive Schooling on Adult Incarceration Rates among U.S. Cohorts of African Americans and Whites Since 1930," *Criminology* 44 (2006): 73–103.

142. R. Kelly Raley, "A Shortage of Marriageable Men? A Note on the Role of Cohabitation in Black-White Differences in Marriage Rates," *American Sociological Review* 61 (1996): 973–983.

143. Julie Phillips, "Variation in African-American Homicide Rates: An Assessment of Potential Explanations," *Criminology* 35 (1997): 527–559.

144. Roy Austin, "Progress toward Racial Equality and Reduction of Black Criminal Violence," *Journal of Criminal Justice* 15 (1987): 437–459.

145. Reynolds Farley and William Frey, "Changes in the Segregation of Whites from Blacks during the 1980s: Small Steps toward a More Integrated Society," *American Sociological Review* 59 (1994): 23–45.

146. Marvin Wolfgang, Robert Figlio, and Thorsten Sellin, *Delinquency in a Birth Cohort* (Chicago: University of Chicago Press, 1972).

147. See Thorsten Sellin and Marvin Wolfgang, *The Measurement of Delinquency* (New York: Wiley, 1964), p. 120.

148. Paul Tracy and Robert Figlio, "Chronic Recidivism in the 1958 Birth Cohort," paper presented at the annual meeting of the American Society of Criminology, Toronto, October 1982; Marvin Wolfgang, "Delinquency in Two Birth Cohorts," in *Perspective Studies of Crime and Delinquency,* eds. Katherine Teilmann Van Dusen and Sarnoff Mednick (Boston: Kluwer-Nijhoff, 1983), pp. 7–17. The following sections rely heavily on these sources.

149. Lyle Shannon, *Criminal Career Opportunity* (New York: Human Sciences Press, 1988).

150. D. J. West and David P. Farrington, *The Delinquent Way of Life* (London: Hienemann, 1977).

151. Michael Schumacher and Gwen Kurz, *The 8% Solution: Preventing Serious Repeat Juvenile Crime* (Thousand Oaks, CA: Sage, 1999).

152. Peter Jones, Philip Harris, James Fader, and Lori Grubstein, "Identifying Chronic Juvenile Offenders," *Justice Quarterly* 18 (2001): 478–507.

153. Lila Kazemian and Marc LeBlanc, "Differential Cost Avoidance and Successful Criminal Careers," *Crime and Delinquency* 53 (2007): 38–63.

154. Rudy Haapanen, Lee Britton, and Tim Croisdale, "Persistent Criminality and Career Length," *Crime and Delinquency* 53 (2007): 133–155.

155. See generally Wolfgang, Thornberry, and Figlio, eds., *From Boy to Man, from Delinquency to Crime.*

156. Paul Tracy and Kimberly Kempf-Leonard, *Continuity and Discontinuity in Criminal Careers* (New York: Plenum Press, 1996).

157. Kimberly Kempf-Leonard, Paul Tracy, and James Howell, "Serious, Violent, and Chronic Juvenile Offenders: The Relationship of Delinquency Career Types to Adult Criminality," *Justice Quarterly* 18 (2001): 449–478.

158. R. Tremblay, R. Loeber, C. Gagnon, P. Charlebois, S. Larivee, and M. LeBlanc, "Disruptive Boys with Stable and Unstable High Fighting Behavior Patterns during Junior Elementary School," *Journal of Abnormal Child Psychology* 19 (1991): 285–300.

159. Jennifer White, Terrie Moffitt, Felton Earls, Lee Robins, and Phil Silva, "How Early Can We Tell? Predictors of Childhood Conduct Disorder and Adolescent Delinquency," *Criminology* 28 (1990): 507–535.

160. John Laub and Robert Sampson, "Unemployment, Marital Discord, and Deviant Behavior: The Long-Term Correlates of Childhood Misbehavior," paper presented at the annual meeting of the American Society of Criminology, Baltimore, November 1990; rev. version.

161. Michael Ezell and Amy D'Unger, "Offense Specialization among Serious Youthful Offenders: A Longitudinal Analysis of a California Youth Authority Sample" (Durham, NC: Duke University, 1998, unpublished report).

Victims and Victimization

CHAPTER OBJECTIVES

1. Be familiar with the concept of victimization
2. Be familiar with the costs of victimization
3. Be able to discuss the problems of crime victims
4. Know the nature of victimization
5. Recognize that there are age, gender, and racial patterns in the victimization data
6. Be familiar with the term "victim precipitation"
7. Be able to discuss the association between lifestyle and victimization
8. List the routine activities associated with victimization risk
9. Be able to discuss the various victim assistance programs

© AP Images/Tina Fineberg

On February 25, 2006, Imette St. Guillen stopped in for a late night drink at The Falls bar, a popular New York City nightspot. Later that evening, the bar's manager asked the bouncer, Darryl Littlejohn, to escort Imette out after she stayed past the 4 A.M. closing time.[1] Later he recalled hearing the pair argue before they disappeared through a side door. Sometime during the next 17 hours, Imette was raped and killed and her bound body left on the side of a desolate Brooklyn roadway. Police investigators soon set their sights on Littlejohn, a felon with prior convictions for robbery, drugs, and gun possession. He was indicted for murder when blood found on plastic ties that were used to bind Imette's hands behind her back matched Littlejohn's DNA.

Imette St. Guillen was a brilliant and beautiful young woman loved by her family and friends. She attended the Boston Latin School in Massachusetts and graduated magna cum laude *from George Washington University in 2003 as a member of Phi Beta Kappa. At the time of her death, she was a graduate student at John Jay College of Criminal Justice in New York City, where she would have completed her master's degree in May 2006. "New York was Imette's home," her sister, Alejandra St. Guillen, told reporters. "She loved the city and its people . . . Imette was a good person, a kind person. Her heart was full of love. With Imette's death, the world lost someone very special too soon."[2]*

The St. Guillen murder case illustrates the importance of understanding the victim's role in the crime process. Why do people become targets of predatory criminals? Do people become victims because of their lifestyle and environment? Did Imette contribute to her attack by staying out late at night, drinking, and being alone? Imette's friends, who had been with her earlier in the evening, had left her in the early morning hours because they considered The Falls bar neighborhood safe. If Imette had been with friends to guard her, would she be alive today? And is this a matter of unfairly "blaming the victim" for her risky behavior? Can someone actually deflect or avoid criminal behavior or is it a matter of fate and chance? What can be done to protect victims, for instance, should a convicted criminal be employed in a bar and asked to escort patrons? And, failing that, what can be done to help them in the aftermath of crime?

Criminologists who focus their attention on crime victims refer to themselves as victimologists. This chapter examines victims and their relationship to the criminal process. First, using available victim data, we analyze the nature and extent of victimization. We then discuss the relationship between victims and criminal offenders. During this discussion, we look at the various theories of victimization that attempt to explain the victim's role in the crime problem. Finally, we examine how society has responded to the needs of victims and discuss the special problems they still face.

PROBLEMS OF CRIME VICTIMS

The National Crime Victimization Survey (NCVS) indicates that the annual number of victimizations in the United States is about 23 million.[3] Being the target or victim of a rape, robbery, or assault is a terrible burden that can have considerable long-term consequences.[4] The costs of victimization can include such things as damaged property, pain and suffering to victims, and the involvement of the police and other agencies of the justice system. In this section we explore some of the effects of these incidents.

Economic Loss

When the costs of goods taken during property crimes is added to productivity losses caused by injury, pain, and emotional trauma, the cost of victimization is estimated to be in the hundreds of billions of dollars.

System Costs Part of the economic loss due to victimization is the cost to American taxpayers of maintaining the justice system. Violent crime by juveniles alone costs the United States $158 billion each year.[5] This estimate includes some of the costs incurred by federal, state, and local governments to assist victims of juvenile violence, such as medical treatment for injuries and services for victims, which amounts to about $30 billion. The remaining $128 billion is due to losses suffered by victims,

such as lost wages, pain, suffering, and reduced quality of life. Not included in these figures are the costs incurred trying to reduce juvenile violence, which include early prevention programs, services for juveniles, and the juvenile justice system.

Juvenile violence is only one part of the crime picture. If the cost of the justice system, legal costs, treatment costs, and so on are included, the total loss due to crime amounts to $450 billion annually, or about $1,800 per U.S. citizen. Crime produces social costs that must be paid by nonvictims as well. For example, each heroin addict is estimated to cost society more than $135,000 per year; an estimated half-million addicts cost society about $68 billion per year.[6]

Individual Costs In addition to these societal costs, victims may suffer long-term losses in earnings and occupational attainment. Victim costs resulting from an assault are as high as $9,400, and costs are even higher for rape and arson; the average murder costs around $3 million.[7] Research by Ross Macmillan shows that Americans who suffer a violent victimization during adolescence earn about $82,000 less than nonvictims; Canadian victims earn $237,000 less. Macmillan reasons that victims bear psychological and physical ills that inhibit first their academic achievement and later their economic and professional success.[8]

Some victims are physically disabled as a result of serious wounds sustained during episodes of random violence, including a growing number that suffer paralyzing spinal cord injuries. If victims have no insurance, the long-term effects of the crime may have devastating financial as well as emotional and physical consequences.[9]

System Abuse

The suffering endured by crime victims does not end when their attacker leaves the scene of the crime. They may suffer more victimization by the justice system.

While the crime is still fresh in their minds, victims may find that the police interrogation following the crime is handled callously, with innuendos or insinuations that they were somehow at fault. Victims have difficulty learning what is going on in the case; property is often kept for a long time as evidence and may never be returned.

The system can be especially harsh on rape victims, some of whom report that the treatment they receive from legal, medical, and mental health services is so destructive that they cannot help feeling "re-raped."[10] Research by Courtney Ahrens found that rape survivors who speak out about their assault experiences are often punished for doing so when they are subjected to negative reactions from people who were supposed to give them support, leading some rape survivors to stop talking about their experiences to anyone at all. Ahrens uncovered three routes to silence: (1) negative reactions from professionals led survivors to question whether future disclosures would be effective; (2) negative reactions from friends and family reinforced feelings of self-blame; and (3) negative reactions from either source reinforced uncertainty about whether their experiences qualified as rape.[11] But if the victim finds the justice system personnel sympathetic and responsive, she or he will develop confidence in the agencies of justice and be more willing to turn to them and report future victimizations.[12]

Long-Term Stress

Victims may suffer stress and anxiety long after the incident is over and the justice process has been completed. Posttraumatic stress disorder (PTSD)—a condition whose symptoms include depression, anxiety, and self-destructive behavior—is a common problem especially when the victim does not receive adequate support from family and friends.[13]

Adolescent Stress It is widely assumed that younger children are less likely to be injured in attacks than older teens and adults, but in fact the opposite may be true.[14] Recent research by David Finkelhor and his colleagues at the University of New Hampshire Crimes against Children Research Center found that younger children's victimization by peers and siblings was similar to that experienced by older youth. Both groups suffered similar injuries, were just as likely to be hit with an object that could cause injury, and were victimized on multiple occasions.[15]

These younger victims are also more prone to suffer stress. Adolescent victims are particularly at risk to PTSD.[16] Kids who have undergone traumatic sexual experiences later suffer psychological deficits.[17] Mark Shelvin and his associates found that a history of childhood trauma, including rape and molestation, was significantly associated with visual, auditory, and tactile hallucinations. Kids who were repeatedly traumatized increased their experience with the three types of hallucinations, clearly indicating that childhood abuse can have a devastating effect on long-term mental health.[18]

Many run away to escape their environment, which puts them at risk for juvenile arrest and involvement with the justice system.[19] Others suffer posttraumatic mental problems, including acute stress disorders, depression, eating disorders, nightmares, anxiety, suicidal ideation, and other psychological problems.[20] Stress, however, does not end in childhood. Children who are psychologically, sexually, or physically abused are more likely to suffer low self-esteem and be more suicidal as adults.[21] They are also placed at greater risk to be re-abused as adults than those who escaped childhood victimization.[22] The re-abused carry higher risks for psychological and physical problems, ranging from sexual promiscuity to increased HIV infection rates.[23] Abuse as a child may lead to despair, depression, and even homelessness as an adult. One study of homeless women found that they were much more likely than other women to report childhood physical abuse, childhood sexual abuse, adult physical assault, previous sexual assault in adulthood, and a history of mental health problems.[24]

Relationship Stress Spousal abuse takes a particularly heavy toll on victims. Numerous research efforts show that victims of spousal abuse suffer an extremely high prevalence of psychological problems, including but not limited to depression, generalized anxiety disorder (GAD), panic disorder, substance use disorders, borderline personality disorder, antisocial personality disorder, posttraumatic stress disorder (an emotional disturbance following exposure to stresses outside the range of normal human experience), anxiety disorder, and obsessive-compulsive disorder (an extreme preoccupation with certain thoughts and compulsive performance of certain behaviors).[25] One reason may be that abusive spouses are as likely to abuse their victims psychologically with threats and intimidation as they are to use physical force; psychological abuse can lead to depression and other long-term disabilities.[26]

Fear

Many people fear crime, especially the elderly, the poor, and minority group members.[27] Their fear is escalated by lurid news accounts of crime and violence.[28] A recent study (2007) by Matthew Lee and Erica DeHart showed that news stories of a local serial killer can cause a chill felt throughout the city. About half the people they surveyed experienced an increase in their *fear of crime* that prompted them to protect themselves and their family by implementing some sort of protective measure, such as carrying mace or pepper spray or adding a security device to their home.[29]

While hearing about crime causes fear, those who experience it are even more likely to be fearful and change their behaviors. Victims of violent crime are the most deeply affected, fearing a repeat of their attack. Many go through a fundamental life change, viewing the world more suspiciously and as a less safe, controllable, and meaningful place. Some develop a generalized fear of crime and worry about being revictimized. For example, if they have been assaulted, they may develop fears that their house will be burglarized.[30] These people are more likely to suffer psychological stress for extended periods of time.[31]

Crime can have devastating effects on its victims, who may take years to recover from the incident. In a moving book, *Aftermath: Violence and the Remaking of a Self*, rape victim Susan Brison recounts the difficult time she had recovering from her ordeal. The trauma disrupted her memory, cutting off events that happened before the rape from those that occurred afterward, and eliminated her ability to conceive of a happy or productive future. Although sympathizers encouraged her to forget the past, she found that confronting it could be therapeutic.[32]

Even if they have escaped attack themselves, hearing about another's victimization may make people timid and cautious.[33] If they don't fear for themselves, they become concerned for others—their wives or husbands, children, elderly parents, and siblings.[34]

Antisocial Behavior

There is growing evidence of a correlation between crime and victimization. Kids who are victims share many of the same characteristics as those who are delinquent, such as antisocial behavior tendencies and impulsive personalities.[35] As adults, victims are more likely to commit crimes themselves.[36] People who were physically or sexually abused, especially young males, are much more likely to smoke, drink, and take drugs than are nonabused youth. Incarcerated offenders report significant amounts of posttraumatic stress disorder as a result of prior victimization, which may in part explain their violent and criminal behaviors.[37]

© David McNew/Getty Images

Victims sometimes suffer long-term fear and trauma. Abused children may suffer into their adulthood. At a press conference outside the Los Angeles County Courthouse, where a record $660 million settlement between the Archdiocese of Los Angeles and victims of sexual abuse by clergy members was approved by a judge on July 16, 2007, Esther Miller shows a photo of Father Michael Nocita, the priest who allegedly abused her. The proposed settlement, plus $114 million in related settlements to which the church has agreed, increases the archdiocese's financial liability to over $774 million, the biggest payout since the church sex abuse scandal broke in Boston in 2001. The archdiocese reportedly plans to raise the $660 million through the sale of some of its buildings, insurance payments, investments, and loans and contributions from some of the religious orders. In Boston, the church settled for $157 million; in Portland, Oregon, it made a $129 million settlement; and in 2005, the diocese in Orange County, California, paid $100 million for sex abuse claims. Five dioceses facing large settlements have filed for bankruptcy protection. After the settlement was announced, Cardinal Roger Michael Mahony apologized to victims, many of whom were children when they were sexually abused by clergy in the Los Angeles archdiocese, and acknowledged he made mistakes handling the scandal.

Victims may seek revenge against the people who harmed them or who they believe are at fault for their problems. In some cases, these feelings become generalized to others who share the same characteristics of their attackers (e.g., men, Hispanics).[38] As a result their reactions become displaced, and they may lash out at people who are not their attackers.

The abuse–crime phenomenon is referred to as the **cycle of violence**.[39] Research shows that both boys and girls are more likely to engage in violent behavior if they were the targets of physical abuse and were exposed to violent behavior among adults they know or live with or were exposed to weapons.[40]

WWW The mission of the **National Center for Victims of Crime** is to help victims of crime rebuild their lives: "We are dedicated to serving individuals, families, and communities harmed by crime." Access their website at academic.cengage.com/criminaljustice/siegel.

THE NATURE OF VICTIMIZATION

How many crime victims are there in the United States, and what are the trends and patterns in victimization? According to the NCVS, about 23 million criminal victimizations occur each year.[41] While this total is significant, it represents a decade-long decline in criminal victimization that began in 1993. Since then the violent crime rate decreased 58 percent, from 50 to 21 victimizations per 1,000 persons age 12 or older (Figure 3.1). Property crime declined 52 percent, from 319 to 154 per 1,000 households (Figure 3.2).

connections

As discussed in Chapter 2, the NCVS is currently the leading source of information about the nature and extent of victimization. It employs a highly sophisticated and complex sampling methodology to collect data annually from thousands of citizens. Statistical techniques then estimate victimization rates, trends, and patterns that occur in the entire U.S. population.

While the number and rate of victimization have declined, patterns in the victimization survey findings are stable and repetitive, suggesting that victimization is not random but is a function of personal and ecological factors. The stability of these patterns allows us to make judgments about the nature of victimization; policies can then be created in an effort to reduce the victimization rate. Who are victims? Where does victimization take place? What is the relationship between victims and criminals? The following sections discuss some of the most important victimization patterns and trends.

The Social Ecology of Victimization

The NCVS shows that violent crimes are slightly more likely to take place in an open, public area (such as a street, a park, or a field), in a school building, or at a commercial establishment such as a tavern during the daytime or early evening hours than in a private home during the morning or late evening hours. The more serious violent crimes, such as rape and aggravated assault, typically take place after 6 P.M. Approximately two-thirds of

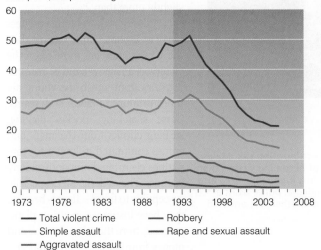

Figure 3.1 Violent Crime Victimization Rates

The NCVS reveals long-term declines in victimization to the lowest per capita rates in 30 years.

Rate per 1,000 persons age 12 or older

— Total violent crime — Robbery
— Simple assault — Rape and sexual assault
— Aggravated assault

Note: The violent crimes included are rape, robbery, aggravated and simple assault, and homicide. The NCVS redesign was implemented in 1993; the area with the lighter shading is before the redesign and the darker area after the redesign.

Source: Shannan Catalano, *Criminal Victimization 2005* (Washington, DC: Bureau of Justice Statistics, 2006).

rapes and sexual assaults occur at night—6 P.M. to 6 A.M. Less serious forms of violence, such as unarmed robberies and personal larcenies like purse snatching, are more likely to occur during the daytime. Neighborhood characteristics affect the chances of victimization. Those living in the central city have

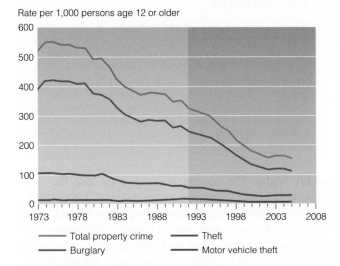

Figure 3.2 Property Crime Victimization Rates

Rate per 1,000 persons age 12 or older

— Total property crime — Theft
— Burglary — Motor vehicle theft

Note: Property crimes include burglary, theft, and motor vehicle theft. The NCVS redesign was implemented in 1993; the area with the lighter shading is before the redesign and the darker area after the redesign.

Source: Shannan Catalano, *Criminal Victimization 2005* (Washington, DC: Bureau of Justice Statistics, 2006).

significantly higher rates of theft and violence than suburbanites; people living in rural areas have a victimization rate almost half that of city dwellers. The risk of murder for both men and women is significantly higher in disorganized inner-city areas where gangs flourish and drug trafficking is commonplace.

Not surprisingly, the chances of becoming a crime victim are most common in areas frequented by the most crime-prone elements of society. Since teenage males are the group most likely to engage in crime, schools unfortunately are the locale of a great deal of victimization. The most recent surveys of school crime show that while victim rates are declining, about 5 percent of students now experience a crime at school each year—about 4 percent reported a crime of theft and 1 percent reported having been a violence victim at school. This equals an estimated 1.2 million crimes of theft against students and about 740,000 violent crimes, including an estimated 150,000 of the most serious violent victimizations (rape, sexual assault, robbery, aggravated assault). Students also reported that about two-thirds of the serious violent crimes they experienced did not occur at school.[42] The risk of school victimization is not lost on students: about 6 percent of students age 12 to 18 reported that they avoided school activities or one or more places in school because they thought someone might attack or harm them.

The Victim's Household

The NCVS tells us that within the United States, larger, African American, western, and urban homes are the most vulnerable to crime. In contrast, rural, white homes in the Northeast are the least likely to contain crime victims or be the target of theft offenses, such as burglary or larceny. People who own their homes are less vulnerable than renters.

Recent population movement and changes may account for decreases in crime victimization. U.S. residents have become extremely mobile, moving from urban areas to suburban and rural areas. In addition, family size has been reduced; more people than ever before are living in single-person homes (about one-quarter of the population). It is possible that the decline in household victimization rates during the past decades can be explained by the fact that smaller households in less populated areas have a lower victimization risk.

Victim Characteristics

Social and demographic characteristics also distinguish victims and nonvictims. The most important of these factors are gender, age, social status, and race.

Gender Gender affects victimization risk. Males are more likely than females to be the victims of violent crime. Men are almost twice as likely as women to experience robbery and 50 percent more likely to be the victim of assault; women are much more likely than men to be victims of rape or sexual assault. For all crimes, males are more likely to be victimized than females. However, the gender differences in the violence victimization rate

Both personal characteristics and environmental factors influence victimization risk. Males, minority group members, and city dwellers have a greater chance of becoming victims than women, European Americans, and people living in rural areas. Living in a high-crime area also increases the likelihood of becoming a crime victim. Here, Kokomo, Indiana, police assist a victim of an attempted robbery. One man was wounded by police and another was arrested following a four-hour standoff at a local residence.

appear to be narrowing (Figure 3.3), a phenomenon related to increasing gender equality in contemporary society.[43]

Females are most often victimized by someone they know, whereas males are more likely to be victimized by a stranger. Of those offenders victimizing females, about two-thirds are described as someone the victim knows or is related to. In contrast, only about half of male victims are attacked by a friend, relative, or acquaintance.

Age Victim data reveal that young people face a much greater victimization risk than do older people. As Figure 3.4 shows, victim risk diminishes rapidly after age 25 and becomes negligible after age 65.

The elderly, who are thought of as the helpless targets of predatory criminals, are actually much safer than their grandchildren. People over 65, who make up about 15 percent of the population, account for only 1 percent of violent victimizations; teens 12 to 19, who also make up 15 percent of the population,

typically account for more than 30 percent of victimizations. Teens 16 to 19 suffer the most personal victimizations, at around 44 per 1,000, whereas people over 65 experience slightly more than 2.

Although the elderly are less likely to become crime victims than the young, they are most often the victims of a narrow band of criminal activities from which the young are more immune. Frauds and scams, purse snatching, pocket picking, stealing checks from the mail, and crimes committed in long-term care settings claim predominantly elderly victims. The elderly are especially susceptible to fraud schemes because they have insurance, pension plans, proceeds from the sale of homes, and money from Social Security and savings that make them attractive financial targets. Because many elderly live by themselves and are lonely, they remain more susceptible to telephone and mail fraud. Unfortunately, once victimized the elderly have less opportunity to either recover their lost money or to earn enough to replace it.[44] Elder abuse is a particularly important issue because of shifts in the U.S. population; the Bureau of the Census predicts that by 2030 the population over age 65 will nearly triple to more than 70 million people, and older people will make up more than 20 percent of the population (up from 12.3 percent in 1990). The saliency of elder abuse is underscored by reports from the National Center on Elder Abuse, which show an increase of 150 percent in reported cases of elder abuse nationwide since 1986.[45]

connections

The association between age and victimization is undoubtedly tied to lifestyle: adolescents often stay out late at night, go to public places, and hang out with other kids who have a high risk of criminal involvement. Teens also face a high victimization risk because they spend a great deal of time in the most dangerous building in the community—the local school. As Chapter 2 indicated, adolescents have the highest crime rates. It is not surprising that people who associate with these high-crime-rate individuals (other adolescents) have the greatest victimization risk.

Social Status The poorest Americans are also the most likely victims of violent and property crime. For example, homeless people, who are among the poorest individuals in America, suffer very high rates of assault.[46] This association occurs across all gender, age, and racial groups. Although the poor are more likely to suffer violent crimes, the wealthy are more likely targets of personal theft crimes such as pocket picking and purse snatching. Perhaps the affluent—sporting more expensive attire and driving better cars—attract the attention of thieves.

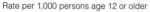

Figure 3.3 Violent Crime Victimization and Gender

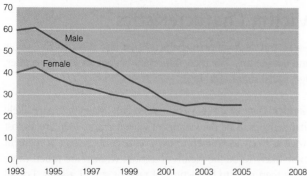

Rate per 1,000 persons age 12 or older

Source: Shannan Catalano, *Criminal Victimization 2005* (Washington, DC: Bureau of Justice Statistics, 2006).

Figure 3.4 **Age and Violent Crime Victimization**

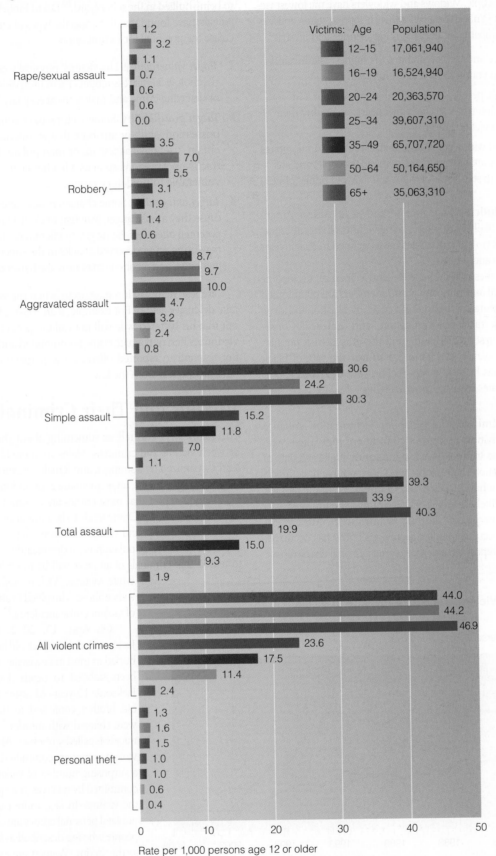

Victims: Age | Population
12–15 | 17,061,940
16–19 | 16,524,940
20–24 | 20,363,570
25–34 | 39,607,310
35–49 | 65,707,720
50–64 | 50,164,650
65+ | 35,063,310

Rape/sexual assault
1.2
3.2
1.1
0.7
0.6
0.6
0.0

Robbery
3.5
7.0
5.5
3.1
1.9
1.4
0.6

Aggravated assault
8.7
9.7
10.0
4.7
3.2
2.4
0.8

Simple assault
30.6
24.2
30.3
15.2
11.8
7.0
1.1

Total assault
39.3
33.9
40.3
19.9
15.0
9.3
1.9

All violent crimes
44.0
44.2
46.9
23.6
17.5
11.4
2.4

Personal theft
1.3
1.6
1.5
1.0
1.0
0.6
0.4

Rate per 1,000 persons age 12 or older

Source: Shannan Catalano, *Criminal Victimization 2005* (Washington, DC: Bureau of Justice Statistics, 2006).

Marital Status Marital status also influences victimization risk. Never-married males and females are victimized more often than married people. Widows and widowers have the lowest victimization risk. This association between marital status and victimization is probably influenced by age, gender, and lifestyle:

▮ Adolescence and teens who have the highest victimization risk, are too young to have been married.

▮ Young single people go out in public more often and sometimes interact with high-risk peers, increasing their exposure to victimization.

▮ Widows and widowers suffer much lower victimization rates because they are older, interact with older people, and are more likely to stay home at night and to avoid public places.

Race and Ethnicity As Figure 3.5 shows, (a) African Americans are more likely than whites to be victims of violent crime, and (b) serious violent crime rates have declined in recent years for both blacks and whites.

Why do these discrepancies exist? Because of income inequality, racial and minority group members are often forced to live in deteriorated urban areas beset by alcohol and drug abuse, poverty, racial discrimination, and violence. Consequently, their lifestyle places them in the most at-risk population group. However, as Figure 3.5 shows, the rate of black victimization has been in steep decline, and the racial gap in victimization rates seems to be narrowing.

Repeat Victimization Does prior victimization enhance or reduce the chances of future victimization? Individuals who have been crime victims have a significantly higher chance of future victimization than people who have not been victims.[47] Households that have experienced victimization in the past are the ones most likely to experience it again in the future.[48]

What factors predict chronic victimization? Most repeat victimizations occur soon after a previous crime has occurred, suggesting that repeat victims share some personal characteristic that makes them a magnet for predators.[49] For example, children who are shy, physically weak, or socially isolated may be prone to being bullied in the schoolyard.[50] David Finkelhor and Nancy Asigian have found that three specific types of characteristics increase the potential for victimization:

▮ *Target vulnerability.* The victims' physical weakness or psychological distress renders them incapable of resisting or deterring crime and makes them easy targets.

▮ *Target gratifiability.* Some victims have some quality, possession, skill, or attribute that an offender wants to obtain, use, have access to, or manipulate. Having attractive possessions such as a leather coat may make one vulnerable to predatory crime.

▮ *Target antagonism.* Some characteristics increase risk because they arouse anger, jealousy, or destructive impulses in potential offenders. Being gay or effeminate, for example, may bring on undeserved attacks in the street; being argumentative and alcoholic may provoke barroom assaults.[51]

Repeat victimization may occur when the victim does not take defensive action. For example, if an abusive husband finds out that his battered wife will not call the police, he repeatedly victimizes her; or if a hate crime is committed and the police do not respond to reported offenses, the perpetrators learn they have little to fear from the law.[52]

Victims and Their Criminals

The victim data also tell us something about the relationship between victims and criminals. Males are more likely to be violently victimized by a stranger, and females are more likely to be victimized by a friend, an acquaintance, or an intimate.

Victims report that most crimes are committed by a single offender over age 20. Crime tends to be intraracial: black offenders victimize blacks, and whites victimize whites. However, because the country's population is predominantly white, it stands to reason that criminals of all races will be more likely to target white victims. Victims report that substance abuse is involved in about one-third of violent crime incidents.[53]

On April 15, 2002, the body of Jackson Carr, a six-year-old boy, was found buried in mud in Lewisville, Texas; he had been stabbed to death. Later that day, Jackson's 15-year-old sister and 10-year-old brother confessed to the crime and were charged with murder.[54] (Sibling homicide is called siblicide.) Although many violent crimes are committed by strangers, a surprising number of violent crimes are committed by relatives or acquaintances of the victims. In fact, more than half of all nonfatal personal crimes are committed by people who are described as being known to the victim. Women are especially vulnerable to people they know. More than

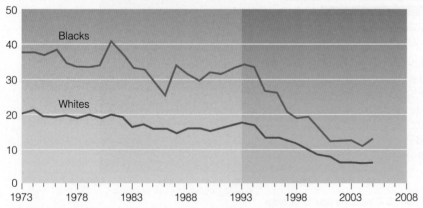

Figure 3.5 Violent Crime Rates by Race of Victim

Rate per 1,000 persons age 12 and over

Source: Bureau of Justice Statistics, www.ojp.usdoj.gov/bjs/glance/race.htm.

six in ten rape or sexual assault victims state the offender was an intimate, a relative, a friend, or an acquaintance. Women are more likely than men to be robbed by a friend or acquaintance; 74 percent of males and 43 percent of females state the individuals who robbed them were strangers.

THEORIES OF VICTIMIZATION

For many years criminological theory focused on the actions of the criminal offender; the role of the victim was virtually ignored. But more than 50 years ago scholars began to realize that the victim is not a passive target in crime but someone whose behavior can influence his or her own fate, someone who "shapes and molds the criminal."[55] These early works helped focus attention on the role of the victim in the crime problem and led to further research efforts that have sharpened the image of the crime victim. Today a number of different theories attempt to explain the cause of victimization; the most important are discussed here.

Victim Precipitation Theory

According to victim precipitation theory, some people may actually initiate the confrontation that eventually leads to their injury or death. Victim precipitation can be either active or passive.

Active precipitation occurs when victims act provocatively, use threats or fighting words, or even attack first.[56] In 1971, Menachem Amir suggested female victims often contribute to their attacks by dressing provocatively or pursuing a relationship with the rapist.[57] Although Amir's findings are controversial, courts have continued to return not-guilty verdicts in rape cases if a victim's actions can in any way be construed as consenting to sexual intimacy.[58]

In contrast, passive precipitation occurs when the victim exhibits some personal characteristic that unknowingly either threatens or encourages the attacker. The crime can occur because of personal conflict—for example, when two people compete over a job, promotion, love interest, or some other scarce and coveted commodity. A woman may become the target of intimate violence when she increases her job status, and her success results in a backlash from a jealous spouse or partner.[59] Although the victim may never have met the attacker or even know of his or her existence, the attacker feels menaced and acts accordingly.[60]

Passive precipitation may also occur when the victim belongs to a group whose mere presence threatens the attacker's reputation, status, or economic well-being. For example, hate crime violence may be precipitated by immigrant group members arriving in the community to compete for jobs and housing. Research indicates that passive precipitation is related to power: if the target group can establish themselves economically or gain political power in the community, their vulnerability will diminish. They are still a potential threat, but they become too formidable a target to attack; they are no longer passive precipitators.[61] By implication, economic power reduces victimization risk.

Lifestyle Theory

Some criminologists believe people may become crime victims because their lifestyle increases their exposure to criminal offenders. Victimization risk is increased by such behaviors as associating with young men, going out in public places late at night, and living in an urban area. Conversely, one's chances of victimization can be reduced by staying home at night, moving to a rural area, staying out of public places, earning more money, and getting married. The basis of lifestyle theory is that crime is not a random occurrence but rather a function of the victim's lifestyle. For example, due to their lifestyle and demographic makeup, college campuses contain large concentrations of young women who may be at greater risk for rape and other forms of sexual assault than women in the general population. Single women who drink frequently and have a prior history of being sexually assaulted are most likely to be assaulted on campus.[62]

High-Risk Lifestyles People who have high-risk lifestyles—drinking, taking drugs, getting involved in crime—maintain a much greater chance of victimization.[63] Groups that have an extremely risky life, such as young runaways living on the street, are at high risk for victimization; the more time they are exposed to street life, the greater their risk of becoming crime victims.[64] Teenage males have an extremely high victimization risk because their lifestyle places them at risk both at school and once they leave the school grounds.[65] They spend a great deal of time hanging out with friends and pursuing recreational fun.[66] Their friends may give them a false ID so they can go drinking in the neighborhood bar, or they may hang out in taverns at night, which places them at risk because many fights and assaults occur in places that serve liquor.

Exposure to violence and associating with violent peers enmeshes young men in a lifestyle that increases their victimization risk. One way for young males to avoid victimization is to choose their companions wisely. If they limit their male friends and hang out with girls they will lower their chances of victimization.[67] The perils of a deviant lifestyle do not end in adolescence and will haunt the risk taker into their adulthood. Kids who take drugs and carry weapons in their adolescence maintain a greater chance of being shot and killed as adults.[68]

Lifestyle risks continue into young adulthood. College students who spend several nights each week partying and who take recreational drugs are much more likely to suffer violent crime than those who avoid such risky academic lifestyles.[69] As adults, those who commit crimes increase their chances of becoming the victims of homicide.[70]

What lures victims into a high-risk lifestyle even though they realize it is fraught with danger? As you may recall, victims share personality traits also commonly found in law violators, namely impulsivity and low self-control. Perhaps their impetuous and reckless nature leads some people to seek out risky situations that put them in greater danger than they might have imagined.[71]

Victims and Criminals One element of lifestyle that may place people at risk for victimization is ongoing involvement in a criminal career. Analysis of data from the Rochester and

Pittsburgh Youth Studies—two ongoing longitudinal surveys tracking thousands of at-risk youth—indicates that kids who became victims of serious crime were more likely than non-victims to have participated in such criminal activities as gang/group fights, serious assaults, and drug dealing. They are also more likely to have associated with delinquent peers.

Carrying a weapon was another surefire way to become a crime victim. Males who carried weapons were approximately three times more likely to be victimized than those who did not carry weapons.[72] Another study of high school youth, conducted by Pamela Wilcox, David May, and Staci Roberts, also found that kids who carry weapons to school are much more likely to become crime victims than those who avoid weapons. They found that carrying a weapon may embolden youths and encourage them to become involved in risk-taking behavior that they would not have attempted otherwise. In short, while some kids carry weapons for self-defense, having a gun in their possession may actually increase the likelihood of their (a) getting involved in crime and (b) becoming a crime victim themselves.[73]

These data indicate that criminals and victims may not be two separate and distinct groups. Rather, the risk of victimization is directly linked to the high-risk lifestyle of young, weapon-toting gang boys.

Deviant Place Theory

According to **deviant place theory**, the greater their exposure to dangerous places, the more likely people will become victims of crime and violence.[74] Victims do not encourage crime but are victim prone because they reside in socially disorganized high-crime areas where they have the greatest risk of coming into contact with criminal offenders, irrespective of their own behavior or lifestyle.[75] The more often victims visit dangerous places, the more likely they will be exposed to crime and violence.[76] Neighborhood crime levels, then, may be more important for determining the chances of victimization than individual characteristics. Consequently, there may be little reason for residents in lower-class areas to alter their lifestyle or take safety precautions because personal behavior choices do not influence the likelihood of victimization.[77]

Deviant places are poor, densely populated, highly transient neighborhoods in which commercial and residential property exist side by side.[78] The commercial property provides criminals with easy targets for theft crimes, such as shoplifting and larceny. Successful people stay out of these stigmatized areas; they are homes for "demoralized kinds of people" who are easy targets for crime: the homeless, the addicted, the retarded, and the elderly poor.[79] People who live in more affluent areas and take safety precautions significantly lower their chances of becoming crime victims; the effect of safety precautions is less pronounced in poor areas. Residents of poor areas have a much greater risk of becoming victims because they live near many motivated offenders; to protect themselves, they have to try harder to be safe than the more affluent.[80]

Sociologist William Julius Wilson has described how people who can afford to leave dangerous areas do so. He suggests that affluent people realize that criminal victimization can be avoided by moving to an area with greater law enforcement and lower crime rates. Because there are significant interracial income differences, white residents are able to flee inner-city high-crime areas, leaving members of racial minorities behind to suffer high victimization rates.[81]

Routine Activities Theory

Routine activities theory was first articulated in a series of papers by Lawrence Cohen and Marcus Felson.[82] They concluded that the volume and distribution of predatory crime (violent crimes against a person and crimes in which an offender attempts to steal an object directly) are closely related to the interaction of three variables that reflect the routine activities of the typical American lifestyle (see Figure 3.6):

▌ The availability of **suitable targets**, such as homes containing easily salable goods

▌ The absence of **capable guardians**, such as police, homeowners, neighbors, friends, and relatives

▌ The presence of **motivated offenders**, such as a large number of unemployed teenagers

The presence of these components increases the likelihood that a predatory crime will take place. Targets are more likely to be victimized if they are poorly guarded and exposed to a large group of motivated offenders such as teenage boys.[83] As targets increase in value and availability, so too should crime rates. Conversely, as the resale value of formerly pricey goods such as iPods and cell phones declines, so too should burglary rates.[84]

Increasing the number of motivated offenders and placing them in close proximity to valuable goods will increase victimization levels. Even after-school programs, designed to reduce criminal activity, may produce higher crime rates because they lump together motivated offenders—teen boys with vulnerable victims (other teen boys).[85] Young women who drink to excess in bars and frat houses may elevate their risk of **date rape** because (a) they are perceived as easy targets, and (b) their attackers can rationalize the attack because they view intoxication as a sign of immorality ("She's loose, so I didn't think she'd care").[86] Conversely, people can reduce their chances of victimization if they adopt a lifestyle that limits their exposure to danger: by getting married, having children, and moving to a small town.[87]

Guardianship Even the most motivated offenders may ignore valuable targets if they are well guarded. Despite containing valuable commodities, private homes and/or public businesses may be considered off-limits by seasoned criminals if they are well protected by capable guardians and efficient security systems.[88]

Criminals are also aware of police guardianship. In order to convince them that "crime does not pay," more cops can be put on the street. Proactive, aggressive law enforcement officers who quickly get to the scene of the crime help deter criminal activities.[89]

Hot Spots Motivated people—such as teenage males, drug users, and unemployed adults—are the ones most likely to commit

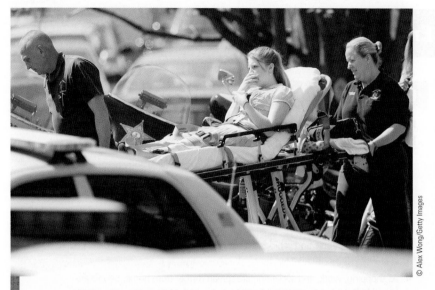

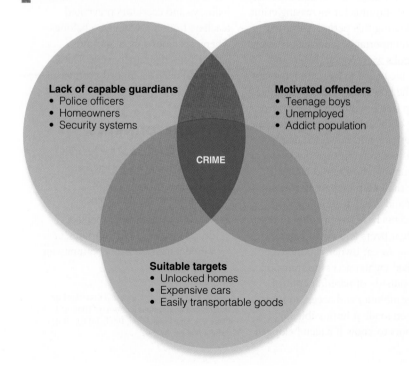

commit crime. Even the most desperate criminal might hesitate to attack a well-defended target, whereas a group of teens might rip off an unoccupied home on the spur of the moment.[91] In hot spots for crime, therefore, an undefended yet attractive target becomes an irresistible objective for motivated criminals. Given these principles, it is not surprising that people who (a) live in high-crime areas and (b) go out late at night (c) carrying valuables such as an expensive watch and (d) engage in risky behavior such as drinking alcohol, (e) without friends or family to watch or help them, have a significant chance of becoming crime victims.[92]

Lifestyle, Opportunity, and Routine Activities Routine activities theory is bound up in opportunity and lifestyle. A person's living arrangements can affect victim risk; people who live in unguarded areas are at the mercy of motivated offenders. Lifestyle affects the opportunity for crime because it controls a person's proximity to criminals, time of exposure to criminals, attractiveness as a target, and ability to be protected.[93]

Criminal opportunities (such as suitable victims and targets) abound in urban environments where facilitators (such as guns and drugs) are also readily found. Environmental factors, such as physical layout and cultural style, may either facilitate or restrict criminal opportunity. Motivated offenders living in these urban hot spots continually learn about criminal opportunities from peers, the media, and their own perceptions; such information may either escalate their criminal motivation or warn them of its danger.[94]

Empirical Support Cohen and Felson argue that crime rates increased between 1960 and 1980 because the number of adult caretakers at home during the day (guardians) had decreased as a result of increased female participation in the workforce. While mothers are at work and children in daycare, homes are left unguarded. A recent study by Steven Messner and his associates found that between the years of 1967 and 1998, as unemployment rates increased, juvenile homicide arrest rates decreased, a finding that supports the effects of adult supervision on juvenile crime predicted by routine activities theory.[95]

Similarly, with the growth of suburbia during the 1960s, traditional urban neighborhoods were in transition and/or decline, and the number of such familiar guardians as family, neighbors, and friends had diminished. At the same time, the volume of easily transportable wealth increased, creating a greater

A young woman is carried out by emergency rescuers during the funeral service of Virginia Tech shooting victim Reema Samaha on April 23, 2007, in McLean, Virginia. Samaha graduated from Westfield High School, the same school attended by gunman Seung-Hui Cho. How would routine activities theory explain the Virginia Tech shooting? What aspects of the theory could be applied to such a seemingly senseless killing?

crime. If they congregate in a particular neighborhood, it becomes a "hot spot" for crime and violence. People who live in these hot spots elevate their chances of victimization. For example, people who live in public housing projects may have high victimization rates because their fellow residents, mostly indigent, are extremely motivated to commit crime.[90] Yet motivated criminals must have the opportunity to find suitable undefended targets before they

Figure 3.6 Routine Activities Theory: The Interaction of Three Factors

Lack of capable guardians
- Police officers
- Homeowners
- Security systems

Motivated offenders
- Teenage boys
- Unemployed
- Addict population

CRIME

Suitable targets
- Unlocked homes
- Expensive cars
- Easily transportable goods

The Criminological Enterprise

CRIME AND EVERYDAY LIFE

A core premise of routine activities theory is that all things being equal, the greater the opportunity to commit crime, the higher the crime and victimization rate. This thesis is cogently presented by Marcus Felson in *Crime and Everyday Life*. Using a routine activities perspective, Felson shows why he believes U.S. crime rates are so high and why U.S. citizens suffer such high rates of victimization.

According to Felson, there are always impulsive, motivated offenders who are willing to take the chance, if conditions are right, of committing crime for profit. Therefore, crime rates are a function of changing social conditions. Crime in the United States grew as the country changed from a nation of small villages and towns to one of large urban environments. In a village, not only could a thief be easily recognized, but the commodities stolen could be identified long after the crime occurred. Cities provided the critical population mass to allow predatory criminals to hide and evade apprehension. After the crime, criminals could blend into the crowd, disperse their loot, and make a quick escape using the public transportation system.

The modern-day equivalent of the urban center is the shopping mall. Here, strangers converge in large numbers and youths "hang out." The interior is filled with people, so drug deals can be concealed in the pedestrian flow. Stores have attractively displayed goods, which encourage shoplifting and employee pilferage. Substantial numbers of cars are parked in areas that make larceny and car theft virtually undetectable. Cars that carry away stolen merchandise have an undistinguished appearance. Who notices people placing items in a car in a shopping mall lot? Also, shoppers can be attacked in parking lots as people go in isolation to and from their cars.

EXHIBIT 3A

How Development of the Divergent Metropolis Has Increased Crime Levels

1. It has become more difficult to protect people from criminal entry because homes have been dispersed over larger areas, huge parking lots have been created, and building heights lowered.

2. There are fewer people in each household and consequently less intrapersonal and intrafamily supervision.

3. By spreading people and vehicles over larger areas as they travel and park, people are more exposed to attack.

4. As shopping, work, and socializing are spread further from home, people are forced to leave their immediate neighborhood, and, as strangers, they become more vulnerable to attack.

5. By spreading vast quantities of retail goods throughout huge stores and malls, with fewer employees to watch over them, the divergent metropolis creates a retail environment that invites people of all ages to shoplift.

6. Commuting to the inner city for work requires that millions of dollars' worth of vehicles be left in parking lots without supervision.

Felson believes these changes in the structure and function of society have been responsible for changes in the crime rates. He concludes that rather than change people, crime prevention strategies must be established to reduce the opportunity to commit crime.

Why did crime and delinquency rates increase dramatically between 1960 and 1990? According to Felson, structural changes in American society were the stimulus for increasing crime rates. During this period, suburbs grew in importance, and the divergent metropolis was created. Labor and family life began to be scattered away from the household, decreasing guardianship (see Exhibit 3A). The convenience of microwave ovens, automatic dishwashers, and increased emphasis on fast-food offerings freed adolescents from common household chores. Rather than help prepare the family dinner and wash dishes afterward, adolescents have the freedom to meet with their peers and avoid parental controls. As car ownership increased, teens had greater access to transportation outside of parental control. Greater mobility and access to transportation made it impossible for neighbors to know if a teen belonged

in an area or was an intruder planning to commit a crime. As schools became larger and more complex, they provided ideal sites for crime. The many hallways and corridors prevented teachers from knowing who belongs where; spacious school grounds reduced teacher supervision. These structural changes helped produce a 30-year crime wave.

CRITICAL THINKING

1. What technological changes influence crime rates? The Internet? Video and computer games? Cell phones? ATM machines?

2. Would increased family contact decrease adolescent crime rates, or would it increase the opportunity for child abuse?

Source: Marcus Felson, *Crime and Everyday Life: Insights and Implications for Society* (Thousand Oaks, CA: Pine Forge Press, 1994; 3rd ed., 2002), Exhibit A at pp. 57–59.

VICTIMIZATION THEORIES

	Major Premise	Strengths of the Theory	Research Focus of the Theory
Victim Precipitation	The major premise of victim precipitation theory is that victims trigger criminal acts by their provocative behavior. Active precipitation involves fighting words or gestures. Passive precipitation occurs when victims unknowingly threaten their attacker.	The strength of the theory is that it explains multiple victimizations: if people precipitate crime, it follows that they will become repeat victims if their behavior persists over time.	The research focuses of the theory are the victim's role, crime provocation, and the victim–offender relationship.
Lifestyle	The major premise of lifestyle theory is that victimization risk is increased when people have a high-risk lifestyle. Placing oneself at risk by going out to dangerous places results in increased victimization.	The strength of the theory is that it explains victimization patterns in the social structure. Males, young people, and the poor have high victimization rates because they have a higher-risk lifestyle than females, the elderly, and the affluent.	The research focuses of the theory are personal activities, peer relations, place of crime, and type of crime.
Deviant Place	The major premise of deviant place theory is that victims do not encourage crime but are victim prone because they reside in socially disorganized high-crime areas where they have the greatest risk of coming into contact with criminal offenders, irrespective of their own behavior or lifestyle.	The strength of the theory is that it shows why people with conventional lifestyles become crime victims in high risk areas. Victimization is a function of place and location and not lifestyle and risk taking.	The research focus of the theory is victimization in high-crime, disorganized neighborhoods.
Routine Activities	The major premise of routine activities theory is that crime rates can be explained by the availability of suitable targets, the absence of capable guardians, and the presence of motivated offenders.	The strengths of the theory are that it can explain crime rates and trends; it shows how victim behavior can influence criminal opportunity; and it suggests that victimization risk can be reduced by increasing guardianship and/or reducing target vulnerability.	The research focuses of the theory are opportunity to commit crime, effect of police and guardians, population shifts, and crime rates.

number of available targets.[96] These structural changes in society led to 30 years of increasing crime rates. To counteract these forces, some communities became better organized, restricted traffic, changed street patterns, and limited neighborhood entrances to control the opportunity to commit crime and reduce the chances of residents' victimization.[97]

Skyrocketing drug use in the 1980s created an excess of motivated offenders, and the rates of some crimes, such as robbery, increased dramatically. Crime rates may have fallen in the 1990s because a robust economy decreased the pool of motivated offenders, and the growing number of police officers increased guardianship.[98] If crime is rational, criminal motivation should be reduced if potential offenders perceive alternatives to crime; in contrast, the perception of opportunities for crime should increase criminal motivation. The Criminological Enterprise feature on crime in everyday life shows how these relationships can be influenced by cultural and structural change.

The various theories of victimization are summarized in Concept Summary 3.1.

CARING FOR THE VICTIM

National victim surveys indicate that almost every American age 12 and over will one day become the victim of a common-law crime, such as larceny or burglary, and in the aftermath suffer financial problems, mental stress, and physical hardship.[99] Surveys show that more than 75 percent of the general public has been victimized by crime at least once in their life; as many as 25 percent of the victims develop posttraumatic stress disorder, and their symptoms last for more than a decade after the crime occurred.[100] The long-term effects of sexual victimization can include years of problem avoidance, social withdrawal, and self-criticism. Helping these victims adjust and improve their coping techniques can be essential to their recovery.[101] Law enforcement agencies, courts, and correctional and human service systems have come to realize that due process and human rights exist for both the defendant and the victim of criminal behavior.

Cynthia Ellis of Richmond touches a photograph of her son, murder victim Da'Mon Jacob, during the 18th Annual Victims March on the Capitol in Sacramento, California, on April 23, 2007. Hundreds of crime victims from across the state gathered at the Capitol to promote greater rights for victims and their families. Can victim advocates make a difference?

EXHIBIT 3.1

The Rights Established under the Crime Victims' Rights Act of 2004

The Crime Victims' Rights Act of 2004, 18 U.S.C. § 3771, provides that officers and employees of the Department of Justice shall make their best efforts to see that crime victims are notified of, and accorded, the following rights:

▌ The right to be reasonably protected from the accused.

▌ The right to reasonable, accurate, and timely notice of any public court proceeding, or any parole proceeding, involving the crime or of any release or escape of the accused.

▌ The right not to be excluded from any such public court proceeding, unless the court, after receiving clear and convincing evidence, determines that testimony by the victim would be materially altered if the victim heard other testimony at that proceeding.

▌ The right to be reasonably heard at any public proceeding in the district court involving release, plea, sentencing, or any parole proceeding.

▌ The reasonable right to confer with the attorney for the government in the case.

▌ The right to full and timely restitution as provided by law.

▌ The right to proceedings free from unreasonable delay.

▌ The right to be treated with fairness and with respect for the victim's dignity and privacy.

Source: Justice for All Act of 2004, the Crime Victims' Rights Act of 2004, 18 U.S.C. § 3771, www.usdoj.gov/usao/eousa/vr/cvra/index.html (accessed March 14, 2007).

The Government's Response to Victimization

Because of public concern over violent personal crime, President Ronald Reagan created a Task Force on Victims of Crime in 1982.[102] This group suggested that a balance be achieved between recognizing the victim's rights and providing the defendant with due process. Recommendations included providing witnesses and victims with protection from intimidation, requiring restitution in criminal cases, developing guidelines for fair treatment of crime victims and witnesses, and expanding programs of victim compensation.[103] Consequently, the Omnibus Victim and Witness Protection Act was passed, which required the use of victim impact statements at sentencing in federal criminal cases, greater protection for witnesses, more stringent bail laws, and the use of restitution in criminal cases.

In 1984 the Comprehensive Crime Control Act and the Victims of Crime Act authorized federal funding for state victim compensation and assistance projects.[104] With these acts, the federal government began to address the plight of the victim and make victim assistance an even greater concern of the public and the justice system. In 2004 the Justice for All Act modified existing federal law and created a new set of rights for victims (Exhibit 3.1), including the right to be protected from the accused in their case and to be informed of their release. Legal expert Michael O'Hear finds that the Crime Victims' Rights Act of 2004 can be viewed as an effort to promote victims' rights as a counterweight to defendants' rights, illustrating both the public's hostility to defendants and its skepticism of the traditional lawyer- and judge-dominated legal system, which they feel is too liberal.[105]

Due to this recognition of the needs of victims, an estimated 2,000 victim-witness assistance programs have developed around the United States.[106] Victim-witness assistance programs are organized on a variety of governmental levels and serve a variety of clients. We will look at the most prominent forms of victim services operating in the United States.[107]

Victim Compensation One of the primary goals of victim advocates has been to lobby for legislation creating crime victim compensation programs.[108] As a result of such legislation, the victim ordinarily receives compensation from the state to pay for damages associated with the crime. Rarely are two compensation schemes alike, however, and many state programs suffer from lack of both adequate funding and proper organization within the criminal justice system. Compensation may be made for medical bills, loss of wages, loss of future earnings, and counseling. In the case of death, the victim's survivors can receive burial expenses and aid for loss of support.[109] Awards are typically in the $100 to $15,000 range. Occasionally programs will provide emergency assistance to indigent victims until compensation is available. Emergency assistance may come in the form of food vouchers or replacement of prescription medicines.

In 1984, the federal government created the Victim of Crime Act (VOCA), which grants money to state compensation boards derived from fines and penalties imposed on federal offenders. The money is distributed each year to the states to fund both their crime victim compensation programs and their victim assistance programs, such as rape crisis centers and domestic violence shelters. Victims of child abuse and victims of domestic violence received most of the funds. VOCA money goes to support victims' medical expenses, gives them economic support for lost wages, helps to compensate for the death of loved ones, and provides mental health counseling.[110]

Victim Advocates Assuring victims' rights can involve an eclectic group of advocacy groups, some independent, others government sponsored, and some self-help. Advocates can be especially helpful when victims need to interact with the agencies of justice. For example, advocates can lobby police departments to keep investigations open as well as request the return of recovered stolen property. They can demand from prosecutors and judges protection from harassment and reprisals by, for example, making "no contact" a condition of bail. They can help victims make statements during sentencing hearings as well as probation and parole revocation procedures. Victim advocates can also interact with news media, making sure that reporting is accurate and that victim privacy is not violated. Victim advocates can be part of an independent agency similar to a legal aid society. If successful, top-notch advocates may eventually open private offices, similar to attorneys, private investigators, or jury consultants.

Some programs assign advocates to help victims understand the operations of the justice system and guide them through the process. Victims of sexual assault may be assigned the assistance of a rape victim advocate to stand by their side as they negotiate the legal and medical systems that must process their case. Research shows that rape survivors who had the assistance of an advocate were significantly more likely to have police reports taken, were less likely to be treated negatively by police officers, and reported less distress from their medical contact experiences.[111]

Court advocates prepare victims and witnesses by explaining court procedures: how to be a witness, how bail works, and what to do if the defendant makes a threat. Lack of such knowledge can cause confusion and fear, making some victims reluctant to testify in court procedures.

Many victim programs also provide transportation to and from court, and advocates may remain in the courtroom during hearings to explain procedures and provide support. Court escorts are particularly important for elderly and disabled victims, victims of child abuse and assault, and victims who have been intimidated by friends or relatives of the defendant. These types of services may be having a positive effect since recent research shows that victims may be now less traumatized by a court hearing than previously believed.[112]

Victim Counseling Numerous programs provide counseling and psychological support to help victims recover from the long-term trauma associated with a violent victimization. Clients are commonly referred to the local network of public and private social service agencies that can provide emergency and long-term assistance with transportation, medical care, shelter, food, and clothing. In addition, more than half of victim programs provide crisis intervention to victims, many of whom feel isolated, vulnerable, and in need of immediate services. Some programs counsel at their offices, and others visit victims' homes, the crime scene, or a hospital. Helping victims adjust is often a difficult process and recent research has found little evidence that counseling efforts are as successful as previously hoped.[113]

Public Education More than half of all victim programs include public education programs that help familiarize the general public with their services and with other agencies that assist crime victims. In some instances, these are primary education programs, which teach methods of dealing with conflict without resorting to violence. For example, school-based programs present information on spousal and dating abuse followed by discussions of how to reduce violent incidents.[114]

Victim–Offender Reconciliation Programs Victim–offender reconciliation programs (VORPs) use mediators to facilitate face-to-face encounters between victims and their attackers. The aim is to engage in direct negotiations that lead to restitution agreements and, possibly, reconciliation between the two parties involved.[115] Hundreds of programs are currently in operation, and they handle many thousands of cases per year. Designed at first to address routine misdemeanors such as petty theft and vandalism, programs now commonly hammer out restitution agreements in more serious incidents such as residential burglary and even attempted murder.

Trisha Meili, author of *I Am the Central Park Jogger*, acknowledges the applause of people gathered in the Capitol Rotunda in Frankfort, Kentucky, after delivering a speech at the Crime Victims' Rights Day ceremony. Meili speaks to groups around the country about her recovery after a brutal attack while jogging in New York's Central Park in 1989. Educating people about how to avoid victimization may help them avoid similar attacks.

Reconciliation programs are based on the concept of restorative justice, which rejects punitive correctional measures in favor of viewing crimes of violence and theft as interpersonal conflicts that need to be settled in the community through noncoercive means. See Chapter 8 for more on this approach.

connections

Victim Impact Statements Most jurisdictions allow victims to make an impact statement before the sentencing judge. This gives the victim an opportunity to tell of his or her experiences and describe the ordeal; in the case of a murder trial, the surviving family can recount the effect the crime has had on their lives and well-being.[116] The effect of victim/witness statements on sentencing has been the topic of some debate. Some research finds that victim statements result in a higher rate of incarceration, but others find that the statements are insignificant.[117] Those who favor the use of impact statements argue that because the victim is harmed by the crime, the victim has a right to influence the outcome of the case. After all, the public prosecutor is allowed to make sentencing recommendations because the public has been harmed by the crime. Logically the harm suffered by the victim legitimizes his or her right to make sentencing recommendations.[118]

Victims and Self-Protection

Although the general public mostly approves of the police, fear of crime and concern about community safety have prompted some to become their own "police force," taking an active role in community protection and citizen crime control groups.[119] The more crime in an area, the greater the amount of fear and the more likely residents will be to engage in self-protective measures.[120]

Research indicates that a significant number of crimes may not be reported to police simply because victims prefer to take matters into their own hands.[121] One manifestation of this trend is the concept of **target hardening**, or making one's home and business crime-proof through locks, bars, alarms, and other devices.[122] Other commonly used crime prevention techniques include a fence or barricade at the entrance; a doorkeeper, guard, or receptionist in an apartment building; an intercom or phone to gain access to the building; surveillance cameras; window bars; warning signs; and dogs chosen for their ability to guard the house. The use of these measures is inversely proportional to perception of neighborhood safety: people who fear crime are more likely to use crime prevention techniques. Although the true relationship is still unclear, there is mounting evidence that people who protect their homes are less likely to be victimized by property crimes.[123] One study conducted in the Philadelphia area found that people who install burglar alarms are less likely to suffer burglary than those who forgo similar preventive measures.[124]

Fighting Back Some people take self-protection to its ultimate end by preparing to fight back when criminals attack them. How successful are victims when they resist? Research indicates that victims who fight back often frustrate their attackers but also face increased odds of being physically harmed during the attack.[125] In some cases, fighting back decreases the odds of a crime being completed but increases the victim's chances of injury.[126] Resistance may draw the attention of bystanders and make a violent crime physically difficult to complete, but it can also cause offenders to escalate their violence.[127]

What about the use of firearms for self-protection? Again, there is no clear-cut answer. Each year, 2.5 million times, victims use guns for defensive purposes, a number that is not surprising considering that about one-third of U.S. households contain guns.[128] Gary Kleck has estimated that armed victims kill between 1,500 and 2,800 potential felons each year and wound between 8,700 and 16,000. Kleck's research shows, ironically, that by fighting back victims kill far more criminals than the estimated 250 to 1,000 killed annually by police.[129] Kleck has found that the risk of collateral injury is relatively rare and that potential victims should be encouraged to fight back.[130] In a recent study conducted with colleague Jongyeon Tark, Kleck reviewed more than 27,000 contact crime incidents and found that when compared to nonresistance, self-protection significantly reduced the likelihood of property loss and injury and that the most forceful tactics, including resistance with a gun, appear to have the strongest effects in reducing the risk of injury. Importantly, the research indicated that resistance did not contribute to injury in any meaningful way. The conclusion: it is better to fight than flee.[131]

"Stand Your Ground" Should people carry guns for self-protection? The jury is still out on this issue so it depends on whom you ask! Nonetheless, 15 states have passed laws that allow crime victims to use deadly force in certain situations in which they might have formerly been charged with a crime.[132] Florida's law, enacted on October 1, 2005, allows the use of deadly force when a person reasonably believes it necessary to prevent the commission of a "forcible felony," including carjacking, robbery, or assault.

The traditional "castle doctrine" required that people could only use deadly force in their own home when they reasonably believed that their lives were in danger. The new law allows the average citizen to use deadly force when they reasonably believe that their homes or vehicles have been illegally invaded. The Florida law authorizes the use of defensive force by anyone "who is not engaged in an unlawful activity and who is attacked in any other place where he or she has a right to be." Furthermore, under the law, such a person has no duty to retreat and can stand his or her ground and meet force with force. The statute also grants civil and criminal immunity to anyone found to have had such a reasonable belief.[133]

Community Organization Not everyone is capable of buying a handgun or semiautomatic weapon and doing battle with predatory criminals. An alternative approach has been for communities to organize on the neighborhood level against crime. Citizens have been working independently and in co-operation with local police agencies in neighborhood patrol and block watch programs. These programs organize local citizens in urban areas to patrol neighborhoods, watch for suspicious people, help secure the neighborhood, lobby for improvements (such as increased lighting), report crime to police, put out community newsletters, conduct home security surveys, and serve as a source for crime information or tips.[134] Although such programs are welcome additions to police services, there is little evidence that they appreciably affect the crime rate. There is also concern that their effectiveness is spottier in low-income, high-crime areas, which need the most crime prevention assistance.[135] Block watches and neighborhood patrols seem more successful when they are part of general-purpose or multi-issue community groups rather than when they focus directly on crime problems.[136]

Victims' Rights

More than 20 years ago, legal scholar Frank Carrington suggested that crime victims have legal rights that should assure them of basic services from the government.[137] According to Carrington, just as the defendant has the right to counsel and a fair trial, society is also obliged to ensure basic rights for law-abiding citizens. These rights range from adequate protection from violent crimes to victim compensation and assistance from the criminal justice system.

Because of the influence of victims' rights advocates, every state now has a set of legal rights for crime victims in its code of laws, often called a Victims' Bill of Rights.[138] These generally include the right:

▪ To be notified of proceedings and the status of the defendant.

▪ To be present at criminal justice proceedings.

▪ To make a statement at sentencing, and to receive restitution from a convicted offender.

▪ To be consulted before a case is dismissed or a plea agreement entered.

▪ To a speedy trial.

▪ To keep the victim's contact information confidential.

Not only has the victims' rights movement caught on in the United States, it has also had an impact in Europe. The European Union member nations have agreed in principle to a set of rules that creates minimum standards for the protection of victims of crime. These guarantee that all victims should:

▪ Be treated with respect

▪ Have their entitlement to a real and appropriate role in criminal proceedings recognized

▪ Have the right to be heard during proceedings, and the right to supply evidence

▪ Receive information on: the type of support available; where and how to report an offence; criminal proceedings and their role in them; access to protection and advice; entitlement to compensation; and, if they wish, the outcomes of their complaints including sentencing and release of the offender

▪ Have communication safeguards: that is, member states should take measures to minimize communication difficulties in criminal proceedings

▪ Have access to free legal advice concerning their role in the proceedings and, where appropriate, legal aid

▪ Receive payment of expenses incurred as a result of participation in criminal proceedings

▪ Receive reasonable protection, including protection of privacy

▪ Receive compensation in the course of criminal proceedings

▪ Receive penal mediation in the course of criminal proceedings where appropriate

▪ Benefit from various measures to minimize the difficulties faced where victims are resident in another member state, especially when organizing criminal proceedings[139]

A final, albeit controversial, element of the victims' rights movement is the development of offender registration laws that require that the name and sometimes addresses of known sex offenders be posted by law enforcement agencies. Today almost every state has adopted sex offender laws and the federal government runs a National Sex Offender Public Registry with links to every state.[140] Sex offender registration is indelibly linked to the death of Megan Kanka, an incident described in the Profiles in Crime feature "Jesse Timmendequas and Megan's Law."

🖱 **WWW** Go to academic.cengage.com/criminaljustice/siegel to learn more about the following services:

▪ It is the mission of the **Crime Victims Board of New York** to provide compensation to innocent victims of crime in a timely, efficient, and compassionate manner; to fund direct services to crime victims via a network of community-based programs; and to advocate for the rights and benefits of all innocent victims of crime.

▪ The **Office for Victims of Crime (OVC)** was established by the 1984 Victims of Crime Act (VOCA) to oversee diverse programs that benefit victims of crime. The OVC provides substantial funding to state victim assistance and compensation programs and supports training designed to educate criminal justice and allied professionals regarding the rights and needs of crime victims.

▪ The **Victim-Offender Reconciliation Program (VORP) Information and Resource Center** provides information on programs and training and provides technical assistance.

▪ The **National Organization for Victim Assistance** is a private, nonprofit organization of victim and witness assistance programs and practitioners, criminal justice agencies and professionals, mental health professionals, researchers, former victims and survivors, and others committed to the recognition and implementation of victim rights and services.

JESSE TIMMENDEQUAS AND MEGAN'S LAW

© AP Images/Charles Rex Arbogast

Richard and Maureen Kanka thought that their daughter Megan was safe in their quiet, suburban neighborhood in Hamilton Township, New Jersey. Then, on July 29, 1994, their lives were shattered when their 7-year-old daughter Megan went missing. Maureen Kanka searched the neighborhood and met 33-year-old Jesse Timmendequas, who lived across the street. Timmendequas told her that he had seen Megan earlier that evening while he was working on his car. The police were called in and soon focused their attention on Timmendequas's house when they learned that he and two other residents were convicted sex offenders who had met at a treatment center and decided to live together upon their release. Timmendequas, who appeared extremely nervous when questioned, was asked to accompany police back to their headquarters, where he confessed to luring Megan into his home by inviting her to see a puppy, then raping her and strangling her to death.

Timmendequas had served six years in prison for aggravated assault and attempted sexual assault on another child. The fact that a known sex offender was living anonymously in the Kankas' neighborhood turned Megan's death into a national crusade to develop laws that require sex offenders to register with local police when they move into a neighborhood and require local authorities to provide community notification of the sex offender's presence. New York State's Sex Offender Registration Act is typical of these efforts, commonly known as "Megan's Law." Becoming effective on January 21, 1996, the statute requires that sex offenders in New York are classified by the risk of reoffense. A court determines whether an offender is a level 1 (low risk), 2 (moderate risk), or 3 (high risk). The court also determines whether an offender should be given the designation of a sexual predator, sexually violent offender, or predicate sex offender. Offenders are required to be registered for 20 years or life. Level 1 offenders with no designation must register for 20 years. Level 1 offenders with a designation, as well as level 2 and level 3 offenders regardless of whether they have a designation, must register for life. Local law enforcement agencies are notified whenever a sex offender moves into their jurisdiction. That agency may notify schools and other "entities with vulnerable populations" about the presence of a level 2 or level 3 offender if the offender poses a threat to public safety. The act established a toll-free telephone information line that citizens can call to inquire whether a person is listed in the registry and access information on sex offenders living in their neighborhoods. On the federal level, the Jacob Wetterling Crimes Against Children Law, passed in May 1996, requires states to pass some version of "Megan's Law" or lose federal aid. At least 47 states plus the District of Columbia have complied. Jesse Timmendequas was sentenced to death on June 20, 1997, and is currently on death row.

The case of Megan Kanka illustrates both the risk children face from sexual predators and the efforts being made by the justice system to limit that risk. To some civil liberty groups, such as the American Civil Liberties Union, registration laws go too far because they will not prevent sex offenders from committing crimes and because they victimize rehabilitated ex-offenders and their families. Should the rights of the victim take precedent over the privacy of the offender?

Sources: New York State Sex Offender Registry and the Sex Offender Registration Act (SORA), http://criminaljustice.state.ny.us/nsor/ (accessed March 14, 2007), New York State Correction Law Article 6-C (Section 168 et seq.); CourtTV Library, *New Jersey v. Timmendequas*, www.courttv.com/archive/casefiles/verdicts/kanka.html (accessed March 14, 2007).

THINKING LIKE A CRIMINOLOGIST

The director of the state's department of human services has asked you to evaluate a self-report survey of adolescents age 10 to 18. She has provided you with the following information on physical abuse:

> *Adolescents experiencing abuse or violence are at high risk of immediate and lasting negative effects on health and well-being. Of the high school students surveyed, an alarming one in five (21 percent) said they had been physically abused. Of the older students, age 15 to 18, 29 percent said they had been physically abused. Younger students also reported significant rates of abuse: 17 percent responded "yes" when asked whether they had been physically abused. Although girls were far less likely to report abuse than boys, 12 percent said they had been physically abused. Most abuse occurs at home, occurs more than once, and the abuser is usually a family member. More than half of those physically abused had tried alcohol and drugs, and 60 percent had admitted to a violent act. Nonabused children were significantly less likely to abuse substances, and only 30 percent indicated they had committed a violent act.*

 Writing Exercise Write a brief paper (two double-spaced pages) explaining how you would interpret these data, what factors might influence their validity, and your interpretation of the association between abuse and delinquency.

 Doing Research on the Web To help formulate your recommendations, review these Web-based resources:

▯ The National Council on Child Abuse and Family Violence (NCCAFV) maintains a website with links to documents on child abuse and violence.

▯ In Canada, the National Clearinghouse on Family Violence maintains information on abuse and violence.

These websites can be accessed via academic.cengage.com/criminaljustice/siegel.

SUMMARY

▯ Criminologists now consider victims and victimization a major focus of study. About 24 million U.S. citizens are victims of crime each year. Like the crime rate, the victimization rate has been in sharp decline.

▯ The social and economic costs of crime are in the billions of dollars. Victims suffer long-term consequences such as experiencing fear and posttraumatic stress disorder.

▯ Research shows that victims are more likely to engage in antisocial behavior than nonvictims.

▯ Like crime, victimization has stable patterns and trends. Violent-crime victims tend to be young, poor, single males living in large cities, although victims come in all ages, sizes, races, and genders.

▯ Females are more likely to be victimized by someone they know than are males.

▯ Adolescents maintain a high risk of being physically and sexually victimized. Their victimization has been linked to a multitude of subsequent social problems.

▯ Many victimizations occur in the home, and many victims are the target of relatives and loved ones.

▯ Victim precipitation theory holds that victims provoke criminals, through either active or passive precipitation.

▯ Lifestyle theory suggests that victims put themselves in danger by engaging in high-risk activities, such as going out late at night, living in a high-crime area, and associating with high-risk peers.

▯ Deviant place theory argues that victimization risk is related to neighborhood crime rates.

▯ The routine activities theory maintains that a pool of motivated offenders exists and that these offenders will take advantage of unguarded, suitable targets.

▯ Numerous programs help victims by providing court services, economic compensation, public education, and crisis intervention. Most states have created a Victims' Bill of Rights.

■ Rather than depend on the justice system, some victims have attempted to help themselves through community organization for self-protection.

■ CENGAGENOW™ is an easy-to-use online resource that helps you study in less time to get the grade you want—NOW. CengageNOW™ Personalized Study (a diagnostic study tool containing valuable text-specific resources)

lets you focus on just what you don't know and learn more in less time to get a better grade. If your textbook does not include an access code card, you can go to www.ichapters.com to purchase CengageNOW™.

KEY TERMS

victimologists (70)
victimization (70)
posttraumatic stress disorder (PTSD) (71)
obsessive-compulsive disorder (71)
cycle of violence (72)
elder abuse (74)
chronic victimization (76)

siblicide (76)
victim precipitation theory (77)
active precipitation (77)
passive precipitation (77)
lifestyle theory (77)
deviant place theory (78)
routine activities theory (78)
suitable targets (78)

capable guardians (78)
motivated offenders (78)
date rape (78)
victim-witness assistance programs (82)
victim compensation (82)
crisis intervention (82)
restitution agreements (83)
target hardening (84)

CRITICAL THINKING QUESTIONS

1. Considering what we learned in this chapter about crime victimization, what measures can you take to better protect yourself from crime?

2. Do you agree with the assessment that schools are some of the most dangerous locations in the community? Did you find your high school to be a dangerous environment?

3. Does a person bear some of the responsibility for his or her victimization if the person maintains a lifestyle that contributes to the chances of becoming a crime victim? That is, should we "blame the victim"?

4. Have you ever experienced someone "precipitating" crime? If so, did you do anything to help the situation?

NOTES

1. New England News, "Authorities Develop Case Against Bouncer in Grad Student Slaying," 24 March 2006, www1.whdh.com/news/articles/local/BO16577/ (accessed May 9, 2007).
2. Ibid.
3. Shannan Catalano, *Criminal Victimization 2005* (Washington, DC: Bureau of Justice Statistics, 2006).
4. Arthur Lurigio, "Are All Victims Alike? The Adverse, Generalized, and Differential Impact of Crime," *Crime and Delinquency* 33 (1987): 452–467.
5. Children's Safety Network Economics and Insurance Resource Center, "State Costs of Violence Perpetrated by Youth," www.edarc.org/pubs/tables/youth-viol.htm (accessed March 14, 2007).
6. George Rengert, *The Geography of Illegal Drugs* (Boulder, CO: Westview, 1996), p. 5.
7. Ted R. Miller, Mark A. Cohen, and Brian Wiersema, *Victim Costs and Consequences: A New Look* (Washington, DC: National Institute of Justice, 1996), p. 9, table 2.
8. Ross Macmillan, "Adolescent Victimization and Income Deficits in Adulthood: Rethinking the Costs of Criminal Violence from a Life-Course Perspective," *Criminology* 38 (2000): 553–588.
9. James Anderson, Terry Grandison, and Laronistine Dyson, "Victims of Random Violence and the Public Health Implication: A Health Care or Criminal Justice Issue?" *Journal of Criminal Justice* 24 (1996): 379–393.
10. Rebecca Campbell and Sheela Raja, "Secondary Victimization of Rape Victims: Insights from Mental Health Professionals Who Treat Survivors of Violence," *Violence and Victims* 14 (1999): 261–274.
11. Courtney Ahrens, "Being Silenced: The Impact of Negative Social Reactions on the Disclosure of Rape," *American Journal of Community Psychology* 38 (2006): 263–274.
12. Min Xie, Greg Pogarsky, James Lynch, and David McDowall, "Prior Police Contact and Subsequent Victim Reporting: Results from the NCVS," *Justice Quarterly* 23 (2006): 481–501.
13. Angela Scarpa, Sara Chiara Haden, and Jimmy Hurley, "Community Violence Victimization and Symptoms of Posttraumatic Stress Disorder: The Moderating Effects of Coping and Social Support," *Journal of Interpersonal Violence* 21 (2006): 446–469.
14. Dean Kilpatrick, Benjamin Saunders, and Daniel Smith, *Youth Victimization: Prevalence and Implications* (Washington, DC: National Institute of Justice, 2003).
15. David Finkelhor, Heather Turner, and Richard Ormrod, "Kid's Stuff: The Nature and Impact of Peer and Sibling Violence on Younger and Older Children," *Child Abuse and Neglect* 30 (2006): 1,401–1,421.
16. Catherine Grus, "Child Abuse: Correlations with Hostile Attributions," *Journal of Developmental and Behavioral Pediatrics* 24 (2003): 296–298.
17. Kim Logio, "Gender, Race, Childhood Abuse, and Body Image among Adolescents," *Violence Against Women* 9 (2003): 931–955.
18. Mark Shevlin, Martin Dorahy, and Gary Adamson, "Childhood Traumas and Hallucinations: An Analysis of the National Comorbidity Survey," *Journal of Psychiatric Research* 41 (2007): 222–228.
19. Jeanne Kaufman and Cathy Spatz Widom, "Childhood Victimization, Running Away, and Delinquency," *Journal of Research*

in Crime and Delinquency 36 (1999): 347–370.

20. N. N. Sarkar and Rina Sarkar, "Sexual Assault on Woman: Its Impact on Her Life and Living in Society," *Sexual and Relationship Therapy* 20 (2005): 407–419.

21. Michael Wiederman, Randy Sansone, and Lori Sansone, "History of Trauma and Attempted Suicide among Women in a Primary Care Setting," *Violence and Victims* 13 (1998): 3–11; Susan Leslie Bryant and Lillian Range, "Suicidality in College Women Who Were Sexually and Physically Abused and Physically Punished by Parents," *Violence and Victims* 10 (1995): 195–215; William Downs and Brenda Miller, "Relationships between Experiences of Parental Violence During Childhood and Women's Self-Esteem," *Violence and Victims* 13 (1998): 63–78; Sally Davies-Netley, Michael Hurlburt, and Richard Hough, "Childhood Abuse as a Precursor to Homelessness for Homeless Women with Severe Mental Illness," *Violence and Victims* 11 (1996): 129–142.

22. Jane Siegel and Linda Williams, "Risk Factors for Sexual Victimization of Women," *Violence Against Women* 9 (2003): 902–930.

23. Michael Miner, Jill Klotz Flitter, and Beatrice Robinson, "Association of Sexual Revictimization with Sexuality and Psychological Function," *Journal of Interpersonal Violence* 21 (2006): 503–524.

24. Lana Stermac and Emily Paradis, "Homeless Women and Victimization: Abuse and Mental Health History among Homeless Rape Survivors," *Resources for Feminist Research* 28 (2001): 65–81.

25. Gregory Stuart, Todd M. Moore, Kristina Coop Gordon, Susan Ramsey, and Christopher Kahler, "Psychopathology in Women Arrested for Domestic Violence," *Journal of Interpersonal Violence* 21 (2006): 376–389; Caron Zlotnick, Dawn Johnson, and Robert Kohn, "Intimate Partner Violence and Long-Term Psychosocial Functioning in a National Sample of American Women," *Journal of Interpersonal Violence* 21 (2006): 262–275.

26. K. Daniel O'Leary, "Psychological Abuse: A Variable Deserving Critical Attention in Domestic Violence," *Violence and Victims* 14 (1999): 1–21.

27. Ron Acierno, Alyssa Rheingold, Heidi Resnick, and Dean Kilpatrick, "Predictors of Fear of Crime in Older Adults," *Journal of Anxiety Disorders* 18 (2004): 385–396.

28. Mirka Smolej and Janne Kivivuori, "The Relation Between Crime News and Fear of Violence," *Journal of Scandinavian Studies in Criminology and Crime Prevention* 7 (2006): 211–227.

29. Matthew Lee and Erica DeHart, "The Influence of a Serial Killer on Changes in Fear of Crime and the Use of Protective Measures: A Survey-Based Case Study of Baton Rouge," *Deviant Behavior* 28 (2007): 1–28.

30. Pamela Wilcox Rountree, "A Reexamination of the Crime–Fear Linkage," *Journal of*

Research in Crime and Delinquency 35 (1998): 341–372.

31. Robert Davis, Bruce Taylor, and Arthur Lurigio, "Adjusting to Criminal Victimization: The Correlates of Postcrime Distress," *Violence and Victimization* 11 (1996): 21–34.

32. Susan Brison, *Aftermath: Violence and the Remaking of a Self* (Princeton, NJ: Princeton University Press, 2001).

33. Susan Popkin, Victoria Gwlasda, Dennis Rosenbaum, Jean Amendolla, Wendell Johnson, and Lynn Olson, "Combating Crime in Public Housing: A Qualitative and Quantitative Longitudinal Analysis of the Chicago Housing Authority's Anti-Drug Initiative," *Justice Quarterly* 16 (1999): 519–557.

34. Karen Snedker, "Altruistic and Vicarious Fear of Crime: Fear for Others and Gendered Social Roles," *Sociological Forum* 21 (2006): 163–195.

35. Jared Dempsey, Gary Fireman, and Eugene Wang, "Transitioning Out of Peer Victimization in School Children: Gender and Behavioral Characteristics," *Journal of Psychopathology and Behavioral Assessment* 28 (2006): 271–280.

36. Timothy Ireland and Cathy Spatz Widom, *Childhood Victimization and Risk for Alcohol and Drug Arrests* (Washington, DC: National Institute of Justice, 1995).

37. Brigette Erwin, Elana Newman, Robert McMackin, Carlo Morrissey, and Danny Kaloupek, "PTSD, Malevolent Environment, and Criminality among Criminally Involved Male Adolescents," *Criminal Justice and Behavior* 27 (2000): 196–215.

38. Ulrich Orth, Leo Montada, and Andreas Maercker, "Feelings of Revenge, Retaliation Motive, and Posttraumatic Stress Reactions in Crime Victims," *Journal of Interpersonal Violence* 21 (2006): 229–243.

39. Cathy Spatz Widom, *The Cycle of Violence* (Washington, DC: National Institute of Justice, 1992), p. 1.

40. Steve Spaccarelli, J. Douglas Coatsworth, and Blake Sperry Bowden, "Exposure to Serious Family Violence among Incarcerated Boys: Its Association with Violent Offending and Potential Mediating Variables," *Violence and Victims* 10 (1995): 163–180; Jerome Kolbo, "Risk and Resilience among Children Exposed to Family Violence," *Violence and Victims* 11 (1996): 113–127.

41. Victim data used in these sections are from Catalano, *NVCS, 2005.*

42. J. DeVoe, K. Peter, M. Noonan, T. Snyder, and K. Baum, *Indicators of School Crime and Safety: 2006*, U.S. Departments of Education and Justice (Washington, DC: U.S. Government Printing Office, 2006).

43. Victoria Titterington, "A Retrospective Investigation of Gender Inequality and Female Homicide Victimization," *Sociological Spectrum* 26 (2006): 205–231.

44. Lamar Jordan, "Law Enforcement and the Elderly: A Concern for the 21st Century,"

FBI Law Enforcement Bulletin 71 (2002): 20–24.

45. Robert C. Davis and Juanjo Medina-Ariza, *Results from an Elder Abuse Prevention Experiment in New York* (Washington, DC: National Institute of Justice, September 2001).

46. Tracy Dietz and James Wright, "Age and Gender Differences and Predictors of Victimization of the Older Homeless," *Journal of Elder Abuse and Neglect* 17 (2005): 37–59.

47. Karin Wittebrood and Paul Nieuwbeerta, "Criminal Victimization during One's Life Course: The Effects of Previous Victimization and Patterns of Routine Activities," *Journal of Research in Crime and Delinquency* 37 (2000): 91–122; Janet Lauritsen and Kenna Davis Quinet, "Repeat Victimizations among Adolescents and Young Adults," *Journal of Quantitative Criminology* 11 (1995): 143–163.

48. Denise Osborn, Dan Ellingworth, Tim Hope, and Alan Trickett, "Are Repeatedly Victimized Households Different?" *Journal of Quantitative Criminology* 12 (1996): 223–245.

49. Graham Farrell, "Predicting and Preventing Revictimization," in *Crime and Justice: An Annual Review of Research*, eds. Michael Tonry and David Farrington, vol. 20 (Chicago: University of Chicago Press, 1995), pp. 61–126.

50. Ibid., p. 61.

51. David Finkelhor and Nancy Asigian, "Risk Factors for Youth Victimization: Beyond a Lifestyles/Routine Activities Theory Approach," *Violence and Victimization* 11 (1996): 3–19.

52. Graham Farrell, Coretta Phillips, and Ken Pease, "Like Taking Candy: Why Does Repeat Victimization Occur?" *British Journal of Criminology* 35 (1995): 384–399.

53. Christopher Innes and Lawrence Greenfeld, *Violent State Prisoners and Their Victims* (Washington, DC: Bureau of Justice Statistics, 1990).

54. Associated Press, "Texas Siblings Accused of Killing 6-Year-Old Brother," *New York Times*, 16 April 2002.

55. Hans Von Hentig, *The Criminal and His Victim: Studies in the Sociobiology of Crime* (New Haven: Yale University Press, 1948), p. 384.

56. Marvin Wolfgang, *Patterns of Criminal Homicide* (Philadelphia: University of Pennsylvania Press, 1958).

57. Menachem Amir, *Patterns in Forcible Rape* (Chicago: University of Chicago Press, 1971).

58. Susan Estrich, *Real Rape* (Cambridge, MA: Harvard University Press, 1987).

59. Edem Avakame, "Female's Labor Force Participation and Intimate Femicide: An Empirical Assessment of the Backlash Hypothesis," *Violence and Victim* 14 (1999): 277–283.

60. Martin Daly and Margo Wilson, *Homicide* (New York: Aldine de Gruyter, 1988).

61. Rosemary Gartner and Bill McCarthy, "The Social Distribution of Femicide in Urban Canada, 1921–1988," *Law and Society Review* 25 (1991): 287–311.

62. Bonnie Fisher, Francis Cullen, and Michael Turner, *The Sexual Victimization of College Women* (Washington, DC: National Institute of Justice, 2001).

63. Lening Zhang, John W. Welte, and William F. Wieczorek, "Deviant Lifestyle and Crime Victimization," *Journal of Criminal Justice* 29 (2001): 133–143.

64. Dan Hoyt, Kimberly Ryan, and Mari Cauce, "Personal Victimizaton in a High-Risk Environment: Homeless and Runaway Adolescents," *Journal of Research in Crime and Delinquency* 36 (1999): 371–392.

65. See generally Gary Gottfredson and Denise Gottfredson, *Victimization in Schools* (New York: Plenum Press, 1985).

66. Gary Jensen and David Brownfield, "Gender, Lifestyles, and Victimization: Beyond Routine Activity Theory," *Violence and Victims* 1 (1986): 85–99.

67. Dana Haynie and Alex Piquero, "Pubertal Development and Physical Victimization in Adolescence," *Journal of Research in Crime and Delinquency* 43 (2006): 3–35.

68. Rolf Loeber, Mary DeLamatre, George Tita, Jacqueline Cohen, Magda Stouthamer-Loeber, and David Farrington, "Gun Injury and Mortality: The Delinquent Backgrounds of Juvenile Offenders," *Violence and Victim* 14 (1999): 339–351; Adam Dobrin, "The Risk of Offending on Homicide Victimization: A Case Control Study," *Journal of Research in Crime and Delinquency* 38 (2001): 154–173.

69. Bonnie Fisher, John Sloan, Francis Cullen, and Chunmeng Lu, "Crime in the Ivory Tower: The Level and Sources of Student Victimization," *Criminology* 36 (1998): 671–710.

70. Dobrin, "The Risk of Offending on Homicide Victimization."

71. Christopher Schreck, Eric Stewart, and Bonnie Fisher, "Self-control, Victimization, and Their Influence on Risky Lifestyles: A Longitudinal Analysis Using Panel Data," *Journal of Quantitative Criminology* 22 (2006): 319–340.

72. Rolf Loeber, Larry Kalb, and David Huizinga, *Juvenile Delinquency and Serious Injury Victimization* (Washington, DC: Office of Juvenile Justice and Delinquency Prevention, 2001).

73. Pamela Wilcox, David May, and Staci Roberts, "Student Weapon Possession and the 'Fear and Victimization Hypothesis': Unraveling the Temporal Order," *Justice Quarterly* 23 (2006): 502–529.

74. Maryse Richards, Reed Larson, and Bobbi Viegas Miller, "Risky and Protective Contexts and Exposure to Violence in Urban African American Young Adolescents," *Journal of Clinical Child and Adolescent Psychology* 33 (2004): 138–148.

75. James Garofalo, "Reassessing the Lifestyle Model of Criminal Victimization," in *Positive Criminology*, eds. Michael Gottfredson and Travis Hirschi (Newbury Park, CA: Sage, 1987), pp. 23–42.

76. Richards, Larson, and Miller, "Risky and Protective Contexts and Exposure to Violence in Urban African American Young Adolescents."

77. Terance Miethe and David McDowall, "Contextual Effects in Models of Criminal Victimization," *Social Forces* 71 (1993): 741–759.

78. Rodney Stark, "Deviant Places: A Theory of the Ecology of Crime," *Criminology* 25 (1987): 893–911.

79. Ibid., p. 902.

80. Pamela Wilcox Rountree, Kenneth Land, and Terance Miethe, "Macro–Micro Integration in the Study of Victimization: A Hierarchical Logistic Model Analysis across Seattle Neighborhoods," paper presented at the annual meeting of the American Society of Criminology, Phoenix, November 1993.

81. William Julius Wilson, *The Truly Disadvantaged* (Chicago: University of Chicago Press, 1990); see also Allen Liska and Paul Bellair, "Violent-Crime Rates and Racial Composition: Convergence over Time," *American Journal of Sociology* 101 (1995): 578–610.

82. Lawrence Cohen and Marcus Felson, "Social Change and Crime Rate Trends: A Routine Activities Approach," *American Sociological Review* 44 (1979): 588–608.

83. Teresa LaGrange, "The Impact of Neighborhoods, Schools, and Malls on the Spatial Distribution of Property Damage," *Journal of Research in Crime and Delinquency* 36 (1999): 393–422.

84. Melanie Wellsmith and Amy Burrell, "The Influence of Purchase Price and Ownership Levels on Theft Targets: The Example of Domestic Burglary," *British Journal of Criminology* 45 (2005): 741–764.

85. Denise Gottfredson and David Soulé, "The Timing of Property Crime, Violent Crime, and Substance Use among Juveniles," *Journal of Research in Crime and Delinquency* 42 (2005): 110–120.

86. Georgina Hammock and Deborah Richardson, "Perceptions of Rape: The Influence of Closeness of Relationship, Intoxication, and Sex of Participant," *Violence and Victimization* 12 (1997): 237–247.

87. Wittebrood and Nieuwbeerta, "Criminal Victimization during One's Life Course," pp. 112–113.

88. Brandon Welsh and David Farrington, "Surveillance for Crime Prevention in Public Space: Results and Policy Choices in Britain and America," *Criminology and Public Policy* 3 (2004): 701–730.

89. Richard Timothy Coupe and Laurence Blake, "The Effects of Patrol Workloads and Response Strength on Arrests at Burglary Emergencies," *Journal of Criminal Justice* 33 (2005): 239–255.

90. Don Weatherburn, Bronwyn Lind, and Simon Ku, "'Hotbeds of Crime?' Crime and Public Housing in Urban Sydney," *Crime and Delinquency* 45 (1999): 256–271.

91. Andy Hochstetler, "Opportunities and Decisions: Interactional Dynamics in Robbery and Burglary Groups," *Criminology* 39 (2001): 737–763.

92. Richard Felson, "Routine Activities and Involvement in Violence as Actor, Witness, or Target," *Violence and Victimization* 12 (1997): 209–223.

93. Terance Miethe and Robert Meier, *Crime and Its Social Context: Toward an Integrated Theory of Offenders, Victims, and Situations* (Albany: State University of New York Press, 1994).

94. Ronald Clarke, "Situational Crime Prevention," in *Building a Safer Society, Strategic Approaches to Crime Prevention*, vol. 19 of *Crime and Justice, A Review of Research*, eds. Michael Tonry and David Farrington (Chicago: University of Chicago Press, 1995), pp. 91–151.

95. Steven Messner, Lawrence Raffalovich, and Richard McMillan, "Economic Deprivation and Changes in Homicide Arrest Rates for White and Black Youths, 1967–1998: A National Time-Series Analysis," *Criminology* 39 (2001): 591–614.

96. Lawrence Cohen, Marcus Felson, and Kenneth Land, "Property Crime Rates in the United States: A Macrodynamic Analysis, 1947–1977, with Ex-Ante Forecasts for the Mid-1980s," *American Journal of Sociology* 86 (1980): 90–118.

97. Patrick Donnelly and Charles Kimble, "Community Organizing, Environmental Change, and Neighborhood Crime," *Crime and Delinquency* 43 (1997): 493–511.

98. Simha Landau and Daniel Fridman, "The Seasonality of Violent Crime: The Case of Robbery and Homicide in Israel," *Journal of Research in Crime and Delinquency* 30 (1993): 163–191.

99. Patricia Resnick, "Psychological Effects of Victimization: Implications for the Criminal Justice System," *Crime and Delinquency* 33 (1987): 468–478.

100. Dean Kilpatrick, Benjamin Saunders, Lois Veronen, Connie Best, and Judith Von, "Criminal Victimization: Lifetime Prevalence, Reporting to Police, and Psychological Impact," *Crime and Delinquency* 33 (1987): 479–489.

101. Cassidy Gutner, Shireen Rizvi, Candice Monson, and Patricia Resick, "Changes in Coping Strategies, Relationship to the Perpetrator, and Posttraumatic Distress in Female Crime Victims," *Journal of Traumatic Stress* 19 (2006): 813–823.

102. U.S. Department of Justice, *Report of the President's Task Force on Victims of Crime* (Washington, DC: U.S. Government Printing Office, 1983).

103. Ibid., pp. 2–10; and "Review on Victims—Witnesses of Crime," *Massachusetts Lawyers Weekly*, 25 April 1983, p. 26.

104. Robert Davis, *Crime Victims: Learning How to Help Them* (Washington, DC: National Institute of Justice, 1987).

105. Michael M. O'Hear, "Punishment, Democracy, and Victims," *Federal Sentencing Reporter* 19 (2006): 1.

106. Peter Finn and Beverly Lee, *Establishing a Victim-Witness Assistance Program* (Washington, DC: U.S. Government Printing Office, 1988).

107. This section leans heavily on Albert Roberts, "Delivery of Services to Crime Victims: A National Survey," *American Journal of Orthopsychiatry* 6 (1991): 128–137; see also Albert Roberts, *Helping Crime Victims: Research, Policy, and Practice* (Newbury Park, CA: Sage, 1990).

108. Randall Schmidt, "Crime Victim Compensation Legislation: A Comparative Study," *Victimology* 5 (1980): 428–437.

109. Ibid.

110. National Association of Crime Victim Compensation Boards, http://nacvcb.org/ (accessed May 9, 2007).

111. Rebecca Campbell, "Rape Survivors' Experiences with the Legal and Medical Systems: Do Rape Victim Advocates Make a Difference?" *Violence Against Women* 12 (2006): 30–45.

112. Ulrich Orth and Andreas Maercker, "Do Trials of Perpetrators Retraumatize Crime Victims?" *Journal of Interpersonal Violence* 19 (2004): 212–228.

113. Barbara Sims, Berwood Yost, and Christina Abbott, "The Efficacy of Victim Services Programs," *Criminal Justice Policy Review* 17 (2006): 387–406.

114. Pater Jaffe, Marlies Sudermann, Deborah Reitzel, and Steve Killip, "An Evaluation of a Secondary School Primary Prevention Program on Violence in Intimate Relationships," *Violence and Victims* 7 (1992): 129–145.

115. Andrew Karmen, "Victim–Offender Reconciliation Programs: Pro and Con," *Perspectives of the American Probation and Parole Association* 20 (1996): 11–14.

116. Rachelle Hong, "Nothing to Fear: Establishing an Equality of Rights for Crime Victims through the Victims' Rights Amendment," *Notre Dame Journal of Legal Ethics and Public Policy* (2002): 207–225; see also

Payne v. Tennessee, 111 S.Ct. 2597, 115 L. Ed.2d 720 (1991).

117. Robert Davis and Barbara Smith, "The Effects of Victim Impact Statements on Sentencing Decisions: A Test in an Urban Setting," *Justice Quarterly* 11 (1994): 453–469; Edna Erez and Pamela Tontodonato, "The Effect of Victim Participation in Sentencing on Sentence Outcome," *Criminology* 28 (1990): 451–474.

118. Douglas E. Beloof, "Constitutional Implications of Crime Victims as Participants," *Cornell Law Review* 88 (2003): 282–305.

119. Sara Flaherty and Austin Flaherty, *Victims and Victims' Risk* (New York: Chelsea House, 1998).

120. Pamela Wilcox Rountree and Kenneth Land, "Burglary Victimization, Perceptions of Crime Risk, and Routine Activities: A Multilevel Analysis across Seattle Neighborhoods and Census Tracts," *Journal of Research in Crime and Delinquency* 33 (1996): 1,147–1,180.

121. Leslie Kennedy, "Going It Alone: Unreported Crime and Individual Self-Help," *Journal of Criminal Justice* 16 (1988): 403–413.

122. Ronald Clarke, "Situational Crime Prevention: Its Theoretical Basis and Practical Scope," in *Annual Review of Criminal Justice Research*, eds. Michael Tonry and Norval Morris (Chicago: University of Chicago Press, 1983).

123. See generally Dennis P. Rosenbaum, Arthur J. Lurigio, and Robert C. Davis, *The Prevention of Crime: Social and Situational Strategies* (Belmont, CA: Wadsworth, 1998).

124. Andrew Buck, Simon Hakim, and George Rengert, "Burglar Alarms and the Choice Behavior of Burglars," *Journal of Criminal Justice* 21 (1993): 497–507; for an opposing view, see James Lynch and David Cantor, "Ecological and Behavioral Influences on Property Victimization at Home: Implications for Opportunity Theory," *Journal of Research in Crime and Delinquency* 29 (1992): 335–362.

125. Alan Lizotte, "Determinants of Completing Rape and Assault," *Journal of Quantitative Criminology* 2 (1986): 213–217.

126. Polly Marchbanks, Kung-Jong Lui, and James Mercy, "Risk of Injury from Resisting Rape," *American Journal of Epidemiology* 132 (1990): 540–549.

127. Caroline Wolf Harlow, *Robbery Victims* (Washington, DC: Bureau of Justice Statistics, 1987).

128. Gary Kleck, "Guns and Violence: An Interpretive Review of the Field," *Social Pathology* 1 (1995): 12–45, at 17.

129. Ibid.

130. Gary Kleck, "Rape and Resistance," *Social Problems* 37 (1990): 149–162.

131. Jongyeon Tark and Gary Kleck, "Resisting Crime: The Effects of Victim Action on the Outcomes of Crimes," *Criminology* 42 (2004): 861–909.

132. Adam Liptak, "15 States Expand Right to Shoot in Self-Defense," *New York Times*, 7 August 2006, p. 1.

133. Patrik Jonsson, "Is Self-Defense Law Vigilante Justice? Some say proposed laws can help deter gun violence. Others worry about deadly confrontations," *Christian Science Monitor*, 24 February 2006.

134. James Garofalo and Maureen McLeod, *Improving the Use and Effectiveness of Neighborhood Watch Programs* (Washington, DC: National Institute of Justice, 1988).

135. Peter Finn, *Block Watches Help Crime Victims in Philadelphia* (Washington, DC: National Institute of Justice, 1986).

136. Ibid.

137. See Frank Carrington, "Victim's Rights Litigation: A Wave of the Future," in *Perspectives on Crime Victims*, eds. Burt Galaway and Joe Hudson (St. Louis: Mosby, 1981).

138. National Center for Victims of Crime, www.ncvc.org/policy/issues/rights/ (accessed March 14, 2007).

139. Council Framework Decision of 15 March 2001 on the Standing of Victims in Criminal Proceedings, http://eur-lex.europa.eu/smartapi/cgi/sga_doc?smartapi!celexapi!prod!CELEXnumdoc&lg=EN&numdoc=32001F0220&model=guichett (accessed March 14, 2007); Proposal for a Council Directive on Compensation to Crime Victims, http://europa.eu.int/eur-lex/en/com/pdf/2002/com2002_0562en01.pdf (accessed March 14, 2007).

140. U.S. Department of Justice, Dru Sjodin, National Sex Offender Public Registry, www.nsopr.gov (accessed March 14, 2007).

PART TWO

THEORIES OF CRIME CAUSATION

An important goal of the criminological enterprise is to create valid and accurate theories of crime causation. A theory can be defined as an abstract statement that explains why certain things do (or do not) happen. A valid theory must have the ability to (a) predict future occurrences or observations of the phenomenon in question and (b) be validated or tested through experiment or some other form of empirical observation.

Criminologists have sought to collect vital facts about crime and interpret them in a scientifically meaningful fashion. By developing empirically verifiable statements, or hypotheses, and organizing them into theories of crime causation, they hope to identify the causes of crime.

Since the late nineteenth century, criminological theory has pointed to various underlying causes of crime. The earliest theories generally attributed crime to a single underlying cause: atypical body build, genetic abnormality, insanity, physical anomalies, or poverty. Later theories attributed crime causation to multiple factors: poverty, peer influence, school problems, and family dysfunction.

In this section, theories of crime causation are grouped into six chapters. Chapters 4 and 5 focus on theories that view crime as based on individual traits. They hold that crime is either a free will choice made by an individual, a function of personal psychological or biological abnormality, or both. Chapters 6, 7, and 8 investigate theories based in sociology and political economy. These theories portray crime as a function of the structure, process, and conflicts of social living. Chapter 9 is devoted to theories that combine or integrate these various concepts into a cohesive, complex, developmental view of crime.

Rational Choice Theory

CHAPTER OBJECTIVES

1. Be familiar with the concept of rational choice
2. Know the work of Beccaria
3. Be familiar with the concept of offense-specific crime
4. Be familiar with the concept of offender-specific crime
5. Be able to discuss why violent and drug crimes are rational
6. Know the various techniques of situational crime prevention
7. Be able to discuss the association between punishment and crime
8. Be familiar with the concepts of certainty, severity, and speed of punishment
9. Know what is meant by specific and general deterrence
10. Be able to discuss the issues involving the use of incapacitation
11. Understand the concept of just desert

Just before Christmas in 2004, more than 150,000 fax machines around the country spat out a mysterious message addressed to a "Dr. Mitchel" and came from a financial planner named simply "Chris." Though it was clearly the wrong number, a lot of people were intrigued because the note was about a hot stock that "Chris" wanted the good doctor to buy immediately:

> *"I have a stock for you that will tripple [sic] in price just like the last stock I gave you 'SIRI' did. I can't get you on either phone. Either call me, or call Linda to place the new trade. We need to buy IFLB now."*

Soon after the mystery fax was sent, shares of IFLB (Infinium Labs, a video gaming company now called Phantom Entertainment) started to increase, jumping 160 percent in four days and trading at six times its previous volume. Two other stocks mentioned in alternate versions of the fax—Data Evolution and Soleil Film—saw similar increases. Unfortunately for the investors who jumped on the tip, there was no "Dr. Mitchel," no "Chris," no "Linda," and no real stock tip. It was all part of a scam to buy shares of the stocks in advance while prices were cheap, blanket the nation with bogus faxes, and pocket a tidy profit after the prices rose. It all worked according to plan: in less than two months, the conspirators made almost $400,000 on just two of the stocks.

Eventually the press got wind of the faxes and published stories about the scam. The Securities and Exchange Commission opened an investigation, tracing the fax calls to a Florida company run by Michael Pickens, who was arrested and charged with securities fraud in July 2005. Michael pleaded guilty in October 2006. On December 20, 2007, Pickens was sentenced to five years' probation and was ordered to take part in a substance abuse program and pay restitution of $1.2 million in connection with the fraud. One irony of the case was that Pickens is the son of multibillionaire oil investor T. Boone Pickens, one of the nation's richest men.[1]

The "pump and dump" stock market scheme orchestrated by Michael Pickens required knowledge, planning, and ingenuity. Criminals involved in such schemes carefully plan their activities, buy the proper equipment, try to avoid detection, and then attempt to squirrel their criminal profits in some hidden bank account. Their calculated actions suggest that the decision to commit crime can involve rational and detailed planning and decision making, designed to maximize personal gain and avoid capture and punishment. Some criminologists go so far as suggesting that the source of all criminal violations—whether committing a robbery, selling drugs, attacking a rival, or filing a false tax return—rests upon rational decision making. Such a decision may be based on a variety of personal reasons, including greed, revenge, need, anger, lust, jealousy, thrill-seeking, or vanity. But the final decision to commit a crime is only made after the potential offender carefully weighs the benefits and consequences of their planned action and decides that the benefits of crime are greater than its consequences:

■ A jealous boyfriend concludes that the risk of punishment is worth the satisfaction of punching a rival in the nose.

■ The greedy shopper considers the chance of apprehension by store detectives so small that she takes a "five-finger discount" on a new sweater.

■ The drug dealer concludes that the huge profit from a single shipment of cocaine far outweighs the possible costs of apprehension.

■ The schoolyard bully carefully selects his next victim, someone weak, unpopular, and who probably won't fight back.

■ The college student downloads a program that allows her to illegally copy music onto her iPod.

But while we can easily assume that international drug dealers, white-collar criminals such as Michael Pickens, and organized crime figures use planning, organization, and rational decision making to commit their crimes, can we also assume that such common crimes as theft, fraud, and even murder are a function of detailed planning and decision making? Before college students take music off the Web they must first not only acquire knowledge, expertise, and skill, but also decide that the money they save is worth the risk of detection. But what about the college student who gets into a bar fight or decides to have sex with an unconscious girl at a frat party? Are these crimes calculated and shrewd or random and senseless? Some criminologists would answer that they believe all criminal behavior, no matter how destructive or seemingly irresponsible, is actually a matter of thought and decision making. As a group they are referred to as rational choice theorists.

This chapter reviews the philosophical underpinnings of rational choice theory, tracing it back to the classical school of criminology. We then turn to more recent theoretical models that flow from the concept of choice. These models hold that because criminals are rational, their behavior can be controlled or deterred by the fear of punishment; desistance can then be explained by a growing and intense fear of criminal sanctions. These views include situational crime control, general deterrence

theory, specific deterrence theory, and incapacitation. Finally, the chapter briefly reviews how choice theory has influenced criminal justice policy.

THE DEVELOPMENT OF RATIONAL CHOICE THEORY

Rational choice theory has its roots in the classical school of criminology developed by the Italian social thinker Cesare Beccaria.[2] As you may recall from Chapter 1, Beccaria and other utilitarian philosophers suggest that (a) people choose all behavior, including criminal behavior; (b) their choices are designed to bring them pleasure and reduce pain; (c) criminal choices can be controlled by fear of punishment; and (d) the more severe, certain, and swift the punishment, the greater its ability to control criminal behavior. In keeping with his utilitarian views, Beccaria called for fair and certain punishment to deter crime. He believed people are egotistical and self-centered, and therefore they must be motivated by the fear of punishment, which provides a tangible motive for them to obey the law and suppress the "despotic spirit" that resides in every person.[3]

Beccaria believed that, to deter people from committing more serious offenses, crime and punishment must be proportional; if not, people would be encouraged to commit more serious offenses. For example, if robbery, rape, and murder were all punished by death, robbers or rapists would have little reason to refrain from killing their victims to eliminate them as witnesses to the crime. Today, this is referred to as the concept of marginal deterrence—if petty offenses were subject to the same punishment as more serious crimes, offenders would choose the worse crime because the resulting punishment would be about the same.[4]

The Classical Theory of Crime

Beccaria's ideas and writings inspired social thinkers to believe that criminals choose to commit crime and that crime can be controlled by judicious punishment. His vision was widely accepted throughout Europe and the United States.[5]

In Britain, philosopher Jeremy Bentham (1748–1833) helped popularize Beccaria's views in his writings on utilitarianism. Bentham believed that people choose actions on the basis of whether they produce pleasure and happiness and help them avoid pain or unhappiness.[6] The purpose of law is to produce and support the total happiness of the community it serves. Because punishment is in itself harmful, its existence is justified only if it promises to prevent greater evil than it creates. Punishment, therefore, has four main objectives:

1. To prevent all criminal offenses

2. When it cannot prevent a crime, to convince the offender to commit a less serious crime

3. To ensure that a criminal uses no more force than is necessary

4. To prevent crime as cheaply as possible[7]

This vision was embraced by France's postrevolutionary Constituent Assembly (1789) in its Declaration of the Rights of Man:

> [T]he law has the right to prohibit only actions harmful to society. . . . The law shall inflict only such punishments as are strictly and clearly necessary . . . no person shall be punished except by virtue of a law enacted and promulgated previous to the crime and applicable to its terms.

Similarly, a prohibition against cruel and unusual punishment was incorporated in the Eighth Amendment to the U.S. Constitution.

Beccaria's writings have been credited as the basis of the elimination of torture and severe punishment in the nineteenth century. The practice of incarcerating criminals and structuring prison sentences to fit the severity of crime was a reflection of his classical criminology.

By the end of the nineteenth century, the popularity of the classical approach began to decline, and by the middle of the twentieth century, this perspective was neglected by mainstream criminologists. During this period, positivist criminologists focused on internal and external factors—poverty, IQ, education, home life—which were believed to be the true causes of criminality. Because these conditions could not be easily manipulated, the concept of punishing people for behaviors beyond their control seemed both foolish and cruel. Although classical principles still controlled the way police, courts, and correctional agencies operate, most criminologists rejected classical criminology as an explanation of criminal behavior.

Contemporary Choice Theory Emerges

Beginning in the mid-1970s, there was renewed interest in the classical approach to crime. First, the rehabilitation of known criminals—considered a cornerstone of positivist policy—came under attack. According to positivist criminology, if crime was caused by some social or psychological problem, such as poverty, then crime rates could be reduced by providing good jobs and economic opportunities. Despite some notable efforts to provide such opportunities, a number of national surveys (the best known being Robert Martinson's "What Works?") failed to find examples of rehabilitation programs that prevented future criminal activity.[8] A well-publicized book, *Beyond Probation*, by Charles Murray and Louis Cox, went as far as suggesting that punishment-oriented programs could suppress future criminality much more effectively than those that relied on rehabilitation and treatment efforts.[9]

A significant increase in the reported crime rate, as well as serious disturbances in the nation's prisons, frightened the general public. The media depicted criminals as callous and dangerous rather than as needy people deserving of public sympathy. Some criminologists began to suggest that it made more sense to frighten these cold calculators with severe punishments than to waste public funds by futilely trying to improve entrenched social conditions linked to crime, such as poverty.[10]

Thinking About Crime Beginning in the late 1970s, a number of criminologists began producing books and monographs expounding the theme that criminals are rational actors who plan their crimes, fear punishment, and deserve to be penalized for their misdeeds. In a 1975 book that came to symbolize renewed interest in classical views, *Thinking about Crime*, political scientist James Q. Wilson debunked the positivist view that crime was a function of external forces, such as poverty, that could be altered by government programs. Instead, he argued, efforts should be made to reduce criminal opportunity by deterring would-be offenders and incarcerating known criminals. People who are likely to commit crime, he maintained, lack inhibition against misconduct, value the excitement and thrills of breaking the law, have a low stake in conformity, and are willing to take greater chances than the average person. If they could be convinced that their actions will bring severe punishment, only the totally irrational would be willing to engage in crime.[11] Wilson made this famous observation:

> Wicked people exist. Nothing avails except to set them apart from innocent people. And many people, neither wicked nor innocent, but watchful, dissembling, and calculating of their chances, ponder our reaction to wickedness as a clue to what they might profitably do.[12]

Here Wilson is saying that unless we react forcefully to crime, those "sitting on the fence" will get a clear message—crime pays.

Impact on Crime Control Coinciding with the publication of Wilson's book was a conservative shift in U.S. public policy, which resulted in Ronald Reagan's election to the presidency in 1980. Political decision makers embraced Wilson's ideas as a means to bring the crime rate down. Tough new laws were passed, creating mandatory prison sentences for drug offenders; the nation's prison population skyrocketed. Critics decried the disproportionate number of young minority men being locked up for drug law violations.[13] Today, about 60 percent of the prison population is African American or Hispanic.[14] Despite liberal anguish, conservative views of crime control have helped shape criminal justice policy for the past two decades.[15] Many Americans, some of whom are passionate opponents of abortion on the grounds that it takes human life, became, ironically, ardent supporters of the death penalty![16] This "get tough" attitude was supported by the fact that while the prison population has grown to new heights, the crime rate has been in a steep decline.

From these roots, a more contemporary version of classical theory has evolved. It is based on intelligent thought processes and criminal decision making.[17] This new view of rational choice is somewhat different from the original classical theory that portrayed criminals as people who tried to maximize their pleasure and minimize pain. If they were caught committing crime it was because they were sloppy thinkers and imperfect in their decision making. In contrast, the contemporary version views the decision to commit crime as being shaped by human emotions and thought process. It recognizes that other influences have an impact on

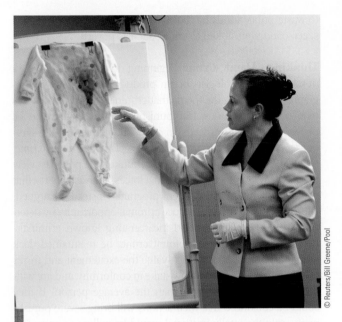

The blood-covered sleeper recovered from the body of Lillian Entwistle at the Entwistle home is shown during the murder trial of Neil Entwistle at Middlesex Superior Court, in Woburn, Massachusetts on June 16, 2008. Convicted of murdering his wife and infant daughter, Entwistle received a life sentence. Massachusetts is a non-death penalty state. Is it possible that this tragedy could have been avoided if the threat of capital punishment were present? Or are depraved criminals such as Neil Entwistle irrational and immune to fear of death? Could a truly "rational" person kill his wife and baby girl? Are such crimes inherently "irrational"?

criminal decision making, including social relationships, individual traits and capabilities, and environmental characteristics. So, this new version of rational choice theory assumes that human behavior is both "willful and determined."[18]

www Go to academic.cengage.com/criminaljustice/siegel to:

- Learn about **Beccaria's life history and the formulation of his ideas**, as well as find some useful links

- Find out more about the life of **Jeremy Bentham**

- Read a famous talk given by **James Wilson, "Two Nations,"** the 1997 Francis Boyer lecture delivered at the annual dinner of the American Enterprise Institute

- Read what the American Civil Liberties Union has to say about the **death penalty**; even if the death penalty were an effective deterrent, some critics believe it presents ethical problems that make its use morally dubious

THE CONCEPTS OF RATIONAL CHOICE

According to this contemporary rational choice approach, law-violating behavior occurs when an offender decides to risk breaking the law after considering both personal factors (i.e., the need for money, revenge, thrills, and entertainment) and situational factors (i.e., how well a target is protected and the efficiency of the local police force). People who believe that the risks of crime outweigh the rewards may decide to go straight. If they think they are likely to get arrested and punished, they are more likely to seek treatment and turn their lives around than risk criminal activities.[19]

Before choosing to commit a crime, reasoning criminals carefully select targets and their behavior is systematic and selective. For example, burglars seem to choose targets based on their value, novelty, and resale potential. A relatively new piece of electronic gear, such as an iPhone or Xbox, may be a prime target because it has not yet saturated the market and still retains high value.[20] The decision to commit crime is enhanced by the promise of easy gain with low risk.

In contrast, the decision to forego crime is reached when the potential criminal believes that risks outweigh rewards. People will forego crime if after a careful evaluation of the circumstances they conclude that:

- They stand a good chance of being caught and punished.

- They fear the consequences of punishment.

- They risk losing the respect of their peers, damaging their reputations, and experiencing feelings of guilt or shame.[21]

- The risk of apprehension outweighs the profit and/or pleasure of crime.[22]

Risk evaluations may cover a wide range of topics: What's the chance of getting caught? How difficult will it be to commit the crime? Is the profit worth the effort? Should I risk committing crime in my own neighborhood where I know the territory, or is it worth traveling to a strange place in order to increase my profits?[23]

People who decide to get involved in crime weigh the chances of arrest (based on their past experiences) plus the subjective psychic rewards of crime, including the excitement and social status it brings and perceived opportunities for easy gains. If the rewards are great, the perceived risk small, and the excitement high, the likelihood of committing additional crimes increases.[24] For example, those who report having successfully shoplifted also say they will do it again in the future; past experience has taught them the rewards of illegal behavior.[25]

Criminals then are people who share the same ambitions as conventional citizens but have decided to cut corners and use illegal means to achieve their goals (see the Profiles in Crime feature "Looting the Public Treasury"). Many criminal offenders retain conventional American values of striving for success, material attainment, and hard work.[26] When Philippe Bourgois studied crack dealers in East Harlem in New York City, he found that their motivations were not dissimilar from the "average citizen": They were upwardly mobile, scrambling around to obtain their "piece of the pie."[27] If they commit crime, it is because they have chosen an illegal path to obtain the goals that might otherwise have been out of reach.

PROFILES IN CRIME

LOOTING THE PUBLIC TREASURY

After graduating from UCLA, Albert Robles served terms as mayor, councilman, and deputy city manager of South Gate, California, an industrial community about 12 miles outside downtown Los Angeles. Soon after Robles became city treasurer in 1997, he plotted to rule the city purely for his own benefit. He even proclaimed himself "King of South Gate" and referred to the city as his "fiefdom." Once in power, Robles got involved in a number of convoluted illegal schemes, including:

▌ Using the city's treasury as his "private piggy bank for himself, his family, and his friends" (according to acting U.S. Attorney George Cardona), costing South Gate more than $35 million and bringing it to the verge of bankruptcy

▌ Firing city hall employees at will, replacing them with supporters who had little experience

▌ Recruiting and bankrolling unqualified local supporters for city council until he controlled the council

▌ Threatening anyone who stood in his way (suspiciously, one of his adversaries on the city council was shot in the head)

Robles and his corrupt cronies then cooked up schemes to line their own pockets with the public's cash. In one such scheme, Robles coerced businesses to hire a financial consultant, Edward Espinoza, in order to win various city contracts, including senior housing and sewer rehabilitation projects. As part of this plan, Robles and Espinoza set up a shell corporation that raked in some $2.4 million—more than $1.4 million

of which went straight into Robles's pockets. He used part of the money to buy a $165,000 beach condo in Baja for his mother; he also forked over $55,000 for "platinum membership" in a motivational group. In another scheme, Robles steered a $48 million refuse and recycling contract to a company in exchange for more than $30,000 in gifts and campaign contributions.

In February 2003, Robles was targeted by a federal grand jury looking into the handling of federal loans and grants. FBI and IRS investigators pored over city records to uncover his illegal schemes. The citizens of South Gate ultimately voted Robles and his cronies out of office (but not before he racked up huge legal bills at the city's expense), and he was convicted at trial in July 2005. Two of his business associates—including Espinoza—also went to prison.

Robles's illegal acts were the product of careful plotting and planning. They were motivated by greed and not need. To some criminologists, stories like these confirm the fact that many crimes are a matter of rational choice.

Sources: Federal Bureau of Investigation, "Corruption in City Hall: The Crooked Reign of 'King' Albert," January 8, 2007, www.fbi.gov/page2/jan07/cityhall010807.htm (accessed July 3, 2008); Hector Becerra, "Robles Sentenced to 10 Years," *Los Angeles Times*, 29 November 2006, p.1.

---

connections

Lack of conventional opportunity is a persistent theme in sociological theories of crime. The frustration caused by a perceived lack of opportunity explains the high crime rates in lower-class areas. Chapter 6 discusses strain and cultural deviance theories, which provide alternative explanations of how lack of opportunity is associated with crime.

Crime Is Both Offense- and Offender-Specific

Rational choice theorists view crime as being both offense- and offender-specific.[28] That a crime is **offense-specific** means that

offenders will react selectively to the characteristics of an individual criminal act. Take for instance the decision to commit a burglary. The thought process might include:

▌ Evaluating the target yield

▌ Probability of security devices

▌ Police patrol effectiveness

▌ Availability of a getaway car

▌ Ease of selling stolen merchandise

▌ Presence of occupants

▌ Neighbors who might notice a break-in

▌ Presence of guard dogs

▌ Presence of escape routes

▌ Entry points and exits

The fact that a crime is offender-specific means that criminals are not simply automatons who, for one reason or another, engage in random acts of antisocial behavior. Before deciding to commit crime, individuals must decide whether they have the prerequisites to commit a successful criminal act. These might include evaluation of:

◾ Whether they possess the necessary skills to commit the crime

◾ Their immediate need for money or other valuables

◾ Whether legitimate financial alternatives to crime exist, such as a high-paying job

◾ Whether they have available resources to commit the crime

◾ Their fear of expected apprehension and punishment

◾ Option of alternative criminal acts, such as selling drugs

◾ Physical ability, including health, strength, and dexterity

Note the distinction made here between crime and criminality.[29] Crime is an event; criminality is a personal trait. Professional criminals do not commit crime all the time, and even ordinary citizens may, on occasion, violate the law. Some people considered "high risk" because they are indigent or disturbed may never violate the law, whereas others who are seemingly affluent and well adjusted may risk criminal behavior given enough provocation and/or opportunity. What conditions promote crime and enhance criminality?

Structuring Criminality

A number of personal factors condition people to choose crime. Among the more important factors are economic opportunity, learning and experience, and knowledge of criminal techniques.

Economic Opportunity In a recent issue of *Boston Magazine*, a university lecturer with a master's degree from Yale and a doctorate in cultural anthropology wrote a first-person account of how she took another job to pay the bills: call girl.[30] Rather than living on the meager teaching salary she was offered, the "Ivy League Hooker" chose to make the tax-free $140 per hour for her services (she charged $200, handing over $60 to the escort service that arranged her dates). She left the "business" when she became financially self-sufficient.

The Ivy League hooker is not alone. Perceptions of economic opportunity influence the decision to commit crime. Some people may engage in criminal activity simply because they need the money to support their lifestyle and perceive few other potential income sources. Sociologists Christopher Uggen and Melissa Thompson found that people who begin taking hard drugs also increase their involvement in crime, taking in from $500 to $700 per month. Once they become cocaine and heroin users, the benefits of other criminal enterprise become overwhelmingly attractive: how else can a drug user earn enough to support their habit?[31]

Crime also becomes attractive when an individual becomes convinced that it will result in excessive profits with few costs. Research shows that criminals may be motivated to commit crime when they know others who have made "big scores" and are quite successful at crime. Although the prevailing wisdom is that crime does not pay, a small but significant subset of criminals actually enjoy earnings of close to $50,000 per year from crime, and their success may help motivate other would-be offenders.[32] However, offenders are likely to desist from crime if they believe that their future criminal earnings will be relatively low and that attractive and legal opportunities to generate income are available.[33] In this sense, rational choice is a function of a person's perception of conventional alternatives and opportunities.

connections

The role of economic needs in the motivation of white-collar criminals is discussed in Chapter 12. Research shows that even consistently law-abiding people may turn to criminal solutions when faced with overwhelming economic needs. They make the rational decision to commit crimes to solve some economic crisis.

Learning and Experience Learning and experience may be important elements in structuring the choice of crime.[34] Career criminals may learn the limitations of their powers; they know when to take a chance and when to be cautious. Experienced criminals may turn from a life of crime when they develop a belief that the risk of crime is greater than its potential profit.[35] Patricia Morgan and Karen Ann Joe's three-city study (San Francisco, San Diego, and Honolulu) of female drug abusers found that experience helped dealers avoid detection. One dealer, earning $50,000 per year, explained her strategy this way:

> I stayed within my goals, basically . . . I don't go around doing stupid things. I don't walk around telling people I have drugs for sale. I don't have people sitting out in front of my house. I don't have traffic in and out of my house . . . I control the people I sell to.[36]

Morgan and Joe found that these female dealers consider drug distribution a positive experience that gives them economic independence, self-esteem, increased ability to function, professional pride, and the ability to maintain control over their lives. These women often seemed more like yuppies opening a boutique than out-of-control addicts:

> I'm a good dealer. I don't cut my drugs, I have high-quality drugs insofar as it's possible to get high-quality drugs. I want to be known as somebody who sells good drugs, but doesn't always have them, as opposed to someone who always has them and sometimes the drugs are good.[37]

Here we see how experience in the profession shapes criminal decision making.

Knowledge of Criminal Techniques Criminals report learning techniques that help them avoid detection, a sure sign of rational thinking and planning. Some are specialists, who learn to be professional car thieves or bad check artists. Others are generalists who sell drugs one day and commit burglaries the next. In his studies of drug dealers, criminologist Bruce Jacobs found that crack dealers learn how to stash crack cocaine in some undisclosed location so that they are not forced to carry large amounts of product on their persons. Dealers carefully evaluate the security of their sales area before setting up shop.[38] Most consider the middle of a long block the best place for drug deals because they can see everything in both directions; police raids can be spotted before they develop.[39] If a buyer seems dangerous or unreliable, the dealer would require that they do business in spaces between apartment buildings or in back lots. Although dealers lose the tactical edge of being on a public street, they gain a measure of protection because their associates can watch over the deal and come to the rescue if the buyer tries to "pull something."[40] Similar detection avoidance schemes were found by Gordon Knowles in his study of crack dealers in Honolulu, Hawaii. Knowles found that drug dealers often use pornographic film houses as their base of operations because they offer both privacy and convenience.[41]

When Jacobs, along with Jody Miller, studied female crack dealers, they discovered a variety of defensive moves used by the dealers to avoid detection.[42] One of these techniques, called *stashing*, involved learning how to hide drugs on their person, in the street, or at home. One dealer told Jacobs and Miller how she hid drugs in the empty shaft of a curtain rod; another wore hollow earmuffs to hide crack. Because a female officer is required to conduct body cavity searches on women, the dealers had time to get rid of their drugs before they got to the station house. Dealers are aware of legal definitions of possession. One said she stashed her drugs 250 feet from her home because that was beyond the distance (150 feet) at which police considered a person legally to be in "constructive possession" of drugs.

Criminals who learn the proper techniques may be able to prolong their criminal careers. Jacobs found that these offenders use specific techniques to avoid being apprehended by police. They play what they call the "peep game" before dealing drugs, scoping out the territory to make sure the turf is free from anything out of place that could be a potential threat (such as police officers or rival gang members).[43] One crack dealer told Jacobs:

> There was this red Pontiac sittin' on the corner one day with two white guys inside. They was just sittin' there for an hour, not doin' nothin'. Another day, diff'rent people be walkin' up and down the street you don't really recognize. You think they might be kin of someone but then you be askin' around and they [neighbors] ain't never seen them before neither. When ya' see strange things like that, you think somethin' be goin' on [and you don't deal].[44]

Drug dealers told Jacobs that they also carefully consider whether they should deal alone or in groups; large groups draw more attention from police but can offer more protection. Drug-dealing gangs and groups can help divert the attention of police: if their drug dealing is noticed by detectives, a dealer can slyly walk away or dispose of evidence while confederates distract the cops.[45]

connections

Rational choice theory dovetails with routine activities theory, which you learned about in Chapter 3. Although not identical, these approaches both claim that crime rates are a normal product of criminal opportunity. Both suggest that criminals consider such elements as guardianship and target attractiveness before they decide to commit crimes. The routine activities and rational choice views also agree that criminal opportunity is a key element in the criminal process. The overlap between these two viewpoints may help criminologists suggest means for effective crime control.

Structuring Crime

Criminal decision making is not only based on an assessment of personal needs and capabilities, but also on a rational assessment of the criminal event. Decisions must be made about what, where, when, and whom to target.

Choosing the Type of Crime. The choice of crime may be dictated by market conditions. Generalists may alter their criminal behavior according to shifting opportunity structures: they may rob the elderly on the first of the month when they know that Social Security checks have been cashed, switch over to shoplifting if a new fence moves into the neighborhood, and, if a supply becomes available, sell a truckload of hijacked cigarettes to neighborhood convenience stores.

Sometimes the choice of crime is structured by the situational factors. Eric Baumer and his associates found that cities whose population of crack cocaine users is on the increase also experience an increase in their robbery rates and a corresponding decrease in burglary rates. Baumer reasons that crack users need to purchase drugs quickly and are in no position to plan a burglary and take the time to sell their loot; street robberies are designed to provide a quick influx of cash that meets their lifestyle needs.[46]

Choosing the Time and Place of Crime There is evidence of rationality in the way criminals choose the time and place of their crimes. Because criminals often go on foot or use public transportation, they are unlikely to travel long distances to commit crimes and are more likely to drift toward the center of a city than move toward outlying areas.[47] Some may occasionally commute to distant locations to commit crimes if they believe the payoff is greater, but most prefer to stay in their own neighborhood where they are familiar with the terrain.[48] They will only travel to unfamiliar areas if they believe the new location contains a worthy target and lax law enforcement. They may be encouraged to travel when the police are cracking down in their own neighborhood and the "heat is on."[49] Evidence is accumulating that predatory criminals are in fact aware of law enforcement capabilities and consider them closely before deciding to commit crimes. Communities with the reputation of employing aggressive crime-fighting cops are less likely to attract potential offenders than areas perceived to have passive law enforcers.[50]

Two people were killed and another critically injured during the Nashville, Tennessee, robbery shown in this security camera picture. Are such acts random and unplanned or are they the product of planning and choice? The robbers wore masks so that they would not be recognized in person or in video images. Convenience stores typically have a lot of cash on hand and are not well guarded, making them attractive targets for calculating criminals such as these.

Selecting the Target of Crime Criminals may also be well aware of target vulnerability. When they choose targets they may shy off if they sense danger. In a series of interviews with career property offenders, Kenneth Tunnell found that burglars avoid targets if they feel there are police in the area or if "nosy neighbors" might be suspicious and cause trouble.[51] Paul Bellair found that robbery levels are relatively low in neighborhoods where residents keep a watchful eye on their neighbors' property.[52]

Predatory criminals seek out easy targets who can't or won't fight back and avoid those who seem menacing and dangerous. Not surprisingly they tend to shy away from potential victims who they believe are "armed and dangerous."[53] The search for suitable victims may bring them in contact with people who themselves engage in deviant or antisocial behaviors.[54] Perhaps predatory criminals sense that people with "dirty hands" make suitable targets because they are unlikely to want to call police or get entangled with the law.

In some instances, however, targets are chosen in order to send a message rather than to generate capital. Bruce Jacobs and Richard Wright conducted in-depth interviews with street robbers who target drug dealers and found that their crimes are a response to one of three types of violations:[55]

▌ *Market-related* violations emerge from disputes involving partners in trade, rivals, or generalized predators.

▌ *Status-based* violations involve encounters in which the grievant's essential character or normative sensibilities have been challenged.

▌ *Personalistic* violations flow from incidents in which the grievant's autonomy or belief in a just world have been jeopardized

Robbery in this instance is an instrument used to settle scores, display dominance, and stifle potential rivals.

IS CRIME RATIONAL?

It is relatively easy to show that some crimes are the product of rational, objective thought, especially when they involve an ongoing criminal conspiracy centered on economic gain. When prominent bankers in the savings and loan industry were indicted for criminal fraud, their elaborate financial schemes exhibited not only signs of rationality but brilliant, though flawed, financial expertise.[56] The stock market manipulations of Enron and WorldCom executives, the drug dealings of international cartels, and the gambling operations of organized crime bosses all demonstrate a reasoned analysis of market conditions, interests, and risks. Even small-time wheeler-dealers, such as the female drug dealers discussed earlier in the chapter, are guided by their rational assessment of the likelihood of apprehension and take pains to avoid detection. But what about common crimes of theft and violence? Are these rational acts or unplanned, haphazard, and spontaneous?

Is Theft Rational?

Some common theft-related crimes—larcenies, shoplifting, purse snatchings—seem more likely to be random acts of criminal opportunity than well-thought-out conspiracies. However, there is evidence that even these seemingly unplanned events may be the product of careful risk assessment, including environmental, social, and structural factors. For example, there are professional shoplifters, referred to as **boosters**, who use complex methods in order to avoid detection. They steal with the intention of reselling stolen merchandise to professional fences, another group of criminals who use cunning and rational decision making in their daily activities.

Burglars' crimes seem to be motivated by rational choice and show evidence of planning and thought. Burglars carefully choose the neighborhood location of their crimes. They seem to avoid areas where residents protect their homes with alarms, locks, and other methods of "target hardening" or where residents watch out for one another and try to control unrest or instability in their communities.[57] Most burglars prefer to commit crimes in permeable neighborhoods, those with a greater than usual number of access streets from traffic arteries into the neighborhood.[58] These areas are chosen for theft and break-ins because they are familiar and well traveled, they appear more open and vulnerable, and they offer more potential escape routes.[59] Burglars appear to monitor car and pedestrian traffic and avoid selecting targets on heavily traveled streets.[60] Corner homes, usually near traffic lights or stop signs, are the ones most likely to be burglarized: stop signs give criminals a legitimate reason to stop their cars and look for an attractive target.[61] Secluded homes, such as those at the end of a cul-de-sac or surrounded by wooded areas, also make suitable targets.[62] Professionals also report being concerned about target convenience. They are more apt to choose familiar burglary sites that are located in easily accessible and open areas.[63]

Burglars also seem to choose the right "working hours." They prefer working between 9 A.M. and 11 A.M. and in mid-afternoon, when adults are either at work or dropping off or picking up kids at school.[64] Burglars avoid Saturdays because most families are at home; Sunday morning during church hours is considered a prime time for weekend burglaries.[65] Some find out which families have star high school athletes because those that do are sure to be at the weekend game, leaving their houses unguarded.[66]

Burglars also seem choosy when they select targets. They avoid freestanding buildings because they can more easily be surrounded by police; they like to select targets that are known to do a primarily cash business, such as bars, supermarkets, and restaurants.[67]

Burglars also seem to know the market and target goods that are in demand. British authorities report that carefully planned burglaries seem to be on the decline presumably because goods that were the target a few years back—video recorders and DVD players—are now so cheap that they are not worth stealing; in British terms, they are barely worth "nicking." Flat screen TVs may be valuable, but those that are the most valuable have become so large that they are impractical to steal.[68] As a result, the planned professional burglary is on a decline in Britain at the same time that street muggings are on the rise.

Is Drug Use Rational?

Did Lindsay Lohan make an objective, rational choice to abuse alcohol and potentially sabotage her career? Did emerging star Heath Ledger make a rational choice when he abused prescription drugs to the point that it killed him? Is it possible that drug users and dealers, a group not usually associated with clear thinking, make rational choices?

Research does in fact show that from its onset drug use is controlled by rational decision making. Users report that they begin taking drugs when they believe that the benefits of substance abuse outweigh its costs (e.g., they believe that drugs will provide a fun, exciting, thrilling experience). Their entry into substance abuse is facilitated by their perception that valued friends and family members endorse and encourage drug use and abuse substances themselves.[69]

In adulthood, heavy drug users and dealers show signs of rationality and cunning in their daily activity, approaching drug dealing as a business proposition. Research conducted by Leanne Fiftal Alarid and her partners shows that women drawn into dealing drugs learn the trade in a businesslike manner. One young dealer told them how she learned the techniques of the trade from an older male partner:

> He taught me how to "recon" [reconstitute] cocaine, cutting and repacking a brick from 91 proof to 50 proof, just like a business. He treats me like an equal partner, and many of the friends are business associates. I am a catalyst. . . . I even get guys turned on to drugs.[70]

Note the business terminology used. This coke dealer could be talking about an IT training course at a major corporation! If criminal acts are treated as business decisions, in which profit and loss potential must be carefully calculated, then crime must indeed be a rational event. The Criminological Enterprise feature Planning Violence: Murder for Hire," takes a look at two interesting murder-for-hire schemes that backfired.

© AP Images/Mary Ann Chastain

Is drug use rational? Former South Carolina Treasurer Thomas Ravenel is followed by the news media on March 14, 2008, as he leaves a Columbia, South Carolina, court after a federal judge sentenced him to 10 months in prison. Ravenel plead guilty to conspiracy to possess with intent to distribute cocaine. Is it possible that a successful, highly educated person such as Ravenel (he graduated from The Citadel in Charleston and later received his M.B.A. from the University of South Carolina) made a rational choice to abuse cocaine? Or do you instead believe that drug abuse is the product of uncontrollable personal demons?

PLANNING VIOLENCE: MURDER FOR HIRE

While violent acts always seem irrational on the surface they may actually involve careful planning and thought. Nowhere are elements of preparation and design more apparent than in elaborate plots involving murder for hire.

Take the case of Paul William Driggers, 54, an Idaho man who offered $10,000 for someone to kill his ex-wife because he was facing child molestation and gun charges and because he wanted his children back. Driggers contacted an associate in prison and asked to be put in touch with a person who could do a job for him. He got the name of a third man who was then living in California. In April 2006, using the name "Huey," Driggers contacted the California man

and induced him to come to Idaho to discuss a "business proposition." Driggers and the man met at a Coeur d'Alene restaurant and discussed a number of illegal things they could do, including counterfeiting, producing precursor chemicals for the manufacture of methamphetamine, identity theft, and false charity campaigns. After the two left the restaurant, Driggers told the California man that he wanted his ex-wife killed and offered the man $10,000 for the murder. Instead of committing the crime, the California man contacted state police. When the two later met in a Lowe's parking lot, the California man was wearing a wire. Driggers showed him photographs of his ex-wife, and the two discussed the details of the murder, including using walkie-talkies to communicate, and how to dispose of the body. Driggers was

convicted of attempted murder on February 23, 2007.

The Drigger's case is not unique. Richard Kaplan, a former New Brunswick official who plotted to kill his wife, was already serving a federal prison sentence for accepting more than $30,000 in bribes. While in prison he pursued a murder-for-hire plot through a fellow inmate. Rather than commit the crime, the inmate alerted authorities and became a cooperating witness in an FBI undercover investigation. Kaplan wanted his wife dead because of money issues and the belief that she was planning to get a divorce. Not long after arriving at the prison, he began telling a fellow inmate that he wanted to find someone who could kill his wife and make it look like an accident. He told the inmate he was willing to pay $25,000 for the murder.

Is Violence Rational?

Brandon Wilson, 21, slashed the throat of Matthew Cecchi, a 9-year-old California boy, then stabbed him in the back and left him to bleed to death on the floor of a public restroom. At trial, he claimed that he was not responsible for his actions, that he was high on LSD, and said that the voice of God told him to kill a child. After his conviction on murder charges, Wilson told the jury that he would "do it again in a second if I had the chance." When the jury later met to consider the death penalty, Wilson told them, "My whole purpose in life is to help destroy your society. You people are here as representatives of that society. As such, you should do everything in your power to rid the world of me, execute me." Granting his wish, the jury foreman told reporters, "If there was ever a case that deserved the death penalty, this one fits."[71]

Though seemingly a demented child killer, Brandon Wilson's statements indicate that he is a rational and calculating killer who may have carefully chosen his victim. Is it possible that violent acts, through which the offender gains little material benefit, are the product of reasoned decision making? Yes, it is, according to crime experts such as Richard Felson, who argues that violence is a matter of choice and serves specific goals:

- *Control*. The violent person may want to control their victim's behavior and life.

- *Retribution*. The perpetrator may want to punish someone without calling the police or using the justice system to address their grievances. They take the law into their own hands.

- *Deterrence*. The attacker may want to stop someone from repeating acts that they consider hostile or provocative.

- *Reputation*. An attack may be motivated by the need to enhance reputation and create self-importance in the eyes of others.

Felson also recognizes that the violent act may have multiple goals. But in any case, even violence may be a product of rational decision making.[72]

Rational Robbers Street robbers also are likely to choose victims who are vulnerable, have low coercive power, and do not pose any threat.[73] In their survey of violent felons, James Wright and Peter Rossi found that robbers avoid victims who may be armed and dangerous. About three-fifths of all felons interviewed were more afraid of armed victims than of police; about two-fifths had avoided a victim because they believed the victim was armed; and almost one-third reported that they had been scared off, wounded, or captured by armed victims.[74] It comes as no surprise that cities with higher than average gun-carrying rates generally have lower rates of unarmed robbery.[75]

Robbers also tend to pick the time and day of crimes carefully. When they rob a commercial establishment, they choose the time when there is the most cash on hand to increase their take from the crime. For example, robbery rates increase in the winter partly because the Christmas shopping season means more money in the cash registers of potential targets.[76] Targets are generally found close to robbers' homes or in areas in which

Kaplan allegedly wanted a hit man to kill his wife in a staged car accident where the vehicle would be destroyed. "That's the end of that. . . . So I'm killing two birds with one stone." The inmate hooked Kaplan up with a "hit man" and Kaplan sent a letter to a post office box instructing him that he wanted to go forward with the plan to kill his wife. In order to provide a "down payment," he asked his accountant to send him $2,000 from his out-of-state bank account. He told his accountant that he needed the money to hire a private investigator to check up on his wife and get evidence to use against her if she did in fact file for divorce. On March 30, 2008, he met with the alleged hit man at the federal prison, stated his desire to have his wife murdered, and acknowledged that once the meeting was over, the deal was complete

and there was no going back. Kaplan also told the hit man that he would pay the remaining balance of the murder-for-hire fee after his wife was killed. The hit man turned out to be an FBI agent, who turned the evidence over to the United States Attorney. On August 19, 2008, Kaplan pleaded guilty to using the mail (a facility of interstate commerce) in the commission of murder for hire.

Is violence rational, even murder? Violence does not always involve spontaneous acts motivated by rage, mental illness, or economic desperation. As these cases show, murder can be a highly complex affair that requires planning, preparation, and rational choice.

CRITICAL THINKING

1. Do you agree that these cases illustrate rational thinking? If not, how else

would you explain the conspirators' involvement in an elaborate murder-for-hire scheme?

2. Can you think of other violent crimes that involved elaborate schemes that suggest rational choice?

Sources: United States Department of Justice News Release, "Coeur d'Alene Man Convicted of Attempted Murder-for-Hire: Jury Says Paul Driggers Tried to Have Ex-Wife Killed," February 23, 2007, http://saltlakecity.fbi.gov/dojpressrel/pressrel07/murderforhire022307.htm (accessed September 1, 2008); United States Department of Justice News Release, "Former New Brunswick Official Already Serving Prison Sentence Pleads Guilty to Murder-for-Hire Plot Targeting His Wife," August 19, 2008, http://newark.fbi.gov/dojpressrel/2008/nk081908.htm (accessed September 1, 2008).

they routinely travel. Familiarity with the area gives them ready knowledge of escape routes; this is referred to as their "awareness space."[77] A familiar location allows them to blend in, not look out of place, and not get lost when returning home with their loot.[78]

Rational Killers? Hollywood likes to portray deranged people killing innocent victims at random, but people who carry guns and are ready to use them typically do so for more rational reasons. They may perceive that they live in a dangerous environment and carry a weapon for self-protection. Some are involved in dangerous illegal activities such as drug dealing and carry weapons as part of the job.[79] Even in apparently senseless killings among strangers, the conscious motive is typically revenge for a prior dispute or disagreement among the parties involved or their families.[80] Many homicides are motivated by offenders' desire to avoid retaliation from a victim they assaulted or to avoid future prosecutions by getting rid of witnesses.[81] Although some killings are the result of anger and aggression, others are the result of rational planning.

Even serial murderers, outwardly the most irrational of all offenders, tend to pick their targets with care. Most choose victims who are defenseless or who cannot count on police protection: prostitutes, gay men, hitchhikers, children, hospital patients, the elderly, and the homeless. Rarely do serial killers target weightlifters, martial arts experts, or any other potentially powerful group.[82]

Rational Sex Criminals? One might think that sex crimes are highly irrational, motivated by hate, lust, revenge—emotions

that defy rational planning. But sex criminals report using rational thought and planning when carrying out their crimes. Serial rapists rationally choose their targets. They travel, on average, three miles from their homes to commit their crimes in order to avoid victims who might recognize them later. The desire to avoid detection supersedes the wish to obtain a victim with little effort. Older, more experienced rapists who have extensive criminal histories are willing to travel further; younger rapists who have less experience committing crimes travel less and are therefore more at risk of detection.[83]

Child molesters/rapists report that they volunteer or seek employment in day care centers and other venues where victims can be found. They use their status to gain the trust of children and to be seen as nonthreatening to the child. Within the context of this work environment they can then use subtle strategies of manipulation, such as giving love and attention to gain their victims' trust (e.g., spending a lot of time with them), and they can gradually desensitize the children and gain their cooperation in sexual activity (e.g., through nonsexual touching).[84] These efforts obviously display planning and rationality.

Rational Airplane Hijackers? Certainly the activities of people who hijack airplanes can't be called rational. Or can they? In a recent study, Laura Dugan, Gary LaFree, and Alex Piquero found that even airplane hijackers, a rather unique sort of violent criminal, may be rational decision makers. Hijacking rates declined when airlines employed measures to make it more difficult to commit crime (for example, using metal detectors in airports) or to increase the cost of crime (for example, boosting the punishments for hijacking). Dugan and her associates found that hijacking rates significantly increased soon after a spate of successful hijackings and decreased when antihijacking policies were implemented. The fact that hijackers were deterred by the threat of apprehension and punishment and encouraged by others' success is surely a sign of rational decision making.[85]

ELIMINATING CRIME

For many people, then, crime is attractive; it brings rewards, excitement, prestige, or other desirable outcomes without lengthy work or effort.[86] Whether the motive is economic gain, revenge, or hedonism, crime has an allure that some people cannot resist.[87] Some law violators describe the adrenaline rush that comes from successfully executing illegal activities in dangerous situations as edgework, the "exhilarating, momentary integration of danger, risk, and skill" that motivates people to try a variety of dangerous criminal and noncriminal behaviors.[88] Crime is not some random act but a means that can provide both pleasure and solutions to vexing personal problems. As Michael Gottfredson and Travis Hirschi put it, they derive satisfaction from "money without work, sex without courtship, revenge without court delays."[89]

Considering its allure, how can crime be prevented and/or eliminated? It seems logical that if crime is rational and people choose to commit crime after weighing its rewards and benefits and factoring in their needs and abilities, then it can be controlled or eradicated by convincing potential offenders that:

▌ Crime is a poor choice that will not bring them rewards but instead lead to hardship and deprivation.

▌ Crime is not worth the effort. It is easier to work at a legitimate job than to evade police, outwit alarms, and avoid security.

▌ Crime brings pain that is not easily forgotten. People who experience the pains of punishment will not readily commit more crimes.

Strategies for crime control based on these premises are illustrated in Concept Summary 4.1 (see page 116). The following sections discuss each of these crime reduction or control strategies in some detail.

Situational Crime Prevention

Desperate people may contemplate crime, but only the truly irrational would attack a well-defended, inaccessible target and risk strict punishment. Crime prevention can be achieved by reducing the opportunities people have to commit particular crimes, a practice known as situational crime prevention. According to this concept, in order to reduce criminal activity, planners must be aware of the characteristics of sites and situations that are at risk to crime; the things that draw or push people toward these sites and situations; what equips potential

criminals to take advantage of illegal opportunities offered by these sites and situations; and what constitutes the immediate triggers for criminal actions.[90] Criminal acts will be avoided if (a) potential targets are guarded securely, (b) the means to commit crime are controlled, and (c) potential offenders are carefully monitored.

Situational crime prevention was first popularized in the United States in the early 1970s by Oscar Newman, who coined the term defensible space. This term signifies that crime can be prevented or displaced through the use of residential architectural designs that reduce criminal opportunity, such as well-lit housing projects that maximize surveillance.[91] C. Ray Jeffery wrote *Crime Prevention through Environmental Design*, which extended Newman's concepts and applied them to nonresidential areas, such as schools and factories.[92] According to this view, mechanisms such as security systems, deadbolt locks, high-intensity street lighting, and neighborhood watch patrols should reduce criminal opportunity.[93]

In 1992, Ronald Clarke published *Situational Crime Prevention*, which compiled the best-known strategies and tactics to reduce criminal incidents.[94] Criminologists have suggested using a number of situational crime prevention efforts that might reduce crime rates. One approach is not to target a specific crime but to create an environment that can reduce the overall crime rate by limiting the access to tempting targets for a highly motivated offender group (such as high school students).[95]

Targeting Specific Crimes Situational crime prevention can also involve developing tactics to reduce or eliminate a specific crime problem (such as shoplifting in an urban mall or street-level drug dealing). According to Derek Cornish and Ronald Clarke, situational crime prevention efforts may be divided into five strategies:[96]

▌ Increase the effort needed to commit crime

▌ Increase the risks of committing crime

▌ Reduce the rewards for committing crime

▌ Reduce provocation/induce guilt or shame for committing crime

▌ Reduce excuses for committing crime

Increase Efforts Some of the tactics to increase efforts include target-hardening techniques such as putting unbreakable glass on storefronts, locking gates, and fencing yards. Technological advances can make it more difficult to commit crimes; having an owner's photo on credit cards should reduce the use of stolen cards. The development of new products, such as steering locks on cars, can make it more difficult to commit crimes. Empirical evidence indicates that steering locks have helped reduce car theft in the United States, Britain, and Germany.[97] Installing a locking device on cars that prevents inebriated drivers from starting the vehicle (breath-analyzed ignition interlock device) significantly reduces drunk-driving rates among people with a history of driving while intoxicated.[98] Removing visibility-blocking signs from store windows, installing brighter lights,

EXHIBIT 4.1

Crime Discouragers

	Types of Supervisors and Objects of Supervision		
Level of Responsibility	Guardians (monitoring suitable targets)	Handlers (monitoring likely offenders)	Managers (monitoring amenable places)
Personal (owners, family, friends)	Student keeps eye on own book bag	Parent makes sure child gets home	Homeowner monitors area near home
Assigned (employees with specific assignment)	Store clerk monitors jewelry	Principal sends kids back to school	Doorman protects building
Diffuse (employees with general assignment)	Accountant notes shoplifting	School clerk discourages truancy	Hotel maid impairs trespasser
General (strangers, other citizens)	Bystander inhibits shoplifting	Stranger questions boys at mall	Customer observes parking structure

Source: Marcus Felson, "Those Who Discourage Crime," in John Eck and David Weisburd, *Crime and Place* (Monsey, NY: Criminal Justice Press, 1995), p. 59. Reprinted by permission.

and instituting a pay-first policy can help reduce thefts from gas stations and convenience stores.[99]

Another way to increase effort is to reduce opportunities for criminal activity. Many cities have established curfew laws in an effort to limit the opportunity juveniles have to engage in antisocial behavior.[100] However, curfew laws have not met with universal success.[101] So another approach has been to involve kids in after-school programs that take up their time and reduce their opportunity to get in trouble. An example of this type of program is the Doorsteps Neighbourhood Program in Toronto, Ontario, which is designed to help children in high-risk areas complete their schoolwork as well as providing them with playtime that helps improve their literacy and communication skills. Children who are part of this program enter into routines that increase the effort they must make if they want to get involved in after-school crime and nuisance activities.[102]

Reduce Rewards Target reduction strategies are designed to reduce the value of crime to the potential criminal. These include making car radios removable so they can be kept in the home at night, marking property so that it is more difficult to sell when stolen, and having gender-neutral phone listings to discourage obscene phone calls. Tracking systems, such as those made by the LoJack Corporation, help police locate and return stolen vehicles.

Increase Risk If criminals believe that committing crime is very risky, only the most foolhardy would attempt to commit criminal acts. Managing crime falls into the hands of people Marcus Felson calls crime discouragers.[103] These discouragers can be grouped into three categories: guardians, who monitor targets (such as store security guards); handlers, who monitor potential offenders (such as parole officers and parents); and managers, who monitor places (such as homeowners and doorway attendants). If crime discouragers do their job correctly, the

potential criminal will be convinced that the risk of crime outweighs any potential gains.[104]

Crime discouragers have different levels of responsibility, ranging from highly personal involvement, such as the homeowner protecting her house and the parent controlling his children, to the most impersonal general involvement, such as a stranger who stops someone from shoplifting in the mall (Exhibit 4.1).

Research indicates that crime discouragers can have an impact on crime rates. An evaluation of a police initiative in Oakland, California, found that an active working partnership with residents and businesspeople who have a stake in maintaining order in their places of work or residences can reduce levels of drug dealing while at the same time increasing civil behavior. Collective action and cooperation in solving problems were effective in controlling crime, whereas individual action (such as calling 911) seemed to have little effect.[105]

In addition to crime discouragers, it may be possible to raise the risks of committing crime by creating mechanical devices that increase the likelihood that a criminal will be observed and captured. The Comparative Criminology feature "Reducing Crime through Surveillance" discusses a recent evaluation of such methods in Great Britain and other nations.

Increase Shame/Reduce Provocation Crime may be reduced or prevented if we can communicate to people the wrongfulness of their behavior and how it is harmful to society. We may tell them to "say no to drugs" or that "users are losers." By making people aware of the shamefulness of their actions, we hope to prevent their criminal activities even if chances of detection and punishment are slight.

Some efforts to make people ashamed of their acts are personal and provocative. "John Lists" have been published to shame men involved in hiring prostitutes. Recently, a judge in Hudson, Kansas, ordered a man who admitted molesting an 11-year-old boy to post "A Sex Offender Lives Here" signs on all

Comparative Criminology

REDUCING CRIME THROUGH SURVEILLANCE

Brandon Welsh and David Farrington have been using systematic review and meta-analysis to assess the comparative effectiveness of situational crime prevention techniques. Recently, they evaluated the effectiveness of closed-circuit television (CCTV) surveillance cameras and improved street lighting, techniques that are currently being used around the world.

They found that CCTV surveillance cameras serve many functions and are used in both public and private settings. CCTV can deter would-be criminals who fear detection and apprehension. It can also aid police in the detection and apprehension of suspects, aid in the prosecution of alleged offenders, improve police officer safety and compliance with the law (through, for instance, cameras mounted on the dashboard of police cruisers to record police stops, searches, and so on), and aid in the detection and prevention of terrorist activities. Nowhere is the popularity of CCTV more apparent than in Great Britain, where an estimated 4.2 million CCTV cameras are in operation—1 for every 14 citizens. It has been estimated that the average Briton is caught on camera 300 times each day.

After reviewing 41 studies conducted around the world, Welsh and Farrington found that CCTV interventions have a small but significant desirable effect on crime and are most effective in reducing vehicle crimes. They conclude that effectiveness is significantly correlated with the degree of coverage of the CCTV cameras, which is greatest in car parks (parking lots). However, the effect was most pronounced in the parking lots that employed other situational crime prevention interventions as well, such as improved lighting and security officers.

Importantly, Welsh and Farrington found that CCTV schemes in the United Kingdom showed a sizeable (19 percent) and significant desirable effect on crime, while those in other countries showed no desirable effect on crime. One reason was that all of the sites that used other interventions alongside CCTV were in England. It is possible that CCTV on its own is insufficient to influence an offender's decision to commit a crime or not and it has to be buttressed by other methods such as security fences or guards.

Another important issue is cultural context. In the United Kingdom, there is a high level of public support for the use of CCTV cameras in public settings to prevent crime. In America and other nations, the public is less accepting and more apprehensive of "Big Brother" implications arising from this surveillance technology. Furthermore, in America, resistance to the use of CCTV in public places also takes the form of legal action and constitutional challenges under the U.S. Constitution's Fourth Amendment prohibition against unreasonable searches and seizures. In Sweden, surveillance cameras are highly regulated in public places, with their use requiring in almost all instances a permit from the county administrative board. In Norway, there is a high degree of political scrutiny of public CCTV schemes run by the police.

It could very well be that the overall poor showing of CCTV schemes in countries other than Great Britain is due in part to a lack of public support (and maybe even political support) for the schemes, which, in turn, may result in reduced program funding, the police assigning lower priority to CCTV, and negative media reaction. Each of these factors could potentially undermine the effectiveness of CCTV schemes. In contrast, the British Home Office, which funded many of the British evaluations, wanted to show that CCTV was effective because it had invested so much money in these schemes.

Welsh and Farrington conclude that overall CCTV reduces crime in some circumstances. In light of the mixed results, future CCTV schemes should be carefully implemented in different settings and should employ high quality evaluation designs with long follow-up periods.

CRITICAL THINKING

Would you be willing to have a surveillance camera set up in your home or dorm in order to prevent crime, knowing that your every move was being watched and recorded?

Source: Brandon C. Welsh and David P. Farrington, *Making Public Places Safer: Surveillance and Crime Prevention* (New York: Oxford University Press, 2008).

---

four sides of his home and "A Sex Offender in this Car" in bold yellow lettering on the sides of his automobile.[106] This order is typical for judges who have ordered people convicted of socially unacceptable crimes to advertise their guilt in the hope that they will be too ashamed to recidivate.

Other methods of inducing guilt or shame might include such techniques as posting signs or warnings to embarrass potential offenders or creating mechanisms to identify perpetrators and/or publicize their crimes. For example, caller ID can be used to identify people making obscene phone calls. In one study, Ronald Clarke showed how caller ID in New Jersey resulted in significant reductions in the number of obscene phone calls.[107] Megan's Law requires sex offender registration and notification systems. While these systems have been used for more than a decade, there is little evidence that they reduce sex crimes: research shows that sex offender registration does not have a statistically significant effect on the number of rapes reported at the state level.[108]

Some crimes are the result of extreme provocation (e.g., road rage). It might be possible to reduce provocation by creating programs that reduce conflict. Creating an early closing time in local bars and pubs might limit assaults that are the result of late night drinking. Posting guards outside of schools at recess might prevent childish taunts from escalating into full-blown brawls. Antibullying programs that have been implemented in schools are another method of reducing provocation.

Remove Excuses Crime may be reduced by making it difficult for people to excuse their criminal behavior by saying things like "I did not know that was illegal" or "I had no choice." Some municipalities have set up roadside displays that electronically flash cars' speed rate as they drive by, so that when stopped by police, drivers cannot say they did not know how fast they were going. Litter boxes, brightly displayed, can eliminate the claim that "I just did not know where to throw my trash." Reducing or eliminating excuses also makes it physically easy for people to comply with laws and regulations, thereby reducing the likelihood they will choose crime.

Situational Crime Prevention: Costs and Benefits Some attempts at situational crime prevention have proven highly successful while others have not met their goals. However, it is now apparent that the approach brings with it certain nontransparent or hidden costs and benefits that can either increase effectiveness or undermine success. Before the overall success of this approach can be evaluated, these costs and benefits must be considered. Among the hidden benefits of situational crime control efforts are:

▪ *Diffusion.* Sometimes efforts to prevent one crime help prevent another; in other instances, crime control efforts in one locale reduce crime in another area.[109] This effect is referred to as diffusion of benefits. Diffusion may be produced by two independent effects. Crime control efforts may deter criminals by causing them to fear apprehension. Video cameras set up in a mall to reduce shoplifting can also reduce property damage because would-be vandals fear they will be caught on camera. One recent police program targeting drugs in areas of Jersey City, New Jersey, also reduced public morals crimes because potential offenders were aware of increased police patrols.[110]

▪ *Discouragement.* Sometimes crime control efforts targeting a particular locale help reduce crime in surrounding areas and populations; this is referred to as discouragement. In her study of the effects of the SMART program (a drug enforcement program in Oakland, California, that enforces municipal codes and nuisance abatement laws), criminologist Lorraine Green found that not only did drug dealing decrease in targeted areas but improvement was found in adjacent areas as well. She suggests that the program most likely discouraged buyers and sellers who saw familiar hangouts closed. This sign that drug dealing would not be tolerated probably decreased the total number of people involved in drug activity even though they did not operate in the targeted areas.[111] Another example of this effect can

be found in evaluations of the LoJack auto protection system. LoJack uses a hidden radio transmitter to track stolen cars. As the number of LoJack installations rises, police notice that the sale of stolen auto parts declines. It appears that people in the illegal auto parts business (that is, chop shops) close down because they fear that the stolen cars they buy might contain LoJack.[112] A device designed to protect cars from theft also has the benefit of disrupting the sale of stolen car parts.

While there are hidden benefits to situational crime prevention, there may also be costs that limit their effectiveness:

▪ *Displacement.* A program that seems successful because it helps lower crime rates at specific locations or neighborhoods may simply be redirecting offenders to alternative targets; crime is not prevented but deflected or displaced, and is referred to as crime displacement.[113] Beefed-up police patrols in one area may shift crimes to a more vulnerable neighborhood.[114]

▪ *Extinction.* Sometimes crime reduction programs may produce a short-term positive effect, but benefits dissipate as criminals adjust to new conditions; this is referred to as extinction. As they perceive new threats, criminals learn to dismantle alarms or avoid patrols; they may try new offenses they had previously avoided. And elimination of one crime may encourage commission of another: if every residence in a neighborhood has a foolproof burglar alarm system, motivated offenders may be forced to turn to armed robbery, a riskier and more violent crime.

▪ *Encouragement.* Crime reduction programs may boomerang and increase rather than decrease the potentiality for crime. For example, some situational efforts rely on increasing the risk of crime by installing street lighting, assuming that rational criminals will avoid areas where their criminal activities are more visible. However, as Brandon Welsh and David Farrington note, in some cases street lighting improvement efforts can backfire and increase opportunities for crime. Well-lighted areas may bring a greater number of potential victims and potential offenders into the same physical space. The increased visibility may allow potential offenders to make better judgments of target vulnerability and attractiveness (e.g., they can spot people with jewelry and other valuables). Lighting may make an area more attractive and increase social activity; increasing the number of unoccupied homes makes them available for burglary. Increased illumination may make it easier for offenders to commit crimes and to escape.[115]

Before the effectiveness of situational crime prevention can be accepted, these hidden costs and benefits must be weighed and balanced.

General Deterrence

According to the rational choice view, motivated, rational people will violate the law if left free and unrestricted. General deterrence theory holds that crime rates are influenced and

Police officers search suspects in a night raid in Camden, New Jersey. Camden has an extremely high crime rate and police are determined to deter crime in the area. Can aggressive policing tactics such as night sweeps deter crime or do they just displace crime to other areas of the city? If criminals are rational, they might be wary of police and take steps to avoid contact and escape detection.

controlled by the threat and/or application of criminal punishment. If people fear being apprehended and punished, they will not risk breaking the law. An inverse relationship should then exist between crime rates and the fear of legal sanctions. If, for example, the punishment for a crime is increased and the effectiveness and efficiency of the criminal justice system are improved, then, fearing future punishments, the number of people willing to risk committing crime should decline.

The factors of severity, certainty, and speed of punishment may also influence one another. If a particular crime—say, robbery—is punished severely, but few robbers are ever caught or punished, the severity of punishment for robbery will probably not deter people from robbing. However, if the certainty of apprehension and conviction is increased by modern technology, more efficient police work, or some other factor, then even minor punishment might deter the potential robber.

Deterrence theorists tend to believe that the certainty of punishment seems to have a greater impact than its severity or speed. In other words, people will more likely be deterred from crime if they believe that they will get caught; what happens to them after apprehension seems to have less impact.[116] Nonetheless, all three elements of the deterrence equation are important, and it would be a mistake to emphasize one at the expense of the others. For example, if all resources were given to police agencies to increase the probability of arrest, crime rates might increase because there were insufficient funds for swift prosecution and effective correction.[117]

Perception and Deterrence According to deterrence theory, not only does the actual chance of punishment influence criminality, so too does the *perception of punishment*. A central theme

of deterrence theory is that people who perceive they will be punished for crimes will avoid doing those crimes.[118] Conversely, the likelihood of being arrested or imprisoned will have little effect on crime rates if criminals believe that they have only a small chance of suffering apprehension and punishment.[119]

Because criminals are rational decision makers, if they can be convinced crime will lead to punishment then they will be deterred. To prove this relationship empirically Canadian criminologists Etienne Blais and Jean-Luc Bacher had insurance companies send a written threat to a random sample of insured persons reminding them of the punishment for insurance fraud, and then compared their claims with a control group of people who did not get the threatening letter. The letter was sent to the insured persons at a time when they had the opportunity to exaggerate the value of their claims. Blais and Bacher found that those who got the letter were less likely to pad their claims than were those in the control group.[120] Clearly the warning gave people the perception they would be caught and punished for insurance fraud deterred their illegal activity.

Certainty of Punishment and Deterrence According to deterrence theory, if the probability of arrest, conviction, and sanctioning increase, crime rates should decline. As the certainty of punishment increases, even the most motivated criminal may desist because the risks of crime outweigh its rewards.[121] If people believe that their criminal transgressions will result in apprehension and punishment, then only the truly irrational will commit crime.[122] Considering this association, it is common for crime control efforts to be aimed at convincing rational criminals to avoid the risk of crime. Take for instance Project Safe Neighborhoods, which was the centerpiece of the government's crime policy in President Bush's first term. Safe Neighborhoods relied on media campaigns aimed at convincing people that carrying handguns was a serious crime for which they would be caught, prosecuted, and severely punished with mandatory prison sentences. Evaluations suggest that the program worked and gun crimes declined after the program was instituted.[123]

The Tipping Point Unfortunately for deterrence theory, punishment is not very certain. Only 10 percent of all serious offenses result in apprehension (half go unreported, and police make arrests in about 20 percent of reported crimes). Police routinely do not arrest suspects in personal disputes even when they lead to violence.[124] As apprehended offenders are processed through all the stages of the criminal justice system, the odds of their receiving serious punishment diminish. As a result, some offenders believe they will not be severely punished for their acts and consequently have little regard for the law's deterrent power.

Criminologists maintain that if the certainty of punishment could be increased to critical level, the so-called tipping point, then the deterrent effect would kick in and crime rates decline.[125] Crime persists because we have not reached the tipping point, and most criminals believe that (a) there is only a small chance they will be arrested for committing a particular crime, (b) police officers are sometimes reluctant to make arrests even when they are aware of crime, and (c) even if apprehended there is a good chance of either getting off totally or receiving a lenient punishment such as probation.[126]

One way of increasing the tipping point may be to add police officers. As the number of active, aggressive crime-fighting cops increases, arrests and convictions should likewise increase, and would-be criminals convinced that the risk of apprehension outweighs the benefits they can gain from crime.[127]

While adding cops seems a logical way of reducing crime, this assumption has been questioned ever since a famous experiment was conducted in the early 1970s by the Kansas City, Missouri, Police Department.[128] To evaluate the effectiveness of police patrols, fifteen independent Kansas City police beats or districts were divided into three groups. The first (active) retained a normal police patrol; the second (proactive) was supplied with two to three times the normal amount of patrol forces; the third (reactive) eliminated its preventive patrol entirely, and police officers responded only when summoned by citizens to the scene of a crime.

Surprisingly, these variations in patrol techniques had little effect on the crime patterns. Variations in police patrol techniques appeared to have little effect on citizens' attitudes toward the police, their satisfaction with police, or their fear of future criminal behavior. It is possible that as people traveled around the city they noticed a large number of police officers in one area and relatively few in another; the two effects may have cancelled each other out!

While subsequent research using sophisticated methodological tools found evidence that increased police levels does reduce the level of criminal activity over time, it was hard to shake the influence of the Kansas City study.[129] It had convinced criminologists that the mere presence of patrol officers on the street did not have a deterrent effect.

But what if the officers were engaging in aggressive, focused crime-fighting initiatives, targeting specific crimes such as murder or robbery? Would such activities result in more arrests and a greater deterrent effect?[130] To answer this question, some police departments have instituted crackdowns—sudden changes in police activity designed to increase the communicated threat or actual certainty of punishment. For example, a police task force might target street-level narcotics dealers by using undercover agents and surveillance cameras in known drug-dealing locales. Crackdown efforts have met with mixed reviews.[131] In one well-known study, Lawrence Sherman found that while crackdowns initially deterred crime, crime rates returned to earlier levels once the crackdown ended.[132] Other research efforts have also found that while at first successful as a

crime suppression technique, the initial effect of the crackdown soon wore off after high intensity police activity ended.[133]

Although these results are troubling, there is some evidence that when police combine crackdowns with the use of aggressive problem-solving and community improvement techniques, such as increasing lighting and cleaning vacant lots, crackdowns may be successful in reducing some forms of crime.[134] When the Dallas Police Department established a policy of aggressively pursuing truancy and curfew enforcement they found that the effort actually lowered rates of gang violence.[135] A month-long crackdown and cleanup initiative in seven city neighborhoods in Richmond, Virginia, found that crime rates declined by 92 percent; the effects persisted up to six months after the crackdown ended, and no displacement was observed.[136] Police seem to have more luck deterring crime when they use more focused approaches, such as aggressive problem-solving and community improvement techniques.[137] Merely saturating an area with police may not deter crime, but focusing efforts at a particular problem area may have a deterrent effect.

Severity of Punishment and Deterrence According to general deterrence theory, as the severity of punishment increases, crime rates should decrease. Does this equation hold water? The evidence is decidedly mixed. While some studies have found that increasing sanction levels can control common criminal behaviors, others have not achieved a positive result.[138]

Take the case of enhancing punishment: in order to control handguns, a state might add five years to a sentence if a handgun was used during the crime. However, it is often difficult to determine if such measures actually work. When Daniel Kessler and Steven Levitt evaluated the deterrent effect of California's sentencing enhancement act they found that it did in fact lower crime rates.[139] However, gun crimes also went down in other states that did not enhance or increase their sentences.[140] What appears to be a deterrent effect may be the result of some other factor, such as an improved economy.

It stands to reason that if severity of punishment can deter crime, then fear of the death penalty—the ultimate legal deterrent—should significantly reduce murder rates. Because no one denies its emotional impact, failure of the death penalty to deter violent crime would jeopardize the validity of the entire deterrence concept. Because this topic is so important, it is featured in The Criminological Enterprise, "Does Capital Punishment Deter Murder?" on page 112.

connections

Even if capital punishment proves to be a deterrent, many experts still question its morality, fairness, and legality. Chapter 4 provides further discussion that can help you decide whether the death penalty is an appropriate response to murder.

Morality, Shame, and Humiliation According to criminologist Per-Olof Wikström, morality plays an important role in the decision to commit crime.[141] People will be more easily deterred if they have a strong sense of moral beliefs and are inherently reluctant to engage in behavior in violation of their core values. According to Wikström's "Situational Action Theory," the strength of a *moral belief* can be characterized as "the intensity of the moral emotions: the potency of the feelings of guilt and shame if violating a moral rule (or, at the other extreme, the potency of feelings of virtue and satisfaction if abiding by a rule)." The strength of a *moral habit* can be characterized as "the intervention (force) needed to break the habit" (that is, the external "force" necessary to change a habitual response into a deliberate one).[142] To commit crime, people must *decide* to behave in a way that violates their own sense of morality. Their decision may depend on their perception of consequences in their immediate environment. They may be more apt to choose to do the moral thing if they also fear being caught and punished for their transgressions. So deterrence is helped when people have strong moral values and is undermined when values and beliefs are weak and attenuated.

If people violate their own moral code of good behavior, they may also fear the shame and humiliation of being found out by those people they admire; fear of shame and humiliation may deter crime. Those who fear being rejected by family and peers are reluctant to engage in deviant behavior.[143] These factors manifest themselves in two ways: (1) personal shame over violating the law and (2) the fear of public humiliation if the deviant behavior becomes public knowledge. People who say that their involvement in crime would cause them to feel ashamed are less likely to offend than people who deny fears of embarrassment.[144]

People who are afraid that significant others—such as parents, peers, neighbors, and teachers—will disapprove of their behavior are less likely to commit crime.[145] While shame can be a powerful deterrent, offenders also seem to be influenced by forgiveness and acceptance. They are less likely to repeat their criminal activity if victims are willing to grant them forgiveness.[146]

The fear of exposure and consequent shaming may vary according to the cohesiveness of community structure and the type of crime. Informal sanctions may be most effective in highly unified areas where everyone knows one another and the crime cannot be hidden from public view. The threat of informal sanctions seems to have the greatest influence on instrumental crimes, which involve planning, and not on impulsive or expressive criminal behaviors or those associated with substance abuse.[147]

Speed (Celerity) of Punishment and Deterrence The third leg of Beccaria's equation involves the celerity or speed of punishment: the faster punishment is applied and the more closely it is linked to the crime, the more likely it will serve as a deterrent.[148] The deterrent effect of the law may be neutralized if there is a significant lag between apprehension and punishment. In the American justice system, court delays brought by numerous evidentiary hearings and requests for additional trial

Table 4.1 Time Under Sentence of Death and Execution, by Race

Year of execution	Number executed	Average elapsed time in months from sentence to execution for all inmates
2000	85	137
2001	66	142
2002	71	127
2003	65	131
2004	59	132
2005	60	147
2006	53	145

Source: Bureau of Justice Statistics, *Capital Punishment, 2006—Statistical Tables*, www.ojp.usdoj.gov/bjs/pub/html/cp/2006/tables/cp06st11.htm (accessed July 5, 2008).

preparation time are common trial tactics. As a result, the criminal process can be delayed to a point where the connection between crime and punishment is broken. Take for instance how the death penalty is employed. As Table 4.1 shows, more than 10 years typically elapse between the time a criminal is convicted for murder and their execution. During that period, many death row inmates have repented, matured, and turned their lives around, only to be taken out and executed. Delay in its application may mitigate or neutralize the potential deterrent effect of capital punishment.

The threat of punishment may also be neutralized by the belief that even if caught criminals can avoid severe punishment through plea negotiations. The fact that killers can avoid the death penalty by bargaining for a life sentence may also undermine the deterrent effect of the law.[149]

Research indicates that in general, the deterrence and retributive value of a given criminal sanction steadily decreases as the lag between crime and punishment lengthens. Because criminals "discount" punishments that lag far behind their crimes, how and when punishment is applied can alter its affect. A criminal who is apprehended, tried, and convicted soon after he or she commits the crime will be more deeply affected than one who experiences a significant lag between crime and punishment.[150] Criminologist Raymond Paternoster found that adolescents, a group responsible for a disproportionate amount of crime, may be well aware that the juvenile court is generally lenient about imposing meaningful sanctions on even the most serious juvenile offenders.[151] Even those accused of murder are often convicted of lesser offenses and spend relatively short amounts of time behind bars.[152] Not surprisingly, the more experience a kid has with the juvenile justice system, the less deterrent effect it has: crime-prone youth, ones who have a long history of criminality, know that crimes provide immediate gratification, whereas the threat of punishment is far in the future.[153]

Analyzing General Deterrence Some experts believe that the purpose of the law and justice system is to create a "threat system."[154] That is, the threat of legal punishment should, on the face of it, deter lawbreakers through fear. Nonetheless, as we have already discussed, the relationship between crime rates and deterrent measures is far less clear than choice theorists might expect. Despite efforts to punish criminals and make them fear crime, there is little evidence that the fear of apprehension and punishment alone can reduce crime rates. How can this discrepancy be explained?

- *Rationality.* Deterrence theory assumes a rational offender who weighs the costs and benefits of a criminal act before deciding on a course of action. In many instances, criminals are desperate people who suffer from personality disorders that impair their judgment and render them incapable of making truly rational decisions. Many offenders are under the influence of drugs when they commit crimes, others suffer from mental illness, while many bear the burden of both mental illness and drug abuse.[155] They may be impulsive and imprudent rather than reasoning and calculating.

- *Compulsion.* Not all offenders are equal and it is well known that a relatively small group of chronic offenders commits a significant percentage of all serious crimes. Some psychologists believe this select group suffers from an innate or inherited emotional state that renders them both incapable of fearing punishment and less likely to appreciate the consequences of crime.[156] Research shows that people who are easily aroused sexually also say that they will be more likely to act in a sexually aggressive fashion and not consider the legal consequences of their actions.[157] Their heightened emotional state negates the deterrent effect of the law.

- *Need.* Many offenders are members of what is referred to as the underclass—people cut off from society, lacking the education and skills they need to be in demand in the modern economy.[158] Such desperate people may not be deterred from crime by fear of punishment because, in reality, they perceive few other options for success. Among poor, high-risk groups, such as teens living in economically depressed neighborhoods, the threat of formal sanctions is irrelevant.[159] Young people in these areas have less to lose because their opportunities are few, and they have little attachment to social institutions such as school or family. In their environment, they see many people who appear relatively well-off (the neighborhood drug dealer) committing crimes without getting caught or punished.[160]

- *Greed.* Some may be immune to deterrent effects because they believe the profits from crime are worth the risk of punishment; it may be their only significant chance for gain and profit. When criminologists Alex Piquero and George Rengert studied active burglars, they found that the lure of criminal profits outweighed their fears of capture and subsequent punishment. Perceived risk of punishment may deter some potential and active criminal offenders, but only if they doubt that they can make a "big score" from committing a crime.[161] Greed may encourage some law violators to overestimate the rewards of crime that in reality are often quite meager. When Steven Levitt and Sudhir Alladi Venkatesh studied the financial rewards of being in a drug gang, they found that despite enormous risks to health, life, and freedom, average gang members earned only slightly more than what they could in the legitimate labor market (about $6 to $11 per hour).[162] Why then did they stay in the gang? Members believed that there was a strong potential for future riches if they stayed in the drug business and earned a "management" position (i.e., gang leaders earned a lot more). Deterrence is neutralized because the gang boys' greed causes them to overestimate the potential for future criminal gain versus the probability of apprehension and punishment.[163]

- *Misperception.* Some people are more "deterrable" than others—that is, while some are deterred by the threat of punishment, others seem immune.[164] Perhaps they are poor students of justice system effectiveness. The scope of their assessments may be limited to their immediate surroundings. If they see a lot of cops on the street making arrests, they may be apprehensive, but their fear might simply cause them to shift the location of their criminal activities to a safer environment—crime displacement— rather than deterring future criminal activities. They may rely more on their peers for information than read the latest UCR reports or scan citywide arrest statistics. As a result they hear their friends bragging about big scores and profitable drug deals rather than information showing arrest rates are up. So while increasing punitive measures may work on some offenders, it might have no impact on others and may even make the situation worse.[165]

Specific Deterrence

The general deterrence model focuses on future or potential criminals. In contrast, the theory of **specific deterrence** (also called special or particular deterrence) holds that criminal sanctions should be so powerful that known criminals will never repeat their criminal acts:

- The drunk driver whose sentence is a substantial fine and a week in the county jail should be convinced that the price to be paid for drinking and driving is too great to consider future violations.

- The burglar who spends five years in a tough maximum security prison will find his enthusiasm for theft dampened.

- The tax cheat who is assessed triple damages will think twice before filing a false return.

In principle, punishment works if a connection can be established between the planned action and memories of its consequence; if these recollections are adequately intense, the action will be unlikely to occur again.[166] Yet the connection between experiencing punishment and fearing future punishment is not always as strong as expected.[167]

At first glance, specific deterrence does not seem to work because a majority of known criminals are not deterred by their punishment. Arrest and punishment seem to have little effect on

DOES CAPITAL PUNISHMENT DETER MURDER?

According to deterrence theory, the death penalty—the ultimate deterrent—should deter murder—the ultimate crime. Most Americans approve of the death penalty, including, as Norma Wilcox and Tracey Steele found, convicted criminals who are currently behind bars. But is the public's approval warranted? Does the death penalty actually deter murder?

Empirical research on the association between capital punishment and murder can be divided into three types: immediate impact studies, comparative research, and time-series analysis.

Immediate Impact

If capital punishment is a deterrent, the reasoning goes, then its impact should be greatest after a well-publicized execution. Robert Dann began testing this assumption in 1935 when he chose five highly publicized executions of convicted murderers in different years and determined the number of homicides in the 60 days before and after each execution. Each 120-day period had approximately the same number of homicides, as well as the same number of days on which homicides occurred. Dann's study revealed that an average of 4.4 more homicides occurred during the 60 days following an execution than during those preceding it, suggesting that the overall impact of executions might actually be an increase in the incidence of homicide. Seventy years later when Lisa Stolzenberg and Stewart D'Alessio examined the

effect of the death penalty on the murder rate in Houston, Texas, they also found that even when executions were highly publicized in the local press, they still had little influence on the murder rate.

Comparative Research

Another type of research compares the murder rates in jurisdictions that have abolished the death penalty with the rates of those that employ the death penalty. Studies using this approach have found little difference in the murder rates of adjacent states, regardless of their use of the death penalty; capital punishment did not appear to influence the reported rate of homicide. Research conducted in 14 nations around the world found little evidence that countries with a death penalty have lower violence rates than those without; homicide rates actually decline after capital punishment is abolished, a direct contradiction to its supposed deterrent effect.

Time-Series Studies

Time-series studies look at the long-term association between capital sentencing and murder. If capital punishment is a deterrent, then periods that have an upswing in executions should also experience a downturn in violent crime and murder. Most research efforts have failed to show such a relationship. One test of the deterrent effect of the death penalty in Texas by Jon Sorenson and his colleagues found no association between the frequency of execution during the years 1984 to 1997 and murder rates. Matt Breverlin used data gathered from 1974 to 2001 in all 50 states to demonstrate that the death penalty for juveniles has no

statistically significant deterrent effect. His conclusion is that state-level economic conditions, population density, and incarceration rates have a much greater impact on the juvenile murder rate than the deterrent impact of the death penalty. These findings seem to indicate that the threat and/or reality of execution has relatively little influence on murder rates. Although it is still uncertain why the threat of capital punishment fails as a deterrent, the cause may lie in the nature of homicide itself. Murder is often an expressive "crime of passion" involving people who know each other and who may be under the influence of drugs and alcohol. Those who choose to take a life may be less influenced by the threat of punishment, even death, than those who commit crime for economic gain.

Rethinking the Deterrent Effect of Capital Punishment

In contrast to these results, some recent studies have concluded that executing criminals may, in fact, bring the murder rate down. Those who still maintain that an association exists between capital punishment and murder rate believe that the relationship has been masked or obscured by faulty research methods. Newer studies, using sophisticated data analysis, have been able to uncover a more significant association. For example, criminologist Steven Stack has conducted a number of research studies that show that the immediate impact of a well-publicized execution can lower the murder rate during the following month. James Yunker, using a national data set, has found evidence that there is a deterrent effect of capital punishment now that the pace of

experienced criminals and may even increase the likelihood that first-time offenders will commit new crimes.[168] A sentence to a juvenile justice facility does little to deter a persistent delinquent from becoming an adult criminal.[169] Most prison inmates had prior records of arrest and conviction before their current offenses.[170] About two-thirds of all convicted felons are rearrested within three years of their release from prison, and those

who have been punished in the past are the most likely to recidivate.[171] Incarceration may sometimes slow down or delay recidivism in the short term, but the overall probability of rearrest does not change following incarceration.[172]

According to the theory of specific deterrence, the harsher the punishment, the less likely the chances of recidivism. But research shows that this is not always the case. Offenders executions has accelerated. Economists Hashem Dezhbakhsh, Paul H. Rubin, and Joanna M. Shepherd performed an advanced statistical analysis on county-level homicide data in order to calculate the effect of each execution on the number of homicides that would otherwise have occurred. Using a variety of models (for example, the effect of an execution conducted today on reducing homicides in five years, and so on), they found that each execution leads to an average of 18 fewer murders. In another study, Shepherd claims that the reason some research has not found a deterrent effect is because capital punishment may have differing influence depending on where and how it is used. Each state's murder rate is calculated differently and lumping all state data together masks the deterrent effect of the death penalty. Shepherd found that the use of capital punishment deterred murder in states that conducted more executions than the norm. In contrast, when states that conducted relatively few executions (one or two per year), the average execution either increased the murder rate or had no effect. Shepherd concludes that each execution has two opposing effects: (1) it can contribute to a climate of brutal violence (i.e., the brutalization effect) that tells people it is okay to kill in revenge; (2) it can act as a deterrent and show potential criminals that the state is willing to use the ultimate penalty to punish crimes. However, the deterrent effect takes place only if a state routinely uses executions. Only then do potential criminals become convinced that the state is serious about the punishment and start to reduce their criminal activity.

So on the one hand, the most recent research indicates that the death penalty is being used more frequently, it is possible that the tipping point has been reached, and it is now an effective deterrent measure. On the other hand, capital punishment remains controversial: since 1976, more than 100 people have been wrongfully convicted and sentenced to death in the United States. And according to research sponsored by the Pew Foundation, a majority of death penalty convictions have been overturned, many due to "serious, reversible error," including egregiously incompetent defense counsel, suppression of exculpatory evidence, false confessions, racial manipulation of the jury, "snitch" and accomplice testimony, and faulty jury instructions.

After years of study, the death penalty remains a topic of considerable criminological debate.

CRITICAL THINKING

Even if effective, there is no question the death penalty still carries with it tremendous baggage. For example, when Geoffrey Rapp studied the effect of the death penalty on the safety of police officers, he found that the introduction of capital punishment actually created an extremely dangerous environment for law enforcement officers. Because the death penalty does not have a deterrent effect, criminals are more likely to kill police officers when the death penalty is in place. Tragically, the death penalty may lull officers into a false sense of security, causing them to let down their guard—killing fewer citizens but getting killed more often themselves Given

Rapp's findings, should we still maintain the death penalty?

Sources: Pew Foundation, "Death Penalty," www. pewcenteronthestates.org/topic_category.aspx? category=510 (accessed July 5, 2008); Joanna Shepherd, "Deterrence versus Brutalization: Capital Punishment's Differing Impacts among States," *Michigan Law Review* 104 (2005): 203–253; Matt Beverlin, "A Study of the Deterrence Effect of the Juvenile Death Penalty," paper presented at the annual meeting of the Southern Political Science Association, New Orleans, 2005, 1–34; John Donohue and Justin Wolfers, "Uses and Abuses of Empirical Evidence in the Death Penalty Debate," *Stanford Law Review* 58 (2005): 791–845; Lisa Stolzenberg and Stewart D'Alessio, "Capital Punishment, Execution Publicity, and Murder in Houston, Texas," *Journal of Criminal Law and Criminology* 94 (2004): 351–380; Geoffrey Rapp "The Economics of Shootouts: Does the Passage of Capital Punishment Laws Protect or Endanger Police Officers?" *Albany Law Review* 65 (2002): 1,051–1,084; Robert Dann, "The Deterrent Effect of Capital Punishment," *Friends Social Service Series* 29 (1935); Thorsten Sellin, *The Death Penalty* (Philadelphia: American Law Institute, 1959); Walter Reckless, "Use of the Death Penalty," *Crime and Delinquency* 15 (1969): 43–51; Dane Archer, Rosemary Gartner, and Marc Beittel, "Homicide and the Death Penalty: A Cross-National Test of a Deterrence Hypothesis," *Journal of Criminal Law and Criminology* 74 (1983): 991–1,014; Jon Sorenson, Robert Wrinkle, Victoria Brewer, and James Marquart, "Capital Punishment and Deterrence: Examining the Effect of Executions on Murder in Texas," *Crime and Delinquency* 45 (1999): 481–931; Norma Wilcox and Tracey Steele, "Just the Facts: A Descriptive Analysis of Inmate Attitudes toward Capital Punishment," *Prison Journal* 83 (2003): 464–483; Zhiqiang Liu, "Capital Punishment and the Deterrence Hypothesis: Some New Insights and Empirical Evidence," *Eastern Economic Journal* (Spring 2004); Steven Stack, "The Effect of Well-Publicized Executions on Homicide in California," *Journal of Crime and Justice* 21 (1998): 1–12; James Yunker, "A New Statistical Analysis of Capital Punishment Incorporating U.S. Postmoratorium Data," *Social Science Quarterly* 82 (2001): 297–312; Hashem Dezhbakhsh, Paul H. Rubin, and Joanna M. Shepherd, "Does Capital Punishment Have a Deterrent Effect? New Evidence from Postmoratorium Panel Data," *American Law and Economics Review* 5 (2003): 344–376.

sentenced to prison do not have lower rates of recidivism than those receiving more lenient community sentences for similar crimes. White-collar offenders who receive prison sentences are as likely to recidivate as those who receive community-based sanctions.[173]

In some instances, rather than reducing the frequency of crime, severe punishments may actually increase reoffending

rates.[174] Some states are now employing high security "supermax" prisons that use bare minimum treatment and 23-hours-a-day lockdown. Certainly such a harsh regimen should deter future criminality. But a recent study in the state of Washington that matched on a one-to-one basis supermax prisoners with inmates from more traditional prisons showed that upon release supermax prisoners had significantly higher felony recidivism rates than their nonsupermax controls. Those released directly into the community from a supermax prison committed new offenses sooner than supermax prisoners who were first sent to traditional institutions three months or more before their release.[175]

How is it possible that the harshest treatment increases rather than reduced crime?

▌ Punishment may bring defiance rather than deterrence. People who are harshly treated may want to show that they cannot be broken by the system.

▌ The stigma of harsh treatment labels people and helps lock offenders into a criminal career instead of convincing them to avoid one.

▌ Criminals who are punished may also believe that the likelihood of getting caught twice for the same type of crime is remote: "Lightning never strikes twice in the same spot," they may reason; no one is that unlucky.[176]

Domestic Violence Studies While these results are not encouraging, there are research studies that show that arrest and conviction may under some circumstances lower the frequency of reoffending, a finding that supports specific deterrence.[177] The most famous of these involve arrest and punishment for domestic violence. Yet, they also show that achieving specific deterrent effects may sometimes be elusive. In the classic study, Lawrence Sherman and Richard Berk had police officers in Minneapolis, Minnesota, randomly assign three separate outcomes to domestic assault cases they encountered on their beats:[178]

▌ Advice and mediation only

▌ Remove the assailant from the home for a period of eight hours

▌ Formally arrest the assailant

According to deterrence theory, arrest should have a greater impact than advice and mediation, and in this case it did. Sherman and Berk found that when police took formal action (arrest), the chance of recidivism was substantially less than with less punitive measures, such as warning offenders or ordering offenders out of the house for a cooling-off period. A six-month follow-up found that only 10 percent of those who were arrested repeated their violent behavior, while 19 percent of those advised and 24 percent of those sent away repeated their offenses. Sherman and Berk concluded that a formal arrest was the most effective means of controlling domestic violence, regardless of what happened to the offender in court, and the specific deterrent effect of arrest produced positive long-term outcomes.

The Minneapolis experiment deeply affected police operations around the nation. Atlanta, Chicago, Dallas, Denver, Detroit, New York, Miami, San Francisco, and Seattle, among other large cities, adopted policies encouraging arrests in domestic violence cases. A number of states adopted legislation mandating that police either take formal action in domestic abuse cases or explain in writing their failure to act. Nonetheless, replicating the Minneapolis experiment in five other locales—including Omaha, Nebraska, and Charlotte, North Carolina—

failed to duplicate the original results.[179] In these locales, formal arrest was not a greater deterrent to domestic abuse than warning or advising the assailant.

More recent efforts to link punishment and deterrence in domestic violence cases have also produced inconclusive results. A 2008 examination conducted by Andrew Klein and Terri Tobin of the abuse and criminal careers of 342 men arraigned in the Quincy, Massachusetts, District Court found that batterers were undeterred by arrest, prosecution, probation supervision, incarceration, and treatment. Although only a minority of the men in the study reabused (32 percent) or were arrested for any crime (43 percent) within a year of their first involvement with the justice system, over the next decade the majority (60 percent) were involved in a second incident and almost three-fourths were rearrested for a domestic abuse or non–domestic abuse crime. The implications of the domestic violence research is that even if punishment can produce a short-term specific deterrent effect, it fails to produce longer-term behavior change.[180]

Incapacitation

It stands to reason that if more criminals are sent to prison, the crime rate should go down. Because most people age out of crime, the duration of a criminal career is limited. Placing offenders behind bars during their prime crime years should lessen their lifetime opportunity to commit crime. The shorter the span of opportunity, the fewer offenses they can commit during their lives; hence crime is reduced. This theory, known as the incapacitation effect, seems logical, but does it work? The most recent data (2008) indicate that nationwide almost 1.6 million are in prison and that the inmate population has nearly tripled in 30 years; another 723,000 people are in local jails. The number of American adults is about 230 million, meaning that one in every 99.1 adults is behind bars.[181] Advocates of incapacitation suggest that this growth in the prison/jail population is directly responsible for the decade-long decline in the crime rate: by putting dangerous felons under lock and key for longer periods of time, the opportunity they have to commit crime is significantly reduced and so too is the crime rate.

Belief that strict incarceration can shape criminal choice and reduce crime rates has encouraged states to adopt tough sentencing laws such as the "three strikes and you're out" policy. This sentencing model mandates that people convicted of three felony offenses serve a mandatory life term without parole. Many states already employ habitual offender laws that provide long (or life) sentences for repeat offenders. Three strikes supporters credit the law for a significant drop in California's crime rate, among the sharpest decline in any state. At least 2 million fewer criminal incidents have occurred, including 6,700 fewer homicides, since the state's three strikes law took effect.[182]

Does Incarceration Control Crime? The fact that crime rates have dropped while the prison population has boomed supports those who suggest that incapacitating criminals is an effective crime control policy. This assumption seems logical considering how much crime chronic offenders commit each year and the fact that criminal opportunities are ended once

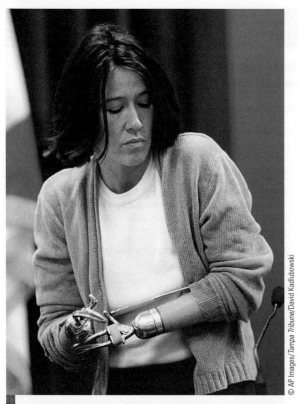

Simply put, if dangerous criminals were incapacitated, they would never have the opportunity to prey upon others. One of the most dramatic examples of the utility of incapacitation is the case of Lawrence Singleton, who in 1978 raped a young California girl, Mary Vincent, and then chopped off her arms with an axe. He served eight years in prison for this vile crime. Upon his release, he moved to Florida, where in 1997 he killed Roxanne Hayes. Vincent is shown here as she testifies at the penalty phase of Singleton's trial; he was sentenced to death. Should a dangerous predator such as Singleton ever be released from incapacitation? Is rehabilitation even a remote possibility?

they are behind bars. While it is difficult to measure precisely, there is at least some evidence that crime rates and incarceration rates are interrelated.[183] Economist Steven Levitt concludes that each person put behind bars results in a decrease of 15 serious crimes per year. He argues that the social benefits associated with crime reduction equal or exceed the social and financial costs of incarceration.[184]

connections

Chapter 2 discussed the factors that control crime rates. What appears to be an incapacitation effect may actually reflect the effect of some other legal phenomena and not the incarceration of so many criminals. If, for example, the crime rate drops as more people are sent to prison, it would appear that incapacitation works. However, crime rates may really be dropping because potential criminals now fear punishment and are being deterred from crime. What appears to be an incapacitation effect may actually be an effect of general deterrence. Similarly, people may be willing to build new prisons because the economy is robust. If the crime rate drops, it may be because of economic effects and not because of prison construction.

While Levitt's argument is persuasive, not all criminologists buy into the incapacitation effect:

- There is little evidence that incapacitating criminals will deter them from future criminality and even more reason to believe they may be more inclined to commit crimes upon release. The more prior incarceration experiences inmates have, the more likely they are to recidivate (and return to prison) within 12 months of their release.[185]

- By its nature, the prison experience exposes young, first-time offenders to higher-risk, more experienced inmates who can influence their lifestyle and help shape their attitudes. Novice inmates also run an increased risk of becoming infected with AIDS and other health hazards, and that exposure reduces their life chances after release.[186] The short-term crime-reduction effect of incapacitating criminals is negated if the prison experience has the long-term effect of escalating frequency of criminal behavior upon release.

- The economics of crime suggest that if money can be made from criminal activity, there will always be someone to take the place of the incarcerated offender. New criminals will be recruited and trained, offsetting any benefit accrued by incarceration. Imprisoning established offenders may likewise open new opportunities for competitors who were suppressed by more experienced criminals. Incarcerating gang members or organized crime figures may open crime and illegal drug markets to new groups and gangs who are even hungrier and more aggressive than the gangs they replaced.

- Most criminal offenses are committed by teens and very young adult offenders who are unlikely to be sent to prison for a single felony conviction. Aging criminals are already past the age when they are likely to commit crime. As a result, a strict incarceration policy may keep people in prison beyond the time they are a threat to society while a new cohort of high-risk adolescents is on the street.[187]

- An incapacitation strategy is terribly expensive. The prison system costs billions of dollars each year. Even if incarceration could reduce the crime rate, the costs would be enormous. Are U.S. taxpayers willing to spend billions more on new prison construction and annual maintenance fees? A strict incarceration policy would result in a growing number of elderly inmates whose maintenance costs, estimated at about $70,000 per year, are three times higher than those of younger inmates. Estimates are that about 16 percent of the prison population is over age 50.[188]

- Relying on incapacitation as a crime control mechanism has resulted in an ever-expanding prison population. Eventually most inmates return to society in a process referred to as reentry. In most states, prison inmates, especially those convicted of drug crimes, have come from comparatively few urban inner-city areas. Their return may contribute to family disruption, undermine social institutions, and create community disorganization. Rather than act as a crime suppressant, incarceration may have the long-term effect of accelerating crime rates.[189]

Three Strikes Laws So while on an individual level there is evidence that a stay in prison can reduce the length of a criminal career, there is some question whether increasing the size of the prison population can have a dramatic effect on crime rates.[190] Take the "three strikes and you're out" laws that require the state courts to hand down mandatory periods of incarceration of up to life in prison to persons who have been convicted of a serious criminal offense on three or more separate occasions. While a policy of placing people convicted of a third felony behind bars for life is politically compelling, many criminologists believe it will not work for these reasons:

▪ Most three-time losers are on the verge of aging out of crime, so why waste money by keeping them behind bars?

▪ Current sentences for violent crimes are already severe.

▪ An expanding prison population will drive up already high prison costs.

▪ There would be racial disparity in sentencing.

▪ Police would be in danger because two-time offenders would violently resist a third arrest knowing they face a life sentence.

▪ The prison population probably already contains the highest-frequency criminals.[191]

Concept Summary 4.1 outlines the various methods of crime control and their effects.

---

connections

As millions of former inmates reenter their old neighborhoods, they may become a destabilizing force, driving up crime rates. Chapter 6 discusses the effect of community disorganization on crime rates and efforts being made to maintain social control.

PUBLIC POLICY IMPLICATIONS OF CHOICE THEORY

From the origins of classical theory to the development of modern rational choice views, the belief that criminals choose to commit crime has influenced the relationship among law, punishment, and crime. Although research on the core principles of choice theory and deterrence theories produces mixed results, these models have had an important impact on crime prevention strategies.

When police patrol in well-marked cars, it is assumed that their presence will deter would-be criminals. When the harsh realities of prison life are portrayed in movies and TV shows, the lesson is not lost on potential criminals. Nowhere is the idea that the threat of punishment can control crime more evident than in the implementation of tough mandatory criminal sentences to control violent crime and drug trafficking.

CONCEPT SUMMARY 4.1

CRIME CONTROL STRATEGIES BASED ON RATIONAL CHOICE

Situational Crime Prevention

▪ This strategy is aimed at convincing would-be criminals to avoid specific targets. It relies on the doctrine that crime can be avoided if motivated offenders are denied access to suitable targets.

▪ Operationalizations of this strategy are home security systems or guards, which broadcast the message that guardianship is great here, stay away; the potential reward is not worth the risk of apprehension.

▪ Problems with the strategy are the extinction of the effect and displacement of crime.

General Deterrence Strategies

▪ These strategies are aimed at making potential criminals fear the consequences of crime. The threat of punishment is meant to convince rational criminals that crime does not pay.

▪ Operationalizations of these strategies are the death penalty, mandatory sentences, and aggressive policing.

▪ Problems with these strategies are that criminals do not fear punishment and the certainty of arrest and punishment is low.

Specific Deterrence Strategy

▪ This strategy refers to punishing known criminals so severely that they will never be tempted to repeat their offenses. If crime is rational, then painful punishment should reduce its future allure.

▪ Operationalizations of this strategy are harsh prisons and stiff fines.

▪ A problem with this strategy is that punishment may increase reoffending rates rather than deter crime.

Incapacitation Strategies

▪ These strategies attempt to reduce crime rates by denying motivated offenders the opportunity to commit crime. If, despite the threat of law and punishment, some people still find crime attractive, then the only way to control their behavior is to incarcerate them for extended periods.

▪ Operationalizations of these strategies are long prison sentences, placing more people behind bars.

▪ A problem with these strategies is that people are kept in prison beyond the years they may commit crime. Minor, nondangerous offenders are also locked up, and this is a very costly strategy.

Despite the ongoing debate about its deterrent effect, some advocates argue that the death penalty can effectively restrict criminality; at least it ensures that convicted criminals never again get the opportunity to kill. Many observers are dismayed because people who are convicted of murder sometimes kill again when released on parole. One study of 52,000 incarcerated murderers found that 810 had been previously convicted of murder and had killed 821 people following their previous release from prison.[192] About 9 percent of all inmates on death row have had prior convictions for homicide. Death penalty advocates argue that if these criminals had been executed for their first offenses, hundreds of people would be alive today.[193] Recent evidence indicating that if used frequently capital punishment can reduce a state's murder rate has encouraged some members of the moral and legal community to suggest that capital punishment is morally justified because it is a life-saving social policy. Writing in the *Stanford Law Review*, Cass Sunstein and Adrian Vermeule conclude that "a government that settles upon a package of crime-control policies that does *not* include capital punishment might well seem, at least prima facie, to be both violating the rights and reducing the welfare of its citizens—just as would a state that failed to enact simple environmental measures promising to save a great many lives."[194]

Just Desert

The concept of criminal choice has also prompted the creation of justice policies referred to as **just desert**. The just desert position has been most clearly spelled out by criminologist Andrew Von Hirsch in his book *Doing Justice*.[195] Von Hirsch suggests the concept of desert as a theoretical model to guide justice policy. This utilitarian view purports that punishment is needed to preserve the social equity disturbed by crime. Nonetheless, he claims, the severity of punishment should be commensurate with the seriousness of the crime.[196] Von Hirsch's views can be summarized in these three statements:

1. Those who violate others' rights deserve to be punished.

2. We should not deliberately add to human suffering; punishment makes those punished suffer.

3. However, punishment may prevent more misery than it inflicts; this conclusion reestablishes the need for desert-based punishment.[197]

Desert theory is also concerned with the rights of the accused. It alleges that the rights of the person being punished should not be unduly sacrificed for the good of others (as with deterrence). The offender should not be treated as more (or less) **blameworthy** than is warranted by the character of his or her offense. For example, Von Hirsch asks the following question: If two crimes, A and B, are equally serious, but if severe penalties are shown to have a deterrent effect only with respect to A, would it be fair to punish the person who has committed crime A more harshly simply to deter others from committing the crime? Conversely, imposing a light sentence for a serious crime would be unfair because it would treat the offender as less blameworthy than he or she is.

If deterrence is not a proper basis, then how do we determine how much punishment is fitting for a particular crime? In other words, how do we assess blame? According to legal scholar Richard Frase, two basic elements determine an offender's degree of blameworthiness: the nature and seriousness of the harm caused or threatened by the crime and the offender's degree of fault in committing the crime. In contemporary society, fault is measured by a number of factors: the offender's intent (e.g., deliberate wrongdoing is considered more serious than criminal negligence); his or her capacity to obey the law (e.g., blameworthiness is tempered by such conditions as mental disease or defect, chemical dependency, or situational factors such as threats or other strong inducements to commit the crime); the offender's motives for committing the crime (which may mitigate or aggravate culpability); and, for multidefendant crimes, the defendant's role in the offense as instigator, leader, follower, primary actor, or minor player.[198] According to Frase, fairness is brought to the justice process by assessing blame in a fair and even-handed manner: fairness to the victim and the victim's family (who might otherwise seek vengeance); fairness to law-abiding persons (who refrained from committing this offense); and fairness to the defendant (who has a right to be punished in proportion to his blameworthiness).

In sum, the just desert model suggests that retribution justifies punishment because people deserve what they get for past deeds. Punishment based on deterrence or incapacitation is wrong because it involves an offender's future actions, which cannot accurately be predicted. Punishment should be the same for all people who commit the same crime. Criminal sentences based on individual needs or characteristics are inherently unfair because all people are equally blameworthy for their misdeeds. The influence of Von Hirsch's views can be seen in sentencing models that give the same punishment to all people who commit the same type of crime.

THINKING LIKE A CRIMINOLOGIST

The attorney general has recently funded a national survey of state sentencing practices. The table provided here shows the most important findings from the survey. Disturbed that almost 20 percent of violent felons do not go to prison, including 17 percent of rapists and even some murderers, the attorney general has asked you to make some recommendations about criminal punishment. Is it possible, she asks, to require that violent criminals serve some time in prison, and could that rule have an impact on crime rates? What could be gained by either increasing punishment or requiring inmates to spend rational time behind bars before their release? Are we being too lenient or too punitive?

Table 4A Felony Sentences in State Courts

Most serious conviction offense	Percentage of felons convicted in state courts during 2004 sentenced to . . .			
	Incarceration		Nonincarceration	
	Prison	Jail	Probation	Other
All offenses	40	30	28	2
Violent offenses	54	24	20	2
Property offenses	37	31	30	2
Drug offenses	37	30	30	3
Weapon offenses	44	28	27	1
Other offenses	34	35	29	2

Note: Detail may not sum to total because of rounding. Data on sentence type were reported for 98% of all cases.
Source: Matthew Durose and Patrick Langan, *Felony Sentences in State Courts, 2004* (Washington DC: Bureau of Justice Statistics, 2007), www.ojp.usdoj.gov/bjs/pub/pdf/fssc04.pdf (accessed June 30, 2008).

 Writing Exercise As someone who has studied choice theory, how would you interpret these data, and what do they tell you about sentencing patterns? How might crime rates be affected if the way we punished offenders was radically changed? Write a letter to the attorney general outlining your recommendations and reasons.

 Doing Research on the Web The Bureau of Justice Statistics sponsors surveys that track cases for up to one year to provide a complete overview of the processing of felony defendants. There is also documentation on the development and use of truth-in-sentencing (TIS) laws that require convicted criminals to serve a longer amount of their sentence behind bars. Read Morgan Reynold's *Crime and Punishment in America* to learn more about the association between crime and expected punishment.

Go to academic.cengage.com/criminaljustice/siegel for the findings of the Bureau of Justice Statistics, to see how TIS laws influence sentencing, and to read *Crime and Punishment in America.*

SUMMARY

▪ Choice theories assume that criminals carefully choose whether to commit criminal acts. Choice theories include rational choice, situational crime

prevention, general deterrence, specific deterrence, and incapacitation.

▪ People are influenced by their fear of the criminal penalties associated with

being caught and convicted for law violations.

▪ The choice approach is rooted in the classical criminology of Cesare Beccaria, who argued that punishment should be certain, swift, and severe enough to deter crime.

■ Today, choice theorists identify offense-specific and offender-specific crimes. Offense-specific means that the characteristics of the crime determine whether it occurs. For example, carefully protecting a home means that it will be less likely to be a target of crime. Offender-specific refers to the personal characteristics of potential criminals. People with specific skills and needs may be more likely to commit crime than others.

■ Research shows that offenders consider their targets carefully before deciding on a course of action. Even violent criminals and drug addicts show signs of rationality.

■ By implication, crime can be prevented or displaced by convincing potential criminals that the risks of violating the law exceed the benefits. Situational crime prevention is the application of security and protective devices that make it more difficult to commit crime or that reduce criminal rewards.

■ Deterrence theory holds that if criminals are indeed rational, an inverse relationship should exist between punishment and crime. The certainty of punishment seems to deter crime. If people do not believe they will be caught, even harsh punishment may not deter crime.

■ Deterrence theory has been criticized on the grounds that it wrongfully assumes that criminals make a rational choice before committing crimes, it ignores the intricacies of the criminal justice system, and it does not take into account the social and psychological factors that may influence criminality. Research does not validate that the death penalty reduces the murder rate.

■ Specific deterrence theory holds that the crime rate can be reduced if known offenders are punished so severely that they never commit crimes again. There is little evidence that harsh punishment actually reduces the crime rate. Most prison inmates recidivate.

■ Incapacitation theory maintains that if deterrence does not work, the best course of action is to incarcerate known offenders for long periods so that they lack criminal opportunity. Research has not proved that increasing the number of people in prison—and increasing prison sentences—will reduce crime rates.

■ Choice theory has been influential in shaping public policy. Criminal law is designed to deter potential criminals and fairly punish those who have been caught in illegal acts. Some courts have changed sentencing policies to adapt to classical principles, and the U.S. correctional system seems to be aimed at incapacitation and specific deterrence.

■ The just desert view is that criminal sanctions should be geared precisely to the seriousness of the crime. People should be punished on the basis of whether they deserve to be punished for what they did and not because punishment may affect or deter their future behavior. The just desert concept argues that the use of punishment to deter or control crime is morally correct because criminals deserve to be punished for their misdeeds.

■ CENGAGENOW™ is an easy-to-use online resource that helps you study in less time to get the grade you want—NOW. CengageNOW™ Personalized Study (a diagnostic study tool containing valuable text-specific resources) lets you focus on just what you don't know and learn more in less time to get a better grade. If your textbook does not include an access code card, you can go to www.ichapters.com to purchase CengageNOW™.

KEY TERMS

rational choice (96)
marginal deterrence (96)
reasoning criminal (98)
offense-specific crime (99)
offender-specific crime (100)
boosters (102)
permeable neighborhood (103)
edgework (106)

situational crime prevention (106)
defensible space (106)
crime discouragers (107)
diffusion of benefits (109)
discouragement (109)
crime displacement (109)
extinction (109)
general deterrence (109)

tipping point (111)
crackdowns (111)
specific deterrence (113)
incapacitation effect (116)
just desert (119)
blameworthy (120)

CRITICAL THINKING QUESTIONS

1. Are criminals rational decision makers, or are they motivated by uncontrollable psychological and emotional drives?

2. Would you want to live in a society where crime rates are low because criminals are subjected to extremely harsh punishments, such as flogging for vandalism?

3. If you were caught by the police while shoplifting, which would you be more afraid of receiving, criminal punishment or having to face your friends or relatives?

4. Is it possible to create a method of capital punishment that would actually deter murder, for example, by televising executions? What might be some of the negative consequences of such a policy?

NOTES

1. Reuters News Service, "T. Boone Pickens' Son Gets Probation in Fraud Case," December 10, 2007, www.cnbc.com/id/22183588/ (accessed June 30, 2008); FBI, "Hot Stock Tip, Anyone? The Case of the Phony Faxes," November 20, 2006, www.fbi.gov/page2/nov06/stock_scam112006.htm (accessed June 16, 2008).

2. Francis Edward Devine, "Cesare Beccaria and the Theoretical Foundations of Modern Penal Jurisprudence," *New England Journal on Prison Law* 7 (1982): 8–21.

3. Ibid.

4. George J. Stigler, "The Optimum Enforcement of Laws," *Journal of Political Economy* 78 (1970): 526–528.

5. Bob Roshier, *Controlling Crime* (Chicago: Lyceum Books, 1989), p. 10.

6. Jeremy Bentham, *A Fragment on Government and an Introduction to the Principle of Morals and Legislation*, ed. Wilfred Harrison (Oxford: Basil Blackwell, 1967).

7. Ibid., p. xi.

8. Robert Martinson, "What Works? Questions and Answers about Prison Reform," *Public Interest* 35 (1974): 22–54.

9. Charles Murray and Louis Cox, *Beyond Probation* (Beverly Hills: Sage, 1979).

10. Ronald Bayer, "Crime, Punishment, and the Decline of Liberal Optimism," *Crime and Delinquency* 27 (1981): 190.

11. James Q. Wilson, *Thinking about Crime*, rev. ed. (New York: Vintage Books, 1983), p. 260.

12. Ibid., p. 128.

13. Michael Tonry, *Malign Neglect: Race, Crime and Punishment in America* (New York: Oxford University Press, 1995).

14. William J. Sabol, Heather Couture, and Paige M. Harrison, *Prisoners in 2006* (Washington, DC: Bureau of Justice Statistics, 2007).

15. John Irwin and James Austin, *It's about Time: America's Imprisonment Binge* (Belmont, CA: Wadsworth, 1997).

16. Kimberly Cook, "A Passion to Punish: Abortion Opponents Who Favor the Death Penalty," *Justice Quarterly* 15 (1998): 329–346.

17. See generally Derek Cornish and Ronald Clarke, eds., *The Reasoning Criminal: Rational Choice Perspectives on Offending* (New York: Springer Verlag, 1986); Philip Cook, "The Demand and Supply of Criminal Opportunities," in *Crime and Justice*, vol. 7, ed. Michael Tonry and Norval Morris (Chicago: University of Chicago Press, 1986), pp. 1–28; Ronald Clarke and Derek Cornish, "Modeling Offenders' Decisions: A Framework for Research and Policy," in *Crime and Justice*, vol. 6, ed. Michael Tonry and Norval Morris (Chicago: University of Chicago Press, 1985), pp. 147–187; and Morgan Reynolds, *Crime by Choice: An Economic Analysis* (Dallas: Fisher Institute, 1985).

18. David A. Ward, Mark C. Stafford, and Louis N. Gray, "Rational Choice, Deterrence, and Theoretical Integration" *Journal of Applied Social Psychology* 36 (2006): 571–585.

19. Hung-en Sung and Linda Richter, "Rational Choice and Environmental Deterrence in the Retention of Mandated Drug Abuse Treatment Clients," *International Journal of Offender Therapy and Comparative Criminology* 51 (2007): 686–702.

20. Melanie Wellsmith and Amy Burrell, "The Influence of Purchase Price and Ownership Levels on Theft Targets: The Example of Domestic Burglary," *British Journal of Criminology* 45 (2005): 741–764.

21. Jeffrey Bouffard, "Predicting Differences in the Perceived Relevance of Crime's Costs and Benefits in a Test of Rational Choice Theory," *International Journal of Offender Therapy and Comparative Criminology* 51 (2007): 461–485.

22. George Rengert and John Wasilchick, *Suburban Burglary: A Time and Place for Everything* (Springfield, IL: Charles C Thomas, 1985).

23. Carlo Morselli and Marie-Noële Royer, "Criminal Mobility and Criminal Achievement," *Journal of Research in Crime and Delinquency* 45 (2008): 4–21.

24. Ross Matsueda, Derek Kreager, and David Huizinga, "Deterring Delinquents: A Rational Choice Model of Theft and Violence," *American Sociological Review* 71 (2006): 95–122.

25. Jeffrey Bouffard, "Predicting Differences in the Perceived Relevance of Crime's Costs and Benefits in a Test of Rational Choice Theory," *International Journal of Offender Therapy and Comparative Criminology* 51 (2007): 461–485.

26. Christopher Uggen and Melissa Thompson, "The Socioeconomic Determinants of Ill-Gotten Gains: Within-Person Changes in Drug Use and Illegal Earnings," *American Journal of Sociology* 109 (2003): 146–187.

27. Philippe Bourgois, *In Search of Respect: Selling Crack in El Barrio* (Cambridge: Cambridge University Press, 1995), p. 326.

28. Derek Cornish and Ronald Clarke, "Understanding Crime Displacement: An Application of Rational Choice Theory," *Criminology* 25 (1987): 933–947.

29. Michael Gottfredson and Travis Hirschi, *A General Theory of Crime* (Stanford, CA: Stanford University Press, 1990).

30. Jeannette Angell, "Confessions of an Ivy League Hooker," *Boston Magazine*, August 2004, pp. 120–134.

31. Uggen and Thompson, "The Socioeconomic Determinants of Ill-Gotten Gains."

32. Pierre Tremblay and Carlo Morselli, "Patterns in Criminal Achievement: Wilson and Abrhamse Revisited," *Criminology* 38 (2000): 633–660.

33. Liliana Pezzin, "Earnings Prospects, Matching Effects, and the Decision to Terminate a Criminal Career," *Journal of Quantitative Criminology* 11 (1995): 29–50.

34. Ronald Akers, "Rational Choice, Deterrence, and Social Learning Theory in Criminology: The Path Not Taken," *Journal of Criminal Law and Criminology* 81 (1990): 653–676.

35. Neal Shover, *Aging Criminals* (Beverly Hills: Sage, 1985).

36. Patricia Morgan and Karen Ann Joe, "Citizens and Outlaws: The Private Lives and Public Lifestyles of Women in the Illicit Drug Economy," *Journal of Drug Issues* 26 (1996): 125–142, at 132.

37. Ibid., p. 136.

38. Bruce Jacobs, "Crack Dealers' Apprehension Avoidance Techniques: A Case of Restrictive Deterrence," *Justice Quarterly* 13 (1996): 359–381.

39. Ibid., p. 367.

40. Ibid., p. 372.

41. Gordon Knowles, "Deception, Detection, and Evasion: A Trade Craft Analysis of Honolulu, Hawaii's Street Crack Cocaine Traffickers," *Journal of Criminal Justice* 27 (1999): 443–455.

42. Bruce Jacobs and Jody Miller, "Crack Dealing, Gender, and Arrest Avoidance," *Social Problems* 45 (1998): 550–566.

43. Jacobs, "Crack Dealers' Apprehension Avoidance Techniques."

44. Ibid., p. 367.

45. Ibid., p. 368.

46. Eric Baumer, Janet Lauritsen, Richard Rosenfeld, and Richard Wright, "The Influence of Crack Cocaine on Robbery, Burglary, and Homicide Rates: A Cross-City, Longitudinal Analysis," *Journal of Research in Crime and Delinquency* 35 (1998): 316–340.

47. Michael Costanzo, William Halperin, and Nathan Gale, "Criminal Mobility and the Directional Component in Journeys to Crime," in *Metropolitan Crime Patterns*, ed. Robert Figlio, Simon Hakim, and George Rengert (Monsey, NY: Criminal Justice Press, 1986), pp. 73–95.

48. Morselli and Royer, "Criminal Mobility and Criminal Achievement."

49. Joseph Deutsch and Gil Epstein, "Changing a Decision Taken under Uncertainty: The Case of the Criminal's Location Choice," *Urban Studies* 35 (1998): 1,335–1,344.

50. Robert Sampson and Jacqueline Cohen, "Deterrent Effects of the Police on Crime: A Replication and Theoretical Extension," *Law and Society Review* 22 (1988): 163–188.

51. Kenneth Tunnell, *Choosing Crime* (Chicago: Nelson-Hall, 1992), p. 105.

52. Paul Bellair, "Informal Surveillance and Street Crime: A Complex Relationship," *Criminology* 38 (2000): 137–167.

53. Gary Kleck and Don Kates, *Armed: New Perspectives on Guns* (Amherst, NY: Prometheus Books, 2001).

54. Elizabeth Ehrhardt Mustaine and Richard Tewksbury, "Predicting Risks of Larceny Theft Victimization: A Routine Activity Analysis Using Refined Lifestyle Measures," *Criminology* 36 (1998): 829–858.

55. Bruce A. Jacobs and Richard Wright, "Researching Drug Robbery," *Crime and Delinquency*, December 2007 Online Edition, http://cad.sagepub.com/cgi/rapidpdf/0011128707307220v1 (accessed June 30, 2008).

56. Associated Press, "Thrift Hearings Resume Today in Senate," *Boston Globe*, 2 January 1991, p. 10.

57. Pamela Wilcox, Tamara Madensen, and Marie Skubak Tillyer, "Guardianship in Context: Implications for Burglary Victimization Risk and Prevention," *Criminology* 45 (2007): 771–803.

58. Garland White, "Neighborhood Permeability and Burglary Rates," *Justice Quarterly* 7 (1990): 57–67.

59. Ibid., p. 65.

60. Matthew Robinson, "Lifestyles, Routine Activities, and Residential Burglary Victimization," *Journal of Criminal Justice* 22 (1999): 27–52.

61. Cromwell, Olson, and Avary, *Breaking and Entering*.

62. Andrew Buck, Simon Hakim, and George Rengert, "Burglar Alarms and the Choice Behavior of Burglars: A Suburban Phenomenon," *Journal of Criminal Justice* 21 (1993): 497–507.

63. Ralph Taylor and Stephen Gottfredson, "Environmental Design, Crime, and Prevention: An Examination of Community Dynamics," in *Communities and Crime*, ed. Albert Reiss and Michael Tonry (Chicago: University of Chicago Press, 1986), pp. 387–416.

64. George Rengert and John Wasilchick, *Space, Time, and Crime: Ethnographic Insights into Residential Burglary* (Washington, DC: National Institute of Justice, 1989); see also Rengert and Wasilchick, *Suburban Burglary*.

65. Paul Cromwell, James Olson, and D'Aunn Wester Avary, *Breaking and Entering, an Ethnographic Analysis of Burglary* (Newbury Park, CA: Sage, 1989), pp. 30–32.

66. Ibid., p. 24.

67. John Gibbs and Peggy Shelly, "Life in the Fast Lane: A Retrospective View by Commercial Thieves," *Journal of Research in Crime and Delinquency* 19 (1982): 229–230.

68. "The Decline of the English Burglary, *The Economist* 371 (May 29, 2004): 59.

69. John Petraitis, Brian Flay, and Todd Miller, "Reviewing Theories of Adolescent Substance Use: Organizing Pieces in the Puzzle," *Psychological Bulletin* 117 (1995): 67–86.

70. Leanne Fiftal Alarid, James Marquart, Velmer Burton, Francis Cullen, and Steven Cuvelier, "Women's Roles in Serious Offenses: A Study of Adult Felons," *Justice Quarterly* 13 (1996): 431–454, at 448.

71. Ben Fox, "Jury Recommends Death for Convicted Child Killer," *Boston Globe*, 6 October 1999, p. 3.

72. Richard B. Felson, *Violence and Gender Reexamined* (Washington, DC: American Psychological Association, 2002).

73. Richard Felson and Steven Messner, "To Kill or Not to Kill? Lethal Outcomes in Injurious Attacks," *Criminology* 34 (1996): 519–545, at 541.

74. James Wright and Peter Rossi, *Armed and Considered Dangerous: A Survey of Felons and Their Firearms* (Hawthorne, NY: Aldine De Gruyter, 1983), pp. 141–159.

75. Gary Kleck and Marc Gertz, "Carry Guns for Protection: Results from the National Self-Defense Survey," *Journal of Research in Crime and Delinquency* 35 (1998): 193–224.

76. Peter Van Koppen and Robert Jansen, "The Time to Rob: Variations in Time and Number of Commercial Robberies," *Journal of Research in Crime and Delinquency* 36 (1999): 7–29.

77. William Smith, Sharon Glave Frazee, and Elizabeth Davison, "Furthering the Integration of Routine Activity and Social Disorganization Theories: Small Units of Analysis and the Study of Street Robbery as a Diffusion Process," *Criminology* 38 (2000): 489–521.

78. Wim Bernasco and Paul Nieuwbeerta, "How Do Residential Burglars Select Target Areas? A New Approach to the Analysis of Criminal Location Choice," *British Journal of Criminology* 45 (2005): 296–315.

79. Alan Lizotte, Marvin Krohn, James Howell, Kimberly Tobin, and Gregory Howard, "Factors Influencing Gun Carrying among Young Urban Males over the Adolescent–Young Adult Life Course," *Criminology* 38 (2000): 811–834.

80. Scott Decker, "Deviant Homicide: A New Look at the Role of Motives and Victim–Offender Relationships," *Journal of Research in Crime and Delinquency* 33 (1996): 427–449.

81. Felson and Messner, "To Kill or Not to Kill?"

82. Eric Hickey, *Serial Murderers and Their Victims* (Pacific Grove, CA: Brooks/Cole, 1991), p. 84.

83. Janet Warren, Roland Reboussin, Robert Hazlewood, Andrea Cummings, Natalie Gibbs, and Susan Trumbetta, "Crime Scene and Distance Correlates of Serial Rape," *Journal of Quantitative Criminology* 14 (1998): 35–58.

84. Benoit Leclerc, Jean Proulx, and André McKibben, "Modus Operandi of Sexual Offenders Working or Doing Voluntary Work with Children and Adolescents," *Journal of Sexual Aggression* 11 (2005): 187–195.

85. Laura Dugan, Gary Lafree, and Alex Piquero, "Testing a Rational Choice Model of Airline Hijackings," *Criminology* 43 (2005): 1,031–1,065.

86. Christopher Birkbeck and Gary LaFree, "The Situational Analysis of Crime and Deviance," *American Review of Sociology* 19 (1993): 113–137; Karen Heimer and Ross Matsueda, "Role-Taking, Role Commitment, and Delinquency: A Theory of Differential Social Control," *American Sociological Review* 59 (1994): 400–437.

87. Peter Wood, Walter Gove, James Wilson, and John Cochran, "Nonsocial Reinforcement and Habitual Criminal Conduct: An Extension of Learning," *Criminology* 35 (1997): 335–366.

88. Jeff Ferrell, "Criminological Versthen: Inside the Immediacy of Crime," *Justice Quarterly* 14 (1997): 3–23, at 12.

89. Michael Gottfredson and Travis Hirschi, *General Theory of Crime*.

90. Patricia Brantingham, Paul Brantingham, and Wendy Taylor, "Situational Crime Prevention as a Key Component in Embedded Crime Prevention," *Canadian Journal of Criminology and Criminal Justice* 47 (2005): 271–292.

91. Oscar Newman, *Defensible Space: Crime Prevention through Urban Design* (New York: Macmillan, 1973).

92. C. Ray Jeffery, *Crime Prevention through Environmental Design* (Beverly Hills: Sage, 1971).

93. See also Pochara Theerathorn, "Architectural Style, Aesthetic Landscaping, Home Value, and Crime Prevention," *International Journal of Comparative and Applied Criminal Justice* 12 (1988): 269–277.

94. Ronald Clarke, *Situational Crime Prevention: Successful Case Studies* (Albany, NY: Harrow and Heston, 1992).

95. Marcus Felson, "Routine Activities and Crime Prevention," in *National Council for Crime Prevention, Studies on Crime and Crime Prevention, Annual Review*, vol. 1 (Stockholm: Scandinavian University Press, 1992), pp. 30–34.

96. Derek Cornish and Ronald Clarke, "Opportunities, Precipitators and Criminal Decisions: A Reply to Wortley's Critique of Situational Crime Prevention," *Crime Prevention Studies* 16 (2003): 41–96; Ronald Clarke and Ross Homel, "A Revised Classification of Situational Prevention Techniques," in *Crime Prevention at a Crossroads*, ed. Steven P. Lab (Cincinnati: Anderson Publishing, 1997).

97. Barry Webb, "Steering Column Locks and Motor Vehicle Theft: Evaluations for Three Countries," in *Crime Prevention Studies*, ed. Ronald Clarke (Monsey, NY: Criminal Justice Press, 1994), pp. 71–89.

98. Barbara Morse and Delbert Elliott, "Effects of Ignition Interlock Devices on DUI Recidivism: Findings from a Longitudinal Study in Hamilton County, Ohio," *Crime and Delinquency* 38 (1992): 131–157.

99. Nancy LaVigne, "Gasoline Drive-Offs: Designing a Less Convenient Environment," in *Crime Prevention Studies*, vol. 2, ed. Ronald Clarke (New York: Criminal Justice Press, 1994), pp. 91–114.

100. Eric Fritsch, Tory Caeti, and Robert Taylor, "Gang Suppression through Saturation Patrol, Aggressive Curfew, and Truancy Enforcement: A Quasi-Experimental Test of the Dallas Anti-Gang Initiative," *Crime and Delinquency* 45 (1999): 122–139.

101. Kenneth Adams, "The Effectiveness of Juvenile Curfews at Crime Prevention," *The Annals of the American Academy of Political and Social Science* 587 (May 2003): 136–159.

102. Brantingham, Brantingham, and Taylor, "Situational Crime Prevention as a Key Component in Embedded Crime Prevention."

103. Marcus Felson, "Those Who Discourage Crime," in *Crime and Place, Crime Prevention Studies*, vol. 4, ed. John Eck and David Weisburd (New York: Criminal Justice Press, 1995), pp. 53–66; John Eck, "Drug Markets and Drug Places: A Case-Control Study of the Spatial Structure of Illicit Drug Dealing," Ph.D. diss., University of Maryland, College Park, 1994.

104. Eck, "Drug Markets and Drug Places," p. 29.

105. Lorraine Green Mazerolle, Colleen Kadleck, and Jan Roehl, "Controlling Drug and Disorder Problems: The Role of Place Managers," *Criminology* 36 (1998): 371–404.

106. "Pervert's Tough Sign-tence," *The Sun*, 26 Mar 2008, www.thesun.co.uk/sol/homepage/news/article960199.ece (accessed June 30, 2008).

107. Ronald Clarke, "Deterring Obscene Phone Callers: The New Jersey Experience," *Situational Crime Prevention*, ed. Ronald Clarke (Albany, NY: Harrow and Heston, 1992), pp. 124–132.

108. Bob Edward Vásquez, Sean Maddan, and Jeffery T. Walker, "The Influence of Sex Offender Registration and Notification Laws in the United States: A Time-Series Analysis," *Crime and Delinquency* 54 (2008): 175–192.

109. Ronald Clarke and David Weisburd, "Diffusion of Crime Control Benefits: Observations of the Reverse of Displacement," in *Crime Prevention Studies*, vol. 2, ed. Ronald Clarke (New York: Criminal Justice Press, 1994).

110. David Weisburd and Lorraine Green, "Policing Drug Hot Spots: The Jersey City Drug Market Analysis Experiment," *Justice Quarterly* 12 (1995): 711–734.

111. Lorraine Green, "Cleaning Up Drug Hot Spots in Oakland, California: The Displacement and Diffusion Effects," *Justice Quarterly* 12 (1995): 737–754.

112. Ian Ayres and Steven D. Levitt, "Measuring Positive Externalities from Unobservable Victim Precaution: An Empirical Analysis of Lojack," *Quarterly Journal of Economics* 113 (1998): 43–78.

113. Robert Barr and Ken Pease, "Crime Placement, Displacement, and Deflection," in *Crime and Justice, A Review of Research*, vol. 12, ed. Michael Tonry and Norval Morris (Chicago: University of Chicago Press, 1990), pp. 277–319.

114. Clarke, *Situational Crime Prevention*, p. 27.

115. Brandon Welsh and David Farrington, "Crime Prevention and Hard Technology: The Case of CCTV and Improved Street Lighting," in *The New Technology of Crime, Law, and Social Control*, ed. James Byrne and Donald Rebovich (Monsey, NY: Criminal Justice Press, 2007).

116. Daniel Nagin and Greg Pogarsky, "An Experimental Investigation of Deterrence: Cheating, Self-Serving Bias, and Impulsivity," *Criminology* 41 (2003): 167–195.

117. Silvia Mendes, "Certainty, Severity, and Their Relative Deterrent Effects: Questioning the Implications of the Role of Risk in Criminal Deterrence Policy," *Policy Studies Journal* 32 (2004): 59–74.

118. Nagin and Pogarsky, "Integrating Celerity, Impulsivity, and Extralegal Sanction Threats into a Model of General Deterrence."

119. Robert Bursik, Harold Grasmick, and Mitchell Chamlin, "The Effect of Longitudinal Arrest Patterns on the Development of Robbery Trends at the Neighborhood Level," *Criminology* 28 (1990): 431–450; Theodore Chiricos and Gordon Waldo, "Punishment and Crime: An Examination of Some Empirical Evidence," *Social Problems* 18 (1970): 200–217.

120. Etienne Blais and Jean-Luc Bacher, "Situational Deterrence and Claim Padding: Results from a Randomized Field Experiment," *Journal of Experimental Criminology* 3 (2007): 337–352.

121. R. Steven Daniels, Lorin Baumhover, William Formby, and Carolyn Clark-Daniels, "Police Discretion and Elder Mistreatment: A Nested Model of Observation, Reporting, and Satisfaction," *Journal of Criminal Justice* 27 (1999): 209–225.

122. Daniel Nagin and Greg Pogarsky, "Integrating Celerity, Impulsivity, and Extralegal Sanction Threats into a Model of General Deterrence: Theory and Evidence," *Criminology* 39 (2001): 865–892.

123. Timothy O'Shea, "Getting the Deterrence Message Out: The Project Safe Neighborhoods Public—Private Partnership," *Police Quarterly* 10 (2007): 288–306.

124. David Klinger, "Policing Spousal Assault," *Journal of Research in Crime and Delinquency* 32 (1995): 308–324.

125. Charles Tittle and Alan Rowe, "Certainty of Arrest and Crime Rates: A Further Test of the Deterrence Hypothesis," *Social Forces* 52 (1974): 455–462.

126. Daniels, Baumhover, Formby, and Clark-Daniels, "Police Discretion and Elder Mistreatment."

127. David Bayley, *Policing for the Future* (New York: Oxford, 1994).

128. George Kelling, Tony Pate, Duane Dieckman, and Charles Brown, *The Kansas City Preventive Patrol Experiment: A Summary Report* (Washington, DC: Police Foundation, 1974).

129. Tomislav V. Kovandzic and John J. Sloan, "Police Levels and Crime Rates Revisited, A County-Level Analysis from Florida (1980–1998)," *Journal of Criminal Justice* 30 (2002): 65–76; Steven Levitt, "Using Electoral Cycles in Police Hiring to Estimate the Effect of Police on Crime," *American Economic Review* 87 (1997): 70–91; Marvell and Moody, "Specification Problems, Police Levels, and Crime Rates."

130. Michael White, James Fyfe, Suzanne Campbell, and John Goldkamp, "The Police Role in Preventing Homicide: Considering the Impact of Problem-Oriented Policing on the Prevalence of Murder," *Journal of Research in Crime and Delinquency* 40 (2003): 194–226.

131. Kenneth Novak, Jennifer Hartman, Alexander Holsinger, and Michael Turner, "The Effects of Aggressive Policing of Disorder on Serious Crime," *Policing* 22 (1999): 171–190.

132. Lawrence Sherman, "Police Crackdowns," *NIJ Reports* (March/April 1990): 2–6, at 2.

133. Jacqueline Cohen, Wilpen Gorr, and Piyusha Singh, "Estimating Intervention Effects in Varying Risk Settings: Do Police Raids Reduce Illegal Drug Dealing at Nuisance Bars?" *Criminology* 42 (2003): 257–292.

134. Anthony Braga, David Weisburd, Elin Waring, Lorraine Green Mazerolle, William Spelman, and Francis Gajewski, "Problem-Oriented Policing in Violent Crime Places: A Randomized Controlled Experiment," *Criminology* 37 (1999): 541–580.

135. Fritsch, Caeti, and Taylor, "Gang Suppression through Saturation Patrol, Aggressive Curfew, and Truancy Enforcement."

136. Michael Smith, "Police-Led Crackdowns and Cleanups: An Evaluation of a Crime Control Initiative in Richmond, Virginia," *Crime and Delinquency* 47 (2001): 60–68.

137. Braga, Weisburd, Waring, Mazerolle, Spelman, and Gajewski, "Problem-Oriented Policing in Violent Crime Places."

138. Nagin and Pogarsky, "Integrating Celerity, Impulsivity, and Extralegal Sanction Threats into a Model of General Deterrence," pp. 884–885.

139. Daniel Kessler and Steven D. Levitt, "Using Sentence Enhancements to Distinguish between Deterrence and Incapacitation," *Journal of Law and Economics* 42 (1999): 343–363.

140. Cheryl Marie Webster, Anthony Doob, and Franklin Zimring, "Proposition 8 and Crime Rates in California: The Case of the Disappearing Deterrent," *Criminology and Public Policy* 5 (2006): 417–448.

141. Per-Olof Wikström, "Linking Individual, Setting and Acts of Crime. Situational Mechanisms and the Explanation of Crime," in *The Explanation of Crime: Contexts, Mechanisms and Development*, ed. Per-Olof Wikström and Robert Sampson (Cambridge: Cambridge University Press, 2006), pp. 61–107.

142. Per-Olof Wikström and Kyle Treiber, "The Role of Self-Control in Crime Causation: Beyond Gottfredson and Hirschi's General Theory of Crime," *European Journal of Criminology* 4 (2007): 237–264 at 246.

143. Donald Green, "Past Behavior as a Measure of Actual Future Behavior: An Unresolved Issue in Perceptual Deterrence Research," *Journal of Criminal Law and Criminology* 80 (1989): 781–804, at 803; Matthew Silberman, "Toward a Theory of Criminal Deterrence," *American Sociological Review* 41 (1976): 442–461; Linda Anderson, Theodore Chiricos, and Gordon Waldo, "Formal and Informal Sanctions: A Comparison of Deterrent Effects," *Social Problems* 25 (1977): 103–114. See also Maynard Erickson and Jack Gibbs, "Objective and Perceptual Properties of Legal Punishment and Deterrence Doctrine," *Social Problems* 25 (1978): 253–264; and Daniel Nagin and Raymond Paternoster, "Enduring Individual Differences and Rational Choice Theories of Crime," *Law and Society Review* 27 (1993): 467–485.

144. Harold Grasmick and Robert Bursik, "Conscience, Significant Others, and Rational Choices: Extending the Deterrence Model," *Law and Society Review* 24 (1990): 837–861, at 854.

145. Harold Grasmick, Robert Bursik, and Karyl Kinsey, "Shame and Embarrassment as Deterrents to Noncompliance with the Law: The Case of an Anti-Littering Campaign," paper presented at the annual meeting of the American Society of Criminology, Baltimore, November 1990, p. 3.

146. Harry Wallace, Julie Juola Exline, and Roy Baumeister, "Interpersonal Consequences of Forgiveness: Does Forgiveness Deter or Encourage Repeat Offenses?" *Journal of Experimental Social Psychology* 44 (2008): 453–460.

147. Thomas Peete, Trudie Milner, and Michael Welch, "Levels of Social Integration in Group Contexts and the Effects of Informal Sanction Threat on Deviance," *Criminology* 32 (1994): 85–105.

148. Richard D. Clark, "Celerity and Specific Deterrence: a Look at the Evidence," *Canadian Journal of Criminology* 30 (1988): 109–122.

149. Charles N. W. Keckler, "Life v. Death: Who Should Capital Punishment Marginally Deter?" *Journal of Law, Economics and Policy* 2 (2006): 101–161.

150. Yair Listokin, "Crime and (with a Lag) Punishment: The Implications of Discounting for Equitable Sentencing," *American Criminal Law Review* 44 (2007): 115–140.

151. Paternoster, "Decisions to Participate in and Desist from Four Types of Common Delinquency."

152. James Williams and Daniel Rodeheaver, "Processing of Criminal Homicide Cases in a Large Southern City," *Sociology and Social Research* 75 (1991): 80–88.

153. Greg Pogarsky, KiDeuk Kim, and Ray Paternoster, "Perceptual Change in the National Youth Survey: Lessons for Deterrence Theory and Offender Decision-Making," *Justice Quarterly* 22 (2005): 1–29.

154. Ernest Van Den Haag, "The Criminal Law as a Threat System," *Journal of Criminal Law and Criminology* 73 (1982): 709–785.

155. James A. Swartz and Arthur J. Lurigio, "Serious Mental Illness and Arrest: The Generalized Mediating Effect of Substance Use," *Crime and Delinquency* 53 (2007): 581–604.

156. David Lykken, "Psychopathy, Sociopathy, and Crime," *Society* 34 (1996): 30–38.

157. George Lowenstein, Daniel Nagin, and Raymond Paternoster, "The Effect of Sexual Arousal on Expectations of Sexual Forcefulness," *Journal of Research in Crime and Delinquency* 34 (1997): 443–473.

158. Ken Auletta, *The Under Class* (New York: Random House, 1982).

159. Foglia, "Perceptual Deterrence and the Mediating Effect of Internalized Norms among Inner-City Teenagers"; Raymond Paternoster, "Decisions to Participate in and Desist from Four Types of Common Delinquency: Deterrence and the Rational Choice Perspective," *Law and Society Review* 23 (1989): 7–29; Raymond Paternoster, "Examining Three-Wave Deterrence Models: A Question of Temporal Order and Specification," *Journal of Criminal Law and Criminology* 79 (1988): 135–163; Raymond Paternoster, Linda Saltzman, Gordon Waldo, and Theodore Chiricos, "Estimating Perceptual Stability and Deterrent Effects: The Role of Perceived Legal Punishment in the Inhibition of Criminal Involvement," *Journal of Criminal Law and Criminology* 74 (1983): 270–297; M. William Minor and Joseph Harry, "Deterrent and Experiential Effects in Perceptual Deterrence Research: A Replication and Extension," *Journal of Research in Crime and Delinquency* 19 (1982): 190–203; Lonn Lanza-Kaduce, "Perceptual Deterrence and Drinking and Driving among College Students," *Criminology* 26 (1988): 321–341.

160. Foglia, "Perceptual Deterrence and the Mediating Effect of Internalized Norms among Inner-City Teenagers," pp. 419–443.

161. Alex Piquero and George Rengert, "Studying Deterrence with Active Residential Burglars," *Justice Quarterly* 16 (1999): 451–462.

162. Steven Levitt and Sudhir Alladi Venkatesh, "An Economic Analysis of a Drug-Selling Gang's Finances," NBER Working Papers 6592 (Cambridge, MA: National Bureau of Economic Research, Inc., 1998).

163. Bill McCarthy, "New Economics of Sociological Criminology," *Annual Review of Sociology* (2002): 417–442.

164. Greg Pogarsky, "Identifying 'Deterrable' Offenders: Implications for Research on Deterrence," *Justice Quarterly* 19 (2002): 431–453.

165. Gary Kleck, Brion Sever, Spencer Li, and Marc Gertz, "The Missing Link in General Deterrence Research," *Criminology* 43 (2005): 623–660.

166. James Q. Wilson and Richard Herrnstein, *Crime and Human Nature* (New York: Simon & Schuster, 1985), p. 494.

167. Alicia Sitren and Brandon Applegate, "Testing the Deterrent Effects of Personal and Vicarious Experience with Punishment and Punishment Avoidance," *Deviant Behavior* 28 (2007): 29–55.

168. Christina Dejong, "Survival Analysis and Specific Deterrence: Integrating Theoretical and Empirical Models of Recidivism," *Criminology* 35 (1997): 561–576.

169. Paul Tracy and Kimberly Kempf-Leonard, *Continuity and Discontinuity in Criminal Careers* (New York: Plenum Press, 1996).

170. Lawrence Greenfeld, *Examining Recidivism* (Washington, DC: U.S. Government Printing Office, 1985).

171. Allen Beck and Bernard Shipley, *Recidivism of Prisoners Released in 1983* (Washington, DC: Bureau of Justice Statistics, 1989).

172. Dejong, "Survival Analysis and Specific Deterrence," p. 573.

173. David Weisburd, Elin Waring, and Ellen Chayet, "Specific Deterrence in a Sample of Offenders Convicted of White-Collar Crimes," *Criminology* 33 (1995): 587–607.

174. Dejong, "Survival Analysis and Specific Deterrence"; Raymond Paternoster and Alex Piquero, "Reconceptualizing Deterrence: An Empirical Test of Personal and Vicarious Experiences," *Journal of Research in Crime and Delinquency* 32 (1995): 251–258.

175. David Lovell, L. Clark Johnson, and Kevin Cain, "Recidivism of Supermax Prisoners in Washington State," *Crime and Delinquency* 53 (2007): 633–656.

176. Greg Pogarsky and Alex R. Piquero, "Can Punishment Encourage Offending? Investigating the 'Resetting' Effect," *Journal*

of *Research in Crime and Delinquency* 40 (2003): 92–117.

177. Doris Layton MacKenzie and Spencer De Li, "The Impact of Formal and Informal Social Controls on the Criminal Activities of Probationers," *Journal of Research in Crime and Delinquency* 39 (2002): 243–276.

178. Lawrence Sherman and Richard Berk, "The Specific Deterrent Effects of Arrest for Domestic Assault," *American Sociological Review* 49 (1984): 261–272;

179. Christopher Maxwell, Joel H. Garner, and Jeffrey A. Fagan, *The Effects of Arrest in Intimate Partner Violence: New Evidence from the Spouse Assault Replication Program* (Washington, DC: National Institute of Justice, 2001); J. David Hirschel, Ira Hutchison, and Charles Dean, "The Failure of Arrest to Deter Spouse Abuse," *Journal of Research in Crime and Delinquency* 29 (1992): 7–33; Franklyn Dunford, David Huizinga, and Delbert Elliott, "The Role of Arrest in Domestic Assault: The Omaha Experiment," *Criminology* 28 (1990): 183–206.

180. Andrew Klein and Terri Tobin, "A Longitudinal Study of Arrested Batterers, 1995–2005: Career Criminals," *Violence Against Women* 14 (2008): 136–157.

181. Pew Charitable Trust, *One in 100: Behind Bars in America 2008* (Washington, DC: Pew Charitable Trusts, 2008), www .pewcenteronthestates.org/uploadedFiles/One%20in%20100.pdf (accessed June 30, 2008).

182. Bobby Caina Calvan, "Calif. Initiative Seeks to Rewrite Three-Strikes Law," *Boston Globe*, 12 July 2004, p.1.

183. William Spelman, "Specifying the Relationship Between Crime and Prisons," *Journal of Quantitative Criminology* 24 (2008): 149–178.

184. Steven Levitt, "Why Do Increased Arrest Rates Appear to Reduce Crime: Deterrence, Incapacitation, or Measurement Error?" *Economic Inquiry* 36 (1998):353–372; see also Thomas Marvell and Carlisle Moody, "The Impact of Prison Growth on Homicide," *Homicide Studies* 1 (1997): 205–233.

185. John Wallerstedt, *Returning to Prison, Bureau of Justice Statistics Special Report* (Washington, DC: U.S. Department of Justice, 1984).

186. James Marquart, Victoria Brewer, Janet Mullings, and Ben Crouch, "The Implications of Crime Control Policy on HIV/AIDS-Related Risk among Women Prisoners," *Crime and Delinquency* 45 (1999): 82–98.

187. Jose Canela-Cacho, Alfred Blumstein, and Jacqueline Cohen, "Relationship between the Offending Frequency of Imprisoned and Free Offenders," *Criminology* 35 (1997): 133–171.

188. Kate King and Patricia Bass, "Southern Prisons and Elderly Inmates: Taking a Look Inside," paper presented at the annual meeting of the American Society of Criminology, San Diego, November 1997.

189. James Lynch and William Sabol, "Prisoner Reentry in Perspective," Urban Institute: www.urban.org/publications/410213.html (accessed June 30, 2008).

190. Rudy Haapanen, Lee Britton, and Tim Croisdale, "Persistent Criminality and Career Length," *Crime and Delinquency* 53 (2007): 133–155.

191. Marc Mauer, testimony before the U.S. Congress, House Judiciary Committee, on "Three Strikes and You're Out," March 1, 1994.

192. Stephen Markman and Paul Cassell, "Protecting the Innocent: A Response to the Bedeau-Radelet Study," *Stanford Law Review* 41 (1988): 121–170, at 153.

193. James Stephan and Tracy Snell, *Capital Punishment, 1994* (Washington, DC: Bureau of Justice Statistics, 1996), p. 8.

194. Cass R. Sunstein and Adrian Vermeule, "Is Capital Punishment Morally Required? Acts, Omissions, and Life-Life Tradeoffs," *Stanford Law Review* 58 (2006): 703–750 at 749.

195. Andrew Von Hirsch, *Doing Justice* (New York: Hill and Wang, 1976).

196. Ibid., pp. 15–16.

197. Ibid.

198. Richard Frase, "Punishment Purposes," *Stanford Law Review* 67 (2005): 67–85.

Trait Theories

On Monday, April 16, 2007, 23-year-old Seung-Hui Cho methodically took the lives of 32 people—27 students and 5 professors—at Virginia Tech before taking his own life.[1] In the aftermath of the tragedy, Cho was described as a loner unable to make social connections. He had been involuntarily institutionalized in a mental health facility. He became fixated on several female students who eventually complained to the police because he was showing up at their rooms and bombarding them with instant messages.[2] In a creative writing class, he read one of his poems in class, and its sinister content so frightened classmates that some did not show up the next time the class met.[3]

Ten months after the Virginia Tech incident, on February 14, 2008, another tragedy occurred at Northern Illinois University. Steven Kazmierczak, a former student who was currently enrolled in the school of social work at the University of Illinois at Urbana-Champaign, entered Cole Hall, a large auditorium-style lecture hall on the NIU campus, armed with a shotgun and three handguns. Standing on the stage he methodically began shooting into the crowded classroom, killing 5 and wounding 16 others before taking his own life. In the aftermath of the incident, Kazmierczak was described as "an outstanding student" who suffered from depression and anxiety. His girlfriend, Jessica Baty, confirmed that Kazmierczak was taking Xanax (an anti-anxiety drug), Ambien (a sleep aid), and Prozac (an antidepressant), but that he had stopped taking the Prozac about three weeks prior to the shooting. "He was anything but a monster," Baty said. "He was probably the nicest, most caring person ever."[4]

These two senseless tragedies remind us that at least in some instances the cause of crime is linked to mental or physical abnormality. How could two college students such as Cho and Kazmierczak engage in mass murder unless they were suffering from some form of mental instability or collapse? In the aftermath of the killings there seemed to be ample evidence that both were under severe psychological stress yet no one was able to foresee or predict their violent actions.

The image of a disturbed, mentally ill offender seems plausible because a generation of Americans has grown up on films and TV shows that portray violent criminals as mentally deranged and physically abnormal. Beginning with Alfred Hitchcock's film *Psycho*, producers have made millions depicting the ghoulish acts of people who at first seem normal and even friendly but turn out to be demented and dangerous. Lurking out there are fanatical patients (*Saw 1–3*), crazed babysitters (*The Hand that Rocks the Cradle*), frenzied airline passengers (*Red Eye*; *Turbulence*), deranged roommates (*Single White Female*), cracked neighbors (*Disturbia*), psychotic tenants (*Pacific Heights*), demented secretaries (*The Temp*), unhinged police (*Maniac Cop*), mad cab drivers (*The Bone Collector*), irrational fans (*The Fan*; *Misery*), abnormal girlfriends (*Fatal Attraction*) and boyfriends (*Fear*), unstable husbands (*Enough*; *Sleeping with the Enemy*) and wives (*Black Widow*), loony fathers (*The Stepfather*), mothers (*Friday the 13th, Part 1*), and grandmothers (*Hush*), unbalanced crime victims (*I Know What You Did Last Summer*), maniacal children (*The Good Son*; *Children of the Corn*), manic vacationers (*Hostel*; *Touristas*), lunatic high school friends (*Scream*) and college classmates (*Scream II*), possessed dolls (*Child's Play 1–5*) and their mates (*Bride of Chucky*), and nutsy teenaged admirers (*The Crush*). Sometimes they even try to kill each other (*Freddy vs. Jason*). No one can ever be safe when the psychologists and psychiatrists who should be treating these disturbed people turn out to be demonic murderers themselves (*Hannibal*; *Silence of the Lambs*; *Red Dragon*). Is it any wonder that we respond to a particularly horrible crime by saying of the perpetrator, "That guy must be crazy" or "She is a monster!"

The view that criminals bear physical and/or mental traits that make them different and abnormal is not restricted to the movie-going public. Since the nineteenth century, some criminologists have suggested that biological and psychological traits may influence behavior. They believe that people may develop physical or mental traits at birth or soon after that affect their social functioning over the life course and influence their behavior choices.[5]

What may appear to some as the effect of environment and socialization may be actually linked to genetically determined physical and/or mental traits. Recent research by Kevin Beaver shows that environmental influences may have less effect on behavior than previously assumed.[6] If environmental influences have relatively little effect, as Beaver found, what does shape behavior choices over the life course? Psychologist Bernard Rimland, for one, argues that childhood behavior problems that are commonly linked to poor environment, disrupted socialization, or inadequate parenting actually stem from neurological abnormality. In his 2008 book, *Dyslogic Syndrome*, Rimland disputes the notion that bad or ineffective parenting is to blame for troubled or disobedient children:

> . . . most "bad" children . . . suffer from toxic physical environments, often coupled with genetic vulnerability, rather than toxic family environments. . . . research clearly shows that the culprits primarily responsible for the dyslogical behavior of millions of America's children are not their parents, but rather the poor-quality food substitutes they eat, the pollutants in the air they breathe, the chemically contaminated water they drink, and other less well-known physical insults that cause malfunctioning brains and bodies. Many of these children are labeled "hyperactive" or "attention disordered." Some are labeled "conduct disordered." Some are labeled "oppositional." Thousands are labeled "depressed" or "bipolar." And many are simply dismissed as hopelessly warped or evil. They struggle at school, they struggle through life, and in their wake they leave a trail of misery—of disrupted and saddened lives. But it's not truly their fault, and it's rarely their parents' fault.[7]

According to another expert on human behavior, Barbara Oakley, some people have a genetically produced Machiavellian core: even after they harm us and do evil deeds, we are willing give them the benefit of the doubt; they are "successfully sinister." Not surprisingly, Oakley believes that Machiavellian behavior is a function of inherited genetic structure. But genes alone do not dictate behavior: environment, experiences, and circumstances interact with genes to shape behavior. Even when these "malignant narcissists" seem successful, their lives are actually troubled and they leave behind a trail of emotional scars on people with whom they come into contact.[8]

So it is possible that inherited and/or developed personal traits and biological makeup, interacting with parenting or social environment, explain the direction of behavioral choices. The fact that each of us has a unique physical makeup and personality structure explains why, when faced with the same life situations, one person commits crime and becomes a chronic offender, whereas another attends school, church, and neighborhood functions and obeys the laws of society. It also explains why without social and environmental triggers even the most troubled people may remain crime free and live a relatively normal life.

To understand this view of crime causation, we begin with a brief review of the development of trait theories.

FOUNDATIONS OF TRAIT THEORY

As you may recall, Cesare Lombroso's work on the "born criminal" identified the primitive, atavistic anomalies that he believed were the direct cause of crime. Lombroso was not alone in his views on the biological basis of crime. A contemporary, Raffaele Garofalo (1852–1934), shared the belief that certain physical characteristics indicate a criminal nature: "a lower degree of sensibility to physical pain, seems to be demonstrated by the readiness with which prisoners submit to the operation of tattooing."[9]

Enrico Ferri (1856–1929) added a social dimension to Lombroso's work and argued that criminals should not be held personally or morally responsible for their actions because forces outside their control caused criminality.[10]

Advocates of the inheritance school such as Henry Goddard, Richard Dugdale, and Arthur Estabrook traced several generations of crime-prone families (referred to by pseudonyms the "Jukes" and the "Kallikaks"), finding evidence that criminal tendencies were based on genetics.[11] Their conclusion: traits deemed socially inferior could be passed down from generation to generation through inheritance. Modern scholars point out that these families lived in severe poverty, so that social rather than biological factors may have been at the root of their problems.[12]

The body build or somatotype school, developed more than 50 years ago by William Sheldon, held that criminals manifest distinct physiques that make them susceptible to particular types of antisocial behavior. Three types of body builds were identified:

- *Mesomorphs* have well-developed muscles and an athletic appearance. They are active, aggressive, sometimes violent, and the most likely to become criminals.

- *Endomorphs* have heavy builds and are slow moving. They are known for lethargic behavior rendering them unlikely to commit violent crime and more willing to engage in less strenuous criminal activities such as fencing stolen property.

- *Ectomorphs* are tall, thin, and less social and more intellectual than the other types.[13]

The work of Lombroso and his contemporaries is regarded today as a historical curiosity, not scientific fact. Their research methodology has been discredited because they did not use control groups from the general population to compare results. Many of the traits they assumed to be inherited are not really genetically determined but could be caused by deprivation in surroundings and diet. Even if most criminals shared some biological traits, they might be products not of heredity but of some environmental condition, such as poor nutrition or health care. Unusual appearance, and not behavior, may have prompted people to be labeled and punished by the justice system. In his later writings, even Lombroso admitted that the born criminal was just one of many criminal types.

Because of these deficiencies the validity of biological/psychological explanations of criminality became questionable and, for a time, disregarded by the criminological mainstream. At midcentury, sociology dominated the study of crime and scholarship, and any suggestion that antisocial behavior may have an individual-level cause was treated with enmity.[14] Some criminologists have gone as far as to label this position as biophobia, the view that no serious consideration should be given to biological factors when attempting to understand human nature.[15]

Sociobiology

What seems no longer tenable at this juncture is any theory of human behavior which ignores biology and relies exclusively on socio-cultural learning. . . . Most social scientists have been wrong in their dogmatic rejection and blissful ignorance of the biological parameters of our behavior.[16]

In the early 1970s, spurred by the publication of *Sociobiology*, by biologist Edmund O. Wilson, the biological basis for crime once again emerged into the limelight.[17] Sociobiology differs from earlier theories of behavior in that it stresses that biological and genetic conditions affect how social behaviors are learned and perceived. These perceptions, in turn, are linked to existing environmental structures. Sociobiologists view the gene as the ultimate unit of life that controls all human destiny. Although they believe that environment and experience also have an impact on behavior, their main premise is that most actions are controlled by a person's "biological machine." Most important, people are controlled by the innate need to have their genetic material survive and dominate others. Consequently, they do everything in their power to ensure their own survival and that of others who share their gene pool (relatives, fellow citizens, and so forth). Even when they come to the aid of others, which is called reciprocal altruism, people are motivated by the belief that their actions will be reciprocated and that their gene survival capability will be enhanced.

The study of sociobiology revived interest in finding a biological basis for crime and delinquency. If, as it suggests, biological (genetic) makeup controls human behavior, it follows that it should also be responsible for determining whether a person chooses law-violating or conventional behavior. This view of crime causation is referred to as trait theory.

Contemporary Trait Theories

Trait theorists today do not suggest that a single biological or psychological attribute is thought to adequately explain all criminality. Rather, each offender is considered unique, physically and mentally; consequently, there must be different explanations for each person's behavior. Some may have inherited criminal tendencies, others may be suffering from nervous system (neurological) problems, and still others may have a blood chemistry disorder that heightens their antisocial activity. Criminologists who focus on the individual see many explanations for crime, because, in fact, there are many differences among criminal offenders.

Trait theorists are not overly concerned with legal definitions of crime; they do not try to explain why people violate particular statutory laws such as car theft or burglary. To them, these are artificial legal concepts based on arbitrary boundaries (i.e., speeding may be arbitrarily defined as exceeding 65 miles per hour in some areas, 70 in others). Instead, trait theorists focus on basic human behavior and drives—attachment, aggression, violence, impulsivity—that are linked to antisocial behavior patterns. They also recognize that human traits may not alone produce criminality and that crime-producing interactions involve both personal traits—such as intelligence, personality, and chemical and genetic makeup—and environmental factors, such as family life, educational attainment, economic factors, and neighborhood conditions. Physical or mental traits are, therefore, but one part of a large pool of environmental, social, and personal factors that account for criminality. Some people may have a predisposition toward aggression, but environmental stimuli can either suppress or trigger antisocial acts.

Even the most committed trait theorists recognize that environmental conditions in disadvantaged inner-city areas may have a powerful influence on antisocial behavior. Many people who reside in these areas experience poverty, racism, frustration, and anger, yet relatively few become delinquents and even fewer mature into adult criminals. Because not all humans are born with equal potential to learn and achieve (**equipotentiality**), the combination of physical traits and the environment produces individual behavior patterns. Trait theorists argue that those who do become chronic offenders suffer some biological/psychological condition or trait that renders them incapable of resisting social pressures and problems.[18] As biocriminologists Anthony Walsh and Lee Ellis conclude, "If there is one takeaway lesson from studying biological bases of behavior, it is that the more we study them the more we realize how important the environment is."[19]

Trait theories have gained recent prominence because of what is now known about chronic recidivism and the development of criminal careers. If only a small percentage of all offenders go on to become persistent repeaters, then it is possible that what sets them apart from the criminal population is an abnormal biochemical makeup, brain structure, or genetic constitution.[20] Even if criminals do "choose crime," the fact that some repeatedly make that choice could well be linked to their physical and mental makeup. All people may be aware of and even fear the sanctioning power of the law, but some are unable to control their urges and passions.

Trait theories can be divided into two major subdivisions: one that stresses psychological functioning and another that stresses biological makeup. Although there is often overlap between these views (i.e., brain functioning may have a biological basis), each branch has its unique characteristics and will be discussed separately.

BIOLOGICAL TRAIT THEORIES: BIOSOCIAL THEORY

Rather than view the criminal as a person whose behavior is controlled solely by conditions determined at birth, most biocriminologists believe that physical, environmental, and social conditions work in concert to produce human behavior. Because of this integrated approach, this view is commonly referred to as **biosocial theory** (see Figure 5.1). The following subsections will examine some of the more important schools of thought within biosocial theory.[21] First, we look at the biochemical factors that are believed to affect behavior. Then the relationship of brain function and crime will be considered, followed by an analysis of genetics and crime. Finally, evolutionary views of crime causation are evaluated.

Biochemical Conditions and Crime

Some trait theorists believe biochemical conditions, including both those that are genetically predetermined and those acquired through diet and environment, control and influence antisocial behavior.[22] The influence of damaging chemical and biological contaminants may begin even before birth if the mother's diet either lacks or has an excess of important nutrients (such as manganese) that may later cause developmental problems in their offspring.[23] Maternal alcohol abuse and smoking during gestation have long been linked to prenatal damage and subsequent antisocial behavior in adolescence.[24] Once recent study by Lisa Gatzke-Kopp and Theodore Beauchaine examined relations between maternal smoking and child behavior among 133 women and their children aged 7 to 15.[25] The researchers compared women who smoked during pregnancy with (a) those who did not smoke, and (b) those who did not smoke but experienced significant secondhand exposure. Gatzke-Kopp and Beauchaine found that exposure to smoke was associated with increased psychopathology in offspring and that exposure to secondhand cigarette

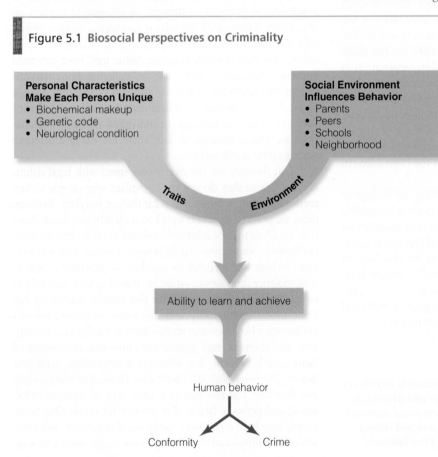

Figure 5.1 Biosocial Perspectives on Criminality

Personal Characteristics Make Each Person Unique
- Biochemical makeup
- Genetic code
- Neurological condition

Social Environment Influences Behavior
- Parents
- Peers
- Schools
- Neighborhood

Traits   Environment

Ability to learn and achieve

Human behavior

Conformity   Crime

While some crimes are rational and seem to be the product of planning and thought, others seem irrational and random. If crime were not assumed to be a function of biological and mental personal traits why would criminal offenders be evaluated by mental health professionals? Take the case of Leeland Eisenberg, shown here at the Strafford County house of corrections Dover, New Hampshire, during his video arraignment in Rochester District Court on December 3, 2007. District Court Judge Daniel Cappiello ordered a mental evaluation for Eisenberg, who was accused of taking workers hostage at a Hillary Rodham Clinton campaign office after his demands to speak to the presidential candidate about health care were denied. The justice system recognizes that the cause of crime may have biological/psychological underpinnings.

smoke during pregnancy predicted conduct disorder symptoms even when controlling for such influences as income, parental antisocial tendencies, prematurity, low birth weight, and poor parenting practices.

In sum, exposure to harmful chemicals and poor diet in utero, at birth, and beyond may then affect people throughout their life course. Some of the more important biochemical factors that have been linked to criminality are set out in detail here.

Chemical and Mineral Influences Biosocial criminologists maintain that minimum levels of minerals and chemicals are needed for normal brain functioning and growth, especially in the early years of life. Research conducted over the past decade shows that an over- or undersupply of certain chemicals and minerals—including sodium, mercury potassium, calcium, amino acids, monoamines, and peptides—can lead to depression, mania, cognitive problems, memory loss, and abnormal sexual activity.[26] Common food additives such as calcium propionate, which is used to preserve bread, have been linked to problem behaviors.[27] Even some commonly used medicines may have detrimental side effects. There has been recent research

linking sildenafil, more commonly known as Viagra, with aggressive and violent behavior. While the cause is still unknown, it is possible that sildenafil exerts various biochemical and physiologic effects in the brain and that it affects information processing.[28]

In some instances the influence of chemicals and minerals is direct. Research now shows that people who start drinking by the age of 14 are five times more likely to become alcoholics than people who hold off on drinking until the age of 21. It is possible that early exposure of the brain to alcohol may short-circuit the growth of brain cells, impairing the learning and memory processes that protect against addiction. Thus, early ingestion of alcohol will have a direct influence on behavior.[29]

In other cases, the relationship between biochemical makeup and antisocial behavior is indirect. Chemical and mineral imbalance leads to cognitive and learning deficits and problems, and these factors in turn are associated with antisocial behaviors.[30] Research shows that excessive intake of certain metals such as iron and manganese may be linked to neurological dysfunctions such as intellectual impairment and attention deficit hyperactivity disorder (ADHD). These neurological conditions are believed to be a precursor of delinquent and criminal behaviors.[31] In a recent international study, Hong Kong researchers D. K. L. Cheuk and Virginia Wong measured the blood mercury levels of 52 children diagnosed with ADHD and compared them to another group of 59 non-ADHD adolescents. After controlling for numerous personal and social factors, Cheuk and Wong found that the ADHD children had significantly higher mercury levels than the controls. While the sample size they used was small, they were able to conclude that mercury poisoning, both prenatal and after birth, can have a detrimental effect on cognitive functions and cause behavioral problems later in life that have been associated with crime and delinquency.[32]

Diet and Crime If biochemical makeup can influence behavior, then it stands to reason that food intake and diet are related to crime.[33] Those biocriminologists who believe in a diet–aggression association claim that in every segment of society there are violent, aggressive, and amoral people whose improper food, vitamin, and mineral intake may be responsible for their antisocial behavior. If diet could be improved, they believe, the frequency of violent behavior would be reduced.[34]

In some instances, the absence in the diet of certain chemicals and minerals—including sodium, potassium, calcium, amino acids, magnesium, monoamines, and peptides—can lead to depression, mania, cognitive problems, memory loss, and abnormal sexual activity.[35] In contrast, research shows that excessive amounts of harmful substances such as food dyes and artificial colors and/or flavors seem to provoke hostile, impulsive, and otherwise antisocial behaviors.[36] Take for instance a recent study that tested 153 3-year-olds and 144 children between the ages of 8 and 9 by exposing them to three different drink combinations:

▪ "Mix A" contained the additives sunset yellow, carmoisine, tartrazine, ponceau 4R, and sodium benzoate, chemicals typically found in two single-serving bags of candy.

▪ "Mix B" contained sunset yellow, carmoisine, quinoline yellow, allura red, and sodium benzoate, equaled to what is in two to four bags of candy.

▪ The third drink was a placebo with no additives.

Using a carefully planned experimental design, the researchers found that Mix A markedly worsened the younger children's hyperactivity scores, and that both Mix A and Mix B affected older children adversely.[37]

One area of diet that has received a great deal of attention is the association between high intakes of carbohydrates and sugar and antisocial behavior. Experiments have been conducted in which children's diets were altered so that sweet drinks were replaced with fruit juices, table sugar with honey, molasses substituted for sugar in cooking, and so on; results indicate that these changes can reduce aggression levels.[38] Although these results are impressive, a number of biologists have questioned this association, and some recent research efforts have failed to find a link between sugar consumption and violence.[39] In one important study, a group of researchers had 25 preschool children and 23 school-age children described as sensitive to sugar follow a different diet for three consecutive three-week periods. One diet was high in sucrose, the second substituted aspartame (NutraSweet) for a sweetener, and the third relied on saccharin. Careful measurement of the subjects found little evidence of cognitive or behavioral differences that could be linked to diet. If anything, sugar seemed to have a calming effect on the children.[40]

In sum, while some research efforts allege a sugar–violence association, others suggest that many people who maintain diets high in sugar and carbohydrates are not violent or crime prone. In some cases, in fact, sugar intake has been found to possibly reduce or curtail violent tendencies.[41] Recent experimental research conducted in the United States and abroad has found that diet and crime may be significantly related. The Comparative Criminology feature "Diet and Crime: An International Perspective" reviews some of these findings.

Glucose Metabolism/Hypoglycemia Research shows that persistent abnormality in the way the brain metabolizes glucose (sugar) can be linked to antisocial behaviors such as substance abuse.[42] Hypoglycemia occurs when glucose in the blood falls below levels necessary for normal and efficient brain functioning. The brain is sensitive to the lack of blood sugar because it is the only organ that obtains its energy solely from the combustion of carbohydrates. Thus, when the brain is deprived of blood sugar, it has no alternate food supply to call upon, and brain metabolism slows down, impairing function. Symptoms of

hypoglycemia include irritability, anxiety, depression, crying spells, headaches, and confusion.

Research studies have linked hypoglycemia to outbursts of antisocial behavior and violence.[43] Several studies have related assaults and fatal sexual offenses to hypoglycemic reactions.[44] Hypoglycemia has also been connected with a syndrome characterized by aggressive and assaultive behavior, glucose disturbance, and brain dysfunction. Some attempts have been made to measure hypoglycemia using subjects with a known history of criminal activity. Studies of jail and prison inmate populations have found a higher than normal level of hypoglycemia.[45] High levels of reactive hypoglycemia have been found in groups of habitually violent and impulsive offenders.[46]

Hormonal Influences Criminologist James Q. Wilson, in his book *The Moral Sense*, concludes that hormones, enzymes, and neurotransmitters may be the key to understanding human behavior. According to Wilson, they help explain gender differences in the crime rate. Males, he writes, are biologically and naturally more aggressive than females, while women are naturally more nurturing due to the fact they are ones who bear and raise children.[47] Hormone levels also help explain the aging-out process. Levels of testosterone, the principal male steroid hormone, decline during the life cycle and may explain why violence rates diminish over time.[48]

A number of biosocial theorists are now evaluating the association between violent behavior episodes and hormone levels, and the findings suggest that abnormal levels of male sex hormones (androgens) do in fact produce aggressive behavior.[49] In particular, in one recent study Lee Ellis and his associates found that self-reported violent criminality was positively correlated with masculine mannerisms, masculine body appearance, physical strength, strength of sex drive, low-deep voice, upper body strength, lower body strength, and amount of body hair.[50] Other androgen-related male traits include sensation seeking, impulsivity, dominance, and lesser verbal skills; all of these androgen-related male traits are related to antisocial behaviors.[51] There is a growing body of evidence suggesting that hormonal changes are also related to mood and behavior and, concomitantly, that adolescents experience more intense mood swings, anxiety, and restlessness than their elders.[52] An association between hormonal activity and antisocial behavior is suggested because rates of both factors peak in adolescence.[53]

One area of concern has been testosterone, the most abundant androgen, which controls secondary sex characteristics, such as facial hair and voice timbre. Excessive levels of testosterone have been linked to violence and aggression.[54] Studies of prisoners show that testosterone levels are higher in men who commit violent crimes than in the general population.

Hormonal differences may be a key to understanding gender differences in the crime rate. Females may be biologically protected from deviant behavior in the same way they are immune from some diseases that strike males.[55] Girls who have high levels of testosterone or are exposed to testosterone *in utero* may become more aggressive in adolescence.[56]

Conversely, boys who were prenatally exposed to steroids that decrease androgen levels display decreased aggressiveness in adolescence. Gender differences in the crime rate then may be explained by the relative difference in androgens between the two sexes.

Hormonal changes may also be able to explain regional and temporal differences in the crime rate. We know that violent crime rates vary from month to month in a seasonal pattern peaking in the summer, and that crime rates are higher in the warmer West and South regions than the cooler Northeast and Midwest. Evidence also shows that impulsive work-related behavior such as strikes and quitting jobs are more likely to occur during the summer. How can these phenomena be explained? It is possible they are due to the side effects of stress hormones such as adrenaline, which the body generates to cope with thermal heat stress. As heat rises, people get irritable, and the body produces excess hormones, which are directly related to aggression and antisocial behaviors.[57]

How Hormones Influence Behavior Hormones cause areas of the brain to become less sensitive to environmental stimuli. High androgen levels require people to seek excess stimulation and to be willing to tolerate pain in their quest for thrills. Androgens are linked to brain seizures that, under stressful conditions, can result in emotional volatility. Androgens affect the brain structure itself. They influence the left hemisphere of the neocortex, the part of the brain that controls sympathetic feelings toward others.[58] Here are some of the physical reactions produced by hormones that have been linked to violence:

▪ A lowering of average resting arousal under normal environmental conditions to a point that individuals are motivated to seek unusually high levels of environmental stimulation and are less sensitive to harmful aftereffects resulting from this stimulation

▪ A lowering of seizure thresholds in and around the limbic system, increasing the likelihood that stressful environmental factors will trigger strong and impulsive emotional responses

▪ A rightward shift in neocortical functioning, resulting in an increased reliance on the brain hemisphere that is most closely integrated with the limbic system and is least prone to reason in logical-linguistic forms or to respond to linguistic commands[59]

These effects promote violence and other serious crimes by causing people to seek greater levels of environmental stimulation and to tolerate more punishment, increasing impulsivity, emotional volatility, and antisocial emotions.[60]

Drugs that decrease testosterone levels are now being used to treat male sex offenders.[61] The female hormones, estrogen and progesterone, have been administered to sex offenders to decrease their sexual potency.[62] The long-term side effects of this treatment and the potential dangers are still unknown.[63]

Premenstrual Syndrome Hormonal research has not been limited to male offenders. The suspicion has long existed that the onset of the menstrual cycle triggers excessive amounts of the female sex hormones, which affect antisocial, aggressive behavior. This condition is commonly referred to as premenstrual syndrome, or PMS.[64] The link between PMS and delinquency was first popularized more than 35 years ago by Katharina Dalton, whose studies of English women indicated that females are more likely to commit suicide and be aggressive and otherwise antisocial just before or during menstruation.[65] Based on her findings, lawyers began using PMS as a legal criminal defense that was accepted in courts in England and the United States.[66]

Dalton's research is often cited as evidence of the link between PMS and crime, but methodological problems make it impossible to accept her findings at face value. There is still significant debate over any link between PMS and aggression. Some doubters argue that the relationship is spurious; it is equally likely that the psychological and physical stress of aggression brings on menstruation and not vice versa.[67]

Diana Fishbein, a noted expert on biosocial theory, concludes that there is in fact an association between elevated levels of female aggression and menstruation. Research efforts, she argues, show (a) that a significant number of incarcerated females committed their crimes during the premenstrual phase and (b) that at least a small percentage of women appear vulnerable to cyclical hormonal changes, which makes them more prone to anxiety and hostility.[68] While the debate is ongoing, it is important to remember that the overwhelming majority of females who do suffer anxiety reactions prior to and during menstruation do not actually engage in violent criminal behavior; so any link between PMS and crime is tenuous at best.[69]

Allergies Allergies are defined as unusual or excessive reactions of the body to foreign substances.[70] For example, hay fever is an allergic reaction caused when pollen cells enter the body and are fought or neutralized by the body's natural defenses. The result of the battle is itching, red eyes and active sinuses.

Cerebral allergies cause an excessive reaction in the brain, whereas neuroallergies affect the nervous system. Neuroallergies and cerebral allergies are believed to cause the allergic person to produce enzymes that attack wholesome foods as if they were dangerous to the body.[71] They may also cause swelling of the brain and produce sensitivity in the central nervous system, conditions linked to mental, emotional, and behavioral problems. Research indicates a connection between allergies and hyperemotionality, depression, aggressiveness, and violent behavior.[72]

Neuroallergy and cerebral allergy problems have also been linked to hyperactivity in children, a condition also linked to antisocial behavior. The foods most commonly involved in producing such allergies are cow's milk, wheat, corn, chocolate, citrus, and eggs; however, about 300 other foods have been identified as allergens. The potential seriousness of the problem has been raised by studies linking the average consumption of one suspected cerebral allergen, corn, to cross-national homicide rates.[73]

Environmental Contaminants When the Centers for Disease Control and Prevention (CDC) conducted a very extensive

Comparative Criminology

DIET AND CRIME: AN INTERNATIONAL PERSPECTIVE

Can what you eat control your behavior? Some recent experimental studies conducted around the world have shown that diet and crime may have a significant association.

▮ Research conducted in the United States, Britain, Canada, Australia, and Argentina seems to link homicide rates and omega-6 fats found in corn, safflower, soybean, cottonseed, and sunflower oils. National Institutes of Health scientists found that murder rates were 20 times higher in countries with the highest omega-6 intake, compared with those with the lowest. Within these countries, homicide rates rose over time in direct proportion to increasing omega-6 consumption.

▮ A recent study conducted in India found that violent criminals have lower overall cholesterol levels than members of the general population.

▮ Adrian Raine and his colleagues charted the long-term effects of a two-year diet enrichment program for 3-year-olds in the African nation of Mauritania. One hundred randomly selected children were placed in the program, which provided them with nutritious lunches, physical exercise, and enhanced education. They were then compared with a control group made up of children who did not participate in the program. By age 17, kids who had been malnourished before they entered the nutrition program had higher scores on physical and psychological well-being than malnourished kids who had not been in the program. By age 23, the malnourished kids who had been in the program 20 years earlier still did better on personality tests and had lower levels of self-reported crimes than the malnourished children who not been placed in the program. Overall, the results showed that providing children with nutritious diets and enriched environments is associated with greater mental health and reduced antisocial activities later in life.

▮ Bernard Gesch and his associates studied the behavior of 231 inmates at a British maximum security prison. Half of the group received daily capsules containing vitamins, minerals, and essential fatty acids, such as omega-3 and omega-6, while the other half took placebo pills. Antisocial behavior among inmates was recorded before and during distribution of the dietary supplements. Gesch found that the supplement group broke prison rules 25 percent less than those on the placebo. The greatest reduction was for serious offenses—instances of fighting, assaulting guards, or taking hostages dropped 37 percent. There was, however, no significant change in the control group.

▮ A Finnish study of 115 depressed outpatients being treated with antidepressants found that those who responded fully to treatment had higher levels of vitamin B12 in their blood at the beginning of treatment and six months later. Depression has been linked to antisocial activities. The researchers speculated that vitamin B12 deficiency leads to the accumulation of the amino acid homocysteine, which has been linked to depression.

▮ Carlos Iribarren and associates examined the relationship between omega-3 intake and hostility. Using a sample of 3,600 young adults living in urban environments around the United States, Iribarren and colleagues controlled for a wide range of factors and found that a higher consumption of the omega-3 fatty acid docosahexaenoic acid (DHA), or of omega-3-rich fish in general, was related to significantly lower levels of hostility.

▮ In Holland, the Justice Ministry's National Agency of Correctional Institutions (DJI) carried out a study in close cooperation with the Radboud University of Nijmegen to determine the association between diet and behavior among institutionalized offenders. Between 2005 and 2007, 221 juvenile and adult offenders from eight institutions were the subjects: 116 offenders received nutritional supplements and 105 received placebos. The nutritional supplements contained vitamins, minerals, and essential fatty acids. The prisoners used the

evaluation of chemical and mineral contamination in the United States just a few years ago, it found that despite some significant improvements there are still many dangerous substances in the environment, including lead, copper, cadmium, mercury, and inorganic gases, such as chlorine and nitrogen dioxide.[74] Prolonged exposure to these substances can cause severe illness or death; at more moderate levels, they have been linked to emotional and behavioral disorders.[75] Among the suspects that have been linked to developmental delays and emotional problems are chemicals used in the agricultural business in insecticides and pesticides. One such substance, chlorpyrifos, is now banned for residential use but is still allowed for agriculture and commercial enterprises. Recent research by Virginia Rauh and her colleagues found that children exposed to large amounts of chlorpyrifoss before birth maintain an increased risk for personal problems such as attention deficit hyperactivity disorder. Highly exposed children were significantly more likely to score lower on measures of psychomotor products for between one and three months. The number of reports and offences recorded was used to measure their levels of aggression and how often they breached regulations. Additionally, aggression was measured by using questionnaires and through observation of the prisoners. Psychiatric complaints, including fear and despondency, were also recorded. The study found small but nevertheless significant differences between the two groups, indicating that diet may indeed have an important influence on aggression. While behavioral differences were recorded, psychological differences between the groups were insignificant.

▪ A recent British review of existing research on the association between diet and crime conducted by Courtney Van de Weyer found that a combination of nutrients was significantly associated with good mental health and well-being, as follows:

• Polyunsaturated fatty acids (particularly the omega-3 types found in oily fish and some plants)
• Minerals, such as zinc (in whole grains, legumes, meat, and milk), magnesium (in green leafy vegetables, nuts, and whole grains), and iron (in red meat, green leafy vegetables, eggs, and some fruit)
• Vitamins, such as folate (in green leafy vegetables and fortified cereals), a range of B vitamins (whole grain products, yeast, and dairy products), and antioxidant vitamins such as C and E (in a wide range of fruits and vegetables)

▪ People eating diets that lack one or more of this combination of polyunsaturated fats, minerals, and vitamins, and/or contain too much saturated fat (or other elements, including sugar and a range of food and agricultural chemicals) seem to be at higher risk of developing the following conditions:

• Attention deficit hyperactivity disorder (ADHD)
• A range of depressive conditions
• Schizophrenia
• Dementia, including Alzheimer's disease

▪ People are eating too much saturated fat, sugar, and salt and not enough vitamins and minerals. This diet is not only fueling obesity, cardiovascular disease, diabetes, and some cancers, but may also be contributing to rising rates of mental ill-health and antisocial behavior.

Though more research is needed before the scientific community reaches a consensus on the specific association between diet and crime, there is mounting evidence that vitamins, minerals, chemicals, and other nutrients from a diet rich in fruits, vegetables, and whole grains can improve brain function, basic intelligence, and academic performance. In contrast, those lacking in proper diet seem at greatest risk to antisocial behaviors.

CRITICAL THINKING

1. If biocriminologists are correct in their thinking about diet and crime, should schools be required to provide a proper and nutritious lunch for all children?

2. How would a biocriminologist explain the aging-out process? Hint: Do people eat better as they mature? What about after they get married? How would biocriminologists explain regional differences in the crime rate? Do people in New England eat better than those in the far West?

Sources: Dutch Ministry of Justice, "Further Study Required into Food and Aggression Relationship," press release, February 7, 2007, http://english .justitie.nl/currenttopics/pressreleases/archives2007/ 70704further-study-required-into-food-and-aggression-relationship.aspx (accessed July 9, 2008); Nandini Chakrabarti and V. K. Sinha, "A Study of Serum Lipid Profile and Serum Apolipoproteins A1 and B in Indian Male Violent Criminal Offenders," *Criminal Behaviour and Mental Health* 16 (2006): 177–182; Courtney Van de Weyer, "Changing Diets, Changing Minds: How Food Affects Mental Well Being and Behaviour," *Sustain: The Alliance for Better Food and Farming,* www.sustainweb.org/publications/ (accessed July 9, 2008); Adrian Raine, Kjetil Mellingen, Jianghong Liu, Peter Venables, and Sarnoff Mednick, "Effects of Environmental Enrichment at Age Three to Five Years on Schizotypal Personality and Antisocial Behavior at Ages Seventeen and Twenty-Three Years," *American Journal of Psychiatry* 160 (2003): 1–9; Gloria McVeigh, "Calming Foods," *Prevention* 77 (2005); Jukka Hintikka, Tommi Tolmunen, Antti Tanskanen, and Heimo Viinamäki, "High Vitamin B12 Level and Good Treatment Outcome May Be Associated in Major Depressive Disorder," *BMC Psychiatry* 3 (2003): 17–18; C. Iribarren, J. H. Markovitz, D. R. Jacobs, Jr., P. J. Schreiner, M. Daviglus, and J. R. Hibbeln, "Dietary Intake of Omega-3, Omega-6 Fatty Acids and Fish: Relationship with Hostility in Young Adults—The CARDIA Study," *European Journal of Clinical Nutrition* 58 (2004): 24–31; C. Bernard Gesch, Sean M. Hammond, Sarah E. Hampson, Anita Eves, and Martin J. Crowder, "Influence of Supplementary Vitamins, Minerals, and Essential Fatty Acids on the Antisocial Behaviour of Young Adult Prisoners: Randomized, Placebo-Controlled Trial," *British Journal of Psychiatry* 181 (2002): 22–28.

and mental development.[76] These outcomes have been linked to antisocial behavior.

connections

The link between neurological deficiencies such as ADHD and antisocial behavior will be discussed more fully later in this chapter.

Lead Levels A number of recent research studies have suggested that lead ingestion is linked to aggressive behaviors on both a macro or group/nation level and on a micro or individual case level.[77]

On a macro level, areas with the highest concentrations of lead also report the highest levels of homicide.[78] Examining changes in lead levels in the United States, Britain, Canada, France, Australia, Finland, Italy, West Germany, and New Zealand

Benita Nahimana (foreground left), 3, plays with her sister Sophia and neighbor Gloria on the chipped-paint wood floor in their old apartment with parents Regina and Razaro nearby. Now in a new home, Benita is still recovering from being exposed to lead poisoning in the apartment. Some criminologists believe that early and prolonged exposure to lead is related to antisocial behavior in adolescence.

(lead levels changed when nations phased out lead-containing paint and gasoline), economist Rick Nevin found that long-term worldwide trends in crime levels correlate significantly with changes in environmental levels of lead. Nevin discovered that children exposed to higher levels of lead during the preschool developmental years engaged in higher rates of offending when they reached their late teens and early 20s. His conclusion: 65 to 90 percent or more of the substantial variation in violent crime in all these countries was explained by lead. In the United States, juvenile arrest rates skyrocketed in the 1960s, an increase that tracked the increase in the use of leaded gas usage after World War II. As the use of leaded gas declined, so too did crime rates.[79]

On a micro level, research finds that even limited exposure to lead can have a deleterious influence on a child's development and subsequent behavior and correlates significantly with neurological conditions such as hyperactivity.[80] Delinquents are almost four times more likely to have high bone lead levels than children in the general population.[81] Criminologist Deborah Denno investigated the behavior of more than 900 African American youth and found that lead poisoning was one of the most significant predictors of male delinquency and persistent adult criminality.[82] Herbert Needleman and his associates have conducted a number of studies indicating that youths who had high lead concentrations in their bones were much more likely to report attention problems, delinquency, and aggressiveness than those who were lead free.[83] Recent research shows that almost any elevated level of lead ingestion is related to lower IQ scores, a factor linked to aggressive behavior.[84] There is also evidence linking lead exposure to mental illnesses, such as schizophrenia, which have been linked to antisocial behaviors.[85]

The CDC survey found that among children ages 1 to 5, the average blood lead level was about 2.2 percent, which was down from 4.4 percent a decade ago. While the improvement is welcome, exposure of children to lead in homes containing lead-based paint and lead-contaminated dust remains a serious public health concern.[86] Research also shows that lead effects may actually begin in the womb due to the mother's dietary consumption of foods that are high in lead content, such as seafood.[87] Improved prenatal care may help mothers avoid the danger of lead exposure and reduce long-term crime rates.

Neurophysiological Conditions and Crime

Some researchers focus their attention on neurophysiology, the study of brain activity.[88] They believe neurological and physical abnormalities are acquired as early as the fetal or prenatal stage or through birth delivery trauma and that they control behavior throughout the life span.[89]

Studies conducted in the United States and in other nations have indicated that the relationship between impairment in executive brain functions (such as abstract reasoning, problem-solving skills, and motor behavior skills) and aggressive behavior is significant.[90] Children who suffer from measurable neurological deficits at birth are believed to also suffer from a number of antisocial traits throughout their life course, ranging from habitual lying to antisocial violence.[91]

The association between neurological disorder and antisocial behaviors may take a number of different paths:

▪ *Direct association*. Neurological deficits may be a direct cause of antisocial behavior, including violent offending.[92] The presence of brain abnormality causes irrational and destructive behaviors. Clinical analysis of convicted murderers by Peer Briken and colleagues found that a significant number (31 percent) showed evidence of brain abnormalities, including epilepsy, traumatic brain injury, childhood encephalitis or meningitis causing brain damage, genetic disorders, and unspecified brain damage.[93] In addition, the subjects with brain abnormalities were significantly more likely to commit multiple murders.

▪ *Indirect association*. Being in possession of a neurological impairment leads to the development of personality traits that are linked to antisocial behaviors. For example, impulsivity and lack of self-control have been linked to antisocial behavior. While the prevailing wisdom is that self-control is a product of socialization and upbringing, there is now evidence that self-control may in fact be regulated and controlled by the prefrontal cortex of the brain.[94] Under this scenario, neurological impairment reduces impulse- and self-control and leads to damaging behavioral choices.

■ *Interactive cause.* Neurological deficits may interact with another trait or social condition to produce antisocial behaviors. Take, for instance, research conducted by Adrian Raine, which found that kids who had experienced birth complications indicative of neurological impairment and had also experienced maternal rejection as they matured were more likely to engage in criminal offending than boys who did not experience these symptoms.[95] The combination of neurological dysfunction and maternal rejection had a more powerful influence on behavior than either of these conditions alone.

Measuring Neurological Impairment There are numerous ways to measure neurological functioning, including memorization and visual awareness tests, short-term auditory memory tests, and verbal IQ tests. These tests have been found to distinguish criminal offenders from noncriminal control groups.[96]

Traditionally, the most important measure of neurophysiological functioning is the electroencephalograph (EEG), which records the electrical impulses given off by the brain.[97] It represents a signal composed of various rhythms and transient electrical discharges, commonly called brain waves, which can be recorded by electrodes placed on the scalp. The frequency is given in cycles per second, measured in hertz (Hz), and usually ranges from 0.5 to 30 Hz. Studies using the EEG find that violent criminals have far higher levels of abnormal EEG recordings than nonviolent or one-time offenders. Although about 5 percent of the general population have abnormal EEG readings, about 50 to 60 percent of adolescents with known behavior disorders display abnormal recordings.[98] Behaviors highly correlated with abnormal EEG included poor impulse control, inadequate social adaptation, hostility, temper tantrums, and destructiveness.[99] Studies of adults have associated slow and bilateral brain waves with hostile, hypercritical, irritable, nonconforming, and impulsive behavior.[100]

Newer brain scanning techniques, using electronic imaging such as positron emission tomography (PET), brain electrical activity mapping (BEAM), single photon emission computed tomography (SPECT), and the superconducting quantum interference device (SQUID), have made it possible to assess which areas of the brain are directly linked to antisocial behavior.[101] Violent criminals have been found to have impairment in the prefrontal lobes, thalamus, hypothalamus, medial temporal lobe, superior parietal, and left angular gyrus areas of the brain.[102] Some research using PET shows that domestic violence offenders have lower metabolism in the right hypothalamus and decreased correlations between cortical and subcortical brain structures than a group of control subjects.[103] Another recent study by Daniel Amen and his colleagues employed SPECT to test a sample of people convicted of an impulsive murder. They found that these offenders suffer from a condition that reduces blood flow to a region of the brain involved with planning and self-control. Because this area of the brain is believed to control anger management, those who suffer the reduced blood flow may be limited in their self-control, planning, and understanding of future consequences when challenged or forced to concentrate.[104]

It is possible that antisocial behavior is influenced by what is referred to as prefrontal dysfunction, a condition that occurs when demands on brain activity overload the prefrontal cortex and result in a lack of control over antisocial behaviors. Because the prefrontal lobes have not fully developed in adolescence, it is not surprising that this is the time that violent behavior peaks.[105]

Minimal Brain Dysfunction (MBD) MBD is related to an abnormality in cerebral structure. It has been defined as an abruptly appearing, maladaptive behavior that interrupts an individual's lifestyle and life flow. In its most serious form, MBD has been linked to serious antisocial acts, an imbalance in the urge-control mechanisms of the brain, and chemical abnormality. Included in the category of minimal brain dysfunction are several abnormal behavior patterns: dyslexia, visual perception problems, hyperactivity, poor attention span, temper tantrums, and aggressiveness. One type of minimal brain dysfunction is manifested through episodic periods of explosive rage. This form of the disorder is considered an important cause of such behavior as spouse beating, child abuse, suicide, aggressiveness, and motiveless homicide. One perplexing feature of this syndrome is that people who are afflicted with it often maintain warm and pleasant personalities between episodes of violence. Some studies measuring the presence of MBD in offender populations have found that up to 60 percent exhibit brain dysfunction on psychological tests.[106] Criminals have been characterized as having a dysfunction of the dominant hemisphere of the brain.[107] Researchers using brain wave data have predicted with 95 percent accuracy the recidivism of violent criminals.[108] More sophisticated brain scanning techniques, such as PET, have also shown that brain abnormality is linked to violent crime.[109]

Learning Disabilities One specific type of MBD that has generated considerable interest is learning disability (LD), a disorder in one or more of the basic psychological processes involved in understanding or using spoken or written language. Learning disabled children usually exhibit poor motor coordination (for example, problems with poor hand-eye coordination, trouble climbing stairs, clumsiness), have behavior problems (lack of emotional control, hostility, cannot stay on task), and have improper auditory and vocal responses (do not seem to hear, cannot differentiate sounds and noises).[110] Though learning disabilities are quite common (approximately 10 percent of all youths have some form of learning disorders), estimates of LD among youths who engage in antisocial behavior is far higher.[111]

What is the link between antisocial behavior and learning disabilities? There are two popular explanations:

■ *Susceptibility rationale* argues that the link is caused by certain side effects of learning disabilities, such as impulsiveness, poor ability to learn from experience, and inability to take social cues.

■ *School failure rationale* assumes that the frustration caused by the LD produces poor school performance leading to a negative self-image and acting-out behavior.

Some recent research conducted by Tomer Einat and Amela Einat in Israel might help settle this issue. They found that a far higher percentage of Israeli prison inmates (69.6 percent) were characterized as learning disabled, as opposed to an estimated 10 to 15 percent of the general Israeli population. Among the inmates, learning disabilities were correlated both with low level of education (i.e., dropping out of school at an early age) and early age of criminal onset. Their conclusion: people with learning disabilities who give up school at early stages due to their disabilities are more likely to initiate a criminal career at an early age, as compared to individuals—with or without learning disabilities—who do not leave school. Helping LD kids adjust to school may also help them avoid criminal careers.[112]

Attention Deficit Hyperactivity Disorder (ADHD) Many parents have noticed that their children do not pay attention to them—they run around and do things in their own way. Sometimes this inattention is a function of age; in other instances, it is a symptom of attention deficit hyperactivity disorder (ADHD), in which a child shows a developmentally inappropriate lack of attention, impulsivity, and hyperactivity. The various symptoms of ADHD are described in Exhibit 5.1.

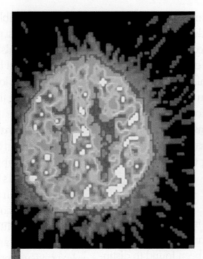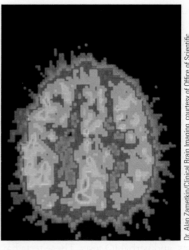

Dr. Alan Zametkin/Clinical Brain Imaging, courtesy of Office of Scientific Information, NIMH

This scan compares a normal brain (left) and an ADHD brain (right). Areas of orange and white demonstrate a higher rate of metabolism, while areas of blue and green represent an abnormally low metabolic rate. Why is ADHD so prevalent in the United States today? Some experts believe that our immigrant forebears, risk takers who impulsively left their homelands for life in a new world, may have brought with them a genetic predisposition for ADHD.

EXHIBIT 5.1

Symptoms of Attention Deficit Hyperactivity Disorder (ADHD)

Lack of Attention

- Frequently fails to finish projects
- Does not seem to pay attention
- Does not sustain interest in play activities
- Cannot sustain concentration on schoolwork or related tasks
- Is easily distracted

Impulsivity

- Frequently acts without thinking
- Often "calls out" in class
- Does not want to wait his or her turn in lines or games
- Shifts from activity to activity
- Cannot organize tasks or work
- Requires constant supervision

Hyperactivity

- Constantly runs around and climbs on things
- Shows excessive motor activity while asleep
- Cannot sit still; is constantly fidgeting
- Does not remain in his or her seat in class
- Is constantly on the go like a "motor"

Source: Adapted from American Psychiatric Association, *Diagnostic and Statistical Manual of Mental Disorders*, 4th ed. (Washington, DC: American Psychiatric Press, 1994).

About 3 percent of U.S. children (most often boys, but the condition can also affect girls) are believed to suffer from this disorder, and it is the most common reason children are referred to mental health clinics. ADHD has been associated with poor school performance, grade retention, placement in special needs classes, bullying, stubbornness, and lack of response to discipline. Although the origin of ADHD is still unknown, suspected causes include neurological damage, prenatal stress, and even reactions to food additives and chemical allergies. Some psychologists believe that the syndrome is essentially a chemical problem, specifically, an impairment in the chemical system that supports rapid and efficient communication in the brain's management system.[113]

There are also ties to family turmoil: parents of ADHD children are more likely to be divorced or separated, and ADHD children are much more likely to move to new locales than non-ADHD children.[114] It may be possible then that emotional turmoil either produces symptoms of ADHD or, if they already exist, causes them to intensify.

A series of research studies now links ADHD to the onset and sustenance of a delinquent career.[115] Children with ADHD are more likely to use illicit drugs, alcohol, and cigarettes in adolescence; to be arrested; to be charged with a felony; and to have multiple arrests than non-ADHD youths. There is some evidence that ADHD youths who also exhibit early signs of MBD and conduct disorder (e.g., fighting) are the most at risk for persistent antisocial behaviors continuing into adulthood.[116] Many ADHD children also suffer from conduct disorder (CD) and continually engage in aggressive and antisocial behavior in early childhood. The disorders are sustained over the life course: children diagnosed as ADHD are more likely to be suspended from school and engage in criminal behavior as adults. This ADHD–crime association is important because symptoms of ADHD seem stable through adolescence into adulthood.[117] Hyperactive/ADHD children are at greater risk for adolescent antisocial activity and drug use/abuse that persists into adulthood.[118]

How is ADHD treated? Today, the most typical treatment is doses of stimulants, such as Ritalin, which ironically help control emotional and behavioral outbursts. Other therapies, such as altering diet and food intake, are now being investigated.[119] However, treatment is not always effective. While some treated children with ADHD improve, many do not and continue to show a greater occurrence of externalizing (acting-out) behaviors and significant deficits in areas such as social skills, peer relations, and academic performance over the life course. A recent study by Stephen Hinshaw and his associates compared groups of ADHD and non-ADHD girls and found that even after treatment about four-fifths of the ADHD girls required social services such as special education, tutoring, or psychotherapy, compared to only one-seventh of the comparison girls; 50 percent of the ADHD girls exhibited oppositional defiant disorder, compared to only 7 percent of the control group.[120]

Tumors, Lesions, Injury, and Disease The presence of brain tumors and lesions has also been linked to a wide variety of psychological problems, including personality changes, hallucinations, and psychotic episodes.[121] Persistent criminality has been linked to lesions in the frontal and temporal regions of the brain, which play an important role in regulating and inhibiting human behavior, including formulating plans and controlling intentions.[122] Clinical evaluation of depressed and aggressive psychopathic subjects showed a significant number (more than 75 percent) had dysfunction of the temporal and frontal regions of the brain.[123]

There is evidence that people with tumors are prone to depression, irritability, temper outbursts, and even homicidal attacks. Clinical case studies of patients suffering from brain tumors indicate that previously docile people may undergo behavior changes so great that they attempt to seriously harm their families and friends. When the tumor is removed, their behavior returns to normal.[124] In addition to brain tumors, head injuries caused by accidents, such as falls or auto crashes, have been linked to personality reversals marked by outbursts of antisocial and violent behavior.[125]

A variety of central nervous system diseases have also been linked to personality changes. Some of these conditions include cerebral arteriosclerosis, epilepsy, senile dementia, Wernicke-Korsakoff's syndrome, and Huntington's chorea. Associated symptoms of these diseases are memory deficiency, orientation loss, and affective (emotional) disturbances dominated by rage, anger, and increased irritability.[126]

Brain Chemistry Neurotransmitters are chemical compounds that influence or activate brain functions. Those studied in relation to aggression include dopamine, norepinephrine, serotonin, monoamine oxidase, and GABA.[127] Evidence exists that abnormal levels of these chemicals are associated with aggression. For example, several researchers have reported inverse correlations between serotonin concentrates in the blood and impulsive and/or suicidal behavior.[128] Recent studies of habitually violent Finnish criminals show that low serotonin (5-hydroxytryptamine, 5-HT) levels are associated with poor impulse control and hyperactivity. In addition, a relatively low concentration of 5-hydroxyindoleactic acid (5-HIAA) is predictive of increased irritability, sensation seeking, and impaired impulse control.[129]

What is the link between brain chemistry and crime? Prenatal exposure of the brain to high levels of androgens can result in a brain structure that is less sensitive to environmental inputs. Affected individuals seek more intense and varied stimulation and are willing to tolerate more adverse consequences than individuals not so affected.[130] Such exposure also results in a rightward shift in (brain) hemispheric functioning and a concomitant diminution of cognitive and emotional tendencies. One result of this tendency is that left-handers are disproportionately represented in the criminal population since the movement of each hand tends to be controlled by the hemisphere of the brain on the opposite side of the body.

It has also been suggested that individuals with a low supply of the enzyme monoamine oxidase (known either by the acronym MOMA and/or MAO) engage in behaviors linked with violence and property crime, including defiance of punishment, impulsivity, hyperactivity, poor academic performance, sensation seeking and risk taking, and recreational drug use.[131] Abnormal levels of MAO may explain both individual and group differences in the crime rate. For example, females have higher levels of MAO than males, a condition that may explain gender differences in the crime rate.[132]

The brain and neurological system can produce natural or endogenous opiates that are chemically similar to the narcotics opium and morphine. It has been suggested that the risk and thrills involved in crime cause the neurological system to produce increased amounts of these natural narcotics. The result is an elevated mood state, perceived as an exciting and rewarding experience that acts as a positive reinforcement for crime.[133] The brain then produces its own natural high as a reward for risk-taking behavior. Some people achieve this high by rock climbing and skydiving; others engage in crimes of violence.

Because this linkage has been found, it is not uncommon for violence-prone people to be treated with antipsychotic drugs such as Haldol, Stelazine, Prolixin, and Risperdal, which help control levels of neurotransmitters (such as serotonin/dopamine); these are sometimes referred to as **chemical restraints** or **chemical straitjackets**.

Arousal Theory

It has long been suspected that obtaining thrills is a crime motivator. Adolescents may engage in crimes such as shoplifting and vandalism simply because they offer the attraction of "getting away with it"; from this perspective, delinquency is a thrilling demonstration of personal competence. According to sociologist Jack Katz, there are immediate gratifications from criminality, which he labels the "seductions of crime." These are situational inducements that directly precede the commission of a crime and draw offenders into law violations. For example, someone challenges their authority and they vanquish their

The Criminological Enterprise

TEENAGE BEHAVIOR: IS IT THE BRAIN?

Teenagers and adults often don't see eye to eye, and new brain research is now shedding light on some of the reasons why so much conflict exists. Although adolescence is often characterized by increased independence and a desire for knowledge and exploration, it also is a time when the brain matures at different rates, and the resulting instability can result in high-risk behaviors, vulnerability to substance abuse, and mental distress.

Recent imaging studies in humans show that brain development and connectivity are not complete until the late teens or early twenties. It is becoming clear that the status of brain chemical systems and connectivity between brain regions make teenagers different from both the young child and the fully mature adult. In other words, as if you did not already know, there really is a big difference between the teenage and adult brains!

Brain Structure and Aggression

One area of teen brain functioning that has piqued the interests of neurscientists is aggression. Adolescent aggressive behavior can be divided into two types: proactive and reactive. Proactive aggressors plan how they're going to hurt and bully others. Reactive aggression, however, is not premeditated; it occurs in response to an upsetting trigger from the environment.

Research psychiatrist Frank Guido finds that aggressive teen behavior may be linked to the amygdala, an area of the brain that processes information regarding threats and fear. Aggressive behavior may also be associated with a lessening of activity in the frontal lobe, a brain region linked to decision-making and impulse control. Guido's research indicates that reactively aggressive adolescents—most commonly boys—frequently misinterpret their surroundings, feel threatened, and act inappropriately aggressive. They tend to strike back when being teased, blame others when getting into a fight, and overreact to accidents.

---

opponent with a beating; or they want to do something exciting, so they break into and vandalize a school building.

According to Katz, choosing crime can help satisfy personal needs for thrills and excitement. For some people, shoplifting and vandalism are attractive because getting away with crime is a thrilling demonstration of personal competence; Katz calls this "sneaky thrills." Even murder can have an emotional payoff. Killers behave like the avenging gods of mythology, choosing to have life-or-death control over their victims.[134]

How can Katz's findings be explained? According to **arousal theory**, for a variety of genetic and environmental reasons, there is variation in response to environmental stimuli. People seek to maintain a preferred or optimal level of arousal: too much stimulation leaves us anxious and stressed out; too little makes us feel bored and weary. There is variation in the way the brain processes sensory input. Some nearly always feel comfortable with little stimulation, others require a high degree of environmental input to feel comfortable. The latter are "sensation seekers," who seek out stimulating activities, which may include aggressive, violent behavior patterns.[135]

Evidence that some people may have lower levels of arousal comes from studies on resting heart rate levels conducted by Adrian Raine and his associates, who found that antisocial children have lower resting heart rates than the general population. Raine speculates that some people lack fear and are nonresponsive to the threat of punishment, a condition that allows them to feel relatively comfortable while engaging in antisocial encounters. People who have low arousal levels will seek out risky situations and become more involved with criminal behavior

as an avenue toward thrill seeking. Because lack of fear and thrill-seeking behavior are characteristics of adult psychopaths, antisocial children might therefore develop into psychopaths as adults.[136]

The factors that determine a person's level of arousal are not fully determined, but suspected sources include:

- *Brain chemistry (and brain structure)*. Some people have brains with many more nerve cells with receptor sites for neurotransmitters than others.

- *Heart rate*. Another view is that people with low heartbeat rates are more likely to commit crime because they seek stimulation to increase their feelings of arousal to normal levels.[137]

- *Autonomic nervous system*. Some biosocial theorists link arousal to the autonomic nervous system as measured by skin conductance response. People with abnormally exaggerated skin conductivity may react with above average negative emotional intensity to stimulus that would have little effect on the average person. As a result, provocations that some people might merely shrug off are viewed as highly confrontational, inflammatory, insulting, and deserving of an aggressive reply.[138]

In sum, brain structure, chemistry and development are believed to exert a strong influence on human behavior. The Criminological Enterprise feature "Teenage Behavior: Is It the Brain?" shows that the relationship may be more universal than we would like to believe.

Their behavior is emotionally "hot," defensive, and impulsive. To find out why, Guido and his colleagues recruited two groups of male adolescents: one group diagnosed with "reactive-affective-defensive-impulsive" (RADI) behavior and the other group without any history of mental illness or aggression problems. While being scanned by a brain imaging machine, both sets of teenagers were asked to perform tasks that involved reacting to age-appropriate, fear-inducing images. The tasks also tested the teenagers' impulsivity. Preliminary data reveal that the brains of RADI teenagers exhibited greater activity in the amygdala and lesser activity in the frontal lobe in response to the images than the brains of the teenagers in the control group.

Guido's research helps explain what goes on in the brains of some teenage boys who respond with inappropriate anger and aggression to perceived threats. It is possible that rather than having a social or environmental basis, antisocial behavior is a function of how the brain influences decision-making and impulse control.

CRITICAL THINKING

1. If teen aggression is linked to brain chemistry and structure, what is the purpose of such crime-reducing policies as providing summer jobs for at-risk kids or providing counseling for those who have already violated the law?

2. Do you believe that crime declines with age because changes in the brain structure lessen in adulthood? Could differences between the teen brain and adult brain really explain age-related differences in antisocial behavior or is something else to blame?

Sources: Society for Neuroscience News Release, November 5, 2007, "Studies Identify Brain Areas and Chemicals Involved in Aggression; May Speed Development of Better Treatment," www.sfn.org/index.cfm?pagename=news_110507d (accessed July 10, 2008); Society for Neuroscience News Release, "New Research Sheds Light on Brain Differences in Adolescents, Understanding Their Impulsive, Risk-Taking Behavior," November 6, 2007, www.sfn.org/index.cfm?pagename=news_110607b (accessed July 10, 2008).

Genetics and Crime

Early biological theorists believed that criminality ran in families. Although research on deviant families is not taken seriously today, modern biosocial theorists are still interested in the role of genetics. Some believe antisocial behavior characteristics and mental disorders may be inherited. According to this view, (a) antisocial behavior is inherited, (b) the genetic makeup of parents is passed on to children, and (c) genetic abnormality is linked to a variety of antisocial behaviors.[139]

This view, while controversial, is not strange or unusual. There is evidence that animals can be bred to have aggressive traits: pit bull dogs, fighting bulls, and fighting cocks have been selectively mated to produce superior predators. Although no similar data exist with regard to people, a growing body of research is focusing on the genetic factors associated with human behavior. There is evidence that personality traits such as extraversion, openness, agreeableness, and conscientiousness are genetically determined.[140] There are also data suggesting that human traits associated with criminality have a genetic basis.[141] The relationship may be either direct or indirect. A direct association might include possessing particular genes highly correlated with crime or, conversely, having genes that make one crime avoidant.[142] An indirect association occurs when genetic makeup is associated with a personality/physical trait that is linked to antisocial behavior. Personality conditions linked to aggression (such as psychopathy, impulsivity, and neuroticism) and psychopathology (such as schizophrenia) have been found to be heritable.[143]

This line of reasoning was cast in the spotlight in the 1970s when genetic testing showed that Richard Speck, the convicted killer of eight nurses in Chicago, allegedly had an abnormal XYY chromosomal structure (XY is normal in males). There was much public concern that all people with XYYs were potential killers and should be closely controlled. Civil libertarians expressed fear that all XYYs could be labeled dangerous and violent regardless of whether they had engaged in violent activities.[144] When it was disclosed that neither Speck nor most violent offenders actually had an extra Y chromosome, interest in the XYY theory dissipated.[145] However, the Speck case drew researchers' attention to looking for a genetic basis of crime.

Researchers have carefully explored the heritability of criminal tendencies by looking at a variety of factors. Some of the most important are described here.

Parental Deviance If criminal tendencies are inherited, then it stands to reason that the children of criminal parents should be more likely to become law violators than the offspring of conventional parents. A number of studies have found that parental criminality and deviance do, in fact, have a powerful influence on delinquent behavior.[146] Some of the most important data on parental deviance were gathered by Donald J. West and David P. Farrington as part of a long-term study of English youth called the Cambridge Study in Delinquent Development (CSDD). Now directed by Farrington, this research has followed a group of about 1,000 males from the time they were 8 years old until today when many are in their 30s and older. The boys in the study have been repeatedly interviewed and their school and police records evaluated. These cohort data indicate that a significant number of delinquent youths have criminal fathers.[147] While 8.4 percent of the sons of noncriminal fathers eventually became chronic offenders, about 37 percent of youths with criminal fathers were multiple offenders.[148] More recent analysis of the data confirms that delinquent youth grow up to become the parents of antisocial children.[149]

In another important analysis, Farrington found that one type of parental deviance, schoolyard aggression or bullying, may be both inter- and intragenerational. Bullies have children who bully others, and these "second-generation bullies" grow up to become the fathers of children who are also bullies, in a never-ending cycle.[150] Farrington's findings are supported by data from the Rochester Youth Development Study (RYDS), a longitudinal analysis that has been monitoring the behavior of 1,000 area youths since 1988. Though their data does not allow them to definitively determine whether it is a result of genetics or socialization, the RYDS researchers have also found an intergenerational continuity in antisocial behavior.[151]

The cause of intergenerational deviance is still uncertain. It is possible that environmental, genetic, psychological, or child-rearing factors are responsible for the linkage between generations. The link might also have some biological basis. Research on the sons of alcoholic parents shows that these boys suffer many neurological impairments related to chronic delinquency.[152] These results may indicate that (a) prolonged parental alcoholism causes genetic problems related to developmental impairment or (b) the children of substance-abusing parents are more prone to suffer neurological impairment before, during, or after birth.

The quality of family life may be key in determining children's behavior. Criminal parents should be the ones least likely to have close, intimate relationships with their offspring. Research shows that substance-abusing and/or criminal parents are the ones most likely to use harsh and inconsistent discipline, a factor closely linked to delinquent behavior.[153]

There is no certainty about the nature and causal relationship between parental and child deviance. Data from the CSDD may help shed some light on the association. Recent analysis shows that parental conflict and authoritarian parenting were related to early childhood conduct problems in two successive generations. In addition, males who were poorly supervised by their parents were themselves poor supervisors as fathers. These findings indicate that parenting styles may help explain antisocial behavior in children and that style is passed down from one generation to the next. In addition, CSDD data found that antisocial males tend to partner with antisocial female peers and breed antisocial children. In sum, then, the CSDD data indicate that the intergenerational transmission of antisocial behaviors may have both genetic and experiential dimensions.[154] Nonetheless, recent evidence indicates that at least part of the association is genetic in nature.[155] It is also possible that the association is related to the labeling process and family stigma: social control agents may be quick to fix a delinquent label on the children of known law violators; "the acorn," the reasoning goes, "does not fall far from the tree."[156]

Sibling Similarities It stands to reason that if the cause of crime is in part genetic, then the behavior of siblings should be similar because they share genetic material. Research does show that if one sibling engages in antisocial behavior, so do his/her brothers and sisters. The effect is greatest among same-sex siblings.[157] Sibling pairs who report warm, mutual relationships and share friends are the most likely to behave in a similar fashion; those who maintain a close relationship also have similar rates of crime and drug abuse.[158]

While the similarity of siblings' behavior seems striking, what appears to be a genetic effect may also be explained by other factors:

- Siblings who live in the same environment are influenced by similar social and economic factors.
- Deviant siblings may grow closer because of shared interests.
- Younger siblings who admire their older siblings may imitate the elders' behavior.
- The deviant sibling forces or threatens the brother or sister into committing criminal acts.
- Siblings living in a similar environment may develop similar types of friends; it is peer behavior that is the critical influence. The influence of peers may negate any observed interdependence of sibling behavior.[159]

Twin Behavior As mentioned above, because siblings are usually brought up in the same household and share common life experiences, any similarity in their antisocial behavior might be a function of environmental influences and experiences and not genetics at all. To guard against this, biosocial theorists have compared the behavior of same-sex twins and again found concordance in their behavior patterns.[160]

However, an even more rigorous test of genetic theory involves comparison of the behavior of identical monozygotic (MZ) twins with fraternal dizygotic (DZ) twins; while the former have an identical genetic makeup, the latter share only about 50 percent of their genetic combinations. Research has shown that MZ twins are significantly closer in their personal characteristics, such as intelligence, than are DZ twins.[161]

The earliest studies conducted on the behavior of twins detected a significant relationship between the criminal activities of MZ twins and a much lower association between those of DZ twins. A review of relevant studies conducted between 1929 and 1961 found that 60 percent of MZ twins shared criminal behavior patterns (if one twin was criminal, so was the other), whereas only 30 percent of DZ twin behavior was similarly related.[162] These findings may be viewed as powerful evidence that a genetic basis for criminality exists.

There have been several research efforts confirming the significant correspondence of twin behavior in activities ranging from frequency of sexual activity to crime.[163] David Rowe and D. Wayne Osgood analyzed the factors that influence self-reported delinquency in a sample of twin pairs and concluded that genetic influences actually have significant explanatory power: if one member of a twin pair was delinquent, so was the other, and the effect was greater among MZ twins.[164] In another recent study, Sara Jaffee and colleagues found a strong genetic association in the development of conduct disorder—for example, persistent lying, bullying, violence, physical cruelty, and stealing. There was significantly more concordance among MZ twins than DZ twins.[165]

Other relevant findings include:

▪ There is a significantly higher risk for suicidal behavior among monozygotic twin pairs than dizygotic twin pairs.[166]

▪ Differences in concordance between MZ and DZ twins have been found in tests measuring psychological dysfunctions, such as conduct disorders, impulsivity, and antisocial behavior.[167]

▪ MZ twins are closer than DZ twins in such crime-relevant measures as level of aggression and verbal skills.[168]

▪ Both members of MZ twin pairs who suffer child abuse are more likely to engage in later antisocial acivity more often than DZ pairs.[169]

▪ Using samples of same-sex twin pairs, psychiatrist Essi Viding and colleagues found a powerful hereditary influence on levels of callous, unemotional behavior in children.[170]

One famous study of twin behavior still underway is the Minnesota Twin Family Study. This research compares the behavior of MZ and DZ twin pairs who were raised together with others who were separated at birth and in some cases did not even know of each other's existence. The study shows some striking similarities in behavior and ability for twin pairs raised apart. An MZ twin reared away from a co-twin has about as good a chance of being similar to the co-twin in terms of personality, interests, and attitudes as one who has been reared with his or her co-twin. The conclusion: identical twins are genetically wired to be similar; any differences in their behaviors or activities would be forced upon them by their living conditions (see Exhibit 5.2).[171]

In addition, some experts, including David Rowe, conclude that individuals who share genes are alike in personality regardless of how they are reared; in contrast, the environment has little effect on the personality of twins.[172]

Evaluating Genetic Research Twin studies also have their detractors. Some opponents suggest that available evidence provides little conclusive proof that crime is genetically predetermined. Not all research efforts have found that MZ twin pairs are more closely related in their criminal behavior than DZ or ordinary sibling pairs, and some that have found an association note that it is at best "modest."[173] Those who oppose the genes–crime relationship point to the inadequate research designs and weak methodologies of supporting research. The newer, better-designed research studies, critics charge, provide less support than earlier, less methodically sound studies.[174]

EXHIBIT 5.2

Findings from the Minnesota Twin Family Study

▪ MZ twins become *more* similar with respect to abilities such as vocabularies and arithmetic scores as they age. As DZ (fraternal) twins get older, they become less similar with respect to vocabularies and arithmetic scores.

▪ A P300 is a tiny electrical response (a few millionths of a volt) that occurs in the brain when a person detects something that is unusual or interesting. For example, if a person were shown nine circles and one square, a P300 brain response would appear after seeing the square because it's different. Identical (MZ) twin children have very similar looking P300s. By comparison, children who are fraternal (DZ) twins do not show as much similarity in their P300s. These results indicate that the way the brain processes information may be greatly influenced by genes.

▪ An EEG is a measure of brain activity or brain waves that can be used to monitor a person's state of arousal. MZ twins tend to produce strikingly similar EEG spectra; DZ twins show far less similarity.

▪ MZ twins tend to have more similar ages at the time of death than DZ twins do. That is, MZ twins are more likely to die at about the same age, and DZ twins are more likely to die at different ages.

Source: Minnesota Study of Twins Reared Apart, www.psych.umn.edu/psylabs/mtfs/special.htm (accessed July 10, 2008).

Even if the behavior similarities between MZ twins are greater than those between DZ twins, the association may be explained by environmental factors. MZ twins are more likely to look alike and to share physical traits than DZ twins, and they are more likely to be treated similarly. Similarities in their shared behavior patterns may therefore be a function of socialization and/or environment and not heredity.[175]

It is also possible that what appears to be a genetic effect picked up by the twin research is actually the effect of sibling influence on criminality referred to as the contagion effect: genetic predispositions and early experiences make some people, including twins, susceptible to deviant behavior, which is transmitted by the presence of antisocial siblings in the household.[176]

The contagion effect may explain in part the higher concordance of deviant behaviors found in identical twins as compared to fraternal twins or mere siblings. The relationship between identical twins may be stronger and more enduring than other sibling pairs so that contagion and not genetics explains their behavioral similarities. According to Marshall Jones and Donald Jones, the contagion effect may also help explain why the behavior of twins is more similar in adulthood than adolescence.[177] Youthful misbehavior is influenced by friends and peer group relationships. As adults, the influence of peers may wane as people marry and find employment. In contrast, twin influence is everlasting; if one twin is antisocial, it legitimizes and supports the criminal behavior in his or her co-twin. This effect may grow even stronger in adulthood because twin relations are more enduring than any other. What seems to be a genetic effect may actually be the result of sibling interaction with a brother or sister who engages in anti-social activity.

Adoption Studies One way of avoiding the pitfalls of twin studies is to focus attention on the behavior of adoptees. It seems logical that if the behavior of adopted children is more closely aligned to that of their biological parents than to that of their adoptive parents, then the idea of a genetic basis for criminality would be supported. If, on the other hand, adoptees are more closely aligned to the behavior of their adoptive parents than their biological parents, an environmental basis for crime would seem more valid.

Several studies indicate that some relationship exists between biological parents' behavior and the behavior of their children, even when their contact has been nonexistent.[178] In what is considered the most significant study in this area, Barry Hutchings and Sarnoff Mednick analyzed 1,145 male adoptees born in Copenhagen, Denmark, between 1927 and 1941. Of these, 185 had criminal records.[179] After following 143 of the criminal adoptees and matching them with a control group of 143 noncriminal adoptees, Hutchings and Mednick found that the criminality of the biological father was a strong predictor of the child's criminal behavior. When both the biological and the adoptive fathers were criminals, the probability that the youth would engage in criminal behavior greatly increased: 24.5 percent of the boys whose adoptive and biological fathers were criminals had been convicted of a criminal law violation. Only 13.5 percent of those whose biological and adoptive fathers were not criminals had similar conviction records.[180]

A more recent analysis of Swedish adoptees also found that genetic factors are highly significant, accounting for 59 percent of the variation in their petty crime rates. Boys who had criminal parents were significantly more likely to violate the law. Environmental influences and economic status were significantly less important, explaining about 19 percent of the variance in crime. Nonetheless, having a positive environment, such as being adopted into a more affluent home, helped inhibit genetic predisposition.[181]

The genes–crime relationship is controversial because it implies that the propensity to commit crime is present at birth and cannot be altered. It raises moral dilemmas. If *in utero* genetic testing could detect a gene for violence, and a violence gene was found to be present, what could be done as a precautionary measure?

Evolutionary Theory

Some criminologists believe the human traits that produce violence and aggression are produced through the long process of human evolution.[182] According to this evolutionary view, the competition for scarce resources has influenced and shaped the human species.[183] Over the course of human existence, people whose personal characteristics enable them to accumulate more than others are the most likely to breed and dominate the species. People have been shaped to engage in actions that promote their well-being and ensure the survival and reproduction of their genetic line. Males who are impulsive risk-takers may be able to father more children because they are reckless in their social relationships and have sexual encounters with numerous partners. If, according to evolutionary theories, such behavior patterns are inherited, impulsive behavior becomes intergenerational, passed down from father to son. It is not surprising then that human history has been marked by war, violence, and aggression.

Violence and Evolution In their classic book *Homicide*, Martin Daly and Margo Wilson suggest that violent offenses are often driven by evolutionary and reproductive factors. High rates of spouse abuse in modern society may be a function of aggressive men seeking to control and possess mates. When females are murdered by their spouses, the motivating factor is typically fear of infidelity and the threat of attachment to a new partner. Infidelity challenges male dominance and future reproductive rights. It comes as no surprise that in some cultures, including our own, sexual infidelity discovered in progress by the aggrieved husband is viewed legally as a provocation that justifies retaliatory killing.[184] Men who feel most threatened over the potential of losing mates to rivals are the ones most likely to engage in sexual violence. Research shows that women in common-law marriages, especially those who are much younger than their husbands, are at greater risk than older married women. Abusive males may fear the potential loss of their younger mates, especially if they are not bound by a marriage contract, and may use force for purposes of control and possession.[185]

Armed robbery is another crime that may have evolutionary underpinnings. Though most robbers are caught and severely punished, it remains an alluring pursuit for men who want to both show their physical prowess and display resources with which to conquer rivals and attract mates. Violent episodes are far more common among men who are unemployed and unmarried—in other words, those who may want to demonstrate their allure to the opposite sex but who are without the benefit of position or wealth.[186]

Gender and Evolution Evolutionary concepts have been linked to gender-based differences in the crime rate. To ensure survival of the gene pool (and the species), it is beneficial for a male of any species to mate with as many suitable females as possible since each can bear his offspring. In contrast, because of the long period of gestation, females require a secure home and a single, stable nurturing partner to ensure their survival. Because of these differences in mating patterns, the most aggressive males mate most often and have the greatest number of offspring. Therefore, over the history of the human species, aggressive males have had the greatest impact on the gene pool. The descendants of these aggressive males now account for the disproportionate amount of male aggression and violence.[187]

Crime rate differences between the genders, then, may be less a matter of socialization than inherent differences in mating patterns that have developed over time.[188] Among young men, reckless, life-threatening "risk-proneness" is especially likely to evolve in cultures that force males to find suitable mates to ensure their ability to reproduce. Unless they are aggressive with potential mates and potential rivals for those suitable mates, they are doomed to remain childless.[189]

Other evolutionary factors may have influenced gender differences. Feminists have suggested that with the advent of agriculture and trade in prehistory, women were forced into a position of high dependence and limited power. They began to compete among themselves to secure partners who could provide necessary resources. As a result of these early evolutionary developments, intergender competition became greatest during periods of resource deprivation—times when women become most dependent on a male for support. These trends can still be observed. For example, during times of high female unemployment, female–female aggression rates increase as women compete with each other for men who can provide them with support. In contrast, as rates of social welfare increase, female–female aggression rates diminish because the state serves as a readily available substitute for a male breadwinner.[190]

Evaluation of the Biosocial Branch of Trait Theory

Biosocial perspectives on crime have raised some challenging questions. Critics find some of these theories to be racist and dysfunctional. If there are biological explanations for street crimes, such as assault, murder, or rape, the argument goes, and if, as the official crime statistics suggest, the poor and minority-group members commit a disproportionate number of such acts, then by implication biological theory says that members of these groups are biologically different, flawed, or inferior.

Some biological explanations for the geographic, social, and temporal patterns in the crime rate are problematic. Furthermore, biological theory seems to divide people into criminals and noncriminals on the basis of their genetic and physical makeup, ignoring self-reports indicating that almost everyone has engaged in some type of illegal activity during his or her lifetime.

Biosocial theorists counter that their views should not be confused with Lombrosian, deterministic biology. Rather than suggest that there are born criminals and noncriminals, they maintain that some people carry the potential to be violent or antisocial and that environmental conditions can sometimes trigger antisocial responses.[191] This would explain why some otherwise law-abiding citizens engage in a single, seemingly unexplainable antisocial act, and conversely, why some people with long criminal careers often engage in conventional behavior. It also explains why there are geographic and temporal patterns in the crime rate: people who are predisposed to crime may simply have more opportunities to commit illegal acts in the summer in Los Angeles and Atlanta than in the winter in Bedford, New Hampshire, and Minot, North Dakota, or perhaps their hormonal levels become activated as the temperature rises.

The biosocial view is that behavior is a product of interacting biological and environmental events.[192] Physical impairments may make some people "at risk" to crime, but it is when they are linked to social and environmental problems, such as family dysfunction, that they trigger criminal acts.[193] For example, Avshalom Caspi and his associates found that girls who reach physical maturity at an early age are the ones most likely to engage in delinquent acts. This finding might suggest a relationship between biological traits (hormonal activity) and crime. However, the Caspi research found that the association may also have an environmental basis. Physically mature girls are the ones most likely to have prolonged contact with a crime-prone group: older adolescent boys.[194] Here, the combination of biological change, social relationships, and routine opportunities may predict crime rates.

The most significant criticism of biosocial theory has been the lack of adequate empirical testing. In most research efforts, sample sizes are relatively small and nonrepresentative. A great deal of biosocial research is conducted with samples of adjudicated offenders who have been placed in clinical treatment settings. Methodological problems make it impossible to determine whether findings apply only to offenders who have been convicted of crimes and placed in treatment or to the population of criminals as a whole.[195] More research is needed to clarify the relationships proposed by biosocial researchers and to silence critics. Concept Summary 5.1 summarizes the various biosocial theories of crime.

PSYCHOLOGICAL TRAIT THEORIES

Andrew Luster, an heir to the Max Factor cosmetic fortune, lived a privileged life of sun and fun in a beach house in an exclusive community near Santa Barbara. However, Andrew had a darker side, which came to light on July 17, 2000, when he was arrested after a young woman accused him of drugging her with the "date rape" drug GHB and then having sex with her while she was unconscious. When police served a warrant on his home, they found tapes indicating Luster had a habit of drugging women and raping them while they were comatose. Halfway through the trial, Luster jumped bail, disappeared, and was declared a fugitive from justice. In his absence, the jury found him guilty on 86 of the 87 counts, and he was eventually sentenced to more than 100 years in prison. Five months later, he was captured in the resort town of Puerto Vallarta, Mexico, by bounty hunter Duane "Dog" Chapman. On July 3, 2003, an appellate court denied Luster's appeal of his guilty verdicts because he had jumped bail.

How can we explain the bizarre behavior of Andrew Luster? Why would a wealthy, handsome man drug and rape

BIOSOCIAL THEORIES OF CRIME

Biochemical

▮ The major premise of the theory is that crime, especially violence, is a function of diet, vitamin intake, hormonal imbalance, or food allergies.

▮ The strengths of the theory are that it explains irrational violence; it shows how the environment interacts with personal traits to influence behavior.

▮ The research focuses of the theory are diet, hormones, enzymes, environmental contaminants, and lead intake.

Neurological

▮ The major premise of the theory is that criminals and delinquents often suffer brain impairment, as measured by the EEG. Attention deficit hyperactivity disorder and minimal brain dysfunction are related to antisocial behavior.

▮ The strengths of the theory are that it explains irrational violence; it shows how the environment interacts with personal traits to influence behavior.

▮ The research focuses of the theory are ADD, ADHD, learning disabilities, brain injuries, and brain chemistry.

Genetic

▮ The major premise of the theory is that criminal traits and predispositions are inherited. The criminality of parents can predict the delinquency of children.

▮ The strengths of the theory are that it explains why only a small percentage of youth in high-crime areas become chronic offenders.

▮ The research focuses of the theory are twin behavior, sibling behavior, and parent–child similarities.

Evolutionary

▮ The major premise of the theory is that as the human race evolved, traits and characteristics have become ingrained. Some of these traits make people aggressive and predisposed to commit crime.

▮ The strengths of the theory are that it explains high violence rates and aggregate gender differences in the crime rate.

▮ The research focuses of the theory are gender differences and understanding human aggression.

unsuspecting women? Could his acts possibly be the result of calculation and planning, or are they the product of some mental aberration or personality disturbance?

The second branch of trait theories focuses on the psychological aspects of crime, including the associations among intelligence, personality, learning, and criminal behavior.

Assistant Special Agent in Charge for the Los Angeles Federal Bureau of Investigation Ralph Boelter speaks to reporters along with Ventura County Sheriff Bob Brooks during a news conference on June 18, 2003, in Ventura, California, following the capture of Max Factor heir Andrew Luster in Puerto Vallarta, Mexico. Luster, who fled to Mexico during his trial for 87 criminal counts, including rape, was convicted in absentia and sentenced to 124 years in prison. Luster's crimes seem motivated more by psychological abnormality than environment, socialization, or choice.

Psychological theories of crime have a long history. In *The English Convict*, Charles Goring (1870–1919) studied the mental characteristics of 3,000 English convicts.[196] He found little difference in the physical characteristics of criminals and noncriminals, but he uncovered a significant relationship between crime and a condition he referred to as defective intelligence, which involves such traits as feeble-mindedness, epilepsy, insanity, and defective social instinct.[197] Goring believed criminal behavior was inherited and could, therefore, be controlled by regulating the reproduction of families who produced mentally defective children.

Gabriel Tarde (1843–1904) is the forerunner of modern-day learn- ing theorists.[198] Tarde believed people learn from one another through a process of imitation. Tarde's ideas are similar to modern social learning theorists who believe that both interpersonal and observed behavior, such as a movie or television, can influence criminality.

Since the pioneering work of people like Tarde and Goring, psychologists, psychiatrists, and other mental health professionals have long played an active role in formulating criminological theory. In their quest to understand and treat all varieties of abnormal mental conditions, psychologists have encountered clients whose behavior falls within categories society has labeled as criminal, deviant, violent, and antisocial.

This section is organized along the lines of the predominant psychological views most closely associated with the causes of criminal behavior. Some psychologists view antisocial behavior from a **psychoanalytic** or **psychodynamic perspective**: their focus is on early childhood experience and its effect on personality. In contrast, **behaviorism** stresses social learning and behavior modeling as the keys to criminality. **Cognitive theory** analyzes human perception and how it affects behavior.

Psychodynamic Theory

Psychodynamic (or psychoanalytic) psychology was originated by Viennese psychiatrist Sigmund Freud (1856–1939) and has since remained a prominent segment of psychological theory.[199]

Freud believed that we all carry with us residue of the most significant emotional attachments of our childhood, which then guide future interpersonal relationships. Today the term "psychodynamic" refers to a broad range of theories that focus on the influence of instinctive drives and forces and the importance of developmental processes in shaping personality. Contemporary psychodynamic theory places greater emphasis on conscious experience and its interaction with the unconscious, in addition to the role that social factors play in development. Nonetheless, it still focuses on the influence of early childhood experiences on the development of personality, motivation, and drives.

connections

Chapter 1 discussed how some of the early founders of psychiatry, including Philippe Pinel and Benjamin Rush, tried to develop an understanding of the "criminal mind." Later theories suggested that mental illness and insanity were inherited and that deviants were inherently mentally damaged by reason of their inferior genetic makeup.

Elements of Psychodynamic Theory According to the classic version of the theory, the human personality contains a three-part structure. The **id** is the primitive part of an individual's mental makeup present at birth. It represents unconscious biological drives for sex, food, and other life-sustaining necessities. The id follows the **pleasure principle**: it requires instant gratification without concern for the rights of others.

The **ego** develops early in life, when a child begins to learn that his or her wishes cannot be instantly gratified. The ego is that part of the personality that compensates for the demands of the id by helping the individual guide his or her actions to remain within the boundaries of social convention. The ego is guided by the **reality principle**: it takes into account what is practical and conventional by societal standards.

The **superego** develops as a result of incorporating within the personality the moral standards and values of parents, community, and significant others. It is the moral aspect of an

EXHIBIT 5.3

Freud's Model of the Personality Structure

Personality Structure	Guiding Principle	Description
Id	Pleasure principle	Unconscious biological drives; requires instant gratification
Ego	Reality principle	Helps the personality refine the demands of the id; helps person adapt to conventions
Superego	The conscience	The moral aspect of the personality

individual's personality; it passes judgments on behavior. The superego is divided into two parts: **conscience** and **ego ideal**. Conscience tells what is right and wrong. It forces the ego to control the id and directs the individual into morally acceptable and responsible behaviors, which may not be pleasurable. Exhibit 5.3 summarizes Freud's personality structure.

Psychosexual Stages of Human Development The most basic human drive present at birth is **eros**, the instinct to preserve and create life. The other is the death instinct (**thanatos**), which is expressed as aggression.

Eros is expressed sexually. Consequently, very early in their development, humans experience sexuality, which is expressed by seeking pleasure through various parts of the body. During the first year of life, a child attains pleasure by sucking and biting; Freud called this the **oral stage**. During the second and third years of life, the focus of sexual attention is on the elimination of bodily wastes—the **anal stage**. The **phallic stage** occurs during the third year when children focus their attention on their genitals. Males begin to have sexual feelings for their mothers (the **Oedipus complex**) and girls for their fathers (the **Electra complex**). **Latency** begins at age 6. During this period, feelings of sexuality are repressed until the genital stage begins at puberty; this marks the beginning of adult sexuality.

If conflicts are encountered during any of the psychosexual stages of development, a person can become **fixated** at that point. This means, as an adult, the fixated person will exhibit behavior traits characteristic of those encountered during infantile sexual development. For example, an infant who does not receive enough oral gratification during the first year of life is likely as an adult to engage in such oral behavior as smoking, drinking, or drug abuse or to be clinging and dependent in personal relationships. Thus, according to Freud, the roots of adult behavioral problems can be traced to problems developed in the earliest years of life.

The Psychodynamics of Antisocial Behavior Psychologists have long linked criminality to abnormal mental states produced by early childhood trauma. For example, Alfred Adler (1870–1937), the founder of individual psychology, coined the term **inferiority complex** to describe people who have feelings of

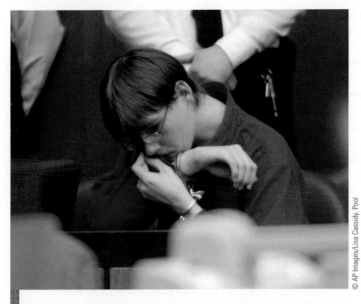

Psychologists recognize that a variety of mental disorders may be linked to antisocial behavior. Some suffer a deficit in emotional cognition that prevents them from being aware of their feelings or being able to understand or talk about their thoughts and emotions. John Odgren cries during his hearing at Middlesex (Massachusetts) Superior Court on March 26, 2007. Odgren was charged with killing fellow student James Alenson at Lincoln-Sudbury Regional High School. Odgren, who has a form of autism known as Asperger's Syndrome, fatally stabbed the 15-year-old Alenson for no apparent reason.

inferiority and compensate for them with a drive for superiority. Controlling others may help reduce personal inadequacies. Erik Erikson (1902–1984) described the identity crisis as a period of serious personal questioning people undertake in an effort to determine their own values and sense of direction. Adolescents undergoing an identity crisis might exhibit out-of-control behavior and experiment with drugs and other forms of deviance.

The psychoanalyst whose work is most closely associated with criminality is August Aichorn.[200] After examining many delinquent youths, Aichorn concluded that societal stress, though damaging, could not alone result in a life of crime unless a predisposition existed that psychologically prepared youths for antisocial acts. This mental state, which he labeled latent delinquency, is found in youngsters whose personality requires them to act in these ways:

▌ Seek immediate gratification (to act impulsively)

▌ Consider satisfying their personal needs more important than relating to others

▌ Satisfy instinctive urges without considering right and wrong (that is, they lack guilt)

The psychodynamic model of the criminal offender depicts an aggressive, frustrated person dominated by events that occurred early in childhood. Perhaps because they may have suffered unhappy experiences in childhood or had families that could not provide proper love and care, criminals suffer from weak or damaged egos that make them unable to cope with conventional society. Weak egos are associated with immaturity, poor social skills, and excessive dependence on others. People with weak egos may be easily led into crime by antisocial peers and

drug abuse. Some offenders have underdeveloped super-egos and consequently lack internalized representations of those behaviors that are punished in conventional society. They commit crimes because they have difficulty understanding the consequences of their actions.[201]

Offenders may suffer from a garden variety of mood and/or behavior disorders. They may be histrionic, depressed, antisocial, or narcissistic.[202] They may suffer from conduct disorders, which include long histories of antisocial behavior, or mood disorders characterized by disturbance in expressed emotions. Among the latter is bipolar disorder, in which moods alternate between periods of wild elation and deep depression.[203] Some offenders are driven by an unconscious desire to be punished for prior sins, either real or imaginary. As a result, they may violate the law to gain attention or to punish their parents.

According to this view, crime is a manifestation of feelings of oppression and people's inability to develop the proper psychological defenses and rationales to keep these feelings under control. Criminality enables troubled people to survive by producing positive psychic results: it helps them to feel free and independent, and it gives them the possibility of excitement and the chance to use their skills and imagination. Crime also provides them with the promise of positive gain; it allows them to blame others for their predicament (for example, the police), and it gives them a chance to rationalize their sense of failure ("If I hadn't gotten into trouble, I could have been a success").[204]

Attachment Theory Attachment theory, a view most closely associated with psychologist John Bowlby, is also connected to the psychodynamic tradition. Bowlby believed that the ability to form attachments—that is, emotionally bond to another person—has important lasting psychological implications that follow people across the life span. Attachments are formed soon after birth, when infants bond with their mothers. They will become frantic, crying and clinging to prevent separation or to reestablish contact with a missing parent. Bowlby noted that this behavior was not restricted to humans and occurs in all mammals, indicating that separation anxiety may be instinctual or evolutionary. After all, attachment figures, especially the mother, provide support and care, and without attachment an infant would be helpless and could not survive. Bowlby also challenged Freud's view of the development of the ego and superego, claiming that at birth these were bound up in the relationship with one's mother:

It is not surprising that during infancy and early childhood these functions are either not operating at all or are doing so most imperfectly. During this phase of life, the child is therefore dependent on his mother performing them for him. She orients him in space and time, provides his environment, permits the satisfaction of some impulses, restricts others. She is his ego and his super-ego. Gradually he learns these arts himself, and as he does, the skilled parent transfers the roles to him. This is a slow, subtle and continuous process, beginning when he first learns to walk and feed himself, and not ending completely until maturity is reached. . . . Ego and super-ego development are thus inextricably bound up with the child's primary human relationships.[205]

Bowlby's most important finding was that to grow up mentally healthy, "the infant and young child should experience a warm, intimate, and continuous relationship with his mother (or permanent mother substitute) in which both find satisfaction and enjoyment."[206]

According to this view, failing to develop proper attachment may cause people to fall prey to a number of psychological disorders. Psychologists believe that children with attachment problems lack trust and respect for others. They often display many psychological symptoms, some which resemble attention deficit hyperactivity disorder (ADHD). They may be impulsive and have difficulty concentrating and consequently experience difficulty in school. As adults, they often have difficulty initiating and sustaining relationships with others and find it difficult to sustain romantic relationships. Criminologists have linked people having detachment problems with a variety of antisocial behaviors, including sexual assault and child abuse.[207] It has been suggested that boys disproportionately experience disrupted attachment and that these disruptions are causally related to disproportionate rates of male offending.[208]

Mood Disorders and Crime Psychologists recognize a variety of mental disorders that may be linked to antisocial behavior. Adolescents who are frequently uncooperative and hostile and who seem to be much more difficult than other children the same age may be suffering from a psychological condition known as *disruptive behavior disorder (DBD)*, which can take on two distinct forms: *oppositional defiant disorder (ODD)* and *conduct disorder (CD)*.[209] Children suffering from ODD experience an ongoing pattern of uncooperative, defiant, and hostile behavior toward authority figures that seriously interferes with the youngsters' day-to-day functioning. Symptoms of ODD may include frequent loss of temper and constant arguing with adults; defying adults or refusing adult requests or rules; deliberately annoying others; blaming others for mistakes or misbehavior; being angry and resentful; being spiteful or vindictive; swearing or using obscene language; or having low self-esteem. The person with ODD is moody and easily frustrated and may abuse drugs as a form of self-medication.[210]

CD is typically considered a more serious group of behavioral and emotional problems.[211] Children and adolescents with CD have great difficulty following rules and behaving in socially acceptable ways. They are often viewed by other children, adults, and social agencies as severely antisocial. Research shows that they are frequently involved in such activities as bullying, fighting, committing sexual assaults, and cruelty to animals.

What causes CD? Numerous biosocial and psychological factors are suspected. There is evidence, for example, that interconnections between the frontal lobes and other brain regions may influence CD. There is also research showing that levels of serotonin can influence the onset of CD and that CD has been shown to aggregate in families, suggesting a genetic basis of the disorder.[212]

ODD and CD are not the only mood disorders associated with antisocial behavior. Some people find it impossible to cope with feelings of oppression or depression. Research shows that people who are clinically depressed are more likely to engage in a garden variety of illegal acts.[213] Some people suffer from **alexithymia**, a deficit in emotional cognition that prevents them from being aware of their feelings or being able to understand or talk about their thoughts and emotions; they seem robotic and emotionally dead.[214] Others may suffer from eating disorders and are likely to use fasting, vomiting, and drugs to lose weight or to keep from gaining weight.[215]

Crime and Mental Illness The most serious forms of psychological disturbance will result in mental illness referred to as **psychosis**, which include severe mental **disorders**, such as depression, bipolar disorder (manic depression), and **schizophrenia**—characterized by extreme impairment of a person's ability to think clearly, respond emotionally, communicate effectively, understand reality, and behave appropriately. Schizophrenics may hear nonexistent voices, hallucinate, and make inappropriate behavioral responses. People with severe mental disorders exhibit illogical and incoherent thought processes and a lack of insight into their behavior. For example, they may see themselves as agents of the devil, avenging angels, or the recipients of messages from animals and plants.

David Berkowitz (the "Son of Sam" or the "44-caliber killer"), a notorious serial killer who went on a rampage from 1976 to 1977, exhibited these traits when he claimed that his killing spree began when he received messages from a neighbor's dog. **Paranoid schizophrenics**, such as Eugene Weston, who went on a shooting rampage in the U.S. Capitol building in 1998, suffer complex behavior delusions involving wrongdoing or persecution—they think everyone is out to get them.

There is evidence that law violators suffer from a disproportionate amount of mental health problems and personality disturbance.[216] Female offenders seem to have more serious mental health symptoms, including schizophrenia, paranoia, and obsessive behaviors, than male offenders.[217] It is not surprising that abusive mothers have been found to have mood and personality disorders and a history of psychiatric diagnoses.[218] Juvenile murderers have been described in clinical diagnosis as "overtly hostile," "explosive or volatile," "anxious," and "depressed."[219] Studies of men accused of murder found that 75 percent could be classified as having some mental illness, including schizophrenia.[220] Also, the reported substance abuse among the mentally ill is significantly higher than that of the general population.[221] Kids growing up in homes where parents suffer mental illness are much more likely to be at risk for family instability, poverty, and other factors that are related to future delinquency and crime. So not only may mental illness be a cause of crime but its effect may be intergenerational.[222]

The diagnosed mentally ill appear in arrest and court statistics at a rate disproportionate to their presence in the population.[223] There is also evidence that the mentally ill are prone to attack their caregivers: doctors working with mental patients are significantly more likely to be attacked by patients than any other health care provider.[224]

ANDREA YATES

Andrea (Kennedy) Yates was born on July 2, 1964, in Houston, Texas. She seemed to have a successful, normal life, being the class valedictorian, captain of the swim team, and a member of the National Honor Society. She graduated from the University of Texas School of Nursing in Houston and worked as a registered nurse at a University of Texas–run facility. She met and married Rusty Yates, and the couple began to raise a family. Though money was tight and living conditions cramped, the couple had five children in the first eight years of their marriage. The pressure began to take a toll on Andrea, and her mental health deteriorated. On June 17, 1999, after attempting suicide by taking an overdose of pills, she was placed in Houston's Methodist Hospital psychiatric unit and diagnosed with a major depressive disorder. Even though she was medicated with powerful antipsychotics such as Haldol, Andrea continued to have psychotic episodes and was hospitalized for severe depression. Her losing battle with mental illness culminated in an act that shocked the nation. On June 20, 2001, she systematically drowned all five of her children, including her eldest, seven-year-old Noah, who tried to escape after seeing his siblings dead, but was dragged back into the bathroom by his mother and drowned also.

At trial, Yates's defense team attempted to show that she suffered from delusional depression and postpartum mood swings that can sometimes evoke psychosis. Though she drowned her children one by one, even chasing down Noah to drag him to the tub, did she really have any awareness that what she was doing was wrong? Postpartum depression affects about 40 percent of all mothers and in its mildest forms leaves new mothers feeling "blue" for a few weeks; more serious cases can last more than a year and involve fatigue, withdrawal, and eating disorders. The

most serious form, which Andrea Yates is believed to have suffered, is a psychosis that produces hallucinations, delusions, feelings of worthlessness, and inadequacy. Though very uncommon, postpartum psychosis increases the likelihood of both suicide and infanticide if left untreated. Despite her long history of mental illness and psychiatric testimony suggesting she lacked the capacity to understand her actions, the jury found her guilty of murder on March 12, 2002, ordering a life sentence instead of the death penalty sought by the prosecution.

Andrea's conviction was later overturned when a Texas appeals court ruled that an expert witness, Dr. Park Dietz, made a false statement during the trial. (He claimed she might have been influenced by an episode of *Law and Order*, though no such episode ever aired; it was actually *L.A. Law* that dealt with a case of a mother killing her children.) At the time of this writing Andrea remains in a psychiatric facility.

The Andrea Yates case illustrates the association between mental illness and crime. Who could claim that a woman as disturbed as Andrea *chose* to kill her own children? While the jury may have reached that verdict, it was constrained by the legal definition of insanity that relies on the immediate events that took place and not Andrea's long-term mental state that produced this horrible crime.

Sources: "Andrea Yates: Ill or Evil?" CourtTV Crime Library, www.crime library.com/notorious_murders/women/andrea_yates/ (accessed July 10, 2008); CNN, "The Case of Andrea Yates," www.cnn.com/SPECIALS/2001/yates/ (accessed July 10, 2008).

Nor is this relationship unique to the United States. Forensic criminologist Henrik Belfrage studied mental patients in Sweden and found that 40 percent of those discharged from institutional care had a criminal record as compared to less than 10 percent of the general public.[225] Another Swedish study found that about 1 in 20 serious crimes in that country were committed by people with severe mental illness. Australian men diagnosed with schizophrenia are four times more likely than the general population to be convicted for serious violence.[226] And a recent Danish study found a significant positive relationship between mental disorders such as schizophrenia and criminal violence.[227] Similarly, a study of German inmates found a significant amount of mental illness in both male and female prisoners.[228]

A recent review of the existing literature on the relationship between psychopathology and delinquent behavior concluded that delinquent adolescents have higher rates of clinical mental disorders when compared to adolescents in the general population.[229] In sum, people who suffer paranoid or delusional feelings, and who believe that others wish them harm or that their mind is dominated by forces beyond their control, seem to be violence prone.[230] The Andrea Yates murder case, set out in the Profiles in Crime feature, was one of the most widely followed stories linking mental illness to crime.

Is the Link Valid? Despite this evidence, there are still questions about whether mental illness is a direct cause of crime and violence. The mentally ill may be more likely to withdraw or harm themselves than to act aggressively toward others.[231] Mentally disordered inmates who do recidivate upon release appear to do so for the same reasons as the mentally sound—extensive criminal histories, substance abuse, and family dysfunction—rather than as a result of their illness.[232]

It is also possible that the link between mental illness and crime is spurious and an artifact of some intervening factor: the factors that cause mental turmoil also cause antisocial behaviors. People who suffer child abuse are more likely to have mental anguish and commit violent acts; child abuse is the actual cause of both problems.[233]

Mentally ill people may be more likely to lack financial resources than the mentally sound. Living in a stress-filled, urban environment may produce both symptoms of mental illness and crime.[234] It is not surprising then that mentally ill people, forced to live in deteriorated neighborhoods, are much more likely to be crime victims than the mentally sound.[235]

A recent Swedish study found that schizophrenic patients are very likely to live in neighborhoods characterized by high levels of disorder, fear of crime, and victimization. The association was circular: the presence of large numbers of mentally ill people helped increase neighborhood fear, leading to neighborhood deterioration, lowered values, and the influx of more diagnosed mentally ill people seeking cheap housing. Segregating the mentally ill may result in worsening of the illness as well as increasing the deterioration of local areas.[236]

It is also possible that the link is caused by the treatment of the mentally ill: the police may be more likely to arrest the mentally ill, giving the illusion that they are crime prone.[237] However, some recent research by Paul Hirschfield and his associates gives only mixed support to this view. Although some mental health problems increase the risk of arrest, others bring out more cautious or compassionate police responses that may result in treatment rather than arrest.[238]

The mental illness–crime link may be a function of resources: a lack of resources may inhibit the mentally ill from obtaining the proper treatment, which, if made available, would result in reduced criminality. For example, a recent study conducted in North Carolina compared the outcomes for mentally ill patients who received outpatient treatment with an untreated comparison group; treatment significantly reduced arrest probability (12 percent versus 45 percent).[239] Further research is needed to clarify this important relationship.

Behavioral Theory

Psychological behavior theory maintains that human actions are developed through learning experiences. Rather than focusing on unconscious personality traits or cognitive development patterns produced early in childhood, behavior theorists are concerned with the actual behaviors people engage in during the course of their daily lives. The major premise of behavior theory is that people alter their behavior according to the reactions it receives from others. Behavior is supported by rewards and extinguished by negative reactions or punishments. Behavioral theory is quite complex with many different subareas. With respect to criminal activity, the behaviorist views crimes, especially violent acts, as learned responses to life situations that do not necessarily represent psychologically abnormal responses.

Social Learning Theory Social learning is the branch of behavior theory most relevant to criminology.[240] Social learning theorists, most notably Albert Bandura, argue that people are not actually born with the ability to act violently but that they learn to be aggressive through their life experiences.

These experiences include personally observing others acting aggressively to achieve some goal or watching people being rewarded for violent acts on television or in movies. People learn to act aggressively when, as children, they model their behavior after the violent acts of adults. Later in life, these violent behavior patterns persist in social relationships. For example, the boy who sees his father repeatedly strike his mother with impunity is the one most likely to grow up to become a battering parent and husband.

Though social learning theorists agree that mental or physical traits may predispose a person toward violence, they believe that activating a person's violent tendencies is achieved by factors in the environment. The specific forms that aggressive behavior takes, the frequency with which it is expressed, the situations in which it is displayed, and the specific targets selected for attack are largely determined by social learning. However, people are self-aware and engage in purposeful learning. Their interpretations of behavior outcomes and situations influence the way they learn from experiences. One adolescent who spends a weekend in jail for drunk driving may find it the most awful experience of her life—one that teaches her to never drink and drive again. Another person, however, may find it an exciting experience about which he can brag to his friends.

Social Learning and Violence Social learning theorists view violence as something learned through a process called behavior modeling. In modern society, aggressive acts are usually modeled after three principal sources:

- *Family interaction.* Studies of family life show that aggressive children have parents who use similar tactics when dealing with others. For example, the children of wife batterers are more likely to use aggressive tactics themselves than children in the general population, especially if the victims (their mothers) suffer psychological distress from the abuse.

- *Environmental experiences.* People who reside in areas in which violence is a daily occurrence are more likely to act violently than those who dwell in low-crime areas whose norms stress conventional behavior.

- *Mass media.* Films and television shows commonly depict violence graphically. Moreover, violence is often portrayed as an acceptable behavior, especially for heroes who never have to face legal consequences for their actions. For example, David Phillips found the homicide rate increases significantly immediately after a heavyweight championship prizefight.[241]

The Criminological Enterprise feature "Violent Media/Violent Behavior?" has more on the effects of the media and violent behavior.

The Criminological Enterprise

VIOLENT MEDIA/ VIOLENT BEHAVIOR?

Does the media influence behavior? Does broadcast violence cause aggressive behavior in viewers? This has become a hot topic because of the persistent theme of violence on television and in films. Critics have called for drastic measures, ranging from banning TV violence to putting warning labels on heavy metal albums out of fear that listening to hard-rock lyrics produces delinquency.

If there is in fact a TV–violence link, the problem is indeed alarming. Systematic viewing of TV begins at 2.5 years of age and continues at a high level during the preschool and early school years. The Kaiser Foundation study, *Zero to Six: Electronic Media in the Lives of Infants, Toddlers, and Preschoolers*, found that children 6 and under spend an average of two hours a day using screen media such as TV and computers, about the same amount of time they spend playing outside and significantly more than the amount they spend reading or being read to (about 39 minutes per day). Nearly half of children 6 and under have used a computer, and just under a third have played video games. Even the youngest children—those under 2—are exposed to electronic media for more than two hours per day; more than 40 percent of those under 2 watch TV every day. Marketing research indicates that adolescents ages 11 to 14 view violent horror movies at a higher rate than any other age group. Children this age use older peers and siblings and apathetic parents to gain access to R-rated films. Most U.S. households now have cable TV, which features violent films and shows unavailable on broadcast networks. Even children's programming is saturated with violence.

A University of Pennsylvania study found that children's programming contained an average of 32 violent acts per hour, that 56 percent had violent characters, and that 74 percent had characters who became the victims of violence (though "only 3.3 percent had characters who were actually killed"). In all, the average child views 8,000 TV murders before finishing elementary school.

The fact that children watch so much violent TV is not surprising considering the findings of a well-publicized study conducted by UCLA researchers, who found that at least 10 network shows made heavy use of violence. Of the 161 television movies monitored (every one that aired that season), 23 raised concerns about their use of violence, violent theme, violent title, or inappropriate portrayals of a scene. Of the 118 theatrical films monitored (every one that aired that season), 50 raised concerns about their use of violence.

On-air promotions also reflect a continuing, if not worsening, problem. Some series may contain several scenes of violence, each of which is appropriate within its context. An advertisement for that show, however, will feature only those violent scenes without any of the context. Even some children's television programming had worrisome signs, featuring "sinister combat" as the theme of the show. The characters are usually happy to fight and frequently do so with little provocation. There have been numerous anecdotal cases of violence linked to TV and films. For example, in a famous incident, John Hinckley shot President Ronald Reagan due to his obsession with actress Jodie Foster, which developed after he watched her play a prostitute in the violent film *Taxi Driver*. The film depicted an attempted assassination of a political figure; Hinckley viewed the film at least 15 times.

While not all experts believe that media violence is a direct *cause* of violent behavior (because if it was there would be millions of daily incidents in which viewers imitated the aggression they watched on TV or in movies), many do agree that media violence *contributes* to aggression. Developmental psychologist John Murray carefully reviewed existing research on the effect of TV violence on children and reached the conclusion that viewing media violence is related to both short- and long-term increases in aggressive attitudes, values, and behaviors; the effects of media violence are both real and strong. Similarly, Brad Bushman and Craig Anderson have found that watching violence on TV is correlated to aggressive behaviors.

There is also evidence that kids who watch TV are more likely to persist in aggressive behavior as adults. A recent study conducted by researchers at Columbia University found that kids who watch more than an hour of TV each day show an increase in assaults, fights, robberies, and other acts of aggression later in life and into adulthood. One reason is that TV viewing may create changes in personality and cognition that produce long-term behavioral changes. Dimitri Christakis and his associates found that for every hour of television watched daily between the ages of 1 and 3, the risk of developing attention problems increased by 9 percent over the life course; attention problems have been linked to antisocial behaviors.

There are several explanations for the effects of television and film violence on behavior:

▪ Media violence can provide aggressive "scripts" that children store in memory. Repeated exposure to these scripts can increase their retention and lead to changes in attitudes.

▪ Children learn from what they observe. In the same way they learn

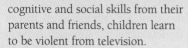

cognitive and social skills from their parents and friends, children learn to be violent from television.

▌ Television violence increases the arousal levels of viewers and makes them more prone to act aggressively. Studies measuring the galvanic skin response of subjects—a physical indication of arousal based on the amount of electricity conducted across the palm of the hand—show that viewing violent television shows led to increased arousal levels in young children.

▌ Watching television violence promotes such negative attitudes as suspiciousness and the expectation that the viewer will become involved in violence. Those who watch television frequently come to view aggression and violence as common and socially acceptable behavior.

▌ Television violence allows aggressive youths to justify their behavior. It is possible that, instead of causing violence, television helps violent youths rationalize their behavior as a socially acceptable and common activity.

▌ Television violence may disinhibit aggressive behavior, which is normally controlled by other learning processes. *Disinhibition* takes place when adults are viewed as being rewarded for violence and when violence is seen as socially acceptable. This contradicts previous learning experiences in which violent behavior was viewed as wrong.

Debating the Media–Violence Link

While this research is quite persuasive, not all criminologists accept that watching TV and movies or playing violent video games contributes to violent behavior. Just because kids who are exposed to violent media also engage in violent behaviors is not proof of a causal connection. It is also possible that kids who are violent later seek out violent media. What would we expect violent gang boys to watch on TV? *Hannah Montana*? There is little evidence that areas that experience the highest levels of violent TV viewing also have rates of violent crime that are above the norm. Millions of children watch violence every night but do not become violent criminals. If violent TV shows did, indeed, cause interpersonal violence, then there should be few ecological and regional patterns in the crime rate, but there are many. Put another way, how can regional differences in the violence rate be explained considering the fact that people all across the nation watch the same TV shows and films? Nor can the violence–media link explain recent crime trends. Despite a rampant increase in violent TV shows, films, and video games, the violence rate among teens has been in a significant decline.

One reason for the ongoing debate may be that media violence may affect one subset of the population but have relatively little effect on others. Sociologist George Comstock has identified attributes that make some people especially prone to the effects of media violence:

▌ Predisposition for aggressive or antisocial behavior

▌ Rigid or indifferent parenting

▌ Unsatisfactory social relationships

▌ Low psychological well-being

▌ Having been diagnosed as suffering from DBDs (disruptive behavior disorders)

So if the impact of media on behavior is not in fact universal, it may have the greatest effect on those who are the most socially and psychological vulnerable.

CRITICAL THINKING

1. Should the government control the content of TV shows and limit the amount of weekly violence? How could the national news be shown if violence were omitted? What about boxing matches or hockey games?

2. How can we explain the fact that millions of kids watch violent TV shows and remain nonviolent? If there is a TV–violence link, how can we explain the fact that violence rates may have been higher in the Old West than they are today? Do you think violent gang kids stay home and watch TV shows?

Sources: George Comstock, "A Sociological Perspective on Television Violence and Aggression," *American Behavioral Scientist* 51 (2008): 1,184–1,211; John Murray, "Media Violence: The Effects Are Both Real and Strong," *American Behavioral Scientist* 51 (2008): 1,212–1,230; Tom Grimes and Lori Bergen, "The Epistemological Argument Against a Causal Relationship Between Media Violence and Sociopathic Behavior Among Psychologically Well Viewers," *American Behavioral Scientist* 51 (2008): 1,137–1,154; Victoria Rideout, Elizabeth Vandewater, and Ellen Wartella, *Zero to Six: Electronic Media in the Lives of Infants, Toddlers and Preschoolers* (Menlo Park, CA: Kaiser Foundation, 2003); Dimitri Christakis, Frederick Zimmerman, David DiGiuseppe, and Carolyn McCarty, "Early Television Exposure and Subsequent Attentional Problems in Children," *Pediatrics* 113 (2004): 708–713; Jeffery Johnson, Patricia Cohen, Elizabeth Smailes, Stephanie Kasen, and Judith Brook, "Television Viewing and Aggressive Behavior During Adolescent and Adulthood," *Science* 295 (2002): 2,468–2,471; Craig Anderson and Brad J. Bushman, "The Effects of Media Violence on Society," *Science* 295 (2002): 2,377–2,379; Brad Bushman and Craig Anderson, "Media Violence and the American Public," *American Psychologist* 56 (2001): 477–489; UCLA Center for Communication Policy, *Television Violence Monitoring Project* (Los Angeles).

Social learning theorists have tried to determine what triggers violent acts. One position is that a direct, pain-producing physical assault will usually trigger a violent response. Yet the relationship between painful attacks and aggressive responses has been found to be inconsistent. Whether people counterattack in the face of physical attack depends, in part, on their skill in fighting and their perception of the strength of their attackers. Verbal taunts and insults have also been linked to aggressive responses. People who are predisposed to aggression by their learning experiences are likely to view insults from others as a challenge to their social status and to react with violence. Still another violence-triggering mechanism is a perceived reduction in one's life conditions. Prime examples of this phenomenon are riots and demonstrations in poverty-stricken ghetto areas. Studies have shown that discontent also produces aggression in the more successful members of lower-class groups who have been led to believe they can succeed but then have been thwarted in their aspirations. While it is still uncertain how this relationship is constructed, it is apparently complex. No matter how deprived some individuals are, they will not resort to violence. It seems evident that people's perceptions of their relative deprivation have different effects on their aggressive responses.

In summary, social learning theorists have said that the following four factors may contribute to violent and/or aggressive behavior:

▎ *An event that heightens arousal*. Such as a person frustrating or provoking another through physical assault or verbal abuse.

▎ *Aggressive skills*. Learned aggressive responses picked up from observing others, either personally or through the media.

▎ *Expected outcomes*. The belief that aggression will somehow be rewarded. Rewards can come in the form of reducing tension or anger, gaining some financial reward, building self-esteem, or gaining the praise of others.

▎ *Consistency of behavior with values*. The belief, gained from observing others, that aggression is justified and appropriate, given the circumstances of the current situation.

Cognitive Theory

One area of psychology that has received increasing recognition in recent years has been the cognitive school. Psychologists with a cognitive perspective focus on mental processes and how people perceive and mentally represent the world around them and solve problems. The pioneers of this school were Wilhelm Wundt (1832–1920), Edward Titchener (1867–1927), and William James (1842–1920). Today, there are several subdisciplines within the cognitive area. The **moral development** branch is concerned with the way people morally represent and reason about the world. **Humanistic psychology** stresses self-awareness and "getting in touch with feelings." The **information processing** branch focuses on the way people process, store,

encode, retrieve, and manipulate information to make decisions and solve problems.

Moral and Intellectual Development Theory The moral and intellectual development branch of cognitive psychology is perhaps the most important for criminological theory. Jean Piaget (1896–1980), the founder of this approach, hypothesized that people's reasoning processes develop in an orderly fashion, beginning at birth and continuing until they are 12 years old and older.[242] At first, children respond to the environment in a simple manner, seeking interesting objects and developing their reflexes. By the fourth and final stage, the formal operations stage, they have developed into mature adults who can use logic and abstract thought.

Lawrence Kohlberg first applied the concept of moral development to issues in criminology.[243] He found that people travel through stages of moral development during which their decisions and judgments on issues of right and wrong are made for different reasons. It is possible that serious offenders have a moral orientation that differs from that of law-abiding citizens. Kohlberg classified people according to the stage on this continuum at which their moral development ceased to grow. Kohlberg and his associates conducted studies in which criminals were found to be significantly lower in their moral judgment development than noncriminals of the same social background.[244] Since his pioneering efforts, researchers have continued to show that criminal offenders are more likely to be classified in the lowest levels of moral reasoning (Stages 1 and 2), whereas noncriminals have reached a higher stage of moral development (Stages 3 and 4).[245]

Recent research indicates that the decision not to commit crimes may be influenced by one's stage of moral development. People at the lowest levels report that they are deterred from crime because of their fear of sanctions. Those in the middle consider the reactions of family and friends. Those at the highest stages refrain from crime because they believe in duty to others and universal rights.[246]

Moral development theory suggests that people who obey the law simply to avoid punishment or have outlooks mainly characterized by self-interest are more likely to commit crimes than those who view the law as something that benefits all of society. Those at higher stages of moral reasoning tend to sympathize with the rights of others and are associated with conventional behaviors, such as honesty, generosity, and nonviolence. Subsequent research has found that a significant number of noncriminals display higher stages of moral reasoning than criminals and that engaging in criminal behavior leads to reduced levels of moral reasoning, which in turn produces more delinquency in a never ending loop.[247]

connections

The deterrent effect of informal sanctions and feelings of shame discussed in Chapter 4 may hinge on the level of a person's moral development. The lower one's state of moral development, the less impact informal sanctions may have; increased moral development and informal sanctions may be better able to control crime.

Information Processing When cognitive theorists who study information processing try to explain antisocial behavior, they do so in terms of mental perception and how people use information to understand their environment. When people make decisions, they engage in a sequence of cognitive thought processes:

1. Encode information so that it can be interpreted.

2. Search for a proper response.

3. Decide on the most appropriate action.

4. Act on the decision.[248]

Not everyone processes information in the same way, and the differences in interpretation may explain the development of radically different visions of the world.

According to this cognitive approach, people who use information properly, who are better conditioned to make reasoned judgments, and who can make quick and reasoned decisions when facing emotion-laden events are the ones best able to avoid antisocial behavior choices.[249] In contrast, crime-prone people may have cognitive deficits and use information incorrectly when they make decisions.[250] Law violators may lack the ability to perform cognitive functions in a normal and orderly fashion.[251] Some may be sensation seekers who are constantly looking for novel experiences, whereas others lack deliberation and rarely think through problems. Some may give up easily, whereas others act without thinking when they get upset.[252]

People with inadequate cognitive processing perceive the world as stacked against them; they believe they have little control over the negative events in their life.[253] Chronic offenders come to believe that crime is an appropriate means to satisfy their immediate personal needs, which take precedence over more distant social needs such as obedience to the law.[254] They have a distorted view of the world that shapes their thinking and colors their judgments. Because they have difficulty making the right decision while under stress, they pursue behaviors that they perceive as beneficial and satisfying, but that turn out to be harmful and detrimental.[255] They may take aggressive action because they wrongly believe that a situation demands forceful responses when it actually does not. They find it difficult to understand or sympathize with other people's feelings and emotions, which leads them to blame their victims for their problems.[256] Thus, the sexual offender believes their target either led them on or secretly wanted the forcible sex to occur: "She was asking for it."[257]

Shaping Perceptions People whose cognitive processes are skewed or faulty may be relying on mental scripts learned in childhood that tell them how to interpret events, what to expect, how they should react, and what the outcome of the interaction should be.[258] Hostile children may have learned improper scripts by observing how others react to events; their own parents' aggressive and inappropriate behavior would have considerable impact. Some may have had early and prolonged exposure to violence (for example, child abuse), which increases their sensitivity to slights and maltreatment. Oversensitivity to rejection by their peers is a continuation of sensitivity to rejection by their parents.[259] Violent behavior responses learned in childhood become a stable behavior because the scripts that emphasize aggressive responses are repeatedly rehearsed as the child matures.[260]

To violence-prone kids, people seem more aggressive than they actually are and seem to intend them ill when there is no reason for alarm. According to information processing theory, as these children mature, they use fewer cues than most people to process information. Some use violence in a calculating fashion as a means of getting what they want; others react in an overly volatile fashion to the slightest provocation. Aggressors are more likely to be vigilant, on edge, or suspicious. When they attack victims, they may believe they are defending themselves, even though they are misreading the situation.[261]

Adolescents who use violence as a coping technique with others are also more likely to exhibit other social problems, such as drug and alcohol abuse.[262] There is also evidence that delinquent boys who engage in theft are more likely to exhibit

Zachariah Blanton (center), 17, is led into the Jackson County Courthouse in Brownstown, Indiana, by sheriff's deputies on July 26, 2006. Blanton was tried on charges of murder, attempted murder, and criminal recklessness for a series of highway shootings that killed a man in southern Indiana. Blanton had been on a hunting trip with relatives but got into an argument and drove off in anger shortly before the attacks. He drove to a nearby overpass, aimed his rifle over the trunk of his vehicle, and fired at trucks on Interstate 65. Can such incidents of random and seemingly unprovoked violence be a product of impaired judgment and cognitive dysfunction?

cognitive deficits than nondelinquent youth. For example, they have a poor sense of time, leaving them incapable of dealing with or solving social problems in an effective manner.[263] Information processing theory has been used to explain the occurrence of date rape. Sexually violent males believe that when their dates say "no" to sexual advances the women are really "playing games" and actually want to be taken forcefully.[264]

Errors in cognition and information processing have been used to explain the behavior of child abusers. Distorted thinking patterns that abusers express include the following:

▌ *Child as a sexual being*. Children are perceived as being able to and wanting to engage in sexual activity with adults and also as not harmed by such sexual contact.[265]

▌ *Nature of harm*. The offender perceives that sexual activity does not cause harm (and may in fact be beneficial) to the child.

▌ *Entitlement*. The child abuser perceives that he is superior and more important than others and hence is able to have sex with whomever, and whenever, he wants.

▌ *Dangerous world*. An offender perceives that others are abusive and rejecting, and he must fight to regain control.

▌ *Uncontrollable*. The world is perceived as uncontrollable, and circumstances are outside of his control.

Treatment based on how people process information takes into account that people are more likely to respond aggressively to a provocation because thoughts tend to intensify the insult or otherwise stir feelings of anger. Cognitive therapists, during the course of treatment, attempt to teach explosive people to control aggressive impulses by viewing social provocations as problems demanding a solution rather than retaliation. Programs are aimed at teaching problem-solving skills that may include self-disclosure, role-playing, listening, following instructions, joining in, and using self-control.[266]

Therapeutic interventions designed to make people better problem solvers may involve such measures as (a) enhancing coping and problem-solving skills; (b) enhancing relationships with peers, parents, and other adults; (c) teaching conflict resolution and communication skills and methods for resisting peer pressure related to drug use and violence; (d) teaching consequential thinking and decision-making abilities; (e) modeling prosocial behaviors, including cooperation with others, self-responsibility, respecting others, and public speaking efficacy; and (f) teaching empathy.[267]

Treatment interventions based on learning social skills are relatively new, but there are some indications that this approach can have long-term benefits for reducing criminal behavior.[268]

The various psychological theories of crime are set out in Concept Summary 5.2.

 **www** Go to academic.cengage.com/criminaljustice/siegel to learn more about the following:

▌ A collection of links to libraries, museums, and biographical materials related to **Sigmund Freud and his works**.

▌ The **National Mental Health Association (NMHA)**,

the country's oldest and largest nonprofit organization addressing all aspects of mental health and mental illness. It is dedicated to improving the mental health of all individuals and achieving victory over mental illnesses.

▌ A site devoted to the relationship between **mental illness and crime**.

▌ The life and work of **Albert Bandura**.

PSYCHOLOGICAL TRAITS AND CHARACTERISTICS

In addition to creating theories of behavior and development, psychologists also study psychological traits and characteristics that define an individual and shape how they function in the world. Certain traits have become associated with psychological problems and the development of antisocial behavior trends.

Two of the most critical—personality and intelligence—are discussed in detail in the following sections.

Personality and Crime

Personality can be defined as the reasonably stable patterns of behavior, including thoughts and emotions, that distinguish one person from another.[269] One's personality reflects a characteristic way of adapting to life's demands and problems. The way we behave is a function of how our personality enables us to interpret life events and make appropriate behavioral choices. Can the cause of crime be linked to personality?

The association between personality traits and crime has a long history. Sheldon Glueck and Eleanor Glueck identified a number of personality traits that they believe characterize antisocial youth:[270]

self-assertiveness	sadism
defiance	lack of concern for others
extroversion	feeling unappreciated
ambivalence	distrust of authority
impulsiveness	poor personal skills
narcissism	mental instability
suspicion	hostility
destructiveness	resentment[271]

connections

The Glueck research is representative of the view that antisocial people maintain a distinct set of personal traits, which makes them particularly sensitive to environmental stimuli. Once dismissed by mainstream criminologists, the section on life course theories in Chapter 9 shows how the Gluecks' views still influence contemporary criminological theory.

Psychologist Hans Eysenck linked personality to crime when he identified two traits that he associated with antisocial behavior: *extroversion-introversion* and *stability-instability*. Extreme introverts are overaroused and avoid sources of stimulation; in contrast, extreme extroverts are unaroused and seek sensation. Introverts are slow to learn and be conditioned; extroverts are impulsive individuals who lack the ability to examine their own motives and behaviors. Those who are unstable, a condition Eysenck calls "neuroticism," are anxious, tense, and emotionally unstable.[272] People who are both neurotic and extroverted lack self-insight and are impulsive and emotionally unstable; they are unlikely to have reasoned judgments of life events. While extrovert neurotics may act self-destructively (e.g., abusing drugs), more stable people will be able to reason that such behavior is ultimately harmful and life threatening. Eysenck believes that personality is controlled by genetic factors and is heritable.

A number of research efforts have found an association between the personality traits identified by Eysenck and repeat and chronic criminal offending.[273] Other suspected traits include

impulsivity, hostility, and aggressiveness.[274] Callous, unemotional traits in very young children can be a warning sign for future psychopathy and antisocial behavior.[275] Personality defects have been linked not only to aggressive antisocial behaviors such as assault and rape, but also to white-collar and business crimes.[276]

According to this view, the personality is the key to understanding antisocial behavior. The more severe the disorder, the greater the likelihood that the individual will engage in serious and repeat antisocial acts.[277] Take for instance sadistic personality disorder, defined as a repeat pattern of cruel and demeaning behavior. People suffering from this type of extreme personality disturbance seem prone to engage in serious violent attacks, including homicides motivated by sexual sadism.[278]

The Antisocial Personality *The Diagnostic and Statistical Manual of the American Psychiatric Association* (APA) defines the antisocial personality as a pervasive pattern of disregard for, and violation of, the rights of others that begins in childhood or early adolescence and continues into adulthood. In addition, those suffering from this disease usually exhibit at least three of the following behaviors:

- Failure to conform to social norms with respect to lawful behaviors as indicated by repeatedly performing acts that are grounds for arrest
- Deceitfulness, as indicated by repeatedly lying, use of aliases, or conning others for personal profit or pleasure
- Impulsivity or failure to plan ahead
- Irritability and aggressiveness, as indicated by repeated physical fights or assaults
- Reckless disregard for safety of self or others
- Consistent irresponsibility, as indicated by repeated failure to sustain consistent work behavior or honor financial obligations
- Lack of remorse, as indicated by being indifferent to or rationalizing having hurt, mistreated, or stolen from another[279]

The terms psychopath and sociopath are commonly used to describe people who have an antisocial personality (though the APA considers them antiquated and obsolete). Though these terms are often used interchangeably, some psychologists distinguish between sociopaths and psychopaths, suggesting that the former are a product of a destructive home environment whereas the latter are a product of a defect or aberration within themselves.[280] This condition is discussed in The Criminological Enterprise feature "The Psychopath."

Research on Personality Since maintaining a deviant personality has been related to crime and delinquency, numerous attempts have been made to devise accurate measures of personality and determine whether they can predict antisocial behavior. One of the most widely used psychological tests is the Minnesota Multiphasic Personality Inventory, commonly called the MMPI. This test has subscales designed to

THE PSYCHOPATH

Some violent offenders may have a disturbed character structure commonly referred to as psychopathy, sociopathy, or antisocial personality. Psychopaths exhibit a low level of guilt and anxiety and persistently violate the rights of others. Although they may exhibit superficial charm and above-average intelligence, this often masks a disturbed personality that makes them incapable of forming enduring relationships with others and continually involves them in such deviant behaviors as violence, risk taking, substance abuse, and impulsivity.

From an early age, many psychopaths have had home lives that were filled with frustrations, bitterness, and quarreling. Antisocial youths exhibit low levels of guilt and anxiety and persistently violate the rights of others. Their intelligence may alter their criminal career development, and render it quite different from that of nonpsychopathic criminals; high intelligence appears to enhance the destructive potential of a psychopath while intelligence may mediate the criminality of the non-psychopath.

As a result of this instability and frustration, these individuals developed personalities that became unreliable, unstable, demanding, and egocentric. Most psychopaths are risk-taking, sensation seekers who are constantly involved in a garden variety of antisocial behaviors. Some may become almost addicted to thrill seeking, resulting in repeated and dangerous risky behaviors. They are often described as grandiose, egocentric, manipulative, forceful, and cold-hearted, with shallow emotions and the inability to feel remorse, empathy with others, or anxiety over their misdeeds. When they commit antisocial acts, they are less likely to feel shame or empathize with their victims. Hervey Cleckley, a leading authority on psychopathy, described them as follows:

> [Psychopaths are] chronically antisocial individuals who are always in trouble, profiting neither from experience nor punishment, and maintaining no real loyalties to any person, group, or code. They are frequently callous and hedonistic, showing marked emotional immaturity, with lack of responsibility, lack of judgment and an ability to rationalize their behavior so that it appears warranted, reasonable and justified.

Considering these personality traits, it is not surprising that research studies show that people evaluated as psychopaths are significantly more prone to criminal and violent behavior when compared to nonpsychopathic control groups. Psychopaths tend to continue their criminal careers long after other offenders burn out or age out of crime. They are continually in trouble with the law and, therefore, are likely to wind up in penal institutions. After reviewing available data, forensic psychologist James Blair and his colleagues conclude that approximately 15 to 25 percent of U.S. prison inmates meet diagnostic criteria for psychopathy. Once they are released, former inmates who suffer from psychopathy are three times more likely to reoffend within a year of release than other prisoners, and four times more likely to reoffend violently.

The Cause of Psychopathy

Though psychologists are still not certain of the cause of psychopathy, a number of factors are believed to contribute to its development.

Traumatic Socialization

Some explanations focus on family experiences, suggesting that the influence of an unstable parent, parental rejection, lack of love during childhood, and inconsistent discipline may be related to psychopathy. Children who lack the opportunity to form an attachment to a mother figure in the first three years of life, who suffer sudden separation from the mother figure, or who see changes in the mother figure are most likely to develop psychopathic personalities. According to this view, the path runs from antisocial parenting to psychopathy to criminality. Psychologist David Lykken suggests that psychopaths have an inherited "low fear quotient," which inhibits their fear of punishment. All people have a natural or innate fear of certain stimuli, such as spiders, snakes, fires, or strangers. Psychopaths, as a rule, have few fears. Normal socialization processes depend on punishing antisocial behavior to inhibit future transgressions. Someone who does not fear punishment is simply harder to socialize.

Neurological Disorder

Psychopaths may suffer from lower than normal levels of arousal. Research studies show that psychopaths have lower skin conductance levels and fewer

measure many different personality traits, including psychopathic deviation (Pd scale), schizophrenia (Sc), and hypomania (Ma).[281] Research studies have detected an association between scores on the Pd scale and criminal involvement.[282] Another frequently administered personality test, the California Personality Inventory (CPI), has also been used to distinguish deviants from nondeviant groups.[283] The Multidimensional Personality Questionnaire (MPQ) allows researchers to assess such personality traits as control, aggression, alienation, and well-being.[284] Evaluations using this scale indicate that adolescent offenders who are crime prone maintain "negative emotionality," a tendency to experience aversive affective states, such as anger, anxiety, and irritability. They also are predisposed to weak personal constraints, and they have difficulty controlling impulsive behavior urges. Because they are both impulsive and spontaneous responses than normal subjects. There may be a link between psychopathy and autonomic nervous system (ANS) dysfunction. The ANS mediates physiological activities associated with emotions and is manifested in such measurements as heartbeat rate, blood pressure, respiration, muscle tension, capillary size, and electrical activity of the skin (called galvanic skin resistance). Psychopaths may be less capable of regulating their activities than other people. While some people may become anxious and afraid when facing the prospect of committing a criminal act, psychopaths in the same circumstances feel no such fear. James Ogloff and Stephen Wong conclude that their reduced anxiety levels result in behaviors that are more impulsive and inappropriate and in deviant behavior, apprehension, and incarceration.

Brain Structure

Another view is that psychopathy is related to an abnormal brain structure. One suspect is dysfunction in the limbic inhibitory system, manifested through damage to the frontal and temporal lobes of the brain. Consequently, psychopaths may need greater than average stimulation to bring them up to comfortable levels (similar to arousal theory, discussed earlier).

Yet another view is that psychopathy is bound up in an impairment of the amygdala, the part of the brain that plays a crucial role in processing emotions. As James Blair and his colleagues suggest, amygdala dysfunction gives rise to

impairments in aversive conditioning, instrumental learning, and the processing of fearful and sad expressions. These impairments interfere with socialization; people with impaired amygdalae do not learn to avoid actions that cause harm to other individuals. Because of this deficiency, psychopaths have problems distinguishing and processing people's facial expressions. When Quinton Deeley and his colleagues compared facial recognition ability of psychopaths with a control group, they found that the former were significantly less likely to recognize and emotionally respond to facial and other signals of distress. This inability may help explain the lack of emotional empathy observed among people with antisocial personalities.

Chronic Offending

The antisocial personality concept seems to jibe with what is known about chronic offending. As many as 80 percent of high-end chronic offenders exhibit sociopathic behavior patterns. Though comprising about 4 percent of the total male population and less than 1 percent of the total female population, they are responsible for half of all serious felony offenses committed annually. Not all high-rate chronic offenders are sociopaths, but enough are to support a strong link between personality dysfunction and long-term criminal careers.

CRITICAL THINKING

1. Should people diagnosed as psychopaths be separated and treated even if they have not yet committed a crime?

2. Should psychopathic murderers be spared the death penalty because they lack the capacity to control their behavior?

Sources: Cengiz Basoglu, Umit Semiz, Ozgur Oner, Huseyin Gunay, Servet Ebrinc, Mesut Cetin, Onur Sildiroglu, Ayhan Algul, Alpay Ates, and Guner Sonmez, "A Magnetic Resonance Spectroscopy Study of Antisocial Behaviour Disorder, Psychopathy and Violent Crime among Military Conscripts," *Acta Neuropsychiatrica* 20 (2008): 72–77; Rolf Holmqvist, "Psychopathy and Affect Consciousness in Young Criminal Offenders," *Journal of Interpersonal Violence* 23 (2008): 209–224; James Blair, Derek Mitchell, and Karina Blair, *The Psychopath: Emotion and the Brain* (New York: Blackwell Publishing, 2005); Quinton Deeley, Eileen Daly, Simon Surguladze, Nigel Tunstall, Gill Mezey, Dominic Beer, Anita Ambikapathy, Dene Robertson, Vincent Giampietro, Michael Brammer, Amory Clarke, John Dowsett, Tom Fahy, Mary L. Phillips, and Declan G. Murphy, "Facial Emotion Processing in Criminal Psychopathy," *British Journal of Psychiatry* 189 (2006): 533–539; Gisli Gudjonsson, Emil Einarsson, Ólafur Örn Bragason, and Jon Fridrik Sigurdsson, "Personality Predictors of Self-Reported Offending in Icelandic Students," *Psychology, Crime and Law* 12 (2006): 383–393; Sue Kellett and Harriet Gross, "Addicted to Joyriding? An Exploration of Young Offenders' Accounts of Their Car Crime," *Psychology, Crime and Law* 12 (2006): 39–59; Peter Johansson and Margaret Kerr, "Psychopathy and Intelligence: A Second Look," *Journal of Personality Disorders* 19 (2005): 357–369; Kent Kiehl, Andra Smith, Adrianna Mendrek, Bruce Forster, Robert Hare, and Peter F. Liddle, "Temporal Lobe Abnormalities in Semantic Processing by Criminal Psychopaths as Revealed by Functional Magnetic Resonance Imaging," *Psychiatry Research: Neuroimaging* 130 (2004): 27–42; David Lykken, "Psychopathy, Sociopathy, and Crime," *Society* 34 (1996): 30–38; Hervey Cleckley, "Psychopathic States," in *American Handbook of Psychiatry*, ed. S. Aneti (New York: Basic Books, 1959), pp. 567–569.

aggressive, crime-prone people are quick to take action against perceived threats.

Evidence that personality traits predict crime and violence is important because it suggests that the root cause of crime can be found in the forces that influence human development at an early stage of life. If these results are valid, rather than focus on job creation and neighborhood improvement, crime control efforts might be better focused on helping families raise children who are reasoned and reflective and enjoy a safe environment.

Intelligence and Crime

Intelligence refers to a person's ability to reason, comprehend ideas, solve problems, think abstractly, understand complex ideas, learn from experience, and discover solutions to complex problems. It was long believed that people who maintain a below-average intelligence quotient (IQ) were at risk for criminality. Criminals were believed to have inherently substandard intelligence, and thus, they seemed naturally inclined to commit more crimes than more intelligent persons. Furthermore, it was thought that if authorities could determine which individuals had low IQs, they might identify potential criminals before they committed socially harmful acts.

During the early twentieth century, social scientists had a captive group of subjects in juvenile training schools and penal institutions, and they began to measure the correlation between IQ and crime by testing adjudicated offenders. Thus, inmates of penal institutions were used as a test group around which numerous theories about intelligence were built, leading ultimately to the nature-versus-nurture controversy that is still going on today. These concepts are discussed in some detail in the following sections.

Nature Theory Nature theory argues that intelligence is largely determined genetically, that ancestry determines IQ, and that low intelligence, as demonstrated by low IQ, is linked to criminal behavior. When the newly developed IQ tests were administered to inmates of prisons and juvenile training schools in the first decades of the 20th century, the nature position gained support because a very large proportion of the inmates scored low on the tests. During his studies in 1920, Henry Goddard found that many institutionalized persons were what he considered "feebleminded"; he concluded that at least half of all juvenile delinquents were mental defectives.[285] In 1926, William Healy and Augusta Bronner tested groups of delinquent boys in Chicago and Boston and found that 37 percent were subnormal in intelligence. They concluded that delinquents were five to ten times more likely to be mentally deficient than normal boys.[286] These and other early studies were embraced as proof that low IQ scores identified potentially delinquent children and that a correlation existed between innate low intelligence and deviant behavior. IQ tests were believed to measure the inborn genetic makeup of individuals, and many criminologists accepted the idea that individuals with substandard IQs were predisposed toward delinquency and adult criminality.

Nurture Theory The rise of culturally sensitive explanations of human behavior in the 1930s led to the nurture school of intelligence. Nurture theory states that intelligence must be viewed as partly biological but primarily sociological. Because intelligence is not inherited, low-IQ parents do not necessarily produce low-IQ children.[287] Nurture theorists discredited the notion that people commit crimes because they have low IQs. Instead, they postulated that environmental stimulation from parents, relatives, social contacts, schools, peer groups, and innumerable others create a child's IQ level and that low IQs result from an environment that also encourages delinquent and criminal behavior. Thus, if low IQ scores are recorded among criminals, these scores may reflect criminals' cultural background, not their mental ability. Studies challenging the assumption that people automatically committed criminal acts because they had below-average IQs began to appear as early as the 1920s. John Slawson studied 1,543 delinquent boys in New York institutions and compared them with a control group

of New York City boys in 1926.[288] Slawson found that although 80 percent of the delinquents achieved lower scores in abstract verbal intelligence, delinquents were about normal in mechanical aptitude and nonverbal intelligence. These results indicated the possibility of cultural bias in portions of the IQ tests. He also found that there was no relationship between the number of arrests, the types of offenses, and IQ.

Though many early criminologists believed there was a link between intelligence and crime, in 1931, Edwin Sutherland evaluated IQ studies of criminals and delinquents and noted significant variation in the findings, which disproved any notion that criminals were "feebleminded."[289] Sutherland's research all but put an end to the belief that crime was caused by "feeblemindedness"; the IQ–crime link was ignored in the criminological literature.

More than 40 years later, the respected criminologists Travis Hirschi and Michael Hindelang resurrected the IQ–crime debate. They reexamined existing research data and concluded that the weight of evidence shows that IQ is a more important factor than race and socioeconomic class for predicting criminal and delinquent involvement.[290] Rejecting the notion that IQ tests are race and class biased, they concluded that major differences exist between criminals and noncriminals within similar racial and socioeconomic class categories. They proposed the idea that low IQ increases the likelihood of criminal behavior through its effect on school performance. That is, youths with low IQs do poorly in school, and school failure and academic incompetence are highly related to delinquency and later to adult criminality.

Hirschi and Hindelang's inferences have been supported by research conducted by both U.S. and international scholars.[291] *The Bell Curve*, Richard Herrnstein and Charles Murray's influential albeit controversial book on intelligence, comes down firmly for an IQ–crime link. Their extensive review of the available literature shows that people with lower IQs are more likely to commit crime, get caught, and be sent to prison.[292]

Some studies have found a direct IQ–delinquency link among samples of adolescent boys.[293] When Alex Piquero examined violent behavior among groups of children in Philadelphia, he found that scores on intelligence tests were the best predictors of violent behavior and could be used to distinguish between groups of violent and nonviolent offenders.[294] Others find that the IQ–crime link is an indirect one: low intelligence leads to poor school performance, which enhances the chances of criminality.[295] The IQ–crime relationship has also been found in cross-national studies conducted in a number of countries, including Sweden, Denmark, and Canada.[296]

IQ and Crime Reconsidered The Hirschi-Hindelang research increased interest and research on the association between IQ and crime, but the issue is far from settled and is still a matter of significant debate. While the studies cited above found an IQ–crime association, others suggest that IQ level has negligible influence on criminal behavior.[297] An evaluation of existing knowledge on intelligence conducted by the American Psychological Association concluded that the strength of an IQ–crime link was "very low."[298] Those who question the IQ–crime link suggest that any association may be based on spurious data and inadequate research methodologies:

▌ IQ tests are biased and reflect middle class values. As a result, socially disadvantaged people do poorly on IQ tests and members of that group are also the ones most likely to commit crime. The low-IQ–crime association is spurious: people who suffer disadvantages such as poverty and limited educational resources do poorly on IQ tests and also commit crime.

▌ The measurement of intelligence is often varied and haphazard, and results may depend on the particular method used. The correlation between intelligence and antisocial behavior using IQ tests as a measure of aptitude is slight; it is stronger if attendance in special programs or special schools is used as an indicator of intellectual ability.[299]

▌ People with low IQs are stigmatized and negatively labeled by middle class decision makers such as police officers, teachers, and guidance counselors. It is not a low IQ that causes criminal behavior—the stigma that people with low IQs suffer pushes them into criminality.

▌ Research using official record data may be flawed. It is possible that criminals with high IQ are better able to avoid detection and punishment than low IQ people. Research using data from arrestees may omit the more intelligent members of the criminal subclass. And even if they are caught, high IQ offenders are less likely to be convicted and punished. Because their favorable treatment helps higher IQ offenders avoid the pains of criminal punishment, it lessens their chances of recidivism.

▌ Maintaining a low IQ may influence some criminal patterns, such as arson and sex crimes, but not others, such as theft offenses.[300]

Even if it can be shown that known offenders have lower IQs than the general population, it is difficult to explain many patterns in the crime rate: Why are there more male than female criminals? (Are females smarter than males?) Why do crime rates vary by region, time of year, and even weather patterns? Why does aging out occur? IQs do not increase with age, so why should crime rates fall?

The various psychological perspectives, characteristics, and attributes are outlined in Figure 5.2.

 www To read all about **IQ testing and intelligence**, go to academic.cengage.com/criminaljustice/siegel.

PUBLIC POLICY IMPLICATIONS OF TRAIT THEORY

For most of the twentieth century, biological and psychological views of criminality have influenced crime control and prevention policy. The result has been front-end or primary

Figure 5.2 Psychological Perspectives on Criminality

Theory	Cause
PSYCHODYNAMIC (psychoanalytic)	**Intrapsychic processes** • Unconscious conflicts • Mood disorders • Psychosis • Lack of attachment • Sexuality
BEHAVIORAL	**Learning processes** • Learning experiences • Stimulus • Rewards and punishments • Direct/indirect observation
COGNITIVE	**Information processing** • Thinking • Planning • Memory • Perception • Ethical values

Characteristic	Cause
PERSONALITY	**Personality processes** • Antisocial personality • Sociopath/psychopath temperament • Abnormal affect, lack of emotional depth
INTELLIGENCE	**Intellectual processes** • Low IQ • Poor school performance • Decision-making ability

prevention programs that seek to treat personal problems before they manifest themselves as crime. To this end, thousands of family therapy organizations, substance abuse clinics, and mental health associations operate throughout the United States. Teachers, employers, relatives, welfare agencies, and others make referrals to these facilities. These services are based on the premise that if a person's problems can be treated before they become overwhelming, some future crimes will be prevented. Secondary prevention programs provide treatment such as psychological counseling to youths and adults who are at risk for law violation. Tertiary prevention programs may be a requirement of a probation order, part of a diversionary sentence, or aftercare at the end of a prison sentence.

Biologically oriented therapy is also being used in the criminal justice system. Programs have altered diets, changed lighting, compensated for learning disabilities, treated allergies, and so on.[301] More controversial has been the use of mood-altering chemicals, such as lithium, pemoline, imipramine, phenytoin, and benzodiazepines, to control behavior. Another practice that has elicited concern is the use of psychosurgery (brain surgery) to control antisocial behavior. Surgical procedures have been used to alter the brain structure of convicted sex offenders in an effort to eliminate or control their sex drives. Results are still preliminary, but some critics argue that these procedures are without scientific merit.[302]

Numerous psychologically based treatment methods range from individual counseling to behavior modification. For example, treatment based on how people process information takes into account that people are more likely to respond aggressively to provocation if thoughts intensify the insult or otherwise stir feelings of anger. Cognitive therapists attempt to teach explosive people to control aggressive impulses by viewing social provocations as problems demanding a solution rather than retaliation. Therapeutic interventions designed to make people better problem solvers may involve measures that enhance

- Coping and problem-solving skills
- Relationships with peers, parents, and other adults
- Conflict resolution and communication skills, and methods for resisting peer pressure related to drug use and violence
- Consequential thinking and decision-making abilities
- Prosocial behaviors, including cooperation with others, self-responsibility, respecting others, and public-speaking efficacy
- Empathy[303]

While it is often difficult to treat people with severe mental and personality disorders, there is evidence that positive outcomes can be achieved with the right combination of treatment modalities.[304]

THINKING LIKE A CRIMINOLOGIST

The American Psychiatric Association believes a person should not be held legally responsible for a crime if his or her behavior meets the following standard developed by legal expert Richard Bonnie:

A person charged with a criminal offense should be found not guilty by reason of insanity if it is shown that as a result of mental disease or mental retardation he was unable to appreciate the wrongfulness of his conduct at the time of the offense.

As used in this standard, the terms *mental disease* and *mental retardation* include only those severely abnormal mental conditions that grossly and demonstrably impair a person's perception or understanding of reality and that are not attributable primarily to the voluntary ingestion of alcohol or other psychoactive substances.

 Writing Exercise As a criminologist with expertise on trait theories of crime, do you agree with this standard? Write a brief paper (two pages double-spaced) explaining your view of the APA's standard, and what modifications, if any, you suggest to include other categories of offenders who are not excused by this definition.

 Doing Research on the Web Before you give your opinion, check out the website of the American Psychiatric Association and see what their position is on the insanity defense. To learn more about the structure of mental illness and how it relates to crime, visit the Health Canada website. Both websites can be easily accessed through academic.cengage .com/criminaljustice/siegel.

SUMMARY

- The earliest positivist criminologists were biologists. Led by Cesare Lombroso, these early researchers believed that some people manifested primitive traits that made them born criminals. Today their research is debunked because of poor methodology, testing, and logic.

- Biological views fell out of favor in the early twentieth century. In the 1970s, spurred by the publication of Edmund O. Wilson's *Sociobiology*, several criminologists again turned to study of the biological basis of criminality. For the most part, the effort has focused on the cause of violent crime.

■ One area of interest is biochemical factors, such as diet, allergies, hormonal imbalances, and environmental contaminants (such as lead).

■ Neurophysiological factors, such as brain disorders, ADHD, EEG abnormalities, tumors, and head injuries, have been linked to crime. Criminals and delinquents often suffer brain impairment, as measured by the EEG. Attention deficit hyperactivity disorder and minimal brain dysfunction are related to antisocial behavior.

■ Some biocriminologists believe that the tendency to commit violent acts is inherited. Research has been conducted with twin pairs and adopted children to determine whether genes are related to behaviors.

■ An evolutionary branch holds that changes in the human condition, which have taken millions of years to evolve, may help explain crime rate differences. As the human race evolved, traits and characteristics have become ingrained.

■ There are also psychologically based theories of crime. The psychodynamic view, developed by Sigmund Freud, links aggressive behavior to personality conflicts arising from childhood.

■ According to psychodynamic theory, unconscious motivations developed early in childhood propel some people into destructive or illegal behavior.

■ The development of the unconscious personality early in childhood influences behavior for the rest of a person's life.

■ Criminals have weak egos and damaged personalities.

■ According to some psychoanalysts, psychotics are aggressive, unstable people who can easily become involved in crime.

■ Attachment theory holds that the ability to form attachments—that is, to emotionally bond to another person— has important lasting psychological implications that follow people across the life span.

■ Attachments are formed soon after birth, when infants bond with their mothers.

■ According to this view, failing to develop proper attachment may cause people to fall prey to a number of psychological disorders.

■ Psychologists believe that children with attachment problems lack trust and respect for others.

■ Criminologists have linked people having detachment problems with a variety of antisocial behaviors, including sexual assault and child abuse.

■ Behaviorists view aggression as a learned behavior. Children who are exposed to violence and see it rewarded may become violent as adults.

■ People commit crime when they model their behavior after others they see being rewarded for the same acts. Behavior is reinforced by rewards and extinguished by punishment.

■ Learning may be either direct and experiential or observational, such as watching TV and movies.

■ Cognitive psychology is concerned with human development and how people perceive the world. Cognitive theory stresses knowing and perception. Some people have a warped view of the world.

■ Criminality is viewed as a function of improper information processing. Individual reasoning processes influence behavior. Reasoning is influenced by the way people perceive their environment.

■ There is evidence that people with abnormal or antisocial personalities are crime prone.

■ Psychological traits such as personality and intelligence have been linked to criminality. One important area of study has been the antisocial personality, a person who lacks emotion and concern for others.

■ While some criminologists find a link between intelligence and crime, others dispute any linkage between IQ level and law-violating behaviors.

■ The controversial issue of the relationship of IQ to criminality has been resurrected once again with the publication of research studies purporting to show that criminals have lower IQs than noncriminals.

■ CENGAGENOW™ is an easy-to-use online resource that helps you study in less time to get the grade you want—NOW. CengageNOW™ Personalized Study (a diagnostic study tool containing valuable text-specific resources) lets you focus on just what you don't know and learn more in less time to get a better grade. If your textbook does not include an access code card, you can go to www.ichapters.com to purchase CengageNOW™.

KEY TERMS

Machiavellian *(130)*
inheritance school *(131)*
somatotype *(131)*
biophobia *(131)*
reciprocal altruism *(131)*
trait theory *(131)*
equipotentiality *(132)*
biosocial theory *(132)*
hypoglycemia *(136)*
androgens *(136)*

testosterone *(136)*
neocortex *(136)*
premenstrual syndrome (PMS) *(137)*
cerebral allergies *(137)*
neuroallergies *(137)*
neurophysiology *(138)*
electroencephalograph (EEG) *(139)*
learning disability *(139)*
attention deficit hyperactivity disorder (ADHD) *(140)*

conduct disorder (CD) *(140)*
chemical restraints *(141)*
chemical straitjackets *(141)*
arousal theory *(142)*
contagion effect *(145)*
defective intelligence *(148)*
psychoanalytic or psychodynamic perspective *(149)*
behaviorism *(149)*
cognitive theory *(149)*

id *(149)*
pleasure principle *(149)*
ego *(149)*
reality principle *(149)*
superego *(149)*
conscience *(149)*
ego ideal *(149)*
eros *(149)*
thanatos *(149)*
oral stage *(149)*
anal stage *(149)*
phallic stage *(149)*
Oedipus complex *(149)*
Electra complex *(149)*
latency *(149)*
fixated *(149)*

inferiority complex *(149)*
identity crisis *(150)*
latent delinquency *(150)*
bipolar disorder *(150)*
attachment theory *(150)*
alexithymia *(151)*
psychosis *(151)*
disorders *(151)*
schizophrenia *(151)*
paranoid schizophrenic *(151)*
social learning *(153)*
behavior modeling *(153)*
moral development *(156)*
humanistic psychology *(156)*
information processing *(156)*
personality *(159)*

sadistic personality disorder *(159)*
psychopath *(159)*
sociopath *(159)*
Minnesota Multiphasic Personality
   Inventory (MMPI) *(159)*
California Personality Inventory (CPI)
   (160)
Multidimensional Personality
   Questionnaire (MPQ) *(160)*
intelligence *(161)*
nature theory *(162)*
nurture theory *(162)*
primary prevention programs *(163)*
secondary prevention programs *(163)*
tertiary prevention programs *(163)*

CRITICAL THINKING QUESTIONS

1. What should be done with the young children of violence-prone criminals if in fact research could show that the tendency to commit crime is inherited?

2. After considering the existing research on the subject, would you recommend that young children be forbidden from eating foods with a heavy sugar content?

3. Knowing what you do about trends and patterns in crime, how would you counteract the assertion that people who commit crime are physically or mentally abnormal? For example, how would you explain the fact that crime is more likely to occur in western and urban areas than in eastern or rural areas?

4. Aside from becoming a criminal, what other career paths are open to psychopaths?

5. Research shows that kids who watch a lot of TV in adolescence are more likely to behave aggressively in adulthood. This has led some to conclude that TV watching is responsible for adult violence. Can this relationship be explained in another way?

NOTES

1. Ian Urbina and Manny Fernardez, "Memorial Services Held in U.S. and Around World," *New York Times*, 21 April 2007.
2. Raymond Hernandez, "A Friend, a 'Good Listener' and a Victim in a Day of Tragedy," *New York Times*, 17 April 2007.
3. Ibid.
4. Abbie Boudreau and Scott Zamost, "Girlfriend: Shooter Was Taking Cocktail of Three Drugs," CNN, 20 February 2008, www.cnn.com/2008/CRIME/02/20/shooter .girlfriend/ (accessed July 5, 2008).
5. Dalton Conley and Neil Bennett, "Is Biology Destiny? Birth Weight and Life Chances," *American Sociological Review* 654 (2000): 458–467.
6. Kevin Beaver, "Nonshared Environmental Influences on Adolescent Delinquent Involvement and Adult Criminal Behavior," *Criminology* 46 (2008): 341–369.
7. Bernard Rimland, *Dyslogic Syndrome: Why Today's Children are "Hyper," Attention Disordered, Learning Disabled, Depressed, Aggressive, Defiant, or Violent—And What We Can Do About It* (London: Jessica Kingsley Publishers, 2008).
8. Barbara Oakley, *Evil Genes: Why Rome Fell, Hitler Rose, Enron Failed and My Sister Stole My Mother's Boyfriend* (Amherst, NY: Prometheus Books, 2007).
9. Raffaele Garofalo, *Criminology*, trans. Robert Miller (Boston: Little, Brown, 1914), p. 92.
10. Enrico Ferri, *Criminal Sociology* (New York: D. Appleton, 1909).
11. See Richard Dugdale, *The Jukes* (New York: Putnam, 1910); Arthur Estabrook, *The Jukes in 1915* (Washington, DC: Carnegie Institute of Washington, 1916); Henry H. Goddard, *The Kallikak Family: A Study in the Heredity of Feeble-Mindedness* (New York: Macmillan, 1912).
12. Stephen Jay Gould, *The Mismeasure of Man*, rev. ed. (New York: Norton, 1996).
13. William Sheldon, *Varieties of Delinquent Youth* (New York: Harper Bros., 1949).
14. John Laub and Robert Sampson, "The Sutherland-Glueck Debate: On the Sociology of Criminological Knowledge," *American Journal of Sociology* 96 (1991): 1,402–1,440.
15. Lee Ellis, "A Discipline in Peril: Sociology's Future Hinges on Curing Biophobia," *American Sociologist* 27 (1996): 21–41.
16. Pierre van den Bergle, "Bringing the Beast Back In: Toward a Biosocial Theory of Aggression," *American Sociological Review* 39 (1974): 779.
17. Edmund O. Wilson, *Sociobiology* (Cambridge, MA: Harvard University Press, 1975).
18. Anthony Walsh, "Behavior Genetics and Anomie/Strain Theory," *Criminology* 38 (2000): 1,075–1,108.
19. Anthony Walsh and Lee Ellis, "Shoring Up the Big Three: Improving Criminological Theories with Biosocial Concepts," paper

presented at the annual meeting of the American Society of Criminology, San Diego, November 1997, p. 16.

20. Israel Nachshon, "Neurological Bases of Crime, Psychopathy and Aggression," in *Crime in Biological, Social and Moral Contexts*, ed. Lee Ellis and Harry Hoffman (New York: Praeger, 1990), p. 199. Herein cited as *Crime in Biological Contexts*.

21. Leonard Hippchen, "Some Possible Biochemical Aspects of Criminal Behavior," *Journal of Behavioral Ecology* 2 (1981): 1–6; Sarnoff Mednick and Jan Volavka, "Biology and Crime," in *Crime and Justice*, ed. Norval Morris and Michael Tonry (Chicago: University of Chicago Press, 1980), pp. 85–159; Saleem Shah and Loren Roth, "Biological and Psychophysiological Factors in Criminality," in *Handbook of Criminology*, ed. Daniel Glazer (Chicago: Rand McNally, 1974), pp. 125–140.

22. See generally Adrian Raine, *The Psychopathology of Crime* (San Diego: Academic Press, 1993); see also Leonard Hippchen, *The Ecologic-Biochemical Approaches to Treatment of Delinquents and Criminals* (New York: Van Nostrand Reinhold, 1978).

23. Jonathon Ericson, Francis Crinella, K. Alison Clarke-Stewart, Virginia Allhusen, Tony Chan, and Richard T. Robertson, "Prenatal Manganese Levels Linked to Childhood Behavioral Disinhibition," *Neurotoxicology and Teratology* 29 (2007): 181–187; Joseph Hibbeln, John Davis, Colin Steer, Pauline Emmett, Imogen Rogers, Cathy Williams, and Jean Golding, "Maternal Seafood Consumption in Pregnancy and Neurodevelopmental Outcomes in Childhood (ALSPAC Study): An Observational Cohort Study," *Lancet* 369 (2007): 578–585.

24. Lauren Wakschlag, Kate Pickett, Kristen Kasza, and Rolf Loeber, "Is Prenatal Smoking Associated with a Developmental Pattern of Conduct Problems in Young Boys?" *Journal of the American Academy of Child and Adolescent Psychiatry* 45 (2006): 461–467; "Diet and the Unborn Child: The Omega Point," *The Economist*, January 19, 2006.

25. Lisa M. Gatzke-Kopp and Theodore Beauchaine, "Direct and Passive Prenatal Nicotine Exposure and the Development of Externalizing Psychopathology," *Child Psychiatry and Human Development* 38 (2007): 255–269.

26. K. Murata, P. Weihe, E. Budtz-Jorgensen, P. J. Jorgensen, and P. Grandjean, "Delayed Brainstem Auditory Evoked Potential Latencies in 14-Year-Old Children Exposed to Methylmercury," *Journal of Pediatrics* 144 (2004): 177–183; Eric Konofal, Samuele Cortese, Michel Lecendreux, Isabelle Arnulf, and Marie Christine Mouren, "Effectiveness of Iron Supplementation in a Young Child with Attention-Deficit/Hyperactivity Disorder," *Pediatrics* 116 (2005): 732–734.

27. Sue Dengate and Alan Ruben, "Controlled Trial of Cumulative Behavioural Effects of a Common Bread Preservative," *Journal of Pediatrics and Child Health* 38 (2002): 373–376.

28. Harold Milman and Suzanne Arnold, "Neurologic, Psychological, and Aggressive Disturbances with Sildenafil," *Annals of Pharmacotherapy* 36 (2002): 1,129–1,134.

29. F. T. Crews, A. Mdzinarishvili, D. Kim, J. He, and K. Nixon, "Neurogenesis in Adolescent Brain Is Potently Inhibited by Ethanol," *Neuroscience* 137 (2006): 437–445.

30. G. B. Ramirez, O. Pagulayan, H. Akagi, A. Francisco Rivera, L. V. Lee, A. Berroya, M. C. Vince Cruz, and D. Casintahan, "Tagum Study II: Follow-Up Study at Two Years of Age after Prenatal Exposure to Mercury," *Pediatrics* 111 (2003): 289–295.

31. Gail Wasserman, Xinhua Liu, Faruque Parvez, Habibul Ahsan, Diane Levy, Pam Factor-Litvak, Jennie Kline, Alexander van Geen, Vesna Slavkovich, Nancy J. Lolacono, Zhongqi Cheng, Yan Zheng, and Joseph Graziano, "Water Manganese Exposure and Children's Intellectual Function in Araihazar, Bangladesh," *Environmental Health Perspectives* 114 (2006): 124–129; Eric Konofal, Michel Lecendreux, Isabelle Arnulf, and Marie-Christine Mouren, "Iron Deficiency in Children with Attention-Deficit/Hyperactivity Disorder," *Archives of Pediatric and Adolescent Medicine* 158 (2004): 1,113–1,115; Konofal et al., "Effectiveness of Iron Supplementation in a Young Child with Attention-Deficit/Hyperactivity Disorder."

32. D. K. L. Cheuk and Virginia Wong, "Attention Deficit Hyperactivity Disorder and Blood Mercury Level: A Case-Control Study in Chinese Children," *Neuropediatrics* 37 (2006): 234–240.

33. Alexandra Richardson and Paul Montgomery, "The Oxford-Durham Study: A Randomized Controlled Trial of Dietary Supplementation with Fatty Acids in Children with Developmental Coordination Disorder," *Pediatrics* 115 (2005): 1,360–1,366.

34. Ronald Prinz and David Riddle, "Associations between Nutrition and Behavior in 5-Year-Old Children," *Nutrition Reviews Supplement* 44 (1986): 151–158.

35. M. Mousain-Bosc, M. Roche, A. Polge, D. Pradai-Prat, J. Rapin, and J. P. Bali, "Improvement of Neurobehavioral Disorders in Children Supplemented with Magnesium-Vitamin B6, Part I, Attention Deficit Hyperactivity Disorder," *Magnesium Research* 19 (2006) 46–52.

36. Karen Lau, W. Graham McLean, Dominic P. Williams, and C. Vyvyan Howard "Synergistic Interactions between Commonly Used Food Additives in a Developmental Neurotoxicity Test," *Toxicological Science* 90 (2006): 178–187.

37. Donna McCann, Angelina Barrett, Alison Cooper, Debbie Crumpler, Lindy Dalen, Kate Grimshaw, Elizabeth Kitchin, Kris Lok, Lucy Porteous, Emily Prince, Edmund Sonuga-Barke, John O Warner, and Jim Stevenson, "Food Additives and Hyperactive Behaviour in 3-Year-Old and 8/9-Year-Old Children in the Community: A Randomised, Double-Blinded, Placebo-Controlled Trial," *Lancet* 370 (2007): 1,560–1,567.

38. Stephen Schoenthaler and Walter Doraz, "Types of Offenses which Can Be Reduced in an Institutional Setting Using Nutritional Intervention," *International Journal of Biosocial Research* 4 (1983): 74–84.

39. H. Bruce Ferguson, Clare Stoddart, and Jovan Simeon, "Double-Blind Challenge Studies of Behavioral and Cognitive Effects of Sucrose-Aspartame Ingestion in Normal Children," *Nutrition Reviews Supplement* 44 (1986): 144–158; Gregory Gray, "Diet, Crime and Delinquency: A Critique," *Nutrition Reviews Supplement* 44 (1986): 89–94.

40. Mark Wolraich, Scott Lindgren, Phyllis Stumbo, Lewis Steginik, Mark Appelbaum, and Mary Kiritsy, "Effects of Diets High in Sucrose or Aspartame on the Behavior and Cognitive Performance of Children," *New England Journal of Medicine* 330 (1994): 303–306.

41. Dian Gans, "Sucrose and Unusual Childhood Behavior," *Nutrition Today* 26 (1991): 8–14.

42. Diana Fishbein, "Neuropsychological Function, Drug Abuse, and Violence, a Conceptual Framework," *Criminal Justice and Behavior* 27 (2000): 139–159.

43. D. Hill and W. Sargent, "A Case of Matricide," *Lancet* 244 (1943): 526–527.

44. E. Podolsky, "The Chemistry of Murder," *Pakistan Medical Journal* 15 (1964): 9–14.

45. J. A. Yaryura-Tobias and F. Neziroglu, "Violent Behavior, Brain Dysrhythmia and Glucose Dysfunction: A New Syndrome," *Journal of Orthopsychiatry* 4 (1975): 182–188.

46. Matti Virkkunen, "Reactive Hypoglycemic Tendency among Habitually Violent Offenders," *Nutrition Reviews Supplement* 44 (1986): 94–103.

47. James Q. Wilson, *The Moral Sense* (New York: Free Press, 1993).

48. Walter Gove, "The Effect of Age and Gender on Deviant Behavior: A Biopsychosocial Perspective," in *Gender and the Life Course*, ed. A. S. Rossi (New York: Aldine, 1985), pp. 115–144.

49. Alan Booth and D. Wayne Osgood, "The Influence of Testosterone on Deviance in Adulthood: Assessing and Explaining the Relationship," *Criminology* 31 (1993): 93–118.

50. Lee Ellis, Shyamal Das, and Hasan Buker, "Androgen-Promoted Physiological Traits

and Criminality: A Test of the Evolutionary Neuroandrogenic Theory," *Personality and Individual Differences* 44 (2008): 701–711.

51. Anthony Walsh, "Genetic and Cytogenetic Intersex Anomalies: Can They Help Us to Understand Gender Differences in Deviant Behavior?" *International Journal of Offender Therapy and Comparative Criminology* 39 (1995): 151–166.

52. Christy Miller Buchanan, Jacquelynne Eccles, and Jill Becker, "Are Adolescents the Victims of Raging Hormones? Evidence for Activational Effects of Hormones on Moods and Behavior at Adolescence," *Psychological Bulletin* 111 (1992): 62–107.

53. Alex Piquero and Timothy Brezina, "Testing Moffitt's Account of Adolescent-Limited Delinquency," *Criminology* 39 (2001): 353–370.

54. Booth and Osgood, "The Influence of Testosterone on Deviance in Adulthood."

55. Walsh, "Genetic and Cytogenetic Intersex Anomalies: Can They Help Us to Understand Gender Differences in Deviant Behavior?"

56. Celina Cohen-Bendahan, Jan Buitelaar, Stephanie van Goozen, Jacob Orlebeke, and Peggy Cohen-Kettenis, "Is There an Effect of Prenatal Testosterone on Aggression and Other Behavioral Traits? A Study Comparing Same-Sex and Opposite-Sex Twin Girls," *Hormones and Behavior* 47 (2005): 230–237

57. John Simister and Cary Cooper, "Thermal Stress in the U.S.A.: Effects on Violence and on Employee Behaviour," *Stress and Health: Journal of the International Society for the Investigation of Stress* 21 (2005): 3–15.

58. Lee Ellis, "Evolutionary and Neurochemical Causes of Sex Differences in Victimizing Behavior: Toward a Unified Theory of Criminal Behavior and Social Stratification," *Social Science Information* 28 (1989): 605–636.

59. For a general review, see Lee Ellis and Phyllis Coontz, "Androgens, Brain Functioning, and Criminality: The Neurohormonal Foundations of Antisociality," in *Crime in Biological Contexts*, pp. 162–193.

60. Ibid., p. 181.

61. Robert Rubin, "The Neuroendocrinology and Neuro-Chemistry of Antisocial Behavior," in *The Causes of Crime, New Biological Approaches*, ed. Sarnoff Mednick, Terrie Moffitt, and Susan Stack (Cambridge: Cambridge University Press, 1987), pp. 239–262.

62. J. Money, "Influence of Hormones on Psychosexual Differentiation," *Medical Aspects of Nutrition* 30 (1976): 165.

63. Mednick and Volavka, "Biology and Crime."

64. For a review of this concept, see Anne E. Figert, "The Three Faces of PMS: The Professional, Gendered, and Scientific Structuring of a Psychiatric Disorder," *Social Problems* 42 (1995): 56–72.

65. Katharina Dalton, *The Premenstrual Syndrome* (Springfield, IL: Charles C Thomas, 1971).

66. M. S. Zeedyk and F. E. Raitt, "Biology in the Courtroom: PMS in Legal Defenses," *Psychology, Evolution and Gender* 1 (1999): 123–143.

67. Julie Horney, "Menstrual Cycles and Criminal Responsibility," *Law and Human Nature* 2 (1978): 25–36.

68. Diana Fishbein, "Selected Studies on the Biology of Antisocial Behavior," in *New Perspectives in Criminology*, ed. John Conklin (Needham Heights, MA: Allyn & Bacon, 1996), pp. 26–38.

69. Ibid.; Karen Paige, "Effects of Oral Contraceptives on Affective Fluctuations Associated with the Menstrual Cycle," *Psychosomatic Medicine* 33 (1971): 515–537.

70. H. E. Amos and J. J. P. Drake, "Problems Posed by Food Additives," *Journal of Human Nutrition* 30 (1976): 165.

71. Ray Wunderlich, "Neuroallergy as a Contributing Factor to Social Misfits: Diagnosis and Treatment," in *Ecologic-Biochemical Approaches to Treatment of Delinquents and Criminals*, ed. Leonard Hippchen (New York: Von Nostram Reinhold, 1978), pp. 229–253.

72. See, for example, Paul Marshall, "Allergy and Depression: A Neurochemical Threshold Model of the Relation between the Illnesses," *Psychological Bulletin* 113 (1993): 23–39.

73. A. R. Mawson and K. J. Jacobs, "Corn Consumption, Tryptophan, and Cross-National Homicide Rates," *Journal of Orthomolecular Psychiatry* 7 (1978): 227–230.

74. Centers for Disease Control, "CDC Releases Most Extensive Assessment Ever of Americans' Exposure to Environmental Chemicals," Centers for Disease Control press release, 31 January 2003.

75. Núria Ribas-Fitó, Maties Torrent, Daniel Carrizo, Jordi Júlvez, Joan O. Grimalt, and Jordi Sunyer, "Exposure to Hexachlorobenzene during Pregnancy and Children's Social Behavior at 4 Years of Age," *Environmental Health Perspectives* 115 (2007): 447–450.

76. Virginia Rauh, Robin Garfinkel, Frederica Perera, Howard Andrews, Lori Hoepner, Dana Barr, Ralph Whitehead, Deliang Tang, and Robin Whyatt, "Impact of Prenatal Chlorpyrifos Exposure on Neurodevelopment in the First 3 Years of Life Among Inner-City Children," *Pediatrics* 118 (2006): 1,845–1,859.

77. David C. Bellinger, "Lead," *Pediatrics* 113 (2004): 1,016–1,022.

78. Paul Stretesky and Michael Lynch, "The Relationship between Lead Exposure and Homicide," *Archives of Pediatric Adolescent Medicine* 155 (2001): 579–582.

79. Rick Nevin, "Understanding International Crime Trends: The Legacy of Preschool Lead Exposure," *Environmental Research* 104 (2007): 315–336.

80. Joel Nigg, G. Mark Knottnerus, Michelle Martel, Molly Nikolas, Kevin Cavanagh, Wilfried Karmaus, and Marsha D. Rappley, "Low Blood Lead Levels Associated with Clinically Diagnosed Attention-Deficit/Hyperactivity Disorder and Mediated by Weak, Cognitive Control," *Biological Psychiatry* 63 (2008): 325–331.

81. Jeff Evans, "Asymptomatic, High Lead Levels Tied to Delinquency," *Pediatric News* 37 (2003): 13.

82. Deborah Denno, "Considering Lead Poisoning as a Criminal Defense," *Fordham Urban Law Journal* 20 (1993): 377–400.

83. Herbert Needleman, Christine McFarland, Roberta Ness, Stephen Fienberg, and Michael Tobin, "Bone Lead Levels in Adjudicated Delinquents: A Case Control Study," *Neurotoxicology and Teratology* 24 (2002): 711–717; Herbert Needleman, Julie Riess, Michael Tobin, Gretchen Biesecker, and Joel Greenhouse, "Bone Lead Levels and Delinquent Behavior," *Journal of the American Medical Association* 275 (1996): 363–369.

84. Todd A. Jusko, Charles R. Henderson Jr., Bruce P. Lanphear, Deborah A. Cory-Slechta, Patrick J. Parsons, and Richard L. Canfield, "Blood Lead Concentrations <10 µg/dL and Child Intelligence at 6 Years of Age," *Environ Health Perspectives* 116 (2008): 243–248.

85. Mark Opler, Alan Brown, Joseph Graziano, Manisha Desai, Wei Zheng, Catherine Schaefer, Pamela Factor-Litvak, and Ezra S. Susser, "Prenatal Lead Exposure, [Delta]-Aminolevulinic Acid, and Schizophrenia," *Environmental Health Perspectives* 112 (2004): 548–553.

86. Centers for Disease Control, "CDC Releases Most Extensive Assessment Ever of Americans' Exposure to Environmental Chemicals."

87. Emily Oken, Robert O. Wright, Ken P. Kleinman, David Bellinger, Chitra J. Amarasiriwardena, Howard Hu, Janet W. Rich-Edwards, and Matthew W. Gillman, "Maternal Fish Consumption, Hair Mercury, and Infant Cognition in a U.S. Cohort," *Environmental Health Perspectives* 113 (2005): 1,376–1,380.

88. Terrie Moffitt, "The Neuropsychology of Juvenile Delinquency: A Critical Review," in *Crime and Justice, An Annual Review*, vol. 12, ed. Norval Morris and Michael Tonry (Chicago: University of Chicago Press, 1990), pp. 99–169.

89. Terrie Moffitt, Donald Lynam, and Phil Silva, "Neuropsychological Tests Predicting Persistent Male Delinquency," *Criminology* 32 (1994): 277–300; Elizabeth Kandel and Sarnoff Mednick, "Perinatal Complications Predict Violent Offending," *Criminology* 29 (1991): 519–529; Sarnoff Mednick,

Ricardo Machon, Matti Virkkunen, and Douglas Bonett, "Adult Schizophrenia Following Prenatal Exposure to an Influenza Epidemic," *Archives of General Psychiatry* 44 (1987): 35–46; C. A. Fogel, S. A. Mednick, and N. Michelson, "Hyperactive Behavior and Minor Physical Anomalies," *Acta Psychiatrica Scandinavia* 72 (1985): 551–556.

90. Jean Seguin, Robert Pihl, Philip Harden, Richard Tremblay, and Bernard Boulerice, "Cognitive and Neuropsychological Characteristics of Physically Aggressive Boys," *Journal of Abnormal Psychology* 104 (1995): 614–624; Deborah Denno, "Gender, Crime and the Criminal Law Defenses," *Journal of Criminal Law and Criminology* 85 (1994): 80–180.

91. Yaling Yang, Adrian Raine, Todd Lencz, Susan Bihrle, Lori LaCasse, and Patrick Colletti, "Prefrontal White Matter in Pathological Liars," *British Journal of Psychiatry* 187 (2005): 320–325.

92. Pallone and Hennessy, "Brain Dysfunction and Criminal Violence," p. 25.

93. Peer Briken, Niels Habermann, Wolfgang Berner, and Andreas Hill, "The Influence of Brain Abnormalities on Psychosocial Development, Criminal History and Paraphilias in Sexual Murderers," *Journal of Forensic Sciences* 50 (2005): 1–5.

94. Kevin Beaver, John Paul Wright, and Matthew Delisi, "Self-Control as an Executive Function: Reformulating Gottfredson and Hirschi's Parental Socialization Thesis," *Criminal Justice and Behavior* 34 (2007): 1,345–1,361.

95. Adrian Raine, P. Brennan, and S. Mednick, "Interaction Between Birth Complications and Early Maternal Rejection in Predisposing to Adult Violence: Specificity to Serious, Early Onset Violence," *American Journal of Psychiatry* 154 (1997): 1,265–1,271.

96. Deborah Denno, *Biology, Crime and Violence: New Evidence* (Cambridge: Cambridge University Press, 1989).

97. Diana Fishbein and Robert Thatcher, "New Diagnostic Methods in Criminology: Assessing Organic Sources of Behavioral Disorders," *Journal of Research in Crime and Delinquency* 23 (1986): 240–267.

98. See generally David Rowe, *Biology and Crime* (Los Angeles: Roxbury Press, 2001).

99. R. W. Aind and T. Yamamoto, "Behavior Disorders of Childhood," *Electroencephalography and Clinical Neurophysiology* 21 (1966): 148–156.

100. See generally Jan Volavka, "Electroencephalogram among Criminals," in *The Causes of Crime, New Biological Approaches*, ed. Sarnoff Mednick, Terrie Moffitt, and Susan Stack (Cambridge: Cambridge University Press, 1987), pp. 137–145; Z. A. Zayed, S. A. Lewis, and R. P. Britain, "An Encephalographic and Psychiatric Study of 32 Insane Murderers,"

British Journal of Psychiatry 115 (1969): 1,115–1,124.

101. Nathaniel Pallone and James Hennessy, "Brain Dysfunction and Criminal Violence," *Society* 35 (1998): 21–27; P. F. Goyer, P. J. Andreason, and W. E. Semple, "Positronic Emission Tomography and Personality Disorders," *Neuropsychopharmacology* 10 (1994): 21–28.

102. Adrian Raine, Monte Buchsbaum, and Lori LaCasse, "Brain Abnormalities in Murderers Indicated by Positron Emission Tomography," *Biological Psychiatry* 42 (1997): 495–508.

103. David George, Robert Rawlings, Wendol Williams, Monte Phillips, Grace Fong, Michael Kerich, Reza Momenan, John Umhau, and Daniel Hommer, "A Select Group of Perpetrators of Domestic Violence: Evidence of Decreased Metabolism in the Right Hypothalamus and Reduced Relationships between Cortical/Subcortical Brain Structures in Positron Emission Tomography," *Psychiatry Research: Neuroimaging* 130 (2004): 11–25.

104. Daniel G. Amen, Chris Hanks, Jill Prunella, and Aisa Green, "An Analysis of Regional Cerebral Blood Flow in Impulsive Murderers Using Single Photon Emission Computed Tomography," *Journal of Neuropsychiatry and Clinical Neurosciences* 19, (2007): 304–309.

105. Adrian Raine, "The Role of Prefrontal Deficits, Low Autonomic Arousal, and Early Health Factors in the Development of Antisocial and Aggressive Behavior in Children," *Journal of Child Psychology and Psychiatry* 43 (2002): 417–434.

106. D. R. Robin, R. M. Starles, T. J. Kenney, B. J. Reynolds, and F. P. Heald, "Adolescents Who Attempt Suicide," *Journal of Pediatrics* 90 (1977): 636–638.

107. R. R. Monroe, *Brain Dysfunction in Aggressive Criminals* (Lexington, MA: D.C. Heath, 1978).

108. L. T. Yeudall, *Childhood Experiences as Causes of Criminal Behavior* (Senate of Canada, Issue no. 1, Thirteenth Parliament, Ottawa, 1977).

109. Raine, Buchsbaum, and LaCasse, "Brain Abnormalities in Murderers Indicated by Positron Emission Tomography."

110. Cited in Charles Post, "The Link between Learning Disabilities and Juvenile Delinquency: Cause, Effect, and 'Present Solutions,'" *Juvenile and Family Court Journal* 31 (1981): 59.

111. Joel Zimmerman, William Rich, Ingo Keilitz, and Paul Broder, "Some Observations on the Link between Learning Disabilities and Juvenile Delinquency," *Journal of Criminal Justice* 9: 9–17 (1981); J. W. Podboy and W. A. Mallory, "The Diagnosis of Specific Learning Disabilities in a Juvenile Delinquent Population," *Juvenile and Family Court Journal* 30: 11–13 (1978).

112. Tomer Einat and Amela Einat, "Learning Disabilities and Delinquency: A Study of Israeli Prison Inmates," *International Journal of Offender Therapy and Comparative Criminology*, October 1, 2007, http://ijo.sagepub.com/cgi/rapidpdf/0306624X07307352v1 (accessed July 5, 2008).

113. Thomas Brown, *Attention Deficit Disorder: The Unfocused Mind in Children and Adults* (New Haven, CT: Yale University Press, 2005).

114. Simon, "Does Criminal Offender Treatment Work?"

115. Terrie Moffitt and Phil Silva, "Self-Reported Delinquency, Neuropsychological Deficit, and History of Attention Deficit Disorder," *Journal of Abnormal Child Psychology* 16 (1988): 553–569.

116. Molina Pelham, Jr., "Childhood Predictors of Adolescent Substance Use in a Longitudinal Study of Children with ADHD," *Journal of Abnormal Psychology* 112 (2003): 497–507; Peter Muris and Cor Meesters, "The Validity of Attention Deficit Hyperactivity and Hyperkinetic Disorder Symptom Domains in Nonclinical Dutch Children," *Journal of Clinical Child and Adolescent Psychology* 32 (2003): 460–466.

117. Elizabeth Hart et al., "Criterion Validity of Informants in the Diagnosis of Disruptive Behavior Disorders in Children: A Preliminary Study," *Journal of Consulting and Clinical Psychology* 62 (1994): 410–414.

118. Russell Barkley, Mariellen Fischer, Lori Smallish, and Kenneth Fletcher, "Young Adult Follow-Up of Hyperactive Children: Antisocial Activities and Drug Use," *Journal of Child Psychology and Psychiatry* 45 (2004): 195–211.

119. Karen Harding, Richard Judah, and Charles Gant, "Outcome-Based Comparison of Ritalin[R] versus Food-Supplement Treated Children with AD/HD," *Alternative Medicine Review* 8 (2003): 319–330.

120. Stephen Hinshaw, Elizabeth Owens, Nilofar Sami, and Samantha Fargeon, "Prospective Follow-Up of Girls with Attention-Deficit/Hyperactivity Disorder into Adolescence: Evidence for Continuing Cross-Domain Impairment," *Journal of Consulting and Clinical Psychology* 74 (2006), 489–499.

121. Rita Shaughnessy, "Psychopharmacotherapy of Neuropsychiatric Disorders," *Psychiatric Annals* 25 (1995): 634–640.

122. Yeudall, "A Neuropsychosocial Perspective of Persistent Juvenile Delinquency and Criminal Behavior," p. 4; F. A. Elliott, "Neurological Aspects of Antisocial Behavior," in *The Psychopath: A Comprehensive Study of Antisocial Disorders and Behaviors*, ed. W. H. Reid (New York: Brunner/Mazel, 1978), pp. 146–189.

123. Ibid., p. 177.

124. H. K. Kletschka, "Violent Behavior Associated with Brain Tumor," *Minnesota Medicine* 49 (1966): 1,853–1,855.

125. V. E. Krynicki, "Cerebral Dysfunction in Repetitively Assaultive Adolescents," *Journal of Nervous and Mental Disease* 166 (1978): 59–67.

126. C. E. Lyght, ed., *The Merck Manual of Diagnosis and Therapy* (West Point, FL: Merck, 1966).

127. Reiss and Roth, *Understanding Violence*, p. 119.

128. M. Virkkunen, M. J. DeJong, J. Bartko, and M. Linnoila, "Psychobiological Concomitants of History of Suicide Attempts among Violent Offenders and Impulsive Fire Starters," *Archives of General Psychiatry* 46 (1989): 604–606.

129. Matti Virkkunen, David Goldman, and Markku Linnoila, "Serotonin in Alcoholic Violent Offenders," *The Ciba Foundation Symposium, Genetics of Criminal and Antisocial Behavior* (Chichester, England: Wiley, 1995).

130. Lee Ellis, "Left- and Mixed-Handedness and Criminality: Explanations for a Probable Relationship," in *Left-Handedness, Behavioral Implications and Anomalies*, ed. S. Coren (Amsterdam: Elsevier, 1990): 485–507.

131. M. Skondras, M. Markianos, A. Botsis, E. Bistolaki, and G. Christodoulou, "Platelet Monoamine Oxidase Activity and Psychometric Correlates in Male Violent Offenders Imprisoned for Homicide or Other Violent Acts," *European Archives of Psychiatry and Clinical Neuroscience* 254 (2004): 380–386.

132. Lee Ellis, "Monoamine Oxidase and Criminality: Identifying an Apparent Biological Marker for Antisocial Behavior," *Journal of Research in Crime and Delinquency* 28 (1991): 227–251.

133. Walter Gove and Charles Wilmoth, "Risk, Crime and Neurophysiologic Highs: A Consideration of Brain Processes that May Reinforce Delinquent and Criminal Behavior," in *Crime in Biological Contexts*, pp. 261–293.

134. Jack Katz, *Seduction of Crime: Moral and Sensual Attractions of Doing Evil* (New York: Basic Books, 1988), pp. 12–15.

135. Lee Ellis, "Arousal Theory and the Religiosity-Criminality Relationship," in *Contemporary Criminological Theory*, ed., Peter Cordella and Larry Siegel (Boston, MA: Northeastern University, 1996), pp. 65–84.

136. Adrian Raine, Patricia Brennan, and Sarnoff Mednick, "The Interaction between Birth Complications and Early Maternal Rejection in Predisposing to Adult Violence: Specificity to Serious, Early Onset Violence," *American Journal of Psychiatry* 154 (1997): 1,265–1,271.

137. Adrian Raine, Peter Venables, and Sarnoff Mednick, "Low Resting Heart Rate at Age 3 Years Predisposes to Aggression at Age

11 Years: Evidence from the Mauritius Child Health Project," *Journal of the American Academy of Adolescent Psychiatry* 36 (1997): 1,457–1,464.

138. Daniel Hart, Nancy Eisenberg, and Carlos Valiente, "Personality Change at the Intersection of Autonomic Arousal and Stress," *Psychological Science* 18 (2007): 492–497.

139. Anita Thapar, Kate Langley, Tom Fowler, Frances Rice, Darko Turic, Naureen Whittinger, John Aggleton, Marianne Van den Bree, Michael Owen, and Michael O'Donovan, "Catechol O-methyltransferase Gene Variant and Birth Weight Predict Early-Onset Antisocial Behavior in Children with Attention-Deficit/Hyperactivity Disorder," *Archives of General Psychiatry* 62 (2005): 1,275–1,278.

140. Kerry Jang, W. John Livesley, and Philip Vernon, "Heritability of the Big Five Personality Dimensions and Their Facets: A Twin Study," *Journal of Personality* 64 (1996): 577–589.

141. David Rowe, "As the Twig Is Bent: The Myth of Child-Rearing Influences on Personality Development," *Journal of Counseling and Development* 68 (1990): 606–611; David Rowe, Joseph Rogers, and Sylvia Meseck-Bushey, "Sibling Delinquency and the Family Environment: Shared and Unshared Influences," *Child Development* 63 (1992): 59–67.

142. Brian Boutwell and Kevin Beaver, "A Biosocial Explanation of Delinquency Abstention," *Criminal Behaviour and Mental Health* 18 (2008): 59–74.

143. Gregory Carey and David DiLalla, "Personality and Psychopathology: Genetic Perspectives," *Journal of Abnormal Psychology* 103 (1994): 32–43.

144. T. R. Sarbin and L. E. Miller, "Demonism Revisited: The XYY Chromosome Anomaly," *Issues in Criminology* 5 (1970): 195–207.

145. Mednick and Volavka, "Biology and Crime," p. 93.

146. For an early review, see Barbara Wooton, *Social Science and Social Pathology* (London: Allen & Unwin, 1959); John Laub and Robert Sampson, "Unraveling Families and Delinquency: A Reanalysis of the Gluecks' Data," *Criminology* 26 (1988): 355–380.

147. D. J. West and D. P. Farrington, eds., "Who Becomes Delinquent?" in *The Delinquent Way of Life* (London: Heinemann, 1977); D. J. West, *Delinquency, Its Roots, Careers, and Prospects* (Cambridge, MA: Harvard University Press, 1982).

148. West, *Delinquency*, p. 114.

149. Carolyn Smith and David Farrington, "Continuities in Antisocial Behavior and Parenting across Three Generations," *Journal of Child Psychology and Psychiatry* 45 (2004): 230–247.

150. David Farrington, "Understanding and Preventing Bullying," in *Crime and Justice*, vol. 17, ed. Michael Tonry (Chicago: University of Chicago Press, 1993), pp. 381–457.

151. Terence Thornberry, Adrienne Freeman-Gallant, Alan Lizotte, Marvin Krohn, and Carolyn Smith, "Linked Lives: The Intergenerational Transmission of Antisocial Behavior," *Journal of Abnormal Child Psychology* 31 (2003): 171–185.

152. Philip Harden and Robert Pihl, "Cognitive Function, Cardiovascular Reactivity, and Behavior in Boys at High Risk for Alcoholism," *Journal of Abnormal Psychology* 104 (1995): 94–103.

153. Laub and Sampson, "Unraveling Families and Delinquency," p. 370.

154. Smith and Farrington, "Continuities in Antisocial Behavior and Parenting across Three Generations."

155. David Rowe and David Farrington, "The Familial Transmission of Criminal Convictions," *Criminology* 35 (1997): 177–201.

156. D. P. Farrington, Gwen Gundry, and D. J. West, "The Familial Transmission of Criminality," in *Crime and the Family*, ed. Alan Lincoln and Murray Straus (Springfield, IL: Charles C Thomas, 1985), pp. 193–206.

157. Abigail Fagan and Jake Najman, "Sibling Influences on Adolescent Delinquent Behaviour: An Australian Longitudinal Study," *Journal of Adolescence* 26 (2003): 547–559.

158. David Rowe and Bill Gulley, "Sibling Effects on Substance Use and Delinquency," *Criminology* 30 (1992): 217–232; see also David Rowe, Joseph Rogers, and Sylvia Meseck-Bushey, "Sibling Delinquency and the Family Environment: Shared and Unshared Influences," *Child Development* 63 (1992): 59–67.

159. Dana Haynie and Suzanne Mchugh, "Sibling Deviance in the Shadows of Mutual and Unique Friendship Effects?" *Criminology* 41 (2003): 355–393.

160. Louise Arseneault, Terrie Moffitt, Avshalom Caspi, Alan Taylor, Fruhling Rijsdijk, Sara Jaffee, Jennifer Ablow, and Jeffrey Measelle, "Strong Genetic Effects on Cross-Situational Antisocial Behaviour among 5-Year-Old Children According to Mothers, Teachers, Examiner-Observers, and Twins' Self-Reports," *Journal of Child Psychology and Psychiatry* 44 (2003): 832–848.

161. David Rowe, "Sibling Interaction and Self-Reported Delinquent Behavior: A Study of 265 Twin Pairs," *Criminology* 23 (1985): 223–240; Nancy Segal, "Monozygotic and Dizygotic Twins: A Comparative Analysis of Mental Ability Profiles," *Child Development* 56 (1985): 1,051–1,058.

162. Ibid.

163. Michael Lyons, Karestan Koenen, Francisco Buchting, Joanne Meyer, Lindon Eaves, Rosemary Toomey, Seth Eisen, Jack

Goldberg, Stephen Faraon, Rachel Ban, Beth Jerskey, and Ming Tsuang, "A Twin Study of Sexual Behavior in Men," *Archives of Sexual Behavior* 33 (2004): 129–136.

164. David Rowe, "Genetic and Environmental Components of Antisocial Behavior: A Study of 265 Twin Pairs," *Criminology* 24 (1986): 513–532; David Rowe and D. Wayne Osgood, "Heredity and Sociological Theories of Delinquency: A Reconsideration," *American Sociological Review* 49 (1984): 526–540.

165. Sara Jaffee, Avshalom Caspi, Terrie Moffitt, Kenneth Dodge, Michael Rutter, Alan Taylor, and Lucy Tully, "Nature × Nurture: Genetic Vulnerabilities Interact with Physical Maltreatment to Promote Conduct Problems," *Development and Psychopathology* 17 (2005): 67–84.

166. Ping Qin, "The Relationship of Suicide Risk to Family History of Suicide and Psychiatric Disorders," *Psychiatric Times* 20 (2003): 13. Available at www .psychiatrictimes.com/display/article/ 10168/48641 (accessed July 5, 2008).

167. Jane Scourfield, Marianne Van den Bree, Neilson Martin, and Peter McGuffin, "Conduct Problems in Children and Adolescents: A Twin Study," *Archives of General Psychiatry* 61 (2004): 489–496; Jeanette Taylor, Bryan Loney, Leonardo Bobadilla, William Iacono, and Matt McGue, "Genetic and Environmental Influences on Psychopathy Trait Dimensions in a Community Sample of Male Twins," *Journal of Abnormal Child Psychology* 31 (2003): 633–645.

168. Ginette Dionne, Richard Tremblay, Michel Boivin, David Laplante, and Daniel Perusse, "Physical Aggression and Expressive Vocabulary in 19-Month-Old Twins," *Developmental Psychology* 39 (2003): 261–273.

169. Jaffee et al., "Nature × Nurture: Genetic Vulnerabilities Interact with Physical Maltreatment to Promote Conduct Problems."

170. Essi Viding, James Blair, Terrie Moffitt, and Robert Plomin, "Evidence for Substantial Genetic Risk for Psychopathy in 7-Year-Olds," *Journal of Child Psychology and Psychiatry* 46 (2005): 592–597.

171. Thomas Bouchard, "Genetic and Environmental Influences on Intelligence and Special Mental Abilities," *American Journal of Human Biology* 70 (1998): 253–275; some findings from the Minnesota study can be accessed from the website: www.psych.umn.edu/psylabs/mtfs/ (accessed July 5, 2008).

172. David Rowe, *The Limits of Family Influence: Genes, Experiences and Behavior* (New York: Guilford Press, 1995), p. 64.

173. Gregory Carey, "Twin Imitation for Antisocial Behavior: Implications for Genetic and Family Environment Research," *Journal of Abnormal Psychology* 101 (1992): 18–25; David Rowe and

Joseph Rodgers, "The Ohio Twin Project and ADSEX Studies: Behavior Genetic Approaches to Understanding Antisocial Behavior," paper presented at the annual meeting of the American Society of Criminology, Montreal, Canada, November 1987.

174. Glenn Walters, "A Meta-Analysis of the Gene–Crime Relationship," *Criminology* 30 (1992): 595–613.

175. Alice Gregory, Thalia Eley, and Robert Plomin, "Exploring the Association between Anxiety and Conduct Problems in a Large Sample of Twins Aged 2–4," *Journal of Abnormal Child Psychology* 32 (2004): 111–123.

176. Marshall Jones and Donald Jones, "The Contagious Nature of Antisocial Behavior," *Criminology* 38 (2000): 25–46.

177. Jones and Jones, "The Contagious Nature of Antisocial Behavior," p. 31.

178. R. J. Cadoret, C. Cain, and R. R. Crowe, "Evidence for a Gene–Environment Interaction in the Development of Adolescent Antisocial Behavior," *Behavior Genetics* 13 (1983): 301–310.

179. Barry Hutchings and Sarnoff A. Mednick, "Criminality in Adoptees and Their Adoptive and Biological Parents: A Pilot Study," in *Biological Bases in Criminal Behavior*, ed. S. A. Mednick and K. O. Christiansen (New York: Gardner Press, 1977).

180. For similar results, see Sarnoff Mednick, Terrie Moffitt, William Gabrielli, and Barry Hutchings, "Genetic Factors in Criminal Behavior: A Review," in *Development of Antisocial and Prosocial Behavior*, ed. Dan Olweus (New York: Academic Press, 1986), pp. 3–50; Sarnoff Mednick, William Gabrielli, and Barry Hutchings, "Genetic Influences in Criminal Behavior: Evidence from an Adoption Cohort," in *Perspective Studies of Crime and Delinquency*, ed. Katherine Teilmann Van Dusen and Sarnoff Mednick (Boston: Kluver-Nijhoff, 1983), pp. 39–57; Michael Bohman, "Predisposition to Criminality: Swedish Adoption Studies in Retrospect," in *Genetics of Criminal and Antisocial Behavior*, pp. 99–114.

181. Lawrence Cohen and Richard Machalek, "A General Theory of Expropriative Crime: An Evolutionary Ecological Approach," *American Journal of Sociology* 94 (1988): 465–501.

182. For a general review, see Martin Daly and Margo Wilson, "Crime and Conflict: Homicide in Evolutionary Psychological Theory," in *Crime and Justice, An Annual Edition*, ed. Michael Tonry (Chicago: University of Chicago Press, 1997), pp. 51–100.

183. Ibid.

184. Martin Daly and Margo Wilson, *Homicide* (New York: Aldine de Gruyter, 1988), p. 194.

185. Margo Wilson, Holly Johnson, and Martin Daly, "Lethal and Nonlethal Violence against Wives," *Canadian Journal of Criminology* 37 (1995): 331–361.

186. Daly and Wilson, *Homicide*, pp. 172–173.

187. Lee Ellis, "The Evolution of Violent Criminal Behavior and Its Nonlegal Equivalent," in *Crime in Biological, Social, and Moral Contexts*, ed. Lee Ellis and Harry Hoffman (New York: Praeger, 1990), pp. 63–65.

188. David Rowe, Alexander Vazsonyi, and Aurelio Jose Figuerdo, "Mating-Effort in Adolescence: A Conditional Alternative Strategy," *Personal Individual Differences* 23 (2002): 105–115.

189. Ibid.

190. Anne Campbell, Steven Muncer, and Daniel Bibel, "Female–Female Criminal Assault: An Evolutionary Perspective," *Journal of Research in Crime and Delinquency* 35 (1998): 413–429.

191. Deborah Denno, "Sociological and Human Developmental Explanations of Crime: Conflict or Consensus," *Criminology* 23 (1985): 711–741.

192. Israel Nachshon and Deborah Denno, "Violence and Cerebral Function," in *The Causes of Crime, New Biological Approaches*, ed. Sarnoff Mednick, Terrie Moffitt, and Susan Stack (Cambridge: Cambridge University Press, 1987), pp. 185–217.

193. Raine, Brennan, Mednick, and Mednick, "High Rates of Violence, Crime, Academic Problems, and Behavioral Problems in Males with Both Early Neuromotor Deficits and Unstable Family Environments."

194. Avshalom Caspi, Donald Lynam, Terrie Moffitt, and Phil Silva, "Unraveling Girls' Delinquency: Biological, Dispositional, and Contextual Contributions to Adolescent Misbehavior," *Developmental Psychology* 29 (1993): 283–289.

195. Glenn Walters and Thomas White, "Heredity and Crime: Bad Genes or Bad Research," *Criminology* 27 (1989): 455–486, at 478.

196. Charles Goring, *The English Convict: A Statistical Study, 1913* (Montclair, NJ: Patterson Smith, 1972).

197. Edwin Driver, "Charles Buckman Goring," in *Pioneers in Criminology*, ed. Hermann Mannheim (Montclair, NJ: Patterson Smith, 1970), p. 440.

198. Gabriel Tarde, *Penal Philosophy*, trans. R. Howell (Boston: Little, Brown, 1912).

199. See generally Donn Byrne and Kathryn Kelly, *An Introduction to Personality* (Englewood Cliffs, NJ: Prentice Hall, 1981).

200. August Aichorn, *Wayward Youth* (New York: Viking Press, 1935).

201. See generally D. A. Andrews and James Bonta, *The Psychology of Criminal Conduct* (Cincinnati, OH: Anderson, 1994), pp. 72–75.

202. Paige Crosby Ouimette, "Psychopathology and Sexual Aggression in Nonincarcerated Men," *Violence and Victimization* 12 (1997): 389–397.

203. Robert Krueger, Avshalom Caspi, Phil Silva, and Rob McGee, "Personality Traits Are Differentially Linked to Mental Disorders: A Multitrait-Multidiagnosis Study of an Adolescent Birth Cohort," *Journal of Abnormal Psychology* 105 (1996): 299–312.

204. Seymour Halleck, *Psychiatry and the Dilemmas of Crime* (Berkeley: University of California Press, 1971).

205. John Bowlby, "Maternal Care and Mental Health," World Health Organization Monograph (WHO Monographs Series No. 2). (Geneva: World Health Organization, 1951), p. 53.

206. Ibid., p. 13.

207. Eric Wood and Shelley Riggs, "Predictors of Child Molestation: Adult Attachment, Cognitive Distortions, and Empathy," *Journal of Interpersonal Violence* 23 (2008): 259–275.

208. Karen L. Hayslett-McCall and Thomas J. Bernard, "Attachment, Masculinity, and Self-Control: A Theory of Male Crime Rates," *Theoretical Criminology* 6 (2002): 5–33.

209. Jeffrey Burke, Rolf Loeber, and Boris Birmaher, "Oppositional Defiant Disorder and Conduct Disorder: A Review of the Past 10 Years, Part II," *Journal of the American Academy of Child and Adolescent Psychiatry* 41 (2002): 1,275–1,294.

210. Ellen Kjelsberg, "Gender and Disorder Specific Criminal Career Profiles in Former Adolescent Psychiatric In-Patients," *Journal of Youth and Adolescence* 33 (2004): 261–270.

211. Richard Rowe, Julie Messer, Robert Goodman, and Howard Meltzer, "Conduct Disorder and Oppositional Defiant Disorder in a National Sample: Developmental Epidemiology," *Journal of Child Psychology and Psychiatry and Allied Disciplines* 45 (2004): 609–621.

212. Paul Rohde, Gregory N. Clarke, David E. Mace, Jenel S. Jorgensen, and John R. Seeley, "An Efficacy/Effectiveness Study of Cognitive-Behavioral Treatment for Adolescents with Comorbid Major Depression and Conduct Disorder," *Journal of the American Academy of Child and Adolescent Psychiatry* 43 (2004): 660–669.

213. Minna Ritakallio, Riittakerttu Kaltiala-Heino, Janne Kivivuori, Tiina Luukkaala, and Matti Rimpelä, "Delinquency and the Profile of Offences among Depressed and Non-Depressed Adolescents," *Criminal Behaviour and Mental Health* 16 (2006): 100–110.

214. Grégoire Zimmermann, "Delinquency in Male Adolescents: The Role of Alexithymia and Family Structure," *Journal of Adolescence* 29 (2006): 321–332.

215. Ching-hua Ho, J. B Kingree, and Martie Thompson, "Associations between Juvenile Delinquency and Weight-Related Variables: Analyses from a National Sample of High School Students," *International Journal of Eating Disorders* 39 (2006): 477–483.

216. Michael Pullmann, Jodi Kerbs, Nancy Koroloff, Ernie Veach-White, Rita Gaylor, and DeDe Sieler, "Juvenile Offenders with Mental Health Needs: Reducing Recidivism Using Wraparound," *Crime and Delinquency* 52 (2006): 375–397; Jennifer Beyers and Rolf Loeber, "Untangling Developmental Relations between Depressed Mood and Delinquency in Male Adolescents," *Journal of Abnormal Child Psychology* 31 (2003): 247–267.

217. Dorothy Espelage, Elizabeth Cauffman, Lisa Broidy, Alex Piquero, Paul Mazerolle, and Hans Steiner, "A Cluster-Analytic Investigation of MMPI Profiles of Serious Male and Female Juvenile Offenders," *Journal of the American Academy of Child and Adolescent Psychiatry* 42 (2003): 770–777.

218. Richard Famularo, Robert Kinscherff, and Terence Fenton, "Psychiatric Diagnoses of Abusive Mothers, A Preliminary Report," *Journal of Nervous and Mental Disease* 180 (1992): 658–660.

219. James Sorrells, "Kids Who Kill," *Crime and Delinquency* 23 (1977): 312–320.

220. Richard Rosner, "Adolescents Accused of Murder and Manslaughter: A Five-Year Descriptive Study," *Bulletin of the American Academy of Psychiatry and the Law* 7 (1979): 342–351.

221. Richard Wagner, Dawn Taylor, Joy Wright, Alison Sloat, Gwynneth Springett, Sandy Arnold, and Heather Weinberg, "Substance Abuse among the Mentally Ill," *American Journal of Orthopsychiatry* 64 (1994): 30–38.

222. Susan Phillips, Alaattin Erkanli, Gordon Keeler, Jane Costello, and Adrian Angold, "Disentangling the Risks: Parent Criminal Justice Involvement and Children's Exposure to Family Risks," *Criminology and Public Policy* 5 (2006): 677–702.

223. Bruce Link, Howard Andrews, and Francis Cullen, "The Violent and Illegal Behavior of Mental Patients Reconsidered," *American Sociological Review* 57 (1992): 275–292; Ellen Hochstedler Steury, "Criminal Defendants with Psychiatric Impairment: Prevalence, Probabilities and Rates," *Journal of Criminal Law and Criminology* 84 (1993): 354–374.

224. Richard Friedman, "Violence and Mental Illness—How Strong Is the Link?" *New England Journal of Medicine* 355 (2006): 2,064–2,066.

225. Henrik Belfrage, "A Ten-Year Follow-Up of Criminality in Stockholm Mental Patients: New Evidence for a Relation between Mental Disorder and Crime," *British Journal of Criminology* 38 (1998): 145–155.

226. C. Wallace, P. Mullen, P. Burgess, S. Palmer, D. Ruschena, and C. Browne, "Serious Criminal Offending and Mental Disorder: Case Linkage Study," *British Journal of Psychiatry* 174 (1998): 477–484.

227. Patricia Brennan, Sarnoff Mednick, and Sheilagh Hodgins, "Major Mental Disorders and Criminal Violence in a Danish Birth Cohort," *Archives of General Psychiatry* 57 (2000): 494–500.

228. Stefan Watzke, Simone Ullrich, and Andreas Marneros, "Gender- and Violence-Related Prevalence of Mental Disorders in Prisoners," *European Archives of Psychiatry and Clinical Neuroscience* 256 (2006): 414–421.

229. Robert Vermeiren, "Psychopathology and Delinquency in Adolescents: A Descriptive and Developmental Perspective," *Clinical Psychology Review* 23 (2003): 277–318.

230. John Monahan, *Mental Illness and Violent Crime* (Washington, DC: National Institute of Justice, 1996).

231. Robin Shepard Engel and Eric Silver, "Policing Mentally Disordered Suspects: A Reexamination of the Criminalization Hypothesis," *Criminology* 39 (2001): 225–352; Marc Hillbrand, John Krystal, Kimberly Sharpe, and Hilliard Foster, "Clinical Predictors of Self-Mutilation in Hospitalized Patients," *Journal of Nervous and Mental Disease* 182 (1994): 9–13.

232. James Bonta, Moira Law, and Karl Hanson, "The Prediction of Criminal and Violent Recidivism among Mentally Disordered Offenders: A Meta-Analysis," *Psychological Bulletin* 123 (1998): 123–142.

233. Eric Silver, "Mental Disorder and Violent Victimization: The Mediating Role of Involvement in Conflicted Social Relationships," *Criminology* 40 (2002): 191–212.

234. Stacy DeCoster and Karen Heimer, "The Relationship between Law Violation and Depression: An Interactionist Analysis," *Criminology* 39 (2001): 799–837.

235. Alexander McFarlane, Geoff Schrader, Clara Bookless, and Derek Browne, "Prevalence of Victimization, Posttraumatic Stress Disorder and Violent Behaviour in the Seriously Mentally Ill," *Australian and New Zealand Journal of Psychiatry* 40 (2006): 1,010–1,015; Eric Silver, "Extending Social Disorganization Theory: A Multilevel Approach to the Study of Violence among Persons with Mental Illness," *Criminology* 38 (2000): 1,043–1,074.

236. B. Lögdberg, L. L. Nilsson, M. T. Levander, and S. Levander, "Schizophrenia, Neighbourhood, and Crime," *Acta Psychiatrica Scandinavica* 110 (2004): 92–97.

237. Courtenay Sellers, Christopher Sullivan, Bonita Veysey, and Jon Shane, "Responding to Persons with Mental Illnesses: Police Perspectives on Specialized and Traditional Practices," *Behavioral Sciences and the Law* 23 (2005):647–657.

238. Paul Hirschfield, Tina Maschi, Helene Raskin White, Leah Goldman Traub, and Rolf Loeber, "Mental Health and Juvenile Arrests: Criminality, Criminalization, or Compassion?" *Criminology* 44 (2006): 593–630.

239. Jeffrey Wanson, Randy Borum, Marvin Swartz, Virginia Hidaym, H. Ryan Wagner, and Barbara Burns, "Can Involuntary Outpatient Commitment Reduce Arrests among Persons with Severe Mental Illness?" *Criminal Justice and Behavior* 28 (2001): 156–189.

240. This discussion is based on three works by Albert Bandura: *Aggression: A Social Learning Analysis* (Englewood Cliffs, NJ: Prentice Hall, 1973); *Social Learning Theory* (Englewood Cliffs, NJ: Prentice Hall, 1977); and "The Social Learning Perspective: Mechanisms of Aggression," in *Psychology of Crime and Criminal Justice*, ed. Hans Toch (New York: Holt, Rinehart & Winston, 1979), pp. 198–236.

241. David Phillips, "The Impact of Mass Media Violence on U.S. Homicides," *American Sociological Review* 48 (1983): 560–568.

242. See generally Jean Piaget, *The Moral Judgment of the Child* (London: Kegan Paul, 1932).

243. Lawrence Kohlberg, *Stages in the Development of Moral Thought and Action* (New York: Holt, Rinehart & Winston, 1969).

244. L. Kohlberg, K. Kauffman, P. Scharf, and J. Hickey, *The Just Community Approach in Corrections: A Manual* (Niantic: Connecticut Department of Corrections, 1973).

245. Scott Henggeler, *Delinquency in Adolescence* (Newbury Park, CA: Sage, 1989), p. 26.

246. Carol Veneziano and Louis Veneziano, "The Relationship between Deterrence and Moral Reasoning," *Criminal Justice Review* 17 (1992): 209–216.

247. Quinten Raaijmakers, Rutger Engels, and Anne Van Hoof, "Delinquency and Moral Reasoning in Adolescence and Young Adulthood," *International Journal of Behavioral Development* 29 (2005): 247–258; Scott Henggeler, *Delinquency in Adolescence* (Newbury Park, CA: Sage, 1989), p. 26.

248. K. A. Dodge, "A Social Information Processing Model of Social Competence in Children," in *Minnesota Symposium in Child Psychology*, vol. 18, ed. M. Perlmutter (Hillsdale, NJ: Erlbaum, 1986), pp. 77–125.

249. Adrian Raine, Peter Venables, and Mark Williams, "Better Autonomic Conditioning and Faster Electrodermal Half-Recovery Time at Age 15 Years as Possible Protective Factors against Crime at Age 29 Years," *Developmental Psychology* 32 (1996): 624–630.

250. Jean Marie McGloin and Travis Pratt, "Cognitive Ability and Delinquent Behavior among Inner-City Youth: A Life-Course Analysis of Main, Mediating, and Interaction Effects," *International Journal of Offender Therapy and Comparative Criminology* 47 (2003): 253–271.

251. Elizabeth Cauffman, Laurence Steinberg, and Alex Piquero, "Psychological, Neuropsychological, and Physiological Correlates of Serious Antisocial Behavior in Adolescence: The Role of Self-Control," *Criminology* 43 (2005): 133–176.

252. Donald Lynam and Joshua Miller, "Personality Pathways to Impulsive Behavior and Their Relations to Deviance: Results from Three Samples," *Journal of Quantitative Criminology* 20 (2004): 319–341.

253. Shadd Maruna, "Desistance from Crime and Explanatory Style: A New Direction in the Psychology of Reform," *Journal of Contemporary Criminal Justice* 20 (2004): 184–200.

254. Tony Ward and Claire Stewart, "The Relationship between Human Needs and Criminogenic Needs," *Psychology, Crime and Law* 9 (2003): 219–225.

255. David Ward, Mark Stafford, and Louis Gray, "Rational Choice, Deterrence, and Theoretical Integration," *Journal of Applied Social Psychology* 36 (2006): 571–585.

256. Coralijn Nas, Bram Orobio de Castro, and Willem Koops, "Social Information Processing in Delinquent Adolescents," *Psychology, Crime and Law* 11 (2005): 363–375.

257. Elizabeth Kubik and Jeffrey Hecker, "Cognitive Distortions About Sex and Sexual Offending: A Comparison of Sex Offending Girls, Delinquent Girls, and Girls from the Community" *Journal of Child Sexual Abuse* 14 (2005): 43–69.

258. L. Huesman and L. Eron, "Individual Differences and the Trait of Aggression," *European Journal of Personality* 3 (1989): 95–106.

259. Rolf Loeber and Dale Hay, "Key Issues in the Development of Aggression and Violence from Childhood to Early Adulthood," *Annual Review of Psychology* 48 (1997): 371–410.

260. Judith Baer and Tina Maschi, "Random Acts of Delinquency: Trauma and Self-Destructiveness in Juvenile Offenders," *Child and Adolescent Social Work Journal* 20 (2003): 85–99.

261. J. E. Lochman, "Self and Peer Perceptions and Attributional Biases of Aggressive and Nonaggressive Boys in Dyadic Interactions," *Journal of Consulting and Clinical Psychology* 55 (1987): 404–410.

262. Kathleen Cirillo, B. E. Pruitt, Brian Colwell, Paul M. Kingery, Robert S. Hurley, and Danny Ballard, "School Violence: Prevalence and Intervention Strategies for At-Risk Adolescents," *Adolescence* 33 (1998): 319–331.

263. Leilani Greening, "Adolescent Stealers' and Nonstealers' Social Problem-Solving Skills," *Adolescence* 32 (1997): 51–56.

264. D. Lipton, E. C. McDonel, and R. McFall, "Heterosocial Perception in Rapists," *Journal of Consulting and Clinical Psychology* 55 (1987): 17–21.

265. Vincent Marziano, Tony Ward, Anthony Beech, and Philippa Pattison, "Identification of Five Fundamental Implicit Theories Underlying Cognitive Distortions in Child Abusers: A Preliminary Study," *Psychology, Crime and Law* 12 (2006): 97–105.

266. *Understanding Violence*, p. 389.

267. Cirillo, Pruitt, Colwell, Kingery, Hurley, and Ballard, "School Violence."

268. See generally Walter Mischel, *Introduction to Personality*, 4th ed. (New York: Holt, Rinehart & Winston, 1986).

269. D. A. Andrews and J. Stephen Wormith, "Personality and Crime: Knowledge and Construction in Criminology," *Justice Quarterly* 6 (1989): 289–310; Donald Gibbons, "Comment—Personality and Crime: Non-Issues, Real Issues, and a Theory and Research Agenda," *Justice Quarterly* (1989): 311–324.

270. Sheldon Glueck and Eleanor Glueck, *Unraveling Juvenile Delinquency* (Cambridge, MA: Harvard University Press, 1950).

271. See generally Hans Eysenck, *Personality and Crime* (London: Routledge and Kegan Paul, 1977).

272. Hans Eysenck and M. W. Eysenck, *Personality and Individual Differences* (New York: Plenum, 1985).

273. Catrien Bijleveld and Jan Hendriks, "Juvenile Sex Offenders: Differences between Group and Solo Offenders," *Psychology, Crime and Law* 9 (2003): 237–246; Joshua Miller and Donald Lynam, "Personality and Antisocial Behavior," *Criminology* 39 (2001): 765–799; Edelyn Verona and Joyce Carbonell, "Female Violence and Personality," *Criminal Justice and Behavior* 27 (2000): 176–195.

274. Hans Eysenck and M. W. Eysenck, *Personality and Individual Differences* (New York: Plenum, 1985).

275. Essi Viding, James Blair, Terrie Moffitt, and Robert Plomin, "Evidence for Substantial Genetic Risk for Psychopathy in 7-Year-Olds," *Journal of Child Psychology and Psychiatry* 46 (2005): 592–597.

276. Gerhard Blickle, Alexander Schlegel, Pantaleon Fassbender, and Uwe Klein, "Some Personality Correlates of Business White-Collar Crime," *Applied Psychology: An International Review* 55 (2006): 220–233.

277. Andreas Hill, Niels Habermann, Wolfgang Berner, and Peer Briken, "Sexual Sadism and Sadistic Personality Disorder in Sexual Homicide," *Journal of Personality Disorders* 20 (2006): 671–684.

278. Andreas Hill, Niels Habermann, Wolfgang Berner, and Peer Briken, "Sexual Sadism and Sadistic Personality Disorder in Sexual Homicide," *Journal of Personality Disorders* 20 (2006): 671–684.

279. American Psychiatric Association, *Diagnostic and Statistical Manual of Mental Disorders* (Washington, DC: American Psychiatric Association, 1994).

280. See generally R. Starke Hathaway and Elio Monachesi, *Analyzing and Predicting Juvenile Delinquency with the MMPI* (Minneapolis: University of Minnesota Press, 1953).

281. R. Starke Hathaway, Elio Monachesi, and Lawrence Young, "Delinquency Rates and Personality," *Journal of Criminal Law, Criminology, and Police Science* 51 (1960): 443–460; Michael Hindelang and Joseph Weis, "Personality and Self-Reported Delinquency: An Application of Cluster Analysis," *Criminology* 10 (1972): 268; Spencer Rathus and Larry Siegel, "Crime and Personality Revisited," *Criminology* 18 (1980): 245–251.

282. See generally Edward Megargee, *The California Psychological Inventory Handbook* (San Francisco: Jossey-Bass, 1972).

283. Avshalom Caspi, Terrie Moffitt, Phil Silva, Magda Stouthamer-Loeber, Robert Krueger, and Pamela Schmutte, "Are Some People Crime-Prone? Replications of the Personality–Crime Relationship across Countries, Genders, Races and Methods," *Criminology* 32 (1994): 163–195.

284. Edwin Sutherland, "Mental Deficiency and Crime," in *Social Attitudes,* ed. Kimball Young (New York: Henry Holt, 1931).

285. William Healy and Augusta Bronner, *Delinquency and Criminals: Their Making and Unmaking* (New York: Macmillan, 1926).

286. Joseph Lee Rogers, H. Harrington Cleveland, Edwin van den Oord, and David Rowe, "Resolving the Debate over Birth Order, Family Size and Intelligence," *American Psychologist* 55 (2000): 599–612.

287. John Slawson, *The Delinquent Boys* (Boston: Budget Press, 1926).

288. Edwin Sutherland, "Mental Deficiency and Crime," in *Social Attitudes*, ed. Kimball Young (New York: Henry Holt, 1931), chap. 15.

289. Travis Hirschi and Michael Hindelang, "Intelligence and Delinquency: A Revisionist Review," *American Sociological Review* 42 (1977): 471–586.

290. Travis Hirschi and Michael Hindelang, "Intelligence and Delinquency: A Revisionist Review," *American Sociological Review* 42 (1977): 471–586.

291. Donald Lynam, Terrie Moffitt, and Magda Stouthamer-Loeber, "Explaining the Relation between IQ and Delinquency: Class, Race, Test Motivation, School Failure or Self-Control," *Journal of Abnormal Psychology* 102 (1993): 187–196.

292. Susan Pease and Craig T. Love, "Optimal Methods and Issues in Nutrition Research in the Correctional Setting," *Nutrition Reviews Supplement* 44 (1986): 122–131.

293. Alex Piquero, "Frequency, Specialization, and Violence in Offending Careers," *Journal of Research in Crime and Delinquency* 37 (2000): 392–418.

294. James Q. Wilson and Richard Herrnstein, *Crime and Human Nature* (New York: Simon & Schuster, 1985), p. 148.

295. Ibid., p. 171.

296. Lorne Yeudall, Delee Fromm-Auch, and Priscilla Davies, "Neuropsychological Impairment of Persistent Delinquency," *Journal of Nervous and Mental Diseases* 170 (1982): 257–265; Hakan Stattin and Ingrid Klackenberg-Larsson, "Early Language and Intelligence Development and Their Relationship to Future Criminal Behavior," *Journal of Abnormal Psychology* 102 (1993): 369–378; H. D. Day, J. M. Franklin, and D. D. Marshall, "Predictors of Aggression in Hospitalized Adolescents," *Journal of Psychology* 132 (1998): 427–435.

297. Camilla Hagelstam and Helinä Häkkänen, Adolescent Homicides in Finland: Offence and Offender Characteristics," *Forensic Science International* 164 (2006): 110–115.

298. Richard Herrnstein and Charles Murray, *The Bell Curve, Intelligence and Class Structure in American Life* (New York: Free Press, 1994).

299. Murray Simpson, M. K Simpson, and J. Hogg, "Patterns of Offending among People with Intellectual Disability: A Systematic Review Part I: Methodology and Prevalence Data," *Journal of Intellectual Disability Research* 45 (2001): 384–396.

300. Ibid.

301. Mark O'Callaghan and Douglas Carroll, "The Role of Psychosurgical Studies in the Control of Antisocial Behavior," in *The Causes of Crime: New Biological Approaches*, ed. Sarnoff Mednick, Terrie Moffitt, and Susan Stack (Cambridge: Cambridge University Press, 1987), pp. 312–328.

302. Reiss and Roth, *Understanding and Preventing Violence*, p. 389.

303. Cirillo, Pruitt, Colwell, Kingery, Hurley, and Ballard, "School Violence."

304. Martin Olsson, Kjell Hansson, and Marianne Cederblad, "A Long-Term Follow-Up of Conduct Disorder Adolescents into Adulthood," *Nordic Journal of Psychiatry* 60 (2006): 469–479.

Social Structure Theories

CHAPTER OBJECTIVES

1. Be familiar with the concept of social structure
2. Have knowledge of the socioeconomic structure of American society
3. Be able to discuss the concept of social disorganization
4. Be familiar with the works of Shaw and McKay
5. Know the various elements of ecological theory
6. Be able to discuss the association between collective efficacy and crime
7. Know what is meant by the term "anomie"
8. Be familiar with the concept of strain
9. Understand the concept of cultural deviance
10. Explain the meaning of the terms "focal concerns" and "conduct norms"

© AP Images/Edgard Garrido

The tiny country of El Salvador (population 6.6 million) is home to more than 40,000 gang members. Rather than being a homegrown phenomenon, gangs are actually a U.S import. How did this happen? In the early 1990s, hundreds of members of two of Los Angeles's largest gangs, the 18th Street Gang and the MS-13 gang, who had illegally made their home in the United States, were deported back to El Salvador. The deportees brought L.A. gang culture with them to a country already swamped with weapons from an ongoing civil war. Now on their home turf, gang boys recruited thousands of local teenagers into their reconstituted gangs. Joining a gang gave these poor, urban teenagers a powerful sense of identity and belonging. They were also free now to show their courage and manhood by engaging in a never-ending turf war with one another.

Ironically, both gangs were started in Los Angeles by Salvadorans fleeing a civil war. When they first arrived in L.A. they were preyed upon by preexisting Mexican gangs. The MS-13 gang was formed as a means of self-protection. The gang's name— Mara Salvatrucha—most likely refers to a mara, slang for "army ant," and salvatrucha, local slang for tough, streetwise Salvadorans; the "13" is a common L.A. gang reference. Over time, both gangs' ranks grew and members entered a variety of rackets, from extortion to drug trafficking. When law enforcement cracked down and deported members, the deportees quickly created outposts in El Salvador and throughout Central America. The Salvadoran government has responded by criminalizing gang membership and arresting thousands. But government efforts have not stemmed the tide of recruitment and the gangs appear to be more popular than ever.[1] Gang membership has continued to grow and the gangs have returned to set up branches in the United States. Some experts believe that the 10,000-member MS-13 is now the nation's most dangerous gang, while the 18th Street Gang, with over 20,000 members, is the largest.

Both MS-13 and the 18th Street Gang are part of a significant national gang population. The federal government sponsors the National Youth Gang Survey (NYGS) to measure gang activity around the United States. The most recent NYGS found that a significant majority of urban areas report the presence of gangs and that gangs exist in all levels of the social strata, from rural counties to metropolitan areas.[2] The most recent count found an estimated 760,000 gang members, and 24,000 gangs were active in more than 2,900 jurisdictions around the United States.

Teen gangs have become an ever-present fixture of the American urban experience. Gang members are heavily armed, dangerous, and more violent than nonmembers. They are about ten times more likely to carry handguns than nongang members, and gun-toting gang members commit about ten times more violent crimes than nonmembers; gang homicides seem to be on an upswing. Nowhere is the gang problem more serious than in Los Angeles, where a single gang can have up to 20,000 members.

To criminologists it comes as no surprise that gangs develop in poor, deteriorated urban neighborhoods. Many kids in these areas grow up hopeless and alienated, believing that they have little chance of being part of the American Dream.[3] Joining a gang holds the promise of economic rewards and status enhancements, which the conventional world simply cannot provide.

This association between social conditions and crime is not lost on criminologists, many of whom conclude that criminals are indigent and desperate people rather than abnormal, calculating, or evil. Raised in deteriorated parts of town, they lack the social support and economic resources available to more affluent members of society. According to this view, it is *social forces*—and not individual traits—that cause crime. To understand criminal behavior, we must analyze the influence of these destructive social forces.

As you may recall (Chapter 1), the social environment and its influence on human behavior has been the primary focus of criminology since the early twentieth century, when sociologists Robert Ezra Park (1864–1944), Ernest W. Burgess (1886–1966), Louis Wirth (1897–1952), and their colleagues were teaching and conducting criminological research in the sociology department at the University of Chicago. Their influence was such that most criminologists have been trained in sociology, and criminology courses are routinely taught in departments of sociology. What is their vision and how do they connect criminality with a person's place in the social structure?

connections

Concern about the ecological distribution of crime, the effect of social change, and the interactive nature of crime itself has made sociology the foundation of modern criminology. This chapter reviews sociological theories that emphasize the relationship between social status and criminal behavior. In Chapter 7 the focus shifts to theories that emphasize socialization and its influence on crime and deviance; Chapter 8 covers theories based on the concept of social conflict.

SOCIOECONOMIC STRUCTURE AND CRIME

People in the United States live in a stratified society. Social strata are created by the unequal distribution of wealth, power, and prestige. Social classes are segments of the population whose members have a relatively similar portion of desirable things and who share attitudes, values, norms, and an identifiable lifestyle. In U.S. society, it is common to identify people as upper-, middle-, and lower-class citizens, with a broad range of economic variations existing within each group. The upper-upper class is reserved for a small number of exceptionally well-to-do families who maintain enormous financial and social resources. Today, the poorest fifth (20 percent) of all U.S. households earn about $10,000 per year and receive only 3 percent of the country's aggregate income, the smallest share ever (see Table 6.1). In contrast, the top fifth (20 percent) of households earn more than $150,000 per year, a record high; the top 20 percent collect more than 50 percent of all household income, the most in history.[4]

Nor is the wealth concentration effect unique to the United States; it is a worldwide phenomenon. According to the most recent World Wealth Report, there are about 8 million high net worth individuals in the world today (people with more than $1 million in assets excluding their primary residence); they have a net worth of more than $30.8 trillion, and their numbers are steadily growing.[5]

In contrast, the indigent have scant, if any, resources and suffer socially and economically as a result. And while the United States is the richest country in the world, the most recent federal data indicate that the number and rate of people living in poverty has risen since 2000[6] (Figure 6.1). More than 37 million Americans now live in poverty.

Lower-class areas are scenes of inadequate housing and health care, disrupted family lives, underemployment, and despair. Members of the lower class also suffer in other ways. They are more prone to depression, less likely to have achievement motivation, and less likely to put off immediate gratification for future gain. For example, they may be less willing to stay in

Table 6.1 Mean and Share of Household Income

	Mean Household Income	Share of Household Income
Lowest fifth	$10,655	3.4%
Second fifth	27,357	8.6
Third fifth	46,301	14.6
Fourth fifth	72,825	23.0
Highest fifth	159,583	50.4

Source: Income, Poverty and Health Insurance in the United States: 2005 (P60-231) (Washington, DC: U.S. Census Department, 2006), www.census.gov/prod/2006pubs/p60-231.pdf (accessed June 3, 2007).

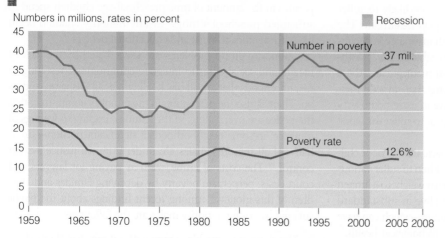

Figure 6.1 Number in Poverty and Poverty Rate

Numbers in millions, rates in percent

Recession

Sources: U.S. Census Bureau, *Current Population Survey, 1960 to 2006 Annual Social and Economic Supplements*; Jennifer Cheeseman Day, *Population Projections of the United States by Age, Sex, Race, and Hispanic Origin: 1995 to 2050*, U.S. Bureau of the Census, Current Population Reports, P25-1130, U.S. Government Printing Office, Washington, DC, 1996.

school because the rewards for educational achievement are in the distant future.

The poor are constantly bombarded by the media with advertisements linking material possessions to self-worth, but they are often unable to attain desired goods and services through conventional means. Though they are members of a society that extols material success above any other, they are unable to satisfactorily compete for such success with members of the upper classes. As a result, they may turn to illegal solutions to their economic plight: they may deal drugs for profit, steal cars and sell them to "chop shops," or commit armed robberies for desperately needed funds. They may become so depressed that they take alcohol and drugs as a form

of self-tranquilization, and because of their poverty, they may acquire the drugs and alcohol through illegal channels.

The Underclass

In 1966, sociologist Oscar Lewis argued that the crushing lifestyle of lower-class areas produces a **culture of poverty**, which is passed from one generation to the next.[7] Apathy, cynicism, helplessness, and mistrust of social institutions such as schools, government agencies, and the police mark the culture of poverty. This mistrust prevents members of the lower class from taking advantage of the meager opportunities available to them. Lewis's work was the first of a group that described the plight of **at-risk** children and adults. In 1970, Swedish economist Gunnar Myrdal described a worldwide **underclass** that was cut off from society, its members lacking the education and skills needed to be effectively in demand in modern society.[8]

Economic disparity will continually haunt members of the underclass and their children over the course of their life span. Even if they value education and other middle-class norms, their desperate life circumstances (e.g., high unemployment and nontraditional family structures) may prevent them from developing the skills, habits, and lifestyles that lead first to educational success and later to success in the workplace.[9] Their ability to maintain social ties in the neighborhood become weak and attenuated, further weakening a neighborhood's cohesiveness and its ability to regulate the behavior of its citizens.[10]

Child Poverty

The timing of poverty also seems to be relevant. Findings suggest that poverty during early childhood may have a more severe impact on behavior than poverty during adolescence and adulthood.[11] This is particularly important today because, as Figure 6.2 shows, children have a higher poverty rate, almost 18 percent, than any other age group.

Children are hit especially hard by poverty. Hundreds of studies have documented the association between family poverty and children's health, achievement, and behavior impairments.[12] Children who grow up in

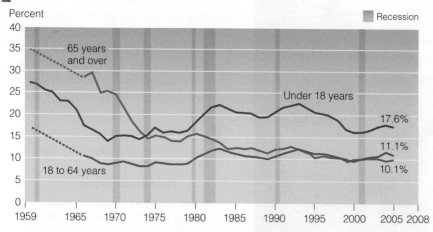

Figure 6.2 Poverty Rates by Age

Percent

Recession

Sources: U.S. Census Bureau, *Current Population Survey, 1960 to 2006 Annual Social and Economic Supplements*; Jennifer Cheeseman Day, *Population Projections of the United States by Age, Sex, Race, and Hispanic Origin: 1995 to 2050*, U.S. Bureau of the Census, Current Population Reports, P25-1130, U.S. Government Printing Office, Washington, DC, 1996; www.aza.org/RC/RC_Trends/Documents/2020TrendsReport.pdf (accessed July 26, 2007).

low-income homes are less likely to achieve in school and are less likely to complete their schooling than children with more affluent parents.[13] Poor children are also more likely to suffer from health problems and to receive inadequate health care. The number of U.S. children covered by health insurance is declining and will continue to do so for the foreseeable future.[14] Without health benefits or the means to afford medical care, these children are likely to have health problems that impede their long-term development. Children who live in extreme poverty or who remain poor for multiple years appear to suffer the worst outcomes.

Besides their increased chance of physical illness, poor children are much more likely than wealthy children to suffer various social and physical ills, ranging from low birth weight to a limited chance of earning a college degree. Many live in substandard housing—high-rise, multiple-family dwellings—which can have a negative influence on their long-term psychological health.[15] Adolescents in the worst neighborhoods share the greatest risk of dropping out of school and becoming teenage parents.

Minority Group Poverty

The burdens of underclass life are often felt most acutely by minority group members. While whites use their economic, social, and political advantages to live in sheltered gated communities protected by security guards and police, minorities are denied similar protections and privileges.[16] According to the U.S. Census Bureau, about 25 percent of African Americans and 22 percent of Hispanics live in poverty as compared to 8 percent of non-Hispanic whites and 11 percent of Asians.[17]

The rates of child poverty in the United States also vary significantly by race and ethnicity. Latino and African American children are more than twice as likely to be poor as Asian and white children. Minority children are four times less likely to have health insurance as other kids. There are large ethnic disparities in the amount of time preschool-age children spend in structured preschool settings. Clearly minority children begin life with significant social and educational deficits.[18]

Minority group problems are exacerbated by the lack of meaningful social effort to integrate communities, resulting in neighborhoods that are all black, all white, all Hispanic, and so on. There is also the perception in the minority community that the police are overzealous in their duties, leading to feelings of injustice; in some neighborhoods a significant portion—up to half—of all minority males are under criminal justice system control.[19] The costs of crime, such as paying for lawyers and court costs, perpetuate poverty by depriving families and children of this money.[20] Among recent findings about the plight suffered by young minority males are the following:

▌ The share of young black men without jobs has climbed relentlessly, with only a slight pause during the economic peak of the late 1990s. In 2000, 65 percent of black male high school dropouts in their 20s were jobless—that is, unable to find work, not seeking it, or incarcerated. Today, the share had grown to 72 percent, compared with 34 percent of white and 19 percent of Hispanic dropouts. Even when high school graduates were included, half of black men in their 20s are jobless, up from 46 percent in 2000.

▌ Incarceration rates have climbed and reached historic highs in the past few years. In 1995, 16 percent of black men in their 20s who did not attend college were in jail or prison; today, 21 percent are incarcerated. By their mid-30s, six in ten black men who dropped out of school have spent time in prison.

▌ In the inner cities, more than half of all black men do not finish high school.[21]

Some experts believe that interracial crime rate differentials can be explained by differences in standard of living: If interracial economic disparity would end, so too might differences in the crime rate.[22] The issue of minority poverty is explored further in the Race, Culture, Gender, and Criminology feature "There Goes the Neighborhood," which discusses the works of William Julius Wilson, one of the nation's leading experts on race and culture.

www Go to academic.cengage.com/ criminaljustice/siegel to learn more about the following topics:

▌ The **World Wealth Report**.

▌ **Kids Count**, a project of the Annie E. Casey Foundation, is a national and state-by-state effort to track the relative status of children in the United States.

▌ The **Northwestern University/University of Chicago Joint Center for Poverty Research** examines what it means to be poor and live in America.

© Mario Tama/Getty Images

About 25 percent of children in the United States live in poverty. These children are less likely to achieve in school or to complete their education. They are more likely to have health problems and to receive inadequate health care. Children living in poverty suffer a variety of social and physical ills, ranging from low birth weight to dropping out of school to becoming teenage parents.

THERE GOES THE NEIGHBORHOOD

William Julius Wilson, one of the nation's most prominent sociologists, has produced an impressive body of work that details racial problems and racial politics in American society. In 1987, he provided a description of the plight of the lowest levels of the underclass, which he labeled the truly disadvantaged. Wilson portrayed members of this group as socially isolated people who dwell in urban inner cities, occupy the bottom rung of the social ladder, and are the victims of discrimination. They live in areas in which the basic institutions of society—family, school, housing—have long since declined. Their decline triggers similar breakdowns in the strengths of inner-city areas, including the loss of community cohesion and the ability of people living in the area to control the flow of drugs and criminal activity. For example, in a more affluent area, neighbors might complain to parents that their children were acting out. In distressed areas, this element of informal social control may be absent because parents are under stress or all too often absent. These effects magnify the isolation of the underclass from mainstream society and promote a ghetto culture and behavior.

Because the truly disadvantaged rarely come into contact with the actual source of their oppression, they direct their anger and aggression at those with whom they are in close and intimate contact, such as neighbors, businesspeople, and landlords. Members of this group, plagued by under- or unemployment, begin to lose self-confidence, a feeling supported by the plight of kin and friendship groups who also experience extreme economic marginality. Self-doubt is a neighborhood norm, overwhelming those forced to live in areas of concentrated poverty.

In his important book, *When Work Disappears*, Wilson assesses the effect of joblessness and underemployment on residents in poor neighborhoods on Chicago's south side. He argues that for the first time since the nineteenth century, most adults in inner-city ghetto neighborhoods are not working during a typical week. He finds that inner-city life is only marginally affected by the surge in the nation's economy, which has been brought about by new industrial growth connected with technological development. Poverty in these inner-city areas is eternal and unchanging and, if anything, worsening as residents are further shut out of the economic mainstream.

Wilson focuses on the plight of the African American community, which had enjoyed periods of relative prosperity in the 1950s and 1960s. He suggests that as difficult as life was in the 1940s and 1950s for African Americans, they at least had a reasonable hope of steady work. Now, because of the globalization of the economy, those opportunities have evaporated. This development is important because in the past growth in the manufacturing sector fueled upward mobility and provided the foundation of today's African American middle class. Those opportunities no longer exist as manufacturing plants have moved to inaccessible rural and overseas locations where the cost of doing business is lower. With manufacturing opportunities all but obsolete in the United States, service and retail establishments, which depended on blue-collar spending, have similarly disappeared, leaving behind an economy based on welfare and government supports. In less than 20 years, formerly active African American communities have become crime-infested inner-city neighborhoods.

The hardships faced by residents in Chicago's south side are not unique to that community. Beyond sustaining inner-city poverty, the absence of employment opportunities has torn at the social fabric of the nation's inner-city neighborhoods. Work helps socialize young people into the wider society, instilling in them such desirable values as hard work, caring, and respect for others. When work becomes scarce, however, the discipline and structure it provides are absent. Community-wide underemployment destroys social cohesion, increasing the presence of neighborhood social problems ranging from drug use to educational failure. Schools in these areas are unable to teach basic skills and because desirable employment is lacking, there are few adults to serve as role models. In contrast to more affluent suburban households where daily life is organized around job and career demands, children in inner-city areas are not socialized in the workings of the mainstream economy.

In *The Bridge over the Racial Divide: Rising Inequality and Coalition Politics*, Wilson expands on his views of race in contemporary society. He argues that despite economic gains, there is a growing inequality in American society, and ordinary families, of all races and ethnic origins, are suffering. Whites, Latinos, African Americans, Asians, and Native Americans must therefore begin to put aside their differences and concentrate more on what they have in common—their aspirations, problems, and hopes. There needs to be mutual cooperation across racial lines.

One reason for this set of mutual problems is that the government tends to aggravate rather than ease the financial stress being placed on ordinary families. Monetary policy, trade policy, and tax policy are harmful to working-class families. A multiracial citizens' coalition could pressure national public officials to focus on the interests of ordinary people. As long as middle- and working-class groups are fragmented along racial lines, such pressure is impossible.

Wilson finds that racism is becoming more subtle and harder to detect. Whites believe that blacks are responsible for their inferior economic status because of their cultural traits. Because even affluent whites fear corporate downsizing, they are unwilling to vote for governmental assistance to the poor because it means

(continued)

(continued)

more taxes and lower corporate profits, a condition that threatens their jobs. Whites are continuing to be suburban dwellers, further isolating poor minorities in central cities and making their problems distant and unimportant. Wilson continues to believe that the changing marketplace, with its reliance on sophisticated computer technologies, is continually decreasing demand for low-skilled workers, which impacts African Americans more negatively than other better educated and affluent groups.

Wilson argues for a cross-race, class-based alliance of working- and middle-class Americans to pursue policies that will benefit them rather than the affluent. These include full employment, programs to help families and workers in their private lives, and a reconstructed "affirmative opportunity" program that benefits African Americans without antagonizing whites.

In his most recent work, *There Goes the Neighborhood*, Wilson, along with Richard P. Taub, assesses racial relations

in four Chicago neighborhoods. The picture he paints is quite bleak. He finds that racism is still an active part of people's lives though its motif is changing. People are unusually hostile when outsiders move into their enclave. If they have a choice they move, if not they are angry and sullen. In a white middle-class neighborhood, people are angry when black and Latino newcomers arrive, believing they threaten property values and neighborhood stability. Whites and Latinos are able to reach common ground on only one social issue: preventing kids from being bused to a black school district. People seem unfazed about using offensive racist language to express their feelings and feel superior to other groups and races. Racism seems to cloak social anxiety: people worried about jobs and health care take their frustrations out on others. Wilson as always comes up with a prescription for positive change: strengthen neighborhood social organizations and people will be less likely to flee. Race relations can be improved if people from diverse backgrounds can

come together to reach common goals such as school improvement. Society as a whole must be willing to help out and repair inner-city ghetto areas. Without such help, racial and class tensions spread throughout the city.

CRITICAL THINKING

1. Is it unrealistic to assume that a government-sponsored public works program can provide needed jobs in this era of budget cutbacks?

2. What are some of the hidden costs of unemployment in a community setting?

3. How would a biocriminologist explain Wilson's findings?

Sources: William Julius Wilson and Richard Taub, *There Goes the Neighborhood: Racial, Ethnic, and Class Tensions in Four Chicago Neighborhoods and Their Meaning for America* (New York: Knopf, 2006); William Julius Wilson, *The Truly Disadvantaged* (Chicago: University of Chicago Press, 1987); *When Work Disappears: The World of the Urban Poor* (New York: Alfred Knopf, 1996); *The Bridge over the Racial Divide: Rising Inequality and Coalition Politics* (Wildavsky Forum Series, 2) (Berkeley: University of California Press, 1999).

SOCIAL STRUCTURE THEORIES

The problems caused by poverty and income inequality are not lost on criminologists. They recognize that the various sources of crime data show that crime rates are highest in neighborhoods characterized by poverty and social disorder. Although members of the middle and upper classes sometimes engage in crime, these are generally nonviolent acts, such as embezzlement and fraud, which present little danger to the general public. In contrast, lower-class crime is often the violent, destructive product of youth gangs and marginally and underemployed young adults. The real crime problem is essentially a lower-class phenomenon, which breeds criminal behavior that begins in youth and continues into young adulthood. Kids growing up poor and living in households that lack economic resources are much more likely to get involved in serious crime than their wealthier peers.[23] To explain this phenomenon, criminologists have formulated social structure theories. As a group, they suggest that social and economic forces operating in deteriorated lower-class areas are the

key determinant of criminal behavior patterns. Social forces begin to affect people while they are relatively young and continue to influence them throughout their lives. Though not all youthful offenders become adult criminals, those who are exposed to a continual stream of violence in deteriorated inner-city neighborhoods are the ones most likely to persist in their criminal careers.[24]

Social structure theorists challenge those who suggest that crime is an expression of some personal trait or individual choice. They argue that people living in equivalent social environments tend to behave in a similar, predictable fashion. If the environment did not influence human behavior, then crime rates would be distributed equally across the social structure, which they are not.[25] Because crime rates are higher in lower-class urban centers than in middle-class suburbs, social forces must be operating in blighted urban areas that influence or control behavior.[26]

There are three independent yet overlapping branches within the social structure perspective—social disorganization, strain theory, and cultural deviance theory (outlined in Figure 6.3):

▌ **Social disorganization theory** focuses on the conditions within the urban environment that affect crime rates. A disorganized area is one in which institutions of social

Figure 6.3 The Three Branches of Social Structure Theory

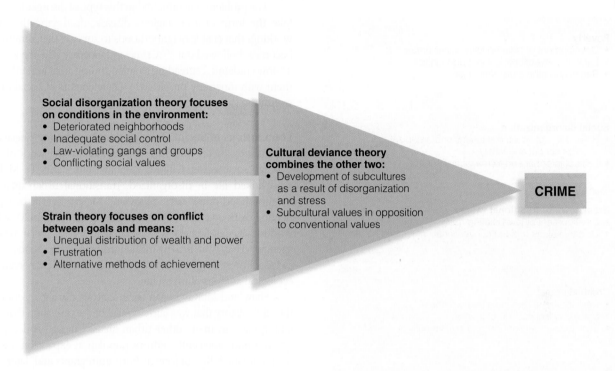

control—such as the family, commercial establishments, and schools—have broken down and can no longer carry out their expected or stated functions. Indicators of social disorganization include high unemployment, school drop-out rates, deteriorated housing, low-income levels, and large numbers of single-parent households. Residents in these areas experience conflict and despair, and, as a result, antisocial behavior flourishes.

▌ **Strain theory** holds that crime is a function of the conflict between the goals people have and the means they can use to obtain them legally. Most people in the United States desire wealth, material possessions, power, prestige, and other life comforts. And although these social and economic goals are common to people in all economic strata, strain theorists insist that the ability to obtain these goals is class dependent. Members of the lower class are unable to achieve these symbols of success through conventional means. Consequently, they feel anger, frustration, and resentment, which is referred to as **strain**. Lower-class citizens can either accept their condition and live out their days as socially responsible, if unrewarded, citizens, or they can choose an alternative means of achieving success, such as theft, violence, or drug trafficking.

▌ **Cultural deviance theory**, the third variation of structural theory, combines elements of both strain and social disorganization. According to this view, because of strain and social isolation, a unique lower-class culture develops in disorganized neighborhoods. These independent **subcultures** maintain a unique set of values and beliefs that are in conflict with conventional social norms. Criminal behavior is an expression of conformity to lower-class subcultural values

and traditions and not a rebellion from conventional society. Subcultural values are handed down from one generation to the next in a process called **cultural transmission**.

Although each of these theories is distinct in critical aspects, each approach has at its core the view that socially isolated people, living in disorganized neighborhoods, are the ones most likely to experience crime-producing social forces. Each branch of social structure theory will now be discussed in some detail.

Social Disorganization Theory

Social disorganization theory links crime rates to neighborhood ecological characteristics. Communities where the fabric of social life has become frayed and torn are unable to provide essential services to their residents, such as education, health care, and proper housing. Residents in these crime-ridden neighborhoods want to leave the community at the earliest opportunity. Because they want out, they become uninterested in community matters. As a result, these neighborhoods are destabilized. There is constant population turnover; people are not interested in investing in these communities. Because housing is deteriorated the neighborhood becomes mixed-use (i.e., residential and commercial property exist side by side).

Because the area is undergoing stress, the normal sources of *social control* common to most neighborhoods—the family, school, personal ties, interest of the business community, law enforcement, and social service agencies—become weak and disorganized. Personal relationships are strained because neighbors are constantly relocating to better areas. Resident turnover further weakens communication and blocks the establishment

Figure 6.4 Social Disorganization Theory

Poverty
- Development of isolated lower-class areas
- Lack of conventional social opportunities
- Racial and ethnic discrimination

▽

Social disorganization
- Breakdown of social institutions and organizations such as school and family
- Lack of informal and formal social control

▽

Breakdown of traditional values
- Development of law violating gangs and groups
- Deviant values replace conventional values and norms

▽

Criminal areas
- Neighborhood becomes crime prone
- Stable pockets of crime develop
- Lack of external support and investment

▽

Cultural transmission
Adults pass norms (focal concerns) to younger generation, creating stable lower-class culture

▽

Criminal careers
Most youths age out of delinquency, marry, and raise families, but some remain in life of crime

A policewoman searches the schoolbag of a young girl in the graffiti-covered Cabrini Green Housing Project. Because socially disorganized areas are undergoing stress, the normal sources of social control common to most neighborhoods—the family, school, personal ties, interest of the business community, law enforcement, and social service agencies—become weak and disorganized. When social control can be maintained, the likelihood of crime and violence decreases.

of common goals. The result: any attempt at community-level problem solving ends in frustration.[27]

The problems encountered in this type of disorganized area take the form of a contagious disease, destroying the inner workings that enable neighborhoods to survive; the community becomes "hollowed out."[28] Crime and violence take the form of a "slow epidemic," spreading to surrounding areas and infecting them with inner-city problems.[29] The elements of social disorganization theory are shown in Figure 6.4.

Foundations of Social Disorganization Theory Social disorganization theory was first popularized by the work of two Chicago sociologists, Clifford R. Shaw and Henry D. McKay, who linked life in disorganized, transitional urban areas to neighborhood crime rates. Shaw and McKay began their pioneering work on crime in Chicago during the early 1920s while working as researchers for a state-supported social service agency.[30] They were heavily influenced by Chicago School sociologists Ernest Burgess and Robert Park, who had pioneered the ecological analysis of urban life.

Shaw and McKay began their analysis during a period in the city's history that was fairly typical of the transition that was taking place in many other urban areas. Chicago had experienced a mid-nineteenth-century population expansion, fueled by a dramatic influx of foreign-born immigrants and, later, migrating southern families. Congregating in the central city, the newcomers occupied the oldest housing areas and therefore faced numerous health and environmental hazards.

Sections of the city started to physically deteriorate. This condition prompted the city's wealthy, established citizens to become concerned about the moral fabric of Chicago society. The belief was widespread that immigrants from Europe and the rural South were crime prone and morally dissolute. In fact, local groups were created with the very purpose of "saving" the children of poor families from moral decadence.[31] It was popular to view crime as the property of inferior racial and ethnic groups.

Transitional Neighborhoods Shaw and McKay explained crime and delinquency within the context of the changing urban environment and ecological development of the city. They saw that Chicago had developed into distinct neighborhoods (natural areas), some affluent and others wracked by extreme poverty. These poverty-ridden, **transitional neighborhoods** suffered high rates of population turnover and were incapable of inducing residents to remain and defend the neighborhoods against criminal groups.

Low rents in these areas attracted groups with different racial and ethnic backgrounds. Newly arrived immigrants from Europe and the South congregated in these transitional neighborhoods. Their children were torn between assimilating into a new culture and abiding by the traditional values of their parents. They soon found that informal social control mechanisms that had restrained

© Ralf-Finn Hestoft/Corbis

behavior in the "old country" or rural areas were disrupted. These urban areas were believed to be the spawning grounds of young criminals.

In transitional areas, successive changes in the population composition, disintegration of traditional cultures, diffusion of divergent cultural standards, and gradual industrialization of the area result in dissolution of neighborhood culture and organization. The continuity of conventional neighborhood traditions and institutions is broken, leaving children feeling displaced and without a strong or definitive set of values.

Concentric Zones Shaw and McKay identified the areas in Chicago that had excessive crime rates. Using a model of analysis pioneered by Ernest Burgess, they noted that distinct ecological areas had developed in the city, comprising a series of five concentric circles, or zones, and that there were stable and significant differences in interzone crime rates (Figure 6.5). The areas of heaviest concentration of crime appeared to be the transitional inner-city zones, where large numbers of foreign-born citizens had recently settled.[32] The zones furthest from the city's center had correspondingly lower crime rates.

Analysis of these data indicated a surprisingly stable pattern of criminal activity in the various ecological zones over a 65-year period. Shaw and McKay concluded that, in the transitional neighborhoods, multiple cultures and diverse values, both conventional and deviant, coexist. Children growing up in the street culture often find that adults who have adopted a deviant lifestyle are the most financially successful people in the neighborhood: for example, the gambler, the pimp, or the drug dealer. Required to choose between conventional and deviant lifestyles, many inner-city kids saw the value in opting for the latter. They join with other like-minded youths and form law-violating gangs and cliques. The development of teenage law-violating groups is an essential element of youthful misbehavior in lower-class areas. The values that inner-city youths adopt are often in conflict with existing middle-class norms, which demand strict obedience to the legal code. Consequently, a value conflict occurs that sets the delinquent youth and his or her peer group even further apart from conventional society. The result is a more solid embrace of deviant goals and behavior. To justify their choice of goals, these youths seek support by recruiting new members and passing on the delinquent tradition.

Shaw and McKay's statistical analysis confirmed their theoretical suspicions. Even though crime rates changed, they found that the highest rates were always in Zones I and II (central city and a transitional area). The areas with the highest crime rates retained high rates even when their ethnic composition changed (in the areas Shaw and McKay examined, from German and Irish to Italian and Polish).[33]

The Legacy of Shaw and McKay Social disorganization concepts articulated by Shaw and McKay have remained a prominent fixture of criminological scholarship and thinking for more than 75 years. While cultural and social conditions have changed and American society today is much more heterogeneous and mobile than during Shaw and McKay's time, the most important elements of their findings still hold up:[34]

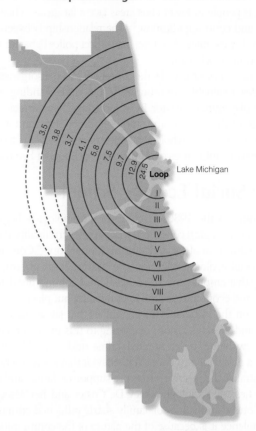

Figure 6.5 Shaw and McKay's Concentric Zones Map of Chicago

Note: Arabic numerals represent the rate of male delinquency.

Source: Clifford R. Shaw, et al., *Delinquency Areas* (Chicago: University of Chicago Press, 1929), p. 99.

▪ Crime rates are sensitive to the destructive social forces operating in lower-class urban neighborhoods.

▪ Environmental factors, rather then individual differences, are the root cause of crime. Personal abnormality or inferiority has little to do with crime rates.

▪ Crime is a constant fixture in poverty areas regardless of racial and/or ethnic makeup.

▪ Neighborhood disintegration and the corresponding erosion of social control are the primary causes of criminal behavior; community values, norms, and cohesiveness affect individual behavior choices.

Despite these noteworthy achievements, the validity of some of Shaw and McKay's positions have been challenged. Some critics have faulted their assumption that neighborhoods are essentially stable, suggesting that there is a great deal more fluidity and transition than assumed by Shaw and McKay.[35] There is also concern about their reliance on police records to calculate neighborhood crime rates. Relying on official data means that findings may be more sensitive to the validity of police-generated data than they are true interzone crime rate differences. Numerous studies indicate that police use extensive discretion when arresting people and that social status is one factor that influences their decisions.[36] It is possible that people in middle-class neighborhoods commit many criminal acts that never show up in official statistics, whereas people in lower-class areas face a far greater chance of arrest and court adjudication.[37] The relationship between ecology and crime rates, therefore, may reflect police behavior more than criminal behavior.

These criticisms aside, the concept of social disorganization provides a valuable contribution to our understanding of the causes of criminal behavior. By introducing a new variable—the ecology of the city—to the study of crime, Shaw and McKay paved the way for a whole generation of criminologists to focus on the social influences of criminal and delinquent behavior.

The Social Ecology School

Beginning in the 1980s, a group of criminologists began to study the ecological conditions that support criminality, changing the direction of social disorganization theory.[38] Contemporary social ecologists developed a "purer" form of structural theory that emphasizes the association of community deterioration and economic decline to criminality but places less emphasis on the value and norm conflict that lay at the core of Shaw and McKay's vision. According to this more contemporary view, living in deteriorated, crime-ridden neighborhoods exerts a powerful influence over behavior that is strong enough to neutralize the positive effects of a supportive family and close social ties. As sociologist Stacy De Coster and her associates point out, if individual or family status influence criminality and violence it is because of the nature of the communities in which disadvantaged persons and families reside and not the strength of family relationships themselves.[39] In the following sections, some of the more recent social ecological research is discussed in detail.

Community Deterioration Social ecologists have focused their attention on the association between crime rates and community deterioration: disorder, poverty, alienation, disassociation, and fear of crime.[40] They find that neighborhoods with a high percentage of deserted houses and apartments experience high crime rates; abandoned buildings serve as a "magnet for crime."[41] Areas in which houses are in poor repair, boarded up, and burned out, and whose owners are best described as "slumlords," are also the location of the highest violence rates and gun crime.[42] These are neighborhoods in which retail establishments often go bankrupt, are abandoned, and deteriorate physically.[43]

Poverty becomes "concentrated" in deteriorated areas.[44] As working- and middle-class families flee, elements of the most disadvantaged population are consolidated within inner-city poverty areas. As the working and middle classes move out, they take with them their financial and institutional resources and support. Businesses are disinclined to locate in poverty areas; banks become reluctant to lend money for new housing or businesses.[45] Areas of poverty concentration experience significant income and wealth disparities, nonexistent employment opportunities, inferior housing patterns, and unequal access to health care; not surprisingly, they also experience high rates of crime.[46]

Minority group members living in these areas are hit particularly hard. They are also exposed to race-based disparity such as income inequality and institutional racism.[47] Black crime rates, more so than white, seem to be influenced by the shift of high-paid manufacturing jobs overseas and their replacement with lower-paid service sector jobs. Both African American men and women seem less able to prosper in a service economy than white men and women, and over time the resulting economic disadvantage translates into increased levels of violence.[48] In desperation, some turn to armed robbery as a means of economic survival. More often than not, these desperate acts go awry, and the result is gun play and death. And because victims may be white there appears to be a racial motivation. However, what appear to be racially motivated crimes may be more a function of economic factors (i.e., the shift of jobs overseas) rather than interracial hate or antagonism.[49]

Chronic Unemployment The association between unemployment and crime is still unsettled: aggregate crime rates and aggregate unemployment rates seem weakly related. In other words, crime rates sometimes rise during periods of economic prosperity and fall during periods of economic decline.[50] Yet, as Shaw and McKay claimed, neighborhoods that experience chronic unemployment also encounter social disorganization and crime.[51] How can these divergent trends be explained?

One possibility is that even though short-term national economic trends may have little effect on crime, long-term *local unemployment* rates may have a more significant impact on conditions at the community or neighborhood level.[52] Take the situation in Milwaukee.[53] Since 1998, Wisconsin has lost nearly 90,000 manufacturing jobs and the city of Milwaukee has suffered the brunt of the slowdown. The unemployment rate hovers around 7 percent, up from 2.6 percent in 1998, and nearly double the national average. In inner-city neighborhoods, nearly 60 percent of working-age males are without jobs. With only half of adults earning more than a high school diploma, the city's residents aren't well matched for the white-collar positions most common today. During this period of economic transition, the city has experienced a significant increase in violent crime, especially murder. Hopefully, as the economy evolves and expands, crime rates may be reduced.

How does job loss lead to crime? Unemployment destabilizes households, and unstable families are the ones most likely to produce children who put a premium on violence and aggression as a means of dealing with limited opportunity. This lack of opportunity perpetuates higher crime rates, especially when large groups or cohorts of people of the same age compete for relatively scant resources.[54]

Limited employment opportunities also reduce the stabilizing influence of parents and other adults, who may have once been able to counteract the allure of youth gangs. Sociologist Elijah Anderson's analysis of Philadelphia neighborhood life found that "old heads" (i.e., respected neighborhood residents) who at one time played an important role in socializing youth have been displaced by younger street hustlers and drug dealers. While the old heads complain that these newcomers may not have earned or worked for their fortune in the "old-fashioned way," the old heads also admire and envy these kids whose gold chains and luxury cars advertise their wealth amid poverty.[55] The old heads may admire the fruits of crime, but they disdain the violent manner in which they were acquired.

Community Fear In neighborhoods where people help one another, residents are less likely to fear crime and be afraid of becoming a crime victim.[56] People feel safe in neighborhoods that are orderly and in repair.[57] In contrast, those living in neighborhoods that suffer social and physical incivilities—rowdy youth, trash and litter, graffiti, abandoned storefronts, burned-out buildings, littered lots, strangers, drunks, vagabonds, loiterers, prostitutes, noise, congestion, angry words, dirt, and stench—are much more likely to be fearful. Put another way, disorder breeds fear.[58] Fear is based on experience. Residents who have already been victimized are more fearful of the future than those who have escaped crime.[59] People become afraid when they are approached by someone in the neighborhood selling drugs. They become afraid when they see neighborhood kids hanging out in community parks and playgrounds or when gangs proliferate in the neighborhood.[60] They may fear that their children will also be approached and seduced into the drug life.[61] The presence of such incivilities, especially when accompanied by relatively high crime rates, convinces residents that their neighborhood is dangerous; becoming a crime victim seems inevitable.[62] Eventually they become emotionally numb, and as their exposure to crime increases, they experience indifference to the suffering of others.[63]

Fear can become contagious. People tell others when they have been victimized, spreading the word that the neighborhood is getting dangerous and that the chances of future victimization are high.[64] They dread leaving their homes at night and withdraw from community life.

> ## connections
>
> Fear of repeat victimization may be both instinctual and accurate. Remember that in Chapter 3 we discussed the fact that some people may be "victim prone" and fated to suffer repeated victimization over the life course.

When people live in areas where the death rates are high and life expectancies are short, they may alter their behavior out of fear. They may feel, "Why plan for the future when there is a significant likelihood that I may never see it?" In such areas, young boys and girls may psychologically assimilate by taking risks and discounting the future. Teenage birthrates soar and so do violence rates.[65] For these children, the inevitability of death skews their perspective of how they live their lives.

When fear grips a neighborhood, business conditions begin to deteriorate, population mobility increases, and a "criminal element" begins to drift into the area.[66] In essence, the existence of fear incites more crime, increasing the chances of victimization, producing even more fear, in a never-ending loop.[67] Fear is often associated with other community-level factors:

1. *Race and fear.* Fear of crime is also bound up in anxiety over racial and ethnic conflicts. Fear becomes most pronounced in areas undergoing rapid and unexpected racial and age-composition changes, especially when they are out of proportion to the rest of the city.[68] Whites become particularly fearful when they sense that they are becoming a racial minority in their neighborhood.[69]

   The fear experienced by whites may be based on racial stereotypes, but it may also be caused by the premonition that they will become less well protected because police do not provide adequate services in predominantly African American neighborhoods.[70]

   Whites are not the only group to experience race-based fear. Minority group members may experience greater levels of fear than whites, perhaps because they may have fewer resources to address ongoing social problems.[71] Fear can be found among other racial and ethnic groups, especially when they believe they are in the minority and vulnerable to attack. In their study of race relations in Florida, Ted Chiricos and his associates found that whites feel threatened by Latinos and blacks but only in South Florida where whites are outnumbered by those two groups; in contrast, Latinos are threatened by blacks but only outside of South Florida where Latinos are the minority.[72]

2. *Gangs and fear.* Gangs flourish in deteriorated neighborhoods with high levels of poverty, lack of investment, high unemployment rates, and population turnover.[73] Unlike any other crime, however, gang activity is frequently undertaken out in the open, on the public ways, and in full view of the rest of the community.[74] Brazen criminal activity undermines community solidarity because it signals that the police must be either corrupt or inept. The fact that gangs are willing to openly engage in drug sales and other types of criminal activity shows their confidence that they have silenced or intimidated law-abiding people in their midst. The police and the community alike become hopeless about their ability to restore community stability, producing greater levels of community fear.

3. *Mistrust and fear.* People who report living in neighborhoods with high levels of crime and civil disorder become suspicious and mistrusting.[75] They develop a sense of powerlessness, which amplifies the effect of neighborhood disorder and increases levels of mistrust. Some residents become so suspicious of authority that they develop a siege mentality in which the outside world is considered the enemy out to destroy the neighborhood. Elijah Anderson found that residents in the African American neighborhoods he studied believed in the existence of a secret plan to eradicate the population by such strategies as permanent unemployment, police brutality, imprisonment, drug distribution, and AIDS.[76] White officials and political leaders were believed to have hatched this conspiracy, and it was demonstrated by the lax law enforcement efforts in poor areas. Residents felt that police cared little about black-on-black crime because it helped reduce the population. Rumors abounded that federal government agencies, such as the CIA, controlled the drug trade and used profits to fund illegal overseas operations.

This siege mentality results in mistrust of critical social institutions, including business, government, and schools. Government officials seem arrogant and haughty. Residents become self-conscious, worried about garnering any respect, and are particularly attuned to anyone who disrespects them. Considering this feeling of mistrust, when police ignore crime in poor areas or, conversely, when they are violent and corrupt, anger flares, and people take to the streets and react in violent ways.[77]

Community Change In our postmodern society, urban areas undergoing rapid structural changes in racial and economic composition also seem to experience the greatest change in crime rates. In contrast, stable neighborhoods, even those with a high rate of poverty, experience relatively low crime rates and have the strength to restrict substance abuse and criminal activity.[78]

Recent studies recognize that change, not stability, is the hallmark of inner-city areas. A neighborhood's residents, wealth, density, and purpose are constantly evolving. Even disorganized neighborhoods acquire new identifying features. Some may become multiracial, while others become racially homogeneous. Some areas become stable and family oriented, while in others, mobile, never-married people predominate.[79]

As areas decline, residents flee to safer, more stable localities. Those who can move to more affluent neighborhoods find that their lifestyles and life chances improve immediately and continue to do so over their life span.[80] Those who cannot leave because they cannot afford to live in more affluent communities face an increased risk of victimization.

High population turnover can have a devastating effect on community culture because it thwarts communication and information flow.[81] In response to this turnover, a culture may develop that dictates standards of dress, language, and behavior to neighborhood youth that are in opposition to those of conventional society. All these factors are likely to produce increased crime rates.

The Cycles of Community Change During periods of population turnover, communities may undergo changes that undermine their infrastructure. Urban areas seem to have life cycles, which begin with building residential dwellings and are followed by a period of decline, with marked decreases in socioeconomic status and increases in population density.[82] Later stages in this life cycle include changing racial or ethnic makeup, population thinning, and finally, a renewal stage in which obsolete housing is replaced and upgraded (i.e., gentrification). Areas undergoing such change seem to experience an increase in their crime rates.[83]

As communities go through cycles, neighborhood deterioration precedes increasing rates of crime and delinquency.[84] Neighborhoods most at risk for crime rate increases contain large numbers of single-parent families and unrelated people living together, have gone from having owner-occupied to renter-occupied units, and have an economic base that has lost semi-skilled and unskilled jobs (indicating a growing residue of discouraged workers who are no longer seeking employment).[85] These ecological disruptions strain existing social control mechanisms and inhibit their ability to control crime and delinquency.

Community change may also have racial overtones. Because of racial differences in economic well-being, those "left behind" are all too often minority citizens.[86] Those who cannot move find themselves surrounded by a constant influx of new residents. Whites may feel threatened as the number of minorities in the population increases and competes with them for jobs and political power.[87] According to the racial threat hypothesis as the percentage of minority group members in the population increases, so too does the crime rate. Why does this phenomenon occur? In changing neighborhoods, adults may actually encourage the law-violating behavior of youths. They may express attitudes that justify violence as a means of protecting their property and way of life by violently resisting newcomers.[88] They may also demand more money be spent on police and other justice agencies. As racial prejudice increases, the call for law and order aimed at controlling the minority population grows louder.[89]

Collective Efficacy

Cohesive communities, whether urban or rural, with high levels of social control and social integration, where people know one another and develop interpersonal ties, may also develop collective efficacy: mutual trust, a willingness to intervene in the supervision of children, and the maintenance of public order.[90] It is the cohesion among neighborhood residents combined with shared expectations for informal social control of public space that promotes collective efficacy.[91] Residents in these areas are able to enjoy a better life because the fruits of cohesiveness can be better education, health care, and housing opportunities.[92]

In contrast, residents of socially disorganized neighborhoods find that efforts at social control are weak and attenuated. People living in economically disadvantaged areas are significantly more likely to perceive their immediate surroundings in more negative terms (i.e., higher levels of incivilities) than those living in areas that maintain collective efficacy.[93] When community social control efforts are blunted, crime rates increase, further weakening neighborhood cohesiveness.[94]

There are actually three forms of collective efficacy:

1. *Informal social control.* Some elements of collective efficacy operate on the primary or private level and involve peers, families, and relatives. These sources exert informal control by either awarding or withholding approval, respect, and admiration. Informal control mechanisms include direct criticism, ridicule, ostracism, desertion, or physical punishment.[95]

   The most important wielder of informal social control is the family, which may keep at-risk kids in check through such mechanisms as corporal punishment, withholding privileges, or ridiculing lazy or disrespectful behavior. The importance of the family to apply informal social control takes on greater importance in neighborhoods with few social ties among adults and limited collective efficacy. In these areas parents cannot call upon neighborhood resources to take up the burden of controlling children and face the burden of providing adequate supervision.[96]

The family is not the only force of informal social control. In some neighborhoods, people are committed to preserving their immediate environment by confronting destabilizing forces such as teen gangs.[97] By helping neighbors become more resilient and self-confident, adults in these areas provide the external support systems that enable youth to desist from crime. Residents teach one another that they have moral and social obligations to their fellow citizens; children learn to be sensitive to the rights of others and to respect differences.

In some areas, neighborhood associations and self-help groups form.[98] The threat of skyrocketing violence rates may draw people together to help each other out. While criminologists believe that crime rates are lower in cohesive neighborhoods, it is also possible that an escalating crime rate may bring people closer together to fight a common problem.[99] Some neighbors may get involved in informal social control through surveillance practices, for example, by keeping an eye out for intruders when their neighbors go out of town. Informal surveillance has been found to reduce the levels of some crimes such as street robberies; however, if robbery rates remain high, surveillance may be terminated because people become fearful for their safety.[100]

2. *Institutional social control.* Social institutions such as schools and churches cannot work effectively in a climate of alienation and mistrust. Unsupervised peer groups and gangs, which flourish in disorganized areas, disrupt the influence of those neighborhood control agents that do exist.[101]

People who reside in these neighborhoods find that involvement with conventional social institutions, such as schools and afternoon programs, is often attenuated or blocked.[102] Children are at risk for recruitment into gangs and law-violating groups when there is a lack of effective public services. Gangs become an attractive alternative when adolescents have little to do after school and must rely on out-of-home care rather than more structured school-based programs.[103] As a result, crime may flourish and neighborhood fear increases, conditions that decrease a community's cohesion and thwart the ability of its institutions to exert social control over its residents.[104]

To combat these influences, communities that have collective efficacy attempt to utilize their local institutions to control crime. Sources of institutional social control include businesses, stores, schools, churches, and social service and volunteer organizations.[105] When these institutions are effective, crime rates decline.[106] Some institutions, such as recreation centers for teens, have been found to lower crime rates because they exert a positive effect; others, such as taverns and bars, can help destabilize neighborhoods and increase the rate of violent crimes such as rape and robbery.[107]

3. *Public social control.* Stable neighborhoods are also able to arrange for external sources of social control. If they can draw on outside help and secure external resources—a process referred to as public social control—they are better able to reduce the effects of disorganization and maintain lower levels of crime and victimization.[108] Racial differences in crime and violence rates may be explained in part by the ability of citizens in affluent, predominantly white neighborhoods to use their economic resources, and the political power they bring, to their own advantage. They demand and receive a level of protection in their communities that is not enjoyed in less affluent minority communities.[109]

The level of policing, one of the primary sources of public social control, may vary from neighborhood to neighborhood. The police presence is typically greatest when community organizations and local leaders have sufficient political clout to get funding for additional law enforcement personnel. An effective police presence sends a message that the area will not tolerate deviant behavior. Because they can respond vigorously to crime, the police prevent criminal groups from gaining a toehold in the neighborhood.[110] Criminals and drug dealers avoid such areas and relocate to easier and more appealing targets.[111] In contrast, crime rates are highest in areas where police are mistrusted because they engage in misconduct, for example, use of excessive force, or because they are seemingly indifferent to neighborhood problems.[112]

In more disorganized areas, the absence of political powerbrokers limits access to external funding and protection.[113] Without outside funding, a neighborhood may lack the ability to get back on its feet.[114] In these areas there are fewer police, and those that do patrol the area are less motivated and their resources are stretched tighter. These communities cannot mount an effective social control effort because as neighborhood disadvantage increases, its level of informal social control decreases.[115]

The government can also reduce crime by providing economic and social supports through publicly funded social support and welfare programs. Though welfare is often criticized by conservative politicians as being a government handout, there is evidence of a significant negative association between the amount of welfare money people receive and crime rates.[116] Government assistance may help people improve their social status by providing them with the financial resources to clothe, feed, and educate their children while at the same time reducing stress, frustration, and anger. Using government subsidies to reduce crime is controversial and not all research has found that it actually works as advertised.[117]

People living in disorganized areas may also be able to draw on resources from their neighbors in more affluent surrounding communities, helping to keep crime rates down.[118] This phenomenon may explain, in part, why violence rates are high in poor African American neighborhoods cut off from outside areas for support.[119]

The Effect of Collective Efficacy The ramifications of having adequate controls are critical. In areas where collective efficacy remains high, children are less likely to become involved with deviant peers and engage in problem behaviors.[120] In these more stable areas, kids are able to use their wits to avoid violent confrontations and to feel safe in their own neighborhood, a

SOCIAL DISORGANIZATION THEORIES

Theory	Major Premise	Strengths	Research Focus
Shaw and McKay's Concentric Zones Theory	Crime is a product of transitional neighborhoods that manifest social disorganization and value conflict.	Identifies why crime rates are highest in slum areas. Points out the factors that produce crime. Suggests programs to help reduce crime.	Poverty; disorganization, gangs, neighborhood change; community context of crime.
Social Ecology Theory	The conflicts and problems of urban social life and communities, including fear, unemployment, deterioration, and siege mentality, influence crime rates.	Accounts for urban crime rates and trends. Identifies community-level factors that produce high crime rates.	Social control; fear; collective efficacy; unemployment.

concept referred to as **street efficacy**.[121] In contrast, adolescents who live in neighborhoods with concentrated disadvantage and low collective efficacy, lose confidence in their ability to avoid violence. And as research by sociologist Patrick Sharkey has shown, this is important because adolescents with high levels of street efficacy are less likely to resort to violence themselves or to associate with delinquent peers.[122]

Collective efficacy has other benefits. When residents are satisfied that their neighborhoods are good places to live they feel a sense of obligation to maintain order and are more willing to work hard to encourage informal social control. In areas where social institutions and processes—such as police protection—are working adequately, residents are willing to intervene personally to help control unruly children and uncivil adults.[123]

In contrast, in disorganized areas, the population is transient and people want to leave as soon as they can afford to find better housing. Interpersonal relationships remain superficial, and people are less willing to help out neighbors or exert informal controls over their own or neighbors' children. Social institutions such as schools and churches cannot work effectively in a climate of alienation and mistrust.[124] Children who live in these neighborhoods find that involvement with conventional social institutions, such as schools and afternoon programs, is blocked; they are instead at risk for recruitment into gangs.[125] These problems are stubborn and difficult to overcome. And even when an attempt is made to revitalize a disorganized neighborhood by creating institutional support programs such as community centers and better schools, the effort may be countered by the ongoing drain of deep-rooted economic and social deprivation.[126]

According to the social ecology school, then, the quality of community life, including levels of change, fear, incivility, poverty, and deterioration, has a direct influence on an area's crime rate. It is not some individual property or trait that causes people to commit crime but the quality and ambience of the community in which they reside. Conversely, in areas that have high levels of social control and collective efficacy, crime rates have been shown to decrease—no matter what the economic situation. Concept Summary 6.1 sets out the features of social disorganization theory.

wwww Go to academic.cengage.com/criminaljustice/siegel to read:

▪ A famous *Atlantic Magazine* article titled "Broken Windows," which discusses the concept of **community deterioration and crime**.

▪ An article showing the association between **collective efficacy and crime**.

STRAIN THEORIES

As a group, strain theorists believe that most people share similar values and goals. They want to earn money, have a nice home, drive a great car, and wear stylish clothes. They also want to care for their families and educate their children. Unfortunately, the ability to achieve these personal goals is stratified by socioeconomic class. While the affluent may live out the American Dream, the poor are shut out from achieving their goals. Because they can't always get what they want, they begin to feel frustrated and angry; a condition which is referred to as strain.

Strain is related to criminal motivation. People who feel economically and socially humiliated may perceive the right to humiliate others in return.[127] Psychologists warn that under these circumstances those who consider themselves "losers" begin to fear and envy "winners" who are doing very well at their expense. If they fail to take risky aggressive tactics, they are surely going to lose out in social competition and have little chance of future success.[128] These generalized feelings of **relative deprivation** are precursors to high crime rates.[129]

According to the strain view, sharp divisions between the rich and poor create an atmosphere of envy and mistrust that may lead to violence and aggression.[130] People who feel deprived because of their race or economic class standing eventually develop a sense of injustice and discontent. The less fortunate begin to distrust the society that has nurtured social inequality and obstructed their chances of progressing

John Ziebell yells at Immigration Day protest marchers as they pass by his home in New Haven, Connecticut, on May 1, 2007. Ziebell was angry because, he said, he was unemployed and has been unable to find a job. According to strain theory, conflict results when, because of rapid changes in society, a gulf develops between personal goals and the means available to achieve them. The result: alienation and conflict.

Figure 6.6 The Basic Components of Strain Theory

Poverty
Relative deprivation
Feelings of inadequacy
Siege mentality

Maintenance of conventional rules and norms
Despite adversity, people remain loyal to conventional values and rules of dominant middle-class culture.

Strain
People who desire conventional success but lack means and opportunity will experience strain and frustration.

Formation of gangs and groups
People form law-violating groups to seek alternative means of achieving success.

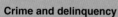

Crime and delinquency
People engage in antisocial acts to achieve success and relieve their feelings of strain.

Criminal careers
Feelings of strain may endure, sustaining criminal careers.

by legitimate means. The constant frustration that results from these feelings of inadequacy produces pent-up aggression and hostility and, eventually, leads to violence and crime. The effect of inequality may be greatest when the impoverished population believes they are becoming less able to compete in a society where the balance of economic and social power is shifting further toward the already affluent. Under these conditions, the likelihood that the poor will choose illegitimate life-enhancing activities increases.[131] The basic components of strain theory are set out in Figure 6.6.

Strain theories come in two distinct formulations:

▐ *Structural strain*. Using a sociological lens, structural strain suggests that economic and social sources of strain shape collective human behavior.

▐ *Individual strain*. Using a psychological reference, individual strain theories suggest that individual life experiences cause some people to suffer pain and misery, feelings which are then translated into antisocial behaviors.

The Concept of Anomie

The roots of strain theories can be traced to Émile Durkheim's notion of anomie (from the Greek *a nomos*, "without norms").

According to Durkheim, an anomic society is one in which rules of behavior (i.e., values, customs, and norms) have broken down or become inoperative during periods of rapid social change or social crisis such as war or famine. Anomie is most likely to occur in societies that are moving from a preindustrial society, which is held together by traditions, shared values, and unquestioned beliefs (i.e., **mechanical solidarity**) to a postindustrial social system, which is highly developed and dependent upon the division of labor. In this modern society, people are connected by their interdependent needs for one another's services and production (i.e., **organic solidarity**). The shift in traditions and values creates social turmoil. Established norms begin to erode and lose meaning. If a division occurs between what the population expects and what the economic and productive forces of society can realistically deliver, a crisis situation develops that can manifest itself in normlessness or anomie. This condition can be found in modern day Russia as it shifts from a Communist to free enterprise system without the social support and guarantees the population has come to expect.[132]

Anomie undermines society's social control function. Every society works to limit people's goals and desires. If a society becomes anomic, it can no longer establish and maintain control over its population's wants and desires. Because people find it difficult to control their appetites, their demands become unlimited. Under these circumstances, obedience to legal codes may be strained, and alternative behavior choices, such as crimes, may be inevitable.

Merton's Theory of Anomie

Durkheim's ideas were applied to criminology by sociologist Robert Merton in his **theory of anomie**.[133] Merton used a modified version of the concept of anomie to fit social, economic, and cultural conditions found in modern U.S. society.[134] He found that two elements of culture interact to produce potentially anomic conditions: culturally defined goals and socially approved means for obtaining them. Contemporary society stresses the goals of acquiring wealth, success, and power. Socially permissible means include hard work, education, and thrift.

In the United States, Merton argued, legitimate means to acquire wealth are stratified across class and status lines. Those with little formal education and few economic resources soon find that they are denied the ability to legally acquire wealth—the preeminent success symbol. When socially mandated goals are uniform throughout society and access to legitimate means is bound by class and status, the resulting strain produces anomie among those who are locked out of the legitimate opportunity structure. Consequently, they may develop criminal or delinquent solutions to the problem of attaining goals.

Social Adaptations Merton argued that each person has his or her own concept of the goals of society and the means at his or her disposal to attain them. Table 6.2 shows Merton's diagram of the hypothetical relationship between social goals, the means for getting them, and the individual actor. Here is a brief description of each of these modes of adaptation:

▌ *Conformity.* Conformity occurs when individuals both embrace conventional social goals and also have the means at their disposal to attain them. The conformist desires wealth and success and can obtain them through education and a high paying job. In a balanced, stable society, this is the most common social adaptation. If a majority of its people did not practice conformity, the society would cease to exist.

▌ *Innovation.* Innovation occurs when an individual accepts the goals of society but rejects or is incapable of attaining them through legitimate means. Many people desire material goods and luxuries but lack the financial ability to attain them. The resulting conflict forces them to adopt innovative solutions to their dilemma: they steal, sell drugs, or extort money. Of the five adaptations, innovation is most closely associated with criminal behavior.

If successful, innovation can have serious, long-term social consequences. Criminal success helps convince otherwise law-abiding people that innovative means work better and faster than conventional ones. The prosperous drug dealer's expensive car and flashy clothes give out the message that crime pays. Merton claims, "The process thus enlarges the extent of anomie within the system, so that others, who did not respond in the form of deviant behavior to the relatively slight anomie which they first obtained, come to do so as anomie is spread and is intensified."[135]

Table 6.2 Typology of Individual Modes of Adaptation

Modes of Adaptation	Cultural Goals	Institutionalized Means
I. Conformity	+	+
II. Innovation	+	−
III. Ritualism	−	+
IV. Retreatism	−	−
V. Rebellion	±	±

Source: Robert Merton, "Social Structure and Anomie," in *Social Theory and Social Structure* (Glencoe, IL: Free Press, 1957).

This explains why crime is initiated and sustained in certain low-income ecological areas.

▌ *Ritualism.* Ritualists are less concerned about accumulating wealth and instead gain pleasure from practicing traditional ceremonies regardless of whether they have a real purpose or goal. The strict set of manners and customs in religious orders, feudal societies, clubs, and college fraternities encourage and appeal to ritualists. Ritualists should have the lowest level of criminal behavior because they have abandoned the success goal, which is at the root of criminal activity.

▌ *Retreatism.* Retreatists reject both the goals and the means of society. Merton suggests that people who adjust in this fashion are "in the society but not of it." Included in this category are "psychotics, psychoneurotics, chronic autists, pariahs, outcasts, vagrants, vagabonds, tramps, chronic drunkards, and drug addicts." Because such people are morally or otherwise incapable of using both legitimate and illegitimate means, they attempt to escape their lack of success by withdrawing—either mentally or physically.

▌ *Rebellion.* Rebellion involves substituting an alternative set of goals and means for conventional ones. Revolutionaries who wish to promote radical change in the existing social structure and who call for alternative lifestyles, goals, and beliefs are engaging in rebellion. Rebellion may be a reaction against a corrupt and hated government or an effort to create alternate opportunities and lifestyles within the existing system.

Evaluation of Anomie Theory According to anomie theory, social inequality leads to perceptions of anomie. To resolve the goals–means conflict and relieve their sense of strain, some people innovate by stealing or extorting money, others retreat into drugs and alcohol, others rebel by joining revolutionary groups, and still others get involved in ritualistic behavior by joining a religious cult.

Merton's view of anomie has been one of the most enduring and influential sociological theories of criminality. By linking deviant behavior to the success goals that control social behavior, anomie theory attempts to pinpoint the cause of the conflict that produces personal frustration and consequent criminality. By acknowledging that society unfairly distributes the legitimate means to achieving success, anomie theory helps explain the existence of high-crime areas and the apparent predominance of delinquent

Merton describes a number of adaptations to the anomie caused by the disjunction of goals and means. Here, children stand among the tents set up in a shantytown being built in the Liberty City neighborhood in Miami, Florida, October 24, 2006. Several organizations and individuals occupied the public land to build the shantytown to serve the needs of the poor African American community in the wake of a government housing scandal. The lot had been vacant for years since the city of Miami purchased, and subsequently demolished, the low-rent apartment complex that had been located at the site. Which of Merton's adaptations best describes this social action?

Macro-Level Theory: Institutional Anomie Theory

An important addition to the strain literature is the book *Crime and the American Dream*, by Steven Messner and Richard Rosenfeld.[139] Their macro-level version of anomie theory views antisocial behavior as a function of cultural and institutional influences in U.S. society, a model they refer to as **institutional anomie theory**. Messner and Rosenfeld agree with Merton's view that the success goal is pervasive in American culture. They refer to this as the **American Dream**, a term they employ as both a goal and a process. As a goal, the American Dream involves accumulating material goods and wealth via open individual competition. As a process, it involves both being socialized to pursue material success and believing that prosperity is an achievable goal in American culture. In the United States, the capitalist system encourages innovation in pursuit of monetary rewards. Businesspeople such as Bill Gates, Warren Buffett, and Donald Trump are considered national heroes and leaders. Anomic conditions occur because the desire to succeed at any cost drives people apart, weakens the collective sense of community, fosters ambition, and restricts desires to achieve anything that is not material wealth. Achieving a "good name" and respect is not sufficient. Capitalist culture "exerts pressures toward crime by encouraging an anomic cultural environment, an environment in which people are encouraged to adopt an 'anything goes' mentality in the pursuit of personal goals . . . [and] the anomic pressures inherent in the American dream are nourished and sustained by an institutional balance of power dominated by the economy."[140]

What is distinct about American society, according to Messner and Rosenfeld, and what most likely determines the exceedingly high national crime rate, is that anomic conditions have been allowed to "develop to such an extraordinary degree."[141] There do not seem to be any alternatives that would serve the same purpose or strive for the same goal.

Impact of Anomie Why does anomie pervade American culture? According to Messner and Rosenfeld, it is because capitalist culture promotes intense pressures for economic success. Prosocial, noneconomic institutions that might otherwise control the exaggerated emphasis on financial success, such as religious or charitable institutions, have been rendered powerless or obsolete. As a result, the value structure of society is dominated by economic realities that weaken institutional social control. In other words, people are so interested in making money

and criminal behavior among the lower class. By suggesting that social conditions, not individual personalities, produce crime, Merton greatly influenced the direction taken to reduce and control criminality during the latter half of the twentieth century.

A number of questions are left unanswered by anomie theory.[136] Merton does not explain why people choose to commit certain types of crime. For example, why does one anomic person become a mugger and another deals drugs? Anomie may be used to explain differences in crime rates, but it cannot explain why most young criminals desist from crime as adults. Does this mean that perceptions of anomie dwindle with age? Is anomie short-lived?

Critics have also suggested that people pursue a number of different goals, including educational, athletic, and social success. Juveniles may be more interested in immediate goals, such as having an active social life or being a good athlete, than in long-term "ideal" achievements, such as monetary success. Achieving these goals is not a matter of social class alone; other factors, including athletic ability, intelligence, personality, and family life, can either hinder or assist goal attainment.[137] Anomie theory also assumes that all people share the same goals and values, which is false.[138]

Some contemporary theories are grounded on Merton's visionary concepts. Some of these are macro-level theories that hold that the success goal integrated within American society influences the nature and extent of the aggregate crime rate. There are also individual micro-level versions of the theory, which focus on how an individual is effected by feelings of alienation and strain.

that their behavior cannot be controlled by the needs of family or the restraints of morality.

There are three reasons social institutions have been undermined. First, noneconomic functions and roles have been devalued. Performance in other institutional settings—the family, school, or community—is assigned a lower priority than the goal of financial success. Few students go to college to study the classics; most want to major in a field with good job prospects. Second, when conflicts emerge, noneconomic roles become subordinate to and must accommodate economic roles. The schedules, routines, and demands of the workplace take priority over those of the home, the school, the community, and other aspects of social life. A parent given the opportunity for a promotion thinks nothing of uprooting his family and moving them to another part of the country. And third, economic language, standards, and norms penetrate into noneconomic realms. Economic terms become part of the common vernacular. People want to get to the "bottom line"; spouses view themselves as "partners" who "manage" the household. Retired people say they want to "downsize" their household; we "outsource" home repairs instead of doing them ourselves. Corporate leaders run for public office promising to "run the country like a business." People join social clubs to make connections and "network," not to make close friends.

According to Messner and Rosenfeld, the relatively high U.S. crime rates can be explained by the interrelationship between culture and institutions. The dominance of the American Dream mythology ensures that many people will develop wishes and desires for material goods that cannot be satisfied by legitimate means. People are willing to do anything to get ahead, from cheating on tests to get higher grades to engaging in corporate fraud and tax evasion.[142] Those who cannot succeed become willing to risk everything, including a prison sentence.

The American Dream mythos may have a different effect on people depending on their place in the social structure. In their analysis of survey data, Stephen Cernkovich and his associates found that the American Dream mythology had a greater effect on whites than African Americans. Cernkovich reasons that whites may have greater expectations of material success than African Americans, whose aspirations have been tempered by a long history of racial and economic deprivation. When whites experience strain, they are more apt to react with anger and antisocial behavior.[143]

Institutional Effects At the institutional level, the dominance of economic concerns weakens the informal social control exerted by the family, church, and school. These institutions have lost their ability to regulate behavior and have instead become a conduit for promoting material success. Parents push their kids to succeed at any cost; schools encourage kids to get into the best colleges by any means possible; religious institutions promote their wealth and power.[144] Crime rates may rise even in a healthy economy because national prosperity heightens the attractiveness of monetary rewards, encouraging people to gain financial success by any means possible, including illegal ones. Meanwhile, the importance of social institutions as a means of exerting social control is reduced. In this "culture of competition," self-interest prevails and generates amorality, acceptance of inequality, and disdain for the less fortunate.[145]

The Messner-Rosenfeld version of anomie strain may be a blueprint for crime reduction strategies: If citizens are provided with an economic safety net, they may be able to resist the influence of economic deprivation and commit less crime. Nations that provide such resources—welfare, pension benefits, health care—have significantly lower crime rates.[146] In contrast, crime and violence rates are highest in nations that experience high levels of income inequality.[147]

Micro-Level Theory: General Strain Theory

Sociologist Robert Agnew's general strain theory (GST) helps identify the micro-level or individual influences of strain. Whereas Merton explains social class differences in the crime rate, Agnew explains why individuals who feel stress and strain are more likely to commit crimes. Agnew also offers a more general explanation of criminal activity among all elements of society rather than restricting his views to lower-class crime.[148]

Multiple Sources of Stress Agnew suggests that criminality is the direct result of negative affective states—the anger, frustration, and adverse emotions that emerge in the wake of negative and destructive social relationships. He finds that negative affective states are produced by a variety of sources of strain (Figure 6.7):

- *Failure to achieve positively valued goals.* This category of strain, similar to what Merton speaks of in his theory of anomie, is a result of the disjunction between aspirations and expectations. This type of strain occurs when people aspire for wealth and fame but, lacking financial and educational resources, assumes that such goals are impossible to achieve. These people, wracked by despair, who feel few opportunities for success, are at risk for crime.[149]

- *Disjunction of expectations and achievements.* Strain can also be produced when there is a disjunction between expectations and achievements. When people compare themselves to peers who seem to be doing a lot better financially or socially (such as making more money or getting better grades), even those doing relatively well feel strain. For example, when a high school senior is accepted at a good college but not a "prestige school" like some of her friends, she will feel strain. Perhaps she is not being treated fairly because the "playing field" is tilted against her; "other kids have connections," she may say. Yet perceptions of inequity may result in many adverse reactions, ranging from running away from its source to lowering the benefits of others through physical attacks or vandalizing their property.

- *Removal of positively valued stimuli.* Strain may occur because of the actual or anticipated removal or loss of a positively valued stimulus from the individual. Divorce can produce strain, as can the death of a loved one, moving to a new neighborhood, or getting a new job. The loss of positive stimuli may lead to criminality when a person tries to

Figure 6.7 Elements of General Strain Theory (GST)

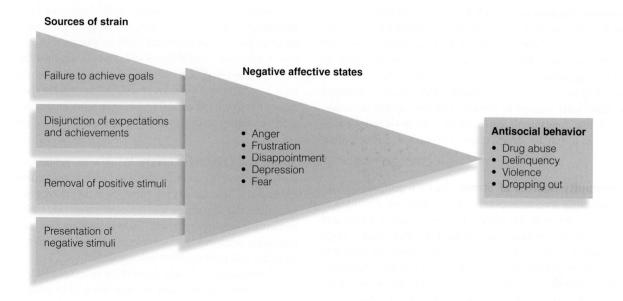

Sources of strain

Failure to achieve goals

Disjunction of expectations and achievements

Removal of positive stimuli

Presentation of negative stimuli

Negative affective states

- Anger
- Frustration
- Disappointment
- Depression
- Fear

Antisocial behavior

- Drug abuse
- Delinquency
- Violence
- Dropping out

prevent the loss, retrieve what has been lost, obtain substitutes, or seek revenge against those responsible for the loss.[150]

The effect of removal of positive stimuli may be class bound. Middle-class people are less able to cope with the removal of positive stimulus. Perhaps when you are expected to succeed because of your class position failure is harder to swallow; those who have limited opportunities and lower expectations may be able to take failure in stride.[151]

Presentation of negative stimuli. While the GST recognizes that the removal of positive stimuli produce strain, it relies more heavily on the effects of negative or noxious stimuli. Included within this category are such pain-inducing social interactions as child abuse and neglect, crime victimization, physical punishment, family and peer conflict, school failure, and interaction with stressful life events ranging from family breakup, unemployment, moving, feelings of dissatisfaction with friends and school to verbal threats and air pollution.[152] Becoming the target of racism and discrimination may also trigger the anger and aggression predicted by Agnew.[153]

Another important source of negative stimuli is to experience violent crime firsthand. Agnew himself found evidence that the strain associated with becoming a crime victim and anticipating future victimization may cause people to embrace antisocial behavior.[154] People who are victims of violent crimes may develop angry emotionality that translates into anger and subsequent antisocial behaviors.[155]

The effect of negative stimuli is not always a one-shot deal but may be ongoing. Some people who feel constantly picked on and maltreated by others will become detached and sullen. And even though they are angry and disengaged, they may be forced to interact with the source of strain, such as their boss, on a regular basis. Because this is unpleasant, they get angry and frustrated and plan corrective action: they

can assault or seek revenge against the source of their strain or even self-medicate by using drugs and alcohol).[156]

According to Agnew, the greater the intensity and frequency of strain experiences, the greater their impact and the more likely they are to cause criminality. Each type of strain will increase the likelihood of experiencing such negative emotions as disappointment, depression, fear, and, most important, anger. Anger increases perceptions of being wronged and produces a desire for revenge, energizes individuals to take action, and lowers inhibitions. Violence and aggression seem justified if you have been wronged and are righteously angry.

Because it produces these emotions, strain can be considered a predisposing factor for criminality when it is chronic and repetitive and creates a hostile, suspicious, and aggressive attitude. Individual strain episodes may serve as a situational event or trigger that produces crime, such as when a particularly stressful event ignites a violent reaction. Strain may predispose people toward antisocial behaviors rather than cause them to commit a specific act to relieve strain. So the person who feels strain because of financial need may be as likely to beat up a rival as he is to rob a liquor store.[157]

Sources of Strain

There are a variety of sources of strain. Sometimes it can be a particular individual who is causing problems, such as a peer group rival. When individuals identify a target to blame for their problems, they are more likely to respond with retaliatory action (for example, "Joe stole my wife away by lying about me, so I beat him up!"). Sometimes the source of strain is difficult to pinpoint (for example, "I feel depressed because of the way the world is going"); this type of ambiguous strain is unlikely to produce an aggressive response.[158]

Social Sources of Strain People may begin to feel strain because of their membership in a peer or social group. The relationship may be reciprocal. People who report feelings of stress and anger are more likely to interact with others who are similarly stressed out.[159] Peer group membership has its benefits, such as friendship, companionship, and support, but such groups also force members into behavior patterns (such as using drugs) that can be the source of unwelcome stress. Feelings of strain and being overwhelmed may become magnified as individuals attempt to comply with peer group demands. People may, for example, get involved in an unwanted shoplifting spree to pay for drugs, creating even more stress in their lives.[160]

Community Sources of Strain The GST generally focuses on individual level sources of strain, yet there are distinct ecological variations in the crime rate. Some regions, cities, and neighborhoods are more crime prone than others. Can ecological differences produce "negative affective states" in large segments of the population, which account for these differences? Agnew suggests that there are, in fact, community-level factors, such as blocked opportunities and lack of social support, that produce feelings of strain. According to Agnew, communities contribute to strain in several ways:

▮ They influence the goals people pursue and the ability people have to meet these goals.

▮ They influence feelings of relative deprivation and exposure to aversive stimuli, including family conflict, incivility, and economic deprivation.

▮ They influence the likelihood that angry, strain-filled individuals will interact with one another.

Consequently, not only does GST predict deviance on an individual level, but it can also account for community-level differences in the crime rate.

Coping with Strain

Not all people who experience strain fall into a life of crime and eventually resort to criminality. Some are able to marshal their emotional, mental, and behavioral resources to cope with the anger and frustration produced by strain. Coping ability may be a function of both individual traits and personal experiences over the life course. Personal temperament, prior learning of antisocial attitudes and behaviors, and association with criminal peers who reinforce anger are among other factors affecting the ability to cope. People who are impulsive and lack attachments to others are less able to cope than those who are bonded to others and maintain higher levels of self-control.[161] Those high in negative emotionality and low in constraint will be more likely to react to strain with antisocial behaviors.[162] In contrast, those people who can call on family, friends, and social institutions for help and support are better able to cope with strain.[163]

Although it may be socially disapproved, criminality can provide relief and satisfaction for someone living an otherwise stress-filled life. Using violence for self-protection may increase feelings of self-worth among those who feel inadequate or intellectually insecure. Violent responses may also be used in response to negative stimuli, such as violence.[164]

Some defenses are cognitive; individuals may be able to rationalize frustrating circumstances. Not getting the career they desire is "just not that important"; they may be poor, but the "next guy is worse off"; and if things didn't work out, then they "got what they deserved." Others seek behavioral solutions: they run away from adverse conditions or seek revenge against those who caused the strain. Others will try to regain emotional equilibrium with techniques ranging from physical exercise to drug abuse.

Strain and Criminal Careers While some people can effectively cope with strain, how does GST explain both chronic offending and the stability of crime over the life course? GST recognizes that certain people have traits that may make them particularly sensitive to strain. These include an explosive temperament, being overly sensitive or emotional, low tolerance for adversity, and poor problem-solving skills.[165]

Aggressive people who have these traits are likely to have poor interpersonal skills and are more likely to be treated negatively by others; their combative personalities make them feared and disliked. These people are likely to live in families whose caretakers share similar personality traits. They are also more likely to reject conventional peers and join deviant groups. Such individuals are subject to a high degree of strain over the course of their lives.

Crime peaks during late adolescence because this is a period of social stress caused by the weakening of parental supervision and the development of relationships with a diverse peer group. Many young people going through the trauma of family breakup and frequent changes in family structure find themselves feeling a high degree of strain. They may react by becoming involved in precocious sexuality or by turning to substance abuse to mask the strain. For example, research shows that young girls of any social class are more likely to bear out-of-wedlock children if they themselves experienced an unstable family life.[166] Adolescence is also a period during which hormone levels peak, and the behavior moderating aspects of the brain have not fully developed—two factors that make adolescent males susceptible to environmental sources of strain.[167]

As they mature, children's expectations increase; some find that they are unable to meet academic and social demands. Adolescents are very concerned about their standing with peers. Those deficient in these areas may find they are social outcasts, another source of strain. In adulthood, crime rates drop because these sources of strain are reduced, new sources of self-esteem emerge, and adults seem more likely to bring their goals in line with reality.

connections

Explaining continuity and change in offending rates over the life course has become an important goal of criminologists. Analysis of latent trait and life course theories in Chapter 9 provides some recent thinking on this topic.

STRAIN THEORIES

Theory	Major Premise	Strengths	Research Focus
Anomie Theory	People who adopt the goals of society but lack the means to attain them seek alternatives, such as crime.	Points out how competition for success creates conflict and crime. Suggests that social conditions and not personality can account for crime. Explains high lower-class crime rates.	Frustration; anomie; effects of failure to achieve goals.
Institutional Anomie Theory	The desire to accumulate wealth and material goods pervade all aspects of American life.	Explains why crime rates are so high in American culture.	Frustration; effects of materialism.
General Strain Theory	Strain has a variety of sources. Strain causes crime in the absence of adequate coping mechanisms.	Identifies the complexities of strain in modern society. Expands on anomie theory. Shows the influence of social events on behavior over the life course. Explains middle-class crimes.	Strain; inequality; negative affective states; influence of negative and positive stimuli.

Evaluating GST

Agnew's work is important because it both clarifies the concept of strain and directs future research agendas. The model has been shown to predict crime and deviance within a number of subject, racial, gender, and age groups.[168] It also addresses the dynamic nature of criminal behavior: levels of strain vary over the life course and so do crime rates. As levels of strain increase, so does involvement in antisocial activities; as strain levels decrease, so do individual crime rates. Feelings of strain then appear to play a key role in offending continuity and change.[169]

One of the biggest question marks about GST is its ability to adequately explain gender differences in the crime rate. Females experience as much or more strain, frustration, and anger as males, but their crime rate is much lower. Is it possible that there are gender differences either (a) in the relationship between strain and criminality or (b) in the ability to cope with the effects of strain? Not all sources of strain produce the anger envisioned by Agnew.[170] Although females may experience more strain, males may be more deeply affected by interpersonal stress.[171]

There is evidence that stress influences both males and females equally; however, the degree to which it leads to criminal behavior is much higher among males than females.[172] When presented with similar types of strain, males and females respond with a different constellation of negative emotions.[173] Females may be socialized to internalize stress, blaming themselves for their problems; males may take the same type of strain and relieve it by striking out at others and deflecting criticism with aggression.[174] Consequently, males may resort to criminality in the face of stressors of any magnitude, but only extreme levels of strain produce violent reactions from women.[175] Males may also seek out their peers when they are faced with strain,

whereas females are less inclined to confide in others. Male bonding with peers may actually increase their involvement with deviant behavior, a risk that is avoided by females. More effort is certainly needed to understand the cross-gender impact of strain.[176]

These issues aside, general strain theory has proven to be an enduring vision of the cause of criminality. Researchers have continued to show that people who perceive strain are the ones most likely to engage in delinquent activity.[177] Concept Summary 6.2 sets out the features of strain theory.

 www To read more about the work of **Émile Durkheim**, go to academic.cengage.com/criminaljustice/siegel.

CULTURAL DEVIANCE THEORIES

The third branch of social structure theory combines the effects of social disorganization and strain to explain how people living in deteriorated neighborhoods react to social isolation and economic deprivation. Because their lifestyle is draining, frustrating, and dispiriting, members of the lower class create an independent subculture with its own set of rules and values. Middle-class culture stresses hard work, delayed gratification, formal education, and being cautious; the lower-class subculture stresses excitement, toughness, risk taking, fearlessness, immediate gratification, and "street smarts." The lower-class subculture is an attractive alternative because the urban poor find that it is impossible to meet the behavioral demands of middle-class society.

According to cultural deviance theory, gangs flourish in an environment where there is strain and social disorganization. They provide an alternative for neighborhood kids who feel they can never make it in the legitimate world. Here, Los Angeles gang police officers question a 17-year-old gang member caught associating with another member and violating his probation on August 4, 2006, in Los Angeles, California. The boy was handcuffed and taken to the Rampart police station for a hearing with a probation officer. Local residents have a deep-seated resentment of the LAPD. The area is known for its violent gangs, which compete for the lucrative drug trade. Los Angeles's violent crime rates, traditionally among the highest in California, have recently fallen as gangs have shifted to outlying counties where real estate prices are more affordable. Does that mean that crime-producing inner-city norms and values will be spreading to surrounding areas and infecting them with inner-city problems?

Unfortunately, subcultural norms often clash with conventional values. People who have close personal ties to the neighborhood, especially when they are to deviant networks such as gangs and criminal groups, may find that community norms interfere with their personal desire for neighborhood improvement. So when the police are trying to solve a gang-related killing, neighbors may find that their loyalty to the gang boy and his family outweighs their desire to create a more stable crime-free community by giving information to the police.[178] Figure 6.8 outlines the elements of cultural deviance theory.

Conduct Norms

The concept that the lower class develops a unique culture in response to strain can be traced to Thorsten Sellin's classic 1938 work, *Culture Conflict and Crime*, a theoretical attempt to link cultural adaptation to criminality.[179] Sellin's main premise is that criminal law is an expression of the rules of the dominant culture. The content of the law, therefore, may create a clash between conventional, middle-class rules and splinter groups, such as ethnic and racial minorities who are excluded from the social mainstream. These groups maintain their own set of conduct norms—rules governing the day-to-day living conditions within these subcultures.[180] Conduct norms can be found in almost any culture and are not the property of any particular group, culture, or political structure.

Complicating matters is the fact that most of us belong to several social groups. In a complex society, the number of groups people belong to—family, peer, occupational, and religious—is quite large. "A conflict of norms is said to exist when more or less divergent rules of conduct govern the specific life situation in which a person may find himself."[181] According to Sellin, **culture conflict** occurs when the rules expressed in the criminal law clash with the demands of group conduct norms. To make his point, Sellin cited the case of a Sicilian father in New Jersey who killed the 16-year-old boy who seduced his daughter and then expressed surprise at being arrested. He claimed that he had "merely defended his family honor in a traditional way."[182]

Focal Concerns

In his classic 1958 paper, "Lower Class Culture as a Generating Milieu of Gang Delinquency," Walter Miller identified the unique value system that defines lower-class culture.[183] Conformance to these **focal concerns** dominates life among the lower class. According to Miller, clinging to lower-class focal concerns promotes illegal or violent behavior. Toughness may mean displaying fighting prowess; street smarts may lead to drug deals; excitement may result in drinking, gambling, or drug abuse. Focal concerns do not necessarily represent a rebellion against middle-class values; rather, these values have evolved specifically to fit conditions in lower-class areas. The major lower-class focal concerns are set out in Exhibit 6.1.[184] The Profiles in Crime feature "A Life in the Drug Trade" illustrates how lower-class focal concerns shape behavior in the inner city.

It is this adherence to the prevailing cultural demands of lower-class society that causes urban crime. Research, in fact, shows that members of the lower class value toughness and want to show they are courageous in the face of provocation.[185] A reputation for toughness helps them acquire social power while at the same time insulating them from becoming victims. Violence is also seen as a means to acquire the accouterments of wealth (nice clothes, flashy cars, or access to clubs), control or humiliate another person, defy authority, settle drug-related "business" disputes, attain retribution, satisfy the need for thrills or risk taking, and respond to challenges to one's manhood.[186]

To some criminologists, the influence of lower-class focal concerns and culture seem as relevant today as when first identified by Miller almost 50 years ago. The Race, Culture, Gender, and Criminology feature "The Code of the Streets" discusses a recent version of the concept of cultural deviance.

Theory of Delinquent Subcultures

Albert Cohen first articulated the theory of delinquent subcultures in his classic 1955 book, *Delinquent Boys*.[187] Cohen's central position was that delinquent behavior of lower-class youths

EXHIBIT 6.1

Miller's Lower-Class Focal Concerns

Trouble

In lower-class communities, people are evaluated by their actual or potential involvement in making trouble. Getting into trouble includes such behavior as fighting, drinking, and sexual misconduct. Dealing with trouble can confer prestige—for example, when a man establishes a reputation for being able to handle himself well in a fight. Not being able to handle trouble, and having to pay the consequences, can make a person look foolish and incompetent.

Toughness

Lower-class males want local recognition of their physical and spiritual toughness. They refuse to be sentimental or soft and instead value physical strength, fighting ability, and athletic skill. Those who cannot meet these standards risk getting a reputation for being weak, inept, and effeminate.

Smartness

Members of the lower-class culture want to maintain an image of being streetwise and savvy, using their street smarts, and having the ability to outfox and out-con the opponent. Though formal education is not admired, knowing essential survival techniques, such as gambling, conning, and outsmarting the law, is a requirement.

Excitement

Members of the lower class search for fun and excitement to enliven an otherwise drab existence. The search for excitement may lead to gambling, fighting, getting drunk, and sexual adventures. In between, the lower-class citizen may simply "hang out" and "be cool."

Fate

Lower-class citizens believe their lives are in the hands of strong spiritual forces that guide their destinies. Getting lucky, finding good fortune, and hitting the jackpot are all slum dwellers' daily dreams.

Autonomy

Being independent of authority figures, such as the police, teachers, and parents, is required; losing control is an unacceptable weakness, incompatible with toughness.

Source: Walter Miller, "Lower-Class Culture as a Generating Milieu of Gang Delinquency," *Journal of Social Issues* 14 (1958): 5–19.

Figure 6.8 Elements of Cultural Deviance Theory

Poverty
Lack of opportunity
Anomie

Socialization
Lower-class youths are socialized to value middle-class goals and ideas. However, their environment inhibits future success.

Subculture
Blocked opportunities prompt formation of groups with alternative lifestyles and values.

Deviant values
The new subculture maintains values considered deviant by the normative culture.

Crime and delinquency
Obeying subcultural values involve youth in criminal behaviors such as drug use and violence.

Criminal careers
Some gang members can parlay their status into criminal careers; others become drug users or commit violent assault.

---

is actually a protest against the norms and values of middle-class U.S. culture. Because social conditions make them incapable of achieving success legitimately, lower-class youths experience a form of culture conflict that Cohen labels status frustration.[188] As a result, many of them join together in gangs and engage in behavior that is "nonutilitarian, malicious, and negativistic."[189]

Cohen viewed the delinquent gang as a separate subculture, possessing a value system directly opposed to that of the larger society. He describes the subculture as one that "takes its norms from the larger culture, but turns them upside down. The delinquent's conduct is right by the standards of his subculture precisely because it is wrong by the norms of the larger cultures."[190]

According to Cohen, the development of the delinquent subculture is a consequence of socialization practices found in the ghetto or inner-city environment. These children lack the basic skills necessary to achieve social and economic success in the demanding U.S. society. They also lack the proper education and therefore do not have the skills upon which to build a knowledge or socialization foundation. He suggests that lower-class parents are incapable of teaching children the necessary techniques for entering the dominant middle-class culture. The consequences of this deprivation include developmental handicaps, poor speech and communication skills, and inability to delay gratification.

Middle-Class Measuring Rods One significant handicap that lower-class children face is the inability to positively impress authority figures, such as teachers, employers, or supervisors. Cohen calls the standards set by these authority figures middle-class measuring rods. The conflict and frustration lower-class youths experience when they fail to meet these standards is a primary cause of delinquency. For example, the fact that a lower-class student is deemed by those in power to be substandard

A LIFE IN THE DRUG TRADE

In summer 2004, a dramatic murder trial took place in New York City that aptly illustrates how lower-class cultural concerns—the code of the streets—clash with the rules and values of American culture and how deviant cultures can exist side by side with middle-class culture.

Two Bronx men, Alan Quiñones and Diego Rodriguez, were accused of heroin trafficking and killing a police informant. The trial hinged on the testimony of one of their confederates—Hector Vega, a key government witness who had previously pleaded guilty to taking part in the murder. He described in vivid detail how he watched the defendants beat the victim, Edwin Santiago, as he lay handcuffed on the floor of a Bronx apartment. He told the jury how the defendants Quiñones and Rodriguez spit in Santiago's face to show what they thought of police informants. Santiago's body was found mutilated and burned beyond recognition on June 28, 1999.

During the trial, Vega gave the jury a detailed lesson in retail drug operations. In the Bronx, beatings, slashings, and shootings are routinely used to enforce what he called "the drug law": "If people deserved it, I beat them up." He showed them a tattoo on his upper right arm that meant "Money, Power, Respect." Vega, 31, also told the jury that he headed a group of heroin vendors who did business from his "spot," his sales area, between Daly and Honeywell Avenues in the Bronx. He said he had learned the trade from a stepfather, a building superintendent who he said had a second job as a narcotics entrepreneur: "I always knew about the drug business. I was raised around it."

As a mid-level drug dealer, Vega received heroin on consignment from big-time drug wholesalers and turned it over in $100 packages to people he called his "managers," who in turn found "runners" to sell it on the street. His job was to "make sure everybody is working, and I will make sure everything is running correctly." Vega received a "commission" of about 35 percent of all sales in his organization; he estimated that he made a total of at least $500,000 in the five years before his arrest.

Vega told how he used strict rules to run his organization. He did not sell between 1 and 3 P.M. because of "school hours." He did not allow anyone to sell at his spot without his approval, or steal drugs from him, or pass him a counterfeit bill, or taint the quality of drugs sold under his name. If that happened, he said, "I'd be looking like a fool. The drug spot will go down." When Manny, one of his workers, stole one package of heroin, Vega slashed his face with a box cutter. When the wound did not immediately bleed, "I didn't see nothing cut, I didn't see anything I did, so I did it a second time," he said, until he saw blood. Angered by a counterfeit bill he received from a crack addict, "I punched him in the face, I kicked him, I threw him on the floor and kicked him again." He disciplined one stranger who cheated him by hitting the man in the back of the head with a three-foot tree branch. Police informants were given special treatment. "In the drug world, in the drug law, we say that snitches get stitches," he said. "In jail you cut their face. In the street, you beat them. You kill them."

Vega testified that the defendants Quiñones and Rodriguez were heroin wholesalers and that he began buying drugs from them a few months before Santiago's death. After he learned that Quiñones suspected Santiago of working undercover for the police, he helped him lure Santiago to the apartment of a girlfriend where the beatings and murder took place. For his cooperation, Vega faced a 15-year sentence rather than the death penalty.

Source: Julia Preston, "Witness Gives Details of Life as Drug Dealer," *New York Times*, 12 July 2004.

---

or below the average of what is expected can have an important impact on his or her future life chances. A school record may be reviewed by juvenile court authorities and by the military. Because a military record can influence whether or not someone is qualified for certain jobs, it is quite influential.[191] Negative evaluations become part of a permanent file that follows an individual for the rest of his or her life. When he or she wants to improve, evidence of prior failures is used to discourage advancement.

The Formation of Deviant Subcultures Cohen believes lower-class boys who suffer rejection by middle-class decision makers usually elect to join one of three existing subcultures:

the corner boy, the college boy, or the delinquent boy. The corner boy role is the most common response to middle-class rejection. The corner boy is not a chronic delinquent but may be a truant who engages in petty or status offenses, such as precocious sex and recreational drug abuse. His main loyalty is to his peer group, on which he depends for support, motivation, and interest. His values, therefore, are those of the group with which he is in close personal contact. The corner boy, well aware of his failure to achieve the standards of the American Dream, retreats into the comforting world of his lower-class peers and eventually becomes a stable member of his neighborhood, holding a menial job, marrying, and remaining in the community.

Race, Culture, Gender, and Criminology

THE CODE OF THE STREETS

A widely cited view of the interrelationship of culture and behavior is Elijah Anderson's concept of the "code of the streets." He sees that life circumstances are tough for the "ghetto poor"—lack of jobs that pay a living wage, stigma of race, fallout from rampant drug use and drug trafficking, and alienation and lack of hope for the future. Living in such an environment places young people at special risk of crime and deviant behavior.

There are two cultural forces running through the neighborhood that shape their reactions. *Decent values* are taught by families committed to middle-class values and representing mainstream goals and standards of behavior. Though they may be better off financially than some of their street-oriented neighbors, they are generally "working poor." They value hard work and self-reliance and are willing to sacrifice for their families; they harbor hopes for a better future for their children. Most go to church and take a strong interest in education. Some see their difficult situation as a test from God and derive great support from their faith and from the church community.

In opposition, *street values* are born in the despair of inner-city life and are in opposition to those of mainstream society. The street culture has developed what Anderson calls a code of the streets, a set of informal rules setting down both proper attitudes and ways to respond if challenged. If the rules are violated, there are penalties and sometimes violent retribution.

At the heart of the code is the issue of respect—loosely defined as being "treated right." The code demands that disrespect be punished or hard-won respect be lost. With the right amount of respect, a person can avoid being bothered in public. If he is bothered, not only may he be in physical danger, but he has been disgraced or "dissed" (disrespected). Some forms of dissing, such as maintaining eye contact for too long, may seem pretty mild. But to street kids who live by the code, these actions become serious indications of the other person's intentions and a warning of imminent physical confrontation.

These two orientations—decent and street—socially organize the community. Their coexistence means that kids who are brought up in decent homes must be able to successfully navigate the demands of the street culture. Even in decent families, parents recognize that the code must be obeyed or at the very least negotiated; it cannot simply be ignored.

The Respect Game

Young men in poor inner-city neighborhoods build their self-image on the foundation of respect. Having "juice" (as respect is sometimes called on the street) means that they can take care of themselves even if it means resorting to violence. For street youth, losing respect on the street can be damaging and dangerous. Once they have demonstrated that they can be insulted, beaten up, or stolen from, they become an easy target. Kids from decent families may be able to keep their self-respect by getting good grades or a scholarship. Street kids do not have that luxury. With nothing to fall back on, they cannot walk away from an insult. They must retaliate with violence.

One method of preventing attacks is to go on the offensive. Aggressive, violence-prone people are not seen as easy prey. Robbers do not get robbed, and street fighters are not the favorite targets of bullies. A youth who communicates an image of not being afraid to die and not being afraid to kill has given himself a sense of power on the street.

Anderson's work has been well received by the criminological community. A number of researchers have found that the "code of the streets" does in fact exist and that Anderson's observations are in fact valid. Jeffery Fagan's interviews with 150 young men who had experiences with violent crimes while living in some of New York City's toughest neighborhoods found that many alternated their demeanor between "decent" and "street" codes of behavior. Both orientations existed side by side within the same individuals. The street code's rules for getting and maintaining respect through aggressive behavior forced many "decent" youths to situationally adopt a tough demeanor and perhaps behave violently in order to survive an otherwise hostile and possibly dangerous environment.

CRITICAL THINKING

1. Does the code of the street, as described by Anderson, apply in the neighborhood in which you were raised? That is, is it universal?

2. Is there a form of "respect game" being played out on college campuses? If so, what is the substitute for violence?

Sources: Elijah Anderson, *Code of the Street: Decency, Violence, and the Moral Life of the Inner City* (New York: Norton, 2000); Elijah Anderson, "Violence and the Inner-City Street Code," in *Violence and Children in the Inner City,* ed. Joan McCord (New York: Cambridge University Press, 1998), pp. 1–30; Elijah Anderson, "The Code of the Streets," *Atlantic Monthly* 273 (May 1994): 80–94; Timothy Brezina, Robert Agnew, Francis T. Cullen, and John Paul Wright, "The Code of the Street: A Quantitative Assessment of Elijah Anderson's Subculture of Violence Thesis and Its Contribution to Youth Violence Research," *Youth Violence and Juvenile Justice* 2 (2004): 303–328; Jeffrey Fagan, *Adolescent Violence: A View from the Street,* NIJ Research Preview (Washington, DC: National Institute of Justice, 1998).

The college boy embraces the cultural and social values of the middle class. Rather than scorning middle-class measuring rods, he actively strives to be successful by those standards. Cohen views this type of youth as one who is embarking on an almost hopeless path, since he is ill-equipped academically, socially, and linguistically to achieve the rewards of middle-class life.

The delinquent boy adopts a set of norms and principles in direct opposition to middle-class values. He engages in short-run hedonism, living for today and letting "tomorrow take care of itself."[192] Delinquent boys strive for group autonomy. They resist efforts by family, school, or other sources of authority to control their behavior. They may join a gang because it is perceived as autonomous, independent, and the focus of "attraction, loyalty, and solidarity."[193] Frustrated by their inability to succeed, these boys resort to a process Cohen calls reaction formation. Symptoms of reaction formation include overly intense responses that seem disproportionate to the stimuli that trigger them. For the delinquent boy, this takes the form of irrational, malicious, and unaccountable hostility to the enemy, which in this case are "the norms of respectable middle-class society."[194] Reaction formation causes delinquent boys to overreact to any perceived threat or slight. They sneer at the college boy's attempts at assimilation and scorn the corner boy's passivity. The delinquent boy is willing to take risks, violate the law, and flout middle-class conventions.

Cohen's work helps explain the factors that promote and sustain a delinquent subculture. By introducing the concepts of status frustration and middle-class measuring rods, Cohen makes it clear that social forces and not individual traits promote and sustain a delinquent career. By introducing the corner boy, college boy, delinquent boy triad, he helps explain why many lower-class youth fail to become chronic offenders: there is more than one social path open to indigent youth.[195] His work is a skillful integration of strain and social disorganization theories and has become an enduring element of the criminological literature.

Theory of Differential Opportunity

In their classic work *Delinquency and Opportunity*, written over 40 years ago, Richard Cloward and Lloyd Ohlin combined strain and social disorganization principles into a portrayal of a gang-sustaining criminal subculture.[196] Cloward and Ohlin agreed with Cohen and found that independent delinquent subcultures exist within society. They consider a delinquent subculture to be one in which certain forms of delinquent activity are essential requirements for performing the dominant roles supported by the subculture.[197]

Youth gangs are an important part of the delinquent subculture. Although not all illegal acts are committed by gang youth, they are the source of the most serious, sustained, and costly criminal behaviors. Delinquent gangs spring up in disorganized areas where youths lack the opportunity to gain success through conventional means.

True to strain theory principles, Cloward and Ohlin portray inner-city kids as individuals who want to conform to middle-class values but lack the means to do so.[198]

Differential Opportunities The centerpiece of the Cloward and Ohlin theory is the concept of differential opportunity, which states that people in all strata of society share the same success goals but that those in the lower class have limited means of achieving them. People who perceive themselves as failures within conventional society will seek alternative or innovative ways to gain success. People who conclude that there is little hope for advancement by legitimate means may join with like-minded peers to form a gang. Gang members provide the emotional support to handle the shame, fear, or guilt they may develop while engaging in illegal acts. Delinquent subcultures then reward these acts that conventional society would punish. The youth who is considered a failure at school and is only qualified for a menial job at a minimum wage can earn thousands of dollars plus the respect of his or her peers by joining a gang and engaging in drug deals or armed robberies.

Cloward and Ohlin recognize that the opportunity for both successful conventional and criminal careers is limited. In stable areas, adolescents may be recruited by professional criminals, drug traffickers, or organized crime groups. Unstable areas, however, cannot support flourishing criminal opportunities. In these socially disorganized

Kids may join gangs because they are looking for acceptance and respect. The gang may serve as a surrogate family. By providing an alternative, community programs hope to entice kids away from gangs. Some programs have a religious theme. The Venerable Khon Sao, a Buddhist monk, teaches Cambodian youths, many of them gang members, how to pray at a Buddhist temple in Lowell, Massachusetts. In conjunction with the police department, the temple has begun a program that teaches the teens the fundamentals of Buddhist thought two evenings a week. In the classes, the youths learn how to pray, meditate, and act peacefully.

neighborhoods, adult role models are absent, and young criminals have few opportunities to join established gangs or to learn the fine points of professional crime. Cloward and Ohlin's most important finding, then, is that all opportunities for success, both illegal and conventional, are closed for the most "truly disadvantaged" youth.

Because of differential opportunity, kids are likely to join one of three types of gangs:

- *Criminal gangs*. Criminal gangs exist in stable lower-class areas in which close connections among adolescent, young adult, and adult offenders create an environment for successful criminal enterprise.[199] Youths are recruited into established criminal gangs that provide a training ground for a successful criminal career. Gang membership provides a learning experience in which the knowledge and skills needed for success in crime are acquired. During this "apprenticeship stage," older, more experienced members of the criminal subculture hold youthful "trainees" on tight reins, limiting activities that might jeopardize the gang's profits (for example, engaging in nonfunctional, irrational violence). Over time, new recruits learn the techniques and attitudes of the criminal world and how to "cooperate successfully with others in criminal enterprises."[200] To become a fully accepted member of the criminal gang, novices must prove themselves reliable and dependable in their contacts with their criminal associates.

- *Conflict gangs*. Conflict gangs develop in communities unable to provide either legitimate or illegitimate opportunities. These highly disorganized areas are marked by transient residents and physical deterioration. Crime in this area is "individualistic, unorganized, petty, poorly paid, and unprotected."[201] There are no successful adult criminal role models from whom youths can learn criminal skills. When such severe limitations on both criminal and conventional opportunity intensify frustrations of the young, violence is used as a means of gaining status. The image of the conflict gang member is the swaggering, tough adolescent who fights with weapons to win respect from rivals and engages in unpredictable and destructive assaults on people and property. Conflict gang members must be ready to fight to protect their own and their gang's integrity and honor. By doing so, they acquire a "rep," which provides them with a means for gaining admiration from their peers and consequently helps them develop their own self-image. Conflict gangs, according to Cloward and Ohlin, "represent a way of securing access to the scarce resources for adolescent pleasure and opportunity in underprivileged areas."[202]

- *Retreatist gangs*. Retreatists are double failures, unable to gain success through legitimate means and unwilling to do so through illegal ones. Some retreatists have tried crime or violence but are too clumsy, weak, or scared to be accepted in criminal or violent gangs. They then retreat into a role on the fringe of society. Members of the retreatist subculture constantly search for ways of getting high—alcohol, pot, heroin, unusual sexual experiences, music. They are always "cool," detached from relationships with the conventional world. To feed their habit, retreatists develop a "hustle"—pimping, conning, selling drugs, and committing petty crimes. Personal status in the retreatist subculture is derived from peer approval.

Evaluating Social Structure Theories

The social structure approach has significantly influenced both criminological theory and crime prevention strategies. Its core concepts seem to be valid in view of the relatively high crime and delinquency rates and gang activity occurring in the deteriorated inner-city areas of the nation's largest cities.[203] The public's image of the disorganized inner city includes roaming bands of violent teenage gangs, drug users, prostitutes, muggers, and similar frightening examples of criminality. All of these are present today in inner-city areas.

Critics of the approach charge that we cannot be sure that it is lower-class culture itself that promotes crime and not some other force operating in society. They deny that residence in urban areas alone is sufficient to cause people to violate the law.[204] It is possible, they counter, that lower-class crime rates may be an artifact of bias in the criminal justice system. Lower-class areas seem to have higher crime rates because residents are arrested and prosecuted by agents of the justice system who, as members of the middle class, exhibit class bias.[205] Class bias is often coupled with discrimination against minority group members, who have long suffered at the hands of the justice system.

Even if the higher crime rates recorded in lower-class areas are valid, it is still true that most members of the lower class are not criminals. The discovery of the chronic offender indicates that a significant majority of people living in lower-class environments are not criminals and that a relatively small proportion of the population commits most crimes. If social forces alone could be used to explain crime, how can we account for the vast number of urban poor who remain honest and law abiding? Given these circumstances, law violators must be motivated by some individual mental, physical, or social process or trait.[206]

It is also questionable whether a distinct lower-class culture actually exists. Several researchers have found that gang members and other delinquent youths seem to value middle-class concepts, such as sharing, earning money, and respecting the law, as highly as middle-class youths. Criminologists contend that lower-class youths also value education as highly as middle-class students do.[207] Public opinion polls can also be used as evidence that a majority of lower-class citizens maintain middle-class values. National surveys find that people in the lowest income brackets want tougher drug laws, more police protection, and greater control over criminal offenders.[208] These opinions seem similar to conventional middle-class values rather than representative of an independent, deviant subculture. While this evidence contradicts some of the central ideas of social structure theory, the discovery of stable patterns of lower-class crime, the high crime rates found in disorganized inner-city areas, and the rise of teenage gangs and groups support a close association between

CULTURAL DEVIANCE THEORIES

Theory	Major Premise	Strengths	Research Focus
Miller's Focal Concern Theory	Citizens who obey the street rules of lower-class life (focal concerns) find themselves in conflict with the dominant culture.	Identifies the core values of lower-class culture and shows their association to crime.	Cultural norms; focal concerns.
Cohen's Theory of Delinquent Gangs	Status frustration of lower-class boys, created by their failure to achieve middle-class success, causes them to join gangs.	Shows how the conditions of lower-class life produce crime. Explains violence and destructive acts. Identifies conflict of lower class with middle class.	Gangs; culture conflict; middle-class measuring rods; reaction formation.
Cloward and Ohlin's Theory of Opportunity	Blockage of conventional opportunities causes lower-class youths to join criminal, conflict, or retreatist gangs.	Shows that even illegal opportunities are structured in society. Indicates why people become involved in a particular type of criminal activity. Presents a way of preventing crime.	Gangs; cultural norms; culture conflict; effects of blocked opportunity.

crime rates and social class position. Concept Summary 6.3 sets out the features of cultural deviance theories.

PUBLIC POLICY IMPLICATIONS OF SOCIAL STRUCTURE THEORY

Social structure theory has had a significant influence on public policy. If the cause of criminality is viewed as a schism between lower-class individuals and conventional goals, norms, and rules, it seems logical that alternatives to criminal behavior can be provided by giving inner-city dwellers opportunities to share in the rewards of conventional society.

One approach is to give indigent people direct financial aid through welfare and Aid to Dependent Children (ADC). Although welfare has been curtailed through the Federal Welfare Reform Act of 1996, research shows that crime rates decrease when families receive supplemental income through public assistance payments.[209]

There are also efforts to reduce crime by improving the community structure in high-crime inner-city areas. Crime prevention efforts based on social structure precepts can be traced back to the Chicago Area Project, supervised by Clifford R. Shaw. This program attempted to organize existing community structures to develop social stability in otherwise disorganized lower-class neighborhoods. The project sponsored recreation programs for children in the neighborhoods, including summer camping. It campaigned for community improvements in such areas as education, sanitation, traffic safety, physical conservation, and law enforcement. Project members also worked with police and court agencies to supervise and treat gang youth and adult

offenders. In a 25-year assessment of the project, Solomon Kobrin found that it was successful in demonstrating the feasibility of creating youth welfare organizations in high-delinquency areas.[210] Kobrin also discovered that the project made a distinct contribution to ending the isolation of urban males from the mainstream of society.

Social structure concepts, especially Cloward and Ohlin's views, were a critical ingredient in the Kennedy and Johnson administrations' "War on Poverty," begun in the early 1960s. Rather than organizing existing community structures, as Shaw's Chicago Area Project had done, this later effort called for an all-out attack on the crime-producing structures of inner-city areas. War on Poverty programs included the Job Corps, VISTA (the urban Peace Corps), Head Start and Upward Bound (educational enrichment programs), Neighborhood Legal Services, and the largest community organizing effort, the Community Action Program. War on Poverty programs were sweeping efforts to change the social structure of the inner-city area. They sought to reduce crime by developing a sense of community pride and solidarity in poverty areas and by providing educational and job opportunities for crime-prone youths. Some War on Poverty programs—Head Start, Neighborhood Legal Services, and the Community Action Program—have continued to help people.

Today Operation Weed and Seed is the foremost structural theory based crime reduction strategy. Its aim is to prevent, control, and reduce violent crime, drug abuse, and gang activity in targeted high-crime neighborhoods across the country. Weed and Seed sites range in size from several neighborhood blocks to 15 square miles.[211] The strategy involves a two-pronged approach. First, law enforcement agencies and prosecutors cooperate in "weeding out" criminals who participate in violent crime and drug abuse and attempt to prevent their return to the targeted area. Then, participating agencies begin "seeding," which brings human services to the area, encompassing prevention, intervention, treatment, and neighborhood revitalization. A community-orientated policing component bridges weeding and seeding strategies. Officers obtain helpful information from area residents for weeding efforts while they aid residents in obtaining information about community revitalization and seeding resources. Operation Weed and Seed is an example of a modern-day crime control approach that relies on changing neighborhood structure to reduce crime rates.

THINKING LIKE A CRIMINOLOGIST

You are a criminologist from a local university who is serving as an advisor to the mayor of Central City, an industrial town with a population of 300,000. The mayor, up for reelection, is disappointed that efforts by the local police force to reduce public disorder and crime rates through a community police program do not seem to be working. He has recently read a report issued by the federal government suggesting that the key to reducing neighborhood crime is to create a sense of "collective efficacy" in city neighborhoods. The report defined collective efficacy as "cohesion among neighborhood residents combined with shared expectations for informal social control of public space." The report, written by criminologists Robert Sampson and Stephen Raudenbush, found that when the rules of comportment are unclear and people mistrust one another, they are unlikely to take action against disorder and crime. When there is cohesion and mutual trust among neighbors, the likelihood is greater that they will share a willingness to intervene for the common good. They found that in neighborhoods where this sense of collective efficacy was strong, rates of violence were low, regardless of neighborhood composition or socioeconomic conditions. Collective efficacy also appeared to deter disorder: where it was strong, observed levels of physical and social disorder were low. The mayor wants to apply these concepts to Central City, and he has asked for your help.

 Writing Assignment Write a memo to the mayor stating your recommendations for reducing crime in Central City (about two pages in length). The problem is twofold: (1) How can collective efficacy be improved? (2) What test will show whether improvements in collective efficacy levels are responsible for lower violent crime rates?

 Doing Research on the Web To help formulate your recommendations, review these Web-based resources:

▪ Read the report by Robert J. Sampson and Stephen W. Raudenbush, "Disorder in Urban Neighborhoods: Does It Lead to Crime?" at the National Institute of Justice website.

▪ Read a second report linking collective efficacy to violence entitled *Neighborhood Inequality, Collective Efficacy, and the Spatial Dynamics of Urban Violence* by Jeffrey D. Morenoff, Robert J. Sampson, and Stephen W. Raudenbush.

These reports can be accessed via academic.cengage.com/criminaljustice/siegel.

SUMMARY

▪ Sociology has been the main orientation of criminologists because they know that crime rates vary among elements of the social structure, that society goes through changes that affect crime, and that social interaction relates to criminality.

▪ Social structure theories suggest that people's places in the socioeconomic structure influence their chances of becoming criminals.

▪ Poor people are more likely to commit crimes because they are unable to achieve monetary or social success in any other way.

▪ Social structure theory includes three schools of thought: social disorganization theories, strain theories, and cultural deviance theories.

- Social disorganization theory suggests that the urban poor violate the law because they live in areas in which social control has broken down. The origin of social disorganization theory can be traced to the work of Clifford R. Shaw and Henry D. McKay. Shaw and McKay concluded that disorganized areas, marked by divergent values and transitional populations, produce criminality. Modern social ecology theory looks at such issues as community fear, unemployment, and deterioration.

- Strain theories view crime as resulting from the anger people experience over their inability to achieve legitimate social and economic success.

- Strain theories hold that most people share common values and beliefs, but the ability to achieve them is differentiated by the social structure.

- The best-known strain theory is Robert Merton's theory of anomie, which describes what happens when people have inadequate means to satisfy their goals.

- Steven Messner and Richard Rosenfeld show that the core values of American culture produce strain.

- Robert Agnew suggests that strain has multiple sources and is linked to anger and frustration that people endure when their goals and aspirations are frustrated or when they lose something they value.

- Cultural deviance theories hold that a unique value system develops in lower-class areas.

- Lower-class values approve of behaviors such as being tough, never showing fear, and defying authority. People perceiving strain will bond together in their own groups or subcultures for support and recognition.

- Albert Cohen links the formation of subcultures to the failure of lower-class citizens to achieve recognition from middle-class decision makers, such as teachers, employers, and police officers.

- Richard Cloward and Lloyd Ohlin have argued that crime results from lower-class people's perception that their opportunity for success is limited. Consequently, youths in low-income areas may join criminal, conflict, or retreatist gangs.

- CENGAGENOW™ is an easy-to-use online resource that helps you study in less time to get the grade you want—NOW. CengageNOW™ Personalized Study (a diagnostic study tool containing valuable text-specific resources) lets you focus on just what you don't know and learn more in less time to get a better grade. If your textbook does not include an access code card, you can go to www.ichapters.com to purchase CengageNOW™.

 ## KEY TERMS

stratified society (178)
culture of poverty (179)
at-risk (179)
underclass (179)
truly disadvantaged (181)
social structure theory (182)
social disorganization theory (182)
strain theory (183)
strain (183)
cultural deviance theory (183)
subcultures (183)
cultural transmission (183)

transitional neighborhoods (184)
incivilities (187)
siege mentality (187)
gentrification (187)
collective efficacy (187)
street efficacy (190)
relative deprivation (190)
mechanical solidarity (191)
organic solidarity (191)
theory of anomie (192)
institutional anomie theory (193)
American Dream (193)

general strain theory (GST) (194)
negative affective states (194)
conduct norms (198)
culture conflict (198)
focal concerns (198)
status frustration (199)
middle-class measuring rods (199)
corner boy (200)
college boy (202)
delinquent boy (202)
reaction formation (202)
differential opportunity (202)

 ## CRITICAL THINKING QUESTIONS

1. Is there a "transition" area in your town or city? Does the crime rate remain constant in this neighborhood regardless of the racial, ethnic, or cultural composition of its residents?

2. Do you believe a distinct lower-class culture exists? Do you know anyone who has the focal concerns Miller talks about? Did you experience elements of these focal concerns while you were in high school? Will emerging forms of communication such as the Internet reduce cultural differences and create a more homogenous society, or are subcultures resistant to such influences?

3. Do you agree with Agnew that there is more than one cause of strain? If so, are there other sources of strain that he did not consider?

4. How would a structural theorist explain the presence of middle-class crime?

5. How would biosocial theories explain the high levels of violent crime in lower-class areas?

NOTES

1. Arian Campo-Flores, "The Most Dangerous Gang in the United States," *Newsweek* 28 March 2006; Ricardo Pollack, "Gang Life Tempts Salvador Teens," BBC News, http://news.bbc.co.uk/1/hi/world/americas/4201183.stm (accessed May 30, 2007).

2. Arlen Egley, Jr., and Christina E. Ritz, *Highlights of the 2004 National Youth Gang Survey* (Washington, DC: Office of Juvenile Justice and Delinquency Prevention, 2006).

3. Steven Messner and Richard Rosenfeld, *Crime and the American Dream* (Belmont, CA: Wadsworth, 1994), p. 11.

4. Sam Roberts, *Who We Are Now: The Changing Face of America in the Twenty-First Century* (New York: Times Books, Henry Holt, 2004).

5. "High Net Worth Wealth Grows Strongly at Over 8%, Surpassing $30 Trillion in 2004, According to Merrill Lynch and Capgemini," *World Wealth Report*, 9 June 2005.

6. Carmen DeNavas-Walt, Bernadette D. Proctor, and Cheryl Hill Lee, *Income, Poverty and Health Insurance in the United States: 2005* (P60-231) (Washington, DC: U.S. Census Department, 2006), www.census.gov/prod/2006pubs/p60-231.pdf (accessed May 30, 2007).

7. Oscar Lewis, "The Culture of Poverty," *Scientific American* 215 (1966): 19–25.

8. Gunnar Myrdal, *The Challenge of World Poverty* (New York: Vintage Books, 1970).

9. James Ainsworth-Darnell and Douglas Downey, "Assessing the Oppositional Culture Explanation for Racial/Ethnic Differences in School Performances," *American Sociological Review* 63 (1998): 536–553.

10. Barbara Warner, "The Role of Attenuated Culture in Social Disorganization Theory," *Criminology* 41 (2003): 73–97.

11. Jeanne Brooks-Gunn and Greg J. Duncan, "The Effects of Poverty on Children," *Future of Children* 7 (1997): 34–39.

12. Brooks-Gunn and Duncan, "The Effects of Poverty on Children."

13. Greg Duncan, W. Jean Yeung, Jeanne Brooks-Gunn, and Judith Smith, "How Much Does Childhood Poverty Affect the Life Chances of Children?" *American Sociological Review* 63 (1998): 406–423.

14. Ibid., p. 409.

15. Gary Evans, Nancy Wells, and Annie Moch, "Housing and Mental Health: A Review of the Evidence and a Methodological and Conceptual Critique," *Journal of Social Issues* 59 (2003): 475–501.

16. Maria Velez, Lauren Krivo, and Ruth Peterson, "Structural Inequality and Homicide: An Assessment of the Black-White Gap in Killings," *Criminology* 41 (2003): 645–672.

17. DeNavas-Walt, Proctor, and Lee, *Income, Poverty and Health Insurance in the United States: 2005.*

18. UCLA Center for Health Policy Research, "The Health of Young Children in California: Findings from the 2001 California Health Interview Survey" (Los Angeles, UCLA Center for Health Policy Research, 2003).

19. John Hagan, Carla Shedd, and Monique Payne, "Race, Ethnicity, and Youth Perceptions of Criminal Injustice," *American Sociological Review* 70 (2005): 381–407.

20. Eric Lotke, "Hobbling a Generation: Young African-American Men in Washington, D.C.'s Criminal Justice System—Five Years Later," *Crime and Delinquency* 44 (1998): 355–366.

21. Ronald Mincy, ed., *Black Males Left Behind* (Washington, DC: Urban Institute, 2006); Erik Eckholm, "Plight Deepens for Black Men, Studies Warn," *New York Times*, 20 March 2006.

22. Thomas McNulty and Paul Bellair, "Explaining Racial and Ethnic Differences in Serious Adolescent Violent Behavior," *Criminology* 41 (2003): 709–748; Julie A. Phillips, "White, Black, and Latino Homicide Rates: Why the Difference?" *Social Problems* 49 (2002): 349–374.

23. David Bjerk, "Measuring the Relationship Between Youth Criminal Participation and Household Economic Resources," *Journal of Quantitative Criminology* 23 (2007): 23–39.

24. Justin Patchin, Beth Huebner, John McCluskey, Sean Varano, and Timothy Bynum, "Exposure to Community Violence and Childhood Delinquency," *Crime and Delinquency* 52 (2006): 307–332.

25. David Brownfield, "Social Class and Violent Behavior," *Criminology* 24 (1986): 421–438.

26. See Charles Tittle and Robert Meier, "Specifying the SES/Delinquency Relationship," *Criminology* 28 (1990): 271–295, at 293.

27. See Ruth Kornhauser, *Social Sources of Delinquency* (Chicago: University of Chicago Press, 1978), p. 75.

28. Jonathan Crane, "The Epidemic Theory of Ghettos and Neighborhood Effects on Dropping Out and Teenage Childbearing," *American Journal of Sociology* 96 (1991): 1,226–1,259; see also Rodrick Wallace, "Expanding Coupled Shock Fronts of Urban Decay and Criminal Behavior: How U.S. Cities Are Becoming 'Hollowed Out,'" *Journal of Quantitative Criminology* 7 (1991): 333–355.

29. Jeffrey Fagan and Garth Davies, "The Natural History of Neighborhood Violence," *Journal of Contemporary Criminal Justice* 20 (2004): 127–147.

30. Clifford R. Shaw and Henry D. McKay, *Juvenile Delinquency and Urban Areas*, rev. ed. (Chicago: University of Chicago Press, 1972).

31. Anthony Platt, *The Child Savers: The Invention of Delinquency* (Chicago: University of Chicago Press, 1968).

32. Shaw and McKay, *Juvenile Delinquency and Urban Areas*, p. 52.

33. Ibid., p. 171.

34. Claire Valier, "Foreigners, Crime and Changing Mobilities," *British Journal of Criminology* 43 (2003): 1–21.

35. For a discussion of these issues, see Robert Bursik, "Social Disorganization and Theories of Crime and Delinquency: Problems and Prospects," *Criminology* 26 (1988): 521–539.

36. Robert Sampson, "Effects of Socioeconomic Context of Official Reaction to Juvenile Delinquency," *American Sociological Review* 51 (1986): 876–885.

37. Jeffrey Fagan, Ellen Slaughter, and Eliot Hartstone, "Blind Justice? The Impact of Race on the Juvenile Justice Process," *Crime and Delinquency* 33 (1987): 224–258; Merry Morash, "Establishment of a Juvenile Police Record," *Criminology* 22 (1984): 97–113.

38. For a general review, see James Byrne and Robert Sampson, eds., *The Social Ecology of Crime* (New York: Springer Verlag, 1985).

39. Stacy De Coster, Karen Heimer, and Stacy Wittrock, "Neighborhood Disadvantage, Social Capital, Street Context, and Youth Violence," *Sociological Quarterly* (2006): 723–753.

40. See generally Bursik, "Social Disorganization and Theories of Crime and Delinquency," pp. 519–551.

41. William Spelman, "Abandoned Buildings: Magnets for Crime?" *Journal of Criminal Justice* 21 (1993): 481–493.

42. Keith Harries and Andrea Powell, "Juvenile Gun Crime and Social Stress: Baltimore, 1980–1990," *Urban Geography* 15 (1994): 45–63.

43. Ellen Kurtz, Barbara Koons, and Ralph Taylor, "Land Use, Physical Deterioration, Resident-Based Control, and Calls for Service on Urban Streetblocks," *Justice Quarterly* 15 (1998): 121–149.

44. Paul Stretesky, Amie Schuck, and Michael Hogan, "Space Matters: An Analysis of Poverty, Poverty Clustering, and Violent Crime," *Justice Quarterly* 21 (2004): 817–841.

45. Jeffrey Morenoff, Robert Sampson, and Stephen Raudenbush, "Neighborhood Inequality, Collective Efficacy, and the Spatial Dynamics of Urban Violence," *Criminology* 39 (2001): 517–560.

46. Gregory Squires and Charis Kubrin, "Privileged Places: Race, Uneven Development and the Geography of Opportunity in Urban America," *Urban Studies* 42 (2005): 47–68.

47. Karen Parker and Matthew Pruitt, "Poverty, Poverty Concentration, and Homicide," *Social Science Quarterly* 81 (2000): 555–582.

48. Karen Parker, "Industrial Shift, Polarized Labor Markets, and Urban Violence: Modeling the Dynamics between the Economic Transformation and Disaggregated Homicide," *Criminology* 42 (2004): 619–645.

49. Tim Wadsworth and Charis Kubrin, "Structural Factors and Black Interracial Homicide: A New Examination of the Causal Process," *Criminology* 42 (2004): 647–672.

50. Steven Messner, Lawrence Raffalovich, and Richard McMillan, "Economic Deprivation and Changes in Homicide Arrest Rates for White and Black Youths, 1967–1998: A National Time Series Analysis," *Criminology* 39 (2001): 591–614.

51. Steven Messner and Kenneth Tardiff, "Economic Inequality and Levels of Homicide: An Analysis of Urban Neighborhoods," *Criminology* 24 (1986): 297–317.

52. Adam Dobrin, Daniel Lee, and Jamie Price, "Neighborhood Structure Differences between Homicide Victims and Nonvictims," *Journal of Criminal Justice* 33 (2005): 137–143; G. David Curry and Irving Spergel, "Gang Homicide, Delinquency, and Community," *Criminology* 26 (1988): 381–407; Darrell Steffensmeier and Dana Haynie, "Gender, Structural Disadvantage, and Urban Crime: Do Macrosocial Variables Also Explain Female Offending Rates?" *Criminology* 38 (2000): 403–438; Richard McGahey, "Economic Conditions, Organization, and Urban Crime," in *Communities and Crime*, eds. Albert Reiss and Michael Tonry (Chicago: University of Chicago Press, 1986), pp. 231–270.

53. Kathleen Kingsbury, "The Next Crime Wave," *Time*, 11 December (2006).

54. Scott Menard and Delbert Elliott, "Self-Reported Offending, Maturational Reform, and the Easterlin Hypothesis," *Journal of Quantitative Criminology* 6 (1990): 237–268.

55. Elijah Anderson, *Streetwise: Race, Class and Change in an Urban Community* (Chicago: University of Chicago Press, 1990), pp. 243–244.

56. Matthew Lee and Terri Earnest, "Perceived Community Cohesion and Perceived Risk of Victimization: A Cross-National Analysis," *Justice Quarterly* 20 (2003): 131–158.

57. Joseph Schafer, Beth Huebner, and Timothy Bynum, "Fear of Crime and Criminal Victimization: Gender-Based Contrasts," *Journal of Criminal Justice* 34 (2006): 285–301.

58. Xu Yili, Mora Fiedler, and Karl Flaming, "Discovering the Impact of Community Policing," *The Journal of Research in Crime and Delinquency* 42 (2005): 147–186.

59. Stephanie Greenberg, "Fear and Its Relationship to Crime, Neighborhood Deterioration, and Informal Social Control," in *The Social Ecology of Crime*, eds. James Byrne and Robert Sampson (New York: Springer Verlag, 1985), pp. 47–62.

60. Pamela Wilcox, Neil Quisenberry, and Shayne Jones, "The Built Environment and Community Crime Risk Interpretation," *Journal of Research in Crime and Delinquency* 40 (2003): 322–345.

61. C. L. Storr, C.-Y. Chen, and J. C. Anthony, "'Unequal Opportunity': Neighborhood Disadvantage and the Chance to Buy Illegal Drugs," *Journal of Epidemiology and Community Health* 58 (2004): 231–238.

62. Pamela Wilcox Rountree and Kenneth Land, "Burglary Victimization, Perceptions of Crime Risk, and Routine Activities: A Multilevel Analysis across Seattle Neighborhoods and Census Tracts," *Journal of Research in Crime and Delinquency* 33 (1996): 147–180.

63. Tim Phillips and Philip Smith, "Emotional and Behavioural Responses to Everyday Incivility," *Journal of Sociology* 40 (2004): 378–399.

64. Wesley Skogan, "Fear of Crime and Neighborhood Change," in *Communities and Crime*, eds. Albert Reiss and Michael Tonry (Chicago: University of Chicago Press, 1986), pp. 191–232.

65. Margo Wilson and Martin Daly, "Life Expectancy, Economic Inequality, Homicide, and Reproductive Timing in Chicago Neighborhoods," *British Journal of Medicine* 314 (1997): 1,271–1,274.

66. Skogan, "Fear of Crime and Neighborhood Change."

67. Ibid.

68. Ralph Taylor and Jeanette Covington, "Community Structural Change and Fear of Crime," *Social Problems* 40 (1993): 374–392.

69. Ted Chiricos, Michael Hogan, and Marc Gertz, "Racial Composition of Neighborhood and Fear of Crime," *Criminology* 35 (1997): 107–131.

70. Ibid., p. 125.

71. Jodi Lane and James Meeker, "Social Disorganization Perceptions, Fear of Gang Crime, and Behavioral Precautions among Whites, Latinos, and Vietnamese," *Journal of Criminal Justice*, 32 (2004): 49–62.

72. Ted Chiricos, Ranee McEntire, and Marc Gertz, "Social Problems, Perceived Racial and Ethnic Composition of Neighborhood and Perceived Risk of Crime," *Social Problems* 48 (2001): 322–341.

73. G. David Curry and Irving Spergel, "Gang Homicide, Delinquency, and Community," *Criminology* 26 (1988): 381–407.

74. Lawrence Rosenthal, "Gang Loitering and Race," *Journal of Criminal Law and Criminology* 91 (2000): 99–160.

75. Catherine E. Ross, John Mirowsky, and Shana Pribesh, "Powerlessness and the Amplification of Threat: Neighborhood Disadvantage, Disorder, and Mistrust," *American Sociological Review* 66 (2001): 568–580.

76. Anderson, *Streetwise: Race, Class, and Change in an Urban Community*, p. 245.

77. William Terrill and Michael Reisig, "Neighborhood Context and Police Use of Force," *Journal of Research in Crime and Delinquency* 40 (2003): 291–321.

78. Bridget Freisthler, Elizabeth Lascala, Paul Gruenewald, and Andrew Treno, "An Examination of Drug Activity: Effects of Neighborhood Social Organization on the Development of Drug Distribution Systems" *Substance Use and Misuse*, 40 (2005): 671–686.

79. Finn-Aage Esbensen and David Huizinga, "Community Structure and Drug Use: From a Social Disorganization Perspective," *Justice Quarterly* 7 (1990): 691–709.

80. Micere Keels, Greg Duncan, Stefanie Deluca, Ruby Mendenhall, and James Rosenbaum, "Fifteen Years Later: Can Residential Mobility Programs Provide a Long-Term Escape from Neighborhood Segregation, Crime, and Poverty?" *Demography* 42 (2005): 51–72.

81. Wesley Skogan, *Disorder and Decline: Crime and the Spiral of Decay in American Neighborhoods* (New York: Free Press, 1990), pp. 15–35.

82. Robert Bursik and Harold Grasmick, "Decomposing Trends in Community Careers in Crime," paper presented at the annual meeting of the American Society of Criminology, Baltimore, November 1990.

83. Ralph Taylor and Jeanette Covington, "Neighborhood Changes in Ecology and Violence," *Criminology* 26 (1988): 553–589.

84. Leo Scheurman and Solomon Kobrin, "Community Careers in Crime," in *Communities and Crime*, eds. Albert Reiss and Michael Tonry (Chicago: University of Chicago Press, 1986), pp. 67–100.

85. Ibid.

86. Allen Liska and Paul Bellair, "Violent-Crime Rates and Racial Composition: Convergence over Time," *American Journal of Sociology* 101 (1995): 578–610.

87. Patricia McCall and Karen Parker, "A Dynamic Model of Racial Competition, Racial Inequality, and Interracial Violence," *Sociological Inquiry* 75 (2005): 273–294.

88. Janet Heitgerd and Robert Bursik, "Extracommunity Dynamics and the Ecology of Delinquency," *American Journal of Sociology* 92 (1987): 775–787.

89. Steven Barkan and Steven Cohn, "Why Whites Favor Spending More Money to Fight Crime: The Role of Racial Prejudice," *Social Problems* 52 (2005): 300–314.

90. Jeffrey Michael Cancino, "The Utility of Social Capital and Collective Efficacy: Social Control Policy in Nonmetropolitan Settings," *Criminal Justice Policy Review* 16 (2005): 287–318; Chris Gibson, Jihong Zhao, Nicholas Lovrich, and Michael Gaffney, "Social Integration, Individual Perceptions of Collective Efficacy, and Fear of Crime in Three Cities," *Justice Quarterly* 19 (2002): 537–564.

91. Robert J. Sampson and Stephen W. Raudenbush, *Disorder in Urban Neighborhoods: Does It Lead to Crime?* (Washington, DC: National Institute of Justice, 2001).

92. Andrea Altschuler, Carol Somkin, and Nancy Adler, "Local Services and Amenities, Neighborhood Social Capital, and Health," *Social Science and Medicine* 59 (2004): 1,219–1,230.

93. Michael Reisig and Jeffrey Michael Cancino, "Incivilities in Nonmetropolitan Communities: The Effects of Structural Constraints, Social Conditions, and Crime," *Journal of Criminal Justice* 32 (2004): 15–29.

94. Robert Sampson, Jeffrey Morenoff, and Felton Earls, "Beyond Social Capital: Spatial Dynamics of Collective Efficacy for Children," *American Sociological Review* 64 (1999): 633–660.

95. Donald Black, "Social Control as a Dependent Variable," in *Toward a General Theory of Social Control*, ed. D. Black (Orlando: Academic Press, 1990).

96. Jennifer Beyers, John Bates, Gregory Pettit, and Kenneth Dodge, "Neighborhood Structure, Parenting Processes, and the Development of Youths' Externalizing Behaviors: A Multilevel Analysis," *American Journal of Community Psychology* 31 (2003): 35–53.

97. Ralph Taylor, "Social Order and Disorder of Street Blocks and Neighborhoods: Ecology, Microecology, and the Systemic Model of Social Disorganization," *Journal of Research in Crime and Delinquency* 34 (1997): 113–155.

98. April Pattavina, James Byrne, and Luis Garcia, "An Examination of Citizen Involvement in Crime Prevention in High-Risk versus Low- to Moderate-Risk Neighborhoods," *Crime and Delinquency* 52 (2006): 203–231.

99. Steven Messner, Eric Baumer, and Richard Rosenfeld, "Dimensions of Social Capital and Rates of Criminal Homicide," *American Sociological Review* 69 (2004): 882–905.

100. Paul Bellair, "Informal Surveillance and Street Crime: A Complex Relationship," *Criminology* 38 (2000): 137–170.

101. Skogan, *Disorder and Decline*.

102. Robert Sampson and W. Byron Groves, "Community Structure and Crime: Testing Social Disorganization Theory," *American Journal of Sociology* 94 (1989): 774–802; Denise Gottfredson, Richard McNeill, and Gary Gottfredson, "Social Area Influences on Delinquency: A Multilevel Analysis," *Journal of Research in Crime and Delinquency* 28 (1991): 197–206.

103. Jodi Eileen Morris, Rebekah Levine Coley, and Daphne Hernandez, "Out-of-School Care and Problem Behavior Trajectories among Low-Income Adolescents: Individual, Family, and Neighborhood," *Child Development* 75 (2004): 948–965.

104. Ruth Triplett, Randy Gainey, and Ivan Sun, "Institutional Strength, Social Control, and Neighborhood Crime Rates," *Theoretical Criminology* 7 (2003): 439–467; Fred Markowitz, Paul Bellair, Allen Liska, and Jianhong Liu, "Extending Social Disorganization Theory: Modeling the Relationships between Cohesion, Disorder, and Fear," *Criminology* 39 (2001): 293–320.

105. Robert Bursik and Harold Grasmick, "The Multiple Layers of Social Disorganization," paper presented at the annual meeting of the American Society of Criminology, New Orleans, November 1992.

106. George Capowich, "The Conditioning Effects of Neighborhood Ecology on Burglary Victimization," *Criminal Justice and Behavior* 30 (2003): 39–62.

107. Ruth Peterson, Lauren Krivo, and Mark Harris, "Disadvantage and Neighborhood Violent Crime: Do Local Institutions Matter?" *Journal of Research in Crime and Delinquency* 37 (2000): 31–63.

108. Maria Velez, "The Role of Public Social Control in Urban Neighborhoods: A Multi-Level Analysis of Victimization Risk," *Criminology* 39 (2001): 837–864.

109. Velez, Krivo, and Peterson, "Structural Inequality and Homicide."

110. David Klinger, "Negotiating Order in Patrol Work: An Ecological Theory of Police Response to Deviance," *Criminology* 35 (1997): 277–306.

111. Rodney Stark, "Deviant Places: A Theory of the Ecology of Crime," *Criminology* 25 (1987): 893–911.

112. Robert Kane, "Compromised Police Legitimacy as a Predictor of Violent Crime in Structurally Disadvantaged Communities," *Criminology* 43 (2005): 469–498.

113. Robert Sampson, "Neighborhood and Community," *New Economy* 11 (2004): 106–113.

114. Robert Bursik and Harold Grasmick, "Economic Deprivation and Neighborhood Crime Rates, 1960–1980," *Law and Society Review* 27 (1993): 263–278.

115. Delbert Elliott, William Julius Wilson, David Huizinga, Robert Sampson, Amanda Elliott, and Bruce Rankin, "The Effects of Neighborhood Disadvantage on Adolescent Development," *Journal of Research in Crime and Delinquency* 33 (1996): 389–426.

116. James DeFronzo, "Welfare and Homicide," *Journal of Research in Crime and Delinquency* 34 (1997): 395–406.

117. John Worrall, "Reconsidering the Relationship between Welfare Spending and Serious Crime: A Panel Data Analysis with Implications for Social Support Theory," *Justice Quarterly* 22 (2005): 364–391.

118. Robert Sampson, Jeffrey Morenoff, and Felton Earls, "Beyond Social Capital: Spatial Dynamics of Collective Efficacy for Children," *American Sociological Review* 64 (1999): 633–660.

119. Thomas McNulty, "Assessing the Race-Violence Relationship at the Macro Level: The Assumption of Racial Invariance and the Problem of Restricted Distribution," *Criminology* 39 (2001): 467–490.

120. Delbert Elliott, William Julius Wilson, David Huizinga, Robert Sampson, Amanda Elliott, and Bruce Rankin, "The Effects of Neighborhood Disadvantage on Adolescent Development," *Journal of Research in Crime and Delinquency* 33 (1996): 389–426 at 414.

121. Patrick Sharkey, "Navigating Dangerous Streets: The Sources and Consequences of Street Efficacy," *American Sociological Review* 71 (2006): 826–846.

122. Ibid.

123. Eric Silver and Lisa Miller, "Sources of Informal Social Control in Chicago Neighborhoods," *Criminology* 42 (2004): 551–585.

124. Bursik and Grasmick, "Economic Deprivation and Neighborhood Crime Rates, 1960–1980."

125. Robert Sampson and W. Byron Groves, "Community Structure and Crime: Testing Social Disorganization Theory," *American Journal of Sociology* 94 (1989): 774–802; Denise Gottfredson, Richard McNeill, and Gary Gottfredson, "Social Area Influences on Delinquency: A Multilevel Analysis," *Journal of Research in Crime and Delinquency* 28 (1991): 197–206.

126. Peterson, Krivo, and Harris, "Disadvantage and Neighborhood Violent Crime."

127. John Braithwaite, "Poverty Power, White-Collar Crime, and the Paradoxes of Criminological Theory," *Australian and New Zealand Journal of Criminology* 24 (1991): 40–58.

128. Wilson and Daly, "Life Expectancy, Economic Inequality, Homicide, and Reproductive Timing in Chicago Neighborhoods."

129. Judith Blau and Peter Blau, "The Cost of Inequality: Metropolitan Structure and Violent Crime," *American Sociological Review* 147 (1982): 114–129.

130. P. M. Krueger, S. A. Huie, R. G. Rogers, and R. A. Hummer, "Neighborhoods and Homicide Mortality: An Analysis of Race/Ethnic Differences," *Journal of Epidemiology and Community Health* 58 (2004): 223–230.

131. Gary LaFree and Kriss Drass, "The Effect of Changes in Intraracial Income Inequality and Educational Attainment on Changes in Arrest Rates for African Americans and Whites, 1957 to 1990," *American Sociological Review* 61 (1996): 614–634; Taylor and Covington, "Neighborhood Changes in Ecology and Violence," p. 582; Richard Block, "Community Environment and Violent Crime," *Criminology* 17 (1979): 46–57; Robert Sampson, "Structural Sources of Variation in Race-Age-Specific Rates of Offending across Major U.S. Cities," *Criminology* 23 (1985): 647–673; Richard Rosenfeld, "Urban Crime Rates: Effects of Inequality, Welfare Dependency, Region and Race," in *The Social Ecology of Crime*, eds. James Byrne and Robert Sampson (New York: Springer Verlag, 1985), pp. 116–130.

132. Sang-Weon Kim and William Pridemore, "Poverty, Socioeconomic Change, Institutional Anomie, and Homicide," *Social Science Quarterly* 86 (2005): 1377–1398.

133. Robert Merton, *Social Theory and Social Structure*, enlarged ed. (New York: Free Press, 1968).

134. For an analysis, see Richard Hilbert, "Durkheim and Merton on Anomie: An Unexplored Contrast in Its Derivatives," *Social Problems* 36 (1989): 242–256.

135. Ibid., p. 243.

136. Albert Cohen, "The Sociology of the Deviant Act: Anomie Theory and Beyond," *American Sociological Review* 30 (1965): 5–14.

137. Robert Agnew, "The Contribution of Social Psychological Strain Theory to the Explanation of Crime and Delinquency," in *Advances in Criminological Theory*, vol. 6, *The Legacy of Anomie*, eds. Freda Adler and William Laufer (New Brunswick, NJ: Transaction Press, 1995), pp. 111–122.

138. These criticisms are articulated in Messner and Rosenfeld, *Crime and the American Dream*, p. 60.

139. Messner and Rosenfeld, *Crime and the American Dream*.

140. Ibid., p. 61.

141. Steven Messner and Richard Rosenfeld, "An Institutional-Anomie Theory of the Social Distribution of Crime," paper presented at the annual meeting of the American Society of Criminology, Phoenix, November 1993.

142. Lisa Mufti, "Advancing Institutional Anomie Theory," *International Journal of Offender Therapy and Comparative Criminology* 50 (2006): 630–653.

143. Stephen Cernkovich, Peggy Giordano, and Jennifer Rudolph, "Race, Crime, and the American Dream," *Journal of Research in Crime and Delinquency* 37 (2000): 131–170.

144. Jon Gunnar Bernburg, "Anomie, Social Change, and Crime: A Theoretical Examination of Institutional-Anomie Theory," *British Journal of Criminology* 42 (2002): 729–743.

145. John Hagan, Gerd Hefler, Gabriele Classen, Klaus Boehnke, and Hans Merkens, "Subterranean Sources of Subcultural Delinquency Beyond the American Dream," *Criminology* 36 (1998): 309–340.

146. Jukka Savolainen, "Inequality, Welfare State and Homicide: Further Support for the Institutional Anomie Theory," *Criminology* 38 (2000): 1,021–1,042.

147. Kate Pickett, Jessica Mokherjee, and Richard Wilkinson, "Adolescent Birth Rates, Total Homicides, and Income Inequality in Rich Countries," *American Journal of Public Health* 95 (2005): 1,181–1,183.

148. Robert Agnew, "Foundation for a General Strain Theory of Crime and Delinquency," *Criminology* 30 (1992): 47–87.

149. Stephen Baron, "Street Youth, Strain Theory, and Crime," *Journal of Criminal Justice* 34 (2006): 209–223.

150. Cesar Rebellon, "Reconsidering the Broken Homes/Delinquency Relationship and Exploring Its Mediating Mechanism(s)," *Criminology* 40 (2002): 103–135.

151. G. Roger Jarjoura, "The Conditional Effect of Social Class on the Dropout–Delinquency Relationship," *Journal of Research in Crime and Delinquency* 33 (1996): 232–255.

152. Robert Agnew and Helene Raskin White, "An Empirical Test of General Strain Theory," *Criminology* 30 (1992): 475–499; John Hoffman and Alan Miller, "A Latent Variable Analysis of General Strain Theory," *Journal of Quantitative Criminology* 13 (1997): 111–113; Raymond Paternoster and Paul Mazerolle, "General Strain Theory and Delinquency: A Replication and Extension," *Journal of Research in Crime and Delinquency* 31 (1994): 235–263.

153. Ronald Simons, Yi Fu Chen, and Eric Stewart, "Incidents of Discrimination and Risk for Delinquency: A Longitudinal Test of Strain Theory with an African American Sample," *Justice Quarterly* 20 (2003): 827–854.

154. Robert Agnew, "Experienced, Vicarious, and Anticipated Strain: An Exploratory Study on Physical Victimization and Delinquency," *Justice Quarterly* 19 (2002): 603–633.

155. Carter Hay and Michelle Evans, "Violent Victimization and Involvement in Delinquency: Examining Predictions from General Strain Theory," *Journal of Criminal Justice* 34 (2006): 261–274,

156. Sherod Thaxton and Robert Agnew, "The Nonlinear Effects of Parental and Teacher Attachment on Delinquency: Disentangling Strain from Social Control Explanations," *Justice Quarterly* 21 (2004): 763–791.

157. Stacy De Coster and Lisa Kort-Butler, "How General Is General Strain Theory?" *Journal of Research in Crime and Delinquency* 43 (2006): 297–325.

158. Paul Mazerolle and Alex Piquero, "Linking General Strain with Anger: Investigating the Instrumental, Escapist, and Violent Adaptations to Strain," paper presented at the annual meeting of the American Society of Criminology, Boston, November 1995.

159. Paul Mazerolle, Velmer Burton, Francis Cullen, T. David Evans, and Gary Payne, "Strain, Anger, and Delinquent Adaptations Specifying General Strain Theory," *Journal of Criminal Justice* 28 (2000): 89–101; Paul Mazerolle and Alex Piquero, "Violent Responses to Strain: An Examination of Conditioning Influences," *Violence and Victimization* 12 (1997): 323–345.

160. George E. Capowich, Paul Mazerolle, and Alex Piquero, "General Strain Theory, Situational Anger, and Social Networks: An Assessment of Conditioning Influences," *Journal of Criminal Justice* 29 (2001): 445–461.

161. Carter Hay and Michelle Evans, "Violent Victimization and Involvement in Delinquency: Examining Predictions from General Strain Theory."

162. Robert Agnew, Timothy Brezina, John Paul Wright, and Francis T. Cullen, "Strain, Personality Traits, and Delinquency: Extending General Strain Theory," *Criminology* 40 (2002): 43–71.

163. Wan-Ning Bao, Ain Haas, and Yijun Pi, "Life Strain, Coping, and Delinquency in the People's Republic of China," *International Journal of Offender Therapy and Comparative Criminology* 51 (2007): 9–24.

164. Timothy Brezina, "The Functions of Aggression: Violent Adaptations to Interpersonal Violence," paper presented at the annual meeting of the American Society of Criminology, San Diego, November 1997.

165. Agnew, Brezina, Wright, and Cullen, "Strain, Personality Traits, and Delinquency"; Robert Agnew, "Stability and Change in Crime over the Life Course: A Strain Theory Explanation," in *Advances in Criminological Theory*, vol. 7, *Developmental Theories of Crime and Delinquency*, ed. Terence Thornberry (New Brunswick, NJ: Transaction Books, 1995), pp. 113–137.

166. Lawrence Wu, "Effects of Family Instability, Income, and Income Instability on the Risk of Premarital Birth," *American Sociological Review* 61 (1996): 386–406.

167. Anthony Walsh, "Behavior Genetics and Anomie/Strain Theory," *Criminology* 38 (2000): 1,075–1,108.

168. Michael Ostrowsky and Steven Messner, "Explaining Crime for a Young Adult Population: An Application of General Strain Theory," *Journal of Criminal Justice* 33 (2005): 463–476.

169. Lee Ann Slocum, Sally Simpson, and Douglas Smith, "Strained Lives and Crime: Examining Intra-Individual Variation in Strain and Offending in a Sample of Incarcerated Women," *Criminology* 43 (2005): 1,067–1,110.

170. Lisa Broidy, "A Test of General Strain Theory," *Criminology* 39 (2001): 9–36.

171. Robert Agnew and Timothy Brezina, "Relational Problems with Peers, Gender and Delinquency," *Youth and Society* 29 (1997): 84–111.

172. John Hoffmann and S. Susan Su, "The Conditional Effects of Stress on Delinquency and Drug Use: A Strain Theory in Assessment of Sex Differences," *Journal of Research in Crime and Delinquency* 34 (1997): 46–78.

173. Lisa Broidy, "The Role of Gender in General Strain Theory," paper presented at the annual meeting of the American Society of Criminology, Boston, November 1995.

174. Lisa Broidy and Robert Agnew, "Gender and Crime: A General Strain Theory Perspective," *Journal of Research in Crime and Delinquency* 34 (1997): 275–306.

175. Robbin Ogle, Daniel Maier-Katkin, and Thomas Bernard, "A Theory of Homicidal Behavior among Women," *Criminology* 33 (1995): 173–193.

176. Nicole Leeper Piquero and Miriam Sealock, "Gender and General Strain Theory: A Preliminary Test of Broidy and Agnew's Gender/GST Hypothesis," *Justice Quarterly* 21 (2004): 125–158.

177. Teresa LaGrange and Robert Silverman, "Investigating the Interdependence of Strain and Self-Control," *Canadian Journal of Criminology and Criminal Justice* 45 (2003): 431–464.

178. Christopher Browning, Seth Feinberg, and Robert D. Dietz, "The Paradox of Social Organization: Networks, Collective Efficacy, and Violent Crime in Urban Neighborhoods," *Social Forces* 83 (2004): 503–534.

179. Thorsten Sellin, *Culture Conflict and Crime*, Bulletin No. 41 (New York: Social Science Research Council, 1938).

180. Ibid., p. 22.

181. Ibid., p. 29.

182. Ibid., p. 68.

183. Walter Miller, "Lower-Class Culture as a Generating Milieu of Gang Delinquency," *Journal of Social Issues* 14 (1958): 5–19.

184. Ibid., pp. 14–17.

185. Fred Markowitz and Richard Felson, "Social-Demographic Attitudes and Violence," *Criminology* 36 (1998): 117–138.

186. Jeffrey Fagan, *Adolescent Violence: A View from the Street*, NIJ Research Preview (Washington, DC: National Institute of Justice, 1998).

187. Albert Cohen, *Delinquent Boys* (New York: Free Press, 1955).

188. Ibid., p. 25.

189. Ibid., p. 28.

190. Ibid.

191. Clarence Schrag, *Crime and Justice American Style* (Washington, DC: U.S. Government Printing Office, 1971), p. 74.

192. Cohen, *Delinquent Boys*, p. 30.

193. Ibid., p. 31.

194. Ibid., p. 133.

195. J. Johnstone, "Social Class, Social Areas, and Delinquency," *Sociology and Social Research* 63 (1978): 49–72; Joseph Harry, "Social Class and Delinquency: One More Time," *Sociological Quarterly* 15 (1974): 294–301.

196. Richard Cloward and Lloyd Ohlin, *Delinquency and Opportunity* (New York: Free Press, 1960).

197. Ibid., p. 7.

198. Ibid., p. 85.

199. Ibid., p. 171.

200. Ibid., p. 23.

201. Ibid., p. 73.

202. Ibid., p. 24.

203. Finn-Aage Esbensen and David Huizinga, "Gangs, Drugs and Delinquency in a Survey of Urban Youth," *Criminology* 31 (1993): 565–587.

204. For a general criticism, see Kornhauser, *Social Sources of Delinquency*.

205. Charles Tittle, "Social Class and Criminal Behavior: A Critique of the Theoretical Foundations," *Social Forces* 62 (1983): 334–358.

206. James Q. Wilson and Richard Herrnstein, *Crime and Human Nature* (New York: Simon & Schuster, 1985).

207. Kenneth Polk and F. Lynn Richmond, "Those Who Fail," in *Schools and Delinquency*, eds. Kenneth Polk and Walter Schafer (Englewood Cliffs, NJ: Prentice Hall, 1974), p. 67.

208. Kathleen Maguire and Ann Pastore, *Sourcebook of Criminal Justice Statistics, 1996* (Washington, DC: U.S. Government Printing Office, 1996), pp. 150–166.

209. James DeFronzo, "Welfare and Burglary," *Crime and Delinquency* 42 (1996): 223–230.

210. Solomon Kobrin, "The Chicago Area Project—25-Year Assessment," *Annals of of the American Academy of Political and Social Science* 322 (1959): 20–29.

211. Community Capacity Development Office website: www.ojp.usdoj.gov/ccdo/nonflash .html (accessed April 23, 2007).

Social Process Theories

CHAPTER OBJECTIVES

1. Be familiar with the concept of socialization
2. Discuss the effect of schools, family, and friends on crime
3. Be able to discuss the differences between the concepts of social learning, social control, and social reaction
4. Be familiar with the concept of differential association
5. Be able to discuss what is meant by a definition toward criminality
6. Understand the concept of neutralization
7. Be able to discuss the relationship between self-concept and crime
8. Know the elements of the social bond
9. Describe the labeling process and how it leads to criminal careers
10. Be familiar with the concepts of primary and secondary deviance
11. Show how the process of labeling leads to criminal careers

Teenager Genarlow Wilson was an honor student and a gifted athlete, attractive, popular, *and outgoing. He had a 3.2 grade point average, was all-conference in football, voted 11th-grade prom prince, and his senior year was capped off with a special honor when he was elected Douglas County High's first-ever homecoming king. Genarlow is now serving a sentence in a Georgia prison. His crime: Engaging in consensual sex when he was 17 years old with a girl two years younger. Wilson was convicted of* aggravated child molestation even though he and the girl were both minors at the time and the sex was clearly consensual.

Wilson engaged in oral sex with the girl during a wild party involving a bunch of kids, marijuana, and alcohol, all captured on videotape. The tapes made it clear the sex was voluntary and not coerced. Though the prosecutor favored leniency, Wilson refused a plea bargain because it would mean admitting he was a sexual predator, a charge he vehemently denied and that no one, including the prosecutor, believed was true. Ironically, if the couple had had sexual intercourse, it would have been considered a misdemeanor, but since oral sex was involved, the crime was considered a felony. An additional irony in the case: After Wilson was convicted the Georgia law was changed, making consensual oral sex between minors a misdemeanor as well. But the new law did not apply retroactively. Instead of using his college scholarship, Wilson was sent to prison.[1]

Genarlow Wilson's case shows how social interactions and process shape crime. He did not consider himself a criminal and even in court denied his culpability. Here is an exchange he had with the prosecutor during the trial:

Genarlow: *. . . Aggravated child molestation is when like a 60-year–some old man likes messing with 10-year-old girls. I'm 17, the girl was 15, sir. You call that child molestation, two years apart?*
Barker: *I didn't write the law.*
Genarlow: *I didn't write the law, either.*
Barker: *That's what the law states is aggravated child molestation, Mr. Wilson, not me.*
Genarlow: *Well, sir, I understand you're just doing your job. I don't blame you. . . . But do you think it's fair? . . . Would you want your son on trial for something like this?[2]*

Should Genarlow Wilson have been labeled a "sexual predator"? If he had engaged in a different type of sex act, the case would never have been made public. The law itself was designed to protect young girls from being abused by much older men, and not members of their own peer group with whom they were socializing freely. And if the act itself was so bad, why was it decriminalized a short time later? The bottom line: if the party had occurred a few months later, Genarlow Wilson would have been playing football at Georgia State University, and not sent to Georgia State Prison!

Genarlow Wilson was in fact labeled a sexual predator and sent to prison because those in power, who define the law and control its process, decided that his behavior constituted a serious crime, a felony. They could have just as easily ignored the action and let him go. It would have been just another case of teens behaving badly. But even powerful decision makers can change their minds and reassess labels. On June 9, 2007, a Georgia judge threw out Genarlow's 10-year sentence and amended it to misdemeanor aggravated child molestation with a 12-month term, plus credit for time served. Under the ruling, Genarlow, who has been behind bars for more than two years, would not be required to register as a sex offender. In making his decision, the Georgia judge stated:

> If this court or any court cannot recognize the injustice of what has occurred here, then our court system has lost sight of the goal our judicial system has always strived to accomplish . . . justice being served in a fair and equal manner. . . . The fact that Genarlow Wilson has spent two years in prison for what is now classified as a misdemeanor, and without assistance from this court, will spend eight more years in prison, is a grave miscarriage of justice.[3]

So now Genarlow Wilson, imprisoned for years after he was labeled as a dangerous sexual predator, has been relabeled as a *victim* of the same justice process that had destroyed his life and reputation.

SOCIALIZATION AND CRIME

To some criminologists, an individual's relationship with critical elements of the social process is the key to understanding the onset and continuation of a criminal career. They believe that criminality is a function of socialization, the interactions people have with various organizations, institutions, and processes of society. Most people are influenced by their family relationships, peer group associations, educational experiences, and interactions with authority figures, including teachers, employers, and agents of the justice system. If these relationships are positive and supportive, people can succeed within the rules of society; if these relationships are dysfunctional and destructive, conventional success may be impossible, and criminal solutions may become a feasible alternative. Taken together, this view of crime is referred to as social process theory.

The influence of social process theories has endured because the relationship between social class and crime is still uncertain. Most residents of inner-city areas refrain from criminal activity, and few of those who do commit crimes remain persistent chronic offenders into their adulthood. If poverty were the sole cause of crime, then indigent adults would be as criminal as indigent teenagers. The association between economic status and crime has been called problematic because class position alone cannot explain crime rates.[4] Today, more than 37 million Americans live below the poverty line. Even if we were to assume that all criminals come from the lower class—which they do not—it is evident that the great majority of the most indigent Americans do not commit criminal acts even though they may have a great economic incentive to do so. Relatively few people living in the most deteriorated areas become persistent offenders, and most who do desist from crime despite the continuing pressure of poverty and social decay. Some other force, then, must be at work to explain why the majority of at-risk individuals do not become persistent criminal offenders and to explain why some who have no economic or social reason to commit crime do so anyway.

Criminologists have long studied the critical elements of socialization to determine how they contribute to a burgeoning criminal career. Prominent among these elements are the family, the peer group, and the school.

Family Relations

For some time, family relationships have been considered a major determinant of behavior.[5] In fact, there is abundant evidence that parenting factors, such as the ability to communicate and to provide proper discipline, may play a critical role in determining whether people misbehave as children and even later as adults.

Youth who grow up in households characterized by conflict and tension, and where there is a lack of familial love and support, are susceptible to the crime-promoting forces in the environment.[6] Even those children living in so-called high-crime areas will be better able to resist the temptations of the streets if they receive fair discipline, care, and support from parents who provide them with strong, positive role models. Nonetheless, living in a disadvantaged neighborhood places terrific strain on family functioning, especially in single-parent families that experience social isolation from relatives, friends, and neighbors. Children who are raised within such distressed families are at risk for delinquency.[7]

The relationship between family structure and crime is critical when the high rates of divorce and single parents are considered. Table 7.1 shows that today about 32 percent of children live in single-family homes and that there are significant racial differences in family structure.[8] Family disruption or change can have a long-lasting impact on children. Research conducted in both the United States and abroad shows that children raised in homes with one or both parents absent may be prone to antisocial behavior.[9] It is not surprising that the number of single-parent households in the population is significantly related to arrest rates.[10]

The Effects of Divorce Why is the effect of divorce or separation so devastating? Even if single mothers (or fathers) can make

Table 7.1 Children in Single-Parent Families, by Race

United States	
Non-Hispanic White	23%
Black or African American	65%
American Indian	49%
Asian and Pacific Islander	17%
Hispanic or Latino	36%
Total	32%

Source: Annie E. Casey Foundation, Kids Count, 2006, www.kidscount.org/sld/compare_results.jsp?i=722 (accessed June 9, 2007).

up for the loss of a second parent, it is difficult to do so and the chances of failure increase. Single parents may find it difficult to provide adequate supervision, exposing children to the negative effects of antisocial peers.[11] Poorly supervised youths may be more prone to act impulsively and are therefore less able to employ self-control to restrain their activities.[12]

Living in a single-parent household has been linked to educational failure. Children living with a single parent may receive less encouragement and less help with schoolwork. Poor school achievement and limited educational aspirations have been associated with delinquent behavior. Also, because they are receiving less attention as a result of having just one parent, these children may be more prone to rebellious acts, such as running away and truancy.[13] Children in two-parent households, on the other hand, are more likely to want to go on to college than kids in single-parent homes.[14]

Because their incomes may decrease substantially in the aftermath of marital breakup, some divorced mothers are forced to move to residences in deteriorated neighborhoods that may place children at risk of crime and drug abuse. In poor neighborhoods single parents cannot call upon neighborhood resources to take up the burden of controlling children, and, as a result, a greater burden is placed on families to provide adequate supervision.[15] Some groups (i.e., Hispanics, Asians) have been raised in cultures where divorce is rare and parents have less experience in developing child-rearing practices that buffer the effects of family breakup on adolescent problem behavior.[16]

When a mother remarries, it does not seem to mitigate the effects of divorce on youth. Children living with a stepparent exhibit as many problems as youth in single-parent families and considerably more problems than those who are living with both biological parents.[17]

Family Deviance A number of studies have found that parental deviance has a powerful influence on children's future behavior. Kids look up to and are influenced by their parents, so it comes as no surprise that they are willing to model their behavior along parental lines.[18] When parents drink, take drugs, and commit crimes, the effects can be both devastating and long term. In fact, research shows the effect is intergenerational: the children of deviant parents produce delinquent children themselves.[19]

Some of the most important data on the influence of parental deviance were gathered by British criminologist David Farrington, whose longitudinal research data were gathered in the long-term Cambridge Study in Delinquent Development (CSDD). Some of the most important results include:

- A significant number of delinquent youths have criminal fathers. About 8 percent of the sons of noncriminal fathers became chronic offenders, compared to 37 percent of youths with criminal fathers.[20]

- School yard bullying may be both inter- and intragenerational. Bullies have children who bully others, and these "second-generation bullies" grow up to become the fathers of children who are also bullies (see Chapter 9 for more on bullying in the school yard).[21] Thus, one family may have a grandfather, father, and son who are or were school yard bullies.[22]

- Children whose parents go to prison are much more likely to be at risk for delinquency than children of nonincarcerated parents.[23]

> **connections**
>
> Sampson and Laub's research will be discussed more fully in Chapter 9. Although deviant parents may encourage offending, Sampson and Laub believe that life experiences can either encourage crime-prone people to offend or conversely aid them in their return to a conventional lifestyle.

Parental Efficacy While poor parenting and parental deviance may increase exposure to criminality, children raised by parents who have excellent parenting skills, who are supportive and can effectively control their children in a noncoercive fashion, are more insulated from crime-producing forces in society.[24] Effective parenting can help neutralize the effect of both individual (e.g., emotional problems) and social (e.g., delinquent peers) forces that promote delinquent behaviors.[25] Even young people who are at risk to delinquency because of personality problems or neurological syndromes, such as ADHD, have a much better prognosis if they receive effective, supportive parenting.[26]

Research shows that antisocial behavior will be reduced if parents provide the type of structure that integrates children into families, while giving them the ability to assert their individuality and regulate their own behavior—a phenomenon referred to as **parental efficacy**.[27] In some cultures emotional support from the mother is critical, whereas in others the father's support remains the key factor.[28]

A number of studies support the link between the quality of family life and delinquency. Children who feel inhibited with their parents and refuse to discuss important issues with them are more likely to engage in deviant activities. Children who report having troubled home lives also exhibit lower levels of self-esteem and are more prone to antisocial behaviors.[29] One reason for poor communication is parents who rely on authoritarian disciplinary practices, holding a "my way or the

Children raised by parents who have excellent parenting skills, who are supportive, and who can effectively control their children in a noncoercive fashion are more insulated from crime-producing forces in society. Effective parenting can help neutralize the effect of both individual and social forces that promote delinquent behaviors. Parental efficacy means that parents provide the type of structure that integrates children into families, while giving them the ability to assert their individuality and regulate their own behavior.

highway" orientation. Telling kids that "as long as you live in my house you will obey my rules" does little to improve communications and may instead produce kids who are rebellious and crime prone.[30]

While the prevailing wisdom is that bad parents produce bad kids, some recent research by David Huh and his colleagues found that the relationship may not be what it seems. To find out what he discovered, read Exhibit 7.1.

Child Abuse and Crime There is also a suspected link between crime and child abuse, neglect, and sexual abuse.[31] Numerous studies conducted in the United States and abroad show that there is a significant association between child maltreatment and serious self-reported and official delinquency, even when taking into account gender, race, and class.[32] Children, both males and females, black or white, who experience abuse, neglect, or sexual abuse are believed to be more crime prone and suffer from other social problems such as depression, suicide attempts, substance abuse, and self-injurious behaviors.[33]

Educational Experience

The educational process and adolescent achievement in school have been linked to criminality. Studies show that children who do poorly in school, lack educational motivation, and feel alienated are the most likely to engage in criminal acts.[34] Children who fail in school have been found to offend more frequently than those who are successful in school. These children commit more serious and violent offenses and persist in their offending into adulthood.[35]

Schools contribute to criminality when they label problem youths and set them apart from conventional society. One way in which schools perpetuate this stigmatization is the "track system," which identifies some students as college bound and others as academic underachievers or potential dropouts.[36] Those children placed in tracks labeled advanced placement, college prep, or honors will develop positive self-images and achievement motivation, whereas those assigned to lower level or general courses of study may believe academic achievement is closed to someone of their limited skills.

Another significant educational problem is that many students leave high school without gaining a diploma. According to a recent report by the nonprofit Urban Institute, the national graduation rate is 68 percent, with nearly one-third of all public high school students failing to graduate. Institute researchers found tremendous racial gaps in graduation rates. Students from historically disadvantaged minority groups (American Indian, Latino, African American) have little more than a 50-50 chance of finishing high school with a diploma; by comparison, graduation rates for whites and Asians are 75 and 77 percent nationally.[37] These results are disturbing because research indicates that many school dropouts, especially those who have been expelled, face a significant chance of entering a criminal career.[38] In contrast, doing well in school and developing attachments to teachers have been linked to crime resistance.[39]

Peer Relations

Psychologists have long recognized that the peer group has a powerful effect on human conduct and can have a dramatic influence on decision making and behavior choices.[40] Peer influence on behavior has been recorded in different cultures and may be a universal norm.[41]

Though experts have long debated the exact relationship between peer group interaction and delinquency, there is little question that some kids are particularly susceptible to peer influence.[42] The more antisocial the peer group, the more likely its members will engage in delinquency; nondelinquent friends will help moderate delinquency.[43] One recent study found that kids involved in delinquency are five times more likely than nonoffenders to associate with delinquent peers.[44]

While there is agreement that the association between peers and criminality exists, there is some debate over the path of the relationship:

■ Delinquent friends cause law-abiding youth to get in trouble. Kids who fall in with a bad crowd are at risk for delinquency.[45] For girls, a "bad crowd" usually means teenage boys! It may not be surprising that delinquent girls are significantly more likely than their nondelinquent peers to identify males as their closest friends.[46] For girls, hanging out with males may be a precursor to antisocial behavior.[47]

■ Antisocial youths seek out and join up with like-minded friends; deviant peers sustain and amplify delinquent careers.[48] Those who choose aggressive or violent friends are more likely to begin engaging in antisocial behavior themselves and suffer psychological deficits.[49] A number of research efforts have found that boys who go through puberty at an early age are more likely to later engage in violence, property crimes, drug use, and precocious sexual behavior.[50] The boys who mature early are the most likely to develop strong attachments to delinquent friends and to be influenced by peer pressure.[51]

■ As children move through their life course, antisocial friends help youths maintain delinquent careers and obstruct the aging-out process.[52] In contrast, noncriminal friends moderate criminality.[53] When (and if) adulthood brings close and sustaining ties to conventional friends, marriage, and family, levels of deviant behavior decline.[54]

Troubled youths choose delinquent peers out of necessity rather than desire. The social baggage they cart around prevents them from developing associations with conventional peers. Because they are impulsive, they may join cliques whose members are dangerous and get them into trouble.[55] Deviant peers do not cause straight kids to go bad, but they amplify the likelihood of a troubled kid getting further involved in antisocial behaviors.[56]

Many kids have religious affiliations or belong to other institutions that teach moral values that may help shield them from delinquency. Here, Natalie Kruger (15) gives a high-five to youth leader Adrian Martin at a food distribution center in Stone Mountain, Georgia, as other teenagers from Eastminster Presbyterian Church gather around them after the group finished stocking items they brought from their church. The teens joined their peers nationwide for "World Vision," a 30-hour fast during which they also donated food and necessities to organizations that distribute them to the needy.

© AP Images/John Amis

Institutional Involvement and Belief

Peers, schools, and family are not the only sources of socialization. Many kids have religious affiliations or belong to other institutions that teach moral values. It follows that people who hold high moral values and beliefs, who have learned to distinguish "right from wrong," and who regularly attend religious services should also eschew crime and other antisocial behaviors. Religion binds people together and forces them to confront the consequences of their behavior. Committing crimes would violate the principles of all organized religions.

Sociologists Travis Hirschi and Rodney Stark found in a classic study that, contrary to expectations, the association between religious attendance and belief and delinquent behavior patterns is negligible and insignificant.[57] However, some research efforts have reached an opposite conclusion, finding that attending religious services significantly helps reduce crime.[58] Kids living in disorganized high-crime areas who attend religious services are better able to resist illegal drug use.[59]

Interestingly, participation seems to be a more significant inhibitor of crime than merely having religious beliefs and values.[60]

The Effects of Socialization on Crime

To many criminologists, the elements of socialization described up to this point are the chief determinants of criminal behavior. According to this view, people living in even the most deteriorated urban areas can successfully resist inducements to crime if they have a positive self-image, learn moral values, and have the support of their parents, peers, teachers, and neighbors. The girl with a positive self-image who is chosen for a college scholarship has the warm, loving support of her parents and is viewed by friends and neighbors as someone who is "going places." She is less likely to adopt a criminal way of life than another adolescent who is abused at home, lives with criminal parents, and whose bond to her school and peer group is shattered because she is labeled a troublemaker.[61] The boy who has learned criminal behavior from his parents and siblings and then joins a neighborhood gang is much more likely to become an adult criminal than his next-door neighbor who idolizes his hard-working, deeply religious parents. It is socialization, not the social structure, which determines life chances. The more social problems encountered during the socialization process, the greater the likelihood that youths will encounter difficulties and obstacles as they mature, such as being unemployed or becoming a teenage mother.

Theorists who believe that an individual's socialization determines the likelihood of criminality adopt the social process approach to human behavior. The social process approach has several independent branches (Figure 7.1):

▌ Social learning theory suggests that people learn the techniques and attitudes of crime from close and intimate relationships with criminal peers; crime is a learned behavior.

▌ Social control theory maintains that everyone has the potential to become a criminal but that most people are controlled by their bonds to society. Crime occurs when the forces that bind people to society are weakened or broken.

▌ Social reaction theory (labeling theory) says people become criminals when significant members of society label them as such, and some accept those labels as a personal identity. The Genarlow Wilson case illustrates the effect of negative labeling.

Put another way, social learning theory assumes people are born good and learn to be bad; social control theory assumes people are born bad and must be controlled in order to be good; social reaction theory assumes that, whether good or bad, people are controlled by the reactions of others. Each of these independent branches will be discussed separately.

Figure 7.1 The Social Processes That Control Human Behavior

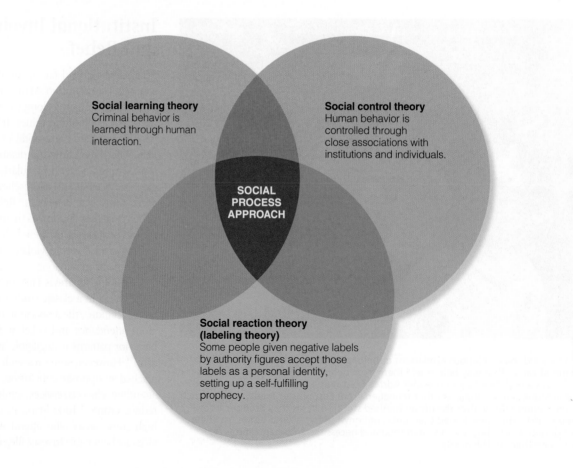

Social learning theory
Criminal behavior is learned through human interaction.

Social control theory
Human behavior is controlled through close associations with institutions and individuals.

SOCIAL PROCESS APPROACH

Social reaction theory (labeling theory)
Some people given negative labels by authority figures accept those labels as a personal identity, setting up a self-fulfilling prophecy.

www Go to academic.cengage.com/criminaljustice/siegel to access the following:

- The **Institute for Child and Family**, whose goal is to stimulate and coordinate the cross-disciplinary work required to make progress on the most difficult child and family policy issues facing the United States.

- **United Family Services**, a website devoted to family issues of all types.

SOCIAL LEARNING THEORY

Social learning theorists believe crime is a product of learning the norms, values, and behaviors associated with criminal activity. Social learning can involve the actual techniques of crime—how to hot-wire a car or roll a joint—as well as the psychological aspects of criminality—how to deal with the guilt or shame associated with illegal activities. This section briefly reviews the three most prominent forms of social learning theory: differential association theory, differential reinforcement theory, and neutralization theory.

Differential Association Theory

One of the most prominent social learning theories is Edwin H. Sutherland's differential association theory. Often considered the preeminent U.S. criminologist, Sutherland first put forth his theory in his 1939 text, *Principles of Criminology*.[62] The final version of the theory appeared in 1947. When Sutherland died in 1950, Donald Cressey, his long-time associate, continued his work. Cressey was so successful in explaining and popularizing his mentor's efforts that differential association remains one of the most enduring explanations of criminal behavior.

Sutherland's research on white-collar crime, professional theft, and intelligence led him to dispute the notion that crime was a function of the inadequacy of people in the lower classes.[63] To Sutherland, criminality stemmed neither from individual traits nor from socioeconomic position; instead, he believed it to be a function of a learning process that could affect any individual in any culture. Acquiring a behavior is a social learning process, not a political or legal process. Skills and motives conducive to crime are learned as a result of contacts with procrime values, attitudes, and definitions and other patterns of criminal behavior.

Principles of Differential Association The basic principles of differential association are explained as follows:[64]

- *Criminal behavior is learned.* This statement differentiates Sutherland's theory from prior attempts to classify criminal behavior as an inherent characteristic of criminals. By suggesting that delinquent and criminal behavior is learned, Sutherland implied that it can be classified in the same manner as any other learned behavior, such as writing, painting, or reading.

- *Learning is a by-product of interaction.* Criminal behavior is learned as a by-product of interacting with others. Sutherland believed individuals do not start violating the law simply by living in a criminogenic environment or by manifesting personal characteristics, such as low IQ or family problems, associated with criminality. People actively participate in the learning process as they interact with other individuals. Romantic partners who engage in antisocial activities may influence their partner's behavior, suggesting that partners learn from one another.[65] Thus, criminality cannot occur without the aid of others; it is a function of socialization.

- *Learning occurs within intimate groups.* Learning criminal behavior occurs within intimate personal groups. People's contacts with their most intimate social companions—family, friends, peers—have the greatest influence on their deviant behavior and attitude development. Relationships with these influential individuals color and control the way people interpret everyday events. For example, research shows that children who grow up in homes where parents abuse alcohol are more likely to view drinking as being socially and physically beneficial.[66] The intimacy of these associations far outweighs the importance of any other form of communication—for example, movies or television. Even on those rare occasions when violent motion pictures seem to provoke mass criminal episodes, these outbreaks can be more readily explained as a reaction to peer group pressure than as a reaction to the films themselves.

- *Criminal techniques are learned.* Learning criminal behavior involves acquiring the techniques of committing the crime, which are sometimes very complicated and sometimes very simple. This requires learning the specific direction of motives, drives, rationalizations, and attitudes. Some children may meet and associate with criminal "mentors" who teach them how to be successful criminals and gain the greatest benefits from their criminal activities.[67] They learn the proper way to pick a lock, shoplift, and obtain and use narcotics. In addition, novice criminals learn to use the proper terminology for their acts and then acquire "proper" reactions to law violations. For example, getting high on marijuana and learning the proper way to smoke a joint are behavior patterns usually acquired from more experienced companions. Moreover, criminals must learn how to react properly to their illegal acts, such as when to defend them, rationalize them, or show remorse for them.

- *Perceptions of legal code influence motives and drives.* The specific direction of motives and drives is learned from perceptions of various aspects of the legal code as being favorable or unfavorable. The reaction to social rules and laws is not uniform across society, and people constantly come into contact with others who maintain different views on the utility of obeying the legal code. Some people they admire may openly disdain or flout the law or ignore its substance. People experience what Sutherland calls *culture conflict* when they are exposed to different and opposing attitudes toward what is right and wrong, moral and immoral.

The conflict of social attitudes and cultural norms is the basis for the concept of differential association.

- *Differential associations may vary in frequency, duration, priority, and intensity.* Whether a person learns to obey the law or to disregard it is influenced by the quality of social interactions. Those of lasting *duration* have greater influence than those that are brief. Similarly, *frequent* contacts have greater effect than rare and haphazard contacts. Sutherland did not specify what he meant by *priority*, but Cressey and others have interpreted the term to mean the age of children when they first encounter definitions of criminality. Contacts made early in life probably have a greater and more far-reaching influence than those developed later on. Finally, *intensity* is generally interpreted to mean the importance and prestige attributed to the individual or groups from whom the definitions are learned. For example, the influence of a father, mother, or trusted friend far outweighs the effect of more socially distant figures.

- *The process of learning criminal behavior by association with criminal and anticriminal patterns involves all of the mechanisms involved in any other learning process.* This suggests that learning criminal behavior patterns is similar to learning nearly all other patterns and is not a matter of mere imitation.

- *Criminal behavior is an expression of general needs and values, but it is not excused by those general needs and values because noncriminal behavior is also an expression of those same needs and values.* This principle suggests that the motives for criminal behavior cannot logically be the same as those for conventional behavior. Sutherland rules out such motives as desire to accumulate money or social status, personal frustration, or low self-concept as causes of crime because they are just as likely to produce noncriminal behavior, such as getting a better education or working harder on a job. It is only the learning of deviant norms through contact with an excess of definitions favorable toward criminality that produces illegal behavior.

A person becomes a criminal when he or she perceives more favorable than unfavorable consequences to violating the law (Figure 7.2). According to Sutherland's theory, individuals become law violators when they are in contact with people, groups, or events that produce an excess of definitions favorable toward criminality and are isolated from counteracting forces. A definition favorable toward criminality occurs, for example,

Figure 7.2 Differential Associations

Differential associations

Play fair.

Don't be a bully.

Forgive and forget.

Turn the other cheek.

Evil is always punished.

Honesty is the best policy.

Ideas that prohibit crime

Drinking is OK.

The end justifies the means.

I don't get mad I get even.

Don't let anyone push you around.

People should take drugs if they want to.

Ideas that justify crime

when a person is exposed to friends sneaking into a theater to avoid paying for a ticket or talking about the virtues of getting high on drugs. A definition unfavorable toward crime occurs when friends or parents demonstrate their disapproval of crime. Neutral behavior, such as reading a book, is neither positive nor negative with respect to law violation. Cressey argues that neutral behavior is important; for example, when a child is occupied doing something neutral, it prevents him or her from being in contact with those involved in criminal behaviors.[68]

In sum, differential association theory holds that people learn criminal attitudes and behavior while in their adolescence from close and trusted friends and/or relatives. A criminal career develops if learned antisocial values and behaviors are not at least matched or exceeded by conventional attitudes and behaviors. Criminal behavior, then, is learned in a process that is similar to learning any other human behavior.

Testing Differential Association Theory Despite the importance of differential association theory, research devoted to testing its assumptions has been relatively sparse. It has proven difficult to conceptualize the principles of the theory so that they can be empirically tested. For example, social scientists find it difficult to evaluate such vague concepts as "definition toward criminality." It is also difficult to follow people over time, establish precisely when definitions toward criminality begin to outweigh prosocial definitions, and determine if this imbalance produces criminal behavior.

Despite these limitations, several notable research efforts have supported the core principles of this theory. These generally show a correlation between (a) having deviant friends, (b) holding deviant attitudes, and (c) committing deviant acts.[69] People who report having attitudes that support deviant behavior are also likely to engage in deviant behavior.[70] In a classic work, criminologist James Short surveyed institutionalized youths and found that they had, in fact, maintained close associations with delinquent youths prior to their law-violating acts.[71] Association with deviant peers has been found to sustain the deviant attitudes that support crime both in group settings and in solo ventures.[72] Mark Warr found that antisocial children who maintain delinquent friends over a long duration are much more likely to persist in their delinquent behavior than those without such peer support.[73] Scales measuring differential association have been significantly correlated with criminal behaviors among samples taken in other nations and cultures.[74]

Differential association also seems especially relevant in trying to explain the onset of substance abuse and a career in the drug trade. This requires learning proper techniques and attitudes from an experienced user or dealer.[75] In his interview study of low-level drug dealers, Kenneth Tunnell found that many novices were tutored by a more experienced criminal dealer who helped them make connections with buyers and sellers. One told him:

> I had a friend of mine who was an older guy, and he introduced me to selling marijuana to make a few dollars. I started selling a little and made a few dollars. For a young guy to be making a hundred dollars or so, it was a lot of money. So I got kind of tied up in that aspect of selling drugs.[76]

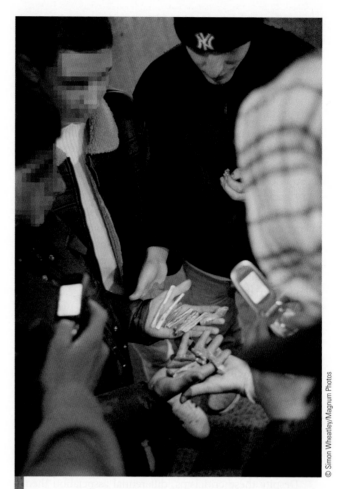

Differential association theory suggests that people learn the techniques and attitudes necessary to commit crime. Criminal knowledge is gained through experience, and after considering the outcomes of their past experiences, potential offenders decide which criminal acts will be profitable and which are dangerous and should be avoided. Here, a young man is shown photographing a drug deal on his cell phone. Is it possible that he is documenting the experience to learn and keep a record of the best techniques of drug dealing?

© Simon Wheatley/Magnum Photos

Tunnell found that making connections is an important part of the dealer's world. Adolescent drug users are likely to have intimate relationships with a peer friendship network that supports their substance abuse and teaches them how to deal within the drug world.[77]

Differential association may also be used to explain the gender difference in the crime rate. Males are more likely to socialize with deviant peers than females and, when they do, are more deeply influenced by peer relations.[78] Females are shielded by their unique moral sense, which makes caring about people and avoiding social harm a top priority. Males, in contrast, have a more cavalier attitude toward others and are more interested in their own self-interests. They are therefore more susceptible to the influence of deviant peers.[79]

Analysis of Differential Association Theory There have been a number of important critiques of the theory. According to the *cultural deviance critique*, differential association is invalid because it suggests that criminals are people "properly" socialized into a deviant subculture; that is, they are taught criminal norms by significant others. Supporters counter that differential association also recognizes that individuals can embrace criminality because they have been improperly socialized into the normative culture.[80]

Differential association theory also fails to explain why one youth who is exposed to delinquent definitions eventually succumbs to them, while another, living under the same conditions, is able to avoid criminal entanglements. It fails to account for the origin of delinquent definitions. How did the first "teacher" learn delinquent attitudes and definitions in order to pass them on? Another apparently valid criticism of differential association is that it assumes criminal and delinquent acts to be rational and systematic. This ignores spontaneous and wanton acts of violence and damage that appear to have little utility or purpose, such as the isolated psychopathic killing or serial rapist.

Another critique concerns the relationship between deviant peers and criminality. It is possible that youths learn about crime and then commit criminal acts, but it is also possible that experienced delinquents and criminals seek out like-minded peers after they engage in antisocial acts and that the internalization of deviant attitudes follows, rather than precedes, criminality ("birds of a feather flock together").[81] Research on gang boys shows that they are involved in high rates of criminality before they join gangs, indicating that the group experience facilitates their antisocial behavior rather than playing a role in its creation.[82]

Despite these criticisms, differential association theory maintains an important place in the study of criminal behavior. For one thing, it provides a consistent explanation of all types of delinquent and criminal behavior. Unlike social structure theories, it is not limited to the explanation of a single facet of antisocial activity, such as lower-class gang activity. The theory can also account for the extensive delinquent behavior found even in middle- and upper-class areas, where youths may be exposed to a variety of prodelinquent definitions from such sources as overly opportunistic parents and friends.

Differential Reinforcement Theory

Differential reinforcement theory is another attempt to explain crime as a type of learned behavior. First proposed by Ronald Akers in collaboration with Robert Burgess in 1966, it is a version of the social learning view that employs both differential association concepts along with elements of psychological learning theory.

connections

Psychological learning theories were first discussed in Chapter 5. These trait theories maintain that human actions are developed through learning experiences. Behavior is supported by rewards and extinguished by negative reactions or punishments. In contrast, sociological learning theory holds that behavior is constantly being shaped by life experiences.

According to Akers, the same process is involved in learning both deviant and conventional behavior. People learn to be neither "all deviant" nor "all conforming" but rather strike a balance between the two opposing poles of behavior. This balance is usually stable, but it can undergo revision over time.[83]

A number of learning processes shape behavior. Direct conditioning, also called differential reinforcement, occurs when behavior is reinforced by being either rewarded or punished while interacting with others. When behavior is punished, this is referred to as negative reinforcement. This type of reinforcement can be distributed by using either negative stimuli (punishment) or loss of a positive reward. Whether deviant or criminal behavior has been initiated or persists depends on the degree to which it has been rewarded or punished and the rewards or punishments attached to its alternatives.

According to Akers, people learn to evaluate their own behavior through their interactions with significant others and groups in their lives. These groups control sources and patterns of reinforcement, define behavior as right or wrong, and provide behaviors that can be modeled through observational learning. The more individuals learn to define their behavior as good or at least as justified, rather than as undesirable, the more likely they are to engage in it. Adolescents who join a drug-abusing peer group whose members value drugs and alcohol, encourage their use, and provide opportunities to observe people abusing substances will be encouraged, through this social learning experience, to use drugs themselves.

Akers's theory posits that the principal influence on behavior comes from "those groups which control individuals' major sources of reinforcement and punishment and expose them to behavioral models and normative definitions."[84] The important groups are the ones with which a person is in differential association—peer and friendship groups, schools, churches, and similar institutions. Within the context of these critical groups, according to Akers, "deviant behavior can be expected to the extent that it has been differentially reinforced over alternative behavior . . . and is defined as desirable or justified."[85] Once people are indoctrinated into crime, their behavior can be reinforced by being exposed to deviant behavior models, associating with deviant peers, and lacking negative sanctions from parents or peers. The deviant behavior, originally executed by imitating someone else's behavior, is sustained by social support. It is possible that differential reinforcements help establish criminal careers and are a key factor in explaining persistent criminality.

Testing Differential Reinforcement The principles of differential reinforcement have been subject to empirical review by Akers and other criminologists.[86] In an important test of his theory, Akers and his associates surveyed 3,065 male and female adolescents on drug- and alcohol-related activities and their perception of variables related to social learning and differential reinforcement. Items in the scale included the respondents' perceptions of esteemed peers' attitudes toward drug and alcohol abuse, the number of people they admired who actually used controlled substances, and whether people they admired would reward or punish them for substance abuse. Akers found a strong association between drug and alcohol abuse and social learning variables: those who believed they would be rewarded for deviance by those they respect were the ones most likely to engage in deviant behavior.[87]

Akers also found that the learning–deviant behavior link is not static. The learning experience continues within a deviant group as behavior is both influenced by and exerts influence over group processes. For example, adolescents may learn to smoke because their friends are smoking and, therefore, approve of this behavior. Over time, smoking influences friendships and peer group memberships as smokers seek out one another for companionship and support.[88]

Differential reinforcement theory is an important perspective that endeavors to determine the cause of criminal activity. It considers how the content of socialization conditions crime. Because not all socialization is positive, it accounts for the fact that negative social reinforcements and experiences can produce criminal results. This concurs with research that demonstrates that parental deviance is related to adolescent antisocial behavior.[89] Parents may reinforce their children's deviant behavior by supplying negative social reinforcements. Akers's work also fits well with rational choice theory because they both suggest that people learn the techniques and attitudes necessary to commit crime. Criminal knowledge is gained through experience. After considering the outcome of their past experiences, potential offenders decide which criminal acts will be profitable and which are dangerous and should be avoided.[90] Integrating these perspectives, people make rational choices about crime because they have learned to balance risks against the potential for criminal gain.

Neutralization Theory

Neutralization theory is identified with the writings of David Matza and his associate Gresham Sykes.[91] They view the process of becoming a criminal as a learning experience in which potential delinquents and criminals master techniques that enable them to counterbalance or neutralize conventional values and drift back and forth between illegitimate and conventional behavior. One reason this is possible is the subterranean value structure of American society. Subterranean values are morally tinged influences that have become entrenched in the culture but are publicly condemned. They exist side by side with conventional values and while condemned in public may be admired or practiced in private. Examples include viewing pornographic films, drinking alcohol to excess, and gambling on sporting events. In American culture, it is common to hold both subterranean and conventional values; few people are "all good" or "all bad."

Matza argues that even the most committed criminals and delinquents are not involved in criminality all the time; they also attend schools, family functions, and religious services. Their behavior can be conceived as falling along a continuum between total freedom and total restraint. This process, which he calls drift, refers to the movement from one extreme of behavior to another, resulting in behavior that is sometimes unconventional, free, or deviant and at other times constrained and sober.[92] Learning techniques of neutralization enables a person to temporarily "drift away" from conventional behavior and get

involved in more subterranean values and behaviors, including crime and drug abuse.[93]

Sykes and Matza base their theoretical model on these observations:[94]

- *Criminals sometimes voice a sense of guilt over their illegal acts.* If a stable criminal value system existed in opposition to generally held values and rules, it would be unlikely that criminals would exhibit any remorse for their acts, other than regret at being apprehended.

- *Offenders frequently respect and admire honest, law-abiding people.* Really honest people are often revered; and if for some reason such people are accused of misbehavior, the criminal is quick to defend their integrity. Those admired may include sports figures, priests and other clergy, parents, teachers, and neighbors.

- *Criminals draw a line between those whom they can victimize and those whom they cannot.* Members of similar ethnic groups, churches, or neighborhoods are often off limits. This practice implies that criminals are aware of the wrongfulness of their acts.

- *Criminals are not immune to the demands of conformity.* Most criminals frequently participate in many of the same social functions as law-abiding people—for example, in school, church, and family activities.

Because of these factors, Sykes and Matza conclude that criminality is the result of the neutralization of accepted social values through the learning of a standard set of techniques that allow people to counteract the moral dilemmas posed by illegal behavior.[95]

Techniques of Neutralization Sykes and Matza suggest that people develop a distinct set of justifications for their law-violating behavior. These neutralization techniques enable them to temporarily drift away from the rules of the normative society and participate in subterranean behaviors. These techniques of neutralization include the following patterns:

- *Deny responsibility.* Young offenders sometimes claim their unlawful acts were simply not their fault. Criminals' acts resulted from forces beyond their control or were accidents.

- *Deny injury.* By denying the wrongfulness of an act, criminals are able to neutralize illegal behavior. For example, stealing is viewed as borrowing; vandalism is considered mischief that has gotten out of hand. Delinquents may find that their parents and friends support their denial of injury. In fact, they may claim that the behavior was merely a prank, helping affirm the offender's perception that crime can be socially acceptable.

- *Deny the victim.* Criminals sometimes neutralize wrongdoing by maintaining that the victim of crime "had it coming." Vandalism may be directed against a disliked teacher or neighbor; or homosexuals may be beaten up by a gang because their behavior is considered offensive. Denying the victim may also take the form of ignoring the rights of an absent or unknown victim: for example, stealing from the unseen owner of a department store. It becomes morally acceptable for the criminal to commit such crimes as vandalism when the victims, because of their absence, cannot be sympathized with or respected.

▮ *Condemn condemners.* An offender views the world as a corrupt place with a dog-eat-dog code. Because police and judges are on the take, teachers show favoritism, and parents take out their frustrations on their kids, it is ironic and unfair for these authorities to condemn his or her misconduct. By shifting the blame to others, criminals are able to repress the feeling that their own acts are wrong.

▮ *Appeal to higher loyalties.* Novice criminals often argue that they are caught in the dilemma of being loyal to their own peer group while at the same time attempting to abide by the rules of the larger society. The needs of the group take precedence over the rules of society because the demands of the former are immediate and localized (Figure 7.3).

In sum, the theory of neutralization presupposes a condition that allows people to neutralize unconventional norms and values by using such slogans as "I didn't mean to do it," "I didn't really hurt anybody," "They had it coming to them," "Everybody's picking on me," and "I didn't do it for myself." These excuses allow people to drift into criminal modes of behavior.

Testing Neutralization Theory Attempts have been made to verify the assumptions of neutralization theory empirically, but the results have been inconclusive.[96] One area of research has been directed at determining whether there really is a need for law violators to neutralize moral constraints. The thinking behind this research is this: if criminals hold values *in opposition* to accepted social norms, then there is really no need to neutralize. So far, the evidence is mixed. Some studies show that law violators approve of criminal behavior, such as theft and violence, and still others find evidence that even though they may be active participants themselves criminals voice disapproval of illegal behavior.[97] Some studies indicate that law violators approve of social values such as honesty and fairness; others come to the opposite conclusion.[98] The Criminological Enterprise feature "When Being Good Is Bad" focuses on this issue.

In addition to youthful delinquent behaviors, the adoption of neutralization techniques have also been used to explain the onset of white-collar crime.[99] Businessmen may find it easier to cut corners by claiming that "the government exaggerates dangers to the consumer" (denial of injury) or the "markets are generally safe so the corporate producers should not have to take blame for the few injuries that occur" (denial of responsibility), or "the bottom line is all that matters" (appeal to higher loyalty). The need to get ahead in the corporate world may help them neutralize the moral constraints that their parents may have taught them in adolescence, such as play fair, don't cheat, take responsibility.

The theory of neutralization, then, is a major contribution to the literature of crime and delinquency. It can account for the aging-out process: youths can forgo criminal behavior as adults because they never really rejected the morality of normative society. It helps explain the behavior of the occasional or non-chronic delinquent, who is able to successfully age out of crime. Because teens are not committed to criminality, as they mature they simply drift back into conventional behavior patterns. While they are young, justifications and excuses neutralize guilt and enable individuals to continue to feel good about themselves.[100] In contrast, people who remain criminals as adults may be using newly learned techniques to neutralize the wrongfulness of their actions and avoid guilt. For example, psychotherapists accused of sexually exploiting their clients blame the victim for "seducing them"; some claim there was little injury caused by the sexual encounter; others seek scapegoats to blame for their actions.[101]

Are Learning Theories Valid?

Learning theories make a significant contribution to our understanding of the onset of criminal behavior. Nonetheless, the general learning model has been subject to some

▮ **Figure 7.3 Techniques of Neutralization**

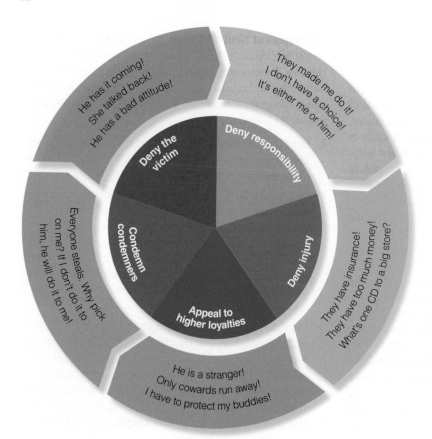

The Criminological Enterprise

WHEN BEING GOOD IS BAD

In their neutralization theory, Sykes and Matza claim that neutralizations provide offenders with a means of preserving a noncriminal self-concept even as they engage in crime and deviance. Sykes and Matza's vision assumes that most criminals believe in conventional norms and values and must use neutralizations in order to shield themselves from the shame attached to criminal activity. Recent research by criminologist Volkan Topalli finds that Sykes and Matza may have ignored the influential street culture that exists in highly disadvantaged neighborhoods. Using data gleaned from 191 in-depth interviews with active criminals in St. Louis, Missouri, Topalli finds that street criminals living in disorganized, gang-ridden neighborhoods "disrespect authority, lionize honor and violence, and place individual needs above those of all others." Rather than having to neutralize conventional values in order to engage in deviant ones, these offenders do not experience guilt that requires neutralizations; they are "guilt free." There is no need for them to "drift" into criminality, Topalli finds, because their allegiance to nonconventional values and lack of guilt perpetually leave them in a state of openness to crime.

Rather than being contrite or ashamed, the offenders Topalli interviewed took great pride in their criminal activities and abilities. Bacca, a street robber who attacked a long-time neighbor without provocation, exemplified such sentiments:

Actually I felt proud of myself just for robbing him, just for doing what I did I felt proud of myself. I didn't feel like I did anything wrong, I didn't feel like I lost a friend 'cause the friends I do have . . . are lost, they're dead. I feel like I don't have anything to lose. I wanted to do just what I wanted to do.

Topalli refers to streetwise offenders such as Bacca as "hardcores," who experience no guilt for their actions and operate with little or no regard for the law. They have little contact with agents of formal social control or conventional norms because their crimes are not directed toward conventional society— they rob drug dealers. Most hardcores maintain no permanent home, staying in various residences as their whim dictates. Their lifestyles are almost entirely dominated by the street ethics of violence, self-sufficiency, and opportunism. Obsessed with a constant need for cash, drugs, and alcohol in order to "keep the party going," on the one hand, and limited by self-defeating and reckless spending habits on the other, they often engage in violent crime to bankroll their street life activities. They do not have to neutralize conventional values because they have none.

Rather than neutralizing conventional values, hard-core criminals often have to neutralize deviant values: they are expected to be "bad" and have to explain good behavior. Even if they themselves are the victims of crime, they can never help police or even talk to them, a practice defined as snitching and universally despised and discouraged. Smokedog, a carjacker and drug dealer, described the anticipated guilt of colluding with the police in this way, "You know I ain't never told on nobody and I ain't never gonna tell on nobody 'cause I would feel funny in the world if I told on somebody. You know, I would feel funny, I would have regrets about what I did."

Street criminals are also expected to seek vengeance if they are the target of theft or violence. If they don't, their self-image is damaged and they look weak and ineffective. If they decide against vengeance, they must neutralize their decision by convincing themselves that they are being merciful, respecting direct appeals by their target's family and friends. T-dog, a young drug dealer and car thief, told Topalli how he neutralized the decision not to seek revenge by allowing his uncle to "calm him down." The older man, a robber and drug dealer himself, intervened before T-dog could leave his house armed with two 9mm automatics: "That's basically what he told me, 'Calm down.' He took both my guns and gave me a little .22 to carry when I'm out to put me back on my feet. Gave me an ounce of crack and a pound of weed. That's what made me let it go." In other cases, offenders claimed the target was just not worth the effort, reserving their vengeance for those who were worthy opponents.

Do these findings indicate that neutralization theory is invalid? Topalli concludes that the strength of the theory is its emphasis on cognitive processes that occur prior to offending. He suggests that neutralization theory's current emphasis on a conventional cultural value orientation must be expanded to accommodate the values of the street culture.

CRITICAL THINKING

1. Are there deviant norms and values that you have to neutralize in order to engage in conventional behaviors? What neutralizations have you come up with in order to save face when your friends wanted to engage in some forms of deviance but you decided not to take the risk?

2. Do you agree with Topalli that kids in disorganized neighborhoods shun conventional values? Or do you agree with Sykes and Matza that everyone shares conventional norms and values?

Source: Volkan Topalli, "When Being Good Is Bad: An Expansion of Neutralization Theory," *Criminology* 43 (2005): 797–836.

criticism. One complaint is that learning theorists fail to account for the origin of criminal definitions. How did the first "teacher" learn criminal techniques and definitions? Who came up with the original neutralization technique?

Learning theories also imply that people systematically learn techniques that enable them to be active and successful criminals, but they fail to adequately explain spontaneous and wanton acts of violence and damage and other expressive crimes that appear to have little utility or purpose. Principles of differential association can easily explain shoplifting, but is it possible that a random shooting is caused by excessive deviant definitions? It is estimated that about 70 percent of all arrestees were under the influence of drugs and alcohol when they committed their crime. Do "crack heads" pause to neutralize their moral inhibitions before mugging a victim? Do drug-involved kids stop to consider what they have "learned" about moral values?[102]

Little evidence exists substantiating that people learn the techniques that enable them to become criminals before they actually commit criminal acts. It is equally plausible that people who are already deviant seek out others with similar lifestyles. Early onset of deviant behavior is now considered a key determinant of criminal careers. It is difficult to see how extremely young adolescents had the opportunity to learn criminal behavior and attitudes within a peer group setting.

Despite these criticisms, learning theories maintain an important place in the study of delinquent and criminal behavior. Unlike social structure theories, these theories are not limited to the explanation of a single facet of antisocial activity—for example, lower-class gang activity—they may be used to explain criminality across all class structures. Even corporate executives may be exposed to a variety of procriminal definitions and learn to neutralize moral constraints.

wwww Edwin H. Sutherland served as the 29th president of the American Sociological Society. His presidential address, "White-Collar Criminality," was delivered at the organization's annual meeting in Philadelphia in December 1939. To read Sutherland's groundbreaking talk on white-collar crime, go to academic.cengage.com/criminaljustice/siegel.

SOCIAL CONTROL THEORY

Social control theories maintain that all people have the potential to violate the law and that modern society presents many opportunities for illegal activity. Criminal activities, such as drug abuse and car theft, are often exciting pastimes that hold the promise of immediate reward and gratification.

Considering the attractions of crime, the question control theorists pose is, Why do people obey the rules of society? A choice theorist would respond that it is the fear of punishment; structural theorists would say that obedience is a function of having access to legitimate opportunities; learning theorists

would explain that obedience is acquired through contact with law-abiding parents and peers. In contrast, social control theorists argue that people obey the law because behavior and passions are being controlled by internal and external forces. Because they have been properly socialized, most people have developed a strong moral sense, which renders them incapable of hurting others and violating social norms. They develop a **commitment to conformity**, which requires that they obey the rules of society.[103] Properly socialized people believe that getting caught at criminal activity will hurt a dearly loved parent or jeopardize their chance at a college scholarship, or perhaps they feel that their job will be forfeited if they get in trouble with the law. In other words, people's behavior, including criminal activity, is controlled by their attachment and commitment to conventional institutions, individuals, and processes. On the other hand, those who have not been properly socialized, who lack a commitment to others or themselves, are free to violate the law and engage in deviant behavior. Those who are "uncommitted" are not deterred by the threat of legal punishments because they have little to lose.[104]

Self-Concept and Crime

Early versions of control theory speculated that control was a product of social interactions. Maladaptive social relations produced weak self-concept and poor self-esteem, rendering young people at risk to crime. In contrast, youths who felt good about themselves and maintained a positive attitude were able to resist the temptations of the streets. As early as 1951, sociologist Albert Reiss described how delinquents had weak egos.[105] Scott Briar and Irving Piliavin noted that youths who believe criminal activity will damage their self-image and their relationships with others will be most likely to conform to social rules; they have a commitment to conformity. In contrast, those less concerned about their social standing are free to violate the law.[106] In his **containment theory**, pioneering control theorist Walter Reckless argued that a strong self-image insulates a youth from the pressures and pulls of criminogenic influences in the environment.[107] In a series of studies conducted within the school setting, Reckless and his colleagues found that nondelinquent youths are able to maintain a positive self-image in the face of environmental pressures toward delinquency.[108]

While these works are critical to the field, Travis Hirschi's vision of social control, articulated in his highly influential 1969 book *Causes of Delinquency*, is now the dominant version of the theory.[109]

connections

Tying social control and self-concept to crime helps to explain why some people, but not all, in disadvantaged areas are crime prone. It also suggests means to reduce crime rates: for example, by providing self-concept enhancing opportunities for relatively disadvantaged youth or helping mothers and fathers improve their parenting skills.

Hirschi's Social Bond Theory

In his insightful work, Hirschi links the onset of criminality to the weakening of the ties that bind people to society. He assumes that all individuals are potential law violators, but they are kept under control because they fear that illegal behavior will damage their relationships with friends, parents, neighbors, teachers, and employers. Without these social ties or bonds, and in the absence of sensitivity to and interest in others, a person is free to commit criminal acts. Hirschi does not view society as containing competing subcultures with unique value systems. Most people are aware of the prevailing moral and legal code. He suggests, however, that in all elements of society people vary in how they respond to conventional social rules and values. Among all ethnic, religious, racial, and social groups, people whose bond to society is weak may fall prey to criminogenic behavior patterns.

connections

Though his work has achieved a prominent place in criminological literature, Hirschi, along with Michael Gottfredson, has restructured his concept of control by integrating biosocial, psychological, and rational choice theory ideas into a "general theory of crime." This theory of self-control is discussed more fully in Chapter 9.

Elements of the Social Bond Hirschi argues that the social bond a person maintains with society is divided into four main elements: attachment, commitment, involvement, and belief (Figure 7.4).

■ *Attachment.* Attachment refers to a person's sensitivity to and interest in others.[110] Without a sense of attachment, psychologists believe a person becomes a psychopath and loses the ability to relate coherently to the world. The acceptance of social norms and the development of a social conscience depend on attachment to and caring for other human beings. Hirschi views parents, peers, and schools as the important social institutions with which a person should maintain ties. Attachment to parents is the most important. Even if a family is shattered by divorce or separation, a child must retain a strong attachment to one or both parents. Without this attachment, it is unlikely that feelings of respect for others in authority will develop.

■ *Commitment.* Commitment involves the time, energy, and effort expended in conventional lines of action, such as getting an education and saving money for the future. If people build a strong commitment to conventional society, they will be less likely to engage in acts that will jeopardize their hard-won position. Conversely, the lack of commitment to conventional values may foreshadow a condition in which risk-taking behavior, such as crime, becomes a reasonable behavior alternative. The association may be reciprocal. Kids who drink and engage in deviant behavior are more likely to fail in school; kids who fail in school are more likely to later drink and engage in deviant behavior.[111]

■ *Involvement.* Heavy involvement in conventional activities leaves little time for illegal behavior. When people become involved in school, recreation, and family, Hirschi believes,

Figure 7.4 Elements of the Social Bond

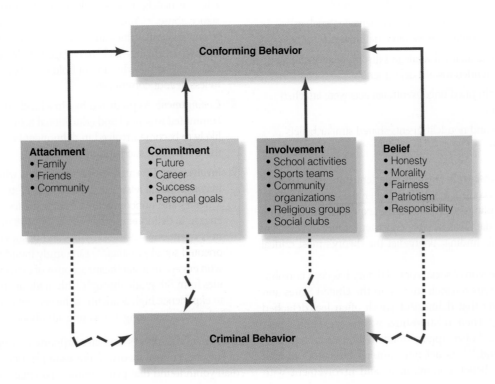

it insulates them from the potential lure of criminal behavior, whereas idleness enhances it.

- *Belief.* People who live in the same social setting often share common moral beliefs; they may adhere to such values as sharing, sensitivity to the rights of others, and admiration for the legal code. If these beliefs are absent or weakened, individuals are more likely to participate in antisocial or illegal acts.

Hirschi further suggests that the interrelationship of social bond elements controls subsequent behavior. For example, people who feel kinship and sensitivity to parents and friends should be more likely to adopt and work toward legitimate goals. A person who rejects such social relationships is more likely to lack commitment to conventional goals. Similarly, people who are highly committed to conventional acts and beliefs are more likely to be involved in conventional activities.

Testing Social Bond Theory One of Hirschi's most significant contributions was his attempt to test the principal hypotheses of social bond theory. He administered a detailed self-report survey to a sample of more than 4,000 junior and senior high school students in Contra Costa County, California.[112] In a detailed analysis of the data, Hirschi found considerable evidence to support the control theory model. Among Hirschi's more important findings are the following:

- Youths who were strongly attached to their parents were less likely to commit criminal acts.
- Commitment to conventional values, such as striving to get a good education and refusing to drink alcohol and "cruise around," was indicative of conventional behavior.
- Youths involved in conventional activity, such as homework, were less likely to engage in criminal behavior.
- Youths involved in unconventional behavior, such as smoking and drinking, were more delinquency prone.
- Youths who maintained weak and distant relationships with people tended toward delinquency.
- Those who shunned unconventional acts were attached to their peers.
- Delinquents and nondelinquents shared similar beliefs about society.

Supporting Research Hirschi's data lent important support to the validity of control theory. Even when the statistical significance of his findings was less than he expected, the direction of his research data was notably consistent. Only in very rare instances did his findings contradict the theory's most critical assumptions.

Hirschi's version of social control theory has been corroborated by numerous research studies, in the United States and abroad, showing that delinquent youth often feel detached from society.[113] Their relationships within the family, peer group, and school often appear strained, indicative of a weakened social bond.[114] Associations among indicators of lack of attachment, belief, commitment, and involvement with measures of delinquency have tended to be positive and significant.[115] In contrast, strong positive attachments help control delinquency.[116]

- *Attachment.* Research indicates that, as Hirschi predicts, young people who are attached to their families and friends are less likely to get involved in a deviant peer group and consequently less likely to engage in criminal activities.[117] Teens who are attached to their parents are also able to develop the social skills that equip them both to maintain harmonious social ties and to escape life stresses such as school failure.[118] In contrast, family detachment—including intrafamily conflict, abuse of children, and lack of affection, supervision, and family pride—are predictive of delinquent conduct.[119]

  Attachment to education is equally important. Youths who are detached from the educational experience are at risk of criminality; those who are committed to school are less likely to engage in delinquent acts.[120] Youths who fail at school and are detached from the educational experience are at risk of criminality; those who seem attached to school are less likely to engage in delinquent acts.[121] In a recent study of adolescent motherhood, Trina Hope, Esther Wilder, and Toni Terling Watt discovered that adolescent mothers who keep their babies reduce deviant activities such as smoking and marijuana use. The birth of a child serves as a mechanism of social control and reduces the likelihood of delinquent behavior. Attachment to a child, even during difficult circumstances, may produce the behavior change predicted by Hirschi.[122]

- *Belief.* There is support for Hirschi's view that holding positive beliefs is inversely related to criminality. Children who are involved in religious activities and hold conventional religious beliefs are less likely to become involved in substance abuse.[123] Young people who live in areas marked by strong religious values and who hold strong religious beliefs themselves are less likely to engage in delinquent activities than adolescents who do not hold such beliefs or who live in less devout communities.[124]

- *Commitment.* As predicted by Hirschi, children who are committed to school and educational achievement are less likely to become involved in delinquent behaviors than those who lack such commitment.[125]

- *Involvement.* Research shows that youths who are involved in conventional leisure activities, such as supervised social activities and noncompetitive sports, are less likely to engage in delinquency than those who are involved in unconventional leisure activities and unsupervised, peer-oriented social pursuits.[126] One study found that students who engage in a significant amount of extracurricular activities from 8th grade through 12th grade are more likely to experience high academic achievement and prosocial behaviors extending into young adulthood.[127]

Cross-national surveys have also supported the general findings of Hirschi's control theory.[128] For example, one study of Canadian youth found that perceptions of parental attachment were

PROFILES IN CRIME

ALPHA DOG

Twenty-five-year-old Jesse James Hollywood (his real name) was living a comfortable life in Brazil, teaching English and living in a fashionable neighborhood, when he was arrested in November of 2005 and sent back to California, where he faces charges of kidnapping and killing a 15-year-old boy.

Though Hollywood never held a job, by age 19 he was able to purchase a Mercedes and a $200,000 house in West Hills, California. His place became a popular spot for local kids who came and went at all hours of the day. Jesse was a popular guy, an outgoing kid who, despite being short in stature, was an excellent athlete. How was Jesse able to do all this? Unbeknownst to many, he was a large-scale marijuana dealer.

Jesse's world began to unravel when he came up with a scheme to get money owed to him by Benjamin Markowitz, 22, one of his customers. Hollywood went to Markowitz's family home on August 6, 2000, in order to kidnap him and hold him for ransom. According to authorities, on the way there, Jesse and his friends spotted Markowitz's 15-year-old stepbrother, Nicholas, whom they forced into a van and transported to the home of another accomplice. After being held captive for a few days, Nick Markowitz was made to walk a mile into the Los Padres National Forest before being shot nine times with a high-powered assault rifle and buried in a shallow grave. His body was discovered four days later by hikers. While four other kids were tried and convicted in the case, Hollywood escaped and became the subject of an international manhunt, his mug shot plastered on the FBI's website. He wound up in Brazil, where he used fake papers that identified him as Michael Costa Giroux, a native of Rio de Janeiro. In 2005, Brazilian authorities deported him as an illegal alien. A 2007 film, *Alpha Dog*, starring Bruce Willis, Justin Timberlake, and Sharon Stone, is based on the case. He is currently awaiting trial for the murder.

Jesse James Hollywood grew up in an affluent family and seemed to be popular and successful. How could he have become involved in an awful, violent crime? How would a control theorist explain his actions?

Sources: Tim Uehlinger, "The Long Hunt for Jesse James Hollywood," *Dateline*, April 12, 2006, www.msnbc.msn.com/id/12207033/ (accessed June 9, 2007; Ted Rowlands, "'Hollywood' Faces Murder Charge," April 19, 2006, www.cnn.com/2006/US/04/19/rowlands.hollywoodmurder/ (accessed June 9, 2007).

---

the strongest predictor of delinquent or law-abiding behavior. Teens who are attached to their parents may develop the social skills that equip them both to maintain harmonious social ties and to escape life stresses such as school failure.[129]

The Profiles in Crime feature describes a case that may rest on a frayed and tattered bond to society.

Opposing Views A great deal of scholarly research has been conducted to corroborate social control theory by replicating Hirschi's original survey techniques.[130] There has been significant empirical support for Hirschi's work, but there are also those who question some or all of its elements. Here are some elements that have come under criticism and need further study:

▮ *Friendship.* One significant criticism concerns Hirschi's contention that delinquents are detached loners whose bond to their family and friends has been broken. Some critics have questioned whether delinquents (a) do have strained relations with family and peers and (b) may be influenced by close relationships with deviant peers and family members. A number of research efforts do show that

delinquents maintain relationships with deviant peers and are influenced by members of their deviant peer group.[131] Delinquents, however, may not be "lone wolves" whose only personal relationships are exploitive; their friendship patterns seem quite close to those of conventional youth.[132] In fact, some types of offenders, such as drug abusers, may maintain even more intimate relations with their peers than nonabusers.[133]

▮ *Not all elements of the bond are equal.* Hirschi makes little distinction between the importance of each element of the social bond, yet research evidence suggests that there may be differences. Some adolescents who report high levels of "involvement," which Hirschi suggests should reduce delinquency, are involved in criminal behavior. As kids get involved in behaviors outside the home, it is possible that parental control weakens, and youths have greater opportunity to commit crime.[134] When asked, children report that concepts such as "involvement" and "belief have relatively little influence over behavior patterns."[135]

▮ *Deviant peers and parents.* Hirschi's conclusion that any form of social attachment is beneficial, even to deviant peers and parents, has also been disputed. Rather than deter delinquency attachment to deviant peers, it may support and nurture antisocial behavior. In a now classic study, criminologist Michael Hindelang found that attachment to delinquent peers escalated rather than restricted criminality.[136] In a similar fashion, a number of research efforts have found that youths attached to drug-abusing parents are more likely to become drug users themselves.[137] Attachment to deviant family members, peers, and associates may help motivate youths to commit crime and facilitate their antisocial acts.[138]

▌ *Restricted in scope.* There is some question as to whether the theory can explain all modes of criminality (as Hirschi maintains) or is restricted to particular groups or forms of criminality. Control variables seem better able to explain minor delinquency (such as alcohol and marijuana abuse) than more serious criminal acts and associations (such as the association between child abuse and violence).[139] Research efforts have found control variables are more predictive of female than male behavior.[140] Perhaps girls are more deeply influenced by the quality of their bond to society.

▌ *Changing bonds.* Social bonds seem to change over time, a phenomenon ignored by Hirschi.[141] It is possible that at one age level, weak bonds (to parents) lead to delinquency, while at another, strong bonds (to peers) lead to delinquency.

▌ *Crime and social bonds.* It is possible that Hirschi miscalculated the direction of the relationship between criminality and a weakened social bond.[142] Social bond theory projects that a weakened bond leads to delinquency, but it is possible that the chain of events may flow in the opposite direction: kids who break the law find that their bond to

parents, schools, and society eventually becomes weak and attenuated.[143]

Although these criticisms need to be addressed with further research, the weight of existing empirical evidence supports control theory, and it has emerged as one of the preeminent theories in criminology. For many criminologists, it is perhaps the most important way of understanding the onset of youthful misbehavior.

 **wwww** To read more about **Hirschi's work**, go to academic.cengage.com/criminaljustice/siegel.

SOCIAL REACTION THEORY

Social reaction theory, commonly called labeling theory (the two terms are used interchangeably here), explains how criminal careers form based on destructive social interactions and encounters. Its roots are found in the **symbolic interaction theory** of sociologists Charles Horton Cooley and George Herbert Mead, and later, Herbert Blumer.[144] Symbolic interaction theory holds that people communicate via symbols—gestures, signs, words, or images—that stand for or represent something else.

People interpret symbolic gestures from others and incorporate them in their self-image. Symbols are used by others to let people know how well they are doing and whether they are liked or appreciated. How people view reality then depends on the content of the messages and situations they encounter, the subjective interpretation of these interactions, and how they shape future behavior. There is no objective reality. People interpret the reactions of others, and this interpretation assigns meaning. Because interpretation changes over time, so do the meanings of concepts and symbols.

Social reaction theory picks up on these concepts of *interaction* and *interpretation.*[145] Throughout their lives, people are given a variety of symbolic labels and ways to interact with others. These labels represent behavior and attitude characteristics; labels help define not just one trait but the whole person. People labeled insane are also assumed to be dangerous, dishonest, unstable, violent, strange, and otherwise unsound. Valued labels, including smart, honest, and hard-working, suggest overall competence. These labels can improve self-image and social standing. Research shows that people who are labeled with one positive trait, such as being physically attractive, are assumed to maintain other traits, such as being intelligent and competent.[146] In contrast, negative labels—including troublemaker, mentally ill, and stupid— help stigmatize the recipients of these labels

According to labeling theory, perceptions guide behavior. Would you want to invite this guy to lunch with your family? He is The Scary Guy (his real name) and he spends his time teaching students and adults about what they can do to change the world by taking responsibility for their own behavior. His mission is to eliminate hate, violence, and prejudice worldwide. He is shown here bringing home his message at Valencia Middle School in Tucson, Arizona. What do you think of him now?

© AP Images

and reduce their self-image. Those who have accepted these labels are more prone to engage in delinquent behaviors than those whose self-image has not been so tarnished.[147]

Both positive and negative labels involve subjective interpretation of behavior: a troublemaker is merely someone people label as troublesome. There need not be any objective proof or measure indicating that the person is actually a troublemaker. Though a label may be a function of rumor, innuendo, or unfounded suspicion, its adverse impact can be immense.

If a devalued status is conferred by a significant other—teacher, police officer, elder, parent, or valued peer—the negative label may cause permanent harm. The degree to which a person is perceived as a social deviant may affect his or her treatment at home, at work, at school, and in other social situations. Children may find that their parents consider them a bad influence on younger brothers and sisters. School officials may limit them to classes reserved for people with behavioral problems. Likewise, when adults are labeled as criminal, ex-con, or drug addict, they may find their eligibility for employment severely restricted. Furthermore, if the label is bestowed as the result of conviction for a criminal offense, the labeled person may be subjected to official sanctions ranging from a mild reprimand to incarceration.

Beyond these immediate results, labeling advocates maintain that, depending on the visibility of the label and the manner and severity with which it is applied, a person will have an increasing commitment to a deviant career. As one national commission put it: "Thereafter he may be watched; he may be suspect . . . he may be excluded more and more from legitimate opportunities."[148] Labeled people may find themselves turning to others similarly stigmatized for support and companionship. Isolated from conventional society, they may identify themselves as members of an outcast group and become locked into a deviant career. Figure 7.5 illustrates this process.

Interpreting Crime

Labeling theorists use an interactionist definition of crime. In a defining statement, sociologist Kai Erickson argues, "Deviance is not a property inherent in certain forms of behavior, it is a property conferred upon those forms by the audience which directly or indirectly witnesses them."[149] Crime and deviance, therefore, are defined by the social audience's reaction to people and their behavior and the subsequent effects of that reaction; they are not defined by the moral content of the illegal act itself.[150]

In another famous statement, Howard Becker sums up the importance of the audience's reaction:

> Social groups create deviance by making rules whose infractions constitute deviance, and by applying those rules to particular people and labeling them as outsiders. From this point of view, deviance is not a quality of the act a person commits, but rather a consequence of the application by others of rules and sanctions to an "offender." The deviant is one to whom the label has successfully been applied; deviant behavior is behavior that people so label.[151]

In its purest form, social reaction theory argues that such crimes as murder, rape, and assault are only bad or evil because people label them as such. After all, the difference between an

Figure 7.5 The Labeling Process

Initial criminal act
People commit crimes for a number of reasons.

Detection by the justice system
Arrest is influenced by racial, economic, and power relations.

Decision to label
Some are labeled "official" criminals by police and court authorities.

Creation of a new identity
Those labeled are known as troublemakers, criminals, and so on, and are shunned by conventional society.

Acceptance of labels
Labeled people begin to see themselves as outsiders (secondary deviance, self-labeling).

Deviance amplification
Stigmatized offenders are now locked into criminal careers.

excusable act and a criminal one is often a matter of legal definition, which changes from place to place and from year to year. Acts such as abortion, marijuana use, possession of a handgun, and gambling have been legal at some points and places in history and illegal at others.

Becker refers to people who create rules as *moral entrepreneurs*. An example of a moral entrepreneur today might be members of an ultra-orthodox religious group who target the gay lifestyle and mount a campaign to prevent gays from adopting children or participating in same-sex marriages.[152]

Differential Enforcement

An important principle of social reaction theory is that the law is differentially applied, benefiting those who hold economic and social power and penalizing the powerless. The probability of being brought under the control of legal authority is a function of a person's race, wealth, gender, and social standing. A core concept of social reaction theory is that police officers are more likely to suspect, question, search, and arrest males, minority group members, and those in the lower class and to use their discretionary powers to give beneficial treatment to more favored groups.[153] The term racial profiling has been used to signify that police suspicion is often directed at minority group males. Minorities and the poor are more likely to be prosecuted for criminal offenses and to receive harsher punishments when convicted.[154] Judges may sympathize with white defendants and help them avoid criminal labels, especially if they seem to come from "good families," whereas minority defendants are not afforded that luxury.[155]

This evidence is used to support the labeling concept that personal characteristics and social interactions are more important variables in developing criminal careers than merely violating the law. Social reaction theorists also argue that the content of the law reflects power relationships in society. They point to the evidence that white-collar crimes—economic crimes usually committed by members of the upper class—are most often punished by a relatively small fine and rarely result in a prison sentence. This treatment contrasts with long prison sentences given to those convicted of "street crimes," such as burglary or car theft, which are the province of the lower, powerless classes.[156]

In sum, a major premise of social reaction theory is that the law is differentially constructed and applied, depending on the offenders. It favors the powerful members of society who direct its content and penalizes people whose actions represent a threat to those in control, such as minority group members and the poor who demand equal rights.[157]

Consequences of Labeling

This labeling process is important because once they are stigmatized as troublemakers, adolescents begin to reassess their self-image. Parents who label their children as troublemakers promote deviance amplification. Labeling alienates parents from their children, and negative labels reduce children's self-image and increase delinquency; this process is referred to as reflected appraisals.[158] Parental labeling is extremely damaging because it may cause adolescents to seek deviant peers whose behavior amplifies the effect of the labeling.[159]

As they mature, children are in danger of receiving repeated, intensive, official labeling, which has been shown to produce self-labeling and to damage identities.[160] Kids who perceive that they have been negatively labeled by significant others such as peers and teachers are also more likely to self-report delinquent behavior and to adopt a deviant self-concept.[161] They are likely to make deviant friends and join gangs, associations that escalate their involvement in criminal activities.[162] If their deviant activities land them in court the effects can be devastating. An official label increases the risk of their later dropping out of high school. Rather than deterring crime, court intervention increases the likelihood of future criminality.[163] Ironically, the official labeling process may take a greater toll on novice criminals than on more experienced offenders—a consequence that indicates the power of negative labels.[164]

As these youth become adults, the labeling process continues to take its toll. Male drug users labeled as addicts by social control agencies eventually become self-labeled and increase their drug use.[165] People arrested in domestic violence cases, especially those with a low stake in conformity (for example, those who are jobless and unmarried), increase offending after being given official labels.[166] And once in prison, inmates labeled high risk are more likely to have disciplinary problems than those who are spared such negative labels.[167]

Labels are believed to produce stigma. The labeled deviant becomes a social outcast who may be prevented from enjoying a higher education, well-paying jobs, and other social benefits. Such alienation leads to a low self-image.

Joining Deviant Cliques When people are labeled as deviant, they may join up with similarly outcast delinquent peers who facilitate their behavior.[168]

Eventually, antisocial behavior becomes habitual and automatic.[169] The desire to join deviant cliques and groups may stem from a self-rejecting attitude ("At times, I think I am no good at all"), which eventually results in a weakened commitment to conventional values and behaviors. In turn, these people may acquire motives to deviate from social norms. Facilitating this attitude and value transformation is the bond social outcasts form with similarly labeled peers in the form of a deviant subculture.[170]

Membership in a deviant subculture often involves conforming to group norms that conflict with those of conventional society. Deviant behaviors that defy conventional values can serve a number of different purposes. Some acts are defiant, designed to show contempt for the source of the negative labels. Other acts are planned to distance the transgressor from further contact with the source of criticism (for example, an adolescent runs away from critical parents).[171]

Retrospective Reading On January 19, 2007, area residents were shocked to learn that John Odgren, a student at upscale Lincoln-Sudbury Regional High School in Massachusetts, had stabbed a fellow student to death. Within days, the media reported that Odgren had often boasted of violence, that he kept a gun at home, and had bragged to fellow students that he once tried to kill someone. Odgren asked kids, "How many people have you killed in the virtual world?" and told them, "I once tried to kill a person for real." He seemed fascinated by violent books and told friends about part of a book he liked that described the dripping sound of blood. He visited websites that taught bomb making skills. After the murder, the public learned that the teenager had been diagnosed with Asperger syndrome, a mild form of autism, and a hyperactivity disorder, and had been taking several medications. He had been enrolled in a special ed program called Great Opportunities, which "provides a welcoming place for students whose significant emotional and/or psychiatric disabilities have interfered with their ability to access public education without the intensive support provided at GO."[172]

After someone is labeled because of some unusual or inexplicable act, such as the stabbing described above, people begin to reconstruct the culprit's identity so that the act and the label become understandable (e.g., "we always knew there was something wrong with that boy"). It is not unusual for the media to lead the way and interview boyhood friends of an assassin or serial killer. On the 11 o'clock news we can hear them report that the suspect was withdrawn, suspicious, and negativistic as a youth, expressing violent thoughts and ideation, a loner, troubled, and so on. Yet, until now no one was suspicious and nothing was done. This is referred to as retrospective reading, a process in which the past of the labeled person is reviewed and reevaluated to fit his or her current status. By conducting a retrospective reading, we can now understand what prompted his current behavior; therefore, the label must be accurate.[173]

Dramatization of Evil Labels become the basis of personal identity. As the negative feedback of law enforcement agencies, parents, friends, teachers, and other figures amplifies the force of the original label, stigmatized offenders may begin to reevaluate their own identities. If they are not really evil or bad, they may ask themselves, why is everyone making such a fuss? Frank Tannenbaum, a social reaction theory pioneer, referred to this process as the dramatization of evil. With respect to the consequences of labeling delinquent behavior, Tannenbaum stated:

> The process of making the criminal, therefore, is a process of tagging, defining, identifying, making conscious and self-conscious; it becomes a way of stimulating, suggesting and evoking the very traits that are complained of. If the theory of relation of response to stimulus has any meaning, the entire process of dealing with the young delinquent is mischievous insofar as it identifies him to himself or to the environment as a delinquent person. The person becomes the thing he is described as being.[174]

Primary and Secondary Deviance

One of the best-known views of the labeling process is Edwin Lemert's concept of primary deviance and secondary deviance.[175] According to Lemert, primary deviance involves norm violations or crimes that have very little influence on the actor and can be quickly forgotten. For example, a college student takes a "five-finger discount" at the campus bookstore. He successfully steals a textbook, uses it to get an A in a course, goes on to graduate, is admitted into law school, and later becomes a famous judge. Because his shoplifting goes unnoticed, it is a relatively unimportant event that has little bearing on his future life.

In contrast, secondary deviance occurs when a deviant event comes to the attention of significant others or social control agents who apply a negative label. The newly labeled offender then reorganizes his or her behavior and personality around the consequences of the deviant act. The shoplifting student is caught by a security guard and expelled from college. With his law school dreams dashed and his future cloudy, his options are limited; people who know him say he "lacks character," and he begins to share their opinion. He eventually becomes a drug dealer and winds up in prison (Figure 7.6).

Secondary deviance involves resocialization into a deviant role. The labeled person is transformed into one who, according to Lemert, "employs his behavior or a role based upon it as a means of defense, attack, or adjustment to the overt and covert problems created by the consequent social reaction to him."[176]

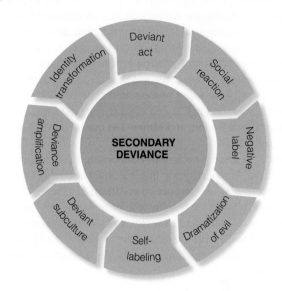

Figure 7.6 Secondary Deviance

Secondary deviance produces a deviance amplification effect. Offenders feel isolated from the mainstream of society and become firmly locked within their deviant role. They may seek out others similarly labeled to form deviant subcultures or groups. Ever more firmly enmeshed in their deviant role, they are locked into an escalating cycle of deviance, apprehension, more powerful labels, and identity transformation. Lemert's concept of secondary deviance expresses the core of social reaction theory: deviance is a process in which one's identity is transformed. Efforts to control the offenders, whether by treatment or punishment, simply help lock them in their deviant role.

Research on Social Reaction Theory

Research on social reaction theory can be classified into two distinct categories. The first focuses on the characteristics of offenders who are chosen for labels. The theory maintains that these offenders should be relatively powerless people who are unable to defend themselves against the negative labeling. The second type of research attempts to discover the effects of being labeled. Labeling theorists predict that people who are negatively labeled should view themselves as deviant and commit increasing amounts of criminal behavior.

Who Gets Labeled? The poor and powerless people are victimized by the law and justice system; labels are not equally distributed across class and racial lines. Critics charge that although substantive and procedural laws govern almost every aspect of the American criminal justice system, discretionary decision making controls its operation at every level. From the police officer's decision on whom to arrest to the prosecutor's decisions on whom to charge and for how many and what kind of charges, to the court's decision on whom to release or on whom to permit bail, to the grand jury's decision on indictment, to the judge's decision on the length of the sentence, discretion works to the detriment of minorities, including African Americans, Latinos, Asian Americans, and Native Americans.[177]

Although these arguments are persuasive, little definitive evidence exists that the justice system is inherently unfair and biased. Procedures such as arrest, prosecution, and sentencing seem to be more often based on legal factors, such as prior record and severity of the crime, than on personal characteristics, such as class and race.[178] However, it is possible that discriminatory practices in the labeling process are subtle and hidden. For example, in a thorough review of sentencing disparity, Samuel Walker, Cassia Spohn, and Miriam DeLone identify what they call contextual discrimination. This term refers to judges' practices in some jurisdictions of imposing harsher sentences on African Americans only in some instances, such as when they victimize whites and not other African Americans.[179] They may also be more likely to impose prison sentences on racial minorities in "borderline" cases for which whites get probation. According to their view, racism is very subtle and hard to detect, but it still exerts an influence in the distribution of criminal sanctions.

Labeling Effects Considerable evidence indicates social sanctions lead to self-labeling and deviance amplification.[180] Children negatively labeled by their parents routinely suffer a variety of problems, including antisocial behavior and school failure.[181] This process has been observed in the United States and abroad, indicating that the labeling process is universal, especially in nations in which a brush with the law brings personal dishonor, such as China and Japan.[182]

Empirical evidence supports the view that labeling plays a significant role in persistent offending.[183] Although labels may not cause adolescents to initiate criminal behaviors, experienced criminals are significantly more likely to continue offending if they believe their parents and peers view them in a negative light; they now have a "damaged identity."[184] Maintaining a damaged identity after official labeling may, along with other negative social reactions from society, produce a "cumulative disadvantage," which provokes some adolescents into repeating their antisocial behaviors.[185] Using longitudinal data obtained from youths ages 13 to 22, Jön Gunnar Bernburg and Marvin Krohn found evidence that, rather than deterring future offending, the "cumulative disadvantage" created by official intervention actually increases the probability that a labeled person will get involved in subsequent antisocial behavior. A label triggers exclusionary processes that limit conventional opportunities, such as educational attainment and employment. Kids who were labeled in adolescence were much more likely to engage in crime in early adulthood unless they were able to overcome labels and do well in school and obtain meaningful employment opportunities.[186]

Is Labeling Theory Valid?

Labeling theory has been the subject of academic debate in criminological circles. Those who criticize it point to its inability to specify the conditions that must exist before an act or individual is labeled deviant—that is, why some people are labeled and others remain "secret deviants."[187]

There is also some question about the real cost of being labeled. In an in-depth analysis of research on the crime-producing effects of labels, criminologist Charles Tittle found little evidence that stigma produces crime.[188] Tittle claims that many criminal careers occur without labeling; that labeling often comes after, rather than before, chronic offending; and that criminal careers may not follow even when labeling takes place. Getting labeled by the justice system and having an enduring criminal record then may have little effect on people who have been burdened with social and emotional problems since birth.[189]

While these criticisms are telling, criminologists Raymond Paternoster and Leeann Iovanni have identified features of the labeling perspective that are important contributions to the study of criminality:[190]

- The labeling perspective identifies the role played by social control agents in the process of crime causation. Criminal behavior cannot be fully understood if the agencies and individuals empowered to control and treat it are neglected.

- Labeling theory recognizes that criminality is not a disease or pathological behavior. It focuses attention on the social interactions and reactions that shape individuals and their behavior.

- Labeling theory distinguishes between criminal acts (primary deviance) and criminal careers (secondary deviance) and shows that these concepts must be interpreted and treated differently.

Labeling theory is also important because of its focus on interaction as well as the situations surrounding the crime. Rather than viewing the criminal as a robot-like creature whose actions are predetermined, it recognizes that crime is often the result of complex interactions and processes. The decision to commit crime involves actions of a variety of people, including peers, the victim, the police, and other key characters. Labels may expedite crime because they guide the actions of all parties involved in these criminal interactions. Actions deemed innocent when performed by one person are considered provocative when someone who has been labeled as deviant engages in them. Similarly, labeled people may be quick to judge, take offense, or misinterpret behavior of others because of past experience.

Labeling theory is also supported by research showing that convicted criminals who are placed in treatment programs aimed at reconfiguring their self-image may be able to develop revamped identities and desist from crime. Some are able to go through "redemption rituals" in which they are able to cast off their damaged identities and develop new ones. As a result, they develop an improved self-concept, which reflects the positive reinforcement they receive while in treatment.[191]

EVALUATING SOCIAL PROCESS THEORIES

The branches of social process theory—social learning, social control, and social reaction—are compatible because they suggest that criminal behavior is part of the socialization process.

When interactions with critically important social institutions and processes—the family, schools, justice system, peer groups, employers, and neighbors—are troubled and disturbed, people may turn to criminal solutions for their problems, a process sociologist Robert Agnew uncovered when he studied offenders' "storylines" (see The Criminological Enterprise feature).

Though there is some disagreement about the relative importance of those influences and the form they take, there seems to be little question that social interactions shape the behavior, beliefs, values, and self-image of the offender. People who have learned deviant social values, find themselves detached from conventional social relationships, or are the subject of stigma and labels from significant others will be the most likely to fall prey to criminal behavior. These negative influences can affect people in all walks of life, beginning in their youth and continuing through their majority. The major strength of the social process view is the vast body of empirical data showing that delinquents and criminals are people who grew up in dysfunctional families, who had troubled childhoods, and who failed at school, at work, and in marriage. Prison data show that these characteristics are typical of inmates.

Although persuasive, these theories do not always account for the patterns and fluctuations in the crime rate. If social process theories are valid, for example, people in the West and South must be socialized differently from those in the Midwest and New England because these latter regions have much lower crime rates. How can the fact that crime rates are lower in October than in July be explained if crime is a function of learning or control? How can social processes explain why criminals escalate their activity or why they desist from crime as they age? Once a social bond is broken, how can it be "reattached"? Once crime is "learned," how can it be "unlearned"?

Concept Summary 7.1 sets out the premises, strengths, and research focus of social process theories.

PUBLIC POLICY IMPLICATIONS OF SOCIAL PROCESS THEORY

Social process theories have had a major influence on policy-making since the 1950s. Learning theories have greatly influenced the way criminal offenders are dealt with and treated. The effect of these theories has mainly been felt by young offenders, who are viewed as being more salvageable than "hardened" criminals. If people become criminal by learning definitions and attitudes toward criminality, advocates of the social learning approach argue that they can "unlearn" them by being exposed to definitions toward conventional behavior. It is common today for residential and nonresidential programs to offer treatment programs that teach offenders about the harmfulness of drugs, how to forgo delinquent behavior, and how to stay in school. If learning did not affect behavior, such exercises would be futile.

Control theories have also influenced criminal justice and other public policy. Programs have been developed to increase people's commitment to conventional lines of action. Some work at creating and strengthening bonds early in life before the onset of criminality. The educational system has been the scene of numerous programs designed to improve basic skills and create an atmosphere in which youths will develop a bond to their schools. The most famous of these efforts is the Head Start Program. Today, Head Start is administered by the Head Start Bureau; the Administration on Children, Youth, and Families (ACFY); the Administration for Children and Families (ACF); and the Department of Health and Human Services (DHHS). It receives annual funding of almost $7 billion, enrolls close to 1 million children, and provides support to more than 1,600 individual programs.[192]

Control theories have focused on the family and have played a key role in putting into operation programs designed to strengthen the bond between parent and child. Others attempt to repair bonds that have been broken and frayed. Examples of this approach are the career, work furlough, and educational opportunity programs being developed in the nation's prisons. These programs are designed to help inmates maintain a stake in society so they will be less willing to resort to criminal activity on their release.

Labeling theorists caution against too much intervention. Rather than ask social agencies to attempt to rehabilitate people having problems with the law, they argue, "less is better." Put another way, the more institutions try to "help" people, the more these people will be stigmatized and labeled. For example, a special education program designed to help problem readers may cause them to label themselves and others as slow or stupid. Similarly, a mental health rehabilitation program created with the best intentions may cause clients to be labeled as crazy or dangerous.

The influence of labeling theory can be viewed in the development of diversion and restitution programs. **Diversion programs** are designed to remove both juvenile and adult offenders from the normal channels of the criminal justice process by placing them in programs designed for rehabilitation. A college student whose drunken driving causes injury to a pedestrian may, before a trial occurs, be placed for six months in an alcohol treatment program. If he successfully completes the program, charges against him will be dismissed. Thus, he avoids the stigma of a criminal label. Such programs are common throughout the nation. Often, they offer counseling, medical advice, and vocational, educational, and family services.

Another label-avoiding innovation that has gained popularity is restitution. Rather than face the stigma of a formal trial, an offender is asked to either pay back the victim of the crime for any loss incurred or do some useful work in the community in lieu of receiving a court-ordered sentence.

Despite their good intentions, stigma-reducing programs have not met with great success. Critics charge that they substitute one kind of stigma for another—for instance, attending a mental health program in place of a criminal trial. In addition, diversion and restitution programs usually screen out violent offenders and repeat offenders. Finally, there is little hard evidence that the recidivism rate of people placed in alternative programs is less than that of people sent to traditional programs.

STORYLINES

Criminologist Robert Agnew, who is already well known for his general strain theory (see Chapter 6), has identified a new concept—storylines—to help explain why people commit crimes. He finds that when criminals are asked why they offend, they typically tell a story explaining why they engaged in crime. These stories describe the events and conditions leading up to the crime. They claim that some unusual or unplanned event led to their taking criminal actions to solve their problems: they were insulted by a rival and sought revenge; they lost money gambling and had to break into a car to steal the CD player; some guy was hitting on their girl so they gave him a beatdown. A storyline is a temporally limited, interrelated set of events and conditions that increases the likelihood that individuals will engage in a crime or a series of related crimes.

Storylines begin with a particular event; that is, "something happens" to the individual that upsets his life. This event *temporarily* affects the characteristics of the individual, the individual's interactions with others, and/or the settings encountered by the individual in ways that increase the likelihood of crime. In particular, the event leads to a *temporary* increase in strain, reduction in social control, and an increase in the social learning of criminal techniques and attitudes. The storyline ends when some event restores the individual's normal level of functioning, ending the temporary drama in their lives.

What are some typical stories that are told?

1. **A Desperate Need for Money.** Offenders often report that they engage in crime during those periods when they have a desperate need for money. *Something has happened* that creates a *temporary, but desperate need for money* and the individual *believes that there are no good legitimate options for obtaining such money*. Usually cited for this turn of events are unexpected expenses, poor budgeting between paydays, temporary employment problems, the temporary loss of other sources of financial support, demands that debts be repaid, gambling losses, drug binges, and the pressure to pay legal fines or fees. So this storyline might go: "I knew the Knicks were going to beat the Celtics, so I borrowed $500 for a bet, and then they lost on a lucky shot. I had to pay the loan back so I stole my brother-in-law's plasma TV and sold it on the street."

2. **An Unresolved Dispute.** This storyline begins when *someone does or says something that the individual does not like*, or challenges and/or threatens a core identity value or status. The individual experiences one or more negative emotions, such as anger and humiliation, and then finds someone to blame for this negative treatment. This type of storyline often has a romantic twist: "I thought someone was hitting on my girl, because she was acting very strange. I thought she was trying to hook up with someone and I was really upset. Then I saw this guy with her. I was afraid she was going to be unfaithful, so I hit him in the face with a pipe."

3. **A Brief, but Close Involvement with a Criminal Other(s).** Individuals often develop close associations with criminal others over long periods of time, but sometimes the associations are more fleeting—lasting only hours, days, or weeks. This storyline can have a number of elements. The individual *gets involved with another individual or group* who *entices them into committing a crime they would never have committed on their own*. Success in a crime might lead to invitations for other crimes. Using this storyline, a person might say, "I was in a bar drinking when these guys I met told me that I could get some great weed for only $100 an ounce. I usually don't do things like that, but the price seemed so good I couldn't pass it up."

4. **A Brief, Tempting Opportunity for Crime.** Individuals may develop or encounter tempting opportunities for crime that last from several hours to weeks. This storyline has two key elements. *Something happens* that causes individuals to *perceive the costs of crime as low and the benefits as high over a period of time*. This storyline might be, "I know this guy who is working as a security guard in a electronics store. He will sell me video games for $10 each that I know I can peddle on the street for $30. He can get me 50 games next week. Why pass up an easy $1,000? And besides, I can't get in trouble because I didn't really take the stuff myself."

And of course individuals may experience more than one storyline at a time, each one contributing to or influencing another: a kid runs away from home, creating a desperate need for money; this gets him into disputes with other kids on the street, putting him in temporary contact with antisocial peers and creates tempting opportunities for crime.

Agnew believes that storylines are the key to understanding the immediate cause of crime. The ebb and flow of storylines, partly a function of luck and chance, help explain why some people commit crime, then stop, only to start again. They also help us understand the context of crime, why it occurs in some situations and not others. A person may commit a violent act when they are in the midst of a domestic crisis, but resolve the same situation peacefully at another point in their life.

CRITICAL THINKING

1. What storylines do college students use when they cheat on tests? Smoke pot? Get drunk at a frat party? Are they similar to Agnew's vision?

2. If people use storylines to get involved in crime, are there ones that prevent or inhibit illegal activities?

Source: Robert Agnew, "Storylines as a Neglected Cause of Crime," *Journal of Research in Crime and Delinquency* 43 (2006): 119–147.

SOCIAL PROCESS THEORIES

Theory	Major Premise	Strengths	Research Focus
SOCIAL LEARNING THEORIES			
Differential Association Theory	People learn to commit crime from exposure to antisocial definitions.	Explains onset of criminality. Explains the presence of crime in all elements of social structure. Explains why some people in high-crime areas refrain from criminality. Can apply to adults and juveniles.	Measuring definitions toward crime; influence of deviant peers and parents.
Differential Reinforcement Theory	Criminal behavior depends on the person's experiences with rewards for conventional behaviors and punishment for deviant ones. Being rewarded for deviance leads to crime.	Adds psychological learning theory principles to differential association. Links sociological and psychological principles.	The cause of criminal activity; how the content of socialization conditions crime.
Neutralization Theory	Youths learn ways of neutralizing moral restraints and periodically drift in and out of criminal behavior patterns.	Explains why many delinquents do not become adult criminals. Explains why youthful law violators can participate in conventional behavior.	Identifying the neutralizations people use to commit crime without jeopardizing their cherished beliefs and values.
SOCIAL CONTROL THEORY			
Hirschi's Control Theory	A person's bond to society prevents him or her from violating social rules. If the bond weakens, the person is free to commit crime.	Explains the onset of crime; can apply to both middle- and lower-class crime. Explains its theoretical constructs adequately so they can be measured. Has been empirically tested.	Measuring the association between commitment, attachment, involvement, belief, and crime.
SOCIAL REACTION THEORY			
Labeling Theory	People enter into law-violating careers when they are labeled for their acts and organize their personalities around the labels.	Explains the role of society in creating deviance. Explains why some juvenile offenders do not become adult criminals. Develops concepts of criminal careers.	Determining whether self-concept is related to crime. Showing how the differential application of labels produces crime; measuring the effect of stigma.

THINKING LIKE A CRIMINOLOGIST

The governor has asked you to help her deal with the state's emerging gang problem. The head of the state police views the gang problem as part of a criminal conspiracy designed to provide profits for highly motivated young criminals. Kids turn to gangs, he argues, as a method of obtaining desired goods and services, either directly through theft and extortion or indirectly through the profits generated by drug dealing and weapons sales. He argues that the best method to control this rational choice is to increase police gang control units and pass legislation heavily penalizing gang activity.

As a social process theorist, you believe the gang is a refuge for young men and women who have learned criminal attitudes and behaviors at home. Many have weak ties to their parents and families. Many do poorly in school. You are aware of research that shows that significant numbers of gang members have been sexually abused at home and that their homes are very likely to include drug users and people arrested for crimes. Considering these data, you believe joining a gang can be an assertion of independence not only from the family but also from cultural and class constraints; the gang is a substitute institution that can provide meaning and identity.

Writing Assignment Write a paper (about 500 words) describing gang control programs you suggest the governor implement. Do you believe a "get tough" program would actually work, or might it backfire? How would you convince the governor that your ideas are valid?

Doing Research on the Web Before you tackle the writing exercise above, review these Web-based resources:

- Visit the Street Gang Resource Center, Know Gangs, and Michigan State University Criminal Justice Resources: Gangs.
- Read a general overview of gangs in America and information on the National Youth Gang Center.

These websites can be accessed via academic.cengage.com/criminaljustice/siegel.

SUMMARY

- Social process theories view criminality as a function of people's interaction with various organizations, institutions, and processes in society.

- People in all walks of life have the potential to become criminals if they maintain destructive social relationships. Improper socialization is a key component of crime.

- Social process theories say that the way people are socialized controls their behavior choices, and there is strong evidence that social relations influence behavior.

- Children growing up with conflict, abuse, and neglect are at risk for crime and delinquency. As well, educational failure has been linked to criminality.

- Adolescents who associate with deviant peers are more likely to engage in crime than those who maintain conventional peer group relations. Kids who are socialized to have proper values and beliefs are less likely to get involved in crime than those without normative belief systems.

- Social process theory has three main branches. Social learning theory stresses that people learn how to commit

crimes. Social control theory analyzes the failure of society to control criminal tendencies. Social reaction or labeling theory maintains that negative labels produce criminal careers.

- Social learning theory suggests that people learn criminal behaviors much as they learn conventional behavior.

- Differential association theory, formulated by Sutherland, holds that criminality is a result of a person perceiving an excess of definitions in favor of crime over definitions that uphold conventional values.

- Differential reinforcement theory recasts differential association in terms of reward and punishment.

- Sykes and Matza's theory of neutralization stresses that youths learn behavior rationalizations that enable them to overcome societal values and norms and break the law.

- Social control theories maintain that behavior is a function of the attachment that people feel toward society. People who have a weak commitment to conformity are free to commit crime.

- Control theory maintains that all people have the potential to become criminals,

but a strong positive self-concept aids the commitment to conventional action. A strong self-image may insulate people from crime.

- Hirschi's social bond theory describes the social bond as containing elements of attachment, commitment, involvement, and belief. Weakened bonds allow youths to behave antisocially.

- Social reaction or labeling theory holds that criminality is promoted by becoming negatively labeled by significant others. Such labels as criminal, ex-con, and junkie isolate people from society and lock them into lives of crime.

- Labels create expectations that the labeled person will act in a certain way; labeled people are always watched and suspected. Eventually these people begin to accept their labels as personal identities, locking them further into lives of crime and deviance.

- Lemert suggests that people who accept labels are involved in secondary deviance while primary deviants are able to maintain an undamaged identity.

- Some critics have charged that labeling theory lacks credibility as a description of crime causation. However, supporters reply that it helps explain the continuity of crime and the maintenance of a criminal career.

- Social process theories have greatly influenced social policy. They have controlled treatment orientations as well as community action policies.

- CENGAGENOW™ is an easy-to-use online resource that helps you study in less time to get the grade you want—NOW.

CengageNOW™ Personalized Study (a diagnostic study tool containing valuable text-specific resources) lets you focus on just what you don't know and learn more in less time to get a better grade. If your textbook does not include an access code card, you can go to www.ichapters.com to purchase CengageNOW™.

KEY TERMS

social process theory (214)
parental efficacy (215)
social control theory (218)
social reaction theory (labeling theory) (218)
differential association theory (219)
differential reinforcement theory (222)
direct conditioning (222)

differential reinforcement (222)
negative reinforcement (222)
neutralization theory (223)
subterranean values (223)
drift (223)
commitment to conformity (226)
containment theory (226)
social bond (227)
symbolic interaction theory (230)

racial profiling (232)
reflected appraisals (232)
stigma (232)
retrospective reading (233)
dramatization of evil (233)
primary deviance (233)
secondary deviance (233)
contextual discrimination (234)
diversion programs (235)

CRITICAL THINKING QUESTIONS

1. Do negative labels cause crime? Or do people who commit crime become negatively labeled? That is, are labels a cause of crime or a result?

2. Once weakened, can a person's bonds to society become reattached? What social processes might help reattachment?

3. Can you devise a test of Sutherland's differential association theory? How would you go about measuring an excess of definitions toward criminality?

4. Can you think of ways you may have supported your peers' or siblings' antisocial behavior by helping them learn criminal techniques or attitudes?

5. Do you recall neutralizing any guilt you might have felt for committing a criminal or illegal act? Did your neutralizations come before or after you committed the act in question?

NOTES

1. Wright Thompson, "Outrageous Injustice," ESPN Online http://sports.espn.go.com/espn/eticket/story?page=wilson (accessed June 9, 2007); "Free Genarlow Wilson Now," *New York Times*, 21 December 2006, www.nytimes.com/2006/12/21/opinion/21thu4.html?ei=5088&en=d3a8cf6d030c60b7&ex=1324357200& (accessed June 9, 2007).
2. Chandra Thomas, "Why Is Genarlow Wilson in Prison?" *Atlanta Magazine Online*, www.atlantamagazine.com/article.php?id=158 (accessed April 23, 2007).
3. Shannon McCaffrey, "10-Year Sentence for Teen Sex Thrown Out," *San Jose Mercury News*, 9 June 2007, www.mercurynews.com/portlet/article/html/fragments/print_article.jsp?articleId=6113992&siteId=568 (accessed July 19, 2007).
4. Charles Tittle and Robert Meier, "Specifying the SES/Delinquency Relationship," *Criminology* 28 (1990): 271–299, at 274.
5. Sheldon Glueck and Eleanor Glueck, *Unraveling Juvenile Delinquency* (Cambridge, MA: Harvard University Press, 1950); Ashley Weeks, "Predicting Juvenile Delinquency," *American Sociological Review* 8 (1943): 40–46.
6. Diana Formoso, Nancy Gonzales, and Leona Aiken, "Family Conflict and Children's Internalizing and Externalizing Behavior: Protective Factors," *American Journal of Community Psychology* 28 (2000): 175–199.
7. Roslyn Caldwell, Jenna Silverman, Noelle Lefforge, and Clayton Silver, "Adjudicated Mexican-American Adolescents: The Effects of Familial Emotional Support on Self-Esteem, Emotional Well-Being, and Delinquency," *American Journal of Family Therapy* 32 (2004): 55–69.
8. Annie E. Casey Foundation, Kids Count, 2006, www.aecf.org/kidscount/sld/compare_results.jsp?i=722 (accessed April 23, 2007).
9. Andre Sourander, Henrik Elonheimo, Solja Niemelä, Art-Matti Nuutila, Hans Helenius, Lauri Sillanmäki, Jorma Piha, Tuulk Tamminen, Kirsti Kumpulkinen, Irma Moilanen, and Frederik Almovist, "Childhood Predictors of Male Criminality: A Prospective Population-Based Follow-up Study from Age 8 to Late Adolescence," *Journal of the American Academy of Child and Adolescent Psychiatry* 45 (2006): 578–586.
10. Jukka Savolainen, "Relative Cohort Size and Age-Specific Arrest Rates: A Conditional Interpretation of the Easterlin Effect," *Criminology* 38 (2000): 117–136.
11. Cesar Rebellon, "Reconsidering the Broken Homes/Delinquency Relationship and Exploring Its Mediating Factors," *Criminology* 40 (2002): 103–136.
12. James Unnever, Francis Cullen, and Robert Agnew, "Why Is 'Bad' Parenting Criminogenic? Implications from Rival Theories," *Youth Violence and Juvenile Justice* 4 (2006): 3–33.
13. L. Edward Wells and Joseph Rankin, "Families and Delinquency: A Meta-Analysis of the Impact of Broken Homes," *Social Problems* 38 (1991): 71–90.

14. Nan Marie Astone and Sara McLanahan, "Family Structure, Parental Practices, and High School Completion," *American Sociological Review* 56 (1991): 309–320.

15. Jennifer Beyers, John Bates, Gregory Pettit, and Kenneth Dodge, "Neighborhood Structure, Parenting Processes, and the Development of Youths' Externalizing Behaviors: A Multilevel Analysis," *American Journal of Community Psychology* 31 (2003): 35–53.

16. En-Ling Pan and Michael Farrell, "Ethnic Differences in the Effects of Intergenerational Relations on Adolescent Problem Behavior in U.S. Single-Mother Families," *Journal of Family Issues* 27 (2006): 1137–1158.

17. Paul Amato and Bruce Keith, "Parental Divorce and the Well-Being of Children: A Meta-Analysis," *Psychological Bulletin* 110 (1991): 26–46.

18. Unnever, Cullen, and Agnew, "Why Is 'Bad' Parenting Criminogenic?"

19. Daniel Shaw, "Advancing Our Understanding of Intergenerational Continuity in Antisocial Behavior," *Journal of Abnormal Child Psychology* 31 (2003): 193–199.

20. Donald J. West and David P. Farrington, eds., "Who Becomes Delinquent?" in *The Delinquent Way of Life* (London: Heinemann, 1977); Donald J. West, *Delinquency: Its Roots, Careers, and Prospects* (Cambridge, MA: Harvard University Press, 1982).

21. David Farrington, "Understanding and Preventing Bullying," in Michael Tonry, ed., *Crime and Justice*, vol. 17 (Chicago: University of Chicago Press, 1993), pp. 381–457.

22. Carolyn Smith and David Farrington, "Continuities in Antisocial Behavior and Parenting across Three Generations," *Journal of Child Psychology and Psychiatry* 45 (2004): 230–247.

23. Joseph Murray and David Farrington, "Parental Imprisonment: Effects on Boys' Antisocial Behaviour and Delinquency through the Life-Course," *Journal of Child Psychology and Psychiatry* 46 (2005): 1,269–1,278.

24. John Paul Wright and Francis Cullen, "Parental Efficacy and Delinquent Behavior: Do Control and Support Matter?" *Criminology* 39 (2001): 677–706.

25. Christopher Sullivan, "Early Adolescent Delinquency: Assessing the Role of Childhood Problems, Family Environment, and Peer Pressure," *Youth Violence and Juvenile Justice* 4 (2006): 291–313.

26. Andrea Chronis, Heather Jones, Benjamin Lahey, Paul Rathouz, William Pelham, Jr., Stephanie Hall Williams, Barbara Baumann, and Heidi Kipp, "Maternal Depression and Early Positive Parenting Predict Future Conduct Problems in Young Children with Attention-Deficit/Hyperactivity Disorder," *Developmental Psychology* 43 (2007): 70–82.

27. Carter Hay, "Parenting, Self-Control, and Delinquency: A Test of Self-Control Theory," *Criminology* 39 (2001): 707–736.

28. Sonia Cota-Robles and Wendy Gamble, "Parent-Adolescent Processes and Reduced Risk for Delinquency: The Effect of Gender for Mexican American Adolescents," *Youth and Society* 37 (2006): 375–392.

29. Robert Vermeiren, Jef Bogaerts, Vladislav Ruchkin, Dirk Deboutte, and Mary Schwab-Stone, "Subtypes of Self-Esteem and Self-Concept in Adolescent Violent and Property Offenders," *Journal of Child Psychology and Psychiatry* 45 (2004): 405–411.

30. Jacinta Bronte-Tinkew, Kristin Moore, and Jennifer Carrano, "The Father-Child Relationship, Parenting Styles, and Adolescent Risk Behaviors in Intact Families," *Journal of Family Issues* 27 (2006): 850–881.

31. Murray A. Straus, "Spanking and the Making of a Violent Society: The Short- and Long-Term Consequences of Corporal Punishment," *Pediatrics* 98 (1996): 837–843.

32. Carolyn Smith and Terence Thornberry, "The Relationship between Childhood Maltreatment and Adolescent Involvement in Delinquency," *Criminology* 33 (1995): 451–479.

33. Kristi Holsinger and Alexander Holsinger, "Differential Pathways to Violence and Self-Injurious Behavior: African American and White Girls in the Juvenile Justice System," *Journal of Research in Crime and Delinquency* 42 (2005): 211–242; Eric Slade and Lawrence Wissow, "Spanking in Early Childhood and Later Behavior Problems: A Prospective Study of Infants and Young Toddlers," *Pediatrics* 113 (2004): 1,321–1,330; Fred Rogosch and Dante Cicchetti, "Child Maltreatment and Emergent Personality Organization: Perspectives from the Five-Factor Model," *Journal of Abnormal Child Psychology* 32 (2004): 123–145.

34. *The Forgotten Half: Pathways to Success for America's Youth and Young Families* (Washington, DC: William T. Grant Foundation, 1988); Lee Jussim, "Teacher Expectations: Self-Fulfilling Prophecies, Perceptual Biases, and Accuracy," *Journal of Personality and Social Psychology* 57 (1989): 469–480.

35. Eugene Maguin and Rolf Loeber, "Academic Performance and Delinquency," in *Crime and Justice: A Review of Research,* vol. 20, ed. Michael Tonry (Chicago: University of Chicago Press, 1996), pp. 145–264.

36. Jeannie Oakes, *Keeping Track, How Schools Structure Inequality* (New Haven, CT: Yale University Press, 1985).

37. Christopher B. Swanson, *Who Graduates? Who Doesn't? A Statistical Portrait of Public High School Graduation, Class of 2001* (Washington, DC: Urban Institute, 2004).

38. G. Roger Jarjoura, "Does Dropping Out of School Enhance Delinquent Involvement? Results from a Large-Scale National Probability Sample," *Criminology* 31 (1993): 149–172; Terence Thornberry, Melaine Moore, and R. L. Christenson, "The Effect of Dropping Out of High School on Subsequent Criminal Behavior," *Criminology* 23 (1985): 3–18.

39. Carolyn Smith, Alan Lizotte, Terence Thornberry, and Marvin Krohn, *Resilient Youth: Identifying Factors that Prevent High-Risk Youth from Engaging in Delinquency and Drug Use* (Albany, NY: Rochester Youth Development Study, 1994), pp. 19–21.

40. Irving Janis, *Groupthink: Psychological Studies of Policy Decisions and Fiascoes* (Boston: Houghton Mifflin, 1982).

41. Zhang and Messner, "Family Deviance and Delinquency in China."

42. Maury Nation and Craig Anne Heflinger, "Risk Factors for Serious Alcohol and Drug Use: The Role of Psychosocial Variables in Predicting the Frequency of Substance Use Among Adolescents," *American Journal of Drug and Alcohol Abuse* 32 (2006): 415–433; Robert Agnew and Timothy Brezina, "Relational Problems with Peers, Gender, and Delinquency," *Youth and Society* 29 (1997): 84–111.

43. Sara Battin, Karl Hill, Robert Abbott, Richard Catalano, and J. David Hawkins, "The Contribution of Gang Membership to Delinquency beyond Delinquent Friends," *Criminology* 36 (1998): 93–116.

44. Paul Friday, Xin Ren, Elmar Weitekamp, Hans-Jürgen Kerner, and Terrance Taylor, "A Chinese Birth Cohort: Theoretical Implications," *Journal of Research in Crime and Delinquency* 42 (2005): 123–146.

45. Kate Keenan, Rolf Loeber, Quanwu Zhang, Magda Stouthamer-Loeber, and Welmoet Van Kammen, "The Influence of Deviant Peers on the Development of Boys' Disruptive and Delinquent Behavior: A Temporal Analysis," *Development and Psychopathology* 7 (1995): 715–726.

46. Brett Johnson Solomon, "Other-Sex Friendship Involvement among Delinquent Adolescent Females," *Youth Violence and Juvenile Justice* 4 (2006): 75–96.

47. Nation and Heflinger, "Risk Factors for Serious Alcohol and Drug Use: The Role of Psychosocial Variables in Predicting the Frequency of Substance Use Among Adolescents."

48. Terence Thornberry and Marvin Krohn, "Peers, Drug Use, and Delinquency," in *Handbook of Antisocial Behavior*, eds. David Stoff, James Breiling, and Jack Maser (New York: Wiley, 1997), pp. 218–233; Thomas Dishion, Deborah Capaldi, Kathleen Spracklen, and Fuzhong Li, "Peer Ecology of Male Adolescent Drug Use," *Development and Psychopathology* 7 (1995): 803–824.

49. Sylvie Mrug, Betsy Hoza, and William Bukowski, "Choosing or Being Chosen by Aggressive-Disruptive Peers: Do They Contribute to Children's Externalizing and Internalizing Problems?" *Journal of Abnormal Child Psychology* 32 (2004): 53–66.

50. Kevin Beaver and John Paul Wright, "Biosocial Development and Delinquent Involvement," *Youth Violence and Juvenile Justice* 3 (2005): 168–192.

51. Richard Felson and Dana Haynie, "Pubertal Development, Social Factors, and Delinquency Among Adolescent Boys," *Criminology* 40 (2002): 967–989.

52. Mark Warr, "Age, Peers, and Delinquency," *Criminology* 31 (1993): 17–40.

53. Sara Battin, Karl Hill, Robert Abbott, Richard Catalano, and J. David Hawkins, "The Contribution of Gang Membership to Delinquency beyond Delinquent Friends," *Criminology* 36 (1998): 93–116.

54. Mark Warr, "Life-Course Transitions and Desistance from Crime," *Criminology* 36 (1998): 502–536.

55. Stephen W. Baron, "Self-Control, Social Consequences, and Criminal Behavior: Street Youth and the General Theory of Crime," *Journal of Research in Crime and Delinquency* 40 (2003): 403–425.

56. Daneen Deptula and Robert Cohen, "Aggressive, Rejected, and Delinquent Children and Adolescents: A Comparison of Their Friendships," *Aggression and Violent Behavior* 9 (2004): 75–104.

57. Travis Hirschi and Rodney Stark, "Hellfire and Delinquency," *Social Problems* 17 (1969): 202–213.

58. Colin Baier and Bradley Wright, "If You Love Me, Keep My Commandments: A Meta-Analysis of the Effect of Religion on Crime," *Journal of Research in Crime and Delinquency* 38 (2001): 3–21; Byron Johnson, Sung Joon Jang, David Larson, and Spencer De Li, "Does Adolescent Religious Commitment Matter? A Reexamination of the Effects of Religiosity on Delinquency," *Journal of Research in Crime and Delinquency* 38 (2001): 22–44.

59. Sung Joon Jang and Byron Johnson, "Neighborhood Disorder, Individual Religiosity, and Adolescent Use of Illicit Drugs: A Test of Multilevel Hypothesis," *Criminology* 39 (2001): 109–144.

60. T. David Evans, Francis Cullen, R. Gregory Dunaway, and Velmer Burton, Jr., "Religion and Crime Reexamined: The Impact of Religion, Secular Controls, and Social Ecology on Adult Criminality," *Criminology* 33 (1995): 195–224.

61. Walter Miller, *Violence by Youth Gangs and Youth Groups as a Crime Problem in Major American Cities* (Washington, DC: U.S. Government Printing Office, 1975).

62. Edwin H. Sutherland, *Principles of Criminology* (Philadelphia: Lippincott, 1939).

63. See, for example, Edwin Sutherland, "White-Collar Criminality," *American Sociological Review* 5 (1940): 2–10.

64. See Edwin Sutherland and Donald Cressey, *Criminology,* 8th ed. (Philadelphia: Lippincott, 1970), pp. 77–79.

65. Dana Haynie, Peggy Giordano, Wendy Manning, and Monica Longmore, "Adolescent Romantic Relationships and Delinquency Involvement," *Criminology* 43 (2005): 177–210.

66. Sandra Brown, Vicki Creamer, and Barbara Stetson, "Adolescent Alcohol Expectancies in Relation to Personal and Parental Drinking Patterns," *Journal of Abnormal Psychology* 96 (1987): 117–121.

67. Carlo Morselli, Pierre Tremblay, and Bill McCarthy, "Mentors and Criminal Achievement," *Criminology* 44 (2006): 17–43.

68. Ibid.

69. Matthew Ploeger, "Youth Employment and Delinquency: Reconsidering a Problematic Relationship," *Criminology* 35 (1997): 659–675.

70. Paul Vowell and Jieming Chen, "Predicting Academic Misconduct: A Comparative Test of Four Sociological Explanations," *Sociological Inquiry* 74 (2004): 226–249.

71. James Short, "Differential Association as a Hypothesis: Problems of Empirical Testing," *Social Problems* 8 (1960): 14–25.

72. Andy Hochstetler, Heith Copes, and Matt DeLisi, "Differential Association in Group and Solo Offending," *Journal of Criminal Justice* 30 (2002): 559–566.

73. Warr, "Age, Peers, and Delinquency."

74. Clayton Hartjen and S. Priyadarsini, "Gender, Peers, and Delinquency," *Youth and Society* 34 (2003): 387–414.

75. Denise Kandel and Mark Davies, "Friendship Networks, Intimacy, and Illicit Drug Use in Young Adulthood: A Comparison of Two Competing Theories," *Criminology* 29 (1991): 441–467.

76. Kenneth Tunnell, "Inside the Drug Trade: Trafficking from the Dealer's Perspective," *Qualitative Sociology* 16 (1993): 361–381, at 367.

77. Krohn and Thornberry, "Network Theory," pp. 123–124.

78. Daniel Mears, Matthew Ploeger, and Mark Warr, "Explaining the Gender Gap in Delinquency: Peer Influence and Moral Evaluations of Behavior," *Journal of Research in Crime and Delinquency* 35 (1998): 251–266.

79. Ibid.

80. Ronald Akers, "Is Differential Association/ Social Learning Cultural Deviance Theory?" *Criminology* 34 (1996): 229–247; for an opposing view, see Travis Hirschi, "Theory without Ideas: Reply to Akers," *Criminology* 34 (1996): 249–256.

81. Robert Burgess and Ronald Akers, "A Differential Association–Reinforcement Theory of Criminal Behavior," *Social Problems* 14 (1966): 128–147.

82. Mons Bendixen, Inger Endresen, and Dan Olweus, "Joining and Leaving Gangs: Selection and Facilitation Effects on Self-Reported Antisocial Behaviour in Early Adolescence," *European Journal of Criminology* 3 (2006): 85–114.

83. Ronald Akers, *Deviant Behavior: A Social Learning Approach*, 2nd ed. (Belmont, CA: Wadsworth, 1977).

84. Ronald Akers, Marvin Krohn, Lonn Lanza-Kaduce, and Marcia Radosevich, "Social Learning and Deviant Behavior: A Specific Test of a General Theory," *American Sociological Review* 44 (1979): 638.

85. Ibid.

86. Marvin Krohn, William Skinner, James Massey, and Ronald Akers, "Social Learning Theory and Adolescent Cigarette Smoking: A Longitudinal Study," *Social Problems* 32 (1985): 455–471.

87. L. Thomas Winfree, Christine Sellers, and Dennis L. Clason, "Social Learning and Adolescent Deviance Abstention: Toward Understanding the Reasons for Initiating, Quitting, and Avoiding Drugs," *Journal of Quantitative Criminology* 9 (1993): 101–125.

88. Ronald Akers and Gang Lee, "A Longitudinal Test of Social Learning Theory: Adolescent Smoking," *Journal of Drug Issues* 26 (1996): 317–343.

89. Gary Jensen and David Brownfield, "Parents and Drugs," *Criminology* 21 (1983): 543–554.

90. Ronald Akers, "Rational Choice, Deterrence and Social Learning Theory in Criminology: The Path Not Taken," *Journal of Criminal Law and Criminology* 81 (1990): 653–676.

91. Gresham Sykes and David Matza, "Techniques of Neutralization: A Theory of Delinquency," *American Sociological Review* 22 (1957): 664–670; David Matza, *Delinquency and Drift* (New York: Wiley, 1964).

92. Matza, *Delinquency and Drift*, p. 51.

93. Sykes and Matza, "Techniques of Neutralization," pp. 664–670; see also David Matza, "Subterranean Traditions of Youths," *Annals of the American Academy of Political and Social Science* 378 (1961): 116.

94. Sykes and Matza, "Techniques of Neutralization," pp. 664–670.

95. Ibid.

96. Ian Shields and George Whitehall, "Neutralization and Delinquency among Teenagers," *Criminal Justice and Behavior* 21 (1994): 223–235; Robert A. Ball, "An Empirical Exploration of Neutralization Theory," *Criminologica* 4 (1966): 22–32. See also M. William Minor, "The Neutralization of Criminal Offense," *Criminology* 18 (1980): 103–120; Robert Gordon, James Short, Desmond Cartwright, and Fred Strodtbeck, "Values and Gang Delinquency: A Study of Street Corner Groups," *American Journal of Sociology* 69 (1963): 109–128.

97. Robert Agnew, "The Techniques of Neutralization and Violence," *Criminology* 32 (1994): 555–580; Michael Hindelang, "The Commitment of Delinquents to Their Misdeeds: Do Delinquents Drift?" *Social Problems* 17 (1970): 500–509; Robert Regoli and Eric Poole, "The Commitment of Delinquents to Their Misdeeds: A Reexamination," *Journal of Criminal Justice* 6 (1978): 261–269.

98. Larry Siegel, Spencer Rathus, and Carol Ruppert, "Values and Delinquent Youth: An Empirical Reexamination of Theories of Delinquency," *British Journal of Criminology* 13 (1973): 237–244.

99. Nicole Leeper Piquero, Stephen Tibbetts, and Michael Blankenship, "Examining the Role of Differential Association and Techniques of Neutralization in Explaining Corporate Crime," *Deviant Behavior* 26 (2005): 159–188.

100. John Hamlin, "Misplaced Role of Rational Choice in Neutralization Theory," *Criminology* 26 (1988): 425–438.

101. Mark Pogrebin, Eric Poole, and Amos Martinez, "Accounts of Professional Misdeeds: The Sexual Exploitation of Clients by Psychotherapists," *Deviant Behavior* 13 (1992): 229–252.

102. Eric Wish, *Drug Use Forecasting 1990* (Washington, DC: National Institute of Justice, 1991).

103. Scott Briar and Irving Piliavin, "Delinquency: Situational Inducements and Commitment to Conformity," *Social Problems* 13 (1965–1966): 35–45.

104. Lawrence Sherman and Douglas Smith, with Janell Schmidt and Dennis Rogan, "Crime, Punishment, and Stake in Conformity: Legal and Informal Control of Domestic Violence," *American Sociological Review* 57 (1992): 680–690.

105. Albert Reiss, "Delinquency as the Failure of Personal and Social Controls," *American Sociological Review* 16 (1951): 196–207.

106. Briar and Piliavin, "Delinquency: Situational Inducements and Commitment to Conformity."

107. Walter Reckless, *The Crime Problem* (New York: Appleton-Century-Crofts, 1967), pp. 469–483.

108. Among the many research reports by Reckless and his colleagues are Frank Scarpitti, Ellen Murray, Simon Dinitz, and Walter Reckless, "The Good Boy in a High Delinquency Area: Four Years Later," *American Sociological Review* 23 (1960): 555–558; Walter Reckless, Simon Dinitz, and Ellen Murray, "The Good Boy in a High Delinquency Area," *Journal of Criminal Law, Criminology, and Police Science* 48 (1957): 12–26; Reckless, Dinitz, and Murray, "Self-Concept as an Insulator against Delinquency," *American Sociological Review* 21 (1956): 744–746; Walter Reckless and Simon Dinitz, "Pioneering with Self-Concept as a Vulnerability Factor in Delinquency," *Journal of Criminal Law, Criminology, and Police Science* 58 (1967): 515–523; Walter Reckless, Simon Dinitz, and Barbara Kay, "The Self-Component in Potential Delinquency and Potential Non-Delinquency," *American Sociological Review* 22 (1957): 566–570.

109. Travis Hirschi, *Causes of Delinquency* (Berkeley: University of California Press, 1969).

110. Ibid., p. 231.

111. Robert Crosnoe, "The Connection Between Academic Failure and Adolescent Drinking in Secondary School," *Sociology of Education* 79 (2006): 44–60.

112. Hirschi, *Causes of Delinquency*, pp. 66–74.

113. Øzden Øzbay and Yusuf Ziya Øzcan, "A Test of Hirschi's Social Bonding Theory," *International Journal of Offender Therapy and Comparative Criminology* 50 (2006): 711–726; Michael Wiatrowski, David Griswold, and Mary K. Roberts, "Social Control Theory and Delinquency," *American Sociological Review* 46 (1981): 525–541.

114. Patricia Van Voorhis, Francis Cullen, Richard Mathers, and Connie Chenoweth Garner, "The Impact of Family Structure and Quality on Delinquency: A Comparative Assessment of Structural and Functional Factors," *Criminology* 26 (1988): 235–261.

115. Marc LeBlanc, "Family Dynamics, Adolescent Delinquency, and Adult Criminality,"

paper presented at the Society for Life History Research conference, Keystone, Colorado, October 1990, p. 6.

116. Bobbi Jo Anderson, Malcolm Holmes, and Erik Ostresh, "Male and Female Delinquents' Attachments and Effects of Attachments on Severity of Self-Reported Delinquency," *Criminal Justice and Behavior* 26 (1999): 435–452.

117. Helen Garnier and Judith Stein, "An 18-Year Model of Family and Peer Effects on Adolescent Drug Use and Delinquency," *Journal of Youth and Adolescence* 31 (2002): 45–56.

118. Teresa LaGrange and Robert Silverman, "Perceived Strain and Delinquency Motivation: An Empirical Evaluation of General Strain Theory," paper presented at the annual meeting of the American Society of Criminology, Boston, November 1995.

119. Van Voorhis, Cullen, Mathers, and Garner, "The Impact of Family Structure and Quality on Delinquency."

120. Thomas Vander Ven, Francis Cullen, Mark Carrozza, and John Paul Wright, "Home Alone: The Impact of Maternal Employment on Delinquency," *Social Problems* 48 (2001): 236–257; Patricia Jenkins, "School Delinquency and the School Social Bond," *Journal of Research in Crime and Delinquency* 34 (1997): 337–367.

121. Patricia Jenkins, "School Delinquency and the School Social Bond," *Journal of Research in Crime and Delinquency* 34 (1997): 337–367.

122. Trina Hope, Esther Wilder, and Toni Terling Watt, "The Relationships among Adolescent Pregnancy, Pregnancy Resolution, and Juvenile Delinquency," *Sociological Quarterly* 44 (2003): 555–576.

123. John Cochran and Ronald Akers, "An Exploration of the Variable Effects of Religiosity on Adolescent Marijuana and Alcohol Use," *Journal of Research in Crime and Delinquency* 26 (1989): 198–225.

124. Mark Regnerus and Glen Elder, "Religion and Vulnerability among Low-Risk Adolescents," *Social Science Research* 32 (2003): 633–658; Mark Regnerus, "Moral Communities and Adolescent Delinquency: Religious Contexts and Community Social Control," *Sociological Quarterly* 44 (2003): 523–554.

125. Michael Cretacci, "Religion and Social Control: An Application of a Modified Social Bond of Violence," *Criminal Justice Review* 28 (2003): 254–277.

126. Robert Agnew and David Peterson, "Leisure and Delinquency," *Social Problems* 36 (1989): 332–348.

127. Jonathan Zaff, Kristin Moore, Angela Romano Papillo, and Stephanie Williams, "Implications of Extracurricular Activity Participation during Adolescence on Positive Outcomes," *Journal of Adolescent Research* 18 (2003): 599–631.

128. Marianne Junger and Ineke Haen Marshall, "The Interethnic Generalizability of Social Control Theory: An Empirical Test," *Journal of Research in Crime and Delinquency* 34 (1997): 79–112; Josine Junger-Tas, "An Empirical Test of Social Control Theory,"

Journal of Quantitative Criminology 8 (1992): 18–29.

129. LaGrange and Silverman, "Perceived Strain and Delinquency Motivation."

130. Kimberly Kempf, "The Empirical Status of Hirschi's Control Theory," in *Advances in Criminological Theory*, eds. Bill Laufer and Freda Adler (New Brunswick, NJ: Transaction Books, 1992).

131. Vander Ven, Cullen, Carrozza, and Wright, "Home Alone: The Impact of Maternal Employment on Delinquency," p. 253.

132. Peggy Giordano, Stephen Cernkovich, and M. D. Pugh, "Friendships and Delinquency," *American Journal of Sociology* 91 (1986): 1170–1202.

133. Denise Kandel and Mark Davies, "Friendship Networks, Intimacy, and Illicit Drug Use in Young Adulthood: A Comparison of Two Competing Theories," *Criminology* 29 (1991): 441–467.

134. Velmer Burton, Francis Cullen, T. David Evans, R. Gregory Dunaway, Sesha Kethineni, and Gary Payne, "The Impact of Parental Controls on Delinquency," *Journal of Criminal Justice* 23 (1995): 111–126.

135. Kimberly Kempf Leonard and Scott Decker, "The Theory of Social Control: Does It Apply to the Very Young?" *Journal of Criminal Justice* 22 (1994): 89–105.

136. Michael Hindelang, "Causes of Delinquency: A Partial Replication and Extension," *Social Problems* 21 (1973): 471–487.

137. Gary Jensen and David Brownfield, "Parents and Drugs," *Criminology* 21 (1983): 543–554; see also M. Wiatrowski, D. Griswold, and M. Roberts, "Social Control Theory and Delinquency," *American Sociological Review* 46 (1981): 525–541.

138. Leslie Samuelson, Timothy Hartnagel, and Harvey Krahn, "Crime and Social Control among High School Dropouts," *Journal of Crime and Justice* 18 (1990): 129–161.

139. Cesar Rebellon and Karen van Gundy, "Can Control Theory Explain the Link between Parental Physical Abuse and Delinquency? A Longitudinal Analysis," *Journal of Research in Crime and Delinquency* 42 (2005): 247–274; Marvin Krohn and James Massey, "Social Control and Delinquent Behavior: An Examination of the Elements of the Social Bond," *Sociological Quarterly* 21 (1980): 529–543.

140. Jill Leslie Rosenbaum and James Lasley, "School, Community Context, and Delinquency: Rethinking the Gender Gap," *Justice Quarterly* 7 (1990): 493–513.

141. Randy LaGrange and Helene Raskin White, "Age Differences in Delinquency: A Test of Theory," *Criminology* 23 (1985): 19–45.

142. Robert Agnew, "Social Control Theory and Delinquency: A Longitudinal Test," *Criminology* 23 (1985): 47–61.

143. Alan E. Liska and M. D. Reed, "Ties to Conventional Institutions and Delinquency: Estimating Reciprocal Effects," *American Sociological Review* 50 (1985): 547–560.

144. George Herbert Mead, *Mind, Self and Society* (Chicago: University of Chicago Press,

1934); George Herbert Mead, *The Philosophy of the Act* (Chicago: University of Chicago Press, 1938); Charles Horton Cooley, *Human Nature and the Social Order* (New York: Schocken, 1964, first published 1902); Herbert Blumer, *Symbolic Interactionism: Perspective and Method* (Englewood Cliffs, NJ: Prentice Hall, 1969).

145. Bruce Link, Elmer Streuning, Francis Cullen, Patrick Shrout, and Bruce Dohrenwend, "A Modified Labeling Theory Approach to Mental Disorders: An Empirical Assessment," *American Sociological Review* 54 (1989): 400–423.

146. Linda Jackson, John Hunter, and Carole Hodge, "Physical Attractiveness and Intellectual Competence: A Meta-Analytic Review," *Social Psychology Quarterly* 58 (1995): 108–122.

147. Mike Adams, Craig Robertson, Phyllis Gray-Ray, and Melvin Ray, "Labeling and Delinquency," *Adolescence* (2003): 171–186.

148. *President's Commission on Law Enforcement and the Administration of Youth Crime, Task Force Report: Juvenile Delinquency and Youth* (Washington, DC: U.S. Government Printing Office, 1967), p. 43.

149. Kai Erickson, "Notes on the Sociology of Deviance," *Social Problems* 9 (1962): 397–414.

150. Edwin Schur, *Labeling Deviant Behavior* (New York: Harper & Row, 1972), p. 21.

151. Howard Becker, *Outsiders, Studies in the Sociology of Deviance* (New York: Macmillan, 1963), p. 9.

152. Laurie Goodstein, "The Architect of the 'Gay Conversion' Campaign," *New York Times*, 13 August 1998, p. A10.

153. Christy Visher, "Gender, Police Arrest Decision, and Notions of Chivalry," *Criminology* 21 (1983): 5–28.

154. Marjorie Zatz, "Race, Ethnicity and Determinate Sentencing," *Criminology* 22 (1984): 147–171.

155. Christina DeJong and Kenneth Jackson, "Putting Race into Context: Race, Juvenile Justice Processing, and Urbanization," *Justice Quarterly* 15 (1998): 487–504.

156. Roland Chilton and Jim Galvin, "Race, Crime and Criminal Justice," *Crime and Delinquency* 31 (1985): 3–14.

157. Joan Petersilia, "Racial Disparities in the Criminal Justice System: A Summary," *Crime and Delinquency* 31 (1985): 15–34.

158. Ross Matsueda, "Reflected Appraisals: Parental Labeling, and Delinquency: Specifying a Symbolic Interactionist Theory," *American Journal of Sociology* 97 (1992): 1,577–1,611.

159. Xiaoru Liu, "The Conditional Effect of Peer Groups on the Relationship between Parental Labeling and Youth Delinquency," *Sociological Perspectives* 43 (2000): 499–515.

160. Suzanne Ageton and Delbert Elliott, *The Effect of Legal Processing on Self-Concept* (Boulder, CO: Institute of Behavioral Science, 1973).

161. Adams, Robertson, Gray-Ray, and Ray, "Labeling and Delinquency."

162. Jón Gunnar Bernburg, Marvin Krohn, and Craig Rivera, "Official Labeling, Criminal Embeddedness, and Subsequent Delinquency: A Longitudinal Test of Labeling Theory," *Journal of Research in Crime and Delinquency* 43 (2006): 67–88.

163. Lee Michael Johnson, Ronald Simons, and Rand Conger, "Criminal Justice System Involvement and Continuity of Youth Crime," *Youth and Society* 36 (2004): 3–29.

164. Gary Sweeten, "Who Will Graduate? Disruption of High School Education by Arrest and Court Involvement," *Justice Quarterly* 23 (2006): 462–480.

165. Melvin Ray and William Downs, "An Empirical Test of Labeling Theory Using Longitudinal Data," *Journal of Research in Crime and Delinquency* 23 (1986): 169–194.

166. Sherman and Smith, with Schmidt and Rogan, "Crime, Punishment, and Stake in Conformity."

167. Lawrence Bench and Terry Allen, "Investigating the Stigma of Prison Classification: An Experimental Design," *Prison Journal* 83 (2003): 367–382.

168. Bernburg, Krohn, and Rivera, "Official Labeling, Criminal Embeddedness, and Subsequent Delinquency: A Longitudinal Test of Labeling Theory."

169. Heimer and Matsueda, "Role-Taking, Role-Commitment, and Delinquency."

170. See, for example, Howard Kaplan and Hiroshi Fukurai, "Negative Social Sanctions, Self-Rejection, and Drug Use," *Youth and Society* 23 (1992): 275–298; Howard Kaplan and Robert Johnson, "Negative Social Sanctions and Juvenile Delinquency: Effects of Labeling in a Model of Deviant Behavior," *Social Science Quarterly* 72 (1991): 98–122; Howard Kaplan, Robert Johnson, and Carol Bailey, "Deviant Peers and Deviant Behavior: Further Elaboration of a Model," *Social Psychology Quarterly* 30 (1987): 277–284.

171. Howard Kaplan, *Toward a General Theory of Deviance: Contributions from Perspectives on Deviance and Criminality* (College Station: Texas A&M University, n.d.).

172. Michael Levenson and Brian R. Ballou, "Teen Reportedly Talked of Trying to Kill," *Boston Globe*, 21 January 21, p. 1.

173. John Lofland, *Deviance and Identity* (Englewood Cliffs, NJ: Prentice Hall, 1969).

174. Frank Tannenbaum, *Crime and the Community* (New York: Columbia University Press, 1938), pp. 19–20.

175. Edwin Lemert, *Social Pathology* (New York: McGraw-Hill, 1951).

176. Ibid., p. 75.

177. Bruce Western, *Punishment and Inequality in America* (New York: Russell Sage Foundation, 2006); Sara Steen, Rodney Engen, and Randy Gainey, "Images of Danger and Culpability: Racial Stereotyping, Case Processing, and Criminal Sentencing," *Criminology* 43 (2005): 435–468; Stephanie Bontrager, William Bales, and Ted Chiricos, "Race, Ethnicity, Threat and the Labeling of Convicted Felons," *Criminology* 43 (2005): 589–622.

178. John Wooldredge, "Neighborhood Effects on Felony Sentencing," *Journal of Research in Crime and Delinquency* 44 (2007): 238–263.

179. Samuel Walker, Cassia Spohn, and Miriam DeLone, *The Color of Justice, Race, Ethnicity, and Crime in America* (Belmont, CA: Wadsworth, 1996), pp. 145–146.

180. Howard Kaplan and Robert Johnson, "Negative Social Sanctions and Juvenile Delinquency: Effects of Labeling in a Model of Deviant Behavior," *Social Science Quarterly* 72 (1991): 98–122.

181. Ruth Triplett, "The Conflict Perspective, Symbolic Interactionism, and the Status Characteristics Hypothesis," *Justice Quarterly* 10 (1993): 540–558.

182. Lening Zhang, "Official Offense Status and Self-Esteem among Chinese Youths," *Journal of Criminal Justice* 31 (2003): 99–105.

183. Charles Tittle, "Two Empirical Regularities (Maybe) in Search of an Explanation: Commentary on the Age/Crime Debate," *Criminology* 26 (1988): 75–85.

184. Robert Sampson and John Laub, "A Life-Course Theory of Cumulative Disadvantage and the Stability of Delinquency," in *Developmental Theories of Crime and Delinquency*, ed. Terence Thornberry (New Brunswick, NJ: Transaction Press, 1997): 133–161; Douglas Smith and Robert Brame, "On the Initiation and Continuation of Delinquency," *Criminology* 4 (1994): 607–630.

185. Robert Sampson and John Laub, "A Life-Course Theory of Cumulative Disadvantage and the Stability of Delinquency," in *Developmental Theories of Crime and Delinquency*, ed. Terence Thornberry (New Brunswick, NJ: Transaction Books, 1997), pp. 133–161.

186. Jón Gunnar Bernburg and Marvin Krohn, "Labeling, Life Chances, and Adult Crime: The Direct and Indirect Effects of Official Intervention in Adolescence on Crime in Early Adulthood," *Criminology* 41 (2003): 1,287–1,319.

187. Jack Gibbs, "Conceptions of Deviant Behavior: The Old and the New," *Pacific Sociological Review* 9 (1966): 11–13.

188. Charles Tittle, "Labeling and Crime: An Empirical Evaluation," in *The Labeling of Deviance: Evaluating a Perspective*, ed. Walter Gove (New York: Wiley, 1975), pp. 157–179.

189. Megan Kurlychek, Robert Brame, and Shawn Bushway, "Enduring Risk? Old Criminal Records and Predictions of Future Criminal Involvement," *Crime and Delinquency* 53 (2007): 64–83.

190. Raymond Paternoster and Leeann Iovanni, "The Labeling Perspective and Delinquency: An Elaboration of the Theory and an Assessment of the Evidence," *Justice Quarterly* 6 (1989): 358–394.

191. Shadd Maruna, Thomas Lebel, Nick Mitchell, and Michelle Maples, "Pygmalion in the Reintegration Process: Desistance from Crime through the Looking Glass," *Psychology, Crime, and Law* 10 (2004): 271–281.

192. Head Start statistics can be found at www.acf.hhs.gov/programs/hsb/ (accessed June 4, 2007).

Social Conflict, Critical Criminology, and Restorative Justice

In 2007, the Home Depot Company, the nation's largest home improvement retailer with more than 2,000 stores and 350,000 employees, made national headlines not because of its products but because of an executive pay package. News leaked out that Robert Nardelli, its chief executive officer, had stepped down and was leaving the company with a $210 million severance package.[1] Though Home Depot claimed that Nardelli's departure was a "mutually agreed upon" decision, many attributed it to the poor performance of the company's stock. Regardless of the cause, the fact that Nardelli walked away with a $210 million package that included stock options and other compensation seemed shocking, even in a society where lavish executive pay packages have become the norm. Nardelli had been with the company for only seven years. In August 2007, Nardelli was named CEO of the new Chrysler Corporation.

While the Nardelli case is extreme, the average CEO of a Standard & Poor's 500 company now makes more than $13 million in total compensation each year. At a time when many working families are struggling and more than 37 million Americans live in poverty, CEOs' lucrative pay packages are quite disturbing to some commentators.[2]

And to make matters worse, thousands of companies are believed to have backdated stock options in order to sweeten their top executives' pay packages.[3] A stock option gives the holder the right to purchase a share of stock at a set price, known as the exercise price, at any time during a certain period, usually 10 years. If the market price rises above the exercise price, the holder can buy stock at the exercise price, sell at the market price, and pocket the difference. So if you have the right to buy the stock at $25 per share and the stock goes to $100, you can sell and keep the $75 difference. If you have options to buy a million shares or so, that can amount to some serious money. Most companies' options plans require them to set the exercise price equal to the market price on the date of grant. Backdating the day of the grant can change the exercise price to a much lower number, and automatically increase the holder's potential profit.[4]

To some criminologists the vast difference between executive and worker compensation illustrates the inherent inequities in the capitalist system. While the poor suffer inadequate health care, education, and domicile, the wealthy are able to lock themselves within gated communities and enjoy the finest food, clothing, and shelter. This level of income inequality is one of the main sources of social conflict that wracks contemporary society and is a breeding ground for crime.

Conflict comes in many forms, occurs at many levels of society, and involves a whole slew of adversaries: workers and bosses, the United States and its overseas enemies, religious zealots and apostates, citizens and police. It occurs within cities, neighborhoods, and even within the family.

Conflict can be destructive when it leads to war, violence, and death; it can be functional when it results in positive social change. Conflict promotes crime by creating a social atmosphere in which the law is a mechanism for controlling dissatisfied, have-not members of society while the wealthy maintain their power. This is why crimes that are the province of the wealthy, such as illegal corporate activities, are sanctioned much more leniently than those, such as burglary, that are considered lower-class activities.

Criminologists who view crime as a function of social conflict and economic rivalry have been known by a number of titles, such as conflict, Marxist, or radical criminologists, but here we will refer to them as critical criminologists and their field of study as critical criminology. Many, but not all, apply the type of socioeconomic analysis first used by Karl Marx to identify the economic structures in society that control all human relations. Critical criminologists reject the notion that law is designed to maintain a tranquil, fair society and that criminals are malevolent people who wish to trample the rights of others. They consider acts of racism, sexism, imperialism, unsafe working conditions, inadequate child care, substandard housing, pollution of the environment, and war-making as a tool of foreign policy, to be "true crimes." The crimes of the helpless—burglary, robbery, and assault—are more expressions of rage over unjust economic conditions than actual crimes.[5] By focusing on how the capitalist state uses law to control the lower classes, Marxist thought serves as the basis for critical theory.

Contemporary critical criminologists try to explain crime within economic and social contexts and to express the connection between social class, crime, and social control.[6] They are concerned with issues such as these:

▌ The role government plays in creating a criminogenic environment

▌ The relationship between personal or group power and the shaping of criminal law

▌ The prevalence of bias in justice system operations

▌ The relationship between a capitalist, free enterprise economy and crime rates

Critical criminologists often take the broader view, opposing racism, sexism, and genocide, rather than focusing on burglary, robbery, and rape.[7] This chapter reviews critical criminology. It covers its development and principle ideas, and then looks at policies that have been embraced by critical thinkers, which focus on peace and restoration rather than punishment and exclusion. Figure 8.1 illustrates the various independent branches of social conflict theory.

MARXIST THOUGHT

As you may recall (Chapter 1), Karl Marx (1818–1883) identified the economic structures in society that control all human relations. Marx's view of society was shaped by the economic trends and structures of that period. He lived in an era of unrestrained capitalist expansion.[8] The tools of the Industrial Revolution had become regular features of society by 1850. Mechanized factories, the use of coal to drive steam engines, and modern transportation all inspired economic development. Production had shifted from cottage industries to large factories. Industrialists could hire workers on their own terms; as a result, conditions in factories were atrocious. Owners and government agents, who were the agents of capitalists, ruthlessly suppressed trade unions that promised workers salvation from these atrocities.

Marx's early career as a journalist was interrupted by government suppression of the newspaper where he worked because of the paper's liberal editorial policy. He then moved to Paris, where he met Friedrich Engels (1820–1895), who would become his friend and economic patron. By 1847, Marx and Engels had joined with a group of primarily German socialist revolutionaries known as the Communist League.

Productive Forces and Productive Relations

In 1848, Marx issued his famous *Communist Manifesto*. In this document, Marx focused his attention on the economic conditions perpetuated by the capitalist system. He stated that its development had turned workers into a dehumanized mass who lived an existence that was at the mercy of their capitalist employers. He wrote of the injustice of young children being sent to work in mines and factories from dawn to dusk. He focused on the people who were being beaten down by a system that demanded obedience and cooperation and offered little in return. These oppressive conditions led Marx to conclude that the character of every civilization is determined by its mode of production—the way its people develop and produce material goods (materialism).

Marx identified the economic structures in society that control all human relations. Production has two components: (1) productive forces, which include such things as technology, energy sources, and material resources, and (2) productive relations, which are the relationships that exist among the people producing goods and services. The most important relationship in industrial culture is between the owners of the means of production, the capitalist bourgeoisie, and the people who do the actual labor, the proletariat.

Throughout history, society has been organized this way: master–slave, lord–serf, and now capitalist–proletariat. According

Figure 8.1 The Branches of Social Conflict Theory

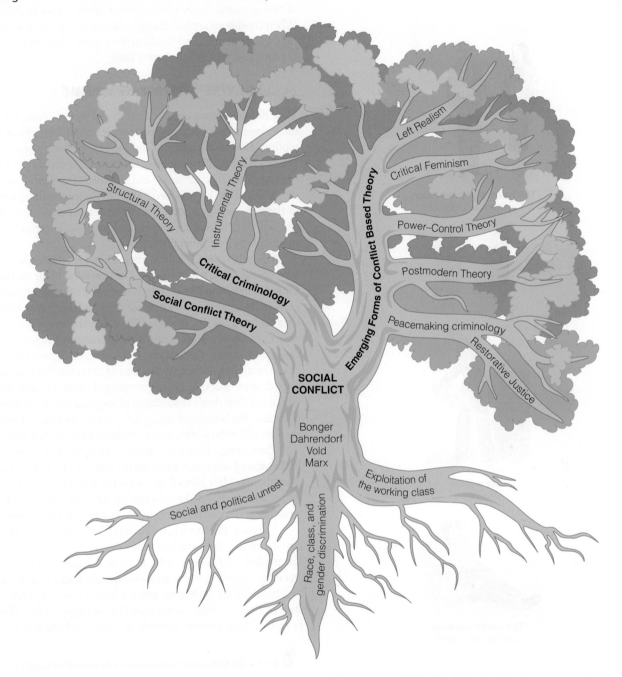

to Marx, capitalist society is subject to the development of a rigid class structure with the capitalist bourgeoisie at the top, followed by the working proletariat, who actually produce goods and services, and at the bottom, the fringe, nonproductive members who produce nothing and live, parasitically, off the work of others—the lumpen proletariat (Figure 8.2).

In Marxist theory, the term "class" does not refer to an attribute or characteristic of a person or a group; rather, it denotes position in relation to others. Thus, it is not necessary to have a particular amount of wealth or prestige to be a member of the capitalist class; it is more important to have the power to exploit others economically, legally, and socially. The political and economic philosophy of the dominant class influences all aspects of life. Consciously or unconsciously, artists, writers, and teachers bend their work to the whims of the capitalist system. Thus, the economic system controls all facets of human life. Consequently, people's lives revolve around the means of production.

As Marx said:

In all forms of society, there is one specific kind of production which predominates over the rest, whose relations thus assign rank and influence to the others. It is a general illumination which bathes all the other colours and modifies their particularity. It is a particular ether which determines the specific gravity of every being which has materialized within it.[9]

Figure 8.2 The Marxist View of Class

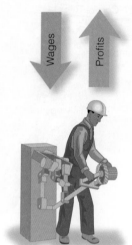

The owners of production
Capitalist bourgeoisie

Wages

Profits

The worker
Proletariat

The nonproductive
Lumpen proletariat

Marx believed societies and their structures were not stable and, therefore, could change through slow evolution or sudden violence. If social conflicts are not resolved, they tend to destabilize society, leading to social change.

The ebb and flow of the capitalist business cycle creates social conflicts that contain the seeds of its own destruction. Marx predicted that from its ashes would grow a socialist state in which the workers themselves would own the means of production. In his analysis, Marx used the **dialectic method**, based on the analysis developed by the philosopher Georg Hegel (1770–1831). Hegel argued that for every idea, or **thesis**, there exists an opposing argument, or **antithesis**. Since neither position can ever be truly accepted, the result is a merger of the two ideas, a

synthesis. Marx adapted this analytic method for his study of class struggle. History, argued Marx, is replete with examples of two opposing forces whose conflict promotes social change. When conditions are bad enough, the oppressed will rise up to fight the owners and eventually replace them. Thus, in the end, the capitalist system will destroy itself.

A Marxist Vision of Crime

Marx did not write a great deal on the subject of crime, but he mentioned it in a variety of passages scattered throughout his writing. He viewed crime as the product of law enforcement policies akin to a labeling process theory.[10] He also saw a connection between criminality and the inequities found in the capitalist system. He reasoned: "There must be something rotten in the very core of a social system which increases in wealth without diminishing its misery, and increases in crime even more rapidly than in numbers."[11]

His collaborator, Friedrich Engels, however, did spend some time on the subject in his work, *The Condition of the Working Class in England in 1844*.[12] Engels portrayed crime as a function of social demoralization—a collapse of people's humanity reflecting a decline in society. Workers, demoralized by capitalist society, are caught up in a process that leads to crime and violence. According to Engels, workers are social outcasts, ignored by the structure of capitalist society and treated as brutes.[13] Left to their own devices, working people committed crime because their choice is a slow death of starvation or a speedy one at the hands of the law. The brutality of the capitalist system, he believed, turns workers into animal-like creatures without a will of their own.

The writings of Karl Marx greatly influenced the development of the view of crime that rested on the concept of social conflict. Even though Marx himself did not write much on the topic of crime, his views on the relationship between the economic structure and social behavior deeply influenced other thinkers.

The concept of social conflict was first applied to criminology by three distinguished scholars: Willem Bonger, Ralf Dahrendorf, and George Vold. In some instances, their works share the Marxist view that industrial society is wracked by conflict between the proletariat and the bourgeoisie; in other instances, their writings diverge from Marxist dogma. The writing of each of these pioneers is briefly described in Exhibit 8.1.

www Go to academic.cengage.com/criminaljustice/siegel to:

- Read about **Marx and his vision**.
- Review an in-depth interview with **Ralf Dahrendorf**.

CREATING A CRITICAL CRIMINOLOGY

The social ferment of the 1960s gave birth to critical criminology. In 1968, a group of British sociologists formed the National Deviancy Conference (NDC). With about 300 members, this

Willem Bonger, Ralf Dahrendorf, and George Vold on Crime

Willem Bonger

Bonger believed that society is divided into have and have-not groups, not on the basis of people's innate ability, but because of the system of production that is in force. In every society that is divided into a ruling class and an inferior class, penal law serves the will of the ruling class. Even though criminal laws may appear to protect members of both classes, hardly any act is punished that does not injure the interests of the dominant ruling class. Crimes, then, are considered to be antisocial acts because they are harmful to those who have the power at their command to control society. Under capitalism, the legal system discriminates against the poor by defending the actions of the wealthy. Because the proletariat are deprived of the materials that are monopolized by the bourgeoisie they are more likely to violate the law.

Ralf Dahrendorf

Dahrendorf argued that modern society is organized into what he called **imperatively coordinated associations.** These associations comprise two groups: those who possess authority and use it for social domination and those who lack authority and are dominated. Society is a plurality of competing interest groups. He proposed a unified conflict theory of human behavior, which can be summarized as follows:

▪ Every society is at every point subject to processes of change; social change is everywhere.

▪ Every society displays at every point dissent and conflict; social conflict is everywhere.

▪ Every element in a society renders a contribution to its disintegration and change.

▪ Every society is based on the coercion of some of its members by others.

George Vold

Vold argued that laws are created by politically oriented groups who seek the government's assistance to help them defend their rights and protect their interests. If a group can marshal enough support, a law will be created to hamper and curb the interests of some opposition group. Every stage of the process—from passing the law, to prosecuting the case, to developing relationships between inmate and guard, parole agent and parolee—is marked by conflict. Criminal acts are a consequence of direct contact between forces struggling to control society.

Sources: Willem Bonger, *Criminality and Economic Conditions*, abridged ed. (Bloomington: Indiana University Press, 1969, first published 1916); Ralf Dahrendorf, *Class and Class Conflict in Industrial Society* (Palo Alto, CA: Stanford University Press, 1959); George Vold, *Theoretical Criminology* (New York: Oxford University Press, 1958).

The NDC called attention to ways in which social control might actually cause deviance rather than just respond to antisocial behavior. Many conference members became concerned about the political nature of social control.

In 1973, critical theory was given a powerful academic boost when British scholars Ian Taylor, Paul Walton, and Jock Young published *The New Criminology*.[14] This brilliant, thorough, and well-constructed critique of existing concepts in criminology called for the development of new methods of criminological analysis and critique. *The New Criminology* became the standard resource for scholars critical of both the field of criminology and the existing legal process. Since its publication there has been a tradition for critical criminologists to turn their attention to the field itself, questioning the role criminology plays in supporting the status quo and aiding in the oppression of the poor and powerless.[15]

U.S. scholars were also influenced during the late 1960s and early 1970s by the widespread unrest and social change that shook the world. The war in Vietnam, prison struggles, and the civil rights and feminist movements produced a climate in which criticism of the ruling class seemed a natural by-product. Mainstream, positivist criminology was criticized as being overtly conservative, pro-government, and antihuman. Critical criminologists scoffed when their fellow scholars used statistical analysis of computerized data to describe criminal and delinquent behavior. Several influential scholars embraced the idea that the social conflict produced by the unequal distribution of power and wealth was at the root cause of crime. William Chambliss and Robert Seidman wrote the well-respected treatise *Law, Order and Power*, which documented how the justice system protects the rich and powerful.[16] Chambliss and Seidman's work showed how control of the political and economic system affects the way criminal justice is administered and that the definitions of crime used in contemporary society favor those who control the justice system.

In another influential work, *The Social Reality of Crime*, Richard Quinney also proclaimed that in contemporary society criminal law represents the interests of those who hold power.[17] Where there is conflict between social groups—the wealthy and the poor—those who hold power will create laws that benefit themselves and keep rivals in check. Law is not an abstract body of rules that represents an absolute moral code; rather, law is an integral part of society, a force that represents a way of life and a method of doing things. Crime is a function of power relations and an inevitable result of social conflict. Criminals are not simply social misfits but people who have come up short in the struggle for success and are seeking alternative means of achieving wealth, status, or even survival.

As a group these social thinkers began to show how in our postindustrial, capitalist society the economic system invariably produces haves and have-nots.[18] The mode of production shapes social life. Because economic competitiveness is the essence of capitalism, conflict increases and eventually destabilizes both social institutions and social groups.[19]

---

organization sponsored several national symposia and dialogues. Members came from all walks of life, but at its core the NDC was a group of academics who were critical of the positivist criminology being taught in British and American universities. More specifically, they rejected the conservative stance of criminologists and their close financial relationship with government funding agencies.

Contemporary Critical Criminology

From these early roots a robust critical criminology was formed. At first, these alternative forms of criminology were considered Marxist and radical. They have morphed into a critical criminology that is antiestablishment and questioning of the socioeconomic structures that produce crime and criminality.[20]

Today, critical criminologists devote their attention to a number of important themes and concepts. One is the use and misuse of power, or the ability of persons and groups to determine and control the behavior of others and to shape public opinion to meet their personal interests. Because those in power shape the content of the law, it comes as no surprise that their behavior is often exempt from legal sanctions. Those who deserve the most severe sanctions (wealthy white-collar criminals whose crimes cost society millions of dollars) usually receive lenient punishments while those whose relatively minor crimes are committed out of economic necessity (petty thieves and drug dealers) receive stricter penalties, especially if they are minority group members who lack social and economic power.[21]

Critical criminologists also critique the field of criminology, questioning the role criminologists play in supporting the status quo and aiding in the oppression of the poor and powerless.[22] After all, criminologists may spend their time creating effective crime control mechanisms that swell the nation's prisons with indigent and desperate people while corporate executives make fat profits.

Critical criminologists have also been deeply concerned about the current state of the American political system and the creation of what they consider to be an American Empire abroad. Ironically, recent events such as the war in Iraq and the efforts to penalize immigrants and close U.S. borders have energized critical thinkers; their vision seems as pertinent today as it was during its heyday in the 1960s and 1970s.[23] The conservative agenda, they believe, calls for the dismantling of welfare and health programs, lowering of labor costs through union busting, tax cuts that favor the wealthy, ending affirmative action, and reducing environmental control and regulation. Some try to show how racism still pervades the American system and manifests itself in a wide variety of social practices ranging from the administration of criminal justice to the "whitening" of the teaching force because selection rests upon a racially skewed selection process.[24]

Because corporations are now more powerful than ever, at the expense of government, spending is being cut on social programs and raised on military expansion. The rapid buildup of the prison system and passage of draconian criminal laws that threaten civil rights and liberties—the war on drugs, the death penalty, "three strikes laws," and the Patriot Act—are other elements of the conservative agenda. Tax cuts for the wealthy mean less money for social programs. The war on drugs has resulted in million of people being incarcerated, most of whom are poor and powerless. Critical criminologists believe that they are responsible for informing the public about the dangers of these developments.[25]

connections

The USA Patriot Act will be discussed further in Chapter 10 within the context of legal efforts to thwart terrorism. While some welcome its provisions that make it easier for the government to monitor people considered dangerous, critical thinkers fear loss of individual freedom at the expense of state power.

Critical criminologists have turned their attention to the threat competitive capitalism presents to the working class. In addition to perpetuating male supremacy and racism, they believe that modern global capitalism helps destroy the lives of workers in less developed countries. Capitalists hailed China's entry into the World Trade Organization in 2001 as a significant economic event. However, critical thinkers point out that the economic boom has significant costs: the average manufacturing wage in China is 20 to 25 cents per hour; many thousands of workers are killed at work each year and millions more disabled.[26]

HOW CRITICAL CRIMINOLOGISTS DEFINE CRIME

According to critical theorists crime is a political concept designed to protect the power and position of the upper classes at the expense of the poor. Some, but not all, would include in a list of "real" crimes such acts as violations of human rights due to racism, sexism, and imperialism and other violations of human dignity and physical needs and necessities. Part of the critical agenda, argues criminologist Robert Bohm, is to make the public aware that these behaviors "are crimes just as much as burglary and robbery."[27]

The nature of a society controls the direction of its criminality; criminals are not social misfits but products of the society and its economic system. "Capitalism," claims Bohm, "as a mode of production, has always produced a relatively high level of crime and violence."[28] According to Michael Lynch and W. Byron Groves, three implications follow from this view:

1. Each society produces its own types and amounts of crime.

2. Each society has its own distinctive ways of dealing with criminal behavior.

3. Each society gets the amount and type of crime that it deserves.[29]

This analysis tells us that criminals are not a group of outsiders who can be controlled by increased law enforcement. Criminality, instead, is a function of social and economic organization. To control crime and reduce criminality, societies must remove the social conditions that promote crime.

In our advanced technological society, those with economic and political power control the definition of crime and the manner in which the criminal justice system enforces the law.[30] Consequently, the only crimes available to the poor are the severely sanctioned "street crimes": rape, murder, theft, and mugging. Members of the middle class cheat on their taxes and engage in petty corporate crime (employee theft), acts that generate social disapproval but are rarely punished severely. The wealthy are involved in acts that should be described as crimes but are not, such as racism, sexism, and profiteering. Although regulatory laws control illegal business activities, these are rarely enforced, and violations are lightly punished. One reason is that an essential feature of capitalism is the need to expand business and create new markets. This goal often comes in conflict with laws designed to protect the environment and creates clashes with those who seek their enforcement. In our postindustrial society the need for expansion usually triumphs. For example, corporate spokespeople and their political allies will brand environmentalists as "tree huggers" who stand in the way of jobs and prosperity.[31]

The rich are insulated from street crimes because they live in areas far removed from crime. Those in power use the fear of crime as a tool to maintain their control over society. The poor are controlled through incarceration, and the middle class is diverted from caring about the crimes of the powerful by their fear of the crimes of the powerless.[32] Ironically, they may have more to lose from the economic crimes committed by the rich than the street crimes of the poor. Stock market swindles and savings and loan scams cost the public billions of dollars but are typically settled with fines and probationary sentences.

Because private ownership of property is the true measure of success in American society (as opposed to being, say, a worthy person), the state becomes an ally of the wealthy in protecting their property interests. As a result, theft-related crimes are often punished more severely than are acts of violence because although the former may be interclass the latter are typically intraclass.

HOW CRITICAL CRIMINOLOGISTS VIEW THE CAUSE OF CRIME

Critical thinkers believe that the key crime-producing element of modern corporate capitalism is the effort to create surplus value—the profits produced by the laboring classes that are accrued by business owners. Once accumulated, surplus value can be either reinvested or used to enrich the owners. To increase the rate of surplus value, workers can be made to toil harder for less pay, be made more efficient, or be replaced by machines or technology. Therefore, economic growth does not benefit all elements of the population, and in the long run it may produce the same effect as a depression or recession.

As the rate of surplus value increases, more people are displaced from productive relationships, and the size of the marginal population swells. As corporations downsize to increase profits, high-paying labor and managerial jobs are lost to computer-driven machinery. Displaced workers are forced into service jobs at minimum wage. Many become temporary employees without benefits or a secure position.

As more people are thrust outside the economic mainstream, a condition referred to as marginalization, a larger portion of the population is forced to live in areas conducive to crime. Once people are marginalized, commitment to the system declines, producing another criminogenic force: a weakened bond to society.[33] This process is illustrated in Figure 8.3.

The government may be quick to respond during periods of economic decline because those in power assume that poor economic conditions breed crime and social disorder. When unemployment is increasing, public officials assume the worst and devote greater attention to the criminal justice system, perhaps

---

Figure 8.3 Surplus Value and Crime

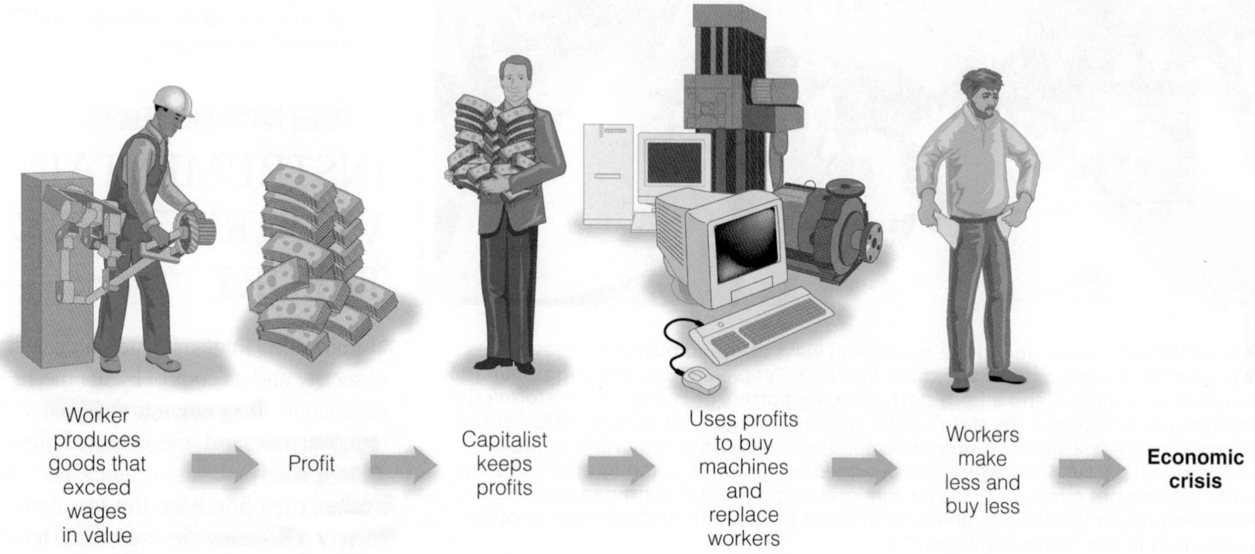

Worker produces goods that exceed wages in value → Profit → Capitalist keeps profits → Uses profits to buy machines and replace workers → Workers make less and buy less → **Economic crisis**

building new prisons to prepare for the coming "crime wave."[34] Empirical research confirms that economic downturns are indeed linked to both crime rate increases and government activities such as passing anticrime legislation.[35] As the level of surplus value increases, so too do police expenditures, most likely because of the perceived or real need for the state to control those on the economic margin.[36]

Globalization

The new global economy is a particularly vexing development for critical theorists and their use of the concept of surplus value. Globalization, which usually refers to the process of creating transnational markets and political and legal systems, has shifted the focus of critical inquiry to a world perspective.

Globalization began when large companies decided to establish themselves in foreign markets by adapting their products or services to the local culture. The process took off with the fall of the Soviet Union, which opened new European markets. The development of China into a super industrial power encouraged foreign investors to take advantage of China's huge supply of workers. As the Internet and communication revolution unfolded, companies were able to establish instant communications with their far-flung corporate empires, a technological breakthrough that further aided trade and foreign investments. A series of transnational corporate mergers (such as Daimler Chrysler) and takeovers (such as Ford and Volvo) produced ever-larger transnational corporations.

Some experts believe globalization can improve the standard of living in third world nations by providing jobs and training, but critical theorists question the altruism of multinational corporations. Their motives are exploiting natural resources, avoiding regulation, and taking advantage of desperate workers. When these giant corporations set up a factory in a developing nation, it is not to help the local population but to get around environmental laws and take advantage of needy workers who may be forced to labor in substandard conditions. Globalization has replaced imperialism and colonization as a new form of economic domination and oppression.

Conflict thinkers David Friedrichs and Jessica Friedrichs warn that globalization presents a four-pronged threat to the world economy:

1. Growing global dominance and the reach of the free-market capitalist system, which disproportionately benefits wealthy and powerful organizations and individuals.

2. Increasing vulnerability of indigenous people with a traditional way of life to the forces of globalized capitalism.

3. Growing influence and impact of international financial institutions (such as the World Bank) and the related relative decline of power of local or state-based institutions.

4. Nondemocratic operation of international financial institutions.[37]

Globalization may have a profound influence on the concept of surplus value. Workers in the United States may be replaced in high-paying manufacturing jobs not by machines but by foreign workers. Instant communication via the Internet and global communications, a development that Marx could not have foreseen, will speed the effect immeasurably. Globalization will have a profound effect on both the economy and eventually on crime rates.

 wwww The theory of **surplus value** can be quite complex. Read more about it at academic.cengage.com/criminaljustice/siegel.

Globalization has changed the traditional ways of doing business, creating prosperity in some nations and chaos in others. People are now moving from nation to nation seeking jobs and a fresh start. Here, supporters of immigration reform rally for immigrants' rights at the state capitol in Salem, Oregon, on April 9, 2006. Several thousand people gathered to support expanding immigrants' rights and to protest congressional bill HR 4437, which was designed to tighten U.S. immigration. The sign reads "We are not criminals." Should immigration policies be tightened to protect American jobs, or should immigrants be allowed to enter the United States in order to take part in the "American Dream"?

© Richard Clement/Reuters/Landov

INSTRUMENTAL VS. STRUCTURAL THEORY

Not all critical thinkers share a similar view of society and its control by the means of production. Instrumental theorists view criminal law and the criminal justice system solely as instruments for controlling the poor, have-not members of society. They view the state as the tool of capitalists. In contrast, structural theorists believe that the law is not the exclusive domain of the rich; rather, it is used to maintain the long-term interests of the capitalist system and to control members of any class who threaten its existence.

Instrumental Theory

According to the instrumental view, the law and justice system serve the powerful and rich and enable them to impose their morality and standards of behavior on the entire society. Those who wield economic power are able to extend their self-serving definition of illegal or criminal behavior to encompass those who might threaten the status quo or interfere with their quest for ever-increasing profits.[38] The concentration of economic assets in the nation's largest industrial firms translates into the political power needed to control tax laws to limit the firms' tax liabilities.[39] Some have the economic clout to hire top attorneys to defend them against antitrust actions, making them almost immune to regulation.

The poor, according to this branch of critical theory, may or may not commit more crimes than the rich, but they certainly are arrested and punished more often. Under the capitalist system, the poor are driven to crime because a natural frustration exists in a society in which affluence is well publicized but unattainable. When class conflict becomes unbearable, frustration can spill out in riots, such as the one that occurred in Los Angeles on April 29, 1992, which was described as a "class rebellion of the underprivileged against the privileged."[40] Because of class conflict, a deep-rooted hostility is generated among members of the lower class toward a social order they are not allowed to shape and whose benefits are unobtainable.[41]

Instrumental theorists consider it essential to demystify law and justice—that is, to unmask its true purpose. Criminological theories that focus on family structure, intelligence, peer relations, and school performance keep the lower classes servile by showing why they are more criminal, less intelligent, and more prone to school failure and family problems than the middle class. Demystification involves identifying the destructive intent of capitalist inspired and funded criminology. Instrumental theory's goal for criminology is to show how capitalist law preserves ruling-class power.[42]

Structural Theory

Structural theorists disagree with the view that the relationship between law and capitalism is unidirectional, always working for the rich and against the poor.[43] If law and justice were purely instruments of the wealthy, why would laws controlling corporate crimes, such as price-fixing, false advertising, and illegal restraint of trade, have been created and enforced?

To a structuralist, the law is designed to keep the system operating efficiently, and anyone, worker or owner, who rocks the boat is targeted for sanction. For example, antitrust legislation is designed to prevent any single capitalist from dominating the system. If the free enterprise system is to function, no single person can become too powerful at the expense of the economic system as a whole. Structuralists would regard the

efforts of the U.S. government to break up Microsoft as an example of a conservative government using its clout to keep the system on an even keel. The long prison sentences given to corporate executives who engage in insider trading are a warning to capitalists that they must play by the rules.

RESEARCH ON CRITICAL CRIMINOLOGY

Critical criminologists rarely use standard social science methodologies to test their views because many believe the traditional approach of measuring research subjects is antihuman and insensitive.[44] Critical thinkers believe that the research conducted by mainstream liberal and positivist criminologists is often designed to unmask weak, powerless members of society so they can be better dealt with by the legal system. They are particularly offended by purely empirical studies, such as those designed to show that minority group members have lower IQs than whites or that the inner city is the site of the most serious crime whereas middle-class areas are relatively crime free. Critical scholars are more likely to examine historical trends and patterns rather than to do surveys and crunch numbers. For example, to examine the changes in criminal law, historian Michael Rustigan analyzed historical records to show that law reform in nineteenth-century England was largely a response to pressure from the business community to increase punishment for property law violations to protect their rapidly increasing wealth.[45] Other research has focused on topics such as how the relationship between convict work and capitalism evolved during the nineteenth century. During this period, prisons became a profitable method of centralized state control over lower-class criminals, whose labor was exploited by commercial concerns. These criminals were forced to labor to pay off wardens and correctional administrators.[46]

Empirical research, however, is not considered totally incompatible with critical criminology, and there have been some important efforts to test its fundamental assumptions. One area of critical research involves examining the criminal justice system to see if it operates as an instrument of class oppression or as a fair, even-handed social control agency. Research has found that jurisdictions with significant levels of economic disparity are also the most likely to have large numbers of people killed by police officers. Police may act more forcefully in areas where class conflict creates the perception that extreme forms of social control are needed to maintain order.[47]

connections

The enforcement of laws against illegal business activities such as price fixing, restraint of trade, environmental crimes, and false advertising is discussed in Chapter 12. Although some people are sent to prison for these white-collar offenses, many offenders are still punished with a fine or economic sanction.

© AP Images/Chris Gardner

MUMIA ABU-JAMAL

Mumia Abu-Jamal (born Wesley Cook on April 24, 1954) began his journalism career with the radical Black Panther Party in the 1960s. By the time he was 15, Mumia was appointed minister of information for the Philadelphia branch. After the Panther party disbanded, Mumia used his writing and speaking talent to become a local broadcaster, even winning a Peabody Award for his coverage of the Pope's visit; in 1980 he became president of the Philadelphia Association of Black Journalists.

Then Mumia Abu-Jamal's life was turned upside down when he was charged with first-degree murder in the killing of Philadelphia police officer Daniel Faulkner. According to authorities, on December 9, 1981, Faulkner, 25, stopped a car for driving the wrong way down the street. Calling for backup, he approached the car and asked the driver, William Cook, to exit the vehicle. A struggle ensued. According to prosecutors, Mumia Abu-Jamal, Cook's older brother, was sitting in a taxicab across the street watching the events unfold. Mumia approached Officer Faulkner and shot him in the back. Faulkner was able to draw his gun and fire one return shot that struck Mumia in the upper abdomen. Having fired this shot, Officer Faulkner fell to the sidewalk. While Faulkner lay helpless, Mumia approached him and shot him numerous times at close range, killing him instantly.

At trial, four eyewitnesses testified that they saw Mumia kill Faulkner, experts testified that the gun that killed Faulkner was Mumia's, and jurors heard that a wounded Mumia was found at the scene of the crime. He was convicted and sentenced to death. Despite the conviction, the case has become a *cause celebre* for many reasons. Supporters claim that many procedural irregularities occurred during the trial and that the conviction of Abu-Jamal

violated his constitutional rights to a fair trial. Among other things, he was denied the right to represent himself at trial. Others claim that Mumia was targeted and framed because of his radical political activities. The prosecution hid evidence, intimidated witnesses, and illegally excused potential African American jurors.

Mumia has now been on death row for more than 20 years. The case has attracted the attention of anti-death–penalty activists from all over the world. Mumia himself has continued his political activism, published a book, *Live from Death Row*, completed B.A. and M.A. degrees, and made frequent radio broadcasts. The French have made him an honorary citizen of Paris, and organizations including Amnesty International, Human Rights Watch, the European Parliament, and the Diet of Japan have demanded that he be awarded a new trial because of the problems in the original case.

Critical criminologists view the Mumia Abu-Jamal case as an indicator of the social conflict that infects the nation's social and political systems. People are targeted because of their political views, minorities cannot get a fair trial, and people who are viewed as a threat to the system may find themselves behind bars or even on death row. Conflict rather than consensus rules and shapes society.

Sources: Mumia Abu-Jamal's Freedom Journal, www.mumia.org/freedom .now (accessed June 5, 2007); Amnesty International, "Mumia Abu-Jamal: Amnesty International Calls for Retrial," February 17, 2000, http://web .amnesty.org/library/Index/engAMR510202000 (accessed June 5, 2007); "A Life in the Balance: The Case of Mumia Abu-Jamal," www .amnestyusa.org/regions/americas/document.do?id= EB6C736A7369F3D78025686C00526C98 (accessed June 5, 2007).

Empirical research also shows, as predicted by critical theory, that a suspect's race is an important factor in shaping justice system decision making. Using data from a national survey, Ronald Weitzer and Steven Tuch found that about 40 percent of African American respondents claimed they were stopped by police because of their race, as compared to just 5 percent of whites; almost 75 percent of young African American men, ages 18 to 34, said they were victims of profiling.[48] Recent research by Albert Meehan and Michael Ponder found that police are more likely to use racial profiling to stop black motorists as they travel further into the boundaries of predominantly white neighborhoods: black motorists driving in an all-white neighborhood set up a red flag because they are "out of place."[49] It is not

surprising to critical theorists that police brutality complaints are highest in minority neighborhoods, especially those that experience relative deprivation (African American residents earn significantly less money than the European American majority).[50] The conflict between police and the minority community can result in violence and charges of racism, a topic explored in the Profiles in Crime feature "Mumia Abu-Jamal."

Criminal courts are also more likely to dole out harsh punishments to members of powerless, disenfranchised groups.[51] Both white and black offenders have been found to receive stricter sentences if their personal characteristics (single, young, urban, male) show them to be members of the "dangerous classes."[52] Unemployed racial minorities may be perceived as "social dynamite" who present a real threat to society and must be controlled and incapacitated.[53] Race also plays a role in prosecution and punishment. African American defendants are more likely to be prosecuted under habitual offender statutes if they commit crimes where there is a greater likelihood of a white victim—for example, larceny and burglary—than if they commit violent crimes that are largely intraracial; where there is a perceived "racial threat," punishment is enhanced.[54] Critical analysis also shows that despite legal controls, the use of the death penalty also seems to be skewed against racial minorities.[55]

Considering these examples of how conflict controls the justice process, it is not surprising when analysis of national population trends and imprisonment rates shows that as the percentage of minority group members increases in a population, the imprisonment rate does likewise.[56] Similarly, states with a substantial minority population have a much higher imprisonment rate than those with predominantly white populations.[57]

Some critical researchers have attempted to show how capitalism influences the distribution of punishment. Robert Weis found that the expansion of the prison population is linked to the need for capitalists to acquire a captive and low-paid labor force to compete with overseas laborers and domestic immigrant labor. Employing immigrants has its political downside because it displaces "American" workers and antagonizes their legal representatives. In contrast, using prison labor can be viewed as a humanitarian gesture. Weiss also observes that an ever-increasing prison population is politically attractive because it masks unemployment rates. Many inmates were chronically unemployed before their imprisonment; incarcerating the chronically unemployed allows politicians to claim they have lowered unemployment. When the millions of people who are on probation and parole and who must maintain jobs are added to the mix, the correctional system is now playing an increasingly important role in suppressing wages and maintaining the profitability of capitalism.[58]

CRITIQUE OF CRITICAL CRIMINOLOGY

Critical criminology has been sharply criticized by some members of the criminological mainstream, who charge that its contribution has been "hot air, heat, but no real light."[59] In turn, critical thinkers have accused mainstream criminologists of being culprits in developing state control over individual lives and selling out their ideals for the chance to receive government funding.

Mainstream criminologists have also attacked the substance of critical thought. Some argue that critical theory simply rehashes the old tradition of helping the underdog, in which the poor steal from the rich to survive.[60] In reality, most theft is for luxury, not survival. While the wealthy do commit their share of illegal acts, these are nonviolent and leave no permanent injuries.[61] People do not live in fear of corrupt businessmen and stock traders; they fear muggers and rapists.

Other critics suggest that critical theorists unfairly neglect the capitalist system's efforts to regulate itself—for example, by instituting antitrust regulations and putting violators in jail. Similarly, they ignore efforts to institute social reforms aimed at helping the poor.[62] There seems to be no logic in condemning a system that helps the poor and empowers them to take on corporate interests in a court of law. Even inherently conservative institutions such as police departments have made attempts at self-regulation when they become aware of class- and race-based inequality such as the use of racial profiling in making traffic stops.[63]

Some argue that critical thinkers refuse to address the problems and conflicts that exist in socialist countries, such as the gulags and purges of the Soviet Union under Stalin. Similarly, they fail to explain why some highly capitalist countries, such as Japan, have extremely low crime rates. Critical criminologists are too quick to blame capitalism for every human vice without adequate explanation or regard for other social and environmental factors.[64] In so doing, they ignore objective reality and refuse to acknowledge that members of the lower classes tend to victimize one another. They ignore the plight of the lower classes, who must live in crime-ridden neighborhoods, while condemning the capitalist system from the security of the "ivory tower."

EMERGING FORMS OF CRITICAL CRIMINOLOGY

Critical criminologists are exploring new avenues of inquiry that fall outside the traditional models of conflict and critical theories. The following sections discuss in detail some recent developments in the conflict approach to crime.

Left Realism

Some critical scholars are now addressing the need for the left wing to respond to the increasing power of right-wing conservatives. They are troubled by the emergence of a strict "law and order" philosophy, which has as its centerpiece a policy of punishing juveniles severely in adult court. At the same time, they find the focus of most left-wing scholarship—the abuse of power by the ruling elite—too narrow. It is wrong, they argue, to ignore inner-city gang crime and violence, which often target indigent people.[65] The approach of left realism is most often connected to the writings of British scholars John Lea and Jock Young. In their well-respected 1984 work, *What Is to Be Done about Law and Order?* they reject the utopian views of idealists who portray street criminals as revolutionaries.[66] They take the more "realistic" approach that street criminals prey on the poor and disenfranchised, thus making the poor doubly abused, first by the capitalist system and then by members of their own class.

Lea and Young's view of crime causation borrows from conventional sociological theory and closely resembles the relative deprivation approach, which posits that experiencing poverty in the midst of plenty creates discontent and breeds crime. As they put it, "The equation is simple: relative deprivation equals discontent; discontent plus lack of political solution equals crime."[67]

In a more recent book, *Crime in Context: A Critical Criminology of Market Societies* (1999), Ian Taylor recognizes that anyone who expects an instant socialist revolution to take place is simply engaging in wishful thinking.[68] He uses data from both Europe and North America to show that the world is currently in the midst of multiple crises that are shaping all human interaction, including criminality. These crises include lack of job creation, social inequality, social fear, political incompetence and failure, gender conflict, and family and parenting issues. These crises have led to a society in which the government seems incapable of creating positive social change: people have become more fearful and isolated from one another and some are excluded from the mainstream because of racism and discrimination; manufacturing jobs have been exported overseas to nations that pay extremely low wages; and fiscal constraints inhibit the possibility of reform. These problems often fall squarely on the shoulders of young black men, who suffer from exclusion and poverty and who now feel the economic burden created by the erosion of manufacturing jobs due to the globalization of the economy. In response, they engage in a form of hypermasculinity, which helps increase their crime rates.[69]

Crime Protection Left realists argue that crime victims in all classes need and deserve protection; crime control reflects community needs. They do not view police and the courts as inherently evil tools of capitalism whose tough tactics alienate the lower classes. In fact, they recognize that these institutions offer life-saving public services. The left realists wish, however, that police would reduce their use of force and increase their sensitivity to the public.[70] They want the police to be more responsive to community needs, end racial profiling, and improve efforts at self-regulation and enforcement through citizen review boards and other control mechanisms.

Preemptive deterrence is an approach in which community organization efforts eliminate or reduce crime before police involvement becomes necessary. The reasoning behind this approach is that if the number of marginalized youths (those who feel they are not part of society and have nothing to lose by committing crime) could be reduced, then delinquency rates would decline.[71]

Although implementing a socialist economy might help eliminate the crime problem, left realists recognize that something must be done to control crime under the existing capitalist system. To develop crime control policies, left realists not only welcome critical ideas but also build on the work of strain theorists, social ecologists, and other mainstream views. Community-based efforts seem to hold the greatest promise of crime control.

Left realism has been criticized by critical thinkers as legitimizing the existing power structure: by supporting existing definitions of law and justice, it suggests that the "deviant" and not the capitalist system causes society's problems. Critics question whether left realists advocate the very institutions that "currently imprison us and our patterns of thought and action."[72] In rebuttal, left realists say that it is unrealistic to speak of a socialist state lacking a police force or a system of laws and justice. They believe the criminal code does, in fact, represent public opinion.

Critical Feminist Theory

Like so many theories in criminology, most of the efforts of critical theorists have been devoted to explaining male criminality.[73] To remedy this theoretical lapse, a number of feminist writers have attempted to explain the cause of crime, gender differences in crime rates, and the exploitation of female victims from a critical perspective.

Critical feminism views gender inequality as stemming from the unequal power of men and women in a capitalist society, which leads to the exploitation of women by fathers and husbands. Under this system, women are considered a commodity worth possessing, like land or money.[74]

The origin of gender differences can be traced to the development of private property and male domination of the laws of inheritance, which led to male control over property and power.[75] A patriarchal system developed in which men's work was valued and women's work was devalued. As capitalism prevailed, the division of labor by gender made women responsible for the unpaid maintenance and reproduction of the current and future labor force, which was derisively called "domestic work." Although this unpaid work done by women is crucial and profitable for capitalists, who reap these free benefits, such labor is exploitative and oppressive for women.[76] Even when women gained the right to work for pay, they were exploited as cheap labor. The dual exploitation of women within the household and in the labor market means that women produce far greater surplus value for capitalists than men.

Patriarchy, or male supremacy, has been and continues to be supported by capitalists. This system sustains female oppression at home and in the workplace.[77] Although the number of traditional patriarchal families is in steep decline, in those that still exist, a wife's economic dependence ties men more securely to wage-earning jobs, further serving the interests of capitalists by undermining potential rebellion against the system.

Patriarchy and Crime Critical feminists link criminal behavior patterns to the gender conflict created by the economic and social struggles common in postindustrial societies. In *Capitalism, Patriarchy, and Crime*, James Messerschmidt argues that capitalist society is marked by both patriarchy and class conflict. Capitalists control the labor of workers, and men control women both economically and biologically.[78] This "double marginality" explains why females in a capitalist society commit fewer crimes than males. Because they are isolated in the family, they have fewer opportunities to engage in elite deviance (white-collar and economic crimes). Although powerful females as well as males will commit white-collar crimes, the female crime rate is restricted because of the patriarchal nature of the capitalist system.[79] Women are also denied access to male-dominated street crimes.

Because capitalism renders lower-class women powerless, they are forced to commit less serious, nonviolent, self-destructive

Critical feminists view gender inequality as a function of female exploitation by men. Women have become a "commodity" worth possessing, like land or money. The origin of gender differences can be traced to the development of private property and men's domination over the laws of inheritance, which led to their control over property and power. Are these teen prostitutes—shown here waiting to be booked at the Maricopa, Arizona, jail—a by-product of this view of women as commodities, which was engendered by the capitalist system?

women is an especially economical way to demonstrate manhood. Would a weak, effeminate male ever attack a woman?

Feminist writers have supported this view by maintaining that in contemporary society men achieve masculinity at the expense of women. In the best-case scenario, men must convince others that in no way are they feminine or have female qualities. For example, they are sloppy and don't cook or do housework because these are "female" activities. More ominously, men may work at excluding, hurting, denigrating, exploiting, or otherwise abusing women. Even in all-male groups men often prove their manhood by treating the weakest member of the group as "woman-like" and abusing him accordingly. Men need to defend themselves at all costs from being contaminated with femininity, and these efforts begin in children's play groups and continue into adulthood and marriage.[85]

crimes, such as abusing drugs. Recent efforts of the capitalist classes to undermine the social support of the poor has hit women particularly hard. The end of welfare, concentration on welfare fraud, and cutbacks to social services, all have directly and uniquely affected women.[80]

Powerlessness also increases the likelihood that women will become targets of violent acts.[81] When lower-class males are shut out of the economic opportunity structure, they try to build their self-image through acts of machismo; such acts may involve violent abuse of women. This type of reaction accounts for a significant percentage of female victims who are attacked by a spouse or intimate partner. According to this view, female victimization should decline as women's place in society is elevated, and they are able to obtain more power at home, in the workplace, and in government. Empirical research seems to support this view. A recent (2004) cross-national study of educational and occupational status of women shows that in nations where the status of women is generally high, sexual violence rates are significantly lower than in nations where women do not enjoy similar educational and occupational opportunities.[82] Women's victimization rates decline as they are empowered socially, economically, and legally.[83]

In *Masculinities and Crime*, Messerschmidt expands on these themes.[84] He suggests that in every culture males try to emulate "ideal" masculine behaviors. In Western culture, this means being authoritative, in charge, combative, and controlling. Failure to adopt these roles leaves men feeling effeminate and unmanly. Their struggle to dominate women in order to prove their manliness is called "doing gender." Crime is a vehicle for men to "do gender" because it separates them from the weak and allows them to demonstrate physical bravery. Violence directed toward

Exploitation and Criminality Critical feminists also focus on the social forces that shape women's lives and experiences to explain female criminality.[86] They attempt to show how the sexual victimization of girls is a function of male socialization because so many young males learn to be aggressive and to exploit women. Males seek out same-sex peer groups for social support; these groups encourage members to exploit and sexually abuse women. On college campuses, peers encourage sexual violence against women who are considered "teasers," "bar pickups," or "loose women." These derogatory labels allow the males to justify their actions; a code of secrecy then protects the aggressors from retribution.[87]

According to the critical feminist view, exploitation triggers the onset of female delinquent and deviant behavior. When female victims run away and abuse substances, they may be reacting to abuse they have suffered at home or at school. Their attempts at survival are labeled as deviant or delinquent behavior.[88] When the exploited girl finds herself in the arms of the justice system her problems may just be beginning. While boys who get in trouble may be considered "overzealous" youth or kids who just went too far, young girls who get in trouble are seen as in opposition and a threat to acceptable images of femininity; their behavior is considered even more unusual and dangerous than male delinquency.[89]

Power–Control Theory

John Hagan and his associates have created a critical feminist model that uses gender differences to explain the onset of criminality.[90] Hagan's view is that crime and delinquency rates are a function of two factors: (1) class position (power) and (2) family functions (control).[91] The link between these two variables is that, within the family, parents reproduce the power relationships they hold in the workplace; a position of dominance at work is equated with control in the household. As a result, parents' work experiences and class position influence the criminality of children.[92]

In paternalistic families, fathers assume the traditional role of breadwinners, while mothers tend to have menial jobs or remain at home to supervise domestic matters. Within the paternalistic home, mothers are expected to control the behavior of their daughters while granting greater freedom to sons. In such a home, the parent–daughter relationship can be viewed as a preparation for the "cult of domesticity," which makes girls' involvement in delinquency unlikely, whereas boys are freer to deviate because they are not subject to maternal control. Girls growing up in patriarchal families are socialized to fear legal sanctions more than are males; consequently, boys in these families exhibit more delinquent behavior than their sisters. The result is that boys not only engage in more antisocial behaviors but have greater access to legitimate adult behaviors, such as working at part-time jobs or possessing their own transportation. In contrast, without these legitimate behavioral outlets, girls who are unhappy or dissatisfied with their status are forced to seek out risky role exit behaviors, including such desperate measures as running away and contemplating suicide.

In egalitarian families—those in which the husband and wife share similar positions of power at home and in the workplace—daughters gain a kind of freedom that reflects reduced parental control. These families produce daughters whose law-violating behavior mirrors their brothers'. In an egalitarian family, girls may have greater opportunity to engage in legitimate adult status behaviors and less need to enact deviant role exits.[93]

Ironically, Hagan believes that these relationships also occur in female-headed households with absent fathers. Hagan and his associates found that when fathers and mothers hold equally valued managerial positions, the similarity between the rates of their daughters' and sons' delinquency is greatest. By implication, middle-class girls are the most likely to violate the law because they are less closely controlled than their lower-class counterparts. In homes in which both parents hold positions of power, girls are more likely to have the same expectations of career success as their brothers. Consequently, siblings of both sexes will be socialized to take risks and engage in other behavior related to delinquency.

Evaluating Power–Control This power–control theory has received a great deal of attention in the criminological community because it encourages a new approach to the study of criminality, one that includes gender differences, class position, and the structure of the family. Empirical analysis of its premises has generally been supportive. Brenda Sims Blackwell's research supports a key element of power–control theory: Females in paternalistic households have learned to fear legal sanctions more than have their brothers.[94]

Not all research is as supportive.[95] Some critics have questioned its core assumption that power and control variables can explain crime.[96] More specifically, critics fail to replicate the finding that upper-class girls are more likely to deviate than their lower-class peers or that class and power

interact to produce delinquency.[97] Some researchers have found few gender-based supervision and behavior differences in worker-, manager-, or owner-dominated households.[98] Research indicates that single-mother families may be different than two-parent egalitarian families, though Hagan's theory equates the two.[99]

It is possible that the concept of family employed by Hagan may have to be reconsidered. Power–control theorists should consider the multitude of power and control relationships that are emerging in postmodern society: blended families, families where mothers hold managerial positions and fathers are blue-collar workers, and so forth.[100]

Finally, power and control may interact with other personal traits, such as personality and self-control, to shape behavior.[101] Further research is needed to determine whether power–control can have an independent influence on behavior and can explain gender differences in the crime rate.

Peacemaking Criminology

To members of the peacemaking movement, the main purpose of criminology is to promote a peaceful, just society. Rather than standing on empirical analysis of data, peacemaking draws its

Restorative justice advocates want to take coercion out of the justice process, and for that reason they are opposed to the death penalty. At a rally kicking off Amnesty International USA's annual meeting in Austin, Texas, attendees raised black flags in protest and called on Republican Governor Rick Perry and Texas legislators to abolish the death penalty. Can restorative principles be applied to criminals who commit the most violent, heinous crimes, or are they only suitable for petty and first-time offenders?

EMERGING FORMS OF CRITICAL CRIMINOLOGY

Theory	Major Premise	Strengths	Research Focus
Left realism	Crime is a function of relative deprivation; criminals prey on the poor.	Represents a compromise between conflict and traditional criminology.	Deterrence; protection
Critical feminist theory	The capitalist system creates patriarchy, which oppresses women.	Explains gender bias, violence against women, and repression.	Gender inequality; oppression; patriarchy
Power–control theory	Girls are controlled more closely than boys in traditional male-dominated households. There is gender equity in contemporary egalitarian homes.	Explains gender differences in the crime rate as a function of class and gender conflict.	Power and control; gender differences; domesticity
Peacemaking criminology	Peace and humanism can reduce crime; conflict resolution strategies can work.	Offers a new approach to crime control through mediation.	Punishment; non-violence; mediation

inspiration from religious and philosophical teachings ranging from Quakerism to Zen.[102]

Peacemakers view the efforts of the state to punish and control as crime-encouraging rather than crime-discouraging. These views were first articulated in a series of books with an anarchist theme written by criminologists Larry Tifft and Dennis Sullivan in 1980.[103] Tifft argues, "The violent punishing acts of the state and its controlling professions are of the same genre as the violent acts of individuals. In each instance these acts reflect an attempt to monopolize human interaction."[104]

Sullivan stresses the futility of correcting and punishing criminals in the context of our conflict-ridden society: "The reality we must grasp is that we live in a culture of severed relationships, where every available institution provides a form of banishment but no place or means for people to become connected, to be responsible to and for each other."[105] Sullivan suggests that mutual aid rather than coercive punishment is the key to a harmonious society. In *Restorative Justice*, Sullivan and Tifft reaffirm their belief that society must seek humanitarian forms of justice without resorting to brutal punishments:

> By allowing feelings of vengeance or retribution to narrow our focus on the harmful event and the person responsible for it—as others might focus solely on a sin committed and the "sinner"—we tell ourselves we are taking steps to free ourselves from the effects of the harm or the sin in question. But, in fact, we are putting ourselves in a servile position with respect to life, human growth, and the further enjoyment of relationships with others.[106]

Today, advocates of the peacemaking movement, such as Harold Pepinsky and Richard Quinney, try to find humanist solutions to crime and other social problems.[107] Rather than punishment and prison, they advocate such policies as mediation and conflict resolution.[108]

Concept Summary 8.1 summarizes the various emerging forms of critical criminology.

CRITICAL THEORY AND PUBLIC POLICY

At the core of all the varying branches of social conflict theory is the fact that conflict causes crime. If conflict and competition in society could somehow be reduced, it is possible that crime rates would fall. Some critical theorists believe this goal can only be accomplished by thoroughly reordering society so that capitalism is destroyed and a socialist state is created. Others call for a more "practical" application of conflict principles. Nowhere has this been more successful than in applying peacemaking principles in the criminal justice system.

Rather than punish law violators harshly and make them outcasts of society, peacemakers look for ways to bring them back to the community. This peacemaking movement has adopted nonviolent methods and applied them to what is known as restorative justice. Springing both from academia and justice system personnel, the restorative approach relies on nonpunitive strategies for crime prevention and control.[109] The next sections discuss the foundation and principles of restorative justice.

The Concept of Restorative Justice

The term "restorative justice" is often hard to define because it encompasses a variety of programs and practices. According to a leading restorative justice scholar, Howard Zehr, restorative justice requires that society address victims' harms and needs, hold offenders accountable to put right those harms, and involve victims, offenders, and communities in the process of healing. Zehr maintains that the core value of the restoration process can be translated into respect for all, even those who are different from us, even those who seem to be our enemies. At its core, Zehr argues, restorative justice is a set of principles, a philosophy, an alternate set of guiding questions that provide an alternative framework for thinking about wrongdoing.[110] Restorative justice would reject concepts such as "punishment," "deterrence" and "incarceration" and embrace "apology," "rehabilitation," "reparation," "healing," "restoration," and "reintegration."

Restorative justice has grown out of a belief that the traditional justice system has done little to involve the community in the process of dealing with crime and wrongdoing. What has developed is a system of coercive punishments, administered by bureaucrats, that are inherently harmful to offenders and reduce the likelihood offenders will ever become productive members of society. This system relies on punishment, stigma, and disgrace. In his controversial book, *The Executed God: The Way of the Cross in Lockdown America*, theology professor Mark Lewis Taylor discusses the similarities between this contemporary, coercive justice system and that which existed in imperial Rome when Jesus and many of his followers were executed because they were an inspiration to the poor and slave populations. They represented a threat to the ruling Roman power structure. So, too, is our modern justice system designed to keep the downtrodden in their place. Taylor suggests that there should be a movement to reduce such coercive elements of justice as police brutality and the death penalty before our "lockdown society" becomes the model used around the globe.[111]

Advocates of restorative justice argue that rather than today's "lockdown" mentality, what is needed is a justice policy that repairs the harm caused by crime and that includes all parties who have suffered from that harm: the victim, the community, and the offender. They have made an ongoing effort to reduce the conflict created by the criminal justice system when it hands out harsh punishments to offenders, many of whom are powerless social outcasts. Based on the principle of reducing social harm, restorative justice advocates argue that the old methods of punishment are a failure: after all, upwards of two-thirds of all prison inmates recidivate soon after their release. And tragically, not all inmates are released. Some are given life sentences for relatively minor crimes under "three strikes" laws, which mandate such a sentence for a third conviction; some are given "life with no parole" sentences, which are in essence "death sentences."[112]

Reintegrative Shaming

One of the key foundations of the restoration movement is contained in John Braithwaite's influential book *Crime, Shame, and Reintegration*.[113] Braithwaite's vision rests on the concept of shame: the feeling we get when we don't meet the standards we have set for ourselves or that significant others have set for us. Shame can lead people to believe that they are defective, that there is something wrong with them. Braithwaite notes that countries such as Japan, in which conviction for crimes brings an inordinate amount of shame, have extremely low crime rates. In Japan, criminal prosecution proceeds only when the normal process of public apology, compensation, and the victim's forgiveness breaks down.

Shame is a powerful tool of informal social control. Citizens in cultures in which crime is not shameful, such as the United States, do not internalize an abhorrence for crime because when they are punished, they view themselves as mere victims of the justice system. Their punishment comes at the hands of neutral strangers, such as police and judges, who are being paid to act. In contrast, shaming relies on the victim's participation.[114]

Braithwaite divides the concept of shame into two distinct types. The most common form of shaming typically involves stigmatization, an ongoing process of degradation in which the offender is branded as an evil person and cast out of society. Shaming can occur at a school disciplinary hearing or a criminal court trial. Bestowing stigma and degradation may have a general deterrent effect: it makes people afraid of social rejection and public humiliation. As a specific deterrent, stigma is doomed to failure; people who suffer humiliation at the hands of the justice system "reject their rejectors" by joining a deviant subculture of like-minded people who collectively resist social control. Despite these dangers, there has been an ongoing effort to brand offenders and make their shame both public and permanent. For example, most states have passed sex offender registry and notification laws that make public the names of those convicted of sex offenses and warn neighbors of their presence in the community.[115]

But the fear of shame can backfire or be neutralized. When shame is managed well, people acknowledge they made mistakes and suffered disappointments, and try to work out what can be done to make things right; this is referred to as shame management. However, in some cases, to avoid the pain of shaming, people engage in improper shame management, a psychological process in which they deny shame by shifting the blame of their actions to their target or to others.[116] They may blame others, get angry, and take out their frustrations on those whom they can dominate. Improper shame management of this sort has been linked to antisocial acts ranging from school yard bullying to tax evasion.[117]

Massive levels of improper shame management may occur on a societal scale during periods of social upheaval. Because of this, some nations that previously have had low crime rates may experience a surge of antisocial behavior during periods of war and revolution. Rape, an act which may have been unthinkable to most men, suddenly becomes commonplace because of the emergence of narcissistic pride, feeling dominant and arrogant, and developing a sense of superiority over others, in this case your enemy. This sense of hubris fosters aggressive actions and allows combatants to rape women whom they perceive as belonging to an enemy group.[118]

Braithwaite argues that crime control can be better achieved through a policy of reintegrative shaming. Here disapproval is extended to the offenders' evil deeds, while at the same time they are cast as respected people who can be reaccepted by society. A critical element of reintegrative shaming occurs when the offenders begin to understand and recognize their wrongdoing and shame themselves. To be reintegrative, shaming must be brief and controlled and then followed by ceremonies of forgiveness, apology, and repentance.

To prevent crime, Braithwaite charges, society must encourage reintegrative shaming. For example, the women's movement can reduce domestic violence by mounting a crusade to shame spouse abusers.[119] Similarly, parents who use reintegrative shaming techniques in their childrearing practices may improve parent–child relationships and ultimately reduce the delinquent involvement of their children.[120] Because informal social controls may have a greater impact than legal or formal ones, it may not be surprising that the fear of personal shame can have a greater deterrent effect than the fear of legal sanctions. It may also be applied to produce specific deterrence. Offenders can meet with victims so that the offenders can experience shame. Family members and peers can be present to help the offender reintegrate.[121] Such efforts can humanize a system of justice that today relies on repression rather than forgiveness as the basis of specific deterrence.

The Process of Restoration

The restoration process begins by redefining crime in terms of a conflict among the offender, the victim, and affected constituencies (families, schools, workplaces, and so forth). Therefore, it is vitally important that the resolution take place within the context in which the conflict originally occurred rather than being transferred to a specialized institution that has no social connection to the community or group from which the conflict originated. In other words, most conflicts are better settled in the community than in a court.

By maintaining "ownership" or jurisdiction over the conflict, the community is able to express its shared outrage about the offense. Shared community outrage is directly communicated to the offender. The victim is also given a chance to voice his or her story, and the offender can directly communicate his or her need for social reintegration and treatment. All restoration programs involve an understanding between all the parties involved in a criminal act: the victim, the offender, and community. Although processes differ in structure and style, they generally include these elements:

1. The offender is asked to recognize that he or she caused injury to personal and social relations along with a determination and acceptance of responsibility (ideally accompanied by a statement of remorse). Only then can the offender be restored as a productive member of the community.

2. Restoration involves turning the justice system into a "healing" process rather than being a distributor of retribution and revenge.

3. Reconciliation is a big part of the restorative approach. Most people involved in offender–victim relationships actually know one another or were related in some way before the criminal incident took place. Instead of treating one of the involved parties as a victim deserving of sympathy and the other as a criminal deserving of punishment, it is more productive to address the issues that produced conflict between these people.[122]

4. The effectiveness of justice ultimately depends on the stake a person has in the community (or a particular social group). If a person does not value his or her membership in the group, the person will be unlikely to accept responsibility, show remorse, or repair the injuries caused by his or her actions. In contrast, people who have a stake in the community and its principle institutions, such as work, home, and school, find that their involvement enhances their personal and familial well-being.[123]

5. A commitment to both material (monetary) restitution and symbolic reparation (an apology).

6. A determination of community support and assistance for both victim and offender.

The intended result of the process is to repair injuries suffered by the victim and the community while assuring reintegration of the offender.

Restoration Programs Negotiation, mediation, consensus-building, and peacemaking have been part of the dispute resolution process in European and Asian communities for centuries.[124] Native American and Native Canadian people have long used the type of community participation in the adjudication process (for example, sentencing circles, sentencing panels, elders panels) that restorative justice advocates are now embracing.[125]

In some Native American communities, people accused of breaking the law meet with community members, victims (if any), village elders, and agents of the justice system in a sentencing circle. Each member of the circle expresses his or her feelings about the act that was committed and raises questions or concerns. The accused can express regret about his or her actions and a desire to change the harmful behavior. People may suggest ways the offender can make things up to the community and those he or she harmed. A treatment program, such as Alcoholics Anonymous, can be suggested, if appropriate.

Restorative justice is now being embraced on many levels within our society and the justice system:

▪ *Community.* Communities that isolate people and have few mechanisms for interpersonal interaction encourage and sustain crime. Those that implement forms of community dialogue to identify problems and plan tactics for their elimination, guided by restorative justice practices and principles, may create a climate in which violent crime is less likely to occur.[126]

▪ *Schools.* Some schools have embraced restorative justice practices to deal with students who are involved in drug and alcohol abuse without having to resort to more punitive measures such as expulsion. Schools in Minnesota, Colorado, and elsewhere are now trying to involve students in "relational rehabilitation" programs that strive to improve individuals' relationships with key figures in the community who may have been harmed by their actions.[127]

▪ *Police.* Restorative justice has also been implemented by police when crime is first encountered. The new community policing models discussed in Chapter 4 are an attempt to bring restorative concepts into law enforcement. Restorative justice relies on the fact that criminal justice policymakers need to listen and respond to the needs of those who are to be affected by their actions, and community policing relies on policies established with input and exchanges between officers and citizens.[128]

▪ *Courts.* Restorative programs in the courts typically involve diverting the formal court process. These programs encourage meeting and reconciling the conflicts between offenders and victims via victim advocacy, mediation programs, and sentencing circles, in which crime victims and their families are brought together with offenders and their families in an effort

Restoration programs can take many forms. Regina Talbert and Anthony Belcher hand out food and clothing on skid row in Los Angeles, February 16, 2007. The two former addicts are part of the New Directions team, who perform outreach to addicted and alcoholic army, navy, and air force veterans in some of the city's most dangerous neighborhoods. Veterans of U.S. wars, including the current campaigns in Afghanistan and Iraq, are increasingly turning up with alarming signs of PTSD and other serious mental issues. Regina (left), who has been in recovery for nine years, hands out fliers about the New Directions treatment center. Would you consider this a "restoration"-based initiative?

to formulate a sanction that addresses the needs of each party. Victims are given a chance to voice their stories, and offenders can help compensate them financially or provide some service (for example, fixing damaged property).[129] The goal is to enable offenders to appreciate the damage they have caused, to make amends, and to be reintegrated back into society.

Balanced and Restorative Justice (BARJ) A number of restorative justice experts (Gordon Bazemore and his associates) have suggested that restorative justice should be centered on the principle of *balance*.[130] According to this approach, the justice system should give equal weight to:

- *Holding offenders accountable to victims.* Offender accountability refers specifically to the requirement that offenders "make amends" for the harm resulting from their crimes by repaying or restoring losses to victims and the community.

- *Providing competency development for offenders* in the system so they can pursue legitimate endeavors after release. Competency development, the rehabilitative goal for intervention, requires that people who enter the justice system should exit the system more capable of being productive and responsible in the community.

- *Ensuring community safety.* The community protection goal explicitly acknowledges and endorses a longtime public expectation—a safe and secure community.

The balanced approach means that justice policies and priorities should seek to address each of the three goals in *each case* and that *system balance* should be pursued. The goal of achieving balance suggests that no one objective can take precedence over any other without creating a system that is "out of balance" and implies that efforts to achieve one goal (e.g., offender accountability) should not hinder efforts to achieve other goals.

BARJ is founded on the belief that justice is best served when the victim, community, and offender are viewed as equal clients of the justice system who will receive fair and balanced attention, be actively involved in the justice process, and gain tangible benefits from their interactions with the justice system. Most BARJ programs are located today within the juvenile justice system. The Comparative Criminology feature "Restoration in the International Community" discusses some recent innovative community programs based on the principles of restorative justice.

The Challenge of Restorative Justice

Restorative justice holds great promise, but there are also some concerns:

- Is it a political movement or a treatment process? Restorative justice is viewed as an extremely liberal alternative and its advocates often warn of the uneven exercise of state power. Some view it as a social movement rather than a method of rehabilitation.[131] Can it survive in a culture that is becoming increasingly conservative and focused on security rather than personal freedom?

- Restorative justice programs must be wary of the cultural and social differences that can be found throughout our heterogeneous society. What may be considered "restorative" in one subculture may be considered insulting and damaging in another.[132]

- There is still no single definition of what constitutes restorative justice.[133] Consequently, many diverse programs that call themselves restorative-oriented pursue objectives that seem remote from the restorative ideal.

- Restorative justice programs face the difficult task of balancing the needs of offenders with those of their victims. If programs focus solely on victims' needs, they may risk ignoring the offenders' needs and increase the likelihood of reoffending. Declan Roache, a lecturer in law at the London School of Economics, makes the argument that the seductive promise of restorative justice may blind admirers to the benefits of traditional methods and prevent them from understanding or appreciating some of the pitfalls of restoration. There is danger, he warns, in a process that is essentially informal, without lawyers, and with little or no oversight on the outcome. The restoration process gives participants unchecked power without the benefit of procedural safeguards.[134]

RESTORATION IN THE INTERNATIONAL COMMUNITY

While the restorative justice philosophy is catching on in the United States, it is widely practiced abroad. Below are just a few of the many programs found around the world.

South Africa

After 50 years of oppressive white rule in South Africa, the race-dividing apartheid policy was abolished in the early 1990s, and in 1994 Nelson Mandela, leader of the African National Congress (ANC), was elected president. Some black leaders wanted revenge for the political murders carried out during the apartheid era, but Mandela established the Truth and Reconciliation Commission. Rather than seeking vengeance for the crimes, this government agency investigated the atrocities with the mandate of granting amnesty to those individuals who confessed their roles in the violence and could prove that their actions served some political motive rather than being based on personal factors such as greed or jealousy.

Supporters of the commission believed that this approach would help heal the nation's wounds and prevent years of racial and ethnic strife. Mandela, who had been unjustly jailed for 27 years by the regime, had reason to desire vengeance. Yet, he wanted to move the country forward after the truth of what happened in the past had been established. Though many South Africans, including some ANC members, believe that the commission is too lenient, Mandela's attempts at reconciliation have prevailed. The commission is a model of restoration over revenge.

Australia

The justice system in Australia makes use of the conferencing process to divert offenders from the justice system. This offers offenders the opportunity to attend a conference to discuss and resolve their offense instead of being charged and appearing in court. (Those who deny guilt are not offered conferencing.) The conference,

normally lasting one to two hours, is attended by the victims and their supporters, the defendant and his or her supporters, and other concerned parties. The conference coordinator focuses the discussion on condemning the act without condemning the character of the actor. Offenders are asked to tell their side of the story, what happened, how they have felt about the crime, and what they think should be done. The victims and others are asked to describe the physical, financial, and emotional consequences of the crime. This discussion may lead the offenders, their families, and their friends to experience the shame of the act, prompting an apology to the victim. A plan of action is developed and signed by key participants. The plan may include the offender paying compensation to the victim, doing work for the victim or the community, or similar solutions. It is the responsibility of the conference participants to determine the outcomes that are most appropriate for these particular victims and these particular offenders.

All eight states and territories in Australia have used the conference model, but there are five in which conferencing is active. Of these five jurisdictions, all but one (the Australian Capital Territory or ACT) have legislatively established conferencing. South Australia began to use conferences routinely in 1994, Western Australia and the ACT in 1995, and New South Wales in 1998. While Queensland is an active jurisdiction, it is experimenting with several formats of organizational placement and delivery, and conferencing is not available on a statewide basis. Tasmania passed legislation in 1997, which gave statutory authority to establish conferences, but a conferencing program has not yet started. The state of Victoria, like the ACT, is without a statutory scheme, but a community organization, working in partnership with state agencies, uses the conference model in selected cases as a presentencing option.

Ireland

A new strategy for some released sex offenders is being planned in Belfast. Following restorative justice principles, it

places the potential for healing at the center of all activities, and seeks to empower everyone affected by crime—including victims, offenders, and communities—in dealing with its effects.

Based on the primary goal of reducing victimization shared by agencies and individuals alike, this intensive and individualized project involves establishing a circle of volunteers around individual ex-offenders upon their release from custody. These volunteers agree to both befriend the ex-offender on a personal individual level, assisting in their reintegration into the community, and also use their regular contact with the offender to monitor his behavior, holding him accountable to his commitment to not re-offend.

Rather than pushing offenders further outside of mainstream society by making it impossible for them to live in regular housing, a member of the circle meets daily with the ex-offender, for coffee or a movie, or just a chat. All circle members meet weekly to check in and discuss any issues together. An initial "covenant" agreement is signed by all members of the circle, including the ex-offender, which outlines their basic expectations of the circle and indicates their specific commitment to the group.

CRITICAL THINKING

Restorative justice may be the model that best serves alternative sanctions. How can this essentially humanistic approach be sold to the general public that now supports more punitive sanctions? For example, would it be reasonable to expect that using restorative justice with nonviolent offenders frees up resources for the relatively few dangerous people in the criminal population? Explain.

Sources: Leena Kurki, *Incorporating Restorative and Community Justice into American Sentencing and Corrections* (Washington, DC: National Institute of Justice, 1999); Australian Government, Australian Institute of Criminology, "Restorative Justice: An Australian Perspective," www.aic.gov.au/rjustice/australia.html (accessed June 5, 2007); Restorative Justice in Ireland, Nenagh Community Reparation Project, Co. Tipperary: www.extern.org/restorative/ (accessed February 4, 2007); John W. De Gruchy, *Reconciliation: Restoring Justice* (Minneapolis: Fortress, 2002).

Benefits may only work in the short term while ignoring long-term treatment needs. Sharon Levrant and her colleagues suggest that restorative justice programs that feature short-term interactions with victims fail to help offenders learn prosocial ways of behaving. Restorative justice advocates may falsely assume that relatively brief interludes of public shaming will change deeply rooted criminal predispositions.[135]

These are a few of the obstacles that restorative justice programs must overcome to be successful and productive. Yet because the method holds so much promise, criminologists are now conducting numerous demonstration projects to find the most effective means of returning the ownership of justice to the people and the community.[136]

THINKING LIKE A CRIMINOLOGIST

The Nenagh Community Reparation Project in Ireland is managed by a local committee representing different community interests in partnership with the Probation and Welfare Service. It began on the initiative of Judge Michael Reilly, who with the cooperation of the community and various agencies has sought to use reparation in his court. In cases where an offender has admitted guilt, the judge can, at his or her discretion, offer the offender the choice of either the normal course of jail or participation in the community reparation project. At this point the court adjourns for approximately 30 minutes while the probation officer explains the project to the offender. If the offender decides to participate in the project, a meeting will be called in the near future.

This meeting is always attended by the offender, two panel members representing the community, the police officers who have been involved in the case, and the probation officer. If the crime involves victims, they are also invited to attend the meeting, although their participation is not mandatory.

At the meeting, offenders are asked to explain the circumstances of the offense, why it happened, how they felt about it then, and how they feel about their actions now. Together, the group decides how the offender might make reparation to the victim and/or the community for the damage caused by the offense.

Once agreement is reached about the form of the reparation, a contract is drawn up that sets out treatment courses the offender will be expected to take (for example, treatment for alcoholism, substance abuse, anger management, and so on as appropriate). Reparation may include letters of apology to the victim, monetary restitution, and other proportionate and appropriate activities. Contracts generally cover a period of approximately six months and are monitored by the probation officer. If the terms of the contract are successfully completed, the record of the offense will be dropped. If the terms are not met, the case will go back to court and proceed in the normal manner.

Writing Exercise As a criminologist, would you suggest that this program be used in the United States? Write a paper (about 400 words) answering this question and explaining how you think people who do not succeed in the program should be handled. Are there any other approaches you would try with these offenders? If so, explain.

Doing Research on the Web To help formulate your recommendations, review these Web-based resources to begin researching your answer:

- Restorative Justice Online is a nonpartisan source of information on restorative justice.
- The Centre for Restorative Justice, at Simon Frazer University in British Columbia, Canada, in partnership with individuals, the community, and justice agencies, exists to support and promote the principles and practices of restorative justice by providing education, training, evaluation, and research.
- The Department of Justice maintains the *Restorative Justice Notebook.*

Visit all three websites via academic.cengage.com/criminaljustice/siegel.

SUMMARY

- Social conflict theorists view crime as a function of the conflict that exists in society.

- Conflict theorists suggest that crime in any society is caused by class conflict. Laws are created by those in power to protect their rights and interests.

- All criminal acts have political undertones. Richard Quinney has called this concept "the social reality of crime."

- One of conflict theory's most important premises is that the justice system is biased and designed to protect the wealthy.

- Critical criminology tries to explain how the workings of the capitalist system produce inequality and crime. In this view, the state serves the interests of the ruling capitalist class. Criminal law is an instrument of economic oppression. Capitalism demands that the subordinate classes remain oppressed.

- The concept of surplus value means that capitalists exploit workers and keep the excess profits from workers' labors.

- Globalization has meant that capitalists can exploit foreign workers for labor and acquire foreign natural resources to maximize their profits.

- Critical criminology views the competitive nature of the capitalist system as a major cause of crime. The poor commit crimes because of their frustration, anger, and need. The wealthy engage in illegal acts because they are used to competition and because they must do so to keep their positions in society.

- Critical scholars have attempted to show that the law is designed to protect the wealthy and powerful and to control the poor, have-not members of society.

- Critical theorists can be divided into those who are instrumental and those who are structural. The former holds that those in power wield their authority to control society and keep the lower classes in check. The latter maintains that the justice system is designed to maintain the status quo and is used to punish the wealthy if they bend the rules governing capitalism.

- Research on critical theory focuses on how the system of justice was designed and how it operates to further class interests. Quite often, this research uses historical analysis to show how the capitalist classes have exerted control over the police, courts, and correctional agencies.

- Critical criminology has been heavily criticized by consensus criminologists, who suggest that social conflict theories make fundamental errors in their concepts of ownership and class interest.

- New forms of critical theory have been emerging.

- Critical feminist writers draw attention to the influence of patriarchal society on crime.

- According to power–control theory, gender differences in the crime rate can be explained by the structure of the family in a capitalist society.

- Left realism takes a moderate position on crime by showing its rational and destructive nature; the justice system is necessary to protect the lower classes until a socialist society can be developed, which will end crime.

- Postmodern theory looks at the symbolic meaning of law and culture.

- Peacemaking criminology brings a call for humanism to criminology.

- Conflict principles have been used to develop the restorative justice model. This holds that reconciliation rather than retribution should be used to prevent and control crime.

- CENGAGENOW™ is an easy-to-use online resource that helps you study in less time to get the grade you want—NOW. CengageNOW™ Personalized Study (a diagnostic study tool containing valuable text-specific resources) lets you focus on just what you don't know and learn more in less time to get a better grade. If your textbook does not include an access code card, you can go to www.ichapters.com to purchase CengageNOW™.

KEY TERMS

CRITICAL THINKING QUESTIONS

1. How would a conservative reply to a call for more restorative justice? How would a restorative justice advocate respond to a conservative call for more prisons?

2. Considering recent changes in American culture, how would a power–control theorist explain recent drops in the U.S. crime rate? Can it be linked to changes in the structure of the American family?

3. Is conflict inevitable in all cultures? If not, what can be done to reduce the level of conflict in our own society?

4. If Marx were alive today, what would he think about the prosperity enjoyed by the working class in industrial societies? Might he alter his vision of the capitalist system?

5. Has religious conflict replaced class conflict as the most important issue facing modern society? Can anything be done to heal the rifts between people of different faiths?

NOTES

1. Parija B. Kavilanz, "Nardelli out at Home Depot: No. 1 Home Improvement Retailer Gives Ex-CEO $210 Million Package; Vice Chairman Frank Blake Takes the Helm," CNNMoney.com, http://money.cnn.com/2007/01/03/news/companies/home_depot/ (accessed June 9, 2007).

2. AFL-CIO 2005 Executive Pay Packages, www.aflcio.org/corporatewatch/paywatch/pay/index.cfm#_ftnref1 (accessed February 8, 2007).

3. Stephanie Saul, "Study Finds Backdating of Options Widespread," *New York Times*, 17 July 2006, p. 1.

4. Carolyn Said and Kathleen Pender, "Inquiry at Apple—Option Irregularities: Stock Grants to Executives under Scrutiny," *San Francisco Chronicle*, 30 June 2006, p. 1.

5. Michael Lynch and W. Byron Groves, *A Primer in Radical Criminology*, 2nd ed. (Albany, NY: Harrow & Heston, 1989), pp. 32–33.

6. Michael Lynch, "Rediscovering Criminology: Lessons from the Marxist Tradition," in *Marxist Sociology: Surveys of Contemporary Theory and Research*, eds. Donald McQuarie and Patrick McGuire (New York: General Hall, 1994).

7. Andrew Woolford, "Making Genocide Unthinkable: Three Guidelines for a Critical Criminology of Genocide," *Critical Criminology* 14 (2006): 87–106.

8. See generally Karl Marx and Friedrich Engels, *Capital: A Critique of Political Economy*, trans. E. Aveling (Chicago: Charles Kern, 1906); Karl Marx, *Selected Writings in Sociology and Social Philosophy*, trans. P. B. Bottomore (New York: McGraw-Hill, 1956). For a general discussion of Marxist thought, see Lynch and Groves, *A Primer in Radical Criminology*, pp. 6–26.

9. Karl Marx, *Grundrisse: Introduction to the Critique of Political Economy*, trans. Martin Nicolaus (New York: Vintage, 1973), pp. 106–107.

10. Lynch, "Rediscovering Criminology."

11. Karl Marx, "Population, Crime and Pauperism," in *Karl Marx and Friedrich Engels, Ireland and the Irish Question* (Moscow: Progress, 1859, reprinted 1971), p. 92.

12. Friedrich Engels, *The Condition of the Working Class in England in 1844* (London: Allen & Unwin, 1950).

13. Lynch, "Rediscovering Criminology," p. 5.

14. Ian Taylor, Paul Walton, and Jock Young, *The New Criminology: For a Social Theory of Deviance* (London: Routledge & Kegan Paul, 1973).

15. Biko Agozino. "Imperialism, Crime and Criminology: Towards the Decolonisation of Criminology," *Crime, Law and Social Change* 41 (2004): 343–358.

16. William Chambliss and Robert Seidman, *Law, Order, and Power* (Reading, MA: Addison-Wesley, 1971), p. 503.

17. Richard Quinney, *The Social Reality of Crime* (Boston: Little, Brown, 1970).

18. This section borrows heavily from Richard Sparks, "A Critique of Marxist Criminology," in *Crime and Justice*, vol. 2, eds. Norval Morris and Michael Tonry (Chicago: University of Chicago Press, 1980), pp. 159–208.

19. Barbara Sims, "Crime, Punishment, and the American Dream: Toward a Marxist Integration," *Journal of Research in Crime and Delinquency* 34 (1997): 5–24.

20. Gregg Barak, "Revisionist History, Visionary Criminology, and Needs-Based Justice," *Contemporary Justice Review* 6 (2003): 217–225.

21. John Braithwaite, "Retributivism, Punishment, and Privilege," in *Punishment and Privilege*, eds. W. Byron Groves and Graeme Newman (Albany, NY: Harrow & Heston, 1986), pp. 55–66.

22. Agozino. "Imperialism, Crime and Criminology: Towards the Decolonisation of Criminology."

23. Barak, "Revisionist History, Visionary Criminology, and Needs-Based Justice."

24. Kitty Kelley Epstein, "The Whitening of the American Teaching Force: A Problem of Recruitment or a Problem of Racism?" *Social Justice* 32 (2005): 89–102.

25. Tony Platt and Cecilia O'Leary, "Patriot Acts," *Social Justice* 30 (2003): 5–21.

26. Garrett Brown, "The Global Threats to Workers' Health and Safety on the Job," *Social Justice* 29 (2002): 12–25.

27. Robert Bohm, "Radical Criminology: Back to the Basics," paper presented at the annual meeting of the American Society of Criminology, Phoenix, November 1993, p. 2.

28. Ibid., p. 4.

29. Lynch and Groves, *A Primer in Radical Criminology*, p. 7.

30. Jeffery Reiman, *The Rich Get Richer and the Poor Get Prison* (New York: Wiley, 1984), pp. 43–44.

31. Rob White, "Environmental Harm and the Political Economy of Consumption," *Social Justice* 29 (2002): 82–102.

32. Sims, "Crime, Punishment, and the American Dream."

33. Michael Lynch, "Assessing the State of Radical Criminology: Toward the Year 2000," paper presented at the annual meeting of the American Society of Criminology, Phoenix, November 1993.

34. Steven Box, *Recession, Crime, and Unemployment* (London: Macmillan, 1987).

35. David Barlow, Melissa Hickman-Barlow, and W. Wesley Johnson, "The Political Economy of Criminal Justice Policy: A Time-Series Analysis of Economic Conditions, Crime, and Federal Criminal Justice

Legislation, 1948–1987," *Justice Quarterly* 13 (1996): 223–241.

36. Mahesh Nalla, Michael Lynch, and Michael Leiber, "Determinants of Police Growth in Phoenix, 1950–1988," *Justice Quarterly* 14 (1997): 144–163.

37. David Friedrichs and Jessica Friedrichs, "The World Bank and Crimes of Globalization: A Case Study," *Social Justice* 29 (2002): 13–36.

38. Gresham Sykes, "The Rise of Critical Criminology," *Journal of Criminal Law and Criminology* 65 (1974): 211–229.

39. David Jacobs, "Corporate Economic Power and the State: A Longitudinal Assessment of Two Explanations," *American Journal of Sociology* 93 (1988): 852–881.

40. Deanna Alexander, "Victims of the L.A. Riots: A Theoretical Consideration," paper presented at the annual meeting of the American Society of Criminology, Phoenix, November 1993.

41. Richard Quinney, "Crime Control in Capitalist Society," in *Critical Criminology*, eds. Ian Taylor, Paul Walton, and Jock Young (London: Routledge & Kegan Paul, 1975), p. 199.

42. Ibid.

43. John Hagan, *Structural Criminology* (New Brunswick, NJ: Rutgers University Press, 1989), pp. 110–119.

44. Roy Bhaskar, "Empiricism," in *A Dictionary of Marxist Thought*, ed. T. Bottomore (Cambridge, MA: Harvard University Press, 1983), pp. 149–150.

45. Michael Rustigan, "A Reinterpretation of Criminal Law Reform in Nineteenth-Century England," in *Crime and Capitalism*, ed. D. Greenberg (Palo Alto, CA: Mayfield, 1981), pp. 255–278.

46. Rosalind Petchesky, "At Hard Labor: Penal Confinement and Production in Nineteenth-Century America," in *Crime and Capitalism*, ed. D. Greenberg (Palo Alto, CA: Mayfield, 1981), pp. 341–357; Paul Takagi, "The Walnut Street Jail: A Penal Reform to Centralize the Powers of the State," *Federal Probation* 49 (1975): 18–26.

47. David Jacobs and David Britt, "Inequality and Police Use of Deadly Force: An Empirical Assessment of a Conflict Hypothesis," *Social Problems* 26 (1979): 403–412.

48. Ronald Weitzer and Steven Tuch, "Perceptions of Racial Profiling: Race, Class and Personal Experience," *Criminology* 40 (2002): 435–456.

49. Albert Meehan and Michael Ponder, "Race and Place: The Ecology of Racial Profiling African American Motorists," *Justice Quarterly* 29 (2002): 399–431.

50. Malcolm Homes, "Minority Threat and Police Brutality: Determinants of Civil Rights Criminal Complaints in U.S. Municipalities," *Criminology* 38 (2000): 343–368.

51. Darrell Steffensmeier and Stephen Demuth, "Ethnicity and Judges' Sentencing Decisions: Hispanic-Black-White Comparisons," *Criminology* 39 (2001): 145–178; Alan Lizotte, "Extra-Legal Factors in Chicago's Criminal Courts: Testing the Conflict Model of Criminal Justice," *Social Problems* 25 (1978): 564–580.

52. Terance Miethe and Charles Moore, "Racial Differences in Criminal Processing: The Consequences of Model Selection on Conclusions about Differential Treatment," *Sociological Quarterly* 27 (1987): 217–237.

53. Tracy Nobiling, Cassia Spohn, and Miriam DeLone, "A Tale of Two Counties: Unemployment and Sentence Severity," *Justice Quarterly* 15 (1998): 459–485.

54. Charles Crawford, Ted Chiricos, and Gary Kleck, "Race, Racial Threat, and Sentencing of Habitual Offenders," *Criminology* 36 (1998): 481–511.

55. Michael Lenza, David Keys, and Teresa Guess, "The Prevailing Injustices in the Application of the Missouri Death Penalty (1978 to 1996)," *Social Justice* 32 (2005): 151–166.

56. Thomas Arvanites, "Increasing Imprisonment: A Function of Crime or Socioeconomic Factors?" *American Journal of Criminal Justice* 17 (1992): 19–38.

57. David Greenberg and Valerie West, "State Prison Populations and Their Growth, 1971–1991," *Criminology* 39 (2001): 615–654.

58. Robert Weiss, "Repatriating Low-Wage Work: The Political Economy of Prison Labor Reprivatization in the Postindustrial United States," *Criminology* 39 (2001): 253–292.

59. Jack Gibbs, "An Incorrigible Positivist," *Criminologist* 12 (1987): 2–3.

60. Jackson Toby, "The New Criminology Is the Old Sentimentality," *Criminology* 16 (1979): 513–526.

61. Richard Sparks, "A Critique of Marxist Criminology," in *Crime and Justice*, vol. 2, eds. Norval Morris and Michael Tonry (Chicago: University of Chicago Press, 1980), pp. 159–208.

62. Carl Klockars, "The Contemporary Crises of Marxist Criminology," in *Radical Criminology: The Coming Crisis*, ed. J. Inciardi (Beverly Hills, CA: Sage, 1980), pp. 92–123.

63. Matthew Petrocelli, Alex Piquero, and Michael Smith, "Conflict Theory and Racial Profiling: An Empirical Analysis of Police Traffic Stop Data," *Journal of Criminal Justice* 31 (2003): 1–10.

64. Ibid.

65. Anthony Platt, "Criminology in the 1980s: Progressive Alternatives to 'Law and Order,'" *Crime and Social Justice* 21–22 (1985): 191–199.

66. John Lea and Jock Young, *What Is to Be Done About Law and Order?* (Harmondsworth, England: Penguin, 1984).

67. Ibid., p. 88.

68. Ian Taylor, *Crime in Context: A Critical Criminology of Market Societies* (Boulder, CO: Westview Press, 1999).

69. Ibid., pp. 30–31.

70. Richard Kinsey, John Lea, and Jock Young, *Losing the Fight Against Crime* (London: Blackwell, 1986).

71. Martin Schwartz and Walter DeKeseredy, *Contemporary Criminology* (Belmont, CA: Wadsworth, 1993), p. 249.

72. Martin D. Schwartz and Walter S. DeKeseredy, "Left Realist Criminology: Strengths, Weaknesses and the Feminist Critique," *Crime, Law, and Social Change* 15 (1991): 51–72.

73. For a general review of this issue, see Kathleen Daly and Meda Chesney-Lind, "Feminism and Criminology," *Justice Quarterly* 5 (1988): 497–538; Douglas Smith and Raymond Paternoster, "The Gender Gap in Theories of Deviance: Issues and Evidence," *Journal of Research in Crime and Delinquency* 24 (1987): 140–172; and Pat Carlen, "Women, Crime, Feminism, and Realism," *Social Justice* 17 (1990): 106–123.

74. Herman Schwendinger and Julia Schwendinger, *Rape and Inequality* (Newbury Park, CA: Sage, 1983).

75. Daly and Chesney-Lind, "Feminism and Criminology."

76. Janet Saltzman Chafetz, "Feminist Theory and Sociology: Underutilized Contributions for Mainstream Theory," *Annual Review of Sociology* 23 (1997): 97–121.

77. Ibid.

78. James Messerschmidt, *Capitalism, Patriarchy, and Crime* (Totowa, NJ: Rowman & Littlefield, 1986); for a critique of this work, see Herman Schwendinger and Julia Schwendinger, "The World According to James Messerschmidt," *Social Justice* 15 (1988): 123–145.

79. Kathleen Daly, "Gender and Varieties of White-Collar Crime," *Criminology* 27 (1989): 769–793.

80. Gillian Balfour, "Re-imagining a Feminist Criminology," *Canadian Journal of Criminology and Criminal Justice* 48 (2006): 735–752.

81. Jane Roberts Chapman, "Violence against Women as a Violation of Human Rights," *Social Justice* 17 (1990): 54–71.

82. Carrie Yodanis, "Gender Inequality, Violence against Women, and Fear," *Journal of Interpersonal Violence* 19 (2004): 655–675.

83. Victoria Titterington, "A Retrospective Investigation of Gender Inequality and Female Homicide Victimization," *Sociological Spectrum* 26 (2006): 205–236.

84. James Messerschmidt, *Masculinities and Crime: Critique and Reconceptualization of Theory* (Lanham, MD: Rowman & Littlefield, 1993).

85. Angela P. Harris, "Gender, Violence, Race, and Criminal Justice," *Stanford Law Review* 52 (2000): 777–810.

86. Suzie Dod Thomas and Nancy Stein, "Criminality, Imprisonment, and Women's Rights in the 1990s," *Social Justice* 17 (1990): 1–5.

87. Walter DeKeseredy and Martin Schwartz, "Male Peer Support and Woman Abuse: An Expansion of DeKeseredy's Model," *Sociological Spectrum* 13 (1993): 393–413.

88. Daly and Chesney-Lind, "Feminism and Criminology." See also Drew Humphries and Susan Caringella-MacDonald, "Murdered Mothers, Missing Wives: Reconsidering Female Victimization," *Social Justice* 17 (1990): 71–78.

89. Kjersti Ericsson and Nina Jon, "Gendered Social Control: 'A Virtuous Girl' and 'a Proper Boy'," *Journal of Scandinavian Studies in Criminology and Crime Prevention* 9 (2006): 126–141.

90. Hagan, *Structural Criminology*.

91. John Hagan, A. R. Gillis, and John Simpson, "The Class Structure and Delinquency: Toward a Power–Control Theory of Common Delinquent Behavior," *American Journal of Sociology* 90 (1985): 1151–1178; John Hagan, John Simpson, and A. R. Gillis, "Class in the Household: A Power–Control Theory of Gender and Delinquency," *American Journal of Sociology* 92 (1987): 788–816.

92. John Hagan, Bill McCarthy, and Holly Foster, "A Gendered Theory of Delinquency and Despair in the Life Course," *Acta Sociologica* 45 (2002): 37–47.

93. Brenda Sims Blackwell, Christine Sellers, and Sheila Schlaupitz, "A Power–Control Theory of Vulnerability to Crime and Adolescent Role Exits—Revisited," *Canadian Review of Sociology and Anthropology* 39 (2002): 199–219.

94. Brenda Sims Blackwell, "Perceived Sanction Threats, Gender, and Crime: A Test and Elaboration of Power–Control Theory," *Criminology* 38 (2000): 439–488.

95. Christopher Uggen, "Class, Gender, and Arrest: An Intergenerational Analysis of Workplace Power and Control," *Criminology* 38 (2001): 835–862.

96. Gary Jensen, "Power–Control versus Social-Control Theory: Identifying Crucial Differences for Future Research," paper presented at the annual meeting of the American Society of Criminology, Baltimore, November 1990.

97. Gary Jensen and Kevin Thompson, "What's Class Got to Do with It? A Further Examination of Power–Control Theory," *American Journal of Sociology* 95 (1990): 1009–1023. For some critical research, see Simon Singer and Murray Levine, "Power–Control Theory, Gender and Delinquency: A Partial Replication with Additional Evidence on the Effects of Peers," *Criminology* 26 (1988): 627–648.

98. Kevin Thompson, "Gender and Adolescent Drinking Problems: The Effects of Occupational Structure," *Social Problems* 36 (1989): 30–38.

99. Kristin Mack and Michael Leiber, "Race, Gender, Single-Mother Households, and Delinquency: A Further Test of Power-Control Theory," *Youth and Society* 37 (2005): 115–144.

100. See generally Uggen, "Class, Gender, and Arrest."

101. Brenda Sims Blackwell and Alex Piquero, "On the Relationships between Gender, Power Control, Self-Control, and Crime," *Journal of Criminal Justice* 33 (2005): 1–17.

102. Liz Walz, "One Blood," *Contemporary Justice Review* 6 (2003): 25–36.

103. See, for example, Larry Tifft and Dennis Sullivan, "The Struggle to Be Human: Crime, Criminology, and Anarchism," *Contemporary Sociology* 11 (1982): 47; Dennis Sullivan, "The Mask of Love: Corrections in America. Toward a Mutual Aid Alternative," *Journal of Criminal Law and Criminology (1973-)* 71 (1980) 657–658.

104. Larry Tifft, "Foreword," in Sullivan, *The Mask of Love*, p. 6.

105. Sullivan, *The Mask of Love*, p. 141.

106. Dennis Sullivan and Larry Tifft, *Restorative Justice* (Monsey, NY: Willow Tree Press, 2001).

107. Richard Quinney, "The Way of Peace: On Crime, Suffering, and Service," in *Criminology as Peacemaking*, eds. Harold Pepinsky and Richard Quinney (Bloomington: Indiana University Press, 1991), pp. 8–9.

108. For a review of Quinney's ideas, see Kevin B. Anderson, "Richard Quinney's Journey: The Marxist Dimension," *Crime and Delinquency* 48 (2002): 232–242.

109. Kathleen Daly and Russ Immarigeon, "The Past, Present and Future of Restorative Justice: Some Critical Reflections," *Contemporary Justice Review* 1 (1998): 21–45.

110. Howard Zehr, *The Little Book of Restorative Justice* (Intercourse, PA: Good Books, 2002): 1–10.

111. Mark Lewis Taylor, *The Executed God: The Way of the Cross in Lockdown America* (Minneapolis, MN: Fortress Press, 2001).

112. Alfred Villaume, "Life Without Parole" and "Virtual Life Sentences": Death Sentences by Any Other Name," *Contemporary Justice Review* 8 (2005): 265–277.

113. John Braithwaite, *Crime, Shame, and Reintegration* (Melbourne, Australia: Cambridge University Press, 1989).

114. Ibid., p. 81.

115. Anthony Petrosino and Carolyn Petrosino, "The Public Safety Potential of Megan's Law in Massachusetts: An Assessment from a Sample of Criminal Sexual Psychopaths," *Crime and Delinquency* 45 (1999): 140–158.

116. Eliza Ahmed, Nathan Harris, John Braithwaite, and Valerie Braithwaite, *Shame Management through Reintegration* (Cambridge, England: Cambridge University Press, 2001).

117. Eliza Ahmed, "'What, Me Ashamed?' Shame Management and School Bullying," *Journal of Research in Crime and Delinquency* 41 (2004): 269–294.

118. John Braithwaite, "Rape, Shame and Pride," *Journal of Scandinavian Studies in Criminology and Crime Prevention* 7 (2006): 2–16.

119. For more on this approach, see Jane Mugford and Stephen Mugford, "Shame and Reintegration in the Punishment and Deterrence of Spouse Assault," paper presented at the annual meeting of the American Society of Criminology, San Francisco, November 1991.

120. Carter Hay, "An Exploratory Test of Braithwaite's Reintegrative Shaming Theory," *Journal of Research in Crime and Delinquency* 38 (2001): 132–153.

121. Mugford and Mugford, "Shame and Reintegration in the Punishment and Deterrence of Spouse Assault."

122. Gene Stephens, "The Future of Policing: From a War Model to a Peace Model," in *The Past, Present and Future of American Criminal Justice*, eds. Brendan Maguire and Polly Radosh (Dix Hills, NY: General Hall, 1996), pp. 77–93.

123. Rick Shifley, "The Organization of Work as a Factor in Social Well-Being," *Contemporary Justice Review* 6 (2003): 105–126.

124. Kay Pranis, "Peacemaking Circles: Restorative Justice in Practice Allows Victims and Offenders to Begin Repairing the Harm," *Corrections Today* 59 (1997): 74–78.

125. Carol LaPrairie, "The 'New' Justice: Some Implications for Aboriginal Communities," *Canadian Journal of Criminology* 40 (1998): 61–79.

126. Diane Schaefer, "A Disembodied Community Collaborates in a Homicide: Can Empathy Transform a Failing Justice System?" *Contemporary Justice Review* 6 (2003): 133–143.

127. David R. Karp and Beau Breslin, "Restorative Justice in School Communities," *Youth and Society* 33 (2001): 249–272.

128. Paul Jesilow and Deborah Parsons, "Community Policing as Peacemaking," *Policing and Society* 10 (2000): 163–183.

129. Gordon Bazemore and Curt Taylor Griffiths, "Conferences, Circles, Boards, and Mediations: The 'New Wave' of Community Justice Decision Making," *Federal Probation* 61 (1997): 25–37.

130. This section is based on Gordon Bazemore and Mara Schiff, "Paradigm Muddle or Paradigm Paralysis? The Wide and Narrow Roads to Restorative Justice Reform (or, a Little Confusion May Be a Good Thing)," *Contemporary Justice Review* 7 (2004): 37–57.

131. John Braithwaite, "Setting Standards for Restorative Justice," *British Journal of Criminology* 42 (2002): 563–577.

132. David Altschuler, "Community Justice Initiatives: Issues and Challenges in the

U.S. Context," *Federal Probation* 65 (2001): 28–33.

133. Lois Presser and Patricia Van Voorhis, "Values and Evaluation: Assessing Processes and Outcomes of Restorative Justice Programs," *Crime and Delinquency* 48 (2002): 162–189.

134. Declan Roche, *Accountability in Restorative Justice* (Clarendon Studies in Criminology) (London, England: Oxford University Press, 2004).

135. Sharon Levrant, Francis Cullen, Betsy Fulton, and John Wozniak, "Reconsidering Restorative Justice: The Corruption of

Benevolence Revisited?" *Crime* and *Delinquency* 45 (1999): 3–28.

136. Edward Gumz, "American Social Work, Corrections and Restorative Justice: An Appraisal," *International Journal of Offender Therapy and Comparative Criminology* 48 (2004): 449–460.

9

Developmental Theories: Life Course and Latent Trait

CHAPTER OBJECTIVES

1. Be familiar with the concept of developmental theory
2. Know the factors that influence the life course
3. Recognize that there are different pathways to crime
4. Know what is meant by "problem behavior syndrome"
5. Differentiate between "adolescent-limited" and "life course persistent" offenders
6. Be familiar with the "turning points in crime"
7. Be able to discuss the influence of social capital on crime
8. Know what is meant by a latent trait
9. Be familiar with the concepts of impulsivity and self-control
10. Be able to discuss Gottfredson and Hirschi's General Theory of Crime

CANNON

HUNTER

SALAS

VICTORINO

© Volusia County Sheriff's Office via Getty Images

In July of 2004, Troy Victorino and some friends were illegally squatting in a Florida home whose owners were spending the summer in Maine. When their granddaughter, Erin Belanger, a local resident, found them she called the police and had them removed from the premises. The squatters were kicked out, but they left behind an Xbox and clothes and the granddaughter took the items back to her home, which she was sharing with friends. Over the next few days, Troy and his friends threatened Erin and slashed the tires on her car. They warned her that they were going to come back and beat her with a baseball bat when she was sleeping. Then on August 6, 2004, Victorino, accompanied by three accomplices armed with aluminum bats, kicked in the locked front door. The group, who wore black clothes and had scarves on their faces, grabbed knives inside and attacked six victims in different rooms of the three-bedroom house as some of them slept. All six victims, including Erin Belanger, were beaten and stabbed beyond recognition.

Troy Victorino was a career criminal. He had spent 8 of the last 11 years before the killings serving prison sentences for a variety of crimes, including auto theft, battery, arson, burglary, and theft. In 1996, he beat a man so severely that doctors needed 15 titanium plates to rebuild the victim's face. In 1997, a jury convicted him on a charge of aggravated battery and he got a five-year sentence. His mother, Sharon Victorino, sent a letter to the judge before sentencing that said her son was sexually abused at age 2, an ordeal that "led to emotional scars that very few can fathom." Troy had been treated for depression since age 8 and had attempted suicide. "In a matter of a few days, you will be seeing before you my son . . . He will stand before you at 6-foot-6 tall, looking very much like a man," Sharon Victorino wrote. "In actuality, Troy is but a boy."[1]

The week before the attack Victorino was arrested for punching a 28-year-old man in the face over a car debt. Charged with felony battery, he was released after posting $2,500 bail and visited his probation officer for his regular check-in the day before the murders. While he should have been arrested then for violating his probation, his case supervisor failed to take action; in the aftermath of the crime Victorino's probation officer and three of his supervisors were dismissed. After being found guilty as charged, Victorino and Jerone Hunter, one of his co-conspirators, were sentenced to death on August 1, 2006.

How can the violent and abusive actions of a Troy Victorino ever be explained? His history of antisocial acts began in his youth and persisted into his adulthood. Some experts believe that antisocial people like Victorino suffer from an abnormal personal trait, such as a low IQ or impulsive personality, which is present at birth or soon afterward. Yet, if the onset of crime is explained by abnormally low intelligence or a defective personality, why is it that most people **desist** or age out of crime as they mature? It seems unlikely that intelligence increases as young offenders mature or that personality flaws disappear. And why is it that most antisocial people start their criminal career with relatively minor crimes such as shoplifting or smoking marijuana and then commit progressively more serious crimes such as burglary and rape? Even if the onset of criminality can be explained by a single biological or personal trait, some other factor must explain its change, development, and continuance or termination.

Concern over these critical issues has prompted some criminologists to identify, describe, and understand the developmental factors that explain the onset and continuation of a criminal career. Rather than look at a single factor, such as poverty or low intelligence, and suggest that people who maintain this trait are predisposed to crime, **developmental theories** attempt to provide a more global vision of a criminal career encompassing its onset, continuation, and termination.

FOUNDATIONS OF DEVELOPMENTAL THEORY

As you may recall from Chapter 1, the foundation of developmental theory can be traced to the pioneering work of Sheldon Glueck and Eleanor Glueck. While at Harvard University in the 1930s, the Gluecks popularized research on the life cycle of delinquent careers. In a series of longitudinal research studies, they followed the careers of known delinquents to determine the social, biological, and psychological characteristics that predicted persistent offending.[2]

connections

Social process theories lay the foundation for assuming that peer, family, educational, and other interactions, which vary over the life course, influence behaviors. See the first few sections of Chapter 7 for a review of these issues. As you may recall from Chapter 2, a great deal of research has been conducted on the relationship of age and crime and the activities of chronic offenders. This scholarship has prompted interest in the life cycle of crime.

The Gluecks' research was virtually ignored for nearly 30 years as the study of crime and delinquency shifted almost exclusively to social and social-psychological factors (i.e., poverty, neighborhood deterioration, and socialization) that formed the nucleus of structural and process theories. However, during the 1990s, the Glueck legacy was rediscovered in a series of papers by criminologists Robert Sampson and John Laub, who used modern statistical techniques to reanalyze the Gluecks' carefully drawn empirical measurements. Their findings, published in a series of books and articles, fueled the popularity of what is now referred to as the life course approach.[3]

The critical Philadelphia cohort research by Marvin Wolfgang and his associates was another milestone prompting interest in explaining criminal career development.[4] As you may recall, Wolfgang found that while many offenders commit a single criminal act and desist from crime, a small group of chronic offenders engage in frequent and repeated criminal activity and continue to do so across their lifespan. Wolfgang's research focused attention on criminal careers. Criminologists were now asking this fundamental question: what prompts one person to engage in persistent criminal activity while another, who on the surface suffers the same life circumstances, finds a way to steer clear of crime and travel along a more conventional path?

A 1990 review paper by Rolf Loeber and Marc LeBlanc was another important event that generated interest in developmental theory. In this landmark work, Loeber and LeBlanc proposed that criminologists should devote time and effort to understanding some basic questions about the evolution of criminal careers: Why do people begin committing antisocial acts? Why do some stop while others continue? Why do some escalate the severity of their criminality (that is, go from shoplifting to drug dealing to armed robbery) while others deescalate and commit less serious crimes as they mature? If some terminate their criminal activity, what, if anything, causes them to begin again? Why do some criminals specialize in certain types of crime, whereas others are generalists engaging in a variety of antisocial behavior? According to Loeber and LeBlanc's developmental view, criminologists must pay attention to how a criminal career unfolds, how it begins, why it is sustained, and how it comes to an end.[5]

These scholarly advances created enormous excitement among criminologists and focused their attention on criminal career research. As research on criminal careers has evolved, two distinct viewpoints have taken shape: life course view and the latent trait view. **Life course theory** views criminality as a dynamic process, influenced by a multitude of individual characteristics, traits, and social experiences. As people travel through the life course, they are constantly bombarded by changing perceptions and experiences, and as a result their behavior will change directions, sometimes for the better and sometimes for the worse (Figure 9.1). In contrast, **latent trait theories** hold that human development is controlled by a stable propensity or "master trait," present at birth or soon after. Some latent trait theorists maintain that this master trait is inflexible, stable, and unchanging throughout a person's lifetime while others recognize that under some circumstances a latent trait can be altered, influenced, or changed by experiences and interactions (Concept Summary 9.1). In either event, as people travel through their life course, this trait is always there, directing their behavior and shaping the course of their life. Because this master trait is enduring, the ebb and flow of criminal behavior is directed by the impact of external forces such as interpersonal interactions and criminal opportunity; while people don't change, their opportunities and experiences do. Each of these positions is discussed in detail in the following sections.

TWO TYPES OF LATENT TRAITS

Constant Latent Trait	*Evolving Latent Trait*
Inflexible	Flexible
Unchanging	Varying
Influenced by psychological/biological traits and conditions	Influenced by human interaction relationships, contact, and associations

LIFE COURSE FUNDAMENTALS

According to the life course view, even as toddlers, people begin relationships and behaviors that will determine their adult life course. At first they must learn to conform to social rules and function effectively in society. Later they are expected to begin to think about careers, leave their parental homes, find permanent relationships, and eventually marry and begin their own families.[6] These transitions are expected to take place in order—beginning with finishing school, then entering the workforce, getting married, and having children.

Some individuals, however, are incapable of maturing in a reasonable and timely fashion because of family, environmental, or personal problems.[7] In some cases, transitions can occur too early—an adolescent girl who engages in precocious sex gets pregnant and is forced to drop out of high school. In other cases, transitions may occur too late—a

teenage male falls in with the wrong crowd, goes to prison, and finds it difficult to break into the job market upon release; he puts off getting married because of his diminished economic circumstances. Sometimes interruption of one trajectory can harm another. A teenager who has family problems may find that her educational and career development is upset or that she suffers from psychological impairments.[8] Because a transition from one stage of life to another can be a bumpy ride, the propensity to commit crimes is neither stable nor constant: it is a developmental process. A positive life experience may help some criminals desist from crime for a while, whereas a negative one may cause them to resume their activities. Criminal careers are said to be developmental because people are influenced by the behavior of those around them, and they, in turn, influence others' behavior. A youth's antisocial behavior may turn his more conventional friends against him; their rejection solidifies and escalates his antisocial behavior.[9]

Disruption Promotes Criminality

Disruptions in life's major transitions can be destructive and ultimately can promote criminality. Those who are already at risk because of socioeconomic problems or family dysfunction are the most susceptible to these awkward transitions. Criminality, according to this view, cannot be attributed to a single cause, nor does it represent a single underlying tendency.[10] People are influenced by different factors as they mature. Consequently, a factor that may have an important influence at one stage of life (such as delinquent peers) may have little influence later on.[11]

These negative life events can become cumulative: As people acquire more personal deficits, the chances of acquiring additional ones increases.[12] The cumulative impact of these disruptions sustains criminality from childhood into adulthood.[13]

Figure 9.1 Life Course and Latent Trait Theories

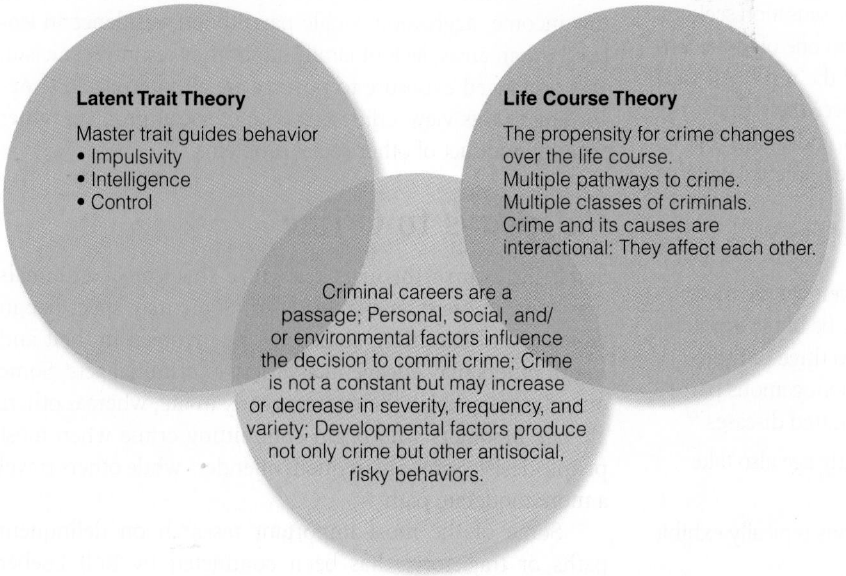

Latent Trait Theory

Master trait guides behavior
- Impulsivity
- Intelligence
- Control

Life Course Theory

The propensity for crime changes over the life course.
Multiple pathways to crime.
Multiple classes of criminals.
Crime and its causes are interactional: They affect each other.

Criminal careers are a passage; Personal, social, and/or environmental factors influence the decision to commit crime; Crime is not a constant but may increase or decrease in severity, frequency, and variety; Developmental factors produce not only crime but other antisocial, risky behaviors.

Changing Life Influences

Life course theories also recognize that as people mature, the factors that influence their behavior change.[14] As people make important life transitions—from child to adolescent, from adolescent to adult, from unwed to married—the nature of social interactions changes.[15]

At first, family relations may be most influential; it comes as no shock to life course theorists when research shows that criminality runs in families and that having criminal relatives is a significant predictor of future misbehaviors.[16] In later adolescence, school and peer relations predominate; in adulthood, vocational achievement and marital relations may be the most critical influences. Some antisocial children who are in trouble throughout their adolescence may manage to find stable work and maintain intact marriages as adults; these life events help them desist from crime. In contrast, less fortunate adolescents who develop arrest records and get involved with the wrong crowd may find themselves limited to menial jobs and at risk for criminal careers.

LIFE COURSE CONCEPTS

From these and similar efforts, a view of crime has emerged that incorporates personal change and growth. The factors that produce crime and delinquency at one point in the life cycle may not be relevant at another; as people mature, the social, physical, and environmental influences on their behavior are transformed. People may show a propensity to offend early in their lives, but the nature and frequency of their activities are often affected by forces beyond their control, which elevate and sustain their criminal activity.[17]

The next sections review some of the more important concepts associated with the developmental perspective and discuss some prominent life course theories.

Problem Behavior Syndrome

Most criminological theories portray crime as the outcome of social problems. Learning theorists view a troubled home life and deviant friends as precursors of criminality; structural theorists maintain that acquiring deviant cultural values leads to criminality. In contrast, the developmental view is that criminality may best be understood as one of many social problems faced by at-risk youth, a view called **problem behavior syndrome (PBS)**. According to this view, crime is one among a group of interrelated antisocial behaviors that cluster together and typically involve family dysfunction, sexual and physical abuse, substance abuse, smoking, precocious sexuality and early pregnancy, educational underachievement, suicide attempts, sensation seeking, and unemployment.[18] People who suffer from one of these conditions typically exhibit many symptoms of the rest.[19] All varieties of criminal behavior, including violence, theft, and drug offenses, may be part of a generalized PBS, indicating that all forms of antisocial behavior have similar developmental patterns (Exhibit 9.1).[20]

Many examples support the existence of PBS:[21]

▌ Adolescents with a history of gang involvement are more likely to have been expelled from school, be binge drinkers, test positively for marijuana, have been in three or more fights in the past six months, have nonmonogamous partners, and test positive for sexually transmitted diseases.[22]

▌ Kids who gamble and take risks at an early age also take drugs and commit crimes.[23]

▌ People who exhibit one of these conditions typically exhibit many of the others.[24]

Those who suffer from PBS are prone to more difficulties than the general population.[25] They find themselves with a range of personal dilemmas ranging from drug abuse to being accident prone, to requiring more health care and hospitalization, to becoming teenage parents, to having mental health problems.[26] PBS has been linked to individual-level personality problems (such as impulsiveness, rebelliousness, and low ego), family problems (such as intrafamily conflict and parental mental disorder), substance abuse, and educational failure.[27] Research shows that social problems such as drug abuse, low income, aggression, single parenthood, residence in isolated urban areas, lack of family support or resources, racism, and prolonged exposure to poverty are all interrelated.[28] According to this view, crime is a type of social problem rather than the product of other social problems.[29]

Pathways to Crime

Some life course theorists recognize that career criminals may travel more than a single road. Some may specialize in violence and extortion; some may be involved in theft and fraud; others may engage in a variety of criminal acts. Some offenders may begin their careers early in life, whereas others are late bloomers who begin committing crime when most people desist. Some are frequent offenders while others travel a more moderate path.[30]

Some of the most important research on delinquent paths or trajectories has been conducted by Rolf Loeber

There is a strong association between parental and children's deviance. In this photo from surveillance videotapes in a Bedford, New Hampshire, store, a woman with her daughter (behind the counter) and her son (at left) are shown in the process of stealing more than $2,000 worth of jewelry. The woman turned herself in after Bedford police made the video public.

as adults, some specialize in a particular criminal activity such as drug trafficking, while others are involved in an assortment of deviant acts—selling drugs, committing robberies and getting involved in break-ins—when the situation arises and the opportunities are present.[32] There may be a multitude of criminal career subgroupings (for example, prostitutes, drug dealers), each with its own distinctive career path.

Age of Onset/Continuity of Crime

Most life course theories assume that the seeds of a criminal career are planted early in life and that early onset of deviance strongly predicts later and more serious criminality.[33] Children who will later become the most serious delinquents begin their deviant careers at a very early (preschool) age, and the earlier the onset of criminality, the more frequent, varied, and sustained the criminal career.[34] If children are aggressive and antisocial during their public school years they are much more likely to be troublesome and exhibit aggressive behavior in adulthood.[35]

Early-onset criminals seem to be more involved in aggressive acts ranging from cruelty to animals to peer-directed violence.[36] In contrast, late starters are more likely to be involved in nonviolent crimes such as theft.[37] Recent research by Daniel Nagin and Richard Tremblay shows that late-onset physical aggression is the exception, not the rule, and that the peak frequency of physical aggression occurs during early childhood and generally declines thereafter.[38]

This finding is quite important because it suggests that the factors that produce long-term violent offending must emerge early in life before environmental influences can have an effect, a finding that contradicts social structure theories. The earlier the onset of crime, the longer its duration.[39] As they emerge into adulthood, persisters report less emotional support, lower job satisfaction, distant peer relationships, and more psychiatric problems than those who desist.[40]

Continuity and Desistance What causes some kids to begin offending at an early age? Research shows that poor parental discipline and monitoring seem to be a key to the early onset of criminality and that these influences may follow kids into their adulthood. The psychic scars of childhood are hard to erase.[41]

Children who are improperly socialized by unskilled parents are the most likely to rebel by wandering the streets

and his associates. Using data from a longitudinal study of Pittsburgh youth, Loeber has identified three distinct paths to a criminal career (Figure 9.2).[31]

1. The **authority conflict pathway** begins at an early age with stubborn behavior. This leads to defiance (doing things one's own way, disobedience) and then to authority avoidance (staying out late, truancy, running away).

2. The **covert pathway** begins with minor, underhanded behavior (lying, shoplifting) that leads to property damage (setting nuisance fires, damaging property). This behavior eventually escalates to more serious forms of criminality, ranging from joyriding, pocket picking, larceny, and fencing to passing bad checks, using stolen credit cards, stealing cars, dealing drugs, and breaking and entering.

3. The **overt pathway** escalates to aggressive acts beginning with aggression (annoying others, bullying), leading to physical (and gang) fighting, and then to violence (attacking someone, forced theft).

The Loeber research indicates that each of these paths may lead to a sustained deviant career. Some people enter two and even three paths simultaneously: They are stubborn, lie to teachers and parents, are bullies, and commit petty thefts. These adolescents are the most likely to become persistent offenders as they mature.

Although some persistent offenders may specialize in one type of behavior, others engage in varied criminal acts and antisocial behaviors as they mature. As adolescents they cheat on tests, bully kids in the school yard, take drugs, commit burglary, steal a car, and then shoplift from a store. Later

Figure 9.2 Loeber's Pathways to Crime

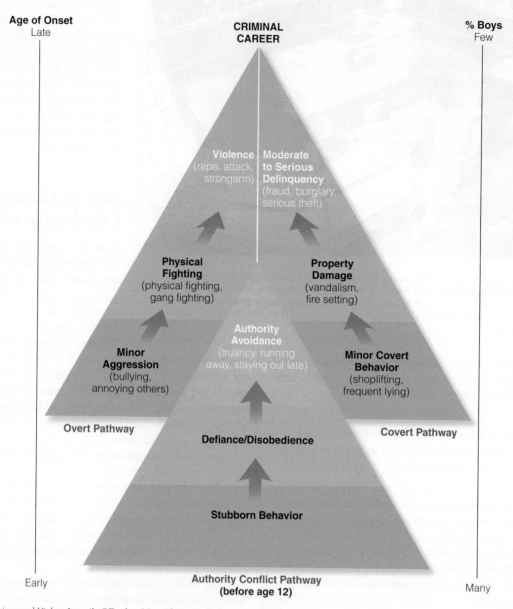

Age of Onset
Late

CRIMINAL CAREER

% Boys
Few

Violence (rape, attack, strongarm)

Moderate to Serious Delinquency (fraud, burglary, serious theft)

Physical Fighting (physical fighting, gang fighting)

Property Damage (vandalism, fire setting)

Authority Avoidance (truancy, running away, staying out late)

Minor Aggression (bullying, annoying others)

Minor Covert Behavior (shoplifting, frequent lying)

Overt Pathway

Covert Pathway

Defiance/Disobedience

Stubborn Behavior

Early

Authority Conflict Pathway (before age 12)

Many

Source: "Serious and Violent Juvenile Offenders," *Juvenile Justice Bulletin,* May 1998.

with deviant peers.[42] Parental influences may be replaced: in middle childhood, social rejection by conventional peers and academic failure sustains antisocial behavior; in later adolescence, commitment to a deviant peer group creates a training ground for crime. While the youngest and most serious offenders may persist in their criminal activity into late adolescence and even adulthood, others are able to age out of crime or desist.

Gender and Desistance As they mature, both males and females who have early experiences with antisocial behavior are the ones most likely to persist throughout their life course. Like

boys, early-onset girls continue to experience difficulties—increased drug and alcohol use, poor school adjustment, mental health problems, poor sexual health, psychiatric problems, higher rates of mortality, criminal behavior, insufficient parenting skills, relationship dysfunction, lower performance in academic and occupational environments, involvement with social service assistance, and adjustment problems—as they enter young adulthood and beyond.[43]

There are also some distinct gender differences. For males, the path runs from early onset in childhood to later problems at work and involvement with substance abuse. For females, the path seems somewhat different: early antisocial behavior leads to relationship problems, depression, tendency to commit suicide, and poor health in adulthood.[44] Males seem to be more deeply influenced by an early history of childhood aggression: males who exhibited chronic physical aggression during the elementary school years exhibit the risk of continued physical violence and delinquency during adolescence; there is less evidence of a linkage between childhood physical aggression and adult aggression among females.[45]

Adolescent-Limiteds and Life Course Persisters

But not all persistent offenders begin at an early age: some begin their journey at different times. Some are precocious, beginning their criminal careers early and persisting into adulthood.[46] Others stay out of trouble in adolescence and do not violate the law until their teenage years. Some offenders may peak at an early age, whereas others persist into adulthood. Some youth maximize their offending rates at a relatively early age and then reduce their criminal activity; others persist into their 20s. Some are high-rate offenders, whereas others offend at relatively low rates.[47] While some kids begin their deviant life course at an early age, others do not. However, some late starters may "catch up" later in their adolescence.

According to psychologist Terrie Moffitt, most young offenders follow one of two paths: **adolescent-limited offenders** may be considered "typical teenagers" who get into minor scrapes and engage in what might be considered rebellious teenage behavior with their friends.[48] As they reach their midteens, adolescent-limited delinquents begin to mimic the antisocial behavior of more troubled teens, only to reduce the frequency of their offending as they mature to around age 18.[49] So while it may be cool for some kids to swagger around and get into trouble during their teenage years, they are ready to settle down and assume more conventional roles as they enter young adulthood.

The second path is the one taken by a small group of **life course persisters** who begin their offending career at a very early age and continue to offend well into adulthood.[50] Moffitt finds that the seeds of life course persistence are planted early in life and may combine the effects of abnormal traits, such as neurological deficits, with severe family dysfunction. Life course persisters are more likely to manifest abnormal personal traits such as low verbal ability, impaired reasoning skills, limited learning ability, and weak spatial and memory functions than adolescent-limited offenders.[51] Individual traits rather than environment seem to have the greatest influence on life course persistence.[52]

It is not surprising, then, that many life course persisters display elements of problem behavior syndrome, including mental health problems, psychiatric pathologies, limited school achievement, ADHD, and health issues.[53]

Research shows that the persistence patterns predicted by Moffitt are valid and accurate.[54] Life course persisters offend more frequently and engage in a greater variety of antisocial acts than other offenders; they also manifest significantly more mental health problems, including psychiatric pathologies, than adolescent-limited offenders.[55]

connections

Moffitt views adolescent-limited kids as following the social learning perspective discussed in Chapter 7. Kids learn that violating the norms of society is an act of independence; some such actions, like smoking and drinking, may be efforts at gaining a pseudomaturity. These acts are neither serious nor violent.

THEORIES OF THE CRIMINAL LIFE COURSE

A number of systematic theories have been formulated that account for onset, continuance, and desistance from crime. As a group they integrate societal level variables such as measures of social control, social learning, and structural models. It is not uncommon for life course theories to interconnect *personal factors* such as personality and intelligence, *social factors* such

According to life course theory, people who engage in antisocial behavior in their adolescence are the ones most likely to persist in that behavior in their adulthood. Here, Quentin Simeon, four-time winner in the Alaska Native Oratory Society annual competition, speaks during the University of Alaska, Anchorage, commencement ceremony on May 7, 2006. Simeon, who was raised in rural Alaska, had been a depressed and troubled teen. He graduated from the honors program with a bachelor's degree as his wife and two daughters watched from the audience. Does his success undermine the validity of the life course view? What factors allow offenders to desist and age out of crime?

EXHIBIT 9.2

Principal Life Course Theories

Name Social Development Model (SDM)

Principal Theorists J. David Hawkins, Richard Catalano

Major Premise Community-level risk factors make some people susceptible to antisocial behaviors. Preexisting risk factors are either reinforced or neutralized by socialization. To control the risk of antisocial behavior, a child must maintain prosocial bonds. Over the life course involvement in prosocial or antisocial behavior determines the quality of attachments. Commitment and attachment to conventional institutions, activities, and beliefs insulate youths from the criminogenic influences in their environment. The prosocial path inhibits deviance by strengthening bonds to prosocial others and activities. Without the proper level of bonding, adolescents can succumb to the influence of deviant others.

Name Interactional Theory

Principle Theorists Terence Thornberry and Marvin Krohn, Alan Lizotte, Margaret Farnworth

Major Premise The onset of crime can be traced to a deterioration of the social bond during adolescence, marked by weakened attachment to parents, commitment to school, and belief in conventional values. The cause of crime and delinquency is bidirectional: weak bonds lead kids to develop friendships with deviant peers and get involved in delinquency. Frequent delinquency involvement further weakens bonds and makes it difficult to reestablish conventional ones. Delinquency-promoting factors tend to reinforce one another and sustain a chronic criminal career. Kids who go through stressful life events such as a family financial crisis are more likely to later get involved in antisocial behaviors and vice versa. Criminality is a developmental process that takes on different meaning and form as a person matures. During early adolescence, attachment to the family is critical; by mid-adolescence, the influence of the family is replaced by friends, school, and youth culture; by adulthood, a person's behavioral choices are shaped by his or her place in conventional society and his or her own nuclear family. Although crime is influenced by these social forces, it also influences these processes and associations. Therefore, crime and social processes are interactional.

Name General Theory of Crime and Delinquency (GTCD)

Primary Theorist Robert Agnew

Major Premise Crime and social relations are reciprocal. Family relationships, work experiences, school performance, and peer relations influence crime. In turn, antisocial acts have a significant impact on family relationships, work experiences, school performance, and peer relations. Engaging in crime leads to a weakened bond with significant others and strengthens the association with criminal peers. Close ties to criminal peers weakens bonds to conventional society.

Crime is most likely to occur when the constraints against crime (e.g., fear of punishment, stake in conformity, self-control) are low and the motivations for crime (e.g., beliefs favorable to crime, exposure to criminals, criminal learning experiences) are high. The way an individual reacts to constraints and motivations is shaped by five key elements of human development, called life domains:

1. *Self.* Irritability and/or low self-control.
2. *Family.* Poor parenting and no marriage or a bad marriage.
3. *School.* Negative school experiences and limited education.
4. *Peers.* Delinquent friends.
5. *Work.* Unemployment or having a bad job.

The structure and impact of each of the life domains are continuously evolving; each has an influence over the other; they are mutually interdependent.

Sources: Robert Agnew, *Why Do Criminals Offend? A General Theory of Crime and Delinquency* (Los Angeles: Roxbury Publishing, 2005); Terence Thornberry, "Toward an Interactional Theory of Delinquency," *Criminology* 25 (1987): 863–891; Richard Catalano, and J. David Hawkins, "The Social Development Model: A Theory of Antisocial Behavior," in *Delinquency and Crime: Current Theories*, ed. J. David Hawkins (New York: Cambridge University Press, 1996): pp. 149–197.

---

as income and neighborhood, *socialization factors* such as marriage and military service, *cognitive factors* such as information processing and attention/perception, and *situational factors* such as criminal opportunity, effective guardianship, and apprehension risk into complex multifactor explanations of human behavior. In this sense they are integrated theories because they incorporate social, personal, and developmental factors into complex explanations of human behavior. They do not focus on the relatively simple question—why do people commit crime?—but on more complex issues: Why do some offenders persist in criminal careers while others desist from or alter their criminal activity as they mature?[56] Why do some people continually escalate their criminal involvement, whereas others slow down and turn their lives around? Are all criminals similar in their offending patterns, or are there different types of offenders

and paths to offending? Life course theorists want to know not only why people enter a criminal way of life but why, once they do, they are able to alter the trajectory of their criminal involvement. One of the more important life course theories, Sampson and Laub's age-graded theory is set out below in some detail. Exhibit 9.2 outlines the principles of some other important life course theories.

Sampson and Laub: Age-Graded Theory

If there are various pathways to crime and delinquency, are there trails back to conformity? In an important 1993 work, *Crime in the Making*, Robert Sampson and John Laub formulated

Figure 9.3 Sampson and Laub's Age-Graded Theory

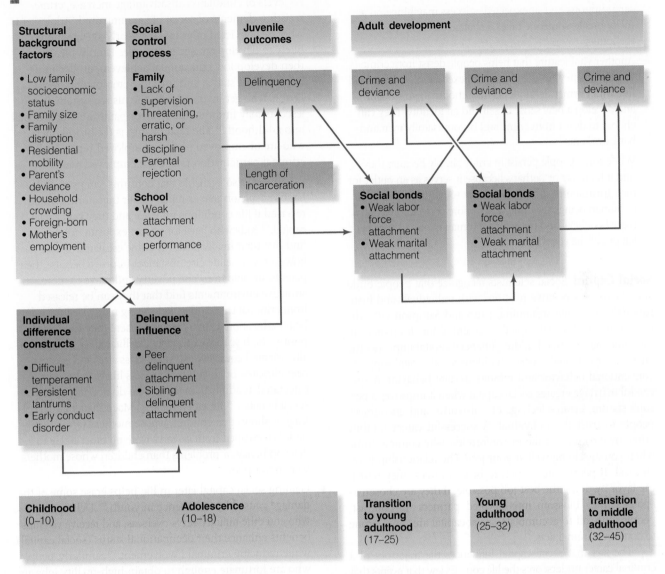

Source: Robert Sampson and John Laub, *Crime in the Making: Pathways and Turning Points through Life* (Cambridge, MA: Harvard University Press, 1993), pp. 244–245.

what they called an *age-graded theory of informal social control* (Figure 9.3). In their pioneering research, Laub and Sampson reanalyzed the data originally collected by the Gluecks more than 40 years before. Using modern statistical analysis, Laub and Sampson relied on this data to formulate a life course/developmental view of crime.[57] Some of the principles of age-graded theory are listed below:

▌ Individual traits and childhood experiences are important to understand the onset of delinquent and criminal behavior. But these alone cannot explain the continuity of crime into adulthood.

▌ Experiences in young adulthood and beyond can redirect criminal trajectories or paths. In some cases people can be turned in a positive direction, while in others negative life experiences can be harmful and injurious.

▌ Repeat negative experiences create a condition called **cumulative disadvantage**. Serious problems in adolescence undermine life chances and reduce employability and social relations. People who increase their cumulative disadvantage risk continued offending.

▌ Positive life experiences and relationships can help a person become reattached to society and allow them to *knife off* from a criminal career path.

▌ Positive life experiences such as gaining employment, getting married, or joining the military create informal social control mechanisms that limit criminal behavior opportunities. These elements of informal social control are called *turning points in crime.*

▌ Two critical elements of informal social control/turning points are marriage and career. Adolescents who are at risk for crime can live conventional lives if they can find good jobs, achieve successful military careers, or enter into a successful marriage. Turning points may be serendipitous and unexpected: success may hinge on a lucky break; someone takes a chance on them; they win the lottery.

- Another vital feature that helps people desist from crime is "human agency" or the purposeful execution of choice and free will. Former delinquents may choose to go straight and develop a new sense of self and an identity. They can choose to desist from crime and become family men and hard workers.[58]

- While some people persist in crime simply because they find it lucrative or perhaps because it serves as an outlet for their frustrations, others choose not to participate because as human beings they find other, more conventional paths more beneficial and rewarding. Human choice cannot be left out of the equation.

Social Capital Social scientists recognize that people build social capital—positive relations with individuals and institutions that are life sustaining. Laub and Sampson view the development of social capital as essential for desistance. In the same manner that building financial capital improves the chances for personal success, building social capital supports conventional behavior and inhibits deviant behavior. A successful marriage creates social capital when it improves a person's stature, creates feelings of self-worth, and encourages people to trust the individual. A successful career inhibits crime by creating a stake in conformity; why commit crime when you are doing well at your job? The relationship is reciprocal. If people are chosen to be employees, they return the favor by doing the best job possible; if they are chosen as spouses, they blossom into devoted partners. In contrast, people who fail to accumulate social capital are more prone to commit criminal acts.[59]

The fact that social capital influences the trajectory of a criminal career underscores the life course view that events that occur in later adolescence and adulthood do in fact influence behavior choices. Life events that occur in adulthood can help either terminate or sustain deviant careers.

Testing Age-Graded Theory There have been a number of research efforts that have supported the basic assumptions of age-graded theory:

- Empirical research now shows that, as predicted by Sampson and Laub, people change over the life course and that the factors that predict delinquency in adolescence, such as a weak bond to parents, may have less of an impact on adult crime when other factors, such as marriage and family, take on greater importance.[60]

- Criminality appears to be dynamic and is affected both by the erosion of informal social control and by interaction with antisocial influences. For example, accumulating deviant peers helps sustain criminality: the more deviant

friends one accumulates over time, the more likely one is to maintain a criminal career.[61]

- As levels of cumulative disadvantage increase, crime-resisting elements of social life are impaired. Adolescents who are convicted of crime at an early age are more likely to develop antisocial attitudes later in life. They then develop low educational achievement, declining occupational status, and unstable employment records.[62] People who get involved with the justice system as adolescents may find that their career paths are blocked well into adulthood.[63] The relationship is reciprocal: men who are unemployed or underemployed report higher criminal participation rates than employed men.[64]

- Evidence is also available that confirms Sampson and Laub's suspicion that criminal career trajectories can be reversed if life conditions improve and they gain social capital.[65] Kids who have long-term exposure to poverty find that their involvement in crime escalates. Those, however, whose life circumstances improve because their parents are able to escape poverty and move to more attractive environments find that they can be released from criminal trajectories. Relocating may place them in better educational environments where they can have a positive high school experience, facilitated by occupationally oriented course work, small class size, and positive peer climates. Such children are less likely to become incarcerated as adults than those who do not enjoy these social benefits.[66] Research by Ross Macmillan and his colleagues shows that children whose mothers were initially poor but escaped from poverty were no more likely to develop behavior problems than children whose mothers were never poor.

- Gaining social capital later in life helps erase some of the damage caused by its absence in youth.[67] Delinquents who enter the military, serve overseas, and receive veterans' benefits enhance their occupational status (social capital) while reducing criminal involvement.[68] Similarly, people who are fortunate enough to obtain high-quality jobs are likely to reduce their criminal activities even if they had a prior history of offending.[69]

The Marriage Factor When they achieve adulthood, adolescents who had significant problems with the law are able to desist from crime if they can establish meaningful social ties that provide informal social control. Of these, none is more important than a successful marriage. People who cannot sustain secure marital relations are less likely to desist from crime. People who can find a spouse who supports them despite knowing about their past misdeeds are the ones most likely to steer away from the path of crime. Marriage both transforms people and reduces their opportunity to commit crimes. It helps cut off a person's past, provides new relationships, creates new levels of supervision, and helps the former offender develop structured routines focused on family life. Happy marriages are life sustaining, and marital quality can even improve over time (as people work less and have fewer parental responsibilities).[70] Spending

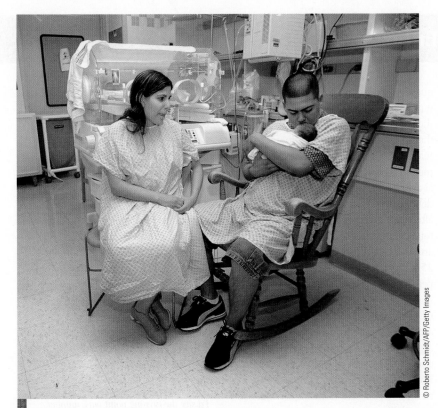

According to Laub and Sampson, getting married and having a family are key elements of social capital and informal social control that allow prior offenders to knife off from crime and live a more conventional lifestyle.

2 percent other races.[75] The research team found former offenders were far less likely to return to crime if they settled down into the routines of a solid marriage. Common-law marriages or living with a partner did not have the same crime-reducing effect as did traditional marriages in which the knot is tied, the union is registered at the courthouse, and there is a general expectation to lead a steady life. Among non-Caucasians, parolees cohabiting without the benefit of marriage actually increased their recidivism rates.

Piquero explains his findings by suggesting that

People who are married often have schedules where they work nine-to-five jobs, come home for dinner, take care of children if they have them, watch television, go to bed, and repeat that cycle over and over again. People who are not married have a lot of free rein to do what they want, especially if they are not employed. There's something about crossing the line of getting married that helps these men stay away from crime. If they don't cross that line, they can continue their lifestyles, which are pretty erratic.[76]

time in marital and family activities also reduces exposure to deviant peers, which in turn reduces the opportunity to become involved in criminal activities.[71] As Mark Warr states:

For many individuals, it seems, marriage marks a transition from heavy peer involvement to a preoccupation with one's spouse. That transition is likely to reduce interaction with former friends and accomplices and thereby reduce the opportunities as well as the motivation to engage in crime.[72]

Even people who have histories of criminal activity and have been convicted of serious offenses reduce the frequency of their offending if they live with spouses and maintain employment when they are in the community.[73] The marriage benefit may also be intergenerational: children who grow up in two-parent families are more likely to later have happy marriages themselves than children who are the product of divorced or never-married parents.[74] If people with marital problems are more crime prone, their children will also suffer a greater long-term risk of marital failure and antisocial activity.

One important new research study further confirms the benefits of marriage as a crime-reducing social event. Researchers Alex Piquero, John MacDonald, and Karen Parker tracked 524 men in their late teens and early 20s for a seven-year period after they were paroled from the California Youth Authority during the 1970s and 1980s. The sample of men, who had been incarcerated for lengthy periods of time, was 48 percent white, 33 percent black, 17 percent Latino, and

While the Piquero research is persuasive, some important questions still need to be answered: Why do some people enter strong marriages while others fail? Does the influence of marriage have an equal effect on men and women? Research by Ronald Simons and his associates found that while marriage significantly improves a woman's life chances, it has less impact on men.[77] However, for both males and females, having an antisocial romantic partner as a young adult increased the likelihood of later criminal behavior, a finding that supports Laub and Sampson.

Future Research Directions Although age-graded theory has received enormous attention, there are still many research questions left unanswered. For example, what is it about a military career that helps reduce future criminality? Does the connection between military service and desistance suggest universal military service as a crime prevention alternative? Why are some troubled youth able to conform to the requirements of a job or career while others cannot? If acquiring social capital—family, friends, education, marriage, and employment—aids in the successful recovery from crime, does the effect produce an actual change in the propensity to commit crime or merely the reduction of criminal opportunity?[78]

Probably the most important issue that must be addressed is whether the relationships that underpin age-graded theory are still valid today. Laub and Sampson's theory relies heavily on the Glueck data collected more than 50 years ago. The Glueck sample lived in a world that was quite

SHARED BEGINNINGS, DIVERGENT LIVES

Why are some delinquents destined to become persistent criminals as adults? John Laub and Robert Sampson have conducted a follow-up to their reanalysis of Sheldon Glueck and Eleanor Glueck's study that matched 500 delinquent boys with 500 nondelinquents. The individuals in the original sample were re-interviewed by the Gluecks at ages 25 and 32. Sampson and Laub located and interviewed the survivors of the delinquent sample, the oldest 70 years old and the youngest 62.

Persistence and Desistance

Laub and Sampson find that delinquency and other forms of antisocial conduct in childhood are strongly related to adult delinquency and drug and alcohol abuse. Former delinquents also suffer consequences in other areas of social life, such as school, work, and family life. For example, delinquents are far less likely to finish high school than are nondelinquents and subsequently are more likely to be unemployed, receive welfare, and experience separation or divorce as adults.

In their latest research, Laub and Sampson address one of the key questions posed by life course theories: is it possible for former delinquents to turn their lives around as adults? They find that most antisocial children do not remain antisocial as adults. For example, of men in the study cohort who survived to age 50, 24 percent had no arrests for delinquent acts of violence and property after age 17 (6 percent had no arrests for total delinquency); 48 percent had no arrests for predatory delinquency after age 25 (19 percent for total delinquency); 60 percent had no arrests for predatory delinquency after age 31 (33 percent for total delinquency); and 79 percent had no arrests for predatory delinquency after age 40 (57 percent for total delinquency). They conclude that desistance from delinquency is the norm and that most, if not all, serious delinquents desist from delinquency.

Why Do Delinquents Desist?

Laub and Sampson's earlier research indicated that building social capital through marriage and jobs were key components of desistance from delinquency. However, in this new round of research, Laub and Sampson were able to find out more about long-term desistance by interviewing 52 men as they approached age 70. The follow-up showed a dramatic drop in criminal activity as the men aged. Between the ages of 17 and 24, 84 percent of the subjects had committed violent crimes; in their 30s and 40s, that number dropped to 14 percent; it fell to just 3 percent as the men reached their 60s and 70s. Property crimes and alcohol- and drug-related crimes also showed significant decreases. They found that men who desisted from crime were rooted in structural routines and had strong social ties to family and community. Drawing on the men's own words, they found that one important element for "going straight" is the "knifing off" of individuals from their immediate environment and offering the men a new script for the future. Joining the military can provide this knifing-off effect, as does marriage or changing one's residence. One former delinquent (age 69) told them:

> I'd say the turning point was, number one, the Army. You get into an outfit, you had a sense of belonging, you made your friends. I think I became a pretty good judge of character. In the Army, you met some good ones, you met some foul balls. Then I met the wife. I'd say probably that would be the turning point. Got married, then naturally, kids come. So now you got to get a better job, you got to make more money. And that's how I got to the Navy Yard and tried to improve myself.

Former delinquents who "went straight" were able to put structure into their lives. Structure often led the men to

different from contemporary society: they did not watch violent video games or TV shows; they used alcohol but were not part of a drug culture; marriage was the norm and the divorce rate was much lower; globalization and job loss were not issues. An important research task is to determine whether the theory's basic premises are still valid considering these structural changes in society. Recent research by Ryan Schroeder and his colleagues show that getting involved in the drug culture has a much more damaging effect on marriage and employment than heavy alcohol abuse.[79] Similarly, joining the military today may have a significantly different meaning and produce significantly different effects than it did for the men in the Glueck sample: recent research indicates that the 12-month prevalence of common mental illnesses in the United States military is estimated to be 26 percent, far above the level in the civilian population. Considering this condition, it is difficult to believe that serving in the military today has the same effect it did 60 years ago.[80]

To answer some of these questions, Laub and Sampson contacted the surviving members of the Glueck cohort. Some of their findings are discussed in The Criminological Enterprise feature "Shared Beginnings, Divergent Lives."

www To read an **assessment of age-graded theory** by Sampson, Laub, and Gary Sweeten, and also one by Laub and Sampson, go to academic.cengage.com/criminaljustice/siegel.

disassociate from delinquent peers, reducing the opportunity to get into trouble. Getting married, for example, may limit the number of nights men can "hang with the guys." As one wife of a former delinquent said, "It is not how many beers you have, it's who you drink with." Even multiple offenders who did time in prison were able to desist with the help of a stabilizing marriage.

Former delinquents who can turn their life around, who have acquired a degree of maturity by taking on family and work responsibilities, and who have forged new commitments are the ones most likely to make a fresh start and find new direction and meaning in life. It seems that men who desisted changed their identity as well, and this, in turn, affected their outlook and sense of maturity and responsibility. The ability to change did not reflect a delinquency "specialty": violent offenders followed the same path as property offenders.

While many former delinquents desisted from delinquency, they still faced the risk of an early and untimely death. Thirteen percent (N=62) of the delinquent as compared to only 6 percent (N=28) of the nondelinquent subjects died unnatural deaths such as violence, cirrhosis of the liver caused by alcoholism, poor self-care, suicide, and so on. By age 65, 29 percent (N=139) of the delinquent and 21 percent (N=95) of the nondelinquent subjects had died from natural causes. Frequent delinquent involvement in adolescence and alcohol abuse were the strongest predictors of an early and unnatural death. So while many troubled youth are able to reform, their early excesses may haunt them across their life span.

Policy Implications

Laub and Sampson find that youth problems—delinquency, substance abuse, violence, dropping out, teen pregnancy—often share common risk characteristics. Intervention strategies, therefore, should consider a broad array of antisocial, criminal, and deviant behaviors and not limit the focus to just one subgroup or delinquency type. Because criminality and other social problems are linked, early prevention efforts that reduce delinquency will probably also reduce alcohol abuse, drunk driving, drug abuse, sexual promiscuity, and family violence. The best way to achieve these goals is through four significant life-changing events: marriage, joining the military, getting a job, and changing one's environment or neighborhood. What appears to be important about these processes is that they all involve, to varying degrees, the following items: a knifing off of the past from the present; new situations that provide both supervision and monitoring as well as new opportunities of social support and growth; and new situations that provide the opportunity for transforming identity. Prevention of delinquency must be a policy at all times and at all stages of life.

CRITICAL THINKING

1. Do you believe that the factors that influenced the men in the original Glueck sample are still relevant for change? For example, considering the current high divorce rate, is marriage still a stabilizing force?

2. Recent reports show that male U.S. veterans are twice as likely to die by suicide than people with no military service, and are more likely to kill themselves with a gun than others who commit suicide. Considering this recent finding, do you agree with Laub and Sampson that military service might be beneficial and help troubled kids turn their lives around?

Sources: John Laub and Robert Sampson, *Shared Beginnings, Divergent Lives: Delinquent Boys to Age 70* (Cambridge, MA: Harvard University Press, 2003); John Laub and Robert Sampson, "Understanding Desistance from Delinquency," in *Delinquency and Justice: An Annual Review of Research*, vol. 28, ed. Michael Tonry (Chicago: University of Chicago Press, 2001), pp. 1–71; John Laub and George Vaillant, "Delinquency and Mortality: A 50-Year Follow-Up Study of 1,000 Delinquent and Nondelinquent Boys," *American Journal of Psychiatry* 157 (2000): 96–102.

LATENT TRAIT THEORIES

In a critical 1990 article, David Rowe, D. Wayne Osgood, and W. Alan Nicewander proposed the concept of latent traits to explain the flow of crime over the life cycle. Their model assumes that a number of people in the population have a personal attribute or characteristic that controls their inclination or propensity to commit crimes.[81] This disposition, or latent trait, may be either present at birth or established early in life, and it can remain stable over time. Suspected latent traits include defective intelligence, damaged or impulsive personality, genetic abnormalities, the physical-chemical functioning of the brain, and environmental influences on brain function such as drugs, chemicals, and injuries.[82]

Regardless of gender or environment, those who maintain one of these suspect traits may be at risk to crime and in danger of becoming career criminals; those who lack the traits have a much lower risk.[83] Because latent traits are stable, people who are antisocial during adolescence are the most likely to persist in crime. The positive association between past and future criminality detected in the cohort studies of career criminals reflects the presence of this underlying stable criminal propensity. That is, if an impulsive personality contributes to delinquency in childhood, it should

EXHIBIT 9.3

Some Important Latent Trait Theories

Name Integrated Cognitive Antisocial Potential (ICAP) Theory

Principal Theorist David Farrington

Latent Trait Antisocial potential

Major Premise People maintain a range of *antisocial potential* (AP), the potential to commit antisocial acts. AP can be viewed as both a long- and short-term phenomenon. Those with high levels of long-term AP are at risk for offending over the life course; those with low AP levels live more conventional lives. Though AP levels are fairly consistent over time, they peak in the teenage years because of the effects of maturational factors—such as increase in peer influence and decrease in family influence—that directly affect crime rates. Long-term AP can be reduced by life-changing events such as marriage. There is also short-term AP when immediate life events may increase a personal antisocial potential so that, in the immediate moment, people may advance their location on the AP continuum. For example, a person with a relatively low long-term AP may suffer a temporary amplification if he is bored, angry, drunk, or frustrated. According to the ICAP theory, the commission of offenses and other types of antisocial acts depends on the interaction between the individual (with his immediate level of AP) and the social environment (especially criminal opportunities and victims).

Name Differential Coercion Theory

Principal Theorist Mark Colvin

Latent Trait Perceptions of coercion

Major Premise Perceptions of coercion begin early in life when children experience punitive forms of discipline—both physical attacks and psychological coercion, including negative commands, critical remarks, teasing, humiliation, whining, yelling, and threats. Through these destructive family interchanges, coercion becomes ingrained and guides reactions to adverse situations that arise in both family and nonfamily settings.

There are two sources of coercion: interpersonal and impersonal. Interpersonal coercion is direct, involving the use or threat of force and intimidation from parents, peers, and significant others. Impersonal coercion involves pressures beyond individual control, such as economic and social pressure caused by unemployment, poverty, or competition among businesses or other groups. High levels of coercion produce criminality, especially when the episodes of coercive behavior are inconsistent and random, because this teaches people that they cannot control their lives. Chronic offenders grew up in homes where parents used erratic control and applied it in an inconsistent fashion.

Name Control Balance Theory

Principal Theorist Charles Tittle

Latent Trait Control/balance

Major Premise The concept of control has two distinct elements: the amount of control one is subject to by others and the amount of control one can exercise over others. Conformity results when these two elements are in balance; control imbalances produce deviant and criminal behaviors.

Those people who sense a deficit of control turn to three types of behavior to restore balance:

1. *Predation* involves direct forms of physical violence, such as robbery, sexual assault, or other forms of assault.

2. *Defiance* challenges control mechanisms but stops short of physical harm: for example, vandalism, curfew violations, and unconventional sex.

3. *Submission* involves passive obedience to the demands of others, such as submitting to physical or sexual abuse without response.

An excess of control can result in crimes of (1) *exploitation*, which involves using others to commit crimes, such as contract killers or drug runners, (2) *plunder*, which involves using power without regard for others, such as committing a hate crime or polluting the environment, or (3) *decadence*, which involves spur of the moment, irrational acts such as child molesting.

Sources: David P. Farrington, "Developmental and Life-Course Criminology: Key Theoretical and Empirical Issues," Sutherland Award address presented at the annual meeting of the American Society of Criminology, Chicago, November 2002, revised March 2003; Charles Tittle, *Control Balance: Toward a General Theory of Deviance* (Boulder, CO: Westview Press, 1995); Mark Colvin, *Crime and Coercion: An Integrated Theory of Chronic Criminality* (New York: Palgrave Press, 2000).

---

also cause the same people to offend as adults because personality traits remain stable over the life span.

But how then can the aging out process be explained? People do commit less crime as they mature. However, declining criminal activity may not be a valid indicator of real behavioral change. Why does this illusion exist? Whereas the propensity to commit crime is stable, the opportunity to commit crime fluctuates over time. People may appear to age out of crime as they mature and develop, simply because there are fewer opportunities to commit crimes and greater inducements to remain "straight." They may marry, have children, and obtain jobs. The former delinquents' newfound adult responsibilities leave them little time to hang with their friends, abuse substances, and get into scrapes with the law. So while their propensity to commit crime remains stable, their opportunity to commit crime has changed.

To understand this concept of stable criminal propensity better, assume that intelligence as measured by IQ tests is a stable latent trait associated with crime. Intelligence remains stable and unchanging over the life course but crime rates decline with age. How can latent trait theory explain this phenomenon? Teenagers have more opportunity to commit crime than adults, so at every level of intelligence, adolescent crime rates will be higher. As they mature, however, teens with both high and low IQs will commit less crime because their adult responsibilities provide them with fewer criminal opportunities. They may get married and raise a family, get a job and buy a home. And like most people, as they age they lose strength and vigor, qualities necessary to commit crime. Though their IQ remains stable and their propensity to commit crime is unchanged, their living environment and biological condition have undergone radical change. Even if they wanted to engage in criminal activities, the former delinquents may lack the opportunity and energy to do so.

Crime and Human Nature

Latent trait theorists were encouraged when two prominent social scientists, James Q. Wilson and Richard Herrnstein, published *Crime and Human Nature* in 1985 and suggested that personal traits—such as genetic makeup, intelligence, and body build—may outweigh the importance of social variables as predictors of criminal activity.[84]

According to Wilson and Herrnstein, all human behavior, including criminality, is determined by its perceived consequences. A criminal incident occurs when an individual chooses criminal over conventional behavior (referred to as *noncrime*) after weighing the potential gains and losses of each: "The larger the ratio of net rewards of crime to the net rewards of noncrime, the greater the tendency to commit the crime."[85]

Wilson and Herrnstein's model assumes that both biological and psychological traits influence the crime–noncrime choice. They see a close link between a person's decision to choose crime and such biosocial factors as low intelligence, mesomorphic body type, genetic influences (parental criminality), and possessing an autonomic nervous system that responds too quickly to stimuli. Psychological traits, such as an impulsive or extroverted personality or generalized hostility, also determine the potential to commit crime.

In their focus on the association between these constitutional and psychological factors and crime, Wilson and Herrnstein seem to be suggesting the existence of an elusive latent trait that predisposes people to commit crime.[86] Their vision helped inspire other criminologists to identify the elusive latent trait that causes criminal behavior. The most prominent latent trait theory is Gottfredson and Hirschi's **General Theory of Crime (GTC)**. Exhibit 9.3 discusses some other important contributions to the latent trait model.

General Theory of Crime

In their important work, *A General Theory of Crime*, Michael Gottfredson and Travis Hirschi modified and redefined some of the principles articulated in Hirschi's original social control theory by adding elements of trait and rational choice theories and shifting the focus from social control to **self-control**.[87]

According to Gottfredson and Hirschi the propensity to commit crime is tied directly to a person's level of self-control. People with limited self-control tend to be impulsive; they are insensitive to other people's feelings, physical (rather than mental), risk-takers, shortsighted, and nonverbal.[88] They have a here-and-now orientation and refuse to work for distant goals; they lack diligence, tenacity, and persistence. People lacking self-control tend to be adventuresome, active, physical, and self-centered. As they mature, they often have unstable marriages, jobs, and friendships.[89] They are less likely to feel shame if they engage in deviant acts and are more likely to find them pleasurable.[90] They are also more likely to engage in dangerous

According to the General Theory of Crime, people who are impulsive and lack self-control are the ones most likely to engage in risky behavior, even if it is not always illegal per se.

behaviors such as drinking, smoking, and reckless driving; all of these behaviors are associated with criminality.[91]

Because those with low self-control enjoy risky, exciting, or thrilling behaviors with immediate gratification, they are more likely to enjoy criminal acts, which require stealth, agility, speed, and power, than conventional acts, which demand long-term study and cognitive and verbal skills. As Gottfredson and Hirschi put it, they derive satisfaction from "money without work, sex without courtship, revenge without court delays."[92]

Gottfredson and Hirschi suggest that crime is not the only outlet for people with an impulsive personality. Even if they do not engage in antisocial behaviors, impulsive people enjoy other risky behaviors such as smoking, drinking, gambling, and illicit sexuality.[93] Although these acts are not illegal, they provide immediate, short-term gratification. It is not surprising then, considering their risky lifestyle, that impulsive people are more prone to be crime victims themselves than their less impulsive peers.[94] Exhibit 9.4 lists the elements of impulsivity.

Low self-control develops early in life and remains stable into and through adulthood.[95] Considering the continuity of criminal motivation, Hirschi and Gottfredson have questioned the utility of the juvenile justice system and of giving more lenient treatment to young delinquent offenders. Why separate youthful and adult offenders legally when the source of their criminality (i.e., impulsivity) is essentially the same?[96]

EXHIBIT 9.4

The Elements of Impulsivity: Signs that a Person Has Low Self-Control

- Insensitive
- Physical
- Shortsighted
- Nonverbal
- Here-and-now orientation
- Unstable social relations
- Enjoys deviant behaviors
- Risk-taker
- Refuses to work for distant goals
- Lacks diligence
- Lacks tenacity
- Adventuresome
- Self-centered
- Shameless
- Imprudent
- Lacks cognitive and verbal skills
- Enjoys danger and excitement

connections

In his original version of control theory, discussed in Chapter 7, Hirschi focused on the social controls that attach people to conventional society and insulate them from criminality. In this newer work, he concentrates on self-control as a stabilizing force. While both views talk about control, they are actually quite different in their concept of control and its formation.

What Causes Impulsivity? Gottfredson and Hirschi trace the root cause of poor self-control to inadequate childrearing practices that begin soon after birth and can influence neural development. Once experiences are ingrained, the brain establishes a pattern of electrochemical activation that remains for life.[97] Parents who refuse or are unable to monitor a child's behavior, to recognize deviant behavior when it occurs, and to punish that behavior will produce children who lack self-control. Children who are not attached to their parents, who are poorly supervised, and whose parents are criminal or deviant themselves are the most likely to develop poor self-control. In a sense, lack of self-control occurs naturally when steps are not taken to stop its development.[98]

While Gottfredson and Hirschi believe that parenting, not heredity, shapes self-control, some recent research efforts do show that an impulsive personality may have physical or social roots, or perhaps both. Children who suffer anoxia (i.e., oxygen starvation) during the birthing process are the ones most likely to lack self-control later in life, suggesting that impulsivity may have a biological basis.[99]

Crime Rate Variations? If individual differences are stable over the life course, how come crime rates vary? Why do people commit less crime as they age? Why are some regions more crime prone than others? Why are some groups more crime prone than others? Does that mean there are between-group differences in self-control? If male crime rates are higher than female rates does that mean men are more impulsive and lacking in self-control? How does the GTC address these issues?

Gottfredson and Hirschi remind us that criminal propensity and criminal acts are separate concepts (Figure 9.4). On one hand, criminal acts, such as robberies or burglaries, are illegal events or deeds that offenders engage in when they perceive them to be advantageous. Burglaries are typically committed by young males looking for cash, liquor, and entertainment; the crime provides "easy, short-term gratification."[100] Crime is rational and predictable; people commit crime when it promises rewards with minimal threat of pain; the threat of punishment can deter crime. If targets are well guarded, crime rates diminish. Only the truly irrational offender would dare to strike under those circumstances.

On the other hand, while criminal offenders are people predisposed to commit crimes, they are not robots who commit crime without restraint; their days are also filled with

Figure 9.4 Gottfredson and Hirschi's General Theory of Crime

Criminal Offender

Impulsive personality
- Physical
- Insensitive
- Risk-taking
- Shortsighted
- Nonverbal

Low self-control
- Poor parenting
- Deviant parents
- Lack of supervision
- Active
- Self-centered

Weakening of social bonds
- Attachment
- Commitment
- Involvement
- Belief

Criminal Opportunity
- Presence of gangs
- Lack of supervision
- Lack of guardianship
- Suitable targets

Criminal Act
- Delinquency
- Smoking
- Drinking
- Underage sex
- Crime

conventional behaviors, such as going to school, parties, concerts, and church. But given the same set of criminal opportunities, such as having a lot of free time for mischief and living in a neighborhood with unguarded homes containing valuable merchandise, crime-prone people have a much higher probability of violating the law than do noncriminals. The propensity to commit crimes remains stable throughout a person's life. Change in the frequency of criminal activity is purely a function of change in criminal opportunity.

If we accept this provision of the GTC, then both criminal propensity and criminal opportunity must be considered to explain criminal participation. So if males and females are equally impulsive but their crime rates vary, the explanation is that males have more opportunity to commit crime. Young teenage girls may be more closely monitored by their parents and therefore lack the freedom to offend. Girls are also socialized to have more self-control than boys: Although females get angry as often as males, many have been taught to blame themselves for such feelings. Females are socialized to fear that anger will harm relationships; males are encouraged to react with "moral outrage," blaming others for their discomfort.[101]

Opportunity can also be used to explain ecological variation in the crime rate. How does the GTC explain the fact that crime rates are higher in the summer than the winter? The number of impulsive people lacking in self-control is no higher in August than it is in December. Gottfredson and Hirschi would argue that seasonal differences are explained by opportunity: during the summer kids are out of school and have more opportunity to commit crime. Similarly, if crime rates are higher in Los Angeles than Minneapolis, it is because either there are more criminal opportunities in this Western city, or because the fast-paced life of L.A. attracts more impulsive people than the laid-back Midwest.

Self-Control and Crime Gottfredson and Hirschi claim that the principles of self-control theory can explain all varieties of criminal behavior and all the social and behavioral correlates of crime. That is, such widely disparate crimes as burglary, robbery, embezzlement, drug dealing, murder, rape, and insider trading all stem from a deficiency of self-control. Likewise, gender, racial, and ecological differences in crime rates can be explained by discrepancies in self-control.

Unlike other theoretical models that explain only narrow segments of criminal behavior (i.e., teenage gang formation), Gottfredson and Hirschi argue that self-control applies equally to all crimes, ranging from murder to corporate theft. White-collar crime rates remain low, they claim, because people who lack self-control rarely attain the positions necessary to commit those crimes. However, relatively few white-collar criminals lack self-control to the same degree and in the same manner as criminals such as rapists and burglars (see the Profiles in Crime feature "James Paul Lewis, Jr.: 'Crimes Against Humanity,'" for an account of someone who may fit this description).

Support for GTC Since the publication of *A General Theory of Crime*, numerous researchers have attempted to test the validity of Gottfredson and Hirschi's theoretical views and a great many

research efforts using a variety of methodologies and subject groups have found empirical support for the basic assumptions of the GTC.[102] The general consensus of this research is that people with low self-control and poor impulse control are the most likely to engage in serious crime.[103] Gottfredson and Hirschi's view has become a cornerstone of contemporary criminological theory.

Importantly, the self-control–crime association has been found across different cultures, nationalities, and ethnicities, supporting its universal status.[104] When Alexander Vazsonyi and his associates analyzed self-control and deviant behavior with samples drawn from a number of different countries including Hungary, Switzerland, the Netherlands, the United States, and Japan, they found that low self-control was significantly related to antisocial behavior and that the association can be seen regardless of culture or national settings.[105] Showing that the self-control–crime association is invariant across cultures is a significant contribution to supporting its validity.

Analyzing the General Theory of Crime By integrating the concepts of socialization and criminality, Gottfredson and Hirschi help explain why some people who lack self-control can escape criminality, and, conversely, why some people who have self-control might not escape. People who are at risk because they have impulsive personalities may forgo criminal careers because there are no criminal opportunities that satisfy their impulsive needs; instead, they may find other outlets for their impulsive personalities. In contrast, if the opportunity is strong enough, even people with relatively strong self-control may be tempted to violate the law; the incentives to commit crime may overwhelm self-control.

Integrating criminal propensity and criminal opportunity can explain why some children enter into chronic offending while others living in similar environments are able to resist criminal activity. It can also help us understand why the corporate executive with a spotless record gets caught up in business fraud. Even a successful executive may find self-control inadequate if the potential for illegal gain is large. The driven executive, accustomed to both academic and financial success, may find that the fear of failure can overwhelm self-control. During tough economic times, the impulsive manager who fears dismissal may be tempted to circumvent the law to improve the bottom line.[106]

Although the General Theory seems persuasive, several questions and criticisms remain unanswered. Among the most important are the following:

▌ *Tautological.* Some critics argue that the theory is tautological or involves circular reasoning: How do we know when people are impulsive? When they commit crimes! Are all criminals impulsive? Of course, or else they would not have broken the law![107]

Gottfredson and Hirschi counter by saying that impulsivity is not itself a propensity to commit crime but a condition that inhibits people from appreciating the long-term consequences of their behavior. Consequently, if given the opportunity, they are more likely to indulge in criminal acts than their nonimpulsive

JAMES PAUL LEWIS, JR.: "CRIMES AGAINST HUMANITY"

On May 26, 2006, James Paul Lewis, Jr., the former director of Orange County, California–based Financial Advisory Consultants (FAC), was sentenced to 30 years in federal prison for running a massive Ponzi scheme that raised more than $300 million and caused more than 1,600 victims to lose more than $156 million of their hard-earned money.

What exactly did James Lewis do to earn a 30-year prison sentence? He offered investors opportunities to invest in two mutual funds. Through false and fraudulent brochures and other promotional material issued by FAC, he told investors that they would earn annual rates of return of up to 18 percent in an Income Fund, which claimed to generate revenue from the leasing of medical equipment, commercial lending, and financing insurance premiums, and 40 percent annual returns in a Growth Fund, which claimed to generate revenue through the purchase and sale of distressed businesses. Instead of investing the investors' money as promised, Lewis used the funds to purchase homes in Villa Park, Laguna Niguel, Palm Desert, San Diego, and Greenwich, Connecticut. He also used investors' money to purchase luxury automobiles for himself, his wife, and his girlfriend. Among other schemes, he used investor money to trade currency futures, managing to lose at least $22 million. To conceal the scheme at FAC, Lewis ran a Ponzi scheme: he took the money of new investors (and new purchases of those who had already bought into the funds) to pay the rates of return promised to investors. In other words, he used the principal to pay the interest! That is, until the money ran out. At one point nearly 3,300 investors had a total balance of $813,932,080 in the funds, but FAC and Lewis's bank accounts held only slightly more than $2 million.

At Lewis's sentencing hearing, United States District Judge Cormac J. Carney ordered him to pay $156 million in restitution. Because many of this victims were elderly, Judge Carney described the scheme as a "crime against humanity." Several victims told the court about their losses, which included life savings and college funds. Many victims described being forced back to work after losing their retirement savings in the scheme.

How would Gottfredson and Hirschi explain Lewis's ongoing criminal activities? Can someone so calculating lack self-control?

Sources: Department of Justice press release, "Operator of Orange County–Based Ponzi Scheme that Caused More than $150 Million in Losses Sentenced to 30 Years in Federal Prison," May 30, 2006, http://losangeles.fbi.gov/dojpressrel/pressrel06/la053006usa.htm (accessed July 20, 2007); Gillian Flaccus, "California Man Gets 30 Years for Ponzi Scheme," *Washington Post*, 27 May 2006, www.washingtonpost.com/wp-dyn/content/article/2006/05/27/AR2006052700250.html (accessed July 20, 2007).

counterparts.[108] According to Gottfredson and Hirschi, impulsivity and criminality are neither identical nor equivalent. Some impulsive people may channel their reckless energies into noncriminal activity, such as trading on the commodities markets or real estate speculation, and make a legitimate fortune for their efforts.

▌ *Different classes of criminals.* As you may recall, Moffitt has identified two classes of criminals—adolescent-limited and life course persistent.[109] Other researchers have found that there may be different criminal paths or trajectories. People offend at a different pace, commit different kinds of crimes, and are influenced by different external forces.[110] For example, most criminals tend to be "generalists" who engage in a garden variety of criminal acts. However, some people "specialize" in violent crimes and others in theft offenses, and these two groups seem quite different in personality and temperament.[111] This would contradict the GTC vision that a single factor causes crime and that there is a single class of offender.

▌ *Ecological differences.* The GTC also fails to address individual and ecological patterns in the crime rate. If crime rates are higher in Los Angeles than in Albany, New York, can it be assumed that residents of Los Angeles are more impulsive than residents of Albany? There is little evidence of regional differences in impulsivity or self-control. Can these differences be explained solely by variation in criminal opportunity? Few researchers have tried to account for the influence of culture, ecology, economy, and so on. Gottfredson and Hirschi might counter that crime rate differences may reflect criminal opportunity: one area may have more effective law enforcement, more draconian laws, and higher levels of guardianship. In their view, opportunity is controlled by economy and culture.

▌ *Racial and gender differences.* Although distinct gender differences in the crime rate exist, there is little evidence that males are more impulsive than females (although females and males differ in many other personality traits).[112] Some research efforts have found gender differences in the association between self-control and crime; the theory predicts no such difference should occur.[113]

Young pictures of Stanley Tookie Williams

© David McNew/Getty Images

One criticism of the General Theory of Crime is that people actually do change over their lifetimes. Here, pictures of cofounder of the Crips gang Stanley "Tookie" Williams show him at an early age. Sentenced to prison for the 1979 murders of four people, Williams spent several years involved with violent activities in prison, but around 1993 changed his behavior and became an antigang activist. Williams coauthored such books as *Life in Prison*, which encourages kids to stay out of gangs, and his memoir *Blue Rage, Black Redemption*. Williams was nominated for the Nobel Peace Prize for his efforts. Do you believe that a gang leader like Tookie Williams can really change, or did his changing life circumstances (i.e., being incarcerated) simply prevent him from committing violent criminal acts? Williams was executed in 2005.

Looking at this relationship from another perspective, males who persist in crime exhibit characteristics that are different than female persisters. Women seem to be influenced by their place of residence, childhood and recent abuses, living with a criminal partner, selling drugs, stress, depression, fearfulness, their romantic relationships, their children, and whether they have suicidal thoughts. In contrast, men are more likely to persist because of their criminal peer associations, carrying weapons, alcohol abuse, and aggressive feelings. Impulsivity alone may not be able to explain why males and females persist or desist.[114]

Similarly, Gottfredson and Hirschi explain racial differences in the crime rate as a failure of childrearing practices in the African American community.[115] In so doing, they overlook issues of institutional racism, poverty, and relative deprivation, which have been shown to have a significant impact on crime rate differentials.

■ *Moral beliefs.* The General Theory also ignores the moral concept of right and wrong, or "belief," which Hirschi considered a cornerstone in his earlier writings on the social bond.[116] Does this mean that learning and assimilating moral values has little effect on criminality? Belief may be the weakest of the bonds associated with crime, and the General Theory reflects this relationship.[117]

■ *Peer influence.* A number of research efforts show that the quality of peer relations either enhances or controls criminal behavior and that these influences vary over time.[118] As children mature, peer influence continues to grow.[119] Research shows that kids who lack self-control also have trouble maintaining relationships with law-abiding peers. They may either choose or be forced to seek out friends who are similarly limited in their ability to maintain self-control. Similarly, as they mature they may seek out romantic relationships with law-violating boyfriends or girlfriends and these entanglements enhance the likelihood that they will get further involved in crime (girls seem more deeply influenced by their delinquent boyfriends than boys by their delinquent girlfriends).[120] This finding contradicts the GTC, which suggests the influence of friends should be stable and unchanging and that a relationship established later in life (making deviant friends) should not influence criminal propensity. Gottfredson and Hirschi might counter that it should come as no surprise that impulsive kids, lacking in self-control, seek out peers with similar personality characteristics.

■ *People change.* One of the most important questions raised about the GTC concerns its assumption that criminal propensity does not change. Is it possible that human personality and behavior patterns remain unaltered over the life course? Research shows that changing life circumstances, such as starting and leaving school, abusing substances and then "getting straight," and starting or ending personal relationships, all influence the frequency of offending.[121] Involvement in organized activities such as karate that teach self-discipline and self-regulation have been shown to improve personality traits in at-risk kids, even those diagnosed with oppositional defiance disorder.[122] As people mature, they may be better able to control their impulsive behavior and reduce their criminal activities.[123]

■ *Effective parenting.* Gottfredson and Hirschi propose that children either develop self-control by the end of early childhood or fail to develop it at all, Research shows, however, that some kids who are predisposed toward delinquency may find their life circumstances improved and their involvement with antisocial behavior diminished if they are exposed to positive and effective parenting that appears later in life.[124] Parenting can influence self-control in later adolescence and kids who receive improved parenting may improve their self-control much later in the life course than predicted by the GTC.[125]

Some of the most significant research on this topic has been conducted by Ronald Simons and his colleagues. Simons has found that boys who were involved in deviant and oppositional behavior during childhood were able to turn their lives around if they later experienced improved parenting, increased school commitment, and/or reduced involvement with deviant peers. So while early childhood antisocial behavior may increase the chances of later criminality, even the most difficult children are at no greater risk for delinquency than are their conventional counterparts if they later experience positive changes in their daily lives and increased ties with significant others and institutions.[126]

Modest relationship. Some research results support the proposition that self-control is a causal factor in criminal and other forms of deviant behavior but that the association is at best quite modest.[127] This would indicate that other forces influence criminal behavior and that low self-control alone cannot predict the onset of a criminal or deviant career. Perhaps antisocial behavior is best explained by a condition that either develops subsequent to the development of self-control or is independent of a person's level of impulsivity.[128] This alternative quality, which may be the real stable latent trait, is still unknown.

Cross-cultural differences. There is some evidence that criminals in other countries do not lack self-control, indicating that the GTC may be culturally limited. Otwin Marenin and Michael Resig actually found equal or higher levels of self-control in Nigerian criminals than in noncriminals.[129] Behavior that may be considered imprudent in one culture may be socially acceptable in another and therefore cannot be viewed as "lack of self-control."[130] There is, however, emerging evidence that the GTC may have validity in predicting criminality abroad.[131]

Misreads human nature. According to Francis Cullen, John Paul Wright, and Mitchell Chamlin, the GTC makes flawed assumptions about human character.[132] It assumes that people are essentially selfish, self-serving, and hedonistic and must therefore be controlled lest they gratify themselves at the expense of others. A more plausible view is that humans are inherently generous and kind; selfish hedonists may be a rare exception.

One of many causes. Research shows that even if lack of self-control is a prerequisite to crime so are other social, neuropsychological, and physiological factors.[133] Social cultural factors have been found to make an independent contribution to criminal offending patterns.[134] Among the many psychological characteristics that set criminals apart from the general population is their lack of self-direction; their behavior has a here-and-now orientation rather than being aimed at providing long-term benefits.[135] Law violators also exhibit lower resting heart rates and perform poorly on tasks that trigger cognitive functions.[136]

Some criminals are not impulsive. Gottfredson and Hirshi assume that criminals are impatient or "present-oriented." They choose to commit crime because the rewards can be enjoyed immediately while the costs or punishments come later or may not come at all. As long as the gains from crime are immediate while the costs of crime are delayed, impulsive present-oriented individuals will commit crimes even if they are not obviously lucrative. However, not all research efforts support this position. As you may recall (Chapter 4), Steven Levitt and Sudhir Alladi Venkatesh found that many young gang boys are willing to wait years to "rise through the ranks" before earning high wages. Their stay in the gang is fueled by the promises of future compensation, a fact that contradicts the GTC. Levitt and Venkatesh conclude that the economic aspects of the decision to join the gang can be viewed as a tournament in which participants vie for large awards that only a small fraction will eventually obtain. Members of the gang accept low wages in the present in the hope that they will advance in the gang and earn well above market wages in the future.[137]

Moreover, gang members seem acutely aware that they are making an investment in the future by foregoing present gains. As one noted:

> You think I wanta be selling drugs on the street my whole life? No way, but I know these n— [above me] are making more money . . . . So you know, I figure I got a chance to move up. But if not, s—, I get me a job doin' something else.[138]

This quotation does not comport with the notion of a super-impulsive young criminal. Even though few gang recruits will ever become gang leaders, they are willing to take the risk in order to earn a future benefit. This finding contradicts Gottfredson and Hirschi's vision of an impulsive criminal who lives for today without worrying about tomorrow.

Self-control may waiver. Gottfredson and Hirschi assume that impulsivity is a singular construct—one is either impulsive or not. However, there may be more than one kind of impulsive personality and it may waiver over time. Some people may be impulsive because they are sensation seekers who are constantly looking for novel experiences, while others lack deliberation and rarely think through problems. Some may give up easily while others act without thinking. Some people may have the ability to persist in self-control while others "get tired" and eventually succumb to their impulses.[139] Think of it this way: a dieter ogles the cheesecake in the fridge all day but has the self-control not to take a slice. Then he wakes hungry in the middle of the night and makes his way into the kitchen, thinking "a little piece of cheesecake won't hurt me." His self-control slips, and his diet goes out the window.

Although questions like these remain, the strength of the GTC lies in its scope and breadth: it attempts to explain all forms of crime and deviance, from lower-class gang delinquency to sexual harassment in the business community.[140] By integrating concepts of criminal choice, criminal

DEVELOPMENTAL THEORIES

Theory	Major Premise	Strengths	Research Focus
LIFE COURSE THEORIES	As people go through the life course, social and personal traits undergo change and influence behavior.	Explains why some at-risk children desist from crime.	Identify critical moments in a person's life course that produce crime.
Interactional Theory	Criminals go through lifestyle changes during their offending career. Crime influences lifestyle and changing lifestyle influences crime.	Combines sociological and psychological theories.	Identify crime-producing interpersonal interactions and their reciprocal effects.
General Theory of Crime and Delinquency (GTCD)	Five critical life domains shape criminal behavior and are shaped by criminal behavior.	Shows that crime and other aspects of social life are interactive and developmental.	Measure the relationship between life domains and crime.
Age-Graded Theory	As people mature, the factors that influence their propensity to commit crime change. In childhood, family factors are critical; in adulthood, marital and job factors are key.	Shows how crime is a developmental process that shifts in direction over the life course.	Identify critical points in the life course that produce crime. Analyze the association between social capital and crime.
LATENT TRAIT THEORIES	A master trait controls human development.	Explains the continuity of crime and chronic offending.	Identify master trait that produces crime.
Integrated Cognitive Antisocial Potential (ICAP) Theory	People with antisocial potential (AP) are at risk to commit antisocial acts. AP can be viewed as both a long- and short-term phenomenon.	Identifies different types of criminal propensity and shows how they may influence behavior in both the short and long term.	Identify the components of long- and short-term AP.
General Theory of Crime	Crime and criminality are separate concepts. People choose to commit crime when they lack self-control. People lacking self-control will seize criminal opportunities.	Integrates choice and social control concepts. Identifies the difference between crime and criminality.	Measure association among impulsivity, low self-control, and criminal behaviors.
Differential Coercion Theory	Individuals exposed to coercive environments develop social-psychological deficits that enhance their probability of engaging in criminal behavior.	Explains why feeling of coercion is a master trait that determines behavior.	Measuring the sources of coercion.
Control Balance Theory	A person's "control ratio" influences his or her behavior.	Explains how the ability to control one's environment is a master trait.	Measuring control balance and imbalance.

opportunity, socialization, and personality, Gottfredson and Hirschi make a plausible argument that all deviant behaviors may originate at the same source. Continued efforts are needed to test the GTC and establish the validity of its core concepts. It remains one of the key developments of modern criminological theory.

A number of other theories have been formulated that propose a master trait controls human development and the propensity to commit crime. Some of the most prominent ones are summarized in Concept Summary 9.2.

www To read an article by Bruce J. Arneklev, Lori Elis, and Sandra Medlicott that **tests the General Theory of Crime**, go to academic.cengage.com/criminaljustice/siegel.

EVALUATING DEVELOPMENTAL THEORIES

Although the differences between the views presented in this chapter may seem irreconcilable, they in fact share some common ground. They indicate that a criminal career must be understood as a passage along which people travel, that it has a beginning and an end, and that events and life circumstances influence the journey. The factors that affect a criminal career may include structural factors, such as income and status; socialization factors, such as family and peer relations; biological factors, such as size and strength; psychological factors, including intelligence and personality; and opportunity factors, such as free time, inadequate police protection, and a supply of easily stolen merchandise.

Life course theories emphasize the influence of changing interpersonal and structural factors (that is, people change along with the world they live in). Latent trait theories place more emphasis on the fact that behavior is linked less to personal change and more to changes in the surrounding world.

These perspectives differ in their view of human development. Do people constantly change, as life course theories suggest, or are they stable, constant, and changeless, as the latent trait view indicates? Are the factors that produce criminality different at each stage of life, as the life course view suggests, or does a master trait—such as control balance, self-control, or coercion—steer the course of human behavior?

It is also possible that these two positions are not mutually exclusive, and each may make a notable contribution to understanding the onset and continuity of a criminal career. In other words, stable individual characteristics—latent traits—may interact with or modify the effects of life course varying social factors to increase their effect and shape the direction of criminal careers.[141] Needless to say, measuring these effects is quite complex and relies on sophisticated research techniques. One research effort by Bradley Entner Wright and his associates found evidence supporting both latent trait and life course theories.[142] Their research, conducted with subjects in New Zealand, indicates that low self-control in childhood predicts disrupted social bonds and criminal offending later in life, a finding that supports latent trait theory. They also found that maintaining positive social bonds helps reduce criminality and that maintaining prosocial bonds could even counteract the effect of low self-control. Latent traits are an important influence on crime, but their findings indicate that social relationships that form later in life appear to influence criminal behavior "above and beyond" individuals' preexisting characteristics.[143] This finding may reflect the fact that there are two classes of criminals: a less serious group who are influenced by life events, and a more chronic group whose latent traits insulate them from any positive prosocial relationships.[144]

PUBLIC POLICY IMPLICATIONS OF DEVELOPMENTAL THEORY

There have been a number of policy-based initiatives based on premises of developmental theory. These typically feature multisystemic treatment efforts designed to provide at-risk kids with personal, social, educational, and family services. For example, one program found that an intervention that promotes academic success, social competence, and educational enhancement during the elementary grades can reduce risky sexual practices and their accompanying health consequences in early adulthood.[145]

Other programs are now employing multidimensional strategies and are aimed at targeting children in preschool through the early elementary grades in order to alter the direction of their life course. Many of the most successful programs are aimed at strengthening children's social-emotional competence and positive coping skills and suppressing the development of antisocial, aggressive behavior.[146] Research evaluations indicate that the most promising multicomponent crime and substance abuse prevention programs for youths, especially those at high risk, are aimed at improving their developmental skills. They may include a school component, an after-school component, and a parent-involvement component. All of these components have the common goal of increasing protective factors and decreasing risk factors in the areas of the family, the community, the school, and the individual.[147] The Boys and Girls Clubs and School Collaborations' Substance Abuse Prevention Program includes a school component called SMART (skills mastery and resistance training) Teachers, an after-school component called SMART Kids, and a parent-involvement component called SMART Parents. Each component is designed to reduce specific risk factors in the children's school, family, community, and personal environments.[148]

Another successful program, Fast Track, is designed to prevent serious antisocial behavior and related adolescent problems in high-risk children entering first grade. The intervention is guided by a developmental approach that suggests that antisocial behavior is the product of the interaction of multiple social and psychological influences:

▌ Residence in low-income, high-crime communities places stressors and influences on children and families that increase their risk levels. In these areas, families characterized by marital conflict and instability make consistent and effective parenting difficult to achieve, particularly with children who are impulsive and of difficult temperament.

▌ Children of high-risk families usually enter the education process poorly prepared for its social, emotional, and cognitive demands. Their parents often are unprepared to relate effectively with school staff, and a poor home–school bond often aggravates the child's adjustment problems. They may be grouped with other children who are similarly unprepared. This peer group may be negatively influenced by disruptive classroom contexts and punitive teachers.

▌ Over time, aggressive and disruptive children are rejected by families and peers and tend to receive less support from teachers. All of these processes increase the risk of antisocial behaviors, in a process that begins in elementary school and lasts throughout adolescence. During this period, peer influences, academic difficulties, and dysfunctional personal identity development can contribute to serious conduct problems and related risky behaviors.[149]

Compared with children in the control group, children in the intervention group displayed significantly less aggressive behavior at home, in the classroom, and on the playground.

By the end of the third grade, 37 percent of the intervention group had become free of conduct problems, in contrast with 27 percent of the control group. By the end of elementary school, 33 percent of the intervention group had a developmental trajectory of decreasing conduct problems, as compared with 27 percent of the control group. Furthermore, placement in special education by the end of elementary school was about one-fourth lower in the intervention group than in the control group.

Group differences continued through adolescence. Court records indicate that by eighth grade, 38 percent of the intervention group boys had been arrested, in contrast with 42 percent of the control group. Finally, psychiatric interviews after ninth grade indicate that the Fast Track intervention has reduced serious conduct disorder by over a third, from 27 percent to 17 percent. These effects generalized across gender and ethnic groups and across the wide range of child and family characteristics measured by Fast Track.

THINKING LIKE A CRIMINOLOGIST

Gary L. Sampson, 41, addicted to alcohol and cocaine, was a deadbeat dad, a two-bit thief, and a bank robber with a long history of violence. On August 1, 2001, he turned himself in to the Vermont State Police after fleeing from a string of three murders he committed in Massachusetts and New Hampshire.

Those who knew Sampson speculated that his murders were a desperate finale to a troubled life. During his early life in New England, he once bound, gagged, and beat three elderly women in a candy store, hijacked cars at knifepoint, and had been medically diagnosed as schizophrenic. In 1977, he married a 17-year-old girl he had impregnated; two months later he was arrested and charged with rape for having "unnatural intercourse with a child under 16." Although he was acquitted of that charge, his wife noticed that Sampson was developing a hair-trigger temper and had become increasingly violent; their marriage soon ended. As the years passed, Sampson had at least four failed marriages, was an absentee father to two children, and became an alcoholic and a drug user; he spent nearly half of his adult life behind bars.

Jumping bail after being arrested for theft from an antique store, he headed south to North Carolina and took on a new identity: Gary Johnson, a construction worker. He took up with Ricki Carter, a transvestite, but their relationship was anything but stable. Sampson once put a gun to Carter's head, broke his ribs, and threatened to kill his family. After his breakup with Carter, Sampson moved in with a new girlfriend, Karen Anderson, and began pulling bank jobs. When the police closed in, Sampson fled north. Needing transportation, he carjacked three vehicles and killed the drivers, one a 19-year-old college freshman who had stopped to give Sampson a hand. In December 2003, Sampson received a death sentence from a jury who was not swayed by his claim that he was mentally unfit.

The governor is unsettled by the verdict. She wants to grant clemency in the case and reduce Sampson's sentence to life in prison. She asks you to help her make the judgment.

 Writing Exercise Write a paper (about 400 words) explaining what advice you would give the governor regarding granting Sampson's clemency. Were his crimes a product of his impaired development? Should he be spared death?

 Doing Research on the Web Before writing your paper, review these Web-based resources:

- Read analyses about using the death penalty for criminals like Sampson in the articles "Science and the Death Penalty" by James P. Rooney and "Give 'Em a Fair Trial . . . Then Hang 'Em" by Colin Kingsbury.

- Also read what U.S. District Court Judge Mark L. Wolf had to say when he sentenced Sampson to death.

- For a conservative take on this issue, go to the National Center for Policy Analysis.

All of these websites can be accessed via academic.cengage.com/criminaljustice/siegel.

SUMMARY

■ Life course theories argue that events that take place over the life course influence criminal choices.

■ The cause of crime constantly changes as people mature. At first, the nuclear family influences behavior; during adolescence, the peer group dominates; in adulthood, marriage and career are critical.

■ There are a variety of pathways to crime: some kids are sneaky, others hostile, and still others defiant.

■ Crime may be part of a variety of social problems, including health, physical, and interpersonal troubles.

■ The social development model finds that living in a disorganized area helps weaken social bonds and sets people off on a delinquent path.

■ According to interactional theory, crime influences social relations, which in turn influence crime; the relationship is interactive. The sources of crime evolve over time.

■ Agnew's General Theory of Crime and Delinquency revolves around five life domains that interact with social factors to produce crime and, in turn, are influenced by crime.

■ Sampson and Laub's age-graded theory holds that the social sources of behavior change over the life course. People who develop social capital are best able to avoid antisocial entanglements. There are important life events or turning points that enable adult offenders to desist from crime. Among the most important are getting married and serving in the military. Laub and Sampson have found that while many criminals desist from crime, they still face other risks such as an untimely death.

■ Latent trait theories hold that some underlying condition present at birth or soon after controls behavior. Suspect traits include low IQ, impulsivity, and personality structure. This underlying trait explains the continuity of offending because, once present, it remains

with a person throughout his or her life. Opportunity to commit crime varies; latent traits remain stable.

■ The General Theory of Crime, developed by Gottfredson and Hirschi, integrates choice theory concepts. People with latent traits choose crime over noncrime; the opportunity for crime mediates their choice.

■ Impulsive people have low self-control and a weak bond to society; they often cannot resist criminal opportunities.

■ Programs that are based on developmental theory are typically multidimensional and multifaceted.

■ CENGAGENOW™ is an easy-to-use online resource that helps you study in less time to get the grade you want—NOW. CengageNOW™ Personalized Study (a diagnostic study tool containing valuable text-specific resources) lets you focus on just what you don't know and learn more in less time to get a better grade. If your textbook does not include an access code card, you can go to www.ichapters.com to purchase CengageNOW™.

 # KEY TERMS

desist (272)
developmental theories (272)
life course theories (272)
latent trait theories (272)
problem behavior syndrome (PBS) (274)
authority conflict pathway (275)

covert pathway (275)
overt pathway (275)
adolescent-limited offenders (277)
life course persisters (277)
integrated theories (278)
age-graded theory (278)

cumulative disadvantage (279)
social capital (280)
latent trait (283)
General Theory of Crime (GTC) (285)
self-control (285)
self-control theory (287)

 # CRITICAL THINKING QUESTIONS

1. Do you consider yourself to have social capital? If so, what form does it take?

2. Someone you know gets a perfect score on the SAT. What personal, family, and social characteristics do you think this individual has? Another person becomes a serial killer. Without knowing this person, what personal, family, and social

characteristics do you think this individual has? If "bad behavior" is explained by multiple problems, is "good behavior" explained by multiple strengths?

3. Do you believe it is a latent trait that makes a person crime prone, or is crime a function of environment and socialization?

4. Do you agree with Loeber's multiple pathways model? Do you know people who have traveled down those paths?

5. Do people really change, or do they stay the same but appear to be different because their life circumstances have changed?

NOTES

1. Fox News, "Xbox Slayings Ringleader Has Criminal History," August 11, 2004, www .foxnews.com/story/0,2933,128674,00 .html (accessed June 9, 2007).

2. See generally Sheldon Glueck and Eleanor Glueck, *500 Criminal Careers* (New York: Knopf, 1930); Glueck and Glueck, *One Thousand Juvenile Delinquents* (Cambridge, MA: Harvard University Press, 1934); Glueck and Glueck, *Predicting Delinquency and Crime* (Cambridge, MA: Harvard University Press, 1967), pp. 82–83; Glueck and Glueck, *Unraveling Juvenile Delinquency* (Cambridge, MA: Harvard University Press, 1950).

3. See generally John Laub and Robert Sampson, "The Sutherland–Glueck Debate: On the Sociology of Criminological Knowledge," *American Journal of Sociology* 96 (1991): 1,402–1,440; John Laub and Robert Sampson, "Unraveling Families and Delinquency: A Reanalysis of the Gluecks' Data," *Criminology* 26 (1988): 355–380.

4. Marvin E. Wolfgang, Robert M. Figlio, and Thorsten Sellin, *Delinquency in a Birth Cohort* (Chicago: University of Chicago Press, 1972).

5. Rolf Loeber and Marc LeBlanc, "Toward a Developmental Criminology," in *Crime and Justice*, vol. 12, eds. Norval Morris and Michael Tonry (Chicago: University of Chicago Press, 1990), pp. 375–473; Loeber and LeBlanc, "Developmental Criminology Updated," in *Crime and Justice*, vol. 23, ed. Michael Tonry (Chicago: University of Chicago Press, 1998), pp. 115–198.

6. Marvin Krohn, Alan Lizotte, and Cynthia Perez, "The Interrelationship between Substance Use and Precocious Transitions to Adult Sexuality," *Journal of Health and Social Behavior* 38 (1997): 87–103, at 88.

7. Jennifer M. Beyers and Rolf Loeber, "Untangling Developmental Relations between Depressed Mood and Delinquency in Male Adolescents,"*Journal of Abnormal Child Psychology* 31 (2003): 247–266.

8. Stephanie Milan and Ellen Pinderhughes, "Family Instability and Child Maladjustment Trajectories during Elementary School," *Journal of Abnormal Child Psychology* 34 (2006): 43–56.

9. Bradley Entner Wright, Avshalom Caspi, Terrie Moffitt, and Phil Silva, "The Effects of Social Ties on Crime Vary by Criminal Propensity: A Life-Course Model of Interdependence," *Criminology* 39 (2001): 321–352.

10. Joan McCord, "Family Relationships, Juvenile Delinquency, and Adult Criminality," *Criminology* 29 (1991): 397–417.

11. Paul Mazerolle, "Delinquent Definitions and Participation Age: Assessing the Invariance Hypothesis," *Studies on Crime and Crime Prevention* 6 (1997): 151–168.

12. Peggy Giordano, Stephen Cernkovich, and Jennifer Rudolph, "Gender, Delinquency, and Desistance: Toward a Theory of Cognitive Transformation?" *American Journal of Sociology* 107 (2002): 990–1,064.

13. John Hagan and Holly Foster, "S/He's a Rebel: Toward a Sequential Stress Theory of Delinquency and Gendered Pathways to Disadvantage in Emerging Adulthood," *Social Forces* 82 (2003): 53–86.

14. G. R. Patterson, Barbara DeBaryshe, and Elizabeth Ramsey, "A Developmental Perspective on Antisocial Behavior," *American Psychologist* 44 (1989): 329–335.

15. Robert Sampson and John Laub, "Crime and Deviance in the Life Course," *American Review of Sociology* 18 (1992): 63–84.

16. David Farrington, Darrick Jolliffe, Rolf Loeber, Magda Stouthamer-Loeber, and Larry Kalb, "The Concentration of Offenders in Families, and Family Criminality in the Prediction of Boys' Delinquency," *Journal of Adolescence* 24 (2001): 579–596.

17. Raymond Paternoster, Charles Dean, Alex Piquero, Paul Mazerolle, and Robert Brame, "Generality, Continuity, and Change in Offending," *Journal of Quantitative Criminology* 13 (1997): 231–266.

18. Magda Stouthamer-Loeber and Evelyn Wei, "The Precursors of Young Fatherhood and Its Effect on Delinquency of Teenage Males," *Journal of Adolescent Health* 22 (1998): 56–65; Richard Jessor, John Donovan, and Francis Costa, *Beyond Adolescence: Problem Behavior and Young Adult Development* (New York: Cambridge University Press, 1991); Xavier Coll, Fergus Law, Aurelio Tobias, Keith Hawton, and Joseph Tomas, "Abuse and Deliberate Self-Poisoning in Women: A Matched Case-Control Study," *Child Abuse and Neglect* 25 (2001): 1,291–1,293.

19. Richard Miech, Avshalom Caspi, Terrie Moffitt, Bradley Entner Wright, and Phil Silva, "Low Socioeconomic Status and Mental Disorders: A Longitudinal Study of Selection and Causation during Young Adulthood," *American Journal of Sociology* 104 (1999): 1,096–1,131; Krohn, Lizotte, and Perez, "The Interrelationship between Substance Use and Precocious Transitions to Adult Sexuality," p. 88; Richard Jessor, "Risk Behavior in Adolescence: A Psychosocial Framework for Understanding and Action," in *Adolescents at Risk: Medical and Social Perspectives*, eds. D. E. Rogers and E. Ginzburg (Boulder, CO: Westview Press, 1992).

20. Deborah Capaldi and Gerald Patterson, "Can Violent Offenders Be Distinguished from Frequent Offenders? Prediction from Childhood to Adolescence," *Journal of Research in Crime and Delinquency* 33 (1996): 206–231; D. Wayne Osgood, "The Covariation among Adolescent Problem Behaviors," paper presented at the annual meeting of the American Society of Criminology, Baltimore, November 1990.

21. For an analysis of more than 30 studies, see Mark Lipsey and James Derzon, "Predictors of Violent or Serious Delinquency in Adolescence and Early Adulthood: A Synthesis of Longitudinal Research," in *Serious and Violent Juvenile Offenders: Risk Factors and Successful Interventions*, eds. Rolf Loeber and David Farrington (Thousand Oaks, CA: Sage, 1998).

22. Gina Wingood, Ralph DiClemente, Rick Crosby, Kathy Harrington, Susan Davies, and Edward Hook III, "Gang Involvement and the Health of African American Female Adolescents," *Pediatrics* 110 (2002): 57.

23. David Husted, Nathan Shapira, and Martin Lazoritz, "Adolescent Gambling, Substance Use, and Other Delinquent Behavior," *Psychiatric Times* 20 (2003): 52–55.

24. Krohn, Lizotte, and Perez, "The Interrelationship between Substance Use and Precocious Transitions to Adult Sexuality," p. 88; Richard Jessor, "Risk Behavior in Adolescence: A Psychosocial Framework for Understanding and Action," in *Adolescents at Risk: Medical and Social Perspectives*, ed. D. E. Rogers and E. Ginzburg (Boulder, CO: Westview, 1992).

25. Terence Thornberry, Carolyn Smith, and Gregory Howard, "Risk Factors for Teenage Fatherhood," *Journal of Marriage and the Family* 59 (1997): 505–522; Todd Miller, Timothy Smith, Charles Turner, Margarita Guijarro, and Amanda Hallet, "A Meta-Analytic Review of Research on Hostility and Physical Health," *Psychological Bulletin* 119 (1996): 322–348; Marianne Junger, "Accidents and Crime," in *The Generality of Deviance*, eds. T. Hirschi and M. Gottfredson (New Brunswick, NJ: Transaction Books, 1993).

26. James Marquart, Victoria Brewer, Patricia Simon, and Edward Morse, "Lifestyle Factors among Female Prisoners with Histories of Psychiatric Treatment," *Journal of Criminal Justice* 29 (2001): 319–328; Rolf Loeber, David Farrington, Magda Stouthamer-Loeber, Terrie Moffitt, Avshalom Caspi, and Don Lynam, "Male Mental Health Problems, Psychopathy, and Personality Traits: Key Findings from the First 14 Years of the Pittsburgh Youth Study," *Clinical Child and Family Psychology Review* 4 (2002): 273–297.

27. Robert Johnson, S. Susan Su, Dean Gerstein, Hee-Choon Shin, and John Hoffman, "Parental Influences on Deviant Behavior in Early Adolescence: A Logistic Response Analysis of Age and Gender-Differentiated Effects," *Journal of Quantitative Criminology* 11 (1995): 167–192; Judith Brook, Martin Whiteman, and Patricia Cohen, "Stage of Drug Use, Aggression, and Theft/Vandalism," in *Drugs, Crime and Other Deviant Adaptations: Longitudinal Studies*, ed. Howard Kaplan (New York: Plenum Press, 1995), pp. 83–96.

28. Helene Raskin White, Peter Tice, Rolf Loeber, and Magda Stouthamer-Loeber, "Illegal Acts Committed by Adolescents under the Influence of Alcohol and Drugs," *Journal of Research in Crime and Delinquency* 39

(2002): 131–153; Candace Kruttschnitt, Jane McLeod, and Maude Dornfeld, "The Economic Environment of Child Abuse," *Social Problems* 41 (1994): 299–312.

29. David Fergusson, L. John Horwood, and Elizabeth Ridder, "Show Me the Child at Seven, II: Childhood Intelligence and Later Outcomes in Adolescence and Young Adulthood," *Journal of Child Psychology and Psychiatry and Allied Disciplines* 46 (2005): 850–859.

30. Margit Wiesner and Ranier Silbereisen, "Trajectories of Delinquent Behaviour in Adolescence and Their Covariates: Relations with Initial and Time-Averaged Factors," *Journal of Adolescence* 26 (2003): 753–771.

31. Rolf Loeber, Phen Wung, Kate Keenan, Bruce Giroux, Magda Stouthamer-Loeber, Wemoet Van Kammen, and Barbara Maughan, "Developmental Pathways in Disruptive Behavior," *Development and Psychopathology* (1993): 12–48.

32. Sheila Royo Maxwell and Christopher Maxwell, "Examining the 'Criminal Careers' of Prostitutes within the Nexus of Drug Use, Drug Selling, and Other Illicit Activities," *Criminology* 38 (2000): 787–809.

33. Alex R. Piquero and He Len Chung, "On the Relationships between Gender, Early Onset, and the Seriousness of Offending," *Journal of Criminal Justice* 29 (2001): 189–206.

34. David Nurco, Timothy Kinlock, and Mitchell Balter, "The Severity of Preaddiction Criminal Behavior among Urban, Male Narcotic Addicts and Two Nonaddicted Control Groups," *Journal of Research in Crime and Delinquency* 30 (1993): 293–316.

35. Hanno Petras, Nicholas Alongo, Sharon Lambert, Sandra Barrueco, Cindy Schaeffer, Howard Chilcoat, and Sheppard Kellam, "The Utility of Elementary School TOCA-R Scores in Identifying Later Criminal Court Violence Among Adolescent Females," *Journal of the American Academy of Child and Adolescent Psychiatry* 44 (2005): 790–797; Hanno Petras, Howard Chilcoat, Philip Leaf, Nicholas Ialongo, and Sheppard Kellam, "Utility of TOCA-R Scores During the Elementary School Years in Identifying Later Violence among Adolescent Males," *Journal of the American Academy of Child and Adolescent Psychiatry* J43 (2004): 88–96.

36. W. Alex Mason, Rick Kosterman, J. David Hawkins, Todd Herrenkohi, Liliana Lengua, and Elizabeth McCauley, "Predicting Depression, Social Phobia, and Violence in Early Adulthood from Childhood Behavior Problems," *Journal of the American Academy of Child and Adolescent Psychiatry* 43 (2004): 307–315; Rolf Loeber and David Farrington, "Young Children Who Commit Crime: Epidemiology, Developmental Origins, Risk Factors, Early Interventions, and Policy Implications," *Development and Psychopathology* 12 (2000): 737–762; Patrick Lussier, Jean Proulx, and Marc LeBlanc, "Criminal Propensity, Deviant Sexual Interests and Criminal Activity of Sexual Aggressors Against Women:

A Comparison of Explanatory Models," *Criminology* 43 (2005): 249–281.

37. Dawn Jeglum Bartusch, Donald Lynam, Terrie Moffitt, and Phil Silva, "Is Age Important? Testing a General versus a Developmental Theory of Antisocial Behavior," *Criminology* 35 (1997): 13–48.

38. Daniel Nagin and Richard Tremblay, "What Has Been Learned from Group-Based Trajectory Modeling? Examples from Physical Aggression and Other Problem Behaviors," *The Annals of the American Academy of Political and Social Science* 602 (2005): 82–117.

39. Mason, Kosterman, Hawkins, Herrenkohi, Lengua, McCauley, "Predicting Depression, Social Phobia, and Violence in Early Adulthood from Childhood Behavior Problems"; Ronald Prinz and Suzanne Kerns, "Early Substance Use by Juvenile Offenders," *Child Psychiatry and Human Development* 33 (2003): 263–268.

40. Glenn Clingempeel and Scott Henggeler, "Aggressive Juvenile Offenders Transitioning into Emerging Adulthood: Factors Discriminating Persistors and Desistors," *American Journal of Orthopsychiatry* 73 (2003): 310–323.

41. David Gadd and Stephen Farrall, "Criminal Careers, Desistance and Subjectivity: Interpreting Men's Narratives of Change," *Theoretical Criminology* 8 (2004): 123–156.

42. G. R. Patterson, L. Crosby, and S. Vuchinich, "Predicting Risk for Early Police Arrest," *Journal of Quantitative Criminology* 8 (1992): 335–355.

43. Holly Hartwig and Jane Myers, "A Different Approach: Applying a Wellness Paradigm to Adolescent Female Delinquents and Offenders," *Journal of Mental Health Counseling* 25 (2003): 57–76.

44. Terrie Moffitt, Avshalom Caspi, Michael Rutter, and Phil Silva, *Sex Differences in Antisocial Behavior: Conduct Disorder, Delinquency, and Violence in the Dunedin Longitudinal Study* (London: Cambridge University Press, 2001).

45. Lisa Broidy, Richard Tremblay, Bobby Brame, David Fergusson, John Horwood, Robert Laird, Terrie Moffitt, Daniel Nagin, John Bates, Kenneth Dodge, Rolf Loeber, Donald Lynam, Gregory Pettit, and Frank Vitaro, "Developmental Trajectories of Childhood Disruptive Behaviors and Adolescent Delinquency: A Six-Site, Cross-National Study," *Developmental Psychology* 39 (2003): 222–245.

46. Ick-Joong Chung, Karl G. Hill, J. David Hawkins, Lewayne Gilchrist, and Daniel Nagin, "Childhood Predictors of Offense Trajectories," *Journal of Research in Crime and Delinquency* 39 (2002): 60–91.

47. Amy D'Unger, Kenneth Land, Patricia McCall, and Daniel Nagin, "How Many Latent Classes of Delinquent/Criminal Careers? Results from Mixed Poisson Regression Analyses," *American Journal of Sociology* 103 (1998): 1,593–1,630.

48. Alex Piquero and Timothy Brezina, "Testing Moffitt's Account of Adolescent-Limited Delinquency," *Criminology* 39 (2001): 353–370.

49. Terrie Moffitt, "Adolescence-Limited and Life-Course Persistent Antisocial Behavior: A Developmental Taxonomy," *Psychological Review* 100 (1993): 674–701.

50. Terrie Moffitt, "Natural Histories of Delinquency," in *Cross-National Longitudinal Research on Human Development and Criminal Behavior*, eds. Elmar Weitekamp and Hans-Jurgen Kerner (Dordrecht, Netherlands: Kluwer, 1994), pp. 3–65.

51. Adrian Raine, Rolf Loeber, Magda Stouthamer-Loeber, Terrie Moffitt, Avshalom Caspi, and Don Lynam, "Neurocognitive Impairments in Boys on the Life-Course Persistent Antisocial Path," *Journal of Abnormal Psychology* 114 (2005): 38–49.

52. Per-Olof Wikstrom and Rolf Loeber, "Do Disadvantaged Neighborhoods Cause Well-Adjusted Children to Become Adolescent Delinquents? A Study of Male Juvenile Serious Offending, Individual Risk and Protective Factors, and Neighborhood Context," *Criminology* 38 (2000): 1,109–1,142.

53. Alex Piquero, Leah Daigle, Chris Gibson, Nicole Leeper Piquero, and Stephen Tibbetts, "Are Life-Course-Persistent Offenders at Risk for Adverse Health Outcomes?" *Journal of Research in Crime & Delinquency* 44 (2007): 185–207.

54. Andrea Donker, Wilma Smeenk, Peter van der Laan, and Frank Verhulst, "Individual Stability of Antisocial Behavior from Childhood to Adulthood: Testing the Stability Postulate of Moffitt's Developmental Theory," *Criminology* 41 (2003): 593–609.

55. Robert Vermeiren, "Psychopathology and Delinquency in Adolescents: A Descriptive and Developmental Perspective," *Clinical Psychology Review* 23 (2003): 277–318; Paul Mazerolle, Robert Brame, Ray Paternoster, Alex Piquero, and Charles Dean, "Onset Age, Persistence, and Offending Versatility: Comparisons across Sex," *Criminology* 38 (2000): 1,143–1,172.

56. Stephen Farrall and Benjamin Bowling, "Structuration, Human Development, and Desistance from Crime," *British Journal of Criminology* 39 (1999): 253–268.

57. Robert Sampson and John Laub, *Crime in the Making: Pathways and Turning Points through Life* (Cambridge, MA: Harvard University Press, 1993); John Laub and Robert Sampson, "Turning Points in the Life Course: Why Change Matters to the Study of Crime," paper presented at the annual meeting of the American Society of Criminology, New Orleans, November 1992.

58. Robert Sampson and John Laub, "A Life-Course View of the Development of Crime," *The Annals of the American Academy of Political and Social Science* 602 (2005): 12–45.

59. Daniel Nagin and Raymond Paternoster, "Personal Capital and Social Control: The Deterrence Implications of a Theory of Criminal Offending," *Criminology* 32 (1994): 581–606.

60. Leonore M. J. Simon, "Social Bond and Criminal Record History of Acquaintance

and Stranger Violent Offenders," *Journal of Crime and Justice* 22 (1999): 131–146.

61. Raymond Paternoster and Robert Brame, "Multiple Routes to Delinquency? A Test of Developmental and General Theories of Crime," *Criminology* 35 (1997): 49–84.

62. Spencer De Li, "Legal Sanctions and Youths' Status Achievement: A Longitudinal Study," *Justice Quarterly* 16 (1999): 377–401.

63. Shawn Bushway, "The Impact of an Arrest on the Job Stability of Young White American Men," *Journal of Research on Crime and Delinquency* 35 (1999): 454–479.

64. Candace Kruttschnitt, Christopher Uggen, and Kelly Shelton, "Individual Variability in Sex Offending and Its Relationship to Informal and Formal Social Controls," paper presented at the annual meeting of the American Society of Criminology, San Diego, November 1997; Mark Collins and Don Weatherburn, "Unemployment and the Dynamics of Offender Populations," *Journal of Quantitative Criminology* 11 (1995): 231–245.

65. Robert Hoge, D. A. Andrews, and Alan Leschied, "An Investigation of Risk and Protective Factors in a Sample of Youthful Offenders," *Journal of Child Psychology and Psychiatry* 37 (1996): 419–424.

66. Richard Arum and Irenee Beattie, "High School Experience and the Risk of Adult Incarceration," *Criminology* 37 (1999): 515–540.

67. Ross Macmillan, Barbara J. McMorris, and Candace Kruttschnitt, "Linked Lives: Stability and Change in Maternal Circumstances and Trajectories of Antisocial Behavior in Children," *Child Development* 75 (2004): 205–220.

68. Robert Sampson and John Laub, "Socioeconomic Achievement in the Life Course of Disadvantaged Men: Military Service as a Turning Point, circa 1940–1965," *American Sociological Review* 61 (1996): 347–367.

69. Christopher Uggen, "Ex-Offenders and the Conformist Alternative: A Job Quality Model of Work and Crime," *Social Problems* 46 (1999): 127–151.

70. Terri Orbuch, James House, Richard Mero, and Pamela Webster, "Marital Quality over the Life Course," *Social Psychology Quarterly* 59 (1996): 162–171; Lee Lillard and Linda Waite, "'Til Death Do Us Part: Marital Disruption and Mortality," *American Journal of Sociology* 100 (1995): 1,131–1,156.

71. Mark Warr, "Life-Course Transitions and Desistance from Crime," *Criminology* 36 (1998): 183–216.

72. Ibid.

73. Doris Layton MacKenzie and Spencer De Li, "The Impact of Formal and Informal Social Controls on the Criminal Activities of Probationers," *Journal of Research in Crime and Delinquency* 39 (2002): 243–278.

74. Pamela Webster, Terri Orbuch, and James House, "Effects of Childhood Family Background on Adult Marital Quality and Perceived Stability," *American Journal of Sociology* 101 (1995): 404–432.

75. Alex Piquero, John MacDonald, and Karen Parker, "Race, Local Life Circumstances, and Criminal Activity over the Life-Course," *Social Science Quarterly* 83 (2002): 654–671.

76. Personal communication with Alex Piquero, September 24, 2002.

77. Ronald Simons, Eric Stewart, Leslie Gordon, Rand Conger, and Glen Elder, Jr., "Test of Life-Course Explanations for Stability and Change in Antisocial Behavior from Adolescence to Young Adulthood," *Criminology* 40 (2002): 401–435.

78. Eloise Dunlap and Bruce D. Johnson, "Family and Human Resources in the Development of a Female Crack-Seller Career," *Journal of Drug Issues* 26 (Winter 1996): 175–198.

79. Ryan Schroeder, Peggy Giordano, and Stephen Cernkovich, "Drug Use and Desistance Processes," *Criminology* 45 (2007): 191–222.

80. James Ridde et al., "Millennium Cohort: The 2001–2003 Baseline Prevalence of Mental Disorders in the U.S. Military," *Journal of Clinical Epidemiology* 60 (2007): 192–201.

81. David Rowe, D. Wayne Osgood, and W. Alan Nicewander, "A Latent Trait Approach to Unifying Criminal Careers," *Criminology* 28 (1990): 237–270.

82. Lee Ellis, "Neurohormonal Bases of Varying Tendencies to Learn Delinquent and Criminal Behavior," in *Behavioral Approaches to Crime and Delinquency*, eds. E. Morris and C. Braukmann (New York: Plenum, 1988), pp. 499–518.

83. David Rowe, Alexander Vazsonyi, and Daniel Flannery, "Sex Differences in Crime: Do Means and Within-Sex Variation Have Similar Causes?" *Journal of Research in Crime and Delinquency* 32 (1995): 84–100.

84. James Q. Wilson and Richard Herrnstein, *Crime and Human Nature* (New York: Simon & Schuster, 1985).

85. Ibid., p. 44.

86. Ibid., p. 171.

87. Michael Gottfredson and Travis Hirschi, *A General Theory of Crime* (Stanford, CA: Stanford University Press, 1990).

88. Gottfredson and Hirschi, *A General Theory of Crime*, p. 90.

89. Ibid., p. 89.

90. Alex Piquero and Stephen Tibbetts, "Specifying the Direct and Indirect Effects of Low Self-Control and Situational Factors in Offenders' Decision Making: Toward a More Complete Model of Rational Offending," *Justice Quarterly* 13 (1996): 481–508.

91. David Forde and Leslie Kennedy, "Risky Lifestyles, Routine Activities, and the General Theory of Crime," *Justice Quarterly* 14 (1997): 265–294.

92. Gottfredson and Hirschi, *A General Theory of Crime*, p. 112.

93. Ibid.

94. Christopher Schreck, Eric Stewart, and Bonnie Fisher, "Self-Control, Victimization, and their Influence on Risky Lifestyles: A Longitudinal Analysis Using Panel Data," *Journal of Quantitative Criminology* 22 (2006): 319–340.

95. Robert Agnew, "The Contribution of Social-Psychological Strain Theory to the Explanation of Crime and Delinquency," *Anomie Theory: Advances in Criminological Theory*, vol. 6, eds. Freda Adler and William Laufer (New Brunswick, NJ: Transaction Books, 1995), pp. 81–96.

96. Travis Hirschi and Michael Gottfredson, "Rethinking the Juvenile Justice System," *Crime and Delinquency* 39 (1993): 262–271.

97. Anthony Walsh and Lee Ellis, "Shoring Up the Big Three: Improving Criminological Theories with Biosocial Concepts," paper presented at the annual meeting of the American Society of Criminology, San Diego, November 1997, p. 15.

98. Dennis Giever, "An Empirical Assessment of the Core Elements of Gottfredson and Hirschi's General Theory of Crime," paper presented at the annual meeting of the American Society of Criminology, Boston, November 1995.

99. Kevin Beaver and John Paul Wright, "Evaluating the Effects of Birth Complications on Low Self-Control in a Sample of Twins," *International Journal of Offender Therapy and Comparative Criminology* 49 (2005): 450–472.

100. Gottfredson and Hirschi, *A General Theory of Crime*, p. 27.

101. For a review of this issue, see Anne Campbell, *Men, Women, and Aggression* (New York: Basic Books, 1993).

102. David Brownfield and Ann Marie Sorenson, "Self-Control and Juvenile Delinquency: Theoretical Issues and an Empirical Assessment of Selected Elements of a General Theory of Crime," *Deviant Behavior* 14 (1993): 243–264; Harold Grasmick, Charles Tittle, Robert Bursik, and Bruce Arneklev, "Testing the Core Empirical Implications of Gottfredson and Hirschi's General Theory of Crime," *Journal of Research in Crime and Delinquency* 30 (1993): 5–29; John Cochran, Peter Wood, and Bruce Arneklev, "Is the Religiosity–Delinquency Relationship Spurious? A Test of Arousal and Social Control Theories," *Journal of Research in Crime and Delinquency* 31 (1994): 92–123; Marc LeBlanc, Marc Ouimet, and Richard Tremblay, "An Integrative Control Theory of Delinquent Behavior: A Validation 1976–1985," *Psychiatry* 51 (1988): 164–176.

103. Daniel Nagin and Greg Pogarsky, "Time and Punishment: Delayed Consequences and Criminal Behavior." *Journal of Quantitative Criminology* 20 (2004): 295–317.

104. Gregory Morris, Peter Wood, and Gregory Dunaway, "Self-Control, Native Traditionalism, and Native American Substance Use: Testing the Cultural Invariance of a General Theory of Crime," *Crime and Delinquency* 52 (2006): 572–598.

105. Alexander Vazsonyi, Janice Clifford Wittekind, Lara Belliston, Timothy Van Loh, "Extending the General Theory of Crime to 'The East': Low Self-Control in Japanese Late Adolescents," *Journal of Quantitative Criminology* 20 (2004): 189–216; Alexander Vazsonyi, Lloyd Pickering, Marianne Junger, and Dick Hessing, "An Empirical Test of a General Theory of Crime: A Four-Nation Comparative Study of Self-Control and the Prediction of Deviance," *Journal of Research in Crime and Delinquency* 38 (2001): 91–131.

106. Michael Benson and Elizabeth Moore, "Are White-Collar and Common Offenders the Same? An Empirical and Theoretical Critique of a Recently Proposed General Theory of Crime," *Journal of Research in Crime and Delinquency* 29 (1992): 251–272.

107. Ronald Akers, "Self-Control as a General Theory of Crime," *Journal of Quantitative Criminology* 7 (1991): 201–211.

108. Gottfredson and Hirschi, *A General Theory of Crime*, p. 88.

109. Moffitt, "Adolescence-Limited and Life-Course Persistent Antisocial Behaviors."

110. Alex Piquero, Robert Brame, Paul Mazerolle, and Rudy Haapanen, "Crime in Emerging Adulthood," *Criminology* 40 (2002): 137–170.

111. Donald Lynam, Alex Piquero, and Terrie Moffitt, "Specialization and the Propensity to Violence: Support from Self-Reports but Not Official Records," *Journal of Contemporary Criminal Justice* 20 (2004): 215–228.

112. Alan Feingold, "Gender Differences in Personality: A Meta Analysis," *Psychological Bulletin* 116 (1994): 429–456.

113. Charles Tittle, David Ward, and Harold Grasmick, "Gender, Age, and Crime/Deviance: A Challenge to Self-Control Theory," *Journal of Research in Crime and Delinquency* 40 (2003): 426–453.

114. Brent Benda, "Gender Differences in Life-Course Theory of Recidivism: A Survival Analysis," *International Journal of Offender Therapy and Comparative Criminology* 49 (2005): 325–342.

115. Gottfredson and Hirschi, *A General Theory of Crime*, p. 153.

116. Ann Marie Sorenson and David Brownfield, "Normative Concepts in Social Control," paper presented at the annual meeting of the American Society of Criminology, Phoenix, November 1993.

117. Brent Benda, "An Examination of Reciprocal Relationship between Religiosity and Different Forms of Delinquency within a Theoretical Model," *Journal of Research in Crime and Delinquency* 34 (1997): 163–186.

118. Delbert Elliott and Scott Menard, "Delinquent Friends and Delinquent Behavior: Temporal and Developmental Patterns," in *Crime and Delinquency: Current Theories*, ed. J. David Hawkins (Cambridge: Cambridge University Press, 1996).

119. Graham Ousey and David Aday, "The Interaction Hypothesis: A Test Using Social Control Theory and Social Learning Theory," paper presented at the annual meeting of the American Society of Criminology, Boston, November 1995.

120. Dana Haynie, Peggy Giordano, Wendy Manning, and Monica Longmore, "Adolescent Romantic Relationships and Delinquency Involvement," *Criminology* 43 (2005): 177–210.

121. Julie Horney, D. Wayne Osgood, and Ineke Haen Marshall, "Criminal Careers in the Short-Term: Intra-Individual Variability in Crime and Its Relations to Local Life Circumstances," *American Sociological Review* 60 (1995): 655–673; Martin Daly and Margo Wilson, "Killing the Competition," *Human Nature* 1 (1990): 83–109.

122. Mark Palermo, Massimo Di Luigi, Gloria Dal Forno, Cinzia Dominici, David Vicomandi, Augusto Sambucioni, Luca Proietti, and Patrizio Pasqualetti, "Externalizing and Oppositional Behaviors and Karate-do: The Way of Crime Prevention," *International Journal of Offender Therapy and Comparative Criminology* 50 (2006): 654–660.

123. Charles R. Tittle and Harold G. Grasmick, "Criminal Behavior and Age: A Test of Three Provocative Hypotheses," *Journal of Criminal Law and Criminology* 88 (1997): 309–342.

124. Callie Harbin Burt, Ronald Simons, and Leslie Simons, "A Longitudinal Test of the Effects of Parenting and the Stability of Self-Control: Negative Evidence for the General Theory of Crime," *Criminology* 44 (2006): 353–396.

125. Carter Hay and Walter Forrest, "The Development of Self-Control: Examining Self-Control Theory's Stability Thesis," *Criminology* 44 (2006): 739–774.

126. Ronald Simons, Christine Johnson, Rand Conger, and Glen Elder, "A Test of Latent Trait versus Life-Course Perspectives on the Stability of Adolescent Antisocial Behavior," *Criminology* 36 (1998): 217–244.

127. Carter Hay, "Parenting, Self-Control, and Delinquency: A Test of Self-Control Theory," *Criminology* 39 (2001): 707–736; Douglas Longshore, "Self-Control and Criminal Opportunity: A Prospective Test of the General Theory of Crime," *Social Problems* 45 (1998): 102–114; Finn-Aage Esbensen and Elizabeth Piper Deschenes, "A Multisite Examination of Youth Gang Membership: Does Gender Matter?" *Criminology* 36 (1998): 799–828.

128. Raymond Paternoster and Robert Brame, "The Structural Similarity of Processes Generating Criminal and Analogous Behaviors," *Criminology* 36 (1998): 633–670.

129. Otwin Marenin and Michael Resig, "A General Theory of Crime and Patterns of Crime in Nigeria: An Exploration of Methodological Assumptions," *Journal of Criminal Justice* 23 (1995): 501–518.

130. Bruce Arneklev, Harold Grasmick, Charles Tittle, and Robert Bursik, "Low Self-Control and Imprudent Behavior," *Journal of Quantitative Criminology* 9 (1993): 225–246.

131. Peter Muris and Cor Meesters, "The Validity of Attention Deficit Hyperactivity and Hyperkinetic Disorder Symptom Domains in Nonclinical Dutch Children," *Journal of Clinical Child and Adolescent Psychology* 32 (2003): 460–466.

132. Francis Cullen, John Paul Wright, and Mitchell Chamlin, "Social Support and Social Reform: A Progressive Crime Control Agenda," *Crime and Delinquency* 45 (1999): 188–207.

133. Alex Piquero, John MacDonald, Adam Dobrin, Leah Daigle, and Francis Cullen, "Self-Control, Violent Offending, and Homicide Victimization: Assessing the General Theory of Crime," *Journal of Quantitative Criminology* 21 (2005): 55–71.

134. Ibid.

135. Richard Wiebe, "Reconciling Psychopathy and Low Self-Control," *Justice Quarterly* 20 (2003): 297–336.

136. Elizabeth Cauffman, Laurence Steinberg, and Alex Piquero, "Psychological, Neuropsychological and Physiological Correlates of Serious Antisocial Behavior in Adolescence: The Role of Self-Control," *Criminology* 43 (2005): 133–176.

137. Steven Levitt and Sudhir Alladi Venkatesh, "An Economic Analysis of a Drug-Selling Gang's Finances," *Quarterly Journal of Economics* 13 (2000): 755–789.

138. Ibid.

139. Mark Muraven, Greg Pogarsky, and Dikla Shmueli, "Self-Control Depletion and the General Theory of Crime," *Journal of Quantitative Criminology* 22 (2006): 263–277.

140. Kevin Thompson, "Sexual Harassment and Low Self-Control: An Application of Gottfredson and Hirschi's General Theory of Crime," paper presented at the annual meeting of the American Society of Criminology, Phoenix, November 1993.

141. Graham Ousey and Pamela Wilcox, "The Interaction of Antisocial Propensity and Life-Course Varying Predictors of Delinquent Behavior: Differences by Method of Estimation and Implications for Theory," *Criminology* 45 (2007): 313–354.

142. Bradley Entner Wright, Avashalom Caspi, Terrie Moffitt, and Phil Silva, "Low Self-Control, Social Bonds, and Crime: Social Causation, Social Selection, or Both?" *Criminology* 37 (1999): 479–514.

143. Ibid., p. 504.

144. Stephen Cernkovich and Peggy Giordano, "Stability and Change in Antisocial Behavior: The Transition from Adolescence to Early Adulthood," *Criminology* 39 (2001): 371–410.

145. Heather Lonczk, Robert Abbott, J. David Hawkins, Rick Kosterman, and Richard Catalano, "Effects of the Seattle Social Development Project on Sexual Behavior, Pregnancy, Birth, and Sexually Transmitted Disease Outcomes by Age 21 Years," *Archive of Pediatrics and Adolescent Medicine* 156 (2002): 438–447.

146. Kathleen Bodisch Lynch, Susan Rose Geller, and Melinda G. Schmidt, "Multi-Year Evaluation of the Effectiveness of a Resilience-Based Prevention Program for Young Children," *Journal of Primary Prevention* 24 (2004): 335–353.

147. This section leans on Thomas Tatchell, Phillip Waite, Renny Tatchell, Lynne Durrant, and Dale Bond, "Substance Abuse Prevention in Sixth Grade: The Effect of a Prevention Program on Adolescents' Risk and Protective Factors," *American Journal of Health Studies* 19 (2004): 54–61.

148. Nancy Tobler and Howard Stratton, "Effectiveness of School Based Drug Prevention Programs: A Meta-Analysis of the Research," *Journal of Primary Prevention* 18 (1997): 71–128.

149. Project overview, Fast Track Data Center: www.pubpol.duke.edu/centers/child/fasttrack/ (accessed August 23, 2008).

PART THREE

CRIME TYPOLOGIES

Criminologists group criminal offenders and/or criminal behaviors into categories or typologies so they may be more easily studied and understood. Are there common traits or characteristics that link offenders together and make them distinct from nonoffenders? Are there common areas between seemingly different acts such as murder and rape?

In this section, we focus on crime typologies. They are clustered into six groups: violent crime (Chapter 10), political crime and terrorism (Chapter 11), economic crimes involving common theft offenses (Chapter 12), enterprise crimes involving white-collar and organized criminals (Chapter 13), public order crimes, such as prostitution and drug abuse (Chapter 14), and cyber crimes (Chapter 15). This format groups criminal behaviors by their focus and consequence: bringing physical harm to others; misappropriating other people's property; violating laws designed to protect public morals; and using technology to commit crime.

Typologies can be useful in classifying large numbers of criminal offenses or offenders into easily understood categories. This text has grouped offenses and offenders on the basis of their legal definitions and their collective goals, objectives, and consequences.

10

Interpersonal Violence

One of the most notorious incidents *of the past decade* began on March 13, 2006, when, after a "performance" at a private residence, three members of Duke University's men's lacrosse team alledgedly raped one of two strippers who had been hired to entertain the team. The three players, David Evans, Reade Seligmann, and Collin Finnerty, were charged with first-degree forcible rape, first-degree sexual offense, and kidnapping.

Media outlets had a field day with the case because the young woman was African American and the players white. The event soon drew national media attention and highlighted racial tensions not only in Durham, North Carolina, where the crime took place, but across the entire nation. The accused boys were wealthy, attractive, and successful. Did they actually believe they could rape a poor young minority woman and get away with the crime because of their power and position? Members of the community demanded justice, the public voiced its outrage, and school officials suspended the accused students and cancelled the lacrosse team's season.

Despite initial shock, public sentiment began to shift as the facts of the case were leaked to the press. There was a lack of physical evidence, the victim's story constantly changed, her character was questioned, there were changes to and inconsistencies in her story, the second stripper did not back up her story, and most damaging, the press got hold of testimony by a lab director that the prosecutor, Durham District Attorney Mike Nifong, deliberately withheld evidence from the defense that might have cleared the suspects (i.e., DNA from other men but not the Duke players were found on the victim's body). On December 22, 2006, Nifong dropped the rape charges against the three indicted players. After ethics charges were filed against him, Nifong asked to be taken off the case, and on January 13, 2007, North Carolina Attorney General Roy Cooper agreed to take over. Soon after, Duke University announced that Collin Finnerty and Reade Seligmann had been invited to return to school while they awaited trial and were eligible to rejoin the team (David Evans had already graduated). On April 11, 2007, all remaining charges were dropped against the three players and in an ironic turnabout, Nifong was brought up on misconduct charges, during which he abruptly resigned his post; he was later stripped of his law license.[1]

The Duke case illustrates the toll violent crime takes on American society. It can divide a community, damage reputations, and cause lifelong harm. It tells people that no matter where they go, they may encounter violent acts. And if the Duke case was a matter of false accusation and overzealous prosecution, it still sends the message that anyone can be accused of violent crime. It may also make it tougher to get a conviction when an actual crime takes place.

Millions of violent crimes occur each year. Some are expressive violence—acts that vent rage, anger, or frustration—and some are instrumental violence—acts designed to improve the financial or social position of the criminal, for example, through an armed robbery or murder for hire. No matter its cause, interpersonal violence takes a terrible toll. It causes people to live in fear, staying home at night and avoiding dangerous neighborhoods. It can also take a toll on communities, disrupting services and driving down real estate values, further destabilizing areas already reeling from the shock of violent crimes.[2]

This chapter explores the concept of violence in some depth. First, it reviews the suggested causes of violent crime. Then it focuses on specific types of interpersonal violence—rape, homicide, assault, robbery, and newly recognized types of interpersonal violence such as stalking and workplace violence. Finally, it briefly examines political violence and terrorism.

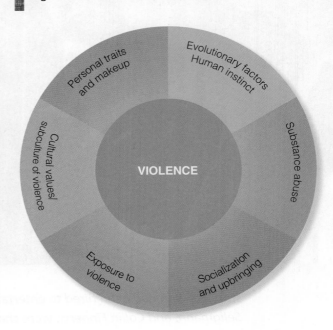

Figure 10.1 Sources of Violence

THE CAUSES OF VIOLENCE

What sets off a violent person? Criminologists have a variety of views on this subject. Some believe that violence is a function of human traits and makeup. Others point to improper socialization and upbringing. Violent behavior may be culturally determined and relate to dysfunctional social values.[3] The various sources of violence are set out in Figure 10.1.

Psychological/Biological Abnormality

On March 13, 1996, an ex–Boy Scout leader named Thomas Hamilton took four high-powered rifles into the primary school of the peaceful Scottish town of Dunblane and slaughtered 16 kindergarten children and their teacher. This horrific crime shocked the British Isles into implementing strict controls on all guns.[4] Bizarre outbursts such as Hamilton's support a link between violence and some sort of mental or biological abnormality.

As you may recall (Chapter 5), some criminologists believe that a significant number of people who are involved in violent episodes may be suffering from severe mental abnormalities.[5] In a classic work, psychologist Dorothy Otnow Lewis shows that youths who kill may be suffering from multiple symptoms of psychological abnormality: neurological impairment (e.g., abnormal EEGs, multiple psychomotor impairments, and severe seizures), low intelligence, and psychotic symptoms such as paranoia,

illogical thinking, and hallucinations.[6] In her book *Guilty by Reason of Insanity*, Lewis finds that death row inmates have a history of mental impairment and intellectual dysfunction.[7]

Lewis's research is not unique. Abnormal personality structures, including such traits as depression, impulsivity, aggression, dishonesty, pathological lying, lack of remorse, borderline personality syndrome, and psychopathology, have all been associated with various forms of violence.[8] It comes as no surprise to psychologists that many murderers kill themselves shortly after committing their crime.[9]

There is also evidence that personality disturbance is linked to some physical trait or characteristic. Neuroscientists claim to have found differences in both the limbic system and the prefrontal cortex of the brain that separates aggressive, violent people from the more level-headed and reasonable. According to this view, if some defect or injury impairs communication between the limbic system and the frontal cortex, a person might not be entirely able to moderate his or her emotional reactions.[10]

Evolutionary Factors/ Human Instinct

Sigmund Freud believed that human behavior is shaped by two instinctual drives: eros, the life instinct, which drives people toward self-fulfillment and enjoyment; and thanatos, the death instinct, which produces self-destruction. Thanatos can be expressed externally (e.g., violence and sadism) or internally (e.g., suicide, alcoholism, or other self-destructive habits).[11]

While rates of violent crime are higher in the United States than in most other Western nations, violence abroad is not unknown. One of the most catastrophic incidents occurred in the village of Dunblane, Scotland, on March 13, 1996, when heavily armed Thomas Hamilton walked onto the grounds of St. Luke's Infant School and began to methodically shoot children in this kindergarten class. Sixteen children and their teacher were killed. The Dunblane massacre prompted the passage of legislation to control handguns in Scotland and England, which failed to please some critics who felt there should be an outright ban on the possession of guns.

In his celebrated book *On Aggression*, anthropologist Konrad Lorenz argued that aggressive energy is produced by inbred instincts that are independent of environmental forces.[12] In the animal kingdom, aggression usually serves a productive purpose—for example, it leads members of grazing species such as zebras and antelopes to spread out over available territory to ensure an ample food supply and the survival of the fittest. Lorenz found that humans possess some of the same aggressive instincts as animals. But among lower species, aggression is rarely fatal; when a conflict occurs, the winner is determined through a test of skill or endurance. This inhibition against killing members of their own species protects animals from self-extinction. Humans, lacking this inhibition against fatal violence, are capable of killing their own kind in war or as a result of interpersonal conflicts such as those arising over finding suitable mates.[13]

Lorenz feared that as technology develops and more lethal weapons are produced, the extinction of the human species becomes a significant possibility.

Substance Abuse

Substance abuse has been associated with violence on both the individual and social levels: substance abusers have higher rates of violence than nonabusers; neighborhoods with high levels of substance abuse have higher violence rates when compared to areas with low use rates.[14] A direct association has been found between community levels of crack cocaine and heroin use and the incidence of street robberies.[15] High use areas may also face social disorganization, poverty, and unemployment, factors that further escalate violence rates.[16]

The link between substance abuse and violence appears in three different formats:[17]

1. *Psychopharmacological relationship.* Violence may be the direct consequence of ingesting mood-altering substances. Experimental evidence shows that high doses of drugs such as PCP and amphetamines produce violent, aggressive behavior.[18] For example, binge drinking has been closely associated with violent crime rates.[19] Heavy drinking reduces cognitive ability, information processing skills, and the ability to process and react to verbal and nonverbal behavior. As a result, miscommunication becomes more likely and the capacity for rational dialogue is compromised.[20] It is not surprising that males involved in sexual assaults often claim that they were drinking and misunderstood their victims' intentions.[21] Drinking becomes particularly dangerous when abusers have access to firearms; guns and alcohol do not mix well.[22]

2. *Economic compulsive behavior.* Drug users resort to violence to obtain the financial resources to support their habit. Studies conducted in the United States and Europe show that addicts commit hundreds of crimes each year.[23]

3. *Systemic link.* Violence escalates when drug-dealing gangs flex their muscle to dominate territory and drive out rivals. Studies of gangs that sell drugs show that their violent activities may result in a significant proportion of all urban homicides.[24]

Socialization and Upbringing

Another view is that improper socialization and upbringing are responsible for the onset of violent acts. Absent or deviant parents, inconsistent discipline, physical abuse, and lack of supervision have all been linked to persistent violent offending.[25]

Although infants demonstrate individual temperaments, who they become may have a lot to do with how they are treated during their early years. Some children are harder to soothe than others; in some cases, difficult infant temperament has been associated with later aggression and behavioral problems.[26] Parents who fail to set adequate limits or to use proper, consistent discipline reinforce a child's coercive behavior.[27] The effects of inadequate parenting and early rejection may affect violent behavior throughout life.[28] There is evidence that children who are maltreated and neglected in early childhood are the ones most likely to be initiated into criminality and thereafter continue or persist in a criminal career.[29]

There are also indications that children who are subject to even minimal amounts of physical punishment may be more likely one day to use violence themselves.[30] Sociologist Murray Straus reviewed the concept of discipline in a series of surveys and found a powerful relationship between exposure to physical punishment and later aggression.[31] The effect of physical punishment may be mediated or neutralized to some extent if parents also provide support, warmth, and care. When kids experience physical punishment in the absence of parental involvement, they feel angry and unjustly treated and are more willing to defy their parents and engage in antisocial behavior.[32]

Abused Children A number of research studies have found that children who are clinically diagnosed as abused later engage in delinquent behaviors, including violence, at a rate significantly greater than that of children who were not abused.[33] Samples of convicted murderers reveal a high percentage of seriously abused youth.[34] The abuse–violence association has been established in many cases in which parents have been killed by their children; sexual abuse is also a constant factor in father (patricide) and mother (matricide) killings.[35] Lewis found in her study of juvenile death row inmates that all had long histories of intense child abuse.[36]

Abuse may have the greatest effect if it is persistent and extends from childhood to adolescence.[37] Children who are physically punished by their parents are likely to physically abuse a sibling and later engage in spouse abuse and other forms of criminal violence.[38] There is evidence that spousal batterers received significantly less love and more punishment from their mothers than did men in a general population comparison group. Abusive childhood experiences may be a key factor in the later development of relationship aggression.[39] Lonnie Athens, a well-known criminologist who links violence to early experiences with child abuse, has coined the phrase violentization process to describe how abused kids are turned into aggressive adults.[40] The stages of this process are described in Exhibit 10.1. Athens recognizes that abuse alone is not a sufficient condition to cause someone to become a dangerous violent criminal. One must complete the full cycle of the "violentization process"—brutalization, belligerence, violent performances, and virulency—to become socialized into violence. Many brutalized children do not go on to become violent criminals, and some later reject the fact that they were abused as youths and redefine their early years as normative.

Exposure to Violence

People who are constantly exposed to violence in the environment may adopt violent methods themselves. Children living in areas marked by extreme violence may eventually

Stages in the Violentization Process

1. **Brutalization Stage.** During this phase of the violentization process, a young victim develops a belligerent, angry demeanor as a result of being mistreated by abusive parents or caretakers. Brutalization can be broader than parental physical or sexual abuse and can result from violent coaching by peers, neighbors, and schoolmates. Although most brutalization occurs early in life, some people can be brutalized as they mature. There are a number of facets in the brutalization stage:

   - *Violent subjugation.* A person is coerced into compliance by physical or verbal force. Coercive violence ends at submission, but retaliatory violence continues regardless of submission, with the goal of gaining long-term submission.

   - *Personal horrification.* An individual is exposed to violence directed at someone else close to him or her, leading to inner conflict and guilt associated with feeling helpless to do anything about the abuse.

   - *Violent coaching.* A brutalizer, through ridicule, threats, or coercion, advises the brutalized individual to depend only on his or her self, encourages defensiveness, and insists that the person has a personal responsibility to commit violence.

2. **Belligerency Stage.** During this stage, the target of brutalization begins to understand his dilemma. At first he may wonder, "Why can't I stop this violence and brutalization?" Then a cognitive process begins in which he concludes that sometimes violence is a necessary evil in the world. He thinks, "Why have I not done anything to stop my own and my intimates' violent subjugation?" Resorting to violence is sometimes necessary in this world.

3. **Violent Performance Stage.** Brutalized youth may become belligerent and angry. When confronted at home, school, or on the street, these belligerent youth respond with violent performances of angry, hostile behavior. The success of their violent confrontations provides them with a sense of power and achievement.

4. **Virulency Stage.** The emerging criminals develop a violent identity that makes them feared; they enjoy intimidating others. Filled with feelings of exultancy, the brutalized youth believe that they can perform even more impressive violent feats in the future. They believe they are now invincible. This process takes violent youths full circle from being the victims of aggression to its initiators; they are now the same people they grew up despising, ready to begin the process with their own children.

Source: Lonnie Athens, *The Creation of Dangerous Violent Criminals* (Urbana: University of Illinois Press, 1992), pp. 27–80.

become desensitized to the persistent brutality.[41] Much of the differences in violent crime rates between whites and racial minorities can be explained by the fact that the latter are often forced to live in high-crime neighborhoods, which increases their risk of exposure to violence.[42] Areas where people have little confidence in the police and are therefore reluctant to call for help, a condition common in the minority community, may also experience higher levels of violent behavior.[43]

Social scientist Felton Earls and his associates conducted the Project on Human Development in Chicago Neighborhoods—a government-funded longitudinal study of pathways to violence among 7,000 Chicago area people in eighty different, randomly selected neighborhoods.[44] Interviews with youths aged 9 to 15 show that large numbers of these children have been victims of or witnesses to violence and that many carry weapons.

Between 30 and 40 percent of the children who reported exposure to violence also displayed significant violent behavior themselves. Earls finds that young teens who witness gun violence are more than twice as likely as nonwitnesses to commit violent crime themselves in the following years.[45] Even a single exposure to firearm violence doubles the chance that a young person will later engage in violent behavior.

Children living in these conditions become "crusted over": they do not let people inside, nor do they express their feelings. They exploit others and in turn are exploited by those older and stronger; as a result, they develop a sense of hopelessness. They find that parents and teachers focus on their failures and problems, not their achievements. Consequently, they are vulnerable to the lure of delinquent gangs and groups.[46]

Cultural Values/Subculture of Violence

Violence may be the product of cultural beliefs, values, and behaviors that develop in poor and disorganized neighborhoods.[47] To explain this phenomenon, criminologists Marvin Wolfgang and Franco Ferracuti formulated the famous concept that some areas contain an independent subculture of violence.[48]

The subculture of violence's norms are separate from society's central, dominant value system. In this subculture, a potent theme of violence influences lifestyles, the socialization process, and interpersonal relationships. Even though the subculture's members share some of the dominant culture's values, they expect that violence will be used to solve social conflicts and dilemmas. In some cultural subgroups, then, violence has become legitimized by custom and norms. It is considered appropriate behavior within culturally defined conflict situations in which an individual who has been offended by a negative outcome in a dispute seeks reparations through violent means—a concept referred to as disputatiousness.[49]

There is evidence that a subculture of violence may be found in areas that experience concentrated poverty and social disorganization.[50] Though most people abhor violence, income inequality and racial disparity may help instill a sense of hopelessness that nourishes pro-violence norms and values.[51] In these areas people are more likely to carry weapons and use them in assaults and robberies. Victims are aware of these tactics and are less likely to fight back forcibly when attacked.[52] However, when pressed to the limit even passive victims may eventually fight back. When Charis Kubrin and Ronald Weitzer studied homicide in St. Louis, Missouri, they discovered that a certain type of killing, referred to as *cultural retaliatory homicide,* is common in neighborhoods that suffer economic disadvantage. In these areas, residents resolve interpersonal conflicts informally—without calling the police—even if it means killing their opponent; neighbors understand and support their violent methods.[53] Because police and other agencies of formal social control are viewed as weak and devalued, understaffed and/or corrupt, people are willing to take matters into their own hands and violence rates increase accordingly.[54]

Peer Group Influences Empirical evidence shows that violence rates are highest in urban areas where subcultural values support teenage gangs whose members typically embrace the use of violence.[55] Gang boys are more likely to own guns and other weapons than non-gang members. They are also more likely to have peers who are gun owners and are more likely to carry guns outside the home.[56] Ominously, major metropolitan areas such as Los Angeles and Chicago are now reporting a significant increase in the number of street gang-related killings.[57]

The association between gang membership and violence has a number of roots. It can result from drug-trafficking activities and turf protection but also stems from personal vendettas and a perceived need for self-protection.[58] Gang boys are much more likely to own guns and associate with violent peers than nonmembers.[59] Those who choose aggressive or violent friends are more likely to begin engaging in antisocial behavior themselves and suffer psychological deficits.[60] The risky gang lifestyle increases the likelihood that boys will themselves become a victim of violent crime. Experiencing victimization brings on retaliation, creating a never-ending cycle of violence begetting even more violence.[61]

While many boys are predisposed toward violence before joining a gang, research shows that once in gangs their violent behavior quickly escalates; after they leave, it significantly declines.[62]

National Values Some nations—including the United States, Sri Lanka, Angola, Uganda, and the Philippines—have relatively high violence rates; others are much more peaceful. According to research by sociologist Jerome Neapolitan, a number of national characteristics are predictive of violence, including a high level of social disorganization, economic stress, high child abuse rates, approval of violence by the government, political corruption, and an inefficient justice system.[63] Children in high-violence nations are likely to be economically deprived and socially isolated, exposed to constant violence, and lacking in hope and respect for the law. Guns are common in these nations because, lacking an efficient justice system, people arm themselves or hire private security forces for protection.[64] In contrast, nations such as Japan have relatively low violence rates because of cultural and economic strengths. Japan boasts a system of exceptionally effective informal social controls that help reduce crime. It also has had a robust economy that may alleviate the stresses that produce violence.[65] The Race, Culture, Gender, and Criminology feature "The Honor Killing of Women and Girls" discusses one type of culturally based violent crime.

Does the United States maintain values that promote violence? According to historian David Courtwright, relatively high

THE HONOR KILLING OF WOMEN AND GIRLS

Honor killing and honor crime involve violence against women and girls, including such acts as beating, battering, or killing, by a family member or relative. The attacks are provoked by the belief or perception that an individual's or family's honor has been threatened because of the actual or perceived sexual misconduct of the female. Honor killings are most common in traditional societies in the Middle East, Southwest Asia, India, China, and Latin America.

Honor killing of a woman or girl by her father, brother, or other male relative may occur because of a suspicion that she engaged in sexual activities before or outside marriage and thus has dishonored the family. Even when rape of a woman or girl has occurred this may be seen as violation of the honor of the family for which the female must be killed. Wives' adultery and daughters' premarital "sexual activity," including rape, are seen as extreme violations of the codes of behavior and thus may result in the death of the female through this so-called "honor" killing. Honor killing/crime is based on the shame that a loss of control of the woman or girl brings to the family and to the male heads of the family.

According to criminologist Linda Williams, men consider honor killings culturally necessary, because any suspicion of sexual activity or suspicion that a girl or a woman was touched by another in a sexual manner is enough to raise questions about the family's honor. Consequently, strict control of women and girls within the home and outside the home is justified. Women are restricted in their activities in the community, religion, and politics. These institutions, in turn, support the control of females. Williams believes that the existence of honor killing is designed for maintaining male dominance. Submissiveness may be seen as a sign of sexual purity and a woman's or girl's attempts to assert her rights can be seen as a violation of the family's honor that needs to be redressed. Rules of honor and threats against females who "violate" such rules reinforce the control of women and have a powerful impact on their lives. Honor killings/crimes serve to keep women and girls from "stepping out of line." The manner in which such behaviors silence women and kill their spirit has led some to label honor killings/crimes more broadly as "femicide."

CRITICAL THINKING

While we may scoff at honor killings, are there elements of American culture and life that you consider harmful to women yet are still tolerated? What can be done to change them?

Sources: Linda M. Williams, "Honor Killings," in *Encyclopedia of Interpersonal Violence*, eds. Claire M. Renzetti and Jeffrey I. Edelson (Thousand Oaks, CA: Sage Publications, 2007); Dan Bilefsky, "How to Avoid Honor Killing in Turkey? Honor Suicide," *New York Times*, 16 July 2006, p. 3; Nadera Shalhoub-Kevorkian, "Reexamining Femicide: Breaking the Silence and Crossing 'Scientific' Borders," *Signs* 28 (2003): 581–608.

---

violence rates in the United States can be traced to a frontier culture that was characterized by racism and preoccupation with personal honor.[66] Westerners drank heavily and frequented saloons and gambling halls, where petty arguments could become lethal because most patrons carried guns and knives. Violent acts often went unpunished because law enforcement agencies were unable or unwilling to take action. The population of the frontier was mostly young bachelors who were sensitive about honor, heavy drinkers, morally indifferent, heavily armed, and unchecked by adequate law enforcement. Many died from disease, but others succumbed to drink and violence. Smoking, gambling, and heavy drinking became a cultural imperative, and those who were disinclined to indulge were considered social outcasts. Courtwright claims that over time gender ratios equalized as more men brought families to the frontier and children of both sexes were born. Many men died, returned home, or drifted elsewhere. By the mid-twentieth century, America's overall male surplus was disappearing, and a balanced population helped bring down the crime rate, but remnants of the frontier mentality still exist in contemporary American society.

www Go to academic.cengage.com/criminaljustice/siegel to:

▌ Read more about the **Dunblane massacre**.

▌ Read the **autobiography of Konrad Lorenz**, who won the Nobel Prize in medicine in 1973.

▌ Visit the **Project on Human Development in Chicago Neighborhoods** website.

FORCIBLE RAPE

Rape (from the Latin *rapere*, to take by force) is defined in common law as "the carnal knowledge of a female forcibly and against her will."[67] It is one of the most loathed, misunderstood, and frightening crimes. Under traditional common-law definitions, rape involves nonconsensual sexual intercourse that a male performs against a female he is neither married to nor cohabitating with.[68] There are of course other forms of sexual assault, including male on male, female on female, and female on male sexual assaults, but these are

Rape has been the subject of books, poems, and paintings. Here is *The Rape of the Sabine Women* by Nicolas Poussin (1594–1665), which hangs in the Louvre in Paris. In early civilization men staked a claim of ownership on women by forcibly abducting and raping them. This practice led to males' solidification of power and their historical domination of women.

not considered within the traditional definition of rape.[69] However, recognizing changing contemporary standards, all but three states have now revised their rape statutes, making them gender neutral.[70] In addition, states now recognize that rape can occur among married couples and people who have been previously sexually intimate.[71]

History of Rape

Rape has been a recognized crime throughout history. It has been the subject of art, literature, film, and theater. Paintings such as the *Rape of the Sabine Women* by Nicolas Poussin, novels such as *Clarissa* by Samuel Richardson, poems such as *The Rape of Lucrece* by William Shakespeare, and films such as *The Accused* have sexual violence as their central theme.

In early civilization rape was common. Men staked a claim of ownership on women by forcibly abducting and raping them. This practice led to males' solidification of power and their historical domination of women.[72] Under Babylonian and Hebraic law, the rape of a virgin was a crime punishable by death. However, if the victim was married, then both she and her attacker were considered equally to blame, and unless her husband intervened, both were put to death.

During the Middle Ages, it was common for ambitious men to abduct and rape wealthy women in an effort to force them into marriage. The practice of "heiress stealing" illustrates how feudal law gave little thought or protection to women and equated them with property.[73] Only in the late fifteenth century, after a monetary economy developed, was forcible sex

outlawed. Thereafter, the violation of a virgin caused an economic hardship on her family, who expected a significant dowry for her hand in marriage. However, the law only applied to the wealthy; peasant women and married women were not considered rape victims until well into the sixteenth century. The Christian condemnation of sex during this period was also a denunciation of women as evil, having lust in their hearts, and redeemable only by motherhood. A woman who was raped was almost automatically suspected of contributing to her attack.

Rape and the Military

The link between the military and rape is inescapable. Throughout recorded history, rape has been associated with armies and warfare. Soldiers of conquering armies have considered sexual possession of their enemies' women one of the spoils of war. Among the ancient Greeks, rape was socially acceptable within the rules of warfare. During the Crusades, even knights and pilgrims, ostensibly bound by vows of chivalry and Christian piety, took time to rape as they marched toward Constantinople.

The belief that women are part of the spoils of war has continued. During World War II the Japanese army forced as many as 200,000 Korean women into frontline brothels, where they were repeatedly raped. In a 1998 Japanese ruling, the surviving Korean women were awarded the equivalent of $2,300 each in compensation.[74] The systematic rape of Bosnian and Kosovar women by Serbian army officers during the civil war in the former Yugoslavia horrified the world during the 1990s. These crimes seemed particularly atrocious because they appeared to be part of an official policy of genocide: rape was deliberately used to impregnate Bosnian women with Serbian children.

On March 9, 1998, Dragoljub Kunarac, 37, a former Bosnian Serb paramilitary commander, admitted before an international tribunal in the Netherlands that he had raped Muslim women during the Bosnian war in 1992. His confession made him the first person to plead guilty to rape as a war crime.[75] Human rights groups have estimated that more than 30,000 women and young girls were sexually abused in the Balkan fighting.

Though shocking, the war crimes discovered in Bosnia have not deterred conquering armies from using rape as a weapon. In 2004 pro-government militias in the Darfur region of Sudan were accused of using rape and other forms of sexual violence "as a weapon of war" to humiliate black African women and girls, as well as the rebels fighting the Sudanese government in Khartoum.[76]

Incidence of Rape

According to the most recent UCR data, about 90,000 rapes or attempted rapes were reported to U.S. police each year, a rate of about 32 per 100,000 inhabitants or more relevantly, 62 per 100,000 females.[77] The rape rate has been in a decade-long decline, and the 2007 totals are significantly below 1992 levels when 84 women per 100,000 were rape victims. The most recent data shows that rape rates declined 4 percent between 2006 and 2007.

Population density influences the rape rate. Metropolitan areas today have rape rates significantly higher than rural areas; nonetheless, urban areas have experienced a much greater drop in rape reports than rural areas. The police make arrests in slightly more than half of all reported rape offenses. Of the offenders arrested, typically about half are under 25 years of age, and about two-thirds are white. The racial and age pattern of rape arrests has been fairly consistent for some time. Finally, rape is a warm-weather crime—most incidents occur during July and August, with the lowest rates occurring during December, January, and February.

These data must be interpreted with caution because rape is a traditionally under-reported crime. As many as 10 percent of all adult women may have been raped during their lifetime.[78] According to the National Crime Victimization Survey (NCVS), almost 200,000 rapes and attempted rapes take place each year, suggesting that fewer than 50 percent of rape incidents are reported to police.[79] Many people fail to report rapes because they are embarrassed, believe nothing can be done, or blame themselves. Some victims of sexual assaults may even question whether they have really been raped; research indicates that when the assault involved a boyfriend, if the woman was severely impaired by alcohol or drugs, or if the act involved oral or digital sex, the women were unlikely to label their situations as being a "real" rape.[80]

Types of Rape and Rapists

Some rapes are planned, others are spontaneous; some focus on a particular victim, whereas others occur almost as an afterthought during the commission of another crime, such as a burglary. Some rapists commit a single crime, whereas others are multiple offenders; some attack alone, and others engage in group or gang rapes.[81] Some use force to attack their target, others prey upon those who are incapacitated by drugs and alcohol.[82] Because there is no single type of rape or rapist, criminologists have attempted to define and categorize the vast variety of rape situations.

Criminologists now recognize that there are numerous motivations for rape and as a result various types of rapists. One of the best-known attempts to classify the personalities of rapists was made by psychologist A. Nicholas Groth, an expert on classifying and treating sex offenders. According to Groth, every rape encounter contains at least one of these three elements: anger, power, and sadism.[83] Consequently, rapists can be classified according to one of the three dimensions described in Exhibit 10.2. In treating rape offenders, Groth found that about 55 percent were of the power type; about 40 percent, the anger type; and about 5 percent, the sadistic type.[84]

Gang Rape Some research studies estimates that as many as 25 percent or more of rapes involve multiple offenders.[85] There is generally little difference in the demographic characteristics of single- or multiple-victim rapes. However, women who are attacked by multiple offenders are subject to more violence, such as beatings and the use of weapons, and the rapes are more likely to be completed than individual rapes. Gang rape victims are more likely to resist and face injury than those attacked by single offenders. They are more likely to call police, to seek therapy, and to contemplate suicide. Gang rapes then, as might be expected, are more severe in violence and outcome.

Serial Rape Some rapists are one-time offenders, but others engage in multiple or serial rapes. Some serial rapists constantly increase their use of force; others do not. Research by Janet Warren and her associates determined that increasers (about 25 percent of serial rapists) tend to be white males who attack multiple victims who are typically older than the norm. During these attacks, the rapist uses excessive profanity and takes more time than during typical rapes. Increasers have a limited criminal history for other crimes, a fact suggesting that their behavior is focused almost solely on sexual violence.[86]

Some serial rapists commit "blitz rapes," in which they attack their victims without warning, whereas others try to "capture" their victims by striking up a conversation or offering them a ride. Others use personal or professional relationships to gain access to their targets.[87]

Acquaintance Rape Acquaintance rape involves someone known to the victim, including family members and friends. Included within acquaintance rapes are the subcategories of *date rape*, which involves a sexual attack during a courting relationship; statutory rape, in which the victim is underage; and **marital rape**, which is forcible sex between people who are legally married to each other.[88] It is difficult to estimate the ratio between rapes involving strangers and those in which victim and assailant are in some way acquainted because women may be more reluctant to report acts involving acquaintances. By some estimates, about 50 percent of rapes involve acquaintances, a number that is not surprising considering the prevalence of negative attitudes toward women and attitudes that support sexual coercion among some groups of young men.[89] Stranger rapes are typically more violent than acquaintance rapes; attackers are more likely to carry a weapon, threaten the victim, and harm her physically. Stranger rapes may also be less likely to be prosecuted than acquaintance rapes because victims may be more reluctant to recount their ordeal at trial if the attack involved a stranger than if their attacker was someone they knew or had been involved with in an earlier relationship.[90]

Date Rape One disturbing trend of rape involves people who are in some form of courting relationship. There is no single form of date rape. Some occur on first dates, others after a relationship has been developing, and still others occur after the couple has been involved for some time. In long-term or close relationships, the male partner may feel he has invested so much time and money in his partner that he is owed sexual relations or that sexual intimacy is an expression that the involvement is progressing. He may make comparisons to other couples who have dated as long and are sexually active.[91] Some use a variety of strategies to coerce sex, including getting their dates drunk, threatening them with termination of the relationship, threatening to disclose negative information, making them feel guilty, or uttering false promises (i.e., "we'll get engaged") to obtain sex.[92]

Date rape is believed to be frequent on college campuses. It has been estimated that 15 to 30 percent of all college women are victims of rape or attempted rape. A recent (2006) survey of college women found that 27 percent of the sample had experienced unwanted sexual contact ranging from kissing and petting to sexual intercourse.[93]

The actual incidence of date rape may be even higher than surveys indicate, because many victims blame themselves and do not recognize the incident as a rape, saying, for example, "I should have fought back harder" or "I shouldn't have gotten drunk."[94] Victims tend to have histories of excessive drinking and prior sexuality, conditions which may convince them that their intemperate and/or immoderate behavior contributed to their own victimization.[95] Some victims do not report rapes because they do not view their experience as a "real rape," which, they believe, involves a strange man "jumping out of the bushes." Other victims are embarrassed and frightened. Many tell their friends about their rape while refusing to let authorities know what happened; reporting is most common in the most serious cases, for example, when a weapon is used; it is less common when drugs and alcohol are involved.[96]

Marital Rape In 1978 Greta Rideout filed rape charges against her husband John. This Oregon case grabbed headlines because it was the first in which a husband was prosecuted for raping his wife while sharing a residence with her. John was acquitted, and the couple briefly reconciled; later, continued violent episodes culminated in divorce and a jail term for John.[97]

Traditionally, a legally married husband could not be charged with raping his wife; this was referred to as the **marital exemption**. The origin of this legal doctrine can be traced to the sixteenth-century pronouncement of Matthew Hale, England's chief justice, who wrote

> But the husband cannot be guilty of rape committed by himself upon his lawful wife, for by their mutual matrimonial consent and contract the wife hath given up herself in this kind unto the husband which she cannot retract.[98]

However, research indicates that many women are raped each year by their husbands as part of an overall pattern of spousal abuse, and they deserve the protection of the law. Many spousal rapes are accompanied by brutal, sadistic beatings and have little to do with normal sexual interests.[99] Not surprisingly, the marital exemption has undergone significant revision. In 1980, only three states had laws against marital rape; today almost every state recognizes marital rape as a crime.[100] Piercing the marital exemption is not unique to U.S. courts; it has also been abolished in Canada, Israel, Scotland, and New Zealand.[101] However, although marital rape is now recognized, most states do not give wives the same legal protection as they would nonmarried couples, and when courts do recognize marital rape, the perpetrators are sanctioned less harshly than are those accused of nonmarital sexual assaults.[102]

Statutory Rape The term "statutory rape" refers to sexual relations between an underage minor and an adult. Although the sex is not forced or coerced, the law says that young people are incapable of giving informed consent, so the act is legally considered nonconsensual. Typically a state's law will define an age of consent above which there can be no criminal prosecution for sexual relations. Although each state is different, most evaluate the age differences between the parties to determine whether an offense has taken place. For example, Indiana law mandates prosecution of men aged 21 or older who have consensual sex with girls younger than 14. In some states, defendants can claim they mistakenly assumed their victims were above the age of consent, whereas in others, "mistake-of-age" defenses are ignored. An American Bar Association (ABA) survey found that prosecution is often difficult in statutory rape cases because the young victims are reluctant to testify. Often parents have given their blessing to the relationships, and juries are reluctant to convict men involved in consensual sex even with young teenaged girls.[103]

The Causes of Rape

What factors predispose some men to commit rape? Criminologists' responses to this question are almost as varied as the crime itself. However, most explanations can be grouped into a few consistent categories.

Evolutionary, Biological Factors One explanation is that rape may be instinctual, developed over the ages as a means of perpetuating the species. In more primitive times, forcible sexual contact may have helped spread genes and maximize offspring. Some believe that these prehistoric drives remain: males still have a natural sexual drive that encourages them to have intimate relations with as many women as possible.[104] The evolutionary view is that the sexual urge corresponds to the unconscious need to preserve the species by spreading one's genes as widely as possible. Men who are sexually aggressive will have a reproductive edge over their more passive peers.[105]

Male Socialization Some researchers argue that rape is a function of modern male socialization. Some men have been socialized to be aggressive with women and believe that the use of violence or force is legitimate if their sexual advances are rebuffed—that is, "women like to play hard to get and expect to be forced to have sex." Those men who have been socialized to believe that "no means yes" are more likely to be sexually aggressive.[106] The use of sexual violence is aggravated if pro-force socialization is reinforced by peer group members who share similar values.[107]

Diana Russell, a leading expert on sexual violence, suggests that rape is actually not a deviant act but one that conforms to the qualities regarded as masculine in U.S. society.[108] Russell maintains that from an early age boys are taught to be aggressive, forceful, tough, and dominating. Men are taught to dominate at the same time that they are led to believe that women want to be dominated. Russell describes the **virility mystique**—the belief that males must separate their sexual feelings from needs for love, respect, and affection. She believes men are socialized to be the aggressors and expect to be sexually active with many women; consequently, male virginity and sexual inexperience are shameful. Similarly, sexually aggressive women frighten some men and cause them to doubt their own masculinity. Sexual insecurity may lead some men to commit rape to bolster their self-image and masculine identity.[109]

Feminists suggest that as the nation moves toward gender equality there may be an immediate increase in rape rates because of increased threats to male virility and dominance. However, in the long term, gender equality will reduce rape rates because there will be an improved social climate toward women.[110]

Psychological Abnormality Another view is that rapists suffer from some type of personality disorder or mental illness. Research shows that a significant percentage of incarcerated rapists exhibit psychotic tendencies, and many others have hostile, sadistic feelings toward women.[111] A high proportion of serial rapists and repeat sexual offenders exhibit psychopathic personality structures.[112] There is evidence linking rape proclivity with **narcissistic personality disorder**, a pattern of traits and behaviors that indicate infatuation and fixation with one's self to the exclusion of all others and the egotistic and ruthless pursuit of one's gratification, dominance, and ambition.[113]

Social Learning This perspective submits that men learn to commit rapes much as they learn any other behavior. For example, sexual aggression may be learned through interaction with peers who articulate attitudes supportive of sexual violence.[114]

Nicholas Groth found that 40 percent of the rapists he studied were sexually victimized as adolescents.[115] A growing body of literature links personal sexual trauma with the desire to inflict sexual trauma on others.[116] Watching violent or pornographic films featuring women who are beaten, raped, or tortured has been linked to sexually aggressive behavior in men.[117] In one startling case, a 12-year-old Providence, Rhode Island, boy sexually assaulted a 10-year-old girl on a pool table after watching television trial coverage of a case in which a woman was similarly raped (the original incident was depicted in a film, *The Accused*, starring Jodie Foster).[118]

Sexual Motivation Most criminologists believe rape is a violent act that is not sexually motivated. Yet it might be premature to dismiss the sexual motive from all rapes.[119] NCVS data reveal that rape victims tend to be young and that rapists prefer younger, presumably more attractive, victims. Data show an association between the ages of rapists and their victims, indicating that men choose rape targets of approximately the same age as consensual sex partners. And, although younger criminals are usually the most violent, older rapists tend to harm their victims more than younger rapists. This pattern indicates that older criminals may rape for motives of power and control, whereas younger offenders may be seeking sexual gratification and may therefore be less likely to harm their victims.

Rape and the Law

Of all violent crimes, none has created such conflict in the legal system as rape. Even if women choose to report sexual assaults to police, they are often initially reluctant because of the sexist fashion in which rape victims are treated by police, prosecutors, and court personnel and the legal technicalities that authorize invasion of women's privacy when a rape case is tried in court.[120] Police officers may be hesitant to make arrests and testify in court when the alleged assaults do not yield obvious signs of violence or struggle (presumably showing the victim strenuously resisted the attack). However, police and courts are now becoming more sensitive to the plight of rape victims and are just as likely to investigate acquaintance rapes as they are **aggravated rapes** involving multiple offenders, weapons, and victim injuries. In some jurisdictions, the justice system takes all rape cases seriously and does not ignore those in which victim and attacker have had a prior relationship or those that did not involve serious injury.[121]

Proving Rape Proving guilt in a rape case is extremely challenging for prosecutors. Although the law does not recognize it, jurors are sometimes swayed by the insinuation that the rape was victim precipitated; thus the blame is shifted from rapist to victim. To get a conviction, prosecutors must establish that the act was forced and violent and that no question of voluntary compliance exists. They may be reluctant to prosecute cases where they have questions about the victim's moral character or if they believe that the victim's demeanor and attitude (i.e., they were dressed provocatively) will turn off the jury and undermine the chance of conviction.[122] Prosecutors may be more willing to bring charges in interracial rape cases because they know that juries are more likely to believe victims and convict defendants in cases involving interracial rape than in intraracial rapes.[123]

As well, there is always fear that a frightened and traumatized victim may identify the wrong man, which happened in the case of Dennis Maher, a Massachusetts man freed after spending more than 19 years in prison for rapes he did not commit. Though three victims provided eyewitness identification at trial, DNA testing proved that Maher could not have been the rapist.[124]

Consent Rape represents a major legal challenge to the criminal justice system for a number of reasons.[125] One issue involves the concept of consent. It is essential to prove that the attack was forced and that the victim did not give voluntary consent to her attacker. In a sense, the burden of proof is on the victim to show that her character is beyond question and that she in no way encouraged, enticed, or misled the accused rapist. On the other hand, some states, such as California and Illinois, now recognize that once given consent can be withdrawn if a woman changes her mind about sex even after relations have begun. Once she says stop, the act must end or else a rape has occurred. Provisions of California's rape law are set out in Exhibit 10.3.

Proving victim dissent is not a requirement in any other violent crime. For example, robbery victims do not have to prove they did not entice their attackers by flaunting expensive jewelry; yet the defense counsel in a rape case can create reasonable doubt about the woman's credibility. A common defense tactic is to introduce suspicion in the minds of the jury that the woman may have consented to the sexual act and later regretted her decision. Conversely, it is difficult for a prosecuting attorney to establish that a woman's character is so impeccable that the absence of consent is a certainty. Such distinctions are important in rape cases because male jurors may be sympathetic to the accused if the victim is portrayed as unchaste. Referring to the woman as "sexually liberated" or "promiscuous" may be enough to result in exoneration of the accused, even if violence and brutality were used in the attack.[126] When Cassia Spohn and David Holleran studied prosecutors' decisions in rape cases, they found that perception of the victim's character was still a critical factor in their decision to file charges. In cases involving acquaintance rape, prosecutors were reluctant to file charges when the victim's character was questioned—for example, when police reports described the victim as sexually active or engaged in sexually oriented occupations such as "stripper." In stranger cases, prosecutors were more likely to take action if a gun or knife was used. And, even if prosecuted and found guilty in a sexual assault case, punishment is significantly reduced if the victim is believed to have negative personal characteristics such as being a transient, a hitchhiker, alone in a bar, or a drug and alcohol abuser.[127] Spohn and Holleran state that prosecutors are still influenced by perceptions of what constitutes "real rape" and who are "real victims."[128]

EXHIBIT 10.3

California Rape Law

(a) Rape is an act of sexual intercourse accomplished with a person not the spouse of the perpetrator. Among the following circumstances sex is considered to be rape:

(1) Where the victim is incapable, because of a mental disorder or developmental or physical disability, of giving legal consent.

(2) Where sex occurred against a person's will by means of force, violence, duress, menace, or fear of immediate and unlawful bodily injury.

(3) Where a victim is prevented from resisting by any intoxicating or controlled substance.

(4) Where a person is at the time unconscious of the nature of the act.

   (A) Was unconscious or asleep.

   (B) Was not aware that the act occurred.

   (C) Was the victim of the perpetrator's fraud

(5) Where a person submits under the wrongful belief that the person committing the act was their spouse.

(6) Where the act is accomplished against the victim's will by threatening to retaliate in the future.

(7) Where the act is accomplished against the victim's will by threatening to use the authority of a public official to incarcerate, arrest, or deport the victim.

(8) It is considered rape if a man continues to have sex with a woman who originally consented but then changed her mind during the sex act.

Source: California PENAL CODE SECTION 261–269, http://caselaw.lp.findlaw.com/cacodes/pen.html; *In re John Z,* 03 C.D.O.S. 129 (2003).

Reform Because of the difficulty rape victims have in obtaining justice, rape laws have been changing around the country. Efforts for reform include changing the language of statutes, dropping the condition of victim resistance, and changing the requirement of use of force to include the threat of force or injury.[129] A number of states and the federal government have replaced rape laws with the more gender-neutral term "crimes of sexual assault."[130] Sexual assault laws outlaw any type of forcible sex, including homosexual rape.[131]

Most states and the federal government have developed shield laws, which protect women from being questioned about their sexual history unless it directly bears on the case. In some instances these laws are quite restrictive, whereas in others they grant the trial judge considerable discretion to admit prior sexual conduct in evidence if it is deemed relevant for the defense. In an important 1991 case, *Michigan v. Lucas*, the U.S. Supreme Court upheld the validity of shield laws and ruled that excluding evidence of a prior sexual relationship between the parties did not violate the defendant's right to a fair trial.[132]

In addition to requiring evidence that consent was not given, the common law of rape required corroboration that the crime of rape actually took place. This involved the need for independent evidence from police officers, physicians, and witnesses that the accused was actually the person who committed the crime, that sexual penetration took place, and that force was present and consent absent. This requirement shielded rapists from prosecution in cases where the victim delayed reporting the crime or in which physical evidence had been compromised or lost. Corroboration is no longer required except under extraordinary circumstances, such as when the victim is too young to understand the crime, has had a previous sexual relationship with the defendant, or gives a version of events that is improbable and self-contradictory.[133]

The federal government may have given rape victims another source of redress when it passed the Violence Against Women Act in 1994. This statute allows rape victims to sue in federal court on the grounds that sexual violence violates their civil rights; the provisions of the act have so far been upheld by appellate courts.[134]

www To read a report on a victim-oriented approach to dealing with **statutory rape**, go to academic.cengage.com/criminaljustice/siegel.

MURDER AND HOMICIDE

Murder is defined in common law as "the unlawful killing of a human being with malice aforethought."[135] It is the most serious of all common-law crimes and the only one that can still be punished by death. Western society's abhorrence of murderers is illustrated by the fact that there is no statute of limitations in murder cases. Whereas state laws limit prosecution of other crimes to a fixed period, usually 7 to 10 years, accused killers can be brought to justice at any time after their crimes were committed. To legally prove that a murder has taken place, most state jurisdictions require prosecutors to show that the accused maliciously intended to kill the victim. "Express or actual malice" is the state of mind assumed to exist when someone kills another person in the absence of any apparent provocation. "Implied or constructive malice" is considered to exist when a death results from negligent or unthinking behavior. In these cases, even though the perpetrator did not wish to kill the victim, the killing resulted from an inherently dangerous act and therefore is considered murder. An unusual example of this concept is the attempted murder conviction of Ignacio Perea, an AIDS-infected Miami man who kidnapped and raped an 11-year-old boy. Perea was sentenced to up to 25 years in prison when the jury agreed with the prosecutor's contention that the AIDS virus is a deadly weapon.[136]

Degrees of Murder

There are different levels or degrees of homicide.[137] *First-degree murder* occurs when a person kills another after premeditation and deliberation. Premeditation means that the killing was considered beforehand and suggests that it was motivated by more than a simple desire to engage in an act of violence. Deliberation means the killing was planned after careful thought rather than carried out on impulse: "To constitute a deliberate and premeditated killing, the slayer must weigh and consider the question of killing and the reasons for and against such a choice;

having in mind the consequences, he decides to and does kill."[138] The planning implied by this definition need not be a long process; it may be an almost instantaneous decision to take another's life. Also, a killing accompanying a felony, such as robbery or rape, usually constitutes first-degree murder (felony murder).

Second-degree murder requires the killer to have malice aforethought but not premeditation or deliberation. A second-degree murder occurs when a person's wanton disregard for the victim's life and his or her desire to inflict serious bodily harm on the victim, ususally with a weapon, results in the victim's death.

Homicide without malice is called manslaughter and is usually punished by anywhere from 1 to 15 years in prison. *Voluntary* or nonnegligent manslaughter refers to a killing, typically without a weapon, committed in the heat of passion or during a sudden quarrel that provoked violence. Although intent may be present, malice is not. Involuntary or negligent manslaughter refers to a killing that occurs when a person's acts are negligent and without regard for the harm they may cause others. Most involuntary manslaughter cases involve motor vehicle deaths—for example, when a drunk driver kills a pedestrian. However, one can be held criminally liable for the death of another in any instance where disregard of safety kills.

One of the most famous cases illustrating the difference between murder and manslaughter occurred on January 26, 2001, when Diane Whipple, a San Francisco woman, died after two large bull mastiff dogs attacked her in the hallway of her apartment building. The dogs' owners—Marjorie Knoller and her husband Robert Noel—were charged with second-degree murder and involuntary manslaughter, respectively. Knoller faced the more severe charge of second-degree murder because she was present during the attack. After the couple's conviction on March 21, 2002, Judge James Warren overturned the murder conviction of Marjorie Knoller and instituted one of manslaughter. He stated that Knoller could not have known that her two dogs would fatally attack Whipple, and therefore the facts did not support the charge of second-degree murder.[139] Nonetheless, the case involved manslaughter, the judge ruled, because the couple knew the dogs were dangerous and did not exercise the proper precautions to ensure they would not attack people. The prosecution appealed the judge's decision, and in a surprising development, on June 1, 2007, the state Supreme Court supported the prosecution when it ruled that a dog owner who knows the animal is a potential killer and exposes other people to the danger may be found guilty of murder. In a unanimous decision, the court ordered Judge Warren to consider restoring the jury's second-degree murder conviction. The appellate court ruled that Knoller, or any other defendant responsible for unintentional but fatal injuries, can be convicted of murder if they acted with "conscious disregard of the danger to human life." On August 22, 2008, Knoller's conviction was reinstated and she could be resentenced to between 15 years to life.[140]

"Born and Alive" One issue that has received national attention is whether a murder victim can be a fetus that has not yet been delivered; this is referred to as feticide. In some instances, fetal harm involves a mother whose behavior endangers an unborn child; in other cases, feticide results from the harmful action of a third party.

Some states have prosecuted women for endangering or killing their unborn fetuses by their drug or alcohol abuse. Some of these convictions have been overturned because the law applies only to a "human being who has been born and is alive."[141] At least 200 women in 30 states have been arrested and charged in connection with harming (though not necessarily killing) a fetus; appellate courts have almost universally overturned such convictions on the basis that they were without legal merit or were unconstitutional.[142] However, in *Whitner v. State*, the Supreme Court of South Carolina ruled that a woman could be held liable for actions during pregnancy that could affect her viable fetus.[143] In holding that a fetus is a "viable person," the court opened the door for a potential homicide prosecution if a mother's action resulted in fetal death.

State laws more commonly allow prosecutions for murder when a third party's actions kill a fetus. Four states (Illinois, Missouri, South Dakota, and West Virginia) extend wrongful death action to the death of any fetus, whereas the remaining states require that the fetus be viable. A viable fetus is able to live outside the mother's body; therefore, the law extends the definition of murder to a fetus that is born alive but dies afterward due to injuries sustained in utero.[144] In a Texas case, a man was convicted of manslaughter in the death of a baby who was delivered prematurely after he caused an auto accident while intoxicated. It was one of the first cases to hold that a person can be held criminally liable for harming an unborn child.[145]

The Nature and Extent of Murder

It is possible to track U.S. murder rate trends from 1900 to the present with the aid of coroners' reports and UCR data. The murder rate peaked in 1933, a time of high unemployment and lawlessness, and then fell until 1958. The homicide rate doubled from the mid-1960s to the late 1970s and then peaked at 10.2 per 100,000 population in 1980. In 2007, almost 17,000 murders were reported to police, a rate of about 5.5 per 100,000 population, half the 1980 level. The murder rate declined 2.7 percent in 2007, reversing a two-year increase.

connections

Is it possible that the recent decline in the murder rate is linked to a relatively mundane factor such as improved health care? Read about Anthony Harris's study on the effects of improved health care on the murder rate in The Criminological Enterprise feature "Explaining Crime Trends" in Chapter 2.

What else do official crime statistics tell us about murder today? Murder tends to be an urban crime. More than half of the homicides occur in cities with a population of 100,000 or more.[146] Almost one-quarter of homicides occur in cities with a population of more than 1 million. Not surprisingly, murder in urban areas is more commonly crime- and gang-related than in less populated areas. Large cities are much more commonly the site of drug-related killings, gang-related murders, and

relatively less likely the location of family-related homicides, including murders of intimates.

Some murders involve very young children, a crime referred to as infanticide (killing older children is called filicide), and others involve senior citizens, referred to as eldercide.[147] The younger the child, the greater the risk of infanticide. At the opposite end of the age spectrum, less than 5 percent of all homicides involve people age 65 or older.

People arrested on murder charges tend to be males (about 90 percent); males are also much more likely to be murder victims. Approximately one-third of murder victims and almost half the offenders are under the age of 25. For both victims and offenders, the rate per 100,000 peaks in the 18- to 24-year-old age group.[148]

Slightly less than half of all victims are African Americans and slightly less than half are white. African Americans are disproportionately represented as both homicide victims and offenders. They are six times more likely to be victimized and eight times more likely to commit homicide than are whites. Murder, like rape, tends to be an intraracial crime; about 90 percent of victims are slain by members of their own race. Similarly, people arrested for murder are generally young (under 35) and male (about 90 percent), and ex-offenders; a significant portion of murderers had prior criminal records.

Murderers typically have a long involvement in crime; few people begin a criminal career by killing someone. When Philip Cook, Jens Ludwig, and Anthony Braga examined all arrests and felony convictions in Illinois between 1990 and 2001, they found that people arrested for homicide were significantly more likely to have been in trouble with the law than the average citizen (that is, the rest of the Illinois population): 42 percent of the murderers had at least 1 prior felony conviction compared with 4 percent of the general population; 71 percent had experienced an arrest compared with 18 percent of average citizens.[149]

Today few would deny that some relationship exists between social and ecological factors and murder. The following section explores some of the more important issues related to these factors.

Murderous Relations

One factor that has received a great deal of attention from criminologists is the relationship between the murderer and the victim.[150] Some murders are expressive, motivated by rage or anger; others are instrumental, the outcome of a botched robbery or drug deal. Murderous relations are also shaped by gender: males more likely to kill others of similar social standing in more public contexts; women kill family members and intimate partners in private locations.[151]

Spousal Relations The rate of homicide among cohabiting couples has declined significantly during the past two decades, a finding that can be attributed to the shift away from marriage in modern society. There are, however, significant gender differences in homicide trends among unmarried people. The number of

Figure 10.2 Murder Transactions

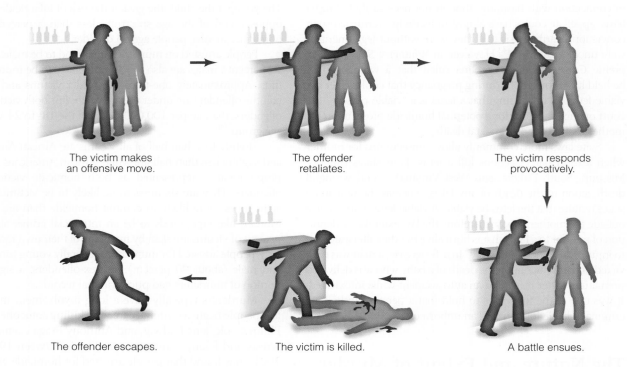

The victim makes an offensive move.

The offender retaliates.

The victim responds provocatively.

A battle ensues.

The victim is killed.

The offender escapes.

unmarried men killed by their partners has declined (mirroring the overall trend in the murder rate), but the number of women killed by the men they live with has increased dramatically.

It is possible that men kill their spouses or partners because they fear losing control and power. Because unmarried people who live together have a legally and socially more open relationship, males in such relationships may be more likely to feel loss of control and exert their power with violence.[152]

Research indicates that most females who kill their mates do so after suffering repeated violent attacks.[153] Perhaps the number of males killed by their partners has declined because alternatives to abusive relationships, such as battered women's shelters, are becoming more prevalent around the United States. Regions that provide greater social support for battered women and that have passed legislation to protect abuse victims also have lower rates of female-perpetrated homicide.[154]

Some people kill their mates because they find themselves involved in a *love triangle*.[155] Interestingly, women who kill out of jealousy aim their aggression at their partners; in contrast, men are more likely to kill their mates' suitors. Love triangles tend to become lethal when the offenders believe they have been lied to or betrayed. Lethal violence is more common when (a) the rival initiated the affair, (b) the killer knew the spouse was already in a steady relationship outside the marriage, and (c) the killer was repeatedly lied to or betrayed.[156]

Personal Relations Most murders occur among people who are acquainted. Although on the surface the killing might have seemed senseless, it often is the result of a long-simmering dispute motivated by revenge, dispute resolution, jealousy, drug deals, racial bias, or threats to identity or status.[157] For example, a prior act of violence, motivated by profit or greed, may generate revenge killing, such as when a buyer robs his dealer during a drug transaction.

How do these murderous relations develop between two people who may have had little prior conflict? In a classic study, David Luckenbill studied *murder transactions* to determine whether particular patterns of behavior are common between the killer and the victim.[158] He found that many homicides follow a sequential pattern. First, the victim makes what the offender considers an offensive move. The offender typically retaliates verbally or physically. An agreement to end things violently is forged with the victim's provocative response. The battle ensues, leaving the victim dead or dying. The offender's escape is shaped by his or her relationship to the victim or the reaction of the audience, if any (Figure 10.2).

Stranger Relations While in the past people tended to kill someone they knew or were related to, over the past decade the number of stranger homicides has increased. Today more than half of murderers are strangers to their victims, a significant increase from years past. Stranger homicides occur most often as felony murders during rapes, robberies, and burglaries. Others are random acts of urban violence that fuel public fear. For example, a homeowner tells a motorist to move his car because it is blocking the driveway, an argument ensues, and the owner gets a pistol and kills the motorist; or consider a young boy who kills a store manager because, he says, "something came into my head to hurt the lady."[159]

Why do stranger killings now make up a greater percentage of all murders than in years past? It is possible that tough new sentencing laws, such as the three strikes laws used in California and other habitual criminal statutes, are responsible. These laws mandate that a "three-time loser" be given a life sentence if convicted of multiple felonies. It is possible, as Tomislav Kovandzic and his associates found, that these laws encourage criminals to kill while committing burglaries and robberies. Why hesitate to kill now because if they are caught they will receive a life sentence anyway.[160]

Student Relations Sadly, violence in schools has become commonplace. About 90 percent of all schools with 1,000 or more students experience a violent incident each year.[161] Violence and bullying have become routine; surveys indicate that more than 16 percent of U.S. schoolchildren have been bullied by other students during the current school term, and approximately 30 percent of 6th- through 10th-grade students reported being involved in some aspect of moderate to frequent bullying, either as a bully, the target of bullying, or both.[162] Sometimes violence and bullying can escalate into a school shooting, such as the Columbine High School massacre, which resulted in the deaths of 15 people.

While relatively rare, these incidents may be expected because up to 10 percent of students report bringing weapons to school on a regular basis.[163] Many of these kids have a history of being abused and bullied; many perceive a lack of support from peers, parents, and teachers.[164] Kids who have been the victims of crime themselves and who hang with peers who carry weapons are the ones most likely to bring guns to school.[165] Troubled kids with little social support but carrying deadly weapons make for an explosive situation.

Research shows that most shooting incidents occur around the start of the school day, the lunch period, or the end of the school day.[166] In most of the shootings (55 percent), a note, threat, or other action indicating risk for violence occurred prior to the event. Shooters were also likely to have expressed some form of suicidal behavior and to have been bullied by their peers.[167]

Serial Murder

For 31 years, Wichita, Kansas's notorious serial killer, known as BTK (for Bind, Torture, Kill), eluded the police. During his murder spree, the BTK killer sent taunting letters and packages to the police and the media. Suddenly, after committing gruesome killings in the 1970s he went underground and disappeared from view. After 25 years of silence he renewed his communications with a local news station. His last communication contained a computer disk, which was traced to 59-year-old Dennis Rader after FBI analysis of deleted data on the disk. Rader later confessed to ten murders in an effort to escape the death penalty.

Criminologists consider a serial killer, such as Rader, to be a person who kills three or more persons in three or more separate events. In between the murders, the serial killer reverts to his normal lifestyle. Rader worked as a supervisor of the Compliance Department at Park City, Kansas, which put him in charge of animal control, housing problems, zoning, general permit enforcement, and a variety of nuisance cases. A married father of two, he served as a county commissioner, a Cub Scout leader, and a member of Christ Lutheran Church where he had been elected president of the Congregation Council. Rader's biography and personal life give few clues to his murderous path, which is perhaps why it took more than three decades to track him down.[168]

Types of Serial Killers There are different types of serial killers. Some wander the countryside killing at random; others hide themselves in a single locale and lure victims to their death.[169] Theodore Bundy, convicted killer of three young women and suspected killer of many others, roamed the country in the 1970s, killing as he went. Wayne Gacy, during the same period, killed more than 30 boys and young men without leaving Chicago.

Some serial killers are sadists who gain satisfaction from torturing and killing.[170] Sadists wish to gain complete control over their victims through humiliation, shame, enslavement, and terror. Dr. Michael Swango, who is suspected of killing between 35 and 60 patients, wrote in his diary of the pleasure he obtained from murder. He wrote of the "sweet, husky, close smell of indoor homicide" and how murders were "the only way I have of reminding myself that I'm still alive."[171]

While Swango obtained pleasure from killing, other health care workers who have committed serial murder rationalize their behavior by thinking they are helping patients end their suffering when they put them to death. Harold Frederick Shipman, Britain's most notorious serial killer, was a general practitioner convicted of 15 murders most involving elderly patients. After he committed suicide in 2004, further investigation found that he actually killed at least 218 patients and perhaps even more.[172]

Another type, the psychopathic killer, is motivated by a character disorder that causes an inability to experience shame, guilt, sorrow, or other normal human emotions; these murderers are concerned solely with their own needs and passions.

Serial murder experts James Alan Fox and Jack Levin have developed the following typology of serial killer motivations:

▪ *Thrill killers* strive for either sexual sadism or dominance. This is the most common form of serial murderer.

Serial killers often resume a "normal" identity in between their murderous activities. Sometimes their occupations and/or professions give them access to the victims they prefer. Charles Cullen, the so-called "Angel of Death," was a male nurse who worked for more than 16 years in health care institutions, a position that gave him access to the 30–40 patients he murdered. After his arrest in 2003, Cullen claimed he was being "merciful" and was merely trying to end their suffering.

- *Mission killers* want to reform the world or have a vision that drives them to kill.
- *Expedience killers* are out for profit or want to protect themselves from a perceived threat.[173]

Female Serial Killers An estimated 10 to 15 percent of serial killers are women. A study by criminologists Belea Keeney and Kathleen Heide investigated the characteristics of a sample of 14 female serial killers and found some striking differences between the way male and female killers carried out their crimes.[174] Males were much more likely than females to use extreme violence and torture. Whereas males used a "hands-on" approach, including beating, bludgeoning, and strangling their victims, females were more likely to poison or smother their victims. Men tracked or stalked their victims, but women were more likely to lure victims to their death. There were also gender-based personality and behavior characteristics. Female killers, somewhat older than their male counterparts, abused both alcohol and drugs; males were not likely to be substance abusers. Women were diagnosed as having histrionic, manic-depressive, borderline, dissociative, and antisocial personality disorders; men were more often diagnosed as having antisocial personalities. Aileen Wuornos, executed for killing seven men, was diagnosed with a severe psychopathic personality, a product most likely of her horrific childhood marred by beatings, alcoholism, rape, incest, and prostitution.[175]

The profile of the female serial killer that emerges is a person who smothers or poisons someone she knows. During childhood she suffered from an abusive relationship in a disrupted family. Female killers' education levels are below average, and if they hold jobs, they are in low-status positions.

Why Do Serial Killers Kill? The cause of serial murder eludes criminologists. Such disparate factors as mental illness, sexual frustration, neurological damage, child abuse and neglect, smothering relationships with mothers (David Berkowitz, the notorious Son of Sam, slept in his parents' bed until he was 10), and childhood anxiety are suspected. Most experts view serial killers as sociopaths who from early childhood demonstrate bizarre behavior, such as torturing animals. Some are sadists who enjoy the sexual thrill of murdering and who are both pathological and destructive narcissists.[176]

This behavior extends to the pleasure they reap from killing, their ability to ignore or enjoy their victims' suffering, and their propensity for basking in the media limelight when apprehended for their crimes. Killing provides a way to fill their emotional hunger and reduce their anxiety levels.[177] Wayne Henley, Jr., who along with Dean Corill killed 27 boys in Houston, offered to help prosecutors find the bodies of additional victims so he could break Chicago killer Wayne Gacy's record of 33 murders.[178]

According to experts Fox and Levin, serial killers enjoy the thrill, the sexual gratification, and the dominance they achieve over the lives of their victims. The serial killer rarely uses a gun because this method is too quick and would deprive him of his greatest pleasure, exalting in his victim's suffering. Levin and Fox dispute the notion that serial killers have some form of biological or psychological problems, such as genetic anomalies or schizophrenia. Even the most sadistic serial murderers are not mentally ill or driven by delusions or hallucinations. Instead, they typically exhibit a sociopathic personality that deprives them of pangs of conscience or guilt to guide their behavior. Serial killers are not insane, they claim, but "more cruel than crazy."[179]

Controlling Serial Killers Serial killers come from diverse backgrounds. To date, law enforcement officials have been at a loss to control random killers who leave few clues, constantly move, and have little connection to their victims. Catching serial killers is often a matter of luck. To help local law enforcement officials, the FBI has developed a profiling system to identify potential suspects. Because serial killers often use the same patterns in each attack they leave a signature that might help in their capture.[180]

In addition, the Justice Department's Violent Criminal Apprehension Program (VICAP), a computerized information service, gathers information and matches offense characteristics on violent crimes around the country.[181] This program links crimes to determine if they are the product of a single culprit.

Mass Murderers

In contrast to serial killings, **mass murder** involves the killing of four or more victims by one or a few assailants within a single event.[182] The murderous incident can last but a few minutes or as long as several hours. In order to qualify as a mass murder, the incident must be carried out by one or a few offenders. Highly organized or institutionalized killings (i.e., as war crimes and large-scale acts of political terrorism, as well as certain acts of highly organized crime rings) while atrocious are not considered mass murder and are motivated by a totally different set of factors. The 2004 brutal and senseless Xbox murders, which involved the killing of six people in Florida by a gang of four men out to avenge the theft of clothes and video games, is a mass murder (see Chapter 9); the genocide of Hitler's Third Reich or a terrorist attack is not.

Mass murderers engage in a single, uncontrollable outburst called "simultaneous killing." Charles Whitman killed 14 people and wounded 30 others from atop the 307-foot tower on the University of Texas campus on August 1, 1966; James Huberty killed 21 people in a McDonald's restaurant in San Ysidro, California, on July 18, 1984; George Hennard, on October 16, 1991, killed 22 people in a Killeen, Texas, cafeteria before committing suicide as police closed in; and Seung-Hui Cho killed 32 people and wounded 25 at Virginia Tech on April 16, 2007.

Fox and Levin define four types of mass murderers:

1. *Revenge killers* seek to get even with individuals or society at large. Their typical target is an estranged wife and "her" children or an employer and "his" employees.

2. *Love killers* are motivated by a warped sense of devotion. They are often despondent people who commit suicide and take others, such as a wife and children, with them.

3. *Profit killers* are usually trying to cover up a crime, eliminate witnesses, and carry out a criminal conspiracy.

4. *Terrorist killers* are trying to send a message. Gang killings tell rivals to watch out; cult killers may actually leave a message behind to warn society about impending doom.[183]

While it often appears that our society has spawned the mass murder, a recent study by Grant Duwe shows that more than 900 mass killings took place between 1900 and 1999 and that mass killings were nearly as common during the 1920s and 1930s as they are today. More of the earlier incidents involved *familicide* (i.e., killing of one's family) and killers were more likely to be older and more suicidal than they are today. The most significant difference between contemporary mass murders and those in the past: more killers use guns today and more incidents involve drug trafficking.[184]

Spree Killers Spree killers engage in a rampage of violence taking place over a period of days or weeks. Unlike mass murderers, their killing is not confined to a single outburst, and unlike serial killers, they do not return to their "normal" identities in between killings. The most notorious spree killing to date occurred in October 2002, in the Washington, D.C., area.[185] John Lee Malvo, 17, a Jamaican citizen, and his traveling companion John Allen Muhammad, 41, an Army veteran with an expert's rating in marksmanship, went on a rampage that left more than 10 people dead.

Some spree killers target a specific group or class. John Paul Franklin targeted mixed race couples, African Americans, and Jews, committing more than 20 murders in 12 states in an effort to instigate a race war (Franklin also shot and paralyzed *Hustler*

publisher Larry Flynt because he published pictures of interracial sex).[186] Others, like the D.C. snipers Malvo and Muhammed, kill randomly and do not seek out a specific class of victim; their targets included the young and old, African Americans and whites, men and women.[187]

WWWW To read about some of the more publicized **school shootings**, go to academic.cengage.com/criminaljustice/siegel.

ASSAULT AND BATTERY

Although many people mistakenly believe the term "assault and battery" refers to a single act, they are actually two separate crimes. *Battery* requires offensive touching, such as slapping, hitting, or punching a victim. *Assault* requires no actual touching but involves either attempted battery or intentionally frightening the victim by word or deed. Although common law originally intended these twin crimes to be misdemeanors, most jurisdictions now upgrade them to felonies either when a weapon is used or when they occur during the commission of a felony (for example, when a person is assaulted during a robbery). In the UCR, the FBI defines serious assault, or aggravated assault, as "an unlawful attack by one person upon another for the purpose of inflicting severe or aggravated bodily injury"; this definition is similar to the one used in most state jurisdictions.[188]

Under common law, battery required bodily injury, such as broken limbs or wounds. However, under modern law, an assault and battery occurs if the victim suffers a temporarily painful blow, even if no injury results. Battery can also involve offensive touching, such as if a man kisses a woman against her will or puts his hands on her body.

Nature and Extent of Assault

The pattern of criminal assault is similar to that of homicide; one could say that the only difference between the two is that the victim survives.[189] Assaults may be common in our society simply because of common life stresses. Motorists who assault each other have become such a familiar occurrence that the term road rage has been coined. There have even been frequent incidents of violent assault among frustrated passengers who lose control while traveling.

Every citizen is bound by the law of assault, even police officers. Excessive use of force can result in criminal charges being filed even if it occurs while police officers are arresting a dangerous felony suspect. Only the minimum amount of force needed to subdue the suspect is allowed by law, and if police use more aggressive tactics than required, they may find themselves the target of criminal charges and civil lawsuits that can run into the millions of dollars.[190]

The FBI records about 860,000 assaults each year, a rate of about 295 per 100,000 inhabitants. Like other violent crimes, the number of assaults has been in decline, down about 25 percent in the past decade. People arrested for assault and those

Figure 10.3 Nonfatal Firearm-Related Violent Crimes

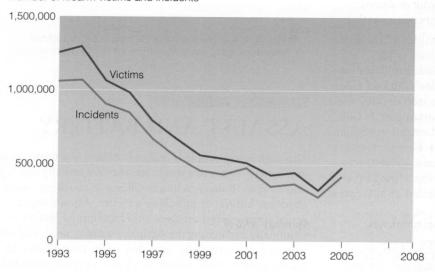

Number of firearm victims and incidents

Source: U.S. Department of Justice, www.ojp.usdoj.gov/bjs/glance/firearmnonfatalno.htm (accessed July 24, 2007).

identified by victims are usually young, male (about 80 percent), and white, although the number of African Americans arrested for assault (about one-third of the total) is disproportionate to their representation in the population. Assault victims tend to be male, but females also face a significant danger. Assault rates are highest in urban areas, during summer, and in southern and western regions. The most common weapons used in assaults are blunt instruments and hands and feet.

The NCVS indicates that only about half of all serious assaults are reported to the police. The NCVS indicates that the number of assault victimizations has been in steep decline, dropping more than 50 percent during the past decade; even weapon-related assaults have dropped sharply (Figure 10.3).

Assault in the Home

Violent attacks in the home are one of the most frightening types of assault. Criminologists recognize that intrafamily violence is an enduring social problem in the United States and abroad.

The UN's World Health Organization (WHO) found that around the world, women often face the greatest risk for violence in their own homes and in familiar settings. Almost half the women who die due to homicide are killed by their current or former husbands or boyfriends; in some countries about 70 percent of all female deaths are domestic homicides. It is possible that nearly one in four women will experience sexual violence by an intimate partner in their lifetime, and most of these are subjected to multiple acts of violence over extended periods of time. In addition to physical abuse, a third to over half of these cases are accompanied by sexual violence; in some countries, up to one-third of adolescent girls report forced

sexual initiation.[191] The WHO report found that the percentage of women assaulted by a spouse or intimate partner varied considerably around the world: less than 3 percent in the United States, Canada, and Australia and up to 38 percent of the married women in the Republic of Korea and 52 percent of Palestinian women on the West Bank and Gaza Strip.[192] In many places assaults and even murders occur because men believe that their partners have been defiled sexually, either through rape or sex outside of marriage. In some societies the only way to cleanse the family honor is by killing the offending female. In Alexandria, Egypt, for example, 47 percent of the women who were killed by a relative were murdered after they had been raped.[193]

Child Abuse One area of intrafamily violence that has received a great deal of media attention is child abuse. This term describes any physical or emotional trauma to a child for which no reasonable explanation, such as an accident or ordinary disciplinary practices, can be found.[194]

Child abuse can result from actual physical beatings administered to a child by hands, feet, weapons, belts, sticks, burning, and so on. Another form of abuse results from neglect—not providing a child with the care and shelter to which he or she is entitled.

Yearly national surveys conducted by the Department of Health and Human Services show that while child abuse rates are in decline the problem is still significant: child protective services (CPS) agencies throughout the United States receive nearly 2 million reports of suspected child abuse or neglect per year. Of these about two-thirds are considered unfounded, which leaves an estimated 900,000 children across the country who are victims of abuse or neglect, or about 12 out of every 1,000 children.[195] The National Child Abuse and Neglect Data System (NCANDS) reported an estimated 1,400 child fatalities occur each year or about 2 children per 100,000 children in the general population.[196] According to David Finkelor and his colleagues there are a variety of reasons for the decline, but the easy availability of psychotropic drugs, which may relieve parental anger and stress, might be the greatest contributor to the decline in reported child abuse.[197]

Causes of Child Abuse Why do parents physically assault their children? Such maltreatment is a highly complex problem with neither a single cause nor a readily available solution. It cuts across ethnic, religious, and socioeconomic lines. Abusive parents cannot be categorized by sex, age, or educational level; they come from all walks of life.[198]

A number of factors have been commonly linked to abuse and neglect:

- Family violence seems to be perpetuated from one generation to another within families. The behavior of abusive parents can often be traced to negative experiences in their own childhood—physical abuse, lack of love, emotional neglect, incest, and so on.

- Blended families, which include children living with an unrelated adult such as a stepparent or another unrelated co-resident, have also been linked to abuse. Children who live with a mother's boyfriend are at much greater risk for abuse than children living with two genetic parents. Some stepparents do not have strong emotional ties to their nongenetic children, nor do they reap emotional benefits from the parent–child relationship.[199]

- Parents may also become abusive if they are isolated from friends, neighbors, or relatives who can help in times of crisis. Potentially abusive parents are often alienated from society; they have carried the concept of the shrinking nuclear family to its most extreme form and are cut off from ties of kinship and contact with other people in the neighborhood.[200]

Sexual Abuse Another aspect of the abuse syndrome is sexual abuse—the exploitation of children through rape, incest, and molestation by parents or other adults. It is difficult to estimate the incidence of sexual abuse, but a number of attempts have been made to gauge the extent of the problem. In a classic study, Diana Russell's survey of women in the San Francisco area found that 38 percent had experienced intra- or extrafamilial sexual abuse by the time they reached age 18.[201] Others have estimated that at least 20 percent of females suffer some form of sexual violence; that is, at least one in five girls suffer sexual abuse.[202]

Although sexual abuse is still prevalent, the number of reported cases has been in a significant decline.[203] However, this trend must be interpreted with caution. While it is possible that the actual number of cases is truly in decline because of the effectiveness of prevention programs, increased prosecution, and public awareness campaigns, declines might be the result of more cases being overlooked because of (a) increased evidentiary requirements to substantiate cases, (b) increased caseworker caution due to new legal rights for caregivers, and (c) increasing limitations on the types of cases that agencies accept for investigation.[204]

Sexual abuse is of particular concern because children who have been abused experience a long list of symptoms, including fear, posttraumatic stress disorder, behavior problems, sexualized behavior, and poor self-esteem.[205] Women who were abused as children are also at greater risk to be reabused as adults than those who avoided childhood victimization.[206] The amount of force used during the abuse, its duration, and its frequency are all related to the extent of the long-term effects and the length of time needed for recovery.

Parental Abuse Parents are sometimes the target of abuse from their own children. Research conducted by Arina Ulman and Murray Straus found:

- The younger the child, the higher the rate of child-to-parent violence (CPV).

- At all ages, more children were violent to mothers than to fathers.

- Both boys and girls hit mothers more often than fathers.

- At all ages, slightly more boys than girls hit parents.

Ulman and Straus found that child-to-parent violence was associated with some form of violence by parents, which could either be husband-to-wife, wife-to-husband, corporal punishment of children, or physical abuse. They suggest that if the use of physical punishment could be eliminated or curtailed, then child-to-parent violence would similarly decline.[207]

Spousal Abuse Spousal abuse has occurred throughout recorded history. Roman men had the legal right to beat their wives for minor acts such as attending public games without permission, drinking wine, or walking outdoors with their faces uncovered.[208] More serious transgressions, such as adultery, were punishable by death. During the later stages of the Roman Empire, the practice of wife beating abated, and by the fourth century, excessive violence on the part of husband or wife was grounds for divorce.[209] During the early Middle Ages, there was a separation of love and marriage.[210] The ideal woman was protected, cherished, and loved from afar. In contrast, the wife, with whom marriage had been arranged by family ties, was guarded jealously and could be punished severely for violating her duties. A husband was expected to beat his wife for "misbehaviors" and might himself be punished by neighbors if he failed to do so.[211]

Through the later Middle Ages and into modern times (from 1400 to 1900), there was little community objection to a man using force against his wife as long as the assault did not exceed certain limits, usually construed as death or disfigurement. By the mid-nineteenth century, severe wife beating fell into disfavor, and accused wife beaters were subject to public ridicule. Nonetheless, limited chastisement was still the rule. By the close of the nineteenth century, England and the United States outlawed wife beating. Yet the long history of husbands' domination of their wives made physical coercion hard to control. Until recent times, the subordinate position of women in the family was believed to give husbands the legal and moral obligation to manage their wives' behavior. Even after World War II, English courts found physical assault a reasonable punishment for a wife who had disobeyed her husband.[212] These ideas form the foundation of men's traditional physical control of women and have led to severe cases of spousal assault.

The Nature and Extent of Spousal Abuse It is difficult to estimate how widespread spousal abuse is today; however, some statistics indicate the extent of the problem. In their classic study of family violence, Richard Gelles and Murray Straus found that 16 percent of surveyed families had experienced husband–wife

Factors That Predict Spousal Abuse

- **Presence of alcohol.** Excessive alcohol use may turn otherwise docile husbands into wife abusers.

- **Access to weapon.** Perpetrator's access to a gun and previous threat with a weapon may lead to abuse.

- **Stepchild in the home.** Having a stepchild living in the home may provoke abuse because the parent may have a more limited bond to the child.

- **Estrangement.** Especially from a controlling partner and subsequent involvement with another partner.

- **Hostility toward dependency.** Some husbands who appear docile and passive may resent their dependence on their wives and react with rage and violence; this reaction has been linked to sexual inadequacy.

- **Excessive brooding.** Obsession with a wife's behavior, however trivial, can result in violent assaults.

- **Social learning.** Some males believe society approves of spouse or mate abuse and use these beliefs to justify their violent behavior. Peer support helps shape their attitudes and behaviors.

- **Socioeconomic factors.** Men who fail as providers and are under economic stress may take their frustrations out on their wives.

- **Flashes of anger.** Research shows that a significant amount of family violence results from a sudden burst of anger after a verbal dispute.

- **Military service.** Spouse abuse among men who have served in the military service is extremely high. Similarly, those serving in the military are more likely to assault their wives than civilian husbands. The reasons for this phenomenon may be the violence promoted by military training and the close proximity in which military families live to one another.

- **Having been battered children.** Husbands who assault their wives were generally battered as children.

- **Unpredictability.** Batterers are unpredictable, unable to be influenced by their wives, and impossible to prevent from battering once an argument has begun.

Sources: Christine Sellers, John Cochran, and Kathryn Branch, "Social Learning Theory and Partner Violence: A Research Note," *Deviant Behavior* 26 (2005) 379–395; Jacquelyn Campbell, Daniel Webster, Jane Koziol-McLain, Carolyn Block, Doris Campbell, Mary Ann Curry, Faye Gary, Nancy Glass, Judith McFarlane, Carolyn Sachs, Phyllis Sharps, Yvonne Ulrich, Susan Wilt, Jennifer Manganello, Xiao Xu, Janet Schollenberger, Victoria Frye, and Kathryn Laughon, "Risk Factors for Femicide in Abusive Relationships: Results from a Multisite Case Control Study," *American Journal of Public Health* 93 (2003): 1,089–1,097; Neil Jacobson and John Mordechai Gottman, *When Men Batter Women: New Insights into Ending Abusive Relationships* (New York: Simon & Schuster, 1998); Kenneth Leonard and Brian Quigley, "Drinking and Marital Aggression in Newlyweds: An Event-Based Analysis of Drinking and the Occurrence of Husband Marital Aggression," *Journal of Studies on Alcohol* 60 (1999): 537–541; Graeme Newman, *Understanding Violence* (New York: Lippincott, 1979).

assaults.[213] In police departments around the country, 60 to 70 percent of evening calls involve domestic disputes.

Nor is violence restricted to marriage: national surveys indicate that between 20 and 40 percent of females experience violence while dating.[214] According to a survey conducted by researchers from the Harvard School of Public Health, one in five high school girls suffered sexual or physical abuse from a boyfriend. The study found that teen girls who had been abused by their boyfriends also were much more likely to use drugs or alcohol, to have unsafe sex, and to acquire eating disorders, among other social problems.[215]

Some of the personal attributes and characteristics of spouse abusers and abusive situations are listed in Exhibit 10.4.

www To read the study on high school dating abuse, go to the **Harvard School of Public Health** website via academic .cengage.com/criminaljustice/siegel.

ROBBERY

The common-law definition of *robbery* (and the one used by the FBI) is "the taking or attempting to take anything of value from the care, custody or control of a person or persons by force or threat of force or violence and/or by putting the victim in fear."[216] A robbery is considered a violent crime because it involves the use of force to obtain money or goods. Robbery is punished severely because the victim's life is put in jeopardy. In fact, the severity of punishment is based on the amount of force used during the crime, not the value of the items taken.

The FBI records almost 50,000 robberies each year, a rate of about 140 per 100,000 population. As with most other violent crimes, there has been a significant reduction in the robbery rate during the past decade; the robbery rate is down almost 40 percent since 1994. However, both the NCVS and UCR recorded significant increases in robbery between 2004 and 2006. However, in 2007 robbery rates declined once again (−1.2 percent). The ecological pattern for robbery is similar to that of other violent crimes, with one significant exception: Northeastern states by far have the highest robbery rate.

Robbery is considered a very serious crime because it can lead to murder. Here, a surveillance photo shows a masked gunman pointing his weapon inside the Illinois Service Federal Savings and Loan during a robbery on May 22, 2007. The robbery of the Chicago South Side bank exploded into gunfire, leaving a teller dead and two other people seriously wounded.

Types of Robberies

■ *Robbery in an open area.* These robberies include street muggings, purse snatchings, and other attacks. Street robberies are the most common type, especially in urban areas where this type of robbery constitutes about 60 percent of reported totals. Street robbery is most closely associated with mugging or yoking, which refers to grabbing victims from behind and threatening them with a weapon. Street muggers often target unsavory characters such as drug dealers or pimps who carry large amounts of cash because these victims would find it awkward to report the crime to the police. Most commit their robberies within a short distance from their homes.

■ *Commercial robbery.* This type of robbery occurs in businesses ranging from banks to liquor stores. Banks are among the most difficult targets to rob, usually because they have more personnel and a higher level of security.

■ *Robbery on private premises.* This type of robbery involves breaking into people's homes. FBI records indicate that this type of robbery accounts for about 10 percent of all offenses.

■ *Robbery after a short, preliminary association.* This type of robbery comes after a chance meeting—in a bar, at a party, or after a sexual encounter.

■ *Robbery after a longer association between victim and offender.* An example of this type of robbery would be an intimate acquaintance robbing his paramour and then fleeing the jurisdiction.

■ *Carjacking.* This is a completed or attempted theft of a motor vehicle by force or threat of force.

Sources: Katie Willis, "Armed Robbery: Who Commits It and Why?" (Canberra: Australian Institute of Criminology, 2006); Patsy Klaus, *Carjackings in the United States, 1992–96* (Washington, DC: Bureau of Justice Statistics, 1999); Peter J. van Koppen and Robert Jansen, "The Road to the Robbery: Travel Patterns in Commercial Robberies," *British Journal of Criminology* 38 (1998): 230–247.

Types of Robbers

■ *Professional robbers.* These robbers have a long-term commitment to crime as a source of livelihood. This type of robber plans and organizes crimes prior to committing them and seeks money to support a hedonistic lifestyle. Some professionals are exclusively robbers, whereas others engage in additional types of crimes. Professionals are committed to robbing because it is direct, fast, and profitable. They hold no other steady job and plan three or four "big scores" a year to support themselves. Planning and skill are the trademarks of the professional robber, who usually operates in groups with assigned roles. Professionals usually steal large amounts from commercial establishments. After a score, they may stop for a few weeks until "things cool off."

■ *Opportunist robbers.* These robbers steal to obtain small amounts of money when an accessible target presents itself. They are not committed to robbery but will steal from cab drivers, drunks, the elderly, and other vulnerable persons if they need some extra spending money. Opportunists are usually teens and gang members who do not plan their crimes. Although they operate within the milieu of the juvenile gang, they are seldom organized and spend little time discussing weapon use, getaway plans, or other strategies.

■ *Addict robbers.* These people steal to support their drug habits. They have a low commitment to robbery because of its danger but a high commitment to theft because it supplies needed funds. The addict is less likely to plan crime or use weapons than the professional robber but is more cautious than the opportunist. Addicts choose targets that present minimal risk; however, when desperate for funds, they are sometimes careless in selecting the victim and executing the crime. They rarely think in terms of the big score; they just want enough money to get their next fix.

■ *Alcoholic robbers.* These people steal for reasons related to their excessive consumption of alcohol. Alcoholic robbers steal (a) when, in a disoriented state, they attempt to get some money to buy liquor or (b) when their condition makes them unemployable and they need funds. Alcoholic robbers have no real commitment to robbery as a way of life. They plan their crimes randomly and give little thought to their victim, circumstance, or escape. For that reason, they are the most likely to be caught.

Sources: Katie Willis, "Armed Robbery: Who Commits It and Why?" (Canberra: Australian Institute of Criminology, 2006); John Conklin, *Robbery and the Criminal Justice System* (New York: Lippincott, 1972), pp. 1–80.

Attempts have been made to classify and explain the nature and dynamics of robbery. One approach is to characterize robberies by type (Exhibit 10.5), and another is to characterize types of robbers based on their specialties (Exhibit 10.6).

As these typologies indicate, the typical armed robber is unlikely to be a professional who carefully studies targets while planning a crime. People walking along the street, convenience stores, and gas stations are much more likely robbery targets than banks or other highly secure environments. Robbers, therefore, seem to be diverted by modest defensive measures, such as having more than one clerk in a store or locating stores in strip malls; they are more likely to try an isolated store.[217]

Acquaintance Robbery

As Exhibit 10.6 suggests, one type of robber may focus on people they know, a phenomenon referred to as **acquaintance robbery**. This seems puzzling because victims can easily identify their attackers and report them to the police. However, despite this threat, acquaintance robbery may be attractive for a number of rational reasons:[218]

■ Victims may be reluctant to report these crimes because they do not want to get involved with the police: They may be involved in crime themselves (drug dealers, for example), or they may fear retaliation if they report the crime. Some victims may be reluctant to gain the label of "rat" or "fink" if they go to the police.

■ Some robberies are motivated by street justice. The robber has a grievance against the victim and settles the dispute by stealing the victim's property. In this instance, robbery may be considered a substitute for an assault: The robber wants retribution and revenge rather than remuneration.[219]

- Because the robber knows the victim personally, the robber has inside information that there will be a "good take." Offenders may target people they know to be carrying a large amount of cash or who just purchased expensive jewelry.

- When a person in desperate need for immediate cash runs out of money, the individual may target people in close proximity simply because they are convenient targets.

When Richard Felson and his associates studied acquaintance robbery, they found that victims were more likely to be injured in acquaintance robberies than in stranger robberies, indicating that revenge rather than reward was the primary motive.[220] Similarly, robberies of family members were more likely to have a bigger payoff than stranger robberies, an indication that the offender was aware that the target had a large amount of cash on hand.

Rational Robbery

Most robbers may be opportunistic rather than professional, but the patterns of robbery suggest that it is not merely a random act committed by an alcoholic or drug abuser. Though most crime rates are higher in the summer, robberies seem to peak during the winter months. One reason may be that the cold weather allows for greater disguise; another reason is that robbers may be attracted to the high amounts of cash people and merchants carry during the Christmas shopping season.[221] Robbers may also be attracted to the winter because days are shorter, affording them greater concealment in the dark.

Robbers also choose vulnerable victims. According to research by criminologist Jody Miller, female armed robbers are likely to choose female targets, reasoning that they will be more vulnerable and offer less resistance.[222] When robbing males, women "set them up" in order to catch them off guard; some feign sexual interest or prostitution to gain the upper hand.[223]

Robbers also seem to be rational when they discuss why they commit crime, who they target, and how they go about their job. When Scott Decker and Richard Wright interviewed active robbers in St. Louis, Missouri, they found that many are motivated by a pressing need for cash.[224] They carefully plan their crimes, choosing victims who can provide the greatest payoff with the least amount of hassle. Some, surprisingly, choose victims who themselves are involved in illegal behavior, most often drug dealers. Ripping off a dealer kills two birds with one stone, providing both money and drugs while at the same time targeting victims who are quite unlikely to call the police. Another ideal target is a married man who is looking for illicit sexual adventures with a prostitute, another victim unlikely to call the police.

Decker and Wright found that robbers have racial, gender, and age preferences in their selection of targets. Some African American robbers prefer white targets because they believe they are too afraid to fight back. Others concentrate on African American victims, who are more likely to carry cash than credit cards. As one interviewee revealed, "White guys can be so paranoid [that] they just want to get away. . . . They're not . . . gonna argue with you." Likewise, intoxicated victims in no condition to fight back were favored targets. Some robbers tend to target women because they feel they are easy subjects; however, others avoid them because they believe they will get emotionally upset and bring unwanted attention. Most agree that the elderly are less likely to put up a fuss than younger, stronger targets.

EMERGING FORMS OF INTERPERSONAL VIOLENCE

Assault, rape, robbery, and murder are traditional forms of interpersonal violence. As more data become available, criminologists have recognized relatively new subcategories within these crime types, such as serial murder and date rape. Additional new categories of interpersonal violence are now receiving attention in criminological literature; the next sections describe three of these forms of violent crime.

Hate Crimes

In the fall of 1998 Matthew Shepard, a gay college student, was kidnapped and severely beaten. He died five days after he was found unconscious on a Wyoming ranch, where he had been left tied to a fence for 18 hours in near freezing temperatures.[225] His two killers, Aaron J. McKinney and Russell A. Henderson, both 22, were sentenced to life in prison after the Shepard family granted them mercy.

It comes as no surprise, considering highly publicized attacks directed against members of the gay community, such as the Shepard killing, that many fear becoming crime victims.[226] Hate crimes or bias crimes are violent acts directed toward a particular person or members of a group merely because the targets share a discernible racial, ethnic, religious, or gender characteristic.[227] Hate crimes can include the desecration of a house of worship or cemetery, harassment of a minority group family that has moved into a previously all-white neighborhood, or a racially motivated murder. For example, on August 23, 1989, Yusuf Hawkins, a black youth, was killed in the Bensonhurst section of Brooklyn, New York, because he had wandered into a racially charged white neighborhood.[228]

Hate crimes usually involve convenient, vulnerable targets who are incapable of fighting back. For example, there have been numerous reported incidents of teenagers attacking vagrants and the homeless in an effort to rid their town or neighborhood of people they consider undesirable.[229] Another group targeted for hate crimes is gay men and women: gay bashing has become common in U.S. cities.

Racial and ethnic minorities have also been the targets of attack. In California, Mexican laborers have been attacked and killed; in New Jersey, Indian immigrants have been the targets of racial hatred.[230] Although hate crimes are often mindless attacks directed toward "traditional" minority victims, political and economic trends may cause this form of violence to be redirected. For example, Asians have been attacked by groups who resent the growing economic power of Japan and Korea as well as the commercial success of Asian Americans.[231] The factors that precipitate hate crimes are listed in Exhibit 10.7.

Hate crimes can have serious consequences. Here, Myrna Francis sits in her vandalized home on August 3, 2006, in York, Pennsylvania. Francis discovered just how much damage three gallons of deck stain can do in the hands of someone motivated by racist hatred. Someone who apparently wanted the black woman to move out of her mostly white neighborhood in the York suburbs broke into her home and did tens of thousands of dollars in damage.

out of active bigotry. They may be young people who get drunk on Saturday night and assault a gay couple or attack an African American man who happens by; they then go back to work or school on Monday. Some are thrill seekers while others may be reacting to the presence of members of a disliked group in their neighborhood. Levin also notes that some people are "sympathizers": they may not attack African Americans but think nothing of telling jokes with racial themes or agreeing with people who despise gays. Finally, there are "spectators" who may not actively participate in bigotry but who do nothing to stop its course. They may even vote for politicians who are openly bigoted because they agree with their tax policies or some other positions, neglecting to process the fact that their vote empowers prejudice and leads to hate.[234]

The Roots of Hate Why do people commit bias crimes? In their book *Hate Crimes*, Jack McDevitt and Jack Levin identify three motivations for hate crimes:

- Thrill-seeking hate crimes. In the same way some kids like to get together to shoot hoops, hatemongers join forces to have fun by bashing minorities or destroying property. Inflicting pain on others gives them a sadistic thrill.

- Reactive (defensive) hate crimes. Perpetrators of these crimes rationalize their behavior as a defensive stand taken against outsiders whom they believe threaten their community or way of life. A gang of teens that attacks a new family in the neighborhood because they are the "wrong" race is committing a reactive hate crime.

- Mission hate crimes. Some disturbed individuals see it as their duty to rid the world of evil. Those on a "mission," like skinheads, the Ku Klux Klan (KKK), and white supremacist groups, may seek to eliminate people who threaten their religious beliefs because they are members of a different faith or threaten "racial purity" because they are of a different race.[232]

More recent research (2002) by McDevitt and Levin with Susan Bennett used data from the Community Disorders Unit (CDU) of the Boston Police Department to uncover a new category of hate crime: retaliatory hate crimes. These offenses are committed in response to a hate crime, whether real or perceived; whether the original incident actually occurred is irrelevant. Their more recent research indicates that most hate crimes can be classified as thrill motivated (66 percent) followed by defensive (25 percent) and retaliative (8 percent). Few cases were mission-oriented offenders.[233]

In his book *The Violence of Hate*, Levin notes that in addition to the traditional hatemongers, hate crimes can be committed by "dabblers"—people who are not committed to hate but drift in and

Nature and Extent of Hate Crime According to the FBI, about 7,000 hate crime incidents occur each year.[235] About half are motivated by racial bigotry, 20 percent by religious intolerance, another 20 percent were the result of a sexual-orientation bias, and about 15 percent are triggered by an ethnicity/national origin bias; the remainder involved a bias against a disability.[236] A recent analysis of 3,000 hate crime cases reported to the police found that about 60 percent of hate crimes involved a violent act, most commonly intimidation or simple assault, and 40 percent of the incidents involved property crimes, most commonly damage, destruction, or vandalism of property.[237] While intimidation was the most common form of hate crime, about 20 percent involve assault with a weapon and a few lead to death.

In crimes where victims could actually identify the culprits, most victims reported that they were acquainted with their attackers or that their attackers were actually friends, coworkers,

---

EXHIBIT 10.7

Factors That Produce Hate Crimes

- Poor or uncertain economic conditions
- Racial stereotypes in films and on television
- Hate-filled discourse on talk shows or in political advertisements
- The use of racial code language such as "welfare mothers" and "inner-city thugs"
- An individual's personal experiences with members of particular minority groups
- Scapegoating—blaming a minority group for the misfortunes of society as a whole

Source: "A Policymaker's Guide to Hate Crimes," *Bureau of Justice Assistance Monograph* (Washington, DC: Bureau of Justice Assistance, 1997).

neighbors, or relatives.[238] Younger victims were more likely to be victimized by people known to them. Hate crimes can occur in many settings, but most are perpetrated in public settings.

Controlling Hate Crimes Because of the extent and seriousness of the problem, a number of legal jurisdictions have made a special effort to control the spread of hate crimes. Boston maintains the Community Disorders Unit, and the New York City Police Department formed the Bias Incident Investigating Unit in 1980. When a crime anywhere in the city is suspected of being motivated by bias, the unit initiates an investigation. The unit also assists victims and works with concerned organizations such as the Commission on Human Rights and the Gay and Lesbian Task Force. These agencies deal with noncriminal bias incidents through mediation, education, and other forms of prevention.[239]

There are also specific hate crime laws that actually originated after the Civil War and that were designed to protect the rights of freed slaves.[240] Today, almost every state jurisdiction has enacted some form of legislation designed to combat hate crimes: 39 states have enacted laws against bias-motivated violence and intimidation; 19 states have statutes that specifically mandate the collection of hate crime data.

Some critics argue that it is unfair to punish criminals motivated by hate any more severely than those who commit similar crimes whose motivation is revenge, greed, or anger. There is also the danger that what appears to be a hate crime, because the target is a minority group member, may actually be motivated by some other factor such as vengeance or monetary gain. In November 2004, Aaron McKinney (who is serving a life sentence for killing Matthew Shepard) told *ABC News* correspondent Elizabeth Vargas that he was high on methamphetamine when he killed Shepard, and that his intent was robbery and not hate. His partner, Russell Henderson, who is appealing his sentence, also claims that the killing was simply a robbery gone bad: "It was not because me and Aaron had anything against gays."[241]

However, in his important book *Punishing Hate: Bias Crimes under American Law*, Frederick Lawrence argues that criminals motivated by bias deserve to be punished more severely than those who commit identical crimes for other motives.[242] He suggests that a society dedicated to the equality of all its people must treat bias crimes differently from other crimes and in so doing enhance the punishment of these crimes.[243]

Some criminals choose their victims randomly; others select specific victims, for example, as in crimes of revenge. Bias crimes are different. They are crimes in which (a) distinct identifying characteristics of the victim are critical to the perpetrator's choice of victim, and (b) the individual identity of the victim is irrelevant.[244] Lawrence views a bias crime as one that would not have been committed but for the victim's membership in a particular group.[245] Bias crimes should be punished more severely because the harm caused will exceed that caused by crimes with other motivations:[246]

▍ Bias crimes are more likely to be violent and involve serious physical injury to the victim.

▍ Bias crimes will have significant emotional and psychological impact on the victim; they result in a "heightened sense of vulnerability," which causes depression, anxiety, and feelings of helplessness.

▍ Bias crimes harm not only the victim but also the "target community."

▍ Bias crimes violate the shared value of equality among citizens and racial and religious harmony in a heterogeneous society.

Recent research by McDevitt and his associates that made use of bias crime records collected by the Boston police supports Lawrence's position. McDevitt found that the victims of bias crime experience more severe post-crime psychological trauma, for a longer period of time, than do victims of similar crimes that are not motivated by hate or bias. Hate crime victims are more likely to suffer intrusive thoughts, feelings of danger, nervousness, and depression at a higher level than nonbias crime victims.[247] Considering the damage caused by bias crimes, it seems appropriate that they be punished more severely than typical common-law crimes.

Legal Controls Should symbolic acts of hate such as drawing a swastika or burning a cross be banned or are they protected by the free speech clause of the First Amendment? The U.S. Supreme Court helped answer this question in the case of *Virginia v. Black* (2003) when it upheld a Virginia statute that makes it a felony "for any person . . . with the intent of intimidating any person or group . . . to burn . . . a cross on the property of another, a highway or other public place," and specifies that "[a]ny such burning . . . shall be prima facie evidence of an intent to intimidate a person or group." The Court ruled that cross burning was intertwined with the Ku Klux Klan and its reign of terror throughout the South. The Court has long held that statements in which the speaker intends to communicate intent to commit an act of unlawful violence to a particular individual or group of individuals is not protected free speech and can be criminalized; the speaker need not actually intend to carry out the threat.[248]

Workplace Violence

Paul Calden, a former insurance company employee, walked into a Tampa cafeteria and opened fire on a table at which his former supervisors were dining. Calden shouted, "This is what you all get for firing me!" and began shooting. When he finished, three were dead and two others were wounded.[249] It has become commonplace to read of irate employees or former employees attacking coworkers or sabotaging machinery and production lines. Workplace violence is now considered one of the leading causes of occupational injury or death.[250] According to the FBI, it can take a number of different forms:

TYPE 1. *Violent acts by criminals who have no other connection with the workplace, but enter to commit robbery or another crime.*

TYPE 2. *Violence directed at employees by customers, clients, patients, students, inmates, or any others for whom an organization provides services.*

TYPE 3. *Violence against coworkers, supervisors, or managers by a present or former employee.*

TYPE 4. *Violence committed in the workplace by someone who doesn't work there, but has a personal relationship with an employee—an abusive spouse or domestic partner.*[251]

Who engages in workplace violence? The typical offender is a middle-aged white male who faces termination in a worsening economy. The fear of economic ruin is especially strong in agencies such as the U.S. Postal Service, where long-term employees fear job loss because of automation and reorganization. In contrast, younger workers usually kill while committing a robbery or another felony.

Creating Workplace Violence A number of factors precipitate workplace violence. One suspected cause is a management style that appears cold and insensitive to workers. As corporations cut their staffs because of some economic downturn or workers are summarily replaced with cost-effective technology, long-term employees may become irate and irrational; their unexpected layoff can lead to violent reactions.[252] The effect is most pronounced when managers are unsympathetic and nonsupportive; their callous attitude may help trigger workplace violence.

Not all workplace violence is triggered by management-induced injustice. In some incidents coworkers have been killed because they refused romantic relationships with the assailants or reported them for sexual harassment. Others have been killed because they got a job the assailant coveted.

Irate clients and customers have also killed because of poor service or perceived slights. While a hospital is designed to help people deal with their clients, patients whose demands are not met may attack those people who are there to be caregivers: health care and social services workers have the highest rate of nonfatal assault injuries. Nurses are three times more likely to experience workplace violence than any other professional group.[253] In one Los Angeles incident, a former patient shot and critically wounded three doctors because his demands for painkillers had gone unheeded.[254] There are a variety of responses to workplace provocations. Some people take out their anger and aggression by attacking their supervisors in an effort to punish the company that dismissed them; this is a form of murder by proxy.[255] Disgruntled employees may also attack family members or friends, misdirecting the rage and frustration caused by their work situation. Others are content with sabotaging company equipment; computer databases are particularly vulnerable to tampering. The aggrieved party may do nothing to rectify the situation; this inaction is referred to as sufferance. Over time, the unresolved conflict may be compounded by other events that cause an eventual eruption.

The Extent of Workplace Violence According to security experts Michael Mantell and Steve Albrecht, the cost of workplace violence for American businesses runs more than $4 billion annually, including lost work time, employee medical benefits, legal expenses, replacing lost employees and retraining new ones, decreased productivity, higher insurance premiums, raised security costs, bad publicity, lost business, and expensive litigation.[256]

These huge costs can be explained by the fact that, on average, violence in the workplace accounts for about 18 percent of all violent crime or, at last count, 1.7 million violent criminal acts, including 1.3 million simple assaults, 325,000 aggravated assaults, 36,500 rapes and sexual assaults, 70,000 robberies, and 900 homicides.[257] Which occupation is most dangerous? Not surprisingly, police officers are at the greatest risk to be victims of workplace violence. Other occupations at risk are correctional officers, taxicab drivers, private security workers, and bartenders. An occupation that is unexpectedly high risk is hospital workers. They average 8.3 assaults per 10,000 employees, which is significantly higher than the rate of nonfatal assaults for all public sector industries—2 per 10,000.[258]

Can Workplace Violence Be Controlled? One approach is to use third parties to mediate disputes. The restorative justice movement (discussed in Chapter 8) advocates the use of mediation to resolve interpersonal disputes. Restorative justice techniques may work particularly well in the workplace, where disputants know one another, and tensions may be simmering over a long period. This may help control the rising tide of workplace violence. Another idea is a human resources approach, with aggressive job retraining and continued medical coverage after layoffs; it is also important to use objective, fair hearings to thwart unfair or biased terminations. Perhaps rigorous screening tests can help identify violence-prone workers so that they can be given anger management training. Most importantly, employers may want to establish policies restricting weapons in the workplace: recent research shows that workplaces where guns were specifically permitted are five to seven times more likely to be the site of a worker homicide than those where all weapons were prohibited.[259]

Stalking

In Wes Craven's popular *Scream* movies, the heroine Sydney (played by Neve Campbell) is stalked by a mysterious adversary who scares her half to death while killing off most of her peer group. Although obviously extreme even by Hollywood standards, the *Scream* movies focus on a newly recognized form of long-term and repeat victimization: stalking.[260]

While it is a complex phenomenon, stalking can be defined as a course of conduct directed at a specific person that involves repeated physical or visual proximity, nonconsensual communication, or verbal, written, or implied threats sufficient to cause fear in a reasonable person.[261]

How big a problem is stalking? Kathleen Basile and her associates used a large national sample of almost 10,000 adults to determine the prevalence of stalking in the United States. Analysis showed about 4.5 percent of adults reported having been stalked. Women had significantly higher prevalence (7 percent) of stalking victimization than did men (2 percent). People who were never married (or who were separated, widowed, or divorced) had significantly higher odds of being stalked than those who were married or had a partner. People aged 55 years or older and those who were retired were least likely to report stalking victimization. Stalking affects nearly 1 in 22 adults or almost 10 million people, approximately 80 percent of whom are women, at sometime during their life.[262]

While this research is disturbing it may actually under-count the problem. Bonnie Fisher and her associates found that about 13 percent of the women in a nationally drawn sample of more than 4,000 college women were the victims of stalking. Considering that there are more than 6.5 million women attending college in the United States, about 700,000 women are being stalked each year on college campuses alone.[263] Though students most likely have a lifestyle that increases the risk of stalking compared to women in the general population, this data make it clear that stalking is a very widespread phenomenon.

connections

The Fisher research found that the likelihood of becoming stalked may be related to the victim's lifestyle and routine activities. Female students who are the victims of stalking tend to date more, go out at night to bars and parties, and live alone. Their lifestyle both brings them into contact with potential stalkers and makes them vulnerable to stalking. For more on routine activities and stalking, go to Chapter 3.

Most victims know their stalker. A recent (2007) meta-analysis of existing research conducted by Brian Spitzberg and William Cupach found that most stalking (79 percent) emerges from preexisting relationships and about half of all stalking emerged specifically from romantic relationships.[264]

Women are most likely to be stalked by an intimate partner—a current spouse, a former spouse, someone they lived with, or even a date. In contrast, men typically are stalked by a stranger or an acquaintance. The typical female victim is stalked because her assailant wants to control her, scare her, or keep her in a relationship. Victims of both genders find that there is a clear relationship between stalking and other emotionally controlling and physically abusive behavior. Some psychologists believe that most stalkers are persons with mental illness who create social and public problems due to their violent behavior.[265]

Stalkers behave in ways that induce fear, but they do not always make overt threats against their victims. Many follow or spy upon their victims, some threaten to kill pets, and others vandalize property. However, as criminologist Mary Brewster found, stalkers who make verbal threats are the ones most likely to later attack their victims.[266] However, it is not uncommon for stalking to end in violence. In their review, Spitzberg and Cupach found that 32 percent of stalking cases involved physical violence and about 12 percent involved sexual violence.[267]

Though stalking is a serious problem, research indicates that many cases are dropped by the courts even though the stalkers often have extensive criminal histories and are frequently the subject of protective orders. A lenient response may be misplaced considering that there is evidence that stalkers repeat their criminal activity within a short time of the lodging of a stalking charge with police authorities.[268] Victims experience its social and psychological consequences long afterward. About one-third seek psychological treatment, and about one-fifth lose time from work; some never return to work.

Why does stalking stop? Most often because the victim moved away or the police got involved or, in some cases, when the stalker met another love interest.

www Go to academic.cengage.com/criminaljustice/siegel to:

▌ Examine the **FBI's hate crime data**.

▌ Read more about the **Boston Community Disorder Unit**.

THINKING LIKE A CRIMINOLOGIST

The FBI is concerned over the recent uptick in the murder rate. The Director wants an explanation for this upward shift after years of decline. What social, economic, and political forces may account for the turnaround? He also wants to determine whether it can be linked to recent data on trends in nonfatal firearm-related violent crimes.

 Writing Exercise As an expert on violent crime in America, you have been asked by the FBI Director to give your opinion on the matter. Going forward, is the American public in for a rising tide of violence and death, or is this a temporary short-term condition? And if there is a danger of rising violence rates, what can be done to reverse its direction? Write a paper (two pages, double-spaced) answering these questions for the Director.

 Doing Research on the Web Before writing your paper, find out more about individual violent crimes around the world by visiting these websites:

▌ Violent Crime News on the Web.

▌ The British Home Office has important information on violent crime.

▌ To read a news story on the recent surge in violent crime, go to CNN.

These websites can be accessed via academic.cengage.com/criminaljustice/siegel.

SUMMARY

■ Violence has become an all too common aspect of modern life. Among the various explanations of sources of violent crime are exposure to violence, personal traits and makeup, evolutionary factors and human instincts, cultural values and a subculture of violence, substance abuse, and socialization and upbringing.

■ Rape, the carnal knowledge of a female forcibly and against her will, has been known throughout history, but the view of rape has evolved. At present, more than 90,000 rapes are reported to U.S. police each year; the actual number of rapes is probably much higher. However, like other violent crimes, the rape rate is in decline.

■ There are numerous forms of rape, including statutory, acquaintance, and date rape. Rape is an extremely difficult charge to prove in court. The victim's lack of consent must be proven;

therefore, it almost seems that the victim is on trial. Rape shield laws have been developed to protect victims from having their personal life placed on trial.

■ Murder is defined as killing a human being with malice aforethought. There are different degrees of murder, and punishments vary accordingly. Like rape, the murder rate and number of annual murders is in decline.

■ Murder can involve a single victim or be a serial killing, mass murder, or spree killing, which involve multiple victims.

■ One important characteristic of murder is that the victim and criminal often know each other. Murder often involves an interpersonal transaction in which a hostile action by the victim precipitates a murderous relationship.

■ Assault involves physically harming another. Assaults often occur in the home,

including child abuse and spouse abuse. There also appears to be a trend toward violence between dating couples.

■ Robbery involves theft by force, usually in a public place. Robbery is considered a violent crime because it can and often does involve violence. Robbery that involves people who know each other is acquaintance robbery.

■ There are newly emerging forms of violent crime, including hate crimes, stalking, and workplace violence.

■ CENGAGENOW™ is an easy-to-use online resource that helps you study in less time to get the grade you want—NOW. CengageNOW™ Personalized Study (a diagnostic study tool containing valuable text-specific resources) lets you focus on just what you don't know and learn more in less time to get a better grade. If your textbook does not include an access code card, you can go to www.ichapters.com to purchase CengageNOW™.

KEY TERMS

expressive violence (302)
instrumental violence (302)
violentization process (304)
crusted over (305)
subculture of violence (305)
disputatiousness (305)
gang rape (308)
serial rape (308)
acquaintance rape (308)
statutory rape (308)
marital rape (309)
marital exemption (309)
virility mystique (310)
narcissistic personality disorder (310)
aggravated rape (310)

consent (311)
shield laws (311)
murder (312)
premeditation (312)
deliberation (312)
felony murder (312)
second-degree murder (312)
manslaughter (312)
nonnegligent manslaughter (312)
involuntary manslaughter (312)
negligent manslaughter (312)
feticide (312)
infanticide (313)
filicide (313)
eldercide (313)

serial killer (315)
mass murder (316)
road rage (317)
child abuse (318)
neglect (318)
sexual abuse (319)
acquaintance robbery (321)
hate or bias crimes (322)
thrill-seeking hate crimes (323)
reactive (defensive) hate crimes (323)
mission hate crimes (323)
retaliatory hate crimes (323)
workplace violence (324)
sufferance (325)
stalking (325)

CRITICAL THINKING QUESTIONS

1. Should different types of rape receive different legal sanctions? For example, should someone who rapes a stranger be punished more severely than someone who is convicted of marital rape or date rape? If your answer is yes, do you also think that someone who kills a stranger should be more severely punished than someone who kills his wife or girlfriend?

2. Is there a subculture of violence in your home city or town? If so, how would you describe its environment and values?

3. There have been significant changes in rape laws regarding issues such as corroboration and shield laws. What other measures would you take to protect the victims of rape when they are forced to testify in court? Should the names of rape victims be published in the press? Do they deserve more protection than those accused of rape?

4. Should hate crimes be punished more severely than crimes motivated by greed, anger, or revenge? Why should crimes be distinguished by the motivations of the perpetrator? Is hate a more heinous motivation than revenge?

5. Do you believe that murder is an interactive event? If so, does that amount to "blaming the victim"? If there is a murder transaction, should we not consider rape, domestic assault, and so forth as "transactions"?

NOTES

1. Susannah Meadows and Evan Thomas, "A Troubled Spring at Duke: A Lacrosse-Team Party Spawns Charges of Rape," *Newsweek*, 10 April 2006, www.msnbc.msn.com/id/12115147/site/newsweek (accessed February 11, 2007); "Accuser Changes Story in Lacrosse Case," *News and Observer*, 11 January 2007, www.newsobserver.com/1185/story/531253.html (accessed June 10, 2007); Sal Ruibal, "Rape Allegations Cast Pall at Duke," *USA Today*, 29 March 2006, www.usatoday.com/sports/college/lacrosse/2006-03-29-duke-fallout_x.htm (accessed April 24, 2007).

2. George Tita, Tricia Petras, and Robert Greenbaum, "Crime and Residential Choice: A Neighborhood Level Analysis of the Impact of Crime on Housing Prices," *Journal of Quantitative Criminology* 22 (2006): 299–317.

3. Robert Nash Parker and Catherine Colony, "Relationships, Homicides, and Weapons: A Detailed Analysis," paper presented at the annual meeting of the American Society of Criminology, Montreal, November 1987.

4. Stryker McGuire, "The Dunblane Effect," *Newsweek*, 28 October 1996, p. 46.

5. Rokeya Farrooque, Ronnie Stout, and Frederick Ernst, "Heterosexual Intimate Partner Homicide: Review of Ten Years of Clinical Experience," *Journal of Forensic Sciences* 50 (2005): 648–651; Miltos Livaditis, Gkaro Esagian, Christos Kakoulidis, Maria Samakouri, and Nikos Tzavaras, "Matricide by Person with Bipolar Disorder and Dependent Overcompliant Personality," *Journal of Forensic Sciences* 50 (2005): 658–661.

6. Dorothy Otnow Lewis, Ernest Moy, Lori Jackson, Robert Aaronson, Nicholas Restifo, Susan Serra, and Alexander Simos, "Biopsychosocial Characteristics of Children Who Later Murder," *American Journal of Psychiatry* 142 (1985): 1,161–1,167.

7. Dorothy Otnow Lewis, *Guilty by Reason of Insanity* (New York: Fawcett Columbine, 1998).

8. Richard Rogers, Randall Salekin, Kenneth Sewell, and Keith Cruise, "Prototypical Analysis of Antisocial Personality Disorder," *Criminal Justice and Behavior* 27 (2000): 234–255; Amy Holtzworth-Munroe and Gregory Stuart, "Typologies of Male Batterers: Three Subtypes and the Differences among Them," *Psychological Bulletin* 116 (1994): 476–497.

9. Katherine Van Wormer and Chuk Odiah, "The Psychology of Suicide-Murder and the Death Penalty," *Journal of Criminal Justice* 27 (1999): 361–370.

10. Daniel Strueber, Monika Lueck, and Gerhard Roth, "The Violent Brain," *Scientific American Mind* 17 (2006): 20–27.

11. Sigmund Freud, *Beyond the Pleasure Principle* (London: Inter-Psychoanalytic Press, 1922).

12. Konrad Lorenz, *On Aggression* (New York: Harcourt Brace Jovanovich, 1966).

13. Nigel Barber, "Why Is Violent Crime So Common in the Americas?" *Aggressive Behavior* 32 (2006): 442–450.

14. Arnie Nielsen, Ramiro Martinez, and Matthew Lee, "Alcohol, Ethnicity, and Violence: The Role of Alcohol Availability for Latino and Black Aggravated Assaults and Robberies," *Sociological Quarterly*, 46 (2005): 479–502.

15. Chris Allen, "The Links Between Heroin, Crack Cocaine and Crime: Where Does Street Crime Fit In?" *British Journal of Criminology* 45 (2005): 355–372.

16. Steven Messner, Glenn Deane, Luc Anselin, and Benjamin Pearson-Nelson, "Locating the Vanguard in Rising and Falling Homicide Rates Across Cities," *Criminology* 43 (2005): 661–696.

17. Paul Goldstein, Henry Brownstein, and Patrick Ryan, "Drug-Related Homicide in New York: 1984–1988," *Crime and Delinquency* 38 (1992): 459–476.

18. Reiss and Roth, *Understanding and Preventing Violence*, pp. 193–194.

19. Robert Brewer and Monica Swahn, "Binge Drinking and Violence," *JAMA: Journal of the American Medical Association* 294 (2005): 16–20.

20. Tomika Stevens, Kenneth Ruggiero, Dean Kilpatrick, Heidi Resnick, and Benjamin Saunders, "Variables Differentiating Singly and Multiply Victimized Youth: Results from the National Survey of Adolescents and Implications for Secondary Prevention," *Child Maltreatment* 10 (2005): 211–223; James Collins and Pamela Messerschmidt, "Epidemiology of Alcohol-Related Violence," *Alcohol Health and Research World* 17 (1993): 93–100.

21. Antonia Abbey; Tina Zawacki, Philip Buck, Monique Clinton, and Pam McAuslan, "Sexual Assault and Alcohol Consumption: What Do We Know about Their Relationship and What Types of Research Are Still Needed?" *Aggression and Violent Behavior* 9 (2004): 271–303.

22. Scott Phillips, Jacqueline Matusko, and Elizabeth Tomasovic, "Reconsidering the Relationship Between Alcohol and Lethal Violence," *Journal of Interpersonal Violence* 22 (2007): 66–84.

23. Martin Grann and Seena Fazel, "Substance Misuse and Violent Crime: Swedish Population Study," *British Medical Journal* 328 (2004): 1,233–1,234; Susanne Rogne Gjeruldsen, Bjørn Myrvang, and Stein Opjordsmoen, "Criminality in Drug Addicts: A Follow-Up Study over 25 Years," *European Addiction Research* 10 (2004): 49–56.

24. Paul Goldstein, Patricia Bellucci, Barry Spunt, and Thomas Miller, "Volume of Cocaine Use and Violence: A Comparison between Men and Women," *Journal of Drug Issues* 21 (1991): 345–367.

25. Todd Herrenkhol, Bu Huang, Emiko Tajima, and Stephen Whitney, "Examining the Link between Child Abuse and Youth Violence," *Journal of Interpersonal Violence* 18 (2003): 1,189–1,208; Pamela Lattimore, Christy Visher, and Richard Linster, "Predicting Rearrest for Violence among Serious Youthful Offenders," *Journal of Research in Crime and Delinquency* 32 (1995): 54–83.

26. Rolf Loeber and Dale Hay, "Key Issues in the Development of Aggression and Violence from Childhood to Early Adulthood," *Annual Review of Psychology* 48 (1997): 371–410.

27. Deborah Capaldi and Gerald Patterson, "Can Violent Offenders Be Distinguished from Frequent Offenders: Prediction from Childhood to Adolescence," *Journal of Research in Crime and Delinquency* 33 (1996): 206–231.

28. Adrian Raine, Patricia Brennan, and Sarnoff Mednick, "Interaction between Birth Complications and Early Maternal Rejection in Predisposing Individuals to

Adult Violence: Specificity to Serious, Early-Onset Violence," *American Journal of Psychiatry* 154 (1997): 1,265–1,271.

29. John Lemmon, "How Child Maltreatment Affects Dimensions of Juvenile Delinquency in a Cohort of Low-Income Urban Youths," *Justice Quarterly* 16 (1999): 357–376.

30. Eric Slade and Lawrence Wissow, "Spanking in Early Childhood and Later Behavior Problems: A Prospective Study of Infants and Young Toddlers," *Pediatrics* 113 (2004): 1,321–1,330.

31. Murray Straus, "Discipline and Deviance: Physical Punishment of Children and Violence and Other Crime in Adulthood," *Social Problems* 38 (1991): 101–123.

32. Ronald Simons, Chyi-In Wu, Kuei-Hsiu Lin, Leslie Gordon, and Rand Conger, "A Cross-Cultural Examination of the Link between Corporal Punishment and Adolescent Antisocial Behavior," *Criminology* 38 (2000): 47–79.

33. Robert Scudder, William Blount, Kathleen Heide, and Ira Silverman, "Important Links between Child Abuse, Neglect, and Delinquency," *International Journal of Offender Therapy* 37 (1993): 315–323.

34. Dorothy Lewis et al., "Neuropsychiatric, Psychoeducational, and Family Characteristics of 14 Juveniles Condemned to Death in the United States," *American Journal of Psychiatry* 145 (1988): 584–588.

35. Charles Patrick Ewing, *When Children Kill* (Lexington, MA: Lexington Books, 1990), p. 22.

36. Lewis, *Guilty by Reason of Insanity*, pp. 11–35.

37. Timothy Ireland, Carolyn Smith, and Terence Thornberry, "Developmental Issues in the Impact of Child Maltreatment on Later Delinquency and Drug Use," *Criminology* 40 (2002): 359–401.

38. Straus, "Discipline and Deviance."

39. Alan Rosenbaum and Penny Leisring, "Beyond Power and Control: Towards an Understanding of Partner Abusive Men," *Journal of Comparative Family Studies* 34 (2003): 7–26.

40. Lonnie Athens, *The Creation of Dangerous Violent Criminals* (Urbana: University of Illinois Press, 1992), pp. 27–80.

41. Eric Stewart, Ronald Simons, and Rand Conger, "Assessing Neighborhood and Social Psychological Influences on Childhood Violence in an African-American Sample," *Criminology* 40 (2002): 801–830.

42. Joanne Kaufman, "Explaining the Race/Ethnicity–Violence Relationship: Neighborhood Context and Social Psychological Processes," *Justice Quarterly* 22 (2005): 224–251; David Farrington, Rolf Loeber, and Madga Stouthamer-Loeber, "How Can the Relationship between Race and Violence by Explained?" in *Violent Crimes: Assessing Race and Ethnic Differences*, ed. D. F. Hawkins (New York: Cambridge University Press, 2003), pp. 213–237.

43. Barbara Warner, "Robberies with Guns: Neighborhood Factors and the Nature of Crime," *Journal of Criminal Justice* 35 (2007): 39–50.

44. Felton Earls, *Linking Community Factors and Individual Development* (Washington, DC: National Institute of Justice, 1998).

45. Jeffrey B. Bingenheimer, Robert T. Brennan, and Felton J. Earls, "Firearm Violence Exposure and Serious Violent Behavior," *Science* 308 (2005): 1,323–1,326; "Witnessing Gun Violence Significantly Increases Likelihood that a Child Will Also Commit Violent Crime; Violence May Be Viewed as Infectious Disease," *AScribe Health News Service*, 26 May 2005.

46. Michael Greene, "Chronic Exposure to Violence and Poverty: Interventions that Work for Youth," *Crime and Delinquency* 39 (1993): 106–124.

47. Robert Baller, Luc Anselin, Steven Messner, Glenn Deane, and Darnell Hawkins, "Structural Covariates of U.S. County Homicide Rates Incorporating Spatial Effects," *Criminology* 39 (2001): 561–590.

48. Marvin Wolfgang and Franco Ferracuti, *The Subculture of Violence* (London: Tavistock, 1967).

49. David Luckenbill and Daniel Doyle, "Structural Position and Violence: Developing a Cultural Explanation," *Criminology* 27 (1989): 419–436.

50. Robert Sampson and William Julius Wilson, "Toward a Theory of Race, Crime, and Urban Inequality," in *Crime and Inequality*, eds. John Hagan and Ruth Peterson (Stanford, CA: Stanford University Press, 1995), p. 51.

51. Liqun Cao, Anthony Adams, and Vickie Jensen, "A Test of the Black Subculture of Violence Thesis," *Criminology* 35 (1997): 367–379.

52. Eric Baumer, Julie Horney, Richard Felson, and Janet Lauritsen, "Neighborhood Disadvantage and the Nature of Violence," *Criminology* 41 (2003): 39–71.

53. Charis Kubrin and Ronald Weitzer, "Retaliatory Homicide: Concentrated Disadvantage and Neighborhood Culture," *Social Problems* 50 (2003): 157–180.

54. Robert J. Kane, "Compromised Police Legitimacy as a Predictor of Violent Crime in Structurally Disadvantaged Communities," *Criminology* 43 (2005): 469–499.

55. Steven Messner, "Regional and Racial Effects on the Urban Homicide Rate: The Subculture of Violence Revisited," *American Journal of Sociology* 88 (1983): 997–1,007; Steven Messner and Kenneth Tardiff, "Economic Inequality and Levels of Homicide: An Analysis of Urban Neighborhoods," *Criminology* 24 (1986): 297–317.

56. Beth Bjerregaard and Alan Lizotte, "Gun Ownership and Gang Membership," *Journal of Criminal Law and Criminology* 86 (1995): 37–58.

57. Fox Butterfield, "Rise in Killings Spurs New Steps to Fight Gangs," *New York Times*, 17 January 2004, p. A1.

58. James Howell, "Youth Gang Homicides: A Literature Review," *Crime and Delinquency* 45 (1999): 208–241.

59. Alan Lizotte and David Sheppard, *Gun Use by Male Juveniles* (Washington, DC: Office of Juvenile Justice and Delinquency Prevention, 2001); Daneen Deptula and Robert Cohen, "Aggressive, Rejected, and Delinquent Children and Adolescents: A Comparison of Their Friendships," *Aggression and Violent Behavior* 9 (2004): 75–104.

60. Sylvie Mrug, Betsy Hoza, and William Bukowski. "Choosing or Being Chosen by Aggressive-Disruptive Peers: Do They Contribute to Children's Externalizing and Internalizing Problems?" *Journal of Abnormal Child Psychology* 32 (2004): 53–66.

61. Daniel Neller, Robert Denney, Christina Pietz, and R. Paul Thomlinson, "Testing the Trauma Model of Violence," *Journal of Family Violence* 20 (2005): 151–159.

62. Rachel Gordon, Benjamin Lahey, Eriko Kawai, Rolf Loeber, Magda Stouthamer-Loeber, and David Farrington, "Antisocial Behavior and Youth Gang Membership," *Criminology* 42 (2004): 55–88.

63. Jerome Neapolitan, "A Comparative Analysis of Nations with Low and High Levels of Violent Crime," *Journal of Criminal Justice* 27 (1999): 259–274.

64. Ibid., p. 271.

65. Aki Roberts and Gary LaFree, "Explaining Japan's Postwar Violent Crime Trends," *Criminology* 42 (2004): 179–210.

66. David Courtwright, "Violence in America," *American Heritage* 47 (1996): 36–52, at 36; David Courtwright, *Violent Land: Single Men and Social Disorder from the Frontier to the Inner City* (Cambridge, MA: Harvard University Press, 1996).

67. William Green, *Rape* (Lexington, MA: Lexington Books, 1988), p. 5.

68. Susan Randall and Vicki McNickle Rose, "Forcible Rape," in *Major Forms of Crime*, ed. Robert Meyer (Beverly Hills: Sage, 1984), p. 47.

69. Barbara Krah, Renate Scheinberger-Olwig, and Steffen Bieneck, "Men's Reports of Nonconsensual Sexual Interactions with Women: Prevalence and Impact," *Archives of Sexual Behavior* 32 (2003): 165–176.

70. Siegmund Fred Fuchs, "Male Sexual Assault: Issues of Arousal and Consent," *Cleveland State Law Review* 51 (2004): 93–108.

71. Raquel Kennedy Bergen and Paul Bukovec, "Men and Intimate Partner Rape: Characteristics of Men Who Sexually Abuse Their Partner," *Journal of Interpersonal Violence* 21 (2006): 1,375–1,384.

72. Susan Brownmiller, *Against Our Will: Men, Women, and Rape* (New York: Simon & Schuster, 1975).

73. Green, *Rape*, p. 6.

74. Yuri Kageyama, "Court Orders Japan to Pay Sex Slaves," *Boston Globe*, 28 April 1998, p. A2.

75. Marlise Simons, "Bosnian Serb Pleads Guilty to Rape Charge before War Crimes Tribunal," *New York Times*, 10 March 1998, p. 8.

76. Marc Lacey, "Amnesty Says Sudan Militias Use Rape as Weapon," *New York Times*, 19 July 2004, p. A9.

77. FBI, *Crime in the United States, 2005*. Crime data in this chapter come from this source and from preliminary 2006 data.

78. Maria Testa, Jennifer Livingston, Carol Vanzile-Tamsen, and Michael Frone, "The Role of Women's Substance Use in Vulnerability to Forcible and Incapacitated Rape," *Journal of Studies on Alcohol* 64 (2003): 756–766.

79. Shannan Catalano, *Criminal Victimization 2005* (Washington, DC: Bureau of Justice Statistics, 2006), p. 2.

80. Carol Vanzile-Tamsen, Maria Testa, and Jennifer Livingston, "The Impact of Sexual Assault History and Relationship Context on Appraisal of and Responses to Acquaintance Sexual Assault Risk," *Journal of Interpersonal Violence* 20 (2005): 813–822; Arnold Kahn, Jennifer Jackson, Christine Kully, Kelly Badger, and Jessica Halvorsen, "Calling It Rape: Differences in Experiences of Women Who Do or Do Not Label Their Sexual Assault as Rape," *Psychology of Women Quarterly* 27 (2003): 233–242.

81. Mark Warr, "Rape, Burglary, and Opportunity," *Journal of Quantitative Criminology* 4 (1988): 275–288.

82. Maria Testa, Jennifer Livingston, and Carol Vanzile-Tamsen, "The Role of Victim and Perpetrator Intoxication on Sexual Assault Outcomes," *Journal of Studies on Alcohol* 65 (2004): 320–329.

83. A. Nicholas Groth and Jean Birnbaum, *Men Who Rape* (New York: Plenum Press, 1979).

84. For another typology, see Raymond Knight, "Validation of a Typology of Rapists," in *Sex Offender Research and Treatment: State-of-the-Art in North America and Europe,* eds. W. L. Marshall and J. Frenken (Beverly Hills: Sage, 1997), pp. 58–75.

85. Sarah Ullman, "A Comparison of Gang and Individual Rape Incidents," *Violence and Victimization* 14 (1999): 123–134.

86. Janet Warren, Roland Reboussin, Robert Hazlewood, Natalie Gibbs, Susan Trumbetta, and Andrea Cummings, "Crime Scene Analysis and the Escalation of Violence in Serial Rape," *Forensic Science International* (1998): 56–62.

87. James LeBeau, "Patterns of Stranger and Serial Rape Offending Factors Distinguishing Apprehended and At-Large Offenders," *Journal of Criminal Law and Delinquency* 78 (1987): 309–326.

88. Bonnie Fisher, Francis Cullen, and Leah Daigle, "The Discovery of Acquaintance Rape," *Journal of Interpersonal Violence* 20 (2005): 493–500.

89. Leah Adams-Curtis and Gordon Forbes, "College Women's Experiences of Sexual Coercion," *Trauma, Violence and Abuse* 5 (2004): 91–122.

90. Cassia Spohn, Dawn Beichner, and Erika Davis-Frenzel, "Prosecutorial Justifications for Sexual Assault Case Rejection: Guarding the 'Gateway to Justice,'" *Social Problems* 48 (2001): 206–235.

91. R. Lance Shotland, "A Model of the Causes of Date Rape in Developing and Close Relationships," in *Close Relationships*, ed. C. Hendrick (Newbury Park, CA: Sage, 1989), pp. 247–270.

92. Kimberly Tyler, Danny Hoyt, and Les Whitbeck, "Coercive Sexual Strategies," *Violence and Victims* 13 (1998): 47–63.

93. Alan Gross, Andrea Winslett, Miguel Roberts, and Carol Gohm, "An Examination of Sexual Violence Against College Women," *Violence Against Women* 12 (2006): 288–300.

94. Allison and Wrightsman, *Rape: The Misunderstood Crime*, p. 64.

95. Amy Buddie and Maria Testa, "Rates and Predictors of Sexual Aggression Among Students and Nonstudents," *Journal of Interpersonal Violence* 20 (2005): 713–725.

96. Bonnie Fisher, Leah Daigle, Francis Cullen, and Michael Turner, "Reporting Sexual Victimization to the Police and Others: Results from a National-Level Study of College Women," *Criminal Justice and Behavior* 30 (2003): 6–39.

97. Allison and Wrightsman, *Rape: The Misunderstood Crime,* pp. 85–87.

98. Cited in Diana Russell, "Wife Rape," in *Acquaintance Rape: The Hidden Crime*, eds. A. Parrot and L. Bechhofer (New York: Wiley, 1991), pp. 129–139, at 129.

99. David Finkelhor and K. Yllo, *License to Rape: Sexual Abuse of Wives* (New York: Holt, Rinehart & Winston, 1985).

100. Allison and Wrightsman. *Rape: The Misunderstood Crime*, p. 89.

101. Associated Press, "British Court Rejects Precedent, Finds a Man Guilty of Raping Wife," *Boston Globe*, 15 March 1991, p. 68.

102. Jill Elaine Hasday, "Contest and Consent: A Legal History of Marital Rape," *California Law Review* 88 (2000): 1,373–1,433.

103. Sharon Elstein and Roy Davis, *Sexual Relationships between Adult Males and Young Teen Girls: Exploring the Legal and Social Responses* (Chicago: American Bar Association, 1997).

104. Donald Symons, *The Evolution of Human Sexuality* (Oxford: Oxford University Press, 1979).

105. Lee Ellis and Anthony Walsh, "Gene-Based Evolutionary Theories in Criminology," *Criminology* 35 (1997): 229–276.

106. Suzanne Osman, "Predicting Men's Rape Perceptions Based on the Belief that 'No' Really Means 'Yes,'" *Journal of Applied Social Psychology* 33 (2003): 683–692.

107. Martin Schwartz, Walter DeKeseredy, David Tait, and Shahid Alvi, "Male Peer Support and a Feminist Routine Activities Theory: Understanding Sexual Assault on the College Campus," *Justice Quarterly* 18 (2001): 623–650.

108. Diana Russell, *The Politics of Rape* (New York: Stein and Day, 1975).

109. Diana Russell and Rebecca M. Bolen, *The Epidemic of Rape and Child Sexual Abuse in the United States* (Thousand Oaks, CA: Sage, 2000).

110. Rachel Bridges Whaley, "The Paradoxical Relationship between Gender Inequality and Rape: Toward a Refined Theory," *Gender and Society* 15 (2001): 531–555.

111. Paul Gebhard, John Gagnon, Wardell Pomeroy, and Cornelia Christenson, *Sex Offenders: An Analysis of Types* (New York: Harper & Row, 1965), pp. 198–205; Richard Rada, ed., *Clinical Aspects of the Rapist* (New York: Grune & Stratton, 1978), pp. 122–130.

112. Stephen Porter, David Fairweather, Jeff Drugge, Huues Herve, Angela Birt, and Douglas Boer, "Profiles of Psychopathy in Incarcerated Sexual Offenders," *Criminal Justice and Behavior* 27 (2000): 216–233.

113. Brad Bushman, Angelica Bonacci, Mirjam van Dijk, and Roy Baumeister, "Narcissism, Sexual Refusal, and Aggression: Testing a Narcissistic Reactance Model of Sexual Coercion," *Journal of Personality and Social Psychology*, 84 (2003): 1,027–1,040.

114. Schwartz, DeKeseredy, Tait, and Alvi, "Male Peer Support and a Feminist Routine Activities Theory."

115. Groth and Birnbaum, *Men Who Rape*, p. 101.

116. See generally Edward Donnerstein, Daniel Linz, and Steven Penrod, *The Question of Pornography* (New York: Free Press, 1987); Diana Russell, *Sexual Exploitation* (Beverly Hills: Sage, 1985), pp. 115–116.

117. Neil Malamuth and John Briere, "Sexual Violence in the Media: Indirect Effects on Aggression against Women," *Journal of Social Issues* 42 (1986): 75–92.

118. Associated Press, "Trial on TV May Have Influenced Boy Facing Sexual-Assault Count," *Omaha World Herald*, 18 April 1984, p. 50.

119. Richard Felson and Marvin Krohn, "Motives for Rape," *Journal of Research in Crime and Delinquency* 27 (1990): 222–242.

120. Laura Monroe, Linda Kinney, Mark Weist, Denise Spriggs Dafeamekpor, Joyce Dantzler, and Matthew Reynolds, "The Experience of Sexual Assault: Findings from a Statewide Victim Needs Assessment," *Journal of Interpersonal Violence* 20 (2005): 767–776.

121. Julie Horney and Cassia Spohn, "The Influence of Blame and Believability Factors on the Processing of Simple versus Aggravated Rape Cases," *Criminology* 34 (1996): 135–163.

122. Mark Whatley, "The Effect of Participant Sex, Victim Dress, and Traditional Attitudes on Causal Judgments for Marital Rape Victims," *Journal of Family Violence* 20 (2005): 191–200; Spohn, Beichner, and Davis-Frenzel, "Prosecutorial Justifications for Sexual Assault Case Rejection."

123. Patricia Landwehr, Robert Bothwell, Matthew Jeanmard, Luis Luque, Roy Brown III, and Marie-Anne Breaux, "Racism in Rape Trials," *Journal of Social Psychology* 142 (2002): 667–670.

124. "Man Wrongly Convicted of Rape Released 19 Years Later," *Forensic Examiner* (May–June 2003): 44.

125. Gerald Robin, "Forcible Rape: Institutionalized Sexism in the Criminal Justice System," *Crime and Delinquency* 23 (1977): 136–153.

126. Associated Press, "Jury Stirs Furor by Citing Dress in Rape Acquittal," *Boston Globe,* 6 October 1989, p. 12.

127. Rodney Kingsworth, Randall MacIntosh, and Jennifer Wentworth, "Sexual Assault: The Role of Prior Relationship and Victim Characteristics in Case Processing," *Justice Quarterly* 16 (1999): 276–302.

128. Cassia Spohn and David Holleran, "Prosecuting Sexual Assault: A Comparison of Charging Decisions in Sexual Assault Cases Involving Strangers, Acquaintances, and Intimate Partners," *Justice Quarterly* 18 (2001): 651–688.

129. Susan Estrich, *Real Rape* (Cambridge, MA: Harvard University Press, 1987), pp. 58–59.

130. See, for example, Mich. Comp. Laws Ann. 750.5200-(1); Florida Statutes Annotated, Sec. 794.011; see generally Gary LaFree, "Official Reactions to Rape," *American Sociological Review* 45 (1980): 842–854.

131. Martin Schwartz and Todd Clear, "Toward a New Law on Rape," *Crime and Delinquency* 26 (1980): 129–151.

132. *Michigan v. Lucas* 90-149 (1991); Comment, "The Rape Shield Paradox: Complainant Protection amidst Oscillating Trends of State Judicial Interpretation," *Journal of Criminal Law and Criminology* 78 (1987): 644–698.

133. Andrew Karmen, *Crime Victims* (Pacific Grove, CA: Brooks/Cole, 1990), p. 252.

134. "Court Upholds Civil Rights Portion of Violence Against Women Act," *Criminal Justice Newsletter* 28 (1 December 1997): 3.

135. Donald Lunde, *Murder and Madness* (San Francisco: San Francisco Book Company, 1977), p. 3.

136. Lisa Baertlein, "HIV Ruled Deadly Weapon in Rape Case," *Boston Globe,* 2 March 1994, p. 3.

137. The legal principles here come from Wayne LaFave and Austin Scott, *Criminal Law* (St. Paul: West, 1986; updated 1993). The definitions and discussion of legal principles used in this chapter lean heavily on this work.

138. LaFave and Scott, *Criminal Law.*

139. Evelyn Nieves, "Woman Gets 4-Year Term in Fatal Dog Attack," *New York Times,* 16 July 2002, p. 1.

140. Bob Egelko, "Murder Conviction Reinstated in S.F. Dog Mauling," *San Francisco Chronicle,* August 23, 2008, www.sfgate.com/cgi-bin/article.cgi?f=/c/a/2008/08/23/BAJC12GPD1.DTL&hw=Robert+Noel&sn=002&sc=103 (accessed September 1, 2008).

141. Pauline Arrillaga, "Jurors Give Drunk Driver 16 Years in Fetus's Death," *Manchester Union Leader,* 22 October 1996, p. B20.

142. Center for Reproductive Law and Policy, *Punishing Women for Their Behavior During Pregnancy* (New York: author, 1996), pp. 1–2.

143. *Whitner v. State of South Carolina,* Supreme Court of South Carolina, Opinion Number 24468, July 15, 1996.

144. Janet Kreps, *Feticide and Wrongful Death Laws* (New York: Center for Reproductive Law and Policy, 1996), pp. 1–2.

145. Arrillaga, "Jurors Give Drunk Driver 16 Years in Fetus's Death."

146. James Alan Fox and Marianne Zawitz, *Homicide Trends in the United States* (Washington, DC: Bureau of Justice Statistics, 2001).

147. Todd Shackelford, Viviana Weekes-Shackelford, and Shanna Beasley, "An Exploratory Analysis of the Contexts and Circumstances of Filicide-Suicide in Chicago, 1965–1994," *Aggressive Behavior* 31 (2005): 399–406.

148. FBI, *Crime in the United States, 2005,* www.fbi.gov/ucr/05cius/offenses/violent_crime/murder_homicide.html (accessed July 22, 2007).

149. Philip Cook, Jens Ludwig, and Anthony Braga, "Criminal Records of Homicide Offenders," *Journal of the American Medical Association* 294 (2005): 598–601.

150. See generally Marc Reidel and Margaret Zahn, *The Nature and Pattern of American Homicide* (Washington, DC: U.S. Government Printing Office, 1985).

151. Terance Miethe and Wendy Regoeczi with Kriss Drass, *Rethinking Homicide: Exploring the Structure and Process Underlying Deadly Situations* (Cambridge, MA: Cambridge University Press, 2004).

152. Angela Browne and Kirk Williams, "Gender, Intimacy, and Lethal Violence: Trends from 1976 through 1987," *Gender and Society* 7 (1993): 78–98.

153. Linda Saltzman and James Mercy, "Assaults between Intimates: The Range of Relationships Involved," in *Homicide: The Victim/Offender Connection,* ed. Anna Victoria Wilson (Cincinnati: Anderson Publishing, 1993), pp. 65–74.

154. Angela Browne and Kirk Williams, "Exploring the Effect of Resource Availability and the Likelihood of Female-Perpetrated Homicides," *Law and Society Review* 23 (1989): 75–94.

155. Richard Felson, "Anger, Aggression, and Violence in Love Triangles," *Violence and Victimization* 12 (1997): 345–363.

156. Ibid., p. 361.

157. Scott Decker, "Deviant Homicide: A New Look at the Role of Motives and Victim–Offender Relationships," *Journal of Research in Crime and Delinquency* 33 (1996): 427–449.

158. David Luckenbill, "Criminal Homicide as a Situational Transaction," *Social Problems* 25 (1977): 176–186.

159. Margaret Zahn and Philip Sagi, "Stranger Homicides in Nine American Cities," *Journal of Criminal Law and Criminology* 78 (1987): 377–397.

160. Tomislav Kovandzic, John Sloan, and Lynne Vieraitis, "Unintended Consequences of Politically Popular Sentencing Policy: The Homicide Promoting Effects of 'Three Strikes' in U.S. Cities (1980–1999)," *Criminology and Public Policy* 3 (2002): 399–424.

161. Jill DeVoe, Katharin Peter, Sally Ruddy, Amanda Miller, Mike Planty, Thomas Snyder, and Michael Rand, *Indicators of School Crime and Safety, 2003* (Washington, DC: U.S. Department of Education and Bureau of Justice Statistics, 2004).

162. Tonja Nansel, Mary Overpeck, and Ramani Pilla, "Bullying Behaviors among US Youth: Prevalence and Association with Psychosocial Adjustment," *Journal of the American Medical Association* 285 (2001): 2,094–3,100.

163. Christine Kerres Malecki and Michelle Kilpatrick Demaray, "Carrying a Weapon to School and Perceptions of Social Support in an Urban Middle School," *Journal of Emotional and Behavioral Disorders* 11 (2003): 169–178.

164. Ibid.

165. Pamela Wilcox and Richard Clayton, "A Multilevel Analysis of School-Based Weapon Possession," *Justice Quarterly* 18 (2001): 509–542.

166. Mark Anderson, Joanne Kaufman, Thomas Simon, Lisa Barrios, Len Paulozzi, George Ryan, Rodney Hammond, William Modzeleski, Thomas Feucht, Lloyd Potter, and the School-Associated Violent Deaths Study Group, "School-Associated Violent Deaths in the United States, 1994–1999," *Journal of the American Medical Association* 286 (2001): 2,695–2,702.

167. Bryan Vossekuil, Marisa Reddy, Robert Fein, Randy Borum, and William Modzeleski, *Safe School Initiative, An Interim Report on the Prevention of Targeted Violence in Schools* (Washington, DC: United States Secret Service, 2000).

168. "BTK Killer Blames "Demon" for Murders," *USA Today,* 7 July 2005, www.usatoday.com/news/nation/2005-07-07-btk-killings_x.htm (accessed April 24, 2007).

169. Alasdair Goodwill and Laurence Alison, "Sequential Angulation, Spatial Dispersion and Consistency of Distance Attack Patterns from Home in Serial Murder, Rape and Burglary," *Journal of Psychology, Crime and Law* 11 (2005): 161–176.

170. Ronald Holmes and Stephen Holmes, *Murder in America* (Thousand Oaks, CA: Sage, 1994) pp. 13–14.

171. "Killing for Pleasure," Court TV Crime Library, www.crimelibrary.com/serial_killers/weird/swango/pleasure_8.html (accessed April 24, 2005.

172. Aneez Esmail, "Physician as Serial Killer—The Shipman Case," *New England Journal of Medicine* 352 (2005): 1,483–1,844.

173. James Alan Fox and Jack Levin, *Overkill: Mass Murder and Serial Killing Exposed* (New York: Plenum, 1994); James Alan Fox, Jack Levin, and Kenna Quinet, *The Will to Kill: Making Sense of Senseless Murder*, 2nd ed. (Boston: Allyn & Bacon, 2004);

174. Belea Keeney and Kathleen Heide, "Gender Differences in Serial Murderers: A Preliminary Analysis," *Journal of Interpersonal Violence* 9 (1994): 37–56.

175. Wade Myers, Erik Gooch, and Reid Meloy, "The Role of Psychopathy and Sexuality in a Female Serial Killer," *Journal of Forensic Sciences* 50 (2005): 652–658.

176. Zelda Knight, "Some Thoughts on the Psychological Roots of the Behavior of Serial Killers as Narcissists: An Object Relations Perspective," *Social Behavior and Personality: An International Journal* 34 (2006): 1,189–1,206.

177. Terry Whitman and Donald Akutagawa, "Riddles in Serial Murder: A Synthesis," *Aggression and Violent Behavior* 9 (2004): 693–703.

178. Holmes and Holmes, *Murder in America*, p. 106.

179. Ibid., p. 17; James Alan Fox and Jack Levin, *Overkill: Mass Murder and Serial Killing Exposed* (New York: Plenum, 1994).

180. Gabrielle Salfati and Alicia Bateman, "Serial Homicide: An Investigation of Behavioural Consistency," *Journal of Investigative Psychology and Offender Profiling* 2 (2005): 121–144.

181. Jennifer Browdy, "VI-CAP System to Be Operational this Summer," *Law Enforcement News*, 21 May 1984, p. 1.

182. James Alan Fox and Jack Levin, "Multiple Homicide: Patterns of Serial and Mass Murder," in *Crime and Justice: An Annual Edition*, vol. 23, ed. Michael Tonry (Chicago: University of Chicago Press, 1998), pp. 407–455; James Alan Fox and Jack Levin, *Overkill: Mass Murder and Serial Killing Exposed* (New York: Plenum, 1994); James Alan Fox, Jack Levin, and Kenna Quinet, *The Will to Kill: Making Sense of Senseless Murder*, 2nd ed. (Boston: Allyn & Bacon, 2004); James Allan Fox and Jack Levin, "A Psycho-Social Analysis of Mass Murder," in *Serial and Mass Murder: Theory, Policy, and Research*, eds. Thomas O'Reilly-Fleming and Steven Egger (Toronto: University of Toronto Press, 1993).

183. James Alan Fox and Jack Levin, "Mass Murder: An Analysis of Extreme Violence," *Journal of Applied Psychoanalytic Studies* 5 (2003): 47–64.

184. Grant Duwe, "The Patterns And Prevalence of Mass Murder in Twentieth-Century America," *Justice Quarterly* 21 (2004): 729–761.

185. Elissa Gootman, "The Hunt for a Sniper: The Victim; 10th Victim Is Recalled as Motivator on Mission," *New York Times*, 14 October 2002, p. A15; Sarah Kershaw, "The Hunt for a Sniper: The Investigation; Endless Frustration but Little Evidence in Search for Sniper," *New York Times*, 14 October 2002, p. A1.

186. "Mugshots, Court TV's Criminal Biography Series, Profiles Racist Serial Killer Joseph Paul Franklin," www.courttv.com/archive/press/Franklin.html (accessed April 24, 2007).

187. Francis X. Clines with Christopher Drew, "Prosecutors to Discuss Charges as Rifle Is Tied to Sniper Killings," *New York Times*, 25 October 2002, p. A1.

188. Federal Bureau of Investigation, *Crime in the United States*, 2005.

189. Keith Harries, "Homicide and Assault: A Comparative Analysis of Attributes in Dallas Neighborhoods, 1981–1985," *Professional Geographer* 41 (1989): 29–38.

190. Kevin Flynn, "Record Payouts in Settlements of Lawsuits against the New York City Police Are Set for Year," *New York Times*, 1 October 1999, p. 12.

191. Etienne Krug, Linda Dahlberg, James Mercy, Anthony Zwi, and Rafael Lozano, *World Report on Violence and Health* (Geneva: World Health Organization, 2002).

192. Ibid., p. 89.

193. Ibid., p. 93.

194. See generally Ruth S. Kempe and C. Henry Kempe, *Child Abuse* (Cambridge, MA: Harvard University Press, 1978).

195. U.S. Department of Health and Human Services, Administration for Children and Families, Children's Bureau, *Child Maltreatment*, 2002 (Washington, DC: U.S. Department of Health and Human Services, 2004).

196. National Clearinghouse on Child Abuse and Neglect, *Child Abuse and Neglect Fatalities: Statistics and Interventions, 2006*, www.childwelfare.gov/pubs/factsheets/fatality.cfm (accessed April 24, 2007).

197. David Finkelhor and Lisa Jones, "Why Have Child Maltreatment and Child Victimization Declined?" *Journal of Social Issues* 62 (2006): 685–716.

198. Wolfner and Gelles, "A Profile of Violence toward Children."

199. Martin Daly and Margo Wilson, "Violence against Step Children," *Current Directions in Psychological Science* 5 (1996): 77–81.

200. Ruth Inglis, *Sins of the Fathers: A Study of the Physical and Emotional Abuse of Children* (New York: St. Martin's, 1978), p. 53.

201. Diana Russell, "The Incidence and Prevalence of Intrafamilial and Extrafamilial Sexual Abuse of Female Children," *Child Abuse and Neglect* 7 (1983): 133–146; see also David Finkelhor, *Sexually Victimized Children* (New York: Free Press, 1979), p. 88.

202. Jeanne Hernandez, "Eating Disorders and Sexual Abuse in Adolescents," paper presented at the annual meeting of the American Psychosomatic Society, Charleston, South Carolina, March 1993; Glenn Wolfner and Richard Gelles, "A Profile of Violence toward Children: A National Study," *Child Abuse and Neglect* 17 (1993): 197–212.

203. Lisa Jones and David Finkelhor, *The Decline in Child Sexual Abuse Cases* (Washington, DC: Office of Juvenile Justice and Delinquency Prevention, 2001).

204. Lisa Jones, David Finkelhor, and Kathy Kopie, "Why Is Sexual Abuse Declining? A Survey of State Child Protection Administrators," *Child Abuse and Neglect* 25 (2001): 1,139–1,141.

205. Eva Jonzon and Frank Lindblad, "Adult Female Victims of Child Sexual Abuse," *Journal of Interpersonal Violence* 20 (2005): 651–666.

206. Jane Siegel and Linda Williams, "Risk Factors for Sexual Victimization of Women," *Violence Against Women* 9 (2003): 902–930.

207. Arina Ulman and Murray Straus, "Violence by Children against Mothers in Relation to Violence between Parents and Corporal Punishment by Parents," *Journal of Comparative Family Studies* 34 (2003): 41–63.

208. R. Emerson Dobash and Russell Dobash, *Violence against Wives* (New York: Free Press, 1979).

209. Julia O'Faolain and Laura Martines, eds., *Not in God's Image: Women in History* (Glasgow: Fontana/Collins, 1974).

210. Laurence Stone, "The Rise of the Nuclear Family in Modern England: The Patriarchal Stage," in *The Family in History*, ed. Charles Rosenberg (Philadelphia: University of Pennsylvania Press, 1975), p. 53.

211. Dobash and Dobash, *Violence against Wives*, p. 46.

212. John Braithwaite, "Inequality and Republican Criminology," paper presented at the annual meeting of the American Society of Criminology, San Francisco, November 1991, p. 20.

213. Richard Gelles and Murray Straus, "Violence in the American Family," *Journal of Social Issues* 35 (1979): 15–39.

214. Miguel Schwartz, Susan O'Leary, and Kimberly Kendziora, "Dating Aggression among High School Students," *Violence and Victimization* 12 (1997): 295–307; James Makepeace, "Social Factor and Victim–Offender Differences in Courtship Violence," *Family Relations* 33 (1987): 87–91.

215. Jay Silverman, Anita Raj, Lorelei Mucci, and Jeanne Hathaway, "Dating Violence against Adolescent Girls and Associated Substance Abuse, Unhealthy Weight Control, Sexual Risk Behavior, Pregnancy, and Suicidality," *Journal of the American Medical Association* 286 (2001): 572–579.

216. FBI, *Crime in the United States*, 2005,

217. James Calder and John Bauer, "Convenience Store Robberies: Security Measures and Store Robbery Incidents," *Journal of Criminal Justice* 20 (1992): 553–566.

218. Richard Felson, Eric Baumer, and Steven Messner, "Acquaintance Robbery," *Journal of Research in Crime and Delinquency* 37 (2000): 284–305.

219. Ibid., p. 287.

220. Ibid.

221. Peter Van Koppen and Robert Jansen, "The Time to Rob: Variations in Time of Number of Commercial Robberies," *Journal of Research in Crime and Delinquency* 36 (1999): 7–29.

222. Jody Miller, "Up It Up: Gender and the Accomplishment of Street Robbery," *Criminology* 36 (1998): 37–67.

223. Ibid., pp. 54–55.

224. Richard Wright and Scott Decker, *Armed Robbers in Action, Stickups and Street Culture* (Boston: Northeastern University Press, 1997).

225. James Brooke, "Gay Student Who Was Kidnapped and Beaten Dies," *New York Times*, 13 October 1998, A1.

226. Melanie Otis, "Perceptions of Victimization Risk and Fear of Crime Among Lesbians and Gay Men," *Journal of Interpersonal Violence* 22 (2007): 198–217.

227. James Garofalo, "Bias and Non-Bias Crimes in New York City: Preliminary Findings," paper presented at the annual meeting of the American Society of Criminology, Baltimore, November 1990.

228. Ronald Powers, "Bensonhurst Man Guilty," *Boston Globe*, 18 May 1990, p. 3.

229. "Boy Gets 18 Years in Fatal Park Beating of Transient," *Los Angeles Times*, 24 December 1987, p. 9B.

230. Ewing, *When Children Kill*, pp. 65–66.

231. Mike McPhee, "In Denver, Attacks Stir Fears of Racism," *Boston Globe*, 10 December 1990, p. 3.

232. Jack Levin and Jack McDevitt, *Hate Crimes: The Rising Tide of Bigotry and Bloodshed* (New York: Plenum Press, 1993).

233. Jack McDevitt, Jack Levin, and Susan Bennett, "Hate Crime Offenders: An Expanded Typology," *Journal of Social Issues* 58 (2002): 303–318.

234. Jack Levin, *The Violence of Hate, Confronting Racism, Anti-Semitism, and other Forms of Bigotry* (Boston: Allyn & Bacon, 2002), pp. 29–56.

235. FBI, *Hate Crime Statistics, 2005* (Washington, DC: FBI, 2006).

236. Ibid.

237. Kevin J. Strom, *Hate Crimes Reported in NIBRS, 1997–99* (Washington, DC: Bureau of Justice Statistics, 2001).

238. Gregory Herek, Jeanine Cogan, and Roy Gillis, "Victim Experiences in Hate Crimes Based on Sexual Orientation," *Journal of Social Issues* 58 (2002): 319–340.

239. Garofalo, "Bias and Non-Bias Crimes in New York City," p. 3.

240. Brian Levin, "From Slavery to Hate Crime Laws: The Emergence of Race and Status-Based Protection in American Criminal Law," *Journal of Social Issues* 58 (2002): 227–246.

241. Felicia Lee, "Gays Angry Over TV Report on a Murder," *New York Times*, 26 November 2004, A3.

242. Frederick M. Lawrence, *Punishing Hate: Bias Crimes under American Law* (Cambridge, MA: Harvard University Press, 1999).

243. Ibid., p. 3.

244. Ibid., p. 9.

245. Ibid., p. 11.

246. Ibid., pp. 39–42.

247. Jack McDevitt, Jennifer Balboni, Luis Garcia, and Joann Gu, "Consequences for Victims: A Comparison of Bias- and Non-Bias-Motivated Assaults," *American Behavioral Scientist* 45 (2001): 697–714.

248. *Virginia v. Black et al.* No. 01-1107. 2003.

249. Carl Weiser, "This Is What You Get for Firing Me," *USA Today*, 28 January 1993, p. 3A.

250. James Alan Fox and Jack Levin, "Firing Back: The Growing Threat of Workplace Homicide," *Annals* 536 (1994): 16–30.

251. FBI, *Workplace Violence: Issues in Response* (Quantico, VA: National Center for the Analysis of Violent Crime, 2001) www.fbi.gov/publications/violence.pdf (accessed April 24, 2007).

252. John King, "Workplace Violence: A Conceptual Framework," paper presented at the annual meeting of the American Society of Criminology, Phoenix, November 1993.

253. Janet R. Copper, "Response to 'Workplace Violence in Health Care: Recognized but Not Regulated,' by Kathleen M. McPhaul and Jane A. Lipscomb (September 30, 2004)," *Online Journal of Issues in Nursing* 10 (2005): 53–55.

254. Associated Press, "Gunman Wounds 3 Doctors in L.A. Hospital," *Cleveland Plain Dealer*, 9 February 1993, p. 1B.

255. Fox and Levin, "Firing Back," p. 5.

256. Michael Mantell and Steve Albrecht, *Ticking Bombs: Defusing Violence in the Workplace* (New York: Irwin, 1994).

257. Detis Duhart, *Workplace Violence, 1993–99* (Washington, DC: Bureau of Justice Statistics, 2001).

258. Centers for Disease Control, National Institute for Occupational Safety and Health, *Violence, Occupational Hazards in Hospitals* (Atlanta: National Institutes of Health, 2002).

259. Dana Loomis, Stephen Marshall, and Myduc Ta, "Employer Policies Toward Guns and the Risk of Homicide in the Workplace," *American Journal of Public Health* 95 (2005): 830–832.

260. The following sections rely heavily on Patricia Tjaden, *The Crime of Stalking: How Big Is the Problem?* (Washington, DC: National Institute of Justice, 1997); see also Robert M. Emerson, Kerry O. Ferris, and Carol Brooks Gardner, "On Being Stalked," *Social Problems* 45 (1998): 289–298.

261. Patrick Kinkade, Ronald Burns, and Angel Ilarraza Fuentes, "Criminalizing Attractions: Perceptions of Stalking and the Stalker," *Crime and Delinquency* 51 (2005): 3–25.

262. Kathleen Basile, Monica Swahn, Jieru Chen, and Linda Saltzman, "Stalking in the United States: Recent National Prevalence Estimates," *American Journal of Preventive Medicine* 31 (2006):172–175.

263. Bonnie Fisher, Francis Cullen, and Michael Turner, "Being Pursued: Stalking Victimization in a National Study of College Women," *Criminology and Public Policy* 1 (2002): 257–309.

264. Brian Spitzberg and William Cupach, "The State of the Art of Stalking: Taking Stock of the Emerging Literature," *Aggression and Violent Behavior* 12 (2007): 64–86.

265. Reid Meloy, "Stalking: The State of the Science," *Criminal Behaviour and Mental Health* 17 (2007): 1–7.

266. Mary Brewster, "Stalking by Former Intimates: Verbal Threats and Other Predictors of Physical Violence," *Violence and Victims* 15 (2000): 41–51.

267. Spitzberg and Cupach, "The State of the Art of Stalking."

268. Carol Jordan, T. K. Logan, and Robert Walker, "Stalking: An Examination of the Criminal Justice Response," *Journal of Interpersonal Violence* 18 (2003): 148–165.

CHAPTER **11**

Political Crime and Terrorism

CHAPTER OUTLINE

Political Crime
The Nature of Political Crimes
The Goals of Political Crime
Becoming a Political Criminal

Types of Political Crimes
Election Fraud
Treason
Espionage
PROFILES IN CRIME: Azzam the American
State Political Crime
PROFILES IN CRIME: Aldrich Hazen Ames
Using Torture
The Criminological Enterprise: Want to Torture? Get a Warrant

Terrorism
Terror Cells
Terrorist and Guerilla
Terrorist and Insurgent
Terrorist and Revolutionary

A Brief History of Terrorism
Religious Roots
Political Roots

Contemporary Forms of Terrorism
Revolutionary Terrorists
Political Terrorists
Nationalist Terrorism
Retributive Terrorism
State-Sponsored Terrorism
Cult Terrorism
Criminal Terrorism

How Are Terror Groups Organized?

What Motivates the Terrorist?
Psychological View
Alienation View
Socialization/Friendship View
Religious/Ideological View
Explaining State-Sponsored Terrorism

Response to Terrorism
Fighting Terrorism with Law Enforcement
Confronting Terrorism with the Law
Political Solutions to Terrorism

CHAPTER OBJECTIVES

1. Be able to define political crime
2. Discuss the motivations and goals of political criminals
3. Find out what accounts for election fraud
4. Distinguish between treason and espionage
5. Be familiar with the term "state-sponsored crime"
6. Distinguish among terrorists, guerillas, and insurgents
7. Know the factors that may cause someone to become a terrorist
8. Be familiar with the background of the contemporary terrorist
9. Be able to discuss federal, local, and state anti-terror initiatives
10. Know the USA Patriot Act and be able to discuss its impact on the American public

On December 27, 2007, Pakistani political leader Benazir Bhutto was assassinated while leaving an election rally in Rawalpindi. While the exact cause of her death is under investigation at this time, there is no question that she was shot at by gunmen who then set off a bomb, killing more than 20 other people and injuring many others. (Some reports indicate that she was hit by shrapnel, others that she was shot, while the Pakistani government claimed she died from a fractured skull caused by hitting her head on part of her car's sunroof.) Bhutto, the daughter of a former prime minister, and educated at Harvard and Oxford universities, had been elected prime minister in 1988 and again in 1993. She had just returned to Pakistan after years in exile in order to run once again for public office. Her death was linked to Baitullah Mehsud, a militant leader who had orchestrated suicide attacks on government, military, and intelligence targets. Mehsud was also known to have run training camps, prepared and dispatched suicide bombers on both sides of the Afghanistan-Pakistan border, and have links to al-Qaeda and other terror groups.

The death of Benazir Bhutto is just one in a continuing string of terrorist acts that have rocked the world since 9/11. As a result, political crime and terrorism have become important areas of criminological inquiry, and many criminologists who previously paid scant attention to the interaction between political motivation and crime have now made it the focus of intense study. This chapter reviews the concept of both violent and nonviolent political crime. We will briefly discuss the concept of political crime, discuss some of its various forms, and then turn to its most extreme variety, terrorism. Because terrorism now occupies the center stage of both world opinion and government policy, it is important for students of criminology to develop a basic understanding of its definition, history, and structure, and review the steps being taken to limit or eliminate its occurrence.

POLITICAL CRIME

While terrorism now occupies the focal point of public concern, it is merely one of many different types of politically motivated crimes. The term **political crime** is used to signify illegal acts that are designed to undermine an existing government and threaten its survival.[1] Political crimes can include both violent and nonviolent acts and range in seriousness from dissent, treason, and espionage to violent acts such as terrorism or assassination.[2]

When an act becomes a political crime and when an actor is considered a political criminal are often extremely subjective. In highly repressive nations, any form of nonsanctioned political activity, including writing a newspaper article critical of the regime, may be considered a political crime, punishable by a prison term or even death. Take for instance the current situation in the central Asian nation of Azerbaijan. According to watchdog group Amnesty International, harassment and ill treatment of opposition journalists by police and other government officials has become routine. The government is bent on silencing rival journalists through arrest and imprisonment on dubious charges or by levying heavy fines following trials for criminal defamation. In contrast, there have been no instances of attacks on progovernment journalists in Azerbaijan.[3] Similarly, people who some label as terrorists and insurrectionists are viewed by others as freedom fighters and revolutionaries. What would have happened to George Washington and Benjamin Franklin had the British won the Revolutionary War? Would they have been hanged for their political crimes or considered heroes and freedom fighters?

The Nature of Political Crimes

The political criminal and political crimes may stem from religious or ideological sources. Because their motivations shift between selfish personal needs and selfless, noble, and/or altruistic desires, political crimes often occupy a gray area between conventional and outlawed behavior. It is easy to condemn interpersonal violent crimes such as rape or murder because their goals are typically selfish and self-centered (e.g., revenge or

profit). In contrast, political criminals may be motivated by conviction rather than greed or anger. While it is true that some political crime involves profit (such as selling state secrets for money), most political criminals do not consider themselves antisocial but instead patriotic and altruistic. They are willing to sacrifice themselves for what they consider to be the greater good. While some concoct elaborate schemes to hide or mask their actions, others are quite brazen, hoping to provoke the government to overreact in their zeal to crack down on dissent. Because state authorities may engage in a range of retaliatory actions that result in human rights violations, even those who support the government may begin to question its activities: maybe the government is corrupt and authoritarian? On the other hand, if the government does nothing, it appears weak and corrupt and unable to protect citizens.

Even those political criminals who profit personally from their misdeeds, such as someone who spies for an enemy nation for financial payoffs, may believe that their acts are motivated by a higher calling than common theft. "My ultimate goal is to weaken or overthrow a corrupt government," they reason, "so selling secrets to the enemy is justified." Political criminals may believe that their acts are criminalized only because the group holding power fears them and wants to curtail their behavior. And while the general public has little objection to laws that control extreme behaviors such as plotting a bloody revolution, they may have questions when a law criminalizes ordinary political dissent or bans political meetings in order to control suspected political criminals.

The Goals of Political Crime

While common criminals may be motivated by greed, vengeance, or jealousy, political criminals have a somewhat different agenda. Rather than personal profit, their acts are aimed at achieving a different set of goals:

▮ *Intimidation*. Some political criminals may want to intimidate or threaten an opponent who does not share their political orientation or views.

▮ *Revolution*. Some political criminals may plot to overthrow the existing government and replace it with one that holds views they find more acceptable.

▮ *Profit*. Another goal of political crime is profit: selling state secrets for personal enrichment or trafficking in stolen arms and munitions.

▮ *Conviction*. Some political criminals are motivated by altruism; they truly believe their crimes will benefit society and are willing to violate the law and risk punishment in order to achieve what they see as social improvement.

▮ *Pseudo-conviction*. These political criminals conceal conventional criminal motivations behind a mask of conviction and altruism. They may form a revolutionary movement out of a hidden desire to engage in violence rather than their stated goal of reforming society. The pseudo-convictional criminal is particularly dangerous because they convince followers to join them in their crimes without fully revealing their true motivations.[4]

Becoming a Political Criminal

Why does someone become a political criminal? There is no set pattern or reason; motivations vary widely. Some use political crime as a stepping stone to public office while others as a method to focus their frustrations. Others hope they can gain respect from their friends and family. Although the motivations for political crime are complex and varied, there does appear to be some regularity in the way ideas are formed. Political crime expert Randy Borum finds that this pattern takes the form of a series of cognitive stages:

▎ Stage 1: *"It's not right."* An unhappy, dissatisfied individual identifies some type of undesirable event or condition. It could be economic (poverty, unemployment, poor living conditions) or social (government-imposed restrictions on individual freedoms, lack of order, or morality) or personal ("I am being cheated out of what is due me"). While the conditions may vary, those involved perceive the experience as "things are not as they should be."

▎ Stage 2: *"It's not fair."* The prospective criminal concludes that the undesirable condition is a product of "injustice"— that is, it does not apply to everyone. A government worker may feel their low pay scale is "not right" and that corporate workers with less skill are making more money and getting more benefits. At the same time, government workers are portrayed as lazy and corrupt. For those who are deprived, this facilitates feelings of resentment and injustice.

▎ Stage 3: *"It's your fault."* Someone or some group must be held accountable for the extremists' displeasure. It always helps to identify a potential target. For example, the underpaid worker may become convinced that minorities get all the good jobs while the worker is suffering financially. Extremist groups spread this propaganda to attract recruits. Americans may be portrayed as rich and undeserving by overseas enemies looking to recruit disenfranchised young men and women to become terrorists.

▎ Stage 4: *"You're evil."* Because good people would not intentionally hurt others, targeted groups are appropriate targets for revenge and/or violence. The disaffected government worker concludes that since his country has let him down it is only fair to sell state secrets to foreign nations for profit or to join a terrorist group or both. Aggression becomes justifiable when aimed against "bad" people, particularly those who intentionally cause harm to others. Second, by casting the target as "evil," it dehumanizes them and makes justifying aggression even easier. So it's not so bad to rig an election, because the opposing candidates are evil and do not deserve to hold office.[5]

connections

Borum's typology seems similar to the techniques of neutralization discussed in Chapter 7. Is it possible that terrorists must neutralize feelings of guilt and shame before planting their bombs? Or do their religious and political beliefs negate any need for psychological process to reduce personal responsibility for violence?

TYPES OF POLITICAL CRIMES

Considering the cognitive stages that produce political crime and terrorism, what are the specific crimes and what form do they take?

Election Fraud

On October 31, 2007, the Federal Election Commission (FEC) announced that it had levied a $1 million fine on Mitchell Wade and MZM, Inc.—the second largest penalty ever paid in the 32-year history of the FEC. According to the FEC, Wade directed corporate contributions to two political candidates, representatives Virgil Goode and Katherine Harris, by funneling cash to employees of MZM, and in some cases their spouses, to make the contributions. In total, Mitchell Wade and his MZM proxies reimbursed, directly and indirectly, $78,000 in contributions to the two candidates.[6] Why were Wade's activities a crime? Because federal law limits an individual's political contributions to $2,300 per candidate and Wade clearly intended to circumvent the law by using proxies for his contributions.[7]

Some political criminals want to shape elections to meet their personal needs. In some instances their goal is altruistic: the election of candidates that reflect their personal political views. In others, their actions are motivated by profit: they are paid by a candidate to rig the election.

Whatever the motive, election fraud is illegal interference with the process of an election. Acts of fraud tend to involve affecting vote counts to bring about a desired election outcome, whether by increasing the vote share of the favored candidate, depressing the vote share of the rival candidates, or both.

In some third world dictatorships, election fraud is the norm and it is common for the ruling party to announce, after party members counted the votes, that they were returned to office with an overwhelming majority. Sometimes allegations of voter fraud by ruling juntas can have disastrous consequences. Take for instance the parliamentary elections that took place in Kenya on December 27, 2007. When it was announced that President Mwai Kibaki had won the presidential election over opposition candidate Raila Odinga, fighting broke out that tore this African nation apart.[8]

Voter fraud has been around since Roman times; a few prominent examples include:

▎ *Intimidation.* Voters can be scared away from the polls through threats or intimidation. Having armed guards posted at polling places may convince people it is dangerous to vote. Lists of registered voters can be obtained and people subjected to threatening calls before the election.

▎ *Disruption.* Bomb threats can be called into voting places in areas that are known to heavily favor the opposing party, with the goal of suppressing the vote. There can be outright sabotage of polling places, ballots, ballot boxes, and voting machines (see Exhibit 11.1).

Police arrest a man suspected of planting a bomb near the parliament house in Kathmandu on May 28, 2008. Two small bombs exploded in Nepal's capital only hours before political parties were due to abolish its once-revered Hindu monarchy at a special assembly session.

■ *Misinformation*. Flyers are sent out to voters registered with the opposition party containing misleading information, such as the wrong election date, or saying that rules have been changed about who is eligible to vote.

■ *Registration fraud*. Political operatives may want to shape the outcome of an election by busing in noneligible voters from other districts. Because many jurisdictions require minimal identification and proof of citizenship, political criminals find it easy to get around residency requirements.

They may provide conspirators with "change of address" forms to allow them to vote in a particular election, when in fact no actual change of address has occurred.

■ *Vote buying*. Securing votes by payment or other rewards or the selling of one's vote is an age-old problem that still exists. One popular method is to buy absentee ballots from people who are in need of cash. The fraudulent voter can then ensure that the vote goes their way, an outcome that cannot be guaranteed if the conspirator casts a secret ballot at a polling place.

Most states have created laws to control and punish vote fraud. The federal government has a number of statutes designed to control and/or restrict fraud, including 18 U.S.C. § 594, which provides:

> *Whoever intimidates, threatens, coerces, or attempts to intimidate, threaten, or coerce, any other person for the purpose of interfering with the right of such other person to vote or to vote as he may choose, or of causing such other person to vote for, or not to vote for, any candidate for the office of President, Vice President, Presidential elector, Member of the Senate, Member of the House of Representatives, Delegate from the District of Columbia, or Resident Commissioner, at any election held solely or in part for the purpose of electing such candidate, shall be fined under this title or imprisoned not more than one year, or both.*

Another provision that applies to voting is 18 U.S.C. § 245(b) (1)(A):

> *Whoever, whether or not acting under color of law, by force or threat of force willfully injures, intimidates or interferes with, or attempts to injure, intimidate or interfere with (1) any person because he is or has been, or in order to intimidate such person or any other person or any class of persons from (A) voting or qualifying to vote, qualifying or campaigning as a candidate for elective office, or qualifying or acting as a poll watcher, or any legally authorized election official, in any primary, special, or general election. . . .*

This provision is in the Civil Rights section of Title 18, the federal criminal code, and it protects the right of all citizens to vote and campaign for office.

EXHIBIT 11.1

Political Violence in Nepal

In Nepal, a 10-year conflict among Maoist insurgents, the police, and the army claimed more than 13,000 lives. In November 2006, Nepal's coalition government and the Communist Party of Nepal (Maoist) signed a comprehensive peace agreement to end the fighting. The Nepali Army and Maoists agreed to participate in elections to create a constituent assembly that would rewrite the country's constitution, including whether it would remain a monarchy. During the election campaign, supporters of all major parties clashed almost daily. On April 6, 2008, the United Nations Mission in Nepal (UNMIN) reported that "election-related violence and intimidation by party workers continues, with frequent and sometimes severe clashes between political parties in many districts." UNMIN said that the Youth Communist League and

other Maoist cadres were involved in the largest proportion of incidents. On April 7, 2008, even as campaigning drew to a close, 12 people were injured in bomb attacks. On April 8, unknown assailants shot dead Rishi Prasad Sharma, a candidate for the Communist Party of Nepal (United Marxist-Leninist). But in spite of clashes and bombings in the weeks leading up the polls, the Nepalese Election Commission said that only 33 of the 21,000 polling booths had to be shut as a result of the violence, an outcome that was actually better than expected.

Sources: Human Rights Watch, "Nepal: Violence Threatens Elections Government and Party Leaders Should Ensure Peaceful Vote," April 9, 2008, www.hrw.org/english/docs/2008/04/08/nepal18476.htm (accessed July 11, 2008); BBC News, "Q&A: Nepal's future," April 11, 2008, http://news.bbc.co.uk/2/hi/south_asia/2707107.stm (accessed July 11, 2008).

Treason

Few people can forget the image of John Walker Lindh, the so-called "American Taliban," when he was captured during the American invasion of Afghanistan. Lindh, who had spent his early years in an affluent Northern California community, converted to Islam and through a convoluted path wound up first in an al-Qaeda training camp and then fighting with the Taliban on the front lines in Afghanistan. He was captured on November 25, 2001, by Afghan Northern Alliance forces, and questioned by CIA agents. Later that day, there was a violent uprising in the prison in which he was being held and during the attack a CIA agent was killed. Walker escaped only to be recaptured seven days later. At his trial, he apologized for fighting alongside the Taliban, saying, "Had I realized then what I know now . . . I never would have joined them" (see Exhibit 11.2). The 21-year-old said Osama bin Laden is against Islam and that he "never understood jihad to mean anti-American or terrorism. . . . I understand why so many Americans were angry when I was first discovered in Afghanistan. I realize many still are, but I hope in time that feeling will change." After a plea agreement, John Walker Lindh was sentenced to 20 years in prison.[9]

Lindh's behavior amounts to what is commonly called treason, an act of disloyalty to one's nation or state. While the crime of treason is well known and the word "traitor" is a generic term, there have actually been fewer than 40 prosecutions for treason in the entire history of the United States and most have resulted in acquittal. In fact, though his behavior might be considered *treasonous*, Lindh was not actually charged or convicted of treason but was charged with serving in the Taliban army and carrying weapons.

While the Lindh case grabbed headlines, the most famous treason case in U.S. history is still the 1807 trial of former Vice President Aaron Burr, a man best known for killing Secretary of the Treasury Alexander Hamilton in 1804 in a duel over a matter of honor. In 1807, Burr was accused of hatching a plot to separate the Western states from the union. When that plot went awry, he conspired to seize Mexico and set up a puppet government with himself as king! Arrested on charges of treason, he was acquitted when the Federal Court, headed by John Marshall, ruled that to be guilty of treason an overt act must be committed; planning is not enough.[10]

Because treason is considered such a heinous crime, and to deter would-be traitors, many nations apply or have applied the death penalty to those convicted of attempting to overthrow the existing government. Treason was considered particularly loathsome under English common law, and until the nineteenth century it was punishable by being "drawn and quartered," a method of execution that involved hanging the offender, removing their intestines while still living, and finally cutting the offender into four pieces for public display. William Wallace, the Scottish patriot made famous in the film *Braveheart*, was so displayed after his execution.

Acts can be considered treasonous in order to stifle political dissent. In eighteenth century England, it was considered treasonous to merely criticize the king or his behavior, and not surprisingly, the American colonists feared giving their own central government that much power. Therefore treason is the only crime mentioned in the United States Constitution, which defines treason as levying war against the United States or "in adhering to their Enemies, giving them Aid and Comfort," and requires the testimony of two witnesses or a confession in open court for conviction. The purpose of this was to limit the government's ability to bring charges of treason against opponents and to make it more difficult to prosecute those who are so charged.

Today, the United States Criminal Code codifies treason as follows:[11]

> . . . *whoever, owing allegiance to the United States, levies war against them or adheres to their enemies, giving them aid and comfort within the United States or elsewhere, is guilty of treason and shall suffer death, or shall be imprisoned not less than five years and fined under this title but not less than $10,000; and shall be incapable of holding any office under the United States.*[12]

Helping or cooperating with the enemy in a time of war (as Lindh did) would be considered treason; so too would be creating or recruiting a military force to help a foreign nation overthrow the government. After World War II, two women—Iva Ikuko Toguri D'Aquino, a Japanese American born in Los Angeles and known as Tokyo Rose, and Mildred Elizabeth Gillars, born in Portland, Maine, and known as Axis Sally—served prison terms for broadcasting for the Axis powers in an effort to demoralize American troops. The first treason charge in the past 50 years was actually levied against a California man, Adam Gadahn, whose case is summarized in the Profiles in Crime feature "Azzam the American."

Espionage

Robert Hanssen was a counterintelligence agent for the FBI assigned to detect and identify Russian spies. A former Chicago police officer, Hanssen's assignment required him to have

---

EXHIBIT 11.2

What Is Jihad?

When John Walker Lindh used the word "jihad" he made reference to a term that has become all too familiar in contemporary society. But the term, which is often assumed to mean "holy war," is more complex than that simple meaning. According to terror expert Andrew Silke, the phrase derives from the Arabic for "struggle," and within Islam there are two forms of jihad: the Greater Jihad and the Lesser Jihad. The Greater Jihad refers to a Muslim's personal struggle to live a good and charitable life and adhere to God's commands. In this sense, jihad is a strictly personal and nonviolent phenomenon. The Lesser Jihad refers to violent struggle on behalf of Islam. Jihadists—literally "those who struggle"—refers to individuals who have volunteered to fight in the Lesser Jihad. Jihadists sometimes call themselves *mujahideen*, meaning "holy warriors."

Source: Andrew Silke, "Holy Warriors: Exploring the Psychological Processes of Jihadi Radicalization," *European Journal of Criminology* 5 (2008): 99–123.

PROFILES IN CRIME

IntelCenter

AZZAM THE AMERICAN

The most recent case in which actual treason has been charged involves a 28-year-old California man, Adam Gadahn, also known as Azzam the American. Gadahn was indicted in 2006 for making a series of propaganda videotapes for al-Qaeda, including one in which he praised the 9/11 hijackers and referred to the United States as "enemy soil."

Gadahn was raised in a counterculture atmosphere on a rural farm. His father, Philip Pearlstein, was the son of a well-known Jewish doctor; his mother was a computer whiz from Pennsylvania. His parents were self-sufficient, raising their son in a cabin with no running water and with electricity produced from solar panels. Though they hoped that by living in isolation and austerity they could avoid the chaotic and destructive elements of contemporary society, Adam Gadahn became heavily involved in the death metal culture. Still feeling empty and alienated, he began studying Islam at age 17, with the Islamic Society of Orange County. He later moved to Pakistan and married an Afghan woman.

Gadahn appeared in a series of videotaped segments that were broadcast between October 2004 and May 2007. In the first tape, Gadahn was shown wearing black sunglasses and a headdress wrapped around his face. He identified himself as Azzam the American and announced his relationship with al-Qaeda. "The streets of America shall run red with blood," he claimed. In a broadcast in 2005, around the fourth anniversary of the 9/11 attacks, Gadahn called the attacks "blessed raids" and discussed the "jihad against America." In 2006, Gadahn appeared in a videotape that also contained statements from Osama bin Laden and Ayman al-Zawahiri and then made another propaganda broadcast that aired on the fifth anniversary of 9/11. On May 29, 2007, Gadahn again made headlines when he issued another video that listed six actions that America must take in order to prevent future terrorist attacks:

▌ "Pull every last one of your soldiers, spies, security advisors, trainers, attachés, . . . out of every Muslim land from Afghanistan to Zanzibar . . ."

▌ "End all support and aid, military, political, economic, or otherwise, to the 56-plus apostate regimes of the

Muslim world, and abandon them to their well-deserved fate . . ."

▌ "End all support, moral, military, economic, political, or otherwise, to the bastard state of Israel, and ban your citizens, Zionist Jews, Zionist Christians, and the rest from traveling to occupied Palestine or settling there. Even one penny of aid will be considered sufficient justification to continue the fight."

▌ "Leave all Muslims alone."

▌ "Impose a blanket ban on all broadcasts to our region."

▌ "Free all Muslim captives from your prisons, detention facilities, and concentration camps, regardless of whether they have been recipients of what you call a fair trial or not."

Gadahn warned, "Your failure to meet our demands . . . means that you and your people will, Allah willing, experience things which will make you forget about the horrors of September 11. . . . This is not a call for negotiations. We do not negotiate with baby killers and war criminals like you." Gadahn also warned George Bush, "You will go down in history not only as the president who embroiled his nation in a series of unwinnable and bloody conflicts in the Islamic world but as the president who set the United States up on its death march." Gadahn is the first person to be charged with treason against the United States in almost 50 years.

Sources: Craig Whitlock, "Converts to Islam Move Up in Cells, Arrests in Europe Illuminate Shift," *Washington Post*, 15 September 2007, p. A10, www.washingtonpost.com/wp-dyn/content/article/2007/09/14/AR2007091402265.html (accessed July 11, 2008); Federal Bureau of Investigation, "American Charged with Treason," October 11, 2006, www.fbi.gov/page2/oct2006/gadahn101106.htm (accessed July 11, 2008); video on Myzine.com, www.myzine.com/play.php?pid=10094 (accessed July 11, 2008); Raffi Khatchadourian, "Azzam the American: The Making of an Al Qaeda Homegrown," *New Yorker*, January 22, 2007, www.newyorker.com/reporting/2007/01/22/070122fa_fact_khatchadourian (accessed July 11, 2008).

access to sensitive top-secret information. In one of the most shocking cases in U.S. history, Hanssen volunteered to become a paid spy for the KGB during the Cold War and over a period of 15 years received at least $1.4 million in cash and diamonds. He was arrested on February 18, 2001, after leaving a package of classified documents for his Russian handlers under a footbridge in a park outside Washington, D.C. During his years as a

double agent, Hanssen not only provided more than 6,000 pages of documents to the Soviet Union but also caused the death of two U.S. double agents whose identities were uncovered with the aid of his secret documents. The Hanssen case, one of the most damaging instances of espionage in U.S. history, was the subject of the 2007 film *Breach*, which starred Chris Cooper as the corrupt agent.[13]

Espionage (more commonly called spying) is the practice of obtaining information about a government, organization, or society that is considered secret or confidential without the permission of the holder of the information. Espionage involves obtaining the information illegally by covertly entering the area where the information is stored, secretly photographing forbidden areas, or subverting through threat or payoff people who know the information and will divulge it through subterfuge.[14]

Espionage is typically associated with spying on potential or actual enemies by a foreign agent who is working for his or her nation's intelligence service. However, there are numerous cases of homegrown spies who are motivated by misguided altruism or belief. Perhaps the most famous international case involved a group of five upper-crust students recruited during the cold war at prestigious Cambridge University in England by Russia's secret service, the KGB. The five were motivated by the belief that capitalism was corrupt and that the Soviet Union offered a better model for society. After graduation, they secured sensitive government posts which gave them access to valuable intelligence they then passed on to the Soviet Union. Two of the conspirators, Guy Burgess and Donald Maclean, were exposed in 1951 and defected to the Soviet Union before they could be captured; Kim Philby, who had worked as a high level intelligence agent, defected to Russia in 1963 but not before passing on information that cost hundreds of lives. The last two members of the ring, Anthony Blunt and John Cairncross, went undetected for many years.[15]

While some spies, like the Cambridge Five, are motivated by ideology, others, like Robert Hanssen, are looking for profit. Government employees in a position of trust may offer to misappropriate state secrets for a payoff from a foreign government. One of the most infamous of these cases, that of CIA double agent Aldrich Ames, is set out in the Profiles in Crime feature.

Industrial Espionage The concept of espionage has been extended to spying involving corporations, referred to as industrial espionage. This involves such unethical or illegal activities as bribing employees to reveal trade secrets such as computer codes or product formulas. The traditional methods of industrial espionage include recruiting agents and inserting them into the target company or breaking into an office to take equipment and information. It can also involve surveillance and spying on commercial organizations in order to determine the direction of their new product line or even what bid they intend to make on a government contract. Such knowledge can provide vast profits when it allows a competitor to save large sums on product development or to win an undeserved contract by underbidding.[16]

Foreign Industrial Espionage Not all corporate espionage is home grown, and some attacks have been carried out by foreign agents. A report of the National Counterintelligence Center lists biotechnology, aerospace, telecommunications, computer software, transportation, advanced materials, energy research, defense, and semiconductor companies as the top targets for foreign economic espionage.[17]

Industrial espionage by foreign agents' efforts has hurt the United States by eroding the U.S. military advantage by enabling foreign militaries to acquire sophisticated capabilities that might otherwise have taken years to develop. Espionage has also undercut the U.S. economy by making it possible for foreign firms to gain a competitive economic edge over U.S. companies.

Many foreign agents did not come to the United States specifically to engage in espionage. But when an opportunity arose, they jumped at the chance in order to satisfy their desire for profits, for academic or scientific acclaim, or out of a sense of patriotism to their home countries.

A number of factors have combined to facilitate private-sector technology theft. Globalization, while generating major gains for the U.S. economy, has given foreigners unprecedented access to U.S. firms and to sensitive technologies. There has also been a proliferation of devices that have made it easy for private-sector experts to illegally retrieve, store, and transfer massive amounts of information, including trade secrets and proprietary data; such devices are increasingly common in the workplace.

In addition to private citizens conducting espionage, foreign government organizations also mount their own operations, including:

- Targeting U.S. firms for technology that would strengthen their foreign defense capabilities

- Posting personnel at U.S. military bases to collect classified information to bolster military modernization efforts

- Employing commercial firms in the United States in a cover effort to target and acquire U.S. technology

- Recruiting students, professors, scientists, and researchers to engage in technology collection

- Making direct requests for classified, sensitive, or export-controlled information

- Forming ventures with U.S. firms in the hope of placing collectors in proximity to sensitive technologies or establishing foreign research[18]

Legal Controls Until 1996, there was no federal statute that explicitly penalized industrial espionage. Recognizing the increasingly important role that intellectual property plays in the well-being of the American economy, Congress enacted the Economic Espionage Act (EEA) of 1996, which criminalizes the theft of trade secrets. The EEA actually contains two separate provisions, one that penalizes foreign agents for stealing American trade secrets and one directed at domestic spying. Some of the key provisions of the EEA are set out in Exhibit 11.3.

Convictions of foreign agents under the Economic Espionage Act have been relatively rare. On December 14, 2006, Fei Ye and Ming Zhong pleaded guilty to two counts each of economic espionage. Ye and Zhong were arrested at the San Francisco International Airport on November 23, 2001, with stolen trade secret information from Sun Microsystems, Inc., and Transmeta Corporation. At their hearing, Ye and Zhong

EXHIBIT 11.3

The Economic Espionage Act of 1996

Provision I

(a) In general. Whoever, intending or knowing that the offense will benefit any foreign government, foreign instrumentality, or foreign agent, knowingly

(1) steals, or without authorization appropriates, takes, carries away, or conceals, or by fraud, artifice, or deception obtains a trade secret;

(2) without authorization copies, duplicates, sketches, draws, photographs, downloads, uploads, alters, destroys, photocopies, replicates, transmits, delivers, sends, mails, communicates, or conveys a trade secret;

(3) receives, buys, or possesses a trade secret, knowing the same to have been stolen or appropriated, obtained, or converted without authorization;

(4) attempts to commit any offense described in any of paragraphs (1) through (3); or

(5) conspires with one or more other persons to commit any offense described in any of paragraphs (1) through (3), and one or more of such person do any act to effect the object of the conspiracy, shall, except as provided in subsection (b), be fined not more than $500,000 or imprisoned not more than 15 years, or both.

Provision II

(a) Whoever, with intent to convert a trade secret, that is related to or included in a product that is produced for or placed in interstate or foreign commerce, to the economic benefit of anyone other than the owner thereof, and intending or knowing that the offense will injure any owner of that trade secret, knowingly

(1) steals, or without authorization appropriates, takes, carries away, or conceals, or by fraud, artifice, or deception obtains such information;

(2) without authorization copies, duplicates, sketches, draws, photographs, downloads, uploads, alters, destroys, photocopies, replicates, transmits, delivers, sends, mails, communicates, or conveys such information;

(3) receives, buys, or possesses such information, knowing the same to have been stolen or appropriated, obtained, or converted without authorization;

(4) attempts to commit any offense described in paragraphs (1) through (3); or

(5) conspires with one or more other persons to commit any offense described in paragraphs (1) through (3), and one or more of such persons do any act to effect the object of the conspiracy, shall, except as provided in subsection (b), be fined under this title or imprisoned not more than 10 years, or both.

Source: The Economic Espionage Act of 1996, 18 U.S.C. §§ 1831–1839.

---

admitted that they intended to utilize the trade secrets in designing a computer microprocessor that was to be manufactured and marketed by a company they established, Supervision, Inc., and would have profited from sales of chips to the city of Hangzhou and the province of Zhejiang in China; their company had applied for funding from the National High Technology Research and Development Program of China. The plea resulted in the first conviction of foreign agents under the Economic Espionage Act, more than 10 years after it was enacted into law.[19]

State Political Crime

While some political crimes are committed by people who oppose the state, others are perpetrated by state authorities against the people they are supposed to serve. Critical criminologists argue that rather than being committed by disaffected people, a great deal of political crime arises from the efforts of the state to either maintain governmental power or to uphold the race, class, and gender advantages of those who support the government. In an industrial society, the state will do everything to protect the property rights of the wealthy while opposing the real interests of the poor. They might even go to war to support the capitalist classes who need the wealth and resources of other nations. The desire for natural resources such as rubber, oil, and metals was one of the primary reasons for Japan's invasion of China and other Eastern nations that sparked their entry into World War II.

It is possible to divide state political crimes into five varieties:[20]

- *Political corruption.* This violation of citizen trust can involve nonviolent crimes such as soliciting bribes (usually money or some other economic benefit, like a gift or service). Politicians, judges, police, and government regulators all engage in corruption that damages public trust in the government and its process. And unfortunately, when corruption is uncovered and the perpetrator brought to justice it is difficult to determine whether a real criminal has been caught or a political opponent framed and punished.

- *Illegal domestic surveillance.* This occurs when government agents listen in on telephone conversations or intercept emails without proper approval in order to stifle dissent and monitor political opponents. Sometimes the true purpose of the surveillance is masked by the need for national security while in reality it is illegal organizational policy and practice that have in some cases been sanctioned by heads of state for political purposes.

- *Human rights violations.* States may treat their citizens in such a fashion as to deny them basic civil rights. Correctional systems have long been suspected of depriving people of civil rights. While prison conditions are notorious in third world nations and inmates are deprived of basic necessities, such human rights violations have also occurred in industrial societies such as the United States. The use of secret prisons to detain terror suspects without trial or indictment might be considered by critics such as the American Civil Liberties Union a human rights violation, and so would be the use of illegal interrogations to obtain confessions or information from suspected terrorists.[21]

- *State violence.* Sometimes state action results in death or disfigurement. While the use of torture and illegal imprisonment is notorious in third world countries, police violence and use of deadly force is not uncommon in Western industrialized nations. In some nations, such as the Russian province of Chechnya, almost all political detainees are subjected to torture, including electric shocks, burnings, and severe beating with boots, sticks, plastic bottles filled

ALDRICH HAZEN AMES

Aldrich Hazen Ames was arrested by the FBI in Arlington, Virginia, on espionage charges on February 24, 1994. At the time of his arrest, Ames was a 31-year veteran of the Central Intelligence Agency (CIA) who had been spying for the Russians since 1985. Arrested with him was his wife, Rosario Ames, who had aided and abetted his espionage activities.

Ames was a CIA case officer who spoke Russian and specialized in the Russian intelligence services, including the KGB, the USSR's foreign intelligence service. His initial overseas assignment was in Ankara, Turkey, where he targeted Russian intelligence officers for recruitment. Later, he worked in New York City and Mexico City. On April 16, 1985, while assigned to the CIA's Soviet/East European Division at CIA Headquarters in Langley, Virginia, he secretly volunteered to KGB officers at the USSR Embassy in Washington, D.C. Shortly thereafter, the KGB paid him $50,000. During the summer of 1985, Ames met several times with a Russian diplomat to whom he passed classified information about CIA and FBI human sources, as well as technical operations targeting the Soviet Union. In December 1985, Ames met with a Moscow-based KGB officer in Bogota, Colombia. In July 1986, Ames was transferred to Rome.

In Rome, Ames continued his meetings with the KGB, including a Russian diplomat assigned to Rome and a Moscow-based KGB officer. At the conclusion of his assignment in Rome, Ames received instructions from the KGB regarding clandestine contacts in the Washington, D.C., area, where he would next be assigned. In the four years after he volunteered, the KGB paid Ames $1.88 million.

Upon his return to Washington, D.C., in 1989, Ames continued to pass classified documents to the KGB, using "dead drops" or prearranged hiding places where he would leave the documents to be picked up later by KGB officers from the USSR Embassy in Washington. In return, the KGB left money and instructions for Ames, usually in other "dead drops."

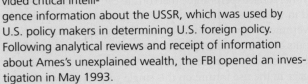

In the meantime, the CIA and FBI learned that Russian officials who had been recruited by them were being arrested and executed. These human sources had provided critical intelligence information about the USSR, which was used by U.S. policy makers in determining U.S. foreign policy. Following analytical reviews and receipt of information about Ames's unexplained wealth, the FBI opened an investigation in May 1993.

FBI special agents and investigative specialists conducted intensive physical and electronic surveillance of Ames during a 10-month investigation. Searches of Ames's residence revealed documents and other information linking Ames to the Russian foreign intelligence service. On October 13, 1993, investigative specialists observed a chalk mark Ames made on a mailbox confirming to the Russians his intention to meet them in Bogota, Colombia. On November 1st, special agents observed him and, separately, his Russian handler in Bogota. When Ames planned foreign travel, including a trip to Moscow, as part of his official duties, a plan to arrest him was approved.

Following guilty pleas by both Ames and his wife on April 28, 1994, Ames was sentenced to incarceration for life without the possibility of parole. Rosario Ames was sentenced on October 20, 1994, to 63 months in prison. Ames also forfeited his assets to the United States, and $547,000 was turned over to the Justice Department's Victims Assistance Fund. Ames is serving his sentence in the federal prison system. Rosario Ames completed her sentence and was released.

Source: FBI, "Famous Cases: Aldrich Hazen Ames," www.fbi.gov/libref/historic/famcases/ames/ames.htm (accessed July 11, 2008).

---

with water or sand, and heavy rubber-coated cables. The rest are subject to psychological pressure, such as threats or imitation of sexual abuse or execution, as well as threats to harm their relatives.[22]

■ *State-corporate crime.* This type of political crime is committed by individuals who abuse their state authority or who fail to exercise it when working with people and organizations in the private sector. These crimes may occur when state institutions such as an environmental agency fail to enforce laws, resulting in the pollution of public waterways. This type of crime is particularly alarming, considering that regulatory laws aimed at controlling private corporations are being scaled back while globalization has made corporations worldwide entities both in production and in advancing the consumption of their products.[23]

Using Torture

On February 23, 2007, Hassan Mustafa Osama Nasr, an Egyptian cleric, made worldwide headlines when he claimed that he had been kidnapped in Italy by American CIA agents and sent to Egypt for interrogation as part of the CIA's "extraordinary rendition." Nasr claimed, "I was subjected to the worst kind of torture in Egyptian prisons. I have scars of torture all over my body." Italy indicted 26 Americans and five Italian agents accused of seizing him and sending him to Egypt without trial or due process.[24]

Of all state political crimes, the use of torture to gain information from suspected political criminals is perhaps the most notorious. Can the torture of a suspected terrorist determined to destroy the government and harm innocent civilians ever be permissible, or is it always an example of state-sponsored political crime? While most people loathe the thought of torturing anyone, some experts argue that torture can sometimes be justified in what they call the ticking bomb scenario. Suppose the government found out that a captured terrorist knew the whereabouts of a dangerous explosive device that was set to go off and kill thousands of innocent people. Would it be permissible to engage in the use torture on this single suspect if it would save the population of a city?

While the ticking bomb scenario has appeal (see The Criminological Enterprise feature "Want to Torture? Get a Warrant"), opponents of torture believe that even imminent danger does not justify state violence. There is a danger that such state-sponsored violence would become calculated and premeditated; torturers would have to be trained, ready, and in place for the ticking bomb argument to work. We couldn't be running around looking for torturers with a bomb set to go off, could we? Because torturers would be part of the government bureaucracy, there is no way to ensure that they would only use their skills in certain morally justifiable cases.[25] What happens if a superior officer tells them to torture someone, but they believe the order is unjustified? Should they follow orders or risk a court-martial for being disobedient? Furthermore, there is very little empirical evidence suggesting that torture provides any real benefits and much more that suggests it can create serious problems. It can damage civil rights and democratic institutions and cause the general public to have sympathy for the victims of torture no matter their evil intent.[26]

Critics have complained that government agencies such as the Central Intelligence Agency (CIA) have used torture without legal authority. Despite its illegality, enemy agents have been detained and physically abused in secret prisons around the world without the benefit of due process. In some cases suspects have been held in foreign countries simply because their governments are not squeamish about using torture during interrogations. Shocking photo evidence of torture from detention facilities at the Guantanamo base in Cuba

supports their charges. Legal scholars have argued that these tactics violate both international treaties and domestic statutes prohibiting torture. Some maintain that the U.S. Constitution limits the authority of an executive agency like the CIA to act against foreigners abroad and also limits physical coercion by the government under the Fifth Amendment Due Process and Self-Incrimination Clauses and the Eighth Amendment prohibition against cruel and unusual punishments. Legally, it is impermissible for United States authorities to engage in indefinite detention or torture regardless of the end, the place, or the victim.[27] Critics of U.S. policy toward terrorists were pleased when on June 12, 2008, in the case of *Boumediene et al. v. Bush, President of the United States, et al.*, the Supreme Court ruled that indefinite detention was constitutionally unacceptable and that terrorists are entitled to process their cases through the court system; the justices ruled that they are eligible for habeas corpus protection. The fact that they have been designated "enemy combatants" does not bar them from the legal process available to U.S. citizens.[28]

The Waterboarding Controversy Can a clear line be drawn between what is considered torture and what constitutes firm but legal interrogation methods? This issue made headlines when it was revealed in 2007 that the CIA made routine use of the waterboarding technique while interrogating suspected terrorists.[29] Waterboarding involves immobilizing a person on

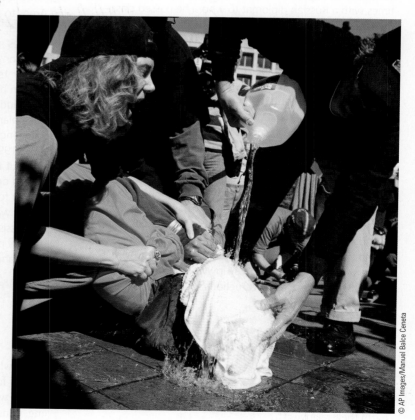

Protestors demonstrate the use of waterboarding on volunteer Maboud Ebrahim Zadeh, November 5, 2007, in front of the Justice Department in Washington, D.C. The demonstration's purpose was to highlight the use of waterboarding as torture in order to protest the nomination of Attorney General Michael Mukasey.

WANT TO TORTURE? GET A WARRANT

According to the ticking bomb scenario, torture can be justified in order to force a political criminal to reveal the location of an explosive device before it can go off and kill many people. While a number of legal and social scholars have debated whether torture can ever be justified in a moral society no matter what the intent, famed social commentator and legal scholar Alan Dershowitz disagrees. He argues that torture can be justified under some circumstances, especially to prevent damaging terror attacks. Moreover, he believes that the "vast majority" of Americans would expect law enforcement agents to engage in time-honored methods of "loosening tongues" if the circumstances demanded it, even though international bodies such as the UN forbid the use of torture no matter how exigent the circumstances. To ensure that torture is not used capriciously, Dershowitz proposes the creation of a "torture warrant" that can only be issued by a judge in cases where (a) there is an absolute need to obtain immediate information in order to save lives and (b) there is probable cause that the suspect has such information and is unwilling to reveal it to law enforcement agents. The suspect would be given immunity from prosecution based on information elicited by the torture; it would only be to save lives. The warrant would limit the torture to nonlethal means, such as sterile needles being inserted beneath the nails to cause excruciating pain without endangering life.

While Dershowitz recognizes that it may sound both awful and absurd for a judge to be issuing a warrant to torture a suspect, in truth every democracy, including our own, has employed torture outside of the law. It is routine for police officers to put tremendous pressure on suspects in order to get them to talk. The "third degree" is all too common, not only on TV shows, but in the back rooms of real police station houses. If it is already used, would it not be better to have it regulated and controlled by the rule of law? If it isn't, law enforcement agents would continue to use torture anyway, only it would fall "below the radar screen of accountability." Which would be more consistent with democratic values?

Dershowitz recognizes that those opposed to the idea of a torture warrant argue that establishing such a precedent would legitimize torture and make it easier to use under any circumstances. But he believes that the opposite would be true: by expressly limiting the use of torture only to the ticking bomb scenario and by requiring an objective and reasoned judge to approve, limit, and monitor the torture, it will be far more difficult to justify its extension to other institutions. The goal of the warrant would be to reduce and limit the amount of torture that would, in fact, be used in an emergency.

Not everyone agrees that in some extreme cases the "ends justify the means." Human Rights Watch, an international group dedicated to protecting the human rights of people around the world, counters Dershowitz by pointing out that while the ticking bomb scenario makes for great philosophical discussion, it rarely arises in real life. Except in movies and TV, interrogators rarely learn that a suspect in custody knows of a particular, imminent terrorist bombing and that they have the knowledge to prevent a catastrophe. Intelligence is rarely, if ever, good enough to provide such specific advance warning. If terrorists knew their plan could be foiled by information provided by a prisoner, why would they not change the plan? While not practical, the ticking bomb scenario can be dangerous because it expands the use of torture to anyone who might have knowledge of unspecified future terrorist attacks: Why are only the victims of an imminent terrorist attack deserving of protection by torture? Why not also use torture to prevent a terrorist attack tomorrow or next week or next year? And why stop with the alleged terrorists themselves? Why not also torture their families or associates—anyone who might provide life-saving information? The slope is very slippery, Human Rights Watch claims.

CRITICAL THINKING

You are a government agent holding a prisoner who has been arrested on suspicion of being a terrorist. You get a call stating that there is a credible threat that a bomb will go off in two hours unless it can be found and defused. The prisoner has knowledge of the bomb's location. How would you get him to reveal the location? Would you consider using torture? Is there a better method?

Sources: Alan M. Dershowitz, *Shouting Fire: Civil Liberties in a Turbulent Age* (New York: Little, Brown, 2002); Dershowitz, "Want to Torture? Get a Warrant," *San Francisco Chronicle*, 22 January 2002; Human Rights Watch, "The Twisted Logic of Torture," January 2005, http://hrw.org/wr2k5/darfurandabughraib/6.htm (accessed July 11, 2008).

his or her back, with the head inclined downward, and pouring water over the face and into the breathing passages. It produces an immediate gag reflex and an experience akin to drowning; the subject believes their death is imminent.

The use of waterboarding is controversial because there seems to be no agreement on whether it is torture or a relatively harmless instrument of interrogation. While official U.S. government policy and government doctrine is vehemently opposed to torture, it has condoned harsh interrogation techniques that combine physical and psychological tactics, including head-slapping, waterboarding, and exposure to extreme cold. Waterboarding even became an issue during the 2008 presidential campaign when Senator John McCain, a former prisoner of war who experienced torture firsthand in a North Vietnamese prison camp, told the press, "All I can say is that it was used in the Spanish Inquisition, it was used in Pol Pot's genocide in Cambodia, and there are reports that it is being used against Buddhist monks today. . . . [Presidential candidates] should know what it is. It is not a complicated procedure. It is torture."[30]

www Go to academic.cengage.com/criminaljustice/siegel to learn more about the following topics:

▌ **Vote fraud** and **election fairness**

▌ Important **espionage cases**

TERRORISM

The political crime that many people are most concerned with is terrorism, and the remainder of this chapter focuses on the history, nature, and extent of terrorism and the methods being employed for its control. Despite its long history, it is often difficult to precisely define terrorism (from the Latin *terrere*, which means to frighten) and to separate terrorist acts from interpersonal crimes of violence. For example, if a group robs a bank to obtain funds for its revolutionary struggles, should the act be treated as terrorism or as a common bank robbery? In this instance, defining a crime as terrorism depends on the kind of legal response the act evokes from those in power. To be considered terrorism, which is a political crime, an act must carry with it the intent to disrupt and change the government and must not be merely a common-law crime committed for greed or egotism.

Because of its complexity, an all-encompassing definition of terrorism is difficult to formulate, although most experts agree that it generally involves the illegal use of force against innocent people to achieve a political objective. According to the U.S. State Department, the term "terrorism" means premeditated, politically motivated violence perpetrated against noncombatant targets by subnational groups or clandestine agents, usually intended to influence an audience. The term "international terrorism" means terrorism involving citizens or the territory of more than one country. A terrorist group is any group practicing, or that has significant subgroups that practice, international terrorism.[31] Exhibit 11.4 sets out a number of definitions of terrorism drafted or used by prominent governmental agencies or organizations.

Terrorism usually involves a type of political crime that emphasizes violence as a mechanism to promote change. Whereas some political criminals sell secrets, spy, and the like, terrorists systematically murder and destroy or threaten such violence to terrorize individuals, groups, communities, or governments into conceding to the terrorists' political demands.[32] Because the terrorist lacks large armies and formidable weapons, their use of subterfuge, secrecy, and hit-and-run tactics is designed to give them a psychological advantage

EXHIBIT 11.4

Definitions of Terrorism

League of Nations Convention (1937)

All criminal acts directed against a State and intended or calculated to create a state of terror in the minds of particular persons or a group of persons or the general public.

UN Resolution Language (1999)

1. *Strongly condemns* all acts, methods and practices of terrorism as criminal and unjustifiable, wherever and by whomsoever committed;

2. *Reiterates* that criminal acts intended or calculated to provoke a state of terror in the general public, a group of persons or particular persons for political purposes are in any circumstance unjustifiable, whatever the considerations of a political, philosophical, ideological, racial, ethnic, religious or other nature that may be invoked to justify them. (GA Res. 51/210, "Measures to Eliminate International Terrorism")

Short Legal Definition Proposed by A. P. Schmid to United Nations Crime Branch (1992)

Act of Terrorism = Peacetime Equivalent of War Crime

Academic Consensus Definition Used by the UN

Terrorism is an anxiety-inspiring method of repeated violent action, employed by (semi-) clandestine individual, group or state actors, for idiosyncratic, criminal or political reasons, whereby—in contrast to assassination—the direct targets of violence are not the main targets. The immediate human victims of violence are generally chosen randomly (targets of opportunity) or selectively (representative or symbolic targets) from a target population, and serve as message generators. Threat- and violence-based communication processes between terrorist (organization), (imperiled) victims, and main targets are used to manipulate the main target (audience[s]), turning it into a target of terror, a target of demands, or a target of attention, depending on whether intimidation, coercion, or propaganda is primarily sought."

United States Department of State

The term "terrorism" means premeditated, politically motivated violence perpetrated against noncombatant (1) targets by subnational groups or clandestine agents, usually intended to influence an audience.

The term "international terrorism" means terrorism involving citizens or the territory of more than one country.

The term "terrorist group" means any group practicing, or that has significant subgroups that practice, international terrorism.

Sources: Patterns of Global Terrorism (Washington: Department of State, 2001): vi; United Nations Office on Drugs and Crime, www.unodc.org/unodc/ (accessed July 8, 2008).

and the power to neutralize the physical superiority of their opponents.

However, it may be erroneous to assume that terrorists have political goals. Some may try to bring about what they consider to be social reform—for example, by attacking women wearing fur coats or sabotaging property during a labor dispute. Terrorism must also be distinguished from conventional warfare because it requires secrecy and clandestine operations to exert social control over large populations.[33]

Terror Cells

Regardless of what organizational structure is used, most groups subdivide their affiliates into **terror cells** for both organizational and security purposes. To enhance security, each cell may be functionally independent so that each member has little knowledge of other cells, their members, locations, and so on. However, individual cell members provide emotional support to one another and maintain loyalty and dedication. Because only the cell leader knows how to communicate with other cells and/or a central command, capture of one cell does not then compromise other group members.

Terrorist cell formations may be based on location, employment, or family membership. Some are formed on the basis of function: some are

A U.S. soldier from Ghost Rider Company, Third Squadron, Second Stryker Cavalry Regiment questions a detained Iraqi man with alleged links to Sunni insurgent groups during the launch of Operation Grim Ghost in the deserts of the Diyala province, northeast of Baghdad, on March 23, 2008. Insurgents are typically organized into all-covert groups who engage in an organized campaign of extreme violence that may often appear to be random and indiscriminate, causing the death of innocent civilians as well as government agents.

fighters, others are political organizers. The number of cells and their composition depend on the size of the terrorist group: local or national groups will have fewer cells than international terrorist groups that may operate in several countries, such as the al-Qaeda group.

Terrorist and Guerilla

The word "terrorist" is often used interchangeably with the term "guerilla," but the terms are quite different. **Guerilla** comes from the Spanish term meaning "little war," which developed out of the Spanish rebellion against French troops after Napoleon's 1808 invasion of the Iberian Peninsula.[34] Terrorists have an urban focus. Operating in small bands, or cadres, of three to five members, they target the property or persons of their enemy, such as members of the ruling class.[35] Guerillas, on the other hand, are located in rural areas and attack the military, the police, and government officials. Their organizations can grow quite large and eventually take the form of a conventional military force. However, guerillas can infiltrate urban areas in small bands, and terrorists can make forays into the countryside; consequently, the terms are sometimes used interchangeably.

Terrorist and Insurgent

During the Iraq war, the term **insurgent** began to be used to describe the forces opposed to American involvement. As commonly used, an insurgency is somewhat different from both guerilla warfare and terrorism. The typical goal of an insurgency is to confront the existing government for control of all or a

portion of its territory, or force political concessions in sharing political power.[36] Insurgents are typically organized into covert groups who engage in an organized campaign of extreme violence, which may often appear to be random and indiscriminate, causing the death of innocent civilians as well as government agents. Insurgents tend to live isolated and stressful lives and enjoy varying levels of wider support.[37]

While insurgents may engage in violence, they do not necessarily need to use terror to meet their aims but can also use nonviolent methods or political tactics. For example, they may set up food distribution centers and schools, providing the population with needed services, and thus gaining control by contrasting their benevolent rule with the government's incompetence and corruption.

When insurgents use violence, it is designed to inspire support and gain converts while at the same time destroying the government's ability to resist. It is easy to recruit supporters once the population believes that the government is incapable of fighting back. On the other hand, some members of the insurgency might shun violence and eventually break away from the mainstream, creating nonviolent splinter groups that operate within the mainstream. They can then operate openly, claiming to sympathize with the violent wing of their organization but just not being part of its structure.

Insurgents, unlike terrorists, require support of a significant portion of the population. While terrorists may operate in small bands with a narrow focus, such as stopping the use of animals in medical research, insurgents represent a popular movement and may also seek external support from other nations to bring pressure on the government. A terror group, in

THE VARIOUS FORMS OF RADICAL POLITICAL GROUPS

	Terrorists	Guerilla	Insurgent	Revolutionary
Description	Groups who engage in premeditated, politically motivated violence perpetrated against noncombatant targets	Armed groups operating in rural areas who attack the military, the police, and other government officials	Groups who engage in armed uprising or revolt against an established civil or political authority	Engages in civil war against sovereign power that holds control of the land
Example	Al-Qaeda, Hamas	Mao's People's Liberation Army, Ho Chi Minh's Viet Cong	Iraqi insurgent groups	American Revolution, French Revolution, Russian Revolution
Goals	Personal, criminal, or political gain or change	Replace or overthrow existing government	Win over population by showing government's incompetence; force government into political concessions and/or power sharing	Gain independence or oust existing government or monarchy
Methods	Small, clandestine cells use systematic violence for purpose of intimidation	Use unconventional warfare and mobile tactics; may grow large and use tactics similar to conventional military force	May use violent (bombings and kidnappings) or nonviolent means (food distribution centers and creating schools)	Can use violent armed conflict or nonviolent methods such as Gandhi used in India

contrast, neither requires nor has active support or sympathy from a large percentage of the population.

Terrorist and Revolutionary

A revolution (from the Latin *revolutio*, "a revolving," and *revolvere*, "turn, roll back") is generally seen as a civil war fought between nationalists and a sovereign power that holds control of the land, or between the existing government and local groups over issues of ideology and power. Historically, the American revolution may be considered an example of a struggle between nationalistic groups and an imperialistic overseas government. Classic examples of ideological rebellions are the French Revolution, which pitted the middle class and urban poor against the aristocracy, and the Russian Revolution of 1917 during which the Czarist government was toppled by the Bolsheviks. More recent ideological revolutions have occurred in China, Cuba, Nicaragua, and Chile, to name but a few.

While some revolutions (such as the American, French, and Russian) rely on armed force, terror activities, and violence, others can be nonviolent, depending on large urban protests and threats. Such was the case when the Shah Mohammad Reza Pahlavi was toppled in Iran after a slew of nonviolent demonstrations, which ended in the 1979 revolution that transformed Iran from a constitutional monarchy into an Islamic republic or theocracy under the rule of Ayatollah Ruhollah Khomeini.

Concept Summary 11.1 distinguishes among the concepts of terrorist, guerilla, insurgent, and revolutionary.

A BRIEF HISTORY OF TERRORISM

Acts of terrorism have been known throughout history. The assassination of Julius Caesar on March 15, 44 BCE, is considered an act of terrorism. Terrorism became widespread at the end of the Middle Ages when political leaders were frequently subject to assassination by their enemies.

Religious Roots

The first terrorist activities were committed by members of minority religious groups who engaged in violence to (a) gain the right to practice their own form of religion, (b) establish the supremacy of their own religion over others, or (c) meet the requirements of the blood-thirsty gods they worshipped.[38]

In some instances, a conquered people used force and violence to maintain their right to worship in their own faith. Zealots, Hebrew warrior groups, were active during the Roman occupation of Palestine in the first century CE. A subgroup of the Zealots, the Sciari (literally translated as *daggermen*), were so named after the long curved knives they favored as a weapon to assassinate Romans or their sympathizers. The Zealots carried out their attacks in broad daylight, typically with witnesses around, in order to send a message that the Roman authorities and those Jews who collaborated with them would not be safe. Ironically, this tactic is still being used by contemporary terrorists. The Zealots and Sciari led the revolt in 66 CE against Roman occupation of the Holy Land, during which they occupied the fortress of Masada. Here they held out for more than seven months before engaging in mass suicide rather than surrender to the Roman legions. The revolt ended badly and the Romans destroyed the Jewish temple and sent the population into exile.

Some religious terrorists want to promote the supremacy of their own sect over a rival group. The (Shi'ite) Muslim Order of the Assassins (*assassin* literally means "hashish-eater," a reference to the commonly held belief that gang members engaged in acts of ritual intoxication and smoked hashish just prior to undertaking their missions) was active in Persia, Syria, and Palestine from 1090 to 1272, killing a great number of their enemies, mainly Sunnis whom they considered apostates, but also Christians who were then the rulers of the kingdom of Jerusalem.[39] The Assassins also were prone to stabbing their victims in an effort to spread their vision of Islam, and carried out missions in public places on holy days in order to publicize their cause. Successful assassinations guaranteed them a place in heaven.

Another form of religious terror is inspired by the requirements of belief. Some religious beliefs have focused on violence, the gods demanding the death of nonbelievers. In India, members of the Thugee cult (from which the modern term "thug" was derived) were devoted to Kali, the goddess of death and destruction. The thugs believed each murder prevented Kali's arrival for 1,000 years, thus sparing the nation from her ferocity. The thugs traveled in gangs of up to 100 with each member having a defined role—some lured unwary travelers, while others strangled the chosen victim. The gang used secret argot and jargon which only they could understand and signs so that members could recognize each other even in the most remote parts of India. Cult members may have killed hundreds of thousands of victims over a 300-year span. They would attach themselves to travelers and when the opportunity arose, strangle them with a noose around their necks, steal their money, and bury their bodies. The killings were highly ritualistic and involved religious rites and prayers. By the mid-nineteenth century the British made it a policy to end Thugee activities, hanged nearly 4,000, and all but eradicated the cult. Thugees represented the last serious religion-inspired terrorist threat until the emergence of Islamic terrorism in the 1980s.

Political Roots

When rulers had absolute power, terrorist acts were viewed as one of the only means of gaining political rights. At times European states encouraged terrorist acts against their enemies. In the sixteenth century, Queen Elizabeth I empowered her naval leaders, including famed captains John Hawkins and Francis Drake, to attack the Spanish fleet and take prizes. These privateers would have been considered pirates had they not operated with government approval. American privateers attacked the British during the Revolutionary War and the War of 1812 and were considered heroes for their actions against the English Navy.

The term "terrorist" first became popular during the French Revolution. Use of the word "terrorism" began in 1795 in reference to the Reign of Terror initiated by the revolutionary government during which agents of the Committee of Public Safety and the National Convention were referred to as terrorists. In response, royalists and opponents of the Revolution employed terrorist tactics in resistance to the Revolutionists. The widespread use of the guillotine is an infamous reminder of this revolutionary violence; urban mobs demanded blood, and many government officials and aristocrats were beheaded in gruesome public spectacles. From the fall of the Bastille on July 14, 1789, until July 1794, thousands suspected of counterrevolutionary activity were killed on the guillotine. Here again, the relative nature of political crime is documented: most victims of the French Reign of Terror were revolutionaries who had been denounced by rival factions, whereas thousands of the hated nobility lived in relative tranquility. The end of the terror was signaled by the death of its prime mover, Maximilien Robespierre, on July 28, 1794, as the result of a successful plot to end his rule. He was executed on the same guillotine to which he had sent almost 20,000 people.

In the hundred years following the French Revolution, terrorism continued to be a political tool around the world. Terrorist acts became the preferred method of political action for national groups in the early years of the twentieth century. In Eastern Europe, the Internal Macedonian Revolutionary Organization campaigned against the Turkish government, which controlled its homeland (Macedonia became part of the former Yugoslavia). Similarly, the protest of the Union of Death Society, or Black Hand, against the Austro-Hungarian Empire's control of Serbia led to the group's assassination of Archduke Franz Ferdinand, which started World War I. Russia was the scene of left-wing revolutionary activity, which killed the czar in 1917 and gave birth to the Marxist state.

After World War I ended, the Treaty of Versailles restructured Europe and broke up the Austro-Hungarian Empire. The result was a hodgepodge of new nations controlled by majority ethnic groups. Self-determination was limited to European nations and ethnic groups and denied to others, especially the colonial possessions of the major European powers, creating bitterness and setting the stage for the long conflicts of the anti-colonial period. The Irish Republican Army, established around 1916, steadily battled British forces from 1919 to 1923, culminating in the Republic of Ireland gaining independence.

Between the world wars, right-wing terrorism existed in Germany, Spain, and Italy. One source of tension, according to author Michael Kellogg, was the virulently anti-Communist exiles (called White Russians) who fled Russia after the 1917 revolution and took up residence in Germany and other Western nations. According to Kellogg, between 1920 and 1923, Adolf Hitler was deeply influenced by the Aufbau (reconstruction), the émigrés' organization. Members of the Aufbau allied with the Nazis to overthrow the legitimate German government and thwart German communists from seizing power. The White Russians deep-seated anti-Semitism may have inspired Hitler to go public with his campaign to kill the European Jews, prompting both the Holocaust and the invasion of Russia, which spelled the eventual doom of Hitler and National Socialism.[40]

During World War II, resistance to the occupying German troops was common throughout Europe. The Germans considered the resistors to be terrorists, but the rest of the world considers them heroes. Meanwhile, in Palestine, Jewish terrorist groups—the Haganah, Irgun, and Stern Gang, whose leaders included Menachem Begin, who later became Israel's prime minister—waged war against the British to force them to allow Jewish survivors of the Holocaust to settle in their traditional homeland. Today, of course, many of these alleged terrorists are considered freedom fighters who laid down their lives for a just cause.

After the war, Arab nationalists felt that they had been betrayed. Believing they were promised postwar independence, they were doubly disappointed; first when the French and British were given authority over their lands, and then especially when the British allowed Zionist immigration into Palestine in keeping with a promise contained in the Balfour Declaration.

Since the end of World War II, the use of terrorism has accelerated its development into a major component of contemporary conflict. Primarily in use immediately after the war as a subordinate element of anticolonial insurgencies, it expanded beyond that role. In the service of various ideologies and aspirations, terrorism sometimes supplanted other forms of conflict completely. It became a far-reaching weapon capable of effects no less global than the intercontinental bomber or missile. It has also proven to be a significant tool of diplomacy and international power for states inclined to use it.

CONTEMPORARY FORMS OF TERRORISM

Today the term "terrorism" encompasses many different behaviors and goals. Some of the more common forms are briefly described here.

Revolutionary Terrorists

Revolutionary terrorists use violence to frighten those in power and their supporters in order to replace the existing government with a regime that holds acceptable political or religious views. Terrorist actions such as kidnapping, assassination, and bombing are designed to draw repressive responses from governments trying to defend themselves. These responses help revolutionaries to expose, through the skilled use of media coverage, the government's inhumane nature. The original reason for the government's harsh response may be lost as the effect of counterterrorist activities is felt by uninvolved people.

Jemaah Islamiyah, an Indonesian terrorist organization aligned with al-Qaeda, is believed to be intent on driving away foreign tourists and ruining the nation's economy so they can usurp the government and set up a pan-Islamic nation in Indonesia and neighboring Malaysia (see Exhibit 11.5).[41]

EXHIBIT 11.5

Jemaah Islamiyah

Jemaah Islamiyah (JI) is a militant Islamic organization located in Southeast Asia devoted to the establishment of fundamentalist Islamic states in countries such as Indonesia, Singapore, Brunei, Malaysia, Thailand, and the Philippines. The name derives from an Arabic phrase meaning "Islamic group" or "Islamic community." The group has its roots in the Darul Islam organization, a violent radical group that advocated the establishment of Islamic law in Indonesia in the 1940s and 1950s as a reaction to Dutch colonial rule and what it perceived as the secular orientation of postcolonial Indonesia.

Jemaah Islamiyah sponsors recruiting, training, indoctrination, and financial support for terror groups in the region and helps link them to kindred organizations such as al-Qaeda, the Abu Sayyaf Group, the Moro Islamic Liberation Front (MILF), the Misuari Renegade/Breakaway Group (MRG/MBG), and the Philippine Raja Solaiman Movement (RSM). Jemaah Islamiyah members have been sent to Afghanistan and southern Philippines for military training where they learned bomb-making and other terror skills.

JI operates through cells with a rather loosely organized structure. The top strategists appear to be mostly Indonesian nationals living in Malaysia, many of whom had gone to Afghanistan to fight the Russians during the Soviet occupation in the 1980s. The second level is made up of field coordinators, responsible for delivering money and explosives and for choosing a local subordinate who can effectively act as team leader of the foot soldiers. At the bottom of the organization are the soldiers who drive the cars, survey targets, and deliver the bombs. They are mostly young men from *pesantrens* (religious boarding schools) or Islamic high schools run by teachers who were involved in the Darul Islam rebellions of the 1950s.

Jemaah Islamiyah has been responsible for numerous attacks that have killed hundreds of civilians in the region. The Bali car bombing on October 12, 2002, in which 202 people died was a coordinated attack designed to destroy the tourist industry, a significant source of income for the government. A suicide bomber using a backpack killed several people in a nightclub frequented by foreign tourists. The survivors ran into the street and were killed by a fertilizer/fuel oil bomb concealed in a parked van. Other attacks linked to Jemaah Islamiyah are the 2003 JW Marriott hotel bombing in Kuningan, Jakarta, the 2004 Australian embassy bombing in Jakarta, and the 2005 Bali terrorist bombing.

Authorities in the region attempted to crack down on the group after the 2002 bombing, arresting more than 200 members. Three of the four main suspects behind the attack were sentenced to death in Indonesia.

Sources: Council on Foreign Relations, "Jemaah Islamiyah," October 3, 2005, www.cfr.org/publication/8948/ (accessed July 12, 2008); GlobalSecurity.org, www.globalsecurity.org/military/world/para/ (accessed July 12, 2008); International Crisis Group, "Indonesia Backgrounder: How the Jemaah Islamiyah Terrorist Network Operates," Executive Summary ICG Asia Report 43, December 11, 2002, www.crisisgroup.org/home/index.cfm?id=1397 (accessed July 12, 2008).

Political Terrorists

Political terrorism is directed at people or groups who oppose the terrorists' political ideology or whom the terrorists define as "outsiders" who must be destroyed. Political terrorists may not want to replace the existing government but to shape it so that it accepts the terrorists' views.

Right-Wing Political Groups Domestic terrorists in the United States can be found across the political spectrum. On the right, they tend to be heavily armed groups organized around such themes as white supremacy, anti-abortion, militant tax resistance, and religious revisionism. Identified groups have included, at one time or another, the Aryan Republican Army, the Aryan Nation, the Posse Comitatus, and the Ku Klux Klan. These groups want to shape U.S. government policy over a range of matters, including ending abortion rights, extending the right to bear arms, and eliminating federal taxation. Anti-abortion groups have demonstrated at abortion clinics, attacked clients, bombed offices, and killed doctors who perform abortions. On October 23, 1998, Dr. Barnett Slepian was shot by a sniper and killed in his Buffalo, New York, home; he was one of a growing number of abortion providers believed to be the victims of terrorists who ironically claim to be "pro-life." Although unlikely to topple the government, these individualistic acts of terror are difficult to predict or control. On April 19, 1995, 168 people were killed during the Oklahoma City bombing, the most severe example of domestic political terrorism in the United States so far.

Left-Wing Political Groups During the turmoil of the 1960s, a number of left-wing political groups emerged to challenge the existing power structure. Some, such as the Black Panther Party—founded in 1966 in Oakland, California, by Bobby Seale and Huey Newton—demanded the right to control community schools, police, and public assistance programs. While many of their activities were productive, such as sponsoring breakfast programs and medical clinics in poor neighborhoods, they also began to openly carry rifles and shotguns while patrolling areas where the Oakland police were rumored to be harassing the community's black citizens. The Panthers' confrontational style led to clashes with police, shootings, and arrests. Because its leaders were faced with criminal charges of varying degrees, the Black Panthers steadily eroded.

Another influential 1960s group, the Students for a Democratic Society (SDS) was founded in Chicago in 1962 and was active on college campuses throughout the sixties protesting the United States' involvement in Vietnam. Though the SDS was nonviolent, a splinter group known as the Weathermen utilized terror tactics to achieve their goals. They were involved in a number of bombings at corporation headquarters and federal institutions, though they typically sent out warnings to evacuate the buildings. The group lost influence when on March 6, 1970, a bomb accidentally exploded in one of their safe houses in New York City. The detonations were so powerful that they collapsed the three-story house, killing three members. The Weathermen disbanded in 1977.

Eco-Terrorism The most active left-leaning domestic political terror groups today are involved in violent actions to protect the environment. Of these groups, the Earth Liberation Front (ELF) is perhaps the best known. Founded in 1994 in Brighton, England, by members of the Earth First! environmental movement, ELF has been active for several years in the United States and abroad. Operating in secret, ELF cells have conducted a series of actions intent on damaging individuals or corporations that they consider a threat to the environment. On October 19, 1998, ELF members claimed responsibility for fires that were set atop Vail Mountain, a luxurious ski resort in Colorado, claiming that the action was designed to stop the resort from expanding into animal habitats (especially that of the mountain lynx); the fires caused an estimated $12 million in damages. On August 22, 2003, members of ELF claimed responsibility for fires that destroyed about a dozen sport utility vehicles at a Chevrolet dealership in West Covina, California.[42] Fires have also been set in government labs where animal research is conducted. Spikes have been driven into trees to prevent logging in fragile areas. Members have conducted arson attacks on property ranging from a Nike shop in a mall north of Minneapolis to new homes on Long Island, New York. On February 7, 2004, ELF group members targeted construction equipment at a 30-acre development site in Charlottesville, Virginia.[43] On March 3, 2008,

The most active left-leaning domestic political terror groups today are involved in violent actions to protect the environment. Firefighters spray water onto burning houses in Woodinville, Washington, where four multimillion-dollar homes burned on March 3, 2008. A sign stating "Built Green? Nope Black! McMansions and R.C.D.s R not green. ELF" was found at the scene.

ELF is believed to have burnt a row of luxury homes in the Seattle area, causing $7 million in damage. While the multi-million dollar homes used green technology such as formalde-hyde-free materials, energy-efficient appliances, and landscaping that included native plants in their construction, the development had drawn opposition because of fear that septic systems could damage critical wetlands needed to protect an aquifer used by about 20,000 people in the area and could harm streams used by Chinook salmon.[44]

Another group, the Animal Liberation Front (ALF) focuses their efforts on protecting animals from being used as food, in clothing, or as experimental subjects. Their philosophy is that animals are entitled to the moral right to possess their own lives and control their own bodies, while rejecting the view that animals are merely capital goods or property intended for the benefit of humans and can be bought, sold, or killed by humans. ALF members conduct actions against scientists who conduct animal research, vandalizing their homes and cars, attacking labs, and setting animals free. They also conduct actions against animal breeding farms and food processing plants. ALF members have raided turkey farms before Thanksgiving and rabbit farms before Easter. Their activities have had significant impact on the commercial aspects of scientific testing, driving up the price of products, such as drugs, which rely on animal experimentation.[45] The ALF position on raising animals in breeding ranches is set out in Exhibit 11.6.

EXHIBIT 11.6

Breeding Ranches and Animal Liberation

A common misconception about fur "ranches" is that the animals do not suffer. This is entirely untrue. These animals suffer a life of misery and frustration, deprived of their most basic needs. They are kept in wire-mesh cages that are tiny, over-crowded, and filthy. Here they are malnourished, suffer contagious diseases, and endure severe stress.

On these farms, the animals are forced to forfeit their natural instincts. Beavers, who live in water in the wild, must exist on cement floors. Minks in the wild, too, spend much of their time in water, which keeps their salivation, respiration, and body temperature stable. They are also, by nature, solitary animals. However, on these farms, they are forced to live in close contact with other animals. This often leads to self-destructive behavior, such as pelt and tail biting. They often resort to cannibalism.

The methods used on these farms reflect not the interests and welfare of the animals but the furriers' primary interest—profit. The end of the suffering of these animals comes only with death, which, in order to preserve the quality of the fur, is inflicted with extreme cruelty and brutality. Engine exhaust is often pumped into a box of animals. This exhaust is not always lethal, and the animals sometimes writhe in pain as they are skinned alive. Another common execution practice, often used on larger animals, is anal electrocution. The farmers attach clamps to an animal's lips and insert metal rods into its anus. The animal is then electrocuted. Decompression chambers, neck snapping, and poison are also used.

Source: Animal Liberation Front, www.animalliberationfront.com/ (accessed July 12, 2008).

Not surprisingly, the FBI and other law enforcement agencies have targeted eco-terror groups such as ELF and ALF. On January 20, 2006, the FBI announced that its Operation Backfire had led to the arrest of 11 people who were accused of 17 attacks, including the $12 million arson of the Vail Ski Resort in 1998 and the sabotage of a high-tension power line near Bend, Oregon, in 1999.[46]

Nationalist Terrorism

Nationalist terrorism promotes the interests of a minority ethnic or religious group that believes it has been persecuted under majority rule and wishes to carve out its own independent homeland.

In Spain, the Basque Fatherland and Liberty (Euzkadi Ta Askatasuna, or ETA) is devoted to establishing a Basque homeland based on Marxist principles in the ethnically Basque areas in northern Spain and southwestern France. ETA was founded in 1959 by Basque Marxist rebels incensed by the efforts of Spanish dictator Francisco Franco to suppress the Basque language and culture. Since then the group has carried out numerous attacks in Spain and some in France. More than 800 people have been killed in ETA attacks since its founding. The group is best known for assassinating high level Spanish officials. In 1973, the group assassinated Admiral Luis Carrero Blanco, the heir apparent to Franco. Spanish King Juan Carlos was also the target of an unsuccessful plot. In addition, the group has targeted lower-level officials, journalists, and businessmen.

In the Middle East, terrorist activities have been linked to the Palestinians' desire to wrest their former homeland from Israel. At first, the Palestinian Liberation Organization (PLO), led by Yasser Arafat, directed terrorist activities against Israel. Now the group Hamas is perpetuating the conflict with Israel and is behind a spate of suicide bombings and terrorist attacks designed to elicit a sharp response from Israel and set back any chance for peace in the region. Hundreds on both sides of the conflict have been killed during terrorist attacks and reprisals. In Lebanon, Hezbollah, an Iranian supported group, is dedicated to fighting Israel and seizing control of the government. Their activities are described in Exhibit 11.7.

The Middle East is not the only source of nationalistic terrorism. The Chinese government has been trying to suppress separatist groups fighting for an independent state in the northwestern province of Xinjiang. The rebels are drawn from the region's Uyghur people, most of whom practice Sufi Islam, speak a Turkic language, and wish to set up a Muslim state called Eastern Turkistan. During the past decade the Uyghur separatists have organized demonstrations, bombings, and political assassinations. The province has witnessed more than 200 attacks since 1990, causing more than 150 deaths.[47] In Russia, Chechen terrorists have been intent on creating a free Chechen homeland and have been battling the Russian government to achieve their goal.

Hezbollah

Hezbollah (from the Arabic, meaning "party of God") is a Lebanese Shi'ite Islamist organization founded in 1982 in response to the presence of Israeli forces in southern Lebanon. At inception, its goals were to both drive Israeli troops out of Lebanon and to form a Shi'ite Islamic republic in Lebanon. Taking its inspiration from Iran, Hezbollah members follow a distinct version of Shia ideology developed by Ayatollah Ruhollah Khomeini, leader of the Islamic Revolution in Iran. Hezbollah has received arms and financial support from Iran, and some observers believe that it is actually a proxy Iranian paramilitary force. Hezbollah is anti-West and anti-Israel and has engaged in a series of terrorist actions including kidnappings, car bombings, and airline hijackings. Some of its most notable attacks directed at U.S. citizens and others include:

- The suicide truck bombings that killed more than 200 U.S. Marines at their barracks in Beirut, Lebanon, in 1983
- The 1985 hijacking of TWA flight 847
- Two major 1990s attacks in Argentina—the 1992 bombing of the Israeli Embassy (killing 29) and the 1994 bombing of a Jewish community center (killing 95)
- A July 2006 raid on a border post in northern Israel in which two Israeli soldiers were taken captive, an action which sparked an Israeli military incursion into Lebanon and the firing of rockets by Hezbollah across the Lebanese border into Israel

In addition to its military/terror campaigns, Hezbollah has attempted to win the hearts and minds of the Lebanese Shi'ite community by providing social services and food to the population. It has also entered the political world, and its candidates have won seats in Lebanon's parliament.

The public face of Hezbollah is Hassan Nasrallah, the group's senior political leader. Originally a military commander, Nasrallah's military and religious training makes him a unique leader. His leadership of Hezbollah's resistance to the Israeli army in the summer of 2006 made him one of the most popular leaders in the Middle East. For over twenty years, Imad Fayez Mugniyah was considered the key planner of Hezbollah's worldwide terrorist operations. On February 13, 2008, Mugniyah was killed in a car bombing in Damascus. Hezbollah officials accused Israel of launching the attacks that killed him, but the Israeli government denied involvement.

Source: Council on Foreign Relations, Hezbollah, www.cfr.org/publication/9155/ (accessed July 12, 2008).

Retributive Terrorism

Some terrorist groups are not nationalist, political, or revolutionary organizations. They do not wish to set up their own homeland or topple a government but rather want to impose their social and religious code on others.[48] **Retributive terrorists** have a number of characteristics that are unique and separate them from guerrillas, revolutionaries, and other terrorists:[49]

- Violence is used as a method of influence, persuasion, or intimidation. The true target of the terrorist act extends far beyond those directly affected by the attack and is designed to lead to some desired behavior on the part of the larger target population or government.

- Victims are usually selected for their maximum propaganda value, usually ensuring a high degree of media coverage. The message is that the target population had better comply with their demands because the terrorists are desperate enough to "do anything." Sometimes this may backfire if the attack results in the death of innocents, especially children, along with the symbolic targets.

- Unconventional military tactics are used, especially secrecy and surprise, as well as targeting civilians, including women and children. Because the goal is to inflict maximum horror, it makes sense to choose targets that contain the largest number of victims from all walks of life. The message: Everyone is a target; no one is safe.

How do retributive terror groups use violence to achieve their goals? According to researchers at the Rand Corporation, there are actually four independent views on the topic:

- *Coercion hypothesis*. Terrorists use violence to cause pain, notably casualties, to frighten the United States and to get us to bend to their will (e.g., withdrawing from the Middle East).

- *Damage hypothesis*. Terrorists want to damage the U.S. economy to weaken its ability to intervene in international affairs.

- *Rally hypothesis*. Violence is used to attract the attention of potential recruits and supporters.

- *Franchise hypothesis*. Jihadists use violence to pursue their own, often local, goals and only receive some support and encouragement from international organizations such as al-Qaeda.[50]

RAND researchers have found that the coercion and damage hypotheses are most consistent with prior attack patterns. Today the retributive terrorist can be categorized into four main groups:

- Al-Qaeda, including the group's strategy, ideology, operations, tactics, finances, changing character, and possible future.

- Terrorist groups that have adopted al-Qaeda's worldview and concept of mass-casualty terrorist attacks, even if the groups are not formally part of al-Qaeda.

- Violent Islamist and non-Islamist terrorist and insurgent groups without known links to al-Qaeda that threaten the United States' interests, friends, and allies. These include Hezbollah and Hamas, along with insurgencies in Iraq, the Philippines, and other countries.

- The nexus between terrorism and organized crime, including the terrorists and insurgents that use criminal organizations and connections to finance their activities. Such actions also tend to weaken and corrupt political and social institutions.[51]

Osama bin Laden and **al-Qaeda** are the paradigm of the new retributive terrorist organization. Rather than fighting for a homeland, their message is a call to take up a cause: There is a war of civilizations in which "Jews and Crusaders" want to destroy Islam and must therefore be defeated. Armed jihad is the individual obligation of every Muslim; terrorism and violence are appropriate methods for defeating even the strongest powers. The end product would be a unified Moslem world, the Caliphate, ruled under Muslim law free of Western influence.

These themes are preached in schools, on the Internet, and disseminated in books, cassette tapes, and pamphlets. Videotapes are distributed in which al-Qaeda's leaders expound on political topics, going as far as calling Western leaders liars and drunkards. As a result of this media strategy, al-Qaeda's messages have penetrated deeply into Muslim communities around the world, finding a sympathetic response among many Muslims who have a sense of helplessness both in the Arab world and in the Western Muslim diaspora. Al-Qaeda appears to have had an impact by offering a sense of empowerment to young men who feel lost in their adopted cultures.[52]

Osama bin Laden's masterminding of the 9/11 bombing was not designed to restore his homeland or bring about a new political state but to have his personal value structure adopted by Muslim nations. His attack may have been designed to create a military invasion of Afghanistan, which he hoped to exploit for his particular brand of revolution, a plan that has succeeded. According to Michael Scott Doran, bin Laden believed his acts would reach the audience that concerned him the most: the *umma*, or universal Islamic community.[53] The media would show Americans killing innocent civilians in Afghanistan, and the *umma* would find it shocking how Americans nonchalantly caused Muslims to suffer and die. The ensuing outrage would open a chasm between the Muslim population of the Middle East and the ruling governments in states allied with the West, such as Saudi Arabia. On October 7, 2001, bin Laden made a broadcast in which he said that the Americans and the British "have divided the entire world into two regions—one of faith, where there is no hypocrisy, and another of infidelity, from which we hope God will protect us."

State-Sponsored Terrorism

State-sponsored terrorism occurs when a repressive government regime forces its citizens into obedience, oppresses minorities, and stifles political dissent. Death squads and the use of government troops to destroy political opposition parties are often associated with political terrorism. Much of what we know about state-sponsored terrorism comes from the efforts of human rights groups such as London-based Amnesty International, whose research shows that tens of thousands of people continue to become victims of security operations that result in disappearances and executions. Political prisoners are now being tortured in about 100 countries, people have disappeared or are being held in secret detention in about 20 countries, and government-sponsored death squads have been operating in more than 35 countries. Countries known for encouraging violent control of dissidents include Brazil, Colombia, Guatemala, Honduras, Peru, Iraq, and the Sudan.

State-sponsored terrorism became a world issue when South and Central American dictatorships in the 1970s and 1980s unleashed state violence against political dissidents through forced disappearance, political imprisonment, torture, blacklisting, and massive exile. The region-wide state repression in this period emerged in response to the rise of the 1960s radical movements, which demanded public reforms and programs to help the lower classes in urban areas and agricultural workers in the countryside. Local authoritarian governments, which used repression to take control of radical political groups, were given financial support by the economic elites who dominated Latin American politics and were fearful of a socialist revolution.[54]

As might be expected, governments claim that repressive measures are needed to control terror and revolutionary groups that routinely use violence. Thus the use of terror is sometimes a way of defending the nation against violence, a conundrum that supports the idea that a state is both protective and destructive.[55]

The Abu Ghraib scandal in Iraq illustrates the difficulty in assigning blame for state-sponsored terrorism. Photos beamed around the world embarrassed the United States when they showed military personnel victimizing suspected insurgents. The government's response was to first condemn those responsible as rogue agents acting on their own, and then to prosecute and imprison the perpetrators. However, some critics, such as criminologist Mark Hamm, suggest that these images constitute the photographic record of a state-sponsored crime.[56] He argues that rather than being the work of a few officers acting independently, the sophisticated interrogation practices at Abu Ghraib were designed and executed by the U.S. Central Intelligence Agency and that the torturing of detainees at Abu Ghraib followed directly from decisions made by top government officials to get tough with prisoner interrogations. So while we condemn state-sponsored violence, it is often difficult to assess blame and even harder to identify who is truly responsible.

Cult Terrorism

In 1995, members of Aum Shinrikyo, a radical religious cult, set off poison gas in a Tokyo subway, killing 12 and injuring more than 3,000. Cult members found modern society too complex to understand, with few clear-cut goals and values.[57]

Some cults like Aum Shinrikyo may be classified as cult terror groups because their leaders demand that followers prove their loyalty through violence or intimidation.[58] These destructive cults are willing to have members commit violence, including murder. Members typically follow a charismatic leader who may be viewed as having godlike powers or even being the reincarnation of an important religious figure. The leader and his or her lieutenants commonly enforce loyalty by severe discipline and by physically preventing members from leaving the group. They may go through doomsday drills and maintain a siege mentality, fearing attacks from the government. It is not uncommon for cult terror groups to begin stockpiling weapons and building defensive barricades. The cult may openly or tacitly endorse individual killings or mass murder, which may be accompanied by mass suicide, either as a further symbolic instrument of their cause or, more commonly, as what they perceive to be justified self-defense, a last resort when the hostile world starts closing in and the leader's authority is threatened.[59]

Criminal Terrorism

Sometimes terrorist groups become involved in common-law crimes such as drug dealing and kidnapping, even selling nuclear materials. According to terrorism expert Chris Dishman, these illegal activities may on occasion become so profitable that they replace the group's original focus. Burmese insurgents continue to actively cultivate, refine, and traffic opium and heroin out of the Golden Triangle (the border between Myanmar [Burma], Thailand, and Laos), and some have even moved into the methamphetamine market.

In December 2001, six men were arrested by Russian security forces as they were making a deal for weapons-grade uranium. Some of the men were members of the Balashikha criminal gang, and they were in possession of two pounds of top-grade radioactive material, which can be used to build weapons. They were asking $30,000 for the deadly merchandise.[60] Since 1990 there have been a half-dozen cases involving theft and transportation of nuclear material and other cases involving people who offered to sell agents material not yet in their possession. These are the known cases; it is impossible to know if client states have already purchased enriched uranium or plutonium.

In some cases there has been close cooperation between organized criminal groups and guerillas. In other instances the relationship is more superficial. For example, the Revolutionary Armed Forces of Colombia (FARC) impose a tax on Colombian drug producers, but evidence indicates that the group cooperates with Colombia's top drug barons in running the trade. In some instances, the line between being a terrorist organization with political support and vast resources and being an organized criminal group engaging in illicit activities for profit becomes blurred. What appears to be a politically motivated action, such as the kidnapping of a government official for ransom, may turn out to be merely a crime for profit.[61]

www Check out the **Animal Liberation Front** website via academic.cengage.com/criminaljustice/siegel.

HOW ARE TERROR GROUPS ORGANIZED?

Terror groups tend to be networked or hierarchical. Newer terrorist organizations tend to be formed as networks, loosely organized groups located in different parts of the city, state, or country (or world) that share a common theme or purpose, but have a diverse leadership and command structure and are only in intermittent communication with one another. While there may be a variety of antigovernment groups operating in the

United States, there is little evidence that they share a single command structure or organizational fabric. These groups have few resources and little experience, so it is critical that they operate under cover and with as little public exposure as possible.

When needed, networked groups can pull factions together for larger scale operations, such as an attack on a military headquarters, or conversely, they can readily splinter off into smaller groups to avoid detection when a counterterrorism operation is underway. The advent of the Internet has significantly improved communications among networked terror groups.

As terror organizations evolve and expand, they may eventually develop a hierarchical organization with a commander at the top of the organization, captains, local area leaders, and so on. Ideological and religious groups tend to gravitate toward this model since a common creed/dogma controls their operations and a singular leader may be needed to define and disseminate group principles and maintain discipline. In a hierarchical model, the leader has the power to increase or decrease levels of violence for political purposes (i.e., they may order their followers to initiate a bombing campaign to influence an election). Schools may be off limits so that the population is not antagonized, or schools may become a target to show that the government cannot protect their children.

The various forms that terror groups take are summarized in Concept Summary 11.2

WHAT MOTIVATES THE TERRORIST?

Before terrorism can be effectively fought, controlled, and eradicated, it is important to understand something about the kind of people who become terrorists, what motivates their behavior, and how their ideas are formed. Unfortunately, this is not an easy task. Terrorism researchers have generally concluded that there is no single personality trait or behavior pattern that distinguishes the majority of terrorists or sets them apart so they can be easily identified and apprehended. Some seem truly disturbed whereas many others have not suffered long-term mental illness or displayed sociopathic traits and/or tendencies. Therefore, early child trauma is not a conclusive predictor of future terrorist activity.[62] As such, there have been a number of competing visions of why terrorists engage in criminal activities such as bombings, shootings, and kidnappings to achieve a political end. There are currently four views of terrorist motivation.

Psychological View

While not all terrorists suffer from psychological deficits, enough do so that the typical terrorist can be described as an emotionally disturbed individual who acts out his or her psychoses within the confines of violent groups. According to this view, terrorist violence is not so much a political instrument as an end in itself; it is the result of compulsion or psychopathology. Terrorists do what they do because of garden variety emotional

TYPES OF TERROR GROUPS

Revolutionary Terrorists	Revolutionary terrorists use violence to frighten those in power and their supporters in order to replace the existing government with a regime that holds acceptable political or religious views.
Political Terrorists	Political terrorism is directed at people or groups who oppose the terrorists' political ideology or whom the terrorists define as "outsiders" who must be destroyed.
Eco-Terrorism	Political eco-terror groups today are involved in violent actions to protect the environment.
Nationalist Terrorism	The actions of nationalist terrorists promote the interests of a minority ethnic or religious group that has been persecuted under majority rule and/or wishes to carve out its own independent homeland.
Retributive Terrorism	Retributive terror groups use violence as a method of influence, persuasion, or intimidation in order to achieve their goal of revenge, retribution, or reprisal for perceived past wrongs.
State-Sponsored Terrorism	Carried out by repressive government regimes, state-sponsored terrorism is designed to force its citizens into obedience, oppress minorities, and stifle political dissent.
Cult Terrorism	Terror cults are those whose leaders demand that followers prove their loyalty through violence or intimidation.
Criminal Terrorism	Terrorist groups become involved in common-law crimes such as drug dealing and kidnapping, even selling nuclear materials to achieve their goals.

problems, including but not limited to self-destructive urges and disturbed emotions combined with problems with authority.[63] As terrorism expert Jerrold M. Post puts it, "Political terrorists are driven to commit acts of violence as a consequence of psychological forces, and . . . their special psychology is constructed to rationalize acts they are psychologically compelled to commit."[64]

The view that terrorists suffer psychological abnormality is quite controversial and some critics suggest that it is spurious; the majority of research on terrorists indicates that most are not psychologically abnormal. Even suicide bombers, a group that should show signs of psychological abnormality, exhibit few signs of the mental problems, such as depression, that are typically found in people who choose to take their own life. After carefully reviewing existing evidence on the psychological state of terrorists, mental health expert Randy Borum concludes:

- Mental illness is not a critical factor in explaining terrorist behavior. Also, most terrorists are not "psychopaths."

- There is no "terrorist personality," nor is there any accurate profile—psychological or otherwise—of the terrorist.

- Histories of childhood abuse and trauma, and themes of perceived injustice and humiliation, often are prominent in terrorist biographies, but do not really help to explain terrorism.[65]

It is also possible that engaging in stressful terrorist activity results in the development of mental disorders and not vice versa.[66] Charles Ruby reviewed the literature on the psychology of terrorists and found little evidence that terrorists are psychologically dysfunctional or pathological. Ruby claims that terrorism is a form of politically motivated violence that is carried out by rational, lucid people who have valid motives; if they had more resources, terrorists would be military officers.[67]

Alienation View

Some experts believe that a lack of economic opportunity and recessionary economies are positively correlated with terrorism.[68] Young men and women are motivated to join terror groups because they are out of the political and social mainstream. Suffering alienation, they lack the tools to compete in a post-technological society. Many are relatively "ordinary" people who, alienated from modern society, believe that a suicide mission will cleanse them from the corruption of the modern world.[69]

According to this view, if terrorists suffer psychological deficiencies it is because they suffer alienation from friends, family, and society.[70] Many have been raised to hate their opponents and learn at an early age that they have been victimized by some oppressor. Terrorists report that they were estranged from their fathers, whom they viewed as economically, socially, or politically weak and ineffective. They are products of dysfunctional families in which the father was absent or, even if present, was a distant and cold figure.[71] Because of this family estrangement, the budding terrorist may have been swayed to join a group or cult by a charismatic leader who serves as an alternative father figure. Some find a sense of belonging in religious schools run by strong leaders who demand strict loyalty from their followers while

Indonesian Muslim cleric Abu Bakar Bashir (foreground) listens to Jemaah Islamiyah terrorist suspect Faiz Abu Bakar Bafana (detained in Singapore), who cries as he testifies by teleconference during Bashir's trial in Jakarta. The cleric, accused of leading a terror network, blamed the United States for orchestrating his treason trial to stop him fighting for the establishment of Islamic law.

indoctrinating them in political causes. This pattern is common among terror groups in Southeast Asia where teachers command strong personal loyalty from their students. This loyalty may be lifelong, as illustrated by the three Jemaah Islamiyah members (see Exhibit 11.5), who testified against their former teacher Abu Bakar Basyir during his terror trial. Despite their willingness to testify for the government, two wept at the sight of their teacher. They repeated that they loved him, but urged him to tell the truth about his activities.[72]

In this sense, terror groups, similar to what happens in urban street gangs, provide a substitute family-like environment, which can nurture a heretofore emotionally underprivileged youth.

Socialization/Friendship View

While alienation and estrangement seem plausible, research shows that terrorist operatives are not poor or lacking in education. Ironically, many terrorists appear to be educated members of the upper class. Osama bin Laden was a multimillionaire when he took up jihad, and at least some of his followers are highly educated and trained. The acts of the modern terrorist— using the Internet; organizing logistically complex and expensive assaults; and writing and disseminating formal critiques, manifestos, and theories—require the training and education of the social elite, not the poor and oppressed.

Marc Sageman studied members of extremist Islamist groups and found that most tend to be well educated as a group; about 60 percent had some form of higher education. More than 75 percent came from upper- or middle-class backgrounds. When they joined a terror organization, the majority had professional occupations (such as doctor or engineer) or semiskilled

employment (such as civil servant); fewer than 25 percent were unemployed or working in unskilled jobs. Surprisingly, Sageman found that almost three-quarters were married and that most had children.[73] These findings suggest that terrorists are not suffering from the social problems usually associated with alienation: poverty, lack of education, and ignorance. Sageman found that the vast majority of Islamic terrorists have close social bonds and social networks. While they may have felt isolated from the rest of society, their tight bonds of family and friendships encouraged them to join terror groups.

Sageman's study found that many jihadist recruits are living in foreign countries when they get involved with terrorist organizations. Feeling homesick, they seek out people with similar backgrounds, whom they find at mosques.[74] If they appear to be motivated by religious fervor, it can be explained that they are merely seeking friends in a foreign land. They live together in apartments in order to share the rent and eat together, typically under strict Muslim dietary laws. As a result, they form groups that solidify their beliefs and create a sense of group solidarity. If one becomes committed to terror, the others follow rather than let him down.

Religious/Ideological View

Another view is that terrorists hold extreme religious and/or ideological beliefs that prompt their behavior. At first they have heightened perceptions of oppressive conditions, believing that they are being victimized by some group or government. Once these potential terrorists recognize that these conditions can be changed by an active governmental reform effort that has not happened, they conclude that they must resort to violence to encourage change. The violence need not be aimed at a specific goal. Rather, terror tactics must help set in motion a series of events that enlists others in the cause and leads to long-term change. "Successful" terrorists believe that their "self-sacrifice" outweighs the guilt created by harming innocent people. Terrorism, therefore, requires violence without guilt; the cause justifies the violence.

Some terrorists are motivated by extreme religious beliefs that often coincide with their ideological views. But how can they justify using violence if they are truly religious since most of the world's religions eschew violence? Islamic terrorists believe that their commitment to God justifies their extreme actions. They regard the actions of people they trust as a testimony to the righteousness of their acts. They trust significant others, and rely on their wisdom, experience, and testimony and accept their expressions of faith. To the terrorists, someone like Osama bin Laden has demonstrated the strength of his faith by living in poverty and giving up a more luxurious and leisurely life in the name of God. When he calls them to jihad, they are likely to follow, even if it means killing those who deny their faith or beliefs. Perceived miracles, such as the defeat of a superpower through faith alone (e.g., the Soviet Afghan war or the fight against the U.S. in Iraq), also increase confidence in the righteousness of the cause. Some have mystical experiences during prayers or dreams that demonstrate the existence of God and reinforce faith. In a videotape in the fall of 2001, Osama bin Laden said that he had banned the reporting of dreams of airplanes flying into buildings prior to September 11 for fear of revealing the plot.[75]

Explaining State-Sponsored Terrorism

How can state-sponsored terror be explained? After all, these violent acts are not directed at a foreign government or overseas adversaries but against natives of one's own country. In her book *Reigns of Terror*, Patricia Marchak finds that people willing to kill or maim their fellow countrymen are likely to be highly susceptible to unquestioning submission to authority. They are conformists who want to be part of the central group and who are quite willing to be part of a state regime. They are vulnerable to ideology that dehumanizes their targets and can utilize propaganda to distance themselves psychologically from those they are terrorizing.[76] So the Nazis had little trouble recruiting people to carry out horrific acts during the Holocaust because many Germans wanted to be part of the popular social/political movement and were easily indoctrinated by the Nazi propaganda that branded Jews as subhuman. Stalin was able to carry out his reign of terror in Russia because his victims were viewed as state enemies who were trying to undermine the Communist regime.

How can these tendencies be neutralized? Marchak sees little benefit to international intervention that results in after-the-fact punishment of the perpetrators, a course of action that was attempted in the former Yugoslavia after death squads had performed "ethnic cleansing" of undesirables. Instead she argues for a prevention strategy that involves international aid and economic development by industrialized nations to those in the third world that are on the verge of becoming collapsed states, the construction of social welfare systems, and the acceptance of international legal norms and standards of human rights.[77]

RESPONSE TO TERRORISM

After the 9/11 attacks, agencies of the criminal justice system began to focus their attention on combating the threat of terror. Even local police agencies created anti-terror programs designed to protect their communities from the threat of attack. How should the nation best prepare itself to thwart potential attacks?

The National Commission on Terrorist Attacks Upon the United States (also known as the 9/11 Commission), an independent, bipartisan commission, was created in late 2002 and given the mission of preparing an in-depth report of the events leading up to the 9/11 attacks. Part of their goal was to create a comprehensive plan to ensure that no further attacks of that magnitude take place.

To monitor the millions of people who cross into America each year, the commission recommended that a single agency should be created to screen border crossings. They also recommended the creation of an investigative agency to monitor all aliens in the United States and to gather intelligence on the way terrorists travel across borders. The commission suggested that people who wanted passports be tagged with **biometric measures** to make them easily identifiable.

In response to the commission report, a **Director of National Intelligence (DNI)** was created and charged with coordinating data from the nation's primary intelligence-gathering agencies. The DNI serves as the principal intelligence adviser to the president and the statutory intelligence advisor to the National Security Council. On February 17, 2005, President George W. Bush named U.S. Ambassador to Iraq John Negroponte to be the first person to hold the post; he was confirmed on April 21, 2005; the current director is Mike McConnell, a former admiral and director of the National Security Agency.

Among the agencies reporting to the DNI is the staff of the newly created National Counterterrorism Center (NCTC), which is staffed by terrorism experts from the CIA, FBI, and the Pentagon; the Privacy and Civil Liberties Board; and the National Counterproliferation Center. The NCTC serves as the primary organization in the United States government for analyzing and integrating all intelligence possessed or acquired by the government pertaining to terrorism and counterterrorism, excepting purely domestic counterterrorism information.

While the 9/11 Commission report outlines what has already been done, what has not been done, and what needs to be done, agencies of the justice system have begun to respond to the challenge.

Fighting Terrorism with Law Enforcement

In the aftermath of the September 11, 2001, attacks, even before the 9/11 Commission made its report, it became obvious that the nation was not prepared to deal adequately with the threat of terrorism. One reason is the very nature of American society. Because we live in a free and open nation, it is extremely difficult to seal the borders and prevent the entry of terrorist groups. In his book *Nuclear Terrorism*, Graham Allison, an expert on nuclear weapons and national security, describes the almost superhuman effort it would take to seal the nation's borders from nuclear attack. Every day, 30,000 trucks, 6,500 rail cars, and 140 ships deliver more than 50,000 cargo containers into the United States. And while fewer than 5 percent ever get screened, those that do are given inspections using external detectors, which may not detect nuclear weapons or fissile material. The potential for terrorists to obtain bombs is significant: there are approximately 130 nuclear research reactors in 40 countries. Two dozen of these have enough highly enriched uranium for one or more nuclear bombs. If terrorists can get their hands on fissile material from these reactors, they could build a crude but working nuclear bomb within a year.

But they may not have to build their own bomb. They may be able to purchase an intact device on the black market. Russia alone has thousands of nuclear warheads and material for many thousands of additional weapons; all of these remain vulnerable to theft. Terrorists may also be able to buy the knowledge to construct bombs. In one well-known incident, Pakistan's leading nuclear scientist, A. Q. Khan, sold comprehensive "nuclear starter kits" that included advanced centrifuge components, blueprints for nuclear warheads, uranium samples in quantities sufficient to make a small bomb, and even provided personal consulting services to assist nuclear development.[78]

Recognizing this problem, law enforcement agencies around the country began to realign their resources to combat future terrorist attacks. In response to 9/11, law enforcement agencies undertook a number of steps: increasing the number of personnel engaged in emergency response planning; updating response plans for chemical, biological, or radiological attacks; and reallocating internal resources or increasing departmental spending to focus on terrorism preparedness.[79] Actions continue to be taken on the federal, state, and local levels.

Federal Law Enforcement One of the most significant changes has been a realignment of the Federal Bureau of Investigation (FBI), the federal government's main law enforcement agency. The FBI has already announced a reformulation of its priorities, making protecting the United States from terrorist attack its number one commitment. It is now charged with coordinating intelligence collection with the Border Patrol, Secret Service, and the CIA. The FBI must also work with and share intelligence with the National Counterterrorism Center (NCTC).

To carry out its newly formulated mission, the FBI is expanding its force of agents. In addition to recruiting candidates with the traditional background in law enforcement, law, and accounting, the Bureau is concentrating on hiring agents with scientific and technological skills as well as foreign-language proficiency in priority areas such as Arabic, Farsi, Pashtun, Urdu, all dialects of Chinese, Japanese, Korean, Russian, Spanish, and Vietnamese, and with other priority backgrounds such as foreign counterintelligence, counterterrorism, and military intelligence. Besides helping in counterterrorism activities, these agents will staff the Cyber Division, which was created in 2001 to coordinate, oversee, and facilitate FBI investigations in which the Internet, online services, and computer systems and networks are the principal instruments or targets of terrorists.

connections

The FBI and its data on crime are discussed in Chapters 2, 10, and 12.

Department of Homeland Security (DHS) Soon after the 2001 attack, President George W. Bush proposed the creation of a new cabinet-level agency called the **Department of Homeland Security (DHS)** and assigned it the following mission:

- Preventing terrorist attacks within the United States
- Reducing America's vulnerability to terrorism
- Minimizing the damage and recovering from attacks that do occur

On November 19, 2002, Congress passed legislation authorizing the creation of the DHS and assigned it the mission of providing intelligence analysis and infrastructure protection, strengthening the borders, improving the use of science and technology to counter weapons of mass destruction, and creating a comprehensive response and recovery division.

Rather than work from ground up, the DHS combined a number of existing agencies into a superagency that carried out the following missions:

- *Border and transportation security.* The Department of Homeland Security is responsible for securing our nation's borders and transportation systems, which include 350 ports of entry. The department manages who and what enters the country, and works to prevent the entry of terrorists and the instruments of terrorism while simultaneously ensuring the speedy flow of legitimate traffic. The DHS also is in charge of securing territorial waters, including ports and waterways.

- *Emergency preparedness and response.* The Department of Homeland Security ensures the preparedness of emergency response professionals, provides the federal government's response, and aids America's recovery from terrorist attacks and natural disasters. The department is responsible for reducing the loss of life and property and protecting institutions from all types of hazards through an emergency management program of preparedness, mitigation, response, and recovery.

- *Chemical, biological, radiological, and nuclear countermeasures.* The department leads the federal government's efforts in preparing for and responding to the full range of terrorist threats involving weapons of mass destruction. To do this, the department sets national policy and establishes guidelines for state and local governments. It directs exercises and drills for federal, state, and local chemical, biological, radiological, and nuclear (CBRN) response teams and plans. The department is assigned to prevent the importation of nuclear weapons and material.

- *Information analysis and infrastructure protection.* The department analyzes information from multiple available sources, including the CIA and FBI, in order to assess the dangers facing the nation. It also analyzes law enforcement and intelligence information.[80]

The DHS has numerous and varied duties. It is responsible for port security and transportation systems and manages airport security with its Transportation Security Administration (TSA). It has its own intelligence section, and it covers every special event in the United States including political conventions.

State Law Enforcement Efforts to Combat Terrorism In the wake of the 9/11 attacks, a number of states have beefed up their intelligence-gathering capabilities and aimed them directly at homeland security. California has introduced the California Anti-Terrorism Information Center (CATIC), a statewide intelligence system designed to combat terrorism. It divides the state into operational zones, and links federal, state, and local information services in one system. Trained intelligence analysts operate within civil rights guidelines and utilize information in a secure communications system; information is analyzed daily.[81] CATIC combines machine-intelligence with information coming from a variety of police agencies. The information is correlated and organized by analysts looking for trends. Rather than simply operating as an information-gathering unit, CATIC is a synthesizing process. It combines open-source public information with data on criminal trends and possible terrorist activities. Processed intelligence is designed to produce threat assessments for each area and to project trends outside the jurisdiction. The CATIC system attempts to process multiple sources of information to predict threats. By centralizing the collection and analytical sections of a statewide system, California's Department of Justice may have developed a method for moving offensively against terrorism.

Local Law Enforcement Federal law enforcement agencies are not alone in responding to the threat of terrorism. And, of course, nowhere is the threat of terrorism being taken more seriously than in New York City, one of the main targets of the 9/11 attacks, which has established a new Counterterrorism Bureau.[82] Teams within the bureau have been trained to examine potential targets in the city and are now attempting to insulate them from possible attack. Viewed as prime targets are the city's bridges, the Empire State Building, Rockefeller Center, and the United Nations headquarters. Bureau detectives are assigned overseas to work with the police in several foreign cities, including cities in Canada and Israel. Detectives have been assigned as liaisons with the FBI and with Interpol in Lyon, France. The city is now recruiting detectives with language skills ranging from Pashtun and Urdu to Arabic, Fujianese, and other dialects. The existing New York City Police Intelligence Division has been revamped, and agents are examining foreign newspapers and monitoring Internet sites. The department is also setting up several backup command centers in different parts of the city in case a terror attack puts headquarters out of operation. Several backup senior command teams have been created so that if people at the highest levels of the department are killed, individuals will already have been tapped to step into their jobs.

The Counterterrorism Bureau has assigned more than 100 city police detectives to work with FBI agents as part of a Joint Terrorist Task Force. In addition, the Intelligence Division's 700 investigators now devote 35 to 40 percent of their resources to counterterrorism, up from about 2 percent before January 2002. The department is also drawing on the expertise of other institutions around the city. For example, medical specialists have been enlisted to monitor daily

developments in the city's hospitals to detect any suspicious outbreaks of illness that might reflect a biological attack. And the police are now conducting joint drills with the New York Fire Department to avoid the problems in communication and coordination that marked the emergency response on September 11.

Confronting Terrorism with the Law

Soon after the September 11 terrorist attacks, the U.S. government enacted several laws focused on preventing further acts of violence against the United States and creating greater flexibility in the fight to control terror activity. Most importantly, Congress passed the USA Patriot Act (USAPA) on October 26, 2001. The bill is over 342 pages long, creates new laws, and makes changes to more than 15 existing statutes. Its aim is to give new powers to domestic law enforcement and international intelligence agencies in an effort to fight terrorism, to expand the definition of terrorist activities, and to alter sanctions for violent terrorism. While it is impossible to discuss every provision of this sweeping legislation here, a few of its more important elements will be examined.

The USA Patriot Act USAPA expands all four traditional tools of surveillance—wiretaps, search warrants, pen/trap orders (installing devices that record phone calls), and subpoenas. The Foreign Intelligence Surveillance Act (FISA), which allows domestic operations by intelligence agencies, is also expanded. USAPA gives greater power to the FBI to check and monitor phone, Internet, and computer records without first needing to demonstrate that they were being used by a suspect or target of a court order.

The government may now serve a single wiretap, or pen/trap order, on any person regardless of whether that person or entity is named in a court order. Prior to this act, telephone companies could be ordered to install pen/trap devices on their networks that would monitor calls coming to a surveillance target and to whom the surveillance target made calls; the USAPA extends this monitoring to the Internet. Law enforcement agencies may now also obtain the email addresses and websites visited by a target, and emails of the people with whom they communicate. It is possible to require that an Internet service provider install a device that records email and other electronic communications on its servers, looking for communications initiated or received by the target of an investigation. Under USAPA, the government does not need to show a court that the information or communication is relevant to a criminal investigation, nor does it have to report where it served the order or what information it received.

The act allows enforcement agencies to monitor cable operators and obtain access to their records and systems. Before the act, a cable company had to give prior notice to the customer, even if that person was a target of an investigation. Information can now be obtained on people with whom the cable subscriber communicates, the content of the person's communications, and the person's subscription records; prior notice is still required if law enforcement agencies want to learn what television programming a subscriber purchases.

The act also expands the definition of "terrorism" and enables the government to monitor more closely those people suspected of "harboring" and giving "material support" to terrorists (Sections 803, 805). It increases the authority of the U.S. attorney general to detain and deport noncitizens with little or no judicial review. The attorney general may certify that he has "reasonable grounds to believe" that a noncitizen endangers national security and is therefore eligible for deportation. The attorney general and secretary of state are also given the authority to designate domestic groups as terrorist organizations and deport any noncitizen who is a member.

Civil Rights and the USA Patriot Act Although law enforcement agencies may applaud these new laws, civil libertarians are troubled because they view the act as eroding civil rights. Some complain that there are provisions that permit the government to share information from grand jury proceedings and from criminal wiretaps with intelligence agencies. First Amendment protections may be violated because the Patriot Act authority is not only limited to true terrorism investigations but covers a much broader range of activity involving reasonable political dissent. Though many critics have called for its repeal, it was reauthorized in 2006 with a slew of provisions insuring that the act did not violate civil rights by limiting its surveillance and wiretap authorizations.[83]

Civil libertarians fear that the Patriot Act gives the government too much power and allows it to monitor the daily activities of ordinary Americans under the guise of national security. It may even allow the government to monitor people's library books. Here, at a press conference at the American Civil Liberties Union in New York, May 30, 2006, librarians George M. Christian, Peter Chase, Janet Nocek, and Barbara Bailey, members of a Connecticut consortium called the Library Connection, speak publicly for the first time about their battle against Patriot Act demands for patrons' library records. The four librarians sought help from the ACLU after the FBI demanded patron records through a National Security Letter. This Patriot Act tool allows the government to demand, without court approval, records of people who are not suspected of any wrongdoing.

Political Solutions to Terrorism

In the long run, it may simply be impossible to defeat terror groups and end terrorism using military, law enforcement, or legal solutions. Using force may play into terrorists' hands and convince people that they are freedom fighters valiantly struggling against a better armed and more ruthless foe. No matter how many terrorists are killed and/or captured, military/deterrence-based solutions may be doomed. Aggressive reprisals will cause terrorist ideology to spread and gain greater acceptance in the underdeveloped world. The resulting anger and alienation will produce more terrorists than can be killed off through violent responses. In contrast, if the terrorist ideology is countered and discredited, the appeal of terror groups such as al-Qaeda will wither and die.

One approach suggested by policy experts is to undermine support for terrorist groups by being benevolent nation builders giving aid to the nations that house terror groups.[84] This is the approach the United States took after World War II to rebuild Germany and Japan (the Marshall Plan) all the while gaining support for its cold war struggle against the Soviet Union. According to the Rand Corporation, a nonprofit research group, the following steps are required to defeat jihadist groups such as al-Qaeda:

▌ Attack the ideological underpinnings of global jihadism

▌ Sever ideological and other links between terrorist groups

▌ Strengthen the capabilities of front-line states to counter local jihadist threats

This approach may work because al-Qaeda's goal of toppling "apostate" regimes in Saudi Arabia, Egypt, and Pakistan and creating an ultraorthodox pan-Islamic government spanning the world does not sit well with large groups of Moslems; their monolithic vision has no room for other Muslim sects such as Shi'ites and Sunni moderates. Therefore, political and social appeals may help fracture local support for al-Qaeda. In addition, the United States should seek to deny sanctuaries to terrorist groups and strengthen the capabilities of foreign governments to deal with terrorist threats, but in an advisory capacity by providing intelligence. In his recent book *Unconquerable Nation*, Brian Michael Jenkins, a noted expert on the topic, identifies the strategic principles he believes are the key to combating terror in contemporary society. These beliefs are summarized in Exhibit 11.8.

www Go to academic.cengage.com/criminaljustice/siegel to access the following websites:

▌ The Office of the **Director of National Intelligence**

▌ The **National Counterterrorism Center** (NCTC)

EXHIBIT 11.8

Countering Terror

- *Destroy the jihadist enterprise.* Jihadists have proven to be flexible and resistant and capable of continued action despite sustained military efforts. They remain the primary threat to U.S. national security and will continue to be so for the foreseeable future. Therefore, they must be destroyed and their ability to operate damaged.

- *Conserve resources for a long war.* The United States must conserve its resources for the long haul. These include blood, natural resources, the will of the American people, and the support of needed allies. This means picking future fights carefully, making security measures both effective and efficient, maintaining domestic support, avoiding extreme measures that alienate the people, and cultivating rather than bullying other countries.

- *Wage more-effective political warfare.* Political solutions must be pragmatic. We must be ready to compromise. Amnesty should be offered to terrorists who have become disillusioned. Local leaders should be accommodated and deals cut to co-opt enemies.

- *Break the cycle of jihadism.* Jihadism is a cycle beginning with recruitment and ending with death, arrest, and/or detention. Combating terror must involve neutralizing terror groups' ability to radicalize and indoctrinate potential recruits before the cycle begins. At the end of the cycle, it must also deal effectively with terror suspects once they have been captured and detained.

- *Impede recruitment.* Recruitment sites must be identified and made dangerous and therefore unusable. Alternatives to terror must be offered. Former, now disillusioned terrorists can be used to denounce terror and counteract its appeal with potential recruits.

- *Encourage defections and facilitate exits.* Potential defectors must be identified and encouraged to quit through the promise of amnesty, cash, job training, and homes.

- *Persuade detainees to renounce terrorism.* Rehabilitation of known terror suspects may be more important than prosecution and imprisonment.

- *Maintain international cooperation.* International cooperation is a prerequisite to success, a precious commodity not to be squandered by bullying, unreciprocated demands, indifference to local realities, or actions that repel even America's closest friends.

- *Reserve the right to retaliate—a muscular deterrent.* Terror groups and their sponsors should know that any attack using weapons of mass destruction will be met with all-out warfare against any group or government known to be or even suspected of being responsible.

Source: Brian Michael Jenkins, *Unconquerable Nation: Knowing Our Enemy, Strengthening Ourselves* (Santa Monica, CA: Rand Corporation, 2006), www.rand.org/pubs/monographs/2006/RAND_MG454.pdf (accessed July 12, 2008).

THINKING LIKE A CRIMINOLOGIST

You have been hired as a terror expert by the newly appointed Director of National Intelligence. She tells you that the United States and its coalition allies have vowed to eliminate the network of al-Qaeda cells thought to have been established throughout the Western world. Already, numerous al-Qaeda and Taliban suspects captured in Afghanistan and elsewhere have been imprisoned on U.S. military bases, including Guantanamo Bay in Cuba. There have been hundreds of arrests made in more than 50 countries, and a number of allies have actually changed their laws to make it easier to apprehend alleged activists. Yet, despite these efforts the threat of terror goes on unabated. The director would like you to make three recommendations, to be implemented immediately, that will help reduce the terrorist threat.

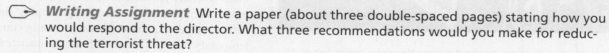

Writing Assignment Write a paper (about three double-spaced pages) stating how you would respond to the director. What three recommendations would you make for reducing the terrorist threat?

Doing Research on the Web Go to academic.cengage.com/criminaljustice/siegel to read about anti-terror activities in the United Kingdom, and read the entire 9/11 Commission report, as well as the FBI's 2004 to 2009 reorganization plan.

SUMMARY

- The term "political crime" is used to signify illegal acts that are designed to undermine an existing government and threaten its survival.

- Political crimes can include both violent and nonviolent acts and range in seriousness from dissent, treason, and espionage to violent acts such as terrorism or assassination.

- The political criminal and political crimes may stem from religious or ideological sources. They often occupy a gray area between conventional and outlawed behavior.

- While common criminals may be motivated by greed, vengeance, or jealousy, political criminals have a somewhat different agenda from common criminals.

- There is no set pattern or reason why someone becomes a political criminal. Some use political crime as a stepping-stone to public office while others as a method to focus their frustrations.

- Some political criminals want to shape elections to meet their personal needs. In some instances the goal is altruistic; in others the motivation is greed and profit.

- Helping or cooperating with the enemy in a time of war would be considered treason.

- Espionage is the practice of obtaining information about a government, organization, or a society that is considered secret or confidential without the permission of the holder of the information.

- Industrial espionage involves unethical or illegal activities such as bribing employees to reveal trade secrets such as computer codes or product formulas.

- While some political crimes are committed by people who oppose the state, others are perpetrated by state authorities against the people they are supposed to serve.

- State political crime has five components: political corruption; illegal domestic surveillance; human rights violations; state violence; and state-corporate crime.

- The use of torture to gain information from suspected political criminals is highly controversial.

- The use of waterboarding has become a national issue as there seems to be no agreement on whether it is torture or a relatively harmless instrument of interrogation.

- The political crime that many people are now most concerned with is terrorism.

- Terrorism is generally defined as the illegal use of force against innocent people to achieve a political objective.

- The term "guerilla" refers to antigovernment forces located in rural areas that attack the military, the police, and government officials.

- The typical goal of an insurgency is to confront the existing government for control of all or a portion of its territory, or force political concessions in sharing political power.

- A revolution is generally seen as a civil war fought between nationalists and a sovereign power that holds control of the land, or between the existing government and local groups over issues of ideology and power.

- Revolutionary terrorists use violence to frighten those in power and their supporters in order to replace the existing government with a regime that holds acceptable political or religious views.

- Political terrorism is directed at people or groups who oppose the terrorists' political ideology or whom the terrorists define as "outsiders" who must be destroyed.

- Nationalist terrorism promotes the interests of a minority ethnic or religious group that believes it has been persecuted under majority rule and wishes to carve out its own independent homeland.

- Retributive terrorists want to impose their social and religious code on others. Al-Qaeda is essentially a retributive terror organization.

- State-sponsored terrorism occurs when a repressive government regime forces its citizens into obedience, oppresses minorities, and stifles political dissent.

- Destructive cults are willing to have members commit violence, including murder.

- Sometimes terrorist groups become involved in common-law crimes such as drug dealing and kidnapping, even selling nuclear materials.

- Terrorism researchers have generally concluded that there is no single personality trait or behavior pattern that distinguishes the majority of terrorists or sets them apart so they can be easily identified and apprehended.

- The National Commission on Terrorist Attacks Upon the United States (also known as the 9/11 Commission) was given the mission of preparing an in-depth report of the events leading up to the 9/11 attacks.

- The Office of the Director of National Intelligence (DNI) is charged with coordinating data from the nation's primary intelligence-gathering agencies.

- The National Counterterrorism Center (NCTC) serves as the primary organization in the United States government for analyzing and integrating all intelligence possessed or acquired by the government pertaining to terrorism and counterterrorism, excepting purely domestic counterterrorism information.

- The FBI has announced a reformulation of its priorities, making protecting the United States from terrorist attack its number one commitment. It is now charged with coordinating intelligence collection with the Border Patrol, Secret Service, and the CIA.

- The Department of Homeland Security (DHS) is the federal agency responsible for preventing terrorist attacks within the United States, reducing America's vulnerability to terrorism, and minimizing the damage and recovering from attacks that do occur.

- The USA Patriot Act (USAPA) was passed to make it easier for law enforcement agencies to conduct anti-terror surveillance.

■ CENGAGENOW™ is an easy-to-use online resource that helps you study in less time to get the grade you want—NOW. CengageNOW™ Personalized Study (a diagnostic study tool containing valuable text-specific resources) lets you focus on just what you don't know and learn more in less time to get a better grade. If your textbook does not include an access code card, you can go to www.ichapters.com to purchase CengageNOW™.

KEY TERMS

political crime *(336)*
election fraud *(337)*
treason *(338)*
espionage *(341)*
state political crime *(342)*
torture *(344)*
ticking bomb scenario *(344)*
habeas corpus *(344)*
terrorism *(346)*

terror cells *(347)*
guerilla *(347)*
insurgent *(347)*
zealot *(348)*
Reign of Terror *(349)*
retributive terror *(353)*
al-Qaeda *(353)*
state-sponsored terror *(354)*

cult terror *(355)*
networks *(355)*
biometric measures *(358)*
Director of National Intelligence (DNI) *(358)*
Department of Homeland Security (DHS) *(359)*
USA Patriot Act (USAPA) *(360)*

CRITICAL THINKING QUESTIONS

1. Would you be willing to give up some of your civil rights in order to aid the war on terror?

2. Should terror suspects arrested in a foreign land be given the same rights and privileges as an American citizen accused of crime?

3. What groups in America might be the breeding ground for terrorist activity in the United States?

4. In light of the 9/11 attack, should acts of terrorism be treated differently from other common-law violent crimes? Should terrorists be executed for their acts even if no one is killed during their attack?

5. Can the use of torture ever be justified? Is the "ticking bomb" scenario valid?

6. A spy gives plans for a new weapon to the enemy. They build the weapon and use it to kill American soldiers. Is the spy guilty of murder?

NOTES

1. Jeffrey Ian Ross, *The Dynamics of Political Crime* (Thousand Oaks, CA: Sage, 2003).
2. Ibid.
3. Amnesty International press release, "Azerbaijan: Rising Tide of Persecution against Independent Journalism," January 24, 2007, http://web.amnesty.org/library/Index/ENGEUR550052007 (accessed July 7, 2008).
4. Stephen Schafer, *The Political Criminal, The Problem of Morality and Crime* (New York: Free Press, 1974): 154–157.
5. Randy Borum, "'Understanding the Terrorist Mind-Set," *FBI Law Enforcement Bulletin*, 72 (2003): 7–10.
6. Federal Election Commission, News Release, "Mitchell Wade and MZM Inc. Agree to Pay $1,000,000 Civil Penalty for Illegal Contribution Reimbursement

Scheme," October 31, 2007, www.fec.gov/press/press2007/20071031mzm.shtml (accessed July 7, 2008).
7. The Bipartisan Campaign Reform Act of 2002 (BCRA, McCain–Feingold Act, Pub.L. 107-155, 116 Stat. 81, enacted 2002-03-27).
8. Amnesty International, "Kenya: Amnesty International Concerned at Police Killings in Election Protests," December 31 2007, www.amnesty.org/en/for-media/press-releases/kenya-amnesty-international-concerned-police-killings-election-protests/ (accessed July 8, 2008).
9. BBC news, "Profile of John Walker Lindh," January 24, 2002, http://news.bbc.co.uk/2/hi/americas/1779455.stm (accessed July 8, 2008).

10. University of Missouri–Kansas City School of Law, Douglas Linder, "The Treason Trial of Aaron Burr," www.law.umkc.edu/faculty/projects/ftrials/burr/burraccount.html (accessed July 8, 2008).
11. John Ziff and Austin Sarat, *Espionage and Treason* (New York: Chelsea House, 1999).
12. United States Criminal Code at 18 U.S.C. § 2381.
13. CNN, "Accused FBI Spy Hanssen Pleads Not Guilty," May 31, 2001, http://archives.cnn.com/2001/LAW/05/31/hanssen.arraignment.02/index.html (accessed July 7, 2008).
14. David Owen, *Hidden Secrets: The Complete History of Espionage and the Technology Used to Support It* (Ontario, Canada, Firefly Books, 2002).

15. BBC News, "Key Cases in Soviet-UK Espionage," January 23, 2006, http://news.bbc.co.uk/2/hi/europe/4639130.stm (accessed July 8, 2008).

16. Hedieh Nasheri, *Economic Espionage and Industrial Spying* (Cambridge, England: Cambridge University Press, 2004).

17. Office of the National Counterintelligence Executive, 2005 Foreign Economic Collection and Industrial Espionage report, www.ncix.gov/publications/reports/fecie_all/FECIE_2005.pdf (accessed July 22, 2008).

18. Ibid.

19. Department of Justice News Release, "Two Men Plead Guilty to Stealing Trade Secrets from Silicon Valley Companies to Benefit China," December 14, 2006, http://sanfrancisco.fbi.gov/dojpressrel/2006/sf121406a.htm (accessed July 7, 2008).

20. Ross, *The Dynamics of Political Crime*.

21. American Civil Liberties Union, "FBI Inquiry Details Abuses Reported by Agents at Guantanamo," January 3, 2007, www.aclu.org/safefree/torture/27816prs20070103.html (accessed July 7, 2008).

22. Human Rights Watch, "Chechnya: Research Shows Widespread and Systematic Use of Torture," http://hrw.org/english/docs/2006/11/13/russia14557_txt.htm (accessed July 7, 2008).

23. Ross, *The Dynamics of Political Crime*.

24. Nadia Abou El-Magd, "Accuser in Case vs. CIA Agents Tells of Torture: Muslim Cleric Says Egyptians Used Electricity," *Boston Globe*, 23 February 2007, A3.

25. Jessica Wolfendale, "Training Torturers: A Critique of the 'Ticking Bomb' Argument," *Social Theory and Practice* 31 (2006): 269–287.

26. Vittorio Bufacchi and Jean Maria Arrigo, "Torture, Terrorism and the State: A Refutation of the Ticking-Bomb Argument," *Journal of Applied Philosophy* 23 (2006): 355–373.

27. Elizabeth Sepper, "The Ties that Bind: How the Constitution Limits the CIA's Actions in the War on Terror," *New York University Law Review* 81 (2006): 1,805–1,843.

28. *Boumediene et al. v. Bush, President of the United States, et al.*, No 06-1195 (June 12, 2008).

29. Scott Shane, David Johnston, and James Risen, "Secret U.S. Endorsement of Severe Interrogations" *New York Times*, 4 October 2007, www.nytimes.com/2007/10/04/washington/04interrogate.html (accessed July 8, 2008).

30. Michael Cooper and Marc Santora, "McCain Rebukes Giuliani on Waterboarding Remark," *New York Times*, 26 October 2007, www.nytimes.com/2007/10/26/us/politics/26giuliani.html (accessed July 7, 2008).

31. Title 22 of the United States Code section 2656f (d) (1999).

32. Paul Wilkinson, *Terrorism and the Liberal State* (New York: Wiley, 1977), p. 49.

33. Jack Gibbs, "Conceptualization of Terrorism," *American Sociological Review* 54 (1989): 329–340, at 330.

34. Robert Friedlander, *Terrorism* (Dobbs Ferry, NY: Oceana Publishers, 1979), p. 14.

35. Daniel Georges-Abeyie, "Political Crime and Terrorism," in *Crime and Deviance: A Comparative Perspective*, ed. Graeme Newman (Beverly Hills: Sage, 1980), pp. 313–333.

36. Terrorism Research, "Differences between Terrorism and Insurgency," www.terrorism-research.com/insurgency/ (accessed July 7, 2008).

37. Andrew Silke, "Holy Warriors: Exploring the Psychological Processes of Jihadi Radicalization," *European Journal of Criminology* 5 (2008): 99–123.

38. Walter Laqueur, *The New Terrorism: Fanaticism and the Arms of Mass Destruction Terrorism and History* (New York: Oxford, 1999).

39. This section relies heavily on Friedlander, *Terrorism*, pp. 8–20.

40. Michael Kellogg, *The Russian Roots of Nazism: White Russians and the Making of National Socialism, 1917–1945* (New York: Cambridge University Press, 2005).

41. Associated Press, "Malaysia Arrests Five Militants," *New York Times*, 15 October 2002, p. A2.

42. Jocelyn Parker, "Vehicles Burn at Dealership: SUV Attacks Turn Violent," *Detroit Free Press*, 23 August 2003, p. 1.

43. "Brutal Elves in the Woods," *Economist* 359 (14 April 2001): 28–30.

44. Steve Miletich, "Hunt Is On: Who Torched the Street of Dreams?" *Seattle Times* 4 March 2008, http://seattletimes.nwsource.com/cgi-bin/PrintStory.pl?document_id=2004258337 (accessed July 7, 2008).

45. Fiona Proffitt, "Costs of Animal Rights Terror," *Science* 304 (18 June 2004): 1,731–1,739.

46. Department of Justice New Release, "Eleven Defendants Indicted on Domestic Terrorism Charges: Group Allegedly Responsible for Series of Arsons in Western States, Acting on Behalf of Extremist Movements," January 20, 2006, www.usdoj.gov/opa/pr/2006/January/06_crm_030.html (accessed July 7, 2008).

47. Chung Chien-Peng, "China's War on Terror," *Foreign Affairs* 81 (July–August 2002): 8–13.

48. Angel Rabasa, Peter Chalk, Kim Cragin, Sara A. Daly, Heather S. Gregg, Theodore W. Karasik, Kevin A. O'Brien, and William Rosenau, *Beyond Al-Qaeda: Part 1, The Global Jihadist Movement* and *Part 2, The Outer Rings of the Terrorist Universe* (Santa Monica, CA: Rand Corporation, 2006).

49. Lawrence Miller, "The Terrorist Mind: A Psychological and Political Analysis, Part I," *International Journal of Offender Therapy and Comparative Criminology* 50 (2006): 121–138.

50. Martin Libicki, Peter Chalk, and Melanie Sisson, *Exploring Terrorist Targeting Preferences* (Santa Monica, CA: Rand Corporation 2007), www.rand.org/pubs/monographs/2007/RAND_MG483.sum.pdf (accessed July 7, 2008).

51. Mark Mazzetti and David Rohde, "Al-Qaeda Chiefs Are Seen to Regain Power," *New York Times*, 19 February 2007, p.1; Sanjeev Gupta, Benedict Clements, Rina Bhattacharya, and Shamit Chakravarti, "Fiscal Consequences of Armed Conflict and Terrorism in Low- and Middle-Income Countries," *European Journal of Political Economy* 20 (2004): 403–421.

52. Ibid.

53. Michael Scott Doran, "Somebody Else's Civil War," *Foreign Affairs* 81 (January–February 2002): 22–25.

54. Gabriela Fried, "Piecing Memories Together after State Terror and Policies of Oblivion in Uruguay: The Female Political Prisoner's Testimonial Project (1997–2004)," *Social Identities* 12 (2006): 543–562.

55. Martin Miller, "Ordinary Terrorism in Historical Perspective," *Journal for the Study of Radicalism* 2 (2008): 125–154.

56. Mark Hamm, "High Crimes and Misdemeanors: George W. Bush and the Sins of Abu Ghraib," *Crime, Media, Culture: An International Journal* 3 (2007): 259–284.

57. Haruki Murakami, *Underground* (New York: Vintage Books, 2001).

58. Lawrence Miller, "The Terrorist Mind: A Psychological and Political Analysis, Part II," *International Journal of Offender Therapy and Comparative Criminology* 50 (2006): 255–268.

59. Ibid.

60. Jeffrey Kluger, "The Nuke Pipeline: The Trade in Nuclear Contraband Is Approaching Critical Mass. Can We Turn Off the Spigot?" *Time*, 17 December 2001, p. 40.

61. Chris Dishman, "Terrorism, Crime, and Transformation," *Studies in Conflict and Terrorism* 24 (2001): 43–56.

62. Stephen J. Morgan, *The Mind of a Terrorist Fundamentalist: The Psychology of Terror Cults* (Awe-Struck E-Books, 2001); Martha Crenshaw, "The Psychology of Terrorism: An Agenda for the 21st Century," *Political Psychology* 21 (June 2000): 405–420.

63. Andrew Silke, "Courage in Dark Places: Reflections on Terrorist Psychology," *Social Research* 71 (2004): 177–198.

64. Jerrold M. Post, "Terrorist Psycho-Logic: Terrorist Behavior as a Product of Psychological Forces," in *Origins of Terrorism: Psychologies, Ideologies Theologies, States of Mind*, ed. Walter Reich (Cambridge: Cambridge University Press, 1990), p. 12.

65. Randy Borum, *Psychology of Terrorism* (Tampa: University of South Florida, 2004), www.ncjrs.gov/pdffiles1/nij/grants/208552.pdf (accessed July 7, 2008).

66. David Weatherston and Jonathan Moran, "Terrorism and Mental Illness: Is There a Relationship?" *International Journal of Offender Therapy and Comparative Criminology* 47 (2003): 698–711.
67. Charles Ruby, "Are Terrorists Mentally Deranged?" *Analyses of Social Issues and Public Policy* 2 (2002): 15–26.
68. Ethan Bueno de Mesquita, "The Quality of Terror," *American Journal of Political Science* 49 (2005): 515–530.
69. Murakami, *Underground*.
70. Jerrold Post, "When Hatred Is Bred in the Bone: Psycho-Cultural Foundations of Contemporary Terrorism," *Political Psychology* 25 (2005): 615–637.
71. This section leans heavily on Anthony Stahelski, "Terrorists Are Made, Not Born: Creating Terrorists Using Social Psychological Conditioning," *Journal of Homeland Security*, March 2004, www.homelandsecurity.org/journal/Articles/stahelski.html (accessed July 7, 2008).
72. Marc Sageman, *Understanding Terror Networks* (Philadelphia: University of Pennsylvania Press, 2004), Ch. 4.
73. Marc Sageman, *Understanding Terror Networks*.
74. Ibid.
75. Ibid.
76. Patricia Marchak, *Reigns of Terror* (Montreal: McGill-Queen's University Press, 2003).
77. Ibid., pp. 153–155.
78. Graham Allison, *Nuclear Terrorism: The Ultimate Preventable Catastrophe* (New York: Times Books, 2004).
79. Rand Corporation, "How Prepared Are State and Local Law Enforcement for Terrorism?" www.rand.org/publications/RB/RB9093/ (accessed July 7, 2008).
80. White House press release, November 11, 2002, www.whitehouse.gov/news/releases/2002/11/20021119-4.html (accessed July 7, 2008). The section on homeland security relies heavily on "The Department of Homeland Security," www.whitehouse.gov/infocus/homeland/ (accessed July 7, 2008).
81. California Anti-Terrorism Information Center (CATIC), www.ag.ca.gov/antiterrorism/ (accessed July 7, 2008).
82. William K. Rashbaum, "Terror Makes All the World a Beat for New York Police," *New York Times*, 15 July 2002, B1; Al Baker, "Leader Sees New York Police in Vanguard of Terror Fight," *New York Times*, 6 August 2002, A2; Stephen Flynn, "America the Vulnerable," *Foreign Affairs* 81 (January–February 2002): 60.
83. U.S. House of Representatives Committee on the Judiciary, http://judiciary.house.gov/Printshop.aspx?Section=232 (accessed July 7, 2008).
84. Rabasa, Chalk, Cragin, Daly, Gregg, Karasik, O'Brien, and Rosenau, *Beyond Al-Qaeda: Parts 1 and 2*.

12

Property Crime

CHAPTER OUTLINE

A Brief History of Theft
Theft in the Nineteenth Century: Train Robbery
and Safecracking

Contemporary Theft
Occasional Thieves
Professional Thieves
Sutherland's Professional Criminal
The Professional Fence
The Criminological Enterprise: Confessions
of a Dying Thief
The Occasional Fence

Larceny/Theft
Larceny Today
PROFILES IN CRIME: Invasion of the Body Snatchers
Shoplifting
Bad Checks
Credit Card Theft
PROFILES IN CRIME: Credit Card Con
Auto Theft
False Pretenses or Fraud
Confidence Games
Embezzlement

Burglary
The Nature and Extent of Burglary
Planning to Burgle
Commercial Burglary
Race, Culture, Gender, and Criminology:
Are There Gender Differences in Burglary?
Careers in Burglary

Arson
The Juvenile Fire Starter
Professional Arson

CHAPTER OBJECTIVES

1. Be familiar with the history of theft offenses
2. Recognize the differences between professional
   and amateur thieves
3. Know the similarities and differences between the
   various types of larceny
4. Understand the different forms of shoplifting
5. Be able to discuss the concept of fraud
6. Know what is meant by a confidence game
7. Understand what it means to burgle a home
8. Know what it takes to be a good burglar
9. Understand the concept of arson

For seven years, dozens of rare maps— often hundreds of years old— were mysteriously disappearing from prestigious libraries around the world. The thefts went unsolved—and in most cases, undetected—until one morning when the head of public services for Yale University's Beinecke Rare Book and Manuscript Library in New Haven, Connecticut, happened to notice an X-Acto knife blade on the floor in the rare documents room. Spotting a man in the stacks, she hurriedly got his name from the library's sign-in register. He was Edward Forbes Smiley III, a well-known rare maps dealer. Yale police conducted video surveillance, and when Smiley left the library, he was followed and arrested at the Yale Center for the British Arts. A search of Smiley's personal property revealed seven rare maps worth more than $700,000. One was a 1614 map that had been removed from the book Advertisements for the Unexperienced Planters of New England, or Anywhere *by Captain John Smith, founder of Jamestown. Another was a "Septentrio vniuersalis descripto" authored by Richard Hakluyt (1552–1616) that had a comparable value of $500,000.*

When interrogated by federal law enforcement agents Smiley admitted stealing and selling 97 rare maps from numerous collections worldwide, worth an estimated $3 million. He was able to lead investigators to most of the dealers and collectors who originally purchased them, but precise identification proved difficult. Many of the libraries weren't even aware they were missing any items since they didn't inventory their books very often. After much painstaking work, 86 of the maps were recovered. On June 29, 2006, Smiley pleaded guilty to numerous charges of art theft. Standing before Judge Janet Bond Arterton, Smiley said he "knowingly and willfully" removed five maps from the Beinecke Library. "I concealed them in my briefcase with the intention of removing them from the library," he said, adding that he knew at the time that his actions were wrong. "I very much regret my actions and apologize to the court and to all the institutions that have been harmed by my conduct." On September 27, 2006, he was sentenced to 42 months in prison and ordered to pay nearly $2 million in restitution. The court left the issue of restitution open in case more maps are found and identified.[1]

Though average citizens may be puzzled and enraged by violent crimes, believing them to be both senseless and cruel, they often view economic crimes with a great deal more ambivalence. Society generally disapproves of crimes involving theft and corruption, but the public seems quite tolerant of the "gentleman bandit," such as Edward Forbes Smiley III, even to the point of admiring such figures. They pop up as characters in popular myths and legends—such as the famed English outlaw Robin Hood—and in films such as *Ocean's Eleven* (2001) and *Ocean's Twelve* (2004), and *Ocean's Thirteen* (2007) in which a suave George Clooney and roguish Brad Pitt lead a band of thieves who loot hundreds of millions of dollars from casinos, galleries, and so on.

How can such ambivalence toward thievery be explained? For one thing, if self-report surveys are accurate, national tolerance toward economic criminals may be prompted by the fact that almost every U.S. citizen has at some time been involved in economic crime. Even those among us who would never consider ourselves lawbreakers may have at one time engaged in petty theft, cheated on our income tax, stolen a textbook from a college bookstore, or pilfered from our place of employment. Consequently, it may be difficult for society to condemn economic criminals without feeling hypocritical.

People may also be somewhat more tolerant of economic crimes because they never seem to seriously hurt anyone—banks are insured, large businesses pass along losses to consumers, stolen cars can be easily replaced and, in most cases, are insured. The true pain of economic crime often goes unappreciated. Convicted offenders, especially businesspeople who commit white-collar crimes involving millions of dollars, often are punished rather lightly.

This chapter is the first of two that reviews the nature and extent of economic crime in the United States. It is divided into two principal sections. The first deals with the concept of professional crime and focuses on different types of professional criminals, including the fence, a buyer and seller of stolen merchandise. The chapter then turns to a discussion of common theft-related offenses or street crime. Included within these general offense categories are such common crimes as auto theft, shoplifting, and credit card fraud. Next, the chapter discusses a more serious form of theft, burglary, which involves forcible entry into a person's home or place of work for the purpose of theft. Finally, the crime of arson is discussed briefly. In Chapter 13 attention will be given to white-collar crimes and economic crimes that involve organizations devoted to criminal enterprise.

A BRIEF HISTORY OF THEFT

As a group, economic crime can be defined as acts in violation of the criminal law designed to bring financial reward to an offender. In U.S. society, the range and scope of criminal activity motivated by financial gain is tremendous: self-report studies show that property crime is widespread among the young in every social class. National surveys of criminal behavior indicate that millions of personal and household thefts occur annually, including auto thefts, shoplifting incidents, embezzlements, burglaries, and larcenies.

Theft, however, is not a phenomenon unique to modern times; the theft of personal property has been known throughout recorded history. The Crusades of the eleventh century inspired peasants and downtrodden noblemen to leave the shelter of their estates to prey on passing pilgrims.[2] Crusaders felt it within their rights to appropriate the possessions of any infidels—Greeks, Jews, or Muslims—they happened to encounter during their travels.

By the thirteenth century, returning pilgrims, not content to live as serfs on feudal estates, gathered in the forests of England and the Continent to poach on game that was the rightful property of their lord or king and, when possible, to steal from passing strangers. By the fourteenth century, many such highwaymen and poachers were full-time livestock thieves, stealing great numbers of cattle and sheep.[3] The fifteenth and sixteenth centuries brought hostilities between England and France in what has come to be known as the Hundred Years' War. Foreign mercenary troops fighting for both sides roamed the countryside; loot and pillage were viewed as a rightful part of their pay. As cities developed and a permanent class of propertyless urban poor was established,[4] theft became more professional. By the eighteenth century, three separate groups of property criminals were active: skilled thieves, smugglers, and poachers.

▌ **Skilled thieves** typically worked in the larger cities, such as London and Paris. This group included pickpockets, forgers, and counterfeiters, who operated freely. They congregated in **flash houses**—public meeting places, often taverns, that served as headquarters for gangs. Here, deals were made, crimes were plotted, and the sale of stolen goods was negotiated.[5]

▌ **Smugglers** were the second group of thieves. They moved freely in sparsely populated areas and transported goods, such as spirits, gems, gold, and spices, without bothering to pay tax or duty.

▌ **Poachers**, the third type of thief, typically lived in the country and supplemented their diet and income with game that belonged to a landlord.

Professional thieves in the larger cities had banded together into gangs to protect themselves, increase the scope of their activities, and help dispose of stolen goods. Jack Wild, perhaps London's most famous thief, perfected the process of buying and selling stolen goods and gave himself the title of Thief-Taker General of Great Britain and Ireland. Before he was hanged, Wild controlled numerous gangs and dealt harshly with any thief who violated his strict code of conduct.[6] During this period, individual theft-related crimes began to be defined by the common law. The most important of these categories are still used today.

Train robbery flourished toward the end of the nineteenth century because professional robbers considered trains easy pickings. Law enforcement was decentralized, and robbers could escape over the border to a neighboring state to avoid detection. Security arrangements were minimal, and robbers could stop, board, and loot trains with little fear of capture. In this nineteenth-century French lithograph designed to depict the danger of the Wild West, masked and armed train robbers frighten passengers on the Rocky Mountain Line.

Theft in the Nineteenth Century: Train Robbery and Safecracking

Train Robbery In the nineteenth century, two new forms of theft appeared. Train robbery hit the nation hard when, in 1866, $700,000 (the equivalent of more than $9 million in today's currency) was taken from an Adams Express car on the New York, New Haven, and Hartford Railroad; it was the first train robbery on record. Also in 1866, the Reno brothers stole $13,000 in their first train holdup. The four brothers and their gang went on to rob a number of banks and trains in southern Indiana and Illinois before being tracked down by the Pinkerton Detective Agency in 1868 (three of the four brothers were lynched by a gang of vigilantes who attacked the jail where they were being held before trial).[7]

Train robbery flourished toward the end of the nineteenth century because professional robbers considered trains easy pickings.[8] Law enforcement was decentralized, and robbers could escape over the border to a neighboring state to avoid detection. Security arrangements were minimal, and robbers could stop, board, and loot trains with little fear of capture. As the threat to trains increased, improvements were initiated in an effort to deter would-be robbers:

- Plainclothes officers were placed on trains and rode unobtrusively among the passengers.
- Baggage cars were equipped with ramps and stalls containing fleet horses that could be used to immediately pursue bandits.
- Cars were made with finer precision and strength to make them impregnable.
- Forensic science made it easier to identify robbers, and improved communication made it easier to capture them.

Federal involvement in train protection extended the ability of law enforcement beyond the county or state in which the robbery occurred. As a result of these innovations, the number of train robberies decreased from twenty-nine in 1900 to seven in 1905; by 1920, train robbers had all but disappeared.[9]

Safecracking Secured boxes and safes have existed for centuries, but it wasn't until early in the twentieth century that use of cast iron became widespread and was used to create solid metal boxes. Safecracking also underwent a dramatic change due to technological changes in the design of safes. In the early 1900s, safes were made of manganese steel because it was resistant to drilling and was fireproof. With the invention and distribution of acetylene torches in the latter part of the nineteenth century, safes constructed of manganese became vulnerable and encouraged safecrackers to commit bold crimes. Safe manufacturers fought back by constructing safes with alternating sheets of copper and steel. The copper diffused heat and made the safe resistant to being torched. In response, safecrackers shifted their approach to attacking safes' locks and locking mechanisms. They developed mechanical devices that either dismantled or destroyed locks. Some burglars developed methods of peeling the laminated layers of the safe apart.

After World War II, safecrackers began using carbide and then diamond drill bits, which tore through metal. Safe manufacturers responded by lining safes with new metals designed to chip or break drill bits. They also developed sophisticated security systems featuring light beams, which would trip an alarm if the beam was interrupted by an intruder. When thieves learned how to neutralize these alarms, they were supplanted by motion detectors and ultrasonic systems, which fill space with sound waves and set off alarms when they are disturbed. Though these systems can be defeated, it requires expensive electronic gear, which most criminals can neither afford nor operate. As a result, the number of safecrackers has declined, and the crime of safe-cracking is relatively rare.[10]

WWW To read more about **Jack Wild** and his times, go to the website of the Old Bailey Court in England via academic.cengage.com/criminaljustice/siegel.

CONTEMPORARY THEFT

Theft is still a popular criminal pastime and millions of property and theft-related crimes occur each year. Most are committed by occasional criminals who do not define themselves by a criminal role or view themselves as committed career criminals; other theft-offenders are in fact skilled professional criminals. The following sections review these two orientations toward property crime.

Occasional Thieves

Occasional offenders are not professional criminals, nor do they make crime their occupation. Many are school-age youths who are unlikely to enter into a criminal career and whose behavior has been described as drifting between conventional and criminal. Added to the pool of amateur thieves are adults who may occasionally violate the criminal law—shoplifters, pilferers, petty thieves—but whose main source of income comes from conventional means and whose self-identity is not criminal. Added together, their behaviors form the bulk of theft crimes.

Occasional thieves do not organize their daily activities around crime nor are they committed to crime as a way of life. Their decision to steal is spontaneous and based on situational inducements.[11] These are short-term influences on a person's behavior that increase risk taking. They include psychological factors, such as an immediate and unsolvable financial problem, and social factors, such as peer pressure to commit a spontaneous criminal act—taking a car for a drunken joyride or breaking into a store or home.

While members of every layer of the economy may at some time experience a situational inducement, the opportunity to solve economic crisis through criminal activity is structured by class: While the poor are forced to engage in low-profit, high-risk crimes, members of the upper class have the opportunity to engage in the more lucrative business-related crimes of price fixing, bribery, and embezzlement.

Occasional thieves have little group support for their acts. Unlike professionals, they do not receive informal peer group support for their crimes. In fact, they will deny any connection to a criminal lifestyle and instead view their transgressions as being "out of character." They may see their crimes as being motivated by necessity. When caught they say they were only "borrowing" the car the police caught them with; they were going to pay for the merchandise they stole from the store, they just "forgot" to go through the checkout line. Because of their lack of commitment to a criminal lifestyle, occasional offenders may be the most likely to respond to the general deterrent effect of the law.

Professional Thieves

In contrast to occasional thieves, professional criminals make a significant portion of their income from crime. Professionals do not delude themselves with the belief that their acts are impulsive, one-time efforts, nor do they employ elaborate rationalizations to excuse the harmfulness of their action ("shoplifting doesn't really hurt anyone"). Consequently, professionals pursue their craft with vigor, attempting to learn from older, experienced criminals the techniques that will earn them the most money with the least risk. Though their numbers are relatively few, professionals engage in crimes that produce the greater losses to society and perhaps cause the more significant social harm.

Professional theft traditionally refers to nonviolent forms of criminal behavior that are undertaken with a high degree of skill for monetary gain and that exploit interests tending to maximize financial opportunities and minimize the possibilities of apprehension. The most typical forms include pocket-picking, burglary, shoplifting, forgery and counterfeiting, extortion, sneak theft, and confidence swindling.[12]

Relatively little is known about the career patterns of professional thieves and criminals. From the literature on crime and delinquency, three patterns emerge:

▪ Youth come under the influence of older, experienced criminals who teach them the trade.

▪ Juvenile gang members continue their illegal activities at a time when most of their peers have "dropped out" to marry, raise families, and take conventional jobs.

▪ Youth sent to prison for minor offenses learn the techniques of crime from more experienced thieves.

In a classic work, *Box Man: A Professional Thief's Journal*, Harry King, a professional thief, relates this story about his entry into crime after being placed in a shelter-care home by his recently divorced mother:

> It was while I was at this parental school that I learned that some of the kids had been committed there by the court for stealing bikes. They taught me how to steal and where to steal them and where to sell them. Incidentally, some of the "nicer people" were the ones who bought bikes from the kids. They would dismantle the bike and use the parts: the wheels, chains, handlebars, and so forth.[13]

Here we can see how would-be criminals may be encouraged in their illegal activities by so-called honest people who are willing to buy stolen merchandise and gain from criminal enterprise.

There is some debate in the criminological literature over who may be defined as a professional criminal. In his classic works, Edwin Sutherland used the term to refer only to thieves

EXHIBIT 12.1

Sutherland's Typology of Professional Thieves

- Pickpocket (cannon)
- Thief in rackets related to confidence games
- Forger
- Extortionist from those engaging in illegal acts (shakedown artist)
- Confidence game artist (con artist)
- Thief who steals from hotel rooms (hotel prowl)
- Jewel thief who substitutes fake gems for real ones (pennyweighter)
- Shoplifter (booster)
- Sneak thief from stores, banks, and offices (heel)

Source: Chic Conwell, *The Professional Thief*, ed. Edwin Sutherland (Chicago: University of Chicago Press, 1937).

who do not use force or physical violence in their crimes and who live solely by their wits and skill.[14] It is more common today for criminologists to use the term to refer to any criminal who identifies with a criminal subculture, who makes the bulk of his or her living from crime, and who possesses a degree of skill in his or her chosen trade.[15] Thus, one can become a professional safecracker, burglar, car thief, or fence. Some criminologists would not consider drug addicts who steal to support their habit as professionals; they lack skill and therefore are amateur opportunists rather than professional technicians. However, some professional criminals take drugs without losing their lofty status in the criminal hierarchy.

Sutherland's Professional Criminal

What we know about the lives of professional criminals has come to us through their journals, diaries, autobiographies, and the first-person accounts they have given to criminologists. The best-known account of professional theft is the life of Chic Conwell, in Edwin Sutherland's classic book *The Professional Thief*.[16] Conwell and Sutherland's concept of professional theft has two critical dimensions.

First, professional thieves engage in limited types of crime, which are described in Exhibit 12.1.[17] Professionals depend solely on their wit and skill. Thieves who use force or commit crimes that require little expertise are not considered worthy of the title "professional." Their areas of activity include "heavy rackets," such as bank robbery, car theft, burglary, and safecracking. You can see that Conwell and Sutherland's criteria for professionalism are weighted heavily toward con games and trickery and give little attention to common street crimes.

The second requirement of professional theft is the exclusive use of wits, *front* (a believable demeanor), and talking ability. Manual dexterity and physical force are of little importance. Professional thieves must acquire status in their profession.

Status is based on their technical skill, financial standing, connections, power, dress, manners, and wide knowledge base. In their world, "thief" is a title worn with pride. Conwell and Sutherland also argue that professional thieves share feelings, sentiments, and behaviors. Of these, none is more important than the code of honor of the underworld; even under the threat of the most severe punishment, a professional thief must never inform (squeal) on his or her fellows. Sutherland and Conwell view professional theft as an occupation with much the same internal organization as that characterizing such legitimate professions as advertising, teaching, or police work. They conclude:

> *A person can be a professional thief only if he is recognized and received as such by other professional thieves. Professional theft is a group way of life. One can get into the group and remain in it only by the consent of those previously in the group. Recognition as a professional thief by other professional thieves is the absolutely necessary, universal and definitive characteristic of the professional thief.*[18]

The Professional Fence

Some experts have argued that Sutherland's view of the professional thief may be outdated because modern thieves often work alone, are not part of a criminal subculture, and were not tutored early in their careers by other criminals.[19] However, some important research efforts show that the principles set down by Sutherland still have value for understanding the behavior of one contemporary criminal type—the **professional fence**—who earns his or her living solely by buying and reselling stolen merchandise. The fence's critical role in criminal transactions has been recognized since the eighteenth century.[20] They act as middlemen who purchase stolen merchandise—ranging from diamonds to auto hubcaps—and resell them to merchants who market them to legitimate customers.[21]

Much of what we know about fences comes from relatively few in-depth studies of the lives and activities of these specialized professional criminals. Carl Klockars examined the life and times of one successful fence who used the alias Vincent Swaggi. Through 400 hours of listening to and observing Swaggi, Klockars found that this highly professional criminal had developed techniques that made him almost immune to prosecution. During the course of a long and profitable career in crime, Swaggi spent only four months in prison. He stayed in business, in part, because of his sophisticated knowledge of the law of stolen property. To convict someone of receiving stolen goods, the prosecution must prove that the accused was in possession of the goods and knew that they had been stolen. Swaggi had the skills to make sure that these elements could never be proved. Also helping Swaggi stay out of the law's grasp were the close working associations he maintained with society's upper classes, including influential members of the justice system. Swaggi helped them purchase stolen items at below-cost, bargain prices. He also helped authorities recover stolen goods and therefore remained in their good graces. Klockars's work strongly suggests that fences customarily cheat their thief-clients and at the same time cooperate with the law.

Sam Goodman, a fence interviewed by sociologist Darrell Steffensmeier, lived in a world similar to Vincent Swaggi's. He

CONFESSIONS OF A DYING THIEF

In their book *Confessions of a Dying Thief*, Darrell Steffensmeier and Jeffery Ulmer provide a close-up view into the dynamics of career criminal Sam Goodman, a veteran thief and fence and quasi-legitimate businessman. Sam had a criminal career that spanned 50 years, beginning in his mid-teens and ending with his death when he was in his sixties. Steffensmeier and Ulmer find that unlike amateur criminals who age out of crime, professional criminals such as Sam, as well as skilled thieves, dealers in stolen goods, bookmakers, con artists, sex merchants, quasi-legitimate businessmen, local racketeers, and Mafiosi frequently persist in their criminality until they are too old or feeble to do otherwise.

Their interviews with Sam show that criminal opportunity is not merely passive: professional criminals actively seek out and create criminal opportunities that are attractive. They support their careers by gaining different types of criminal knowledge:

- *Civil knowledge.* Widely accessible general knowledge that can be put to criminal use.
- *Preparatory knowledge.* Prior familiarity with criminal orientations, language, attitudes, and skills often gained by "hanging around" with criminal associates and observing their lifestyles.
- *Technical knowledge.* More esoteric knowledge or skills that can only be obtained by access to more specialized settings and experienced criminal practitioners.

Sam had a strong commitment to crime throughout the course of his life. The height of his personal commitment to crime was during the middle phase of his career when he was a "big, wide-open" fence. Nonetheless, his favorable attitudes toward crime and other criminals endured into the later "moonlighting" phase of his career when he was less involved in crime. At that point, he also developed more positive attitudes toward legitimate people and associations (such as his employees and legitimate antique dealers). Furthermore, the moonlighting phase of his career saw some changes in Sam's self-definition, as reflected in this assessment in the final weeks of his life (p. 375):

also purchased stolen goods from a wide variety of thieves and suppliers, including burglars, drug addicts, shoplifters, dockworkers, and truck drivers. According to Goodman, to be successful, a fence must meet the following conditions:

- *Upfront cash.* All deals are cash transactions, so an adequate supply of ready cash must always be on hand.
- *Knowledge of dealing—learning the ropes.* The fence must be schooled in the knowledge of the trade, including developing a "larceny sense"; learning to "buy right" at acceptable prices; being able to "cover one's back" and not get caught; finding out how to make the right contacts; and knowing how to "wheel and deal" and how to create opportunities for profit.
- *Connections with suppliers of stolen goods.* The successful fence must be able to engage in long-term relationships with suppliers of high-value stolen goods who are relatively free of police interference. The warehouse worker who pilfers is a better supplier than the narcotics addict, who is more likely to be apprehended and talk to the police.
- *Connections with buyers.* The successful fence must have continuing access to buyers of stolen merchandise who are inaccessible to the common thief. For example, they must make contacts with local pawnshops and other distributors of secondhand goods and be able to move their material without drawing attention from the authorities.[22]
- *Complicity with law enforcers.* The fence must work out a relationship with law enforcement officials who invariably find out about the fence's operations. Steffensmeier found that to stay in business the fence must either bribe officials with good deals on merchandise and cash payments or act as an informer who helps police recover particularly important merchandise and arrest thieves.

For more on Sam Goodman's life, see The Criminological Enterprise feature "Confessions of a Dying Thief."

Fences handle a tremendous variety of products—televisions, cigarettes, stereo equipment, watches, autos, and cameras.[23] In dealing their merchandise, they operate through many legitimate fronts, including art dealers, antique stores, furniture and appliance retailers, remodeling companies, salvage companies, trucking companies, and jewelry stores. When deciding what to pay the thief for goods, the fence uses a complex pricing policy: professional thieves who steal high-priced items are usually given the highest amounts—about 30 to 50 percent of the wholesale price. Furs valued at $5,000 may be bought for $1,500. However, the amateur thief or drug addict who is not in a good bargaining position may receive only 10 cents on the dollar.

Fencing seems to contain many of the elements of professional theft as described by Sutherland: fences live by their wits, never engage in violence, depend on their skill in negotiating, maintain community standing based on connections and power, and share the sentiments and behaviors of their fellows. The only divergence between Sutherland's thief and the fence is the code of honor; it seems likely that the fence is much more willing to cooperate with authorities than most other professional criminals.

I never cared how the cops saw me but I wanted the public to see me in a different light. Not as a guy who did time, not as a burglar, not even as a fence, but as a businessman. As a good Joe. In that way I knew what I done was wrong. . . . If they saw me as a crook, that I could handle. But not a [expletive] bum. I wanted the people to respect me as me. As a businessman taking care of business in my shop.

Deviants, even persistent criminals, are seldom deviant in all or even most aspects of their lives. Sam comfortably rubbed shoulders with thieves, gamblers, and quasi-legitimate businessmen but also courted respectability and pledged allegiance to some major normative standards. Sam was unapologetic about his criminal career. While he realized that his behavior may have violated the law, he took pride in the way he conducted himself and did business, as these deathbed comments illustrate (p. 373):

I do not feel sad about my life. I did what I thought I had to do at the time. But I would not wish my life on somebody else. I made that very goddamn plain to your students—a life in crime can be a bitch. . . . I done wrong, pulled some very rank shit. But helped a whole lot of people, too. If somebody needed something, came into my shop, I more or less gave it away. Anyone that worked for me, I dealt with fairly. Got paid a good dollar and helped them out in little ways.

The life of Sam Goodman shows that while most criminals age out of crime, some do not and remain active throughout their life span.

CRITICAL THINKING

1. Which of the criminological theories best explains Sam Goodman's life and career? For example, how would Sampson and Laub explain his involvement in fencing? Or is his behavior a matter of rational choice?

2. Speculate on the Internet's impact on professional fencing. How do you suppose stolen merchandise can be sold online?

Source: Darrell Steffensmeier and Jeffery Ulmer, *Confessions of a Dying Thief: Understanding Criminal Careers and Illegal Enterprise* (Piscataway, NJ: Transaction-Aldine, 2005).

The Occasional Fence

Professional fences have attracted the attention of criminologists, but like other forms of theft, fencing is not dominated solely by professional criminals. A significant portion of all fencing is performed by amateur or occasional criminals. Novice burglars, such as juveniles and drug addicts, often find it so difficult to establish relationships with professional fences that they turn instead to nonprofessionals to unload the stolen goods.[24]

One type of occasional fence is the part-timer who, unlike professional fences, has other sources of income. Part-timers are often "legitimate" businesspeople who integrate the stolen merchandise into their regular stock. A video store manager who buys stolen DVD players and DVDs and rents them along with his legitimate merchandise is a part-time fence. An added benefit of the illegitimate part of his work is the profit he makes on these stolen items, which is not reported for tax purposes.

Some merchants become actively involved in theft either by specifying the merchandise they want the burglars to steal or by "fingering" victims. Some businesspeople sell merchandise and then describe the customers' homes and vacation plans to known burglars so that they can steal it back!

Associational fences are amateur fences who barter stolen goods for services. These amateurs typically have legitimate professional dealings with known criminals such as bail bond agents, police officers, and attorneys. A lawyer may demand an expensive watch from a client in exchange for legal services. Bartering for stolen merchandise avoids taxes and becomes a transaction in the underground economy.

Neighborhood hustlers buy and sell stolen property as one of the many ways they make a living. They keep some of the booty for themselves and sell the rest in the neighborhood. These dealmakers are familiar figures to neighborhood burglars looking to get some quick cash by selling them stolen merchandise.

Amateur receivers can be complete strangers approached in a public place by someone offering a great deal on valuable commodities. It is unlikely that anyone buying a $2,000 stereo for $200 cash would not suspect that it may have been stolen. Some amateur receivers make a habit of buying suspect merchandise at reasonable prices from a "trusted friend," establishing an ongoing relationship. This practice encourages crime because the criminals know that there will always be someone to buy their merchandise. In addition to the professional fence, the nonprofessional fence may account for a great deal of criminal receiving. Both professional and amateur thieves have a niche in the crime universe.

Criminologists and legal scholars recognize that common theft offenses fall into several categories linked together because they involve the intentional misappropriation of property for personal gain. In fencing, goods are bought from another who is in illegal possession of those goods. In the case of embezzlement, burglary, and larceny, the property is taken through stealth. In other kinds of theft, such as bad checks, fraud, and false pretenses, goods are obtained through deception. Some of the major categories of common theft offenses are discussed in the next sections in some detail.

LARCENY/THEFT

Larceny/theft was one of the earliest common-law crimes created by English judges to define acts in which one person took for his or her own use the property of another.[25] According to common law, larceny was defined as "the trespassory taking and carrying away of the personal property of another with intent to steal."[26] Most state jurisdictions have incorporated the common-law crime of larceny in their legal codes. Today, definitions of larceny often include such familiar acts as shoplifting, passing bad checks, and other theft offenses that do not involve using force or threats on the victim (robbery) or forcibly breaking into a person's home or place of work (burglary).

When it was originally construed, larceny involved taking property that was in the possession of the rightful owners. For example, it would have been considered larceny for someone to go secretly into a farmer's field and steal a cow. Thus, the original common-law definition required a "trespass in the taking"; this meant that for an act to be considered larceny, goods must have been taken from the physical possession of the rightful owner. In creating this definition of larceny, English judges were more concerned with people disturbing the peace than they were with thefts. If someone tried to steal property from another's possession, they reasoned that the act could eventually lead to a physical confrontation and possibly the death of one party or the other, thereby disturbing the peace! Consequently, the original definition of larceny did not include crimes in which the thief had come into the possession of the stolen property by trickery or deceit. It was therefore not considered larceny if someone entrusted with another person's property decided to keep it for themselves.

The growth of manufacturing and the development of the free enterprise system required greater protection for private property. The pursuit of commercial enterprise often required that one person's legal property be entrusted to a second party; therefore larceny evolved to include the theft of goods that had come into the thief's possession through legitimate means.

To get around the element of "trespass in the taking," English judges created the concept of constructive possession. This legal fiction applied to situations in which persons voluntarily and temporarily gave up custody of their property but still believed the property was legally theirs. If a person gave a jeweler her watch for repair, she would still believe she owned the watch even though she had handed it over to the jeweler. Similarly, when a person misplaces his wallet and someone else finds it and keeps it—although identification of the owner can be plainly seen—the concept of constructive possession makes the person who has kept the wallet guilty of larceny.

Larceny Today

Most U.S. state criminal codes separate larceny into **petit** (or **petty**) **larceny** and **grand larceny**. The former involves small amounts of money or property and is punished as a misdemeanor. Grand larceny, involving merchandise of greater value, is a felony punished by a sentence in the state prison. Each state sets its own boundary between grand larceny and petty larceny, but $50 to $100 is not unusual. For example, in Virginia, if the value of the item stolen is $200 or more, the offense is grand larceny; if the value of the item stolen is less than $200, the offense is petit larceny. Grand larceny is punishable by 1–20 years in prison or up to 12 months in jail and/or a fine up to $2,500. Petit larceny is a Class 1 misdemeanor punishable by up to 12 months in jail and/or a fine of up to $2,500.[27]

The distinction between petit and grand larceny can be especially significant in states, such as California, that employ "three strikes" laws mandating that someone convicted of a third felony be given a life sentence. The difference may not be lost on potential criminals: research by John Worrall shows that larceny rates in California have been significantly lowered since passage of the three strikes law.[28]

Larceny/theft is probably the most common criminal offense. According to the FBI about 7 million larcenies are reported to the police annually; this number has declined almost 15 percent during the past decade and the most recent data (2007) indicate that the downward trend seems to be continuing. The average value for property stolen during the commission of a larceny/theft was $764 per offense.[29]

Types of Larceny There are many different varieties of larceny. Figure 12.1 shows the breakdown of larcenies reported to police by type.

Figure 12.1 Types of Larceny Offenses

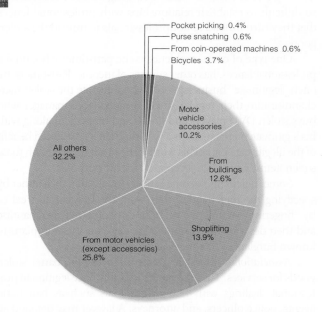

- Pocket picking 0.4%
- Purse snatching 0.6%
- From coin-operated machines 0.6%
- Bicycles 3.7%
- Motor vehicle accessories 10.2%
- All others 32.2%
- From buildings 12.6%
- Shoplifting 13.9%
- From motor vehicles (except accessories) 25.8%

Source: FBI, *Crime in the United States, 2005,* www.fbi.gov/ucr/05cius/offenses/property_crime/larceny-theft.html (accessed June 14, 2007).

INVASION OF THE BODY SNATCHERS

In November 2004, New York police investigated the Daniel George and Son Funeral Home in Brooklyn to check out what they considered to be a routine business dispute. But when they began looking around, they found a sealed room outfitted like an operating room, with a surgical table and overhead lights. They also found FedEx receipts made out to companies that purchase human tissue from cadavers for use in surgical procedures. The department's Major Case Squad was called in and they discovered that a former Manhattan dentist named Michael Mastromarino (pictured) and three other men were running a multimillion-dollar body-snatching business that had looted bones and tissue from more than a thousand corpses. The men then sold the body parts to legitimate companies that supplied hospitals around the United States. Hundreds of people in states as far away as Florida, Nebraska, and Texas received tissue and bone carved from looted corpses, including the cadaver of Alistair Cooke, the late host of PBS's *Masterpiece Theatre*. The tissue was used in such procedures as joint and heart-valve replacements, back surgery, dental implants, and skin grafts. Many of the recipients rushed to doctors to be tested for tainted tissue, and some filed civil lawsuits. (One New Jersey lawyer alone signed up some 200 clients.) Mastromarino was charged with opening graves, body stealing, forgery, grand larceny, and racketeering.

Mastromarino had surrendered his dental license in 2000 because he was addicted to the painkiller Demerol. He started a career as a body harvester, opening Biomedical Tissue Services, an FDA-registered company that appeared completely legitimate. However, he got many of the corpses from Joseph Nicelli, who had been hired by funeral directors in New York, New Jersey, and Philadelphia to embalm bodies in his Brooklyn facility. A single harvested body yielded $7,000 in parts. After Nicelli sold the funeral home, he allegedly continued to help Mastromarino sneak into the secret operating room at night to dissect corpses. To hide their crimes, Mastromarino replaced looted bones with plumbing pipes, and stuffed their surgical gloves and gowns into the bodies before stitching them back together. After robbing the bodies, the men allegedly forged death certificates to hide that the tissue had often been stolen from bodies that would have been rejected as donors, being too old or sick. Some of the recipients were subsequently tested for diseases, including hepatitis. While the Food and Drug Administration claims that the risk of serious infection is fairly remote, an agency advisory also mentions that the "actual infectious risk is unknown." A 41-year-old woman who underwent back surgery on Long Island and two patients in New Jersey say they contracted syphilis from stolen bone tissue.

The body snatchers case illustrates the wide variety of schemes that can involve taking the possessions of another. In this case, the possessions were bodily organs and the victims were dead!

Sources: Michael Powell and David Segal, "In New York, a Grisly Traffic in Body Parts, Illegal Sales Worry Dead's Kin, Tissue Recipients," *Washington Post*, 18 January 2006, p. A03; William Sherman, "Clients Flee Biz Eyed in Ghoul Probe," *New York Daily News*, 13 October 2005.

Most larcenies involve small items of little value. Many of these go unreported, however, especially if the victims were business owners who do not want to take the time to get involved with police. They simply write off the losses as part of doing business. Hotel owners estimate that guests filch $100 million a year in towels, bathrobes, ashtrays, bedspreads, shower heads, flatware, and even television sets and wall paintings.[30]

Other larcenies involve complex criminal conspiracies, and no one, not even the U.S. government, is immune. Thieves steal millions of dollars worth of government equipment and supplies each year. In one incident, the Department of Energy reported more than $20 million in property missing from its site in Rocky Flats, Colorado, including semi-trailers, forklifts, cameras, desks, radios, and more than 1,800 pieces of computer equipment.[31] The Profiles in Crime feature focuses on the so-called "body snatchers case," a very unusual, albeit horrific, case of larceny.

Shoplifting

Shoplifting is a common form of theft involving taking goods from retail stores. Usually shoplifters try to snatch items—jewelry, clothes, records, or appliances—when store personnel are otherwise occupied, hiding the goods on their person. The five-finger discount is an extremely common form of crime. The average shoplifting case for all types of retail is approximately $50. As Table 12.1 shows, between 200 and 300 million shoplifting incidents occur each year and involve somewhere between $11 billion and $15 billion in loss.[32]

Table 12.1 Estimates of Shoplifting Incidents and Losses

Time Frame	Dollars	Incidents
Annually	$11–$15 billion	225–300 million
Daily (365 days)	$31–$41 million	615,000–820,000
Hours (24)	$1.3–$1.7 million	25,000–34,000
Per minute (60)	$21,000–$28,500	425–570

Source: Hayes International, Retail Theft, www.hayesinternational.com/thft_srvys.html (accessed August 26, 2007).

Shoplifting is certainly not unique to the United States. In England, about 5 percent of the population is convicted of shoplifting by age 40. Surveys of retailers in the United Kingdom suggest that there are more than 4 million known shoplifting incidents, 1.3 million apprehended shoplifters, and 800,000 shoplifters reported to the police each year. One reason for the popularity of shoplifting may be lax treatment. Although about one in seven apprehended offenders is eventually convicted in court, fewer than one in twenty shoplifting attempts result in apprehension.[33]

Retail security measures add to the already high cost of this crime, all of which is passed on to the consumer. Some studies estimate that about one in every nine shoppers steals from department stores. Moreover, the increasingly popular discount stores, such as Costco, Wal-Mart, and Target, have a minimum of sales help and depend on highly visible merchandise displays to attract purchasers, all of which makes them particularly vulnerable to shoplifters.

Profile of a Shoplifter   In the early 1960s, Mary Owen Cameron conducted a classic study of shoplifting.[34] In her pioneering effort, Cameron found that about 10 percent of all shoplifters were professionals who derived the majority of their income from shoplifting. Sometimes called boosters or heels, she found that professional shoplifters steal with the intention of reselling stolen merchandise to pawnshops or fences, usually at half the original price.[35]

Cameron found that the majority of shoplifters are amateur pilferers, called snitches in thieves' argot. Snitches are usually respectable people who do not conceive of themselves as thieves but are systematic shoplifters who steal merchandise for their own use. When caught they may try to rationalize or neutralize their behavior. When Paul Cromwell and Quint Thurman interviewed 137 apprehended shoplifters they found widespread use of techniques of neutralizations—statements such as, "I don't know what comes over me. It's like, you know, it's somebody else doing it, not me" (denial of responsibility) or "I like to get nice stuff for my kids, you know. I know it's not O.K., you know what I mean? But I want my kids to dress nice and stuff" (appeal to higher loyalties).[36]

If they are not professionals and want to deny their culpability, why do they steal? Some are impulsive sensation seekers who are driven to shoplift by their psychological need to live on the edge.[37] Others are motivated by rational choice and the desire to get something for nothing. Still another motivation for shoplifting seems to be psychological distress; some amateur shoplifters are looking for a release from anxiety and depression.[38]

Regardless of their motives, snitches are likely to reform if caught because they are not part of a criminal subculture and do not think of themselves as criminals. Cameron reasoned that they are deterred by an initial contact with the law. Getting arrested has a traumatic effect on them, and they will not risk a second offense.

Controlling Shoplifting   One major problem associated with combating shoplifting is that many customers who observe pilferage are reluctant to report it to security agents. Store employees themselves are often loathe to get involved in apprehending a shoplifter. It is also likely that a store owner's decision to prosecute shoplifters will be based on the value of the goods stolen, the nature of the goods stolen, and the manner in which the theft was realized. Shoplifters who planned their crime by using a concealed apparatus, such as a bag pinned to the inside of their clothing, are more apt to be prosecuted than those who impulsively put merchandise into their pockets.[39] The concealment indicates that the crime was premeditated and not a spur of the moment loss of control.

To encourage the arrest of shoplifters, a number of states have passed *merchant privilege laws* designed to protect retailers and their employers from litigation stemming from improper or false arrests of suspected shoplifters. These laws protect but do not immunize merchants from lawsuits. They typically require that arrests be made on reasonable grounds or probable cause, detention be of short duration, and store employees or security guards conduct themselves in a reasonable fashion.

Prevention Strategies   Retail stores are now initiating a number of strategies designed to reduce or eliminate shoplifting. Target removal strategies involve putting dummy or disabled goods on display while the real merchandise is kept under lock and key. Audio equipment with missing parts is displayed, and only after items are purchased are the necessary components installed. Some stores sell from a catalogue while keeping merchandise in stockrooms.

Target hardening strategies involve locking goods in place or having them monitored by electronic systems. Clothing stores may use racks designed to prevent large quantities of garments from being slipped off easily. Store owners may rely on electronic article surveillance (EAS) systems, featuring tags with small electronic sensors that trip sound and light alarms if not removed by employees before the item leaves the store. Security systems now feature source tagging, a process by which manufacturers embed the tag in the packaging or in the product itself. Thieves are hard-pressed to remove or defeat such tags, and retailers save on the time and labor needed to attach the tags at their stores.[40] Situational measures place the most valuable goods in the least vulnerable places, use warning signs to deter potential thieves, and use closed-circuit cameras.

Another approach to shoplifting prevention is to create specialized programs that use methods such as doing community service, paying monetary restitution, writing essays, watching antishoplifting videos, writing apology letters, and being placed in individual and/or family counseling. Evaluations indicate that such programs can be successful in reducing recidivism of young shoplifters.[41]

Bad Checks

Another form of larceny is cashing bad bank checks, knowingly and intentionally drawn on a nonexistent or underfunded bank account, to obtain money or property. In general, for a person to be guilty of passing a bad check, the bank the check is drawn on must refuse payment, and the check casher must fail to make the check good within 10 days after finding out the check was not honored.

Edwin Lemert conducted the best-known study of check forgers more than 40 years ago.[42] Lemert found that the majority of check forgers—he calls them naive check forgers—are amateurs who do not believe their actions will hurt anyone. Most naive check forgers come from middle-class backgrounds and have little identification with a criminal subculture. They cash bad checks because of a financial crisis that demands an immediate resolution—perhaps they have lost money at the horse track and have some pressing bills to pay. Lemert refers to this condition as closure. Naive check forgers are often socially isolated people who have been unsuccessful in their personal relationships. They are risk prone when faced with a situation that is unusually stressful for them. The willingness of stores and other commercial establishments to cash checks with a minimum of fuss to promote business encourages the check forger to risk committing a criminal act. Some of the different techniques used in check fraud schemes, which may cost retail establishments upwards of $1 billion annually, are set out in Exhibit 12.2.

Not all check forgers are amateurs. Lemert found that a few professionals—whom he calls systematic forgers—make a substantial living by passing bad checks. However, professionals constitute a relatively small segment of the total population of check forgers. It is difficult to estimate the number of such forgeries committed each year or the amounts involved. Stores and banks may choose not to press charges because the effort to collect the money due them is often not worth their while. It is also difficult to separate the true check forger from the neglectful shopper.

Credit Card Theft

The use of stolen credit cards is a major problem in U.S. society. It has been estimated that fraud has been responsible for a billion-dollar loss in the credit card industry. Most credit card abuse is the work of amateurs who acquire stolen cards through theft or mugging and then use them for two or three days. However, professional credit card rings may be getting into the act. They collect or buy from employees the names and credit card numbers of customers in retail establishments; then they buy plain plastic cards and have the customers' numbers embossed on them. They create fictitious wholesale companies and apply for and receive authorization to accept credit cards from the customers. They then use the phony cards to charge nonexistent

---

EXHIBIT 12.2

Check Fraud Schemes and Techniques

- *Forged signatures*. Legitimate blank checks with an imitation of the payor signature.
- *Forged endorsements*. The use of a stolen check, which is then endorsed and cashed or deposited by someone other than the payee.
- *Identity assumption*. The use of information about a financial institution customer, such as name, address, financial institution account number, Social Security number, home and work telephone numbers, or employer; criminals use the information to misrepresent themselves as the financial institution customer.
- *Counterfeit checks*. Counterfeit checks are presented based on fraudulent identification or are false checks drawn on valid accounts. Due to the advancement in color copying and desktop publishing capabilities, this is the fastest-growing source of fraudulent checks today.
- *Altered checks*. After a legitimate maker creates a valid check to pay a debt, a criminal takes the good check and uses chemicals or other means to erase the amount or the name of the payee so that new information can be entered. The new information can by added by typewriter, in handwriting, or with a laser printer or check imprinter.
- *Closed account fraud*. This is based on checks being written against closed accounts. This type of fraud generally relies on the float time involved in interfinancial institution transactions.
- *Check kiting*. The process of depositing a check from one bank account into a second bank account without the sufficient funds to cover it.

Sources: Check Fraud Working Group, *Check Fraud: A Guide to Avoiding Losses* (Washington, DC: author), www.occ.treas.gov/chckfrd/chckfrd.pdf (accessed June 14, 2007); National Check Fraud Center, Charleston, SC, www.ckfraud.org (accessed June 14, 2007).

---

purchases on the accounts of the people whose names and card numbers they had collected.

To combat losses from credit card theft, Congress passed a law in 1971 limiting a person's liability to $50 per stolen card. Some states, such as California, have passed specific statutes making it a misdemeanor to obtain property or services by means of cards that have been stolen, forged, canceled, or revoked, or whose use is for any reason unauthorized.[43]

connections

Similar frauds are conducted over the Internet. These will be discussed in Chapter 15.

The problem of credit card misuse is being compounded by thieves who set up bogus Internet sites strictly to trick people into giving them their credit card numbers, which they then use for their own gain. The Profiles in Crime feature discusses one such Internet credit card scheme.[44] The problem is growing so rapidly that a number of new technologies are being prepared aimed at combating credit card number theft over the Internet. One method is to incorporate digital

CREDIT CARD CON

Philip Arcand and his wife, Roberta Galway, lived a life of luxury. They owned two homes, one in British Columbia and one in Las Vegas. They had a Mercedes, a Corvette, and a Ferrari in their driveways. They took frequent trips around the world. All this without having jobs. How did they do it? Through credit card fraud!

Arcand wrote high-pressure scripts to lure in victims, arranged for telemarketing companies to make the pitch, and set up businesses to process the illegal cash flow. The telemarketers claimed to be from a credit card company. They told victims how easy it is to steal a credit card number, especially over the Internet. They offered to sell "protection" policies that would insure that the buyers wouldn't have to pay if thieves ran up a huge tab on account. The telemarketers told the victims that if they didn't get this protection, they would have to foot the bill for any unauthorized charges made if their credit cards were stolen. After making their pitch, the victims were asked: "May we have your credit card number, please?" Later, a charge of between $199 and $389 appeared on their account, even if they didn't sign up for the service.

The scheme was bogus, illegal, and entirely unnecessary because most major credit card companies protect you from fraudulent charges. Still, thousands of Americans were victimized by this scam, the overwhelming majority elderly. In all, they were defrauded out of more than $12 million.

Arcand and Galway were ultimately caught when some of the victims reported their suspicions and complaints to authorities. Arcand was sentenced to 10 years in federal prison; his wife Roberta Galway pleaded guilty and was sentenced to six months in jail.

Source: Federal Bureau of Investigation, "Credit Card Con: Canadian Man Gets 10 Years for $12 Million Telemarketing Scam," www.fbi.gov/page2/nov03/credit112803.htm (accessed April 11, 2006).

signatures into computer operating systems, which can be accessed with a digital key that comes with each computer. Owners of new systems can present three forms of identification to a notary public and trade a notarized copy of their key for a program that will sign files. The basis of the digital signature is a digital certificate, a small block of data that contains a person's "public key." This certificate is signed, in turn, by a certificate authority. This digital certificate will act like a credit card with a hologram and a photograph and identify the user to the distant website and vice versa.[45]

Auto Theft

Motor vehicle theft is another common larceny offense. Yet because of its frequency and seriousness, it is treated as a separate category in the UCR. About 1.2 million motor vehicle thefts, or approximately 416 motor vehicles stolen for every 100,000 inhabitants, now occur each year. Like other property crimes, the number of auto thefts has declined more than 20 percent since 1996 and the downward trend seems to be continuing. Property losses due to motor vehicle theft are now close to $8 billion per year, averaging more than $6,000 per stolen vehicle.[46] These data are considered accurate because almost every state jurisdiction requires owners to insure their vehicles. Auto theft is the most highly reported of all major crimes (80 percent of all auto thefts are reported to police).

A number of attempts have been made to categorize the various forms of auto theft. Distinctions typically are made between theft for temporary personal use, for resale, and for chopping or stripping cars for parts.[47] Typically, auto theft can be divided into the following categories:

- *Joyriding.* Many car thefts are motivated by teenagers' desire to acquire the power, prestige, sexual potency, and recognition associated with an automobile. Joyriders do not steal cars for profit or gain but to experience, even briefly, the benefits associated with owning an automobile.

- *Short-term transportation.* Auto theft for short-term transportation is most similar to joyriding. It involves the theft of a car simply to go from one place to another. In more serious cases, the thief may drive to another city or state and then steal another car to continue the journey.

- *Long-term transportation.* Thieves who steal cars for long-term transportation intend to keep the cars for their personal use. Usually older than joyriders and from a lower-class background, these auto thieves may repaint and otherwise disguise cars to avoid detection.

- *Profit.* Auto theft for profit is motivated by hope for monetary gain. At one extreme are highly organized professionals who resell expensive cars after altering their identification numbers and falsifying their registration papers. At the other end of the scale are amateur auto strippers who steal batteries, tires, and wheel covers to sell them or reequip their own cars.

- *Commission of another crime.* A small portion of auto thieves steal cars to use in other crimes, such as robberies and thefts. This type of auto thief desires both mobility and anonymity.

At one time, joyriding was the predominant motive for auto theft, and most cars were taken by relatively affluent, white, middle-class teenagers looking for excitement.[48] However, because there are more pre- and post-installed security systems, it has become more difficult for amateurs to steal cars. Auto thieves are changing their theft strategies. Experienced thieves now realize it is easier to illegally obtain keys than to try to defeat security systems. Some look for keys left in cars, while others use burglaries and robberies as a method to acquire keys.[49]

While fewer cars are being taken today, fewer stolen cars are being recovered. Part of the reason is that professional car thieves work closely with chop shops, export rings, or both. They want to steal cars and unload them as fast as possible. Export of stolen vehicles has become a global problem, and the emergence of capitalism in eastern Europe has increased the demand for U.S.-made cars.[50] While few experienced thieves want to drive around in a stolen vehicle, they are more than willing to use their profit from selling a stolen car to a chop shop or exporter and then use the proceeds to buy a suitable, legitimate ride.[51]

Which Cars Are Taken Most?   Car thieves show signs of rational choice when they make their target selections. According to the Highway Loss Data Institute (HLDI) the cars with the highest rates of insurance theft claims are versions of the 2003–05 Cadillac Escalade, Mitsubishi Lancer Evolution, and Dodge Ram 1500 quad cab pickup. These three vehicles have claim rates four to five times the average for all vehicles.[52]

While these cars are the ones with the greatest risk of theft per vehicle, widely owned models that have been in production for a few years without many design changes actually stand the greatest risk of theft. These vehicles are popular because their parts are most valued in the secondary market; on the other hand, even luxury models undergo a sharp decline in their theft rate soon after a design change. Enduring models

are also in demand because older cars are more likely to be uninsured, and demand for stolen used parts is higher for these vehicles.

According to the National Insurance Crime Bureau (NICB), the following ten cars are the ones most taken:

1. 1991 Honda Accord
2. 1995 Honda Civic
3. 1989 Toyota Camry
4. 1994 Dodge Caravan
5. 1994 Nissan Sentra
6. 1997 Ford F150 Series
7. 1990 Acura Integra
8. 1986 Toyota Pickup
9. 1993 Saturn SL
10. 2004 Dodge Ram Pickup[53]

According to the NICB, thieves typically choose these vehicles because of the high profit potential when the cars are stripped of their component parts, which are then sold on the black market. These vehicles are popular overseas, and once taken, organized theft rings will illegally export them to foreign destinations. Many of the highly desired cars are never recovered because they are immediately shipped abroad where they command prices three times higher than their U.S. sticker price. The NICB also recognizes that many cars are lost to an owner give-up, which occurs when vehicles that have been reported stolen by their owners are actually driven into ponds, lakes, or quarries, set on fire in sparsely populated areas, or even driven into Mexico and abandoned, with their owners later filing false and fraudulent theft reports. Owner give-ups are often motivated by economic factors. If a person owes more on a vehicle than it is worth, having it stolen allows the owner to walk away from the debt. Similarly, fraudulent theft may seem attractive when the owner has leased the car and the usage has exceeded the terms of the lease, such as excessive mileage or dents.[54]

> **connections**
>
> Chapter 4 discusses the rational choice view of car theft. As you may recall, cars with expensive radios and parts are more often the target of rational thieves.

Stealing Car Parts   Rather than take the entire vehicle, some car thieves specialize in stripping parts at the scene. While theft of expensive audio equipment is not uncommon, another valuable target is blue-white, high-intensity discharge headlights. New ones go for $500 and up per light, sometimes $3,000 per car. Custom rims are also attractive to thieves, especially the "spinners" that keep revolving when the car is stopped. They go from $100 each up to $15,000 for a set of super-luxe models.[55]

Thieves seem to target some cars more than others. Would this 2006 Dodge Ram 1500 truck be a desirable target if you were a car thief?

© AP Images/Nam Y. Huh

About 10 percent of all theft claims involve an air bag. The driver's side bag, mounted in the steering wheel, is the easiest to remove. Insurance industry statistics show that thousands of airbags are stolen each year at a cost of millions of dollars to vehicle owners and their insurers. Airbags have quickly become a primary accessory on the black market for stolen vehicle parts. A new airbag, which retails for approximately $1,000 from a car dealer, costs between $50–200 on the black market. Because of their portability, airbags can be easily removed and installed as "new" by unscrupulous collision repair shops. These dishonest operators will then charge the vehicle owner or their insurer the full price for the replacement, thus committing insurance fraud.[56]

Carjacking You may have read about gunmen approaching a car and forcing the owner to give up the keys; in some cases, people have been killed when they reacted too slowly. This type of auto theft has become so common that it has its own name, carjacking.[57] Carjacking is legally considered a type of robbery because it involves force to steal. According to NCVS data, about 38,000 carjacking victimizations occur annually. During the past decade, that meant that there was an average of 1.7 victimizations per 10,000 persons annually; about 15 people are killed in auto-related crimes each year.[58]

Both victims and offenders in carjackings tend to be young black men. Urban residents are more likely to experience carjacking than suburban or rural residents. About half of all carjackings are typically committed by gangs or groups. These crimes are most likely to occur in the evening, in the central city, in an open area, or in a parking garage. This pattern may reflect the fact that carjacking seems to be a crime of opportunity; it is the culmination of the carjacker's personal needs and desires coinciding with the immediate opportunity for gain. This decision is also shaped by the carjacker's participation in urban street culture.[59]

Weapons, most often guns, were used in about three-quarters of all carjacking victimizations.[60] Despite the presence of weapons, victims resisted the offender in two-thirds of carjackings, and, not surprisingly, about one-third of victims of completed carjackings and about 17 percent of victims of attempted carjackings were injured. Serious injuries, such as gunshot or knife wounds, broken bones, or internal injuries, occurred in about 9 percent of carjackings. More minor injuries, such as bruises and chipped teeth, occurred in about 15 percent of cases.

Combating Auto Theft Auto theft is a significant target of situational crime prevention efforts. One approach to theft deterrence has been to increase the risks of apprehension. Hotlines offer rewards for information leading to the arrest of car thieves. A Michigan-based program, Operation HEAT (Help Eliminate Auto Theft), is credited with recovering more than 900 vehicles, worth $11 million, and resulting in the arrest of 647 people. Another approach has been to place fluorescent decals on windows that indicate that the car is never used between 1 A.M. and 5 A.M.; if police spot a car with the decal being operated during this period, they know it is stolen.[61]

The LoJack system involves installing a hidden tracking device in cars that gives off a signal, enabling the police to pinpoint its location. Research evaluating the effectiveness of this device finds that it has a significant crime reduction capability.[62] Because car thieves cannot tell that LoJack has been installed, it does not reduce the likelihood that a protected car will be stolen. However, cars installed with LoJack have a much higher recovery rate. There may also be a general deterrent effect: areas with high rates of LoJack use experience significant reductions in their auto theft rates. Ironically, LoJack owners actually accrue a smaller than anticipated reward for their foresight than the general public because they have to pay for installation and maintenance of the device. Those without it actually gain more because they benefit from a lower auto theft rate in their community without paying any additional cost.

Other prevention efforts involve making it more difficult to steal cars. Publicity campaigns have been directed at encouraging people to lock their cars. Parking lots have been equipped with theft-deterring closed-circuit TV cameras and barriers. Manufacturers have installed more sophisticated steering column locking devices and other security systems that make theft more difficult.

A study by the Highway Loss Data Institute (HLDI) found that most car theft prevention methods, especially alarms, have little effect on theft rates. The most effective methods appear to be devices that immobilize a vehicle by cutting off the electrical power needed to start the engine when a theft is detected.[63] However, car thieves with modest resources—just a few hundred dollars in off-the-shelf equipment—and some computer knowledge can crack the codes of millions of car keys and suborn these security systems.[64]

False Pretenses or Fraud

The crime of false pretenses, or fraud, involves misrepresenting a fact in a way that causes a victim to willingly give his or her property to the wrongdoer, who then keeps it.[65] In 1757, the English Parliament defined false pretenses to cover an area of law left untouched by larceny statutes. The first false pretenses law punished people who "knowingly and designedly by false pretense or pretenses, [obtained] from any person or persons, money, goods, wares or merchandise with intent to cheat or defraud any person or persons of the same."[66]

False pretenses differs from traditional larceny because the victims willingly give their possessions to the offender, and the crime does not, as does larceny, involve a "trespass in the taking." An example of false pretenses would be an unscrupulous merchant selling someone a chair by claiming it was an antique, but knowing all the while that it was a cheap copy. Another example would be a phony healer selling a victim a bottle of colored sugar water as an elixir that would cure a disease.

Fraud may also occur when people conspire to cheat a third party or institution—for example, by selling fake IDs, tickets, vouchers, tokens, or licenses, which can be used to fraudulently gain services or illegal access. One example of an innovative cheating scheme was instituted by a man named Po Chieng Ma, who conspired to sell answers to the Graduate Management Administration Test (GMAT), the Graduate Record Examinations (GRE), and the Test of English as a Foreign Language (TOEFL) to an estimated 788 customers, each of whom had paid him $2,000 to $9,000. In the scheme, people were paid to take the multiple-choice tests in Manhattan and then call California, where the same tests were to be given, with the answers. The answers were passed on to Ma, who, taking advantage of the three-hour time difference, carved the answers in code on the sides of pencils, which were then given to his customers. Ma pleaded guilty to conspiracy and obstruction of justice and received a four-year prison term for his efforts. In this case, there were many victims, including the testing service, universities, and the students who lost places in school because those who inflated their scores through the scheme were admitted instead.[67]

Confidence Games

Confidence games are run by swindlers who aspire to separate a victim (or "sucker") from his or her hard-earned money. These con games usually involve getting a mark, the target of a con man or woman, interested in some get-rich-quick scheme, which may have illegal overtones. The criminal's hope is that when victims lose their money they will either be too embarrassed or too afraid to call the police. There are hundreds of varieties of con games. The most common is called the pigeon drop.[68] Here, a package or wallet containing money is "found" by a con man or woman. A passing victim is stopped and asked for advice about what to do, since no identification can be found. Another "stranger," who is part of the con, approaches and enters the discussion. The three decide to split the money, but first, to make sure everything is legal, one of the swindlers goes off to consult a lawyer. Upon returning, he or she says that the lawyer claims the money can be split up; first, however, each party must prove he or she has the means to reimburse the original owner, should one show up. The victim then is asked to give some good-faith money for the lawyer to hold. When the victim goes to the lawyer's office to pick up a share of the loot, he or she finds the address bogus and the money gone.

In the new millennium, the pigeon drop has been appropriated by corrupt telemarketers, who contact people over the phone, typically elderly victims, to bilk them out of their savings. The FBI estimates that illicit telephone pitches cost Americans some $40 billion a year. Some common confidence games include:

- Con artists read the obituary column and then send a surviving spouse bills supposedly owed by the person deceased. Or they deliver an item—like a Bible—that they say the deceased relative ordered just before he died.

- A swindler, posing as a bank employee, stops a customer as he or she is about to enter the bank. The swindler claims to be an investigator who is trying to catch a dishonest teller. He asks the customer to withdraw cash to see if he or she got the right amount. After the cash is withdrawn, the swindler asks that it be turned over to them so he can check the serial numbers.

- Pyramid schemes involve the selling of phony franchises. The investor buys a franchise to sell golf clubs or some other commodity paying thousands of dollars. He is asked to recruit some friends to buy more franchises and promised a percentage of the sales of every new franchisee he recruits. Eventually there are hundreds of distributors, few customers, and the merchandise is typically unavailable. Those at the top make lots of money before the pyramid collapses, leaving the individual investors without their cash.

- Shady contractors offer an unusually low price for an expensive job such as driveway repair and then use old motor oil rather than asphalt to make the repairs. The first rain brings disaster. Some offer a low rate but conduct a "free" inspection that turns up several expensive repairs that are actually bogus.

- A business office receives a mailing that looks like an invoice with a self-addressed envelope that makes it look like it comes from the phone company (walking fingers on a yellow background). It appears to be a contract for an ad in the Yellow Pages. On the back, in small print, will be written, "By returning this confirmation, you're signing a contract to be an advertiser in the upcoming, and all subsequent, issues." If the invoice is returned, the business soon finds that it has agreed to a long-term contract to advertise in some private publication that is not widely distributed.

Embezzlement

On December 14, 2006, Linda Wade Dunn, of Coosada, Alabama, was sentenced to 41 months imprisonment for stealing approximately $3,000,000 from her employer, Therapeutic Programs, Inc. (TPI), which provided services to foster children in therapeutic care. From June 1999 through February 2004, Dunn misappropriated approximately $3,005,533 from TPI. How did her scheme work? Dunn, the company bookkeeper, wrote checks on the TPI account and made them payable to herself and to a corporation she controlled. She concealed the theft by altering entries in TPI's records to make it appear that the payees of the checks were legitimate. To cover up her crimes, she intercepted TPI's bank statements, which contained the cancelled checks that would have implicated her in the crime.[69]

Dunn's actions constituted embezzlement, a crime that occurs when someone who is trusted with property fraudulently converts it—that is, keeps it for his or her own use or the use of others. It can be distinguished from fraud on the basis of when the criminal intent was formed. Most U.S. courts require that a serious breach of trust must have occurred before a person can be convicted of embezzlement. The mere act of moving property without the owner's consent, or damaging it or using it, is not considered embezzlement. However, using it up, selling it, pledging it, giving it away, or holding it against the owner's will is considered to be embezzlement.[70]

Embezzlement is not a recent crime. It was mentioned in early Greek culture when, in his writings, Aristotle alluded to theft by road commissioners and other government officials.[71] It was first codified in law by the English Parliament during the sixteenth century to fill a gap in the larceny law.[72] Until then, to be guilty of theft, a person had to take goods from the physical possession of another (trespass in the taking). However, as explained earlier, this definition did not cover instances in which one person trusted another and willfully gave that person temporary custody of his or her property. Store clerks, bank tellers, brokers, and merchants gain lawful possession but not legal ownership of other people's money.

Although it is impossible to know how many embezzlement incidents occur annually, the FBI found that only 19,000 people were arrested for embezzlement in probably an extremely small percentage of all embezzlers. However, the number of people arrested for embezzlement has increased more than 40 percent during the past 25 years, indicating that (a) more employees are willing to steal from their employers, (b) more employers are willing to report instances of embezzlement, or (c) law enforcement officials are more willing to prosecute embezzlers. There has also been a rash of embezzlement-type crimes around the world, especially in third world countries where poverty is all too common and the economy is poor and supported by foreign aid and loans. Government officials and businessmen who have their hands on this money are tempted to convert it for their own use—a scenario that is sure to increase the likelihood of embezzlement.[73]

www Want to avoid **credit card theft**? The Federal Trade Commission has some important tips; access them at academic.cengage.com/criminaljustice/siegel.

BURGLARY

In common law, the crime of burglary is defined as "the breaking and entering of a dwelling house of another in the nighttime with the intent to commit a felony within."[74] Burglary is

Burglary can be combined with other crimes. Suspect Leszek Kuczera (59, center) is escorted by fire marshal Lawrence Pliska (left), NYPD detective Raymond Marino (right), and ATF special agent Bryan Digirolamo (back). Leszek was charged with fourth-degree arson, third-degree burglary, first- and second-degree reckless endangerment, second-degree crime misdemeanor, and petit larceny in regard to a break-in at a Brooklyn, New York, warehouse.

considered a much more serious crime than larceny/theft because it often involves entering another's home, a situation in which the threat of harm to occupants is great. Even though the home may be unoccupied at the time of the burglary, the potential for harm to the occupants is so significant that most state jurisdictions punish burglary as a felony.

The legal definition of burglary has undergone considerable change since its common-law origins. When first created by English judges during the late Middle Ages, laws against burglary were designed to protect people whose homes might be set upon by wandering criminals. Including the phrase "breaking and entering" in the definition protected people from unwarranted intrusions; if an invited guest stole something, it would not be considered a burglary. Similarly, the requirement that the crime be committed at nighttime was added because evening was considered the time when honest people might fall prey to criminals.[75]

In more recent times, state jurisdictions have changed the legal requirements of burglary, and most have discarded the necessity of forced entry. Many now protect all structures, not just dwelling houses. A majority of states have removed the nighttime element from burglary definitions as well. It is common for states to enact laws creating different degrees of burglary. In this instance, the more serious and heavily punished crimes involve a nighttime forced entry into the home; the least serious involve a daytime entry into a nonresidential structure by an unarmed offender. Several gradations of the offense may be found between these extremes.

The Nature and Extent of Burglary

The FBI's definition of burglary is not restricted to burglary from a person's home; it includes any unlawful entry of a structure to commit theft or felony. Burglary is further categorized into three subclasses: forcible entry, unlawful entry where no force is used, and attempted forcible entry. According to the UCR, about 2 million burglaries now occur annually, a decline of more than 14 percent from 1996. Most occur during daylight hours, in residential structures (about two-thirds), and result in a loss of more than $1,700 per burglary.

The NCVS reports that about 3.5 million residential burglaries are either attempted or completed annually. Despite this significant number, the NCVS indicates that the number of burglaries has declined significantly during the past decade. According to the NCVS, those most likely to be burglarized are relatively poor Latino and African American families (annual income under $7,500). Rural owner-occupied and single-family residences had lower burglary rates than urban, renter-occupied and multiple-family dwellings. Households in the northeast were less likely to experience burglary than were households in other regions of the country.

Planning to Burgle

Some burglars are crude thieves who will smash a window and enter a vacant home or structure with minimal preparation; others plan out a strategy. In urban areas and their immediate suburbs, experienced burglars learn to avoid areas of the city in which most residents are renters and not homeowners, reasoning that renters are less likely to be suitable targets than are more affluent homeowners.[76] However, this decision may be shaped by the time of day for which the burglary is planned: when they operate in daylight, experienced burglars minimize the risk of being spotted and apprehended by police by choosing targets in upscale neighborhoods that are set back from the street, provide better cover for their forced entry, and are less likely to be occupied. Homeowners in affluent neighborhoods have higher employment levels so daylight burglaries are a safer, and more lucrative, bet. After dark the patterns seem to change and burglars who operate at night may shift their targets to apartments and townhouses closer to home even though the risk of someone being home is greater.[77] Whether they operate alone or in groups, experienced burglars like to choose targets in neighborhoods they know so that they make their way home undetected if things go awry.[78]

Because it involves planning, risk, and skill, burglary has been a crime long associated with professional thieves who carefully learn their craft. Francis Hoheimer, an experienced professional burglar, has described how he learned the "craft of burglary" from a fellow inmate, Oklahoma Smith, when the two were serving time in the Illinois State Penitentiary. Among Smith's recommendations are these:

> Never wear deodorant or shaving lotion; the strange scent might wake someone up. The more people there are in a house, the safer you are. If someone hears you moving around, they will think it's someone else. . . . If they call, answer in a muffled sleepy voice. . . . Never be afraid of dogs, they can sense fear. Most dogs are friendly, snap your finger, they come right to you.[79]

Despite his elaborate preparations, Hoheimer spent many years in confinement.

Burglars must "master" the skills of their "trade," learning to spot environmental cues "nonprofessionals" fail to notice.[80] They must learn which targets contain valuables worth stealing and which are most likely to prove to be a dry hole. Research shows that burglary rates for student-occupied apartments are actually much lower than rates for other residences in the same neighborhoods; burglars appear to have learned which apartments to avoid.[81]

Most burglars do not like to travel far from their residence, choosing neighborhoods with single-family homes close by.[82] However, experienced burglars are more willing to travel to find rich targets. They have access to transportation that enables them to select a wider variety of targets than younger, more inexperienced thieves.[83] They also seem to be sensitive to police anticrime efforts: When police are active and forceful, burglary rates decline. Experienced burglars may locate to "safer" areas or bide their time and wait for the police to reduce their anticrime initiatives as crime rates decline.[84]

EXHIBIT 12.3

Burglars on the Job

According to active burglars:

- Most avoid occupied residences, considering them high-risk targets.
- Most are not deterred by alarms and elaborate locks; in fact, these devices tell them there is something inside worth stealing.
- Some call occupants from a pay phone, and if the phone is still ringing when they arrive, they know no one is home.
- Once entering a residence, anxiety turns to calm as they first turn to the master bedroom for money and drugs. They also search kitchens believing that some people keep money in a mayonnaise jar.
- Most work in groups, one serving as a lookout while another ransacks the place.
- Some dispose of goods through a professional fence; others try to pawn the goods. Some exchange goods for drugs; some sell them to friends and relatives; and a few keep the stolen items for themselves, especially guns and jewelry.
- Many approach a target masquerading as workmen, such as carpenters or house painters.
- Some stake out residences to learn occupants' routines.
- Tipsters help them select attractive targets.
- Drug dealers are favored targets because they tend to have a lot of cash and drugs, and victims are not going to call the police.
- Targets are often acquaintances.

Source: Richard Wright and Scott Decker, *Burglars on the Job: Streetlife and Residential Break-Ins* (Boston: Northeastern University Press, 1994).

In an important book titled *Burglars on the Job*, Richard Wright and Scott Decker describe the working conditions of active burglars.[85] Most are motivated by the need for cash in order to get high; they want to enjoy the good life, "keeping the party going" without having to work. As Exhibit 12.3 shows, they approach their "job" in a rational workmanlike fashion, but their lives are controlled by their culture and environment. Unskilled and uneducated, urban burglars make the choices they do because there are few conventional opportunities for success.

While most burglars are male, more than 30,000 women are arrested for burglary annually, about 15 percent of the total. What motivates female burglars and how do they differ from males? These are the topics of the Race, Culture, Gender, and Criminology feature "Are There Gender Differences in Burglary?"

Commercial Burglary

Some burglars prefer to victimize commercial property rather than private homes. Of all business establishments, retail stores are burglars' favorite targets. They display merchandise so that burglars know exactly what to look for, where it can be found, and—because the prices are displayed—how much they can hope to gain in resale to a fence. Burglars can legitimately enter a retail store during business hours and gain knowledge about

ARE THERE GENDER DIFFERENCES IN BURGLARY?

Does gender play a role in shaping burglary careers? Are there differences in the way professional male and female burglars approach their craft? Do gender roles influence the burglar lifestyle? To find out, Christopher Mullins and Richard Wright used interviews with 18 active female burglars and 36 males, matched approximately for age. Their findings indicate that significant gender-based differences exist in the way males and females begin and end their offending careers and how they carry out their criminal tasks.

There were similarities in the way most offenders, male or female, were initiated into residential burglary. Burglars of both genders became involved via interaction in intimate groups, such as older friends, family members, or street associates. One told how they got started in burglary:

> [M]e and my brother, we wanted, you know, he came and got me and say he know where a house at to break into. And, uhm, we go there and uh, we just do it . . . me and my brother, he and some more friends.

But there was one key difference between the male and female offenders: the men typically became involved in burglary with male peers; women more often were introduced to crime by their boyfriends. Males are more likely to bring their male peers and family members into their offending networks and resist working with women except their girlfriend or female relative. And when they do include women, they put them in a subservient role, such as a lookout.

Why do they get involved in a burglary career in the first place? Both males and females generally said they got involved in break-ins to finance a party lifestyle centered on drug use and to buy designer clothing and bling-bling jewelry. There were some differences: males reportedly wanted money to pursue sexual conquests; female burglars were far more likely to say that they needed money to buy necessities for their children.

When asked what they were looking for in a prospective residential burglary target, the male and female offenders expressed similar preferences; both wanted to find a dwelling that was (a) unoccupied and (b) contained something of value. Both the men and the women wanted to know something about the people who lived in the residence, be familiar with their day-to-day routine, and to have an idea of the target's valuables. Male offenders used their legitimate jobs as home remodelers, cable television installers, or gardeners to scout potential burglary targets. Female burglars who lacked legitimate entry had to rely on information generated by the men in their immediate criminal social network. Some used sexual attraction to gain the victim's confidence and gather information.

Mullins and Wright also found that men preferred to commit residential burglaries by themselves, while women most often worked with others. Males seemed unwilling to trust accomplices and were also unwilling to share the proceeds. Females, on the other hand, reported that they lacked the knowledge or skills needed to break into a dwelling on their own and were therefore more willing to work with a team.

Finally, when asked what it would take to make them stop committing crime, both male and female offenders claimed that a good job that paid well and involved little or no disciplined subordination to authority would be required to get them to give up their careers in crime. Men also claimed they would probably give up burglary once they settled down and started a family. Because they were dependent on male help, female burglars needed to sever their relationships with criminally involved males in order to reduce their offending. Female burglars were also more sensitive than the males to shaming and ostracism at the hands of their relatives and might quit under family pressure.

Mullins and Wright found that residential burglary is a significantly gender-stratified offense; the processes of initiation, commission, and potential desistance are heavily structured by gender. Women have to negotiate the male-dominated world of burglary to accomplish their crimes. Gender, they find, plays a significant role in shaping opportunity (such as initiation) and the events leading up to residential burglaries (for example, information gathering), while playing a lesser but still important role in molding actual offense commission.

CRITICAL THINKING

1. Do the gender differences in burglary reflect the gender differences found in other segments of society?

2. Do you think gender discrimination helps reduce the female crime rate? If gender equality were achieved, would differences in the crime rate narrow?

Source: Christopher Mullins and Richard Wright, "Gender, Social Networks, and Residential Burglary," *Criminology* 41 (2003): 813–839.

what the store contains and where it is stored; they can also check for security alarms and devices. Commercial burglars perceive retail establishments as quick sources of merchandise that can be easily sold.

Other commercial establishments such as service centers, warehouses, and factories are less attractive targets because it is more difficult to gain legitimate access to plan the theft. The burglar must use a great deal of guile to scope out these places, perhaps posing as a delivery person. In addition, the merchandise is more likely to be used, and it may be more difficult to fence at a premium price.

If burglars choose to attack factories, warehouses, or service centers, the most vulnerable properties are those located far from major thoroughfares and away from pedestrian traffic. Establishments located within three blocks of heavily traveled thoroughfares have been found to be less vulnerable to burglary than those located farther away; commercial establishments in wealthier communities have a higher probability of burglary.[86]

Though alarms have been found to be an effective deterrent to burglary, they are less effective in isolated areas because it takes police longer to respond than on more heavily patrolled thoroughfares, and an alarm is less likely to be heard by a pedestrian who would be able to call for help. Even in the most remote areas, however, burglars are wary of alarms and try to choose targets without elaborate or effective security systems. One study found that the probability of burglary of non-alarmed properties is 4.57 times higher than that of similar property with alarms.[87]

Careers in Burglary

Some criminals make burglary their career and continually develop new and specialized skills to aid their profession. Neal Shover has studied the careers of professional burglars and has uncovered the existence of a particularly successful type which he labels "the good burglar."[88] Professional burglars use this title to characterize colleagues who have distinguished themselves as burglars. Characteristics of the good burglar include:

- Technical competence
- Maintenance of personal integrity
- Specialization in burglary
- Financial success
- The ability to avoid prison sentences

To receive recognition as good burglars, Shover found that novices must develop four key requirements of the trade.

First, they must learn the many skills needed to commit lucrative burglaries. This process may include learning how to gain entry into homes and apartment houses; how to select targets with high potential payoffs; how to choose items with a high resale value; how to open safes properly, without damaging their contents; and how to use the proper equipment, including cutting torches, electric saws, explosives, and metal bars.

Second, the good burglar must be able to team up to form a criminal gang. Choosing trustworthy companions is essential if the obstacles to completing a successful job—police, alarms, and secure safes—are to be overcome.

Third, the good burglar must have inside information. Without knowledge of what awaits them inside, burglars can spend a tremendous amount of time and effort on empty safes and jewelry boxes.

Finally, the good burglar must cultivate fences or buyers for stolen wares. Once the burglar gains access to people who buy and sell stolen goods, he or she must also learn how to successfully sell these goods for a reasonable profit. Evidence of these

skills was discovered in a study of more than 200 career burglars in Australia. Burglars reported that they had developed a number of relatively safe methods for disposing of their loot. Some traded stolen goods directly for drugs; others used fences, legitimate businesses, pawnbrokers, and secondhand dealers as trading partners. Surprisingly, many sold their illegal gains to family or friends. Burglars report that disposing of stolen goods was actually low risk and more efficient than expected. One reason was that in many cases fences and shady businesspeople put in a request for particular items, and the readymade market allowed the stolen merchandise to be disposed of quickly, often in less than one hour. Though the typical markdown was 67 to 75 percent of the price of the goods, most reported that they could still earn a good living, averaging AUS$2,000 per week (about $1,000 in U.S. dollars). Those who benefited most from these transactions were the receivers of stolen property, who make considerable profits and are unlikely to be caught.[89]

According to Shover, a person becomes a good burglar by learning the techniques of the trade from older, more experienced burglars. During this process, the older burglar teaches the novice how to handle such requirements as dealing with defense attorneys, bail bond agents, and other agents of the justice system. Apprentices must be known to have the appropriate character before they are taken under the wing of the old pro. Usually, the opportunity to learn burglary comes as a reward for being a highly respected juvenile gang member; from knowing someone in the neighborhood who has made a living at burglary; or, more often, from having built a reputation for being solid while serving time in prison. Consequently, the opportunity to become a good burglar is not open to everyone.

connections

Shover finds that the process of becoming a professional burglar is similar to the process described in Sutherland's theory of differential association. You can read more about this theory in Chapter 7.

The Burglary "Career Ladder" Paul Cromwell, James Olson, and D'Aunn Wester Avary interviewed 30 active burglars in Texas and found that burglars go through stages of career development. They begin as young *novices* who learn the trade from older, more experienced burglars, frequently siblings or relatives. Novices will continue to get this tutoring as long as they can develop their own markets (fences) for stolen goods. After their education is over, novices enter the *journeyman* stage, characterized by forays in search of lucrative targets and careful planning. At this point, they develop reputations as experienced reliable criminals. Finally, they become *professional* burglars when they have developed advanced skills and organizational abilities that give them the highest esteem among their peers.

The Texas burglars also displayed evidence of rational decision making. Most seemed to carefully evaluate potential costs and benefits before deciding to commit crime. There is evidence that burglars follow this pattern in their choice of burglary sites. Burglars show a preference for corner houses because they are easily observed and offer the maximum number of escape routes.[90] They look for houses that show evidence of long-term care and wealth. Though people may erect fences and other barriers to deter burglars, these devices may actually attract crime because they are viewed as protecting something worth stealing: If there is nothing valuable inside, why go through so much trouble to secure the premises?[91]

Cromwell, Olson, and Avary also found that many burglars had serious drug habits and that their criminal activity was, in part, aimed at supporting their substance abuse.

Repeat Burglary   To what extent do burglars strike the same victim more than once? Research suggests that burglars may in fact return to the scene of the crime to repeat their offenses. One reason is that many burgled items are indispensable (for example, televisions and DVD players); therefore, it is safe to assume that they will quickly be replaced.[92] Research shows that some burglars repeat their acts to steal these replacement goods.[93] Graham Farrell, Coretta Phillips, and Ken Pease have articulated why burglars would most likely try to hit the same target more than once:

▌ It takes less effort to burgle a home or apartment known to be a suitable target than an unknown or unsuitable one.

▌ The burglar is already aware of the target's layout.

▌ The ease of entry of the target has probably not changed, and escape routes are known.

▌ The lack of protective measures and the absence of nosy and intrusive neighbors that made the first burglary a success have probably not changed.

▌ Goods have been observed that could not be taken out the first time.[94]

The repeat burglary phenomenon should mean that homes in close proximity to a burgled dwelling have an increased burglary risk, especially if they are similar in structure to the initial target. But research shows that lack of diversity in the physical construction and general appearance of dwellings in a neighborhood actually helped reduce repeat victimization. Housing diversity allows offenders a choice of targets, and favored targets will be revisited by burglars. If houses are identical, there is no motive for an offender to favor one property over another, and therefore the risk of repeat victimization is limited.[95]

ARSON

Arson is the willful and malicious burning of a home, public building, vehicle, or commercial building. About 70,000 known arsons are now recorded each year. Many of these fires are set by adolescents, causing at least 300 deaths, 2,000 injuries, and more than $300 million in damage; juveniles comprise about 40 percent of all people arrested for arson annually.[96] The average value loss per arson offense is about $15,000; arsons of industrial and manufacturing structures resulted in the highest average dollar losses of more than $350,000 per arson).

Arson has been a common occurrence in America and was even tried as a weapon during the Civil War. In 1864, a small group of Confederate agents attempted to set New York City ablaze by using a liquid called "solidified Greek fire"; the plot failed because they improperly used the chemical.[97] However, arson is not just an American phenomenon. According to the Arson Prevention Bureau, a British group that coordinates a national campaign to reduce arson, every week in England:

▌ There are 2,100 arson attacks.

▌ One or two people die in arson attacks.

A helicopter drops water on a wildfire, March 11, 2007, near Anaheim Hills, California. The fast-moving brush fire scorched 1,000 acres of parched hillside and charred at least two homes, forcing authorities to evacuate more than 200 homes in Orange County. The fire was ignited by flames from a stolen car that was intentionally set ablaze during strong Santa Ana winds.

© AP Images/Kenneth Roberts

- Fifty-five people are injured.
- Four churches or places of worship are damaged or destroyed.
- Twenty schools are damaged or destroyed.
- $60 million in damage and costs result from arson.[98]

There are several motives for arson. Adult arsonists may be motivated by severe emotional turmoil. Some psychologists view fire starting as a function of a disturbed personality. Arson, therefore, should be viewed as a mental health problem and not a criminal act.[99] It is alleged that arsonists often experience sexual pleasure from starting fires and then observing their destructive effects. Although some arsonists may be aroused sexually by their activities, there is little evidence that most arsonists are psychosexually motivated.[100] It is equally likely that fires are started by angry people looking for revenge against property owners or by teenagers out to vandalize property. These findings support the claim that arson should be viewed as a mental health problem, not a criminal act, and that it should be treated with counseling and other therapeutic measures rather than severe punishments.[101]

The Juvenile Fire Starter

Juveniles, the most prolific fire starters, may get involved in arson for a variety of reasons as they mature. Juvenile fire setting has long been associated with psychological abnormality, including depression conduct problems, such as disobedience and aggressiveness, anger, hostility, and resentment over parental rejection.[102] According to research by sociologist Wayne Wooden, juvenile arsonists can be classified in one of four categories:

- *The "playing with matches" fire setter.* This is the youngest fire starter, usually between the ages of 4 and 9, who sets fires because parents are careless with matches and lighters. Proper instruction on fire safety can help prevent fires set by these young children.
- *The "crying for help" fire setter.* This type of fire setter is a 7- to 13-year-old who turns to fire to reduce stress. The source of the stress is family conflict, divorce, death, or abuse. These youngsters have difficulty expressing their feelings of sorrow, rage, or anger and turn to fire as a means of relieving stress or getting back at their antagonists.
- *The "delinquent" fire setter.* Some youth set fires to school property or surrounding areas to retaliate for some slight experienced at school. These kids may break into the school to vandalize property with friends and later set a fire to cover up their activities.
- *The "severely disturbed" fire setter.* This youngster is obsessed with fires and often dreams about them in "vibrant colors." This is the most disturbed type of juvenile fire setter and the one most likely to set numerous fires with the potential for death and damage.[103]

During the past decade, hundreds of jurisdictions across the nation have established programs to address the growing problem of juvenile fire setting. Housed primarily within the fire service, these programs are designed to identify, evaluate, and treat juvenile fire setters to prevent the recurrence of fire-setting behaviors. A promising approach is the FireSafe Families effort in Rhode Island, which combines a training curriculum for fire-safety educators, a training program for community professionals to identify potential behavior that may lead to arson, and a cognitive-behavioral therapy (CBT) program to treat children and their families who are at risk of becoming juvenile fire starters.[104]

Professional Arson

Other arsons are set by professional arsonists who engage in **arson for profit**. People looking to collect insurance money, but who are afraid or unable to set the fire themselves, hire professional arsonists. These professionals have acquired the skills to set fires yet make the cause seem accidental (for example, like an electrical short). Another form is **arson fraud**, which involves a business owner burning his or her property, or hiring someone to do it, to escape financial problems.[105] Over the years, investigators have found that businesspeople are willing to become involved in arson to collect fire insurance or for various other reasons, including but not limited to these:

- Obtaining money during a period of financial crisis
- Getting rid of outdated or slow-moving inventory
- Destroying outmoded machines and technology
- Paying off legal and illegal debt
- Relocating or remodeling a business; for example, when a theme restaurant has not been accepted by customers
- Taking advantage of government funds available for redevelopment
- Applying for government building money, pocketing it without making repairs, and then claiming that fire destroyed the "rehabilitated" building
- Planning bankruptcies to eliminate debts, after the merchandise supposedly destroyed was secretly sold before the fire
- Eliminating business competition by burning out rivals
- Employing extortion schemes that demand that victims pay up or the rest of their holdings will be burned
- Solving labor–management problems; arson may be committed by a disgruntled employee
- Concealing another crime, such as embezzlement

Some recent technological advances may help prove that many alleged arsons were actually accidental fires. There is now evidence of a fire effect called **flashover**. During the course of an ordinary fire, heat and gas at the ceiling of a room can reach 2,000 degrees. This causes clothes and furniture to burst into flame, duplicating the effects of arsonists' gasoline or explosives. It is possible that many suspected arsons are actually the result of flashover.[106]

THINKING LIKE A CRIMINOLOGIST

You are approached by the local police chief, who is quite concerned about high burglary rates in some areas of the city. She is a former student of yours and well aware of recent developments in criminological theory. The chief is a strong advocate of rational choice theory and has already instituted a number of programs based on a deterrence/situational crime prevention model of control. The existing police initiatives include these programs:

- The police offer target hardening measures to repeat victims. They install high-tech security equipment in their homes so that the homes can be monitored on a 24-hour basis. The police plan an advertising campaign to alert would-be offenders that they are on watch at prior target residences.

- A new police initiative identifies repeat burglars in the area and provides intervention designed to supply them with legitimate economic opportunities to reduce their criminal motivation.

- A new school-based program designed to reduce criminal motivation seeks to raise young people's awareness of the dangers of burglary and how it can result in a long prison sentence.

- The police have developed a series of environmental improvements in the target area with a view to minimizing burglary opportunities. These include improved visibility, better access control, and lighting in areas that have relatively high burglary rates. They have also instituted high-visibility police patrols in these areas to deter criminals from committing crimes there.

- A Burglary Control Model House, fitted with low-cost methods of security such as strengthened door/window frames, bolts, locks, and so on, has been built and will be advertised to encourage residents to help themselves avoid burglary.

The chief has asked you to look over these initiatives and comment on their anticipated effectiveness.

 Writing Exercise Write a paper (about 300 words) discussing whether you think there are any possible pitfalls with these initiatives and suggesting, if you can, other policy initiatives that might prove effective in reducing the opportunity to commit burglary and deter potential burglars.

 Doing Research on the Web Before you begin your paper, see what the Metropolitan Police Service—by far the largest of the police services that operate in greater London— suggests, as well as the Burglary Prevention Council. Also, check out a burglary prevention checklist and get some advice on changing the environment to prevent burglary. All of these websites can be accessed through academic.cengage.com/criminaljustice/siegel.

SUMMARY

- Theft offenses are common throughout recorded history. During the Middle Ages, poachers stole game, smugglers avoided taxes, and thieves worked as pickpockets and forgers.

- Economic crimes are designed to financially reward the offender. Opportunistic amateurs commit

the majority of economic crimes. Amateurs steal because of situational inducements.

- Economic crime has also attracted professional criminals. Professionals earn most of their income from crime, view themselves as criminals, and possess skills that aid them in their

law-breaking behavior. A good example of the professional criminal is the fence who buys and sells stolen merchandise.

- Common theft offenses include larceny, fraud, and embezzlement. These are common-law crimes, originally defined by English judges.

- Larceny involves taking the legal possessions of another. Petty larceny is typically theft of amounts under $100; grand larceny usually refers to amounts over $100. Larceny is the most common theft crime and involves such activities as shoplifting, passing bad checks, and stealing or illegally using credit cards.

- Some shoplifters are amateurs who steal on the spur of the moment, while others are professionals who use sophisticated techniques to help them avoid detection.

- The crime of false pretenses, or fraud, is similar to larceny in that it involves the theft of goods or money; it differs in that the criminal tricks victims into voluntarily giving up their possessions.

- Embezzlement involves people taking something that was temporarily entrusted to them, such as bank tellers taking money out of the cash drawer and keeping it for themselves.

- Auto theft usually involves amateur joyriders who borrow cars for short-term transportation and professional auto thieves who steal cars to sell off their parts, which are highly valuable.

- Burglary, a more serious theft offense, was defined in common law as the "breaking and entering of a dwelling house of another in the nighttime with the intent to commit a felony within." This definition has also evolved over time. Today most states have modified their definitions of burglary to include theft from any structure at any time of day.

- Because burglary involves planning and risk, it attracts professional thieves. The most competent have technical ability and personal integrity, specialize in burglary, are financially successful, and avoid prison sentences.

- Professional burglars are able to size up the value of a particular crime and balance it out with the perceived risks. Many have undergone training in the company of older, more experienced burglars. They have learned the techniques to make them good burglars.

- Arson is another serious property crime. Although most arsonists are teenage vandals, there are professional arsonists who specialize in burning commercial buildings for profit.

- CENGAGENOW™ is an easy-to-use online resource that helps you study in less time to get the grade you want—NOW. CengageNOW™ Personalized Study (a diagnostic study tool containing valuable text-specific resources) lets you focus on just what you don't know and learn more in less time to get a better grade. If your textbook does not include an access code card, you can go to www.ichapters.com to purchase CengageNOW™.

KEY TERMS

fence (370)
street crime (370)
economic crime (370)
skilled thieves (370)
flash houses (370)
smugglers (370)
poachers (370)
occasional criminals (371)
professional criminals (371)
situational inducement (371)
professional fence (373)

constructive possession (376)
petit (petty) larceny (376)
grand larceny (376)
shoplifting (377)
snitches (378)
target removal strategies (378)
target hardening strategies (378)
naive check forgers (379)
closure (379)
systematic forgers (379)

carjacking (382)
false pretenses or fraud (382)
confidence games (383)
mark (383)
pigeon drop (383)
embezzlement (383)
good burglar (387)
arson for profit (389)
arson fraud (389)
flashover (389)

CRITICAL THINKING QUESTIONS

1. Differentiate between an occasional and a professional criminal. Which one would be more likely to resort to violence? Which one would be more easily deterred?

2. What crime occurs when a person who owns an antique store sells a client an "original" Tiffany lamp that the seller knows is a fake? Would it still be a crime if the person selling the lamp was not aware that it was a fake? As an antique dealer, should the seller have a duty to determine the authenticity of the products he or she sells?

3. What are the characteristics of good burglars? Can you compare their career path to any other professionals, such as doctors or lawyers? Which theory of criminal behavior best predicts the development of the good burglar?

4. You have been the victim of repeat burglaries. What could you do to reduce the chances of future victimization? (Hint: Buying a gun is not an option!)

NOTES

1. Alison Leigh Cowan, "For Dealer, Stolen Maps Point Way to Prison," *New York Times*, 23 June 2006; Laura Beach, "Edward Forbes Smiley III Admits to Stealing 97 Rare Maps from US and UK Institutions," Antiques and the Arts Online, http://antiquesandthearts.com/TT-2006-06-27-08-24-56p1 (accessed June 12, 2007); David S. Smith, "Smiley Pleads 'Not Guilty' in Yale Map Theft Case," Antiques and the Arts Online, http://antiquesandthearts.com/TT-2005-08-15-17-08-58p1 (accessed June 12, 2007); FBI, Stolen Treasures: The Case of the Missing Maps, September 28, 2006, www.fbi.gov/page2/september06/maps092806.htm (accessed June 12, 2007).

2. Andrew McCall, *The Medieval Underworld* (London: Hamish Hamilton, 1979), p. 86.

3. Ibid., p. 104.

4. J. J. Tobias, *Crime and Police in England, 1700–1900* (London: Gill and Macmillan, 1979).

5. Ibid., p. 9.

6. Marilyn Walsh, *The Fence* (Westport, CT: Greenwood Press, 1977), pp. 18–25.

7. Don DeNevi, *Western Train Robberies* (Millbrae, CA: Celestial Arts, 1976); Harry Sinclair Drago, *Road Agents and Train Robbers: Half a Century of Western Banditry* (New York: Dodd, Mead, 1973).

8. Neal Shover, *Great Pretenders, Pursuits, and Careers of Persistent Thieves* (Boulder, CO: Westview Press, 1996).

9. Ibid., pp. 50–51.

10. Ibid.

11. John Hepburn, "Occasional Criminals," in *Major Forms of Crime*, ed. Robert Meier (Beverly Hills: Sage, 1984), pp. 73–94.

12. James Inciardi, "Professional Crime," in *Major Forms of Crime*, p. 223.

13. Harry King and William Chambliss, *Box Man: A Professional Thief's Journal* (New York: Harper & Row, 1972), p. 24.

14. Edwin Sutherland, "White-Collar Criminality," *American Sociological Review* 5 (1940): 2–10.

15. Gilbert Geis, "Avocational Crime," in *Handbook of Criminology*, ed. D. Glazer (Chicago: Rand McNally, 1974), p. 284.

16. Chic Conwell, *The Professional Thief*, ed. Edwin Sutherland (Chicago: University of Chicago Press, 1937).

17. Ibid., pp. 197–198.

18. Ibid., p. 212.

19. See, for example, Edwin Lemert, "The Behavior of the Systematic Check Forger," *Social Problems* 6 (1958): 141–148.

20. Cited in Walsh, *The Fence*, p. 1.

21. Carl Klockars, *The Professional Fence* (New York: Free Press, 1976); Darrell Steffensmeier, *The Fence: In the Shadow of Two Worlds* (Totowa, NJ: Rowman and Littlefield, 1986); Walsh, *The Fence*, pp. 25–28.

22. Simon Fass and Janice Francis, "Where Have All the Hot Goods Gone? The Role of Pawnshops," *Journal of Research in Crime and Delinquency* 41 (2004): 156–179.

23. Walsh, *The Fence*, p. 34.

24. Paul Cromwell, James Olson, and D'Aunn Avary, "Who Buys Stolen Property? A New Look at Criminal Receiving," *Journal of Crime and Justice* 16 (1993): 75–95.

25. This section depends heavily on a classic book, Wayne LaFave and Austin Scott, *Handbook on Criminal Law* (St. Paul, MN: West Publishing, 1972).

26. Ibid., p. 622.

27. Henrico County Virginia, www.co.henrico.va.us (accessed June 12, 2007).

28. John Worrall, "The Effect of Three-Strikes Legislation on Serious Crime in California," *Journal of Criminal Justice* 32 (2004): 283–296.

29. FBI, Uniform Crime Reports, 2005, www.fbi.gov/ucr/05cius/offenses/property_crime/larceny-theft.html (accessed June 12, 2007).

30. Margaret Loftus, "Gone: One TV," *U.S. News and World Report*, 14 July 1997, p. 61.

31. Timothy W. Maier, "Uncle Sam Gets Rolled," *Insight on the News*, 10 March 1997, p. 13.

32. Hayes International Theft Survey 2005, www.hayesinternational.com/thft_srvys.html (accessed February 25, 2007).

33. David Farrington, "Measuring, Explaining and Preventing Shoplifting: A Review of British Research," *Security Journal* 12 (1999): 9–27.

34. Mary Owen Cameron, *The Booster and the Snitch* (New York: Free Press, 1964).

35. Ibid., p. 57.

36. Paul Cromwell and Quint Thurman, "The Devil Made Me Do It: Use Of Neutralizations by Shoplifters," *Deviant Behavior* 24 (2003): 535–550.

37. Ellen Beate Hansen and Gunnar Breivik, "Sensation Seeking as a Predictor of Positive and Negative Risk Behavior Among Adolescents," *Personality and Individual Differences* 30 (2001): 627–640.

38. Yves Lamontagne, Richard Boyer, Celine Hetu, and Celine Lacerte-Lamontagne, "Anxiety, Significant Losses, Depression, and Irrational Beliefs in First-Offense Shoplifters," *Canadian Journal of Psychiatry* 45 (2000): 64–66.

39. Michael Hindelang, "Decisions of Shoplifting Victims to Invoke the Criminal Justice Process," *Social Problems* 21 (1974): 580–595.

40. Siedfer, "To Catch a Thief, Try This," p. 71.

41. Thomas Kelley, Daniel Kennedy, and Robert Homant, "Evaluation of an Individualized Treatment Program for Adolescent Shoplifters," *Adolescence* 38 (2003): 725–733.

42. Edwin Lemert, "An Isolation and Closure Theory of Naive Check Forgery," *Journal of Criminal Law, Criminology and Police Science* 44 (1953): 297–298.

43. LaFave and Scott, *Handbook on Criminal Law*, p. 672.

44. FBI, "Credit Card Con: Canadian Man Gets 10 Years for $12 Million Telemarketing Scam," www.fbi.gov/page2/nov03/credit112803.htm (accessed April 11, 2006).

45. Peter Wayner, "Bogus Web Sites Troll for Credit Card Numbers," *New York Times*, 12 February 1997, p. A18.

46. FBI, Crime in the United States, 2005, www.fbi.gov/ucr/05cius/offenses/property_crime/motor_vehicle_theft.html (accessed June 12, 2007).

47. Charles McCaghy, Peggy Giordano, and Trudy Knicely Henson, "Auto Theft," *Criminology* 15 (1977): 367–381.

48. Donald Gibbons, *Society, Crime and Criminal Careers* (Englewood Cliffs, NJ: Prentice Hall, 1977), p. 310.

49. Heith Copes and Michael Cherbonneau, "The Key to Auto Theft: Emerging Methods of Auto Theft from the Offenders' Perspective," *British Journal of Criminology*, 46 (2006): 917–934.

50. Kim Hazelbaker, "Insurance Industry Analyses and the Prevention of Motor Vehicle Theft," in *Business and Crime Prevention*, eds. Marcus Felson and Ronald Clarke (Monsey, NY: Criminal Justice Press, 1997), pp. 283–293.

51. Heith Copes, "Streetlife and the Rewards of Auto Theft," *Deviant Behavior* 24 (2003): 309–333.

52. Highway Loss Data Institute, "Cadillac Escalade and Mitsubishi Lancer Evolution Top the List of Highest Insurance Claims for Theft," June 7, 2006, www.iihs.org/news/rss/pr060706.html (accessed March 1, 2007).

53. National Insurance Crime Bureau (NICB), "Hot Wheels: Do You Know Where Your Car Is?" www.nicb.org/cps/rde/xchg/SID-4031FE9A-2CE40A7B/nicb/hs.xsl/72.htm (accessed February 22, 2007).

54. Ibid.

55. "Hot Cars: Parts Crooks Love Best," *BusinessWeek*, 15 September 2003, p. 104.

56. National Insurance Crime Bureau (NICB), Airbag Theft and Fraud: Deflating a Growing Crime Trend, www.nicb.org/pdfs/Airbag.pdf (accessed February 22, 2007).

57. Michael Rand, *Carjacking* (Washington, DC: Bureau of Justice Statistics, 1994), p. 1.

58. Patsy Klaus, *Carjacking, 1993–2002* (Washington, DC: Bureau of Justice Statistics, 2004).

59. Bruce Jacobs, Volkan Topalli, and Richard Wright, "Carjacking, Streetlife, and Offender Motivation," *British Journal of Criminology* 43 (2003): 673–688.

60. Klaus, *Carjacking, 1993–2002*.

61. Ronald Clarke and Patricia Harris, "Auto Theft and Its Prevention," in *Crime and Justice: An Annual Review*, eds. N. Morris and M. Tonry (Chicago: University of Chicago Press, 1992).

62. Ian Ayres and Steven D. Levitt, "Measuring Positive Externalities from Unobservable Victim Precaution: An Empirical Analysis of Lojack," *Quarterly Journal of Economics* 113 (1998): 43–78.

63. Hazelbaker, "Insurance Industry Analyses and the Prevention of Motor Vehicle Theft," p. 289.

64. P. Weiss, "Outsmarting the Electronic Gatekeeper: Code Breakers Beat Security Scheme of Car Locks, Gas Pumps," *Science News* 167 (2005): 86.

65. LaFave and Scott, *Handbook on Criminal Law*, p. 655.

66. 30 Geo. III, C. 24 (1975).

67. Benjamin Weiser, "4-Year Sentence for Mastermind of Scheme to Cheat on Graduate School Tests," *New York Times*, 3 October 1998, p. 8.

68. As described in Charles McCaghy, *Deviant Behavior* (New York: Macmillan, 1976), pp. 230–231.

69. Department of Justice press release, "Local Woman Sentenced for Embezzlement," http://mobile.fbi.gov/dojpressrel/pressrel06/embezzlement121406.htm (accessed June 15, 2007).

70. Ibid., p. 649.

71. Jerome Hall, *Theft, Law and Society* (Indianapolis: Bobbs-Merrill, 1952), p. 36.

72. LaFave and Scott, *Handbook on Criminal Law*, p. 644.

73. Dawit Kiros Fantaye, "Fighting Corruption and Embezzlement in Third World Countries," *Journal of Criminal Law* 68 (April 2004): 170–177.

74. LaFave and Scott, *Handbook on Criminal Law*, p. 708.

75. E. Blackstone, *Commentaries on the Laws of England* (London: 1769), p. 224.

76. Elizabeth Groff and Nancy La Vigne, "Mapping an Opportunity Surface of Residential Burglary," *Journal of Research in Crime and Delinquency* 38 (2001): 257–278.

77. Timothy Coupe and Laurence Blake, "Daylight and Darkness Targeting Strategies and the Risks of Being Seen at Residential Burglaries," *Criminology* 44 (2006): 431–464.

78. Wim Bernasco, "Co-Offending and the Choice of Target Areas in Burglary," *Journal of Investigative Psychology and Offender Profiling* 3 (2006): 139–155.

79. Frank Hoheimer, *The Home Invaders: Confessions of a Cat Burglar* (Chicago: Chicago Review, 1975).

80. Richard Wright, Robert Logie, and Scott Decker, "Criminal Expertise and Offender Decision Making: An Experimental Study of the Target Selection Process in Residential Burglary," *Journal of Research in Crime and Delinquency* 32 (1995): 39–53.

81. Matthew Robinson, "Accessible Targets, but Not Advisable Ones: The Role of 'Accessibility' in Student Apartment Burglary," *Journal of Security Administration* 21 (1998): 28–44.

82. Wim Bernasco and Paul Nieuwbeerta, "How Do Residential Burglars Select Target Areas? A New Approach to the Analysis of Criminal Location Choice," *British Journal of Criminology* 45 (2005): 296–315.

83. Brent Snook, "Individual Differences in Distance Travelled by Serial Burglars," *Journal of Investigative Psychology and Offender Profiling* 1 (2004): 53–66.

84. John Worrall, "Does Targeting Minor Offenses Reduce Serious Crime? A Provisional, Affirmative Answer Based on an Analysis of County-Level Data," *Police Quarterly* 9 (2006): 47–72.

85. Richard Wright and Scott Decker, Burglars on the Job: *Streetlife and Residential Break-Ins* (Boston: Northeastern University Press, 1994).

86. Simon Hakim and Yochanan Shachmurove, "Spatial and Temporal Patterns of Commercial Burglaries," *American Journal of Economics and Sociology* 55 (1996): 443–457.

87. Ibid., pp. 443–456.

88. See generally Neal Shover, "Structures and Careers in Burglary," *Journal of Criminal Law, Criminology and Police Science* 63 (1972): 540–549.

89. Richard Stevenson, Lubica Forsythe, and Don Weatherburn, "The Stolen Goods Market in New South Wales, Australia: An Analysis of Disposal Avenues and Tactics," *British Journal of Criminology* 41 (winter 2001): 101–118.

90. Paul Cromwell, James Olson, and D'Aunn Wester Avary, *Breaking and Entering: An Ethnographic Analysis of Burglary* (Newbury Park, CA: Sage, 1991), pp. 48–51.

91. See M. Taylor and C. Nee, "The Role of Cues in Simulated Residential Burglary: A Preliminary Investigation," *British Journal of Criminology* 28 (1988): 398–401; Julia MacDonald and Robert Gifford, "Territorial Cues and Defensible Space Theory: The Burglar's Point of View," *Journal of Environmental Psychology* 9 (1989): 193–205.

92. Roger Litton, "Crime Prevention and the Insurance Industry," *in Business and Crime Prevention*, p. 162.

93. Ronald Clarke, Elizabeth Perkins, and Donald Smith, Jr., "Explaining Repeat Residential Burglaries: An Analysis of Property Stolen," in *Repeat Victimization*, Crime Prevention Studies, vol. 12, eds. Graham Farrell and Ken Pease (Monsey, NY: Criminal Justice Press, 2001), pp. 119–132.

94. Graham Farrell, Coretta Phillips, and Ken Pease, "Like Taking Candy: Why Does Repeat Victimization Occur?" *British Journal of Criminology* 35 (1995): 384–399, at 391.

95. Michael Townsley, Ross Homel, and Janet Chaseling, "Infectious Burglaries," *British Journal of Criminology* 43 (2003): 615–634.

96. Jeffrey Zaslow, "Dangerous Games—Medical Mystery: Why Some Children Keep Setting Fires—Without Consensus on Cure, Groups Try Safety Lessons, Therapy and Scare Tactics—Sleeping Mom's Singed Hair," *Wall Street Journal*, 27 June 2003, p. A1.

97. Jane Singer, *The Confederate Dirty War: Arson, Bombings, Assassination and Plots for Chemical and Germ Attacks on the Union*, (Jefferson, NC, and London: McFarland & Company, 2005), p. 21.

98. Arson Prevention Bureau of Justice, key facts www.arsonpreventionbureau.org.uk/News/ (accessed October 15, 2003).

99. Nancy Webb, George Sakheim, Luz Towns-Miranda, and Charles Wagner, "Collaborative Treatment of Juvenile Firestarters: Assessment and Outreach," *American Journal of Orthopsychiatry* 60 (1990): 305–310.

100. Vernon Quinsey, Terry Chaplin, and Douglas Unfold, "Arsonists and Sexual Arousal to Fire Setting: Correlations Unsupported," *Journal of Behavior Therapy and Experimental Psychiatry* 20 (1989): 203–209.

101. John Taylor, Ian Thorne, Alison Robertson, and Ginny Avery, "Evaluation of a Group Intervention for Convicted Arsonists with Mild and Borderline Intellectual Disabilities," *Criminal Behaviour and Mental Health* 12 (2002): 282–294.

102. Mark Dadds and Jennifer Fraser, "Fire Interest, Fire Setting and Psychopathology in Australian Children: A Normative Study," *Australian and New Zealand Journal of Psychiatry* 40 (2006): 581–586; Pekka Santtila, Helina Haikkanen, Laurence Alison, Laurence Whyte, and Carrie Whyte, "Juvenile Firesetters: Crime Scene Actions and Offender Characteristics," *Legal and Criminological Psychology* 8 (2003): 1–20.

103. Wayne Wooden, "Juvenile Firesetters in Cross-Cultural Perspective: How Should Society Respond?" *in Official Responses to Problem Juveniles: Some International Reflections*, ed. James Hackler (Onati, Spain: Onati Publications, 1991), pp. 339–348.

104. Scott Turner, "Funding Sparks Effort to Cut Juvenile Arson Rate," *George Street Journal* 27 (31 January 2003): 1.

105. Leigh Edward Somers, *Economic Crimes* (New York: Clark Boardman, 1984), pp. 158–168.

106. Michael Rogers, "The Fire Next Time," *Newsweek*, 26 November 1990, p. 63.

Enterprise Crime: White-Collar and Organized Crime

CHAPTER OBJECTIVES

1. Understand the concept of enterprise crime
2. Be familiar with the various types of white-collar crime
3. Be familiar with the various types of corporate crime
4. Compare corporate crime with individual-level white-collar crimes
5. Discuss the causes of white-collar crime
6. Be able to discuss the different approaches to combating white-collar crime
7. List the elements of white-collar crime enforcement
8. List the different types of illegal behavior engaged in by organized crime figures
9. Describe the evolution of organized crime
10. Explain how the government is fighting organized crime

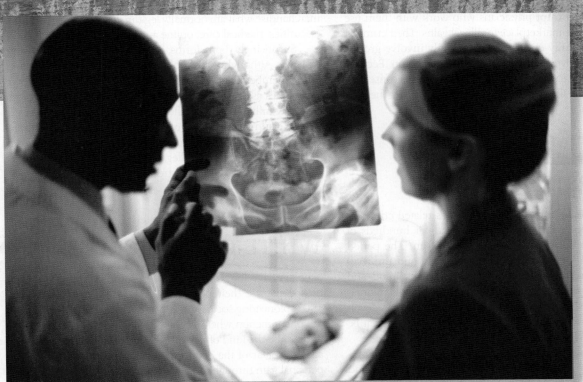

On March 21, 2006, Konstantin Grigoryan, his wife, Mayya Leonidovna Grigoryan, and Eduard Gersheli, Aleksandr Treynker, and Haroutyun Gulderyan were all arrested on charges related to a long-running Medicare fraud scheme that federal authorities believe netted them at least $20 million. The scheme involved defrauding Medicare, the federal health care program, by billing for tests that either were unnecessary or were never performed.

The conspirators paid kickbacks to recruit patients and to submit fraudulent billings to Medicare on behalf of medical service providers, such as medical clinics and diagnostic testing centers. The scheme, commonly referred to as "beneficiary-sharing" or "patient-rotating," involved "marketers" who obtained data about Medicare beneficiaries and sold the information to Medicare providers who then engaged in fraudulent billings. Some marketers, known as "cappers," recruited patients with Medicare coverage and brought them to clinics where they were given unnecessary medical services, including ultrasound examinations and blood tests. The cappers brought in Medicare beneficiaries by car, van, and bus from across California in exchange for kickbacks. Once the patients came into a physician's office, the medical providers allegedly billed the patients' Medicare numbers on the dates of their visits and on many other dates—whether or not any services were in fact provided to the beneficiaries. The conspirators would fabricate the tests so that the patients' files could withstand an audit by Medicare. The criminal scheme caused Medicare to pay out at least $20 million in fraudulent claims from 2000 until 2005. Much of the money was deposited into a maze of bank accounts of "management" and "consulting" companies, including a Panamanian shell corporation with a Swiss account.[1]

Cappers and the corrupt physicians who work with them use their position in the marketplace for illegal gains. Their criminal activities are typically ongoing and typically involve groups of people who provide support, expertise, and so on. Because of their connection to business and commerce and because they conspire to make illegal profits they are referred to here as enterprise crimes.

ENTERPRISE CRIME

While we sometimes think of these business-related crimes as a new phenomenon they have been around for hundreds of years, ever since the industrial revolution began. The period between 1750–1850 witnessed the widespread and unprecedented emergence of financial offences—such as fraud and embezzlement—frequently perpetrated by respectable middle-class offenders as the banking and commercial systems developed. Where there is money, people will steal it, whether it be in the street or in the suite.[2]

In this chapter we divide these crimes of illicit entrepreneurship into two distinct categories: white-collar crime and organized crime. White-collar crime involves illegal activities of people and institutions whose acknowledged purpose is illegal profit through legitimate business transactions. Organized crime involves illegal activities of people and organizations whose acknowledged purpose is profit through illegitimate business enterprise.

Crimes of Business Enterprise

White-collar crime and organized crime are linked here because in each category offenders twist the legal rules of commercial enterprise for criminal purposes. These crimes often overlap. Organized criminals may engage in ongoing fraud schemes and then seek legitimate enterprises to launder money, diversify their sources of income, increase their power and influence, and gain and enhance respectability.[3] Otherwise legitimate businesspeople may turn to organized criminals to help them with economic problems (such as breaking up a strike or dumping hazardous waste products), stifle or threaten competition, and increase their influence.[4] Whereas some corporate executives cheat to improve their company's position in the business world, others are motivated purely for personal gain, acting more like organized criminals than indiscreet businesspeople.[5]

These organizational crimes taint and corrupt the free market system. They mix and match illegal and legal methods and legal and illegal products in all phases of commercial activity. Organized criminals often use illegal marketing techniques (threat, extortion, and smuggling) to distribute otherwise legal products and services (lending money, union activities, selling securities); they also engage in the distribution of products and services (drugs, sex, gambling, and prostitution) that have been outlawed. White-collar criminals use illegal business practices (embezzlement, price fixing, bribery, and so on) to

merchandise what are normally legitimate commercial products (securities, medical care, online auctions).[6]

Surprisingly, both forms of enterprise crime can involve violence. Although the use of force and coercion by organized crime members has been popularized in the media and therefore comes as no shock, that white-collar and high-tech criminals may inflict pain and suffering seems more astonishing. Yet experts claim that hundreds of thousands of occupational deaths occur each year and that "corporate violence" such as unsafe working conditions and illegal pollution annually kills and injures more people than all street crimes combined.[7]

WHITE-COLLAR CRIME

Scholars have long recognized that some unscrupulous businesspeople use their position of trust to fleece the public. In 1907, pioneering sociologist Edward Alsworth Ross recognized the phenomenon when he coined the phrase "the criminaloid" to describe the kind of person who hides behind his or her image as a pillar of the community and paragon of virtue to get personal gain through any means necessary.[8]

In the late 1930s, the distinguished criminologist Edwin Sutherland first used the phrase "white-collar crime" to describe the criminal activities of the rich and powerful. He defined white-collar crime as "a crime committed by a person of respectability and high social status in the course of his occupation."[9] As Sutherland saw it, white-collar crime involved conspiracies by members of the wealthy classes to use their position in commerce and industry for personal gain without regard to the law. Often these actions were handled by civil courts because injured parties were more concerned with recovering their losses than with seeing the offenders punished criminally. Consequently, Sutherland believed that the great majority of white-collar criminals did not become the subject of criminological study. Yet the cost of white-collar crime is probably several times greater than all the crimes customarily regarded as the crime problem. And, in contrast to street crimes, white-collar offenses breed distrust in economic and social institutions, lower public morale, and undermine faith in business and government.[10]

Redefining White-Collar Crime

Although Sutherland's work is considered a milestone in criminological history, his focus was on corporate criminality, including the crimes of the rich and powerful. Contemporary definitions of white-collar crime are typically much broader and include both middle-income Americans and corporate titans who use the marketplace for their criminal activity.[11] Included within recent views of white-collar crime are such acts as income tax evasion, credit card fraud, and bankruptcy fraud. Other white-collar criminals use their positions of trust in business or government to commit crimes. Their activities might include pilfering, soliciting bribes or kickbacks, and embezzlement. Some white-collar criminals set up business for the sole purpose of victimizing the general public. They engage in land swindles (i.e., representing a swamp as a choice building site), securities theft, medical fraud, and so on.

In addition to acting as individuals, some white-collar criminals become involved in criminal conspiracies designed to improve the market share or profitability of their corporations. This type of white-collar crime, which includes antitrust violations, price fixing, and false advertising, is known as corporate crime.[12]

Extent of White-Collar Crime

It is difficult to estimate the extent and influence of white-collar crime on victims because all too often those who suffer the consequences of white-collar crime are ignored by victimologists.[13] The most recent national survey conducted by the National White Collar Crime Center found the following:

▮ About half (46 percent) of households and more than one-third (36 percent) of individuals experience at least one form of white-collar crime victimization each year.

▮ Almost two-thirds (63 percent) of all Americans experience at least one form of white-collar victimization within their lifetimes.

▮ The type of white-collar victimizations that occur most often are product pricing fraud, credit card fraud, unnecessary object repairs, and being directly affected by corporate fraud.

▮ Two-thirds of white-collar victims report the incident to someone (i.e., credit card company, business or person involved, law enforcement, consumer protection agency, personal attorney).

▮ About 30 percent report their victimization to law enforcement or another crime control agency.

This survey data indicate that a significant portion of all U.S. citizens are the victims of white-collar crime at least sometime during their life. It is not surprising then that some estimates of the annual cost of white-collar crime is as high as $660 billion.[14] These losses far outstrip the expense of any other type of crime. Nor is it likely that the full extent of white-collar crime will ever be fully known because many victims (70 percent) are reluctant to report their crime to police, believing that nothing can be done and that getting further involved is pointless.[15] Figure 13.1 illustrates the percentage of individuals who experienced specific white-collar crimes during a single year.

Beyond the monetary cost, white-collar crime often damages property and kills people. Violations of safety standards,

Figure 13.1 Trends in White-Collar Victimization

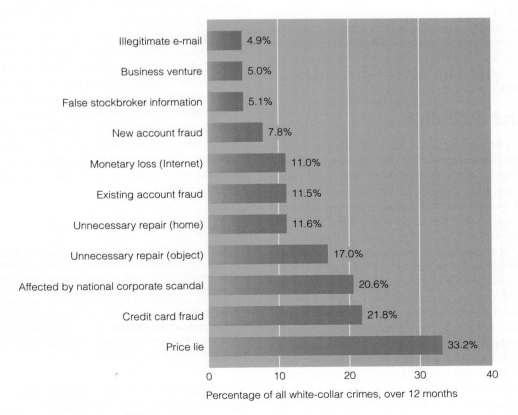

Percentage of all white-collar crimes, over 12 months

- Illegitimate e-mail: 4.9%
- Business venture: 5.0%
- False stockbroker information: 5.1%
- New account fraud: 7.8%
- Monetary loss (Internet): 11.0%
- Existing account fraud: 11.5%
- Unnecessary repair (home): 11.6%
- Unnecessary repair (object): 17.0%
- Affected by national corporate scandal: 20.6%
- Credit card fraud: 21.8%
- Price lie: 33.2%

Source: National White Collar Crime Center, 2006.

pollution of the environment, and industrial accidents due to negligence can be classified as corporate violence. White-collar crime also destroys confidence, saps the integrity of commercial life, and has the potential for devastating destruction. Think of the possible results if nuclear regulatory rules are flouted or if toxic wastes are dumped into a community's drinking water supply.[16]

WWW NAFI, **The National Association of Fraud Investigators**, was established to improve communications and to expand the networking of those in investigation of white-collar crime and related fields, which include but are not limited to law enforcement, insurance investigators, professional investigators, security specialists, bond enforcement agents, attorneys, forensic examiners, tracers/locators, credit card investigators, auto theft investigators, and their international counterparts. Visit NAFI via academic.cengage.com/criminaljustice/siegel.

COMPONENTS OF WHITE-COLLAR CRIME

White-collar crime today represents a range of behaviors involving individuals acting alone and within the context of a business structure. The victims of white-collar crime can be the general public, the organization that employs the offender, or a competing organization. Though there have been numerous attempts to create subcategories or typologies of white-collar criminality, one of the best and most insightful was created more than 25 years ago by criminologist Mark Moore.[17] Moore's typology contains seven elements, ranging from an individual using a business enterprise to commit theft-related crimes to an individual using his or her place within a business enterprise for illegal gain, to business enterprises collectively engaging in illegitimate activity.

Stings and Swindles

For more than a decade, the Gold Club in Atlanta was the hottest spot in town, the destination for conventioneers and businessmen looking for a rowdy night filled with good cigars, strong drinks, and nude dancers.[18] It became the home away from home for well-known professional athletes who stopped by to receive sexual favors from the girls who worked at the club. The federal government filed charges, claiming that the Gold Club manager, Steven Kaplan, was in cahoots with the Gambino organized crime family of New York to overcharge or double bill credit cards of unsuspecting customers. The club owners were also charged with ordering women in their employ to provide sexual services to professional athletes and celebrities to encourage their presence at the club. The scheme depended in part on the victims' reluctance to come forward and press charges, fearing negative publicity. The government won its case when Kaplan pleaded guilty and received a three- to five-year prison sentence and a $5 million fine. Ironically, as part of the deal, the federal government took over the Gold Club, making it the manager of one of the largest strip clubs in the nation!

A sting or swindle involves an ongoing business scheme to cheat clients or customers. Atlanta's Gold Club was closed down after owner Steven E. Kaplan pleaded guilty to one count of racketeering. The federal government took over the strip club after Kaplan pleaded guilty and agreed to forfeit $5 million and spend three to five years in prison. The scheme involved falsely billing customers' credit cards. Perhaps Kaplan felt his victims would be too embarrassed to complain?

Kaplan and his co-conspirators were found guilty of engaging in a **sting or swindle**, a white-collar crime in which people use their institutional or business position to trick others out of their money. Offenses in this category range from fraud involving the door-to-door sale of faulty merchandise to selling bogus or counterfeit products. In 2005 the federal government announced the success of *Operation Bullpen*, aimed at stopping a major swindle in the sports memorabilia industry. Convicted in the investigation was the largest seller in the world of signed celebrity photos: Truly Unique Collectibles, who through their website made millions of dollars selling forged and fraudulent posters, photos, and items. Their celebrity-signed pictures and posters were obtained by "runners," people who happen to catch a celebrity at an event and obtain a signed picture there. Though runners may have obtained one or two signatures from famous athletes, they simply forged many more, claiming all were genuine. The investigation found that the overwhelming number of celebrity-signed photographs and posters being sold throughout the world are sold under this pretense; they are almost all forged.[19]

connections

In Chapter 12, fraud was described as a common theft offense. While these crimes are similar, common fraud involves a crime in which one person uses illegal methods to bilk another out of money, while white-collar fraud involves a person using his or her institutional or business position to reach the same goal. Common-law fraud is typically a short-term transaction whereas white-collar fraud often involves a long-term criminal conspiracy. Although the ends are similar, the means are somewhat different.

The collapse of the Bank of Credit and Commerce International (BCCI) in 1991 is probably the most costly swindle in history, costing depositors an estimated $10 billion. BCCI was the world's seventh largest private bank, with assets of about $23 billion. Investigators believe bank officials made billions of dollars in loans to confederates who had no intention of repaying them; BCCI officers also used false accounting methods to defraud depositors. Its officers helped clients, dictators Saddam Hussein and Ferdinand Marcos, launder money, finance terrorist organizations, and smuggle illegal arms. BCCI officers helped Colombian drug cartel leaders launder drug money so it could be shifted to legitimate banks.[20] After the bank was closed, in addition to the billions in lost deposits, hundreds of millions were spent to pay auditors to liquidate the bank's holdings![21] Despite the notoriety of the BCCI case, investors continue to bite at bogus investment schemes promising quick riches.

Swindling the Desperate When oil prices skyrocketed in 2003 and 2004, one enterprising swindler, Linda Stetler of the Albany, Kentucky-based Vision Oil Company, lured investors into risky schemes by claiming that God (and not geologists) guided her company's oil exploration: "God gave me a vision of three oil wells," she said in a letter sent to potential investors. State regulators found that Stetler and her company engaged in illegal practices, including inadequate disclosures of risks and selling to unsuitable investors. Vision Oil and its agents were fined by the state and ordered to pay restitution to investors.[22]

Swindlers love to target the poor and the desperate, taking advantage of their hope. Religious people are a common target. It is estimated that fake religious organizations bilk thousands of people out of $100 million per year.[23] Swindlers take in worshippers of all persuasions: Jews, Baptists, Lutherans, Catholics, Mormons, and Greek Orthodox have all fallen prey to religious swindles. How do religious swindlers operate? Some create fraudulent charitable organizations and convince devout people to contribute to their seemingly worthwhile cause. Some use religious television and radio shows to sell their products. Others place verses from the scriptures on their promotional literature to comfort hesitant investors.

Another particularly cruel swindle is to prey upon couples desperate to adopt children and use religious organizations or local ministries to conduct their scams. In one Indiana case, Victoria Farahan approached the director of a new local adoption ministry and said she could provide healthy newborns from Hospital 31 in Moscow. Couples were provided with pictures of the babies (which turned out to be pictures of Farahan's own children). Because the scam was run through a religious institution people took it at face value. Before being discovered she was able to bilk couples out $100,000. On July 17, 2006, Farahan pleaded guilty to two counts of mail fraud and five counts of wire fraud.[24]

Chiseling

Chiseling, the second category of white-collar crime, involves regularly cheating an organization, its consumers, or both. Chiselers may be individuals looking to make quick profits in their own businesses or employees of large organizations who decide to cheat on obligations to their company or its clients by doing something contrary to either the law or company policy. Chiseling can involve charging for bogus auto repairs, cheating customers on home repairs, or short-weighting (intentionally tampering with the accuracy of scales used to weigh products) in supermarkets or dairies. In one scheme, some New York City cab drivers routinely tapped the dashboards of their cabs with pens loaded with powerful magnets to zap their meters and jack up the fares.[25] In some cases, workers use their position in an organization to conduct illegal schemes or help others benefit illegally. In one recent case, racetrack tellers at Belmont, Aqueduct, and Saratoga in New York were arrested when it was discovered that they used the flow of cash through betting windows to launder money for drug dealers. The tellers exchanged more than $300,000 in small bills for large ones.[26]

Chiseling may even involve illegal use of information about company policies that have not been disclosed to the public. The secret information can be sold to speculators or used to make money in the stock market. Use of the information violates the obligation to keep company policy secret.

Professional Chiseling It is not uncommon for professionals to use their positions to chisel clients. Pharmacists have been known to alter prescriptions or substitute low-cost generic drugs for more expensive name brands.[27] In one of the most notorious cases in the nation's history, Kansas City pharmacist Robert R. Courtney was charged with fraud when it was discovered that he had been selling diluted mixtures of the cancer medications Taxol, Gemzar, Paraplatin, and Platinol, which are used to treat a variety of illnesses including pancreatic and lung cancer, advanced ovarian and breast cancer, and AIDS-related Kaposi's sarcoma. In one instance, Courtney provided a doctor with only 450 milligrams of Gemzar for a prescription that called for 1,900 mg, a transaction that netted him a profit of $779.[28] After he pleaded guilty, Courtney told authorities that his drug dilution activities were not limited to the conduct he admitted to at the time of his guilty plea. His criminal activities had actually begun in 1992 or even earlier, affected the patients of 400 doctors, involved 98,000 prescriptions, and harmed approximately 4,200 patients.[29] There is no telling how many people died or suffered serious medical complications because of Courtney's criminal conduct.

Securities Chiseling Richard Banville and Harold Howell, two Orange County, California, men, were indicted in 2005 on fraud charges stemming from their operation of a scheme that defrauded elderly and retired victims out of nearly $1.7 million. Banville and Howell operated a company called Trading West, Inc. (TWI), which solicited investments for foreign currency exchange trading. Promising huge returns on investments, they told potential investors that they were really in luck because a world-renowned trader—David Zachary of La Jolla, California—would be doing the trades. Though they promised returns of 10 percent to 40 percent per month, they failed to mention that David Zachary did not really exist. When victims asked to withdraw their monies, Banville and Howell explained that an "early withdrawal penalty" of up to 75 percent of the principal would be assessed, in order to disguise the fact that the scheme diverted victims' monies for the personal benefit of Banville and Howell.[30]

A great deal of chiseling takes place on the commodities and stock markets, where individuals engage in deceptive practices that are prohibited by federal law.[31] Some investment counselors and insurance agents will use their positions to deceive individual clients by misleading them on the quality of their investments; financial organizations cheat their clients by promoting risky investments as being iron-clad safe. Stockbrokers violate accepted practices when they engage in churning the client's account by repeated, excessive, and unnecessary buying and selling of stock.[32] Other broker fraud includes front running, in which brokers place personal orders ahead of a customer's large order to profit from the market effects of the trade, and bucketing, which is skimming customer trading profits by falsifying trade information.[33] Leading market analysts working for distinguished firms such as Salomon Smith Barney (now Smith Barney, a division of Citibank), CSFB (Credit Suisse First Boston), Morgan Stanley, Goldman Sachs, and UBS Warburg, and U.S. Bancorp Piper Jaffray (now Piper Jaffray), and the former Bear Stearns and Lehman Brothers, have been accused of providing false and misleading information in order to pump up the price of stocks to secure business for their firms.[34]

Securities chiseling can also involve using one's position of trust to profit from inside business information, referred to as insider trading. The information can then be used to buy and sell securities, giving the trader an unfair advantage over the general public, which lacks this inside information. As originally conceived, insider trading made it illegal for corporate employees with direct knowledge of market-sensitive information to use that information for their own benefit—for example, by buying stock in a company that they learn will be taken over by the larger concern for which they work. In recent years, the definition of insider trading has been expanded by federal courts to include employees of financial institutions, such as law or banking firms, who misappropriate confidential information on pending corporate actions to purchase stock or give the information to a third party so that party may buy shares in the company. Courts have ruled that such actions are deceptive and violate security trading codes.[35] In one well-known 2007 case of this sort, investigators broke up a $15 million insider trading scam that involved lawyers, registered representatives, compliance personnel, and hedge fund portfolio managers who improperly relied on hundreds of tips during five years of illegal trading. The scam involved insiders at Bear Stearns, Morgan Stanley and Co., and UBS Securities LLC who stole valuable secrets from the companies and employees at Bank of America who accepted illegal payments. This information was used to tip off the conspirators about stock upgrades and downgrades by UBS and impending corporate acquisitions involving Morgan Stanley clients, allowing them to cash in before the news hit the market. The ringleaders charged in the scheme met secretly and used disposable cell phones, secret codes, and cash kickbacks to shield their activities, which netted them each $4 million by executing profitable trades in various brokerage accounts they controlled.[36]

Individual Exploitation of Institutional Position

Another type of white-collar crime involves individuals' exploiting their power or position in organizations to take advantage of other individuals who have an interest in how that power is used. A fire inspector who demands that the owner of a restaurant pay him to be granted an operating license is exploiting his institutional position. In most cases, exploitation occurs when the victim has a clear right to expect a service, and the offender threatens to withhold the service unless an additional payment or bribe is forthcoming.

On the local and state levels, scandals commonly emerge in which liquor license board members, food inspectors, and fire inspectors are named as exploiters. A striking example of exploitation made national headlines when then–San Francisco 49ers co-owner Eddie DeBartolo, Jr., pleaded guilty to concealing an extortion plot by the former governor of Louisiana, Edwin Edwards. According to the authorities, Edwards demanded payments of $400,000 or he would use his influence to prevent DeBartolo from obtaining a license for a riverboat gambling casino.[37] Here a former politician is alleged to have used his still-considerable political clout to demand payment from a businessman desiring to engage in a legitimate business enterprise.

Exploitation can also occur in private industry. Purchasing agents in large companies often demand a piece of the action for awarding contracts to suppliers and distributors. Managing agents in some of New York City's most luxurious buildings have been convicted on charges that they routinely extorted millions of dollars from maintenance contractors and building suppliers. Building managers have been charged with steering repair and maintenance work to particular contractors in exchange for kickbacks totaling millions of dollars.[38] In one case, the FBI arrested executives of Bayship Management Inc. (BSM), one of the largest private ship management companies in the United States. In a sting operation, FBI agents created a bogus undercover marine contracting business, which did business with BSM on government contracts. BSM employees directed the undercover agents to fraudulently inflate the dollar amounts of contracts to cover the cost of bribes! Totally fraudulent contracts were issued for work that was never performed in order to entertain the BSM employees at dinners, golf outings, trips, and for cash payoffs. BSM was "charging" its subcontractors for the right to work on government jobs.[39]

Influence Peddling and Bribery

Sometimes individuals holding important institutional positions sell power, influence, and information to outsiders who have an interest in influencing or predicting the activities of the institution. Offenses within this category include government employees taking kickbacks from contractors in return for awarding them contracts they could not have won on merit, or outsiders bribing government officials, such as those in the Securities and Exchange Commission, who might sell information about future government activities.

Tom DeLay was a major player in the House of Representatives until he was forced out of politics by his involvement in a bribery scandal involving influential Washington, D.C., lobbyist Jack Abramoff. Before he decided not to run for reelection, DeLay was thought to be a target of a U.S. Department of Justice investigation focusing on Abramoff, who allegedly provided DeLay with trips, gifts, and political donations in exchange for favors to Abramoff's lobbying clients. (Clients included the government of the U.S. Commonwealth of the Northern Mariana Islands, Internet gambling services, and several Native American tribes.) Two of DeLay's former political aides, Tony Rudy and Michael Scanlon, as well as Abramoff himself, pleaded guilty in 2006 to charges relating to the investigation.

in return offered special political favors and state business in the dozen years he served in the state's top roles.[41] On January 3, 2006, influential Washington lobbyist Jack Abramoff pleaded guilty to three felony counts: conspiracy, fraud, and tax evasion for bribing public officials, including Bob Ney, a Republican congressman from Ohio. Caught up in the Abramoff scandal was House Majority Leader Tom DeLay, who announced that he was resigning his seat in Congress.[42]

Agents of the criminal justice system have also gotten caught up in official corruption, a circumstance that is particularly disturbing because society expects a higher standard of moral integrity from people empowered to uphold the law and judge their fellow citizens. Police officers have been particularly vulnerable to charges of corruption. Thirty years ago, the Knapp Commission found that police corruption in New York City was pervasive and widespread, ranging from patrol officers accepting small gratuities from local businesspeople to senior officers receiving payoffs in the thousands of dollars from gamblers and narcotics violators.[43] Despite years of effort to eradicate police corruption, instances still abound. In New York City more than 20 officers were alleged to have been patrons of prostitutes working at 335 West 39th Street and a nearby massage parlor; some officers were filmed demanding sex.[44]

One major difference distinguishes influence peddling from the previously discussed exploitation that involves forcing victims to pay for services to which they have a clear right. In contrast, influence peddlers and bribe takers use their institutional positions to grant favors and sell information to which their co-conspirators are not entitled. In sum, in crimes of institutional exploitation, the victim is threatened and forced to pay, whereas the victim of influence peddling is the organization compromised by its employees for their own interests.

Influence Peddling in Government In 2005, Representative Randy "Duke" Cunningham (R-CA) resigned from Congress after confessing to accepting $2.4 million in bribes, including a Rolls-Royce, a yacht, and a 19th-century Louis-Philippe commode. As he entered his guilty plea at a federal courthouse in San Diego, he proclaimed: "In my life, I have known great joy and great sorrow. And now I know great shame."[40]

It has become all too common for elected and appointed government officials to be forced to resign or even to be jailed for accepting bribes to use their influence. The Cunningham case is by no means unique. On April 17, 2006, former Governor George Ryan of Illinois was convicted of steering government contracts to people who were willing to give him kickbacks and bribes. The prosecution said Ryan and his family got fancy vacations, money, and other items worth at least $167,000, and

Influence Peddling in Business Politicians and government officials are not the only ones accused of bribery; business has had its share of scandals. People who hold power in a business may force those wishing to work with the company to pay them some form of bribe or gratuity to gain a contract. In the building industry, a purchasing agent may demand a kickback from contractors hoping to gain a service contract. Sometimes influence peddling can benefit both parties. In the record industry, payola is the routine practice of paying radio stations or DJs to play songs. While the recording companies are forced to pay, they also benefit from having their recording artists receive air time they might not otherwise have gotten. Some large companies have been caught in payola scandals; Sony records paid $10 million to the State of New York to settle a claim that its promoters gave gifts to radio station managers to get songs played.[45]

Business-related bribery is not unique to the United States. In some foreign countries, soliciting bribes to do business is a common, even expected, practice. In European countries, such as Italy and France, giving gifts to secure contracts is a routine practice.[46] It is common for foreign officials to solicit bribes to allow American firms to do business in their countries. In 2007 German prosecutors in Munich, along with the Securities and Exchange Commission and the Justice Department in the United States, charged employees

TYCO, ENRON, AND WORLDCOM: ENTERPRISE CRIME AT THE HIGHEST LEVELS

The Tyco Case

Tyco International Ltd. is a gigantic corporate entity that today operates in all 50 U.S. states and over 100 countries and employs more than 250,000 people. Despite its great success, the U.S. government indicted Tyco's chief executive officer L. Dennis Kozlowski and chief financial officer Marc Swartz, on a variety of fraud and larceny charges including misappropriating $170 million in company funds by hiding unauthorized bonuses and secretly forgiving loans to themselves. Kozlowski and Swartz were also accused of making more than $430 million by lying about Tyco's financial condition in order to inflate the value of their stock.

During their 2004 trial, the government tried to establish a motive by showing jurors elements of their extravagant lifestyle. Kozlowski spent more than $2 million on a party for his wife on the Italian island of Sardinia that featured a performance by singer Jimmy Buffett; young men and women dressed as Roman soldiers and maidens danced and served the guests. He also spent $15 million to furnish an $18 million Tyco-owned apartment on Fifth Avenue in New York City; his expenses included a $15,000 umbrella holder, a $2,200 gilt metal trash basket, and a $6,000 shower curtain.

The defense claimed that the two men were merely highly paid executives and that everything they received was approved by Tyco's board of directors and their accounting firm, PricewaterhouseCoopers. Because there was no stealth, there could be no embezzlement. However, on September 19, 2005, Kozlowski was convicted of looting the company of $150 million and sentenced to 8.3 to 25 years in prison.

The Enron Case

Enron Corporation, an oil and gas trading firm, was one of the largest companies in the United States before it collapsed and cost thousands of employees their life savings and millions of investors their hard-earned money.

Enron was an aggressive energy company that sought to transform itself into the world's biggest energy trader. Enron's share price collapsed when word got out that the company had been setting up shell companies and limited partnerships to conceal debts so they did not show up in the company's accounts.

In one incident, six Enron executives negotiated complex deals in which they made at least $42 million on personal investments totaling $161,000, all the while knowing that the limited partnerships they sold to retirement plans and private foundations were collapsing in value. It is also suspected that Enron engaged in sham transactions in late 2000 that drove up electricity prices in California and helped worsen the energy crisis that plagued the West for more than a year.

Enron's auditors—Arthur Andersen, a prestigious accounting firm—actually shredded key documents to keep them out of the hands of the government. One man involved in the incident, David Duncan, a former Andersen partner who was head of the team that audited Enron, agreed to serve as a government witness after pleading guilty to obstruction of justice. Duncan admitted in court that he "knowingly, intentionally, and corruptly persuaded and attempted to persuade" Andersen employees to withhold records, documents, and other objects from an investigation by the Securities and Exchange Commission (SEC).

In the aftermath of the Enron collapse, key company executives, including chief financial officer (CFO) Andrew Fastow, chief executive officer (CEO) Jeffrey Skilling, and chairman and CEO Kenneth Lay, were charged with conspiracy, securities fraud, wire fraud, bank fraud, and making false statements. Skilling and chief accounting officer Richard Causey were also charged with money laundering and conspiracy. The government claimed that Lay, Skilling, Fastow, Causey, and others oversaw a massive conspiracy to delude investors into believing that Enron was a growing company when, in fact, it was undergoing business setbacks.

The government charges indicate that between 1999 and 2001, these executives used their position of trust to engage in a wide-ranging scheme to deceive the public and the SEC about the true performance of Enron's businesses.

---

of the giant German industrial company Siemens with creating a slush fund worth about $520 million in order to make bribes to secure commercial contracts abroad.[47]

In response to these revelations, Congress passed the Foreign Corrupt Practices Act (FCPA), which makes it a criminal offense to bribe foreign officials or to make other questionable overseas payments. Violations of the FCPA draw strict penalties for both the defendant company and its officers.[48] Moreover, all fines imposed on corporate officers are paid by them, not absorbed by the company. If a domestic company violates the antibribery provisions of the FCPA, a domestic corporation can be fined up to $1 million. Company officers, employees, or stockholders who are convicted of bribery may have to serve a prison sentence of up to five years and pay a $10,000 fine.

Despite the penalties imposed by the FCPA, corporations that deal in foreign trade have continued to give bribes

Their fraud helped inflate Enron's stock price from $30 per share in early 1998 to over $80 per share in January 2001. The three allegedly orchestrated a series of accounting frauds designed to make up the shortfall between what the company actually earned and what was expected by Wall Street analysts. The government contended that even though the company was losing billions of dollars, executives continued to maintain that the company was doing great and would reach its profit targets.

What would motivate the head of one of the nation's largest companies to commit fraud? The most likely reason is greed: between 1998 and 2001, Lay received approximately $300 million from the sale of Enron stock options and restricted stock and made over $217 million in profit; he was also paid more than $19 million in salary and bonuses. More than 35 individuals were charged in connection with Enron's illegal accounting practices. Of these individuals, 23 have pleaded guilty or been convicted, including Fastow, Skilling, and former chairman and CEO Kenneth Lay (whose conviction was vacated due to his death from natural causes). Fastow was sentenced to six years in prison for his role in the accounting scandal and Skilling was sentenced to 24 years and four months in prison, the largest term handed down in connection to the case.

The WorldCom Case

WorldCom CEO Bernie Ebbers was found guilty and received a 25-year sentence for falsifying the company's financial statements by more than $9 billion; WorldCom was forced to file for the largest bankruptcy in U.S. history. One of the most important elements of the case was the more than $400 million that WorldCom loaned or guaranteed to loan Ebbers at an interest rate of 2.15 percent.

Ebbers began his career by creating the LDDS (Long Distance Discount Services), which gained many of America's largest corporations as customers for its voice and data network. He then bought IDB Company and renamed it WorldCom. Through a series of acquisitions, WorldCom became one of the largest Internet hookup and networking companies in the United States; its stock value increased 7,000 percent during the 1990s.

When the market collapsed in 2000, WorldCom was heavily in debt and hemorrhaging money. While people were being laid off, the company made its loans to Ebbers so he could hold on to his company stock, for which he had taken out loans to purchase. Then on June 25, 2002, WorldCom announced that it had illegally treated $3.8 billion in ordinary costs as capital expenditures. The bottom dropped out of the stock, creditors began to sue, and Ebbers was in no position to pay back the loans. The company admitted to overstating profits by a whopping $74.4 billion between 2000 and 2001, including at least $10.6 billion that the firm attributed to account-

ing "errors" as well as "improper" and "inappropriate" accounting. On May 15, 2005, a federal jury in New York convicted Ebbers on all nine counts on which he was charged and Ebbers was sentenced to 25 years in prison.

CRITICAL THINKING

1. Considering the various theories of criminal behavior we have discussed, how would you explain the alleged behavior of millionaire businesspeople such as Bernie Ebbers and Kenneth Lay? Are they impulsive? Do they lack "self-control"? Is there a personality deficit that can explain their behavior?

2. Should white-collar criminals be punished with a prison sentence or would society be better served if all their ill-gotten gains were confiscated?

Sources: Krysten Crawford, CNN, "Ex-WorldCom CEO Ebbers Guilty," 15 March 2006, http://money .cnn.com/2005/03/15/news/newsmakers/ebbers/ index.htm (accessed April 25, 2007); MSNBC, "Ebbers Sentenced to 25 Years in Prison, Ex-WorldCom CEO Guilty of Directing Biggest Accounting Fraud," 13 July 2005, www.msnbc .msn.com/id/8474930 (accessed April 25, 2007); Lynne W. Jeter, *Disconnected: Deceit and Betrayal at WorldCom* (New York: Wiley, 2003); Bethany McLean and Peter Elkind, *The Smartest Guys in the Room: The Amazing Rise and Scandalous Fall of Enron* (New York: Penguin, 2003); Kurt Eichenwald, "Ex-Andersen Partner Pleads Guilty in Record-Shredding," *New York Times*, 12 April 2002, p. C1; John A. Byrne, "At Enron, the Environment Was Ripe for Abuse," *BusinessWeek*, 25 February 2002, p. 12; Peter Behr and Carrie Johnson, "Govt. Expands Charges Against Enron Execs," *Washington Post*, 1 May 2003, p. 1.

to secure favorable trade agreements.[49] Schering-Plough Corporation agreed to pay a civil penalty of $500,000 for violating provisions of the FCPA when it was revealed that an employee of its Polish subsidiary made a payment to a "charitable foundation" headed by a Polish government official. The government charged that these "charitable" payments were designed to influence the official to purchase Schering-Plough's pharmaceutical products for his region's health fund.[50] Other recent cases have involved the DaimlerChrysler auto company (which was investigated after it was discovered that the firm maintained 40 offshore bank accounts used to fund the payment of bribes) and oil companies Amerada Hess, Marathon, and Chevron (because of suspicion that money given to charity in Equatorial Guinea goes directly into the hands of the ruling family in exchange for privileges).[51]

Embezzlement and Employee Fraud

Another type of white-collar crime involves individuals' use of their positions to embezzle company funds or appropriate company property for themselves. Here the company or organization that employs the criminal, rather than an outsider, is the victim of white-collar crime.

Blue-Collar Pilferage Is nothing sacred? Three employees and a friend allegedly stole moon rocks from a NASA laboratory in Houston. FBI agents arrested them after they tried to sell the contraband to an undercover agent in Orlando, Florida. The would-be seller reportedly asked $2,000 per gram for the rocks initially but later bumped the price to $8,000 per gram.[52] While the theft of moon rocks does not happen very often, systematic theft of company property by employees, or pilferage, is common.[53]

While it is difficult to estimate how much employee pilferage occurs each year, Hayes International, a loss prevention outfit, conducts an annual survey of 24 very large retail firms with over 13,000 stores doing $600 billion in sales. The most recent survey found that the number of employees involved in pilferage is on the rise and so too is the value of the merchandise being stolen. Loss prevention efforts have helped increase the amount of money recovered from dishonest employees:[54]

▪ One out of every 26 employees was apprehended for theft from their employer in a single year.

▪ Survey participants now apprehend almost 70,000 dishonest employees each year.

▪ Dollars recovered from dishonest employee apprehensions now total over $50 million each year.

▪ The average dishonest employee case value is more than $700.

Employee theft is most accurately explained by factors relevant to the work setting, such as job dissatisfaction and the workers' belief that they are being exploited by employers or supervisors; economic problems play a relatively small role in the decision to pilfer. So, although employers attribute employee fraud to economic conditions and declining personal values, workers themselves say they steal because of strain and conflict.

Management Fraud Blue-collar workers are not the only employees who commit corporate theft. Management-level fraud is also quite common. Such acts include converting company assets for personal benefit; fraudulently receiving increases in compensation (such as raises or bonuses); fraudulently increasing personal holdings of company stock; retaining one's present position within the company by manipulating accounts; and concealing unacceptable performance from stockholders.[55]

Management fraud has involved some of the nation's largest companies and richest people. The Criminological Enterprise feature "Tyco, Enron, and WorldCom: Enterprise Crime at the Highest Levels" on pages 402–403 focuses on three of the most prominent cases of recent years.

Client Fraud

Client fraud is theft by an economic client from an organization that advances credit to its clients or reimburses them for services rendered. These offenses are linked because they involve cheating an organization (such as a government agency, bank, or insurance company) with many individual clients that the organization supports financially (such as welfare clients or loan applicants), reimburses for services provided (such as an insurance company who pays health care providers), covers losses of (such as claims by insurance policyholders), or extends credit to (as the government does to a taxpayer). Included in this category are insurance fraud, bank fraud credit card fraud, fraud related to welfare and Medicare programs, and tax evasion.

Health Care Fraud It is common for doctors to violate their ethical vows and engage in fraud in obtaining patients and administering their treatment and for patients to try to scam the system for their own benefit. A recent survey of 52 insurers by the National Health Care Anti-Fraud Association (NHCAA) found that they annually recover more than $500 million as a direct result of antifraud activities. While this number is significant it is only a small fraction of the total estimated loss due to health fraud. The NHCAA estimates that of the nation's annual health care outlay, at least 3 percent—or more than $50 billion—is lost to outright fraud. Other estimates by government and law enforcement agencies place the loss as high as 10 percent of annual expenditures—or $170 billion—lost to fraud each year.[56]

A central target of medical fraud is the federal Medicaid program. The Office of Inspector General of the U.S. Department of Health and Human Services estimates that 6 percent of all Medicaid payments (more than $12 billion) should not have been paid due to erroneous billing or payment, inadequate provider documentation of services to back up the claims, and/or outright fraud.[57]

Statewide Medicaid systems have also been the target of enterprise criminals: New York State officials estimate that 10 percent of the entire program—billions of dollars—has been lost due to fraudulent practices.[58]

There are numerous health care–related schemes (see the Profiles in Crime feature). These include:

▪ Billing for services that were never rendered by using genuine patient information to fabricate entire claims or by adding to claims with charges for procedures or services that did not take place.

▪ Billing for more expensive services or procedures than were actually provided or performed, commonly known as "upcoding." This practice requires "inflation" of the patient's diagnosis code to a more serious condition consistent with the false procedure code.

▪ Performing medically unnecessary services solely for the purpose of generating insurance payments. This scheme occurs most often in nerve-conduction and other diagnostic-testing schemes. Some Southern California clinics performed unnecessary, and sometimes harmful,

WHEN THE FLU BUG BITES

Anticipating another tough flu season, some 1,100 employees at a Texas-based oil company lined up last fall to get flu shots during a company-sponsored health fair. Little did they—or their employer—know that after rolling up their sleeves, they'd be injected with water, not vaccine. And they weren't the only ones to receive the fake shots—residents of retirement communities and others in the Houston area got them, too.

It was part of an elaborate scam orchestrated over several months by Iyad Abu El Hawaa and Martha Denise Gonzales, a pair of Houston-area criminals hoping to cash in on the insurance money.

Here's how El Hawaa and Gonzales staged their ruse. First, they set up fake health care offices in three different locations, staffed them with unlicensed "medical practitioners," and hired a few unsuspecting licensed nurses to make the offices look legitimate.

Next, Gonzales used her connections from a job as a doctor's office manager to market bogus flu shots and other health care services to doctors, churches, pharmacies, retirement communities, and others in Texas, Louisiana, Ohio, and Colorado.

El Hawaa and Gonzales then ordered syringes, vials of sterilized water to serve as the fake vaccine, and other medical supplies from legitimate medical suppliers. To cover their tracks and make the vaccine appear—at least on paper—to be legitimate, they forged invoices and other documents.

The nurses hired by the pair unknowingly administered thousands of fake shots. El Hawaa and Gonzales also provided syringes prefilled with the fake vaccine to at least one doctor's office. That put the health of some unsuspecting

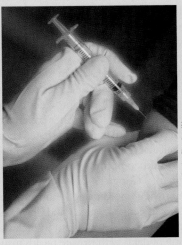

© Darren Greenwood/Design Pics, Inc./Alamy

victims at risk, since the pair frequently didn't bother to use proper hygienic methods to fill the syringes. After the shots were given, El Hawaa and Gonzales created fake medical records, submitted fraudulent claims to Medicare, Medicaid, and various insurance companies, and then sat back and waited for the insurance reimbursement checks to start rolling in.

How were they caught? One of the nurses got suspicious and called the FBI after discovering that there were no vials of vaccine and that the couple could not provide the manufacturer tracking numbers for the vaccine. As federal agents closed in, they caught El Hawaa trying to discard leftover syringes in a dumpster near his office. He and Gonzales were later convicted and sentenced to up to 10 years in prison.

Sources: FBI, "The Case of the Fake Flu Shots: Thousands Injected with Phony Vaccine," October 27, 2006, www.fbi.gov/page2/oct2006/flu_shots102706.htm (accessed April 25, 2007); American Chronicle, "Texas Man Convicted for Distributing Fake Flu Vaccine," 11 September 2006, www.americanchronicle.com/articles/viewArticle.asp?articleID=13430 (accessed April 25, 2007); Harvey Rice, "Guilty Plea Made in Flu Shot Scam: Phony Doctor Faces Prison for Administering Fake Inoculations," *Houston Chronicle*, 6 September 2006, p. 1.

---

surgeries on patients who have been recruited and paid to have these unnecessary surgeries performed.

▌ Misrepresenting noncovered treatments as medically necessary covered treatments for purposes of obtaining insurance payments. This scheme occurs in cosmetic-surgery in which noncovered cosmetic procedures such as nose jobs, tummy tucks, liposuction, or breast augmentations are billed to patients' insurers as deviated-septum repairs, hernia repairs, or lumpectomies.[59]

In addition to individual physicians, some large health care providers have been accused of routinely violating the law to obtain millions in illegal payments. In 1998 the federal government filed suit against two of the nation's largest hospital chains, Columbia/HCA Healthcare Corporation (320 hospitals) and

Quorum Health Group (250 hospitals), alleging that they routinely overstated expenses to bilk Medicare by filing false claims for reimbursement as well as paying kickbacks to doctors for referrals.[60] In 2002, HCA, the nation's largest for-profit hospital chain, pleaded guilty to defrauding government health care programs and received a combination of civil fines and criminal penalties that totaled $1.7 billion. The government has attempted to tighten control over the industry in order to restrict the opportunity for physicians to commit fraud. Health care companies providing services to federal health care programs are also regulated by federal laws that prohibit kickbacks and self-referrals. The Health Insurance Portability and Accountability Act of 1996 (HIPAA) established health care fraud as a independent federal criminal offense, with the basic crime carrying a federal prison term of up to 10 years in addition to significant financial penalties.[61] HIPAA doubles the prison term to up to 20 years should a perpetrator's fraud result in injury to a patient; if the fraud results in a patient's death, the perpetrator can be sentenced to life in federal prison. It is a crime, punishable by up to five years in prison, to provide anything of value, money or otherwise, directly or indirectly, with the intent to induce a referral of a patient or a health care service. Liability attaches to both parties in the transaction—the entity or individual providing the kickbacks and the individual receiving payment of the referral. The law also prohibits physicians and other health care providers from referring beneficiaries in federal health care programs to clinics or other facilities in which the physician or health care provider has a financial interest. It is illegal for a doctor to refer her patients to a blood-testing lab in which she has an ownership share. These practices—kickbacks and self-referrals—are prohibited under federal law because they would compromise a medical professional's independent judgment. Congress also mandated the establishment of a nationwide Coordinated Fraud and Abuse Control Program to coordinate federal, state, and local law enforcement efforts against health care fraud and to include "the coordination and sharing of data" with private health insurers.

Health care fraud is expected to continue to rise as people live longer and produce a greater demand for Medicare benefits. In the future, the utilization of long- and short-term care facilities such as skilled nursing, assisted living, and hospice services will expand substantially. Additionally, fraudulent billings and medically unnecessary services billed to health care insurers are now prevalent throughout the country and are expected to grow in the future.[62]

Bank Fraud Bank fraud can encompass such diverse schemes as check kiting, check forgery, false statements on loan applications, sale of stolen checks, bank credit card fraud, unauthorized use of automatic teller machines (ATMs), auto title fraud, and illegal transactions with offshore banks.[63] Among the schemes used to defraud banks are mortgage frauds in which a group of conspirators fraudulently obtain loans on overvalued or nonexistent property. Some of the more common schemes are set out in Exhibit 13.1.[64]

Tax Evasion Another important aspect of client fraud is tax evasion. Here the victim is the government that is cheated by one of its clients, the errant taxpayer to whom it extended credit by allowing the taxpayer to delay paying taxes on money he or she had already earned. Tax fraud is a particularly challenging area for criminological study because so many U.S. citizens regularly underreport their income, and it is often difficult to separate honest error from deliberate tax evasion.

The basic law on tax evasion is contained in the U.S. Internal Revenue Code, section 7201, which states:

> Any person who willfully attempts in any manner to evade or defeat any tax imposed by this title or the payment thereof shall, in addition to other penalties provided by law, be guilty of a felony and, upon conviction thereof, shall be fined not more than $100,000 or imprisoned not more than five years, or both, together with the costs of prosecution.

To prove tax fraud, the government must find that the taxpayer either underreported his or her income or did not report taxable income. No minimum dollar amount is stated before fraud exists, but the government can take legal action when there is a "substantial underpayment of tax." A second element of tax fraud is "willfulness" on the part of the tax evader. In the major case on this issue, willfulness was defined as a "voluntary, intentional violation of a known legal duty and not the careless disregard for the truth."[65] Finally, to prove tax fraud, the government must show that the taxpayer has purposely attempted to evade or defeat a tax payment. If the offender is guilty of passive neglect, the offense is a misdemeanor. Passive neglect means simply not paying taxes, not reporting income, or not paying taxes when due. On the other hand, affirmative tax evasion, such as keeping double books, making false entries, destroying books or records, concealing assets, or covering up sources of income, constitutes a felony.

Although tax cheating is a serious crime, the great majority of major tax cheats (in some categories, four of five cheaters) are not prosecuted because the IRS lacks the money to enforce the law.[66] Today, the IRS collects more than $2 trillion in revenue and processes more than 224 million tax returns. However, its budget amounts to only 44 cents for each $100 it collects; this is 10 percent less, after adjusting for inflation, than in 1997. In addition, because most IRS resources are devoted to processing tax returns, there is less money for audits, investigations, and collections than there was a decade ago. In 1997 the IRS conducted more than 5,000 tax fraud and other investigations while in 2006 the number dropped to less than 4,000. Not surprisingly the number of people sentenced for tax evasion and other financial crimes dropped from 3,000 to 2,000 during this span. The problem of tax fraud is significant, and honest taxpayers are forced to bear the costs, which may run into the hundreds of billions.

Corporate Crime

Yet another component of white-collar crime involves situations in which powerful institutions or their representatives willfully violate the laws that restrain these institutions from doing social harm or require them to do social good. This is also known as corporate or organizational crime.

Interest in corporate crime first emerged in the early 1900s, when a group of writers, known as muckrakers, targeted the monopolistic business practices of John D. Rockefeller, and other corporate business leaders. In a 1907 article, sociologist E. A. Ross described the "criminaloid": a business leader who while enjoying immunity from the law victimized an unsuspecting public.[67] Edwin Sutherland focused theoretical attention on corporate crime when he began his research on the subject in the 1940s; corporate crime was probably what he had in mind when he coined the phrase "white-collar crime."[68]

Corporate crimes are socially injurious acts committed by people who control companies to further their business interests. The target of their crimes can be the general public, the environment, or even company workers. What

EXHIBIT 13.1

Some Common Bank Fraud Schemes

■ *Property flipping.* Property is purchased, falsely appraised at a higher value, and then quickly sold at a higher value than the market. A home worth $200,000 may be appraised for $800,000 or higher and sold to a co-conspirator who gets a mortgage based on a phony appraisal. The new owner quickly defaults on the loan. This type of scheme typically involves one or more of the following: fraudulent appraisals, doctored loan documentation, and/or inflating buyer income. Kickbacks to buyers, investors, property/loan brokers, appraisers, or title company employees are common in this scheme.

■ *Silent second.* The buyer of a property borrows the down payment from the seller through the issuance of a nondisclosed second mortgage. The primary lender believes the borrower has invested his own money in the down payment, when in fact it is borrowed. The second mortgage may not be recorded to further conceal its status from the primary lender.

■ *Nominee loans/straw buyers.* The identity of the borrower is concealed through the use of a nominee who allows the borrower to use the nominee's name and credit history to apply for a loan.

■ *Fictitious/stolen identity.* A fictitious/stolen identity may be used on the loan application. The applicant may be involved in an identity theft scheme: the applicant's name, personal identifying information, and credit history are used without the true person's knowledge.

■ *Inflated appraisals.* A corrupt home appraiser acts in collusion with a borrower and provides a misleading appraisal report to the lender. The report inaccurately states an inflated property value.

■ *Foreclosure schemes.* The perpetrator identifies homeowners who are at risk of defaulting on loans or whose houses are already in foreclosure. Perpetrators mislead the homeowners into believing that they can save their homes in exchange for a transfer of the deed and up-front fees. The perpetrator profits from these schemes by remortgaging the property or pocketing fees paid by the homeowner.

■ *Equity skimming.* An investor may use a straw buyer, false income documents, and false credit reports to obtain a mortgage loan in the straw buyer's name. Subsequent to closing, the straw buyer signs the property over to the investor in a quit claim deed, which relinquishes all rights to the property and provides no guaranty to title. The investor does not make any mortgage payments and rents the property until foreclosure takes place several months later.

■ *Air loans.* This is a nonexistent property loan where there is usually no collateral. An example of an air loan would be where a broker invents borrowers and properties, establishes accounts for payments, and maintains custodial accounts for escrows. They may set up an office with a bank of telephones, each one used as the employer, appraiser, credit agency, etc., for verification purposes.

■ *Prime bank investment fraud.* In these schemes, victims are told that certain financial instruments (notes, letters of credit, debentures, or guarantees) have been issued by well-known institutions such as the World Bank and offer a risk-free opportunity with high rates of return. Perpetrators often claim that the unusually high rates of return and low risk are the result of a worldwide secret exchange open only to the world's largest financial institutions. Victims are often drawn into prime bank investment frauds because the criminals use sophisticated terms, legal-looking documents, and claim that the investments are insured against loss.

■ *Advanced fee schemes.* In these scams, victims are persuaded to advance relatively small sums of money in the hope of realizing a much larger gain. In securities fraud, victims are told that in order to have the opportunity to be an investor in an initial offering of a promising security, investment (business or land development), or commodity, the victim must first send funds to cover taxes or processing fees.

■ *Hedge fund fraud.* Hedge funds (HFs) are private investment partnerships that routinely accept only high wealth clients willing to invest at least hundreds of thousands of dollars. Historically, these high wealth investors were deemed "financially sophisticated," and, as a result, HFs have been unregulated and are not required to register with any federal or state regulatory agency. More recently, many middle-class investors have been exposed to HFs through ancillary investments such as pensions and endowments. There are over 8,800 HFs currently operating, with over $1.3 trillion in assets under management.

To be found guilty of bank fraud, one must knowingly execute or attempt to execute a scheme to fraudulently obtain money or property from a financial institution. A car dealer would commit bank fraud by securing loans on titles to cars it no longer owned. A real estate owner would be guilty of bank fraud if he or she obtained a false appraisal on a piece of property with the intention of obtaining a bank loan in excess of the property's real worth. Penalties for bank fraud include a maximum fine of $1 million and up to 30 years in prison.

---

makes these crimes unique is that the perpetrator is a legal fiction—a corporation—and not an individual. In reality, it is company employees or owners who commit corporate crimes and who ultimately benefit through career advancement or greater profits. For a corporation to be held criminally liable, the employee committing the crime must be acting within the scope of his employment and must have actual or apparent authority to engage in the particular act in question. **Actual authority** occurs when a corporation knowingly gives authority to an employee; **apparent authority** is satisfied if a third party, such as a customer, reasonably believes the agent has the authority to perform the act in question. Courts have ruled that actual authority may occur even when the illegal behavior is not condoned by the corporation but is nonetheless within the scope of the employee's authority.[69]

Some of the acts included within corporate crime are price fixing and illegal restraint of trade, false advertising, and the use of company practices that violate environmental protection statutes. The variety of crimes contained within this category is great, and they cause vast damage. The following subsections examine some of the most important offenses.

Illegal Restraint of Trade and Price Fixing A restraint of trade involves a contract or conspiracy designed to stifle competition, create a monopoly, artificially maintain prices, or otherwise interfere with free market competition.[70] The control of restraint of trade violations has its legal basis in the **Sherman Antitrust Act**, which subjects to criminal or civil sanctions any person "who shall make any contract or engage in any combination or conspiracy" in restraint of interstate commerce.[71] For violations of its provisions, this federal law created criminal penalties of up to three years imprisonment and $100,000 in fines for individuals and $10 million in fines for corporations.[72] The act outlaws conspiracies between corporations designed to control the marketplace.

In most instances, the act lets the presiding court judge whether corporations have conspired to "unreasonably restrain competition." However, four types of market conditions are considered so inherently anticompetitive that federal courts, through the Sherman Antitrust Act, have defined them as illegal per se, without regard to the facts or circumstances of the case:

- *Division of markets.* Firms divide a region into territories, and each firm agrees not to compete in the others' territories.

- *Tying arrangement.* A corporation requires customers of one of its services to use other services it offers. For example, it would be an illegal restraint of trade if a railroad required that companies doing business with it or supplying it with materials ship all goods they produce on trains owned by the rail line.[73]

- *Group boycott.* An organization or company boycotts retail stores that do not comply with its rules or desires.

- *Price fixing.* A conspiracy to set and control the price of a necessary commodity is considered an absolute violation of the act.

Deceptive Pricing Even the largest U.S. corporations commonly use deceptive pricing schemes when they respond to contract solicitations. Deceptive pricing occurs when contractors provide the government or other corporations with incomplete or misleading information on how much it will actually cost to fulfill the contracts on which they are bidding or use mischarges once the contracts are signed.[74] For example, defense contractors have been prosecuted for charging the government for costs incurred on work they are doing for private firms or shifting the costs on fixed-price contracts to ones in which the government reimburses the contractor for all expenses ("cost-plus" contracts). One well-known example of deceptive pricing occurred when the Lockheed Corporation withheld information that its labor costs would be lower than expected on the C-5 cargo plane. The resulting overcharges were an estimated $150 million. Although the government was able to negotiate a cheaper price for future C-5 orders, it did not demand repayment on the earlier contract. The government prosecutes approximately 100 cases of deceptive pricing in defense work each year, involving 59 percent of the nation's largest contractors.[75]

False Claims Advertising Executives in even the largest corporations sometimes face stockholders' expectations of ever-increasing company profits that seem to demand that sales be increased at any cost. At times executives respond to this challenge by making claims about their products that cannot be justified by actual performance. However, the line between clever, aggressive sales techniques and fraudulent claims is fine. It is traditional to show a product in its best light, even if that involves resorting to fantasy. It is not fraudulent to show a delivery service vehicle taking off into outer space or to imply that taking one sip of beer will make people feel they have just jumped into a freezer. However, it is illegal to knowingly and purposely advertise a product as possessing qualities that the manufacturer realizes it does not have, such as the ability to cure the common cold, grow hair, or turn senior citizens into rock stars (though some rock stars are senior citizens these days).

In 2003 the U.S. Supreme Court, in the case of *Illinois Ex Rel. Madigan v. Telemarketing Associates*, helped define the line separating illegal claims from those that are artistic hyperbole protected by free speech.[76] Telemarketing Associates, a for-profit fundraising corporation, was retained by a charity to solicit donations to aid Vietnam veterans in the state of Illinois. Though donors were told that a significant portion of the money would go to the vets, the telemarketers actually retained 85 percent of all the money collected. The Illinois attorney general filed a complaint in state court, alleging that such representations were knowingly deceptive and materially false. The telemarketers said they were exercising their First Amendment free speech rights when they made their pitch for money.

The Supreme Court disagreed and found that states may charge fraud when fundraisers make false or misleading representations designed to deceive donors about how their donations will be used. The Court held that it is false and misleading for a solicitor to fool potential donors into believing that a substantial portion of their contributions would fund specific programs or services, knowing full well that was not the case.

Worker Safety/Environmental Crimes Much attention has been paid to intentional or negligent environmental pollution caused by many large corporations. The numerous allegations in this area involve almost every aspect of U.S. business. There are many different types of environmental crimes. Some corporations have endangered the lives of their own workers by maintaining unsafe conditions in their plants and mines. It has been estimated that more than 20 million workers have been exposed to hazardous materials while on the job. Some industries have been hit particularly hard by complaints and allegations. The control of workers' safety has been the province of the Occupational Safety and Health Administration (OSHA). OSHA sets industry standards for the proper use of such chemicals as benzene, arsenic, lead, and coke. Intentional violation of OSHA standards can result in criminal penalties.

The major enforcement arm against environmental crimes is the Environmental Protection Agency, which was given full law enforcement authority in 1988. The EPA has successfully prosecuted significant violations across all major environmental statutes, including data fraud cases (for instance, private laboratories submitting false environmental data to state and federal environmental agencies); indiscriminate hazardous waste dumping that resulted in serious injuries and death; industry-wide ocean dumping by cruise ships; oil spills that caused significant damage to waterways, wetlands, and beaches; international smuggling of CFC refrigerants that damage the ozone layer and increase skin cancer risk; and illegal handling of hazardous substances such as pesticides and asbestos that exposed children, the poor, and other especially vulnerable groups to potentially serious illness.[77] Its Criminal Investigation Division (EPA CID) investigates allegations of criminal wrongdoing prohibited by various environmental statutes. Such investigations involve, but are not limited to:

- The illegal disposal of hazardous waste
- The export of hazardous waste without the permission of the receiving country
- The illegal discharge of pollutants to a water of the United States
- The removal and disposal of regulated asbestos-containing materials in a manner inconsistent with the law and regulations
- The illegal importation of certain restricted or regulated chemicals into the United States
- Tampering with a drinking water supply
- Mail fraud
- Wire fraud
- Conspiracy and money laundering relating to environmental criminal activities

Most environmental crime statutes contain overlapping civil, criminal, and administrative penalty provisions, which gives the government latitude in enforcement. Over time, Congress has elevated some violations from misdemeanors to felonies and has increased potential jail sentences and fines for those convicted.[78]

 www Go to academic.cengage.com/criminaljustice/siegel to learn more about the following topics:

- The infamous case of the **Bank of Credit and Commerce International**.
- The FCPA, **Foreign Corrupt Practices Act**, and its provisions.
- **Where to report cases of employee fraud** The National Whistleblower Center is a nonprofit educational advocacy organization that works for the enforcement of environmental laws, nuclear safety, civil rights, and government and industry accountability through the support and representation of employee whistleblowers.

THE CAUSES OF WHITE-COLLAR CRIME

Why do people get involved in risky schemes to use their institutional positions to steal money? Can the same factors that predict other types of criminal offenses also apply to crimes of criminal enterprise? After all, unlike other criminal offenses, white-collar crimes are not committed by teenagers but by otherwise respectable people, many of whom are educated and financially well off. By their very nature, white-collar crimes require that offenders attain a position of power and trust before they can be committed. Therefore, can the theories that predict and explain common-law crime be applied to white-collar crime? This section describes some of the most prominent views of why people commit crimes of criminal enterprise.

Rational Choice: Greed

When Kansas City pharmacist Robert Courtney was asked after his arrest why he substituted improper doses of drugs instead of what doctors had prescribed, he told investigators he cut the drugs' strength "out of greed."[79]

Courtney is not alone. One view of white-collar crime is that greedy people rationally choose to take shortcuts to acquire wealth, believing that the potential profits far outweigh future punishments. Most believe they will not get caught; they are far too clever to be detected by mere civil servants who work for government agencies.

Greed was rampant in the 1980s. Ivan Boesky was a famous Wall Street trader who had amassed a fortune of about $200 million by betting on corporate takeovers, a practice called *arbitrage*. In 1986, he was investigated by the Securities and Exchange Commission for insider trading. To escape serious punishment, he informed on several associates. In exchange for cooperation, Boesky received a sentence of three and a half years in prison and a $100 million fine. Released after serving two years, Boesky was barred from working in the securities business for the remainder of his life.

Caught in the web was billionaire junk bond trader Michael Milken. Indicted by a federal grand jury, Milken pleaded guilty to five securities and reporting violations and was sentenced to 10 years in prison; he served 22 months. He also paid a $200 million fine and another $400 to $800 million in settlements relating primarily to civil lawsuits.

While Boesky and Milken became the symbol of 1980s greed, the lesson of their fall was not easily learned. Billionaire domestic guru Martha Stewart was convicted in 2004 of lying to the government in an insider trading scandal. Stewart was released on March 4, 2005, from a federal women's prison in Alderson, West Virginia, after serving five months and returned to her estate in Katonah, New York, where she finished out the rest of her sentence—five months under house arrest.

Robert R. Courtney, a pharmacist who was convicted of diluting chemotherapy drugs, is a poster boy for white-collar greed. Some of his patients received medicines containing less than 1 percent of the dosages ordered by doctors. Should his acts be considered violent crimes—that is, murder—rather than white-collar enterprise crimes?

Rational Choice: Need

Greed is not the only motivation for white-collar crime; need also plays an important role. Some people turn to crime to fulfill an overwhelming financial or psychological need. Executives may tamper with company books because they feel the need to keep or improve their jobs, satisfy their egos, or support their children. Blue-collar workers may pilfer because they need to keep pace with inflation or buy a new car. Kathleen Daly's analysis of convictions in seven federal district courts indicates that many white-collar crimes involve relatively trivial amounts. Women convicted of white-collar crime typically work in lower-echelon positions, and their acts seem motivated more by economic survival than by greed and power.[80]

Even people in the upper echelons of the financial world, such as Boesky, may carry scars from an earlier needy period in their lives that can be healed only by accumulating ever-greater amounts of money. As one of Boesky's associates put it:

> I don't know what his devils were. Maybe he's greedy beyond the wildest imaginings of mere mortals like you and me. And maybe part of what drives the guy is an inherent insecurity that was operative here even after he had arrived. Maybe he never arrived.[81]

A well-known study of embezzlers by Donald Cressey illustrates the important role need plays in white-collar crime. According to Cressey, embezzlement is caused by what he calls a "nonshareable financial problem." This condition may be the result of offenders' living beyond their means, perhaps piling up gambling debts; offenders feel they cannot let anyone know about such financial problems without ruining their reputations.

Rationalization/Neutralization View

In his research on fraud, Donald Cressey found that the door to solving personal financial problems through criminal means is opened by the rationalizations people develop for white-collar crime: "Some of our most respectable citizens got their start in life by using other people's money temporarily"; "in the real estate business, there is nothing wrong about using deposits before the deal is closed"; "all people steal when they get in a tight spot."[82] Offenders use these and other rationalizations to resolve the conflict they experience over engaging in illegal behavior.

Some white-collar offenders feel free to engage in business crime because they can easily rationalize its effects. Some convince themselves that their actions are not really crimes because the acts involved do not resemble street crimes. A banker who uses his position of trust to lend his institution's assets to a company he secretly controls may see himself as a shrewd businessman, not as a criminal. A pharmacist who chisels customers on prescription drugs may rationalize her behavior by telling herself that it does not really hurt anyone. Further, some businesspeople feel justified in committing white-collar crimes because they believe government regulators do not really understand the business world or the problems of competing in the free enterprise system. Research shows that speech, occupational, and physical therapists working in hospitals, nursing homes, and with home health agencies engage in Medicaid frauds, including cutting sessions short while charging for the entire session or charging individual session rates for group therapy sessions.[83] When interviewed, the workers described using three techniques of neutralization that enabled them to defuse guilt over what they recognized as deviant practices: (1) everyone else does it, (2) it's not my fault or responsibility, and (3) no one is hurt except insurance companies and they are wealthy.

Even when caught, many white-collar criminals cannot see the error of their ways. For example, one offender who was convicted in an electrical industry price fixing conspiracy categorically denied the illegality of his actions. "We did not fix prices," he said; "I am telling you that all we did was recover costs."[84] Some white-collar criminals believe that everyone violates business laws, so it is not so bad if they do so themselves. Rationalizing greed is a common trait of white-collar criminals. Recent research (2007) by Mandeep Dhami shows that neutralization of guilt is possible because significant others give white-collar criminals support: what they did was not so bad, otherwise would they not be condemned by friends and family?[85]

Cultural View

Business culture may also influence white-collar crime. According to this view, some business organizations promote white-collar criminality in the same way that lower-class culture encourages the development of juvenile gangs and street crime. According to the corporate culture view, some business enterprises cause crime by placing excessive demands on employees while at the same time maintaining a business climate tolerant of employee deviance. New employees learn the attitudes and techniques needed to commit white-collar crime from their business peers. Under these circumstances, the attitudes of closest coworkers and the perceived attitudes of executives have a more powerful control over decision making than the attitudes of outsiders—closest friends and business professors—whose more moderate views might have tempered the decision to commit crime.[86]

Business culture may have been responsible for the collapse of Enron. A new CEO had been brought in to revitalize the company, and he wanted to become part of the "new economy" based on the Internet. Layers of management were wiped out, and hundreds of outsiders were recruited. Huge cash bonuses and stock options were granted to top performers. Young managers were given authority to make $5 million decisions without higher approval. It became common for executives to change jobs two or three times in an effort to maximize bonuses and pay. Seminars were conducted showing executives how to hide profits and avoid taxes.[87]

connections

The view that white-collar crime is a learning process is reminiscent of Edwin Sutherland's description of how gang boys learn the techniques of drug dealing and burglary from older youths through differential association. See Chapter 7 for a description of this process.

Those holding the business culture view would point to the Enron scandal as a prime example of what happens when people work in organizations in which the cultural values stress profit over fair play, government scrutiny is limited and regulators are viewed as the enemy, and senior members encourage newcomers to believe that "greed is good."

Self-Control View

In their General Theory of Crime, Travis Hirschi and Michael Gottfredson suggest that the motives that produce white-collar crimes—quick benefits with minimal effort—are the same as those that produce any other criminal behaviors.[88]

White-collar criminals have low self-control and are inclined to follow momentary impulses without considering the long-term costs of such behavior.[89] White-collar crime is relatively rare because, as a matter of course, business executives tend to hire people with self-control, thereby limiting the number of potential white-collar criminals. Hirschi and Gottfredson have collected data showing that the demographic

distribution of white-collar crime is similar to other crimes. For example, gender, race, and age ratios are the same for crimes such as embezzlement and fraud as they are for street crimes such as burglary and robbery.

WHITE-COLLAR LAW ENFORCEMENT SYSTEMS

The Commerce Clause of the U.S. Constitution gives the federal government the authority to regulate white-collar crime. Detection and enforcement are primarily in the hands of administrative departments and agencies, including the FBI, the Internal Revenue Service, the Secret Service, U.S. Customs, the Environmental Protection Agency, and the Securities and Exchange Commission.[90] The decision to pursue criminal rather than civil violations usually is based on the seriousness of the case and the perpetrator's intent, actions to conceal the violation, and prior record. Enforcement generally is reactive (generated by complaints) rather than proactive (involving ongoing investigations or the monitoring of activities). Investigations are carried out by the various federal agencies and the FBI. If criminal prosecution is called for, the case will be handled by attorneys from the criminal, tax, antitrust, and civil rights divisions of the Justice Department. If insufficient evidence is available to warrant a criminal prosecution, the case will be handled civilly or administratively by some other federal agency. The Federal Trade Commission can issue a cease and desist order in antitrust or merchandising fraud cases.

The number of state-funded technical assistance offices to help local prosecutors has increased significantly; more than 40 states offer such services. On the state and local levels, law enforcement officials have made progress in a number of areas, such as controlling consumer fraud. The Environmental Crimes Strike Force in Los Angeles County, California, is considered a model for the control of illegal dumping and pollution.[91] Some of the more common environmental offenses investigated and prosecuted by the task force include:

- The illegal transportation, treatment, storage, or disposal of hazardous waste
- Oil spills
- Fraudulent certification of automobile smog tests[92]

Nonetheless, while local agencies recognize the seriousness of enterprise-type crimes, they rarely have the funds necessary for effective enforcement.[93]

Local prosecutors pursue white-collar criminals more vigorously if they are part of a team effort involving a network of law enforcement agencies.[94] National surveys of local prosecutors find that many do not consider white-collar crimes particularly serious problems. They are more willing to prosecute cases if the offense causes substantial harm and if other agencies fail to act. Relatively few prosecutors participate in

After serving a prison stint for lying to government agents, Martha Stewart was also forced to spend five months in home confinement at her home in Katonah, New York. While some considered her punishment excessive, there are worse things than spending five months at a $16 million estate. Do you think the punishment fit the crime?

interagency task forces designed to investigate white-collar criminal activity.[95]

Controlling White-Collar Crime

In years past, it was rare for a corporate or white-collar criminal to receive a serious criminal penalty.[96] White-collar criminals are often considered nondangerous offenders because they usually are respectable older citizens who have families to support. These "pillars of the community" are not seen in the same light as a teenager who breaks into a drugstore to steal a few dollars. Their public humiliation at being caught is usually deemed punishment enough; a prison sentence seems unnecessarily cruel.

The main reason, according to legal expert Stuart Green, is that perception of white-collar crime is clouded by moral ambiguity. White-collar crimes are typically committed by society's success stories, by the rich and the powerful, and frequently have no visible victim at their root. Both the public and the justice system have had trouble distinguishing criminal fraud from mere lawful exaggeration, tax evasion from "tax avoidance," insider trading from "savvy investing," obstruction of justice from "zealous advocacy," bribery from "horse trading," and extortion from "hard bargaining."[97] Hence, white-collar criminals are treated more leniently than lower-class offenders. People who were shocked when décor diva Martha Stewart did time for some vague white-collar offense would have no problem with the jailing of a lower-class woman who had been caught possessing drugs. Even though both crimes had no discernible victim, Martha's white-collar crime seemed like the more trivial offense.

There have also been charges that efforts to control white-collar crime are biased against specific classes and races: authorities seem to be less diligent when victims are poor or minority group members or the crimes take place in minority areas. When Michael Lynch and his associates studied petroleum refineries' law violations, they found that those polluting black, Latino, and low-income communities receive smaller fines than those refineries in white and affluent communities. They also found that violations of the Clean Air Act, the Clean Water Act, and/or the Resource Conservation and Recovery Act in minority areas received much smaller fines than the same types of violations occurring in white areas ($108,563 versus $341,590).[98]

The prevailing wisdom, then, is that many white-collar criminals avoid prosecution, and those that are prosecuted receive lenient punishment. What efforts have been made to bring violators of the public trust to justice? White-collar criminal enforcement typically involves two strategies designed to control organizational deviance: compliance and deterrence.[99]

Compliance Strategies Compliance strategies aim for law conformity without the necessity of detecting, processing, or penalizing individual violators. At a minimum, they ask for cooperation and self-policing among the business community. Compliance systems attempt to create conformity by giving companies economic incentives to obey the law. They rely on administrative efforts to prevent unwanted conditions before they occur. Compliance systems depend on the threat of economic sanctions or civil penalties to control corporate violators.

One method of compliance is to set up administrative agencies to oversee business activity. The Securities and Exchange Commission regulates Wall Street activities, the Food and Drug Administration regulates drugs, cosmetics, medical devices, meats, and other foods, and the Environmental Protection Agency regulates pollution, dumping, and so on. The legislation creating these agencies usually spells out the penalties for violating regulatory standards. This approach has been used to control environmental crimes by levying heavy fines based on the quantity and quality of pollution released into the environment.[100] It is easier and less costly to be in compliance, the theory goes, than to pay costly fines and risk criminal prosecution for repeat violations. Moreover, the federal government bars people and businesses from receiving government contracts if they have engaged in repeated business law violations.

When compliance fails, and businesspeople violate the law, the institution rather than its individual employees are punished. In 2006, for example, employees of the Longley Jones real estate management company illegally removed and disposed of asbestos in 98 buildings they owned or managed. Longley Jones was charged with one count of conspiracy and seven counts of violating the Clean Air Act. The sentence: the company paid a $3,200 special assessment and a $4 million fine, $3 million of which was suspended if it cleaned up the asbestos at various Longley Jones facilities.[101] Compliance rather than punishment is the goal of the court order.

Another compliance approach is to force corporate boards to police themselves and take more oversight responsibility. In the wake of the Enron and WorldCom debacles, the federal government enacted the Sarbanes-Oxley (SOX) legislation in 2002 to combat fraud and abuse in publicly traded companies.[102] This law limits the nonaudit services auditing firms can perform for publicly traded companies in order to make sure accounting firms do not fraudulently collude with corporate officers; as well, it places greater responsibilities on boards to preserve an organization's integrity and reputation, primarily for U.S. publicly traded companies. It also penalizes any attempts to alter or falsify company records in order to delude shareholders:

> *Sec. 802(a) Whoever knowingly alters, destroys, mutilates, concealing, covers up, falsifies, or makes a false entry in any record, document, or tangible object with the intent to impede, obstruct, or influence the investigation or proper administration of any matter within the jurisdiction of any department or agency of the United States or any case filed under title 11, or in relation to or contemplation of any such matter or case, shall be fined under this title, imprisoned not more than 20 years, or both.*

In sum, compliance strategies attempt to create a marketplace incentive to obey the law. Compliance strategies avoid punishing, stigmatizing, and shaming businesspeople by focusing on the act, rather than the actor, in white-collar crime.[103]

Deterrence Strategies Some criminologists say that the punishment of white-collar crimes should include a retributive component similar to that used in common-law crimes. White-collar crimes, after all, are immoral activities that have harmed social values and deserve commensurate punishment.[104] Even the largest fines and penalties are no more than a slap on the wrist to multibillion-dollar companies. Corporations can get around economic sanctions by moving their rule-violating activities overseas, where legal controls over injurious corporate activities are lax or nonexistent.[105] They argue that the only way to limit white-collar crime is to deter potential offenders through fear of punishment.

Deterrence strategies involve detecting criminal violations, determining who is responsible, and penalizing the offenders to deter future violations.[106] Deterrence systems are oriented toward apprehending violators and punishing them rather than creating conditions that induce conformity to the law.

Deterrence strategies should work—and they have—because white-collar crime by its nature is a rational act whose perpetrators are extremely sensitive to the threat of criminal sanctions. Perceptions of detection and punishment for white-collar crimes appear to be powerful deterrents to future law violations. Although deterrence strategies may prove effective, federal agencies have traditionally been reluctant to throw corporate executives in jail. The government seeks criminal indictments in corporate violations only in "instances of outrageous conduct of undoubted illegality," such as price fixing.[107] The government has also been lenient with companies and individuals that cooperate voluntarily after an investigation has begun; leniency is not given as part of a confession or plea arrangement. Those who comply with the leniency policy are charged criminally for the activity reported.[108]

Is the Tide Turning?

Despite years of neglect, there is growing evidence that white-collar crime deterrence strategies have become normative. In one important case, Adelphia cable operator John Rigas was sentenced to 15 years in prison for bank and securities fraud and his son Timothy Rigas was sentenced to 20 after their conviction on charges that they used company funds to support their extravagant lifestyle. John Rigas took advantage of a shared line of credit with Adelphia, using the company's money—stockholder's money—for personal extravagances.[109]

This get-tough deterrence approach appears to be affecting all classes of white-collar criminals. Although many people believe affluent corporate executives usually avoid serious punishment, public displeasure with such highly publicized white-collar crimes may be producing a backlash that is resulting in more frequent use of prison sentences.[110] With the Enron scandal depriving so many people of their life savings, the general public has become educated as to the damage caused by white-collar criminals and may now consider white-collar crimes as more serious offenses than common-law theft offenses.[111]

Considering this changing vision, it is not surprising that the U.S. Department of Justice Anti-Trust Division is now vigorously pursuing increased jail time for violators as well as more punitive financial penalties. As Figure 13.2 shows, the division has significantly increased the amount of fines it has collected, from $75 million in 2002 to almost $500 million in 2006.

Some commentators now argue that the government may actually be going overboard in its efforts to punish white-collar criminals, especially for crimes that are the result of negligent business practices rather than intentional criminal conspiracy.[112] The U.S. Sentencing Commission has voted to increase penalties for high-dollar fraud and theft offenses.[113] While the Sherman Antitrust Act caps fines at $10 million, the commission's penalties are far more severe. Under these guidelines, corporations convicted of antitrust felonies may result in fines equal to the greater of twice the corporation's illegal financial gain or twice the victim's loss. Both fines and penalties have been increasing, and in one case a food company executive was sentenced to serve more than five years in prison for his

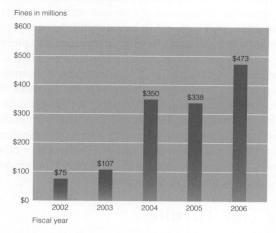

Figure 13.2 Fines in Antitrust Cases Collected by U.S. Department of Justice

Fines in millions

$600
$500
$400 $350
$300 $338
$200
$107
$100 $75
$0
    2002 2003 2004 2005 2006
    Fiscal year

$473

Source: Anti-Trust Division U.S. Department of Justice, www.usdoj.gov/atr/public/press_releases/2006/220465a.htm (accessed June 20, 2007).

role in a bid-rigging scheme; it was the longest single prison sentence ever obtained for an antitrust violation.[114]

www Since 1999, Florida's Department of Environmental Protection has fielded a multiagency Strike Force—led by the department's Division of Law Enforcement—to **investigate pollutant discharges and the release of hazardous material statewide**. Check it out at academic.cengage.com/criminaljustice/siegel.

ORGANIZED CRIME

Organized crime involves ongoing criminal enterprise groups whose ultimate purpose is personal economic gain through illegitimate means. Here a structured enterprise system is set up to continually supply consumers with merchandise and services banned by criminal law but for which a ready market exists: prostitution, pornography, gambling, and narcotics. The system may resemble a legitimate business run by an ambitious chief executive officer, his or her assistants, staff attorneys, and accountants, with thorough, efficient accounts receivable and complaint departments.[115]

Because of its secrecy, power, and fabulous wealth, a great mystique has grown up about organized crime. Its legendary leaders—Al Capone, Meyer Lansky, Lucky Luciano—have been the subjects of books and films. The famous *Godfather* films popularized and humanized organized crime figures; the media often glamorize organized crime figures.[116] Watching the exploits of Tony Soprano and his family life became a national craze.

Most citizens believe organized criminals are capable of taking over legitimate business enterprises if given the opportunity. Almost everyone is familiar with such terms as mob, underworld, Mafia, wise guys, syndicate, or Cosa Nostra,

which refer to organized crime. Although most of us have neither met nor seen members of organized crime families, we feel sure that they exist, and we fear them. This section briefly defines organized crime, reviews its history, and discusses its economic effect and control.

Characteristics of Organized Crime

A precise description of the characteristics of organized crime is difficult to formulate, but here are some of its general traits:[117]

▌ Organized crime is a conspiratorial activity, involving the coordination of numerous people in the planning and execution of illegal acts or in the pursuit of a legitimate objective by unlawful means (e.g., threatening a legitimate business to get a stake in it).

▌ It involves continuous commitment by primary members, although individuals with specialized skills may be brought in as needed. Organized crime is usually structured along hierarchical lines—a chieftain supported by close advisers, lower subordinates, and so on.

▌ Organized crime has economic gain as its primary goal, although power and status may also be motivating factors. Economic gain is achieved through maintenance of a near-monopoly on illegal goods and services, including drugs, gambling, pornography, and prostitution.

▌ Its activities are not limited to providing illicit services. They include such sophisticated activities as laundering illegal money through legitimate businesses, land fraud, and computer crime.

▌ Organized crime employs predatory tactics, such as intimidation, violence, and corruption. It appeals to greed to accomplish its objectives and preserve its gains.

▌ By experience, custom, and practice, organized crime's conspiratorial groups are usually very quick and effective in controlling and disciplining their members, associates, and victims. The individuals involved know that any deviation from the rules of the organization will evoke a prompt response from the other participants. This response may range from a reduction in rank and responsibility to a death sentence.

▌ Organized crime is not synonymous with the Mafia, which is really a common stereotype of organized crime. Although several families in the organization called the Mafia are important components of organized crime activities, they do not hold a monopoly on underworld activities.

▌ It does not include terrorists dedicated to political change. Although violent acts are a major tactic of organized crime, the use of violence does not mean that a group is part of a confederacy of organized criminals.

Activities of Organized Crime

What are the main activities of organized crime? The traditional sources of income are derived from providing illicit materials and using force to enter into and maximize profits in legitimate businesses.[118] Most organized crime income comes from narcotics distribution, loan sharking (lending money at illegal rates), and prostitution. However, additional billions come from gambling, theft rings, pornography, and other illegal enterprises. Organized criminals have infiltrated labor unions and taken control of their pension funds and dues.[119] Hijacking of shipments and cargo theft are other sources of income. Underworld figures fence high-value items and maintain international sales territories. In recent years they have branched into computer crime and other white-collar activities. Organized crime figures have also kept up with the information age by using computers and the Internet to sell illegal material such as pornography.

Organized crime figures are also involved in stock market manipulation. The FBI notes that organized crime groups target "small cap" or "micro cap" stocks, over-the-counter stocks, and other types of thinly traded stocks that can be easily manipulated and sold to elderly or inexperienced investors. The conspirators use offshore bank accounts to conceal their participation in the fraud scheme and to launder the illegal proceeds in order to avoid paying income tax.[120]

Though the mob has been diminished in size and power, it is still flourishing. Michael Coppola, a captain of the Genovese crime family, looks around the court in Somerville, New Jersey, on March 13, 2007, where he faces a first-degree murder charge in connection with the 1977 shooting of John "Johnny Coca Cola" Lardiere. Coppola was on the lam for nearly 11 years, but it now appears he was hiding in plain sight—living the life of a well-heeled gangster, maintaining apartments in New York and San Francisco, and generating income through gambling, extortion, loan sharking, and possibly murder. Authorities allege that Coppola, then a young up-and-comer in the Genovese crime family, was the triggerman who blew away Lardiere in the parking lot of the Red Bull Inn in Somerset County on Easter Sunday morning 30 years ago.

The Concept of Organized Crime

The term "organized crime" conjures up images of strong men in dark suits, machine gun–toting bodyguards, rituals of allegiance to secret organizations, professional "gangland" killings, and meetings of "family" leaders who chart the course of crime much as the board members at General Motors decide on the country's transportation needs. These images have become part of what criminologists refer to as the **alien conspiracy theory** concept of organized crime. According to this vision, organized crime is a direct offshoot of a criminal society—the **Mafia**—that first originated in Italy and Sicily and is still involved in **racketeering** in major U.S. cities. A major premise of the alien conspiracy theory is that the Mafia is centrally coordinated and the various gangs work cooperatively to settle disputes, dictate policy, and assign territory.[121]

The Mob: Cosa Nostra

To some alien conspiracy theorists, "real" organized crime is made up of a national syndicate of 25 or so Italian-dominated crime families that call themselves **Cosa Nostra**. The major families have a total membership of about 1,000 to 2,000 "made men," who have been inducted into organized crime families, and another 17,000 "associates," who are criminally involved with syndicate members. The families control crime in distinct geographic areas. New York City, the most important

organized crime area, alone contains five families—the Gambino, Columbo (formerly Profaci), Lucchese, Bonanno, and Genovese families—named after their founding "godfathers"; in contrast, Chicago contains a single mob organization called the "outfit," which also influences racketeering in such cities as Milwaukee, Kansas City, and Phoenix.[122] The families are believed to be ruled by a "commission" made up of the heads of the five New York families and bosses from Detroit, Buffalo, Chicago, and Philadelphia, which settles personal problems and jurisdictional conflicts and enforces rules that allow members to gain huge profits through the manufacture and sale of illegal goods and services.

Contemporary Organized Crime Groups

A more contemporary vision of organized crime views these groups and gangs as a loose confederation of ethnic and regional crime groups, bound together by a commonality of economic and political objectives.[123] Some of these groups are located in fixed geographical areas. Chicano crime families are found in areas with significant Latino populations, such as California and Arizona. Others are involved in national and even cross-national criminal enterprise. The Hell's Angels motorcycle club is now believed to be one of the leading distributors of narcotics in the United States. Some Italian and Cuban groups operate internationally. Some have preserved their past identity, whereas others are constantly changing organizations. There are several trends among these emerging criminal enterprise groups. First, it is more common to see criminal groups cooperate across ethnic and racial heritage lines. Also, some gangs and criminal enterprises have begun to structure their groups in a hierarchical fashion to be more competitive, and the criminal activities they engage in have become globalized. Finally, more of these criminal enterprises are engaging in white-collar crimes and are co-mingling their illegal activities with legitimate business ventures.[124] As law enforcement pressure has been put on traditional organized crime figures and Mafia dons given long prison sentences, other groups have filled the vacuum.[125]

■ Middle Eastern organized criminals, natives of Lebanon, Egypt, Syria, and other nations in the region, have been active in the United States since the 1970s. These gangs have been known to engage in automobile theft, financial fraud, money laundering, interstate transportation of stolen property, smuggling, drug trafficking, document fraud, health care fraud, identity fraud, cigarette smuggling, and the theft and redistribution of infant formula. Their enterprises rely on extensive networks of international criminal associates and can be highly sophisticated in their criminal operations.

■ Chinese criminal gangs have taken over the dominant role in New York City's heroin market from the traditional Italian-run syndicates. In the United States, Asian criminal enterprises have been identified in more than 50 metropolitan areas. They are most prevalent in Boston, Chicago, Honolulu, Las Vegas, Los Angeles, New Orleans, New York, Newark, Philadelphia, Portland, San Francisco, Seattle, and Washington, D.C.

■ African criminal enterprises have developed quickly since the 1980s and are now targeting international victims and developing criminal networks within more prosperous countries and regions. They are active in several major metropolitan areas in the United States, but are most prevalent in Atlanta, Baltimore, Chicago, Dallas, Houston, Milwaukee, Newark, New York, and Washington, D.C. Of these, Nigerian criminal enterprises are the most commonplace and operate in more than 80 other countries of the world. Engaged in money laundering, drug trafficking, and financial frauds, they specialize in delivering heroin from Southeast and Southwest Asia into Europe and the U.S. and cocaine from South America into Europe and South Africa. The associated money laundering has helped establish Nigerian criminal enterprises on every populated continent of the world.

■ Balkan criminal organizations whose members hale from Serbia, Croatia, Albania, and other nations in southeastern Europe have been active in the United States since the mid-1980s. The various Balkan groups are active in gambling, money laundering, drug trafficking, human smuggling, extortion, violent witness intimidation, robbery, attempted murder, and murder. Balkan organized crime groups have recently expanded into more sophisticated crimes including real estate fraud.

■ Eastern Europe has been the scene of a massive buildup in organized crime since the fall of the Soviet Union. Trading in illegal arms, narcotics, pornography, and prostitution, they operate a multibillion-dollar transnational crime cartel. Some of these groups prey upon women in the poorest areas of Europe—Romania, the Ukraine, Bosnia—and sell them into virtual sexual slavery. Many of these women are transported as prostitutes around the world, some ending up in the United States.

Intensive European enforcement operations conducted with American assistance have helped eliminate some of the major players in the international sex trade. However, it is estimated that 700,000 women are still transported, mostly involuntarily, over international borders each year for the sex trade. One reason for the difficulty in creating effective enforcement is the complicity of local authorities with criminal organizations.[126]

Since 1970, Russian and other eastern European groups have been operating on U.S. soil. Some groups are formed by immigrants from former satellites of the Soviet Union. The FBI established the Yugoslavian/Albanian/Croatian/Serbian (YACS) Crime Group initiative as a response to the increasing threat of criminal activity by people originating from these areas. YACS gangs focus on highly organized and specialized thefts from ATM machines in the New York City area.[127]

In addition, thousands of Russian immigrants are believed to be involved in criminal activity, primarily in Russian enclaves in New York City. Beyond extortion from immigrants, Russian organized crime groups have cooperated with Mafia families in narcotics trafficking, fencing stolen property, money laundering, and other traditional organized crime schemes.[128]

For more on the Russian mob, see the Comparative Criminology feature "Russian Organized Crime."

Controlling Organized Crime

George Vold has argued that the development of organized crime parallels early capitalist enterprises. Organized crime employs ruthless monopolistic tactics to maximize profits; it is also secretive, protective of its operations, and defensive against any outside intrusion.[129] Consequently, controlling its activities is extremely difficult.

Federal and state governments actually did little to combat organized crime until fairly recently. One of the first measures aimed directly at organized crime was the Interstate and Foreign Travel or Transportation in Aid of Racketeering Enterprises Act (Travel Act).[130] The Travel Act prohibits travel in interstate commerce or use of interstate facilities with the intent to promote, manage, establish, carry on, or facilitate an unlawful activity; it also prohibits the actual or attempted engagement in these activities. In 1970 Congress passed the Organized Crime Control Act. Title IX of the act, probably

RUSSIAN ORGANIZED CRIME

In the decade since the collapse of the Soviet Union, criminal organizations in Russia and other former Soviet republics such as the Ukraine have engaged in a variety of crimes: drugs and arms trafficking, stolen automobiles, trafficking in women and children, and money laundering. No area of the world seems immune to this menace, especially not the United States. America is the land of opportunity for unloading criminal goods and laundering dirty money.

Unlike Colombian, Italian, Mexican, or other well-known forms of organized crime, Russian organized crime is not primarily based on ethnic or family structures. Instead, Russian organized crime is based on economic necessity that was nurtured by the oppressive Soviet regime. Here, a professional criminal class developed in Soviet prisons during the Stalinist period that began in 1924—the era of the gulag. These criminals adopted behaviors, rules, values, and sanctions that bound them together in what was called the thieves' world, led by the elite *vory v zakone*, criminals who lived according to the "thieves' law." This thieves' world, and particularly the *vory*, created and maintained the bonds and climate of trust necessary for carrying out organized crime.

The following are some specific characteristics of Russian organized crime in the post-Soviet era:

▪ Russian criminals make extensive use of the state governmental apparatus to protect and promote their criminal activities. For example, most businesses in Russia—legal, quasilegal, and illegal—must operate with the protection of a *krysha* (roof). The protection is often provided by police or security officials employed outside their "official" capacities for this purpose. In other cases, officials are "silent partners" in criminal enterprises that they, in turn, protect.

▪ The criminalization of the privatization process has resulted in the massive use of state funds for criminal gain. Valuable properties are purchased through insider deals for much less than their true value and then resold for lucrative profits.

▪ Criminals have been able to directly influence the state's domestic and foreign policy to promote the interests of organized crime, either by attaining public office themselves or by buying public officials.

Beyond these particular features, organized crime in Russia shares other characteristics that are common to organized crime elsewhere in the world:

▪ Systematic use of violence, including both the threat and the use of force

▪ Hierarchical structure

▪ Limited or exclusive membership

▪ Specialization in types of crime and a division of labor

▪ Military-style discipline, with strict rules and regulations for the organization as a whole

▪ Possession of high-tech equipment, including military weapons

Threats, blackmail, and violence are used to penetrate business management and assume control of commercial enterprises or, in some instances, to fund their own enterprises with money from their criminal activities. As a result of these activities:

▪ Russia has high rates of homicide that are now more than 20 times those in western Europe and approximately three times the rates recorded in the United States. The rates more closely resemble those of a country engaged in civil war or in conflict than those of a country 10 years into a transition.

▪ Corruption and organized crime are globalized. Russian organized crime is active in Europe, Africa, Asia, and North and South America.

▪ Massive money laundering is now common. It allows Russian and foreign organized crime to flourish. In some cases, it is tied to terrorist funding.

The organized crime threat to Russia's national security is now becoming a global threat. Russian organized crime operates both on its own and in cooperation with foreign groups. The latter cooperation often comes in the form of joint money laundering ventures. Russian criminals have become involved in killings for hire in central and western Europe, Israel, Canada, and the United States.

However, in the United States, with the exception of extortion and money laundering, Russians have had little or no involvement in some of the more traditional types of organized crime, such as drug trafficking, gambling, and loan sharking. Instead, these criminal groups are extensively engaged in a broad array of frauds and scams, including health care fraud, insurance scams, stock frauds, antiquities swindles, forgery, and fuel tax evasion schemes. Recently, for example, Russians have become the main purveyors of credit card fraud in the United States. Legitimate businesses, such as the movie business and textile industry, have become targets of criminals from the former Soviet Union, and they are often used for money laundering.

CRITICAL THINKING

The influence of new immigrant groups in organized crime seems to suggest that illegal enterprise is a common practice among "new" Americans. Do you believe that there is some aspect of American culture that causes immigrants to choose a criminal lifestyle? Or does our open culture encourage criminal activities that may have been incubating in people's native lands?

Sources: Louise I. Shelley, "Crime and Corruption: Enduring Problems of Post-Soviet Development," *Demokratizatsiya* 11 (2003): 110–114; James O. Finckenauer and Yuri A. Voronin, *The Threat of Russian Organized Crime* (Washington, DC: National Institute of Justice, 2001).

its most effective measure, has been called the **Racketeer Influenced and Corrupt Organization Act (RICO)**.[131]

RICO did not create new categories of crimes but rather new categories of offenses in racketeering activity, which it defined as involvement in two or more acts prohibited by twenty-four existing federal and eight state statutes. The offenses listed in RICO include state-defined crimes (such as murder, kidnapping, gambling, arson, robbery, bribery, extortion, and narcotic violations) and federally defined crimes (such as bribery, counterfeiting, transmission of gambling information, prostitution, and mail fraud). RICO is designed to limit patterns of organized criminal activity by prohibiting involvement in acts intended to

- Derive income from racketeering or the unlawful collection of debts and use or invest such income
- Acquire through racketeering an interest in or control over any enterprise engaged in interstate or foreign commerce
- Conduct business through a pattern of racketeering
- Conspire to use racketeering as a means of making income, collecting loans, or conducting business

An individual convicted under RICO is subject to 20 years in prison and a $25,000 fine. Additionally, the accused must forfeit to the U.S. government any interest in a business in violation of RICO. These penalties are much more potent than simple conviction and imprisonment.

RICO's success has shaped the way the FBI attacks organized crime groups. They now use the **enterprise theory of investigation (ETI)** model as their standard investigative tool. Rather than investigate crimes after they are committed, under the ETI model the focus is on criminal enterprise and investigation attacks on the structure of the criminal enterprise rather than on criminal acts viewed as isolated incidents.[132] For example, a drug trafficking organization must get involved in such processes as transportation and distribution of narcotics, finance such as money laundering, and communication with clients and dealers. The ETI identifies and then targets each of these areas simultaneously, focusing on the subsystems that are considered the most vulnerable.

The Future of Organized Crime

Joseph Massino's nickname was "the Last Don." The name seemed quite apropos when in 2004 this boss of New York's Bonanno crime family was convicted on charges of murder and racketeering and ordered to pay fines of $9 million and given two consecutive life sentences. Massino's greatest sin, however, may have been violating the Mafia's rule of *omerta*, the traditional "code of silence." While in prison, Massino cooperated with prosecutors, secretly taping a conversation with family *capo* Vincent "Vinnie Gorgeous" Basciano, who was outlining a plan to kill lead prosecutor Greg Andres. Massino's current circumstances are not unique. The heads of the four other New York Mafia families—Lucchese, Colombo, Gambino, and Genovese—also have been convicted and sentenced to prison terms.[133]

The successful prosecution of Massino and other high-ranking organized crime figures are indications that the traditional organized crime syndicates are in decline. Law enforcement officials in Philadelphia, New Jersey, New England, New Orleans, Kansas City, Detroit, and Milwaukee all report that years of federal and state interventions have severely eroded the Mafia organizations in their areas.

What has caused this alleged erosion of Mafia power? First, a number of the reigning family heads are quite old, in their 80s and older, prompting some law enforcement officials to dub them "the Geritol gang."[134] A younger generation of mob leaders is stepping in to take control of the families, and they seem to lack the skill and leadership of the older bosses. In addition, active government enforcement policies have halved what the estimated mob membership was 25 years ago, and a number of the highest-ranking leaders have been imprisoned.

Additional pressure comes from newly emerging ethnic gangs that want to muscle in on traditional syndicate activities, such as drug sales and gambling. For example, Chinese Triad gangs in New York and California have been active in the drug trade, loan sharking, and labor racketeering. Other ethnic crime groups include black and Colombian drug cartels and the Sicilian Mafia, which operates independently of U.S. groups.

The Mafia has also been hurt by changing values in U.S. society. White, ethnic, inner-city neighborhoods, which were the locus of Mafia power, have been shrinking as families move to the suburbs. (It comes as no surprise that fictional character Tony Soprano lived in suburban New Jersey and his daughter went to Columbia.) Organized crime groups have consequently lost their political and social base of operations. In addition, the code of silence that protected Mafia leaders is now broken regularly by younger members who turn informer rather than face prison terms. It is also possible that their success has hurt organized crime families: younger members are better educated than their forebears and are equipped to seek their fortunes through legitimate enterprise.[135]

If traditional organized gangs are in decline, that does not mean the end of organized crime. Russian, Caribbean, and Asian gangs seem to be thriving, and there are always new opportunities for illegal practices. Law enforcement officials believe that Internet gambling sites are tempting targets for enterprise criminals. It is not surprising then that Illinois, Louisiana, Nevada, Oregon, and South Dakota have recently passed laws specifically banning Internet gambling.[136] It is unlikely, considering the demand for illegal goods and services and the emergence of newly constituted crime families, that organized criminal behavior will ever be eradicated.

www Go to academic.cengage.com/criminaljustice/siegel to:

- Learn more about *The Sopranos*.
- Read about **organized crime** and access links to informative sites.

THINKING LIKE A CRIMINOLOGIST

As a criminologist and expert on white-collar crime you are asked to help a legal defense team prepare a sentencing statement in support of Anthony J. Facciabrutto, 33, recently convicted of numerous federal charges.

In 2003, Facciabrutto was charged with mail fraud, money laundering, telemarketing fraud against the elderly, and securities fraud. Facciabrutto owned and operated Facciabrutto Holdings, Inc., a telemarketing company in the Los Angeles area, from 1994 through February 1999. Facciabrutto Holdings, Inc., raised approximately $31 million from more than 800 victims across the United States. Facciabrutto's investors received only a fraction of their total investment in the company. One victim invested in excess of $400,000 and received less than $10,000 in return.

It is alleged that Facciabrutto and the telemarketers he employed sold investments in restaurants and what were marketed as luxury resorts, which never generated profits. The telemarketing operation was, according to the indictment, a scheme where earlier investors were paid "dividend payments" derived from funds obtained from later investors.

Facciabrutto was the chief executive officer for Facciabrutto Holdings, Inc., and is alleged to have paid himself a 40 percent sales commission. Sales managers were paid 25 percent of total sales and salespersons received a 25 percent commission. Facciabrutto allegedly misrepresented sales commissions and made false guarantees to customers. Facciabrutto misrepresented the company's imminent initial public offering, which never occurred. The SEC conducted a civil investigation into Facciabrutto during 1999 and as a result, Facciabrutto was ordered to pay a $3 million judgment. This was his first offense and he claims that overwhelming personal problems drove him to commit crime. Facciabrutto had big personal debts and had borrowed heavily from organized crime figures.

 Writing Exercise Write a brief paper (200 words) explaining how, as a criminologist consulting for his attorney, you would save Facciabrutto from prison.

 Doing Research on the Web Visit academic.cengage.com/criminaljustice/siegel for information on lawyers in white-collar cases, to read an article on deterring white-collar crime, and to check out Cornell University's Legal Information page.

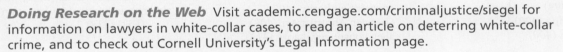

SUMMARY

- Enterprise crime involves illicit entrepreneurship and commerce.

- White-collar and organized crime are linked together because they involve entrepreneurship. Losses from enterprise crime may far outstrip any other type of crime.

- Enterprise crime involves criminal acts that twist the legal rules of commercial enterprise for criminal purposes.

- There are various types of white-collar crime. Stings and swindles involve long-term efforts to cheat people out of their money; chiseling involves regular cheating of an organization or its customers; exploitation involves coercing victims (clients) into paying for services for which they are entitled by threatening consequences if they refuse; influence peddling and bribery involve demanding payment for a service for which the payer is clearly not entitled (the victim here is the organization).

- Embezzlement and employee fraud occur when a person uses a position of trust to steal from an organization.

- Client fraud involves theft from an organization that advances credit, covers losses, or reimburses for services.

- Corporate crime involves various illegal business practices such as price fixing, restraint of trade, and false advertising.

- There are numerous explanations for white-collar crime: some offenders are motivated by greed; others offend due to personal problems.

- Corporate culture theory suggests that some businesses actually encourage employees to cheat or cut corners.

- The self-control view is that white-collar criminals are like any other law violators: impulsive people who lack self-control.

- Little has been done in the past to combat white-collar crime. Most offenders do not view themselves as criminals and therefore do not seem to be deterred by criminal statutes.

- Although thousands of white-collar criminals are prosecuted each year, their numbers are insignificant compared with the magnitude of the problem.

- The government has used various law enforcement strategies to combat white-collar crime. Some involve deterrence, which uses punishment to frighten potential abusers. Others involve economic or compliance strategies, which create economic incentives to obey the law.

- Organized crime supplies gambling, drugs, prostitutes, and pornography to the public. It is immune from prosecution because of public apathy and because of its own strong political connections.

- Organized criminals used to be "white" ethnics, but today other groups have become involved in organized crime activities. The old-line "families" are now more likely to use their criminal wealth and power to buy into legitimate businesses.

- There is debate over the control of organized crime. Some experts believe a national crime cartel controls all activities. Others view organized crime as a group of disorganized, competing gangs dedicated to extortion or to providing illegal goods and services. Efforts to control organized crime have been stepped up. The federal government has used antiracketeering statutes to arrest syndicate leaders. But as long as huge profits can be made, illegal enterprises will continue to flourish.

- CENGAGENOW™ is an easy-to-use online resource that helps you study in less time to get the grade you want—NOW. CengageNOW™ Personalized Study (a diagnostic study tool containing valuable text-specific resources) lets you focus on just what you don't know and learn more in less time to get a better grade. If your textbook does not include an access code card, you can go to www.ichapters.com to purchase CengageNOW™.

KEY TERMS

enterprise crime (396)
white-collar crime (396)
organized crime (396)
corporate crime (397)
sting or swindle (398)
chiseling (399)
insider trading (400)
exploitation (400)

influence peddling (401)
payola (401)
pilferage (404)
organizational crime (406)
actual authority (407)
apparent authority (407)
Sherman Antitrust Act (408)
alien conspiracy theory (415)

Mafia (415)
racketeering (415)
Cosa Nostra (415)
Racketeer Influenced and Corrupt
    Organization Act (RICO) (418)
enterprise theory of investigation
    (ETI) (418)

CRITICAL THINKING QUESTIONS

1. How would you punish a corporate executive whose product killed people if the executive had no knowledge that the product was potentially lethal? What if the executive did know?

2. Is organized crime inevitable as long as immigrant groups seek to become part of the American Dream?

3. Does the media glamorize organized crime? Does it paint an inaccurate picture of noble crime lords fighting to protect their families?

4. Apply traditional theories of criminal behavior to white-collar and organized crime. Which one seems to best predict why someone would engage in these behaviors?

NOTES

1. Department of Justice press release, "Five Arrested in Health Care Fraud Scheme that Collected at Least $20 Million from Medicare Program," March 21, 2006, http://losangeles.fbi.gov/dojpressrel/pressrel06/la032106usa.htm (accessed April 26, 2007).
2. John Locker and Barry Godfrey, "Ontological Boundaries and Temporal Watersheds in the Development of White-Collar Crime," *British Journal of Criminology* 46 (2006): 976–999.
3. Nikos Passas and David Nelken, "The Thin Line between Legitimate and Criminal Enterprises: Subsidy Frauds in the European

Community," *Crime, Law, and Social Change* 19 (1993): 223–243.

4. For a thorough review, see David Friedrichs, *Trusted Criminals* (Belmont, CA: Wadsworth, 1996).

5. Kitty Calavita and Henry Pontell, "Savings and Loan Fraud as Organized Crime: Toward a Conceptual Typology of Corporate Illegality," *Criminology* 31 (1993): 519–548.

6. Mark Haller, "Illegal Enterprise: A Theoretical and Historical Interpretation," *Criminology* 28 (1990): 207–235.

7. Nancy Frank and Michael Lynch, *Corporate Crime, Corporate Violence* (Albany, NY: Harrow & Heston, 1992), p. 7.

8. Edward Alsworth Ross, *Sin and Society: An Analysis of Latter-Day Iniquity* (Boston: Houghton Mifflin Company, 1907): 45–71.

9. Edwin Sutherland, *White-Collar Crime: The Uncut Version* (New Haven, CT: Yale University Press, 1983).

10. Edwin Sutherland, "White-Collar Criminality," *American Sociological Review* 5 (1940): 2–10.

11. David Weisburd and Kip Schlegel, "Returning to the Mainstream," in *White-Collar Crime Reconsidered*, eds. Kip Schlegel and David Weisburd (Boston: Northeastern University Press, 1992), pp. 352–365.

12. Ronald Kramer and Raymond Michalowski, "State-Corporate Crime," paper presented at the annual meeting of the American Society of Criminology, Baltimore, November 1990.

13. Elizabeth Moore and Michael Mills, "The Neglected Victims and Unexamined Costs of White-Collar Crime," *Crime and Delinquency* 36 (1990): 408–418.

14. National Public Survey on White Collar Crime, www.nw3c.org/research/national_public_survey.cfm (accessed April 26, 2007).

15. Natalie Taylor, "Under-Reporting of Crime against Small Business: Attitudes Towards Police and Reporting Practices," *Policing and Society* 13 (2003): 79–90.

16. Gilbert Geis, "White-Collar and Corporate Crime," in *Major Forms of Crime*, ed. Robert Meier (Beverly Hills: Sage, 1984), p. 145.

17. Marshall Clinard and Richard Quinney, *Criminal Behavior Systems: A Typology* (New York: Holt, Rinehart & Winston, 1973), p. 117; Mark Moore, "Notes Toward a National Strategy to Deal with White-Collar Crime," in *A National Strategy for Containing White-Collar Crime*, eds. Herbert Edelhertz and Charles Rogovin (Lexington, MA: Lexington Books, 1980), pp. 32–44.

18. David Firestone, "In Racketeering Trial, Well-Dressed Strip Club Takes the Stage," *New York Times*, 5 May 2001, p. 3.

19. Federal Bureau of Investigation, Operation Bullpen, www.fbi.gov/hq/cid/fc/ec/sm/smoverview.htm (accessed April 26, 2007).

20. Nikos Passas, "Structural Sources of International Crime: Policy Lessons from the BCCI Affair," *Crime, Law and Social Change* 19 (1994): 223–231.

21. Nikos Passas, "Accounting for Fraud: Auditors' Ethical Dilemmas in the BCCI Affair," in *The Ethics of Accounting and Finance*, eds. W. Michael Hoffman, Judith Brown Kamm, Robert Frederick, and Edward Petry (Westport, CT: Quorum Books, 1996), pp. 85–99.

22. Washington State Department of Financial Institutions press release, "Beware of Oil and Gas Schemes, State Securities Regulators Warn Investors, Con Artists May Seek to Exploit Fears over Mideast, Oil Supply," www.dfi.wa.gov/news/oil_gasnr.pdf (accessed April 26, 2007).

23. Earl Gottschalk, "Churchgoers Are the Prey as Scams Rise," *Wall Street Journal* 7 August 1989, p. C1.

24. FBI, "Empty Promises, Empty Cradles: Adoption Scams Bilk Victims, Break Hearts," August 28, 2006, www.fbi.gov/page2/aug06/adoptscams082806.htm (accessed March 26, 2007).

25. Associated Press, "NYC Cab Scam Warning Given," *Boston Globe*, 19 September 1997, p. 13.

26. Richard Pérez-Peña, "Indictments Charge 4 Racetrack Tellers with Laundering Money at Betting Windows," *New York Times*, 20 July 2001, p. A4.

27. Richard Quinney, "Occupational Structure and Criminal Behavior: Prescription Violation of Retail Pharmacists," *Social Problems* 11 (1963): 179–185; see also John Braithwaite, *Corporate Crime in the Pharmaceutical Industry* (London: Routledge and Kegan Paul, 1984).

28. Pam Belluck, "Prosecutors Say Greed Drove Pharmacist to Dilute Drugs" *New York Times*, 18 August 2001, p. 3.

29. Press release, April 22, 2002, Kansas City Division, Federal Bureau of Investigation.

30. U.S. Department of Justice, "Two Men Arraigned in Fraud Scheme that Cost Victims Nearly $1.7 Million," September 7, 2005, www.usdoj.gov/usao/cac/news/pr2005/126.html (accessed April 25, 2007).

31. Anish Vashista, David Johnson, and Muhtashem Choudhury, "Securities Fraud," *American Criminal Law Review* 42 (2005): 877–942.

32. James Armstrong, et al., "Securities Fraud," *American Criminal Law Review* 33 (1995): 973–1,016.

33. Scott McMurray, "Futures Pit Trader Goes to Trial," *Wall Street Journal*, 8 May 1990, p. C1; Scott McMurray, "Chicago Pits' Dazzling Growth Permitted a Free-for-All Mecca," *Wall Street Journal*, 3 August 1989, p. A4.

34. Securities and Exchange Commission press release, "Ten of Nation's Top Investment Firms Settle Enforcement Actions Involving Conflicts of Interest Between Research and Investment Banking. Historic Settlement Requires Payments of Penalties of $487.5 Million, Disgorgement of $387.5 Million, Payments of $432.5 Million to Fund Independent Research, and Payments of $80 Million to Fund Investor Education and Mandates Sweeping Structural Reforms," April 28, 2003.

35. *Carpenter v. United States* 484 U.S. 19 (1987); also see John Boland, "The SEC Trims the First Amendment," *Wall Street Journal*, 4 December 1986, p. 28.

36. The Associated Press, "Prosecutors Crack Insider-Trading Ring" *New York Times*, 2 March 2007.

37. Kevin Sack, "49ers Owner Pleads Guilty in Louisiana Casino Case," *New York Times*, 7 October 1998, p. 1.

38. Charles V. Bagli, "Kickback Investigation Extends to Middle-Class Buildings in New York," *New York Times*, 14 October 1998, p. A19.

39. Press Release, FBI National Press Office, August, 19, 1999.

40. Charles R. Babcock and Jonathan Weisman, "Congressman Admits Taking Bribes, Resigns," *Washington Post*, 29 November 2005, p. 1.

41. Monica Davey and John O'Neil, "Ex-Governor of Illinois Is Convicted on All Charges," *New York Times*, 18 April 2006, p. 1.

42. "DeLay Indicted, Steps Down as Majority Leader," *CNN*, 29 September 2005, www.cnn.com/2005/POLITICS/09/28/delay.indict/index.html (accessed April 26, 2007).

43. *The Knapp Commission Report on Police Corruption* (New York: George Braziller, 1973), pp. 1–3, 170–182.

44. David Kocieniewski and David M. Halbfinger, "New York's Most Respected Officers Led Precinct Where Sex Scandal Festered," *New York Times*, 20 July 1998, p. 1.

45. Disclosure of payments to individuals connected with broadcasts, United States Criminal Code, Title 47, Chapter 5, Subchapter V § 508.

46. Marshall Clinard and Peter Yeager, *Corporate Crime* (New York: Free Press, 1980), p. 67.

47. Carter Dougherty, "Germany Battling Rising Tide of Corporate Corruption," *New York Times*, 15 February 2007.

48. PL No. 95-213, 101-104, 91 Stat. 1494.

49. Thomas Burton, "The More Baxter Hides Its Israeli Boycott Role, the More Flak It Gets," *Wall Street Journal*, 25 April 1991, p. 1.

50. Foreign Corrupt Practices Act Update, "Schering-Plough Settles FCPA Case with SEC for Payments to Charity Headed by Government Official," http://wilmer.admin.hubbardone.com/files/tbl_s29Publications%5CFileUpload5665%5C4421%5CFCPA%2006-30-04.pdf (accessed April 26, 2007).

51. Terence O'Hara, "Chrysler Probe Reflects Trend, U.S. More Vigilant Against Domestic, Foreign Bribery," *Washington Post*, 6 August 2005, p. D01.

52. Adrian Cho, "Hey Buddy . . . Wanna Buy a Moon Rock?" *Science Now*, 7 July 2002, p. 1.

53. Charles McCaghy, *Deviant Behavior* (New York: Macmillan, 1976), p. 178.

54. Hayes International, Highlights from Jack L. Hayes International, Inc.'s 18th Annual Retail Theft Survey," www.hayesinternational.com/thft_srvys.html (accessed April 26, 2007).

55. J. Sorenson, H. Grove, and T. Sorenson, "Detecting Management Fraud: The Role of the Independent Auditor," in *White-Collar Crime, Theory and Research*, eds. G. Geis and E. Stotland (Beverly Hills: Sage, 1980), pp. 221–251.

56. National Health Care Anti-Fraud Association, "About Health Care Fraud," www.nhcaa.org/about_health_care_fraud/ (accessed March 1, 2007).

57. Ibid.

58. Michael Luo and Clifford Levy, "As Medicaid Balloons, Watchdog Force Shrinks," *New York Times*, 19 July 2005, p. A1.

59. National Health Care Anti-Fraud Association, "About Health Care Fraud."

60. Kurt Eichenwald, "Hospital Chain Cheated U.S. on Expenses, Documents Show," *New York Times*, 18 December 1997, p. B1.

61. Health Insurance Portability and Accountability Act of 1996 (HIPAA), United States Code, Title 18, Section 1347.

62. FBI, Financial Crime Report to the Public, 2005, www.fbi.gov/publications/financial/fcs_report052005/fcs_report052005.htm#c1 (accessed March 1, 2007).

63. 18 U.S.C. section 1344 (1994).

64. FBI, Financial Crime Report to the Public, 2006, www.fbi.gov/publications/financial/fcs_report052005/fcs_report052005.htm#c1 (accessed March 1, 2007).

65. *United States v. Bishop*, 412 U.S. 346 (1973).

66. David Cay Johnston, "Departing Chief Says I.R.S. Is Losing War on Tax Cheats," *New York Times*, 5 November 2002, p. 1.

67. Cited in Frank and Lynch, *Corporate Crime, Corporate Violence*, pp. 12–13.

68. Sutherland, "White-Collar Criminality," pp. 2–10.

69. Joseph S. Hall, "Corporate Criminal Liability," *American Criminal Law Review* 35 (1998): 549–560.

70. Kylie Cooper and Adrienne Dedjinou, "Antitrust Violations," *American Criminal Law Review* 42 (2005): 179–221.

71. 15 U.S.C. section 1 (1994).

72. 15 U.S.C. 1–7 (1976).

73. *Northern Pacific Railways v. United States*, 356 U.S. 1 (1958).

74. Tim Carrington, "Federal Probes of Contractors Rise for Year," *Wall Street Journal*, 23 February 1987, p. 50.

75. Ibid.

76. *Illinois Ex Rel. Madigan v. Telemarketing Associates, Inc., et al.* No. 01-1806 (2003).

77. Environmental Protection Agency, Criminal Investigation Division, www.epa.gov/compliance/criminal/index.html (accessed April 26, 2007).

78. Andrew Oliveira, Christopher Schenck, Christopher Cole, and Nicole Janes, "Environmental Crimes (Annual Survey of White Collar Crime)," *American Criminal Law Review* 42 (2005): 347–380.

79. Belluck, "Prosecutors Say Greed Drove Pharmacist to Dilute Drugs," p. 3.

80. Kathleen Daly, "Gender and Varieties of White-Collar Crime," *Criminology* 27 (1989): 769–793.

81. Quoted in Tim Metz and Michael Miller, "Boesky's Rise and Fall Illustrate a Compulsion to Profit by Getting Inside Track on Market," *Wall Street Journal*, 17 November 1986, p. 28.

82. Donald Cressey, *Other People's Money: A Study of the Social Psychology of Embezzlement* (Glencoe, IL: Free Press, 1973), p. 96.

83. Rhonda Evans and Dianne Porche, "The Nature and Frequency of Medicare/Medicaid Fraud and Neutralization Techniques among Speech, Occupational, and Physical Therapists," *Deviant Behavior* 26 (2005): 253–271.

84. Herbert Edelhertz and Charles Rogovin, eds., *A National Strategy for Containing White-Collar Crime* (Lexington, MA: Lexington Books, 1980), Appendix A, pp. 122–123.

85. Mandeep Dhami, "White-Collar Prisoners' Perceptions of Audience Reaction," *Deviant Behavior* 28 (2007): 57–77.

86. Nicole Leeper Piquero, Stephen Tibbetts, and Michael Blankenship, "Examining the Role of Differential Association and Techniques of Neutralization in Explaining Corporate Crime," *Deviant Behavior* 26 (2005): 159–188.

87. John A. Byrne, "At Enron, the Environment Was Ripe for Abuse," *BusinessWeek*, 25 February 2002, p. 14.

88. Travis Hirschi and Michael Gottfredson, "Causes of White-Collar Crime," *Criminology* 25 (1987): 949–974.

89. Michael Gottfredson and Travis Hirschi, *A General Theory of Crime* (Stanford, CA: Stanford University Press, 1990), p. 191.

90. This section relies heavily on Daniel Skoler, "White-Collar Crime and the Criminal Justice System: Problems and Challenges," in *A National Strategy for Containing White-Collar Crime*, eds. Herbert Edelhertz and Charles Rogovin (Lexington, MA: Lexington Books, 1980), pp. 57–76.

91. Theodore Hammett and Joel Epstein, *Prosecuting Environmental Crime: Los Angeles County* (Washington, DC: National Institute of Justice, 1993).

92. Information provided by Los Angeles County District Attorney's Office, April 2003.

93. Ronald Burns, Keith Whitworth, and Carol Thompson, "Assessing Law Enforcement Preparedness to Address Internet Fraud," *Journal of Criminal Justice* 32 (2004): 477–493.

94. Michael Benson, Francis Cullen, and William Maakestad, "Local Prosecutors and Corporate Crime," *Crime and Delinquency* 36 (1990): 356–372.

95. Ibid., pp. 369–370.

96. David Simon and D. Stanley Eitzen, *Elite Deviance* (Boston: Allyn & Bacon, 1982), p. 28.

97. Stuart P. Green, *Lying, Cheating, and Stealing: A Moral Theory of White Collar Crime* (London: Oxford University Press, 2006).

98. Michael Lynch, Paul Stretesky, and Ronald Burns, "Slippery Business," *Journal of Black Studies* 34 (2004): 421–440.

99. This section relies heavily on Albert Reiss, Jr., "Selecting Strategies of Social Control over Organizational Life," in *Enforcing Regulation*, eds. Keith Hawkins and John M. Thomas (Boston: Kluwer Publications, 1984), pp. 25–37.

100. John Braithwaite, "The Limits of Economism in Controlling Harmful Corporate Conduct," *Law and Society Review* 16 (1981–1982): 481–504.

101. Environmental Protection Agency, Office of Criminal Enforcement, Forensics and Training, September 30, 2006, www.epa.gov/compliance/resources/cases/criminal/highlights/2006/longleyjones.pdf (accessed March 7, 2007).

102. Sarbanes-Oxley Act, H.R. 3763-2 (2002).

103. Michael Benson, "Emotions and Adjudication: Status Degradation among White-Collar Criminals," *Justice Quarterly* 7 (1990): 515–528; John Braithwaite, *Crime, Shame, and Reintegration* (Sydney: Cambridge University Press, 1989).

104. Kip Schlegel, "Desert, Retribution and Corporate Criminality," *Justice Quarterly* 5 (1988): 615–634.

105. Raymond Michalowski and Ronald Kramer, "The Space between Laws: The Problem of Corporate Crime in a Transnational Context," *Social Problems* 34 (1987): 34–53.

106. Ibid.

107. Christopher M. Brown and Nikhil S. Singhvi, "Antitrust Violations," *American Criminal Law Review* 35 (1998): 467–501.

108. Howard Adler, "Current Trends in Criminal Antitrust Enforcement," *Business Crimes Bulletin* (April 1996): 1.

109. CNNMoney, "Adelphia Founder Sentenced to 15 Years: John and Timothy Rigas Are Sentenced to Prison Nearly a Year After Their Convictions," 20 June 2005, http://money.cnn.com/2005/06/20/news/newsmakers/rigas_sentencing/index.htm (accessed April 26, 2007).

110. David Weisburd, Elin Waring, and Stanton Wheeler, "Class, Status, and the Punishment of White-Collar Criminals," *Law and Social Inquiry* 15 (1990): 223–243.

111. Sean Rosenmerkel, "Wrongfulness and Harmfulness as Components of Seriousness of White-Collar Offenses," *Journal of Contemporary Criminal Justice* 17 (2001): 308–328.

112. Mark Cohen, "Environmental Crime and Punishment: Legal/Economic Theory and Empirical Evidence on Enforcement of Federal Environmental Statutes," *Journal of*

Criminal Law and Criminology 82 (1992): 1,054–1,109.

113. Russell Mokhiber, "White Collar Crime Penalties," *Multinational Monitor* 22 (2001): 30.

114. Jonathan Lechter, Daniel Posner, and George Morris, "Antitrust Violations," *American Criminal Law Review* 39 (2002): 225–273.

115. See generally President's Commission on Organized Crime, *Report to the President and the Attorney General, The Impact: Organized Crime Today* (Washington, DC: U.S. Government Printing Office, 1986). Herein cited as *Organized Crime Today*.

116. Frederick Martens and Michele Cunningham-Niederer, "Media Magic, Mafia Mania," *Federal Probation* 49 (1985): 60–68.

117. *Organized Crime Today*, pp. 7–8.

118. Alan Block and William Chambliss, *Organizing Crime* (New York: Elsevier, 1981).

119. Alan Block, *East Side/West Side* (New Brunswick, NJ: Transaction Books, 1983), pp. vii, 10–11.

120. Statement for the record of Thomas V. Fuentes, Chief, Organized Crime Section, Criminal Investigative Division, Federal Bureau of Investigation, "Organized Crime before the House Subcommittee on Finance and Hazardous Materials." September 13, 2000.

121. Donald Cressey, *Theft of the Nation* (New York: Harper & Row, 1969).

122. Stanley Einstein, and Menachem Amir, *Organized Crime: Uncertainties and Dilemmas* (Chicago: University of Illinois at Chicago, Office of International Criminal Justice, 1999); William Kleinknecht, *The New Ethnic Mobs: The Changing Face of Organized Crime in America* (New York: Free Press, 1996); Don Liddick, *An Empirical, Theoretical, and Historical Overview of Organized Crime* (Lewiston, NY: Edwin Mellen Press, 1999); Maria Minniti, "Membership Has Its Privileges: Old and New Mafia Organizations," *Comparative Economic Studies* 37 (1995): 31–47.

123. *Organized Crime Today*, p. 11.

124. FBI, "Organized Crime Today," February 20, 2007, www.fbi.gov/page2/feb07/orgcrime022007.htm (accessed April 26, 2007).

125. Ibid.

126. David Binder, "In Europe, Sex Slavery Is Thriving Despite Raids," *New York Times*, 19 October 2002, p. A3.

127. Richard A. Ballezza, "YACS Crime Groups: An FBI Major Crime Initiative," *FBI Law Enforcement Bulletin* 67 (1998): 7–13.

128. Omar Bartos, "Growth of Russian Organized Crime Poses Serious Threat," *CJ International* 11 (1995): 8–9.

129. George Vold, *Theoretical Criminology*, 2nd ed., rev. Thomas Bernard (New York: Oxford University Press, 1979).

130. 18 U.S.C. 1952 (1976).

131. PL 91-452, Title IX, 84 Stat. 922 (1970) (codified at 18 U.S.C. 1961–68, 1976).

132. Richard McFeely, "Enterprise Theory of Investigation," *FBI Law Enforcement Bulletin* 70 (2001): 19–26.

133. National Legal Policy Center, "Bonanno Crime Boss Gets Two Life Terms," August 17, 2005, www.nlpc.org/view.asp?action=viewArticle&aid=975 (accessed April 26, 2007).

134. Selwyn Raab, "A Battered and Ailing Mafia Is Losing Its Grip on America," *New York Times*, 22 October 1990, p. 1.

135. Ibid., p. B7.

136. Rebecca Porter, "Prosecutors, Plaintiffs Aim to Curb Internet Gambling," *Trial* 40 (August 2004): 14.

Public Order Crime: Sex and Substance Abuse

The tastefully crafted Emperor's Club VIP website stated, "Our goal is to make life more peaceful, balanced, beautiful, and meaningful. We honor commitment to our clients as we covet long-term relationships of trust and mutual benefit. Experience for yourself a service of obvious distinction." It provided its "members" with the companionship of young, beautiful women for "total relaxation massage, entertainment purposes, modeling, or private dancing." Site viewers also learned, "We specialize in introductions of: fashion models, pageant winners and exquisite students, graduates and women of successful careers (finance, art, media, etc.) to gentlemen of exceptional standards"; the site proudly proclaimed that its escorts were primed to "make your dreams come true." The site also showed hourly rates based on how many diamonds the young woman deserved: A seven-diamond companion cost more than $3,000 an hour or $31,000 per day.

The Emperor's Club was a high-priced call girl ring. One of the young women, known professionally as "Kristin," was actually 22-year-old Ashley Dupré. Rather than being a highly educated fashion model or career woman, Ashley was a high school drop-out who, after completing her sophomore year in high school, had run away from an abusive home. Ashley knew what it was like to be broke, homeless, and in need of money. She claimed that she became a prostitute because her dream of a singing career hadn't gotten off the ground. Ashley Dupré may have remained an unknown and anonymous "working girl" had it not been for a federal investigation of one of her clients, New York's hard-charging governor Eliot Spitzer, who at one time was considered a future presidential candidate. Known in the club as Client #9, Spitzer had paid $80,000 for services rendered. When a federal investigation uncovered his involvement with the Emperor's Club, the scandal rocked the nation and Spitzer was forced to resign in disgrace.[1]

Societies have long banned or limited behaviors believed to run contrary to social norms, customs, and values. These behaviors are often referred to as public order crimes or victimless crimes, although the latter term can be misleading.[2] Public order crimes involve acts that interfere with the operations of society and the ability of people to function efficiently. Put another way, whereas common-law crimes such as rape or robbery are banned because they cause social harm, other behaviors are outlawed simply because they conflict with social policy, prevailing moral rules, and current public opinion.

Statutes designed to uphold public order usually prohibit the manufacture and distribution of morally questionable goods and services such as erotic material, commercial sex, and mood-altering drugs. They may also ban acts that a few people holding political power consider morally tinged, such as underage drinking. Statutes like these are controversial in part because millions of otherwise law-abiding citizens often engage in these outlawed activities and consequently become criminals. These statutes are also controversial because they selectively prohibit desired goods, services, and behaviors; in other words, they outlaw sin and vice.

This chapter first briefly discusses the relationship between law and morality. Next the chapter addresses public order crimes of a sexual nature: paraphilias, prostitution, and pornography. The chapter concludes by focusing on the abuse of drugs and alcohol.

LAW AND MORALITY

Legislation of moral issues has continually frustrated lawmakers because many of their constituents see little harm in visiting a prostitute or smoking some pot. When a store is robbed or a child assaulted, it is easy to identify the victim and condemn the harm done. It is, however, more difficult to sympathize with or even identify the victims of immoral acts, such as pornography or prostitution, where the parties involved may be willing participants. Some of the "service providers" in the Emperor's Club were paid more for a few days' work than a waitress or teacher makes in a year. The highly paid "models" seemed quite willing to ply their trade. Can we consider them victims? People who employed these women, such as Governor Spitzer, were wealthy and powerful men who freely and voluntarily spent their money for sexual services. Certainly they were not the victim here. If there is no victim, can there be a crime?

To answer this question, we might first consider whether there is actually a victim in so-called victimless crimes. While some young women such as the Emperor's Club's "Kristin" may have voluntarily engaged in highly paid sex work, others have been coerced and forced into the sex trade; they are therefore its victims. Research on prostitution shows that many young runaways and abandoned children are coerced into a life on the streets, where they are cruelly treated and held as virtual captives.[3] It has been estimated that women involved in street prostitution are 60 to 100 times more likely to be murdered than the average woman and that most murders are the result of a dispute over money rather than being sexually motivated.[4] Clearly prostitution carries with it significant professional risk.

Other sexually related offenses, such as pornography, may involve people who voluntarily perform in adult films. But as critics such as Andrea Dworkin point out, women involved in adult films, far from being highly paid stars, are "dehumanized—turned into objects and commodities."[5]

Even if public order crimes do not actually harm their participants, perhaps society as a whole should be considered the victim of these crimes. Is the community harmed when an adult bookstore opens or a brothel is established? Does this signal that a neighborhood is in decline? Does it teach children that deviance is both tolerated and profitable? If women are degraded and sexualized in adult sex films, does that send a message that it is acceptable to demean and/or harm women?

Debating Morality

On February 17, 2006, the front page of the *Dallas Morning News* announced, "Candidate Worked as Prostitute."[6] It seems that Tom Malin, who was campaigning for the District 108 seat in the Texas House of Representatives as an openly gay candidate, had worked as a male escort.[7] Ahead in the race before the story broke, he lost the primary 55 percent to 45 percent. In the aftermath, *The Advocate*, a national gay and lesbian newsmagazine, issued the following statement:

> *Even among many gays and lesbians—and certainly in mainstream culture—sex for pay remains the irredeemable sin. The president can be a recovering alcoholic with a DUI arrest; the vice president can accidentally shoot a man—all is forgiven. But if a person takes money for sex, the taint may be inescapable. Forget about running for office. Forget about a high-profile business career. Forget about acting, modeling, or MTV. It's over. Even many gays will prefer that you take a hike.*

Tom Malin's experience illustrates the concern the public and the media have with issues of morality and values. It is ironic that Malin could be a successful candidate for public office as an openly gay man, something that would have been unthinkable 50 years ago, yet his career was destroyed by his involvement in sex for hire. Although one act considered a violation of social norms only a few years ago is now considered routine and unremarkable, another is still prohibited and shunned by "polite society." Who decides what is acceptable behavior and what is not, and how we distinguish between them, are still matters of great concern to criminologists.

Some scholars argue that acts such as pornography, prostitution, and drug use erode the moral fabric of society and therefore should be prohibited and punished. They are crimes, according to the great legal scholar Morris Cohen, because "it is one of the functions of the criminal law to give expression to the collective feeling of revulsion toward certain acts, even when they are not very dangerous."[8] In his classic statement on the function of morality in the law, legal scholar Sir Patrick Devlin states,

> *Without shared ideas on politics, morals, and ethics no society can exist. . . . If men and women try to create a society in which there is no fundamental agreement about good and evil, they will fail; if having based it on common agreement, the agreement goes, the society will disintegrate. For*

society is not something that is kept together physically; it is held by the invisible bonds of common thought. If the bonds were too far relaxed, the members would drift apart. A common morality is part of the bondage. The bondage is part of the price of society; and mankind, which needs society, must pay its price.[9]

According to this view, so-called victimless crimes are prohibited because one of the functions of criminal law is to express a shared sense of public morality.[10]

Some influential legal scholars have questioned the propriety of legislating morals. H. L. A. Hart states,

It is fatally easy to confuse the democratic principle that power should be in the hands of the majority with the utterly different claim that the majority, with power in their hands, need respect no limits. Certainly there is a special risk in a democracy that the majority may dictate how all should live.[11]

Hart may be motivated by the fact that defining morality may be an impossible task: Who defines morality? Are we not punishing differences rather than social harm? As U.S. Supreme Court Justice William O. Douglas once so succinctly put it, "What may be trash to me may be prized by others."[12] After all, many of the great works of Western art depict nude males and females, some quite young. Are the paintings of Rubens or the sculpture of Michelangelo obscene? The United States Department of Justice spent $8,000 of taxpayers' money on blue drapes to cover two giant, aluminum, art deco statues that had been displayed in its Hall of Justice for more than 70 years. The female statue that represents the Spirit of Justice has its arms raised and a toga draped over its body, but a single breast is completely exposed. The other statue, of a man with a cloth covering his midsection, is called the Majesty of Law. Are these innocent works of art or obscene images that had to be covered to protect the modesty of Justice Department attorneys?[13] You be the judge!

Joseph Gusfield argues that the purpose of outlawing immoral acts is to show the moral superiority of those who condemn the acts over those who partake of them. The legislation of morality "enhances the social status of groups carrying the affirmed culture and degrades groups carrying that which is condemned as deviant."[14] Research indicates that people who define themselves as liberals are also the most tolerant of sexually explicit material. Demographic attributes such as age, educational attainment, and occupational status may also influence views of pornography: the young and better educated tend to be more tolerant than older, less-educated people.[15] Whose views should prevail?

Majority Rule? If a majority of the population chooses to engage in what might objectively be considered immoral or deviant behavior, would it be fair or just to prohibit or control such behavior or render it criminal? According to Hitwise, an Internet monitoring corporation, online porn sites get about three times more visits than the top three web search engines, including Google, Yahoo!, and MSN Search. Adult websites now account for about 20 percent of all Internet visits by

In 2002, the United States Department of Justice spent $8,000 of taxpayers' money on blue drapes to cover the statue of the Spirit of Justice so that former U.S. Attorney General John Ashcroft would not have to appear in public with a semi-nude statue towering above him. Is the statue art or obscenity? Would you have the statue covered? Might there have better things to spend the money on?

U.S. users. Should all obscenity and pornography be legalized if so many people are active users and wish to enjoy its content?[16] And if the law tried to define or limit objectionable material, might it not eventually inhibit free speech and political dissent? Not so, according to social commentator Irving Kristol:

If we start censoring pornography and obscenity, shall we not inevitably end up censoring political opinion? A lot of people seem to think this would be the case—which only shows the power of doctrinaire thinking over reality. We had censorship of pornography and obscenity for 150 years, until almost yesterday, and I am not aware that freedom of opinion in this country was in any way diminished as a consequence of this fact.[17]

Culture Conflicts Cultural clashes may ensue when behavior that is considered normative in one society is deplored by those living in another. For example, Amnesty International estimates that more than 135 million of the world's women have undergone genital mutilation.[18] Custom and tradition are by far the most frequently cited reasons for mutilation, and it is often carried out in a ritual during which the young woman is initiated into adulthood.[19] The surgery is done to ensure virginity, remove sexual sensation, and render the females suitable for marriage; a girl in these societies cannot be considered an adult unless she has undergone genital mutilation. Critics of this practice, led by American author Alice Walker (*The Color Purple*), consider the procedure mutilation and torture; others argue that this ancient custom should be left to the discretion of the indigenous people who consider it part of their culture. "Torture," counters Walker, "is not culture." Can an outsider define the morality of another culture?[20] Amnesty International and the United Nations have worked to end the practice. Because of outside pressure, several African nations south of the Sahara have now instituted bans that are enforced with fines and jail terms. The procedure is now forbidden in Senegal, Egypt, Burkina Faso, the Central African Republic, Djibouti, Ghana, Guinea, and Togo. Other countries, among them Uganda, discourage it. In North Africa, the Egyptian Supreme Court upheld a ban on the practice and also ruled it had no place in Islam.[21] Despite these efforts, thousands of girls are still subject to female circumcision every day in Africa and the Middle East and in Muslim areas all over the world.

Social Harm

Most societies have long banned or limited behaviors that are believed to run contrary to social norms, customs, and values. However, many acts that most of us deem highly immoral and objectionable are not in fact criminal. There is no law against lust, gluttony, avarice, sloth, envy, pride, or anger, although they are considered the *seven deadly sins*. Nor is it a crime in most jurisdictions to ignore the pleas of a drowning person, even though such callous behavior is quite immoral. How then do we distinguish between acts that are criminal and outlawed and those that are merely objectionable but tolerated and legal?

In our society, immoral acts can be distinguished from crimes on the basis of the social harm they cause. Acts that are believed to be extremely harmful to the general public are usually outlawed; those that may only harm the actor are more likely to be tolerated. Yet even this perspective does not always hold sway. Some acts that cause enormous amounts of social harm are perfectly legal. It is well documented that the consumption of tobacco and alcohol is extremely harmful, but these products remain legal to produce and sell; manufacturers continue to sell sports cars and motorcycles that can accelerate to more than 100 mph, but the legal speed limit is usually 65 mph. More people die each year from food-, alcohol-, tobacco-, and auto-related deaths than from all illegal drugs combined. Should drugs be legalized and fast food and fast cars outlawed?

Moral Crusades and Crusaders

In the early West, vigilance committees were set up in San Francisco and other boom towns to pursue cattle rustlers and stagecoach robbers and to dissuade undesirables from moving in. These vigilantes held a strict standard of morality that, when they caught their prey, resulted in sure and swift justice.

The avenging vigilante has remained part of popular culture. Fictional do-gooders who take it on themselves to enforce the law, battle evil, and personally deal with those whom they consider immoral have become enmeshed in the public consciousness. From the Lone Ranger to Spiderman, the righteous vigilante is expected to go on moral crusades without any authorization from legal authorities. Who actually told Spiderman he could destroy half of New York while fighting Dr. Octopus or the Green Goblin? And what about the Justice League? What gives the Martian Manhunter, Wonder Woman, Plastic Man, and their superhero colleagues the right to fight crime in America? The assumption that it is okay to take matters into your own hands if the cause is right and the target is immoral is not lost on the younger generation. Gang boys sometimes take on the street identity of "Batman" or "Superman" so they can battle their rivals with impunity.

Fictional characters are not the only ones who take it upon themselves to fight for moral decency; members of special interest groups are also ready to do battle.[22] During the 1930s, Harry Anslinger, then head of the Federal Bureau of Narcotics, used magazine articles, public appearances, and public testimony to sway public opinion about the dangers of marijuana, which until that time was legal to use and possess.[23] In testimony before the House Ways and Means Committee, considering passage of the Marijuana Tax Act of 1937, Anslinger stated:

> In Florida a 21-year-old boy under the influence of this drug killed his parents and his brothers and sisters. The evidence showed that he had smoked marihuana. In Chicago recently two boys murdered a policeman while under the influence of marihuana. Not long ago we found a 15-year-old boy going insane because, the doctor told the enforcement officers, he thought the boy was smoking marihuana cigarettes. They traced the sale to some man who had been growing marihuana and selling it to these boys all under 15 years of age, on a playground there.[24]

As a result of Anslinger's efforts, a deviant behavior—marijuana use—became a criminal behavior, and previously law-abiding citizens were defined as criminal offenders.

Moral Crusades Today Moral crusades are sometimes designed to draw a bright line between behaviors that are considered morally acceptable and those that right-thinking people would consider deviant and unacceptable. Today, popular targets of moral crusaders are abortion clinics, pornographers, gun dealers, and despoilers of the environment.

Of course, what is right and moral is often in the eye of the beholder. Take for instance the 2004 incident in which shock jock Howard Stern was fined by the Federal Communications Commission (FCC) for "repeated, graphic, and explicit sexual descriptions that were pandering, titillating, or used to shock the audience."[25] The government action prompted the Clear Channel Communications Company to drop Stern's show from their stations. In retaliation, Stern posted on his website transcripts from the *Oprah Winfrey* TV show that used very similar language but was deemed inoffensive by government regulators. Stern was so outraged by the crusade to censor his program that he left public broadcasting for unregulated satellite radio.

In their efforts to protect society, moral crusaders may sometimes engage in illegal and immoral conduct. Abortion foes have resorted to violence and murder to rid the nation of pro-choice health care providers whom they consider immoral, while failing to realize the depravity of their own extreme acts. Some moral crusaders justify their actions by claiming that the very structure of our institutions and beliefs are in danger because of immorality. Andrea Friedman's analysis of antiobscenity campaigns during the cold war era (post–World War II) found that the politics of the times led to images of aggressive or even violent males in comic books and pornography. Moral crusaders argued that this depiction was threatening to family values, which led them to advocate a ban on violent comics and porn magazines.[26]

Opposing the Crusaders In some cases moral crusaders are opposed by organizations committed to stopping their efforts and blunting their "moral crusade." One of these "moral crusades" focuses attention on the gay lifestyle, with the goal of preventing states from legalizing gay marriage and the passage of a constitutional amendment declaring that marriage is between one man and one woman. Their efforts led to passage of the Defense of Marriage Act in 1996, which defined marriage as a union of one man and one woman for the purposes of federal law and preventing the federal government from recognizing same-sex marriages.[27] In return, gay activist groups have campaigned for increasing rights for gay men and women. One important victory occurred in 2003 when the U.S. Supreme Court delivered a historic decision in *Lawrence* v. *Texas*, which made it impermissible for states to criminalize oral and anal sex and all other forms of intercourse that are not heterosexual under statutes prohibiting sodomy, deviant sexuality, or buggery.[28] The *Lawrence* case involved two gay men who had been arrested in 1998 for having sex in the privacy of their Houston home. In overturning their convictions, the Court said this:

> *Although the laws involved . . . here . . . do not more than prohibit a particular sexual act, their penalties and purposes have more far-reaching consequences, touching upon the most private human conduct, sexual behavior, and in the most private of places, the home. They seek to control a personal relationship that, whether or not entitled to formal recognition in the law, is within the liberty of persons to choose without being punished as criminals. The liberty protected by the Constitution allows homosexual persons the right to choose to enter upon relationships in the confines of their homes and their own private lives and still retain their dignity as free persons.*

As a result of the decision, all sodomy laws in the United States are now unconstitutional and unenforceable; acts that were once a crime are now legal. This decision has paved the way for states to rethink their marriage laws. While a majority still ban same-sex marriages, in 2003 Massachusetts's highest court ruled that same-sex couples are legally entitled to wed under the state constitution, and that the state may not "deny the protections, benefits, and obligations conferred by civil marriage to two individuals of the same sex who wish to marry."[29] Connecticut followed suit and legalized same sex marriages in 2008. A number of other states, including New Hampshire, have created legal unions that, while not called marriage, offer all the rights and responsibilities of marriage under state law to same-sex couples.

The debate over gay marriage rages on: Is it fair to prevent one group of loyal tax-paying American citizens from engaging in a behavior that is allowed others who do not share that status or orientation? Are there objective standards of morality or should society respect people's differences? How far should the law go in curbing human behaviors that do not cause social harm? Who controls the law

Moral crusaders wish to shape the law so that it conforms to their personal values and moral beliefs. Here protesters against same-sex marriage circle City Hall in San Francisco, California, on June 16, 2008. Their efforts convinced voters in the November 4, 2008 election to vote for an amendment to the state constitution limiting marriage to heterosexuals only.

© AP Images/Eric Risberg

and should the law be applied to shape morality? Moral crusades such as the one concerning gay marriage and lifestyle sometimes result in the criminalization of acts that crusaders believe threaten the moral fabric of society, present a social harm, and are a danger to the public order. The public order crimes discussed in this chapter are divided into two broad areas. The first relates to what conventional society considers deviant sexual practices: paraphilias, prostitution, and pornography. The second area concerns the use of substances that have been outlawed or controlled because of the alleged harm they cause: drugs and alcohol.

SEXUALLY RELATED OFFENSES

In 2001, the state of Connecticut was rocked when Waterbury Mayor Philip Giordano, a married father of three, was arrested for engaging in sexual relations with minors as young as 9 years old. Giordano was a highly respected officeholder who had been the Republican candidate for the U.S. Senate in the 2000 campaign (he lost to incumbent Joseph Lieberman). During an FBI investigation into city corruption, a 17-year-old girl came forward and charged that Giordano had paid her to have sex with him in his private law office and to watch him have sex with her aunt, Guitana Jones. The teenager told state officials that from the time she was 12, Jones arranged for her to have paid sexual encounters with men (including the mayor); Jones's own daughter, only 8 years old, was also involved.[30] On March 25, 2003, a federal jury convicted Giordano of violating the civil rights of the two young girls. He was also found guilty of conspiracy and of using an interstate device—a cell phone—to arrange the meetings with the girls and received a sentence of 37 years in federal prison.[31]

The Giordano case is particularly shocking because it involves a high public official. And although it is unusual for its sordidness, it is not unique or uncommon. A recent multinational survey concluded that each year in the United States 325,000 children are subjected to some form of sexual exploitation, which includes sexual abuse, prostitution, use in pornography, and molestation by adults.[32] Because of these alarming statistics and also because some sexual practices are believed to cause social harm, some elements of sexual conduct have been made illegal in the United States and abroad.

PARAPHILIAS

In recent years, the archdiocese of Boston has been shaken by allegations that a significant number of its priests have engaged in sexual relations with minor children. Cardinal Bernard Law was forced to step down as leader of the diocese. Numerous churches were closed or sold to help raise money for legal fees and victim compensation. Among the most notorious offenders was Father James Porter, accused of molesting at least 125 children of

both sexes over a 30-year period reaching back to the early 1960s. Porter was sentenced to an 18- to 20-year prison term. The archdiocese eventually turned over the names of nearly 100 priests to prosecutors. As the scandal spread, clergy elsewhere in the United States and abroad resigned amid allegations that they had abused children or failed to stop abuse of which they had knowledge. In Ireland the Most Rev. Brendan Comiskey, the Bishop of Ferns, offered his resignation to the pope, and an archbishop in Wales was forced to resign because he had ignored complaints about two priests later convicted of sexually abusing children. Responding to the crisis, Pope John Paul II called a special meeting of American Catholic leaders in April 2002 to create new policies on sex abuse. The pope issued a statement in which he said that there is "no place in the priesthood . . . for those who would harm the young." He added that sexual abuse by the clergy was not only an "appalling sin" but a crime, and he noted that "many are offended at the way in which church leaders are perceived to have acted in this matter."[33]

Paraphilias have been recorded for thousands of years. From the Greek *para*, "to the side of," and *philos*, "loving," paraphilias are bizarre or abnormal sexual practices involving recurrent sexual urges focused on (a) nonhuman objects (such as underwear, shoes, or leather), (b) humiliation or the experience of receiving or giving pain (such as in sadomasochism or bondage), or (c) children or others who cannot grant consent. More than 2,000-year-old Buddhist texts contain references to sexually deviant behaviors among monastic communities, including sexual activity with animals and sexual interest in corpses. Richard von Krafft-Ebing's *Psychopathia Sexualis*, first published in 1887, was the first text to discuss such paraphilias as sadism, bestiality, and incest.[34]

Some paraphilias, such as wearing clothes normally worn by the opposite sex (transvestite fetishism), can be engaged in by adults in the privacy of their homes and do not involve a third party; these are usually out of the law's reach. Others, however, risk social harm and are subject to criminal penalties. Included in this group of outlawed sexual behaviors are these practices:

- *Asphyxiophilia (autoerotic asphyxia).* By means of a noose, ligature, plastic bag, mask, volatile chemicals, or chest compression, attempting partial asphyxia and oxygen deprivation to the brain to enhance sexual gratification. Almost all cases of asphyxiophilia involve males.

- *Frotteurism.* Rubbing against or touching a nonconsenting person in a crowd, elevator, or other public area.

- *Voyeurism.* Obtaining sexual pleasure from spying on a stranger while he or she disrobes or engages in sexual behavior with another.

- *Exhibitionism.* Deriving sexual pleasure from exposing the genitals to surprise or shock a stranger.

- *Sadomasochism.* Deriving pleasure from receiving pain or inflicting pain on another.

- *Pedophilia.* Attaining sexual pleasure through sexual activity with prepubescent children. Research indicates that more than 20 percent of males report sexual attraction to at least

JOHN EVANDER COUEY AND THE JESSICA LUNSFORD MURDER CASE

On February 24, 2005, 9-year-old Jessica Lunsford was reported missing from her home. When a child is reported missing, the police typically check on all the known sex offenders in the area, which in this case included John Evander Couey, 46, who was not living at the address where he was registered, a legal violation. Police located Couey and searched his room, not finding anything. Couey had a long list of convictions, including burglary, carrying a concealed weapon, disorderly intoxication, driving under the influence, indecent exposure, disorderly conduct, fraud, insufficient funds, and larceny. A habitual drug abuser, in 1991 he had been arrested and charged with "fondling a child under the age of 16."

Nineteen days after Jessica Lunsford was first reported missing, detectives returned to Couey's home and this time found blood on a mattress. Couey had fled but was arrested in Georgia. While in police custody, Couey admitted that he had entered the Lunsford home at around 3 A.M. on February 24, 2005, and found Jessica asleep in her bed. He woke her and ordered her to be quiet. "Don't yell or nothing," he said and told her to follow him back to his sister's house, where he raped her repeatedly and kept her in a closet for three days. When he learned that detectives were searching for him, he panicked and buried her even though she was still alive. He showed investigators the shallow grave where they found Jessica's body inside two tied plastic garbage bags. Her wrists were bound, but she had managed to poke two fingers through the plastic in an attempt to free herself.

Couey was found guilty of murder on March 7, 2007, and a death penalty hearing was held soon after. In closing statements, prosecutor Ric Ridgway called the crime "evil" and asked jurors to remember how Jessica died by suffocating in the hole Couey dug, accompanied only by a

© Brian LaPeter/Pool/Reuters/Landau

stuffed toy she had grabbed as she was being abducted. "She was in pain. In the dark. She was certainly terrified," Ridgway said in his closing statement. "If [Couey] is not the person who deserves the death penalty, who does?"

Defense lawyers pleaded for mercy, arguing that Couey deserved no more than a life sentence in prison because of mental retardation and mental illness, neglect as a child, and the effects of alcohol and drug abuse. "No matter what you do, John Couey is going to die in prison," said defense attorney Alan Fanter. "No child should have to die the way Jessica Lunsford did. But justice is not vengeance." The jury did not buy that argument and sentenced Couey to death on March 14, 2007.

In the aftermath of Jessica Lunsford's abduction, Florida passed legislation that requires increased prison sentences, electronic tracking of all convicted sex offenders on probation, and the mandatory use of state databases by all local probation officials so that known sex offenders cannot avoid the scrutiny of law enforcement. Can such measures control the behavior of pedophiles such as Couey before they kill their innocent victims?

Sources: Court TV Crime Library, Jessica Lunsford, www.crimelibrary.com/serial_killers/predators/jessica_lunsford/9.html (accessed July 14, 2008); *USA Today,* "Judge Throws Out Confession in Jessica Lunsford Case," 30 June 2006, www.usatoday.com/news/nation/2006-06-30-child-confession_x.htm (accessed July 14, 2008); Curt Anderson, "Death Sentence Endorsed in Lunsford Case," *Washington Post,* 15 March 2007, www.washingtonpost.com/wp-dyn/content/article/2007/03/15/AR2007031500518.html (accessed July 14, 2008).

one child, although the rate of sexual fantasies and the potential for sexual contacts are much lower.[35] One of the most horrific cases of pedophilia involved the kidnapping and death of 9-year-old Jessica Lunsford, which is the subject of the Profiles in Crime feature.

Paraphilias that involve unwilling or underage victims are illegal. Most state criminal codes also ban indecent exposure and voyeurism. Others prosecute paraphilias under common-law assault and battery or sodomy statutes. In their extreme examples, paraphilias can lead to sexual assaults in which the victims suffer severe harm.

PROSTITUTION

Eliot Spitzer is not the only well-known politician to get caught up in a prostitution scandal. On July 16, 2007, Louisiana's conservative Republican senator David Vitter apologized to the public after his telephone number showed up in the phone records of Pamela Martin and Associates, an alleged prostitution ring run in the nation's capital by so-called "D.C. Madam" Deborah Jeane Palfrey. "This was a very serious sin in my past for which I am, of course, completely responsible," Vitter said remorsefully. Soon after he issued his statement, Jeanette Maier, a former madam who ran a house of prostitution in New Orleans, claimed Vitter was also a client in her brothel. She told the press: "As far as the girls coming out after seeing David, all they had was nice things to say. It wasn't all about sex. In fact, he just wanted to have somebody listen to him, you know. And I said his wife must not be listening." Frequenting brothels and employing prostitutes is hardly the behavior expected from a married senator known for his strong advocacy of family values.[36] Senator Vitter was not alone in enjoying the services of the D.C. Madam. Also involved in the scandal were Randall L. Tobias, who was forced to step down as deputy secretary of state, and Harlan K. Ullman, the military affairs scholar who created the Pentagon's concept known as "shock and awe."[37] Facing a prison sentence of five or six years, Deborah Jeane Palfrey committed suicide on May 1, 2008.

Prostitution has been known for thousands of years. The term derives from the Latin *prostituere,* which means "to cause to stand in front of." The prostitute is viewed as publicly offering his or her body for sale. The earliest record of prostitution appears in ancient Mesopotamia, where priests engaged in sex to promote fertility in the community. All women were required to do temple duty, and passing strangers were expected to make donations to the temple after enjoying its services.[38]

Modern commercial sex appears to have its roots in ancient Greece, where Solon established licensed brothels in 500 BCE. The earnings of Greek prostitutes helped pay for the temple of Aphrodite. Famous men openly went to prostitutes to enjoy intellectual, aesthetic, and sexual stimulation; prostitutes, however, were prevented from marrying.[39]

During the Middle Ages, though prostitution was a sin under canon law it was widely practiced and considered a method of protecting "respectable" women who might otherwise by attacked by young men. In 1358, the Grand Council of Venice declared that prostitution was "absolutely indispensable to the world."[40] Some church leaders such as St. Thomas Aquinas condoned prostitution; St. Augustine wrote, "If you expel prostitution from society, you will unsettle everything on account of lusts."[41] Nonetheless, prostitution was officially condemned, and working girls were confined to ply their trade in certain areas of the city and required to wear distinctive outfits so they could be easily recognized. Any official tolerance disappeared after the Reformation. Martin Luther advocated abolishing prostitution on moral grounds, and Lutheran doctrine depicted prostitutes as emissaries of the devil who were sent to destroy the faith.[42]

During the early nineteenth century, prostitution was tied to the rise of English breweries: saloons controlled by the companies employed prostitutes to attract patrons and encourage them to drink. This relationship was repeated in major U.S. cities, such as Chicago, until breweries were forbidden to own the outlets that distributed their product.

Today there are many variations, but in general, prostitution can be defined as granting nonmarital sexual access, established by mutual agreement of the prostitutes, their clients, and their employers, for remuneration. This definition is gender-neutral because prostitutes can be straight or gay and male or female.

Prostitutes are referred to by sociologists as "street-level sex workers" whose activities are similar to any other service industry. These conditions are usually present in a commercial sexual transaction:

- *Activity that has sexual significance for the customer.* This includes the entire range of sexual behavior, from sexual intercourse to exhibitionism, sadomasochism, oral sex, and so on.

- *Economic transaction.* Something of economic value, not necessarily money, is exchanged for the activity.

- *Emotional indifference.* The sexual exchange is simply for economic consideration. Although the participants may know each other, their interaction has nothing to do with affection.[43] Men believe that the lack of involvement makes hiring a prostitute less of a hassle and less trouble than becoming involved in a romantic relationship.[44]

Sociologist Monica Prasad observed these conditions when she interviewed both men and women about their motivation to employ a prostitute. Although their choice was shaped by sexuality, she found that their decision was also influenced by pressure from friends to try something different and exciting, the wish for a sexual exchange free from obligations, and curiosity about the world of prostitution. Prasad found that most customers who became "regulars" began to view prostitution merely as a "service occupation."[45]

Incidence of Prostitution Fifty years ago, about two-thirds of non–college-educated men and one-quarter of college-educated men had visited a prostitute.[46] It is likely that the number of men who hire prostitutes has declined sharply; the number of arrests for prostitution has remained stable for the past two decades while the population has increased.[47] How can these changes be accounted for? The sexual revolution has liberalized sexuality so that men are less likely to use prostitutes because legitimate alternatives for sexuality are now available. In addition, the prevalence of sexually transmitted diseases has caused many men to avoid visiting prostitutes for fear of irreversible health hazards.

Despite such changes, the Uniform Crime Report (UCR) indicates that about 80,000 prostitution arrests are made annually, with the gender ratio about 2 to 1 female to male.[48] More alarming is the fact that about 1,200 arrests involved minors under the age of 18, including about 160 kids aged 15 and under. Arguments that criminal law should not interfere with sexual transactions because no one is harmed are undermined by these disturbing statistics.

International Sex Trade

Prostitution flourishes abroad. In some nations it is legal and regulated by the government while others punish prostitution with the death penalty. An example of the former is Germany, which has a flourishing legal sex trade. In 2002, Germany passed a new law removing the prohibition against prostitution and allowed prostitutes to obtain regular work contracts and receive health insurance. In turn, the prostitutes were required to register with the authorities and pay taxes. There is some question whether working prostitutes have taken advantage of the reforms. Nonetheless, all forms of prostitution are quite common in Germany, many sex establishments are quite lavish, and estimated 400,000 people work in the sex trade.[49] In contrast, many Islamic countries punish prostitution with death. In one incident that made international headlines, three women and three men were stoned to death in public in Iran, after a court found them guilty of adultery and prostitution under Islamic laws. The stoning was carried out by local citizens in public in Khazar Abad, a town near the Caspian Sea.[50]

There is also a troubling overseas trade in prostitution in which men from wealthy countries frequent semiregulated sex areas in needy nations such as Thailand in order to procure young girls forced or sold into prostitution—a phenomenon known as *sex tourism*. In addition to sex tours, there has also been a soaring demand for pornography, strip clubs, lap dancing, escorts, and telephone sex in developing countries.[51]

Every year, hundreds of thousands of women and children—primarily from Southeast Asia and eastern Europe—are lured by the promise of good jobs and then forced into brothels or as circuit travelers in labor camps. Most go to wealthy industrialized countries. Japan now has more than 10,000 commercial sex establishments with 150,000 to 200,000 foreign girls trafficked into the country each year.[52] India has experienced a large influx of foreign sex workers who are believed to be the source of the HIV epidemic that is sweeping the country.[53]

It is believed that traffickers import up to 50,000 women and children every year into the United States despite legal prohibitions (in addition to prostitution, some are brought in to work in sweatshops).[54] The international trade in prostitution is the subject of the Comparative Criminology feature "International Trafficking in Prostitution."

Types of Prostitutes

Several different types of prostitutes operate in the United States. As you will see, each group operates in a particular venue.

Streetwalkers Prostitutes who work the streets in plain sight of police, citizens, and customers are referred to as *hustlers*, *hookers*, or *streetwalkers*. Although glamorized by the Julia Roberts character in the film *Pretty Woman* (who winds up with the multimillionaire character played by Richard Gere), streetwalkers are considered the least attractive, lowest paid, most vulnerable men and women in the profession. They are most likely to be impoverished members of ethnic or racial minorities. Many are young runaways who gravitate to major cities to find a new, exciting life and escape from sexual and physical abuse at home.[55] In the United States and abroad, streetwalkers tend to be younger than other prostitutes, start working at a younger age, and have less education. More use money from sex work for drugs and use drugs at work; they are more likely than other prostitutes to be the targets of extreme forms of violence.[56]

Streetwalkers wear bright clothing, makeup, and jewelry to attract customers, and they take their customers to hotels. The term "hooker," however, is not derived from the ability of streetwalkers to hook clients on their charms. It actually stems from the popular name given women who followed Union General "Fighting Joe" Hooker's army during the Civil War.[57] Because streetwalkers must openly display their occupation, they are likely to be involved with the police.

The street life is very dangerous. Interviews conducted with 325 sex workers in Miami by Hilary Surratt and her colleagues found that over 40 percent experienced violence from clients in the prior year: 25 percent were beaten, 13 percent were raped, and 14 percent were threatened with weapons.[58] If they survive and gain experience, street workers learn to adopt sex practices that promote their chances of survival, such as refusing to trade sex for drugs and refusing to service clients they consider too dangerous or distasteful for sex.[59] Teela Sanders's research on the everyday life of British sex workers found that street-level sex workers use rational decision making and learning experiences to reduce the risk of violent victimization. Experienced sex workers are able to come up with protective strategies that help them manage the risk of the profession. Most do not randomly accept all clients and eliminate those they consider dangerous or threatening. They also develop methods to deal with the emotional strain of the work as well as techniques to maintain their privacy and keep their "occupation" hidden from family and neighbors.[60]

Bar Girls B-girls, as they are also called, spend their time in bars, drinking and waiting to be picked up by customers. Although alcoholism may be a problem, B-girls usually work out an arrangement with the bartender so they are served diluted drinks or water colored with dye or tea, for which the customer is charged an exorbitant price. In some bars, the B-girl is given a credit for each drink she gets the customer to buy. It is common to find B-girls in towns with military bases and large transient populations.[61]

Brothel Prostitutes Also called bordellos, cathouses, sporting houses, and houses of ill repute, brothels flourished in the nineteenth and early twentieth centuries. They were large establishments, usually run by madams, that housed several prostitutes. A madam is a woman who employs prostitutes, supervises their behavior, and receives a fee for her services; her cut is usually 40 to 60 percent of the prostitute's earnings. The madam's role may include recruiting women into prostitution and socializing them in the trade.[62]

Brothels declined in importance following World War II. The closing of the last brothel in Texas is chronicled in the play and movie *The Best Little Whorehouse in Texas*. Today the most well-known brothels exist in Nevada, where prostitution is legal outside large population centers (one, the Mustang Ranch, has an official website that sells souvenirs!). Despite their decline, some madams and their brothels have achieved national prominence.

Call Girls The aristocrats of prostitution are call girls. Like the Emperor's Club VIP girls, some charge customers thousands per night and net more than $100,000 per year. Some gain clients through employment in escort services, and others develop independent customer lists. Many call girls come from middle-class backgrounds and service upper-class customers. Attempting to dispel the notion that their service is simply sex for money, they concentrate on making their clients feel important and attractive.

INTERNATIONAL TRAFFICKING IN PROSTITUTION

Trafficking for the purpose of sexual exploitation is now a major international concern. It may be the result of force, coercion, manipulation, deception, abuse of authority, initial consent, family pressure, past and present family and community violence, economic deprivation, or other conditions.

Who Are the Traffickers?

Most traffickers are men, many of whom are involved in organized crime syndicates. Ironically, there is a great deal of cooperation in trafficking, so that in eastern Europe a single gang may include Russians, Moldavians, Egyptians, and Syrians. But while most traffickers are male, women are becoming increasingly involved in the trade. Some were in the sex trade themselves and encouraged by their recruiter/trafficker to return home and recruit other women, often under the scrutiny of people working for the trafficker to make sure they don't try to escape. In some cases, couples work as a team, the woman recruiting the victim and the man involved in transporting the victim abroad. Females contemplating migration may be more inclined to trust another woman rather than a single man, especially if they are wary of traffickers already and assume they are all men.

How common is the practice? Young men and women are trafficked to, from, and through every region in the world. While data is unreliable, estimates of the number of people trafficked internationally each year range from 600,000 men, women, and children to 1.2 million children alone. Despite the differences in these numbers, it is undeniable that a huge amount of trafficking in humans occurs around the globe.

Contributing Factors

Human trafficking is facilitated by social problems and disorder, such as disruptions in the global economy war and social unrest. Trafficking became epidemic in the former Yugoslavia where many women were trafficked and sexually exploited by combatants. Many were forced to provide sexual services for peacekeeping forces and civilian humanitarian personnel and to meet local consumer demand for sexual services. When the region endured economic crisis—with high levels of unemployment, inflation, and economic recession, many local women were trafficked abroad.

Economic crisis hits young girls especially hard. Female victims are often poor and aspire to a better life. They may be forced, coerced, deceived, and psychologically manipulated into industrial or agricultural work, marriage, domestic servitude, organ donation, or sexual exploitation. While victims often come from poorer countries, the market for labor and sex is found in wealthier countries or in countries that, while economically poor, cater to the needs of citizens from wealthy countries, of corporations, or of tourists.

While some individuals are trafficked directly for purposes of prostitution or commercial sexual exploitation, other trafficked persons and even those trafficked for legitimate work may become victims of interpersonal violence. Women trafficked for domestic work in wealthy countries or laborers trafficked for construction, logging, factory, or farm work, are vulnerable to exploitation by their employers. Individuals trafficked for the purpose of labor are usually unfamiliar with their new location and the language spoken there. They often lack formal education and do not know about the human and legal resources that could help them. For these reasons, individuals are vulnerable to the violence of exploitation.

Sex Tourism

Sex tourism is a booming business and many men from wealthy nations engage in sexual activities with trafficked individuals by traveling to destinations where women and children are prostituted. Some countries have recently written laws to prevent their citizens from engaging in sexual activities with minors while traveling outside of their own country. These laws try to deter sex tourism, making travelers reconsider their actions because of the consequences. However, enforcement of these laws may prove difficult due to issues such as jurisdiction and proof, and the practice continues unabated in many parts of the world.

One area of particular concern is child prostitution that flourishes along the German–Czech border. Girls and boys hang out near petrol stations, bus stops, and restaurants on the connecting roads between the two nations. Within towns, they are found in parks, in front of supermarkets and the entrances of gambling halls and houses, and at the railway station. In some areas, the children wait for tourists in cars or by windows. Small babies and children up to 6 years of age are usually offered to tourists by women. Children older than 7 years are usually accompanied by a male adolescent or an adult. Small children can be seen addressing German men asking if they want sex, or begging for money or

Working exclusively via telephone "dates," call girls get their clients by word of mouth or by making arrangements with bellhops, cab drivers, and so on. They either entertain clients in their own apartments or visit clients' hotels and apartments. Upon retiring, a call girl can sell her "date book" listing client names and sexual preferences for thousands of dollars. Despite the lucrative nature of their business, call girls suffer considerable risk by being alone and unprotected with strangers. They often request the business cards of their clients to make sure they are dealing with "upstanding citizens."

food. Many of the children get inside the cars of German tourists and drive away with them. Older children from 8 years on negotiate prices and sexual services. The men usually drive with their victim to a place they are familiar with, where they will not be observed. These places may be on the outskirts of a town, in nearby forests, near parks, in isolated garages, or empty side streets. Or the abusers go with their victims—sometimes accompanied by a pimp—to a nearby flat.

Some of the children were raped or sexually abused before they became involved in commercial sexual exploitation. Poverty, sexual abuse, and family obligation are the main reasons given by children for entering into prostitution. The children usually receive between 5 to 25 euros in payment. Sometimes they just receive sweets. Some sex tourists take the children for a meal or give financial support to their families.

Recruiting Women

While the image of young victims being snatched off the street sends shivers down our spine, forced recruitment, such as kidnapping, is now relatively uncommon. Some traffickers exploit victims' frustration with low salaries in their home countries, while others prey upon a crisis in the victim's family, which requires them to make money abroad. The traffickers then promise the victim to take them abroad and find them traditionally female service sector jobs, such as waitress, salesperson, domestic worker, or au pair/babysitter.

Recruiters, traffickers, and pimps have developed common operating methods. One strategy is advertisements in newspapers offering lucrative job opportunities in foreign countries for low-skilled jobs, such as waitresses and nannies. Another method of recruitment is through "marriage agencies," sometimes called mail-order bride agencies or international introduction services.

But the most common way for women to be recruited is through a friend or acquaintance who gains the woman's confidence. "Second wave" recruiting occurs when a trafficked woman returns home to draft other women. Once a woman has been trafficked and trapped in the sex industry, she has few options. There are few means open to her for escaping the brutality of being forced to have sex with multiple men each day. Once they reach the destination country, travel documents are confiscated, the women are subjected to violence, and threats are made to harm their family members. They are told they owe thousands in travel costs and must pay them off through prostitution. The women get to keep little, if any, of the money and must repay their purchase price and travel and other expenses before they are allowed to leave. They can expect little help from law enforcement authorities, who are either ambivalent or working with the traffickers.

Combating Trafficking

Recently, the United States made stopping the trafficking of women a top priority. In 1998, the "Memorandum on Steps to Combat Violence Against Women and the Trafficking of Women and Girls" was issued, which directed the secretary of state, the attorney general, and the president's Interagency Council on Women to expand their work to stop violence against women to include work against the trafficking of women.

In the former Soviet Union, prevention education projects are aimed at potential victims of trafficking, and nongovernmental organizations have established hotlines for victims or women seeking information about the risks of accepting job offers abroad.

CRITICAL THINKING

1. If put in charge, what would you do to slow or end the international sex trade? Before you answer, remember the saying that prostitution is the oldest profession, which implies that curbing it may prove quite difficult.

2. Should men who hire prostitutes be punished very severely in order to deter them from getting involved in the exploitation of these vulnerable young women?

Sources: Rebecca Surtees, "Traffickers and Trafficking in Southern and Eastern Europe, Considering the Other Side of Human Trafficking," *European Journal of Criminology* 5 (2008): 39–68; Linda Williams and Jennifer Ngo, "Human Trafficking," in *Encyclopedia of Interpersonal Violence,* ed. Claire Renzetti and Jeffrey Edelson (Thousand Oaks, CA: Sage Publications 2007); Cathrin Schauer, "Children in Street Prostitution—Report from the German-Czech Border," publication by ECPAT Germany, UNICEF Germany, Horlemann Editors, Bad Honnef, 2003, www.childcentre.info/ projects/exploitation/germany/dbaFile11447 .doc (accessed July 14, 2008); International Office of Migration (IOM), *Journeys of Jeopardy: A Review of Research on Trafficking on Women and Children in Europe* (Publication No. 11, 2002), www.iom.int/documents/publication/ en/mrs%5F11%5F2002.pdf and www.iom.int/ iomwebsite/Publication/ServletSearchPublication? event=detail&id=5112 (both accessed July 14, 2008); Donna Hughes, "The 'Natasha' Trade: Transnational Sex Trafficking," *National Institute of Justice Journal* (January 2001), www .uri.edu/artsci/wms/hughes/natasha_nij.pdf (accessed July 14, 2008).

Escort Services/Call Houses Some escort services are fronts for prostitution rings. Both male and female sex workers can be sent out after the client calls an ad in the yellow pages. Las Vegas has more than 1,000 listings for adult services in the yellow pages; New York City lists more than 90 escort agencies. While most escort agencies deny that they are involved in prostitution and claim that their employees never provide sexual services, very few are exclusively involved in "social companionship." The Internet makes it easy to find escort services for travelers: a recent Google search found

Prostitution has entered the Internet age, and websites now advertise sex for hire. This placard, taken from the Doll House escort service website and advertising the women who worked there, was used in the trial of its owner, Santiago Steven Maese of Salt Lake City, Utah. On July 12, 2008, Maese was convicted of four counts of exploitation of prostitution as well as other felonies, and faces up to 30 years in prison.

© AP Images/Leah Hogsten, Pool

more than 400,000 listings under "adult escort services" nationwide.

A relatively new phenomenon, call houses, combines elements of the brothel and call girl rings. A madam receives a call from a prospective customer, and if she finds the client acceptable, she arranges a meeting between the caller and a prostitute in her service. The madam maintains a list of prostitutes who are on call rather than living together in a house. The call house insulates the madam from arrest because she never meets the client or receives direct payment.[63]

Circuit Travelers Prostitutes known as circuit travelers move around in groups of two or three to lumber, labor, and agricultural camps. They ask the foremen for permission to ply their trade, service the whole crew in an evening, and then move on. Some circuit travelers seek clients at truck stops and rest areas. Sometimes young girls are forced to become circuit travelers by unscrupulous pimps who force them to work as prostitutes in agricultural migrant camps.[64]

Skeezers Surveys conducted in New York and Chicago have found that a significant portion of female prostitutes have substance abuse problems, and more than half claim that prostitution is how they support their drug habits; on the street, women who barter sex for drugs are called **skeezers**. Not all drug-addicted prostitutes barter sex for drugs, but those that do report more frequent drug abuse and sexual activity than other prostitutes.[65] In a recent study Jessica Edwards, Carolyn Halpern, and Wendee Wechsberg looked into factors that distinguish female crack cocaine users who become skeezers and found that they (a) engaged in more frequent crack use, (b) were more likely to be homeless and unemployed, and (c) suffered more psychological distress than crack users who steered clear of the sex trade.[66] Other research studies find that skeezers are less likely to have a main sexual partner, and more likely to smoke larger quantities of crack. Skeezers have lower self-esteem, greater depression and anxiety, poorer decision-making confidence, more hostility, less social conformity, greater risk-taking behaviors, and more problems growing up, compared to drug users who refrain from trading sex.[67]

Massage Parlors/Photo Studios Some "working girls" are based in massage parlors and photo studios. Although it is unusual for a masseuse to offer all the services of prostitution, oral sex and manual stimulation are common. Most localities have attempted to limit commercial sex in massage parlors by passing ordinances specifying that the masseuse keep certain parts of her body covered and limiting the areas of the body that can be massaged. Some photo studios allow customers to put body paint on models before the photo sessions start.

connections

A new form of prostitution—cyber prostitution—involves the Internet and is discussed in Chapter 15.

Becoming a Prostitute

At age 38, Lt. Cmdr. Rebecca Dickinson had risen from the enlisted ranks in the Navy to its officer corps. She had an assignment to the Naval Academy in Annapolis, Maryland, where she helped teach a leadership course. But faced with money and marital problems, Dickinson contacted the D.C. Madam, Deborah Jeane Palfrey, and worked as a prostitute for some of the richest and most powerful men in Washington. When asked why she did it, she replied, "I needed the money, yes, I did." This desperate Navy officer, whose career was destroyed in the scandal, was paid $130 for a 90-minute session.[68]

Why do such people turn to prostitution? In Dickinson's case, she was a successful career officer who was motivated by an immediate financial need (although she was earning over $75,000 per year from the Navy). But it is more common for male and female street-level sex workers to come from troubled homes marked by extreme conflict and hostility.[69] Many of these children had experienced sexual trauma at an early age.[70] Future prostitutes were initiated into sex by family members at ages as young as 10 to 12 years; they have long histories of sexual exploitation and abuse.[71]

Sexual abuse is not the only social problem that is a forerunner to prostitution. One recent survey of street-level sex workers in Phoenix, Arizona, found that women engaging in prostitution have limited educational backgrounds; most did not complete high school.[72] Girls who get into "the life" report conflict with school authorities, poor grades, and an overly regimented school experience; a significant portion have long histories of drug abuse.[73] Young girls who frequently use drugs and begin using at an early age are most at risk for prostitution to support their habits.[74]

Once they get into the life, personal danger begins to escalate. Girls who may be directed toward prostitution because of childhood sexual abuse are likely to become revictimized as adults.[75] The threat of HIV and STDs is also a daily worry. Recent research directed at the health risks faced by prostitutes found that many suffer from blood-borne viral infections, sexually transmitted diseases, and mental health symptoms. Prostitution was associated with use of emergency care in women and use of inpatient mental health services for men.[76] While some take precautions, such as using or making their clients use condoms, many forego protection if their pimps and brothel owners forbid it or clients refuse to cooperate.[77] Their continuous exposure to danger and violence, both as victims and as witnesses, leads many to self-medication with illegal drugs. Prostitutes then find themselves in a vicious cycle of violence, substance abuse, and AIDS risk.[78]

While most research depicts prostitutes as troubled women who have lived troubled lives, there may be a trend for some young women to enter the sex trade as a rational choice based on economic need. Changing sexual mores help reduce or eliminate the stigma attached to prostitution. There is even evidence that students turn to prostitution to help pay tuition bills.[79] One recent research study conducted in Australia found that the sex industry has become attractive to college students as a way to supplement their income during a time of reduced government aid and increasing educational costs. They view sex work as a "normal" form of employment for students seeking to obtain a higher education.[80]

Child Sexual Abuse and Prostitution Child prostitution is not a recent development. For example, it was routine for poor young girls to serve as prostitutes in nineteenth-century England.[81] In contemporary society, child prostitution has been linked to sexual trauma experienced at an early age.[82] Many have long histories of sexual exploitation and abuse.[83] These early experiences with sex help teach them that their bodies have value and that sexual encounters can be used to obtain affection, power, or money. In a detailed study of child sexual exploitation in North America, Richard J. Estes and Neil Alan Weiner found that the problem of child sexual abuse is much more widespread than has been previously believed or documented.[84] Their research indicated that each year in the United States, 25,000 children are subjected to some form of sexual exploitation, which often begins with sexual assaults by relatives and acquaintances, such as a teacher, coach, or a neighbor. Abusers are nearly always men, and about a quarter of them are married with children.

Once they flee an abusive situation at home, kids are vulnerable to life on the streets. Some get hooked up in the sex trade, starting as strippers and lap dancers and drifting into prostitution and pornography. They remain in the trade because they have lost hope and are resigned to their fate.[85] Some meet pimps who quickly turn them to a life of prostitution and beat them if they do not make their daily financial quotas. Others who fled to the streets exchange sex for money, food, and shelter. Some have been traded between prostitution rings, and others are shipped from city to city and even sent overseas as prostitutes. About 20 percent of sexually exploited children are involved in prostitution rings that work across state lines.

Controlling Prostitution

In the late nineteenth and early twentieth century, efforts were made to regulate prostitution in the United States through medical supervision and the licensing and zoning of brothels in districts outside residential neighborhoods.[86] After World War I, prostitution became associated with disease, and the desire to protect young servicemen from harm helped to end almost all experiments with legalization in the United States.[87] Some reformers attempted to paint pimps and procurers as immigrants who used their foreign ways to snare unsuspecting American girls into prostitution. Such fears prompted passage of the federal Mann Act (1925), which prohibited bringing women into the country or transporting them across state lines for the purposes of prostitution. Often called the "white slave act," it carried a $5,000 fine, five years in prison, or both.[88]

Today, prostitution is considered a misdemeanor, punishable by a fine or a short jail sentence. Most states punish both people engaging in prostitution and those who hire people for sexual activities. Take the Minnesota statute for example:

> *Subd. 3.* Engaging in, hiring, or agreeing to hire an adult to engage in prostitution; penalties. *Whoever intentionally does any of the following may be sentenced to imprisonment for not more than 90 days or to payment of a fine of not more than $1,000, or both:*
>
> *(1) engages in prostitution with an individual 18 years of age or above; or*
>
> *(2) hires or offers or agrees to hire an individual 18 years of age or above to engage in sexual penetration or sexual contact. Except as otherwise provided in subdivision 4, a person who is convicted of violating clause (1) or (2) while acting as a patron must, at a minimum, be sentenced to pay a fine of at least $500.*[89]

In practice, most law enforcement is uneven and aims at confining illegal activities to particular areas in the city.[90] Some local police agencies concerned about prostitution have used high-visibility patrols to discourage prostitutes and their customers, undercover work to arrest prostitutes and drug dealers, and collaboration with hotel and motel owners to identify and arrest pimps and drug dealers.[91]

There has also been an effort to reduce prostitution and protect children forced into the life by punishing sex tourism (see the Comparative Criminology box on international sex trade). The Violent Crime Control and Law Enforcement Act of 1994 included a provision, referred to as the Child Sexual Abuse Prevention Act, which made it a criminal offense to travel abroad for the purpose of engaging in sexual activity with a minor.[92] Some loopholes in the law were closed when President George W. Bush signed the PROTECT Act (Prosecutorial Remedies and Other Tools to end the Exploitation of Children Today) into law in 2003.[93] Despite these efforts, prosecuting sex tourists is often tricky due to the difficulty of gathering evidence of crimes that were committed in other countries and that involve minor children.[94]

Legalize Prostitution?

In some countries, especially in the Muslim world, prostitution carries the death penalty. In others, such as Holland, prostitutes pay taxes and belong to a union. Some countries, such as Australia, allow adults to engage in prostitution but regulate their activities, such as requiring that they must get timely health checkups. Still other countries, such as Brazil, allow women to become prostitutes but criminalize earning money from the work of prostitutes—that is, serving as a pimp. In the United States, prostitution is illegal in all states, though brothels are legal in a number of counties in Nevada (but not in Las Vegas or Reno). A loop hole in the Rhode Island state law allows prostitution in the privacy of a home or business but criminalizes solicitation and operating a brothel.[95]

Feminists have staked out conflicting views of prostitution. One position is that women must become emancipated from male oppression and reach sexual equality. The *sexual equality* view considers the prostitute a victim of male dominance. In patriarchal societies, male power is predicated on female subjugation, and prostitution is a clear example of this gender exploitation.[96] In contrast, for some feminists, the fight for equality depends on controlling all attempts by men or women to impose their will on women. The *free choice view* is that prostitution, if freely chosen, expresses women's equality and is not a symptom of subjugation.

Advocates of both positions argue that the penalties for prostitution should be reduced (decriminalized); neither side advocates outright legalization. Decriminalization would relieve already desperate women of the additional burden of severe legal punishment. In contrast, legalization might be coupled with regulation by male-dominated justice agencies. For example, required medical examinations would mean increased governmental control over women's bodies.

Both positions have had significant influence around the world. In Sweden, feminists have succeeded in getting legislation passed that severely restricts prostitution and criminalizes any effort to buy sexual activities.[97] In contrast, Holland legalized brothels in 2001 but ordered that they be run under a strict set of guidelines.[98]

Should prostitution be legalized? In her book *Brothel*, Alexa Albert, a Harvard-trained physician who interviewed young women working at a legal brothel in Nevada, makes a compelling case for legalization. She found that the women remained HIV-free and felt safer working in a secure environment than alone on city streets. Despite long hours and rules that gave too much profit to the owners, the women actually took pride in their work. In addition to the added security, most earned between $300 and $1,500 per day.[99]

In opposition to this view, Roger Matthews, author of the recent book *Prostitution, Politics and Policy*, provides a detailed framework that opposes legalizing prostitution. It is foolish, he claims, to view prostitution as "sex work" that should be either legalized and/or tolerated and regulated—for example, with areas set up where women can work without fear of arrest, such as Holland's "tolerance zones." After studying street prostitution for more than two decades, Matthews concludes that women on the street are extremely desperate, damaged, and disorganized. Many are involved in substance abuse and experience beating, rape, and other forms of violence on a regular basis. Women who enter prostitution do so after a childhood punctuated with physical and sexual abuse, parental neglect, homelessness, and drug addiction. Prostitution is, he concludes, the world's most dangerous occupation. His solution is to treat the women forced into prostitution as victims and the men who purchase their services as criminals. He applauds Sweden's decision to make buying sexual services a crime, thus criminalizing the "johns" rather than the women in prostitution. When governments legalize prostitution, it leads to a massive expansion of the trade, both legal and illegal.[100]

PORNOGRAPHY

The term **pornography** derives from the Greek *porne*, meaning "prostitute," and *graphein*, meaning "to write." In the heart of many major cities are stores that display and sell books, magazines, and films depicting every imaginable explicit sex act. Suburban video stores also rent and sell sexually explicit DVDs, which make up 15 to 30 percent of the home rental market. The purpose of this material is to provide sexual titillation and excitement for paying customers. Although material depicting nudity and sex is typically legal, protected by the First Amendment's provision limiting governmental control of speech, most criminal codes prohibit the production, display, and sale of legally obscene material.

Obscenity, derived from the Latin *caenum*, for "filth," is defined by Webster's dictionary as "deeply offensive to morality or decency . . . designed to incite to lust or depravity."[101] The problem of controlling pornography centers on this definition of obscenity. Police and law enforcement officials can legally seize only material that is judged obscene. But who, critics ask, is to judge what is obscene? At one time, such novels as *Tropic of Cancer* by Henry Miller, *Ulysses* by James Joyce, and *Lady Chatterley's Lover* by D. H. Lawrence were prohibited because they were considered obscene; today they are considered works of great literary value. Thus, what is obscene today may be considered socially acceptable at a future time. After all, *Playboy* and other adult magazines, sold openly on many college campuses, display nude models in all kinds of sexually explicit poses. Though at one time they were considered racy, today they are relatively tame and you can buy shares of *Playboy* on the New York Stock Exchange.

Allowing individual judgments on what is obscene makes the Constitution's guarantee of free speech unworkable. Could not antiobscenity statutes also be used to control political and social dissent? The uncertainty surrounding this issue is illustrated by Supreme Court Justice Potter Stewart's famous 1964 statement on how he defined obscenity: "I know it when I see it." Because of this legal and moral ambiguity, a global pornography industry is becoming increasingly mainstream, currently generating up to $60 billion per year in revenue. In fact, some Internet pornography companies are now listed on the NASDAQ stock exchange.[102] Nonetheless, while adult material has gone mainstream, courts have long held that the First Amendment was not intended to protect indecency and therefore material considered offensive and obscene can be controlled by the rule of law.[103]

Child Pornography

The use of children in pornography is the most controversial and reprehensible aspect of the business. Each year more than a million children are believed to be used in pornography or prostitution, many of them runaways whose plight is exploited by adults.[104] Sexual exploitation by child pornography rings can cause wide-ranging physical and psychological problems. In cases of extreme, prolonged victimization, children may lock onto the sex group's behavior and become prone to further victimization or even become victimizers themselves.

Child pornography has become widespread on the Internet. In his book, *Beyond Tolerance: Child Pornography on the Internet*, sociologist Philip Jenkins argues that activists are focused on stamping out Internet pornography but that they have not focused on its most dangerous form, kiddie porn, which sometimes involves pictures of girls as young as 4 or 5 in sexual encounters.

When an effort is made to target pedophilic websites, investigators often go in the wrong direction, failing to recognize that most sites are short-lived entities whose addresses are passed around to users. Jenkins suggests that kiddie porn is best combated by more effective law enforcement. Instead of focusing on users, efforts should be directed against suppliers. He also suggests that newsgroups and bulletin boards that advertise and discuss kiddie porn be criminalized.[105]

Does Pornography Cause Violence?

An issue critical to the debate over pornography is whether viewing it produces sexual violence or assaultive behavior. This debate was given added attention when serial killer Ted Bundy claimed his murderous rampage was fueled by reading pornography.

The evidence is mixed. Some studies indicate that viewing sexually explicit material actually has little effect on sexual violence. When Neil Malamuth, Tamara Addison, and Mary Koss surveyed 2,972 male college students, they discovered that frequent use of pornography was not related to sexual aggression. There were only relatively minor differences in sexual aggression between men who report using pornography very frequently when compared to those who said they rarely used it at all. However, men who were both at high risk for sexual aggression and who were very frequent users of pornography were much more likely to engage in sexual aggression than their counterparts who consume pornography less frequently. Put simply, if a person has relatively aggressive sexual inclinations resulting from various personal and cultural factors, exposure to pornography may activate and reinforce associated coercive tendencies and behaviors. But even high levels of exposure to pornography do not turn nonaggressive men into sexual predators.[106]

How might we account for this surprisingly modest association?[107] It is possible that viewing erotic material may act as a safety valve for those whose impulses might otherwise lead them to violence. Convicted rapists and sex offenders report less exposure to pornography than a control group of nonoffenders.[108] Viewing prurient material may have the unintended side effect of satisfying erotic impulses that otherwise might result in more sexually aggressive behavior.

While the pornography–violence link seems modest, there is more evidence that people who are predisposed to violence and exposed to material that portrays violence, sadism, and women enjoying being raped and degraded are also likely to be sexually aggressive toward female victims.[109] Individuals who are already predisposed to sexually offend may become aroused by pornography exposure and have a greater willingness to undertake sexual coercion.[110] For example, men who engage in domestic violence also tend to watch pornography and those who do are more controlling and violent.[111]

Laboratory experiments conducted by a number of leading authorities have found that men exposed to violent pornography are more likely to act aggressively and hold aggressive attitudes toward women.[112] James Fox and Jack Levin find it common for serial killers to collect and watch violent pornography. Some make their own "snuff" films starring their victims.[113] On a macro level, cross-national research indicates that nations that consume the highest levels of pornography also have extremely high rape rates.[114] However, it is still not certain if such material drives people to sexual violence or whether people predisposed to sexual violence are drawn to pornography with a violent theme.

connections

Chapter 5 discusses the effects of media on violence. As you may recall, while there is some evidence that people exposed to violent media will become violent themselves, the association is still being debated.

Pornography and the Law

All states and the federal government prohibit the sale and production of pornographic material. Child pornography is usually a separate legal category that involves either the creation or reproduction of materials depicting minors engaged in actual or simulated sexual activity ("sexual exploitation of minors") or the publication or distribution of obscene, indecent, or harmful materials to minors.[115] Under existing federal law, trafficking in obscenity (18 U.S.C. Sec. 1462, 1464, 1466), child pornography (18 U.S.C. Sec. 2252), harassment (18 U.S.C. Sec. 875(c)), illegal solicitation or luring of minors (18 U.S.C. Sec. 2423(b)), and threatening to injure someone (18 U.S.C. Sec. 875(c)) are all felonies punished by long prison sentences.

While these laws are designed to control obscene material, the First Amendment of the U.S. Constitution protects free speech and prohibits police agencies from limiting the public's right of free expression. This legal protection has sent the government along a torturous road in the attempt to define when material is criminally obscene and eligible for legal control. For example, the Supreme Court held in the twin cases of *Roth v. United States* and *Alberts v. California* that the First Amendment protects all "ideas with even the slightest redeeming social importance—unorthodox ideas, controversial ideas, even ideas hateful to the prevailing climate of opinion, but implicit in the history of the First Amendment is the rejection of obscenity as utterly without redeeming social importance."[116] In the 1966 case of *Memoirs v. Massachusetts*, the Supreme Court again required that for a work to be considered obscene it must be shown to be "utterly without redeeming social value."[117] These decisions left unclear how obscenity is defined. If a highly erotic movie tells a "moral tale," must it be judged legal even if 95 percent of its content is objectionable? A spate of movies made after the *Roth* decision alleged that they were educational so they could not be said to lack redeeming social importance. Many state obscenity cases were appealed to federal courts so judges could decide whether the films totally lacked redeeming social importance. To rectify the situation, the Supreme Court redefined its concept of obscenity in the case of *Miller v. California*:

> The basic guidelines for the trier of fact must be (a) whether the average person applying contemporary community standards would find that the work taken as a whole appeals to the prurient interest; (b) whether the work depicts or describes, in a patently offensive way, sexual conduct specifically defined by the applicable state law; and (c) whether the work, taken as a whole, lacks serious literary, artistic, political or scientific value.[118]

To convict a person of obscenity under the *Miller* doctrine, the state or local jurisdiction must specifically define obscene conduct in its statute, and the pornographer must engage in that behavior. The Court gave some examples of what is considered obscene: "patently offensive representations or descriptions of masturbation, excretory functions and lewd exhibition of the genitals." In subsequent cases the Court overruled convictions for "offensive" or "immoral" behavior; these are not considered obscene. The *Miller* doctrine has been criticized for not spelling out how community standards are to be determined. Obviously,

a plebiscite cannot be held to determine the community's attitude for every trial concerning the sale of pornography. Works that are considered obscene in Omaha might be considered routine in New York, but how can we be sure? To resolve this dilemma, the Supreme Court articulated in *Pope v. Illinois* a reasonableness doctrine: a work is not obscene if a reasonable person applying objective standards would find that the material in question has at least some social value:[119]

> The ideas that a work represents need not obtain majority approval to merit protection, and the value of that work does not vary from community to community based on the degree of local acceptance it has won. The proper inquiry is not whether an ordinary member of any given community would find serious value in the allegedly obscene material, but whether a reasonable person would find such value in the material, taken as a whole.[120]

Controlling Pornography

Sex for profit predates Western civilization. Considering its longevity, there seems to be little evidence that it can be controlled or eliminated by legal means alone. In 1986, the Attorney General's Commission on Pornography advocated a strict law enforcement policy to control obscenity, directing that "the prosecution of obscene materials that portray sexual violence be treated as a matter of special urgency."[121] Since then, there has been a concerted effort by the federal government to prosecute adult-movie distributors. Law enforcement has been so fervent that industry members have filed suit claiming they are the victims of a "moral crusade" by right-wing zealots.[122]

Although politically appealing, controlling sex for profit is difficult because of the public's desire to purchase sexually related material and services. Law enforcement crusades may not necessarily obtain the desired effect. A get-tough policy could make sex-related goods and services scarce, driving up prices and making their sale even more desirable and profitable. Going after national distributors may help decentralize the adult movie and photo business and encourage local rings to expand their activities, for example, by making and marketing videos as well as still photos or distributing them through computer networks.

An alternative approach has been to restrict the sale of pornography within acceptable boundaries. Some municipal governments have tolerated or even established adult entertainment zones in which obscene material can be openly sold. In the case of *Young v. American Mini Theaters*, the Supreme Court permitted a zoning ordinance that restricted theaters showing erotic movies to one area of the city, even though it did not find that any of the movies shown were obscene.[123] The state, therefore, has the right to regulate adult films as long as the public has the right to view them. Some jurisdictions have responded by limiting the sale of sexually explicit material in residential areas and restricting the number of adult stores that can operate in a particular area. For example, New York City has enacted zoning that seeks to break up the concentration of peep shows, topless bars, and X-rated businesses in several neighborhoods, particularly in Times Square.[124] The law forbids sex-oriented businesses within 500 feet of residential zones, schools, churches, or daycare centers. Sex shops cannot be located within 500 feet of each other, so concentrated "red light" districts must be dispersed. Rather than close their doors, sex shops got around the law by adding products like luggage, cameras, T-shirts, and classic films. The courts have upheld the law, ruling that stores can stay in business if no more than 40 percent of their floor space and inventory are dedicated to adult entertainment.[125]

connections

Today, the Internet has become a favored method of delivering adult material and one that defies easy regulation since distribution can be international in scope. The topic of Internet porn will be discussed in Chapter 15.

www Go to academic.cengage.com/criminaljustice/siegel to learn more about the following topics:

▌ The **clergy scandal**

▌ Amnesty International's report on the exploitation of women in Kosovo and Bosnia and their forced entry into the **international sex trade**

▌ *Pope v. Illinois*

SUBSTANCE ABUSE

Who among us can forget that terrible day in January 2008 when the media reported that actor Heath Ledger had died in his New York apartment at the age of 28? His big break came

playing opposite Julia Styles in the teen movie *Ten Things I Hate About You*. He became an international star with his stirring performance as a gay cowboy in Ang Lee's acclaimed film *Brokeback Mountain*. While some in the media speculated about suicide, medical examiners later pinned Ledger's death on an accidental overdose of six drugs—painkillers and sedatives—namely hydrocodone, diazepam, temazepam, alprazolam, and doxylamine, more commonly called Vicodin, Valium, Xanax, Restoril, Unisom, as well as Oxycondone. Three of the six prescription drugs found in Ledger's apartment had been filled in Europe, where the actor was recently filming, police said.

connections

The debate over dangerous prescription drug use has been intensified because they are now easily obtained on the Web. Many suppliers do not require prescriptions. For more on this issue, see the discussion in Chapter 15 on obtaining dangerous drugs via the Web.

Heath Ledger's death is a stark reminder of the dangers of substance abuse, a social problem that spans every segment of society. Large urban areas are beset by drug-dealing gangs, drug users who engage in crime to support their habits, and alcohol-related violence. Rural areas are important staging centers for the shipment of drugs across the country and are often the production sites for synthetic drugs and marijuana farming.[126] Nor is the United States alone in experiencing a problem with substance abuse. Australia reports that almost 20 percent of youths in detention centers and 40 percent of adult prisoners report having used heroin at least once; in Canada, cocaine and crack are considered serious urban problems; South Africa reports increased cocaine and heroin abuse; Thailand has a serious heroin and methamphetamine problem; and British police have found a major increase in heroin abuse.[127]

Another indication of the concern about drugs has been the increasing number of drug-related arrests: from less than half a million in 1977 to more than 1.8 million today.[128] Similarly, the proportion of prison inmates incarcerated for drug offenses has increased by 600 percent since 1986.[129] Clearly the justice system views drug abuse as a major problem and is taking what decision makers regard as decisive measures for its control.

Despite the scope of the drug problem, some still view

Substance abuse can have catastrophic consequences. We were all saddened by the death of talented actor Heath Ledger, whose body is shown here being removed from his Soho apartment by the NYC Medical Examiner team on January 22, 2008. Ledger, 28, was found dead after taking a mixture of prescription medications, including oxycodone, hydrocodone, diazepam, alprazolam, temazepam, and doxylamine. These are the generic names for the painkillers OxyContin and Vicodin, the antianxiety drugs Valium and Xanax, and the sleep aids Restoril and Unisom.

© AP Images/Louis Lanzano

it as another type of victimless public order crime. There is great debate over the legalization of drugs and the control of alcohol. Some consider drug use a private matter and drug control another example of government intrusion into people's private lives. Furthermore, legalization could reduce the profit of selling illegal substances and drive suppliers out of the market.[130] Others see these substances as dangerous, believing that the criminal activity of users makes the term "victimless" nonsensical. Still another position is that the possession and use of all drugs and alcohol should be legalized but that the sale and distribution of drugs should be heavily penalized. This would punish those profiting from drugs and would enable users to be helped without fear of criminal punishment.

When Did Drug Use Begin?

The use of chemical substances to change reality and to provide stimulation, relief, or relaxation has gone on for thousands of years. The opium poppy was first cultivated more than 5,000 years ago and was used by the Persians, Sumerians, Assyrians, Babylonians, and Egyptians. Users discovered that smoking the extract derived from crushing the seed pods yielded a pleasurable, peaceful feeling throughout the body. Known as the *hul gil* or "plant of joy," its use spread quickly around the fertile crescent.[131] The ancient Greeks knew and understood the problem of drug use. At the time of the Crusades, the Arabs were using marijuana. In the Western hemisphere, natives of Mexico and South America chewed coca leaves and used "magic mushrooms" in their religious ceremonies.[132] Drug use was also accepted in Europe well into the twentieth century. Pharmacy records circa 1900 to 1920 show sales of cocaine and heroin solutions to members of the British royal family; records from 1912 show that Winston Churchill, then a member of Parliament, was sold a cocaine solution while staying in Scotland.[133]

In the early years of the United States, opium and its derivatives were easily obtained. Opium-based drugs were used in various patent medicine cure-alls. Morphine was used extensively to relieve the pain of wounded soldiers in the Civil War. By the turn of the century, an estimated 1 million U.S. citizens were opiate users.[134]

Several factors precipitated the current stringent U.S. drug laws. The rural religious creeds of the nineteenth century—especially those of the Methodists, Presbyterians, and Baptists—emphasized individual human toil and self-sufficiency while designating the use of intoxicating substances as an unwholesome surrender to the evils of urban morality. Religious leaders were thoroughly opposed to the use and sale of narcotics. The medical literature of the late 1800s began to designate the use of morphine and opium as a vice, a habit, an appetite, and a disease. Nineteenth- and early twentieth-century police literature described drug users as habitual criminals. Moral crusaders in the nineteenth century defined drug use as evil and directed that local and national entities should outlaw the sale and possession of drugs. Some well-publicized research efforts categorized drug use as highly dangerous.[135] Drug use was also associated with the foreign immigrants recruited to work in factories and mines; they brought with them their national drug habits. Early antidrug legislation appears to be tied to prejudice against immigrating ethnic minorities.[136]

After the Spanish-American War of 1898, the United States inherited Spain's opium monopoly in the Philippines. Concern over this international situation, along with the domestic issues just outlined, led the U.S. government to participate in the First International Drug Conference, held in Shanghai in 1908, and a second one at The Hague in 1912. Participants in these two conferences were asked to strongly oppose free trade in drugs. The international pressure, coupled with a growing national concern, led to the passage of the antidrug laws discussed here.

Alcohol and Its Prohibition

The history of alcohol and the law in the United States has also been controversial and dramatic. At the turn of the twentieth century, a drive was mustered to prohibit the sale of alcohol. This temperance movement was fueled by the belief that the purity of the U.S. agrarian culture was being destroyed by the growth of the city. Urbanism was viewed as a threat to the lifestyle of the majority of the nation's population, then living on farms and in villages. The forces behind the temperance movement were such lobbying groups as the Anti-Saloon League led by Carrie Nation, the Women's Christian Temperance Union, and the Protestant clergy of the Baptist, Methodist, and Congregationalist faiths.[137] They viewed the growing cities, filled with newly arriving Irish, Italian, and Eastern European immigrants, as centers of degradation and wickedness. The propensity of these ethnic people to drink heavily was viewed as the main force behind their degenerate lifestyle. The eventual prohibition of the sale of alcoholic beverages brought about by ratification of the Eighteenth Amendment in 1919 was viewed as a triumph of the morality of middle- and upper-class Americans over the threat posed to their culture by the "new Americans."[138]

Prohibition failed. It was enforced by the Volstead Act, which defined intoxicating beverages as those containing one-half of 1 percent, or more, alcohol.[139] What doomed Prohibition? One factor was the use of organized crime to supply illicit liquor. Also, the law made it illegal only to sell alcohol, not to purchase it; this cut into the law's deterrent capability. Finally, despite the work of Eliot Ness and his "Untouchables," law enforcement agencies were inadequate, and officials were likely to be corrupted by wealthy bootleggers.[140] Eventually, in 1933, the Twenty-First Amendment to the Constitution repealed Prohibition, signaling the end of the "noble experiment."

The Extent of Substance Abuse

Despite continuing efforts at control, the use of mood-altering substances persists around the world. What is the extent of the substance abuse problem today? This question can be answered from both global and individual perspectives. On both fronts, drug use continues at too high a rate, but the trends have been positive: fewer drugs are being marketed; law enforcement has become more efficient at seizing drugs; fewer people are using drugs and using them less frequently than in the past.

A number of national and international surveys attempt to chart trends in drug abuse. Results from some of the most important sources are described in the next sections.

United Nations Global Survey The United Nations conducts an annual World Drug Use Survey that monitors drug cultivation and use around the globe.[141] The most recent report on the world drug problem by the United Nations indicates that the drug epidemic may be abating, drug cultivation is in decline, and law enforcement agencies have become more adept at seizing drug shipments. Among the findings:

▌ Coca cultivation in the Andean countries continues to fall, driven by significant declines in Colombia. Global demand for cocaine has also stabilized, although there have been increases in some European countries.

▌ The production and consumption of amphetamine-type stimulants (ATS) has leveled off, with a clear downward trend in North America and, to a lesser degree, Europe.

▌ Health warnings on higher potency cannabis appear to be getting through. The global production and consumption of cannabis has declined.

▌ Opium production, while significant, is now highly concentrated in Afghanistan's southern provinces, especially in the Taliban-controlled Helmand. If Helmand could be "cured" of its insurgency, drug cultivation should be significantly curtailed.

▌ Despite a massive increase in opium poppy cultivation in Afghanistan, the global area under cultivation for opium is now actually 10 percent lower than in 2000. This decline is mainly due to sustained success in reducing cultivation in Southeast Asia. Poppy cultivation in the so-called "Golden Triangle" has

fallen by some 80 percent since 2000. Southeast Asia is closing a tragic chapter that has blighted the Golden Triangle for decades—the region is now almost opium free.

▌ Drug law enforcement has improved: almost half of all cocaine produced is now being intercepted (up from 24 percent in 1999) and more than a quarter of all heroin (against 15 percent in 1999) shipments are being seized by law enforcement agencies each year. The amount of heroin available to consumers is actually 8 percent lower today than it was in 1990. Improved cooperation among law enforcement bodies has led to improved seizures close to the source of cultivation: about 60 percent of global cocaine seizures take place in South America, the Caribbean, and Central America.

Monitoring the Future (MTF) While the U.N. survey indicates that on a global scale drug cultivation is down and law enforcement efforts improving, it does not tell us much about individual drug use patterns in the United States. To answer this question, a number of yearly surveys of drug use can be examined. One of the most important, the annual Monitoring the Future survey, is conducted by the Institute of Social Research (ISR) at the University of Michigan.[142] Data, collected from the self-report responses of nearly 50,000 high school students in the 8th, 10th, and 12th grades in almost 400 schools across the United States, asks students about their yearly and lifetime drug use experiences.

As Figure 14.1 shows, drug use among American high school seniors (8th and 10th graders were added to the survey in 1991) is much lower now that it was in the 1970s and early 1980s (when their parents were in school). This promising trend in illegal drug use is reflected in trends during the past

Figure 14.1 Trends in Annual Prevalence of Illicit Drug Use

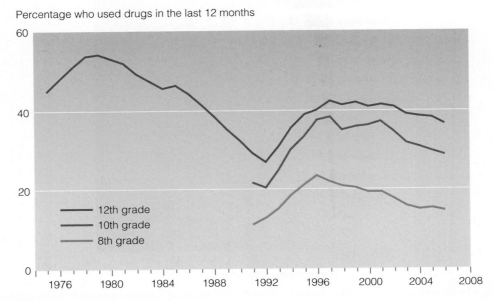

Percentage who used drugs in the last 12 months

Source: The Monitoring the Future Study, University of Michigan.

Table 14.1	Percentage of 8th, 10th, and 12th Graders Who Used Any Illegal Drug During the Past Year	
Grade	1996	2007
8th graders	24%	13%
10th graders	39%	28%
12th graders	42%	36%

Source: Institute of Social Research, *Monitoring the Future*.

decade. According to the most recent survey available, the percentage of U.S. adolescents who use illicit drugs or drink alcohol has been in decline for the past decade.[143] As Table 14.1 shows, students at each grade level experienced declines in their annual drug usage, with the younger respondents reporting the greatest declines.

The only drug showing signs of an increase during the past decade is MDMA (ecstasy). Ecstasy use among teens plummeted in the early 2000s, as concern about the consequences of its use grew. However, the proportion of students seeing great risk in using this drug has been in decline for the past two or three years at all three grade levels, and use has begun to increase, at least in the upper grades.

While the improvement has been impressive, more than 10 percent of 8th graders and more than a third of 12th graders have used some type of illicit drug during the past year. And while drug use is down, many youngsters continue to use drugs and many students have no problem finding illegal drugs on campus.[144]

National Survey on Drug Use and Health Each year the Substance Abuse and Mental Health Services Administration (SAMHSA), a division of the Department of Health and Human Services, conducts the National Survey on Drug Use and Health (NSDUH) (the survey was called the National Household Survey on Drug Abuse—NHSDA—prior to 2002).[145] The NSDUH collects information from a sampling of all U.S. residents of households, noninstitutional group quarters (such as shelters, rooming houses, dormitories), and civilians living on military bases (it excludes homeless people who do not use shelters, military personnel on active duty, and residents of institutional group quarters, such as jails and hospitals).

The most recent NSDUH survey indicates that drug use trends have been relatively stable during the past few years with slight declines in the use of most illegal substances. Nonetheless, an estimated 20 million Americans aged 12 or older had used an illicit drug in the past year, including marijuana/hashish, cocaine (including crack), heroin, hallucinogens, inhalants, or prescription-type psychotherapeutics used nonmedically. As Figure 14.2 shows, marijuana was the most commonly used illicit drug and about 15 million people

Figure 14.2 Past Month Use of Specific Illicit Drugs among Persons Aged 12 or Older

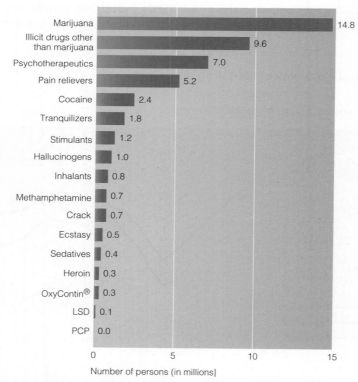

Source: Department of Health and Human Services, 2006 National Survey on Drug Use and Health, www.oas.samhsa.gov/nsduh/2k6nsduh/2k6results.cfm (accessed July 23, 2008).

smoked pot during the past month. About half of all people who said they used a single drug smoked marijuana. Illicit drugs other than marijuana were used by about 10 million people or 47 percent of illicit drug users aged 12 or older; about 20 percent used both marijuana and other drugs.

National Center on Addiction and Substance Abuse (CASA) Survey Surveys conducted by the National Center on Addiction and Substance Abuse at Columbia University provide a less positive view of substance abuse trends, indicating that the problem is still significant. In one effort, entitled "High Society," CASA director Joseph A. Califano, Jr., finds that substance abuse touches almost every American family and is responsible for many of the nation's most devastating social problems, including violent and property crimes, soaring health care costs, family breakup, domestic violence and child abuse, the spread of AIDS, teen pregnancy, poverty, and low productivity (see Exhibit 14.1).

▌ Americans, though comprising only 4 percent of the world's population, consume two-thirds of the world's illegal drugs.

▌ Nearly a quarter of the nation's college students meet the clinical criteria for alcohol and drug abuse and addiction.

▌ Every American child will be offered illegal drugs before graduating from high school, most on several occasions.

▌ The number of teen illegal drug users, which had dropped from its 1979 high of 3.3 million to a low of 1.1 million in 1992, more than doubled to 2.6 million in 2005.

▌ From 1992 to 2003 the number of Americans abusing controlled prescription drugs jumped from 7.8 to 15.1 million.

▌ There has been no significant improvement for decades in alcoholism and alcohol abuse, with the number of alcohol abusers and addicts holding steady at about 16 to 20 million.

▌ One in four Americans will have an alcohol or drug problem at some point in their lives.

▌ 61 million Americans are hooked on cigarettes.

While these data are sobering, the report also notes that a child who reaches age 21 without smoking, using illegal drugs, or abusing alcohol is virtually certain never to do so during their lifetime.

One reason why substance abuse often begins early is that many teens lack parental supervision. One-third of teens and nearly half of 17-year-olds attend house parties where parents are not present and teens are drinking, smoking marijuana, or using cocaine, ecstasy, or prescription drugs. Teens who say parents are not present at the parties they attend are 16 times likelier to say alcohol is available, 15 times likelier to say illegal and prescription drugs are available, and 29 times likelier to say marijuana is available, compared to teens who say parents are always present.

Considering this lack of parental supervision, it is not surprising that CASA finds a significant association between teen drinking and precocious sexuality:

▌ Compared to teens with no sexually active friends, teens who report half or more of their friends are sexually active are more than 6.5 times likelier to drink; 31 times likelier

to get drunk; 22.5 times likelier to have tried marijuana; and more than 5.5 times likelier to smoke.

▌ Teens who spend 25 or more hours a week with a boyfriend/girlfriend are 2.5 times likelier to drink; 5 times likelier to get drunk; 4.5 times likelier to have tried marijuana; and more than 2.5 times likelier to smoke than teens who spend less than 10 hours a week with a boyfriend/girlfriend.

▌ Girls with boyfriends two or more years older are more than twice as likely to drink; almost 6 times likelier to get drunk; 6 times likelier to have tried marijuana; and 4.5 times likelier to smoke than girls whose boyfriends are less than two years older or who do not have a boyfriend.[146]

connections

The problems of self-report surveys were discussed in Chapter 2. While the drug surveys may be beset by problems of missing subjects and subject reliability, they are administered yearly, in a consistent fashion, so that the effects of over- and underreporting and missing subjects should have a consistent effect in every survey year. The surveys have attempted to improve their methodologies to increase validity. For example, the ISR survey now includes 8th and 10th graders in an attempt to survey youths before they drop out of school.

AIDS and Drug Use

Intravenous (IV) drug use is closely tied to the threat of AIDS.[147] Since monitoring the spread of AIDS began in 1981, about one-fourth of all adult AIDS cases reported to the Centers for Disease Control and Prevention in Atlanta have occurred among IV drug users. It is now estimated that as many as one-third of all IV drug users are AIDS carriers.[148]

One reason for the AIDS–drug use relationship is the widespread habit of needle sharing among IV users. One study of Los Angeles drug "shooting galleries" conducted by researcher Douglas Longshore found that about one-quarter of users shoot drugs in these abandoned buildings, private apartments, or other sites, where for a small entry fee injection equipment can be borrowed or rented.[149] Most users (72 percent) shared needles, and although some tried to use bleach as a disinfectant, the majority ignored this safety precaution. Asking for or bringing bleach ruined the moment for some addicts because it reminded them of the risk of AIDS; others were too high to be bothered. As one user told Longshore,

> After I started shooting coke, all hell broke loose, no holds barred, couldn't be bothered to get bleach. That was out of the question. Literally picking needles up that I had no idea who had used. . . . I was just out of my mind insane. [HIV] wasn't a consideration. It was more like, I hope this is going to be okay. You just aren't in your right mind anymore.[150]

Efforts to control drugs by outlawing the over-the-counter sale of hypodermic needles have encouraged needle sharing. Consequently, some jurisdictions have developed outreach programs to help these drug users; others have made an effort to teach users how to clean their needles and syringes; a few states have gone so far as to give addicts sterile needles.[151]

The threat of AIDS may be changing the behavior of recreational and middle-class users, but drug use may still be increasing among the poor, high school dropouts, and other disadvantaged groups. If that pattern is correct, then the recently observed decline in substance abuse may be restricted to one segment of the at-risk population while another is continuing to use drugs at ever-increasing rates.

What Causes Substance Abuse?

What causes people to abuse substances? Although there are many different views on the causes of drug use, most can be characterized as seeing the onset of an addictive career as being either an environmental or a personal matter.

Subcultural View Those who view drug abuse as having an environmental basis concentrate on lower-class addiction. Because a disproportionate number of drug abusers are poor, the onset of drug use can be tied to such factors as racial prejudice, devalued identities, low self-esteem, poor socioeconomic status, and the high level of mistrust, negativism, and defiance found in impoverished areas. Residents feel trapped in a cycle of violence, drug abuse, and despair.[152] Youths in these disorganized areas may join peers to learn the techniques of drug use and receive social support for their habit. Research shows that peer influence is a significant predictor of drug careers that actually grow stronger as people mature.[153] Drug use splits some communities into distinct groups of relatively affluent abstainers and desperately poor abusers.[154]

Psychological View Not all drug abusers reside in lower-class slum areas; the problem of middle-class substance abuse is very real. Consequently, some experts have linked substance abuse to psychological deficits such as impaired cognitive functioning, personality disturbance, and emotional problems that can strike people in any economic class.[155] Research on the psychological characteristics of drug abusers does in fact reveal the presence of a significant degree of personal pathology. Studies have found that addicts suffer personality disorders characterized by a weak ego, low frustration tolerance, anxiety, and fantasies of omnipotence. Many addicts exhibit psychopathic or sociopathic behavior characteristics, forming what is called an addiction-prone personality.[156]

What is the connection between psychological disorder and drug abuse? Drugs may help people deal with unconscious needs and impulses and relieve dependence and depression. People may turn to drug abuse as a form of self-medication in order to reduce the emotional turmoil of adolescence, deal with troubling impulses, or cope with traumatic life experiences. Survivors of sexual assault and physical abuse have been known to turn to drug and alcohol abuse as a coping mechanism.[157] Depressed people may use drugs as an alternative to more radical solutions to their pain, such as suicide.[158]

Genetic Factors Research shows that substance abuse may have a genetic basis.[159] For example, a number of studies comparing alcoholism among identical twins and fraternal twins have found that the degree of concordance (both siblings behaving identically) is twice as high among the identical twin groups.[160]

Taken as a group, studies of the genetic basis of substance abuse suggest that people whose parents were alcoholic or drug dependent have a greater chance of developing a problem than the children of nonabusers, and this relationship occurs regardless of parenting style or the quality of the parent–child relationship.[161] However, not all children of abusing parents become drug dependent themselves, suggesting that even if drug abuse is heritable, environment and socialization must play some role in the onset of abuse.[162]

Social Learning Social psychologists suggest that drug abuse may also result from observing parental drug use. Parental drug abuse begins to have a damaging effect on children as young as 2 years old, especially when parents manifest drug-related personality problems such as depression or poor impulse control.[163] Children whose parents abuse drugs are more likely to have persistent abuse problems than the children of nonabusers.[164]

People who learn that drugs provide pleasurable sensations may be the most likely to experiment with illegal substances; a habit may develop if the user experiences lower anxiety, fear, and tension levels.[165] Having a history of family drug and alcohol abuse has been found to be a characteristic of violent teenage sexual abusers.[166] Heroin abusers report an unhappy childhood that included harsh physical punishment and parental neglect and rejection.[167]

Problem Behavior Syndrome (PBS) For many people, substance abuse is just one of many problem behaviors. Longitudinal studies show that drug abusers are maladjusted, alienated, and emotionally distressed and that drug use is only one among many social problems.[168] Having a deviant lifestyle begins early in life and is punctuated with criminal relationships, family history of substance abuse, educational failure, and alienation. Crack cocaine use has been linked to sexual abuse as children and social isolation as adults.[169] There is robust support for the interconnection of problem drinking and drug abuse, delinquency, precocious sexual behavior, school failure, running away, homelessness, family conflict, and other similar social problems.[170]

Rational Choice Not all people who abuse drugs do so because of personal pathology. Some may use drugs and alcohol because they want to enjoy their effects: get high, relax, improve creativity, escape reality, and increase sexual responsiveness. Research indicates that adolescent alcohol abusers believe that getting high will make them powerful, increase their sexual performance, and facilitate their social behavior; they care little about negative future consequences.[171] Claire Sterk-Elifson's research on middle-class drug-abusing women shows that most were introduced by friends in the context of "just having some fun."[172]

Substance abuse, then, may be a function of the rational but mistaken belief that drugs can benefit the user. The decision to use drugs involves evaluations of personal consequences (such as addiction, disease, and legal punishment) and the expected benefits of drug use (such as peer approval, positive affective states, heightened awareness, and relaxation). Adolescents may begin using drugs because they believe their peers expect them to do so.[173]

Is There a Drug Gateway?

Some experts believe that, regardless of its cause, most people fall into drug abuse slowly, beginning with alcohol and then following with marijuana and more serious drugs as the need for a more powerful high intensifies. A number of research efforts have confirmed this gateway model. James Inciardi, Ruth Horowitz, and Anne Pottieger found a clear pattern of adult involvement in adolescent drug abuse. Kids on crack started their careers with early experimentation with alcohol at age 7, began getting drunk at age 8, had alcohol with an adult present by age 9, and became regular drinkers by the time they were 11 years old.[174] Drinking with an adult present, presumably a parent, was a significant precursor of future substance abuse and delinquency. "Adults who gave children alcohol," they argue, "were also giving

them a head start in a delinquent career."[175] Other research efforts support this view when they find that the most serious drug users have a history of recreational drug and alcohol abuse.[176] Kids who begin using alcohol in adolescence become involved in increasing levels of deviant behavior as they mature.[177]

The drug gateway vision is popular, but not all research efforts find that users progress to ever more potent drugs, and some show that, surprisingly, many hard-core drug abusers never smoked pot or used alcohol.[178] And although many American youths have tried marijuana, few actually progress to crack or heroin abuse.[179]

In sum, there may be no single cause of substance abuse. People may try and continue to use illegal substances for a variety of reasons. As Inciardi points out,

> There are as many reasons people use drugs as there are individuals who use drugs. For some, it may be a function of family disorganization, or cultural learning, or maladjusted personality, or an "addiction-prone" personality. . . . For others, heroin use may be no more than a normal response to the world in which they live.[180]

Types of Drug Users

The general public often groups all drug users together without recognizing that there are many varieties, ranging from adolescent recreational drug users to adults who run large smuggling operations.[181]

Adolescents Who Distribute Small Amounts of Drugs Many adolescents begin their involvement in the drug trade by using and distributing small amounts of drugs; they do not commit any other serious criminal acts. Kenneth Tunnell found in his interviews with low-level drug dealers that many started out as "stash dealers" who sold drugs to maintain a consistent access to drugs for their own consumption; their customers are almost always personal acquaintances, including friends and relatives.[182] They are insulated from the legal system because their activities rarely result in apprehension and sanction.

Adolescents Who Frequently Sell Drugs A small number of adolescents, most often multiple-drug users or heroin or cocaine users, are high-rate dealers who bridge the gap between adult drug distributors and the adolescent user. Frequent dealers often have adults who "front" for them—that is, loan them drugs to sell without upfront cash. The teenagers then distribute the drugs to friends and acquaintances, returning most of the proceeds to the supplier while keeping a commission for themselves. Frequent dealers are more likely to sell drugs in public and can be seen in known drug user hangouts in parks, schools, or other public places. Deals are irregular, so the chances of apprehension are slight.

Teenage Drug Dealers Who Commit Other Delinquent Acts A more serious type of drug-involved youth comprises those who use and distribute multiple substances and also commit both property and violent crimes; many are gang members.[183] Although these youngsters make up about 2 percent of the teenage population, they commit 40 percent of the robberies and assaults and about 60 percent of all teenage felony thefts and drug sales.

These youths are frequently hired by older dealers to act as street-level drug runners. Each member of a crew of three to twelve boys will handle small quantities of drugs, perhaps three bags of heroin, which are received on consignment and sold on the street; the supplier receives 50 to 70 percent of the drug's street value. The crew members also act as lookouts, recruiters, and guards. Between drug sales, the young dealers commit robberies, burglaries, and other thefts.[184]

Adolescents Who Cycle In and Out of the Justice System

Some drug-involved youths are failures at both dealing and crime. They do not have the savvy to join gangs or groups and instead begin committing unplanned, opportunistic crimes that increase their chances of arrest. They are heavy drug users, which both increases apprehension risk and decreases their value for organized drug distribution networks. Drug-involved "losers" can earn a living steering customers to a seller in a "copping" area, "touting" drug availability for a dealer, or acting as a lookout. However, they are not considered trustworthy or deft enough to handle drugs or money. They may bungle other criminal acts, which solidifies their reputation as undesirable.

Drug-Involved Youth Who Continue to Commit Crimes as Adults

Although about two-thirds of substance-abusing youths continue to use drugs after they reach adulthood, about half desist from other criminal activities. Those who persist in both substance abuse and crime as adults exhibit a variety of social and developmental problems. Some evidence also exists that these drug-using persisters have low nonverbal IQs and poor physical coordination.

Outwardly Respectable Adults Who Are Top-Level Dealers

A few outwardly respectable adult dealers sell large quantities of drugs to support themselves in high-class lifestyles. Outwardly respectable dealers are often indistinguishable from other young professionals. Upscale dealers seem to drift into dealing from many different walks of life. Some begin as campus dealers whose lifestyle and outward appearance are indistinguishable from other students (though they are more frequently involved in illegal behavior outside of drug dealing).[185] Frequently they are drawn from professions and occupations that are unstable, have irregular working hours, and accept drug abuse. Former graduate students, musicians, performing artists, and barkeepers are among those who are likely to fit the profile of the adult who begins dealing drugs in his or her 20s. Some use their business skills and drug profits to get into legitimate enterprises or illegal scams. Others drop out of the drug trade because they are the victims of violent crime committed by competitors or disgruntled customers; a few wind up in jail or prison.

Smugglers

Smugglers import drugs into the United States. They are generally men, middle-aged or older, who have strong organizational skills, established connections, capital to invest, and a willingness to take large business risks. Smugglers are a loosely organized, competitive group of individual entrepreneurs. There is a constant flow in and out of the business as some sources become the target of law enforcement activities, new drug sources become available, older smugglers become dealers, and former dealers become smugglers.

Adult Predatory Drug Users Who Are Frequently Arrested

Many users who begin abusing substances in early adolescence continue in drugs and crime in their adulthood. Getting arrested, doing time, using multiple drugs, and committing predatory crimes are a way of life for them. They have few skills, did poorly in school, and have long criminal records. The threat of conviction and punishment has little effect on their criminal activities. These "losers" have friends and relatives involved in drugs and crime. They specialize in robberies, burglaries, thefts, and drug sales. They filter in and out of the justice system and begin committing crimes as soon as they are released. In some populations, at least one-third of adult males are involved in drug trafficking and other criminal acts well into their adulthood.[186]

If they make a "big score," perhaps through a successful drug deal, they may significantly increase their drug use. Their increased narcotics consumption then destabilizes their lifestyle, destroying family and career ties. When their finances dry up, they may become *street junkies*, people whose traditional lifestyle has been destroyed, who turn to petty crime to maintain an adequate supply of drugs. Cut off from a stable source of quality heroin, not knowing from where their next fixes or the money to pay for them will come, looking for any opportunity to make a buck, getting sick or "jonesing," being pathetically unkempt and unable to maintain even the most primitive routines of health or hygiene, street junkies live a very difficult existence. Because they are unreliable and likely to become police informants, street junkies pay the highest prices for the poorest quality heroin; lack of availability increases their need to commit habit-supporting crimes.[187]

Adult Predatory Drug Users Who Are Rarely Arrested

Some drug users are "winners." They commit hundreds of crimes each year but are rarely arrested. On the streets, they are known for their calculated violence. Their crimes are carefully planned and coordinated. They often work with partners and use lookouts to carry out the parts of their crimes that have the highest risk of apprehension. These "winners" are more likely to use recreational drugs, such as coke and pot, than the more addicting heroin or opiates. Some become high-frequency users and risk apprehension and punishment. But for the lucky few, their criminal careers can stretch for up to 15 years without interruption by the justice system. These users are sometimes referred to as *stabilized junkies* who have learned the skills needed to purchase and process larger amounts of heroin. Their addiction enables them to maintain normal lifestyles, although they may turn to drug dealing to create contacts with drug suppliers. They are employable, but earning legitimate income does little to reduce their drug use or dealing activities.[188]

Not all drug-involved people are from the street or were raised in poverty. Some are seemingly respectable adults secretly involved in substance abuse and other crimes. Former New South Wales Aboriginal Affairs Minister Milton Orkopoulos was arrested and charged with 30 offenses, including involvement in child prostitution, sexual assault, and supplying illegal drugs. Here he makes his final walk into the Newcastle Court House in Newcastle, Australia, on March 14, 2008. Orkopoulos was found guilty on 28 counts of child sex and drugs offenses.

Less Predatory Drug-Involved Adult Offenders Most adult drug users are petty criminals who avoid violent crime. These occasional users are people just beginning their addiction, who use small amounts of narcotics, and whose habit can be supported by income from conventional jobs; narcotics have relatively little influence on their lifestyles.[189] They are typically high school graduates and have regular employment that supports their drug use. They usually commit petty thefts or pass bad checks. They stay on the periphery of the drug trade by engaging in such acts as helping addicts shoot up, bagging drugs for dealers, operating shooting galleries, renting needles and syringes, and selling small amounts of drugs. These petty criminal drug users do not have the stomach for a life of hard crime and drug dealing. They violate the law in proportion to the amount and cost of the drugs they are using. Pot smokers have a significantly lower frequency of theft violations than daily heroin users, whose habit is considerably more costly.

Outwardly Respectable Adults Who Are Frequent Users Some drug users continue their activities into their adulthood while others may initiate drug use as part of a new lifestyle developed in their adulthood. While these users may be successful college graduates, they become caught up in the club scene in major cities and get involved in recreational drug use. Some surveys of urban young adults find that almost 40 percent report usage of at least one club drug.[190]

Women Who Are Drug-Involved Offenders Women who are drug-involved offenders constitute a separate type of substance abuser. Although women are far less likely than men to use addictive drugs, research conducted by CASA found that 15 million girls and women use illicit drugs or abuse controlled

prescription drugs, 32 million smoke cigarettes, and 6 million are alcohol abusers and alcoholics. Substance abuse is nondiscriminatory and affects all women—rich, poor, young, old, urban, rural, professional and homemaker.[191]

Though infrequently violent criminals, women who abuse substances are more likely to get involved in prostitution and low-level drug dealing; a few become top-level dealers. Many are pregnant or are already mothers, and because they share needles, they are at high risk of contracting AIDS and passing the HIV virus to their newborn children. They maintain a high risk of victimization. One study of 171 women using crack cocaine found that since initiating crack use, 62 percent of the women reported suffering a physical attack and 32 percent suffered rape; more than half were forced to seek medical care for their injuries.[192]

Drugs and Crime

One of the main reasons for the criminalization of particular substances is the assumed association between drug abuse and crime. Research suggests that many criminal offenders have extensive experience with drug use and that drug users commit an enormous amount of crime; alcohol abuse has also been linked to criminality.[193] Research shows that almost four in ten violent crimes and fatal motor vehicle accidents involve alcohol.[194] A number of sources indicate a strong connection between drug use and crime.

User Surveys Numerous self-report studies have examined the criminal activity of drug users. As a group, they show that people who take drugs have extensive involvement in crime.[195] Youths who abuse alcohol are also the most likely to engage in violence during their life course; violent adolescents report histories of alcohol abuse; adults with long histories of drinking are also more likely to report violent offending patterns.[196] One often-cited study of this type was conducted by sociologist James Inciardi. After interviewing 356 addicts in Miami, Inciardi found that they reported 118,134 criminal offenses during a 12-month period; of these, 27,464 were index crimes.[197] If this behavior is typical, the country's estimated 300,000 to 700,000 heroin users could be responsible for a significant amount of all criminal behavior. An English study using a sample of 100 known abusers found that more than half of the subjects reported involvement in crime in the month prior. The most common offenses were shoplifting, receiving stolen goods, and theft; violence was used relatively rarely (11 percent).[198]

The NSDUH survey found that youths who self-reported delinquent behavior during the past year are also more likely to use illicit drugs in the past month than other youths. Those who reported getting into a serious fight at school or work (21 versus 9 percent), carrying a handgun (35 versus 11 percent), selling illegal drugs (60 versus 9 percent), and stealing or trying to steal something worth $50 or more (44 versus 10 percent) were significantly more likely to use drugs than those who did not engage in such antisocial behaviors.[199]

Arrestee Data According to the most recent National Survey on Drug Use and Health, an estimated 1.2 million adults aged 18 or older were arrested for a serious violent or property offense in the past year. The survey found that of the arrestees,

- Adults who were arrested in the past year for any serious violent or property offense were more likely to have used an illicit drug in the past year than those who were not arrested for a serious offense (60.1 percent versus 13.6 percent).

- Adults who had been arrested for serious violent or property offenses in the past year were more likely than those not arrested for serious offenses to have used marijuana (46.5 percent versus 10 percent) and cocaine, crack cocaine, hallucinogens, methamphetamines, heroin, and prescription drugs nonmedically.[200]

Prison Inmate Surveys Surveys of prison inmates disclose that many are lifelong substance abusers. One recent survey of California inmates found that methamphetamine use was significantly predictive of self-reported violent criminal behavior and general recidivism (i.e., a return to custody for any reason).[201] Bureau of Justice Statistics surveys indicate that about 30 percent of property and 25 percent of drug offenders doing time in state prisons claim they committed crimes for drug money.[202]

The Drug–Crime Connection It is of course possible that most criminals are not actually drug users, but that police are more likely to apprehend muddle-headed substance abusers than clear-thinking abstainers. A second, and probably more plausible, interpretation is that most criminals are in fact substance abusers.

Although the drug–crime connection is powerful, the true relationship is still uncertain because many users have had a history of criminal activity before the onset of their substance abuse.[203] It is possible that:

- Chronic criminal offenders begin to abuse drugs and alcohol *after* they have engaged in crime; that is, crime causes drug abuse.

- Substance abusers turn to a life of crime to support their habits; that is, the economics of drug abuse causes crime. Rich drug users don't commit crime.

- Drug use and crime co-occur in individuals; that is, both crime and drug abuse are caused by some other common factor. For example, risk takers may abuse drugs and also commit crime.[204]

- Drug users engage in activities that involve them with peers who encourage them to commit crime or support their criminal activity.[205] Kids who join gangs are more likely later to abuse substances and commit crime.

- Drug abusers face social problems that lead them to crime. They are more likely to drop out of school, be underemployed, engage in premarital sex, and become unmarried parents.[206] Social problems and not drug use are the cause of crime.

Considering these possible scenarios, it is impossible to make a definitive statement such as "drugs cause crime." However, while it is not certain whether drug use turns otherwise law-abiding citizens into criminals, it certainly amplifies the extent of their criminal activities. And, as addiction levels increase, so do the frequency and seriousness of criminality. While the drug–crime link is still uncertain, drug use interferes with maturation and socialization.

In sum, research testing both the criminality of known narcotics users and the narcotics use of known criminals produces a very strong association between drug use and crime. Even if the crime rate of drug users were actually half that reported in the research literature, users would be responsible for a significant portion of the total criminal activity in the United States. Concept Summary 14.1 summarizes the relationship between drug use and crime.

Drugs and the Law

The federal government first initiated legal action to curtail the use of some drugs early in the twentieth century. In 1906, the Pure Food and Drug Act required manufacturers to list the amounts of habit-forming drugs in products on the labels but did not restrict their use. However, the act prohibited the importation and sale of opiates except for medicinal purposes. In 1914, the Harrison Narcotics Act restricted importation, manufacture, sale, and dispensing of narcotics. It defined *narcotic* as any drug that produces sleep and relieves pain, such as heroin, morphine, and opium. The act was revised in 1922 to allow importation of opium and coca (cocaine) leaves for qualified medical practitioners. The Marijuana Tax Act of 1937 required registration and payment of a tax by all who imported, sold, or manufactured marijuana. Because marijuana was classified as a narcotic, those registering would also be subject to criminal penalty.

In later years, other federal laws were passed to clarify existing drug statutes and revise penalties. For example, the Boggs Act of 1951 provided mandatory sentences for violating federal drug laws. The Durham-Humphrey Act of 1951 made it illegal to dispense barbiturates and amphetamines without a prescription. The Narcotic Control Act of 1956 increased penalties for drug offenders. In 1965, the Drug Abuse Control Act set up stringent guidelines for the legal use and sale of mood-modifying drugs, such as barbiturates, amphetamines, LSD, and any other "dangerous drugs," except narcotics prescribed by doctors and pharmacists. Illegal possession was punished as a misdemeanor and manufacture or sale as a felony. And in 1970, the Comprehensive Drug Abuse Prevention and Control Act set up unified categories of illegal drugs and associated penalties with their sale, manufacture, or possession. The law gave the U.S. attorney general discretion to decide in which category to place any new drug.

THE DRUG–CRIME RELATIONSHIP

Relationship	Definition	Examples
Drug-defined offenses	Violations of laws prohibiting or regulating the possession, use, distribution, or manufacture of illegal drugs	Drug possession or use; marijuana cultivation; cocaine, heroin, or marijuana sales
Drug-related offenses	Offenses in which a drug's pharmacologic effects contribute; offenses motivated by the user's need for money to support continued use; offenses connected to drug distribution itself	Violent behavior resulting from drug effects; stealing to get money to buy drugs; violence against rival drug dealers
Drug-using lifestyle	Drug use and crime are common aspects of a deviant lifestyle; the likelihood and frequency of involvement in illegal activity is increased because drug users may not participate in the legitimate economy and are exposed to situations that encourage crime	A life orientation with an emphasis on short-term goals supported by illegal activities; opportunities to offend resulting from contacts with offenders and illegal markets; criminal skills learned from other offenders

Since then, various federal laws have attempted to increase penalties imposed on drug smugglers and limit the manufacture and sale of newly developed substances. For example, the 1984 Controlled Substances Act set new, stringent penalties for drug dealers and created five categories of narcotic and non-narcotic substances subject to federal laws.[207] The Anti-Drug Abuse Act of 1986 again set new standards for minimum and maximum sentences for drug offenders, increased penalties for most offenses, and created a new drug penalty classification for large-scale offenses (such as trafficking in more than 1 kilogram of heroin), for which the penalty for a first offense was 10 years to life in prison.[208] With then-President George H. W. Bush's endorsement, Congress passed the Anti-Drug Abuse Act of 1988, which created a coordinated national drug policy under a "drug czar," set treatment and prevention priorities, and, symbolizing the government's hard-line stance against drug dealing, imposed the death penalty for drug-related killings.[209]

For the most part, state laws mirror federal statutes. Some states now apply extremely heavy penalties for selling or distributing dangerous drugs, involving long prison sentences of up to 25 years.

Drug Control Strategies

Substance abuse remains a major social problem in the United States. Politicians looking for a safe campaign issue can take advantage of the public's fear of drug addiction by calling for a war on drugs. These wars have been declared even when drug usage is stable or in decline.[210] Can these efforts pay off? Can illegal drug use be eliminated or controlled?

A number of different drug control strategies have been tried with varying degrees of success. Some aim to deter drug use by stopping the flow of drugs into the country, apprehending and punishing dealers, and cracking down on street-level drug deals. Others focus on preventing drug use by educating potential users to the dangers of substance abuse (convincing them to "say no to drugs") and by organizing community groups to work with the at-risk population in their area. Still another approach is to treat known users so they can control their addictions. Some of these efforts are discussed here.

Source Control One approach to drug control is to deter the sale and importation of drugs through the systematic apprehension of large-volume drug dealers, coupled with the enforcement of strict drug laws that carry heavy penalties. This approach is designed to capture and punish known international drug dealers and deter those who are considering entering the drug trade. A major effort has been made to cut off supplies of drugs by destroying overseas crops and arresting members of drug cartels in Central and South America, Asia, and the Middle East, where many drugs are grown and manufactured. The federal government has been in the vanguard of encouraging exporting nations to step up efforts to destroy drug crops and prosecute dealers. However, translating words into deeds is a formidable task. Drug lords are willing and able to fight back through intimidation, violence, and corruption when necessary.

The amount of narcotics grown each year is so vast that even if three-quarters of the opium crop were destroyed, the U.S. market would still require only 10 percent of the remainder to sustain the drug trade. Radically reducing the amount of illegal drugs produced each year might have little effect on U.S. consumption. Drug users in the United States are more able and willing to pay for drugs than anyone else in the world. Even if the supply were reduced, whatever drugs there were would find their way to the United States.

Adding to control problems is the fact that the drug trade is an important source of foreign revenue, and destroying the drug trade undermines the economies of third-world nations.

Even if the government of one nation were willing to cooperate in vigorous drug suppression efforts, suppliers in other nations, eager to cash in on the sellers' market, would be encouraged to turn more acreage over to coca or poppy production. Today, almost every Caribbean country is involved with narcotrafficking and, in the case of Jamaica, large-scale production and export of marijuana. Illicit drug shipments in the region are worth more money than the top five legitimate exports combined. Drug gangs are able to corrupt the political structure and destabilize countries. Drug addiction and violent crime are now common in Jamaica, Puerto Rico, and even small islands like St. Kitts. The corruption of the police and other security forces has reached a crisis point in Jamaica, where an officer can earn the equivalent of half a year's salary by simply looking the other way on a drug deal. In 2006, 1,300 Jamaicans were murdered, in a population of only 3 million—and that was an improvement on the previous year.[211] There are also indications that the drug syndicates may be planting a higher yield variety of coca and improving refining techniques to replace crops lost to government crackdowns.

Adding to the problem of source control is the fact that the United States has little influence in some key drug-producing areas such as Afghanistan and Colombia.[212] War and terrorism also may make source control strategies problematic. After the United States toppled Afghanistan's Taliban government, the remnants began to grow and sell poppies to support their insurgency; Afghanistan now supplies 90 percent of the world's opium.[213] And while the Colombian guerillas may not be interested in joining or colluding with crime cartels, they finance their war against the government by aiding drug traffickers and "taxing" crops and sales.[214]

Interdiction Strategies Law enforcement efforts have also been directed at intercepting drug supplies as they enter the country. Border patrols and military personnel using sophisticated hardware have been involved in massive interdiction efforts; many impressive multimillion-dollar seizures have been made. Yet the U.S. borders are so vast and unprotected that meaningful interdiction is impossible. And even if all importation were shut down, homegrown marijuana and laboratory-made drugs, such as "ice," LSD, and PCP, could become the drugs of choice. Even now, their easy availability and relatively low cost are increasing their popularity among the at-risk population.

Law Enforcement Strategies Local, state, and federal law enforcement agencies have been actively fighting against drugs. One approach is to direct efforts at large-scale drug rings. The long-term consequences have been to decentralize drug dealing and encourage new groups to become major suppliers. Asian, Latin American, and Jamaican groups, motorcycle clubs, and local gangs, such as the Crips and Bloods, are all now involved in large-scale dealing. Colombian syndicates have established cocaine distribution centers on every continent, and Mexican organizations are responsible for large methamphetamine shipments to U.S., Russian, Turkish, Italian, Nigerian, Chinese,

Lebanese, and Pakistani heroin trafficking syndicates, which are now competing for dominance.

Police can also target, intimidate, and arrest street-level dealers and users in an effort to make drug use so much of a hassle that consumption is cut back and the crime rate reduced. Approaches that have been tried include reverse stings, in which undercover agents pose as dealers to arrest users who approach them for a buy.

In terms of weight and availability, there is still no commodity more lucrative than illegal drugs. They cost relatively little to produce and provide large profit margins to dealers and traffickers. At an average street price of $118 per gram in the United States (the current price according to the Office of National Drug Control Policy), a metric ton of pure cocaine is worth more than $100 million; cutting it and reducing purity can double or triple the value.[215] It is difficult for law enforcement agencies to counteract the inducement of drug profits. When large-scale drug busts are made, supplies become scarce and market values increase, encouraging more people to enter the drug trade. There are also suspicions that a displacement effect occurs: stepped-up efforts to curb drug dealing in one area or city simply encourage dealers to seek out friendlier territory.[216]

Punishment Strategies Even if law enforcement efforts cannot produce a general deterrent effect, the courts may achieve the required result by severely punishing known drug dealers and traffickers. A number of initiatives have made the prosecution and punishment of drug offenders a top priority. State prosecutors have expanded their investigations into drug importation and distribution and created special prosecutors to focus on drug dealers. Once convicted, drug dealers can get very long sentences.

However, these efforts often have their downside. Defense attorneys consider delay tactics to be sound legal maneuvering in drug-related cases. Courts are so backlogged that prosecutors are anxious to plea bargain. The consequence of this legal maneuvering is that about 25 percent of people convicted on federal drug charges are granted probation or some other form of community release. Even so, prisons have become jammed with inmates, many of whom were involved in drug-related cases. Many drug offenders sent to prison do not serve their entire sentences because they are released in an effort to relieve prison overcrowding. The mean sentence for drug trafficking is 55 months, but the actual time served is 24 months or about half of the original sentence.[217]

It is unlikely that the public would approve of a drug control strategy that locks up large numbers of traffickers; research indicates that the public already believes drug trafficking penalties are too harsh (while supporting the level of punishment for other crimes).[218] And some critics are disturbed because punishment strategies seem to have a disproportionate effect on minority group members and the impoverished. Some have gone as far as suggesting that government agencies are either ignoring or covering up the toll harsh drug penalties have on society's disadvantaged because it is politically expedient to be a tough defender of the nation's moral climate.[219]

Community Strategies Another type of drug-control effort relies on the involvement of local community groups to lead the fight against drugs. Representatives of various local government agencies, churches, civic organizations, and similar institutions are being brought together to create drug prevention and awareness programs.

Citizen-sponsored programs attempt to restore a sense of community in drug-infested areas, reduce fear, and promote conventional norms and values.[220] These efforts can be classified into one of four distinct categories:[221]

- *Law enforcement–type efforts*. These may include block watches, cooperative police–community efforts, and citizen patrols. Some of these citizen groups are nonconfrontational: they simply observe or photograph dealers, write down their license plate numbers, and then notify police. On occasion, telephone hotlines have been set up to take anonymous tips on drug activity. Other groups engage in confrontational tactics that may even include citizens' arrests. Area residents have gone as far as contracting with private security firms to conduct neighborhood patrols.

- *Use of the civil justice system to discourage offenders*. Landlords have been sued for owning properties that house drug dealers; neighborhood groups have scrutinized drug houses for building code violations. Information acquired from these various sources is turned over to local authorities, such as police and housing agencies, for more formal action.

- *Community-based treatment efforts*. Some of these programs utilize citizen volunteers who participate in self-help support programs. Some such as Narcotics Anonymous or Cocaine Anonymous have more than 1,000 chapters nationally. Other programs provide youths with martial arts training, dancing, and social events as an alternative to the drug life.

- *Enhance the quality of life, improve interpersonal relationships, and upgrade the neighborhood's physical environment*. Activities might include the creation of drug-free school zones, which encourage police to keep drug dealers away from the vicinity of schools. Consciousness-raising efforts include demonstrations and marches to publicize the drug problem and build solidarity among participants. Politicians have been lobbied to get better police protection or tougher laws passed; New York City residents even sent bags filled with crack collected from street corners to the mayor and police commissioner to protest drug dealing. Residents have cleaned up streets, fixed broken streetlights, and planted gardens in empty lots to broadcast the message that they have local pride and do not want drug dealers in their neighborhoods.

These community crime prevention efforts seem appealing, but there is little conclusive evidence that they are an effective drug control strategy. Some surveys indicate that most residents do not participate in programs. There is also evidence that community programs work better in stable, middle-income areas than in those that are crime ridden and disorganized.[222]

Although these findings are discouraging, some studies do find that on occasion deteriorated areas can sustain successful anti-drug programs.[223] Future evaluations of community control efforts should determine whether they can work in the most economically depressed areas.

Education Strategies According to this view, substance abuse would decline if kids could be taught about the dangers of drug use. The most widely known drug education program, Drug Abuse Resistance Education (D.A.R.E.), is an elementary school course designed to give students the skills for resisting peer pressure to experiment with tobacco, drugs, and alcohol. It is unique because it employs uniformed police officers to carry the antidrug message to the students before they enter junior high school. While more than 40 percent of all school districts incorporate assistance from local law enforcement agencies in their drug prevention programming, reviews of the program have not been supportive. Dennis Rosenbaum and his associates found that it had only a marginal impact on student drug use and attitudes.[224] A longitudinal study by psychologist Donald Lynam and his colleagues found that D.A.R.E. had no effect on students' drug use at any time through 10th grade, and a 10-year follow-up failed to find any hidden or delayed "sleeper" effects. At age 20, there were no differences in drug use between those who received D.A.R.E. and those who did not; the only difference was that those who received D.A.R.E. reported slightly lower levels of self-esteem at age 20, an effect that proponents were not aiming for.[225] These evaluations caused D.A.R.E. to revise its curriculum. It is now aimed at older students and relies more on having them question their assumptions about drug use than on listening to lectures on the subject.

Drug-Testing Strategies Drug testing of students, private employees, government workers, and criminal offenders is believed to deter substance abuse. In the workplace, employees are tested to enhance on-the-job safety and productivity. In some industries, such as mining and transportation, drug testing is considered essential because abuse can pose a threat to the public.[226] Business leaders have been enlisted in the fight against drugs. Mandatory drug-testing programs in government and industry are common: more than 40 percent of the country's largest companies, including IBM and AT&T, have drug-testing programs. The federal government requires employee testing in regulated industries such as nuclear energy and defense contracting. About 4 million transportation workers are subject to testing.

Drug testing is also common in government and criminal justice agencies. About 30 percent of local police departments test applicants, and 16 percent routinely test field officers. However, larger jurisdictions serving populations over 250,000 are much more likely to test applicants (84 percent) and field officers (75 percent). Drug testing is also part of the federal government's Drug-Free Workplace Program, which has the goal of improving productivity and safety. Employees most likely to be tested include presidential appointees, law enforcement officers, and people in positions of national security.

One way of eliminating drugs is to create effective community-level drug treatment strategies. Here Tara Ginn receives a certificate of completion from Judge William Morse during a graduation ceremony in Wellness Court in Anchorage, Alaska, on June 2, 2008. Ginn successfully completed a one-year treatment program after being arrested for felony drug possession.

wean patients from the more addicting drugs to those that can be more easily regulated, such as methadone. Methadone is a drug similar to heroin, and addicts can be treated at clinics where they receive methadone under controlled conditions. However, methadone programs have been undermined because some users sell their methadone on the black market, and others supplement their dosages with illegally obtained heroin. Other programs utilize drugs such as Naxalone, which counters the effects of narcotics and eases the trauma of withdrawal, but results have not been conclusive.[231]

Other therapeutic programs attempt to deal with the psychological causes of drug use. Hypnosis, aversion therapy (getting users to associate drugs with unpleasant sensations, such as nausea), counseling, biofeedback, and other techniques are often used.

The long-term effects of treatment on drug abuse are still uncertain. Critics charge that a stay in a residential program can help stigmatize people as addicts even if they never used hard drugs; and in treatment they may be introduced to hard-core users with whom they will associate after release. Users do not often enter these programs voluntarily and have little motivation to change.[232] Relatively few drug-dependent people actually receive the rehabilitation efforts they so desperately need. Unfortunately, those requiring treatment may not often receive the proper care. Many people who need treatment are unaware or in denial. And even those who could be helped soon learn that there are simply more users who need treatment than there are beds in treatment facilities. Many facilities are restricted to users whose health insurance will pay for short-term residential care; when their insurance coverage ends, patients are often released, even though their treatment is incomplete.

Supporters of treatment argue that many addicts are helped by intensive in- and out-patient treatment. As one District of Columbia program shows, clients who complete treatment programs are less likely to use drugs than those who drop out.[233] Although such data support treatment strategies, it is also possible that completers are motivated individuals who would have stopped using drugs even if they had not been treated.

In order to aid in dispensing treatment, state jurisdictions have developed specialized drug courts. These are described in the Policy and Practice in Criminology feature "Drug Courts."

Criminal defendants are now routinely tested at all stages of the justice system, from arrest to parole. The goal is to reduce criminal behavior by detecting current users and curbing their abuse. Can such programs reduce criminal activity? Two evaluations of pretrial drug-testing programs found little evidence that monitoring defendants' drug use influenced their behavior.[227]

Schools have adopted drug testing of students and there is some evidence that random tests can reduce drug use among youth. Those who favor student testing believe it may also help improve the learning environment in schools by diminishing the culture of drugs without sacrificing school morale.[228]

Drug Treatment Strategies A number of approaches are taken to treat known users, getting them clean of drugs and alcohol, and thereby reducing the at-risk population. One approach rests on the assumption that each user is an individual and successful treatment must be geared to the using patterns and personality of the individual offenders in order to build a sense of self.[229] Some programs have placed abusers in regimens of outdoor activities and wilderness training to create self-reliance and a sense of accomplishment.[230] More intensive efforts use group therapy approaches relying on group leaders who have been substance abusers; through such sessions users get the skills and support to help them reject social pressure to use drugs. These programs are based on the Alcoholics Anonymous approach, which holds that users must find within themselves the strength to stay clean and that peer support from those who understand their experiences can help them achieve a drug-free life.

There are also residential programs for the more heavily involved, and a large network of drug treatment centers has been developed. Some detoxification units use medical procedures to

Employment Programs Research indicates that drug abusers who obtain and keep employment will end or reduce the incidence of their substance abuse.[234] Not surprisingly, then, there have been a number of efforts to provide vocational rehabilitation for drug abusers. One approach is the supported work program, which typically involves job-site training, ongoing assessment,

DRUG COURTS

The mission of drug courts is to stop the abuse of alcohol and other drugs and related criminal activity by offenders. Drug courts handle cases involving drug-addicted offenders through an extensive supervision and treatment program. In exchange for successful completion of the program, the court may dismiss the original charge, reduce or set aside a sentence, offer some lesser penalty, or offer a combination of these. The aim is to place nonviolent first offenders into intensive treatment programs rather than in jail or prison. The drug court movement began in Florida in order to address the state's growing problem of prison overcrowding due in large part to an influx of drug-involved offenders. Today there are about 1,700 drug courts operating in the United States, and about 350 more in the planning phases. Currently, 50 states plus the District of Columbia, the Northern Mariana Islands, Puerto Rico, Guam, two federal districts, and 121 tribal programs have drug courts that are in operation or are being planned.

Drug courts address the overlap between the public health threats of drug abuse and crime: crimes are often drug related; drug abusers are frequently involved with the criminal justice system. Drug courts provide an ideal setting to address these problems by linking the justice system with health services and drug treatment providers while easing the burden on the already overtaxed correctional system.

Are drug courts effective? The jury is still out. Research by Denise Gottfredson and her associates conducted in the Baltimore City Drug Treatment Court (BCDTC) found that drug courts did seem to work for reducing crime in a population of offenders who were severely drug addicted. In one study conducted with Lyn Exum, Gottfredson used a carefully designed experimental model in which cases were randomly sent either to the drug court or a traditional court. The researchers found that drug court judges actually impose harsher sentences, but suspended these sentences conditional to compliance with the drug court regimen in drug testing and treatment and attending status hearings. Most importantly, within a 12-month period, 48 percent of drug treatment court clients were arrested for new offenses, compared to 64 percent of the people handled in traditional courts. Among the more serious cases heard, 32 percent of drug court clients versus 57 percent of controls were re-arrested. All things considered, cases handled in a traditional court suffered rearrest at a rate nearly three times that of drug treatment court.

Not all drug courts are equal, and national evaluations suggest that some are more effective than others. One reason may be clientele: drug courts with the lowest recidivism rates (10 percent or less) tend to accept offenders with the least severe problems, mostly alcohol or marijuana, and who are classified by the drug courts as having "minimal" drug problems. In contrast, the drug courts with the highest recidivism rates are willing to handle the more difficult cases involving people addicted to heroin and/or cocaine.

CRITICAL THINKING

1. Are drug courts inherently coercive? Should drug users be forced to go into treatment?

2. Are drug treatment programs doomed to failure because there are so many different types of drug abusers, with entirely different motivations?

Sources: J. Scott Sanford and Bruce Arrigo, "Lifting the Cover on Drug Courts: Evaluation Findings and Policy Concerns," *International Journal of Offender Therapy and Comparative Criminology* 49 (2005): 239–259; John Goldkamp, "The Impact of Drug Courts," *Criminology and Public Policy* 2 (2003): 197–206; Denise Gottfredson, Stacy Najaka, and Brook Kearley, "Effectiveness of Drug Treatment Courts: Evidence from a Randomized Trial," *Criminology and Public Policy* 2 (2003): 171–197; Denise Gottfredson and Lyn Exum, "The Baltimore City Drug Treatment Court: One-Year Results from a Randomized Study," *Journal of Research in Crime and Delinquency* 39 (2002): 337–357; John Roman, Wendy Townsend, and Avinash Singh Bhati, *Recidivism Rates for Drug Court Graduates: Nationally Based Estimates, Final Report* (Washington, DC: Urban Institute, 2003), www.ncjrs.gov/pdffiles1/201229.pdf (accessed July 15, 2008).

and job-site intervention. Rather than teach work skills in a classroom, support programs rely on helping drug abusers deal with real work settings. Other programs that have merit provide training to overcome the barriers to employment and improve work skills, including help with motivation, education, experience, the job market, job-seeking skills, and personal issues.[235]

Concept Summary 14.2 summarizes the various drug control efforts.

Drug Legalization

Considering these problems, some commentators have called for the legalization or decriminalization of restricted drugs. The so-called war on drugs is expensive, costing more than $500 billion over the past 20 years—money that could have been spent on education and economic development. Drug enforcement and treatment now cost federal, state, and local governments about $100 billion per year. The National Center on Addiction and Substance Abuse at Columbia University claims states have spent more than $80 billion on substance abuse and addiction.[236] The federal government is now spending almost $14 billion annually on drug control, up from $7 billion in 1995; this figure does not reflect treatment costs and is expected to increase.[237]

Despite the massive effort to control drugs through prevention, deterrence, education, and treatment strategies, the fight against substance abuse has not proved successful. It is difficult to get people out of the drug culture because of the enormous

DRUG CONTROL STRATEGIES

Control Strategy	Main Focus	Problems/Issues
Source control	Destroy overseas crops and drug labs	Drug profits hard to resist; drug crops in hostile nations are off limits
Interdiction	Seal borders; arrest drug couriers	Extensive U.S. borders hard to control
Law enforcement	Police investigation and arrest of dealers	New dealers are recruited to replace those in prison
Punishment	Deter dealers with harsh punishments	Crowded prisons promote bargain justice
Community development	Help community members deal with drug	Relies on community cohesion and problem solving on the local level
Drug education	Teach kids about the harm of taking	Evaluations do not show that programs are effective
Drug testing	Threaten employees with drug tests	Evaluations do not show that testing deters drug use; people cheat on tests
Treatment	Use of therapy to get people off drugs	Expensive, requires motivation; clients associate with other users
Employment	Provide jobs as an alternative to drugs	Requires that former addicts become steady employees
Legalization	Decriminalize or legalize drugs	Political hot potato; danger of creating more users

profits involved in the drug trade. It has also proved difficult to control drugs by convincing known users to quit; few treatment efforts have been successful. The problem may lie in the fact that there are multiple efforts to control drugs, some relying on enforcement and punishment and others on treatment and rehabilitation. While the former requires drug users to be secretive and discreet in order to avoid detection, the latter demands openness and receptivity to treatment.[238]

Considering this failure, the only course to deal with the drug problem is through decriminalization of drug offenses. Legalization is warranted, according to drug expert Ethan Nadelmann, because the use of mood-altering substances is customary in almost all human societies; people have always wanted, and will find ways of obtaining, psychoactive drugs.[239] Nadelmann heads the Drug Policy Alliance, a national organization dedicated to ending the war against drugs, which they believe has become overzealous in its effort to punish drug traffickers.

Banning drugs creates networks of manufacturers and distributors, many of whom use violence as part of their standard operating procedures. Although some believe that drug use is immoral, Nadelmann questions whether it is any worse than the unrestricted use of alcohol and cigarettes, both of which are addicting and unhealthful. Far more people die each year because they abuse these legal substances than are killed in drug wars or from abusing illegal substances.

Nadelmann also states that just as Prohibition failed to stop the flow of alcohol in the 1920s, while it increased the power of organized crime, the policy of prohibiting drugs is similarly doomed to failure. When drugs were legal and freely available in the early twentieth century, the proportion of Americans using drugs was not much greater than today. Most users led normal lives, probably because of the legal status of their drug use.

If drugs were legalized, the argument goes, price and distribution could be controlled by the government. This would reduce addicts' cash requirements, so crime rates would drop because users would no longer need the same cash flow to support their habits. Drug-related deaths would decline because government control would reduce needle sharing and the spread of AIDS. Legalization would also destroy the drug-importing cartels and gangs. Because drugs would be bought and sold openly, the government would reap a tax windfall both from taxes on the sale of drugs and from income taxes paid by drug dealers on profits that have been part of the hidden economy. Of course, drug distribution would be regulated, like alcohol, keeping drugs away from adolescents, public servants such as police and airline pilots, and known felons. Those who favor legalization point to the Netherlands as a country that has legalized drugs and remains relatively crime free.

The Consequences of Legalization Critics claim the legalization approach might have the short-term effect of reducing the association between drug use and crime, but it might also have grave social consequences. Legalization might increase the nation's rate of drug usage, creating an even larger group of nonproductive, drug-dependent people who must be cared for by the rest of society.[240] If drugs were legalized and freely available, drug users might significantly increase their daily intake. In countries like Iran and Thailand, where drugs are cheap and readily available, the rate of narcotics use is quite high. Historically, the availability of cheap narcotics has preceded drug-use epidemics, as was the case when British and American merchants sold opium in nineteenth-century China.

Furthermore, if the government tried to raise money by taxing legal drugs, as it now does with liquor and cigarettes, that might encourage drug smuggling to avoid tax payments; these "illegal" drugs might then fall into the hands of adolescents.

The Lessons of Alcohol The problems of alcoholism should serve as a warning of what can happen when controlled substances are made readily available. Because women may more easily become dependent on crack than men, the number of drug-dependent babies could begin to match or exceed the number delivered with fetal alcohol syndrome.[241] Drunk-driving fatalities, which today number about 25,000 per year, might be matched by deaths due to driving under the influence of pot or crack. And although distribution would be regulated, it is likely that adolescents would have the same opportunity to obtain potent drugs as they now have to obtain alcoholic beverages.

Decriminalization or legalization of controlled substances is unlikely in the near term, but further study is warranted. What effect would a policy of partial decriminalization (for example, legalizing small amounts of marijuana) have on drug use rates? Would a get-tough policy help to "widen the net" of the justice system and actually deepen some youths' involvement in substance abuse? Can society provide alternatives to drugs that will reduce teenage drug dependency?[242] The answers to these questions have proven elusive.

www Go to academic.cengage.com/criminaljustice/siegel to learn more about the following topics:

- **Cocaine Anonymous** is a fellowship of men and women who share their experience, strength, and hope with one another so that they may solve their common problem and help others to recover from their addiction.

- **Narcotics Anonymous** is a similar organization based on the principles of Alcoholics Anonymous.

THINKING LIKE A CRIMINOLOGIST

The national drug czar asks you to review this policy statement by the Drug Policy Alliance, which is highly critical of the war on drugs:

> *Everyone has a stake in ending the war on drugs. Whether you're a parent concerned about protecting children from drug-related harm, a social justice advocate worried about racially disproportionate incarceration rates, an environmentalist seeking to protect the Amazon rainforest, or a fiscally conservative taxpayer, you have a stake in ending the drug war. U.S. federal, state, and local governments have spent hundreds of billions of dollars trying to make America "drug-free." Yet heroin, cocaine, methamphetamine, and other illicit drugs are cheaper, purer, and easier to get than ever before. Nearly half a million people are behind bars on drug charges—more than all of western Europe (with a bigger population) incarcerates for all offenses. The war on drugs has become a war on families, a war on public health, and a war on our constitutional rights.*
>
> *Many of the problems the drug war purports to resolve are in fact caused by the drug war itself. So-called "drug-related" crime is a direct result of drug prohibition's distortion of immutable laws of supply and demand. Public health problems like HIV and Hepatitis C are all exacerbated by zero tolerance laws that restrict access to clean needles. The drug war is not the promoter of family values that some would have us believe. Children of inmates are at risk of educational failure, joblessness, addiction, and delinquency. Drug abuse is bad, but the drug war is worse.*

Source: Drug Policy Alliance, "What's Wrong with War on Drugs?" www.drugpolicy.org/drugwar/ (accessed July 8, 2008).

 Writing Exercise As the coordinator of the nation's efforts to control drugs, the czar who heads the Office of Drug Control Policy wants you to craft a statement to rebuke this position. What would you say? Write a paper (about 300 words) defending the war on drugs.

 Doing Research on the Web Before you answer, check the drug czar's website; while there, you may want to follow their drug info links, and also check the parents' antidrug site. All can be accessed via academic.cengage.com/criminaljustice/siegel.

SUMMARY

- Public order crimes are acts considered illegal because they conflict with social policy, accepted moral rules, and public opinion.

- There is usually great debate over public order crimes. Some charge that public order crimes are not crimes at all and that it is foolish to legislate morality. Others view such morally tinged acts as prostitution, gambling, and drug abuse as harmful and therefore subject to public control.

- Immoral acts can be distinguished from crimes on the basis of the social harm they cause. Acts that are believed to be extremely harmful to the general public are usually outlawed.

- Moral crusaders attempt to shape the law to match their personal values and beliefs.

- Moral crusades have been aimed at such acts as obscenity and recreational drugs.

- Many public order crimes are sex related.

- Prostitution is a sex-related public order crime. Although prostitution has been practiced for thousands of years and is legal in some areas, most states outlaw commercial sex.

- The international sex trade is a multibillion-dollar business; it involves tricking young girls (primarily from Eastern Europe and Asia) into becoming prostitutes.

- There are a variety of prostitutes, including streetwalkers, B-girls, and call girls.

- Studies indicate that prostitutes come from poor, troubled families and have abusive parents. However, there is little evidence that prostitutes are emotionally disturbed, addicted to drugs, or sexually abnormal.

- Although prostitution is illegal, some cities have set up adult entertainment areas where commercial sex is tolerated by law enforcement agents.

- Pornography involves the sale of sexually explicit material intended to sexually excite paying customers. The depiction of sex and nudity is not illegal, but it does violate the law when it is judged obscene. "Obscenity" is a legal term that today is defined as material offensive to community standards. Thus, each local jurisdiction must decide what pornographic material is obscene. A growing problem is the exploitation of children in obscene materials (kiddie porn), which has been expanded through the Internet.

- The Supreme Court has ruled that local communities can pass statutes outlawing any sexually explicit material. There is no hard evidence that pornography is related to crime or aggression, but data suggest that sexual material with a violent theme is related to sexual violence by those who view it.

- Substance abuse is another type of public order crime. Most states and the federal government outlaw a wide variety of drugs they consider harmful, including narcotics, amphetamines, barbiturates, cocaine, hallucinogens, and marijuana.

- One of the main reasons for the continued ban on drugs is their relationship to crime. Numerous studies have found that drug addicts commit enormous amounts of property and violent crime.

- Alcohol is another commonly abused substance. Although alcohol is legal to possess, it too has been linked to crime. Drunk driving and deaths caused by drunk drivers are growing national problems.

- There are many different strategies to control substance abuse, ranging from source control to treatment. So far, no single method seems effective. Although hotly debated, legalization is unlikely in the near term because so many people already take drugs and because there is an association of drug abuse with crime.

- CENGAGENOW™ is an easy-to-use online resource that helps you study in less time to get the grade you want—NOW. CengageNOW™ Personalized Study (a diagnostic study tool containing valuable text-specific resources) lets you focus on just what you don't know and learn more in less time to get a better grade. If your textbook does not include an access code card, you can go to www.ichapters.com to purchase CengageNOW™.

KEY TERMS

public order crimes *(426)*
victimless crimes *(426)*
social harm *(428)*
vigilantes *(428)*
moral crusaders *(428)*

paraphilias *(430)*
prostitution *(432)*
brothels *(433)*
madam *(433)*
call girls *(433)*

skeezers *(436)*
pornography *(438)*
obscenity *(438)*
temperance movement *(442)*
gateway model *(447)*

CRITICAL THINKING QUESTIONS

1. Under what circumstances, if any, might the legalization or decriminalization of drugs be beneficial to society?

2. Do you consider alcohol a drug? Should greater control be placed on the sale of alcohol?

3. Do TV shows and films glorify drug usage and encourage youths to enter the drug trade? Should all

images on TV of drugs and alcohol be banned?

4. Is prostitution really a crime? Should a man or woman have the right to sell sexual favors if they so choose?

5. Do you believe there should be greater controls placed on the distribution of sexually explicit material on the Internet? Would you approve of the online sale of sexually explicit photos/videos of children if they were artificial images created by computer animation?

6. Which statement is more accurate? (a) Sexually aggressive men are drawn to pornography because it reinforces their preexisting hostile orientation to sexuality. (b) Reading or watching pornography can make men become sexually aggressive.

7. Are there objective standards of morality? Does the existing criminal code reflect contemporary national moral standards? Or are laws banning sexual behaviors and substance abuse the product of a relatively few "moral entrepreneurs" who seek to control other people's behaviors?

NOTES

1. "Emperors Club: All About Eliot Spitzer's Alleged Prostitution Ring," *Huffington Post*, March 10, 2008, www.huffingtonpost.com/2008/03/10/emperors-club-all-about-_n_90768.html (accessed July 7, 2008).

2. Edwin Schur, *Crimes without Victims* (Englewood Cliffs, NJ: Prentice Hall, 1965).

3. Jennifer Williard, *Juvenile Prostitution* (Washington, DC: National Victim Resource Center, 1991).

4. C. Gabrielle Salfati, Alison James, and Lynn Ferguson, "Prostitute Homicides: A Descriptive Study," *Journal of Interpersonal Violence* 23 (2008): 505–543.

5. Andrea Dworkin, quoted in "Where Do We Stand on Pornography," *Ms.* (January–February 1994): 34.

6. Bruce Steele and Sean Kennedy, "Hustle and Grow: Texas Gay Candidate Tom Malin Was Undone by the Revelation of His Past as an Escort. Why Do So Many Young Gay Men Turn to Hustling? And Why Does Sex Work Remain the Unforgivable Sin?" *Advocate* 6 (April 11, 2006): 52.

7. "Ex-Prostitute Candidate Loses District 108 Race," *Dallas Morning News*, 8 March 2006, www.dallasnews.com/s/dws/news/elections/2006/stories/030806dnmetproscand.27b26ab.html (accessed July 7, 2008).

8. Morris Cohen, "Moral Aspects of the Criminal Law," *Yale Law Journal* 49 (1940): 1,017.

9. Sir Patrick Devlin, *The Enforcement of Morals* (New York: Oxford University Press, 1959), p. 20.

10. See Joel Feinberg, *Social Philosophy* (Englewood Cliffs, NJ: Prentice Hall, 1973), Chapters 2 and 3.

11. H. L. A. Hart, "Immorality and Treason," *Listener* 62 (1959): 163.

12. *United States v. 12 200-ft Reels of Super 8mm Film*, 413 U.S. 123 (1973) at 137.

13. *USA Today*, "Justice Department Covers Partially Nude Statues," 29 January 2002, www.usatoday.com/news/nation/2002/01/29/statues.htm (accessed July 7, 2008).

14. Joseph Gusfield, "On Legislating Morals: The Symbolic Process of Designating Deviancy," *California Law Review* 56 (1968): 58–59.

15. John Franks, "The Evaluation of Community Standards," *Journal of Social Psychology* 139 (1999): 253–255.

16. Information provided by Hitwise, Inc., June 4, 2004, www.hitwise.com (accessed July 7, 2008).

17. Irving Kristol, "Liberal Censorship and the Common Culture," *Society* 36 (September 1999): 5.

18. Amnesty International, "Female Genital Mutilation: A Fact Sheet," www.amnestyusa.org/Violence/Womens_Human_Rights/page.do?id=1108439 (accessed July 22, 2008).

19. Barbara Crossette, "Senegal Bans Cutting of Genitals of Girls," *New York Times*, 18 January 1999, p. A11.

20. David Kaplan, "Is It Torture or Tradition?" *Newsweek* (20 December 1993): 124.

21. Crossette, "Senegal Bans Cutting of Genitals of Girls."

22. Howard Becker, *Outsiders* (New York: Macmillan, 1963), pp. 13–14.

23. Edward Brecher, *Licit and Illicit Drugs* (Boston: Little, Brown, 1972), pp. 413–416.

24. Hearings on H.R. 6385, April 27, 28, 29, 30, and May 4, 1937, www.hempfarm.org/Papers/Hearing_Transcript_1.html (accessed July 7, 2008).

25. Federal Communications Commission, "In the Matter of Clear Channel Broadcasting," File No. EB-03-IH-0159 Washington, DC, April 7, 2004, www.fcc.gov/eb/Orders/2004/FCC-04-88A1.html (accessed July 7, 2008).

26. Andrea Friedman, "Sadists and Sissies: Anti-Pornography Campaigns in Cold War America," *Gender and History* 15 (2003): 201–228.

27. US Code, Title 1 § 7. Definition of "marriage" and "spouse."

28. *Lawrence et al. v. Texas*, No. 02-102, June 26, 2003.

29. *Hillary Goodridge et al. vs. Department of Public Health and Another*, SJC-08860, November 18, 2003.

30. Mark Pazniokas, "Mayor Again Denied Bail, Giordano Remains Flight Risk, Judge Says," *Hartford Courant*, 9 November 2001, p. A1; Associated Press, "Waterbury Mayor Paid Teenager for Sex, Reports Say," *New York Times*, 16 August 2001, p.1.

31. Associated Press, "Giordano Guilty in Federal Trial Involving Child Sex Abuse," *Hartford Courant*, 25 March 2003, p. 1.

32. Richard Estes and Neil Alan Weiner, *The Commercial Sexual Exploitation of Children in the U.S., Canada, and Mexico* (Philadelphia: University of Pennsylvania Press, 2001).

33. Charles M. Sennott, "Pope Calls Sex Abuse Crime, Pontiff Says Cases Mishandled, Voices Solidarity with Victims," *Boston Globe*, 24 April 2002, p. A1; Kevin Cullen, "Irish Bishop Quits over Priest Case, Prelate Admits He Failed to Stop Abuse of Children," *Boston Globe*, 2 April 2002, p. A6.

34. W. P. de Silva, "Sexual Variations," *British Medical Journal* 318 (1999): 654–655.

35. Kathy Smiljanich and John Briere, "Self-Reported Sexual Interest in Children: Sex Differences and Psychosocial Correlates in a University Sample," *Violence and Victims* 11 (1996): 39–50.

36. Fox News, "Louisiana Senator David Vitter Apologizes Again for Connection to D.C. Madam Scandal," Monday, July 16, 2007, www.foxnews.com/story/0,2933,289531,00.html (accessed July 7, 2008).

37. Ginger Thompson and Philip Shenon, "Navy Officer Describes Working as a Prostitute," *New York Times*, April 12, 2008, www.nytimes.com/2008/04/12/us/12officer.html (accessed July 7, 2008).

38. See generally V. Bullogh, *Sexual Variance in Society and History* (Chicago: University of Chicago Press, 1958), pp. 143–144.

39. Spencer Rathus, *Human Sexuality* (New York: Holt, Rinehart & Winston, 1983), p. 463.

40. Jeffery Richards, *Sex, Dissidence and Damnation: Minority Groups in the Middle Ages* (New York: Routledge, 1994). p. 125.

41. Ibid., p. 118.

42. Annette Jolin, "On the Backs of Working Prostitutes: Feminist Theory and Prostitution Policy," *Crime and Delinquency* 40 (1994): 60–83.

43. Charles McCaghy, *Deviant Behavior* (New York: Macmillan, 1976), pp. 348–349.

44. Marian Pitts, Anthony Smith, Jeffrey Grierson, Mary O'Brien, and Sebastian Misson, "Who Pays for Sex and Why? An Analysis of Social and Motivational Factors Associated with Male Clients of Sex Workers," *Archives of Sexual Behavior* 33 (2004): 353–358.

45. Monica Prasad, "The Morality of Market Exchange: Love, Money, and Contractual Justice," *Sociological Perspectives* 42 (1999): 181–187.

46. Cited in McCaghy, *Deviant Behavior.*

47. FBI, *Crime in the United States 2005* (Washington, DC: U.S. Government Printing Office, 2006), updated with data from FBI, *Crime in the United States, 2006.*

48. FBI, *Crime in the United States, 2006*, table 29.

49. Mark Landler, "World Cup Brings Little Pleasure to German Brothels," *New York Times*, 3 July 2006, www.nytimes.com/2006/07/03/world/europe/03berlin.html (accessed July 7, 2008).

50. Associated Press, "Iran Stones Six to Death," 26 October 1997, APO 10, www.uri.edu/artsci/wms/hughes/stoned_to_death (accessed July 7, 2008).

51. Elizabeth Bernstein, "The Meaning of the Purchase: Desire, Demand, and the Commerce of Sex," *Ethnography* 2 (2001): 389–420.

52. Shannon Devine, "Poverty Fuels Trafficking to Japan," *Herizons* 20 (2007): 18–22.

53. Jay Silverman, Michele Decker, Humka Gupta, Ayonija Maheshwari, Vipul Patel, and Anita Raj, "HIV Prevalence and Predictors Among Rescued Sex-Trafficked Women and Girls in Mumbai, India," *JAIDS: Journal of Acquired Immune Deficiency Syndromes* 43 (2006): 588–593.

54. David Enrich, "Trafficking in People," *U.S. News and World Report* 131 (23 July 2001): 34.

55. Mark-David Janus, Barbara Scanlon, and Virginia Price, "Youth Prostitution," in *Child Pornography and Sex Rings*, ed. Ann Wolbert Burgess (Lexington, MA: Lexington Books, 1989), pp. 127–146.

56. Teela Sanders and Rosie Campbell, "Designing Out Vulnerability, Building in Respect: Violence, Safety and Sex Work Policy," *British Journal of Sociology* 58 (2007): 1–19.

57. Charles Winick and Paul Kinsie, *The Lively Commerce* (Chicago: Quadrangle Books, 1971), p. 58.

58. Hilary Surratt, James Inciardi, Steven Kurtz, and Marion Kiley, "Sex Work and Drug Use in a Subculture of Violence," *Crime and Delinquency* 50 (2004): 43–60.

59. Lisa Maher, "Hidden in the Light: Occupational Norms among Crack-Using Street-Level Sex Workers," *Journal of Drug Issues* 26 (1996): 143–173.

60. Teela Sanders, *Sex Work: A Risky Business* (Devon, England: Willan Publishing, 2005).

61. Winick and Kinsie, *The Lively Commerce*, pp. 172–173.

62. Paul Goldstein, "Occupational Mobility in the World of Prostitution: Becoming a Madam," *Deviant Behavior* 4 (1983): 267–279.

63. Goldstein, "Occupational Mobility in the World of Prostitution," pp. 267–270.

64. Mireya Navarro, "Group Forced Illegal Aliens into Prostitution, U.S. Says," *New York Times*, 24 April 1998, p. A10.

65. Paul Goldstein, Lawrence Ouellet, and Michael Fendrich, "From Bag Brides to Skeezers: A Historical Perspective on Sex-for-Drugs Behavior," *Journal of Psychoactive Drugs* 24 (1992): 349–361.

66. Jessica Edwards, Carolyn Halpern, and Wendee Wechsberg, "Correlates of Exchanging Sex for Drugs or Money Among Women Who Use Crack Cocaine," *AIDS Education and Prevention* 18 (2006): 420–429.

67. Jan Risser, Sandra Timpson, Sheryl McCurdy, Michael Ross, and Mark Williams, "Psychological Correlates of Trading Sex for Money Among African American Crack Cocaine Smokers," *American Journal of Drug and Alcohol Abuse* 32 (2006): 645–653.

68. Thompson and Shenon, "Navy Officer Describes Working as a Prostitute."

69. Alyson Brown and David Barrett, *Knowledge of Evil: Child Prostitution and Child Sexual Abuse in Twentieth Century England* (Devon, England: Willan, 2002).

70. Jocelyn Brown, Patricia Cohen, Henian Chen, Elizabeth Smailes, and Jeffrey Johnson, "Sexual Trajectories of Abused and Neglected Youths," *Journal of Developmental and Behavioral Pediatrics* 25 (2004): 77–83.

71. Gerald Hotaling and David Finkelhor, *The Sexual Exploitation of Missing Children* (Washington, DC: U.S. Department of Justice, 1988).

72. Lisa Kramer and Ellen Berg, "A Survival Analysis of Timing of Entry into Prostitution: The Differential Impact of Race, Educational Level, and Childhood/Adolescent Risk Factors," *Sociological Inquiry* 73 (2003): 511–529.

73. John Potterat, Richard Rothenberg, Stephen Muth, William Darrow, and Lynanne Phillips-Plummer, "Pathways to Prostitution: The Chronology of Sexual and Drug Abuse Milestones," *Journal of Sex Research* 35 (1998): 333–342.

74. Sheila Royo Maxwell and Christopher Maxwell, "Examining the 'Criminal Careers' of Prostitutes within the Nexus of Drug Use, Drug Selling, and Other Illicit Activities," *Criminology* 38 (2000): 787–809.

75. Michael Miner, Jill Flitter, and Beatrice Robinson, "Association of Sexual Revictimization with Sexuality and Psychological Function," *Journal of Interpersonal Violence* 21 (2006): 503–524.

76. Mandi Burnette, Emma Lucas, Mark Ilgen, Susan Frayne, Julia Mayo, and Julie Weitlauf, "Prevalence and Health Correlates of Prostitution among Patients Entering Treatment for Substance Use Disorders," *Archives of General Psychiatry* 65 (2008): 337–344.

77. Michael Rekart, "Sex-Work Harm Reduction," *Lancet* 366 (2005): 2,123–2,134.

78. Nancy Romero-Daza, Margaret Weeks, and Merrill Singer, "Nobody Gives a Damn if I Live or Die: Violence, Drugs, and Street-Level Prostitution in Inner-City Hartford, Connecticut," *Medical Anthropology* 22 (2003): 233–259.

79. Ron Roberts, Sandra Bergström, and David La Rooy, "UK Students and Sex Work: Current Knowledge and Research Issues," *Journal of Community and Applied Social Psychology* 17 (2007): 141–146.

80. Sarah Lantz, "Students Working in the Melbourne Sex Industry: Education, Human Capital and the Changing Patterns of the Youth Labour Market," *Journal of Youth Studies* 8 (2005): 385–401.

81. Brown and Barrett, *Knowledge of Evil: Child Prostitution and Child Sexual Abuse in Twentieth Century England.*

82. Jocelyn Brown, Patricia Cohen, Henian Chen, Elizabeth Smailes, and Jeffrey Johnson, "Sexual Trajectories of Abused and Neglected Youths," *Journal of Developmental and Behavioral Pediatrics* 25 (2004): 77–83.

83. Gerald Hotaling and David Finkelhor, *The Sexual Exploitation of Missing Children* (Washington, DC: U.S. Department of Justice, 1988).

84. Richard Estes and Neil Alan Weiner, *The Commercial Sexual Exploitation of Children in the U.S., Canada, and Mexico* (Philadelphia: University of Pennsylvania Press, 2001).

85. Shu-ling Hwang and Olwen Bedford, "Juveniles' Motivations for Remaining in Prostitution," *Psychology of Women Quarterly* 28 (2004): 136–137.

86. Barbara G. Brents and Kathryn Hausbeck, "State-Sanctioned Sex: Negotiating Formal and Informal Regulatory Practices in Nevada Brothels," *Sociological Perspectives* 44 (2001): 307–335.

87. Ibid.

88. Mara Keire, "The Vice Trust: A Reinterpretation of the White Slavery Scare in the United States, 1907–1917," *Journal of Social History* 35 (2001): 5–42.

89. Minnesota Statute 609.324, "Other Prostitution Crimes; Patrons, Prostitutes, and Individuals Housing Individuals Engaged in Prostitution; Penalties," www.revisor.leg.state.mn.us/bin/getpub.php?type=s&year=current&num=609.324 (accessed July 8, 2008).

90. Ronald Weitzer, "The Politics of Prostitution in America," in *Sex for Sale*, ed. Ronald Weitzer (New York: Routledge, 2000): 159–180.

91. Sherry Plaster Carter, Stanley Carter, and Andrew Dannenberg, "Zoning Out Crime and Improving Community Health in

Sarasota, Florida: Crime Prevention through Environmental Design," *American Journal of Public Health* 93 (2003): 1,442–1,445.

92. 18 U.S.C. [section] 2423(b) (2000).

93. The Protect Act, Public Law 108-21. April 30, 2003.

94. Sara K. Andrews, "U.S. Domestic Prosecution of the American International Sex Tourist: Efforts to Protect Children from Sexual Exploitation," *Journal of Criminal Law and Criminology* 94 (2004): 415–453.

95. James Joyner, "Loophole Lets Rhode Island Prostitutes Work Indoors," www .outsidethebeltway.com/archives/2005/09/ loophole_lets_ri_prostitutes_work_ indoors/ (accessed July 8, 2008).

96. Andrea Dworkin, *Pornography* (New York: Dutton, 1989).

97. Arthur Gould, "The Criminalisation of Buying Sex: The Politics of Prostitution in Sweden," *Journal of Social Policy* 30 (2001): 437–438.

98. Suzanne Daley, "New Rights for Dutch Prostitutes, but No Gain," *New York Times*, 12 August 2001, p. A4.

99. Alexa Albert, *Brothel: Mustang Ranch and Its Women* (New York: Random House, 2001).

100. Roger Matthews, *Prostitution, Politics and Policy* (London, Routledge-Cavendish, 2008)

101. *Merriam-Webster Dictionary* (New York: Pocket Books, 1974), p. 484.

102. Neil Malamuth, Tamara Addison, and Mary Koss, "Pornography and Sexual Aggression: Are There Reliable Effects and Can We Understand Them?" *Annual Review of Sex Research* 11 (2000): 26–94.

103. Lynn Morgan, "Indecency, Pornography, and the Protection of Children," *Georgetown Journal of Gender and the Law* 7 (2006): 701–721.

104. Albert Belanger et al., "Typology of Sex Rings Exploiting Children," in *Child Pornography and Sex Rings*, ed. Ann Wolbert Burgess (Lexington, MA: Lexington Books, 1984), pp. 51–81.

105. Philip Jenkins, *Beyond Tolerance: Child Pornography Online* (New York: New York University Press, 2001).

106. Neil Malamuth, Tamara Addison, and Mary Koss, "Pornography and Sexual Aggression: Are There Reliable Effects and Can We Understand Them?" *Annual Review of Sex Research* 11 (2000): 26–94.

107. Berl Kutchinsky, "The Effect of Easy Availability of Pornography on the Incidence of Sex Crimes," *Journal of Social Issues* 29 (1973): 95–112.

108. Michael Goldstein, "Exposure to Erotic Stimuli and Sexual Deviance," *Journal of Social Issues* 29 (1973): 197–219.

109. Joetta Carr and Karen VanDeusen, "Risk Factors for Male Sexual Aggression on College Campuses," *Journal of Family Violence* 19 (2004): 279–289; see Edward Donnerstein, Daniel Linz, and Steven Penrod, *The*

Question of Pornography (New York: Free Press, 1987).

110. Michael Seto, Alexandra Maric, and Howard Barbaree, "The Role of Pornography in the Etiology of Sexual Aggression," *Aggression and Violent Behaviour* 6 (2001): 35–53.

111. Catherine Simmons, Peter Lehmann, and Shannon Collier-Tenison, "Linking Male Use of the Sex Industry to Controlling Behaviors in Violent Relationships: An Exploratory Analysis," *Violence Against Women* 14 (2008): 406–417.

112. Edward Donnerstein, "Pornography and Violence against Women," *Annals of the New York Academy of Science* 347 (1980): 277–288; E. Donnerstein and J. Hallam, "Facilitating Effects of Erotica on Aggression against Women," *Journal of Personality and Social Psychology* 36 (1977): 1,270–1,277.

113. James Alan Fox and Jack Levin, "Multiple Homicide: Patterns of Serial and Mass Murder," in *Crime and Justice: An Annual Edition*, vol. 23, ed. Michael Tonry (Chicago: University of Chicago Press, 1998): 418–419.

114. John Court, "Sex and Violence: A Ripple Effect," *Pornography and Aggression*, ed. Neil Malamuth and Edward Donnerstein (Orlando: Academic Press, 1984).

115. "State Laws on Obscenity, Child Pornography, and Harassment," www.lorenavedon.com/ laws.htm (accessed July 8, 2008).

116. *Roth v. United States*, 354 U.S. 476 (1957).

117. *A Book Named "John Cleland's Memoirs of a Woman of Pleasure" v. Attorney General of Massachusetts*, 383 U.S. 413 (1966).

118. *Miller v. California*, 413 U.S. 15 (1973).

119. *Pope v. Illinois*, 481 U.S. 497 (1987).

120. Ibid.

121. *Pornography Commission*, pp. 376–377.

122. Bob Cohn, "The Trials of Adam and Eve," *Newsweek* (7 January 1991): 48.

123. 427 U.S. 50 (1976).

124. Thomas J. Lueck, "At Sex Shops, Fear that Ruling Means the End Is Near," *New York Times*, 25 February 1998, p.1.

125. David Rohde, "In Giuliani's Crackdown on Porn Shops, Court Ruling Is a Setback," *New York Times*, 29 August 1998, p. A11.

126. Ralph Weisheit, "Studying Drugs in Rural Areas: Notes from the Field," *Journal of Research in Crime and Delinquency* 30 (1993): 213–232.

127. "British Officials Report Skyrocketing Heroin Use," *Alcoholism and Drug Abuse Weekly* 10 (August 17, 1998): 7; National Institute on Drug Abuse, Community Epidemiology Work Group, *Epidemiological Trends in Drug Abuse, Advance Report* (Washington, DC: National Institute on Drug Abuse, 1997).

128. FBI, Uniform Crime Report, *Crimes in the United States, 2005*, table 29, www.fbi.gov/ ucr/05cius/data/table_29.html (accessed July 8, 2008).

129. Bureau of Justice Statistics, data from "Correctional Populations in the United States, Annual and Prisoners in 2005," www.ojp.usdoj.gov/bjs/glance/corrtyp.htm (accessed July 8, 2008).

130. Arnold Trebach, *The Heroin Solution* (New Haven, CN: Yale University Press, 1982).

131. James Inciardi, *The War on Drugs* (Palo Alto, CA: Mayfield, 1986), p. 2.

132. See generally David Pittman, "Drug Addiction and Crime," in *Handbook of Criminology*, ed. D. Glazer (Chicago: Rand McNally, 1974), pp. 209–232; Board of Directors, National Council on Crime and Delinquency, "Drug Addiction: A Medical, Not a Law Enforcement, Problem," *Crime and Delinquency* 20 (1974): 4–9.

133. Associated Press, "Records Detail Royals' Turn-of-Century Drug Use," *Boston Globe*, 29 August 1993, p. 13.

134. See Edward Brecher, *Licit and Illicit Drugs* (Boston: Little, Brown, 1972).

135. James Inciardi, *Reflections on Crime* (New York: Holt, Rinehart & Winston, 1978), p. 15.

136. William Bates and Betty Crowther, "Drug Abuse," in *Deviants: Voluntary Actors in a Hostile World*, ed. E. Sagarin and F. Montanino (New York: Foresman and Co., 1977), p. 269.

137. Inciardi, *Reflections on Crime*, pp. 8–10. See also A. Greeley, William McCready, and Gary Theisen, *Ethnic Drinking Subcultures* (New York: Praeger, 1980).

138. Joseph Gusfield, *Symbolic Crusade* (Urbana: University of Illinois Press, 1963), Ch. 3.

139. McCaghy, *Deviant Behavior*, p. 280.

140. Ibid.

141. United Nations, *Office on Drugs and Crime, World Drug Report, 2007*, www.unodc .org/pdf/research/wdr07/WDR_2007.pdf (accessed July 8, 2008).

142. The Monitoring the Future survey is conducted by the Institute for Social Research, University of Michigan, Ann Arbor, www .isr.umich.edu (accessed July 8, 2008).

143. Lloyd Johnston, Patrick O'Malley, Jerald Bachman, and John Schulenberg, Monitoring the Future News Release, "Overall, Illicit Drug Use by American Teens Continues Gradual Decline in 2007," Institute for Social Research, Ann Arbor, MI, December 11, 2007, www.monitoringthefuture.org/ pressreleases/07drugpr.pdf (accessed July 8, 2008).

144. Kristin Finn, "Patterns of Alcohol and Marijuana Use at School," *Journal of Research on Adolescence* 16 (2006): 69–77.

145. Department of Health and Human Services, "Results from the 2006 National Survey on Drug Use and Health," www.oas.samhsa .gov/nsduh/2k6nsduh/2k6Results.cfm (accessed July 8, 2008).

146. National Center on Addiction and Substance Abuse, *National Survey of American Attitudes on Substance Abuse IX: Teen Dating Practices and Sexual Activity* (New York City: author, 2004).

147. See generally Mark Blumberg, ed., *AIDS: The Impact on the Criminal Justice System* (Columbus, OH: Merrill Publishing, 1990).

148. Scott Decker and Richard Rosenfeld, "Intravenous Drug Use and the AIDS Epidemic: Findings for a Twenty-City Sample of Arrestees," paper presented at the annual meeting of the American Society of Criminology, Baltimore, November 1990.

149. Douglas Longshore, "Prevalence and Circumstances of Drug Injection at Los Angeles Shooting Galleries," *Crime and Delinquency* 42 (1996): 21–35.

150. Ibid., p. 30.

151. Mark Blumberg, "AIDS and the Criminal Justice System: An Overview," in *AIDS: The Impact on the Criminal Justice System*, p. 11.

152. Susan James, Janice Johnson, and Chitra Raghavan, "I Couldn't Go Anywhere," *Violence Against Women* 10 (2004): 991–1,015.

153. Marvin Krohn, Alan Lizotte, Terence Thornberry, Carolyn Smith, and David McDowall, "Reciprocal Causal Relationships among Drug Use, Peers, and Beliefs: A Five-Wave Panel Model," *Journal of Drug Issues* 26 (1996): 205–428.

154. Kellie Barr, Michael Farrell, Grace Barnes, and John Welte, "Race, Class, and Gender Differences in Substance Abuse: Evidence of Middle-Class/Underclass Polarization among Black Males," *Social Problems* 40 (1993): 314–326.

155. Peter Giancola, "Constructive Thinking, Antisocial Behavior, and Drug Use in Adolescent Boys with and without a Family History of a Substance Use Disorder," *Personality and Individual Differences* 35 (2003): 1,315–1,331.

156. Jerome J. Platt, *Heroin Addiction and Theory, Research and Treatment: The Addict, the Treatment Process and Social Control* (Melbourne, FL: Krieser Publishing, 1995), p. 127.

157. Daniel Smith, Joanne Davis, and Adrienne Fricker-Elhai, "How Does Trauma Beget Trauma? Cognitions About Risk in Women with Abuse Histories," *Child Maltreatment* 9 (2004): 292–302.

158. Sean Kidd, "The Walls Were Closing In, and We Were Trapped," *Youth and Society* 36 (2004): 30–55.

159. Tracy Hampton, "Genes Harbor Clues to Addiction, Recovery," *Journal of the American Medical Association* 292 (2004): 321–323.

160. D. W. Goodwin, "Alcoholism and Genetics," *Archives of General Psychiatry* 42 (1985): 171–174.

161. Martha Vungkhanching, Kenneth Sher, Kristina Jackson, and Gilbert Parra, "Relation of Attachment Style to Family History of Alcoholism and Alcohol Use Disorders in Early Adulthood," *Drug and Alcohol Dependence* 75 (2004): 47–54.

162. For a thorough review of this issue, see John Petraitis, Brian Flay, and Todd Miller, "Reviewing Theories of Adolescent Substance Use: Organizing Pieces in the Puzzle," *Psychological Bulletin* 117 (1995): 67–86.

163. Judith Brooks and Li-Jung Tseng, "Influences of Parental Drug Use, Personality, and Child Rearing on the Toddler's Anger and Negativity," *Genetic, Social and General Psychology Monographs* 122 (1996): 107–128.

164. Thomas Ashby Wills, Donato Vaccaro, Grace McNamara, and A. Elizabeth Hirky, "Escalated Substance Use: A Longitudinal Grouping Analysis from Early to Middle Adolescence," *Journal of Abnormal Psychology* 105 (1996): 166–180.

165. Denise Kandel and Mark Davies, "Friendship Networks, Intimacy, and Illicit Drug Use in Young Adulthood: A Comparison of Two Competing Theories," *Criminology* 29 (1991): 441–471.

166. J. S. Mio, G. Nanjundappa, D. E. Verlur, and M. D. DeRios, "Drug Abuse and the Adolescent Sex Offender: A Preliminary Analysis," *Journal of Psychoactive Drugs* 18 (1986): 65–72.

167. D. Baer and J. Corrado, "Heroin Addict Relationships with Parents During Childhood and Early Adolescent Years," *Journal of Genetic Psychology* 124 (1974): 99–103.

168. John Wallace and Jerald Bachman, "Explaining Racial/Ethnic Differences in Adolescent Drug Use: The Impact of Background and Lifestyle," *Social Problems* 38 (1991): 333–357.

169. Amy Young, Carol Boyd, and Amy Hubbell, "Social Isolation and Sexual Abuse among Women Who Smoke Crack," *Journal of Psychosocial Nursing* 39 (2001): 16–19.

170. Xiaojin Chen, Kimberly Tyler, Les Whitbeck, and Dan Hoyt, "Early Sexual Abuse, Street Adversity, and Drug Use Among Female Homeless and Runaway Adolescents in the Midwest," *Journal of Drug Issues* 34 (2004): 1–20; John Donovan, "Problem-Behavior Theory and the Explanation of Adolescent Marijuana Use," *Journal of Drug Issues* 26 (1996): 379–404.

171. A. Christiansen, G. T. Smith, P. V. Roehling, and M. S. Goldman, "Using Alcohol Expectancies to Predict Adolescent Drinking Behavior after One Year," *Journal of Counseling and Clinical Psychology* 57 (1989): 93–99.

172. Claire Sterk-Elifson, "Just for Fun? Cocaine Use Among Middle-Class Women," *Journal of Drug Issues* 26 (1996): 63–76, at 69.

173. Icek Ajzen, *Attitudes, Personality and Behavior* (Homewood, IL: Dorsey Press, 1988).

174. James Inciardi, Ruth Horowitz, and Anne Pottieger, *Street Kids, Street Drugs, Street Crime: An Examination of Drug Use and Serious Delinquency in Miami* (Belmont, CA: Wadsworth, 1993), p. 43.

175. Ibid.

176. Cesar Rebellon and Karen Van Gundy, "Can Social Psychological Delinquency Theory Explain the Link Between Marijuana and Other Illicit Drug Use? A Longitudinal Analysis of the Gateway Hypothesis," *Journal of Drug Issues*, Summer 36 (2006): 515–539; Mary Ellen Mackesy-Amiti, Michael Fendrich,

and Paul Goldstein, "Sequence of Drug Use among Serious Drug Users: Typical vs. Atypical Progression," *Drug and Alcohol Dependence* 45 (1997): 185–196.

177. Bu Huang, Helene White, Rick Kosterman, Richard Catalano, and J. David Hawkins, "Developmental Associations between Alcohol and Interpersonal Aggression during Adolescence," *Journal of Research in Crime and Delinquency* 38 (2001): 64–83.

178. Andrew Golub and Bruce Johnson, "The Multiple Paths through Alcohol, Tobacco and Marijuana to Hard Drug Use among Arrestees," paper presented at the annual meeting of the American Society of Criminology, San Diego, November 1997.

179. Andrew Golub and Bruce D. Johnson, *The Rise of Marijuana as the Drug of Choice among Youthful Adult Arrestees* (Washington, DC: National Institute of Justice, 2001).

180. Inciardi, *The War on Drugs*, p. 60.

181. These lifestyles are described in Marcia Chaiken and Bruce Johnson, *Characteristics of Different Types of Drug-Involved Offenders* (Washington, DC: National Institute of Justice, 1988).

182. Kenneth Tunnell, "Inside the Drug Trade: Trafficking from the Dealer's Perspective," *Qualitative Sociology* 16 (1993): 361–381.

183. Lening Zhang, John Welte, and William Wieczorek, "Youth Gangs, Drug Use and Delinquency," *Journal of Criminal Justice* 27 (1999): 101–109.

184. Carolyn Rebecca Block, Antigone Christakos, Ayad Jacob, and Roger Przybylski, *Street Gangs and Crime* (Chicago: Illinois Criminal Justice Information Authority, 1996).

185. Richard Tewksbury and Elizabeth Ehrhardt Mustaine, "Lifestyle of the Wheelers and Dealers: Drug Dealing among American College Students," *Journal of Crime and Justice* 21 (1998): 37.

186. Hilary Saner, Robert MacCoun, and Peter Reuter, "On the Ubiquity of Drug Selling among Youthful Offenders in Washington, D.C., 1985–1991: Age, Period, or Cohort Effect?" *Journal of Quantitative Criminology* 11 (1995): 362–373.

187. Charles Faupel and Carl Klockars, "Drugs–Crime Connections: Elaborations from the Life Histories of Hard-Core Heroin Addicts," *Social Problems* 34 (1987): 54–68.

188. Charles Faupel, "Heroin Use, Crime and Unemployment Status," *Journal of Drug Issues* 18 (1988): 467–479.

189. Faupel and Klockars, "Drugs–Crime Connections."

190. Jeffrey T. Parsons, Perry N. Halkitis, and David S. Bimbi, "Club Drug Use among Young Adults Frequenting Dance Clubs and Other Social Venues in New York City," *Journal of Child and Adolescent Substance Abuse* 15 (2006): 1–14.

191. The National Center on Addiction and Substance Abuse (CASA), *Women Under the Influence* (Baltimore: The Johns University Press, 2006).

192. Russel Falck, Jichuan Wang, and Robert Carlson, "The Epidemiology of Physical Attack and Rape among Crack-Using Women," *Violence and Victims* 16 (2001): 79–89.

193. Marvin Dawkins, "Drug Use and Violent Crime among Adolescents," *Adolescence* 32 (1997): 395–406.

194. U.S. Department of Justice, press release, "Four in Ten Criminal Offenders Report Alcohol as a Factor in Violence," April 5, 1998.

195. Ibid.

196. Bu Huang, Helene White, Rick Kosterman, Richard Catalano, and J. David Hawkins, "Developmental Associations between Alcohol and Interpersonal Aggression during Adolescence," *Journal of Research in Crime and Delinquency* 38 (2001): 64–83; Helene Raskin White and Stephen Hansell, "The Moderating Effects of Gender and Hostility on the Alcohol–Aggression Relationship," *Journal of Research in Crime and Delinquency* 33 (1996): 450–470.

197. James Inciardi, "Heroin Use and Street Crime," *Crime and Delinquency* 25 (1979): 335–346; see also W. McGlothlin, M. Anglin, and B. Wilson, "Narcotic Addiction and Crime," *Criminology* 16 (1978): 293–311.

198. David Best, Clare Sidwell, Michael Gossop, et al., "Crime and Expenditure amongst Polydrug Misusers Seeking Treatment: The Connection between Prescribed Methadone and Crack Use, and Criminal Involvement," *British Journal of Criminology* 41 (2001): 119–126.

199. Overview of Findings from the 2002 National Survey on Drug Use and Health .www.oas.samhsa.gov/nhsda/2k2nsduh/ Overview/2k2Overview.htm (accessed July 8. 2008).

200. National Surveys on Drug Use and Health, "Illicit Drug Use among Persons Arrested for Serious Crimes," www.oas.samhsa .gov/2k5/arrests/arrests.cfm (accessed July 8, 2008).

201. Jerome Cartier, David Farabee, and Michael Prendergast, "Methamphetamine Use, Self-Reported Violent Crime, and Recidivism among Offenders in California Who Abuse Substances," *Journal of Interpersonal Violence* 21 (2006): 435–445.

202. Bureau of Justice Statistics Data, www.ojp .usdoj.gov/bjs/dcf/duc.htm (accessed July 8, 2008).

203. George Speckart and M. Douglas Anglin, "Narcotics Use and Crime: An Overview of Recent Research Advances," *Contemporary Drug Problems* 13 (1986): 741–769; Faupel and Klockars, "Drugs–Crime Connections."

204. Evelyn Wei, Rolf Loeber, and Helene White, "Teasing Apart the Developmental Associations between Alcohol and Marijuana Use and Violence," *Journal of Contemporary Criminal Justice* 20 (2004): 166–183.

205. Susan Martin, Christopher Maxwell, Helene White, and Yan Zhang, "Trends in Alcohol Use, Cocaine Use, and Crime," *Journal of Drug Issues* 34 (2004): 333–360.

206. Marvin Krohn, Alan Lizotte, and Cynthia Perez, "The Interrelationship between Substance Use and Precocious Transitions to Adult Sexuality," *Journal of Health and Social Behavior* 38 (1997): 87–103, at 88.

207. Controlled Substance Act, 21 U.S.C. 848 (1984).

208. Anti-Drug Abuse Act of 1986, PL 99-570, U.S.C. 841 (1986).

209. Anti-Drug Abuse Act of 1988, PL 100-690; 21 U.S.C. 1501; Subtitle A—Death Penalty, Sec. 7001, Amending the Controlled Substances Abuse Act, 21 U.S.C. 848.

210. Eric Jensen, Jurg Gerber, and Ginna Babcock, "The New War on Drugs: Grass Roots Movement or Political Construction?" *Journal of Drug Issues* 21 (1991): 651–667.

211. Orlando Patterson, "The Other Losing War," *New York Times*, 13 January 2007.

212. George Rengert, *The Geography of Illegal Drugs* (Boulder, CO: Westview Press, 1996), p. 2.

213. Fareed Zakaria, "Warlords, Drugs, and Votes; Drugs Have Become the Dominating Feature of Afghanistan's Economy, and Corruption Has Infected Every Aspect of Afghan Political Life," *Newsweek* (9 August 2004): 39.

214. Francisco Gutierrez, "Institutionalizing Global Wars: State Transformations in Colombia, 1978–2002: Colombian Policy Directed at Its Wars, Paradoxically, Narrows the Government's Margin of Maneuver Even as It Tries to Expand It," *Journal of International Affairs* 57 (2003): 135–152.

215. Office of National Drug Control Policy, "Cocaine," www.whitehousedrugpolicy.gov/ drugfact/cocaine/ (accessed July 8, 2008).

216. Mark Moore, *Drug Trafficking* (Washington, DC: National Institute of Justice, 1988).

217. Matthew Durose and Patrick Langan, *Felony Sentences in State Courts, 2002* (Washington, DC: Bureau of Justice Statistics, 2004).

218. Peter Rossi, Richard Berk, and Alec Campbell, "Just Punishments: Guideline Sentences and Normative Consensus," *Journal of Quantitative Criminology* 13 (1997): 267–283.

219. Michael Welch, Russell Wolff, and Nicole Bryan, "Recontextualizing the War on Drugs: A Content Analysis of NIJ Publications and Their Neglect of Race and Class," *Justice Quarterly* 15 (1998): 719–742.

220. Robert Davis, Arthur Lurigio, and Dennis Rosenbaum, eds., *Drugs and the Community* (Springfield, IL: Charles C Thomas, 1993), pp. xii–xv.

221. Saul Weingart, "A Typology of Community Responses to Drugs," in Davis, Lurigio, and Rosenbaum, *Drugs and the Community,* pp. 85–105.

222. Davis, Lurigio, and Rosenbaum, *Drugs and the Community*, pp. xii–xiii.

223. Marianne Zawitz, *Drugs, Crime and the Justice System* (Washington, DC: Bureau of Justice Statistics, 1992), pp. 109–112.

224. Dennis Rosenbaum, Robert Flewelling, Susan Bailey, Chris Ringwalt, and Deanna Wilkinson, "Cops in the Classroom: A Longitudinal Evaluation of Drug Abuse Resistance Education (D.A.R.E.)," *Journal of Research in Crime and Delinquency* 31 (1994): 3–31.

225. Donald R. Lynam, Rich Milich, Rick Zimmerman, Scott Novak, T. K. Logan, Catherine Martin, Carl Leukefeld, and Richard Clayton, "Project D.A.R.E.: No Effects at 10-Year Follow-Up," *Journal of Consulting and Clinical Psychology* 67 (1999): 590–593.

226. Ibid., pp. 115–122.

227. John Goldkamp and Peter Jones, "Pretrial Drug-Testing Experiments in Milwaukee and Prince George's County: The Context of Implementation," *Journal of Research in Crime and Delinquency* 29 (1992): 430–465; Chester Britt, Michael Gottfredson, and John Goldkamp, "Drug Testing and Pretrial Misconduct: An Experiment on the Specific Deterrent Effects of Drug Monitoring Defendants on Pretrial Release," *Journal of Research in Crime and Delinquency* 29 (1992): 62–78.

228. Joseph R. McKinney, "The Effectiveness and Legality of Random Student Drug Testing Programs Revisited," *West's Education Law Reporter* 196 (2006); "Effectiveness of Random Student Drug-Testing Programs, 2005," www.studentdrugtesting.org/ 2005%20McKinney%20survey%20results .pdf (accessed July 8, 2008).

229. Katherine Theall, Kirk Elifson, Claire Sterk, and Eric Stewart, "Criminality among Female Drug Users Following an HIV Risk-Reduction Intervention" *Journal of Interpersonal Violence* 22 (2007): 85–107.

230. See generally Peter Greenwood and Franklin Zimring, *One More Chance* (Santa Monica, CA: Rand, 1985).

231. Tracy Beswick, David David, Jenny Bearn, Michael Gossop, Sian Rees, and John Strang, "The Effectiveness of Combined Naloxone/Lofexidine in Opiate Detoxification: Results from a Double-Blind Randomized and Placebo-Controlled Trial," *American Journal on Addictions* 12 (2003): 295–306.

232. Eli Ginzberg, Howard Berliner, and Miriam Ostrow, *Young People at Risk: Is Prevention Possible?* (Boulder, CO: Westview Press, 1988), p. 99.

233. National Evaluation Data and Technical Assistance Center, *The District of Columbia's Drug Treatment Initiative (DCI)* (Washington, DC: author, February 1998).

234. The following section is based on material found in Jerome Platt, "Vocational Rehabilitation of Drug Abusers," *Psychological Bulletin* 117 (1995): 416–433.

235. Celia Lo, "Sociodemographic Factors, Drug Abuse, and Other Crimes: How They Vary among Male and Female Arrestees," *Journal of Criminal Justice* 32 (2004): 399–409.

236. The National Center on Addiction and Substance Abuse, *Shoveling Up: The Impact*

of Substance Abuse on State Budgets (New York: author, 2001).

237. Office of National Drug Control Policy, *National Drug Control Strategy FY 2009*, Budget Summary, February 2008, www .whitehousedrugpolicy.gov/publications/ policy/09budget/ (accessed July 8, 2008).

238. Barry Goetz, "Pre-Arrest/Booking Drug Control Strategies: Diversion to Treatment, Harm Reduction and Police Involvement,"

Contemporary Drug Problems 33 (2006): 473–520.

239. Ethan Nadelmann, "An End to Marijuana Prohibition," *National Review*, 12 July 2004; Peter Andreas and Ethan Nadelmann, *Policing the Globe: Criminalization and Crime Control in International Relations* (London: Oxford University Press, 2006); Drug Policy Alliance, "What's Wrong with the Drug War?" www.drugpolicy.org/ drugwar/ (accessed July 8, 2008).

240. David Courtwright, "Should We Legalize Drugs? History Answers No," *American Heritage* (February–March 1993): 43–56.

241. James Inciardi and Duane McBride, "Legalizing Drugs: A Gormless, Naive Idea," *Criminologist* 15 (1990): 1–4.

242. Kathryn Ann Farr, "Revitalizing the Drug Decriminalization Debate," *Crime and Delinquency* 36 (1990): 223–237.

Cyber Crime and Technology

CHAPTER OBJECTIVES

1. Understand the concept of cyber crime and why it is becoming so important to study

2. Distinguish among cyber theft, cyber vandalism, and cyber terrorism

3. Know the various types of computer crimes, such as computer frauds, illegal copyright infringement, and Internet securities fraud

4. Be familiar with the terms "identity theft" and "phishing"

5. Know the differences among worms, viruses, Trojan horses, logic bombs, and spam

6. Discuss how the Internet can be used for spying

7. Be able to debate the issue of cyber terrorism

8. Be familiar with the various methods used to control cyber crime

9. Discuss the role technology now plays in the criminal justice system

10. Understand both sides of the debate over the use of technology and infringement of civil liberties

On March 12, 2007, a federal grand jury in Omaha, Nebraska, indicted *Jaisankar Marimuthu, 32, and Chockalingam Ramanathan, 33, residents of Chennai, India, and Thirugnanam Ramanathan, 34, a resident of Malaysia, on charges of conspiracy, fraud, and aggravated identity theft stemming from a high-tech, international fraud scheme designed to hijack online brokerage accounts for profit. The indictment marked the first time that individuals were arrested overseas in connection with an online brokerage intrusion scheme perpetrated in the United States.*

According to the indictment, the defendants, operating primarily from Thailand and India, used their personal online brokerage accounts to purchase shares of several thinly traded stocks. They then hacked into online brokerage accounts of others using stolen usernames and passwords or established new brokerage accounts using stolen identities. Using these accounts, the three allegedly made scores of unauthorized purchases of the same stocks to drive up the market price. Once the share prices were artificially inflated, the defendants sold their own shares for a substantial profit. This "hack, pump, and dump" scheme netted the three more than $2 million.

The defendants used this type of scheme with various stocks between July and November 2006. Because of the scheme's sophistication, the investigation required a cooperative effort of the U.S. Justice Department's Criminal Division, the FBI, and the Securities and Exchange Commission working with international law enforcement. The conspiracy and computer fraud charges in this case each carried a maximum sentence of five years in prison. Wire fraud and securities fraud carry maximum sentences of 20 and 15 years, respectively. Each count of aggravated identity theft adds two years in prison.[1]

Just a few years ago, this complex, global criminal financial enterprise could not have been contemplated, let alone transacted. Innovation brings change and with it new opportunities to commit crime. The technological revolution has provided new tools to misappropriate funds, damage property, and sell illicit material. It has created cyber crime, a new breed of offenses that can be singular or ongoing but typically involve the theft and/or destruction of information, resources, or funds utilizing computers, computer networks, and the Internet.

---

connections

Chapter 13 reviewed the concept of enterprise crime and its motivations, while Chapter 14 covered public order crimes. Cyber crime can be viewed as a type of enterprise crime employing sophisticated technology to achieve illegal profits. It can also involve public order crimes such as the online purchase and sale of pornography and controlled substances. The Internet now enables these previously localized crimes to be conducted on a global scale.

Why is cyber crime rapidly becoming a major social problem? The widespread use of computers and the Internet has ushered in the age of information technology (IT) and made it an intricate part of daily life in most industrialized societies. IT involves computer networking, the Internet, and advanced communications. It is the key to the economic system and will become more important as major industries shift their manufacturing plants to areas of the world where production is much cheaper. IT is responsible for the globalization phenomenon or the process of creating transnational markets, politics, and legal systems—in other words, creating a global economy. The Internet, coupled with ever more powerful computers, is now the chosen medium to provide a wide range of global services, ranging from entertainment and communication to research and education.

The cyber age has also generated an enormous amount of revenue. Spending on IT and telecommunications will grow by more than 6 percent each year, soon reaching about $2 trillion.[2] Today more than 1 billion people are using e-mail and 240 million are mobile Internet users. Magnifying the importance of the Internet is the fact that many critical infrastructure functions are now being conducted online, ranging from banking to control of shipping on the Mississippi River.[3]

This vast network has become a target for illegal activities and enterprise. As a group, these activities are referred to as cyber crime—any criminal act that involves communication, computer and Internet networks. Some cyber criminals use modern technology to sell illegal goods and services, or conversely, to illegally appropriate legitimate products and services. Cyber theft schemes range from illegal copying of copyrighted material to using technology to commit traditional theft-based offenses such as larceny and fraud.

Another type of cyber criminal is motivated less by profit and more by the urge to commit cyber vandalism or technological destruction. They aim their malicious attacks at disrupting, defacing, and destroying technology that they find offensive.

A third type of cyber crime, cyber warfare, is political, involving spying and espionage. It can even involve cyber terrorism, acts aimed at undermining the social, economic, and political system of an enemy nation by destroying its electronic infrastructure and disrupting its economy.

In sum, some cyber criminals are high-tech thieves while others are high-tech vandals; the property they destroy is electronic rather then physical. And some may combine theft and vandalism in political attacks (see Concept Summary 15.1).

This new array of crimes presents a compelling challenge for the justice system and law enforcement community because (a) it is rapidly evolving with new schemes being created daily, (b) it is difficult to detect through traditional law enforcement channels, and (c) its control demands that agents of the justice system develop technical skills that match those of the perpetrators.[4] It may even be possible that the recent crime drop is a result of cyber crime replacing traditional street crime. Instead of robbing a bank at gunpoint, a new group of contemporary thieves finds it easier to hack into accounts and transfer funds to offshore banks. Instead of shoplifting from a brick and mortar store,

---

CONCEPT SUMMARY 15.1

TYPES OF CYBER CRIME

Crime	Definition	Examples
Cyber theft	Use of cyberspace to either distribute illegal goods and services or to defraud people for quick profits	Illegal copyright infringement, identity theft, Internet securities fraud, warez
Cyber vandalism	Use of cyberspace for revenge, destruction, and to achieve a malicious intent	Website defacement, worms, viruses, cyber stalking, cyber bullying
Cyber warfare	An effort by enemy forces to disrupt the intersection where the virtual electronic reality of computers meets the physical world	Logic bombs used to disrupt or destroy "secure" systems or networks, Internet used to communicate covertly with agents around the world

the contemporary cyber thief devises clever schemes to steal from etailers; these crimes are not counted in the UCR or NCVS.

Cyber crimes also present a significant challenge for criminologists because they defy long-held assumptions about the cause of crime. How can we say that crime is a function of social forces, the social environment, or the social structure, when cyber criminals are typically highly educated and technologically sophisticated people who commit their crimes in places far removed from their victims? Cyber crime also demands a degree of self-control and dedication, something a truly impulsive or mentally unstable person would have difficulty achieving. As cyber crime expert Majid Yar explains, it may be that "considerable theoretical innovation" will be required before criminologists can fully understand this phenomenon.[5]

Considering their importance both theoretically and practically, this chapter reviews the various forms of cyber crime. It also looks at how law enforcement agencies are beginning to fight back against cyber criminals and learning to apply some of the emerging technology to deal with traditional crime problems.

Losses due to computer fraud can run into the millions of dollars. Romanian Ione Emil Codarcea, 35, listens during his arraignment in Boston Municipal Court on May 10, 2005. Codarcea, who has ties to the Russian mob, used secretly installed bank card readers and spy cameras to record passwords and steal at least $400,000 from ATM users. Codarcea was being held on $2 million cash bail after he pleaded innocent to charges that included identity fraud, forgery, and larceny.

AP Images/George Rizer, Pool

CYBER THEFT: CYBER CRIMES FOR PROFIT

It is ironic that technological breakthroughs since the dawn of the Industrial Revolution—such as telephones and automobiles—not only brought with them dramatic improvements for society but also created new opportunities for criminal wrongdoing: criminals use the telephone to place bets or threaten victims; cars can be stolen and sold for big profits.[6] The same pattern is now occurring during the IT revolution. The computer and Internet provide opportunities for socially beneficial endeavors—such as education, research, commerce, and entertainment—while at the same time serving as a tool to facilitate illegal activity. The new computer-based technology allows criminals to operate in a more efficient and effective manner. Cyber thieves now have the luxury of remaining anonymous, living in any part of the world (such as the three hackers discussed above), conducting their business during the day or in the evening, working alone or in a group, while at the same time reaching a much wider number of potential victims than ever before. No longer is the con artist or criminal entrepreneur limited to fleecing victims in a particular geographic locale; the whole world can be their target. The technology revolution has opened novel methods for cyber theft that heretofore were nonexistent, ranging from the unlawful distribution of computer software to Internet security fraud.

Cyber thieves conspire to use cyberspace to either distribute illegal goods and services or to defraud people for quick profits. Some of the most common methods are discussed here.

Computer Fraud

Jessica Sabathia, a 31-year-old California woman, pleaded guilty to computer fraud in 2007 as a result of her scheme to embezzle more than $875,000 from North Bay Health Care Group. Sabathia, an accounts payable clerk for North Bay, used her computer to access North Bay's accounting software without the authority of her employer and issued approximately 127 checks payable to herself and others. To conceal the fraud, she then altered the electronic check register to make it appear that the checks had been payable to North Bay's vendors. Jessica cashed several of the checks, and many were deposited into her bank account and the bank accounts of others and used for personal expenses.[7]

Jessica's crime falls under the general category of computer fraud, not a unique offense but rather a common-law crime committed using contemporary technology. Consequently, many computer crimes are prosecuted under such traditional criminal statutes as larceny or fraud. However, not all computer crimes fall under common-law statutes because the property stolen may be intangible (electronic and/or magnetic impulse). Some of these crimes are listed in Exhibit 15.1.

There are a number of recent trends in computer frauds. Internal attacks are now outgrowing external attacks at the world's largest financial institutions. According to a recent global security survey, about 60 percent of U.S. companies report being hit by viruses in the past year; computer network attacks were experienced by 10 percent of international companies.[8]

There has also been a growing trend to commit fraud using devices that rely on IT for their operations. **Automatic teller machines (ATMs)** are now attracting the attention of cyber criminals looking for easy profits.[9] One approach is to use a thin, transparent-plastic overlay on an ATM keypad that captures a user's identification code as it is entered. Though the plastic covering looks like some sort of cover to protect the keys, in fact, microchips in the device record every keystroke. Another transparent device inside the card slot captures card data. While the client completes the transaction, a computer attached to the overlay records all the data necessary to clone the card. Rather than rob an ATM user at gunpoint, the cyber criminal relies on stealth and technological skill to commit the crime.

Distributing Illicit or Illegal Material

The Internet has become a prime source for the delivery of illicit or legally prohibited material. Included within this market are distribution of pornography and obscene material, including kiddie porn and the distribution of dangerous drugs.

Sexually Related Material In March 2008, 22 people—including 12 Americans—were charged with participating in an international child pornography ring. Investigators confiscated more than *400,000* pictures, video files, and other images showing children engaged in sexual behavior. Some of the child victims were as young as 5 years old; many displayed innocent characteristics such as wearing their hair in pigtails. The ring was begun in Australia and had recruited pornographers all over the world, including England, Canada, and Germany.

Though the ring was first discovered and infiltrated in 2006, it took more than two years to get indictments because of its technical sophistication, which included the use of encryption, background checks, and other security measures. One of the men indicted, 54-year-old Raymond Roy of San Juan Capistrano, California, posted videos of Thai children "to give everyone something to do for an afternoon." Another posting made on July 10, 2007, stated, "This one may offend here, so a word of caution, these girls are heavily drugged. Not much action to speak of, the girls are to [*sic*] [expletive deleted] up to move or resist. Three girls, the first one being the youngest, around 8 or 9 [years old]." The 12 men were charged with engaging in a child exploitation enterprise; illegally posting notices seeking to receive, exchange, and distribute child porn across state lines; and obstruction of justice. Several were also charged with producing the pornography—meaning they had contact with the children who were exploited.[10]

The IT revolution has revitalized the porn industry. The Internet is an ideal venue for selling and distributing obscene material; the computer is an ideal device for storage and viewing. It is difficult to estimate the vast number of websites featuring sexual content, including nude photos, videos, live sex acts, and webcam strip sessions among other forms of "adult entertainment."[11] There are some indicators that show the extent of the industry:

▌ Almost 90 percent of porn is created in the United States.

▌ About $3 billion in revenue is generated from U.S. porn sites each year, compared to $9 billion for all movie box office sales.

▌ $89 is spent on porn each second.

▌ 260 new porn sites go online daily.[12]

The number of visits to pornographic sites (mostly by men, though women make up about 30 percent of the viewers) surpasses those made to Internet search engines; some individual sites report as many as 50 million hits per year.

How do adult sites operate today? There are a number of different schemes in operation:[13]

▌ A large firm sells annual subscriptions in exchange for unlimited access to content.

▌ Password services charge an annual fee to deliver access to hundreds of small sites, which share the subscription revenues.

- Large firms provide free content to smaller affiliate sites. The affiliates post the free content and then try to channel visitors to the large sites, which give the smaller sites a percentage of the fees paid by those who sign up.

- Webmasters forward traffic to another porn site in return for a small per-consumer fee. In many cases, the consumer is sent to the other sites involuntarily, which is known in the industry as *mousetrapping*. Web surfers who try to close out a window after visiting an adult site are sent to another web page automatically. This can repeat dozens of times, causing users to panic and restart their computers in order to escape.

- Adult sites cater to niche audiences looking for specific kinds of adult content.

While some sites cater to adult tastes, others cross the legal border by peddling access to obscene material or even kiddie porn. Despite some successful prosecutions, it has been difficult to control Internet pornography. Various federal legislative efforts, including the Communications Decency Act (1996), the Child Online Protection Act (1998), and the Children's Internet Protection Act (2003), have been successfully challenged in the courts under the First Amendment. While enforcement is difficult, the Supreme Court made it easier to enforce Internet pornography laws when, in the case of *United States v. Williams* (No. 06-694, 2008), it ruled that a person offering material as child pornography can be convicted on either of two grounds: (1) for believing that the material depicts real children, or (2) for intending to convince a would-be recipient that the material depicts real children, even if he or she does not actually possess the kiddie porn. While this decision is important, controlling Internet porn is still a challenge. Filtering devices used extensively in schools and libraries fail to block out a lot of obscene material, giving youngsters the opportunity to use computers away from home to surf the net for adult content. It is unlikely that any law enforcement efforts will put a dent in the Internet porn industry.

Distributing Dangerous Drugs In addition to sexual material, the Internet has become a prime purveyor of prescription drugs, some of which can be quite dangerous when they are used to excess or fall into the hands of minors. One national survey found that in a single year (2006–2007) the number of websites that advertise or sell controlled prescription drugs increased 70 percent. There was a 135 percent increase in websites advertising these drugs and a 7 percent increase in sites offering to sell them over the net.[14]

While the sites selling prescription drugs are booming, relatively few require that the patient provide a prescription from his or her doctor, and of those that do, only about half require that the actual prescription be provided; many accept a faxed prescription, giving buyers the opportunity for multiple purchases with a single scrip.

- 33 percent clearly stated that no prescription was needed.

- 53 percent offered an "online consultation," which allowed users to get a prescription and make a purchase.

- 14 percent made no mention of a prescription.[15]

Only 16 percent of all the sites offering controlled prescription drugs required that a prescription be faxed or mailed or that the patient's doctor be contacted for the prescription.

Another problem: there are no controls preventing children from ordering drugs. Children are especially at risk and more than 2 million kids are feared to be abusing a prescription drug. More teens have abused these drugs than many other illegal drugs, including ecstasy, cocaine, crack, and methamphetamine. With access to a credit card, which most kids have, kids can order opioid-based drugs (e.g., Codeine, Demerol, OxyContin, Percocet, and Darvon); depressants (e.g., Xanax, Librium, and Valium), and stimulants (e.g., Adderall, Dexedrine, and Ritalin).[16]

Denial-of-Service Attack

In January 2008, a series of cyber attacks was launched against the Church of Scientology website by a group going by the name of "Anonymous." Declaring war on the church and calling for it to be destroyed, the group coordinated a string of attacks using phone, Internet, and fax methods, which it called "Project Chanology." Members bombarded the church's website with hits so that it would collapse. In addition, they harassed the church with phone calls, sent so-called "black faxes" that use up ink, and engaged in "Google bombing," where the word "Scientology" is linked to other terms such as "dangerous" and "cult" so that people entering the search term "Scientology" get distorted results.[17]

The methods used by the "Anonymous" group is known as a **denial-of-service attack**, typically designed to harass or extort money from legitimate users of an Internet service by threatening to prevent the user having access to the service.[18] Examples include:

- Attempts to flood a computer network, thereby preventing legitimate network traffic

- Attempts to disrupt connections within a computer network, thereby preventing access to a service

- Attempts to prevent a particular individual from accessing a service

- Attempts to disrupt service to a specific system or person

A denial-of-service attack may involve threatening or actually flooding an Internet site with millions of bogus messages or orders so that the services will be tied up and unable to perform as promised. Unless the site operator pays extortion, the attackers threaten to keep up the interference until real consumers become frustrated and abandon the site. Even so-called respectable businesspeople have been accused of launching denial-of-service attacks against rival business interests.[19]

Online gambling casinos—a $7 billion a year industry—have proven particularly vulnerable to attack. Hundreds of attacks have been launched against online casinos located in Costa Rica, the Caribbean, and Great Britain. If the attack coincides with a big sporting event such as the Super Bowl, the casinos may give in and make payments rather than lose revenue and fray customer relations.[20]

Illegal Copyright Infringement

For the past decade, groups of individuals have been working together to illegally obtain software and then "crack" or "rip" its copyright protections, before posting it on the Internet for other members of the group to use; this is called warez.

Frequently, these new pirated copies reach the Internet days or weeks before the legitimate product is commercially available. The government has actively pursued members of the warez community, and some have been charged and convicted under the Computer Fraud and Abuse Act (CFAA), which criminalizes accessing computer systems without authorization to obtain information,[21] and the Digital Millennium Copyright Act (DMCA), which makes it a crime to circumvent antipiracy measures built into most commercial software and also outlaws the manufacture, sale, or distribution of code-cracking devices used to illegally copy software.[22]

File Sharing Another form of illegal copyright infringement involves file-sharing programs that allow Internet users to download music and other copyrighted material without paying the artists and record producers their rightful royalties. Theft through the illegal reproduction and distribution of movies, software, games, and music is estimated to cost U.S. industries $19 billion worldwide each year. Although some students routinely share files and download music, criminal copyright infringement represents a serious economic threat. The United States Criminal Code provides penalties for a first-time offender of five years incarceration and a fine of $250,000.[23] Other provisions provide for the forfeiture and destruction of infringing copies and all equipment used to make the copies.[24]

On June 27, 2005, copyright protection of music and other types of entertainment distributed via the Internet was upheld by the Supreme Court in the case of *MGM Studios, Inc. v. Grokster*, 125 S. Ct. 2764 (2005). The Court unanimously held that software distributors such as Grokster could be sued for inducing copyright infringement if they market file-sharing software that might induce people to illegally copy protected material even if that software could also be used for legitimate purposes. Justice Souter wrote:

> We hold that one who distributes a device with the object of promoting its use to infringe copyright, as shown by the clear expression or other affirmative steps taken to foster infringement, is liable for the resulting acts of infringement by third parties.

As a result of the opinion, on November 7, 2005, Grokster announced that it would suspend its file-sharing service; it was also forced to pay $50 million to the music and recording industries.

Internet Securities Fraud

Fifteen-year-old Jonathan Lebed was charged with securities fraud by the SEC after he repeatedly bought low-cost, thinly traded stocks and then spread hundreds of false and misleading messages concerning them—generally baseless price predictions.

After their values were artificially inflated, Lebed sold the securities at the inflated price. His smallest one-day gain was $12,000 and one day he made $74,000. Lebed agreed to findings of fraud but later questioned whether he had done anything wrong; he was forced to hand over his illicit gains, plus interest, which came to $285,000.[25]

Though he might not agree, young Lebed's actions are considered Internet fraud because they involve using the Internet to intentionally manipulate the securities marketplace for profit. There are three major types of Internet securities fraud today:

- *Market manipulation.* Stock market manipulation occurs when an individual tries to control the price of stock by interfering with the natural forces of supply and demand. There are two principal forms of this crime: the "pump and dump" (described in the opening vignette) and the "cyber smear." In a pump and dump scheme, erroneous and deceptive information is posted online to get unsuspecting investors interested in a stock while those spreading the information sell previously purchased stock at an inflated price. The cyber smear is a reverse pump and dump: negative information is spread online about a stock, driving down its price and enabling people to buy it at an artificially low price before rebuttals by the company's officers reinflate the price.[26]

- *Fraudulent offerings of securities.* Some cyber criminals create websites specifically designed to fraudulently sell securities. To make the offerings look more attractive than they are, assets may be inflated, expected returns overstated, and risks understated. In these schemes, investors are promised abnormally high profits on their investments. No investment is actually made. Early investors are paid returns with the investment money received from the later investors. The system usually collapses, and the later investors do not receive dividends and lose their initial investment. For example, the Tri-West Investment Company solicited investments in "prime bank notes."[27] Visitors to their website were promised an annualized rate of return of 120 percent plus return of their principal at the end of a year, as well as substantial referral fees of 15 percent on all referred investments. The website, which contained alleged testimonials describing instant wealth from early investors, also told visitors that their investments were "guaranteed." Investors contributed $60 million in funds to Tri-West, and some "dividends" were paid. However, no money was actually invested, the dividends were paid from new investments, and most of the cash was siphoned off by the schemers.

- *Illegal touting.* This crime occurs when individuals make securities recommendations and fail to disclose that they are being paid to disseminate their favorable opinions. Section 17(b) of the Securities Act of 1933 requires that paid touters disclose the nature, source, and amount of their compensation. If those who tout stocks fail to disclose their relationship with the company, information misleads investors into believing that the speaker is objective and credible rather than bought and paid for.

Identity Theft

Identity theft occurs when a person uses the Internet to steal someone's identity and/or impersonate the victim to open a new credit card account or conduct some other financial transaction. It is a type of cyber crime that has grown at surprising rates over the past few years.[28]

Identity theft can destroy a person's life by manipulating credit records or stealing from their bank accounts. Identity thieves use a variety of techniques to steal information. They may fill out change of address cards at the post office and obtain people's credit card bills and bank statements. They may then call the credit card issuer and, pretending to be the victim, ask for a change in address on the account. They can then charge numerous items over the Internet and have the merchandise sent to the new address. It may take months for the victim to realize the fraud because the victim is not getting bills from the credit card company.

Some identity theft schemes are extremely elaborate. In one recent scheme, 19 people were indicted on charges that they had created an organization called Shadowcrew to provide stolen credit card numbers and identity documents through an online marketplace. The stolen account numbers were contributed by approved "vendors" who had been granted permission to sell on the Shadowcrew site after being vetted through a complex review process. Shadowcrew members allegedly trafficked in at least 1.7 million stolen credit card numbers and caused total losses in excess of $4 million.[29] While this scheme highlights the seriousness and extent of the problem, relatively little is known about the extent of identity theft and further research is required to better understand this growing cyber crime.[30]

Phishing Some identity thieves create false e-mails or websites that look legitimate but are designed to gain illegal access to a victim's personal information; this is known as phishing (also known as *carding* and *spoofing*).

Some phishers send out e-mails that look like they come from a credit card company or online store telling the victim there is a problem with their account credit or balance. To fix the problem and update their account they are asked to submit their name, address, phone numbers, personal information, credit card account numbers, and Social Security number (SSN). Or the e-mail may direct them to a phony website that purports to be a legitimate company or business enterprise. Once a victim accesses the website they are asked to provide personal information or financial account information to the website so that the problem can be fixed. Some phishing schemes involve job offers. Once the unsuspecting victim fills out the "application," answering personal questions and including their Social Security number, the phisher has them in their grasp. One ingenious scam, referred to as *reshipping*, is discussed in Exhibit 15.2.

Once phishers have a victim's personal information they can do three things. They can gain access to preexisting accounts, banking, credit cards, and buy things using those accounts. They can use the information to open brand new banking accounts and credit cards without the victim's knowledge. Finally, the phishers can implant viruses into their software that forwards the phishing e-mail to other recipients once one person

EXHIBIT 15.2

Reshipping

- The reshipping scheme requires individuals in the United States to receive packages at their residence and subsequently repackage the merchandise for shipment, usually abroad.

- Reshippers are recruited in various ways, most often through employment offers and Internet chat rooms.

- Unknown subjects post help-wanted advertisements at popular Internet job search sites and respondents reply to the online advertisement. As part of the application process, the prospective employee is required to complete an employment application, which requires them to divulge sensitive personal information, such as their date of birth and Social Security number. The "employer" then uses this information to get a credit card in the victim's name.

- The applicant is informed he or she has been hired and will be responsible for forwarding—reshipping—merchandise purchased in the United States to the company's overseas home office. The packages quickly begin to arrive and, as instructed, the employee dutifully forwards the packages to their overseas destination. The reshipper doesn't realize that the recently received merchandise was purchased with fraudulent credit cards—until they are charged for the merchandise they just shipped out of the country.

Source: Internet Crime Complaint Center, www.ic3.gov/crimeschemes .aspx#item-16 (accessed July 15, 2008).

responds to the original e-mail, thereby luring more potential victims into his or her net. Some common phishing scams are listed in Exhibit 15.3.

Phishing e-mails and websites have become even more of a problem now that cyber criminals can easily copy brand names, logos, and corporate personnel insignia directly into the e-mail. The look is so authentic that victims believe the e-mail comes from the advertised company. Most phishers send out spam e-mails to a large number of recipients knowing that some of those recipients will have accounts with the company that they are impersonating.

To meet the increasing threat of phishing and identity theft, Congress passed the Identity Theft and Assumption Deterrence Act of 1998 (Identity Theft Act) to make it a federal crime when anyone:

> *Knowingly transfers or uses, without lawful authority, a means of identification of another person with the intent to commit, or to aid or abet, any unlawful activity that constitutes a violation of Federal law, or that constitutes a felony under any applicable State or local law.[31]*

Violations of the act are investigated by federal investigative agencies such as the U.S. Secret Service, the FBI, and the U.S. Postal Inspection Service. In 2004, the Identity Theft Penalty Enhancement Act was signed into law; the act increases existing penalties for the crime of identity theft, establishes aggravated identity theft as a criminal offense, and establishes mandatory penalties for aggravated identity theft. According to the new law, anyone who knowingly "transfers, possesses, or uses, without lawful authority" someone else's identification

Common Phishing Scams

■ *Account verification scams.* Individuals purchase domain names that are similar to those of legitimate companies, such as *Amazon.Accounts.net*. The real company is Amazon, but it does not have *Accounts* in its domain name. These con artists then send out millions of e-mails asking consumers to verify account information and request Social Security numbers. The victim is directed to a bogus website by clicking the legitimate-looking address.

■ *Sign-in rosters.* There are some companies and governmental agencies (colleges, EDD, state-sponsored programs) that ask you to put your name and SSN on a sign-in roster. Identity thieves may sign up toward the end of a page so that they can copy and collect personal identifying information.

■ *"Help move money from my country," aka Nigerian 419 scam.* A bogus e-mail is sent from an alleged representative of a foreign government asking the victim to help move money from one account to another. Some forms include requests to help a dying woman or free a political prisoner. Some claim that the victim has been the recipient of a legacy or a winning lottery ticket. Nigerian money offers now account for about 12 percent of the scam offers.

■ *Canadian/Netherlands lottery.* Originating from the Netherlands and other foreign countries, these scams usually ask for money to hold the prize until the victim can collect in person.

■ *"Free credit report."* Almost all "free credit report" e-mails are scams. Either the person is trying to find out the victim's Social Security number or the victim is billed for services later on.

■ *"You have won a free gift."* The victim receives an e-mail about a free gift or prize. They just have to send their credit card info to take care of shipping and handling. Responding may result in hundreds of spams or telemarketing calls.

■ *E-mail chain letters/pyramid schemes.* Victims are sent an official looking e-mail requesting cooperation by sending a report to five friends or relatives. Those who respond are then contacted for money in order to keep the chain going.

■ *"Find out everything on anyone."* This e-mail is trying to solicit money by offering a CD or program that victims can use to find out personal information on another person. However, the information is actually is the public domain and can be easily accessed without the program.

■ *Job advertisement scams.* Phishers spoofing legitimate Internet job websites (for instance, spoofing Monster.com) contact a victim promising a high paying job. They solicit personal information, including Social Security numbers.

■ *VISA/MasterCard scam.* A VISA or MasterCard "employee" sends an e-mail asking to confirm unusual spending activity and asks the victim for the code on the back of their credit card.

Source: Identity Theft Resource Center (ITRC), "Scams and Consumer Alerts," www.idtheftcenter.org (accessed July 15, 2008).

Vishing Voice over Internet Protocol (VoIP) is a technology that allows people to make voice calls using a broadband Internet connection instead of a regular (or analog) phone line.[33] Some VoIP services only allow subscribers to call other people using the same service, but others allow you to call anyone who has a telephone number—including local, long distance, mobile, and international numbers. Also, while some VoIP services only work over a computer or a special VoIP phone, others allow traditional phone hookups connected to a VoIP adapter. Cyber thieves have already employed this technology in identity theft schemes.

In one version, the victim receives an e-mail that gives them a number to call. Those who call this "customer service" number (a VoIP account, not a real financial institution) are led through a series of voice-prompted menus that ask for account numbers, passwords, and other critical information. In another version, the victim is contacted over the phone instead of by e-mail. The call is either a live person or a recorded message directing the victim to take action to protect a personal account. The visher may have collected some personal information, including account or credit card numbers, which can create a false sense of security for the victim.[34]

Etailing Fraud

New fraud schemes are evolving to reflect the fact that billions of dollars in goods are sold on the Internet each year. **Etailing fraud** can involve both illegally buying and selling merchandise on the net.

Not only do etail frauds involve selling merchandise, they can also involve buyer fraud. One scam involves purchasing top of the line electronic equipment over the net and then purchasing a second, similar looking but cheaper model of the same brand. The cheaper item is then returned to the etailer after switching bar codes and boxes with the more expensive unit. Because etail return processing centers don't always check returned goods closely they may send a refund for the value of the higher priced model.

In another tactic, called *shoplisting*, a person obtains a legitimate receipt from a store, either buying it from a customer or finding it in the trash, and then steals the identical products and takes them back for a store credit or gift card. The thief then sells the gift card on the net at a discount for quick cash. For example, a thief pays maybe $10 for an unexpired receipt covering $500 of legitimately bought electronics or clothing, shoplifts the listed items, and returns them for a gift card. The card is then sold over the Internet. Not surprisingly, the underground market for receipts has been growing, as many stores have liberalized return policies.[35] Some of the most common fraud schemes are included in Exhibit 15.4. Before you say, "How could anyone fall for this stuff?" remember that each year more than 200,000 people file complaints with the government's Internet fraud center and these scams create more than $240 million in losses![36]

www Established in 1988, the CERT® Coordination Center (CERT/CC) is a center of **Internet security expertise**, located at the Software Engineering Institute, a federally funded research and development center operated by Carnegie Mellon University. Visit this site via academic .cengage.com/criminaljustice/siegel.

will be sentenced to an extra prison term of two years with no possibility of probation. Committing identity fraud while engaged in crimes associated with terrorism—such as aircraft destruction, arson, airport violence, or kidnapping top government officials—will receive a mandatory sentence enhancement of five years.[32]

Most Common Internet Fraud Schemes

Pet Scams

▌ A person sees an online (or offline) ad selling a pet and sends in his money, plus a little extra for delivery costs. But the buyer never gets the pet; the scam artist simply takes the money and runs.

▌ A person is selling a pet. He is sent a check that's actually more than the asking price. When he asks about the overpayment, he's told it's meant for someone else who will be caring for the pet temporarily. He's asked to deposit the check and wire the difference to this other person. But the check bounces and he loses the money he sent to someone who turns out to be a fraudster.

Secret Shoppers and Funds Transfer Scams

▌ A person is hired via the Web to rate experiences while shopping or dining. She is paid by check and asked to wire a percentage of the money to a third party. As with the pet scam, the check is bad and she is out the money she sent. As part of the scam, the fraudsters often use real logos from legitimate companies.

▌ While renting out a property, a person is sent a check that is more than the rental fee and asked to wire the difference to someone else. Or he takes a job that requires him to receive money from a company and redistribute funds to affiliates via wire.

Adoption and Charity Frauds

▌ A person is sent an e-mail that tugs on her heartstrings, asking for a pressing donation to a charity and often using the subject header "Urgent Assistance Is Needed." The name of a real charity is generally used, but the money is really going to a con artist. One set of scams in 2007, for example, used the name of a legitimate British adoption agency to ask for money for orphaned or abandoned children.

Romance Fraud

▌ A person encounters someone in an online dating or social networking site who lives far away or in another country. That person strikes up a relationship with the victim and then wants to meet, but needs money to cover travel expenses. Typically, that's just the beginning—the fraudster may claim to end up in the hospital during the trip or get mugged and need more money, and so forth.

Source: FBI, Internet Crime Report, "The Top Scams of 2007," April 3, 2008, www.fbi.gov/page2/april08/ic3_report040308.html (accessed July 16, 2008).

CYBER VANDALISM: CYBER CRIME WITH MALICIOUS INTENT

The nation was stunned when on March 30, 2008, six teenage girls in Lakeland, Florida, lured a young classmate, a 16-year-old cheerleader, to one girl's home and beat her for over half an hour. The victim suffered black eyes and a concussion. What made the attack an issue of national concern was that it was filmed and put on YouTube. The attackers, seemingly proud of their destructive act, wanted it to be viewed by the public on the Internet. The attack may have been motivated as retaliation for comments the victim posted on her MySpace page about some of the other girls.[37]

Some cyber criminals may not be motivated by greed or profit but by the desire for revenge and destruction, and to achieve a malicious intent. (The denial-of-service attacks launched against the Scientology website, discussed earlier, is an example.) Cyber vandalism ranges from sending destructive viruses and worms to attacks stalking or bullying people using cyberspace as a medium. Cyber vandals may want to damage or deface websites or even, as Exhibit 15.5 reveals, pull a virtual fire alarm!

Swatting

Cyber vandals have developed a new form of "entertainment," called *swatting*: calling 9-1-1 and faking an emergency that draws a response from law enforcement—usually a SWAT team. The callers often tell tales of hostages about to be executed or bombs about to go off. The community is placed in danger as responders rush to the scene, taking them away from real emergencies. And the officers are placed in danger as unsuspecting residents may try to defend themselves. In one case a swatter in Washington state was charged with pretending to be calling from the home of a married California couple, saying he had just shot and murdered someone. A local SWAT team arrived on the scene, and the husband, who had been asleep in his home with his wife and two young children, heard something and went outside to investigate—after first stopping in the kitchen to pick up a knife. What he found was a group of SWAT assault rifles aimed directly at him. Fortunately, the situation didn't escalate, and no one was injured.

Swatters have become more sophisticated in their targets and use of technology. Consider the following Texas case:

Five swatters in several states targeted people who were using online telephone party chat lines (or their family or friends). The swatters found personal details on the victims by accessing telecommunication company information stored on protected computers. Then, by manipulating computer and phone equipment, they called 9-1-1 operators around the country. Using "spoofing technology," the swatters made it look like the calls were actually coming from the victims.

"Swats" that the group committed included using bomb threats at sporting events, causing the events to be delayed; claiming that hotel visitors were armed and dangerous, causing an evacuation of the entire hotel; and making threats against public parks and officials. Between 2002 and 2006, the five swatters called 9-1-1 lines in more than 60 cities nationwide, impacting more than 100 victims, causing a disruption of services for telecommunications providers and emergency responders, and resulting in up to $250,000 in losses.

Source: FBI, "Don't Make the Call: The New Phenomenon of 'Swatting,'" February 4, 2008, www.fbi.gov/page2/feb08/swatting020408.html (accessed July 16, 2008).

CYBER VANDALIZING NASA

In April 2002, Robert Lyttle of San Francisco and Benjamin Stark of St. Petersburg, Florida, hacked into a computer at NASA'S Ames Research Center in Moffett Field, California, and stole information about members of the agency's Astrobiology Institute. They used this information, which was in the form of a spreadsheet, to deface the Institute's home page and post their mission statement. Calling themselves "the Deceptive Duo," Lyttle and Stark stated that their attacks were intended to demonstrate vulnerabilities in the government's computer security systems. They described themselves as anonymous citizens determined to save the country from cyber terrorists by exposing security cracks in critical computer network infrastructures. "Tighten the security before a foreign attack forces you to," the Duo's defacements read. "At a time like this, we cannot risk the possibility of compromise by a foreign enemy." Accompanying the text

was a graphic of two handguns against the backdrop of a tattered American flag. The pair also hacked into the Defense Department's Defense Logistics Information Service website and the agency's Office of Health Affairs. They also tapped into one of the U.S. Navy's databases, which contained classified and unclassified e-mail addresses and phone numbers of a number of Naval officers, and then posted the information on a publicly available website.

Lyttle pleaded guilty to the attacks, and the U.S. District Court in Oakland, California, sentenced him to four months in prison, a payment of restitution of $71,181, and three years of probation. Stark, who also pleaded guilty, was sentenced to two years of probation and ordered to pay restitution of $29,006.

Source: Ethan Butterfield, "Agencies Making Little Progress Against Cybervandalism: Two Men Sentenced to Prison Time, Fined for Breaking into Federal Sites," *Government Computer News* 24 (2005): 14.

Cyber vandals are motivated more by malice than greed:

▌ Some cyber vandals target computers and networks seeking revenge for some perceived wrong.

▌ Some desire to exhibit their technical prowess and superiority.

▌ Some wish to highlight the vulnerability of computer security systems (see the Profiles in Crime feature "Cyber Vandalizing NASA").

▌ Some desire to spy on other people's private financial and personal information (computer voyeurism).

▌ Some want to destroy computer security because they believe in a philosophy of open access to all systems and programs.[38]

What forms does cyber vandalism take?

Worms, Viruses, Trojan Horses, Logic Bombs, and Spam

The most typical use of cyberspace for destructive intent comes in the sending or implanting of disruptive programs, called viruses, worms, trojan horses, logic bombs, and spam.

Viruses and Worms A computer virus is one type of malicious software program (also called malware) that disrupts or destroys existing programs and networks, causing them to perform the task for which the virus was designed.[39] The virus is then spread from one computer to another when a user sends

out an infected file through e-mail, a network, or a disk. Computer worms are similar to viruses but use computer networks or the Internet to self-replicate and send themselves to other users, generally via e-mail, without the aid of the operator.

The damage caused by viruses and worms can be considerable. On March 26, 1999, the Melissa virus disrupted e-mail service around the world when it was posted to an Internet newsgroup, causing more than $80 million in damage. Its creator, David Smith, pleaded guilty to state and federal charges and was later sentenced to 20 months in prison (leniency was granted because he cooperated with authorities in thwarting other hackers).[40] Another damaging piece of malware was the MS Blaster worm—also known as W32.Blaster and W32/Lovsan—which took advantage of a vulnerability in a widely used feature of Microsoft Windows and infected more than 120,000 computers worldwide.[41]

Trojan Horses Some hackers introduce a Trojan horse program into a computer system. The Trojan horse looks like a benign application but contains illicit codes that can damage the system operations. Sometimes hackers with a sense of irony will install a Trojan horse and claim that it is an antivirus program. When it is opened it spreads viruses in the computer system. Though Trojan horses do not replicate themselves like viruses, they can be just as destructive.

Logic Bombs A fourth type of destructive attack which can be launched on a computer system is the logic bomb, a program that is secretly attached to a computer system, monitors the network's work output, and waits for a particular signal such as a date to appear. Also called a *slag code*, it is a type of delayed-action virus that may be set off when a program user makes certain input that sets it in motion. A logic bomb may cause a variety of problems ranging from displaying or printing a spurious message to deleting or corrupting data.

Spam An unsolicited advertisement or promotional material, spam typically comes in the form of an unwanted e-mail message; spammers use electronic communications to send unsolicited messages in bulk. While e-mail is the most common form of spam, it can also be sent via instant messaging and mobile phone messaging, among other media.

Spam can simply be in the form of an unwanted and unwelcome advertisement. For example, it may advertise sexually explicit websites and get into the hands of minors. A more dangerous and malicious form of spam contains a Trojan horse disguised as an e-mail attachment advertising some commodity such as free software or an electronic game. If the recipient downloads or opens the attachment, a virus may be launched that corrupts the victim's computer; the Trojan horse may also be designed to capture important data from the victim's hard drive and send it back to the hacker's e-mail address.

Sending spam can become a crime and even lead to a prison sentence when it causes serious harm to a computer or network.

Website Defacement

Cyber vandals may aim their attention at the websites of their victims. Website defacement is a type of cyber vandalism that occurs when a computer hacker intrudes on another person's website by inserting or substituting codes that expose visitors to the site to misleading or provocative information. Defacement can range from installing humorous graffiti to sabotaging or corrupting the site. In some instances, defacement efforts are not easily apparent or noticeable—for example, when they are designed to give misinformation by substituting or replacing authorized text on a company's web page. The false information may mislead customers and frustrate their efforts to utilize the site or make it difficult for people using search engines to find the site as they surf the net.

Almost all defacement attacks are designed to vandalize web pages rather than bring profit or gain to the intruders (though some defacers may eventually extort money from their targets). Some defacers are simply trying to impress the hacking community with their skills. Others may target a corporation when they oppose its business practices and policies (such as oil companies, tobacco companies, or defense contractors). Some defacement has political goals such as disrupting the website of a rival political party or fund-raising group. Soon after the war in Iraq began, there were approximately 20,000 website defacements, both pro- and antiwar, with most taking place within the first few days of the outset of conflict. Five British government sites were compromised by a hacking group protesting the war with Iraq; graffiti slamming President George W. Bush, Prime Minister Tony Blair, and Israeli Prime Minister Ariel Sharon was posted. In response, the English-language Al Jazeera website, which posted disturbing images of civilian victims, was attacked by hackers.[42]

Content analysis of web page defacements indicate that about 70 percent are pranks instituted by hackers, while the rest have a political motive. Defacers are typically members of an extensive social network who are eager to demonstrate their reasons for hacking and often leave calling cards, greetings, and taunts on web pages.[43]

Website defacement is a significant and major threat to online businesses and government agencies. It can harm the credibility and reputation of the organization and demonstrate that its security measures are inadequate. As a result, clients lose trust and may be reluctant to share information such as credit card numbers and personal information. An e-retailer may lose business if potential clients believe the site is not secure. Financial institutions, such as Web-based banks and brokerage houses, are particularly vulnerable because they rely on security and credibility to protect their clients' accounts.[44]

Cyber Stalking

For two years, Georges DeBeir contacted adolescent girls he met in Internet chat rooms and promised them gifts and money in exchange for sex. Finally he went too far. DeBeir initiated a conversation in a "teensex" chat room with a 14-year-old Baltimore girl named Kathy. After weeks of trading explicit e-mail messages, DeBeir eventually asked Kathy to meet him in person for sex, all the while stressing the importance of keeping their relationship confidential. Unfortunately for DeBeir, "Kathy," was actually an undercover FBI agent working for Innocent Images, a computer crimes unit targeting sexual predators and child pornographers on the Internet. DeBeir was arrested at a Baltimore shopping mall where he had arranged to meet Kathy. He pleaded guilty to one count of traveling interstate with the intent to have sex with a minor, a federal charge that carries with it a maximum sentence of 10 years in prison.[45]

Cyber stalking refers to the use of the Internet, e-mail, or other electronic communication devices to stalk another person.[46] Traditional stalking involves repeated harassing or threatening behavior, such as following a person, appearing at a person's home or place of business, making harassing phone calls, leaving written messages or objects, or vandalizing a person's property. In the Internet age, stalkers, such as Georges DeBeir, can pursue victims through online chat rooms. Pedophiles can use the Internet to establish a relationship with the child, and later make contact for the purpose of engaging in criminal sexual activities. Research by Janis Wolak and her colleagues found that publicity about online "predators" who prey on naive children using trickery and violence is largely inaccurate. Today, Internet predators are more likely to meet, develop relationships with at risk adolescents, and beguile underage teenagers, rather than use coercion and violence.[47]

Not all cyber stalkers are sexual predators. Some send repeated threatening or harassing messages via e-mail and use programs to send messages at regular or random intervals without being physically present at a computer terminal. A cyber stalker may trick other people into harassing or threatening a victim by impersonating their victim on Internet bulletin boards or chat rooms, posting messages that are provocative, such as "I want to have sex." The stalker then posts the victim's name, phone number, or e-mail address hoping that other chat participants will stalk or hassle the victim without the stalker's personal involvement.

Cyber Bullying

Experts define bullying among children as repeated negative acts committed by one or more children against another. These negative acts may be physical or verbal in nature—for example, hitting or kicking, teasing or taunting—or they may involve indirect actions such as manipulating friendships or purposely excluding other children from activities. Implicit in this definition is an imbalance in real or perceived power between the bully and victim. It may come as no surprise that 30 to 50 percent of gay, lesbian, and bisexual young people experience harassment in an educational setting.[48]

Studies of bullying suggest that there are short- and long-term consequences for both the perpetrators and the victims of bullying. Students who are chronic victims of bullying experience more physical and psychological problems than their peers who are not harassed by other children, and they tend not to grow out of the role of victim. Young people mistreated by peers may not want to be in school and may thereby miss out on the benefits of school connectedness as well as educational advancement. Longitudinal studies have found that victims of bullying in early grades also reported being bullied several years later.[49] Chronically victimized students may, as adults, be at increased risk for depression, poor self-esteem, and other mental health problems, including schizophrenia.[50]

While bullying is a problem that remains to be solved, it has now morphed from the physical to the virtual. Because of the creation of cyberspace, physical distance is no longer a barrier to the frequency and depth of harm doled out by a bully to his or her victim.[51] **Cyber bullying** is defined as willful and repeated harm inflicted through the medium of electronic text. Like their real-world counterparts, cyber bullies are malicious aggressors who seek implicit or explicit pleasure or profit through the mistreatment of other individuals. Although power in traditional bullying might be physical (stature) or social (competency or popularity), online power may simply stem from net proficiency. Cyber bullies are able to navigate the net and utilize technology in a way that puts them in a position of power relative to their victim. There are two major formats that bullies can employ to harass their victims: (1) a cyber bully can use a computer and send harassing e-mails or instant messages, post obscene, insulting, and slanderous messages to online bulletin boards, or develop websites to promote and disseminate defamatory content; (2) a cyber bully can use a cell phone to send harassing text messages to the victim.[52]

How common is cyber bullying? One recent survey found that one-third of American youths ages 12 to 17 report being

victims of cyber bullying in the previous 12 months. Of the more than 500 teenagers surveyed, 36 percent reported that mean, threatening, or embarrassing things had been said about them or to them through instant messages, e-mail, social-networking sites, chat rooms, or text messages.[53] While gender and race did not influence cyber bullying, kids who had problems at school, were involved in fights and substance abuse, were computer proficient, and spent more time on-line than average were the ones most likely to be caught up in cyber bullying. Exhibit 15.6 shows some results from another recent national survey of cyber bullying.[54]

Cyber Spying

On July 21, 2005, Carlos Enrique Perez-Melara, the creator and marketer of a spyware program called Loverspy, was indicted by a federal grand jury and charged with such crimes as manufacturing a surreptitious interception device, sending a surreptitious interception device, and advertising a surreptitious interception device.[55]

Loverspy was a computer program designed and marketed by Perez for people to use to spy on others. Prospective purchasers, after paying $89 through a website in Texas, were electronically

---

EXHIBIT 15.6

Cyber Bullying

Sameer Hinduja and Justin Patchin conducted a national survey of approximately 1,500 Internet-using adolescents. Among their most important findings are:

Cyber Bullying Victimization

- 34 percent of respondents reported that they had experienced cyber bullying.
- 13 percent of respondents reported that they had been threatened physically and almost 5 percent reported that they were scared for their safety.

Cyber Bullying Victimization Locations

- The majority of cyber bullying experiences occur in chat rooms (56 percent) or using computer text messages (49 percent).
- 28 percent of respondents who were victims of cyber bullying report being bullied via e-mail.

How Victims of Cyber Bullying Felt

- 34 percent of cyber bullying victims felt frustrated, over 30 percent felt angry, and approximately 22 percent felt sad.
- 35 percent of cyber bullying victims were not bothered by the experience.

Who Victims Tell about the Experience

- Over 40 percent of cyber bullying victims do not tell anyone about the experience.
- Only 14.3 percent of youths told their parent(s), teacher, or another adult.

Source: Sameer Hinduja and Justin Patchin, research summary, "Cyberbullying Victimization. Preliminary Findings from an Online Survey of Internet-Using Adolescents," www.cyberbullying.us (accessed July 16, 2008).

redirected to Perez's computers in San Diego. Purchasers would then select from a menu an electronic greeting card to send to up to five different victims' e-mail addresses. Unbeknownst to the victims, once the e-mail greeting card was opened, Loverspy secretly installed itself on their computer and recorded all their activities, including e-mails sent and received, websites visited, and passwords entered. Loverspy also gave the purchaser the ability to remotely control the victim's computer, including accessing, changing, and deleting files, and turning on web-enabled cameras. Over 1,000 purchasers from the United States and elsewhere purchased Loverspy and used it against more than 2,000 victims.[56]

Perez was indicted for engaging in cyber spying, illegally using the Internet to gather information that is considered private and confidential. Cyber spies have a variety of motivations. Some are people involved in marital disputes who may want to seize the e-mails of their estranged spouse. Business rivals might hire disgruntled former employees, consultants, or outside contractors to steal information from their competitors. These commercial cyber spies target upcoming bids, customer lists, product designs, software source code, voice mail messages, and confidential e-mail messages.[57] Some of the commercial spying is conducted by foreign competitors who seek to appropriate trade secrets in order to gain a business advantage.[58]

While spyware to monitor Internet messages and traffic has become common, spying by government agencies on U.S. citizens remains quite controversial. A case in point was the FBI's web tracking program called Carnivore, whose use was a great concern to civil libertarians. The FBI used the device to obtain e-mail headers and other information without a wiretap under the USA Patriot Act. Under section 216 of the act, the FBI can conduct a limited form of Internet surveillance without first visiting a judge and establishing probable cause that the target has committed a crime. In such cases the FBI is authorized to capture routing information such as e-mail addresses or IP addresses, but not the contents of the communications. The Bureau no longer uses the program and now relies on commercially available applications.[59]

CYBER WARFARE: CYBER CRIME WITH POLITICAL MOTIVES

It is now generally accepted and understood that the developed world is totally dependent upon electronic communication and data storage for its survival. The protection of the key critical technological infrastructure of a nation has been raised in priority so that it is now considered by many countries alongside the other traditional aspects of national defense.[60]

Some cyber criminals are politically motivated. They may be employed by intelligence agencies to penetrate *computer* networks at an enemy nation's most sensitive military bases, defense contractors, and aerospace companies in order to steal

important data. In one well-known cyber espionage case, Chinese agents were able to penetrate computers, enter hidden sections of a hard drive, zip up as many files as possible, and transmit the data to way stations in South Korea, Hong Kong, or Taiwan before sending them to mainland China. The spy ring, known as Titan Rain, is thought to rank among the most pervasive cyber espionage threats ever faced by *computer* networks in the United States. It is believed that the agents have compromised networks ranging from the Redstone Arsenal military base to NASA to the World Bank; the U.S. Army's flight-planning software has also been electronically stolen. Hundreds of Defense Department *computer* systems have been penetrated and similar attacks have been launched against classified systems in Britain, Canada, Australia, and New Zealand.[61] In 2008, the Pentagon issued a report on China's cyber warfare capabilities, acknowledging that hackers in China had penetrated the Pentagon's computer system and that that intrusions, apparently from China, into computer networks used "many of the skills and capabilities that would also be required for computer network attack." While it was not clear if the hackers acted alone or were backed by the Chinese military, there was ample evidence of Chinese interest in cyber espionage as part of their long-term strategy.[62]

Cyber War and Cyber Terror

The justice system must now also be on guard against cyber attacks by terror groups against enemy nations. These attacks integrate terrorist goals with cyber capabilities, a means of attack referred to here as cyber war or cyber terror. While the term may be difficult to define, cyber warfare can be seen as an effort by covert forces to disrupt the intersection where the virtual

© DSK/AFP/Getty Images

In April 2007 two suicide car bomb attacks rocked the city of Algiers in Algeria, damaging the prime minister's office, killing at least 23 people, and injuring more than 160. In an Internet statement, al-Qaeda's branch in North Africa claimed responsibility for the attacks, publishing photographs of what it said were the three suicide bombers. This picture allegedly shows one of the suicide bombers responsible for an attack. The Arabic writing translates to "The Martyr al-Zubair Abu Sajda." Cyber terror and the use of the Internet to further the interests of terror groups and publicize their activities have become part of contemporary life.

electronic reality of computers meets the physical world.[63] Cyber terrorism has been defined as "the premeditated, politically motivated attack against information, computer systems, computer programs, and data which results in violence against noncombatant targets by subnational groups or clandestine agents."[64] Here we use the terms interchangeably.

Terrorist organizations are beginning to understand the destructive power that cyber war can inflict on their enemies even though, ironically, they may come from a region where computer databases and the Internet are not widely used. Terrorist organizations are adapting IT into their arsenal of terror, and agencies of the justice system have to be ready for a sustained attack on the nation's electronic infrastructure.

Warfare and Terror in Cyberspace Cyberspace is a handy battlefield for the terrorist because an attack can strike directly at a target that bombs won't affect: the economy. Because technological change plays a significant role in the development of critical infrastructures, they are particularly vulnerable to attack. And because of rapid technological change, and the interdependence of systems, it is difficult to defend against efforts to disrupt services.[65]

Terror groups may find that waging cyber war has many advantages. There are no borders of legal control, making it difficult for prosecutors to apply laws to some crimes. Terror groups can operate from countries where cyber laws barely exist, making them almost untouchable. Cyber terrorists can also use the Internet and hacking tools to gather information on targets.[66] There is no loss of life and no need to infiltrate "enemy" territory. Terrorists can wage cyber war from anyplace in the world, and the costs are minimal. Nor do terror organizations lack for skilled labor to mount cyber attacks. There are a growing number of highly skilled computer experts available at reasonable costs in developing countries.

Research by Sanjeev Gupta and his associates shows that terror attacks are associated with lower economic growth, higher inflation, and reduced tax revenues. Cyber war may result in a battered economy in which the government is forced to spend more on the military and cut back on social programs and education. These outcomes can weaken target nations and undermine their resolve to continue to resist.[67]

Cyber War Attacks Has the United States already been the target of cyber war attacks? While it may be difficult to separate the damage caused by hackers from deliberate attacks by terrorists, the Center for Strategic and International Studies has uncovered attacks on the National Security Agency, the Pentagon, and a nuclear weapons laboratory; operations were disrupted at all of these sites.[68] The financial service sector is a prime target and has been victimized by information warfare. One survey found that in a single year financial service firms received an average of 1,018 attacks per company, and 46 percent of these firms had at least one server attack during the period.[69]

Computers can be used by terrorist groups to remain connected and communicate covertly with agents around the world. Networks are a cost-effective tool for planning and striking.[70]

They enable terror groups to plan; here are some possible scenarios:

▪ Logic bombs are implanted in an enemy's computer. They can go undetected for years until they are instructed through the Internet to overwhelm a computer system.

▪ Programs are used to allow terrorists to enter "secure" systems and disrupt or destroy the network.

▪ Using conventional weapons, terrorists overload a network's electrical system thereby threatening computer security.[71]

▪ The computer system of a corporation whose welfare is vital to national security—such as Boeing or Raytheon—is breached and disrupted.

▪ Internet-based systems used to manage basic infrastructure needs—such as an oil pipeline's flow or water levels in dams—are attacked and disrupted, posing a danger of loss of life and interruption of services.

Cyber attacks may be directed at the enemy's financial system. In ever-increasing numbers people are spending and investing their money electronically, using online banking, credit card payment, and online brokerage services. The banking/financial system transacts billions of dollars each day through a complex network of institutions and systems. Efficient and secure electronic functioning is required if people are willing to conduct credit and debit card purchases, money transfers, and stock trading. A cyber attack can disrupt these transactions and interfere with the nation's economic well-being.[72]

Terrorists can use the Internet to recruit new members and disseminate information. For example, Islamic militant organizations use the Internet to broadcast anti-Western slogans and information. An organization's charter and political philosophy can be displayed on its website, which can also be used to solicit funds.

One attack method is to release a *botnet* or software robot, also known as a zombie or drone, that allows an unauthorized user to remotely take control of a host computer without the victim's knowledge or permission.[73] Infected computers can be used to launch denial-of-service attacks, send spam and spyware, or commit cyber extortion. In one recent attack, a global telecommunications company with a business unit in Central America experienced several unusual problems, including multiple network outages—some lasting up to six hours—which disrupted businesses and national connectivity, and took automated teller machines offline for extended periods of time. A botnet-based distributed denial-of-service attack had crippled the country's infrastructure.[74]

Some experts question the existence of cyber war, going so far as to claim that not a single case of cyber terrorism has yet been recorded, that hackers are regularly mistaken for terrorists, and cyber defenses are more robust than is commonly supposed. Even so, some of these same skeptics recognize that the potential threat is still there, likely to increase, and steps must be taken to address the dangers ahead.[75]

Funding Terrorist Activities Terrorist groups have used the Internet to conduct white-collar crimes in order to raise funds to buy arms and carry out operations.[76] One method of funding is through fraudulent charitable organizations claiming to support a particular cause such as disaster relief or food services. Charitable organizations in the United States raise more than $130 billion per year. Using bogus charities to raise money is particularly attractive to cyber terrorists because they face far less scrutiny from the government than for-profit corporations and individuals. They may also qualify for financial assistance from government sponsored grant programs. One such bogus group, Holy Land Foundation for Relief and Development (HLFRD) provided more than $12 million to the terrorist group Hamas; in total, HLFRD raised more than $57 million but only reported $36.2 million to the IRS.[77]

Bogus companies have also been used by terrorist groups to receive and distribute money. These shell companies may engage in legitimate activities to establish a positive reputation in the business community but produce bills for nonexistent products that are "paid" by another party with profits from illegal activities, such as insurance fraud or identity theft.[78] If a shell company generates revenues, funds can be distributed by altering financial statements to hide profits and then depositing the profits in accounts that are used directly or indirectly to support terrorist activities. In 2001, a U.S. telecommunications company was indicted on charges of aiding members of al-Qaeda in preparation for the 9/11 terrorist attacks by handling more than $500,000 in transfers monthly.

Another source of terrorist funding, which is discussed less often in the literature, is intellectual property (IP) crime. The illegal sale of counterfeited goods and illegal use of IP to commit other crimes, such as stock manipulation, have been used to support terrorist activities.[79]

THE EXTENT AND COSTS OF CYBER CRIME

How common are cyber crimes and how costly are cyber crimes to American businesses and the general public? The Internet has become a vast engine for illegal profits and criminal entrepreneurs. An accurate accounting of cyber crime will probably never be made because so many offenses go unreported, but there is little doubt that its incidence is growing rapidly.

Though thousands of breaches occur each year, most are not reported to local, state, or federal authorities. Some cyber crime goes unreported because it involves low-visibility acts—such as copying computer software in violation of copyright laws—that simply never get detected.[80] Some businesses choose not to

Theft of intellectual property has become an international issue, and nations around the globe are organizing to thwart cyber thieves. Here, a visitor walks past a salesperson displaying an original copy of antivirus software at the Computers Fair in Kuala Lumpur, Malaysia. Malaysia said it will launch surprise raids on companies nationwide to ferret out illegal software and bring the country's copyright piracy rate down to at least the global average. Each year manufacturers lose around $8 billion from software piracy in the Asia-Pacific region, and Malaysia's local software industry alone lost more than $130 million to piracy in 2004, according to the Business Software Alliance (BSA).

report cyber crime because they fear revealing the weaknesses in their network security systems. However, the information that is available indicates that the profit in cyber crime is vast and continually growing.[81] Losses are now in the billions and rising with the continuing growth of e-commerce. A number of watchdog groups have attempted to decipher estimated costs due to theft, loss of work product, damage to computer networks, and so on.

- *Illegal copying.* The Business Software Alliance (BSA), a professional watchdog group, found in a recent survey that 36 percent of the software installed on computers worldwide (including operating systems, consumer software, and local market software) was pirated, representing a loss of nearly $29 billion. The study found that while $80 billion in software was installed on computers, only $51 billion was legally purchased.[82]

- *Payment fraud.* Credit card fraud on the Internet has increased from $1.6 billion in 2000 to more than $15 billion today.[83]

- *Computer security breaches.* When the Computer Security Institute (CSI) contacted 700 computer security practitioners in U.S. corporations, government agencies, financial institutions, medical institutions, and universities, it found that the average loss from computer security breaches was more than $200,000.[84] The survey showed that such crimes as unauthorized access of computer systems and theft of information have undergone a dramatic increase in recent years. Ironically, while computer theft is increasing, the percentage of organizations reporting computer intrusions to law enforcement has been in decline, presumably because companies fear negative publicity about their security systems.

■ *Phishing and identity theft.* The cost of phishing and identity theft now runs in the billions in the United States. Fifty-seven million U.S. adults think they have received a phishing e-mail. Nearly 1 million users have suffered from identity theft fraud, costing banks and card issuers more than $1 billion annually.[85] The Anti-Phishing Working Group reports that over 15,000 phishing attempts, which used different legitimate brand names, occur each year. A recent survey by the Identity Theft Center indicates that businesses victimized by identity thieves average almost $50,000 in losses.[86]

The United States is not alone in experiencing losses due to identity theft. In Britain, identity fraud is one of the fastest-growing criminal trends and costs the British economy around £1.3 billion per year (more than $2 billion); it takes victims up to 300 hours of effort to regain their former status with banks and credit reference agencies.[87]

■ *Employee abuse.* The Computer Security Institute, an independent security watchdog group, found that 78 percent of employers had detected employee abuse of Internet access privileges (for example, downloading pirated software or inappropriate use of e-mail systems) and 38 percent suffered unauthorized access or misuse on their website.[88] About 25 percent of these reported attacks involved between two and five incidents; 39 percent reported ten or more incidents.[89]

■ *Cyber vandalism.* While corporations are often the target of cyber vandals, the costs and the damage caused is not significant.[90] However, Symantec Corporation conducts an annual Internet Security Threat Report. The latest effort, which makes use of data from over 24,000 security devices deployed in more than 180 countries, shows that online attackers are increasingly using stealthy attacks on personal computers in the pursuit of profit rather than simply to vandalize computer networks. Hackers and malicious-software writers unleashed huge numbers of low-grade attacks designed to advance identity theft, spamming, extortion, and other schemes. There has been a significant increase in attack programs using malicious codes, as cyber vandals hope at least some will get past defenses. Attackers are also targeting their assaults more carefully and using less familiar methods, such as lacing websites with attacks. Personal computers are increasingly the target of attacks because they are considered the weak links in corporate network security and at the same time contain valuable consumer data, such as financial account numbers, passwords, and identifying information.[91]

CONTROLLING CYBER CRIME

The proliferation of cyber crime and its cost to the economy have created the need for new laws and enforcement processes specifically aimed at controlling its new and emerging formulations.

Because technology evolves so rapidly, the enforcement challenges are particularly vexing. There are numerous organizations set up to provide training and support for law enforcement agents. In addition, new federal and state laws have been aimed at particular areas of high-tech crimes.

Congress has treated computer-related crime as a distinct federal offense since the passage of the Counterfeit Access Device and Computer Fraud and Abuse Law in 1984.[92] The 1984 act protected classified U.S. defense and foreign relations information, financial institution and consumer reporting agency files, and access to computers operated for the government. The act was supplemented in 1996 by the National Information Infrastructure Protection Act (NIIPA), which significantly broadened the scope of the law.[93]

Because cyber crime is new, existing laws sometimes are inadequate to address the problem. Therefore new legislation has been drafted to protect the public from this new breed of cyber criminal. For example, before October 30, 1998, when the Identity Theft and Assumption Act of 1998 became law, there was no federal statute that made identity theft a crime. Today, federal prosecutors are making substantial use of the statute and are actively prosecuting cases of identity theft.[94] All states except Vermont and the District of Columbia have passed laws related to identity theft.

In the wake of the 9/11 attacks, the NIIPA has been amended by sections of the USA Patriot Act to make it easier to enforce laws designed to control terrorists and other organized enemies against the nation's computer systems. Subsection 1030(a)(5)(A)(i) of the act criminalizes knowingly causing the transmission of a destructive program, code, or command, and as a result, intentionally causing damage to a protected computer. This section applies regardless of whether the user had authorization to access the protected computer; company insiders and authorized users can be culpable for intentional damage to a protected computer. The act also prohibits intentional access without authorization that results in damage but does not require intent to damage; the attacker can merely be negligent or reckless.

In addition to these main acts, computer-related crimes can also be charged under at least 40 different federal statutes. Supplementing some of the statutes discussed earlier in the chapter, these include the Copyright Act and Digital Millennium Copyright Act, the National Stolen Property Act, the mail and wire fraud statutes, the Electronic Communications Privacy Act, the Communications Decency Act of 1996, the Child Online Protection Act, the Child Pornography Prevention Act of 1996, and the Internet False Identification Prevention Act of 2000.[95] Movie pirates who use the Internet to sell illegally copied films have led the federal government to create the Family Entertainment and Copyright Act of 2005. One part of that statute, known as the ART Act (Artists' Rights and Theft Prevention Act of 2005), criminalizes the use of recording equipment to make copies of films while in movie theaters. The statute also makes it illegal to make a copy of a work in production and put it on the Internet so it will be accessible to members of the public when the individual making the copy knew or should have known the work was intended for commercial distribution.[96]

International Treaties

Because cyber crime is essentially global, international cooperation is required for its control. The Convention on Cybercrime, ratified by the U.S. Senate in August 2006, is the first international treaty that addresses the definition and enforcement of cyber crime. Now signed by 43 nations, it focuses on improving investigative techniques and increasing cooperation among nations. The Convention includes a list of crimes that each signatory state must incorporate into their own law, including such cyber offenses as hacking, distribution of child pornography, and protection of intellectual property rights. It also allows law enforcement agencies new powers, including the ability to require that an Internet service provider monitor a person's online viewing and search choices in real time. The Convention also requires signatory states to cooperate whenever possible in the investigations and prosecution of cyber criminals. The vision is that a common legal framework will eliminate jurisdictional hurdles to facilitate the law enforcement of borderless cyber crimes.[97]

Carrying out this mandate may be difficult to achieve given the legal rights afforded U.S. citizens that may not be realized by residents of other nations. For example, First Amendment protections that restrict the definition of pornography and obscenity in this country may not apply overseas. It is not surprising that watchdog institutions such as the ACLU have condemned the treaty and campaigned against U.S. participation.[98]

Cyber Crime Enforcement Agencies

To enforce cyber laws, the federal government is now operating a number of organizations to control cyber fraud. One approach is to create working groups that coordinate the activities of numerous agencies involved in investigating cyber crime. For example, the Interagency Telemarketing and Internet Fraud Working Group brings together representatives of numerous U.S. attorneys' offices, the FBI, the Secret Service, the Postal Inspection Service, the Federal Trade Commission, the Securities and Exchange Commission, and other law enforcement and regulatory agencies to share information about trends and patterns in Internet fraud schemes.[99]

Specialized enforcement agencies have been created. The Internet Fraud Complaint Center, based in Fairmont, West Virginia, is run by the FBI and the National White-Collar Crime Center. It brings together about 1,000 state and local law enforcement officials and regulators. Its goal is to analyze fraud-related complaints in order to find distinct patterns, develop information on particular cases, and send investigative packages to law enforcement authorities in the jurisdiction that appears likely to have the greatest investigative interest in the matter. The Center now receives more than 200,000 complaints each year, including auction fraud, nondelivery, and credit/debit card fraud, as well as nonfraudulent complaints, such as computer intrusions, spam/unsolicited e-mail, and child pornography.[100] Law enforcement has made remarkable strides in dealing with identity theft as a crime problem over the last several years.

One of the most successful federal efforts is the New York Electronic Crimes Task Force (NYECTF), a partnership between the U.S. Secret Service and a host of other public safety agencies and private corporations. Today, the task force consists of over 250 individual members representing federal, state, and local law enforcement, the private sector, and computer science specialists from 18 different universities. Since 1995, the New York task force has charged over 1,000 individuals with electronic crime losses exceeding $1.0 billion. It has trained over 60,000 law enforcement personnel, prosecutors, and private industry representatives in cyber crime prevention. Its success has prompted similar electronic crime task forces to be set up in Boston, Miami, Charlotte, Chicago, Las Vegas, San Francisco, Los Angeles, and Washington, D.C.[101]

Local Enforcement Efforts

Local police departments are now creating special units to crack down on cyber criminals. In Toronto, Canada, the police department's child-exploitation section concentrates on cracking high profile and difficult cases of Internet child pornography, using inventive and aggressive investigative methods. They estimate there are perhaps 100,000 children depicted in as many as 1 million pictures that circulate via the Internet. The efforts of the four-year-old Toronto police unit have led to 300 arrests so far, and only half have been made in the Toronto area. The unit looks for even the smallest clues to lead them to perpetrators. In one well-known case, investigators homed in on a computer keyboard where the character ñ—unique to Spanish—was visible. In the same series of pictures, they noticed a train ticket that appeared to be European in a child's hand. Sharing the information with Interpol, the international police consortium led to the break-up of a sadistic child-porn ring operating south of Madrid led by a man who had been using his position as a babysitter to gain access to small children.[102]

 WWW To access the Council of Europe's website and to read more about the **Convention on Cybercrime,** go to academic.cengage.com/criminaljustice/siegel.

PREVENTING CRIME WITH TECHNOLOGY

Not only have computers and the Internet been used by criminals and scam artists to fleece the public, but criminal justice agencies are turning the tables by using modern technology to increase their own effectiveness. Information technology now plays a significant role in law enforcement. This effort was given a jump start in 1998, when the federal government, recognizing the vital role information, identification, and communication technologies could and must play in the criminal justice system, enacted the Crime Identification Technology Act of 1998 (CITA), which provided more than a billion dollars in grants to the states to upgrade their IT capabilities in areas such as criminal history record and identification systems and to promote the compatibility and integration of national, state, and local computer systems.[103]

Contemporary IT Programs

There are numerous examples of the blossoming use of IT in law enforcement. Take criminal investigation. Traditionally, to investigate and evaluate a crime scene, police relied on photographic evidence and two-dimensional drawings. However, it can be difficult to visualize the positional relationships of evidence with two-dimensional tools. Now, through a combination of laser and computer technology, high-definition surveying (HDS) creates a virtual crime scene that allows investigators to maneuver every piece of evidence. HDS reflects a laser light off of objects in the crime scene and back to a digital sensor, creating three-dimensional spatial coordinates that are calculated and stored using algebraic equations. The HDS device projects light in a 360-degree horizontal circumference, measuring millions of points, creating a "point cloud." The data points are bounced back to the receiver, collected, converted, and used to create a virtual image of any location. A personal computer can now take the data file and project that site onto any screen.[104]

There have also been new breakthroughs in criminal identification. GE Global Research, among others, is now developing computer vision and image processing technology that will improve the quality of facial images taken from surveillance videos. The underlying video processing technology is composed of face detection, active shape and appearance models, and super-resolution image processing. Once a suspect's face is located in the video, active shape and appearance models lock on to the individual three-dimensional shape of the face in each video frame, allowing it to be rotated to a frontal view. After combining images, super-resolution processing then reconstructs a higher resolution image of the face from several lower resolution video frames. About 10 to 20 video frames are needed to produce a single, higher quality image of the face.[105] Another innovation that pits

Efforts to prevent cyber crime and identify cyber criminals have created new industries and prompted the creation of sophisticated control measures. The display screen of this ATM machine in Dundee, Scotland, asks customers to place a fingertip on the scanner as verification of identity. Scanning fingerprints or irises to verify a customer's identity has yet to penetrate the U.S. banking market because of concerns about expense and privacy. Would the introduction of scanning technology like this make you feel more secure about your personal information and finances?

technology against crime is biometric identification. The Policy and Practice in Criminology feature "Biometric Technology" discusses this new technique.

IT in Corrections

Not only is IT helping to identify criminals, but it is now employed to manage them once they are convicted of crime. Technical experts have identified a number of areas in which correctional management can be aided by information ranging from security in an institution to surveillance after release (see Exhibit 15.7).

EXHIBIT 15.7

Crime Mapping in Corrections

A fight breaks out on the prison yard between two inmates. It quickly escalates as other inmates start to participate. Using sound correctional practices and a quick response, the emergency team is able to quell the disturbance and return all inmates to their cells. The intelligence unit goes to work and is able to determine that the fight was a result of a dispute between two rival gangs within the facility.

Next, the need exists to not only identify the members of each gang, but also determine where they are housed and with whom they associate. This task can be accomplishable in seconds utilizing a new technology called correctional mapping (CORMAP), based on geographic information systems (GIS) principles that are being modified for use in prisons and other multistory buildings. By integrating a combination of computer-assisted drawings (CAD) and GIS, it is now possible to display multilevel living areas in a three-dimensional layout. Each cell on a floor becomes a separate, identifiable living unit, capable of being displayed graphically on a computer screen. Further, it is now possible to display each bed

located within a housing unit and thus identify inmates individually by referencing them to their assigned bed. By establishing this relationship through data linking, CORMAP can instantaneously display all the known information about an inmate simply by clicking on his bed or by entering his name or number.

In the incident example above, any authorized member of an institutional staff with access to a PC could select one of the known participants in the fight and see all of the information currently being stored on a specific individual. This information could include not only his gang affiliation, but also the other members of the gang located within the institution. This type of information could be valuable in assisting the institutional leaders in making informed decisions on what action to take.

Source: National Law Enforcement and Corrections Technology Center (NLECTC), www.justnet.org/virlib/InfoDetail.asp?intInfoID=669 (accessed July 16, 2008).

IT in Corrections

Ground-Penetrating Radar

Ground-penetrating radar (GPR) is able to locate tunnels inmates use to escape. GPR works almost like an old-fashioned Geiger counter, but rather than detecting metal, the system detects changes in ground composition, including voids such as those created by a tunnel.

Heartbeat Monitoring

Now it is possible to prevent escapes by monitoring inmates' heartbeats! The Advanced Vehicle Interrogation and Notification system (AVIAN) works by identifying the shock wave generated by the beating heart, which couples to any surface the body touches. The system takes in all the frequencies of movement, such as the expansion and contraction of an engine or rain hitting the roof, and determines if there is a pattern similar to a human heartbeat.

Backscatter Imaging System for Concealed Weapons

This system utilizes a backscatter imager to detect weapons and contraband. The primary advantage of this device over current walk-through portals is that it can detect nonmetallic as well as metallic weapons. It uses low-power X-rays equal to about five minutes of exposure to the sun at sea level. Although these X-rays penetrate clothing, they do not penetrate the body.

Transmitter Wristbands

These wristbands broadcast a unique serial number via radio frequency every two seconds so that antennas throughout the prison can pick up the signals and pass the data over a local area network to a central monitoring station PC. The wristbands can sound an alert when an inmate gets close to the perimeter fence or when a prisoner does not return from a furlough on time. They can even tag gang members and notify guards when rivals get into contact with each other.

Personal Health Status Monitor

The personal health status monitor uses acoustics to track the heartbeat and respiration of a person in a cell. More advanced health status monitors are now being developed that can monitor five or more vital signs at once, and based on the combination findings, can produce an assessment of the inmate's state of health. This more advanced version of the personal health status monitor may take another decade to develop, but the current version may already help save lives that would otherwise be lost to suicide.

Radar Vital Signs Monitor/Radar Flashlight

The handheld radar flashlight can detect the respiration of a human in a cell from behind a 20-centimeter hollow-core concrete wall or an 8-inch cinder block wall. It instantly gives the user a bar-graph readout that is viewed on the apparatus itself. Other miniature radar detectors give users' heartbeat and respiration readings. The equipment is expected to be a useful tool in searches for people who are hiding, because the only thing that successfully blocks its functioning is a wall made of metal or conducive material.

Under-Vehicle Surveillance System

An under-vehicle surveillance system utilizes a drive-over camera that records a video image of the license plate and the underside of any vehicle entering or leaving the secure perimeter of the prison. This system allows prison staff to check each vehicle for possible escape attempts and keeps a digital recording of every vehicle that enters or exits the prison.

Computer Monitoring Software

A condition of early release may be to have all personal computers monitored. Programs such as Cyber Sentinel, which was originally designed to restrict or monitor the Internet communication of young users, is now being employed to keep track of the web searches and chats of people involved in sexually related crimes.

Automatic Reporting Systems

In a number of jurisdictions, probation automated management (PAM) permits low-risk probationers to report in 24 hours a day, 7 days a week, using their fingerprints as biometric identifiers. This is such a cost-effective measure that it is likely to spread throughout probation departments across the nation.

Sleep Pattern Analysis

Sleep pattern analysis technology, already used by some jurisdictions, can provide preliminary indications of substance abuse and help community corrections officials determine if more testing is warranted. Sleep disruption due to substance abuse can occur in several ways, including altering the sequence and duration of various stages of sleep, total sleep time, and the amount of time needed to fall asleep. The technology consists of a small device, secured to an offender's wrist with a tamper-evident band, that measures sleep quality by recording gross motor activity. Analysis of the data collected may indicate sleep disorders, which potentially could be caused by substance abuse. The device passively collects and records body movement information, and when the offender reports to the probation office or drug court, data can be downloaded and analyzed in a matter of minutes. If data analysis indicates possible substance abuse, the offender can be required to immediately provide a urine specimen for further testing.

Infrared Spectroscopy

Currently in field tests, this technology seeks to modify a glucose-monitoring device into an alcohol-testing product. The device uses a light source, an optical detector, and spectrometers to conduct chemical analysis of tissue and measure alcohol levels. Results, available within just one minute, have accuracy comparable to that of breathalyzers and blood tests. The technology uses infrared spectroscopy to make a nonintrusive examination of a subject's inner forearm; the device also could be modified to examine other parts of the body. The analysis process incorporates a biometric component that identifies an individual's unique tissue structure and tissue chemistry, thus ensuring accurate identification of the person being tested.

Driver Monitoring and Surveillance

This surveillance technology consists of a pair of ankle bracelets that collects data on the unique patterns of movement associated with foot-to-brake, foot-to-gas pedal, acceleration, and deceleration of a motor vehicle. Data analysis can then indicate if and when a subject has been driving. In the case of an individual whose license is restricted, rather than suspended, it can also indicate if the driving took place during a prohibited time (such as outside the normal workday). The bracelets can store and process data for up to 30 days, allowing a community corrections officer to upload data during a scheduled monthly visit. This technology would help corrections professionals deal with a widespread and long-standing problem, as research indicates that up to 75 percent of all drivers with suspended or restricted licenses continue to drive.

Sources: National Law Enforcement and Corrections Technology Center, "Community Corrections Directions," *Tech Beat* (Spring 2007), www.nlectc .org/TECHBeat/spring2007/CommunityCorrections.pdf (accessed July 23, 2008); John Ward, "Jump-Starting Projects to Automatic Correctional Processes," *Corrections Today* 66 (2006): 82–83; John Ward, "Security and Technology: The Human Side," *Corrections Today* 66 (2004): 8; Frank Lu and Laurence Wolfe, "Automated Record Tracking (SWMART) Application," *Corrections Today* 66 (2004): 78–81; Gary Burdett and Mike Rutford, "Technology Improves Security and Reduces Staff in Two Illinois Prisons," *Corrections Today* 65 (2003): 109–110.

BIOMETRIC TECHNOLOGY

Since the terrorist attacks on September 11, 2001, added security measurements have been installed to help protect the country's citizens. Biometrics, the science of using digital technology to identify individuals, has been implemented in many facets of the country's security system. Biometric technology has been installed in airports and immigration centers to ensure that people are not using fake identities for illegal behavior.

Airports

Airports have started to implement the use of biometrics into their systems to prevent nonemployees from entering secured locations. The most popular type of biometrics being used in airports is iris scanning. While you are looking into a camera, a computer scans your eye, records information regarding your iris, and stores the information into a database. Once your eye has been scanned, you are then permitted onto the plane. In order to depart from the plane at your destination, your iris scan must match the one in the database to ensure that you are the person who is supposed to be departing the plane. For those who travel frequently this procedure has proved effective, as it does not requite the individual to continuously stop at checkpoints and have his or her identification checked. The person simply looks into a camera and within seconds is permitted to pass through all the checkpoints.

In addition, an airport in Charlotte, North Carolina, has used the system to keep unwanted individuals from entering secure facilities. With the prior use of swipe cards and/or codes, unauthorized people were able to walk in behind personnel to gain entry into an area; however, this is no longer a problem with the use of biometrics. Employees of the Charlotte airport have their irises scanned and the information gained remains in a database. In order to access the secured areas, personnel must look into a tube and have their match confirmed. Although fingerprints have also been used for this purpose, an iris scan can match over 400 different points of identification compared to only 60 to 70 points in a fingerprint.

Other airports have incorporated another type of biometric technology within their security system: facial recognition. Facial recognition systems measure facial features of people, noting the distance of one feature from another, sizes of features, and so on. An airport in Florida uses a facial recognition system that contains images of the FBI's top ten most wanted criminals, along with other sought-after individuals. Passengers are required to look into cameras to verify that they do not match any of the images in the system. If no matches are found, passengers are permitted to pass through and board their airplane. There is hope that with the continued success of this system, facial recognition systems will help locate fugitives, terrorists, and abducted children who are passing through transportation terminals.

Immigration

The Department of Homeland Security has implemented the United States Visitor and Immigrant Status Indicator Technology (US-VISIT). US-VISIT was developed to provide more security to the nation's airports while keeping

---

Because there are so many areas in which IT can be utilized within corrections, administrators have begun to take advantage of the potential offered by the new technologies to reduce the costs of supervising criminal offenders and to minimize the risk they pose to society. This defines the role of technocorrections. How has IT been applied? A few examples of how IT is being used by institutional and community-based (e.g., probation, parole) corrections are set out in Exhibit 15.8 on page 485.

IT, CRIME, AND CIVIL LIBERTIES

Though the new IT techniques provide the opportunity to increase effectiveness and efficiency within criminal agencies, they come with a price. Some critics believe that they can compromise the privacy and liberty of U.S. citizens who have not engaged in any form of illegal activity. Wary of "Big Brother," the American Civil Liberties Union (ACLU) warns that we are turning into a surveillance society, constantly watched by a plethora of computers, cameras, sensors, wireless communication, GPS, biometrics, and other technologies. And, they warn, there are new technologies on the horizon that can threaten privacy, such as implantable microchips that monitor behavior.[106]

Privacy concerns often focus on surveillance techniques, ranging from traditional closed circuit surveillance cameras to more recent ones such as biometrics. Critics believe that an identification system based on face-recognition technology poses several threats to civil liberties, the most telling being false positives where a person is falsely identified and then investigated, a process which unfairly impinges on the privacy of innocent people. Biometrics can also be used to locate and physically track people, prying into their movements that may have little to do with any crime or terrorist activity.[107] As a result, wary of being watched and recorded by the government, people will alter their activities and actions and, in so doing, lose the right to self-determination of their own behavior.[108]

There are also concerns about the linkage of surveillance information to fast and inexpensive data processing and storage systems.

transportation into and out of the country open. This is accomplished by using biometric scans to determine the identity of all travelers from foreign countries who attempt to enter the United States.

Almost all foreign citizens, regardless of country of origin, who travel into the United States must comply with US-VISIT. The process of registering under the new US-VISIT requirements starts far from U.S. soil. An individual who wishes to travel to the United States must first visit the U.S. consular office in their country and apply for a visa. When they apply they have their biometrics collected in two separate ways. First, photographs are taken of every applicant and those photographs entered into the US-VISIT database along with digital finger scans. The digital finger scans are taken of both the right and left index fingers of the applicant. This information is loaded into a database and then checked to see if it matches any criminals or suspected terrorists already in the system. Once applicants pass the database check they can be issued a visa to travel to the United States. Upon arrival at a U.S. port of entry, the traveler is required to scan their left and right index fingers to determine if the individual at the point of entry is the same as the person who applied for the visa. Entry procedures were started in 115 airports at the beginning of 2004 and today all airports that receive international flights have US-VISIT capabilities. More than a dozen airports within the United States are taking part in the US-VISIT exit procedures, as well as two seaports. The exit procedure requires each traveler to scan their fingers before leaving the country to determine the identity of the individual. So far the system has detected more than 2,000 violators of immigration laws while capturing some 90 million fingerprints. But because the system yielded some false matches, a new 10-finger system is now being deployed at the nation's largest airports at a cost of roughly $300 million.

Homeland Security believes that implementing these new security features will result in fewer criminals or terrorists entering the country, and also reduce the amount of identity theft and fraud that may occur upon entry or exit. However, there are critics who say that the data available to U.S. Customs and Immigration provide too much personal information about travelers and U.S. citizens. Despite privacy concerns, the Department of Homeland Security is set on using the US-VISIT program in conjunction with other government programs to increase the security of the United States.

CRITICAL THINKING

1. Are you afraid that futuristic security methods such as biometric technology will lead to the loss of personal privacy and the erosion of civil liberties?

2. Would you want to be monitored by a computer recognition system as you travel or go about your daily activities?

Sources: Anthony Ramirez, "10 Prints Are Better Than 2, Homeland Security Says," *New York Times*, 26 March 2008, http://topics.nytimes.com/top/reference/timestopics/people/r/anthony_ramirez/ (accessed July 16, 2008); "United States Visitor and Immigrant Status Indicator Technology," Electronic Privacy Information Center, www.epic.org/privacy/us-visit/ (accessed July 16, 2008); US-VISIT, Travel and Transportation, U.S. Department of Homeland Security, www.dhs.gov/xtrvlsec/programs/content_multi_image_0006.shtm (accessed July 16, 2008).

The result is a permanent record that is easily accessed. Every move an individual makes over the course of a day—from using their E-ZPass at a particular exit on the throughway to the items they bought at the drugstore—can be tied across various databases to create a detailed dossier on daily activities.[109] Who should have access to this information and for what purpose is a critical issue.

While these intrusions are troubling, people also want to be protected from harmful criminal activity, ranging from identity theft to terrorism. Protection of civil liberties is important, but so is protection from civil dangers. The level of intrusion and surveillance people will tolerate may depend in large part on their assessment of the risks they face and their willingness to sacrifice civil liberties to reduce these risks.[110] As the threat of terrorism and cyber crime grows, so too may tolerance for invasions of privacy. A number of beliefs seem to sway public opinion about IT—some justify the use of IT in law enforcement while others are voiced by people who wish to restrict its use:

■ *Not much to fear*. Is the government really intent on keeping the public under surveillance? Some commentators view concerns about using IT in criminal justice as misplaced. When they gather data or use IT in surveillance, police agencies may simply be trying to do their job more effectively and not attempting to create a "Big Brother" society. While the media and some civil liberties advocates warn about the loss of privacy, the average citizen has much more to worry about from identity thieves—whose phishing expeditions compromise their financial and personal well-being and security—than from the police.[111]

■ *It really does work*. Modern IT may not be foolproof, but it increases safety. Intrusions into personal space may be warranted if lives are saved. Security cameras, for example, have proliferated in England and are now a vital tool in the government's war on terrorism. While they did not prevent the bombing of the London subway system that killed 56 Londoners in 2005, the images they produced encouraged thousands of tips and led to the arrest of other terrorists in the group, including one who had fled to Italy. While civil liberties groups fear that the success of the surveillance may lead to expanded coverage, that risk is offset by the fact that those bombers will not be able to strike again.[112]

■ *What's the big deal?* While IT makes surveillance and data storage more efficient, it does not gather information that human investigators did not collect in the past. It just does it more efficiently. The new technology is not invading homes but gathering information from public spaces, albeit in the real or electronic world. It is illogical to say that IT should not be used to collect data that any police officer or private citizen is free to observe and record.

■ *IT in criminal justice can be controlled.* There is no question that abuses may occur if law enforcement agents were given free rein to use IT for surveillance and control. However, strict national standards on the use of IT can keep it within acceptable boundaries. A number of national groups, including the American Bar Association (ABA), have already created model rules for IT. The ABA suggests that electronic surveillance must consider the following in order that it not invade people's privacy:

■ The nature of the place, activity, condition, or location to be surveilled

■ The care that has been taken to enhance the privacy of such place, activity, condition, or location

■ The lawfulness of the vantage point, including whether either the surveillance or installation of surveillance equipment requires a physical intrusion

■ The availability and sophistication of the surveillance technology

■ The extent to which the surveillance technology enhances the law enforcement officer's natural senses

■ The extent to which the surveillance of subjects is minimized in time and space

■ The extent to which the surveillance of nonsubjects is likewise minimized

■ Whether the surveillance is covert or overt[113]

As the use of IT in criminal justice proliferates, whether to track and apprehend terrorists, cyber criminals, or common-law felons, its intrusion into the lives of the average citizen will also continue to grow. While civil libertarians warn of its over-reach, the dangers present in contemporary society may override considerations of liberty and privacy.

THINKING LIKE A CRIMINOLOGIST

The president's national security advisor approaches you with a problem. It seems that a tracking device has been developed that can be implanted under the skin, allowing people to be constantly monitored. Implanted at birth, the data surveillance device could potentially cover *everyone*, with a record of every transaction and activity they engage in entered into powerful computers where search engines would keep them under constant surveillance. The surveillance device would enable the government to keep tabs on their whereabouts as well as monitoring their biological activities such as brain waves, heart rate, and so on. The benefits are immense. Once a person becomes a suspect in a crime or is believed to be part of a terrorist cell, he can be easily monitored from a distance without danger to any government agent. Suspects cannot hide or escape detection. Physical readings could be made to determine if they are under stress, using banned substances, and so on.

 Writing Exercise Write a paper expressing your opinion on this device. Is it worthwhile considering the threats faced by America from terrorists and criminals, or does it violate personal privacy and freedom?

 Doing Research on the Web Before you begin writing your paper, go to the American Civil Liberties Union website. They say: "The United States is at risk of turning into a full-fledged surveillance society. The tremendous explosion in surveillance-enabling technologies, combined with the ongoing weakening in legal restraints that protect our privacy, mean that we are drifting toward a surveillance society. The good news is that it can be stopped. Unfortunately, right now the big picture is grim."

You may also want to look at the website of the Center for Democracy and Technology (CDT)—a nonprofit public policy organization dedicated to promoting the democratic potential of today's open, decentralized global Internet. Their mission is to conceptualize, develop, and implement public policies to preserve and enhance free expression, privacy, open access, and other democratic values in the new and increasingly integrated communications medium.

Both websites can be accessed via academic.cengage.com/criminaljustice/siegel.

SUMMARY

- Cyber crime is a new breed of offenses that involves the theft and/or destruction of information, resources, or funds utilizing computers, computer networks, and the Internet.

- Cyber crime presents a challenge for the justice system because it is rapidly evolving, it is difficult to detect through traditional law enforcement channels, and its control demands that agents of the justice system develop technical skills that match those of the perpetrators.

- Cyber crime has grown because information technology (IT) has become part of daily life in most industrialized societies.

- Some cyber crimes use modern technology to accumulate goods and services (cyber theft).

- Cyber vandalism involves malicious attacks aimed at disrupting, defacing, and destroying technology that the attackers find offensive.

- Cyber terrorism is aimed at undermining the social, economic, and political system of an enemy nation by destroying its electronic infrastructure and disrupting its economy.

- Computer fraud is not a unique offense but rather a common-law crime committed using contemporary technology.

- The Internet has become an important source for selling and distributing obscene material.

- While some sites cater to adult tastes, others cross the legal border by peddling access to obscene material or even kiddie porn. It is unlikely that any law enforcement efforts will put a dent in the Internet porn industry.

- A denial-of-service attack is characterized as an attempt to extort money from legitimate users of an Internet service by threatening to prevent the user having access to the service.

- Warez refers to groups of individuals who work together to illegally obtain software and then "crack" or "rip" its copyright protections, before posting it on the Internet for other members of the group to use.

- Another type of illegal copyright infringement involves file-sharing programs that allow Internet users to download music and other copyrighted material without paying the artists and record producers their rightful royalties.

- Internet security fraud involves using the Internet to intentionally manipulate the securities marketplace for profit.

- Identity theft occurs when a person uses the Internet to steal someone's identity and/or impersonate the victim to open a new credit card account or conduct some other financial transaction.

- Identity theft can destroy a person's life by manipulating credit records or stealing from their bank accounts.

- Phishing involves the creation of false e-mails and/or websites that look legitimate but are designed to gain illegal access to a victim's personal information.

- Vishing is a form of phishing utilizing Internet phone protocols.

- Etailing scams involve either the failure to deliver on promised purchases or services or the substitution of cheaper or used material for higher-quality purchases.

- Some cyber criminals may not be motivated by greed or profit but by the desire for revenge, destruction, and to achieve a malicious intent.

- Cyber vandalism ranges from sending destructive viruses and worms to hacker attacks designed to destroy important computer networks.

- A computer virus is one type of malicious software program that disrupts or destroys existing programs and networks, causing them to perform the task for which the virus was designed.

- Computer worms are similar to viruses but use computer networks or the Internet to self-replicate and send themselves to other users, generally via e-mail, without the aid of the operator.

- A Trojan horse looks like a benign application but contains illicit codes that can damage the system operations.

- A logic bomb is a program that is secretly attached to a computer system, monitors the network's work output, and waits for a particular signal such as a date to appear.

- Spam is an unsolicited advertisement or promotional material that typically comes in the form of an unwanted e-mail message.

- Website defacement is a type of cyber vandalism that occurs when a computer hacker intrudes on another person's website by inserting or substituting codes that expose visitors to the site to misleading or provocative information.

- Cyber stalking refers to the use of the Internet, e-mail, or other electronic communications devices to stalk another person. Some cyber stalkers pursue minors through online chat rooms while others harass their victims electronically.

- Cyber bullies harass their victims by posting malicious information on the Internet.

- Cyber spying involves illegally using the Internet to gather information that is considered private and confidential.

- Cyber terrorism can be viewed as an effort by covert forces to disrupt the intersection where the virtual electronic reality of computers meets the physical world.

- Some experts question the existence of cyber terrorism, going so far as to claim that not a single case of cyber terrorism has yet been recorded, that cyber vandals and hackers are regularly mistaken for terrorists, and cyber defenses are more robust than is commonly supposed.

- The Internet has become a vast engine for illegal profits.

- The growth of cyber crime and its cost to the economy has created the need for new laws and enforcement processes specifically aimed at controlling its new and emerging formulations.

- Congress has treated computer-related crime as a distinct federal offense since passage of the Counterfeit Access Device and Computer Fraud and Abuse Law in 1984.

- Because cyber crime is new, existing laws sometimes are inadequate to address the problem. Therefore new legislation has been drafted to protect the public from this new breed of cyber criminal.

- To enforce these laws the federal government is now operating a number of organizations to control cyber fraud. One approach is to create working groups that coordinate the activities of numerous agencies involved in investigating cyber crime.

- Specialized enforcement agencies have been created to crack down on cyber criminals.

- Not only are computers and the Internet being used by criminals and scam artists to fleece the public, but criminal justice agencies are turning the tables by using modern technology to increase their own effectiveness.

- Biometrics is defined as automated methods of recognizing a person based on a physiological or behavioral characteristic.

- Though the new IT techniques provide the opportunity to increase effectiveness and efficiency within criminal agencies, critics believe that they can compromise the privacy and liberty of U.S. citizens who have not engaged in any form of illegal activity.

- A number of factors may tip the balance of public opinion to either support the use of IT in law enforcement or attempt to restrict its use.

- CENGAGENOW™ is an easy-to-use online resource that helps you study in less time to get the grade you want—NOW. CengageNOW™ Personalized Study (a diagnostic study tool containing valuable text-specific resources) lets you focus on just what you don't know and learn more in less time to get a better grade. If your textbook does not include an access code card, you can go to www.ichapters.com to purchase CengageNOW™.

KEY TERMS

cyber crime (468)
information technology (IT) (468)
globalization (468)
cyber theft (468)
cyber vandalism (468)
cyber warfare (468)
cyber terrorism (468)
automatic teller machine (ATM) (470)

denial-of-service attack (471)
warez (472)
identity theft (473)
phishing (473)
etailing fraud (474)
computer virus (476)
malware (476)
computer worms (476)

Trojan horse (476)
logic bomb (476)
spam (477)
website defacement (477)
cyber stalking (477)
cyber bullying (477)
cyber spying (479)

CRITICAL THINKING QUESTIONS

1. Which theories of criminal behavior best explain the actions of cyber criminals, and which ones do you believe fail to explain cyber crime?

2. How would you punish a web page defacer who placed an antiwar message on a government site? Prison? Fine?

3. What guidelines would you recommend for the use of IT in law enforcment?

4. Are we creating a "Big Brother" society and is the loss of personal privacy worth the price of safety?

NOTES

1. U.S. Department of Justice, "Hackers from India Indicted for Online Brokerage Intrusion Scheme that Victimized Customers and Brokerage Firms," March 12, 2007, www.cybercrime.gov/marimuthuIndict.htm (accessed July 5, 2008).
2. Ed Frauenheim, "IDC: Cyberterror and Other Prophecies," CNET News.com, 12 December 2002, http://news.com.com/2100-1001-977780.html (accessed July 5, 2008).
3. Giles Trendle, "An E-Jihad Against Government?" EGOV Monitor, September 2002.
4. "Statement of Michael A. Vatis, Director, National Infrastructure Protection Center, Federal Bureau of Investigation, on Cybercrime before the Senate Judiciary Committee," Criminal Justice Oversight Subcommittee and House Judiciary Committee, Crime Subcommittee, February 29, 2000, www.cybercrime.gov/vatis.htm (accessed July 15, 2008).
5. Majid Yar, Cybercrime and Society (Thousand Oaks, CA: Sage Publications, 2006), p. 19.
6. The President's Working Group on Unlawful Conduct on the Internet, "The Electronic Frontier: The Challenge of

Unlawful Conduct Involving the Use of the Internet," 2000, www.usdoj.gov/criminal/cybercrime/unlawful.htm#EXECSUM (accessed July 15, 2008).

7. U.S. Department of Justice, United States Attorney, Eastern District of California, "Vallejo Woman Admits to Embezzling More than $875,035, Not-for-Profit Organization Victim of Computer Fraud," www.cybercrime.gov/sabathiaPlea.htm (accessed July 15, 2008).

8. *InformationWeek,* Global Security Survey 2007, July 2007, www.cynergistek.com/images/blog/InformationWeek.pdf (accessed July 15, 2008).

9. Chris Richard, "Guard Your Card: ATM Fraud Grows More Sophisticated," *Christian Science Monitor* 95 (2003): 15.

10. Associated Press, "International Child Porn Ring Uncovered," *New York Times,* 4 March 2008.

11. Andreas Philaretou, "Sexuality and the Internet," *Journal of Sex Research* 42 (2005): 180–181.

12. Michael Arrington, Internet Porn Stats Techcrunch, www.techcrunch.com/2007/05/12/internet-pornography-stats/ (accessed July 15, 2008).

13. Jeordan Legon, "Sex Sells, Especially to Web Surfers: Internet Porn a Booming, Billion-Dollar Industry," CNN, 11 December 2003, www.cnn.com/2003/TECH/internet/12/10/porn.business/ (accessed July 15, 2008).

14. National Center on Addiction and Substance Abuse at Columbia University, "You've Got Drugs! IV: Prescription Drug Pushers on the Internet," May 2007, www.casacolumbia.org/articlefiles/531-2008%20You've%20Got%20Drugs%20V.pdf.

15. Ibid.

16. Ibid.

17. Jonathan Richards, "Hackers Declare War on Scientology," Fox News, January 25, 2008, www.foxnews.com/printer_friendly_story/0,3566,325586,00.html (accessed July 15, 2008).

18. This section relies heavily on CERT® Coordination Center, "Denial of Service Attacks," www.cert.org/tech_tips/denial_of_service.html (accessed July 15, 2008).

19. Saul Hansell, "U.S. Tally in Online-Crime Sweep: 150 Charged," *New York Times,* 27 August 2004, p. C1.

20. Stephen Baker and Brian Grow, "Gambling Sites, This Is a Holdup," *BusinessWeek,* 9 August 2004, pp. 60–62.

21. The Computer Fraud and Abuse Act (CFAA), 18 U.S.C. §1030 (1998).

22. The Digital Millennium Copyright Act, Public Law 105-304 (1998).

23. Title 18, United States Code, Section 2319.

24. Title 17, United States Code, Section 506.

25. This section is based on Richard Walker and David M. Levine, "'You've Got Jail': Current Trends in Civil and Criminal Enforcement of Internet Securities Fraud," *American Criminal Law Review* 38 (2001): 405–430.

26. Jim Wolf, "Internet Scams Targeted in Sweep: A 10-Day Crackdown Leads to 62 Arrests and 88 Indictments," *Boston Globe,* 22 May 2001, p. A2.

27. U.S. Department of Justice, "Alleged Leaders of $60 Million Internet Scam Indicted on Fraud and Money Laundering Charges: Massive Internet Investment Fraud Case Involves 15,000 Investors from 60 Countries," January 3, 2003.

28. These sections rely on "Phishing Activity Trends Report, June 2005," "Anti-Phishing Working Group," and "Special Report on 'Phishing'" (2004), U.S. Department of Justice Criminal Division, www.ncjrs.org/spotlight/identity_theft/publications.html#phishing (accessed July 15, 2008).

29. U.S. Department of Justice, "Nineteen Individuals Indicted in Internet 'Carding' Conspiracy," October 28, 2004.

30. Michael White and Christopher Fisher, "Assessing Our Knowledge of Identity Theft: The Challenges to Effective Prevention and Control Efforts," *Criminal Justice Policy Review* 19 (2008): 3–24.

31. Identity Theft and Assumption Deterrence Act, as amended by Public Law 105-318, 112 Stat. 3007 (October 30, 1998).

32. Public Law 108-275 (2004).

33. Federal Communications Commission, "Voice over Internet Protocol," www.fcc.gov/voip/ (accessed July 15, 2007).

34. FBI, "Something Vishy," February 23, 2007, www.fbi.gov/page2/feb07/vishing022307.htm (accessed July 15, 2008).

35. Elizabeth Woyke and Dan Beucke, "Many Not-So-Happy Returns," *BusinessWeek,* 15 August 2005, p. 10.

36. FBI, "Internet Crime Report: The Top Scams of 2007," April 3, 2008, www.fbi.gov/page2/april08/ic3_report040308.html (accessed July 15, 2008).

37. Damien Cave, "Eight Teenagers Charged in Internet Beating Have Their Day on the Web," *New York Times,* 12 April 2008, www.nytimes.com/2008/04/12/us/12florida.html (accessed July 15, 2008).

38. Anne Branscomb, "Rogue Computer Programs and Computer Rogues: Tailoring Punishment to Fit the Crime," *Rutgers Computer and Technology Law Journal* 16 (1990): 24–26.

39. Heather Jacobson and Rebecca Green, "Computer Crimes," *American Criminal Law Review* 39 (2002): 272–326.

40. U.S. Department of Justice, "Creator of 'Melissa' Computer Virus Pleads Guilty to State and Federal Charges," December 9, 1999, www.cybercrime.gov/melissa.htm (accessed July 15, 2008); see also Jacobson and Green, "Computer Crimes," 273–275.

41. Robert Lemos, "'MSBlast' Worm Widespread But Slowing," CNET News.com, 12 August 2003, http://news.com.com/2100-1002-5062655.html (accessed July 15, 2008).

42. "Cyber Threat!" *Middle East* 335 (2003): 38–41.

43. Hyung-jin Woo, Yeora Kim, and Joseph Dominick, "Hackers: Militants or Merry Pranksters? A Content Analysis of Defaced Web Pages," *Media Psychology* 6 (2004): 63–82.

44. Yona Hollander, "Prevent Web Page Defacement," *Internet Security Advisor* 2 (2000): 1–4.

45. Debra Baker, "When Cyber Stalkers Walk," *American Bar Association Journal* 85 (1999): 50–54.

46. U.S. Department of Justice, "Cyberstalking: A New Challenge for Law Enforcement and Industry," a Report from the Attorney General to the Vice President, 1999, www.usdoj.gov/criminal/cybercrime/cyberstalking.htm (accessed July 15, 2008).

47. Janis Wolak, David Finkelhor, Kimberly Mitchell, and Michele Ybarra, "Online 'Predators' and Their Victims: Myths, Realities, and Implications for Prevention and Treatment," *American Psychologist* 63 (2008): 111–128.

48. Kate Gross, "Homophobic Bullying and Schools—Responding to the Challenge," *Youth Studies Australia* 25 (2006): 60.

49. Jane Ireland and Rachel Monaghan, "Behaviors Indicative of Bullying among Young and Juvenile Male Offenders: A Study of Perpetrator and Victim Characteristics," *Aggressive Behavior* 32 (2006): 172–180.

50. Dan Olweus, "A Useful Evaluation Design, and Effects of the Olweus Bullying Prevention Program," *Psychology, Crime and Law* 11 (2005): 389–402.

51. This section leans heavily on Justin Patchin and Sameer Hinduja, "Bullies Move Beyond the Schoolyard: A Preliminary Look at Cyberbullying," *Youth Violence and Juvenile Justice* 4 (2006): 148–169.

52. Sameer Hinduja and Justin Patchin, "Cyberbullying: An Exploratory Analysis of Factors Related to Offending and Victimization," *Deviant Behavior* 29 (2008): 129–156.

53. Jessica Tonn, "Cyber Bullying," *Education Week* 26 (2006): 19.

54. Hinduja and Patchin, "Cyberbullying: An Exploratory Analysis of Factors Related to Offending and Victimization."

55. Manufacturing a Surreptitious Interception Device, Title 18, United States Code, Section 2512(1)(b); Advertising a Surreptitious Interception Device, Title 18, United States Code, Section 2512(1)(c)(i).

56. U.S. Department of Justice, Southern District of California, "Creator and Four Users of Loverspy Spyware Program Indicted," www.cybercrime.gov/perezIndict.htm (accessed July 15, 2008).

57. Tom Yager, "Cyberspying: No Longer a Crime for Geeks Only," *InfoWorld* 22 (2000): 62.

58. Nathan Vardi, "Chinese Take Out," *Forbes* 176 (2005).

59. Kevin Poulsen, "FBI Retires Its Carnivore," *SecurityFocus* (2005): 1–14, www.securityfocus.com/print/news/10307 (accessed July 15, 2008).

60. Clive Carmichael-Jones, "The Enemy Within," VoGon International, www.vogon.us/literature/international/EnemyWithin.pdf (accessed July 15, 2008).

61. Nathan Thornburgh, Matthew Forney, Brian Bennett, Timothy Burger, and Elaine Shannon, "The Invasion of the Chinese Cyberspies (and the Man Who Tried to Stop Them)," *Time*, September 5, 2005, p. 10.

62. Andrew Gray, "Chinese Hackers Worry Pentagon: A Recent Report Expresses Concerns about Technological Advances in Both Cyberspace and Space," *PC World*, March 9, 2008.

63. Barry C. Collin, "The Future of CyberTerrorism: Where the Physical and Virtual Worlds Converge," http://afgen.com/terrorism1.html (accessed July 15, 2008).

64. Mark Pollitt, "Cyberterrorism—Fact or Fancy?" FBI Laboratory, www.cs.georgetown.edu/~denning/infosec/pollitt.html (accessed July 15, 2008).

65. Tomas Hellström, "Critical Infrastructure and Systemic Vulnerability: Towards a Planning Framework," *Safety Science* 45 (2007): 415–430.

66. Mathieu Gorge, "Cyberterrorism: Hype or Reality?" *Computer Fraud and Security* 2 (2007): 9–12.

67. Gupta et al., "Fiscal Consequences of Armed Conflict and Terrorism."

68. Daniel Benjamin, *America and the World in the Age of Terrorism* (Washington, DC: CSIS Press, 2005), pp. 1–216.

69. General Accounting Office, "Critical Infrastructure Protection: Efforts of the Financial Services Sector to Address Cyber Threats," January 2003.

70. Michael Whine, "Cyberspace—A New Medium for Communication, Command, and Control by Extremists," Informaworld, www.informaworld.com/smpp/content~content=a713854363 (accessed July 15, 2008).

71. Yael Shahar, "Information Warfare," IWS: The Information Warfare Site, www.iwar.org.uk/cyberterror/resources/CIT.htm (accessed July 15, 2008).

72. General Accounting Office, "Critical Infrastructure Protection: Efforts of the Financial Services Sector to Address Cyber Threats."

73. Frank Hayes, "Botnet Threat" *Computerworld* 40 (2006): 50.

74. Gale Reference Team, "McAfee Reports Botnets Threaten National Security," *Computer Security Update*, December 1, 2006, pp. 2–4.

75. Gabriel Weimann, "Cyberterrorism: The Sum of All Fears?" *Studies in Conflict and Terrorism* 28 (2005): 129–150.

76. This section leans heavily on John Kane and April Wall, "Identifying the Links between White-Collar Crime and Terrorism," National White Collar Crime Center, 2004, www.ncjrs.gov/pdffiles1/nij/grants/209520.pdf (accessed July 15, 2008).

77. *United States v. Holy Land Foundation for Relief and Development*, http://fl1.findlaw.com/news.findlaw.com/cnn/docs/hlf/ushlf72604ind.pdf (accessed July 15, 2008).

78. Kane and Wall, "Identifying the Links between White-Collar Crime and Terrorism."

79. Loretta Napoleoni, *Modern Jihad: Tracing the Dollars Behind the Terror Networks*, (Sterling, VA: Pluto Press, 2003).

80. Clyde Wilson, "Software Piracy: Uncovering Mutiny on the Cyberseas," *Trial* 32 (1996): 24–31.

81. Deloitte, 2005 Global Security Survey, www.deloitte.com/dtt/cda/doc/content/dtt_financialservices_2005GlobalSecuritySurvey_2005-07-21.pdf (accessed July 15, 2008).

82. Business Software Alliance, "BSA Seventh Annual Global Software Piracy Study," 2003, http://global.bsa.org/idcglobalstudy2007/ (accessed July 15, 2008).

83. Jeanne Capachin and Dave Potterton, "Online Card Payments, Fraud Solutions Bid to Win," *Meridien Research Report*, January 18, 2001.

84. Computer Security Institute, CSI/FBI Computer Crime and Security Survey, 2005, www.gocsi.com (accessed July 15, 2008).

85. Avivah Litan,"Phishing Victims Likely Will Suffer Identity Theft Fraud," Gartner Group, May 14, 2004, www.gartner.com/DisplayDocument?doc_cd=120804 (accessed July 15, 2008).

86. Henry Pontell and Anastasia Tosouni, "Identity Theft: The Aftermath, 2004," with comparisons to "The Aftermath 2003 Survey," Identity Theft Resource Center, 2005.

87. David Porter, "Identity Fraud: The Stealth Threat to UK PLC," *Computer Fraud and Security* (2004): 4–7.

88. Computer Security Institute, "Cybercrime Bleeds U.S. Corporations, Survey Shows; Financial Losses from Attacks Climb for Third Year in a Row," April 7, 2002.

89. Ibid.

90. Lorine Hughes and Gregory DeLone, "Viruses, Worms, and Trojan Horses: Serious Crimes, Nuisance, or Both?" *Social Science Computer Review* 25 (2007): 78–98.

91. Symantec Internet Security Threat Report, "Trends for January–June 07, Volume XII," published September 2007, http://eval.symantec.com/mktginfo/enterprise/white_papers/ent-whitepaper_internet_security_threat_report_xii_exec_summary_09_2007.en-us.pdf (accessed July 15, 2008).

92. Public Law 98-473, Title H, Chapter XXI, [sections] 2102(a), 98 Stat. 1837, 2190 (1984).

93. Public Law 104-294, Title II, [sections] 201, 110 Stat. 3488, 3491-94 (1996).

94. Heather Jacobson and Rebecca Green, "Computer Crime," *American Criminal Law Review* 39 (2002): 273–326; Identity Theft and Assumption Act of 1998 (18 U.S.C. S 1028(a)(7)).

95. Comprehensive Crime Control Act of 1984, PL 98–473, 2101–03, 98 Stat. 1837, 2190 (1984), Adding 18 U.S.C. 1030 (1984); Counterfeit Active Device and Computer Fraud and Abuse Act, Amended by PL 99–474, 100 Stat. 1213 (1986), Codified at 18 U.S.C. 1030 (Supp. V 1987); Computer Abuse Amendments Act 18 U.S.C. Section 1030 (1994); Copyright Infringement Act 17 U.S.C. Section 506(a) 1994; Electronic Communications Privacy Act of 1986 18 U.S.C. 2510–2520 (1988 and Supp. II 1990).

96. Family Entertainment and Copyright Act of 2005, Title 18 United States Code Section 2319B.

97. U.S. State Department Fact Sheet, September 29, 2006, Council of Europe Convention on Cybercrime, www.state.gov/r/pa/prs/ps/2006/73354.htm (accessed July 15, 2008); Council of Europe Convention on Cybercrime, CETS No. 185, http://conventions.coe.int/Treaty/Commun/QueVoulezVous.asp?NT=185&CL=ENG (accessed July 15, 2008).

98. ACLU Memo on the Council of Europe Convention on Cybercrime, June 16, 2004, www.aclu.org/privacy/gen/15746leg20040616.html (accessed July 15, 2008).

99. Bruce Swartz, Deputy Assistant General, Criminal Division, Justice Department, "Internet Fraud Testimony before the House Energy and Commerce Committee," May 23, 2001.

100. IC3 Annual Internet Fraud Report 2006, www.ic3.gov/media/annualreport/2006_IC3Report.pdf (accessed July 15, 2008).

101. "Statement of Mr. Bob Weaver, Deputy Special Agent in Charge, New York Field Office, United States Secret Service, Before the House Financial Services Committee Subcommittee on Financial Institutions and Consumer Credit and the Subcommittee on Oversight and Investigations," U.S. House of Representatives, April 3, 2003, www.iwar.org.uk/ecoespionage/resources/fraud/040303bw.pdf (accessed JUly 15, 2008).

102. Steven Frank, "Toronto's Child Porn Sleuths: A Canadian Team Leads the Way in Tracking Down Global Perpetrators of

Grisly Internet Child Pornography," *Time Canada* 166 (2005): 30.

103. Office of Justice Programs Crime Identification Technology Act, http://it.ojp.gov/fund/files/cita.html (accessed July 15, 2008).

104. Raymond E. Foster, "Crime Scene Investigation," *Government Technology* (March 2005), www.govtech.com/gt/articles/93225 (accessed July 15, 2008).

105. "Recognize the Face," *TechBeat*, Winter 2008, www.justnet.org/techbeat/winter2008/ (accessed July 15, 2008).

106. Jay Stanley and Barry Steinhardt, *Bigger Monster, Weaker Chains: The Growth of an American Surveillance Society* (New York: American Civil Liberties Union, 2003).

107. Margaret Johnson and Neville Holmes, "Biometrics and the Threat to Civil Liberties," *Computer* 37 (2004): 92–94.

108. Benjamin Hale, "Identity Crisis: Face Recognition Technology and Freedom of the Will," *Ethics, Place and Environment* 8 (2005): 141–158.

109. Catherine Yang, Kerry Capell, and Otis Port, "The State of Surveillance," *BusinessWeek*, 8 August 2005, pp. 52–59.

110. W. Kip Viscusi and Richard J. Zeckhauser, "Sacrificing Civil Liberties to Reduce Terrorism Risks," Harvard University, Olin Center for Law, Economics, and Business, 2003, www.law.harvard.edu/programs/olin_center/ (accessed July 15, 2008).

111. Craig Arndt, "The Loss of Privacy and Identity," *Biometric Technology Today* 13 (2005): 6–7.

112. "Today's Debate: Privacy in an Era of Terror (Part I)," *USA Today*, 2 August 2005.

113. American Bar Association, "Technologically Assisted Physical Surveillance, Standard 2-9.1, General Principles," www.abanet.org/crimjust/standards/taps_toc.html (accessed July 15, 2008).

GLOSSARY

acquaintance rape Forcible sex in which offender and victim are acquainted with each other.

acquaintance robbery Robbers who focus their thefts on people they know.

active precipitation The view that the source of many criminal incidents is the aggressive or provocative behavior of victims.

actual authority The authority a corporation knowingly gives to an employee.

actus reus An illegal act. The *actus reus* can be an affirmative act, such as taking money or shooting someone, or a failure to act, such as failing to take proper precautions while driving a car.

adjudication (adult) The determination of guilt or innocence; a judgment concerning criminal charges.

adjudication (juvenile) The juvenile court hearing at which the juvenile is declared a delinquent or status offender, or no finding of fact is made.

adolescent-limited offender Offender who follows the most common criminal trajectory, in which antisocial behavior peaks in adolescence and then diminishes.

adversarial process The procedure used to determine truth in the adjudication of guilt or innocence in which the defense (advocate for the accused) is pitted against the prosecution (advocate for the state), with the judge acting as arbiter of the legal rules. Under the adversarial system, the burden is on the state to prove the charges beyond a reasonable doubt. This system of having the two parties publicly debate has proved to be the most effective method of achieving the truth regarding a set of circumstances. (Under the accusatory, or inquisitorial, system, which is used in continental Europe, the charge is evidence of guilt that the accused must disprove, and the judge takes an active part in the proceedings.)

age-graded theory A developmental theory that posits that (a) individual traits and childhood experiences are important to understand the onset of delinquent and criminal behavior; (b) experiences in young adulthood and beyond can redirect criminal trajectories or paths; (c) serious problems in adolescence undermine life chances; (d) positive life experiences and relationships can help a person knife off

from a criminal career path; (e) positive life experiences such as gaining employment, getting married, or joining the military create informal social control mechanisms that limit criminal behavior opportunities; (f) former criminals may choose to desist from crime because they find more conventional paths more beneficial and rewarding.

aggravated rape Rape involving multiple offenders, weapons, and victim injuries.

aggressive preventive patrol A patrol technique designed to suppress crime before it occurs.

aging out The process by which individuals reduce the frequency of their offending behavior as they age. It is also known as spontaneous remission, because people are believed to spontaneously reduce the rate of their criminal behavior as they mature. Aging out is thought to occur among all groups of offenders.

alexithymia A deficit in emotional cognition that prevents people from being aware of their feelings or being able to understand or talk about their thoughts and emotions; they seem robotic and emotionally dead.

alien conspiracy theory The view that organized crime was imported to the United States by Europeans and that crime cartels have a policy of restricting their membership to people of their own ethnic background.

al-Qaeda (Arabic for "the base") An international fundamentalist Islamist organization comprising independent and collaborative cells, whose goal is reducing Western influence upon Islamic affairs.

alternative sanctions The group of punishments falling between probation and prison; "probation plus." Community-based sanctions, including house arrest and intensive supervision, serve as alternatives to incarceration.

American Dream The goal of accumulating material goods and wealth through individual competition; the process of being socialized to pursue material success and to believe it is achievable.

anal stage In Freud's schema, the second and third years of life, when the focus of sexual attention is on the elimination of bodily wastes.

androgens Male sex hormones.

anomie A condition produced by normlessness. Because of rapidly shifting moral values, the individual has few guides to what is socially acceptable. According to Robert Merton, anomie is a condition that occurs when personal goals cannot be achieved by available means. In Agnew's revision, anomie can occur when positive or valued stimuli are removed or negative or painful ones applied.

antithesis An opposing argument.

apparent authority Authority that a third party, such as a customer, reasonably believes the agent has to perform the act in question.

appeal Taking a criminal case to a higher court on the grounds that the defendant was found guilty because of legal error or violation of constitutional rights; a successful appeal may result in a new trial.

appellate courts Courts that reconsider a case that has already been tried to determine whether the measures used complied with accepted rules of criminal procedure and were in line with constitutional doctrines.

arousal theory A view of crime suggesting that people who have a high arousal level seek powerful stimuli in their environment to maintain an optimal level of arousal. These stimuli are often associated with violence and aggression. Sociopaths may need greater than average stimulation to bring them up to comfortable levels of living; this need explains their criminal tendencies.

arraignment The step in the criminal justice process at which the accused are read the charges against them, asked how they plead, and advised of their rights. Possible pleas are guilty, not guilty, nolo contendere, and not guilty by reason of insanity.

arrest The taking of a person into the custody of the law, the legal purpose of which is to restrain the accused until he or she can be held accountable for the offense at court proceedings. The legal requirement for an arrest is probable cause. Arrests for investigation, suspicion, or harassment are improper and of doubtful legality. The police have the responsibility to use only the reasonable physical force necessary to make an arrest. The summons has been used as a substitute for arrest.

arson The intentional or negligent burning of a home, structure, or vehicle for criminal purposes such as profit, revenge, fraud, or crime concealment.

arson for profit People looking to collect insurance money, but who are afraid or unable to set the fire themselves, hire professional arsonists. These professionals have acquired the skills to set fires, yet make the cause seem accidental.

arson fraud A business owner burns his or her property, or hires someone to do it, to escape financial problems.

assault An attack that may not involve physical contact; includes attempted battery or intentionally frightening the victim by word or deed.

assigned counsel system A list of private bar members who accept cases of indigent criminals on a judge-by-judge, court-by-court, or case-by-case basis. This system is used in less populated areas, where case flow is minimal and a full-time public defender is not needed.

atavistic anomalies According to Lombroso, the physical characteristics that distinguish born criminals from the general population and are throwbacks to animals or primitive people.

at risk Children and adults who lack the education and skills needed to be effectively in demand in modern society.

attachment theory The view that the ability to form attachments, an emotional bond to another person, controls the direction of human behavior.

attention deficit hyperactivity disorder (ADHD) A psychological disorder in which a child shows developmentally inappropriate impulsivity, hyperactivity, and lack of attention.

Auburn system The prison system developed in New York during the nineteenth century that stressed congregate working conditions.

authority conflict pathway The path to a criminal career that begins with early stubborn behavior and defiance of parents.

automatic teller machine (ATM) An automated device that gives banking customers access to their accounts without the need for human intervention.

avertable recidivist A person whose crime would have been prevented if he or she had not been given discretionary release and instead been kept behind bars.

bail The monetary amount for or condition of pretrial release, normally set by a judge at the initial appearance. The purpose of bail is to ensure the return of the accused at subsequent proceedings. If the accused is unable to make bail, he or she is detained in jail. The Eighth Amendment provides that excessive bail shall not be required.

bail bonding agent A person whose business is providing bail to needy offenders, usually at an exorbitant rate of interest.

bail guidelines Standard bail amounts set based on such factors as criminal history and the current charge.

battery A physical attack that includes hitting, punching, slapping, or other offensive touching of a victim.

behavior modeling Process of learning behavior (notably aggression) by observing others. Aggressive models may be parents, criminals in the neighborhood, or characters on television or in video games and movies.

behaviorism The branch of psychology concerned with the study of observable behavior rather than unconscious motives. It focuses on the relationship between particular stimuli and people's responses to them.

bias crimes Violent acts directed toward a particular person or members of a group merely because the targets share a discernible racial, ethnic, religious, or gender characteristic; also called hate crimes.

Bill of Rights The first ten amendments to the U.S. Constitution.

biological determinism A belief that criminogenic traits can be acquired through indirect heredity from a degenerate family whose members suffered from such ills as insanity, syphilis, and alcoholism, or through direct heredity—being related to a family of criminals.

biophobia Sociologists who held the view that no serious consideration should be given to biological factors when attempting to understand human nature.

biosocial theory The view that physical, environmental, and social conditions work in concert to produce human behavior.

bipolar disorder An emotional disturbance in which moods alternate between periods of wild elation and deep depression.

blameworthy The philosophy of justice and punishment that holds that an offender should be treated based solely on the seriousness and character of his or her offense and not for the effect the punishment will have on other people.

blue curtain subculture According to William Westly, the secretive, insulated police culture that isolates the officer from the rest of society.

booking Fingerprinting, photographing, and recording of personal information of a suspect in police custody.

booster Professional shoplifter who steals with the intention of reselling stolen merchandise.

boot camp A short-term militaristic correctional facility in which inmates undergo intensive physical conditioning and discipline.

bourgeoisie In Marxist theory, the owners of the means of production; the capitalist ruling class.

Z. R. Brockway The warden at the Elmira Reformatory in New York, he advocated individualized treatment, indeterminate sentences, and parole. The reformatory program initiated by Brockway included elementary education for illiterates, designated library hours, lectures by local college faculty members, and a group of vocational training shops.

brothel A house of prostitution, typically run by a madam who sets prices and handles "business" arrangements.

brutalization effect The belief that capital punishment creates an atmosphere of brutality that enhances rather than deters the level of violence in society. The death penalty reinforces the view that violence is an appropriate response to provocation.

bucketing A form of stockbroker chiseling in which brokers skim customer trading profits by falsifying trade information.

Bureau of Alcohol, Tobacco, Firearms, and Explosives (ATF) Government agency that has jurisdiction over the sale and distribution of firearms, explosives, alcohol, and tobacco products.

burglary Breaking into and entering a home or structure for the purposes of committing a felony.

California Personality Inventory (CPI) A frequently administered personality test used to distinguish deviants from nondeviant groups.

call girls Prostitutes who make dates via the phone and then service customers in hotel rooms or apartments. Call girls typically have a steady clientele who are repeat customers.

capable guardians Effective deterrents to crime, such as police or watchful neighbors.

capital punishment The use of the death penalty to punish transgressors.

capitalist bourgeoisie The owners of the means of production.

career criminal A person who repeatedly violates the law and organizes his or her lifestyle around criminality.

carjacking Theft of a car by force or threat of force.

cartographic school of criminology An approach developed in Europe in the early nineteenth century making use of social statistics to provide important demographic information on the population, including density, gender, religious affiliations, and wealth. Many of the relationships between crime and social phenomena identified then still serve as a basis for criminology today.

cerebral allergies A physical condition that causes brain malfunction due to exposure to some environmental or biochemical irritant.

chemical restraints Antipsychotic drugs such as Haldol, Stelazine, Prolixin, and Risperdal, which help control levels of neurotransmitters (such as serotonin/dopamine), that are used to treat violence-prone people; also called chemical straitjackets.

chemical straitjackets Another term for chemical restraints; antipsychotic drugs used to treat violence prone people.

Chicago School Group of urban sociologists who studied the relationship between environmental conditions and crime.

child abuse Any physical, emotional, or sexual trauma to a child for which no reasonable explanation, such as an accident, can be found. Child abuse can also be a function of neglecting to give proper care and attention to a young child.

chiseling Crimes that involve using illegal means to cheat an organization, its consumers, or both, on a regular basis.

chivalry hypothesis The idea that low female crime and delinquency rates are a reflection of the leniency with which police treat female offenders.

chronic offender According to Marvin Wolfgang, a delinquent offender who is arrested five or more times before he or she is 18 and who stands a good chance of becoming an adult criminal; such offenders are responsible for more than half of all serious crimes.

chronic victimization Those who have been crime victims maintain a significantly higher chance of future victimization than people who have remained nonvictims. Most repeat victimizations occur soon after a previous crime has occurred, suggesting that repeat victims share some personal characteristic that makes them a magnet for predators.

churning A white-collar crime in which a stockbroker makes repeated trades to fraudulently increase commissions.

classical criminology The theoretical perspective suggesting that (1) people have free will to choose criminal or conventional behaviors; (2) people choose to commit crime for reasons of greed or personal

need; and (3) crime can be controlled only by the fear of criminal sanctions.

cleared crimes Crimes are cleared in two ways: when at least one person is arrested, charged, and turned over to the court for prosecution; or by exceptional means, when some element beyond police control precludes the physical arrest of an offender (for example, the offender leaves the country).

closure A term used by Lemert to describe people from a middle-class background who have little identification with a criminal subculture but cash bad checks because of a financial crisis that demands an immediate resolution.

Code of Hammurabi The first written criminal code, developed in Babylonia around 4,000 years ago.

coercion An act by an individual or individuals against the will or without the permission of another human being. Coercion can be psychological or physical, direct or indirect, interpersonal or impersonal.

coercive ideation The world is conceived as full of coercive forces that can only be overcome through the application of equal or even greater coercive responses.

cognitive theory The study of the perception of reality and of the mental processes required to understand the world in which we live.

cohort A sample of subjects whose behavior is followed over a period of time.

collective efficacy Social control exerted by cohesive communities, based on mutual trust, including intervention in the supervision of children and maintenance of public order.

college boy A disadvantaged youth who embraces the cultural and social values of the middle class and actively strives to be successful by those standards. This type of youth is embarking on an almost hopeless path, because he is ill-equipped academically, socially, and linguistically to achieve the rewards of middle-class life.

commitment to conformity A strong personal investment in conventional institutions, individuals, and processes that prevents people from engaging in behavior that might jeopardize their reputation and achievements.

common law Early English law, developed by judges, that incorporated Anglo-Saxon tribal custom, feudal rules and practices, and the everyday rules of behavior of local villages. Common law became the standardized law of the land in England and eventually formed the basis of the criminal law in the United States.

communist manifesto In this document, Marx focused his attention on the economic conditions perpetuated by the capitalist system. He stated that its development had turned workers into a dehumanized mass who lived an existence that was at the mercy of their capitalist employers.

community-oriented policing (COP) A police strategy that emphasizes fear reduction, community organization, and order maintenance rather than crime fighting.

community service restitution An alternative sanction that requires an offender to work in the community at such tasks as cleaning public parks or helping handicapped children in lieu of an incarceration sentence.

complaint A sworn allegation made in writing to a court or judge that an individual is guilty of some designated (complained of) offense. This is often the first legal document filed regarding a criminal offense. The complaint can be "taken out" by the victim, the police officer, the district attorney, or another interested party. Although the complaint charges an offense, an indictment or information may be the formal charging document.

compurgation In early English law, a process whereby an accused person swore an oath of innocence while being backed up by a group of 12 to 25 "oathhelpers," who would attest to his character and claims of innocence.

computer virus A program that disrupts or destroys existing programs and networks, causing them to perform the task for which the virus was designed.

computer worm A program that attacks computer networks (or the Internet) by self-replicating and sending itself to other users, generally via e-mail without the aid of the operator.

concentration effect As working-class and middle-class families flee inner-city poverty areas, the most disadvantaged population is consolidated in urban ghettos.

concurrent sentences Literally, running sentences together. Someone who is convicted of two or more charges must be sentenced on each charge. If the sentences are concurrent, they begin the same day and are completed after the longest term has been served.

conduct disorder (CD) A psychological condition marked by repeated and severe episodes of antisocial behaviors.

conduct norms Behaviors expected of social group members. If group norms conflict with those of the general culture, members of the group may find themselves described as outcasts or criminals.

confidence game A swindle, usually involving a get-rich-quick scheme, often with illegal overtones, so that the victim will be afraid or embarrassed to call the police.

conflict view The view that human behavior is shaped by interpersonal conflict and that those who maintain social power will use it to further their own needs.

congregate system This prison system included congregate working conditions, the use of solitary confinement to punish unruly inmates, military regimentation, and discipline.

conscience One of two parts of the superego; it distinguishes between what is right and wrong.

consecutive sentences Prison sentences for two or more criminal acts that are served one after the other.

consensus view of crime The belief that the majority of citizens in a society share common ideals and work toward a common good and that crimes are acts that are outlawed because they conflict with the rules of the majority and are harmful to society.

consent In prosecuting rape cases, it is essential to prove that the attack was forced and that the victim did not give voluntary consent to her attacker. In a sense, the burden of proof is on the victim to show that her character is beyond question and that she in no way encouraged, enticed, or misled the accused rapist. Proving victim dissent is not a requirement in any other violent crime.

constable The peacekeeper in early English towns. The constable organized citizens to protect his territory and supervised the night watch.

constructive possession In the crime of larceny, willingly giving up temporary physical possession of property but retaining legal ownership.

contagion effect Genetic predispositions and early experiences make some people, including twins, susceptible to deviant behavior, which is transmitted by the presence of antisocial siblings in the household.

containment theory The idea that a strong self-image insulates a youth from the pressures and pulls of criminogenic influences in the environment.

contextual discrimination A practice in which African Americans receive harsher punishments in some instances (as when they victimize whites) but not in others (as when they victimize other blacks).

continuity of crime The view that crime begins early in life and continues throughout the life course. Thus, the best predictor of future criminality is past criminality.

contract attorney system Providing counsel to indigent offenders by having attorneys under contract to the county handle some or all such cases.

contract system A prison work system in which officials sell the labor of inmates to private businesses.

Control Balance Theory According to Charles R. Tittle, a developmental theory that attributes deviant and criminal behaviors to imbalances between the amount of control that the individual has over others and that others have over him or her.

convict-lease system The system used earlier in the century in which inmates were leased out to private industry to work.

corner boy According to Albert K. Cohen, a role in the lower-class culture in which young men remain in their birth neighborhood, acquire families and menial jobs, and adjust to the demands of their environment.

corporal punishment The use of physical chastisement, such as whipping or electroshock, to punish criminals.

corporate crime White-collar crime involving a legal violation by a corporate entity, such as price fixing, restraint of trade, or hazardous waste dumping.

Cosa Nostra A national syndicate of 25 or so Italian-dominated crime families who control crime in distinct geographic areas.

courtroom work group All the parties in the adversarial process who work together to settle cases with the least amount of effort and conflict.

covert pathway A path to a criminal career that begins with minor underhanded behavior and progresses to fire starting and theft.

crackdown The concentration of police resources on a particular problem area, such as street-level drug dealing, to eradicate or displace criminal activity.

crime A violation of societal rules of behavior as interpreted and expressed by a criminal legal code created by people holding social and political power. Individuals who violate these rules are subject to sanctions by state authority, social stigma, and loss of status.

crime control model A model of criminal justice that emphasizes the control of dangerous offenders and the protection of society. Its advocates call for harsh punishments, such as the death penalty, as a deterrent to crime.

crime discouragers Discouragers can be grouped into three categories: guardians, who monitor targets (such as store security guards); handlers, who monitor potential offenders (such as parole officers and parents); and managers, who monitor places (such as homeowners and doorway attendants).

crime displacement An effect of crime prevention efforts in which efforts to control crime in one area shift illegal activities to another.

crime typology The study of criminal behavior involving research on the links between different types of crime and criminals. Because people often disagree about types of crimes and criminal motivation, no standard exists within the field. Some typologies focus on the criminal, suggesting the existence of offender groups, such as professional criminals, psychotic criminals, occasional criminals, and so on. Others focus on the crimes, clustering them into categories such as property crimes, sex crimes, and so on.

criminal anthropology Early efforts to discover a biological basis of crime through measurement of physical and mental processes.

criminal charge A formal written document identifying the criminal activity, the facts of the case, and the circumstances of the arrest.

criminal justice system The various sequential stages through which offenders pass, from initial contact with the law to final disposition, and the agencies of government—police, courts, and corrections—responsible for apprehending, adjudicating, sanctioning, and treating criminal offenders.

criminality A personal trait of the individual as distinct from a "crime," which is an event.

criminal trial A full-scale inquiry into the facts of the case before a judge, a jury, or both.

criminological enterprise The areas of study and research that taken together make up the field of criminology. Criminologists typically specialize in one of the subareas of criminology, such as victimology or the sociology of law.

criminologists Researchers who use scientific methods to study the nature, extent, cause, and control of criminal behavior.

criminology The scientific study of the nature, extent, cause, and control of criminal behavior.

crisis intervention Emergency counseling for crime victims.

critical criminologists Researchers who view crime as a function of the capitalist mode of production and not the social conflict that might occur in any society regardless of its economic system.

critical criminology The view that capitalism produces haves and have-nots, each engaging in a particular branch of criminality. The mode of production shapes social life. Because economic competitiveness is the essence of capitalism, conflict increases and eventually destabilizes social institutions and the individuals within them.

critical feminist Scholars, both male and female, who focus on the effects of gender inequality and the unequal power of men and women in a capitalist society.

cross-examination The process in which the defense and the prosecution interrogate witnesses during a trial.

cross-sectional survey Survey data derived from all age, race, gender, and income segments of the population measured simultaneously. Because people from every age group are represented, age-specific crime rates can be determined. Proponents believe this is a sufficient substitute for the more expensive longitudinal approach that follows a group of subjects over time to measure crime rate changes.

crusted over Children who have been victims of or witnesses to violence and do not let people inside, nor do they express their feelings. They exploit others and in turn are exploited by those older and stronger; as a result, they develop a sense of hopelessness.

cult terrorists Cults that can be classified as terror groups because their leaders demand that followers prove their loyalty through violence or intimidation. Members typically follow a charismatic leader who may be viewed as having godlike powers or even being the reincarnation of an important religious figure. The leader and his or her lieutenants commonly enforce loyalty by severe discipline and by physically preventing members from leaving the group. They may go through doomsday drills and maintain a siege mentality, fearing attacks from the government. The cult may openly or tacitly endorse individual killings or mass murder, which may be accompanied by mass suicide.

cultural deviance theory Branch of social structure theory that sees strain and social disorganization together resulting in a unique lower-class culture that conflicts with conventional social norms.

cultural transmission The concept that conduct norms are passed down from one generation to the next so that they become stable within the boundaries of a culture. Cultural transmission guarantees that group lifestyle and behavior are stable and predictable.

culture conflict According to Thorsten Sellin, a condition brought about when the rules and norms of an individual's subcultural affiliation conflict with the role demands of conventional society.

culture of poverty The view that people in the lower class of society form a separate culture with its own values and norms that are in conflict with conventional society; the culture is self-maintaining and ongoing.

cumulative disadvantage A condition in which repeated negative experiences in adolescence undermine life chances and reduce employability and social relations. People who increase their cumulative disadvantage risk continued offending.

cyber bullying Willful and repeated harm inflicted through the medium of electronic text.

cyber crime The use of modern technology for criminal purpose.

cyber spying Illegally using the Internet to gather information that is considered private and confidential.

cyber stalking Use of the Internet, e-mail, or other electronic communications devices to stalk another person. Some cyber stalkers pursue minors through online chat rooms; others harass their victims electronically.

cyber terrorism Internet attacks against an enemy nation's technological infrastructure.

cyber theft Use of computer networks for criminal profits. Illegal copyright infringement, identity theft, and Internet securities fraud are examples of cyber theft.

cyber vandalism Use of cyberspace for revenge, destruction, and to achieve a malicious intent. Examples include website defacement, worms, viruses, cyber stalking, and cyber bullying.

cyber warfare Political crime involving spying, espionage, and terrorism, aimed at undermining the social, economic, and political system of an enemy nation by destroying its electronic infrastructure and disrupting its economy.

cycle of violence The idea that victims of crime, especially childhood abuse, are more likely to commit crimes themselves.

date rape Forcible sex during a courting relationship.

day fines Fines geared to the average daily income of the convicted offender in an effort to bring equity to the sentencing process.

deadly force The ability of the police to kill suspects if they resist arrest or present a danger to an officer or the community. The police cannot use deadly force against an unarmed fleeing felon.

death squads Government troops used to destroy political opposition parties.

decadence Spur of the moment, irrational acts such as child molesting.

deconstructionist An approach that focuses on the use of language by those in power to define crime based on their own values and biases; also called postmodernist.

decriminalized Reducing the penalty for a criminal act but not actually legalizing it.

defective intelligence Traits such as feeblemindedness, epilepsy, insanity, and defective social instinct, which Goring believed had a significant relationship to criminal behavior.

defense attorney Legal counsel for the defendant in a criminal case, representing the accused person from arrest to final appeal.

defensible space The principle that crime prevention can be achieved through modifying the physical environment to reduce the opportunity individuals have to commit crime.

defiance Challenging control mechanisms but stopping short of physical harm: for example, vandalism, curfew violations, and unconventional sex.

deliberation Planning a homicide after careful thought, however brief, rather than acting on sudden impulse.

delinquent boy A youth who adopts a set of norms and principles in direct opposition to middle-class values, engaging in short-run hedonism, living for today and letting tomorrow take care of itself.

demystify To unmask the true purpose of law, justice, or other social institutions.

denial-of-service attack Extorting money from an Internet service user by threatening to prevent the user from having access to the service.

Department of Homeland Security (DHS) An agency of the federal government charged with preventing terrorist attacks within the United States, reducing America's vulnerability to terrorism, and minimizing the damage and aiding recovery from attacks that do occur.

deposit bail system A system that allows defendants to post a percentage of their bond (usually 10 percent) with the court; the full amount is required only if the defendant fails to show for trial.

desist To spontaneously stop committing crime.

determinate sentences Fixed terms of incarceration, such as three years' imprisonment. Determinate sentences are felt by many to be too restrictive for rehabilitative purposes; the advantage is that offenders know how much time they have to serve—that is, when they will be released.

deterrence theory The view that if the probability of arrest, conviction, and sanctioning increases, crime rates should decline.

deterrent Preventing crime before it occurs by means of the threat of criminal sanctions.

developmental theory A branch of criminology that examines change in a criminal career over the life course. Developmental factors include biological, social, and psychological change. Among the topics of developmental criminology are desistance, resistance, escalation, and specialization.

deviant behavior Behavior that departs from the social norm.

deviant place theory People become victims because they reside in socially disorganized, high-crime areas where they have the greatest risk of coming into contact with criminal offenders.

dialectic method For every idea, or thesis, there exists an opposing argument, or antithesis. Because neither position can ever be truly accepted, the result is a merger of the two ideas, a synthesis. Marx adapted this analytic method for his study of class struggle.

Differential Association Theory According to Edwin H. Sutherland, the principle that criminal acts are related to a person's exposure to an excess amount of antisocial attitudes and values.

differential opportunity The view that lower-class youths, whose legitimate opportunities are limited, join gangs and pursue criminal careers as alternative means to achieve universal success goals.

differential reinforcement Behavior is reinforced by being either rewarded or punished while interacting with others; also called direct conditioning.

Differential Reinforcement Theory An attempt to explain crime as a type of learned behavior. First proposed by Ronald A. Akers in collaboration with Robert L. Burgess in 1966, it is a version of the social learning view that employs differential association concepts as well as elements of psychological learning theory.

differential social control A process of labeling that may produce a reevaluation of the self, which reflects actual or perceived appraisals made by others.

Differential Social Support and Coercion Theory (DSSCT) According to Mark Colvin, a theory that holds that perceptions of coercion become ingrained and guide reactions to adverse situations that arise in both family and nonfamily settings.

diffusion of benefits An effect that occurs when an effort to control one type of crime has the unexpected benefit of reducing the incidence of another.

direct conditioning Behavior is reinforced by being either rewarded or punished while interacting with others; also called differential reinforcement.

direct examination The questioning of one's own (prosecution or defense) witness during a trial.

directed verdict The right of a judge to direct a jury to acquit a defendant because the state has not proven the elements of the crime or otherwise has not established guilt according to law.

Director of National Intelligence (DNI) Government official charged with coordinating data from the nation's primary intelligence-gathering agencies.

discouragement An effect that occurs when an effort to eliminate one type of crime also controls others, because it reduces the value of criminal activity by limiting access to desirable targets.

discretion The use of personal decision making by those carrying out police, judicial, and sanctioning functions within the criminal justice system.

disorder Any type of psychological problem (formerly labeled neuroses or psychoses), such as anxiety disorders, mood disorders, and conduct disorders.

disposition For juvenile offenders, the equivalent of sentencing for adult offenders. The theory is that disposition is more rehabilitative than retributive. Possible dispositions may be to dismiss the case, release the youth to the custody of his or her parents, place the offender on probation, or send him or her to a correctional institution. For adult defendants found guilty, sentencing usually involves a fine, probation, and/or incarceration.

disputatiousness Behavior within culturally defined conflict situations in which an individual who has been offended by a negative outcome in a dispute seeks reparations through violent means.

diversion programs Programs of rehabilitation that remove offenders from the normal channels of the criminal justice system, thus avoiding the stigma of a criminal label.

division of markets Firms divide a region into territories, and each firm agrees not to compete in the others' territories.

double jeopardy A defendant cannot be prosecuted by a jurisdiction more than once for a single offense.

dramatization of evil As the negative feedback of law enforcement agencies, parents, friends, teachers, and other figures amplifies the force of the original label, stigmatized offenders may begin to reevaluate their own identities. The person becomes the thing he is described as being.

drift According to David Matza, the view that youths move in and out of delinquency and that their lifestyles can embrace both conventional and deviant values.

Drug Enforcement Administration (DEA) The federal agency that enforces federal drug control laws.

dual sovereignty doctrine If a single act violates the laws of two states, the offender may be punished for each offense.

due process model View that focuses on protecting the civil rights of those accused of crime.

early onset A term that refers to the assumption that a criminal career begins early in life and that people who are deviant at a very young age are the ones most likely to persist in crime.

ecological view A belief that social forces operating in urban areas create criminal interactions; some neighborhoods become natural areas for crime.

economic crime An act in violation of the criminal law that is designed to bring financial gain to the offender.

edgework The excitement or exhilaration of successfully executing illegal activities in dangerous situations.

egalitarian families Families in which spouses share similar positions of power at home and in the workplace.

ego The part of the personality, developed in early childhood, that helps control the id and keep people's actions within the boundaries of social convention.

ego ideal Part of the superego; directs the individual into morally acceptable and responsible behaviors, which may not be pleasurable.

elder abuse A disturbing form of domestic violence by children and other relatives with whom elderly people live.

eldercide The murder of a senior citizen.

election fraud Illegal interference with the process of an election. Acts of fraud tend to involve affecting vote counts to bring about a desired election outcome, whether by increasing the vote share of the favored candidate, depressing the vote share of the rival candidates, or both. Varieties of election fraud include intimidation, disruption of polling places, distribution of misinformation such as the wrong election date, registration fraud, and vote buying.

Electra complex A stage of development when girls begin to have sexual feelings for their fathers.

electroencephalograph (EEG) A device that can record the electronic impulses given off by the brain, commonly called brain waves.

electronic monitoring (EM) Offenders wear devices attached to their ankles, wrists, or neck that send signals back to a control office; used to monitor home confinements.

elite deviance White-collar and economic crimes.

embezzlement A type of larceny that involves taking the possessions of another (fraudulent conversion) that have been placed in the thief's lawful possession for safekeeping, such as a bank teller misappropriating deposits or a stockbroker making off with a customer's account.

enterprise crime The use of illegal tactics to gain profit in the marketplace. Enterprise crimes can involve both the violation of law in the course of an otherwise legitimate occupation or the sale and distribution of illegal commodities.

enterprise theory of investigation (ETI) A standard investigation tool of the FBI that focuses on criminal enterprise and investigation attacks on the structure of the criminal enterprise rather than on criminal acts viewed as isolated incidents.

equipotentiality View that all individuals are equal at birth and are thereafter influenced by their environment.

eros The instinct to preserve and create life; eros is expressed sexually.

etailing fraud Illegally buying or selling merchandise on the Internet.

espionage The practice of obtaining information about a government, organization, or society that is considered secret or confidential without the permission of the holder of the information. Commonly called spying.

ex post facto law Those laws that are made to punish actions committed before the existence of such laws and that had not been declared crimes by preceding laws.

exclusionary rule The principle that prohibits using evidence illegally obtained in a trial. Based on the Fourth Amendment "right of the people to be secure in their persons, houses, papers, and effects, against unreasonable searches and seizures," the rule is not a bar to prosecution, as legally obtained evidence may be available that may be used in a trial.

exploitation (of criminals) Using others to commit crimes: for example, as contract killers or drug runners.

exploitation (of victims) Forcing victims to pay for services to which they have a clear right.

expressive crimes Crimes that have no purpose except to accomplish the behavior at hand, such as shooting someone.

expressive violence Violence that is designed not for profit or gain but to vent rage, anger, or frustration.

extinction The phenomenon in which a crime prevention effort has an immediate impact that then dissipates as criminals adjust to new conditions.

false pretenses Illegally obtaining money, goods, or merchandise from another by fraud or misrepresentation.

Federal Bureau of Investigation (FBI) The arm of the U.S. Justice Department that investigates violations of federal law, gathers crime statistics, runs a comprehensive crime laboratory, and helps train local law enforcement officers.

federal courts of appeal Courts that hear appeals from the U.S. district courts.

felony A serious offense that carries a penalty of incarceration in a state prison, usually for one year or more. People convicted of felony offenses lose the right to vote, hold elective office, or maintain certain licenses.

felony murder A homicide in the context of another felony, such as robbery or rape; legally defined as first-degree murder.

fence A buyer and seller of stolen merchandise.

feticide Endangering or killing an unborn fetus.

filicide Murder of an older child.

fine A dollar amount usually exacted as punishment for a minor crime. Although fines are most commonly used in misdemeanors, they are also frequently employed in felonies where the offender benefited financially. Fines may also be combined with other sentencing alternatives, such as probation or confinement.

first-degree murder The killing of another person after premeditation and deliberation.

fixated An adult who exhibits behavior traits characteristic of those encountered during infantile sexual development.

flash houses Public meeting places in England, often taverns, that served as headquarters for gangs.

flashover An effect in a fire when heat and gas at the ceiling of a room reach 2,000 degrees, and clothes and furniture burst into flame, duplicating the effects of arsonists' gasoline or explosives. It is possible

that many suspected arsons are actually the result of flashover.

focal concerns According to Walter Miller, the value orientations of lower-class cultures; features include the needs for excitement, trouble, smartness, and personal autonomy.

foot patrols Police patrols that take officers out of cars and put them on a walking beat to strengthen ties with the community.

forfeiture The seizure of personal property by the state as a civil or criminal penalty.

fraud Taking the possessions of another through deception or cheating, such as selling a person a desk that is represented as an antique but is known to be a copy.

free-venture programs Privately run industries in a prison setting in which the inmates work for wages and the goods are sold for profit.

front running A form of stockbroker chiseling in which brokers place personal orders ahead of a large order from a customer to profit from the market effects of the trade.

gang rape Forcible sex involving multiple attackers.

gatekeepers The police, who initiate contact with law violators and decide whether to formally arrest them and start their journey through the criminal justice system, settle the issue informally (such as by issuing a warning), or simply take no action at all.

gateway model An explanation of drug abuse that posits that users begin with a more benign drug (alcohol or marijuana) and progress to more potent drugs.

gay bashing Violent hate crimes directed toward people because of their sexual orientation.

general deterrence A crime control policy that depends on the fear of criminal penalties. General deterrence measures, such as long prison sentences for violent crimes, are aimed at convincing the potential law violator that the pains associated with crime outweigh its benefits.

General Strain Theory (GST) According to Robert Agnew, the view that multiple sources of strain interact with an individual's emotional traits and responses to produce criminality.

General Theory of Crime (GTC) According to Gottfredson and Hirschi, a developmental theory that modifies social control theory by integrating concepts from biosocial, psychological, routine activities, and rational choice theories.

gentrification A residential renewal stage in which obsolete housing is replaced and upgraded; areas undergoing such change seem to experience an increase in their crime rates.

globalization The process of creating transnational markets, politics, and legal systems in an effort to form and sustain a global economy.

good burglar Professional burglars use this title to characterize colleagues who have distinguished themselves as burglars. Characteristics of the good burglar include technical competence, maintenance of personal integrity, specialization in burglary, financial success, and the ability to avoid prison sentences.

grand jury A group (usually consisting of 23 citizens) chosen to hear testimony in secret and to issue formal criminal accusations (indictments). It also serves an investigatory function.

grand larceny Theft of money or property of substantial value, punished as a felony.

group boycott A company's refusal to do business with retail stores that do not comply with its rules or desires.

guerilla The term means "little war" and developed out of the Spanish rebellion against French troops after Napoleon's 1808 invasion of the Iberian Peninsula. Today the term is used interchangeably with the term "terrorist."

habeas corpus People in custody may seek release by filing a petition for a writ of habeas corpus, a judicial mandate to a prison official ordering that an inmate be brought to the court so it can be determined whether or not that person is imprisoned lawfully and whether he should be released from custody

hands-off doctrine The judicial policy of not interfering in the administrative affairs of a prison.

hate crimes Acts of violence or intimidation designed to terrorize or frighten people considered undesirable because of their race, religion, ethnic origin, or sexual orientation.

heels Professional shoplifters who steal with the intention of reselling stolen merchandise to pawnshops or fences, usually at half the original price.

the hole Solitary confinement used as punishment for prisoners who flout prison rules.

home confinement (HC) Convicted offenders must spend extended periods in their own homes as an alternative to incarceration; also called house arrest or home detention.

homophobia Extremely negative overreaction to homosexuals.

homosexuality Erotic interest in members of one's own sex.

human nature theory A belief that personal traits, such as genetic makeup, intelligence, and body build, may outweigh the importance of social variables as predictors of criminal activity.

humanistic psychology A branch of psychology that stresses self-awareness and "getting in touch with feelings."

hung jury A jury that cannot reach a decision in a criminal case. If a jury is hung, the prosecution can retry the case.

hypermasculine Men who typically have a callous sexual attitude and believe violence is manly. They perceive danger as exciting and are overly sensitive to insult and ridicule. They are also impulsive, more apt to brag about sexual conquests, and more likely to lose control, especially when using alcohol.

hypoglycemia A condition that occurs when glucose (sugar) levels in the blood fall below the necessary level for normal and efficient brain functioning.

id The primitive part of people's mental makeup, present at birth, that represents unconscious biological drives for food, sex, and other life-sustaining necessities. The id seeks instant gratification without concern for the rights of others.

identity crisis A psychological state, identified by Erikson, in which youth face inner turmoil and uncertainty about life roles.

identity theft Using the Internet to steal someone's identity and/or impersonate the victim in order to conduct illicit transactions such as committing fraud using the victim's name and identity

impact statement A victim's statement considered at a sentencing hearing.

imperatively coordinated associations These associations are composed of two groups: those who possess authority and use it for social domination, and those who lack authority and are dominated.

impersonal coercion Pressures beyond individual control, such as economic and social pressure caused by unemployment, poverty, or business competition.

importation model The view that the violent prison culture reflects the criminal culture of the outside world and is neither developed in nor unique to prisons.

incapacitation effect The idea that keeping offenders in confinement will eliminate the risk of their committing further offenses.

incarceration Confinement in jail or prison.

inchoate offenses Incomplete or contemplated crimes such as criminal solicitation or criminal attempts.

incivilities Rude and uncivil behavior; behavior that indicates little caring for the feelings of others.

indeterminate sentence A term of incarceration with a stated minimum and maximum length, such as a sentence to prison for a period of from 3 to 10 years. The prisoner would be eligible for parole after the minimum sentence had been served. Based on the belief that sentences should fit the criminal, indeterminate sentences allow individualized sentences and provide for sentencing flexibility. Judges can set a high minimum to override the purpose of the indeterminate sentence.

index crimes The eight crimes that, because of their seriousness and frequency, the FBI reports the incidence of in the annual Uniform Crime Report. Index crimes include murder, rape, assault, robbery, burglary, arson, larceny, and motor vehicle theft.

indictment A written accusation returned by a grand jury charging an individual with a specified crime, based on the prosecutor's presentation of probable cause.

inevitable discovery rule A rule of law stating that evidence that almost assuredly would be independently discovered can be used in a court of law, even though it was obtained in violation of legal rules and practices.

infanticide The murder of a very young child.

inferiority complex People who have feelings of inferiority and compensate for them with a drive for superiority.

influence peddling Using an institutional position to grant favors and sell information to which their co-conspirators are not entitled.

informal sanctions Disapproval, stigma, or anger directed toward an offender by significant others (parents, peers, neighbors, teachers), resulting in shame, embarrassment, and loss of respect.

information Like an indictment, a formal charging document. The prosecuting attorney makes out the information and files it in court. Probable cause is determined at the preliminary hearing, which, unlike grand jury proceedings, is public and attended by the accused and his or her attorney.

information processing A branch of cognitive psychology that focuses on the way people process, store, encode, retrieve, and manipulate information to make decisions and solve problems.

information technology (IT) All forms of technology used to create, store, retrieve, and exchange data in all its various forms, including electronic, voice, and still image.

inheritance school Advocates of this view trace the activities of several generations of families believed to have an especially large number of criminal members.

inmate subculture The loosely defined culture that pervades prisons and has its own norms, rules, and language.

insider trading Illegal buying of stock in a company based on information provided by someone who has a fiduciary interest in the company, such as an employee or an attorney or accountant retained by the firm. Federal laws and the rules of the Securities and Exchange Commission require that all profits from such trading be returned and provide for both fines and a prison sentence.

institutional anomie theory The view that anomie pervades U.S. culture because the drive for material wealth dominates and undermines social and community values.

instrumental crimes Offenses designed to improve the financial or social position of the criminal.

instrumental theory The view that criminal law and the criminal justice system are capitalist instruments for controlling the lower class.

instrumental violence Violence used in an attempt to improve the financial or social position of the criminal.

insurgent The typical goal of an insurgency is to confront the existing government for control of all or a portion of its territory, or force political concessions in sharing political power. While terrorists may operate in small bands with a narrow focus, insurgents represent a popular movement and may also seek external support from other nations to bring pressure on the government.

integrated theories Models of crime causation that weave social and individual variables into a complex explanatory chain.

intelligence A person's ability to reason, comprehend ideas, solve problems, think abstractly, understand complex ideas, learn from experience, and discover solutions to complex problems.

intensive probation supervision (IPS) A type of intermediate sanction involving small probation caseloads and strict daily or weekly monitoring.

intensive supervision parole (ISP) A type of parole that uses close surveillance and limited caseload sizes. ISP clients are required to have more office and home visits than routine parolees. ISP may also require frequent drug testing, a term in a

community correctional center, and electronic monitoring in the home.

interactionist view The view that one's perception of reality is significantly influenced by one's interpretations of the reactions of others to similar events and stimuli.

interdisciplinary science Involving two or more academic fields.

intermediate sanctions An alternative to prison; these sanctions include fines, forfeiture, home confinement, electronic monitoring, intensive probation supervision, restitution, community corrections, and boot camps.

Internal Revenue Service (IRS) Government agency that enforces violations of income, excise, stamp, and other tax laws.

international terrorism Terrorism involving citizens or the territory of more than one country.

interpersonal coercion The use of force, threat of force, or intimidation by parents, peers, or significant others.

interrogation The questioning of a suspect in police custody.

involuntary manslaughter A homicide that occurs as a result of acts that are negligent and without regard for the harm they may cause others, such as driving under the influence of alcohol or drugs.

jail A place to detain people awaiting trial, hold drunks and disorderly individuals, and confine convicted misdemeanants serving sentences of less than one year.

judge The senior officer in a court of criminal law.

jury array The initial list of persons chosen, which provides the state with a group of citizens potentially capable of serving on a jury; also called a venire.

just desert The philosophy of justice that asserts that those who violate the rights of others deserve to be punished. The severity of punishment should be commensurate with the seriousness of the crime.

justice model A philosophy of corrections that stresses determinate sentences, abolition of parole, and the view that prisons are places of punishment and not rehabilitation.

justice of the peace Established in 1326 in England to assist the shire reeve in controlling the county, these justices eventually took on judicial functions in addition to being peacekeepers.

justification A defense to a criminal charge in which the accused maintains that his or her actions were justified by the circumstances and therefore he or she should not be held criminally liable.

labeling theory Theory that views society as creating deviance through a system of social control agencies that designate certain individuals as deviants. The stigmatized individual is made to feel unwanted in the normal social order. Eventually, the individual begins to believe that the label is accurate, assumes it as a personal identity, and enters into a deviant or criminal career.

landmark decision A decision handed down by the Supreme Court that becomes the law of the land and serves as a precedent for similar legal issues.

larceny Taking for one's own use the property of another, by means other than force or threats on the victim or forcibly breaking into a person's home or workplace; theft.

latency A developmental stage that begins at age 6. During this period, feelings of sexuality are repressed until the genital stage begins at puberty; this marks the beginning of adult sexuality.

latent delinquency A psychological predisposition to commit antisocial acts because of an id-dominated personality that renders an individual incapable of controlling impulsive, pleasure-seeking drives.

latent trait A stable feature, characteristic, property, or condition, present at birth or soon after, that makes some people crime prone over the life course.

latent trait theories Theoretical views that criminal behavior is controlled by a master trait, present at birth or soon after, that remains stable and unchanging throughout a person's lifetime.

law of criminal procedure Judicial precedents that define and guarantee the rights of criminal defendants and control the various components of the criminal justice system.

left realism An approach that views crime as a function of relative deprivation under capitalism and that favors pragmatic, community-based crime prevention and control.

legal code The specific laws that fall within the scope of criminal law.

liberal feminist theory Theory suggesting that the traditionally lower crime rate for women can be explained by their second-class economic and social position. As women's social roles have changed and their lifestyles have become more like those of men, it is believed that their crime rates will converge.

life course persister One of the small group of offenders whose criminal career continues well into adulthood.

life course theories Theoretical views studying changes in criminal offending patterns over a person's entire life.

life domains According to Robert Agnew, the five key elements that influence human behavior involving self, education, work, peers, and family relations.

lifestyle theory People may become crime victims because their lifestyle increases their exposure to criminal offenders.

lineup Witnesses may be brought in to view the suspect in a group of people with similar characteristics and asked to pick out the suspect.

logic bomb A program that is secretly attached to a computer system, monitors the network's work output, and waits for a particular signal such as a date to appear. Also called a slag code, it is a type of delayed-action virus which may be set off when a program user makes certain input that sets it in motion. A logic bomb may cause a variety of problems ranging from displaying or printing a spurious message to deleting or corrupting data.

lumpen proletariat The fringe members at the bottom of society who produce nothing and live, parasitically, off the work of others.

Machiavellian Maintaining a personality that is cleverly deceitful and unscrupulous, characterized by expediency, deceit, and cunning.

madam A woman who employs prostitutes, supervises their behavior, and receives a fee for her services.

Mafia A criminal society that originated in Sicily and is believed to control racketeering in the United States.

mala in se Acts that are outlawed because they violate basic moral values, such as rape, murder, assault, and robbery.

mala prohibitum Acts that are outlawed because they clash with current norms and public opinion, such as tax, traffic, and drug laws.

malware A malicious software program.

mandatory prison term A statutory requirement that a certain penalty shall be set and carried out in all cases on conviction for a specified offense or series of offenses.

manslaughter A homicide without malice.

marginal deterrence The concept that a penalty for a crime may prompt commission of a marginally more severe crime because that crime receives the same magnitude of punishment as the original one.

marginalization Displacement of workers, pushing them outside the economic and social mainstream.

marital exemption The practice in some states of prohibiting the prosecution of husbands for the rape of their wives.

marital rape Forcible sex between people who are legally married to each other.

mark The target of a con man or woman.

Marxist criminologists Criminologists who view crime as a product of the capitalist system.

Marxist criminology The view that crime is a product of the capitalist system; also known as critical criminology or radical criminology.

Marxist feminism The approach that explains both victimization and criminality among women in terms of gender inequality, patriarchy, and the exploitation of women under capitalism.

masculinity hypothesis The view that women who commit crimes have biological and psychological traits similar to those of men.

mass murder The killing of a large number of people in a single incident by an offender who typically does not seek concealment or escape.

mechanical solidarity A characteristic of a pre-industrial society, which is held together by traditions, shared values, and unquestioned beliefs.

mens rea "Guilty mind." The mental element of a crime or the intent to commit a criminal act.

meta-analysis A research technique that uses the grouped data from several different studies.

middle-class measuring rods According to Albert Cohen, the standards by which teachers and other representatives of state authority evaluate lower-class youths. Because they cannot live up to middle-class standards, lower-class youths are bound for failure, which gives rise to frustration and anger at conventional society.

Minnesota Multiphasic Personality Inventory (MMPI) A widely used psychological test that has subscales designed to measure many different personality traits, including psychopathic deviation (Pd scale), schizophrenia (Sc scale), and hypomania (Ma scale).

Miranda **warning** The result of two U.S. Supreme Court decisions (*Escobedo v. Illinois* [378 U.S. 478] and *Miranda v. Arizona* [384 U.S. 436]) that require police officers to inform individuals under arrest of their constitutional right to remain silent and to know that their statements can later be used against them in court, that they can have an attorney present to help them, and that the state will pay for an attorney if they cannot afford to hire one. Although aimed at protecting an individual during in-custody interrogation, the warning must also be given when the investigation shifts from the investigatory to the accusatory stage—that is, when suspicion begins to focus on an individual.

mission hate crimes Violent crimes committed by disturbed individuals who see it as their duty to rid the world of evil.

Missouri Plan A way of picking judges through nonpartisan elections as a means of ensuring judicial performance standards.

modus operandi **(MO)** The working methods of particular offenders.

monetary restitution A sanction requiring that convicted offenders compensate crime victims by reimbursing them for out-of-pocket losses caused by the crime. Losses can include property damage, lost wages, and medical costs.

moral crusaders People who strive to stamp out behavior they find objectionable. Typically, moral crusaders are directed at public order crimes, such as drug abuse or pornography.

moral development The way people morally represent and reason about the world.

moral entrepreneurs Interest groups that attempt to control social life and the legal order in such a way as to promote their own personal set of moral values. People who use their influence to shape the legal process in ways they see fit.

morals squad Plainclothes police officers or detectives specializing in victimless crimes such as prostitution or gambling.

Mosaic Code The laws of the ancient Israelites, found in the Old Testament of the Judeo-Christian Bible.

motivated offenders The potential offenders in a population. According to rational choice theory, crime rates will vary according to the number of motivated offenders.

mug shots Pictures of offenders that can be viewed by victims in an attempt to identify the perpetrator.

Multidimensional Personality Questionnaire (MPQ) A test that allows researchers to assess such personality traits as control, aggression, alienation, and well-being. Evaluations using this scale indicate that adolescent offenders who are crime prone maintain negative emotionality, a tendency to experience aversive affective states such as anger, anxiety, and irritability.

murder The unlawful killing of a human being (homicide) with malicious intent.

naive check forgers Amateurs who cash bad checks because of some financial crisis but have little identification with a criminal subculture.

narcissistic personality disorder A condition marked by a persistent pattern of self-importance, need for admiration, lack of empathy, and preoccupation with fantasies of unlimited success, power, brilliance, beauty, or ideal love.

National Crime Victimization Survey (NCVS) The ongoing victimization study conducted jointly by the Justice Department and the U.S. Census Bureau that surveys victims about their experiences with law violation.

National Incident-Based Reporting System (NIBRS) A program that requires local police agencies to provide a brief account of each incident and arrest within 22 crime patterns, including incident, victim, and offender information.

nature theory The view that intelligence is largely determined genetically and that low intelligence is linked to criminal behavior.

negative affective states According to Robert Agnew, anger, depression, disappointment, fear, and other adverse emotions that derive from strain.

negative reinforcement Using either negative stimuli (punishment) or loss of reward (negative punishment) to curtail unwanted behaviors.

neglect Not providing a child with the care and shelter to which he or she is entitled.

negligent manslaughter A homicide that occurs as a result of acts that are negligent and without regard for the harm they may cause others, such as driving under the influence of alcohol or drugs; also called involuntary manslaughter.

neocortex A part of the human brain; the left side of the neocortex controls sympathetic feelings toward others.

networks When referring to terrorist organizations, networks are loosely organized groups located in different parts of the city, state, or country (or world) that share a common theme or purpose, but have a diverse leadership and command structure and are only in intermittent communication with one another.

neuroallergies Allergies that affect the nervous system and cause the allergic person to produce enzymes that attack wholesome foods as if they were dangerous to the body. They may also cause swelling of the brain and produce sensitivity in the central nervous system—conditions that are linked to mental, emotional, and behavioral problems.

neurophysiology The study of brain activity.

neutralization theory Neutralization theory holds that offenders adhere to conventional values while "drifting" into periods of illegal behavior. In order to drift, people must first overcome (neutralize) legal and moral values.

new generation jails Jails that allow for continuous observation of residents. There are two types: direct and indirect supervision.

nolle prosequi The term used when a prosecutor decides to drop a case after a complaint has been formally made. Reasons for a *nolle prosequi* include insufficient evidence, reluctance of witnesses to testify, police error, and office policy.

nonintervention model The view that arresting and labeling offenders does more harm than good, that youthful offenders in particular should be diverted into informal treatment programs, and that minor offenses should be decriminalized.

nonnegligent manslaughter A homicide committed in the heat of passion or during a sudden quarrel; although intent may be present, malice is not; also called voluntary manslaughter.

normative groups Groups, such as the high school in-crowd, that conform to the social rules of society.

nurture theory The view that intelligence is not inherited but is largely a product of environment. Low IQ scores do not cause crime but may result from the same environmental factors.

obscenity According to current legal theory, sexually explicit material that lacks a serious purpose and appeals solely to the prurient interest of the viewer. While nudity per se is not usually considered obscene, open sexual behavior, masturbation, and exhibition of the genitals is banned in most communities.

obsessive-compulsive disorder An extreme preoccupation with certain thoughts and compulsive performance of certain behaviors.

occasional criminals Offenders who do not define themselves by a criminal role or view themselves as committed career criminals.

Oedipus complex A stage of development when males begin to have sexual feelings for their mothers.

offender classification If the offender is placed on probation, the department diagnoses his or her personality and treatment needs; offenders classified as minimal risks will be given little supervision, perhaps a monthly phone call or visit, whereas those classified as high risk will receive close supervision and intensive care and treatment.

offender-specific crime The idea that offenders evaluate their skills, motives, needs, and fears before deciding to commit crime.

offense-specific crime The idea that offenders react selectively to the characteristics of particular crimes.

oral stage In Freud's schema, the first year of life, when a child attains pleasure by sucking and biting.

ordeal Based on the principle of divine intervention and the then-prevalent belief that divine forces would not allow an innocent person to be harmed, this was a way of determining guilt involving such measures as having the accused place his or her hand in boiling water or hold a hot iron to see if God would intervene and heal the wounds. If the wound healed, the person was found not guilty; conversely, if the wound did not heal, the accused was deemed guilty of the crime for which he or she was being punished.

organic solidarity Postindustrial social systems, which are highly developed and dependent upon the division of labor; people are connected by their interdependent needs for one another's services and production.

organizational crime Crime that involves large corporations and their efforts to control the marketplace and earn huge profits through unlawful bidding, unfair advertising, monopolistic practices, or other illegal means.

organized crime Illegal activities of people and organizations whose acknowledged purpose is profit through illegitimate business enterprise.

overt pathway Pathway to a criminal career that begins with minor aggression, leads to physical fighting, and eventually escalates to violent crime.

paranoid schizophrenics Individuals who suffer complex behavior delusions involving wrongdoing or persecution—they think everyone is out to get them.

paraphilias Bizarre or abnormal sexual practices that may involve recurrent sexual urges focused on objects, humiliation, or children.

parental efficacy Parenting that is supportive, effective, and noncoercive.

parole The early release of a prisoner subject to conditions set by a parole board. Depending on the jurisdiction, inmates must serve a certain proportion of their sentences before becoming eligible for parole. If an inmate is granted parole, the conditions may require him or her to report regularly to a parole officer, refrain from criminal conduct, maintain and support his or her family, avoid contact with other convicted criminals, abstain from using alcohol and drugs, remain within the jurisdiction, and so on. Violations of the conditions of parole may result in revocation of parole, in which case the individual will be returned to prison. The concept behind parole is to allow the release of the offender to community supervision, where rehabilitation and readjustment will be facilitated.

parole grant hearing A meeting of the full parole board or a subcommittee that reviews information, may meet with the offender, and then decides whether the parole applicant has a reasonable chance of succeeding outside prison. Good time credits reduce the minimum sentence and hasten eligibility for parole. In making its decision, the board considers the inmate's offense, time served, evidence of adjustment, and opportunities on the outside.

Part I crimes Another term for index crimes; eight categories of serious, frequent crimes.

Part II crimes All crimes other than index and minor traffic offenses. The FBI records annual arrest information for Part II offenses.

passive precipitation The view that some people become victims because of personal and social characteristics that make them attractive targets for predatory criminals.

paternalistic families Traditional family model in which fathers assume the role of breadwinners, while mothers tend to have menial jobs or remain at home to supervise domestic matters.

patriarchy A society in which men dominate public, social, economic, and political affairs.

payola Bribery of an influential person in exchange for the promotion of a product or service, such giving radio disc jockeys payments to play songs.

peacemaking An approach that considers punitive crime control strategies to be counterproductive and favors the use of humanistic conflict resolution to prevent and control crime.

pedophiles Sexual offenders who target children.

penitentiary State or federally operated facility for the incarceration of felony offenders sentenced by the criminal courts; prison.

penology An aspect of criminology that overlaps with criminal justice; penology involves the correction and control of known criminal offenders.

peremptory challenge The dismissal of a potential juror by either the prosecution or the defense for unexplained, discretionary reasons.

permeable neighborhood Areas with a greater than usual number of access streets from traffic arteries into the neighborhood.

persistence The idea that those who started their delinquent careers early and who committed serious violent crimes throughout adolescence were the most likely to persist as adults.

personality The reasonably stable patterns of behavior, including thoughts and emotions, that distinguish one person from another.

petit (petty) larceny Theft of a small amount of money or property, punished as a misdemeanor.

phallic stage In Freud's schema, the third year, when children focus their attention on their genitals.

phishing Sometimes called carding or brand spoofing, phishing is a scam where the perpetrator sends out e-mails appearing to come from legitimate web enterprises such as eBay, Amazon, PayPal, and America Online in an effort to get the recipient to reveal personal and financial information.

phrenologist A scientist who studied the shape of the skull and bumps on the head to determine whether these physical attributes are linked to criminal behavior; phrenologists believed that external cranial characteristics dictate which areas of the brain control physical activity.

physiognomist A scientist who studied the facial features of criminals to determine whether the shape of ears, nose, and eyes and the distance between them are associated with antisocial behavior.

pigeon drop A con game in which a package or wallet containing money is "found" by a con man or woman. A passing victim is stopped and asked for advice about what to do, and soon another "stranger," who is part of the con, approaches and enters the discussion. The three decide to split the money; but first, one of the swindlers goes off to consult a lawyer. The lawyer claims the money can be split up, but each party must prove he or she has the means to reimburse the original owner, should one show up. The victim then is asked to give some good-faith money for the lawyer to hold. When the victim goes to the lawyer's office to pick up a share of the loot, he or she finds the address bogus and the money gone. In the new millennium, the pigeon drop has been appropriated by corrupt telemarketers, who contact typically elderly victims over the phone to bilk them out of their savings.

pilferage Theft by employees through stealth or deception.

plea bargaining The discussion between the defense counsel and the prosecution by which the accused agrees to plead guilty for certain considerations. The advantage

to the defendant may be a reduction of the charges, a lenient sentence, or (in the case of multiple charges) dropped charges. The advantage to the prosecution is that a conviction is obtained without the time and expense of lengthy trial proceedings.

pleasure principle According to Freud, a theory in which id-dominated people are driven to increase their personal pleasure without regard to consequences.

pledge system An early method of law enforcement that relied on self-help and mutual aid.

plunder Using power without regard for others, such as committing a hate crime or polluting the environment.

poachers Early English thieves who typically lived in the country and supplemented their diet and income with game that belonged to a landlord.

political crime Illegal acts that are designed to undermine an existing government and threaten its survival. Political crimes can include both violent and nonviolent acts and range in seriousness from dissent, treason, and espionage to violent acts such as terrorism or assassination.

poor laws Laws first appearing in England during the early seventeenth century that required that the poor, vagrants, and vagabonds be put to work in public or private enterprise under supervision of a state-appointed master.

population All people who share a particular personal characteristic, such as all high school students or all police officers.

pornography Sexually explicit books, magazines, films, or tapes intended to provide sexual titillation and excitement for paying customers.

positivism The branch of social science that uses the scientific method of the natural sciences and suggests that human behavior is a product of social, biological, psychological, or economic forces.

postmodernist Approach that focuses on the use of language by those in power to define crime based on their own values and biases; also called deconstructionist.

posttraumatic stress disorder (PTSD) Psychological reaction to a highly stressful event; symptoms may include depression, anxiety, flashbacks, and recurring nightmares.

power The ability of people and groups to control the behavior of others, to shape public opinion, and to define deviance.

power–control theory The view that gender differences in crime are a function of economic power (class position, one-earner versus two-earner families) and parental control (paternalistic versus egalitarian families).

precedent A rule derived from previous judicial decisions and applied to future cases; the basis of common law.

predation Direct forms of physical violence, such as robbery, sexual assault, or other forms of physical violence.

preemptive deterrence Efforts to prevent crime through community organization and youth involvement.

preliminary hearings The step at which criminal charges initiated by an information are tested for probable cause; the prosecution presents enough evidence to establish probable cause—that is, a *prima facie* case. The hearing is public and may be attended by the accused and his or her attorney.

premeditation Consideration of a homicide before it occurs.

premenstrual syndrome (PMS) The stereotype that several days prior to and during menstruation females are beset by irritability and poor judgment as a result of hormonal changes.

presentencing investigation An investigation performed by a probation officer attached to a trial court after the conviction of a defendant. The report contains information about the defendant's background, education, previous employment, and family; his or her own statement concerning the offense; the person's prior criminal record; interviews with neighbors or acquaintances; and his or her mental and physical condition (that is, information that would not be made part of the record in the case of a guilty plea or that would be inadmissible as evidence at a trial but could be influential and important at the sentencing stage). After conviction, a judge sets a date for sentencing (usually 10 days to two weeks from the date of conviction), during which time the presentence report is made. The report is required in felony cases in federal courts and in many states, is optional with the judge in some states, and in others is mandatory before convicted offenders can be placed on probation. In the case of juvenile offenders, the presentence report is also known as a social history report.

preventive detention The practice of holding dangerous suspects before trial without bail.

price fixing A conspiracy to set and control the price of a necessary commodity.

primary deviance According to Edwin M. Lemert, deviant acts that do not help redefine the self-image and public image of the offender.

primary prevention programs Treatment programs that seek to correct or remedy personal problems before they manifest themselves as crime.

prison A state or federal correctional institution for incarceration of felony offenders for terms of one year or more.

prisonization process The inmate's assimilation into the prison culture through acceptance of its language, sexual code, and norms of behavior. Those who become the most prisonized will be the least likely to reform on the outside.

proactive policing An aggressive law enforcement style in which patrol officers take the initiative against crime instead of waiting for criminal acts to occur. For example, they stop motor vehicles to issue citations and aggressively arrest and detain suspicious persons.

probable cause The evidentiary criterion necessary to sustain an arrest or the issuance of an arrest or search warrant; less than absolute certainty or "beyond a reasonable doubt" but greater than mere suspicion or hunch. A set of facts, information, circumstances, or conditions that would lead a reasonable person to believe that an offense was committed and that the accused committed that offense. An arrest made without probable cause may be susceptible to prosecution as an illegal arrest under false imprisonment statutes.

probable cause hearing A hearing to determine if there is sufficient evidence to warrant a trial; also called a preliminary hearing.

probation A sentence entailing the conditional release of a convicted offender into the community under the supervision of the court (in the form of a probation officer), subject to certain conditions for a specified time. The conditions are usually similar to those of parole. (Probation is a sentence, an alternative to incarceration; parole is administrative release from incarceration.) Violation of the conditions of probation may result in revocation of probation.

problem behavior syndrome (PBS) A cluster of antisocial behaviors that may include family dysfunction, substance abuse, smoking, precocious sexuality and early pregnancy, educational underachievement, suicide attempts, sensation seeking, and unemployment, as well as crime.

problem-oriented policing (POP) A style of police management that stresses proactive problem solving rather than reactive crime fighting.

productive forces Technology, energy sources, and material resources.

productive relations The relationships that exist among the people producing goods and services.

professional criminals Offenders who make a significant portion of their income from crime.

professional fence An individual who earns his or her living solely by buying and reselling stolen merchandise.

proletariat A term used by Marx to refer to the working class members of society who produce goods and services but who do not own the means of production.

prosecutor Representative of the state (executive branch) in criminal proceedings; advocate for the state's case—the charge—in the adversary trial; for example, the attorney general of the United States, U.S. attorneys, attorneys general of the states, district attorneys, and police prosecutors. The prosecutor participates in investigations both before and after arrest, prepares legal documents, participates in obtaining arrest or search warrants, and decides whether to charge a suspect and, if so, with which offense. The prosecutor argues the state's case at trial, advises the police, participates in plea negotiations, and makes sentencing recommendations.

prosocial bonds Socialized attachment to conventional institutions, activities, and beliefs.

prostitution The granting of nonmarital sexual access for remuneration.

psychoanalytic (psychodynamic) perspective Branch of psychology holding that the human personality is controlled by unconscious mental processes developed early in childhood.

psychopath A person with an antisocial personality disorder, who is aggressive, violent, criminal, amoral, and who lacks empathy with other people.

psychopathic personality A personality characterized by a lack of warmth and feeling, inappropriate behavior responses, and an inability to learn from experience. Some psychologists view psychopathy as a result of childhood trauma; others see it as a result of biological abnormality.

psychosis A mental state in which the perception of reality is distorted. People experiencing psychosis hallucinate, have paranoid or delusional beliefs, change personality, exhibit disorganized thinking, and engage in unusual or bizarre behavior.

public defender system An attorney employed by the state whose job is to provide free legal counsel to indigent defendants.

public order crimes Acts that are considered illegal because they threaten the general well-being of society and challenge its accepted moral principles. Prostitution, drug use, and the sale of pornography are considered public order crimes.

public safety doctrine Evidence can be obtained without a *Miranda* warning if the information the police seek is needed to protect public safety.

racial profiling Selecting suspects on the basis of their ethnic or racial background.

racial threat theory The theory that as the percentage of African Americans in the population increases so too does white fear and demand for increased social control by law enforcement agencies

Racketeer Influenced and Corrupt Organizations (RICO) Act Federal legislation that enables prosecutors to bring additional criminal or civil charges against people whose multiple criminal acts constitute a conspiracy. RICO features monetary penalties that allow the government to confiscate all profits derived from criminal activities. Originally intended to be used against organized criminals, RICO has also been used against white-collar criminals.

racketeering Using an organization to operate or commit ongoing criminal activities, typically extortion, but also other crimes such as drug trafficking and loan sharking committed in an organized manner.

radical criminologists Criminologists who view crime as a product of the capitalist system.

radical criminology The view that crime is a product of the capitalist system; also known as Marxist criminology or critical criminology.

rape Unlawful sexual intercourse with a female without her consent.

rational choice The view that crime is a function of a decision-making process in which the potential offender weighs the potential costs and benefits of an illegal act.

reaction formation According to Albert K. Cohen, rejecting goals and standards that seem impossible to achieve. Because a boy cannot hope to get into college, for example, he considers higher education a waste of time.

reactive (defensive) hate crimes Perpetrators believe they are taking a defensive stand against outsiders whom they believe threaten their community or way of life.

reactive policing Police officers responding only to calls for help.

reality principle According to Freud, the ability to learn about the consequences of one's actions through experience.

reasoning criminal According to the rational choice approach, law-violating behavior occurs when an offender decides to risk breaking the law after considering both personal factors (such as the need for money, revenge, thrills, and entertainment) and situational factors (how well a target is protected and the efficiency of the local police force).

rebuttal evidence Evidence that was not used when the prosecution initially presented its case.

reciprocal altruism According to sociobiology, acts that are outwardly designed to help others but that have at their core benefits to the self.

recognizance Pledge by the accused to return for trial, which may be accepted in lieu of bail.

recovery agent An individual hired by the bonding agent to track down a fugitive in order to recover the lost bond. These modern bounty hunters receive a share of the recovery, and unlike police, bounty hunters can enter a suspect's home without a warrant in most states; also called a skip tracer.

redirect examination Questions asked by the prosecutor about information brought out during cross-examination.

reeve In early England, the senior law enforcement figure in a county, the forerunner of today's sheriff.

reflected appraisals When parents are alienated from their children, their negative labeling reduces their children's self-image and increases delinquency.

reflective role taking According to Ross L. Matsueda and Karen Heimer, the phenomenon that occurs when youths who view themselves as delinquents give an inner voice to their perceptions of how significant others feel about them.

rehabilitation model View that sees criminals as victims of social injustice, poverty, and racism and suggests that appropriate treatment can change them into productive, law-abiding citizens.

Reign of Terror The origin of the term "terrorism," the French Revolution's Reign of Terror began in 1795 and was initiated by the revolutionary government during which agents of the Committee of Public Safety and the National Convention were referred to as terrorists.

reintegrative shaming A method of correction that encourages offenders to confront their misdeeds, experience shame because of the harm they caused, and then be reincluded in society.

relative deprivation The condition that exists when people of wealth and poverty live in close proximity to one another. Some criminologists attribute crime rate differentials to relative deprivation.

release on recognizance (ROR) A nonmonetary condition for the pretrial release of an accused individual; an alternative to monetary bail that is granted after the court determines that the accused has ties in the community, has no prior record of default, and is likely to appear at subsequent proceedings.

removed for cause Removing a juror because he or she is biased, has prior knowledge about a case, or otherwise is unable to render a fair and impartial judgment in a case.

residential community corrections (RCC) A freestanding nonsecure building that is not part of a prison or jail and houses pretrial and adjudicated adults. The residents regularly depart to work, attend school, and/or participate in community corrections activities and programs.

restitution agreement A condition of probation in which the offender repays society or the victim of crime for the trouble the offender caused. Monetary restitution involves a direct payment to the victim as a form of compensation. Community service restitution may be used in victimless crimes and involves work in the community in lieu of more severe criminal penalties.

restorative justice Using humanistic, nonpunitive strategies to right wrongs and restore social harmony.

restorative justice model View that emphasizes the promotion of a peaceful, just society through reconciliation and reintegration of the offender into society.

retaliatory hate crimes A hate crime motivated by revenge for another hate crime, either real or imaginary, which may spark further retaliation.

retributive terror Terror groups who refrain from tying specific acts to direct demands for change. They want to instead redirect the balance between what they believe is good and evil. They see their revolution as existing on a spiritual plane; their mission is to exact retribution against sinners.

retrospective cohort study A study that uses an intact cohort of known offenders and looks back into their early life experiences by checking their educational, family, police, and hospital records.

retrospective reading The reassessment of a person's past to fit a current generalized label.

revocation An administrative act performed by a parole authority that removes a person from parole, or a judicial order by a court removing a person from parole or probation, in response to a violation on the part of the parolee or probationer.

right to counsel The right of a person accused of crime to have the assistance of a defense attorney in all criminal prosecutions.

road rage A term used to describe motorists who assault each other.

robbery Taking or attempting to take something of value by force or threat of force and/or by putting the victim in fear.

role exit behaviors In order to escape from a stifling life in male-dominated families, girls may try to break away by running away and or even attempting suicide.

routine activities theory The view that the volume and distribution of predatory crime are closely related to the interaction of suitable targets, motivated offenders, and capable guardians.

sampling Selecting a limited number of people for study as representative of a larger group.

schizophrenia A type of psychosis often marked by bizarre behavior, hallucinations, loss of thought control, and inappropriate emotional responses. Schizophrenic types include catatonic, which characteristically involves impairment of motor activity; paranoid, which is characterized by delusions of persecution; and hebephrenic, which is characterized by immature behavior and giddiness.

scientific method Using verifiable principles and procedures for the systematic acquisition of knowledge; typically involves formulating a problem, creating a hypothesis, and collecting data through observation and experiment to verify the hypothesis.

search warrant A judicial order, based on probable cause, allowing police officers to search for evidence in a particular place, seize that evidence, and carry it away.

secondary deviance According to Edwin M. Lemert, accepting deviant labels as a personal identity. Acts become secondary when they form a basis for self-concept, as when a drug experimenter becomes an addict.

secondary prevention programs Treatment programs aimed at helping offenders after they have been identified.

second-degree murder A homicide with malice but not premeditation or deliberation, as when a desire to inflict serious bodily harm and a wanton disregard for life result in the victim's death.

selective incapacitation The policy of creating enhanced prison sentences for the relatively small group of dangerous chronic offenders.

self-control A strong moral sense that renders a person incapable of hurting others or violating social norms.

self-control theory According to Gottfredson and Hirschi, the view that the cause of delinquent behavior is an impulsive personality. Kids who are impulsive may find that their bond to society is weak.

self-report survey A research approach that requires subjects to reveal their own participation in delinquent or criminal acts.

semiotics The use of language elements as signs or symbols beyond their literal meaning.

sentencing circle A peacemaking technique in which offenders, victims, and other community members are brought together in an effort to formulate a sanction that addresses the needs of all.

sentencing disparity People convicted of similar criminal acts may receive widely different sentences.

sentencing guidelines Guidelines to control and structure the sentencing process and make it more rational; the more serious the crime and the more extensive the offender's criminal background, the longer the prison term recommended by the guidelines.

serial murder The killing of a large number of people over time by an offender who seeks to escape detection.

serial rape Multiple rapes committed by one person over time.

sexual abuse Exploitation of a child through rape, incest, or molestation by a parent or other adult.

sexual predator law Law that allows authorities to keep some criminals convicted of sexually violent crimes in custody even after their sentences are served.

shame The feeling we get when we don't meet the standards we have set for ourselves or that significant others have set for us.

sheriff The chief law enforcement officer in a county.

Sherman Antitrust Act Law that subjects to criminal or civil sanctions any person "who shall make any contract or engage in any combination or conspiracy" in restraint of interstate commerce.

shield laws Laws designed to protect rape victims by prohibiting the defense attorney from inquiring about their previous sexual relationships.

shire Counties in England and much of Europe in the eleventh century.

shock incarceration A short prison sentence served in boot camp–type facilities.

shock probation A sentence in which offenders serve a short prison term to impress them with the pains of imprisonment before they begin probation.

shoplifting The taking of goods from retail stores.

siblicide Sibling homicide. The median age of sibling homicide offenders is 23, and the median age of their victims is 25. The vast majority of sibling homicide offenders are males (87 percent), and they are most likely to kill their brothers. When lethal violence by brothers against their sisters occurs, it is more likely in juvenile sibling relationships rather than adult sibling relationships (31 percent versus 14 percent). Sisters killing their brothers or sisters are relatively rare events.

siege mentality Residents who become so suspicious of authority that they consider the outside world to be the enemy out to destroy the neighborhood.

situational crime prevention A method of crime prevention that stresses tactics and strategies to eliminate or reduce particular crimes in narrow settings, such as reducing burglaries in a housing project by increasing lighting and installing security alarms.

situational inducement Short-term influence on a person's behavior, such as financial problems or peer pressure, that increases risk taking.

skeezers Prostitutes who trade sex for drugs, usually crack.

skilled thieves Thieves who typically work in the larger cities, such as London and Paris. This group includes pickpockets, forgers, and counterfeiters, who operated freely.

skip tracer An individual hired by the bonding agent to track down a fugitive in order to recover the lost bond. These modern bounty hunters receive a share of the recovery, and unlike police, bounty hunters can enter a suspect's home without a warrant in most states; also called a recovery agent.

smugglers Thieves who move freely in sparsely populated areas and transport goods, such as spirits, gems, gold, and spices, without bothering to pay tax or duty.

snitches Amateur shoplifters who do not self-identify as thieves but who systematically steal merchandise for personal use.

social altruism Voluntary mutual support systems, such as neighborhood associations and self-help groups, that reinforce moral and social obligations.

social bond Ties a person has to the institutions and processes of society. According to Hirschi, elements of the social bond include commitment, attachment, involvement, and belief.

social capital Positive relations with individuals and institutions that are life sustaining.

social code The unwritten prison guidelines that express the values, attitudes, and types of behavior older inmates demand of younger inmates. Passed on from one generation of inmates to another, the inmate social code represents the values of interpersonal relations within the prison.

social conflict theory The view that crime is a function of class conflict and power relations. Laws are created and enforced by those in power to protect their own interests.

social control function The ability of society and its institutions to control, manage, restrain, or direct human behavior.

social control theory The view that people commit crime when the forces that bind them to society are weakened or broken.

social development model (SDM) A developmental theory that attributes criminal behavior patterns to childhood socialization and pro- or antisocial attachments over the life course.

social disorganization theory Branch of social structure theory that focuses on the breakdown of institutions such as the family, school, and employment in inner-city neighborhoods.

social ecologists Criminologists who study the ecological conditions that support criminality.

social ecology Environmental forces that have a direct influence on human behavior.

social harm A view that behaviors harmful to other people and society in general must be controlled. These acts are usually outlawed, but some acts that cause enormous amounts of social harm are perfectly legal, such as the consumption of tobacco and alcohol.

social learning theory The view that human behavior is modeled through observation of human social interactions, either directly from observing those who are close and from intimate contact, or indirectly through the media. Interactions that are rewarded are copied, while those that are punished are avoided.

social process theory The view that criminality is a function of people's interactions with various organizations, institutions, and processes in society.

social psychology The study of human interactions and relationships, emphasizing such issues as group dynamics and socialization.

social reaction theory The view that people become criminals when significant members of society label them as such and they accept those labels as a personal identity. Also known as labeling theory.

social reality of crime The view that the main purpose of criminology is to promote a peaceful, just society.

social structure theory The view that disadvantaged economic class position is a primary cause of crime.

socialization Process of human development and enculturation. Socialization is influenced by key social processes and institutions.

socialization view One view is that people learn criminal attitudes from older, more experienced law violators. Another view is that crime occurs when children develop an inadequate self-image, which renders them incapable of controlling their own misbehavior. Both of these views link criminality to the failure of socialization, the interactions people have with the various individuals, organizations, institutions, and processes of society that help them mature and develop.

sociopath Used interchangeably with *psychopath,* the term refers to someone who is self-serving, hostile, and domineering, though they have superficial charm which they use to dominate and humiliate their victims.

sodomy Illegal sexual intercourse. Sodomy has no single definition, and acts included within its scope are usually defined by state statute.

somatotype A system developed for categorizing people on the basis of their body build.

specific deterrence A crime control policy suggesting that punishment be severe enough to convince convicted offenders never to repeat their criminal activity.

spam An unsolicited advertisement or promotional material, typically in the form of an unwanted e-mail message. While e-mail is the most common form of spam, it can also be sent via instant messaging, Usenet newsgroup, and mobile phone messaging, among other media.

split sentencing A jail term is part of the sentence and is a condition of probation.

stalking A pattern of behavior directed at a specific person that includes repeated physical or visual proximity, unwanted communications, and/or threats sufficient to cause fear in a reasonable person.

stalking statutes Laws that prohibit "the willful, malicious, and repeated following and harassing of another person."

state account system Prisoners produce goods in prison for state use.

state police A law enforcement agency with statewide jurisdiction; the major role of state police is controlling traffic on the highway system, tracing stolen automobiles, and aiding in disturbances and crowd control.

state political crime Political crime that arises from the efforts of the state to either maintain governmental power or to uphold the race, class, and gender advantages of those who support the government. It is possible to divide state political crimes into five varieties: (1) political corruption, (2) illegal domestic surveillance, (3) human rights violations, (4) state violence such as torture, illegal imprisonment, police violence and use of deadly force, and (5) state-corporate crime committed by individuals who abuse their state authority or who fail to exercise it when working with people and organizations in the private sector.

state-sponsored terror Terrorism that occurs when a repressive government regime forces its citizens into obedience, oppresses minorities, and stifles political dissent.

status frustration A form of culture conflict experienced by lower-class youths because social conditions prevent them from achieving success as defined by the larger society.

statutory crimes Crimes defined by legislative bodies in response to changing social conditions, public opinion, and custom.

statutory rape Sexual relations between underage individual and an adult; though not coerced, an underage partner is considered incapable of giving informed consent.

stigma An enduring label that taints a person's identity and changes him or her in the eyes of others.

stigmatize To apply negative labeling with enduring effects on a person's self-image and social interactions.

sting An undercover police operation in which police pose as criminals to trap law violators.

sting or swindle A white-collar crime in which people use their institutional or business position to trick others out of their money.

strain The emotional turmoil and conflict caused when people believe they cannot achieve their desires and goals through legitimate means. Members of the lower class might feel strain because they are denied access to adequate educational opportunities and social support.

strain theorists Criminologists who view crime as a direct result of lower-class frustration and anger.

strain theory Branch of social structure theory that sees crime as a function of the conflict between people's goals and the means available to obtain them.

stratified society Grouping according to social strata or levels. American society is considered stratified on the basis of economic class and wealth.

street crime Common theft-related offenses such as larcenies and burglaries, embezzlement, and theft by false pretenses.

street efficacy A concept in which more cohesive communities with high levels of social control and social integration foster the ability for kids to use their wits to avoid violent confrontations and to feel safe in their own neighborhood. Adolescents with high levels of street efficacy are less likely to resort to violence themselves or to associate with delinquent peers

strict liability crimes Illegal acts whose elements do not contain the need for intent, or *mens rea*; they are usually acts that endanger the public welfare, such as illegal dumping of toxic wastes.

structural theory The view that criminal law and the criminal justice system are means of defending and preserving the capitalist system.

subculture A group that is loosely part of the dominant culture but maintains a unique set of values, beliefs, and traditions.

subculture of violence Norms and customs that, in contrast to society's dominant value system, legitimize and expect the use of violence to resolve social conflicts.

submission Passive obedience to the demands of others, such as submitting to physical or sexual abuse without response.

substantive criminal law A body of specific rules that declare what conduct is criminal and prescribe the punishment to be imposed for such conduct.

subterranean values Morally tinged influences that have become entrenched in the culture but are publicly condemned. They exist side by side with conventional values and while condemned in public may be admired or practiced in private.

sufferance The aggrieved party does nothing to rectify a conflict situation; over time, the unresolved conflict may be compounded by other events that cause an eventual eruption.

suitable target According to routine activities theory, a target for crime that is relatively valuable, easily transportable, and not capably guarded.

superego Incorporation within the personality of the moral standards and values of parents, community, and significant others.

supermax prison An enhanced high-security facility that houses the most dangerous felons in almost total isolation. Also called ultra-max prison.

surety bond The 10 percent the defendant pays to the bonding agent, which serves as the bonding agent's commission.

surplus value The Marxist view that the laboring classes produce wealth that far exceeds their wages and goes to the capitalist class as profits.

surrogate family A common form of adaptation to prison employed by women, this group contains masculine and feminine figures acting as fathers and mothers; some even act as children and take on the role of either brother or sister. Formalized marriages and divorces may be conducted. Sometimes multiple roles are held by one inmate, so that a "sister" in one family may "marry" and become the "wife" in another.

symbolic interaction theory The sociological view that people communicate through symbols. People interpret symbolic communication and incorporate it within their personality. A person's view of reality, then, depends on his or her interpretation of symbolic gestures.

synthesis A merger of two opposing ideas.

systematic forgers Professionals who make a living by passing bad checks.

systematic review A research technique that involves collecting the findings from previously conducted studies, appraising and synthesizing the evidence, and using the collective evidence to address a particular scientific question.

target-hardening strategies Making one's home or business crime proof through the use of locks, bars, alarms, and other devices.

target-removal strategies Displaying dummy or disabled goods as a means of preventing shoplifting.

technical violation Revocation of parole because conditions set by correctional authorities have been violated.

temperance movement An effort to prohibit the sale of liquor in the United States that resulted in the passage of the Eighteenth Amendment to the Constitution in 1919, which prohibited the sale of alcoholic beverages.

terror cells Divisions of terrorist group affiliates, each of which may be functionally independent so that each member has little knowledge of other cells, their members, locations, and so on. The number of cells and their composition depend on the size of the terrorist group. Local or national groups will have fewer cells than international terrorist groups that may operate in several countries, such as the al-Qaeda group.

terrorism The illegal use of force against innocent people to achieve a political objective.

terrorist group Any group practicing, or that has significant subgroups that practice, international terrorism.

tertiary prevention programs Crime control and prevention programs that may be a requirement of a probation order, part of a diversionary sentence, or aftercare at the end of a prison sentence.

testosterone The principal male steroid hormone. Testosterone levels decline during the life cycle and may explain why violence rates diminish over time.

thanatos According to Freud, the instinctual drive toward aggression and violence.

theory of anomie A modified version of the concept of anomie developed by Merton to fit social, economic, and cultural conditions found in modern U.S. society. He found that two elements of culture interact to produce potentially anomic conditions: culturally defined goals and socially approved means for obtaining them.

therapeutic communities (TCs) A treatment approach using a psychosocial, experiential learning process that relies on positive peer pressure within a highly structured social environment.

thesis In the philosophy of Hegel, an original idea or thought.

three strikes Policies whereby people convicted of three felony offenses receive a mandatory life sentence.

thrill-seeking hate crimes Acts by hate-mongers who join forces to have fun by bashing minorities or destroying property; inflicting pain on others gives them a sadistic thrill.

ticking bomb scenario A scenario that some experts argue in which torture can perhaps be justified if the government discovers that a captured terrorist knows the whereabouts of a dangerous explosive device that is set to go off and kill thousands of innocent people.

tipping point The level at which deterrence measures begin to have an appreciable effect on the crime rate.

tithing During the Middle Ages, groups of about ten families who were responsible for maintaining order among themselves and dealing with disturbances, fires, wild animals, and so on.

torture An act that causes severe pain or suffering, whether physical or mental, that is intentionally inflicted on a person for such purposes as obtaining a confession, punishing them for a crime they may have committed, or intimidating or coercing them into a desired action.

trait theory The view that criminality is a product of abnormal biological and/or psychological traits.

transitional neighborhood An area undergoing a shift in population and structure, usually from middle-class residential to lower-class mixed use.

treason An act of disloyalty to one's nation or state.

Trojan horse A computer program that looks like a benign application but contains illicit codes that can damage the system operations. Though Trojan horses do not replicate themselves like viruses, they can be just as destructive.

truly disadvantaged Wilson's term for the lowest level of the underclass; urban, inner-city, socially isolated people who occupy the bottom rung of the social ladder and are the victims of discrimination.

truth-in-sentencing laws Laws that require offenders to serve a substantial portion of their prison sentence behind bars.

turning points According to Laub and Sampson, the life events that alter the development of a criminal career.

tying arrangement A corporation requires customers of one of its services to use other services it offers.

underclass The lowest social stratum in any country, whose members lack the education and skills needed to function successfully in modern society.

Uniform Crime Report (UCR) Large database, compiled by the Federal Bureau of Investigation, of crimes reported and arrests made each year throughout the United States.

USA Patriot Act (USAPA) Legislation giving U.S. law enforcement agencies a freer hand to investigate and apprehend suspected terrorists.

U.S. district courts Trial courts that have jurisdiction over cases involving violations of federal law, such as interstate transportation of stolen vehicles and racketeering.

U.S. marshals Court officers who help implement federal court rulings, transport prisoners, and enforce court orders.

U.S. Supreme Court The court of last resort for all cases tried in the various federal and state courts.

utilitarianism The view that people's behavior is motivated by the pursuit of pleasure and the avoidance of pain.

venire The group called for jury duty from which jury panels are selected.

viatical investments The selling of a death benefit policy, at less than face value, by a terminally ill person to a third party.

vice squad Police officers assigned to enforce morally tinged laws, such as those governing prostitution, gambling, and pornography.

victim compensation The victim ordinarily receives compensation from the state to pay for damages associated with the crime. Rarely are two compensation schemes alike, however, and many state programs suffer from lack of both adequate funding and proper organization within the criminal justice system. Compensation may be made for medical bills, loss of wages, loss of future earnings, and counseling. In the case of death, the victim's survivors can receive burial expenses and aid for loss of support.

victim precipitation theory The idea that the victim's behavior was the spark that ignited the subsequent offense, as when the victim abused the offender verbally or physically.

victimization (by the justice system) While the crime is still fresh in their minds, victims may find that the police interrogation following the crime is handled callously, with innuendos or insinuations that they were somehow at fault. Victims have difficulty learning what is going on in the case; property is often kept for a long time as evidence and may never be returned. Some rape victims report that the treatment they receive from legal, medical, and mental health services is so destructive that they cannot help but feel "re-raped."

victimization survey A statistical survey (such as the NCVS) that measures the amount, nature, and patterns of victimization in the population.

victimless crimes Crimes that violate the moral order but in which there is no actual victim or target. In these crimes, which include drug abuse and sex offenses, it is society as a whole and not an individual who is considered the victim.

victimologist A person who studies the victim's role in criminal transactions.

victim-witness assistance programs Government programs that help crime victims and witnesses; may include

compensation, court services, and/or crisis intervention.

vigilantes Individuals who go on moral crusades without any authorization from legal authorities. The assumption is that it is okay to take matters into your own hands if the cause is right and the target is immoral.

violentization process According to Lonnie Athens, the process by which abused children are turned into aggressive adults. This process takes violent youths full circle from being the victims of aggression to its initiators; they are now the same person they grew up despising, ready to begin the process with their own children.

virility mystique The belief that males must separate their sexual feelings from needs for love, respect, and affection.

voir dire The process in which a potential jury panel is questioned by the prosecution and the defense to select jurors who are unbiased and objective.

voluntary manslaughter A homicide committed in the heat of passion or during a sudden quarrel; although intent may be present, malice is not.

Walnut Street Jail At this institution, most prisoners were placed in solitary cells, where they remained in isolation and did not have the right to work.

warez A term computer hackers and software pirates use to describe a game or application that is made available for use on the Internet in violation of its copyright protection.

watch system In medieval England, men organized in church parishes to guard against disturbances and breaches of the peace at night; they were under the direction of the local constable.

website defacement A type of cyber vandalism that occurs when a computer hacker intrudes on another person's website by inserting or substituting codes that expose visitors to the site to misleading or provocative information. Defacement can range from installing humorous graffiti to sabotaging or corrupting the site.

Wechsler Adult Intelligence Scale One of the standard IQ tests.

Wernicke-Korsakoff disease A deadly neurological disorder.

white-collar crime Illegal acts that capitalize on a person's status in the marketplace. White-collar crimes can involve theft, embezzlement, fraud, market manipulation, restraint of trade, and false advertising.

Wickersham Commission Created in 1931 by President Herbert Hoover to investigate the state of the nation's police forces, a commission that found police training to be inadequate and the average officer incapable of effectively carrying out his duties.

workplace violence Irate employees or former employees attack coworkers or sabotage machinery and production lines; now considered the third leading cause of occupational injury or death.

writ of certiorari An order of a superior court requesting that the record of an inferior court (or administrative body) be brought forward for review or inspection.

zealot The original Zealots were Hebrew warrior groups active during the Roman occupation of Palestine during the first century CE. Today the term commonly refers to a fanatical or over-idealistic follower of a political or religious cause.

CASE INDEX

NAME INDEX

Note: A "nn." following a page reference indicates multiple note numbers on a single page.

Barrett, Angelina, 167n.37
Barrett, David, 460nn.69, 81
Barrios, Lisa, 331n.166
Barrueco, Sandra, 296n.35
Bartko, J., 170n.128
Bartos, Omar, 423n.128
Bartusch, Dawn Jeglum, 296n.37
Basile, Kathleen, 325, 333n.262
Baskin-Sommers, Arielle, 14–15, 27n.38
Basoglu, Cengiz, 161
Bass, Patricia, 126n.188
Bateman, Alicia, 332n.180
Bates, John, 209n.96, 240n.15, 296n.45
Bates, William, 461n.136
Battin, Sara, 240n.43, 241n.53
Bauer, John, 332n.217
Baum, K., 89n.42
Baumeister, Roy, 125n.146, 330n.113
Baumer, Eric, 101, 122n.46, 209n.99,
    329n.52, 332n.218, 333nn.219, 220
Baumhover, Lorin, 124nn.121, 126
Bayer, Ronald, 122n.10
Bayley, David, 124n.127
Bazemore, Gordon, 262, 268nn.129, 130
Beach, Laura, 392n.1
Bean, Lydia, 45
Beasley, Shanna, 331n.147
Beattie, Irenee, 297n.66
Beauchaine, Theodore, 132, 167n.25
Beaver, Kevin, 130, 166n.6, 169n.94,
    170n.142, 240n.50, 297n.99
Beccaria, Cesare, 6, 96, 97, 98, 112
Becerra, Hector, 99
Beck, Allen, 125n.171
Becker, Howard, 18, 27nn.47, 48, 231,
    243n.151, 459n.22
Becker, Jill, 168n.52
Bedord, Olwen, 460n.85
Beech, Anthony, 173n.265
Beer, Dominic, 161
Behr, Peter, 403
Beichner, Dawn, 330nn.90, 122
Beittel, Marc, 115
Belanger, Albert, 461n.104
Belfrage, Henrik, 152, 172n.225
Bell, Paul, 64n.62
Bellair, Paul, 90n.81, 102, 122n.52,
    207n.22, 208n.86, 209nn.100, 104
Bellinger, David C., 168nn.77, 87
Belliston, Lara, 297n.105
Bellucci, Patricia, 328n.24
Belluck, Pam, 421n.28, 422n.79
Beloof, Douglas, 91n.118
Bench, Lawrence, 243n.167
Benda, Brent, 298nn.114, 117
Bendixen, Mons, 241n.82
Benjamin, Daniel, 492n.68
Bennett, Brian, 492n.61
Bennett, Neil, 166n.5
Bennett, Susan, 323, 333n.233
Benson, Michael, 298n.106, 422nn.94,
    95, 103
Bentham, Jeremy, 5–6, 96, 98, 121nn.6, 7
Berg, Ellen, 460n.72
Bergen, Lori, 155

Bergen, Raquel Kennedy, 329n.71
Bergström, Sandra, 460n.79
Berk, Richard, 116, 125n.178, 463n.218
Berliner, Howard, 463n.232
Bern, Jenny, 463n.231
Bernard, Thomas, 64n.51, 172n.208,
    210n.175
Bernasco, Wim, 123n.78, 393nn.78, 82
Bernburg, Jön Gunnar, 210n.144, 234,
    243nn.162, 168, 186
Berner, Wolfgang, 169n.93, 173n.277,
    174n.278
Bernstein, Elizabeth, 460n.51
Berroya, A., 167n.30
Best, Connie, 90n.100
Best, David, 463n.168
Beswick, Tracy, 463n.231
Beucke, Dan, 491n.35
Beutel, Ann, 65n.102
Beverlin, Matt, 115
Beyers, Jennifer, 172n.216, 209n.96,
    240n.15, 295n.7
Bhaskar, Roy, 267n.44
Bhati, Avinash Singh, 455
Bhattacharya, Rina, 365nn.51, 52
Bibel, Daniel, 65n.111, 171n.190
Bieneck, Steffen, 329n.69
Biesecker, Gretchen, 168n.83
Bihrle, Susan, 169n.91
Bijleveld, Catrien, 173n.273
Bilefsky, Dan, 306
Bimbi, David S., 462n.190
Binder, David, 423n.126
Bingenheimer, Jeffrey B., 329n.45
Birkbeck, Christopher, 123n.86
Birmaher, Boris, 172n.209
Birnbaum, Jean, 308, 330n.83
Birt, Angela, 330n.112
Bistolaki, E., 170n.131
Bjerk, David, 207n.23
Bjerregaard, Beth, 63n.31, 329n.56
Black, Donald, 209n.95
Blackstone, E., 393n.75
Blackwell, Brenda Sims, 258, 268nn.93,
    94, 101
Blair, James, 160, 161, 171n.170,
    173n.275
Blair, Karina, 161
Blais, Etienne, 110, 124n.120
Blake, Laurence, 90n.89, 393n.77
Blalock, Hubert, Jr., 66n.127
Blankenship, Michael, 241n.99, 422n.86
Blau, Judith, 64n.79, 209n.129
Blau, Peter, 64n.79, 209n.129
Blickle, Gerhard, 173n.276
Block, Alan, 423nn.118, 119
Block, Carolyn Rebecca, 320, 462n.184
Block, Richard, 209n.131
Blount, William, 329n.33
Blumberg, Mark, 462nn.147, 151
Blumer, Herbert, 27n.46, 230, 243n.144
Blumstein, Alfred, 43, 45, 63n.39,
    126n.187
Bobadilla, Leonardo, 171n.167
Boehnke, Klaus, 210n.145

Boer, Douglas, 330n.112
Bogaerts, Jef, 240n.29
Bohm, Robert, 250, 266nn.27, 28
Bohman, Michael, 171n.180
Boivin, Michel, 171n.168
Bolen, Rebecca M., 330n.109
Bonacci, Angelica, 330n.113
Bond, Dale, 298n.147
Bonett, Douglas, 169n.89
Bonger, Willem, 248, 249
Bonta, James, 171n.201, 172n.232
Bontrager, Stephanie, 243n.177
Bookless, Clara, 172n.235
Booth, Alan, 65n.101, 167n.49, 168n.54
Boruch, Victor, 27n.56
Borum, Randy, 173n.239, 331n.167, 356,
    364n.5, 365n.65
Bothwell, Robert, 331n.123
Botsis, A., 170n.131
Bottcher, Jean, 54, 65n.103
Bouchard, Thomas, 171n.171
Boudreau, Abbie, 166n.4
Bouffard, Jeffrey, 122n.25
Boulerice, Bernard, 169n.90
Boulfard, Jeffrey, 122n.21
Bourgois, Philippe, 98, 122n.27
Boutwell, Brian, 170n.142
Bowden, Blake Sperry, 89n.40
Bowlby, John, 150–151, 172nn.205–206
Bowling, Benjamin, 296n.56
Box, Steven, 65n.110, 266n.34
Boyd, Carol, 462n.169
Boyer, Francis, 98
Boyer, Richard, 392n.38
Braga, Anthony A., 51, 124nn.134, 137,
    313, 331n.149
Bragason, Ólafur Örn, 161
Braithwaite, John, 209n.127, 260,
    266n.21, 268nn.113, 114, 116, 118,
    131, 332n.212, 422nn.100, 103
Braithwaite, Valerie, 268n.116
Brame, Robert, 45, 243nn.184, 189,
    295n.17, 296nn.45, 55, 297n.61,
    298nn.110, 128
Brammer, Michael, 161
Branch, Kathryn, 320
Branscomb, Anne, 491n.38
Brantingham, Patricia, 123nn.90, 102
Brantingham, Paul, 123nn.90, 102
Breaux, Marie-Anne, 331n.123
Brecher, Edward, 459n.23, 461n.134
Breivik, Gunnar, 392n.37
Brems, Christiane, 63n.26
Brennan, Patricia, 169n.95, 170n.136,
    171n.193, 172n.227, 328n.28
Brennan, Robert T., 329n.45
Brents, Barbara G., 460nn.86, 87
Breslin, Beau, 268n.127
Brester, Mary, 333n.266
Breverlin, Matt, 114
Brewer, Robert, 328n.19
Brewer, Victoria, 64n.71, 115, 126n.186,
    295n.26
Brewster, Mary, 326
Brezina, Timothy, 168n.53, 201,

210nn.162, 164, 165, 171, 240n.42, 296n.48
Briar, Scott, 226, 242nn.103, 106
Brick, Michael, 45
Briere, John, 330n.117, 459n.35
Briken, Peer, 138, 169n.93, 173n.277, 174n.278
Brison, Susan, 71, 89n.32
Britain, R. P., 169n.100
Britt, Chester, 463n.227
Britt, David, 267n.47
Britton, Lee, 66n.154, 126n.190
Broder, Paul, 169n.111
Broidy, Lisa, 65n.105, 172n.217, 210nn.170, 173, 174, 296n.45
Bronner, Augusta, 162, 174n..285
Bronte-Tinkew, Jacinta, 240n.30
Brook, Judith, 45, 155, 295n.27
Brooke, James, 333n.225
Brooks, Judith, 462n.163
Brooks-Gunn, Jeanne, 207nn.11–14
Browdy, Jennifer, 332n.181
Brown, Alan, 168n85
Brown, Alyson, 460nn.69, 81
Brown, Charles, 124n.128
Brown, Christopher M., 422n.107
Brown, Garrett, 266n.26
Brown, Jocelyn, 460nn.70, 82
Brown, Roy, III, 331n.123
Brown, Sandra, 241n.66
Brown, Thomas, 169n.113
Browne, Angela, 331nn.152, 154
Browne, C., 172n.226
Browne, Derek, 172n.235
Brownfield, David, 64n.75, 90n.66, 207n.25, 241n.89, 242n.137, 297n.102, 298n.116
Browning, Christopher, 211n.178
Brownmiller, Susan, 329n.72
Brownstein, Henry, 328n.17
Brugess, P., 172n.226
Bryan, Nicole, 463n.219
Bryant, Susan Leslie, 89n.21
Buchanan, Christy Miller, 168n.52
Buchting, Francisco, 170n.163
Buck, Andrew, 91n.124, 123n.62
Buck, Philip, 328n.21
Buddie, Amy, 330n.95
Budtz-Jorgensen, E., 167n.26
Bufacchi, Vittorio, 365n.26
Buitelaar, Jan, 168n.56
Buker, Hasan, 167n.50
Bukovec, Paul, 329n.71
Bukowski, William, 240n.49, 329n.60
Bullogh, V., 459n.38
Bumz, Edward, 269n.136
Burdett, Gary, 485
Burger, Timothy, 492n.61
Burgess, Ernest W., 9, 27nn.24, 25, 178, 184, 185
Burgess, Robert, 222, 241n.81
Burke, Jeffrey, 172n.209
Burnette, Mandi, 460n.76
Burns, Barbara, 173n.239
Burns, Ronald, 333n.261, 422nn.93, 98

Burrell, Amy, 90n.84, 122n.20
Bursik, Robert, 124n.119, 125nn.144–145, 207nn.35, 40, 208nn.82, 88, 209 nn.105, 124, 297n.102, 298n.130
Burt, Callie Harbin, 298n.124
Burton, Thomas, 421n.49
Burton, Velmer, Jr., 64n.77, 65n.102, 123n.70, 210n.159, 241n.60, 242n.134
Buschsbaum, Monte, 169nn.102, 109
Bush, George H. W., 451
Bush, George W., 110, 340, 358, 438, 477
Bushman, Brad, 43, 45, 64n.61, 154, 155, 330n.113
Bushway, Shawn, 45, 243n.189, 297n.63
Buswell, Brenda, 65n.102
Butterfield, Ethan, 476
Butterfield, Fox, 56, 66n.126, 329n.57
Bynum, Timothy, 207n.24, 208n.57
Byrne, Donn, 171n.199
Byrne, James, 207n.38, 209n.98
Byrne, John A., 403, 422n.87

Cadoret, R. J., 171n.178
Caeti, Tory, 123n.100, 124.135
Cain, C., 171n.178
Cain, Kevin, 125n.175
Calavita, Kitty, 421n.5
Calder, James, 332n.217
Caldwell, Roslyn, 239n.7
Califano, Joseph A., Jr., 445
Calnon, Jennifer, 66n.121
Cameron, Mary Owen, 378, 392nn.34, 35
Campbell, Anne, 65nn.102, 111, 171n.190, 297n.101, 463n.218
Campbell, Doris, 320
Campbell, Jacquelyn, 320
Campbell, Rebecca, 88n.10, 91n.111
Campbell, Rose, 460n.56
Campbell, Suzanne, 124n.130
Campo-Flores, Arian, 207n.1
Cancino, Jeffrey, 64n.82, 208n.90
Cancino, Michael, 209n.93
Canela-Cacho, Jose, 126n.187
Canfield, Richard L., 168n.84
Cantor, David, 91n.124
Cao, Liqun, 329n.51
Capachin, Jeanne, 492n.83
Capaldi, Deborah, 240n.48, 295n.20, 328n.27
Capell, Kerry, 493n.109
Capowich, George E., 209n.106, 210n.160
Carbonell, Joyce, 173n.273
Carey, Gregory, 170n.143, 171n.173
Caringella-MacDonald, Susan, 268n.88
Carlen, Pat, 267n.73
Carlson, Robert, 463n.192
Carmichael-Jones, Clive, 470, 492n.60
Carr, Joetta, 461n.109
Carrano, Jennifer, 240n.30
Carrington, Frank, 85, 91n.137
Carrington, Tim, 422nn.74, 75
Carrizo, Daniel, 168n.75
Carroll, Douglas, 174n.301
Carrozza, Mark, 242nn.120, 131

Carter, Sherry Plaster, 460n.91
Carter, Stanley, 460n.91
Cartier, Jerome, 462n.201
Cartwright, Desmond, 241n.96
Casey, Annie E., 239n.8
Casintahan, D., 167n.30
Caspi, Avshalom, 64n.81, 147, 170n.160, 171nn.165, 194, 172n.203, 174n.283, 295nn.9, 19, 26, 296nn.44, 51, 298nn.142, 143
Cassell, Paul, 126n.192
Castro, Bram Orobio de, 173n.256
Catalano, Richard, 240n.43, 241n.53, 278, 298n.145, 462n.177, 463n.196
Catalano, Shannan, 63nn.7, 21, 64n.53, 73, 74, 75, 88n.3, 330n.79
Cauce, Mari, 90n.64
Cauffman, Elizabeth, 65n.105, 172n.217, 173n.251, 298n.136
Cavanagh, Kevin, 168n.80
Cave, Damien, 491n.37
Cecil, Joe, 27n.56
Cederblad, Marianne, 174n.304
Cernkovich, Stephen, 63n.30, 194, 210n.143, 242n.132, 295n.12, 297n.79, 298n.144
Cetin, Mesut, 161
Chafetz, Janet Saltzman, 267nn.76, 77
Chaiken, Marcia, 462n.181
Chakrabarti, Nandini, 137
Chakravarti, Shamit, 365nn.51, 52
Chalk, Peter, 365nn.48, 50, 366n.84
Chambliss, William, 249, 266n.16, 392n.13, 423n.118
Chamlin, Mitchell, 124n.119, 290, 298n.132
Chan, Tony, 167n.23
Chaplin, Terry, 393n.100
Chapman, Jane Roberts, 267n.81
Chappell, Duncan, 63n.8
Charlebois, P., 67n.158
Chaseling, Janet, 393n.95
Chayet, Ellen, 125n.173
Chen, C.-Y., 208n.61
Chen, Henian, 460nn.70, 82
Chen, Jieming, 241n.70
Chen, Jieru, 333n.262
Chen, Xiaojin, 462n.170
Chen, Yi Fu, 210n.153
Cheng, Zhongqi, 167n.31
Cherbonneau, Michael, 392n.49
Chermak, Steven, 66n.131
Chesney-Lind, Meda, 267nn.73, 75, 268n.88
Cheuk, D. K. L., 133, 167n.32
Chien-Peng, Chung, 365n.47
Chilcoat, Howard, 296n.35
Chilton, Roland, 243n.156
Chin, Ko-lin, 13
Chiricos, Theodore, 42, 45, 124nn.119, 143, 125nn.159, 187, 208nn.69, 70, 72, 243n.177, 267n.54
Cho, Adrian, 421n.52
Choudhury, Muhtashem, 421n.31
Christakis, Dimitri, 154, 155

Christakos, Antigone, 462n.184
Christenson, Cornelia, 330n.111
Christenson, R. L., 240n.38
Christiansen, A., 462n.171
Christodoulou, G., 170n.131
Chronis, Andrea, 240n.26
Chung, He Len, 296n.33
Chung, Ick-Joong, 296n.46
Cicchetti, Dante, 240n.33
Cirillo, Kathleen, 173nn.262, 267, 174n.303
Clark, John, 63n.34
Clark, Richard D., 125n.148
Clark-Daniels, Carolyn, 124nn.121, 126
Clarke, Amory, 161
Clarke, Gregory N., 172n.212
Clarke, Robert, 90n.94
Clarke, Ronald, 91n.122, 106, 108, 122nn.17, 28, 123nn.94, 95, 124nn.107, 109, 114, 392n.61, 393n.93
Clarke-Stewart, K. Alison, 167n.23
Clason, Dennis L., 241n.87
Classen, Gabriele, 210n.145
Clavan, Bobby Caina, 125n.182
Clayton, Richard, 331n.165, 463nn.225, 226
Clear, Todd, 331n.131
Cleckley, Hervey, 160, 161
Clements, Benedict, 365nn.51, 52
Cleveland, H. Harrington, 174n.286
Clinard, Marshall, 421nn.17, 46
Clines, Francis X., 332n.187
Clingempeel, Glenn, 296n.40
Clinton, Monique, 328n.21
Cloward, Richard, 202–204, 206, 211nn.196–202
Coatsworth, Douglas J., 89n.40
Cochran, John, 123n.87, 242n.123, 297n.102, 320
Cogan, Jeanine, 333n.238
Cohen, Albert, 198–200, 202, 206, 210n.136, 211nn.187–190, 192–194
Cohen, Jacqueline, 11, 27n.33, 63n.39, 90n.68, 122n.50, 124n.133, 126n.187
Cohen, Lawrence, 78, 79, 90nn.82, 96, 171n.181
Cohen, Mark A., 88.7, 422n.112
Cohen, Morris, 426, 459n.8
Cohen, Patricia, 45, 155, 295n.27, 460n.82
Cohen, Patrick, 460n.70
Cohen, Robert, 241n.56, 329n.59
Cohen-Bendahan, Celina, 168n.56
Cohen-Kettenis, Peggy, 168n.56
Cohn, Bob, 461m.122
Cohn, Ellen, 64nn.59, 63, 65
Cohn, Steven, 208n.89
Cole, Christopher, 422n.78
Coley, Rebekah Levine, 209n.103
Coll, Xavier, 295n.18
Colletti, Patrick, 169n.91
Collier-Tenison, Shannon, 461n.111
Collin, Barry C., 492n.63
Collins, James, 328n.20

Collins, Mark, 297n.64
Colony, Catherine, 328n.3
Colvin, Mark, 284
Colwell, Brian, 173nn.262, 267, 174n.303
Colwell, Lori, 63n.25
Comer, James, 66n.125
Comstock, George, 155
Comte, Auguste, 6
Conger, Rand, 243n.163, 297n.77, 298n.126, 329nn.32, 41
Conklin, John, 321
Conley, Dalton, 166n.5
Conwell, Chic, 373, 392nn.16–18
Cook, Kimberly, 122n.16
Cook, Philip, 50, 51, 122n.17, 313, 331n.149
Cooley, Charles Horton, 17, 230, 243n.144
Coontz, Phyllis, 168nn.59–60
Cooper, Alison, 167n.37
Cooper, Cary, 64n.64, 168n.57
Cooper, Kylie, 422n.70
Cooper, Michael, 365n.30
Copes, Heith, 241n.72, 392nn.49, 51
Copper, Janet R., 333n.253
Cordella, Peter, 170n.135
Cork, Daniel L., 63n.24
Cornish, Derek, 106, 122nn.17, 28, 123n.96
Corrado, J., 462n.167
Cortese, Samuele, 167n.26
Cory-Slechta, Deborah A., 168n.84
Costa, Francis, 295n.18
Costanzo, Michael, 122n.47
Costello, Jane, 172n.222
Cota-Robles, Sonia, 240n.28
Coupe, Richard Timothy, 90n.89, 393n.77
Court, John, 461n.114
Courtwright, David, 305–306, 329n.66, 464n.240
Couzens, Michael, 63n.11
Covington, Jeanette, 208nn.68, 83, 209n.131
Cowan, Alison Leigh, 392n.1
Cox, Louis, 97, 122n.9
Cragin, Kim, 365n.48, 366n.84
Crane, Jonathan, 207n.28
Crawford, Charles, 267n.54
Crawford, Krysten, 403
Creamer, Vicki, 241n.66
Crenshaw, Martha, 365n.62
Cressey, Donald, 4, 16, 27nn.3, 42, 219, 220, 221, 241n.64, 410, 422n.82, 423n.121
Cretacci, Michael, 242n.125
Crews, F. T., 167n.29
Crinella, Francis, 167n.23
Croisdale, Tim, 66n.154, 126n.190
Cromwell, Paul, 122n.61, 123nn.65–66, 378, 387, 392nn.24, 36, 393n.90
Crosby, L., 296n.42
Crosby, Rick, 295n.22
Crosnoe, Robert, 242n.111
Crossette, Barbara, 459nn.19, 22
Crouch, Ben, 126n.186
Crow, Matthew, 57, 66n.134

Crowder, Martin J., 137
Crowe, R. R., 171n.178
Crowther, Betty, 461n.136
Cruise, Keith, 328n.8
Crumpler, Debbie, 167n.37
Cruz, M. C. Vince, 167n.30
Cullen, Francis T., 64n.77, 65n.102, 89n.62, 90n.69, 123n.70, 172n.223, 201, 210nn.159, 162, 165, 239n.12, 240nn.18, 24, 241n.60, 242nn.114, 119, 120, 131, 134, 243n.145, 269n.135, 290, 298nn.132, 133, 134, 330nn.88, 96, 333n.263, 422nn.94, 95
Cullen, Kevin, 459n.33
Cummings, Andrea, 123n.83, 330n.86
Cunningham-Niederer, Michele, 423n.116
Cupach, William, 326, 333nn.264, 267
Curry, G. David, 208nn.52, 73
Curry, Mary Ann, 320
Curtis, Lynn, 66n.125
Cuvelier, Steven, 123n.70
Czaja, Ronald, 63n.33

Dadds, Mark, 393n.102
Dafeamekpoer, Denise Spriggs, 330n.120
Dahlberg, Linda, 13, 332nn.191–193
Dahrendorf, Ralf, 248, 249
Daigle, Leah, 296n.53, 298nn.133, 134, 330nn.88, 96
Dal Forno, Gloria, 298n.122
Dalen, Lindy, 167n.37
D'Alessio, J. Stewart, 65n.88, 66n.128, 114, 115
Daley, Suzanne, 461n.98
Dally, Eileen, 161
Dalton, Katharina, 135, 168n.65
Daly, Kathleen, 267nn.73, 75, 79, 268nn.88, 109, 410, 422n.80
Daly, Martin, 65n.93, 89n.60, 146, 171nn.182–186, 208n.65, 209n.128, 298n.121, 332n.199
Daly, Sara A., 365n.48, 366n.84
Daniels, R. Steven, 124nn.121, 126
Dann, Robert, 114, 115
Dannefer, Dale, 66n.115
Dannenberg, Andrew, 460n.91
Dantzler, Joyce, 330n.120
Darrow, William, 460n.73
Darwin, Charles, 6
Das, Shyamal, 167n.50
Davey, Monica, 421n.41
David, David, 463n.231
Davidson, Laura, 64n.76
Davies, Garth, 207n.29
Davies, Mark, 241n.75, 242n.133, 462n.165
Davies, Priscilla, 174n.296
Davies, Susan, 295n.22
Davies-Netley, Sally, 89n.21
Daviglus, M., 137
Davis, Joanne, 462n.157
Davis, John, 167n.23
Davis, Robert C., 63n.13, 89nn.31, 45, 90n.104, 91nn.117, 123, 463nn.220, 222

Davis, Roy, 330n.103
Davis-Frenzel, Erika, 330nn.90, 122
Davison, Elizabeth, 123n.77
Dawkins, Marvin, 463n.193
Day, H. D., 174n.296
De Coster, Stacy, 186, 207n.39, 210n.157
De Gruchy, John W., 263
De Li, Spencer, 125nn.165, 177, 241n.58, 297nn.62, 73
de Silva, W. P., 459n.34
Dean, Charles, 125n.179, 295n.17, 296n.55
Deane, Glenn, 63n.6, 328n.16, 329n.47
DeBaryshe, Barbara, 295n.14
Deboutte, Dirk, 240n.29
Decker, Michele, 460n.53
Decker, Scott, 45, 123n80, 242nn.135, 322, 331n.157, 333n.224, 385, 393nn.80, 85, 462n.148
DeCoster, Stacy, 172n.234
Dedjinou, Adrienne, 422n.70
Deeley, Quinton, 161
Defina, Robert, 45
DeFronzo, James, 65n.85, 209n.116, 211n.209
DeHart, Erica, 71, 89n.29
DeJong, Christina, 125n.174, 125nn.168, 172, 243n.155
DeJong, M. J., 170n.128
DeKeseredy, Walter, 267n.71, 268n.87, 330nn.107, 114
DeLamatre, Mary, 90n.68
DeLisi, Matt, 169n.94, 241n.72
DeLone, Gregory, 492n.90
DeLone, Miriam, 66n.130, 234, 243n.179, 267n.53
Deluca, Stefanie, 208n.80
Demaray, Michelle Kilpatrick, 331nn.163, 164
Dempsey, Jared, 89n.35
Demuth, Stephen, 66n.132, 267.51
DeNavas-Walt, Carmen, 207nn.6, 17
DeNevi, Don, 392n.7
Dengate, Sue, 167n.27
Denney, Robert, 329n.61
Denno, Deborah, 138, 168n.82, 169nn.90, 96, 171nn.191–192
Dentler, Robert, 64n.73
Deptula, Daneen, 241n.56, 329n.59
DeRios, M. D., 462n.166
Dershowitz, Alan, 345
Derzon, James, 295n.21
Desai, Manisha, 168n.85
Deschenes, Elizabeth Piper, 65n.109, 298n.127
Deutsch, Joseph, 122n.49
Devine, Francis Edward, 121nn.2–3
Devine, Shannon, 460n.52
Devlin, Patrick, 426–427, 459n.9
DeVoe, Jill, 89n.42, 331n.161
Dezhbakhsh, Hashem, 115
Dhami, Mandeep, 410, 422n.85
Di Luigi, Massimo, 298n.122
DiClemente, Ralph, 295n.22

Dieckman, Duane, 124n.128
Dietz, Robert D., 211n.178
Dietz, Tracy, 89n.46
DiGiuseppe, David, 155
DiLalla, David, 170n.143
Dinitz, Simon, 242n.108
Dionne, Ginette, 171n.168
Dirie, Waris, 427
Dishion, Thomas, 240n.48
Dishman, Chris, 355, 365n.61
Dobash, R. Emerson, 332nn.208, 211
Dobash, Russell, 332nn.208, 211
Dobrin, Adam, 90nn.68, 70, 208n.52, 298nn.133, 134
Dodge, Kenneth A., 171n.165, 173n.248, 209n.96, 240n.15, 296n.45
Dohrenwend, Bruce, 243n.145
Dominici, Cinzia, 298n.122
Dominick, Joseph, 491n.43
Donker, Andrea, 296n.54
Donnelly, Patrick, 90n.97
Donnerstein, Edward, 330n.116, 461nn.109, 112
Donohue, John J., III, 42, 43, 45, 115
Donovan, John, 295n.18, 462n.170
Doob, Anthony, 124n.140
Dorahy, Martin, 88n.18
Doran, Michael Scott, 354, 365n.53
Doraz, Walter, 167n.38
Dornfeld, Maude, 296n.28
Dougherty, Carter, 421n.47
Douglas, William O., 427
Downey, Douglas, 207n.9
Downs, William, 89n.21, 243n.165
Dowsett, John, 161
Doyle, Daniel, 329n.49
Drago, Harry Sinclair, 392n.7
Drake, J. J. P., 168n.70
Drass, Kriss, 209n.131, 331n.151
Dressler, Joshua, 23
Drew, Christopher, 332n.187
Driver, Edwin, 171n.197
Drugge, Jeff, 330n.112
Dugan, Laura, 105–106, 123n.85
Dugdale, Richard, 131, 166n.11
Duhart, Detis, 333n.257
Dunaway, R. Gregory, 64n.77, 65n.102, 241n.60, 242n.134, 297n.104
Duncan, Greg J., 207nn.11–14, 208n.80
Dunford, Franklin, 125n.179
D'Unger, Amy, 67n.161, 296n.47
Dunlap, Eloise, 297n.78
Durkheim, Émile, 8, 27nn.8–19, 191, 192
Durose, Matthew, 463n.217
Durrant, Lynne, 298n.147
Duwe, Grant, 317, 332n.184
Dwiggins, Donna, 65n.102
Dworkin, Andrea, 426, 459n.5, 461n.96
Dyson, Laronistine, 88n.9

Earls, Felton, 67n.159, 209nn.94, 118, 305, 329nn.44, 45
Earnest, Terri, 208n.56
Eaves, Lindon, 170n.163
Ebrine, Servet, 161

Eccles, Jacquelynne, 168n.52
Eck, John, 123nn.103, 104
Edelhertz, Herbert, 422n.84
Edwards, Jessica, 436, 460n.66
Egelko, Bob, 331n.140
Eggleston, Carolyn, 65n.102
Egley, Arlen, Jr., 207n.2
Eichenwald, Kurt, 403, 422n.60
Einarsson, Emil, 161
Einat, Amela, 140, 169n.112
Einat, Tomer, 140, 169n.112
Einstein, Stanley, 423n.122
Eisen, Seth, 170n.163
Eisenberg, Nancy, 170n.138
Eitle, David, 66n.128
Eitzen, D. Stanley, 422n.96
El-Magd, Nadia Abou, 365n.24
Elder, Glen, 242n.124, 297n.77, 298n.126
Eley, Thalia, 171n.175
Elifson, Kirk, 463n.229
Elkind, Peter, 403
Ellingworth, Dan, 89n.48
Elliott, Amanda, 209nn.115, 120
Elliott, Delbert, 66n.115, 123n.98, 125n.179, 208n.54, 209nn.115, 120, 243n.160, 298n.118
Elliott, F. A., 169nn.122–123
Ellis, Lee, 132, 134, 166nn.15, 19, 167n.50, 168nn.58–60, 170nn.130, 132, 135, 171n.187, 297nn.82, 97, 330n.105
Elonheimo, Henrik, 239n.9
Elstein, Sharon, 330n.103
Emerson, Robert M., 333n.260
Emmett, Pauline, 167n.23
Endresen, Inger, 241n.82
Engel, Robin Shepard, 66n.121, 172n.231
Engels, Friedrich, 27n.26, 246, 248, 266nn.8, 12
Engels, Rutger, 173n.247
Engen, Rodney, 243n.177
Ennett, Susan, 66n.140
Enrich, David, 160n.54
Epstein, Gil, 122n.49
Epstein, Joel, 422n.91
Epstein, Kitty Kelley, 266n.24
Erez, Edna, 91n.117
Erickson, Kai, 231, 243n.149
Erickson, Maynard, 124n.143
Erickson, Rosemary, 27n.35
Ericson, Jonathon, 167n.23
Ericsson, Kjersti, 268n.80
Erikson, Erik, 150
Erkanli, Alaattin, 172n.222
Ernst, Frederick, 328n.5
Eron, L., 173n.258
Erwin, Brigette, 89n.37
Esagian, Gkaro, 328n.5
Esbensen, Finn-Aage, 65n.109, 208n.79, 211n.203, 298n.127
Esmail, Aneez, 332n.172
Espelage, Dorothy, 65n.105, 172n.217
Estabrook, Arthur, 131
Estes, Richard J., 437, 459n.32, 460n.84
Estrada, Felipe, 64n.69

Estrich, Susan, 89n.58, 331n.129
Evans, David T., 242n.134
Evans, Gary, 207n.15
Evans, Jeff, 168n.81
Evans, Michelle, 210nn.155, 161
Evans, Rhonda, 422n.83
Evans, T. David, 64n.77, 65n.102, 210n.159, 241n.60
Eve, Raymond, 65n.108
Eves, Anita, 137
Ewing, Charles Patrick, 329, 333n.230
Exline, Julie Juola, 125n.146
Exum, Lyn, 455
Eysenck, Hans, 10, 27n.27, 159, 173nn.271, 272, 274
Eysenck, M. W., 173nn.272, 274
Ezell, Michael, 67n.161

Factor-Litvak, Pamela, 167n.31, 168n.85
Fader, James, 66n.152
Fagan, Abigail, 170n.157
Fagan, Jeffery, 125n.179, 201, 207nn.29, 37, 211n.186
Fahy, Tom, 161
Fairweather, David, 330n.112
Falarid, Leanne Fiftal, 65n.102
Falck, Russel, 463n.192
Famularo, Richard, 272n.218
Fantaye, Dawit Kiros, 393n.73
Farabee, David, 462n.201
Faraon, Stephen, 171n.163
Fargeon, Samantha, 169n.120
Farley, Reynolds, 66n.145
Farnworth, Margaret, 64n.73, 278
Farr, Kathryn Ann, 464n.242
Farrall, Stephen, 296nn.41, 56
Farrell, Graham, 89nn.49, 50, 52, 388, 393n.94
Farrell, Michael, 240n.16, 462n.154
Farrington, David P., 13, 39, 63nn.37, 40, 45, 66n.150, 90nn.68, 88, 108, 109, 124n.115, 143, 170nn.147, 149–150, 154–156, 215, 240nn.20, 21, 22, 23, 284, 295nn.16, 26, 296n.36, 329nn.42, 62, 392n.33
Farrooque, Rokeya, 328n.5
Fass, Simon, 392n.22
Fassbender, Pantaleon, 173n.276
Faupel, Charles, 462nn.187–189
Fazel, Seena, 328n.23
Feiedler, Mora, 208n.58
Fein, Robert, 331n.167
Feinberg, Joel, 459n.10
Feinberg, Seth, 211n.178
Feingold, Alan, 298n.112
Fejes-Mendoza, Kathy, 65n.102
Felson, Marcus, 78, 79, 80, 90nn.82, 96, 107, 123nn.95, 103, 211n.185
Felson, Richard, 63n.6, 90n.92, 104, 123nn.72–73, 81, 240n.51, 322, 329n.52, 330n.119, 331nn.155, 156, 332n.218, 333nn.219, 220
Fendrich, Michael, 63n.32, 460n.65, 462n.176
Fenton, Terence, 272n.218

Ferguson, H. Bruce, 167n.39
Fergusson, David, 296nn.29, 45
Fernardez, Manny, 166n.1
Ferracuti, Franco, 11, 27n.31, 305, 329n.48
Ferrell, Jee, 123n.88
Ferri, Enrico, 131, 166n.10
Ferris, Kerry O., 333n.260
Feucht, Thomas, 331n.166
Fienberg, Stephen, 168n.83
Figert, Anne E., 168n.64
Figlio, Robert, 59, 66nn.117, 146, 148, 67n.155, 122n.47, 295n.4
Figuerdo, Aurelio Jose, 171nn.188–189
Finckenauer, James, 13, 27n.57, 417
Finkelhor, David, 71, 76, 88nn.15, 89nn.51, 318, 330n.99, 332nn.197, 201, 203, 204, 460nn.71, 83, 491n.47
Finn, Kristin, 461n.144
Finn, Peter, 90n.106, 91nn.135, 136
Fireman, Gary, 89n.35
Firestone, David, 421n.18
Fischer, Mariellen, 169n.118
Fishbein, Diana, 135, 167n.42, 168nn.68–69, 169n.97
Fisher, Bonnie, 89n.62, 90nn.69, 71, 297n.94, 326, 330nn.88, 96, 333n.263
Fisher, Chrisopher, 491n.30
Fisher, Gene, 45
Flaccus, Gillian, 288
Flaherty, Austin, 91n.119
Flaherty, Sara, 91n.119
Flaming, Karl, 208n.58
Flannery, Daniel, 65nn.102, 108, 297n.83
Flay, Brian, 123n.69, 462n.162
Fletcher, Kenneth, 169n.118
Flewelling, Robert, 63n.35, 66n.140, 463n.224
Flitter, Jill Klotz, 89n.23, 460n.75
Flynn, Kevin, 332n.190
Flynn, Stephen, 366n.82
Fogel, C. A., 169n.89
Foglia, Linda, 125nn.159–160
Fong, Grace, 169n.103
Forbes, Gordon, 330n.89
Forde, David, 297n.91
Formby, William, 124nn.121, 126
Formoso, Diana, 239n.6
Fornango, Robert, 45
Forney, Matthew, 492n.61
Forrest, Walter, 298n.125
Forster, Bruce, 161
Forsythe, Lubica, 393n.89
Foster, Hilliard, 172n.231
Foster, Holly, 268n.92, 295n.13
Foster, Raymond, 493n.104
Fowler, Tom, 170n.139
Fox, Ben, 123n.71
Fox, James Alan, 315–317, 331n.146, 332nn.173, 179, 182, 183, 333nn.250, 255, 439, 461n.113
Fox, Kristan, 66n.129
Francis, Janice, 392n.22

Frank, Guido, 142–143
Frank, Nancy, 421n.7, 422n.67
Frank, Steven, 492n.102
Franklin, J. M., 174n.296
Franks, John, 459n.15
Frase, Richard, 120, 126n.198
Fraser, Jennifer, 393n.102
Frauenheim, Ed, 490n.2
Frayne, Susan, 460n.76
Frazee, Sharon Glave, 123n.77
Freeman-Gallant, Adrienne, 170n.151
Freemon, Melinda, 63n.26
Freisthler, Bridget, 208n.78
Freng, Adrienne, 66n.133
Freud, Sigmund, 7, 149–150, 158, 165, 302, 328n.11
Frey, William, 66n.145
Fricker-Elhai, Adrienne, 462n.157
Friday, Paul, 240n.44
Fridman, Daniel, 90n.98
Fried, Gabriela, 365n.54
Friedlander, Robert, 365nn.34, 39
Friedman, Andrea, 429, 459n.26
Friedrichs, David, 252, 267n.37, 421n.4
Friedrichs, Jessica, 252, 267n.37
Friendman, Richard, 172n.224
Fritsch, Eric, 123n.100m 124.135
Fromm-Auch, Delee, 174n.296
Frone, Michael, 330n.78
Frye, Victoria, 320
Fuchs, Siegmund Fred, 329n.70
Fuentes, Angel Ilarraza, 333n.261
Fuentes, Thomas V., 423n.120
Fukurai, Hiroshi, 243n.170
Fulton, Betsy, 269n.135
Fyfe, James, 124n.130

Gabrielli, William, 171n.180
Gadd, David, 296n.41
Gaffney, Michael, 208n.90
Gagnon, C., 67n.158
Gagnon, John, 330n.111
Gainey, Randy, 209n.104, 243n.177
Gajewski, Francis, 124nn.134, 137
Gale, Nathan, 122n.47
Gall, Franz Joseph, 7
Galving, Jim, 243n.156
Gamble, Wendy, 240n.28
Gans, Dian, 167n.41
Gant, Charles, 169n.119
Garcia, Luis, 209n.98, 333n.247
Gardner, Carol Brooks, 333n.260
Garfinkel, Robin, 168n.76
Garner, Connie Chenoweth, 242nn.114, 119
Garner, Joel H., 125n.179
Garnier, Helen, 242n.117
Garofalo, James, 90n.75, 91n.134, 333nn.227, 239
Garofalo, Raffaele, 130, 166n.9
Gartner, Rosemary, 89n.61, 115
Gary, Faye, 320
Gatzke-Kopp, Lisa M., 132, 167n.25
Gaylor, Rita, 172n.216
Ge, Xiaojia, 65n.87

Gebhard, Paul, 330n.111
Geis, Gilbert, 63n.8, 392n.15, 421n.16
Geller, Susan Rose, 298n.146
Gelles, Richard, 319–320, 332nn.198, 202, 213
George, David, 169n.103
Georges-Abeyie, Daniel, 66n.122, 365n.35
Gerber, Jurg, 463n.210
Gerstein, Dean, 295n.27
Gertz, Marc, 49, 51, 64n.68, 123n.75, 125n.165, 208nn.69, 70, 72
Gesch, Bernard, 136, 137
Giampietro, Vincent, 161
Giancola, Peter, 462n.155
Gibbons, Donald, 173n.269, 392n.48
Gibbs, Jack, 124n.143, 243n.187, 267n.59, 365n.33
Gibbs, John P., 65n.102, 123n.67
Gibbs, Natalie, 123n.83, 330n.86
Gibson, Chris, 208n.90, 296n.53
Giever, Dennis, 297n.98
Gifford, Robert, 393n.91
Gilchrist, Lewayne, 296n.46
Gillis, A. R., 268n.91
Gillis, Roy, 333n.238
Gillman, Matthew W., 168n.87
Ginzberg, Eli, 463n.232
Ginzburg, E., 64n.81
Giordano, Peggy, 63n.30, 210n.143, 241n.65, 242n.132, 295n.12, 297n.79, 298nn.120, 144, 392n.47
Giroux, Bruce, 296n.31
Gjeruldsen, Susanne Rogne, 328n.23
Glass, Nancy, 320
Glick, Barry, 63n.10
Glueck, Eleanor, 10, 27n.29, 159, 173n.270, 239n.5, 272, 279, 281, 282, 295n.2
Glueck, Sheldon, 10, 27n.29, 159, 173n.270, 239n.5, 272, 279, 281, 282, 295n.2
Goddard, Henry, 131, 162
Godfrey, Barry, 420n.2
Goetz, Barry, 464n.238
Gohm, Carol, 330n.93
Gold, Martin, 65n.108
Goldberg, Jack, 171n163
Golding, Jean, 167n.23
Goldkamp, John, 124n.130, 455, 463n.227
Goldman, David, 170n.129
Goldman, M. S., 462n.171
Goldstein, Michael, 461n.108
Goldstein, Paul, 328nn.17, 24, 460nn.62, 63, 65, 462n.176
Golub, Andrew, 462nn.178, 179
Gonzales, Nancy, 239n.6
Gooch, Erik, 332n.175
Gooch, Teresa, 64n.46
Goodman, Robert, 172n.211
Goodstein, Laurie, 243n.152
Goodwill, Alasdair, 331n.169
Goodwin, D. W., 462n.160
Gootman, Elissa, 332n.185
Gordon, Kristina Coop, 89n.25
Gordon, Leslie, 297n.77, 329n.32

Gordon, Rachel, 329n.62
Gordon, Robert, 241n.96
Gorge, Mathieu, 492n.66
Goring, Charles, 148, 171n.196
Gorr, Wilpen, 27n.33, 124n.133
Gossop, Michael, 463nn.168, 231
Gottfredson, Denise, 90nn.65, 85, 209nn.102, 125, 455
Gottfredson, Gary, 90n.65, 209nn.102, 125
Gottfredson, Michael, 52, 63n.19, 65nn.86, 91, 106, 122n.29, 123n.89, 285–290, 297nn.87–89, 92, 93, 96, 100, 298nn.108, 115, 411, 422nn.88, 89, 463n.227
Gottfredson, Stephen, 123n.63
Gottman, John Mordechai, 320
Gottschalk, Earl, 421n.23
Gould, Arthur, 461n.97
Gould, Leroy, 55, 65n.114
Gould, Stephen Jay, 166n.12
Gove, Walter, 123n.87, 167n.48, 170n.133
Goyer, P. F., 169n101
Grandison, Terry, 88n.9
Grandjean, P., 167n.26
Grann, Martin, 328n.23
Grasmick, Harold, 124n.119, 125nn.144–145, 208n.82, 209nn.105, 114, 124, 297n.102, 298nn.113, 123, 130
Gray, Andrew, 192n.62
Gray, Gregory, 167n.39
Gray, Louis N., 122n.18, 173n.255
Gray-Ray, Phyllis, 243nn.147, 161
Graziano, Joseph, 167n.31, 168n.85
Greeley, A., 461nn.137
Green, Aisa, 169n.104
Green, Donald, 124n.143
Green, Lorraine, 109, 124nn.110, 111
Green, Rebecca, 491n.39, 492n.94
Green, Stuart, 412, 422n.97
Green, William, 329nn.67, 73
Greenbaum, Robert, 328n.2
Greenberg, David, 267n.57
Greenberg, Stephanie, 208n.59
Greene, Michael, 329n.46
Greenfeld, Lawrence, 89n.53, 125n.170
Greenhouse, Joel, 168n.83
Greening, Leilani, 173n.263
Greenwood, Peter, 463n.230
Gregg, Heather S., 365nn.48, 366nn.84
Gregory, Alice, 171n.175
Gregory, Carol, 65n.113
Grierson, Jeffrey, 460n.44
Griffiths, Curt Taylor, 268n.129
Grimalt, Joan O., 168n.75
Grimes, Tom, 155
Grimshaw, Kate, 167n.37
Griswold, David, 242nn.113, 137
Groff, Elizabeth, 393n.76
Gross, Alan, 330n.93
Gross, Harriet, 161
Gross, Kate, 491n.48
Gross, Samuel, 15, 27n.39
Groth, A. Nicholas, 308, 310, 330nn.83, 115
Grove, H. D., 422n.55

Groves, Robert M., 63n.24
Groves, W. Byron, 27nn.26, 44, 45, 209nn.102, 125, 250, 266nn.5, 8, 29
Grow, Brian, 491n.20
Grubstein, Lori, 66n.152
Gruenewald, Paul, 208n.78
Grus, Catherine, 88n.16
Gu, Joann, 333n.247
Gudjonsson, Gisli, 161
Guerry, Andre-Michel, 8
Guess, Teresa, 267n.55
Guijarro, Margarita, 295n.25
Gulley, Bill, 170n.158
Gunay, Huseyin, 161
Gundry, Gwen, 170n.156
Gupta, Humka, 460n.53
Gupta, Sanjeev, 365nn.51, 52, 480, 492n.67
Gusfield, Joseph, 427, 459n.14, 461n.138
Gutierrez, Francisco, 463n.214
Gutner, Cassidy, 90n.101
Gwlasda, Victoria, 89n.33

Haapanen, Rudy, 66n.154, 298n.110
Habermann, Niels, 169n.93, 173n.277, 174n.278
Haden, Sara Chiara, 88n.13
Hagan, John, 27n.2, 45, 207n.19, 210n.145, 257–258, 267n.43, 268nn.90–92, 295n.13
Hagelstam, Camilla, 174n.297
Haikkanen, Helina, 393n.102
Hakim, Simon, 91n.124, 122n.47, 123n.62, 393nn.86, 87
Häkkänen, Helinä, 174n.297
Halbfinger, David M., 421n.44
Hale, Benjamin, 493n.108
Hale, Chris, 65n.110
Hale, Matthew, 309
Halkitis, Perry N., 462n.190
Hall, Jerome, 393n.71
Hall, Joseph S., 422n.69
Hallam, J., 461n.112
Halleck, Seymour, 172n.204
Haller, Mark, 421n.6
Hallet, Amanda, 295n.25
Halperin, William, 122n.47
Halpern, Carolyn, 436, 460n.66
Halvorsen, Jessica, 330n.80
Hamlin, John, 241n.100
Hamm, Mark, 354, 365n.56
Hammett, Theodore, 422n.91
Hammock, Georgina, 90n.86
Hammond, Rodney, 331n.166
Hammond, Sean M., 137
Hampson, Sarah E., 137
Hampton, Tracy, 462n.159
Hanks, Chris, 169n.104
Hannon, Lance, 65n.85
Hansell, Saul, 491n.19
Hansell, Stephen, 463n.196
Hansen, Ellen Beate, 392n.37
Hanson, Karl, 172n.232
Hansson, Kjell, 174n.304
Happanen, Rudy, 126n.190

Lin, Kuei-Hsiu, 329n.32
Linbald, Frank, 332n.205
Lind, Bronwyn, 90n.90
Lindgren, Scott, 167n.40
Link, Bruce, 172n.223, 243n.145
Linnoila, M., 170nn.128–129
Linster, Richard, 328n.25
Linz, Daniel, 330n.116, 461n.109
Lipscomb, Jane A., 333n.253
Lipsey, Mark, 295n.21
Liptak, Adam, 91n.132
Lipton, D., 173n.264
Liska, Allen, 90n.81, 208n.86, 209n.104, 242n1.143
Listokin, Yair, 125n.150
Litan, Avivah, 192n.85
Litton, Roger, 393n.92
Liu, Jianghong, 137, 209n.104
Liu, Xiaoru, 243n.159
Liu, Xinhua, 167n.31
Liu, Zhiqiang, 115
Livaditis, Miltos, 328n.5
Livesley, W. John, 170n.140
Livingston, Jennifer, 330nn.78, 80, 82
Lizotte, Alan, 64n.81, 91n.125, 123n.79, 170n.151, 240n.39, 267n.51, 278, 295nn.6, 19, 24, 329nn.56, 59, 462n.153, 463n.206
Lo, Celia, 463n.235
Lochman, J. E., 173n.261
Locker, John, 420n.2
Loeber, Rolf, 65n.102, 67n.158, 90nn.68, 72, 167n.24, 172nn.209, 216, 173nn.238, 259, 240nn.35, 45, 272, 274–275, 295nn.5, 7, 16, 26, 28, 296nn.31, 36, 45, 51, 52, 328n.26, 329nn.42, 62, 463n.204
Lofland, John, 243n.172
Loftus, Margaret, 392n.30
Logan, T. K., 333n.268, 463nn.225, 226
Lögdberg, B., 172n.236
Logie, Robert, 393n.80
Logio, Kim, 88n.17
Lok, Kris, 167n.37
Lolacono, Nancy J., 167n.31
Lombroso, Cesare, 7, 8, 54, 65n.98, 130–131, 147, 164
Lonczk, Heather, 298n.145
Loney, Bryan, 171n.167
Longmore, Monica, 241n.65, 298n.120
Longshore, Douglas, 446, 462nn.149, 150
Loomis, Dana, 333n.259
Lorenz, Konrad, 303, 328n.12
Lotke, Eric, 207n.20
Lott, John, Jr., 51
Love, Craig T., 174n.292
Lovell, David, 125n.175
Lovrich, Nicholas, 208n.90
Lowenstein, George, 125n.157
Lozano, Rafael, 13, 332nn.191–193
Lu, Chunmeng, 90n.69
Lu, Frank, 485
Lucas, Emma, 460n.76
Luckenbill, David, 314, 329n.49, 331n.157
Ludwig, Jens, 50, 51, 313, 331n.149

Lueck, Monika, 328n.10
Lueck, Thomas J., 461n.124
Lui, Kung-Jong, 91n.126
Lunde, Donald, 331n.135
Luo, Michael, 422n.58
Luque, Luis, 331n.123
Lurigio, Arthur J., 88n.4, 89n.31, 91n.123, 125n.155, 463nn.220, 222
Lussier, Patrick, 296n.36
Luther, Martin, 432
Luukkaala, Tiina, 172n.213
Lyght, C. E., 170
Lykken, David, 27n.10, 125n.156, 160, 161
Lynam, Donald, 168n.89, 171n.194, 173nn.252, 273, 174n.291, 295n.26, 296nn.37, 45, 51, 298n.111, 453, 463nn.225, 226
Lynch, James, 88n.12, 91n.124, 126n.189
Lynch, Kathleen Bodisch, 298n.146
Lynch, Michael, 27nn.26, 44, 45, 168n.78, 250, 266nn.5, 6, 8, 10, 13, 29, 33, 267n.36, 412, 421n.7, 422nn.67, 98
Lyons, Michael, 170n.163

Maakestad, William, 422nn.94, 95
MacCoun, Robert, 462n.186
MacDonald, John, 281, 297n.75, 298nn.133, 134
MacDonald, Julia, 393n.91
Mace, David E., 172n.212
Machalek, Richard, 171n.181
Machon, Ricardo, 169n.89
MacIntosh, Randall, 331n.127
Mack, Kristin, 268n.99
MacKenzie, Doris Layton, 125n.177
Mackesy-Amiti, Mary Ellen, 462n.176
Macmillan, Ross, 65n.97, 70, 88n.8, 280, 297n.67
Maddan, Sean, 124n.108
Madensen, Tamara, 122n.57
Maercker, Andreas, 89n.38, 91n.112
Maguin, Eugene, 240n.35
Maguire, Kathleen, 211n.208
Maher, Lisa, 460n.59
Maheshwari, Ayonija, 460n.53
Maier, Timothy W., 392n.31
Maier-Katkin, Daniel, 210n.175
Makepeace, James, 332n.214
Malamuth, Neil, 330n.117, 439, 461nn.102, 106
Malecki, Christine Kerres, 331nn.163, 164
Mallory, W. A., 169n.111
Mandela, Nelson, 263
Manganello, Jennifer, 320
Manning, Wendy, 241n.65, 298n.120
Mantell, Michael, 325, 333n.256
Maples, Michelle, 243n.191
Marchak, Patricia, 358, 366nn.76, 77
Marchbanks, Polly, 91n.126
Marenin, Otwin, 290, 298n.129
Marescialli, Mauro, 13
Marie, Alexandra, 461n.110
Marini, Maragret Mooney, 65n.102
Markianos, M., 170n.131

Markman, Stephen, 126n.192
Markovitz, J. H., 137
Markowitz, Fred, 209n.104, 211n.185
Marneros, Andreas, 172n.228
Marquart, James, 115, 123n.70, 126n.186, 295n.26
Marshall, D. D., 174n.296
Marshall, Ineke Haen, 242n.128, 298n.121
Marshall, Paul, 168n.72
Marshall, Stephen, 333n.259
Martel, Michelle, 168n.80
Martens, Frederick, 423n.116
Martin, Catherine, 463nn.225, 226
Martin, Neilson, 171n.167
Martin, Robert, 51
Martin, Susan, 463n.205
Martines, Laura, 332n.209
Martinez, Amos, 241n.101
Martinez, Ramiro, Jr., 45, 64n.82, 328n.14
Martinson, Robert, 97, 122n.8
Maruna, Shadd, 173n.253, 243n.191
Marvell, Thomas, 51, 124n.129, 125n.184
Marx, Karl, 9, 10, 27n.26, 246–248, 266nn.8, 9, 11
Marziano, Vincent, 173n.265
Maschi, Tina, 173nn.238, 260
Mason, W. Alex, 296nn.36, 39
Massey, James, 241n.86, 242n.139
Massoglia, Michael, 65n.97
Mathers, Richard, 242nn.114, 119
Matheson, Daniel, 27n.39
Matsueda, Ross, 122n.24, 123n.86, 243nn.158, 169
Matthews, Roger, 438, 461n.100
Matusko, Jacqueline, 328n.22
Matza, David, 223, 225, 238, 241nn.91–95
Maudsley, Herny, 7
Mauer, Marc, 126n.191
Maughan, Barbara, 296n.31
Mawson, A. R., 168n.73
Maxwell, Christopher, 125n.179, 296n.32, 460n.74, 463n.205
Maxwell, Sheila Royo, 296n.32, 460n.74
May, David, 78, 90n.73
Mayo, Julia, 460n.76
Mazerolle, Lorraine Green, 123n.105, 124nn.134, 137
Mazerolle, Paul, 172n.217, 210nn.152, 158–160, 295nn.11, 17, 296n.55, 298n.110
Mazzetti, Mark, 365nn.51, 52
McAuslan, Pam, 328n.21
McBride, Duane, 464n.241
McCaffrey, Shannon, 239n.3
McCaghy, Charles, 27n.43, 392n.47, 393n.68, 421n.53, 460nn.43, 46, 461nn.139, 140
McCain, John, 346
McCall, Andrew, 392nn.2, 3
McCall, Patricia, 66n.137, 208n.87, 296n.47
McCann, Donna, 167n.37
McCarthy, Bill, 89n.61, 125n.163, 241nn.67, 68, 268n.92
McCarty, Carolyn, 155

McCauley, Elizabeth, 296nn.36, 39
McClelland, Gary, 27n.41
McCluskey, John, 207n.24
McCord, Joan, 295n.10
McCready, William, 461nn.137
McCue, Colleen, 64nn.46, 47
McCurdy, Sheryl, 460n.67
McDevitt, Jack, 323, 324, 333nn.232, 233, 247
McDonel, C., 173n.264
McDowall, David, 88n.12, 90n.77, 462n.153
McEntire, Ranee, 208n.72
McFall, R., 173n.264
McFarland, Christine, 168n.83
McFarlane, Alexander, 172n.235
McFarlane, Judith, 320
McFeely, Richard, 423n.132
McGahey, RIchard, 208n.52
McGee, Rob, 172n.203
McGloin, Jean Maire, 173n.250
McGlothin, W., 463n.197
McGue, Matt, 171n.167
McGuffin, Peter, 171n.167
McGuire, Stryker, 328n.4
Mchugh, Suzanne, 170
McKay, Henry D., 184–186, 206, 207nn.30, 32, 33
McKenzie, Roderic, 27nn.24, 25
McKibben, André, 123n.84
McKinney, Joseph R., 463n.228
McLanahan, Sara, 240n.14
McLean, Bethany, 403
McLean, W. Graham, 167n.36
McLeod, Jane, 296n.28
McLeod, Maureen, 91n.134
McMackin, Robert, 89n.37
McMillan, Richard, 90n.95, 208n.50
McMorris, Barbara J., 297n.67
McMurray, Scott, 421n.33
McNamara, Grace, 462n.164
McNeill, Richard, 209nn.102, 125
McNulty, Thomas, 207n.22, 209n.119
McPhaul, Kathleen M., 333n.253
McPhee, Mike, 333n.231
McVeigh, Gloria, 137
Mdzinarishvili, A., 167n.29
Mead, George Herbert, 17, 230, 242n.144
Meadows, Susannah, 328n.1
Mears, Daniel, 65n.104, 241nn.78, 79
Measelle, Jeffrey, 170n.160
Medina-Ariza, Juanjo, 89n.45
Mednick, B., 171n.193
Mednick, Sarnoff, 137, 146, 167n.21, 168nn.63, 89, 169nn.89, 95, 170nn.137, 145, 171nn.179–180, 193, 172n.227, 328n.28
Meehan, Albert, 254, 267n.49
Meeker, James, 208n.71
Meesters, Cor, 169n.116, 298n.131
Megargee, Edward, 174n.282
Meier, Robert, 90n.93, 207n.26, 239n.4
Meissner, Christian, 63n.25
Mellingen, Kjetil, 137
Meloy, Reid, 332n.175, 333n.265

Meltzer, Howard, 172n.211
Menard, Scott, 208n.54, 298n.118
Mendenhall, Ruby, 208n.80
Mendes, Silvia, 124n.117
Mendrek, Adrianna, 161
Mercy, James, 13, 51, 91n.126, 331n.153, 332nn.191–193
Merkens, Hans, 210n.145
Mero, Richard, 297n.70
Merton, Robert, 192–194, 206, 210n.133
Meseck-Bushey, Sylvia, 170nn.141, 158
Mesquita, Ethan Bueno de, 366n.68
Messer, Julie, 172n.211
Messerschmidt, James, 256, 257, 267nn.78, 84
Messerschmidt, Pamela, 328n.20
Messner, Steven, 63n.6, 65n.84, 79, 90n.95, 123nn.73, 81, 193, 194, 206, 207n.3, 208nn.50, 51, 209n.99, 210nn.138–141, 168, 240n.41, 328n.16, 329nn.47, 55, 332n.218, 333nn.219, 220
Metz, Tim, 422n.81
Meyer, Joanne, 170n.163
Mezey, Gill, 161
Michalowski, Raymond, 27n.44, 421n.12, 422n.105, 106
Michelson, N., 169n.89
Miech, Richard, 64n.81, 295n.19
Miethe, Terance, 90nn.77, 80, 93, 267n.52, 331n.151
Milan, Stephanie, 295n.8
Miles, William, 63n.31
Miletich, Steve, 365n.44
Mileusnic, Darinka, 27n.41
Milich, Rich, 463nn.225, 226
Miller, Alan, 210n.152
Miller, Amanda, 331n.161
Miller, Bobbi Viegas, 90nn.74, 76
Miller, Brenda, 89n.21
Miller, Darcy, 65n.102
Miller, Jody, 101, 322, 333nn.222, 223
Miller, Joshua, 173nn.252, 273
Miller, Kirk, 63n.33
Miller, L. E., 170n.144
Miller, Lawrence, 365nn.49, 58, 59
Miller, Lisa, 209n.123
Miller, Martin, 365n.55
Miller, Matthew, 43, 45, 51
Miller, Michael, 422n.81
Miller, Susan, 65n.113
Miller, Ted R., 88n.7
Miller, Thomas, 328n.24
Miller, Todd, 123n.69, 295n.25, 462n.162
Miller, Walter, 198, 211nn.183, 184, 241n.61
Mills, Michael, 421n.13
Milman, Harold, 167n.28
Milner, Trudi, 125n.147
Mincy, Ronald, 207n.21
Miner, Michael, 89n.23, 460n.75
Minniti, Maria, 423n.122
Minor, M. William, 125n.159, 241n.96
Mio, J. S., 462n.166
Mirowsky, John, 65n.102, 208n.75

Mischel, Walter, 173n.268
Misson, Sebastian, 460n.44
Mitchell, Derek, 161
Mitchell, Kimberly, 491n.47
Mitchell, Nick, 243n.191
Moch, Annie, 207n.15
Modzeleski, William, 331nn.166, 167
Moffitt, Terrie, 64n.81, 67n.159, 168nn.88–89, 169n.115, 170n.160, 171nn.165, 170, 180, 194, 173n.275, 174nn.283, 291, 277, 288, 295nn.9, 19, 26, 296nn.37, 44, 45, 49–51, 298nn.109, 111, 142, 143
Moilanen, Irma, 239n.9
Mokherjee, Jessica, 210n.147
Mokhiber, Russell, 423n.113
Momenan, Reza, 169n.103
Monachesi, Elio, 174nn.280–281
Monaghan, Rachel, 491n.49
Monahan, John, 172n.230
Money, J., 168n.62
Monroe, Laura, 330n.120
Monroe, Lawrence, 64n.73
Monroe, R. R., 169n.106
Monson, Candice, 90n.101
Montada, Leo, 89n.38
Montgomery, Nicholas, 27n.39
Montgomery, Paul, 167n.33
Moody, Carlisle, 124n.129, 125n.184
Moore, Charles, 267n.52
Moore, Elizabeth, 298n.106, 421n.13
Moore, Kristin, 142n.127, 240n.30
Moore, Mark, 398, 421n.17, 463n.216
Moore, Melanie, 240n.38
Moore, Todd M., 89n.25
Moran, Jonathan, 366n.66
Morenoff, Jeffrey, 207n.45, 209nn.94, 118
Morgan, Lynn, 461n.103
Morgan, Patricia, 100, 122nn.36–37
Morgan, Stephen J., 365n.62
Morris, George, 423n.114
Morris, Gregory, 297n.104
Morris, Jodi Eileen, 209n.103
Morris, Miranda, 65n.106
Morris, Norval, 122n.17
Morrissey, Carlo, 89n.37
Morse, Barbara, 123n.98
Morse, Edward, 295n.26
Morselli, Carlo, 122nn.23, 32, 48, 241nn.67, 68
Mouren, Marie Christine, 167nn.26, 31
Mousain-Bosc, M., 167n.35
Moy, Ernest, 328n.6
Mrug, Sylvie, 240n.49, 329n.60
Mucci, Lorelei, 332n.215
Mufti, Lisa, 210n.142
Mugford, Jane, 268nn.119, 121
Mugford, Stephen, 268nn.119, 121
Mullen, P., 172n.226
Mullings, Janet, 126n.186
Mullins, Christopher, 386
Mulvey, Edward, 63n.36, 65n.94
Muncer, Steven, 65n.111, 171n.190
Muñoz, Ed, 66n.133
Murakami, Haruki, 365n.57, 366n.69

Murata, K., 167n.26
Muraven, Mark, 298n.139
Muris, Peter, 169n.116, 298n.131
Murphy, Declan G., 161
Murray, Charles, 24, 27n.55, 97, 122n.9, 162, 174n.298
Murray, Ellen, 242n.108
Murray, John, 154, 155
Murray, Joseph, 240n.23
Mustaine, Elizabeth Ehrhardt, 122n.54, 462n.185
Muth, Stephen, 460n.73
Myers, Jane, 296n.43
Myers, Wade, 332n.175
Myrdal, Gunnar, 179, 207n.8
Myrvang, Bjørn, 328n.23

Nachshon, Israel, 167n.20, 171n.192
Nadelmann, Ethan, 456, 464n.239
Nagin, Daniel, 45, 124nn.116, 118, 122, 138, 143, 125n.157, 275, 296nn.38, 45, 46, 47, 59, 297n.103
Najaka, Stacy, 455
Najman, Jake, 170n.157
Nalla, Mahesh, 267n.36
Nanjundappa, G., 462n.166
Nansel, Tonja, 331n.162
Napoleoni, Loretta, 492n.79
Nas, Coralijn, 173n.256
Nasheri, Hedieh, 365n.16
Nation, Maury, 240nn.42, 47
Natsuaki, Misaki, 65n.87
Navarro, Mireya, 460n.64
Neal, Daivd, 63n.26
Neapolitan, Jerome, 66n.119, 329nn.63, 64
Nee, C., 393n.91
Needleman, Herbert, 138, 168nn.83
Neilsen, Arnie, 328n.14
Nelken, David, 420n.3
Neller, Daniel, 329n.61
Ness, Roberta, 168n.83
Nevin, Rick, 138, 168n.79
Newman, Elana, 89n.37
Newman, Graeme, 320
Newman, Oscar, 106, 123n.91
Neziroglu, F., 167n.45
Ngo, Jennifer, 435
Nicewander, Alan, 297n.81
Nielsen, Matthew Amie, 45
Niemalä, Solja, 239n.9
Nieuwbeerta, Paul, 89n.47, 90n.87, 123n.78, 393n.82
Nieves, Evelyn, 331n.139
Nigg, Joel, 168n.80
Nikolas, Molly, 168n.80
Nilsson, Anders, 64n.69
Nilsson, L. L., 172n.236
Nisbet, Robert, 27n.15
Nixon, K., 167n.29
Nobiling, Tracy, 66n.130, 267n.53
Noonan, M., 89n.42
Novak, Kenneth, 124n.131
Novak, Scott, 463nn.225, 226
Nurco, David, 296n.34

Nuutila, Art-Matti, 239n.9
Nye, F. Ivan, 49, 64nn.72, 73

Oakes, Jeannie, 240n.36
Oakley, Barbara, 130, 166n.8
O'Brien, Kevin A., 365n.48, 366n.84
O'Brien, Mary, 460n.44
O'Brien, Robert, 63n.14
O'Callaghan, Mark, 174n.301
Odiah, Chuk, 328n.9
O'Donovan, Michael, 170n.139
O'Faolain, Julia, 332n.209
Ogle, Robbin, 210n.175
Ogloff, James, 161
O'Hara, Terence, 421n.51
O'Hear, Michael, 82, 90nn.105
Ohlin, Lloyd, 63n.40, 202–204, 206, 211nn.196–202
Oken, Emily, 168n.87
O'Leary, Cecilia, 266n.25
O'Leary, K. Daniel, 89n.26
O'Leary, Susan, 332n.214
Oliveira, Andrew, 422n.78
Olligschlaeger, Andreas, 27n.33
Olsen, Virgil, 64n.73
Olson, James, 122n.61, 123nn.65–66, 387, 392n.24, 393n.90
Olson, Lynn, 89n.33
Olsson, Martin, 174n.304
Olweus, Dan, 241n.82, 491n.50
O'Malley, Patrick, 63nn.27, 28, 461n.143
O'Neil, John, 421n.41
Oner, Ozgur, 161
Opjordsmoen, Stein, 328n.23
Opler, Mark, 168n.85
Orbuch, Terri, 297nn.70, 74
Orlebeke, Jacob, 168n.56
Ormrod, Richard, 88n.15
Ornstein, Miriam, 63n.35
Orth, Ulrich, 89n.38, 91n.112
Osborn, Denise, 89n.48
Osgood, D. Wayne, 63n.28, 65n.101, 144–145, 167n.49, 168n.54, 171n.164, 283, 295n.20, 297n.81, 298n.121
O'Shea, Timothy, 124n.123
Osman, Suzanne, 330n.106
Ostresh, Erik, 242n.116
Ostrow, Miriam, 463n.232
Ostrowsky, Michael, 210n.168
Otis, Melanie, 333n.226
Ouellet, Lawrence, 460n.65
Ouimet, Marc, 297n.102
Ouimette, Paige Crosby, 172n.202
Ousey, Graham, 298nn.119, 141
Overpeck, Mary, 331n.162
Owen, David, 364n.14
Owen, Michael, 170n.139
Owens, Elizabeth, 169n.120
Özbay, Özden, 242n.113
Özcan, Yusuf Ziya, 242n.113

Pagulayan, O., 167n.30
Paige, Karen, 168n.69
Palermo, Mark, 298n.122
Pallone, Nathaniel J., 169nn.92, 101

Palloni, Alberto, 27n.2
Palmer, S., 172n.226
Pan, En-Ling, 240n.16
Papillo, Angela Romano, 142n.127
Paradis, Emily, 89n.24
Park, Robert Ezra, 9, 27nn.20, 24, 25, 178, 184
Parker, Jocelyn, 365n.42
Parker, Karen, 66nn.128, 137, 208nn.47, 48, 87, 281, 297n.75
Parker, Robert Nash, 64n.70, 328n.3
Parra, Gilbert, 462n.161
Parson, Jeffrey T., 462n.190
Parson, Patrick J., 168n.84
Parsons, Deborah, 268n.128
Parvez, Faruque, 167n.31
Paschall, Mallie, 63n.35, 66n.140
Pasqualetti, Patrizio, 298n.122
Passas, Nikos, 420n.3, 421nn.20, 21
Pastore, Ann, 211n.208
Patchin, Justin, 207n.24, 478, 491nn.51, 52, 54
Pate, Tony, 124n.128
Patel, Vipul, 460n.53
Paternoster, Raymond, 45, 112, 124n.143, 125nn.151, 153, 157, 159, 174, 210n.152, 234, 243n.190, 267n.73, 295n.17, 296nn.55, 59, 297n.61, 298n.128
Patil, Sujata, 27n.39
Pattavina, April, 209n.98
Patterson, Gerald, 295nn.14, 20, 296n.42, 328n.27
Patterson, Orlando, 463n.211
Pattison, Philippa, 173n.265
Paulozzi, Len, 331n.166
Payne, Gary, 210n.159, 242n.134
Payne, Monique, 207n.19
Pazniokas, Mark, 459n.30
Pearson-Nelson, Benjamin, 328n.16
Pease, Ken, 89n.52, 124n.113, 388, 393n.94
Pease, Susan, 174n.292
Peete, Thomas, 125n.147
Pelham, Molina, Jr., 169n.116
Pelham, William, Jr., 240n.26
Pender, Kathellen, 266n.4
Penrod, Steven, 330n.116, 461n.109
Pepinsky, Harold, 259
Perera, Frederica, 168n.76
Perez, Cynthia, 64n.81, 295nn.6, 19, 24, 463n.206
Pérez-Peña, Richard, 421n.26
Perkins, Elizabeth, 393n.93
Perusse, Daniel, 171n.168
Petchesky, Rosalind, 267n.46
Peter, Katharin, 89n.42, 331n.161
Petersilia, Joan, 243n.157
Peterson, David, 242n.126
Peterson, Ruth D., 45, 64n.78, 207n.16, 209nn.107, 109, 126
Petraitis, John, 123n.69, 462n.162
Petras, Hanno, 296n.35
Petras, Tricia, 328n.2
Petrocelli, Matthew, 267nn.63, 64

Petrosino, Anthony, 27n.57, 268n.115
Petrosino, Carolyn, 268n.115
Pettit, Gregory, 209n.96, 240n.15, 296n.45
Pezzin, Liliana, 122n.33
Philaretou, Andreas, 491n.11
Philip, Michael, 66n.123
Phillips, Coretta, 89n.52, 388, 393n.94
Phillips, David, 153, 173n.241
Phillips, Julie, 66n.143, 207n.22
Phillips, Mary L., 161
Phillips, Monte, 169n.103
Phillips, Scott, 328n.22
Phillips, Susan, 172n.222
Phillips, Tim, 208n.63
Phillips-Plummer, Lynanne, 460n.73
Pi, Yijun, 210n.163
Piaget, Jean, 156, 173n.242
Pickering, Lloyd, 297n.105
Pickett, Kate, 167n.24, 210n.147
Pietz, Christina, 329n.61
Piha, Jorma, 239n.9
Pihl, Robert, 169n.90, 170n.152
Piliavin, Irving, 242nn.103, 106
Pilla, Ramini, 331n.162
Pinderhughes, Ellen, 295n.8
Pinel, Philippe, 7
Piquero, Alex, 90n.67, 105–106, 113,
    123n.85, 125nn.161, 174, 176,
    162, 168n.53, 172n.217, 173n.251,
    174n.293, 210nn.158–160,
    267nn.63, 64, 268n.101, 281,
    295n.17, 296nn.33, 48, 53, 55,
    297nn.75, 76, 90, 298nn.110, 111,
    133, 134, 136
Piquero, Nicole Leeper, 210n.176,
    241n.99, 296n.53, 422n.86
Pittman, David, 461n.132
Pitts, Marian, 460n.44
Planty, Mike, 331n.161
Platt, Antony (Tony), 207n.31, 266n.25,
    267n.65
Platt, Jerome J., 462n.156, 463n.234
Ploeger, Matthew, 65n.104, 241nn.69,
    78, 79
Plomin, Robert, 171nn.170, 175, 173n.275
Podboy, J. W., 169n.111
Podolsky, E., 167n.44
Pogarsky, Greg, 88n.12, 124nn.116, 118,
    122, 138, 125nn.153, 164, 176,
    297n.103, 298n.139
Pogrebin, Mark, 241n.101
Polge, A., 167n.35
Polk, Kenneth, 211n.207
Pollack, Otto, 65n.99
Pollack, Ricardo, 207n.1
Pollitt, Mark, 492n.64
Pomeroy, Wardell, 330n.111
Ponder, Michael, 254, 267n.49
Pontell, Henry, 421n.5, 492n.86
Poole, Eric, 241nn.97, 101
Popkin, Susan, 89n.33
Porche, Dianne, 422n.83
Port, Otis, 493n.109
Porteous, Lucy, 167n.37
Porter, David, 492n.87

Porter, Rebecca, 423n.136
Porter, Stephen, 330n.112
Posner, Daniel, 423n.114
Post, Charles, 169n.110
Post, Jerrold M., 356, 365n.64, 366n.70
Potter, Lloyd, 331n.166
Potterat, John, 460n.73
Potterton, Dave, 492n.83
Pottieger, Anne, 447, 462nn.174, 175
Poulsen, Kevin, 492n.59
Powell, Andrea, 207n42
Powell, Michael, 377
Powers, Ronald, 333n.228
Pradai-Prat, D., 167n.35
Pranis, Kay, 268n.124
Prasad, Monica, 432, 460n.45
Pratt, Travis, 173n.250
Prendergast, Michael, 462n.201
Presser, Lois, 269n.133
Preston, Julia, 105, 200
Pribesh, Shana, 208n.75
Price, Jamie, 208n.52
Price, Virginia, 460n.55
Pridemore, William, 209n.132
Prince, Emily, 167n.37
Prinz, Ronald, 167n.34, 296n.39
Prioietti, Luca, 298n.122
Priyadarsini, S., 241n.74
Proctor, Bernadette D., 207nn.6, 17
Proffitt, Fiona, 365n.45
Proulx, Jean, 123n.84, 296n.36
Pruitt, B. E., 173nn.262, 267, 174n.303
Pruitt, Matthew, 208n.47
Prunella, Jill, 169n.104
Przybylski, Roger, 462n.184
Pugh, Meredith, 63n.30, 64n.80, 242n.132
Pullmann, Michael, 172n.216

Qin, Ping, 171n.166
Quetelet, L. A. J. (Adolphe), 8, 27nn.16–17
Quigley, Brian, 320
Quinet, Kenna Davis, 89n.47, 332nn.173,
    182
Quinney, Richard, 249, 259, 265, 266n.17,
    267nn.41, 42, 268n.107, 421nn.17,
    27
Quinsey, Vernon, 393n.100
Quisenberry, Neil, 208n.60

Raab, Selwyn, 423nn.134, 135
Raaijmakers, Quinten, 173n.247
Rabasa, Angel, 365n.48, 366n.84
Radosevich, Marcia, 65n.114,
    241nn.84, 85
Raffalovich, Lawrence, 90n.95, 208n.50
Rafter, Nicole Hahn, 27nn.8–9, 13, 14, 28
Raghavan, Chitra, 462n.152
Raine, Adrian, 136, 137, 139, 142,
    167n.22, 169nn.91, 95, 102, 105,
    109, 170nn.136–137, 171n.193,
    173n.249, 296n.51, 328n.28
Raitt, F. E., 168n.66
Raj, Anita, 332n.215, 460n.53
Raja, Sheela, 88n.10
Raley, R. Kelly, 66n.142

Ramirez, Anthony, 487
Ramirez, G. B., 167n.30
Ramsey, Elizabeth, 295n.14
Ramsey, Susan, 89n.25
Rand, Michael, 63n.21, 64n.53, 331n.161,
    392n.57
Randall, Susan, 329n.68
Range, Lillian, 89n.21
Rankin, Bruce, 209nn.115, 120
Rankin, Joseph, 63n.23, 239n.13
Rapin, J., 167n.35
Rapp, Geoffrey, 115
Rappley, Marsha D., 168n.80
Rashbaum, William K., 366n.82
Ratcliffe, Jerry, 64n.48
Rathouz, Paul, 240n.26
Rathus, Spencer, 63n.34, 174n.281,
    241n.98, 459n.39
Raudenbush, Stephen, 207n.45, 209n.91
Rauh, Virginia, 136, 168n.76
Rawlings, Robert, 169n.103
Ray, Melvin, 243nn.147, 161, 165
Reagan, Ronald, 82, 97
Rebellon, Cesar, 210n.150, 239n.11,
    242n.139, 462n.176
Reboussin, Roland, 123n.83, 330n.86
Reckless, Walter, 9, 115, 226, 242nn.107, 108
Reddy, Marisa, 331n.167
Reed, M. D., 242n1.143
Regnerus, Mark, 242n.124
Regoeczi, Wendy, 331n.151
Regoli, Robert, 241n.97
Reidel, Marc, 331n.150
Reiman, Jeffrey, 266n.30
Reisig, Michael, 208n.77, 209n.93
Reiss, Albert, 170n.127, 174n.302, 226,
    242n.105, 328n.18, 422n.9
Reitzel, Deborah, 91n.114
Rekart, Michael, 460n.77
Ren, Xin, 240n.44
Rengert, George, 88n.6, 91n.124, 113,
    122nn.22, 47, 123nn.62, 64,
    125n.161, 463n.212
Rengifo, Andres, 45
Rennison, Callie Marie, 63n.22
Resick, Patricia, 65n.106, 90n.101
Resig, Michael, 290, 298n.129
Resnick, Heidi, 89n.27, 328n.20
Resnick, Patricia, 90n.99
Ress, Sian, 463n.231
Restifo, Nicholas, 328n.6
Reuter, Peter, 462n.186
Reynolds, B. J., 169n.106
Reynolds, Matthew, 330n.120
Reynolds, Morgan, 122n.17
Rheingold, Alyssa, 89n.27
Ribas-Fitó, Núria, 168n.75
Rice, Frances, 170n.139
Rice, Stephen, 66n.128
Rich, William, 169n.111
Rich-Edwards, Janet W., 168n.87
Richard, Chris, 491n.9
Richards, Jeffery, 459nn.40, 41
Richards, Jonathan, 491n.17
Richards, Maryse, 90nn.74, 76

Schwartz, Miguel, 332n.214
Schwendinger, Herman, 63n.44, 267 nn.74, 78
Schwendinger, Julia, 63n.44, 267nn.74, 78
Scott, Austin, 331nn.137, 138, 392nn.25, 26, 393nn.65, 72, 74
Scott, Peter, 27n.11
Scourfield, Jane, 171n.167
Scudder, Robert, 329n.33
Scuro, Pedro, 13
Sealock, Miriam, 66n.118, 210n.176
Seelers, Courtenay, 172n.237
Seeley, John R., 172n.212
Segal, David, 377
Segal, Nancy, 170nn.161–162
Seguin, Jean, 169n.90
Seidman, David, 63n.11
Seidman, Robert, 249, 266n.16
Sellers, Christine, 241n.87, 268n.93, 320
Sellin, Thorsten, 59, 66nn.146, 147, 115, 198, 211nn.179–182, 295n.4
Semiz, Umit, 161
Semple, W. E., 169n.101
Sennott, Charles M., 459n.33
Sepper, Elizabeth, 365n.27
Serra, Susan, 328n.6
Seto, Michael, 461n.110
Sever, Brion, 125n.165
Sewell, Kenneth, 328n.8
Shachmurove, Yochanan, 393nn.86, 87
Shackelford, Todd, 331n.147
Shah, Saleem, 167n.21
Shahar, Yael, 492n.71
Shalhoub-Kevorkian, Nadera, 306
Shane, Jon, 172n.237
Shane, Scott, 365n.29
Shannon, Elaine, 492n.61
Shannon, Lyle, 66n.149
Shapira, Nathan, 295n.23
Sharkey, Patrick, 190, 209nn.121, 122
Sharpe, Kimberly, 172n.231
Sharps, Phyllis, 320
Shaughnessy, Rita, 169n.121
Shaw, Clifford R., 184–186, 204, 206, 207nn.30, 32, 33
Shaw, Daniel, 240n.19
Shedd, Carla, 207n.19
Sheldon, William, 131, 166n.13
Shelley, Louise, 417
Shelly, Peggy, 123n.67
Shelton, Kelly, 297n.64
Shelvin, Mark, 71
Shenon, Philip, 459n.37, 460n.68
Shepherd, Joanna M., 115
Sheppard, David, 329n.59
Sher, Kenneth, 462n.161
Sherman, Lawrence, 63n.10, 116, 124n.132, 125n.178, 242n.104, 243n.166
Sherman, William, 377
Shevlin, Mark, 88n.18
Shields, Ian, 241n.96
Shifley, Rick, 268n.123
Shin, Hee-Choon, 295n.27
Shipley, Bernard, 125n.171

Shmueli, Dikla, 298n.139
Short, James, 49, 64nn.72, 73, 221, 241nn.71, 96
Shotland, R. Lance, 330n.91
Shover, Neal, 387, 392nn.8–10, 393n.88
Shower, Neal, 122n.35
Showers, Carolin, 65n.102
Shrout, Patrick, 243n.145
Sidwell, Clare, 463n.168
Siedfer, Jill Jordan, 392n.40
Siegel, Jane, 89n.22, 332n.206
Siegel, Larry, 63nn.8, 34, 170n.135, 174n.281, 241n.98
Sieler, DeDe, 172n.216
Sigurdsson, Jon Fridrik, 161
Silbereisen, Ranier, 296n.30
Silberman, Matthew, 124n.143
Sildiroglu, Onur, 161
Silke, Andrew, 339, 365n.37, 365n.63
Sillanmä, Lauri, 239n.9
Silva, Phil, 64n.81, 67n.159, 168n.89, 169n.115, 171n.194, 172n.203, 174n.283, 295nn.9, 19, 296nn.37, 44, 298nn.142, 143
Silver, Clayton, 239n.7
Silver, Eric, 172nn.231, 233, 235, 209n.123
Silverman, Ira, 329n.33
Silverman, Jay, 332n.215, 460n.53
Silverman, Jeanna, 239n.7
Silverman, Robert, 211n.177, 242nn.118, 129
Simeon, Jovan, 167n.39
Simister, John, 64n.64, 168n.57
Simmons, Catherine, 461n.111
Simon, David, 422n.96
Simon, Leonore, 63n.29, 169n.114, 297n.60
Simon, Patricia, 295n.26
Simon, Rita James, 27n.35, 65n.107
Simon, Thomas, 331n.166
Simons, Leslie, 298n.124
Simons, Marlise, 330n.75
Simons, Ronald, 210n.153, 243n.163, 281, 290, 297n.77, 298nn.124, 126, 329nn.32, 41
Simos, Alexander, 328n.6
Simpson, John, 268n.91
Simpson, M. K., 174nn.299–300
Simpson, Murray, 174nn.299–300
Simpson, Sally, 66n.118, 210n.169
Sims, Barbara, 91n.113, 266nn.19, 32
Singer, Jane, 393n.97
Singer, Merrill, 460n.78
Singer, Simion, 268n.97
Singh, Piyusha, 124n.133
Singhvi, Nikhil S., 422n.107
Sinha, V. K., 137
Sisson, Melanie, 365n.50
Sitren, Alicia, 125n.167
Sjodin, Dru, 91n.140
Skinner, William, 241n.86
Skogan, Wesley, 208nn.64, 66, 67, 81, 209n.101
Skoler, Daniel, 422n.90

Skondras, M., 170n.131
Slade, Eric, 240n.33, 329n.30
Slaughter, Ellen, 207n.37
Slavkovich, Vesna, 167n.31
Slawson, John, 162, 174n.287
Sloan, John, 90n.69, 124n.129, 331n.160
Sloat, Alison, 172n.221
Slocum, Lee Ann, 210n.169
Smailes, Elizabeth, 45, 155, 460nn.70, 82
Small, Albion W., 8
Smallish, Lori, 169n.118
Smart, Carol, 65n.110
Smeenk, Wilma, 296n.54
Smiljanich, Kathy, 459n.35
Smith, Andra, 161
Smith, Anthony, 460n.44
Smith, Barbara, 91n.117
Smith, Brad, 66n.133
Smith, Carolyn, 170nn.149, 151, 154, 240nn.22, 32, 39, 295n.25, 329n.37, 462n.153
Smith, Daniel, 88n.14, 462n.157
Smith, David S., 392n.1
Smith, Donald, Jr., 393n.93
Smith, Douglas, 64nn.74, 76, 210n.169, 242n.104, 243nn.166, 184, 267n.73
Smith, G. T., 462n.171
Smith, Judith, 207nn.13, 14
Smith, M. Dwayne, 64n.71
Smith, Michael, 124n.136
Smith, Philip, 208n.63
Smith, Timothy, 295n.25
Smith, William, 123n.77
Smolej, Mirka, 27n.32, 62n.2, 89n.28
Snedker, Karen, 89n.34
Snell, Tracy, 126n.193
Snook, Brent, 393n.83
Snyder, Thomas, 89n.42, 331n.161
Solomon, Brett Johnson, 240n.46
Somers, Leigh, 393n.105
Somkin, Carol, 209n.92
Sommers, Ira, 14–15, 27n.38
Sonmez, Guner, 161
Sonuga-Barke, Edmund, 167n.37
Sorenson, Ann Marie, 297n.102, 298n.116
Sorenson, J. E., 422n.55
Sorenson, Jon, 114, 115
Sorenson, T., 422n.55
Sorrells, James, 172n.219
Soulé, David, 90n.85
Sourander, Andre, 239n.9
Souter, David Hackett, 472
Spaccarelli, Steve, 89n.40
Sparks, Richard, 266n.18, 267n.61
Speck, Richard, 143
Speckart, George, 463n.203
Spelman, William, 124nn.134, 137, 125n.183, 207n.41
Spergel, Irving, 208nn.52, 73
Spitzberg, Brian, 326, 333nn.264, 267
Spohn, Cassia, 66n.130, 234, 243n.179, 267n.53, 311, 330nn.90, 121, 122, 331n.128
Spracklen, Kathleen, 240n.48
Springett, Gwynneth, 172n.221

Spunt, Barry, 328n.24
Spurzheim, Johann K., 7
Squires, George, 207n.46
St. Augustine, 432
Stack, Steven, 114, 115
Stafford, Mark C., 122n.18, 173n.255
Stahelski, Anthony, 366n.71
Stalin, Joseph, 255
Stanley, Jay, 493n.106
Stark, Rodney, 90nn.78, 79, 209n.111, 217, 241n.57
Starles, R. M., 169n.106
Stattin, Hakan, 174n.296
Steele, Bruce, 459n.6
Steele, Tracey, 114, 115
Steen, Sara, 243n.177
Steer, Colin, 167n.23
Steffensmeier, Darrell, 46, 55, 64nn.55–57, 65nn.90, 100, 110, 112, 208n.52, 267n.51, 373–375, 392n.21
Steffensmeier, Renee Hoffman, 65n.110
Stegink, Lewis, 167n.40
Stein, Judith, 242n.117
Stein, Nancy, 268n.86
Steinberg, Laurence, 173n.251, 298n.136
Steiner, Hans, 172n.217
Steinhardt, Barry, 493n.106
Stephan, James, 126n.193
Stephens, Gene, 13, 268n.122
Sterk, Claire, 463n.229
Sterk-Elifson, Claire, 39, 63nn.41, 42, 447, 462n.172
Stermac, Lana, 89n.24
Stetson, Barbara, 241n.66
Steury, Ellen Hochstedler, 172n.223
Stevens, Tomika, 328n.20
Stevenson, Jim, 167n.37
Stevenson, Richard, 393n.89
Stewart, Claire, 173n.254
Stewart, Eric, 90n.71, 210n.153, 297nn.77, 94, 329n.41, 463n.229
Stewart, Potter, 439
Stice, Eric, 216
Stigler, George J., 121n.4
Stobbe, Mike, 51
Stoddart, Clare, 167n.39
Stolzenberg, Lisa, 65n.88, 66n.128, 114, 115
Stone, Emily, 64n.46
Stone, Laurence, 332n.210
Storr, C. L., 208n.61
Stout, Ronnie, 328n.5
Stouthamer-Loeber, Magda, 90n.68, 174nn.283, 291, 240n.45, 295nn.16, 18, 26, 28, 296nn.31, 51, 329nn.42, 62
Stowell, Jacob, 64n.82
Strang, John, 463n.231
Stratton, Howard, 298n.148
Straus, Murray A., 240n.31, 319–320, 329nn.31, 38, 332nn.207, 213
Stretesky, Paul, 168n.78, 207n.44, 422n.98
Streuning, Elmer, 243n.145
Strodtbeck, Fred, 241n.96
Strom, Kevin J., 333n.237

Strueber, Daniel, 328n.10
Stuart, Gregory, 89n.25, 328n.8
Stults, Brian, 66n.128
Stumbo, Phyllis, 167n.40
Su, S. Susan, 210n.172, 295n.27
Sudermann, Marlies, 91n.114
Sullivan, Christopher, 172n.237, 240n.25
Sullivan, Dennis, 259, 268nn.103, 105, 106
Sun, Ivan, 209n.104
Sung, Hung-en, 122n.19
Sunstein, Cass R., 119, 126n.194
Sunyer, Jordi, 168n.75
Surguladze, Simon, 161
Surratt, Hilary, 433, 460n.58
Surtees, Rebecca, 435
Susser, Ezra S., 168n.85
Sutherland, Edwin, 4, 9, 10, 14, 16, 27nn.3, 42, 162, 174nn.284, 288, 219, 220, 226, 238, 241nn.62–64, 372–373, 392n.14, 396, 406, 421nn.9, 10, 422n.68
Swahn, Monica, 328n.19, 333n.262
Swanson, Christopher B., 240n.37
Swartz, Bruce, 492n.99
Swartz, James A., 125n.155
Swartz, Marvin, 173n.239
Sweeten, Gary, 243n.164
Sykes, Gresham, 223, 225, 238, 241nn.91, 93–95, 267n.38
Symons, Donald, 330n.104

Ta, Myduc, 333n.259
Tait, David, 330nn.107, 114
Tajima, Emiko, 328n.25
Takagi, Paul, 267n.46
Tamminen, Tuulk, 239n.9
Tang, Deliang, 168n.76
Tannenbaum, Frank, 233, 243n.174
Tanskanen, Antti, 137
Tarde, Gabriel, 148, 171n.198
Tardiff, Kenneth, 208n.51, 329n.55
Tark, Jongyeon, 51, 84, 91n.131
Tatchell, Renny, 298n.147
Tatchell, Thomas, 298n.147
Taub, Richard P., 182
Taylor, Alan, 170n.160, 171n.165
Taylor, Bruce, 63n.13, 89n.31
Taylor, Dawn, 172n.221
Taylor, Ian, 249, 256, 266n.14, 267nn.68, 69
Taylor, Jeanette, 171n.167
Taylor, John, 393n.101
Taylor, Mark Lewis, 260, 268n.111, 393n.91
Taylor, Natalie, 421n.15
Taylor, Ralph, 123n.63, 207n43, 208nn.68, 83, 209nn.97, 131
Taylor, Robert, 123n.100, 124n.135
Taylor, Terrance, 240n.44
Taylor, Wendy, 123nn.90, 102
Teplin, Linda, 27n.41
Terrill, William, 208n.77
Testa, Maria, 330nn.78, 80, 82, 95
Tewksbury, Richard, 122n.54, 462n.185

Thapar, Anita, 170n.139
Thatcher, Robert, 169n.97
Thaxton, Sherod, 210n.156
Theall, Katherine, 463n.229
Theerathorn, Pochara, 123n.93
Theisen, Gary, 461nn.137
Thomas, Chandra, 239n.2
Thomas, Evan, 328n.1
Thomas, Melvin, 66n.139
Thomas, Stephen, 45
Thomas, Suzie Dod, 268n.86
Thomas, W. I., 9, 17
Thomlinson, R. Paul, 329n.61
Thompson, Carol, 422n.93
Thompson, Ginger, 459n.37, 460n.68
Thompson, Kevin, 268nn.97, 98
Thompson, Martie, 172n.215
Thompson, Melissa, 100, 122nn.26, 31
Thompson, Wright, 239n.1
Thornberry, Terence, 63n.31, 64n.73, 66n.117, 67n.155, 170n.151, 240nn.32, 38, 39, 48, 241n.77, 278, 295n.25, 329n.37, 462n.153
Thornburg, Nathan, 492n.61
Thorne, Ian, 393n.101
Thrasher, Frederick, 27n.22
Thurman, Quint, 378, 392n.36
Tibbetts, Stephen, 241n.99, 296n.53, 297n.90, 422n.86
Tice, Peter, 295n.28
Tifft, Larry, 63n.34, 259, 268nn.103, 104, 106
Tillyer, Marie Skubak, 122n.57
Timpson, Sandra, 460n.67
Tita, George, 90n.68, 328n.2
Titchener, Edward, 156
Titterington, Victoria, 89n.43, 267n.83
Tittle, Charles, 64n.74, 124n.125, 207n.26, 211n.205, 234, 239n.4, 243nn.183, 188, 284, 297n.102, 298nn.113, 123, 130
Tjaden, Patricia, 333n.260
Tobias, Aurelio, 295n.18
Tobias, J. J., 392nn.4, 5
Tobin, Kimberly, 123n.79
Tobin, Michael, 168n.83
Tobin, Terri, 116, 125n.180
Tobler, Nancy, 298n.148
Tolmunen, Tommi, 137
Tomas, Joseph, 295n.18
Tomaskovic-Devey, Donald, 63n.33
Tomasovic, Elizabeth, 328n.22
Tonn, Jessica, 491n.53
Tonry, Michael, 13, 122nn.13, 17
Tontodonato, Pamela, 91n.117
Toomey, Rosemary, 170n.163
Topalli, Volkan, 225, 392n.59
Torrent, Maties, 168n.75
Tosouni, Anastasia, 492n.86
Towns-Miranda, Luz, 393n.99
Townsend, Wendy, 455
Townsley, Michael, 393n.95
Tracy, Paul, 60, 66nn.117, 148, 67nn.156, 157, 125n.169
Trapani, Catherine, 65n.102

Traub, Leah Goldman, 173n.238
Trebach, Arnold, 461n.130
Treiber, Kyle, 124n.142
Tremblay, Pierre, 122n.32, 241nn.67, 68
Tremblay, Richard, 67n.158, 169n.90,
    171n.168, 275, 296n.38, 296n.45,
    297n.102
Trendle, Giles, 490n.3
Treno, Andrew, 208n.78
Trickett, Alan, 89n.48
Triplett, Ruth, 209n.104, 243n.181
Tristan, Jennifer, 216
Trumbetta, Susan, 123n.83, 330n.86
Tseng, Li-Jung, 462n.163
Tsuang, Ming, 171n.163
Tuch, Steven, 66n.135, 254, 267n.48
Tully, Lucy, 171n.165
Tunnell, Kenneth, 102, 122n.51, 221,
    241n.76, 447, 462n.182
Tunstall, Nigel, 161
Turic, Darko, 170n.139
Turner, Charles, 295n.25
Turner, Heather, 88n.15
Turner, Michael, 89n.62, 124n.131,
    330n.96, 333n.263
Turner, Scott, 393n.104
Turpin-Petrosino, Carolyn, 27n.57
Tyler, Kimberly, 330n.92, 462n.170
Tzavaras, Nikos, 328n.5

Uehlinger, Tim, 229
Uggen, Christopher, 100, 122nn.26, 31,
    268nn.95, 100, 297nn.64, 69
Ullman, Sarah, 330n.85
Ullrich, Simone, 172n.228
Ulman, Arina, 319, 332n.207
Ulmer, Jeffery, 375
Ulrich, Yvonne, 320
Umhau, John, 169n.103
Unfold, Douglas, 393n.100
Unnever, James, 239n.12, 240n.18
Urbina, Ian, 166n.1

Vaccaro, Donato, 462n.164
Vaillant, George, 283
Valiente, Carlos, 170n.138
Valier, Claire, 307n.34
Van de Weyer, Courtney, 137
van den Bergle, Pierre, 166n.16
Van den Bree, Marianne, 170n.139,
    171n.167
Van Den Haag, Ernest, 125n.154
van den Oord, Edwin, 174n.286
van der Laan, Peter, 296n.54
van Geen, Alexander, 167n.31
van Goozen, Stephanie, 168n.56
Van Gundy, Karen, 242n.139, 462n.176
Van Hoof, Anne, 173n.247
Van Kammen, Welmoet, 240n.45, 296n.31
van Kijk, Mirjam, 330n.113
van Koppen, Peter J., 123n.76, 321, 333n.221
Van Loh, Timothy, 297n.105
Van Voorhis, Patricia, 242nn.114, 119,
    269n.133
Van Wormer, Katherine, 328n.9

Vander Ven, Thomas, 242nn.120, 131
VanDeusen, Karen, 461n.109
Vandewater, Elizabeth, 155
Vanzile-Tamsen, Carol, 330nn.78, 80, 82
Varano, Sean, 207n.24
Vardi, Nathan, 492n.58
Vargas, Elizabeth, 324
Vashista, Anish, 421n.31
Vasquez, Bob Edward, 124n.108
Vatis, Michael A., 490n.3
Vazsonyi, Alexander, 65nn.102, 108,
    171nn.188–189, 287, 297nn.83, 105
Veach-White, Ernie, 172n.216
Velez, Maria, 207n.16, 209nn.108, 109
Venables, Peter, 170n.137, 173n.249
Veneziano, Carol, 173n.246
Veneziano, Louis, 173n.246
Venkatesh, Sudhir Alladi, 113, 125n.162,
    290, 298nn.137, 138
Verhulst, Frank, 296n.54
Verlur, D. E., 462n.166
Vermeiren, Robert, 172n.229, 240n.29,
    296n.55
Vermeule, Adrian, 119, 126n.194
Vernon, Philip, 170n.140
Verona, Edelyn, 173n.273
Veronen, Lois, 90n.100
Veysey, Bonita, 65n.84, 172n.237
Vicomandi, David, 298n.122
Victor, Timothy, 27n.56
Viding, Essi, 145, 171n.170, 173n.275
Vieraitis, Lynne, 51, 331n.160
Vigdor, E. R., 51
Viinamaki, Heimo, 137
Villaume, Alred, 268n.112
Villemez, Wayne, 64n.74
Virkkunen, Matti, 167n.46, 169n.89,
    170nn.128, 129
Viscusi, W. Kip, 493n.110
Visher, Christy, 243n.153, 328n.25
Vitaro, Frank, 296n.45
Volavka, Jan, 167n.21, 168n.63, 169n.100,
    170n.145
Vold, George, 248, 249, 416, 423
Von, Judith, 90n.100
Von Hentig, Hans, 89n.55
Von Hirsch, Andrew, 119–120,
    126nn.195–197
Voronin, Yuri A., 417
Voss, Harwin, 55, 65n.114
Vossekuil, Bryan, 331n.167
Vowell, Paul, 241n.70
Vuchinich, S., 296n.42
Vungkhanching, Martha, 462n.161

Wade, Emily, 216
Wadsworth, Tim, 208n.49
Wagner, Charles, 393n.99
Wagner, H. Ryan, 173n.239
Wagner, Richard, 172n.221
Waite, Linda, 297n.70
Waite, Phillip, 298n.147
Wakschlag, Lauren, 167n.24
Waldo, Gordon, 124nn.119, 143,
    125n.159

Walker, Alice, 428
Walker, Jeffery T., 124n.108
Walker, Richard, 491n.25
Walker, Robert, 333n.268
Walker, Samuel, 234, 243n.179
Wall, April, 492nn.76, 78
Wallace, C., 172n.226
Wallace, Harry, 125n.146
Wallace, John, 462n.168
Wallace, Roderick, 207n.28
Wallerstedt, John, 126n.185
Walsh, Anthony, 132, 166nn.18, 19,
    168nn.51, 55, 210n.167, 297n.97,
    330n.105
Walsh, Marilyn, 392nn.6, 23
Walters, Glenn, 171n.195
Walton, Paul, 249, 266n.14
Walz, Liz, 268n.102
Wang, Eugene, 89n.35
Wang, Jichuan, 463n.192
Wang, Morgan, 64n.61
Wanson, Jeffrey, 173n.239
War, Tony, 173n.265
Ward, David A., 122n.18, 173n.255,
    298n.113
Ward, John, 485
Ward, Tony, 173n.254
Waring, Elin, 124nn.134, 137, 125n.173,
    422n.110
Warner, Barbara, 63n.38, 207n.10,
    329n.43
Warner, John O., 167n.37
Warr, Mark, 65n.104, 221, 240n.52,
    241nn.54, 73, 78, 79, 281, 297nn.71,
    72, 330n.81
Warren, Janet, 123n.83, 308, 330n.86
Wartella, Ellen, 155
Wasilchick, John, 122n.22,
    123n.64
Wasserman, Gail, 167n.31
Waters, Glenn, 171n.174
Watt, Toni Terling, 228, 242n.122
Watzke, Stefan, 172n.228
Wayner, Peter, 392n.45
Weatherburn, Don, 90n.90, 297n.64,
    393n.89
Weatherston, David, 366n.66
Webb, Barry, 123n.97
Webb, Nancy, 393n.99
Webb, Vincent, 45
Weber, Eugen, 27n.6
Webster, Cheryl Marie, 124n.140
Webster, Daniel, 320
Webster, Pamela, 297nn.70, 74
Wechsberg, Wendee, 436, 460n.66
Weekes-Shackelford, Viviana, 331n.147
Weeks, Margaret, 460n.78
Wei, Evelyn, 295n.18
Weihe, P., 167n.26
Weimann, Gabriel, 492n.75
Weinberg, Heather, 172n.221
Weiner, Neil Alan, 437, 459n.32, 460n.84
Weingart, Saul, 463n.221
Weis, Joseph, 63n.39, 65n.110, 174n.281
Weis, Robert, 255

SUBJECT INDEX

ABA (American Bar Association), 309, 488
abortion, 42–43, 351
Abramoff, Jack, 401
Abu Ghraib scandal, 354
Abu-Jamal, Mumia, 254
abuse. *See* child abuse; sexual crimes/abuse
account verification scams, 474
ACLU (American Civil Liberties Union), 86, 361, 483, 486
acquaintance rape, 308–309
acquaintance robbery, 321–322
active precipitation, 77
actual authority, 407
"actual malice," 312
actus reus, 22, 23
ADC (Aid to Dependent Children), 204
addict robbers, 321
addiction-prone personality, 446
ADHD (attention deficit hyperactivity disorder), 133, 140–141, 151, 215
adolescent-limited offender, 277, 288
adolescents. See teenagers
adoption frauds, 399, 475
adoption studies, 146
adult drug dealers, 448–449
adult escort services, 433, 435–436
advanced fee schemes, 407
Advanced Vehicle Interrogation and Notification system (AVIAN), 485
advertising, false claims, 408
advertising spam, 477
Advocate, The (magazine), 426
Afghanistan, 339, 350, 354, 443, 452
African Americans
    community deterioration and, 186
    "driving while black" phenomenon, 37, 56, 264
    minority group poverty, 180
    modern plight of young male, 256
    race and crime, 55–59
    racism and discrimination against, 56, 254, 255
    self-control and impulsivity in, 289
    as underemployed, 181
African criminal enterprises, 416
Aftermath (Brison), 71
after-school programs, 107
age
    in crime patterns/trends, 42, 46, 52–53
    sexual motivation in rape, 310
    and victimization, 74, 75, 313, 322, 325–326
age of onset, 275–277
age-graded theory, 278–282, 291, 294
aggravated assault, 30, 31, 44, 317
aggravated rape, 310

aggression, 133–137, 141–143, 146, 155, 156, 303
    See also strain theories
aging out
    causes of, 275–276, 282–283
    cognitive theory and, 158
    and the General Theory of Crime, 289
    hormonal influences, 134
    overview on, 53
    strain and, 196
    See also developmental theory
Aid to Dependent Children (ADC), 204
AIDS and drug use, 445, 446, 449, 456
air bag theft, 382
air loan fraud, 407
airplane hijacking, 105–106
airport security, 486
alcohol consumption
    abuse and dependence, 445, 457
    and crime, 8, 52–53, 303, 449, 456
    date rape and, 309
    in gateway model, 447
    onset and addiction, 133
    prohibition of, 442
    school failure/delinquent behavior, 227
    self-reporting, 45
    situation crime prevention and, 106
    by teenagers, 444
    and victimization, 70, 77, 78
alcoholic robbers, 321
alexithymia, 151
alien conspiracy theory, 415
alien smugglers, 21
alienation view of terrorism, 356–357
All God's Children (Butterfield), 56
allergies, 135
al-Qaeda, 339, 340, 348, 350, 353–354, 361, 363, 479
amateur receivers, 375
American Bar Association (ABA), 309, 488
American Civil Liberties Union (ACLU), 86, 361, 483, 486
American Dream, 190, 193, 194, 200
American Psychiatric Association (APA), 159
American Psychological Association, 162
Ames, Aldrich Hazen, 341, 343
Amnesty International, 427, 428
amphetamine-type stimulants (ATS), 443
amygdala dysfunction, 161
anal stage, 149
androgens, 134–135, 141
anger rape, 308
animal breeding ranches, 352
Animal Liberation Front (ALF), 352, 355
anomie, 8, 191–194, 197

Anonymous group, 471
anoxia, 286
antiabortion terrorists, 351, 429
Anti-Drug Abuse Act of 1986, 451
Anti-Drug Abuse Act of 1988, 451
Anti-Phishing Working Group, 482
antisocial behavior
    androgen-related male traits, 134–135
    the antisocial personality, 159–161
    cognitive and learning deficits and, 133
    by crime victims, 71–72
    in developmental criminology, 10
    diet and, 136–137
    neurological disorders, 138–139
    parental efficacy and, 215–216
    peer relations, 217
    in principal life course theories, 278
    psychodynamics of, 149–150
    of the psychopath, 160, 161
    psychosurgery for, 164
    in trait theories, 131–132
antisocial potential (AP), 284
antithesis, 248
apparent authority, 407
apprehension rates, 110–111
Arab nationalists, 350
arbitrage, 409
Arcand, Philip, 380
arousal theory, 141–142, 155, 156, 160–161
arson, 19, 20, 30–32, 388–389
arson for profit, 389
arson fraud, 389
ART Act (Artists' Rights and Theft Prevention Act of 2005), 482
Arthur Andersen, 402
artificial intelligence, 39
Artists' Rights and Theft Prevention Act of 2005 (ART Act), 482
Asian crime statistics, 12, 13
asphyxiophilia, 430
assassination, 335–336
Assassins (Muslim Order of the), 349
assault
    aggravated, 30, 31, 44, 317
    criminal law history and, 19, 20
    firearms and, 49
    in the home, 318–320
    nature and extent of, 317–318
    as Part I crime, 30, 31
    statistics on, 41, 317–318
assault weapons, 50
associational fences, 375
Assumption Deterrence Act of 1998 (Identity Theft Act), 473, 482
atavistic anomalies, 7

central nervous system diseases, 141
cerebral allergies, 135
CFAA (Computer Fraud and Abuse Act), 472
charitable organization scams, 475, 480–481
check fraud, 379
chemical influences, 133, 134, 136, 137, 140
chemical restraints/straitjackets, 141
Chicago Area Project, 204
Chicago School Group, 8–9
child abuse
    causes and statistics, 318–319
    cognition and information processing, 158
    international crime trends, 13
    link to crime by victims of, 153, 216, 304
    neglect, 216, 218
    See also sexual abuse of children
Child Online Protection Act of 1998, 471
child pornography, 439, 440, 470, 471, 483
child poverty, 179–180
child prostitution, 437
Child Sexual Abuse Prevention Act, 438
children and the media, 154
Children's Internet Protection Act of 2000, 471
child-to-parent violence, 319
Chinese crime trends, 12, 13
Chinese criminal gangs, 416, 418
chiseling, 399–400
chivalry hypothesis, 54
Cho, Seung-Hui, 129, 130
choice theory. *See* rational choice theory
chronic offenders
    crime patterns and, 59–60
    developmental theory on, 10
    factors encouraging, 100–101
    inadequate cognitive processing, 157
    and the incapacitation effect, 116–117
    labeling effects, 234
    life course persisters, 277
    psychopaths as, 161
    specific deterrence and, 113–116
    strain and, 196
    three strikes policy, 57, 60, 116
    trait theory and, 132
    See also developmental theory
"chronic six percent," 59
chronic unemployment, 186–187
chronic victimization, 76
Church of Scientology, 471, 475
CIA (U.S. Central Intelligence Agency), 343, 344
cigarette smoking mothers, 132–133
circuit travelers, 436
cities. *See* urbanization/urban landscape
civil liberties, 361, 479, 486–488
class conflict, 10, 11, 17, 18, 25
    See also social classes
class-crime relationship, 49, 52
classical criminology, 5–6, 11, 96–97

Clean Air Act, 412, 413
clearance rates, 31, 32
clergy scandals, 430
climate. *See* weather
closed-circuit television (CCTV) surveillance cameras, 108
closure, 379
cocaine
    crack cocaine, 43, 101, 447, 450, 457
    cultivation and use, 443–445, 450
    dealing, 103, 452
    history of use, 442
    as recreational drug, 448
Cocaine Anonymous, 453
Codarcea, Emil, 469
Code of Hammurabi, 18
code of honor (thieves), 370, 373, 374
code of silence (Mafia), 418
code of the streets, 201
coercion, 284
coercion hypothesis, 353
coercive violence, 304
cognitive differences, 55
cognitive theory, 149, 156–158
cohort research, 38, 59, 60, 143–144
collective efficacy, 188–190
college boy subculture, 200, 202
college campus interpersonal crime, 309, 326
Columbia/HCA Healthcare Corporation (HCA), 405
Commerce Clause (U.S. Constitution), 411
commercial robbery, 321
commitment, 227, 228
commitment to conformity, 226
commodity market chiseling, 400
common law, 19, 20, 376
Communications Decency Act of 1996, 471
Communist Manifesto (Marx), 9, 246
community. *See* neighborhood
Community Action Program, 204
community deterioration, 186
community fear, 187–188
comparative research, 114
compliance strategies, 412–413
Comprehensive Crime Control Act, 82
Comprehensive Drug Abuse Prevention and Control Act of 1970, 450
compurgation, 18
computer data mining, 39–41
computer fraud, 469–470
Computer Fraud and Abuse Act (CFAA), 472
computer information theft, 470
computer monitoring software, 485
Computer Security Institute (CSI), 481, 482
computer virus, 476
computer vision and image processing technology, 484
computer worm, 476
computer-assisted personal interviewing (CAPI), 35
computer-related crimes. *See* cyber crime
con artist, 373, 383

concentric zones theory, 184–186, 190
Condition of the Working Class in England in 1844 (Engels), 248
conduct disorder (CD), 140, 145, 150, 151
conduct norms, 198
conferencing process, 263
Confessions of a Dying Thief (Steffensmeier and Ulmer), 374
confidence games, 373, 383
conflict, 246–248
conflict criminology. See critical criminology
conflict gangs, 203
conflict resolution, 259
conflict view, 17–18, 25
conformity, 192
conscience, 149
consensus view, 16–18, 25, 265
consent, 311
conservative agenda, 250, 255
conspiracy, 20
"constructive malice," 312
constructive possession, 376
contagion effect, 46–47, 145
containment theory, 226
contextual discrimination, 234
continuity of crime, 60
contractual relationships, 22
Control Balance Theory, 284, 291
control strategies. *See* deterrence
Controlled Substances Act of 1984, 451
Convention on Cybercrime, 483
conventional values, 223–226
convergence, 55, 58–59
"copping" area, 448
Coppola, Michael, 415
copyright infringement, 472
CORMAP (correctional mapping), 484
corner boy subculture, 200
corporate crime, 397, 401–403, 406–411, 470, 479
corporate culture theory, 411
correctional mapping (CORMAP), 484
Cosa Nostra, 415
Couey, John Evander, 431
Counterfeit Access Device and Computer Fraud and Abuse Law of 1984, 482
counterfeit checks, 379
Counterterrorism Bureau (NYC), 360
court advocates, 83
court system. *See* justice system
Courtney, Robert R., 399, 409, 410
covert pathway, 275
crack cocaine, 43, 101, 447, 450, 457
crackdown, 111
credit card theft/fraud, 379–380, 384, 397, 474, 481
Crime, Shame, and Reintegration (Braithwaite), 260
Crime Analysis Tactical Clearing House (CATCH), 41
Crime and Everyday Life (Felson), 80
Crime and Human Nature (Wilson and Hernnstein), 285
Crime and Personality (Eysenck), 10

delinquent subcultures theory, 198–200, 202, 204

demystify, 253

denial-of-service attack, 471, 480

Denmark adoption study, 146

Department of Homeland Security (DHS), 359, 363, 486, 487

depression, 136, 151

desert theory, 119–120

desistance, 60, 272, 280
    See also aging out; developmental theory

deterrence
    arson, 389
    in classical criminology, 6, 11
    in contemporary criminal law, 19
    controlling prostitution, 437–438
    crime statistics role in, 11
    cyber crime, 482–483
    drug control, 451–455
    ethics and research methodology, 24
    general deterrence, 109–113, 120–121
    in-school programs, 292
    of larceny/theft, 109, 378–379, 382
    of pornography, 440–441
    preemptive deterrence, 256
    primary prevention programs, 163
    secondary prevention programs, 163
    security system, 78, 84, 385, 387
    situational crime prevention, 106–109
    social controls for, 188–189
    specific deterrence, 113–116
    target hardening, 84, 102, 106–107, 378
    technology for, 483–485
    tertiary prevention programs, 163
    victims and self-protection, 84
    white-collar crime, 412–413

deterrence theory, 10, 14

development. *See* human development

developmental theory
    basics of, 10, 11, 272
    biosocial factors and, 285, 290–292
    evaluating, 291–292
    life course fundamentals, 273–274
    psychological traits in, 285, 290, 292
    public policy implications of, 283, 292–293
    See also latent trait theories; life course theories

deviance amplification effect, 233, 234

deviant behavior, 4–5, 16

deviant cliques, 217, 232

deviant place theory, 78, 81, 87

Diagnostic and Statistical Manual of the American Psychiatric Association (APA), 159

dialectic method, 248

Dickinson, Rebecca, 436

diet, 132–137

Differential Association Theory, 219–222, 237

differential coercion theory, 284, 291

differential enforcement, 231–232

differential opportunity theory, 202–204

Differential Reinforcement Theory, 222–223, 237

diffusion of benefits, 109

Digital Millennium Copyright Act (DMCA), 472

direct conditioning, 222–223, 237

Director of National Intelligence (DNI), 358, 363

Dirie, Waris, 427

discipline. *See* punishment

discouragement, 109

discrimination, 56, 62, 234

disgruntled employee violence, 324, 325

disinhibiting, 155

disorders, 151

disorganization. *See* social disorganization theory

disputatiousness, 305

disruptive behavior disorder (DBD), 151, 155

"dissing," 201

diversion programs, 235

Division of Labor in Society, The (Durkheim), 8

division of markets, 408

divorce, 214–215

DMCA (Digital Millennium Copyright Act), 472

DNI (Director of National Intelligence), 358, 363

dog owner manslaughter, 312

"doing gender," 257

Doing Justice (Von Hirch), 120

domestic surveillance, 342

domestic violence
    evolutionary theory on, 146
    gun control and, 50
    overview on, 318–320
    relationship stress, 71
    special assistance following, 32
    specific deterrence for, 116
    spousal homicide, 313–314
    by victims of child abuse, 304
    See also child abuse

Doorsteps Neighborhood Program (Toronto), 107

"double marginality," 256

dramatization of evil, 233

drift, 223–225

Driggers, Paul William, 104

driver monitoring and surveillance, 485

driving while black (DWB) phenomenon, 37, 56, 254

driving while intoxicated (DWI), 106

dropouts, 44, 216–217

drug abuse
    AIDS and, 445, 446, 449, 456
    cohort study involving, 39
    control strategies, 5, 451–456
    and crime, 43, 100, 101, 449–450
    deviance and, 4
    drug courts, 455
    gateway model, 447
    impact on marriage and employment, 282
    international crime trends, 443, 451–452, 456, 457

and the law, 450–451
    legalization of drugs, 442, 455–457
    linked to violence, 14–15, 303
    prescription drugs, 471
    by prostitutes, 436, 437, 449
    as public order crime, 16, 18
    rationality of, 103
    self-reporting, 45
    types of, 447–449
    victimization and, 77–81
    See also cocaine; drug dealing

Drug Abuse Control Act of 1965, 450

Drug Abuse Resistance Education (D.A.R.E.), 453

drug control, 5, 451–456

drug courts, 455

"drug czar," 451

drug dealing
    cocaine, 103, 452
    control strategies, 451–453
    criminal mentors, 221
    criminal terrorism, 355
    gang involvement in, 43, 447–448, 452
    international crime trends, 443, 451–452, 456, 457
    legalization of drugs, 455–457
    life in the drug trade, 200
    online drug distribution, 471
    by organized crime, 414, 416
    rational choice in, 100, 101, 103
    robbery and, 321, 322, 385
    types of dealers, 447–448

drug gateway, 447

drug testing, 453–454, 456

drunk driving, 106, 457

Duncan, David, 402

Dunn, Linda Wade, 383

Dupré, Ashley, 425

duress defense, 23

Durham-Humphrey Act of 1951, 450

DWB (driving while black), 37, 56, 254

dysfunctional families. *See* family dissolution/dysfunction

Dyslogic Syndrome (Rimland), 130

DZ (dizygotic) twins, 144, 145

early childhood. See human development

early onset, 59–60

Earth Liberation Front (ELF), 351–352

EAS (electronic article surveillance) systems, 378

Eastern European crime trends, 416, 434–435

eating disorders, 151

Ebbers, Bernie, 403

ecological view, 9, 11

ecology of crime
    and General Theory of Crime, 286–288
    and the incapacitation effect, 117
    interpersonal violence, 308, 320
    location, 9, 287, 288
    patterns associated with, 47–48, 72–73, 185–186, 235, 384
    time of day, 47, 72–73, 384, 385
    See also weather

economic compulsive behavior, 303
economic crimes, 370
  See also organized crime; property crime; white-collar crime
economic disparity, 178–182, 190, 194, 245–246
Economic Espionage Act (EEA) of 1996, 341–342
economic forces. *See* conflict view; socio-economic conditions
economic loss, 70
economic opportunity, 100
eco-terrorism, 351–352, 356
ecstasy, 444, 445
ectomorphs, 131
edgework, 106
education. *See* schools
Edwards, Edwin, 400
EEA (Economic Espionage Act) of 1996, 341–342
EEG (electroencephalograph), 139, 148
effective parenting, 215–216, 286, 289–290
egalitarian families, 258
ego, 149–151
ego ideal, 149
Eighth Amendment rights, 97, 344
El Salvadorian gangs, 177
elder abuse, 74
eldercide, 313
elderly, victimization of the, 74, 383
election fraud, 337–338
Electra complex, 149
electroencephalograph (EEG), 139, 148
electronic article surveillance (EAS) systems, 378
elite deviance. *See* white-collar crime
e-mail chain letter, 474
email surveillance, 360
embezzlement, 19, 383–384, 404, 410
emotional cognition deficit, 151
Emperor's Club, 425, 426
empirical research, 253, 254
employee drug-testing strategies, 453–454, 456
employee fraud, 404, 409
employee Internet-access abuse, 482
employment, and desistance, 280, 281
employment programs, 454–456
endomorphs, 131
England. *See* Great Britain
English common law, 19
English Convict, The (Goring), 148
Enron Corporation, 402–403, 411, 413
enterprise crimes, 396
  See also organized crime; white-collar crime
enterprise theory of investigation (ETI), 418
entrapment defense, 23
environment, 8, 132, 144, 146, 153
environmental contaminants, 135–137
environmental crimes, 47, 396, 398, 408–409, 411–414

Environmental Crimes Strike Force (Los Angeles), 411
EPA (Environmental Protection Agency), 409, 411, 412
equipotentiality, 132
equity skimming fraud, 407
eros, 149
escort services, 433, 435–436
Espinoza, Edward, 99
espionage, 339–342, 363
ETA (Euzkadi Ta Askatasuna), 352
etailing fraud, 474–475
ethical issues in criminology, 23–24
ethnicity, 44, 45, 76
ETI (enterprise theory of investigation), 418
European crime trends, 12, 13, 45, 85
Evano, Ronald and Mary, 33
Evans, David, 301
evolutionary theory, 146–148, 302–303, 310
Executed God, The (Taylor), 260
exhibitionism, 430, 431
expedience serial killers, 316
experimental research, 38–39
exploitation crimes, 284, 400, 434–435, 470
"express malice," 312
expressive crimes, 49
extinction, 109
extortion, 373, 412
extroversion, 159

facial recognition systems, 486
failure to act, 22
false claims advertising, 408
false pretenses. *See* fraud
familicide, 317
family
  family deviance, 143–144, 146, 215
  as informal social control, 188, 228
  patriarchal, 256
  power-control theory, 257–258
  siblings, 43, 144
  socialization and crime, 214–216
  See also parents
family dissolution/dysfunction
  disrupting development, 273, 274, 278
  family deviance, 143–144, 146, 215
  involvement in terrorist groups, 356
  link to ADHD, 140
  and the psychopath, 160
  race and crime rates, 57–58
  single-parent families, 44, 214–215, 258
  strain and, 196, 214
Family Entertainment and Copyright Act of 2005, 482
family problem factor, 60, 153
Farahan, Victoria, 399
Fast Track, 292–293
Fastow, Andrew, 402, 403
FBI. *See* U.S. Federal Bureau of Investigation
FCPA (Foreign Corrupt Practices Act), 402–403, 409

fear of crime, 71, 187–188, 302, 326
fear quotient, 160, 161
Federal Bureau of Investigation's Uniform Crime Report. See UCR
federal drug abuse statutes, 450–451
Federal Gun Control Act of 1968, 50
federal political crime statutes, 338, 339
Federal Violent Crime Control and Law Enforcement Act of 1994, 50
Federal Welfare Reform Act of 1996, 204
feeblemindedness, 162
felony, 19
felony murder, 312
Female Offender, The (Lombroso), 54
femicide, 306
feminist views, 55, 256–257, 438
fences, 370, 373–376, 387
fetal alcohol syndrome, 457
feticide, 312–313
fictitious identity fraud, 407
Fifth Amendment rights, 344
file sharing, 472
filicide, 313
finger scanning, 486–487
Finnerty, Collin, 301
Finnish biosocial studies, 136, 141
firearms
  alcohol and violent crime, 303
  assault weapons, 50
  backscatter imaging system detection, 485
  crime data and, 43, 49
  gun control debate, 50–51
  handguns, 43, 49–51
  possession by gangs, 43
  and victimization, 78, 84
FireSafe Families (Rhode Island), 389
First Amendment rights, 324, 361, 408, 438–440, 471, 483
first-degree murder, 20, 312
FISA (Foreign Intelligence Surveillance Act), 360
five-finger discount, 31, 102, 142, 373, 377–379
fixation, 149
flash houses, 370
flashover, 389
focal concern theory, 198, 199, 204
food additives, 133, 134, 137
forcible rape
  California rape law, 311
  causes of, 309–310
  clearance of, 31
  as common-law crime, 19, 20
  date rape, 78, 158
  definition of, 306–307
  firearms in, 49
  history of, 307
  international crime trends, 12–13
  justice system abuse following, 70
  and the law, 310–312
  and the military, 307
  as Part I crime, 30, 31
  pornography link to, 439
  rational choice in, 105

schizophrenia, 151–153
school behavior/performance factors
    African American male, 180
    bullying, 144, 215, 315
    and chronic offending, 60, 282
    high-school dropouts, 44, 216–217
    leading to learning disabilities (LD),
        139–140
    shaping the life course, 292
school crime, 43, 73, 129
schools
    attachment to, 227, 228
    college campus rape, 309
    the educational experience, 216–217
    in-school prevention/intervention
        programs, 292–293
    labeling in, 232
    in restorative justice, 261
    substance-abuse prevention strategies,
        453, 456
scientific method, 4, 6, 7, 253
Scream (movie), 325
SDM (social development model), 278
SEC (U.S. Securities and Exchange
    Commission), 401, 402, 411, 412
Second Amendment rights, 50
secondary deviance, 233, 234
secondary prevention programs, 163
second-degree murder, 312
"secret deviants," 234
secret shopper scams, 475
Securities Act of 1933, 472
securities chiseling, 399–400
securities fraud, 95–96, 407, 415,
    467, 472
security breaches, 481–482
security systems, 78, 84, 385, 387,
    486–487
"seduction of crime," 141
segregation, 57, 62
self-concept, 226
self-control, 138–139, 285–290, 292
self-control theory, 287, 411
    See also GTC (General Theory of Crime)
self-defense, 23, 50, 51, 78, 84
self-referrals, 406
self-report survey, 24, 35–37, 45–46,
    53–56, 449–450
Seligmann, Reade, 301
sentencing circle, 261
sentencing practices, 57, 233–234, 246,
    250
separation anxiety, 150–151
September 11 attacks, 336, 340, 354,
    358–360, 482, 486
serial murder, 105, 315–316
serial rape, 308
sex offenders
    registration of, 85, 108, 260
    restorative justice in Ireland, 263
    sexual predator laws, 21
    types of forcible rape, 308
    undercover exposure of, 3
sex tourism, 433, 434–435, 437–438
sex trade, 416, 426, 433–435, 437–438

sex-oriented businesses zoning ordinances,
    440–441
sexual abuse of children
    by Catholic priests, 430
    child pornography, 439, 440, 470, 471,
        483
    cyber stalking, 3, 477
    international statistics, 13
    leading to careers in prostitution,
        436–437
    linked to substance abuse, 446, 447
    pedophilia, 430–431
    rationality of, 105
    sexual tourism, 434–435, 437–438
sexual arousal, 113, 310, 316, 389
sexual crimes/abuse
    cognitive deficits, 158
    crime-prone victims of, 216
    cyber stalking, 477–478
    international trends in, 13
    labeling and, 214
    leading to criminal acts, 310
    long-term trauma following, 70, 71, 81,
        446
    overview on, 319
    paraphilias, 430–431
    patriarchy and crime, 257
    pornography link to, 439
    rationality in, 105
    and sadistic personality disorder, 159
    sexual arousal/motivation in, 113, 310
    as underreported, 35
    victim advocates, 83
    See also forcible rape; prostitution; sex
        offenders
sexual equality, 438
sexual purity, 306
sexually related material distribution, 427,
    470–471, 483
Shadowcrew, 473
shame, 107, 112, 260–261, 263, 264
Shepard, Matthew, 322, 324
Sherman Antitrust Act, 408, 413
shield laws, 311
shifting blame, 223, 224
"shooting galleries," 446
shoplifting, 31, 102, 142, 373, 377–379
shoplisting, 474
shopping mall crime, 80
short-term transportation theft, 383
siblicide, 76
siblings, 43, 144
siege mentality, 187–188
Siemens, 401–402
sign-in rosters, 474
sildenafil, 133
silent second mortgage fraud, 407
sin. *See* morality
single photon emission computed tomogra-
    phy (SPECT), 139
single-parent families, 44, 214–215, 258
"Situational Action Theory," 112
situational crime prevention, 106–109, 118
Situational Crime Prevention (Clarke), 106
situational inducement, 372

skeezers, 436
skilled thieves, 370
Skilling, Jeffrey, 402, 403
skills mastery and resistance training
    (SMART), 292
slag code, 477
sleep pattern analysis, 485
SMART (skills mastery and resistance train-
    ing), 292
Smiley, Edward Forbes , III, .70, 369
Smith, David, 476
smugglers, 370, 448
sneak thief, 373
"sneaky thrills," 142
snitches, 378
social adaptations, 192
social bond, 227, 278
social bond theory, 227–230
social capital, 280
social change crimes, 336, 337
social classes
    bias in IQ test, 162, 163
    and the consensus view of crime, 16
    crime and social structure, 178–180, 190
    crime patterns and, 47, 49, 52
    differential enforcement, 231–232
    under Hammurabi Code, 18
    lower class, 178–183, 197, 198
    middle class, 178, 186, 195, 197–200,
        202, 203
    racism and economic disparity, 178–182
    substance abuse, 446, 447
    underclass, 179–182
    and victimization, 74
    in white-collar crimes, 396, 412, 413
    See also conflict view; critical
        criminology
social conditions. *See* socioeconomic
    conditions
social conflict, 246–248
    See also critical criminology
social control, 15, 16, 19, 183, 188–189,
    231–234
social control theory, 218, 226–230, 235,
    237
social development model (SDM), 278
social disorganization theory
    concentric zones theory, 184–186, 190
    overview of, 182–184, 206
    the social ecology school, 186–190
social disparity, 57
social ecology/ecologists, 186–190
social facts, 14
social goals, 192–194
social harm, 16, 428
social institutions, 189, 190, 193–194,
    217–218
social isolation, 179, 181
social learning theories
    basics of, 148–149, 153, 237
    differential association theory, 219–222,
        237
    differential reinforcement theory,
        222–223, 237
    evaluating, 224, 226

neutralization theory, 223–226, 237, 410
    in the social process approach, 218
    substance abuse causes, 446–447
    on violence, 153, 156, 310, 320
social policy. *See* justice policy
social positivism, 8
social process theories
    evaluating, 234–235
    overview of, 218–219, 237–239
    public policy implications of, 235
    social control theory, 226–230
    social reaction theory, 230–234
    socialization and crime, 214–218
    storylines, 236
    See also social learning theories
social psychology, 9, 10
social reaction theory, 218, 230–235, 237
Social Reality of Crime (Quinney), 249
social structure theory
    evaluating, 185–186, 203–204
    overview on, 182–183
    public policy implications, 204–205
    socioeconomic structure and crime, 42,
        46, 80, 178–180
    the truly disadvantaged, 181–182
    See also cultural deviance theories; so-
        cial disorganization theory; strain
        theories
social theory, 4, 14
socialism, 246, 255, 256
socialization
    and crime, 214–219
    gender and development, 54–55
    impact on terrorism, 357
    nuture theory, 162
    psychopaths and traumatic, 160
    rape and male, 310
    shaping criminal behavior, 130
    and violent crime, 303–304
    See also human development
socialization view, 9, 11
sociobiology, 131, 164–165
Sociobiology (Wilson), 131, 164
socioeconomic conditions
    chronic offending, 60
    crime and social structure, 178–180
    crime patterns/trends, 44–47, 49, 52
    disrupting development, 273
    gang membership, 178
    general deterrence, 113
    impact on workplace violence, 324, 325
    influence on crime rates, 42, 47, 48, 57
    involvement in terrorist activities, 356,
        357
    liberal feminist theory, 55
    mentally ill criminals, 153
    producing violent subculture, 305
    prostitution to address, 436–437
    race and social disparity, 57
    in trait theory, 132
    victimization rates, 74, 78
    white-collar crime, 410
    See also critical criminology; social struc-
        ture theory
sociology of law, 4, 14, 16

sociopath, 159, 316
sodomy, 21–22, 429
software robot, 480
software theft/code-cracking, 470, 481
solicitation, 20
somatotype school, 131
Sopranos (TV show), 414, 418
source control, 451–452, 456
South African restorative justice, 263
Southeast Asian drug trade, 443, 452
spam, 477
specific (special) deterrence, 113–116, 118
SPECT (single photon emission computed
        tomography), 139
Spitzer, Eliot, 425, 426
spoofing, 473–475
sporting houses, 433, 437, 438
spousal abuse. *See* domestic violence
spousal homicide, 313–314
spree killers, 317
spying, 339–342, 363
St. Guillen, Imette, 69–70
stabilized junkies, 448
stalking, 21, 325–326
standard of living, 180
Stark, Benjamin, 476
"stash dealers," 447
state political crime, 342–344
state secrets, 336
state violence, 342–343
state-corporate crime, 343
state-sponsored terrorism, 354, 356, 358
statistics. *See* crime data
status frustration, 199
status-based violations, 102
statutory crimes (*mala prohibitum*), 19
statutory rape, 31, 308–309
Stern, Howard, 429
Stetler, Linda, 399
Stevens, Douglas Richard, 3–4
Stewart, Martha, 409, 412
stigma/stigmatization
    attempts to combat, 235
    drug treatment programs, 454
    in interactionist view, 18
    from labeling, 232
    link to crime, 234
    low IQ, 163
    as shaming, 260
sting operations, 398–399
stock market chiseling, 400
stock market manipulation, 95–96, 397,
        407, 415
stolen identity fraud, 407
storylines, 235, 236
strain, 183
strain theories
    components of, 183, 190–191, 206
    concept of anomie, 191–193, 197
    macro-level theory (institutional anomie
        theory), 193–194, 197
    micro-level theory (general strain the-
        ory), 194–197
stranger relations murder, 315
stratified society, 178

straw buyer, 407
"straw" purchasers, 51
street crime, 232, 251, 321, 370
street efficacy, 190
street junkies, 448
street values, 201, 225
"street-level sex workers," 432
streetwalkers, 433
stress, 71
strict liability crimes, 23
structural strain, 191
structural theory, 9, 11, 253
structure of society
    and crime trends, 42, 46, 80
        effects of street lighting, 106, 108, 109
    in situational crime prevention, 106
student relations murders, 315
student stalking, 326
Students for a Democratic Society (SDS),
        351
subculture, 183, 199, 305–306, 373, 446
subculture of violence, 305–306
subjectivity, 17
submission, 284
substance abuse
    causes of, 446–447
    and chronic offending, 60
    dangers of, 441–442
    deviance and, 4
    extent of, 442–445
    factor in arrest rates, 226
    gateway theory, 447
    history of, 442
    initiation into, 221–223
    parental efficacy and, 216
    sexuality and, 445
    and violent crime, 303
    See also alcohol consumption; drug
        abuse
substantive criminal law, 16
subterranean values, 223
sufferance, 325
sugar consumption, 134
suicide bombers, 356
suitable targets, 78, 79
superego, 149–151
supermax prisons, 115–116
surplus value, 251
surveillance, 108, 342, 360–361, 378,
        485–488
survey research, 34–38
Swaggi, Vincent, 373
Swango, Michael, 315
Swartz, Marc, 402
swatting, 475
Sweden, 146, 152, 153, 438
swindles/swindlers, 383, 398–399
Symantec Corporation, 482
symbolic interaction theory, 230
symbolic reparation, 261
synthesis, 248
system abuse, 70–71
system balance, 262
systematic forgers, 379
systematic rape, 307

systematic review, 39
systemic link, 303

target-hardening strategies, 84, 102, 106–107, 378
target-removal strategies, 378
targets, 76, 84, 102, 104–107, 386–388
tautological theory, 287
tax evasion, 406, 412
technological destruction, 468
technology, 252, 468, 479, 483–488
teen pregnancy, 45, 228
teenagers
  brain development in, 142–143
  curfew laws, 107
  drug use/dealing by, 443–445, 447–448, 456, 457
  victimization of, 71, 73, 74
  violent media engagement, 154
  See also juvenile delinquency
Telemarketing Associates, 408
television violence, 43–44, 154–155
temperance movement, 442, 456
temperature and crime rates, 47–48, 147, 235, 287
temporal patterns. See weather
terror cells, 347
terrorism
  cult terrorists, 349, 354–356
  cyber, 479–481
  definitions of, 346, 348
  forms of, 348, 350–355
  group organization, 355
  history of, 348–350
  motivation for, 355–358
  overview on, 346–348, 363
  response to, 358–362
  terrorist groups online, 355, 357, 359, 360
  See also Muslim terrorists
terrorist killers, 317
tertiary prevention programs, 163
testosterone, 134
thanatos, 149, 302
theft. *See* larceny/theft
theft rings, 415
theory construction and testing, 14, 16
theory of anomie, 192–193
therapy organizations, 163
There Goes the Neighborhood (Wilson), 182
thesis, 248
thieves, 372–376
Thinking about Crime (Wilson), 97
three strikes
  aimed at chronic offenders, 60, 116
  larceny categories, 376
  link to stranger relations murders, 315
  racial threat effect, 57
  shortcomings of, 118
  viewed by restorative justice, 260
thrill serial killers, 315
thrill-seeking hate crimes, 323
Thugee cult, 349
ticking bomb scenario, 344, 345
time of day, 47, 72–73, 384, 385

time-series studies, 114
Timmendequas, Jesse, 85, 86
tipping point, 111, 115
Titan Rain, 479
torture, 344–346
"torture warrant," 345
"touting" drugs, 448
trade restraint, 408
Trading West Inc. (TWI), 399–400
traffic violations, 30
trafficking in prostitution, 416, 433–435, 437
train robbery, 371
trait theory
  foundations of, 11, 130–132
  psychological traits and characteristics, 158–163
  the psychopath, 160–161
  public policy implications of, 163–164
  See also biosocial theory; psychological trait theories
transitional neighborhoods, 184–185
transmitter wristbands, 485
Travel Act (Interstate and Foreign Travel or Transportation in Aid of Racketeering Enterprises Act), 416
treason, 339, 340
treatment, 163, 164, 235, 453, 454, 456
trespass in taking, 376, 382–384
trial by ordeal/combat, 18–19
Tri-West Investment Company, 472
Trojan horse, 476, 477
truly disadvantaged, 181–182, 203
Truly Unique Collectibles, 398
Truth and Reconciliation Commission (South Africa), 263
truth-in-sentencing laws, 60
turning points in crime, 279–280
twin behavior, 144–145
Tyco International Ltd., 402
tying arrangement, 408

UCR (Uniform Crime Report)
  on burglary, 384
  evaluating the, 31–33, 37
  on gender, 53
  on interpersonal violence, 308, 313
  overview of the, 30–34, 37
  on prostitution, 432
umma (universal Islamic community), 354
Unconquerable Nation (Jenkins), 361
underclass, 179–182
underemployment, 181
underreported crime, 32, 35
under-vehicle surveillance system, 485
unemployment, 42, 79, 181, 186–187, 255
unified conflict theory, 249
Uniform Crime Report. *See* UCR
Union of Death Society, 349
United Nations definition of terrorism, 346
United Nations Mission in Nepal (UNMIN), 338
United Nations Survey of Criminal Justice Systems (UNCJS), 12

United Nations World Drug Use Survey, 443
United Nations World Health Organization (WHO), 12, 13, 318
United States Visitor and Immigrant Status Indicator Technology (US-VISIT), 486–487
University of Michigan Institute for Social Research (ICR), 36
"upcoding," 404
Urban Institute, 216
urbanization/urban landscape
  anomie and, 8
  concentric zones theory, 184–186, 190
  crime level increase and, 80
  cycles of, 188
  interpersonal violence, 308, 313
  social ecology, 9
  social isolation in, 181
  temperance movement response to, 442
  and victimization, 73, 78–80
  See also social structure theory
U.S. Bureau of Justice Statistics, 30, 34, 38, 450
U.S. Central Intelligence Agency (CIA), 343, 344
U.S. Constitution
  Commerce Clause of the, 411
  Eighth Amendment rights, 97, 344
  Fifth Amendment rights, 344
  First Amendment rights, 483, 324, 361, 408, 438–440, 471
  Fourth Amendment rights, 108
  Second Amendment rights, 50
U.S. Department of Health and Human Services, 318
U.S. Department of Homeland Security (DHS), 359, 363, 486, 487
U.S. Department of Justice, 401, 411, 413
U.S. Department of State, 346
U.S. Environmental Protection Agency (EPA), 411, 412
U.S. Federal Bureau of Investigation
  crime date collection by, 30
  cyber spying by the, 479
  fighting terrorism/political crime, 343, 359, 363
  interpersonal violence statistics, 317–318, 320, 323
  on property crime, 376, 383, 384
  regional crime rate data, 48
U.S. Food and Drug Administration, 412
U.S. Securities and Exchange Commission (SEC), 401, 402, 411, 412
U.S. Sentencing Commission, 413–414
U.S. Supreme Court
  dog owner manslaughter ruling, 312
  First Amendment and hate crimes, 324
  on obscenity, 439, 440, 458
  reliance on criminologists, 14
  software file sharing case, 472
USA Patriot Act (USAPA) of 2001, 360–361, 363, 479, 482
USB Securities LLC scam, 400
utilitarianism, 5–6, 96
Uyghur separatists, 352

PHOTO CREDITS

This page constitutes an extension of the copyright page. We have made every effort to trace the ownership of all copyrighted material and to secure permission from copyright holders. In the event of any question arising as to the use of any material, we will be pleased to make the necessary corrections in future printings. Thanks are due to the following authors, publishers, and agents for permission to use the material indicated.

Chapter 1. 3: © Gueorqui Pinkhassov/ Magnum Photos; **6:** T. H. Matteson, "The Trial of George Jacobs, August 5, 1692." Oil on canvas. 39 × 53 inches. #1,246. Peabody Essex Museum, Salem, MA; **7:** © The Image Works; **15:** © Stan Honda/ AFP/Getty Images; **17:** © Nicholas Kamm/ AFP/Getty Images; **21:** © AP Images/Jane Rosenberg.

Chapter 2. 29: © AP Images/Jacqueline Larma; **36:** © AP Images/David Kidwell; **39:** © AP Images/Greg Cooper; **47:** © AP Images/Tucson Police Department; **52:** © AP Images/Jose Luis Magana; **54:** © David De Lossy/Photodisc/Getty Images; **56:** © AP Images/Steve Yeater.

Chapter 3. 69: © AP Images/Tina Fineberg; **72:** © David McNew/Getty Images; **74:** © AP Images/*Kokomo Tribune*/ Tim Bath; **79:** © AP Images/Alex Wong; **82:** © AP Images/Rich Pedroncelli; **83:** © AP Images/Ed Reinke; **86:** inset, © AP Images/Charles Rex Arbogast.

Chapter 4. 95: © Reuters/Jeff Zelevansky; **98:** © Reuters/Bill Greene/Pool; **99:** inset, © AP Images/Nick Ut; **102:** © AP Images/ Nashville Police Department; **103:** © AP Images/Mary Ann Chastain; **110:** © Reuters/ Shannon Stapleton; **117:** © AP Images/*Tampa Tribune*/David Kadlubowski.

Chapter 5. 129: © AP Images/Amy Sancetta; **133:** © AP Images/Pool/*Foster's Daily Democrat*/Mike Ross; **138:** © AP Images/Jim Cole; **140:** Dr. Alan Zametkin/ Clinical Brain Imaging, Courtesy of Office of Scientific Information, NIMH; **148:** © AP Images/Mark J. Terrill; **150:** © AP Images/ Lisa Cassidy, Pool; **152:** inset, © David J. Phillip/Pool/Reuters/Corbis; **157:** © AP Images/Michael Conroy.

Chapter 6. 177: © AP Images/Edgard Garrido; **180:** © Mario Tama/Getty Images; **184:** © Ralf-Finn Hestoft/Corbis; **191:** © AP Images/Bob Child; **193:** © Joe Raedle/Getty Images; **198:** © Robert Nickelsberg/Getty Images; **202:** © Spencer Platt/Getty Images.

Chapter 7. 213: © AP Images/Gregory Smith; **216:** © AP Images/Steve Helber; **217:** © AP Images/John Amis; **221:** © Simon Wheatley/Magnum Photos; **229:** inset, © AP Images/Federal Police/HO; **230:** © AP Images/John Miller.

Chapter 8. 245: © AP Images/Gene Blythe; **252:** © Richard Clement/Reuters/Landov; **254:** inset, © AP Images/Chris Gardner; **257:** © A. Ramey/PhotoEdit; **258:** © AP Images/Harry Cabluck; **262:** © Charles Ommanney/Getty Images.

Chapter 9. 271: © Volusia County Sheriff's Office via Getty Images; **275:** © AP Images/ Consignment Gallery release via Bedford, N.H. Police Dept; **277:** © AP Images/ *Anchorage Daily News*/Bill Roth; **281:** © Roberto Schmidt/AFP/Getty Images; **285:** © Gabriele Stabile/Getty Images; **289:** © David McNew/Getty Images.

Chapter 10. 301: © AP Images/Chuck Burton; **303:** © AP Images/Gwen Mayor; **307:** Nicolas Poussin, c. 1637–38. "The Rape of the Sabines," Louvre, Paris, France/ Bridgeman Art Library; **316:** © AP Images/ Kathy Johnson; **320:** © AP Images/FBI, HO-File; **323:** © AP Images/*York Daily Record*/Bil Bowden.

Chapter 11. 335: © AP Photo/Wally Santana; **338:** © Reuters/Gopal Chitrakar; **340:** inset, © AP Images/IntelCenter; **343:** inset, © AP Images/Mark Wilson; **344:** © AP Images/Manuel Balce Ceneta; **347:** © David Furst/AFP/Getty Images; **351:** © AP Images/Elaine Thompson; **357:** © Bay Ismoyo/AFP/Getty Images; **361:** © AP Images/Shiho Fukada.

Chapter 12. 369: © AP Images/Bob Child; **371:** © Mary Evans Picture Library/The Image Works; **377:** inset, © Seth Wenig/ Landov; **381:** © AP Images/Nam Y. Huh; **384:** © AP Images/Dima Gavrysh; **388:** © AP Images/Kenneth Roberts.

Chapter 13. 395: © Stockbyte/Getty Images; **398:** © Erik S. Lesser/Getty Images; **401:** © Chip Somodevilla/Getty Images; **405:** inset, Darren Greenwood/ Design Pics, Inc./Alamy; **410:** © AP Images/KMBC-TV; **412:** © AP Images/Louis Lanzano; **415:** © AP Images/Mike Derer/ Pool.

Chapter 14. 425: © Timothy A. Clary/ AFP/Getty Images; **427:** © AP Images/ Kamenko Pajic; **429:** © AP Images/Eric Risberg; **431:** inset, © Brian LaPeter/Pool/ Reuters/Landov; **436:** © AP Images/Leah Hogsten/Pool; **441:** © AP Images/Louis Lanzano; **449:** © AP Image/Dean Lewins; **454:** © AP Photo/*Anchorage Daily New*/ Bill Roth.

Chapter 15. 467: © Associated Press/AP Images; **469:** © AP Images/George Rizer, Pool; **479:** © DSK/AFP/Getty Images; **481:** © AP Photo/Andy Wong; **484:** © AP Images/Martin Cleaver.

Repeated iconic images (cracked gray wall) © Medioimages/Photodisc/Getty Images; (orange rock formation) © Michael Medford/Riser/Getty Images

Inside Cover Front. Casare Lombroso: Stock Montage, Inc.; Cesare Beccaria: © The Granger Collection, New York; Jeremy Benthan: © The Granger Collection, New York; Emile Durkheim: © Bettmann/ Corbis; Karl Marx: Stock Montage, Inc.; Sheldon and Eleanor Glueck: Courtesy of Art & Visual Materials, Special Collections Department, Harvard Law School Library.

Preface. xiv: © AP Images/Gerald Herbert

Table of Contents. 1. vi: © Nicholas Kamm/AFP/Getty Images; **2. vii:** © AP Images/Jose Luis Magana; **3. vii:** bottom, © David McNew/Getty Images; **4. vii:** right, © AP Images/Nashville Police Department; **viii:** top, © Reuters/Shannon Stapleton; **5. viii:** bottom, © AP Images/ Lisa Cassidy, Pool; **7. ix:** © AP Images/ John Amis; **10. x:** middle, © AP Images/ *York Daily Record*/Bil Bowden; **11. x:** top, AP Images/IntelCenter; **13. xi:** left, © Chip Somodevilla/Getty Images; **14. xi:** right, © AP Images/Eric Risberg; **15. xii:** © AP Photo/Andy Wong.

TO THE OWNER OF THIS BOOK:

I hope that you have found *Criminology: Theories, Patterns, and Typologies,* Tenth Edition, useful. So that this book can be improved in a future edition, would you take the time to complete this sheet and return it?
Thank you.

School and address: _____

_____

Department: _____

Instructor's name: _____

1. What I like most about this book is: _____

_____

_____

2. What I like least about this book is: _____

_____

_____

3. My general reaction to this book is: _____

_____

_____

4. The name of the course in which I used this book is: _____

_____

5. Were all of the chapters of the book assigned for you to read? _____

   If not, which ones weren't? _____

6. In the space below, or on a separate sheet of paper, please write specific suggestions for improving this book and anything else you'd care to share about your experience in using this book.

_____

_____

_____

_____

_____

_____

TAPE HERE.
DO NOT STAPLE.

TAPE HERE.
DO NOT STAPLE.

FOLD HERE

WADSWORTH
CENGAGE Learning

NO POSTAGE
NECESSARY
IF MAILED
IN THE
UNITED STATES

BUSINESS REPLY MAIL
FIRST-CLASS MAIL   PERMIT NO. 34   BELMONT CA

POSTAGE WILL BE PAID BY ADDRESSEE

Attn: Carolyn Henderson Meier,

Criminal Justice Editor

Wadsworth Cengage Learning
10 Davis Drive
Belmont, CA   94002-9801

FOLD HERE

OPTIONAL:

Your name:_____ Date: _____

May we quote you, either in promotion for *Criminology: Theories, Patterns, and Typologies*, Tenth
Edition, or in future publishing ventures?

Yes: _____   No: _____

Sincerely yours,

Larry J. Siegel

Time Line of Criminological Theories

Theory	1775	1800	1825	1850	1875	1900	1925	1939
ORIGIN Classical Theory		Beccaria *On Crimes and Punishments* (1764)				Kant *Philosophy of Law* (1887)	Brockway *The American Reformatory* (1910)	Mabbott *Punishment* (1939)
CONTEMPORARY THEORY (Rational) Choice Theory (p.98)		Bentham *Moral Calculus* (1789)	Bentham *The Rationale of Punishment* (1830)					
ORIGIN Positivist Theory		Gall *Cranioscopy/Phrenology* (1800)			Lombroso *Criminal Man* (1863)	Garofalo *Criminology* (1885)	Kretschmer *Physique and Character* (1921)	Hooton *American Criminal* (1939)
CONTEMPORARY THEORY Biosocial Theory (p.132)					Dugdale *The Jukes* (1877)	Ferri *Criminal Sociology* (1884)	Goring *The English Convict* (1913)	
ORIGIN Positivist Theory					Maudsley *Pathology of Mind* (1867)	Tarde *Penal Philosophy* (1912)	Freud *General Introduction to Psychoanalysis* (1920)	
CONTEMPORARY THEORY Psychological Trait Theory (p.147)		Pinel *Treatise on Insanity* (1800)					Healy *The Individual Deliquent* (1915)	
ORIGIN Marxist Theory				Marx *Communist Manifesto* (1848)			Bonger *Criminality and Economic Conditions* (1916)	Rusche & Kircheimer *Punishment and Social Structure* (1939)
CONTEMPORARY THEORY Critical Criminology (p.248)								
ORIGIN Sociological Theory			Quetelet *The Propensity of Crime* (1831)			Durkheim *The Division of Labor in Society* (1893)	Park, Burgess, & McKenzie *The City* (1925)	Merton *Social Structure and Anomi* (1938)
CONTEMPORARY THEORY Social Structure Theory (p.182)							Shaw et al. (1925) *Delinquency Areas* Thrasher *The Gang* (1926)	Sellin *Culture, Conflict and Crime* (1938)
ORIGIN Sociological Theory							Mead *The Psychology of Punitive Justice* (1917)	Sutherland *Principles of Criminology* (1939)
CONTEMPORARY THEORY Social Learning Theory (p.235)							Sutherland *Criminology* (1924)	Sutherland *The Professional Thief* (1937)
ORIGIN Multifactor/Integrated Theory							Glueck & Glueck *500 Criminal Careers* (1930)	
CONTEMPORARY THEORY Life Course Theory (p.277)								
ORIGIN Multifactor/Integrated Theory								
CONTEMPORARY THEORY Latent Trait Theory (p.283)								

1775   1800   1825   1850   1875   1900   1925   1939

Time Line of Criminological Theories (continued)

Andenaes
General Preventive Effects of Punishment (1966)

Martinson
What Works (1974)

Cohen & Felson
Routine Activities (1979)

Clarke
Situational Crime Prevention (1992)

Packer
The Limits of Criminal Sanction (1968)

Newman
Defensible Space (1973)

J. Q. Wilson
Thinking About Crime (1975)

Katz
Seductions of Crime (1988)

Montagu
Man and Aggression (1968)

Jeffery
Crime Prevention (1971)

E. O. Wilson
Sociobiology (1975)

Mednick & Volavka
Biology and Crime (1980)

Rowe
The Limits of Family Influence (1995)

Sheldon
Varieties of Delinquent Youth (1949)

Dalton
The Premenstrual Syndrome (1971)

Ellis
Evolutionary Sociobiology (1989)

Friedlander
Psychoanalytic Approach to Delinquency (1947)

Eysenck
Crime and Personality (1964)

Bandura
Aggression (1973)

Hirschi & Hindelang
Intelligence and Delinquency (1977)

Henggeler
Delinquency in Adolescence (1989)

Moffitt
Neuropsychology of Crime (1992)

Wilson & Daly
Evolutionary Psychology (1997)

Murray & Herrnstein
The Bell Curve (1994)

Vold
Theoretical Criminology (1958)

Chambliss & Seidman
Law, Order and Power (1971)

Lea & Young
Left Realism (1984)

Hagan
Structural Criminology (1989)

Braithwaite
Crime, Shame, and Reintegration (1989)

Dahrendorf
Class and Class Conflict in Industrial Society (1959)

Taylor, Walton, & Young
The New Criminology (1973)

Daly & Chesney-Lind
Feminist Theory (1988)

Quinney & Pepinsky
Criminology as Peacemaking (1991)

Cloward & Ohlin
Delinquency and Opportunity (1960)

Kornhauser
Social Sources of Delinquency (1978)

Wilson
The Truly Disadvantaged (1987)

Agnew
General Strain Theory (1992)

Courtwright
Violent Land (1996)

Lewis
The Culture of Poverty (1966)

Blau & Blau
The Cost of Inequality (1982)

Messner & Rosenfeld
Crime and the American Dream (1994)

Lemert
Social Pathology (1951)

Hirschi
Causes of Delinquency (1969)

Schur
Labeling Deviant Behavior (1972)

Akers
Deviant Behavior (1977)

Kaplan
General Theory of Deviance (1992)

Becker
Outsiders (1963)

Heimer & Matsueda
Differential Social Control (1994)

Glueck & Glueck
Unraveling Juvenile Delinquency (1950)

West & Farrington
Delinquent Way of Life (1977)

Thornberry
Interactional Theory (1987)

Sampson & Laub
Crime in the Making (1993)

Weis
Social Development Theory (1981)

Moffitt
Adolescence-Limited and Life-Course Persistent Antisocial Behavior (1995)

Hathaway & Monachesi
Analyzing and Predicting Juvenile Delinquency with the MMPI (1953)

Wolfgang, Figlio, & Sellin
Delinquency in Birth Cohorts (1972)

Wilson & Herrnstein
Crime and Human Nature (1985)

Tittle
Control Balance: Toward a General Theory of Deviance (1995)

Eysenck
Crime and Personality (1964)

Gottfredson & Hirschi
General Theory of Crime (1990)

1947   1969   1975   1980   1991   1995   1997